Ruth Bader Ginsburg at the Supreme Court

Oral Arguments, Majority Opinions and Dissents

EDITED BY ROSS UBER

Ruth Bader Ginsburg at the Supreme Court

Second Edition, October 2019

Edited by Ross Uber (mammoth.publishing@gmail.com)

Library of Congress Control Number: 2019907392

ISBN (paperback): 9780578525587

ISBN (ebook): 9780578525594

Contents

Oral Arguments before the Supreme Court

Selected Majority Opinions

Selected Dissents

Oral Arguments before the Supreme Court

- SHARRON A. FRONTIERO & JOSEPH FRONTIERO v. ELLIOT L. RICHARDSON, SECRETARY OF DEFENSE, et al. - *Amicus Curiae (American Civil Liberties Union) on behalf of the Appellee, by special leave of the Court*

- MEL KAHN v. ROBERT L. SHEVIN, et al. - *Appellee*

- CASPAR WEINBERGER, SECRETARY OF HEALTH, EDUCATION, AND WELFARE v. STEPHEN WIESENFELD - *Appellee*

- EDWIN EDWARDS, GOVERNOR OF LOUISIANA, et al. v. MARSHA B. HEALY, et al. - *Appellee*

- JOSEPH CALIFANO, SECRETARY OF HEALTH, EDUCATION, AND WELFARE v. LEON GOLDFARB - *Appellee*

- BILLY DUREN v. MISSOURI - *Petitioner*

SHARRON A. FRONTIERO & JOSEPH FRONTIERO v. ELLIOT L. RICHARDSON, SECRETARY OF DEFENSE, et al.

Facts of the Case: Sharron Frontiero, a lieutenant in the United States Air Force, wanted a dependent's allowance for her husband. Federal law stipulated that the wives of military members automatically became dependents. Husbands of female members of the military, however, were not accepted as dependents unless they were dependent on their wives for over half of their support. Therefore, Frontiero's request for dependent status for her husband was denied.

Question: Did the federal law violate the Fifth Amendment's Due Process Clause, requiring different qualification criteria for male and female military spousal dependency, by unconstitutionally discriminating against women?

Conclusion: Yes. The Court decided that the statute in question clearly stated "dissimilar treatment for men and women who are similarly situated," violating the Due Process Clause and the equal protection requirements that it implied. However, a majority could not agree on the standard of review. The plurality opinion written by Justice William J. Brennan, Jr., applying a strict standard of review to the sex-based classification as it would to racial classification, found that the government's interest in administrative convenience couldn't justify discriminatory practices. But a concurring opinion by Justice Lewis F. Powell and joined by Chief Justice Warren E. Burger and Justice Harry A. Blackmun wouldn't go so far as to hold sex discrimination to the same standard as race, choosing instead to argue that statutes drawing lines between the sexes alone necessarily involved the "very kind of arbitrary legislative choice forbidden by the Constitution," a view employed in the Court's prior decision in Reed v. Reed. Justice Potter Stewart concurred separately that the statutes created unfair discrimination in violation of the Constitution. Justice William H. Rehnquist dissented to affirm the reasoning of the lower court opinion.

Burger Majority	Stewart Majority	White Majority
Douglas Majority	Marshall Majority	Blackmun Majority
Brennan Majority	Powell Majority	Rehnquist Dissent

Frontiero v. Richardson Oral Arguments - January 17, 1973

Warren E. Burger

We'll hear arguments next in 71-1694, Frontiero against Laird. Mr. Levin.

Joseph J. Levin, Jr.

Mr. Chief Justice and may it please the Court. This is a sex discrimination case. After a short statement of the facts here, I will seek to refute the Government's statistical analysis of the case and point to what we consider to be then substantiability of the Government's interest in continuing this particular sex discrimination. Following this, I will speak briefly about the merits of judging sex classifications by what we consider to be an intermediate test. Professor Ginsburg to my left will then speak on the merits of judging these cases by standard of strict scrutiny. A year after entering the Armed Forces in 1968, Lieutenant Sharron Frontiero married Joseph Frontiero. Because of the statutes which are at issue here, any male member of the Armed Forces would have automatically become entitled to certain housing allowance benefits and medical benefits. Lieutenant Frontiero did not. The statutes giving males in the Armed Forces the irrebuttable presumption, that their spouses are dependent, and grant benefits regardless of the wives' actual financial dependency. A female must prove that her spouse is in fact dependent upon her for more than one-half of his support. In this case, Lieutenant Frontiero earns more than three times as much as her husband Joseph. Her income is approximately $8,200. His income is just a little in excess of $2,800. But because Joseph's individual expenses are low, his small income meets more than half of his personal expenses. Now, Sharron was therefore denied any supplemental benefits in both housing and medical for her spouse. It's undisputed that under these statutes, the ones which are at issue here that male Armed Forces member would have received this housing and medical benefits. So we have a two-fold discrimination. The first is procedural. Women are forced to the burdens and uncertainties of proving that their spouses are in fact dependent upon them while males are given the benefits automatically and irrefutably. But more importantly, there's a substantive discrimination here. Males whose wives are not financially dependent upon them, nevertheless receive these housing and medical benefits. Women in precisely the same circumstances, identical circumstances do not receive the benefits. And the Government really seeks to explain a way this discrimination by saying that it's only a procedural difference. And that since women earn less than men that they can presume for the sake, and I'm talking about women in the general population that they can presume for the sake of administrative convenience or administrative ease that the male spouses are financially dependent. We have three relatively simple answers to the Government's contention that lower income shows dependency. First of all, earning levels don't alone necessarily indicate dependency only because --

Warren E. Burger

Did they indicate a general tendency, do you think?

Joseph J. Levin, Jr.

I think that earning level, not necessary even a general tendency I would think that you could say that in the whole population that it does indicate a tendency that men earn more than women, and we don't dispute that. We don't dispute that at all. But the only reason that Joseph Frontiero's expense that the -- only because his expenses are low as he is technically not one-half financially dependent upon his wife, Sharron Frontiero, which is the criteria and the standard that women are forced to submit to under these statutes. And this is -- in spite of the fact that his income is less than one-third of her income. So, though we feel that income and expenses are relevant in this case, the Government wants to take into account only income. If they really believe that income is the only predictor of dependency then why not make that the standard for determining dependency. Instead, they take a biological class, women, and they ascribe the status to the entire class without reservation. If they believe that lower income equals dependency then let them protect their own interest by making that, that is income the criterion and in the sex discrimination they could do this with a narrowly drawn statute. Now, we doubt that what the Government refers to in its brief as, if I recall correctly, economic facts of life are really facts at all. Their own statistics is set out on page 51 of our own blue brief show that Armed Forces males actually are earn less than females. Now, if lower income equals dependency then the majority of Armed Forces males who are now granted in irrefutable presumption, would not be able to prove their spouses dependent. Now, they say that our use of this kind of comparison is unfair kind of like mixing apples and oranges.

Potter Stewart

This is a median income of Armed Forces males and --

Joseph J. Levin, Jr.

Of Armed Forces males, yes, sir.

Potter Stewart

The reason is there is a higher percentage of non-commissioned and commissioned officers among the female?

Joseph J. Levin, Jr.

I don't --

Potter Stewart

Well, that would have to be the reason, wouldn't it?

Joseph J. Levin, Jr.

It very well could be.

Potter Stewart

And we're dealing here with military personnel whose spouses are civilians, are we not?

Joseph J. Levin, Jr.

Yes sir. But let's --

Potter Stewart

Are we not?

Joseph J. Levin, Jr.

-- let's assume that the Government is correct in what they say that we should not have used this case.

Potter Stewart

Does these case involved only military personnel whose spouses are civilians?

Joseph J. Levin, Jr.

Yes, sir. It would.

Potter Stewart

That's right.

Joseph J. Levin, Jr.

That's correct. Now, let's say that the Government is correct in what they have to say about our analysis that way. They suggest that we should instead use the figure for all women instead of just women in the working population. Well, let's do that. Now the census shows that for all women and this is for everyone over the age of 14, regardless of whether or not they are employed that for all women as a median income of $2,400. And if we lump the military male's median income which is $3,700 with the median income for the female, we come up with a $6,100 lump sum median. Now, the dependency standard we recall is one-half in fact or one-half dependency.

For a woman to fail to provide, that is the wife of an Air Force or any Armed Services member for him -- for her to fail to provide, one-half of her own support, she would have to have expenses that total $4,800 which would be over 80% of the entire family's income. Now, we don't think that the Government can prove or saying here that service family's wives such spendthrifts, I don't believe this anyway to prove it. But this whole analytical approach of statistics is extremely misleading. We don't think that it has any particular relevance in this case because the crucial aspect of it is the substantive inequality which results here. And that is that when you get right down to the bottom that males who cannot prove their wives dependent, nevertheless, receive the benefits. Women in the identical position do not and there's no way to cure that. There's no way to cure that in Sharron Frontiero's case.

Potter Stewart

What are we talking about the terms of numbers? I suppose what 98-99% of the military personnel are males or is that to a higher percentage?

Joseph J. Levin, Jr.

I don't have access to these percentages. As I recall the figures are that there are approximately a million five married male service members and that there are somewhere in excess of, I am talking the Government new figures, are somewhere in excess of 6,000 married female service members, that's --

Potter Stewart

So would this percentage of -- somewhat comparable to that I mentioned?

Joseph J. Levin, Jr.

They very well could be. I have not computed this, but I would say that that was --

Potter Stewart

Because I understood that the good part of the Government's argument is based upon administrative simplicity, is it not?

Joseph J. Levin, Jr.

Mr. Justice, the only part of the Government's argument, their entire argument is based upon administrative convenience. And that is all that they have alleged. To them, that's the only justification and we don't say that this is an illegitimate end because of course it isn't. But it in itself cannot justify the discrimination that exists here. If it did then any arbitrary cut off in benefits would be constitutional. In Shapiro versus Thompson, in Reed versus Reed, we feel that this Court explicitly rejected administrative convenience as justifying this kind of discrimination. And the court in Shapiro explicitly stated that this interest was insufficient regardless of whether measured against the rational basis or the compelling state interest standard. Now, the Government has proposed that the minimal standard of review be used here. The amicus, American Civil Liberties Union has proposed that the -- and will argue that the strict standard of suspect classification is appropriate for this case. Now, we suggest. We, as appellant suggest that the strict standard applicable in the -- that the strict standard here does not pose a choice between polar alternatives. We agree wholeheartedly with what Mr. Justice Powell had to say in Weber versus Aetna. That regardless of the test employed here, that the essential inquiry is inevitably a deal what legitimate state interest does the classification promote and what fundamental personal rights, might the classification endanger. Now here, the classification that we're talking about surrounds employment benefits and this is an area of discrimination in which women had been discriminated against -- been the object of discrimination, I think and that's well documented. The Government's approach employs sort of reverse bootstraps theory where their reasoning is that traditional discrimination and employment should be rewarded by further discrimination and employment benefits, if you look at the figures that they attempt to use. Now, we got stack up against the woman's right to be free from these inequalities and what the Government stacks up against the right of women to be free inequalities is the ease of administration. That's the only thing that they really advanced in this case.

William H. Rehnquist

Well, Mr. Levin, you say that it's a personal right you claim here, following the analysis in Weber. But it's a personal right to more money, isn't it? Well, what more you are claiming now?

Joseph J. Levin, Jr.

It's a personal right. It's a personal right, Mr. Justice Rehnquist to be free from discrimination and employment. And it --

William H. Rehnquist

Well, but you can argue any equal protection that way. You are saying in effect, I want to be free from this discrimination that I claim exists. But I would think if you follow the Weber analogy, you got to see what it is your claiming, what you would get if your claim were sustained?

Warren E. Burger

Which is more money?

Joseph J. Levin, Jr.

Yes, sir. I think so too. But I think with the right that I'm talking about and I think that the kind of personal right that Court is talking about and Mr. Justice Powell is talking about for the Court in Weber was – was the right to be -- for group to be free from discrimination, here that's the right for women as a group to be free from discrimination and that you got to look at the facts involved in that case. You have to look at the facts and you have to determine whether or not the Government has advanced to sufficient or legitimate is the language is here, governmental interest. For example, evidence might be adduced to show that a sex difference which related to performance in combat would be a legitimate governmental interest. That might be. I am not saying it would be but it might be and here, the Air Force certainly doesn't claim that the general earning differentials that you see in the population as a whole would justify discrimination, sex discrimination in basic pay. So, it certainly couldn't justify sex to discrimination in fringe benefits. We think that Mr. Justice Powell's analysis in Webber is a legitimate method for determining what standard to be used in this case. It's stronger than the minimal scrutiny standard which the Government proposes. We feel that a burden should be placed on both the Government, the Government to show illegitimate governmental interest and on the appellant to show that there is discrimination. We think that there should be equal burdens here. The test should be stronger than it is --

Potter Stewart

There used to be an old-fashioned idea that a statute enacted by the Congress or statute enacted by the legislature of the state was presumptively constitutional. We don't hear much about that anymore but --

Joseph J. Levin, Jr.

Your Honor, --

Potter Stewart

I think that -- when I went to law school, that's what the doctrine was.

Joseph J. Levin, Jr.

Well, I think that, that is fine except when the state is classifying different groups and especially when they are classifying a group which is traditionally been the object of discrimination, and consequently, the lower standard in sex discrimination cases, the minimal scrutiny standard simply isn't sufficient.

Potter Stewart

Now, it gets so that statutes enacted in that area is only so to step one, isn't it?

Joseph J. Levin, Jr.

Step one owe it before its test.

Potter Stewart

Yes.

Joseph J. Levin, Jr.

Well, I think the legislature should consider this in passing legislation and they should make sure that you don't have invidious discrimination.

Potter Stewart

The rule construction to which I referred was sort of based upon the hypothesis that Congress would consider the Constitution before it enacted legislation.

Joseph J. Levin, Jr.

Yes, sir. Well, --

Potter Stewart

That was the basis of that rule statutory construction, that the Congress could read the Constitution as well as other people.

Joseph J. Levin, Jr.

Appellants in this case would say that apparently, the Congress did not pay too much attention to the Constitution in enacting these particular provisions.

Warren E. Burger

But does this record show whether the petitioner was a volunteer or was drafted into the Army?

Joseph J. Levin, Jr.

Petitioner was in a sense a volunteer. She -- the Air Force put her through some portion of her schooling and in return she was obligated to serve in the Air Force. So it's six of one, half a dozen of another, I would say that probably a volunteer. I have used more time than I should have. I'd like Professor Ginsburg to speak the appellant's respective position of strict view that is going to argue and felt that it was essential in this case that she be given an opportunity to present oral argument to the Court.

Warren E. Burger

Very well. Mrs. Ginsburg.

Ruth Bader Ginsburg

Mr. Chief Justice and may it please the Court.

Amicus views this case as kin to Reed v. Reed 404 U.S. The legislative judgment in both derives from the same stereotype.

The man is or should be the independent partner in a marital unit.

The woman with an occasional exception is dependent, sheltered from bread winning experience.

Appellees stated in answer to interrogatories in this case that they remained totally uninformed on the application of this stereotype to serve as families that is they do not know whether the proportion of wage-earning wives of servicemen is small, large, or middle size.

What is known is that by employing the sex criterion, identically situated persons are treated differently.

The married serviceman gets benefits for himself, as well as his spouse regardless of her income.

The married servicewoman is denied medical care for her spouse and quarter's allowance for herself as well as her spouse even if as in this case, she supplies over two-thirds the support of the marital unit.

For these reasons, amicus believes that the sex-related means employed by Congress fails to meet the rationality standard.

It does not have a fair and substantial relationship to the legislative objective so that all similarly circumstanced persons shall be treated alike.

Nonetheless, amicus urges the Court to recognize in this case what it has in others, that it writes not only for this case and this day alone, but for this type of case.

As is apparent from the decisions cited at pages 27 to 34 of our brief, in lower federal as well as state courts, the standard of review in sex discrimination cases is to say the least confused.

A few courts have ranked sex as a suspect criterion.

Others, including apparently the court below in this case, seem to regard the Reed decision as a direction to apply minimal scrutiny and there are various shades between.

The result is that in many instances, the same or similar issues are decided differently depending upon the court's view of the stringency of review appropriate.

To provide the guidance so badly needed and because recognition is long overdue, amicus urges the Court to declare sex a suspect criterion.

This would not be quite the giant step appellee suggests.

As Professor Gunther observed in an analysis of last term's equal protection decisions published in the November 1972 Harvard Law Review, it appears that in Reed, some special suspicion of sex as a classifying factor entered into the Court's analysis.

Appellees concede that the principle ingredient involving strict scrutiny is present in the sex criterion.

Sex like race is a visible, immutable characteristic bearing no necessary relationship to ability.

Sex like race has been made the basis for unjustified or at least unproved assumptions, concerning an individual's potential to perform or to contribute to society.

But appellees point out that although the essential ingredient rendering a classification suspect is present, sex-based distinctions unlike racial distinctions do not have an especially disfavored constitutional history.

It is clear that the core purpose of the Fourteenth Amendment was to eliminate invidious racial discrimination.

But why did the framers of the Fourteenth Amendment regard racial discrimination as odious.

Because a person's skin color bears no necessary relationship to ability, similarly as appellees' concede, a person's sex bears no necessary relationship to ability.

Moreover, national origin and alienage have been recognized as suspect classifications, although the new comers to our shores was not the paramount concern of the nation when the Fourteenth Amendment was adopted.

But the main thrust of the argument against recognition of sex as a suspect criterion centers on two points.

First, women are a majority.

Second, legislative classification by sex does not, it is asserted, imply the inferiority of women.

With respect to the numbers argument, the numerical majority was denied even the right to vote until 1920.

Women today face discrimination in employment as pervasive and more subtle than discrimination encountered by minority groups.

In vocational and higher education, women continue to face restrictive quotas no longer operative with respect to other population groups.

Their absence is conspicuous in Federal and State Legislative, Executive, and Judicial Chambers in higher civil service positions and in appointed posts in federal, state, and local government.

Surely, no one would suggest that race is not a suspect criterion in the District of Columbia because the black population here outnumbers the white.

Moreover, as Mr. Justice Douglas has pointed out most recently in Hadley against Alabama 41 Law Week 3205, Equal Protection and Due Process of law apply to the majority as well as to the minorities.

Due to sex classifications listed by appellees imply a judgment of inferiority.

Even the Court below suggested that they do.

That court said it would be remiss if it failed to notice lurking in the background the subtle injury inflicted on servicewomen, the indignity of being treated differently so many of them feel.

Sex classifications do stigmatize when as in Goesaert against Cleary 235 U.S., they exclude women from an occupation thought more appropriate to men.

The sex criterion stigmatizes when it is used to limit hours of work for women only.

Hours regulations of the kind involved in Muller against Oregon though perhaps reasonable on the turn of the century conditions, today protect women from competing for extra remuneration, higher paying jobs, promotions.

The sex criterion stigmatizes when as in Hoyt against Florida 368 U.S, it assumes that all women are preoccupied with home and children and therefore should be spared the basic civic responsibility of serving on a jury.

These distinctions have a common effect.

They help keep woman in her place, a place inferior to that occupied by men in our society.

Appellees recognize that there is doubt as to the contemporary validity of the theory that sex classifications do not brand the female sex as inferior.

But they advocate a hold the line position by this Court unless and until the equal rights amendment comes into force.

Absent the equal rights amendment, appellees assert, no close scrutiny of sex based classifications is warranted.

This Court should stand pat on legislation of the kind involved in this case.

Legislation making a distinction, servicewomen regard as the most frozen equity, the greatest irritant and the most discriminatory provision relating to women in the middle -- in the military service.

But this Court has recognized that the notion of what constitutes equal protection does change.

Proponents as well as opponents of the equal rights amendment believe that clarification of the application of equal protection to the sex criterion is needed and should come from this Court.

Proponents believe that appropriate interpretation of the Fifth and Fourteenth Amendments would secure equal rights and responsibilities for men and women.

But they also stressed that such interpretation was not yet discernible and in any event the amendment would serve an important function in removing even the slightest doubt that equal rights for men and women is fundamental constitutional principle.

In asking the Court to declare sex a suspect criterion, amicus urges a position forcibly stated in 1837 by Sara Grimke, noted abolitionist and advocate of equal rights for men and women.

She spoke not elegantly, but with unmistakable clarity.

She said, "I ask no favor for my sex.

All I ask of our brethren is that they take their feet off our necks."

In conclusion, amicus joins appellants in requesting that this Court reverse the judgment entered below and remand the case with instructions to grant the relief requested in appellants complaint.

Thank you.

Warren E. Burger

Thank you Mrs. Ginsburg. Mr. Huntington.

Samuel Huntington

Mr. Chief Justice and may it please the Court. A position of the Government in this case is first that there is a rational basis for the different treatment of male and female members of the Armed Forces in the statute here under review. And second, that the rational basis standard is the proper standard for determining the validity of those statutes. I would like to first address myself to the statutes and then discuss the appropriate standard of review. I think it would be useful to begin by reviewing the actual impact of the housing allowance and medical care statutes here in issue. The housing allowance statute is 37 U.S.C. 403 grants a basic housing allowance to each member of the military for whom on-base housing is not available. In addition, each such member is entitled to an increased housing allowance if he has one or more dependents as defined by 37 U.S.C. 401. Under the scale which is now in existence, for example, a lieutenant in Pay Grade II would be entitled to $138.60 for -- per month for housing without dependents and $175.80 with dependents, a difference of $37.20. Now, the particular issue here of course concerns under what circumstances a member of the Armed Forces may claim a spouse as a dependent. And the general rule under the statute is that wives of male members qualified automatically for dependency benefits, whereas husbands of female members qualify only if dependent in fact on their wives for over half of their support.

Potter Stewart

Does this housing allowance run right through all of the commissioned and non-commissioned ranks?

Samuel Huntington

Yes, it applies to everyone.

Potter Stewart

There is an amount, I know, but --?

Samuel Huntington

There is an amount. Yes.

Potter Stewart

Thank you.

Samuel Huntington

I would like to point out, now first --

Potter Stewart

Except those for whom housing is provided by the Government?

Samuel Huntington

Yes, right. Housing is available and --

Potter Stewart

For the person and his family, and his or her family?

Samuel Huntington

Right. I would like to point out that under --

Byron R. White

Well, as you put it, the discrimination is against the men, is that it?

Samuel Huntington

Well, I didn't mean to imply that. No, it's --[Attempt to Laughter] The -- I'd like to point out that under 37 U.S.C. 420 in the case of an inter-service marriage, neither the husband nor the wife may claim his or her spouse as a dependent. Now, this fact has considerable importance here for a significant majority of married women in the Armed Force are married to military men. Now while the record is silent on this matter, the Senate Report issued on the proposals in Congress last year to amend these statutes contained a letter from the general counsel of the Department of Defense which is in point. In the letter, at page 4 of the report that's Senate Report 92-1218, it is noted that a recently completed survey of married women in the Air Force show that 25% of the officers were married, but that only 4% of the officers were married to civilians and the percentage of all women in the Air Force married to civilians is even smaller. In not being able to claim their husbands as dependents, military women married to military men are not discriminated against since their husbands could not claim them either. Similarly, a female member --

Thurgood Marshall

[Voice Overlap] But the only way for the woman to get equality as to put a husband as none.

Samuel Huntington

Well, that would be --[Laughter]

Thurgood Marshall

Is that right?

Samuel Huntington

One way, yes. Well, this is also true that these women who married the military men are not discriminated with respect to medical benefits because under 10 U.S.C. 1074 both the husband and the wife would qualify for medical benefits. Well, in short then the only women who are treated differently then their male counterparts are those women who are married to civilian. Now, in our view, one does not have to search far to discover a rational basis for Congress' decision to treat married men and married women differently with respect to dependency benefits. We start with the basic purpose of the two statutes. And the basic purpose is to provide housing allowance and medical benefits for dependents in order to establish a compensation pattern which would attract career personnel into the Armed Forces. In Congress' view, this would enable the military to compete with the civilian sector of the economy for married people. Now in establishing these benefits, Congress had to determine what proof of dependency it would require. Now, an examination of this statute shows that where it was very likely that a military person would be supporting certain relatives, dependency benefits were conferred automatically where it would be less likely or unusual that a military member would be supporting a person, proof of dependency was required. Thus, under 37 U.S.C. 401, a serviceman's wife and minor children automatically qualify for dependency benefits, whereas, his older children and his parents would qualify only if dependent in fact. And since women, generally do not provide the main support for their husbands, children, or parents, servicewomen were required to establish to establish dependency in fact in each case. Let me state this in other way. Taking the over one million married military men as a group, a significant majority of their wives are the dependent upon them. Under these circumstances, it is rational to decide to grant all married men dependency benefits for their wives automatically rather than undertaking the heavy administrative burden of determining dependency in fact in each case. On the other hand, taking the one or two thousand military women who are married to civilians as a group, an overwhelming majority of their husbands are not dependent upon them. Under these circumstances, it is rational to examine individually the few instances where a military woman might have a dependent husband.

Potter Stewart

We're talking --

Thurgood Marshall

On your rational relationship, are you going to square this with Reed against Reed as some?

Samuel Huntington

Yes, we think Reed against Reed is distinguishable. Let me just addressed myself to the statistical basis for a statement that the majority of women are dependent upon their husbands. The ACLU cites in their brief the fact that 60% of all women living with their husbands are gainfully employed. Well, the converse of this fact of course is that 40% of all married women are not employed. Moreover, of those who work, as other figures cited in the ACLU brief indicate, only a portion work full time. In preparing this for this argument I looked at the --

Byron R. White

You mean like a 90% or what ir do you know it?

Samuel Huntington

Well, I think the figure in their brief was that 43% of women are in the labor force and 18% work full time.

Byron R. White

18%.

Samuel Huntington

That's at page 45 of the ACLU brief. In the statistical abstract of the United States which is a document which is cited in our brief is a table that shows that in 1970, in white families where both the husband and wife worked and the husband is under 35; the main contribution of the wife to the total family income was 27.1%. That's at the table at page 327 of the statistical abstract. In comparable, black families, the main contribution the wife was slightly higher at 33.4%. In short, there can be no question but that husbands still provide the primary income in most families. In many families, they provide the only income. In the remaining families, their aggregate contribution to the total family income, totally eclipses the aggregate contribution of working wives. Now, if that is true today, we submit that 23 years ago and 17 years ago when the statutes here were passed, it was even true to a greater extent. Now on the other side of the coin, it can hardly be disputed that most men are not dependent upon their wives. As we note in our brief, almost all married work and in families were both the husband and the wife work, the husband's income is generally well above the wife's.

Byron R. White

Is there some danger of fraud in these areas as part of the Government's aim or let's assume that you are trying to determine if the parents or older children are dependent, do you just take an affidavit or what do you do?

Samuel Huntington

They fill out a form listing their expenses.

Byron R. White

That will be the end of it, isn't it?

Samuel Huntington

I beg your pardon?

Byron R. White

That's the end of it, isn't it?

Samuel Huntington

That, I believe that probably is.

Byron R. White

What is the -- is that the large administrative burden you're talking about?

Samuel Huntington

Well, for a million and a half men to have to examine a million and a half forms, I submit would be an administrative burden to --

Byron R. White

But I mean, I agree it's a burden but I'm just trying to find out how much of the burden it is. It's just --

Samuel Huntington

Well --

Byron R. White

-- making an affidavit, and then somebody will have to read them, I suppose.

Samuel Huntington

Making an affidavit and then somebody reading it and making a determination as to whether it's justified, I think that's -- that is exactly what's involved. I suppose that if evidence came to the Military's attention that the affidavit was false then you would have to investigate further.

Byron R. White

But wouldn't it be the other -- how about -- how about letting the women claim -- you could treat women the same as men the other way I suppose.

Potter Stewart

[Voice Overlap] of all administration.

Samuel Huntington

You mean deny them benefits altogether? Not even give them a chance to show that they --

Byron R. White

Well, treat them like --

Samuel Huntington

Or treat them the way the men; well, certainly Congress could do that --

Thurgood Marshall

That is the whole argument?

Samuel Huntington

-- and the proposal before Congress in the last Congress and it probably be resubmitted at this time is to amend the statute to treat women exactly the same way. What I'm saying here is --

Warren E. Burger

Would that include a requirement to show a dependency?

Samuel Huntington

No, that would -- there would be no requirement -- dependency benefits for spouse and minor children would be conferred automatically both on men and --

Warren E. Burger

The Senate Bill would give the petitioners exactly what they're asking for here?

Samuel Huntington

Oh, yes, that's right. But we submit that while that may be a good suggestion and Congress may adopt it but there is rational basis, for the classification made in the statutes, and it is the difference statistical characteristics of married military men as a group compared with not married military women as a group which justify the different treatment here.

Thurgood Marshall

Those contentions haven't been consistent I'm sure, aren't they, for 40 years?

Samuel Huntington

You mean consistent for 40 years? No, as I --

Thurgood Marshall

Of course, they vary every year.

Samuel Huntington

Well the statistics I gave were for the current year or in the last couple of years.

Thurgood Marshall

And that would not what the statute was based on?

Samuel Huntington

The statute was based on the situation 20 years ago and as --

Thurgood Marshall

Is there any evidence in the legislative history that they consider those factors?

Samuel Huntington

No, there is not. The legislative history simply indicates that --

Thurgood Marshall

Women are women and men are men.

Samuel Huntington

The statute was designed to give dependent -- to give benefits for dependence. Now what I am stating --

Thurgood Marshall

Do I understand the legislative history other than there should be a distinction made between men and women in the Armed Services? Is there anything else in the legislative history on this statute other than that?

Samuel Huntington

Well, it's not even that. I mean the statute speaks for itself on that point. The only thing in the legislative history is that by giving allowances for dependents, you would compensate military personnel better so that you could compete with the civilian sector of the economy. Now, I still say that it is apparent that Congress wrestled with the question of how do you determine who's the dependent. And that it was rational for them to determine that in the case of men you assume that wives are dependent automatically because treating the class of men as a whole that is generally true. Treating the class of women it is -- it is generally not true.

Thurgood Marshall

We base it on the whole general class of women and the whole general class of men.

Samuel Huntington

Right, but we submit that there is a --

Thurgood Marshall

And that's a rational basis.

Samuel Huntington

We submit it's a rational basis.

Thurgood Marshall

That's a rational basis.

Samuel Huntington

Yes.

Thurgood Marshall

It is!

Samuel Huntington

We submit it is a rational basis because there's statistical differences between the two classes which justify --

Thurgood Marshall

What's the good difference is that Congress consider. You said not.

Samuel Huntington

I said the legislative history doesn't indicate that they – they -- they looked at it. The legislative history is fairly silent. I say, you don't have to go very far to find an underlying rational here. I think that this is fairly apparent. I don't believe this is the type of case where you have to strain your imagination to dream up some conceivable rational behind the statute. I think the rational as I've indicated is one which if it doesn't lead back from the statute is one which is fairly apparent.

Thurgood Marshall

Women are women and men are men and you can draw that difference and that difference only in based money on.

Samuel Huntington

Well, I would submit simply that there are statistical differences here which do justify the different treatment. I'd like to turn now to the Reed and Reed case. In that case, as you will recall the Court reviewed an Idaho statute which provided that when competing applications to administer an estate were filed by a man and a woman in the same priority group, the man was to be given preference and appointed. Now there is no evidence in the record that men as a class were better administrators than women and the Court rejected the contention that measure was justified to save litigation costs. In short, there are no differences in the two classes of applicants, men and women which justify the discrimination. By contrast, there are very real and relevant statistical differences between married military men as a class and married women which justify the, in our view justify the classifications under review in this case. I would like to turn now to the question of the appropriate standard to be applied under the due process clause of the Fifth Amendment to determine the validity of these statutes. To begin with, as this Court has held a numerous cases, traditional principles of equal protection developed under the Fourteenth Amendment are relevant in considering a tax under the Fifth Amended alleging that federal statutes unjustifiably discriminate between different classes of individuals. Now as already as been touched upon here today, the traditional equal protection tests is the rational basis test. Although originally developed in cases involving statutes regulating business, the test has been applied in recent years to cases involving economic and social benefits. Now as both Mr. Levin and Professor Ginsburg have pointed out, the Court has imposed a stricter standard of review with respect to statutory classifications in two types of cases; those involving classifications which affect fundamental personal rights and those involving inherently suspect classifications. As far as the personal rights are concerned, I would disagree with Mr. Levin that personal rights of the type which bring in to play this, the standard are involved here, the rights are two dependency benefits. These are the same type of economic benefits which were under review in the Dandridge case and I think it's not the type of personal rights which were under consideration in the Weber case which involved the relationship between illegitimate children and legitimate children within the family unit. The rights here so we would say that the stricter review if it's going to apply at all in this case, it must be because sex is a suspect classification. Let me just comment briefly on Professor Gunther's article in the Harvard Law Review. He suggested there that in recent cases, this Court has not been limited simply to one, the polar extremes. But that in reviewing statutes the Court has been taking a fairly close look even when applying the rational basis test to determine whether there is in fact some Government interest involved which can -- which is readily apparent and you don't have to stretch the imagination to come up with it. We would submit that in this case, the classifications here would stand scrutiny under that type of approach. I would like to turn now to Professor Ginsburg's argument that classifications based on sex are suspect for equal protection and due process purposes. To begin with, as Professor Ginsburg acknowledges, this Court has never treated classifications based on sex as inherently suspect. And only last term in Reed against Reed applied the traditional rational basis test. In our view, the Court should not now abandon the traditional test and treat sex classifications as suspect. Just last week in the Crest (ph) decision, which upheld the $50 filing fee for requirement as a pre-condition to discharge and bankruptcy, the Court referred to the suspect criteria of race, nationality, and alienage. Now, race classifications of course have an especially disfavored status in our constitutional history. And each of the three classifications in the words of Justice Blackmun in Graham against Richardson involves and I quote "a discreet and insular minority for whom heightened judicial solicitude is appropriate." Now these minorities generally lack the political power to protect their own interest. Now, we are not contending that women have achieved equal political power with men. The statistics cited by Professor Ginsburg as to the number of women in high government positions in state and federal legislatures are certainly not in dispute, they're very small. What we do suggest is that because they are a numerical majority in the population as a whole, they have been exercising substantial and growing political influence upon state and federal legislatures. At the federal level, as summarized in the ACLU's brief, there has been considerable legislative activity in amending statutes containing classifications based on sex. Proposed legislation to amend these statutes as I've already stated, was before Congress last year and undoubtedly will be before Congress this year. And also of course the equal rights amendment which was passed last year is evidence -- is an indication of the influence that women who favor the amendment have been able to exert. There is another reason for not expanding the category of suspect classifications to include women. Unlike classifications based on race, nationality, or alienage, classifications based on sex frequently are not arbitrary, but reflect the actual differences between the sexes which are relevant to the purpose of the statutes containing the classifications. Now, we contend here that the dependency statutes, for example, do not discriminate against women because of their femininity. They treat women differently because women as a class are less likely to have dependents than men. Similarly, the Florida statute upheld that Hoyt against Florida did not excuse women from jury duty because they were inferior, but excused them because of the fact that women as class were more likely than men to have family responsibilities, making it impractical for them to serve as jurors. Application of the rational basis test permits the Courts to consider statutes on a case by case basis to determine which classifications are based on valid factual or physiological differences between the sexes and which classifications like the one struck down in Reed and Reed are arbitrary and not based on sex differences. On the other hand, denominating sex classifications as suspect would subject all statutes containing sex classifications to strict review and could result in invalidating many of them whether or not individual classifications reflect acknowledged factual or physiological differences.

Warren E. Burger

But when you talk about generality of women as being less likely to have dependents, you mean dependents in this narrow sense, financially?

Samuel Huntington

Dependence as defined -- yes, dependence --

Warren E. Burger

In terms of children?

Samuel Huntington

No, in terms of dependent spouses, that's what I mean. Well, in closing, let me simply state that we have no quarrel with the drive of any women to achieve equality by attacking statutes enacted in a different era that may reflect antiquated notions of the respective roles of the sexes. We submit, however, that the plea for across the board change rather than case by case consideration is better addressed to the legislature rather than to the courts. In conclusion, the judgment of the District Court should be affirmed. Thank you.

Byron R. White

Could I ask you -- if we agreed with the other side, what do you understand the consequence would be?

Samuel Huntington

I understand the consequence would be that you would extend the same benefits to women. I think --

Byron R. White

What would we strike down?

Samuel Huntington

You would strike down the portion of the statute which says that women have to establish dependency in fact in order to claim their wife as a --

Byron R. White

Or we strike that provision down which provides for their allowance then how do they get the allowance?

Samuel Huntington

No, you wouldn't strike. You would only strike down the part that requires them to establish dependency in fact in order to claim --

Byron R. White

Well, if you just strike down the discrimination, the other way of doing it would be to say that the -- is that the male must prove --

Samuel Huntington

The males must -- well, I would think that would definitely not be the preferable alternative.

Byron R. White

I didn't say preferable, I wondered how do you know which one?

Samuel Huntington

Well, I think the -- I think the inquiry here would be what Congress would have wished had it been faced with the situation of not being able to make this classification and I think that the conclusion would have to be that they would wish that the --

Byron R. White

Could we just strike down that particular part of the statute of the provision, just those particular words?

Samuel Huntington

That's right. Yes.

Warren E. Burger

And then we construe all the other relevant statutes to mean and then women wherever it says men or --

Samuel Huntington

Well, just in this narrow context.

Warren E. Burger

I am talking about in these statutes.

Samuel Huntington

In Section -- in 43 -- 37 U.S.C. 401.

Warren E. Burger

So, we strike down one statute and rework some others? Or at least --

Samuel Huntington

Well, no, just within the definition part itself would be the only -- if you simply said that the same standard have to apply to women as applies to men.

Byron R. White

Well, a --

Warren E. Burger

Well, couldn't we just as easily, why couldn't we just as easily say that since the allowances if that were the conclusion are discriminatory, all allowances are stricken?

Samuel Huntington

Well, I think that would fly right in the face of the purpose of Congress in adopting the dependency benefits statutes to be --

Warren E. Burger

Any more so than except as to numbers?

Samuel Huntington

Oh, yes, but well I think the numbers [Attempt to Laughter] are quite relevant when you're talking about a million and a half men and only a couple of a thousand women married to civilians.

Warren E. Burger

You don't want us to strike the allowances for men?

Samuel Huntington

No, we don't want you to strike that and we don't want you to require that the men's applications for dependency allowances be examined in each case.

Byron R. White

Well, in fact in 401 the definition says that a dependent is a -- of a member of the service is one, his spouse; two, is unmarried minor child.

Samuel Huntington

Well, if you just struck the --

Byron R. White

And then down below it says however, the first is not a dependent of a female member unless he is in fact dependent on her for over half his support. Now, what do we strike down?

Samuel Huntington

That sentence.

Byron R. White

That sentence. Well, then there are no provisions for a man being independent, because up above, it's just a female member, his spouse.

Samuel Huntington

Well, I think "his" means her in this context. At least in certain areas --[Laughter]

Byron R. White

Obviously, I mean if the Constitution discriminated what, is that it?

Warren E. Burger

Right.

Samuel Huntington

Well, if the statute has always been construed to --

Byron R. White

Well, it doesn't, is it so? That means his, it means his because --

Samuel Huntington

Well, I mean take the next one, his unmarried legitimate child.

Byron R. White

Well, so we do have to change the meaning of "his" in one, don't we?

Warren E. Burger

We have to make it really his or hers?

Byron R. White

We have to make it his or hers?

Samuel Huntington

Then why do a complete job. You can do it but the way --[Laughter] -- but the way the statute has been construed is interchangeable with her and his.

Thurgood Marshall

Well, should we assume that petitioners cases in this case are not in favor of cutting out all of the allowances that the wife gets.

Samuel Huntington

Well, you could certainly assume that and we're not suggesting that you do that. Thank you.

Warren E. Burger

You have three minutes left, Mr. Levin if you wish to use it.

Joseph J. Levin, Jr.

I would do answer Mr. Justice White about which provision of the statute should be struck.

Warren E. Burger

Rewritten?

Joseph J. Levin, Jr.

First of all, I think you don't get into any trouble by striking that portion that begins however and in support.

Byron R. White

Why not?

Joseph J. Levin, Jr.

Because I don't believe that "his" means his in the masculine --

Byron R. White

It means not -- now doesn't it?

Joseph J. Levin, Jr.

No, sir. It doesn't mean it now. Because the only limitation you have is down here is not a dependent of a female member unless he is in fact dependent on her for over one-half the --

Warren E. Burger

What page of what document?

Joseph J. Levin, Jr.

I am looking at page 23 (a) of the appendix.

Warren E. Burger

Of the appendix?

Joseph J. Levin, Jr.

Yes, sir. Last paragraph.

Warren E. Burger

Hmm.

Joseph J. Levin, Jr.

But I certainly wouldn't construe "his" in the masculine or feminine sense.

Byron R. White

Or we need to strike that one sentence? That's what we're talking about?

Joseph J. Levin, Jr.

I believe that that would extend the benefits to all, yes sir. I think the Government has misconstrued the basic question here and the basic purpose of the statute. The basic purpose of these statutes in the legislative history shows this is to extend these benefits to men and women, that's the language that the legislature use and the proponents of the legislation used. And the idea was to encourage re-enlistment of men and women and it said more than once, so that is the legislative history. Anything else, would be inconsistent with the basic purpose of the statutes. I think we lose sight of the issue that no matter how many figures are thrown after the court that nevertheless you get right down to rock-bottom, women who are identically situated to men as in the case of Lieutenant Frontiero don't receive either housing benefits or medical benefits and there can't be no justification for that kind of situation. The Government talked in terms of forms that have to be filled out. Well, I know for military experience that there are hundred forms that have to be filled out when you go in. Men, all service people have to inform the Government as to how many dependents they have and a variety of other items in order to determine initially what kind of payments they might be eligible to receive. So you're not asking for any, if you extend it all the way around, you certainly wouldn't be asking for any extension. You just have to require a quality of root, I prefer to call it that. This Senate Bill has been discussed by the Government, of course, is speculative and it's only perspective as I read it would not apply whatsoever to assist Lieutenant Frontiero and her husband. I think in Reed versus Reed that the lower court there talked in terms of a difference and the experience of men and women and attempted to justify the classification that way. Well, statistics in that case could just as easily have shown that more than in any business world than are women and that con -- and have more and consequently, they have more experience of the classification would then be justified, once again, under the administrative convenience justification. I think you get into a problem when you try and ask the question what is the definition of dependency. The Government seems to want to use one-half dependent in the case of women who are seeking to have their husbands as dependents but to use another classification that is just general dependency of bread winning in the case of men, and we think that this cannot in any way be justified.

Warren E. Burger

Thank you.

The case is submitted.

MEL KAHN v. ROBERT L. SHEVIN, et al.

Facts of the Case: Since 1941, Florida state law granted a $500 property tax exemption for widows but not for widowers. Widower Mel Kahn applied to the Dade County Tax Assessor's Office for the property tax exemption, and was denied. Kahn sued in circuit court and sought a declaratory judgment. The circuit court decided that the statute was gender-based and therefore violated the Equal Protection Clause of the Fourteenth Amendment. The Florida Supreme Court reversed and decided that the gender classification had a "fair and substantial relation" to the purpose of the legislation.

Question: Is the Equal Protection Clause of the Fourteenth Amendment violated by the Florida statute that only provides property tax exemptions to widows?

Conclusion: No. The 6-3 majority opinion was delivered by Justice William O. Douglas. The Supreme Court held that single women face significantly more hardship in the job market than single men, and the disparity is especially true for surviving spouses. While widowers can generally continue in the job they held previously, many widows enter the job market for the first time or after a long absence. Based on these differences, the Court held that the gender classification in the Florida statute has a "fair and substantial relation" to the legislation's purpose of easing the financial impact of the loss of a spouse. Justice William J. Brennan, Jr. wrote a dissenting opinion in which he argued classifications based on characteristics over which individuals have no control, such as gender, must be subject to strict judicial scrutiny. In such cases, the government must prove not only that such classifications serve a compelling government interest, but also that the interest cannot be served by any other classification. In this case, he argued that the purpose of the legislation could be achieved without gender-based discrimination. Justice Thurgood Marshall joined in the dissent. Justice Byron R. White, in his separate dissent, wrote that gender-based classifications require significant justification that Florida didn't provide.

Burger Majority	Stewart Majority	White Dissent
Douglas Majority	Marshall Dissent	Blackmun Majority
Brennan Dissent	Powell Majority	Rehnquist Majority

Kahn v. Shevin Oral Arguments - February 25, 1974

Warren E. Burger

We will hear arguments next in 73-78, Kahn against Shevin. Mrs. Ginsburg, you may proceed whenever you're ready.

Ruth Bader Ginsburg

Mr. Chief Justice --

Warren E. Burger

If you'd like to lower the lectern, you've quite the liberty to do so

Ruth Bader Ginsburg

Mr. Chief Justice and may it please the Court.

Appellant Mel Kahn, a Florida resident is a widower.

In January 1971, based on his status as a surviving spouse, he applied to the Dade County Tax Assessor for a property tax exemption.

The statute under which widower Kahn sought exemption provided, a widow, along with the disabled persons is entitled to exempt $500 yearly from her property tax.

Mel Khan was denied the claimed exemption solely on the ground of his sex.

Requesting judicial review, he alleged that the statute under which he claimed exemption have been interpreted and applied in conflict with the equal protection guarantee of the Fourteenth Amendment.

Warren E. Burger

Actually he didn't allege that in the trial, didn't he expressly say he didn't want to raise this federal question there?

Ruth Bader Ginsburg

In the original complaint, he suggested that he might save at the federal question till a later time but then the federal question was raised and decided with the agreement of all parties.

William H. Rehnquist

But he didn't simply say he might say but he said he wanted to say that, didn't he?

Ruth Bader Ginsburg

Yes.

But apparently, with the understanding of the court and the agreement of both sides, the federal question was heard and decided both in the trial court and in the Florida Supreme Court.

Appellant sought a declaration that the exemption provision is unconstitutional insofar as it excludes widowers.

On cross motions for summary judgment, the Court of First Instance held that the statute by according exemption to all widows and excluding all widowers discriminated arbitrarily between widowed persons and therefore violated the equal protection guarantees of the State and Federal Constitution.

On appeal, the Florida Supreme Court reversed.

The Florida Supreme Court held that the distinction between surviving spouses though based solely on gender did not deny to any person the equal protection of the laws.

It is appellant's position that the gender based distinction upheld by the Florida Supreme Court discriminates invidiously in two respects.

First, most obviously, it discriminates against men who have lost their wives more subtly but as surely it discounts the contribution made to the marital unit and the family academy by the female partner for her death, occasions no exemption for the surviving spouse.

By defining the exempt person as widow, rather than surviving spouse, this provision now covering the blind and the totally disabled along with the widow is keen to a classification delineated by the president of one of our nation's leading educational institutions.

Anticipating an increase in conscription not too many years ago, this distinguished educator complained, "We shall be left with the blind, the lame, and the women."

This Court's decision in Reed v. Reed 404 U.S. and its judgment in Frontiero v. Richardson 411 U.S. indicate genuine concern to analyze sex classifications free from the generalizations of the Victorian age.

Appellant maintains that the Reed standard is not met by a surviving spouse, tax exemption that uses gender as the sole criterion for qualification or if need is the concern then sex should not be a substitute for an income test.

And if widowed state is the concern, then it is irrational to distinguish between taxpayers based on their sex.

Far from constituting a rational shorthand but distinguishing between taxpayers on the basis of need or life situation.

A widow's only classification is a crude device that originated in and today perpetuates Victorian assumptions concerning the station of men and women.

To resolve this case, the Court need not go beyond the scrutiny employed in Reed and followed by the Tenth Circuit in Moritz v. Commissioner 469 F. 2d.

The decision in Reed and the judgment in Frontiero indicate the Court's clear willingness to give sex classifications more than surface examination.

However, if the Court wants to consider application of a suspect classification doctrine then it must face the fact that problems of race and sex discrimination are often different and that neither women nor blacks are aided by lumping the two together for all purposes.

Thus far, this Court has applied the label suspect classification only in opinions involving discrimination, hostile to groups not dominant in society.

But whatever may be said for a one-way suspect classification doctrine in cases involving racial discrimination, a one-way approach in sex discrimination cases would be fought with danger for women because of the historic tendency of jurors to rationalize any special treatment of women as benignly in their favor.

With respect to race, the effects of officially sanctioned segregation are still very much with us but complex doctrines directed to the continuing impact of racial segregation are not necessarily applicable to sex discrimination.

The difference is perhaps best illustrated with respect to the educational experience.

Most public education is co-educational though females have been segregated and restricted in some areas, most notably vocational training and athletics.

But generally, females participate with males in academic programs, in elementary and high school and in fact, tend to do better there than males.

For many females, this record of achievement continues into college and university.

For example, females outscore males on the law school admissions test.

The problem for women is that along the way, an attitude is instilled insidiously.

This attitude is described in a nutshell in graffiti etched on a college library carrel in the early 1950s.

The epigram reads, "Study hard, get good grades, get your degree, get married, have three kids, die, and be buried."

From the first drop line, the sex of the writer is impossible to determine from the second, her sex is impossible to mistake.

To cure the problem, thought so acutely by the young woman who wrote those words and so many others like her, the law must stop using sex as a shorthand for functional description.

It must deal with the parent not the mother, with the homemaker not the housewife, and with the surviving spouse not the widow.

To appreciate the character of the challenged classification, the widow's only exemption must be viewed in historical context.

The exemption became part of Florida's law in 1885.

At that time, indeed, well into the 20th century, Florida Law routinely differentiated between the roles of men and women and particularly married men and married women.

Women could not vote nor did they serve on juries for example.

Well, past the middle of the 20th century, in fact up till 1968, a Florida married woman could not transfer even her own interest in real property without her husband's consent.

Not surprisingly, the married woman was deemed worthy of special solicitude.

On the death of the person, the law regarded as her guardian, her superior not her peer.

While the widows only exemption was designed with the 19th century status of married woman in mind.

The Florida Supreme Court found contemporary justification for it in this unquestionable fact.

Women workers as a class do not earn as much as man.

This well known and still wide earnings gap according to the Florida Supreme Court supplies a fair and substantial basis for the tax classification widow rather than surviving spouse.

But beyond doubt, a widow's only exemption has no impact whatever on the conditions responsible for the earnings gap.

Warren E. Burger

It is not clear. You are arguing that sex ought not to be treated as a suspect classification?

Ruth Bader Ginsburg

I am arguing that if first, that it is not necessary to deal with that question in this case.

But second, that if sex is treated as a suspect classification which I think properly it is, then the Court must be aware that the arguments that we give special scrutiny only to lines that appear to disfavoring women will be ultimately harmful to women because the history has been --

Warren E. Burger

So it's suspect class?

Ruth Bader Ginsburg

It is the classification.

It is the criterion sex that is suspect.

Not female but the criterion sex.

Warren E. Burger

Generally, isn't it the fact that the Court has found classification to be suspect when it involves a discriminatory classification against a minority group?

Ruth Bader Ginsburg

Yes.

Warren E. Burger

Is that accurate?

Ruth Bader Ginsburg

In this Court's precedent, the suspect label has been used --

Warren E. Burger

Because the paradigm is race?

Ruth Bader Ginsburg

Yes, and national --

Warren E. Burger

(Voice Overlap) minority race?

Ruth Bader Ginsburg

Yes.

And what was looked at --

Warren E. Burger

Alienage is another? Possibly, right?

Ruth Bader Ginsburg

Alienage, yes.

Warren E. Burger

So the suspect classification is not only with respect to discriminatory classification against a minority group, is that correct?

Ruth Bader Ginsburg

That is how it has been used in this Court's precedent.

Warren E. Burger

Traditionally, up till now?

Ruth Bader Ginsburg

Yes.

Warren E. Burger

And your point, I gather, is that I don't know if you mentioned it but women first of all are not a minority group, and secondly, since courts have been in the habit to view any classification of women as beneficent --

Ruth Bader Ginsburg

Yes.

Warren E. Burger

-- provision of course should be on guard and not --

Ruth Bader Ginsburg

Yes, my point is that the women -- what will aid woman most is not looking to see whether a classification is benign or invidious but whether it is a sex criterion, as a shorthand for what should be a functional criteria.

Warren E. Burger

Right. In other words, you don't want it whether it helps -- even when it helps?

Ruth Bader Ginsburg

My question is if it ever does one.

Yes.

Warren E. Burger

But even if it does, you would assume on that assumption --

Ruth Bader Ginsburg

But I have not yet found any such classification in the law that genuinely helps from the very short-sided view point perhaps such as this one?

Yes.

But long run?

No.

I think that what women need is first of all a removal of exclusions and restricted quotas.

They are the only population group that today still faces outright exclusions and restrictive quotas and then what is necessary is the welcome sign.

A notice that in the professions, in trades and occupations women are now as welcomed as men.

But the notion that they need special favored treatment because they are women I think has been – what has helped to keep women in a special place, and has kept them away from equal opportunity for so long.

In other words, take this exemption.

It's not the purpose of this exemption to eliminate discrimination against women.

It isn't the purpose to eliminate discrimination in pay or to equalize training, study, job opportunities for them.

In contrast to these widows exemption are measures that are realistically designed to promote equal opportunity free from gender based discrimination, Title VII of the Civil Rights Act of 1964 for example.

These measures focus on eliminating sex typing of this very order as the essential task.

Nor, can an exemption of this kind be regarded as a rational welfare measure to alleviate the effects of past discrimination against women.

As a welfare measure, supposedly directed to the authority of women property owners to pay taxes, the exemption is incredibly designed that encompasses the independently wealthy widow and at the same time it excludes the women who encounters perhaps the sharpest discrimination.

The female had a household who never marry and some, the classification is obviously unrelated to any biological difference between men and women.

It is not fairly and substantially related to the need or life situation of the individual men or women but it is very much related to underestimation of the women's contribution to the family economy.

Significantly, the Florida Supreme Court on other days has demonstrated its understanding of the very real and substantial economic contribution made by the female partner whether it's homemaker to gainful employment or as increasingly the case through productive effort both in and outside the home.

In --

Warren E. Burger

But insofar as the statute does not differentiate among various widows or various categories of widows. It's very typical of tax legislation generally, isn't it?

Ruth Bader Ginsburg

Yes, the --

Warren E. Burger

I mean certainly, the federal income tax which gives every taxpayer an exemption of $750 for each dependent regardless of his circumstances or the dependents' circumstances. If he is below certain age, he is certainly very blunt instrument. And insofar as this --

Ruth Bader Ginsburg

Yes.

Warren E. Burger

-- as this legislation fails to discriminate as among various categories of widows, you don't really attack it, do you?

Ruth Bader Ginsburg

The classification surviving spouse is well-known classification in both state and federal tax law.

It does reflect the legislature's recognition that loss of a spouse is a unique episode in a person's life and I am not challenging the classification surviving spouse.

Warren E. Burger

No, my point was. Perhaps, I didn't express it very well. You, a few moments ago, spoke and said that the legislation is applicable whether the widow be a millionairess or whether she be a poor working widow or whether she had children or no children, and so on. I didn't really understand that your basic attack upon this legislation was premised upon that fact.

Ruth Bader Ginsburg

That's right.

I am not suggesting that the tax assessor call in each individual exempt person and see if that person really needs the exemption, not at all.

Warren E. Burger

I don't think so.

Ruth Bader Ginsburg

But I am suggesting is that the sex criterion is invalid.

Thurgood Marshall

Mrs. Ginsburg, assume and argue that being said -- how do you get into relief in this case?

Ruth Bader Ginsburg

Well --

Thurgood Marshall

Assuming that we declare the statute unconstitutional.

Ruth Bader Ginsburg

Yes. Well, if this Court --

Thurgood Marshall

Who gets any relief then?

Ruth Bader Ginsburg

Mel Khan gets the tax exemption for the tax year in question.

Thurgood Marshall

How?

Ruth Bader Ginsburg

First, --

Thurgood Marshall

I said, if we declare the statute unconstitutional.

Ruth Bader Ginsburg

Insofar as it discriminates against widowers, I think that, if you declare the gender line unconstitutional which is the only thing that the Court has been requested to do, then the Florida Supreme Court should be free to consider where the total demolition of this exemption or repairing it to fit the Constitutional requirements is preferred.

Thurgood Marshall

Assuming that they just ended and nobody gets other than --

Ruth Bader Ginsburg

For the future. Widower concept is exemption --

Thurgood Marshall

Well, does this case in this Court which says that that's not for the courts to do the case of Cummings (ph) against the Board of Education in Georgia 1914 or so.

Ruth Bader Ginsburg

Yes, I am sorry that I am not familiar with that.

Thurgood Marshall

Well, it's a case where -- it's just like this, you want to knock out and then this Court said that if you do that and nobody gets anything, that's not the proper place with equity court to act.

Ruth Bader Ginsburg

I am asking this Court to take the same approach that was taken in Frontiero last semester, where a group of service spouses, in that case husbands, did not qualify for the exemption because the statute excluded them and all this Court held was that the state was unconstitutional insofar as it excluded that class.

Thurgood Marshall

And this Court has plenty of jurisdictions over the federal jurisdiction over the federal army?

Ruth Bader Ginsburg

Yes, but ultimately --

Thurgood Marshall

And we do not have it on the State of Florida.

Ruth Bader Ginsburg

Ultimately, of course that is a question for the Florida Supreme Court to answer and it can answer that question for itself. But it would be --

Thurgood Marshall

Then you'd be perfectly satisfied if the end result of this case is that would it get nothing?

Ruth Bader Ginsburg

No, I do not think that that would be the reasonable approach for either the Florida Supreme Court or the Florida legislature to take.

There's a Florida problem here that --

Warren E. Burger

Of course if everybody – if the end result is that everybody is the exemption that's the same as nobody getting an exemption.

Ruth Bader Ginsburg

That all widowed persons get the exemption and we're talking about a very small addition, since there are about four times as many widows.

Warren E. Burger

Many more widows than widowers.

Ruth Bader Ginsburg

-- in Florida as widowers I suppose that a reasonable legislature looking at that logic class and wanting the exemption for that logic class would extend it to this much smaller group by than

(Voice Overlap)

Warren E. Burger

My brother Marshall suggests that is the question ultimately up to the Supreme Court and/or legislature of Florida.

Ruth Bader Ginsburg

That's quite correct.

Yes.

All we ask of this Court --

Warren E. Burger

Unlike Frontiero in that respect.

Ruth Bader Ginsburg

We ask this Court to declare the statute defective in that it excludes widowers, and the remaining relief would be inappropriate question for the Florida Supreme Court.

Warren E. Burger

Mrs. Ginsburg, pursuing this discussion, do I understand you to say that the Florida court would have not only authority but I think on page 26 of your brief you said it's a responsible court it would in effect rewrite this statute contrary to what you concede to be as plain language and intent that a court would do that rather than the Florida legislation?

Ruth Bader Ginsburg

The court has two choices in that situation.

It can either nullify the statute in which case it is totally toward the legislature's will or it can modify the statute to meet the constitutional equal protection requirement.

If it guesses the wrong way in either direction, the legislature of course has the final word.

But the court faced with the question, should we take this exemption away from the three quarters of the population, the widow population that now gets it, rather than extend it to the one-quarter that doesn't in order to preserve what the legislature did do.

It seems to me, it's eminently more destructive of the legislative will to say that we remove this exemption altogether than to say we'll keep what you wanted and then just add this much smaller group.

Warren E. Burger

I might agree with that. Excuse Mr. Chief Justice, I am going to say I could be persuaded, I think, to agree that it would be more constructive if you prevail here for the legislation in the end to equalize it. But I was curious by your suggestion that the court itself could rewrite a perfectly plain statute conceded by you to be plain.

Ruth Bader Ginsburg

A number of state courts have done just that.

We have cited Small against Feezy (ph) for example.

Warren E. Burger

We gone that far but I didn't know it gone that far?

Ruth Bader Ginsburg

These were all cases where a statute was constitutionally infirm because of under inclusion.

A group had been left out and then it was the court's choice to determine whether it wanted to knock out the provision altogether or to do well as Mr. Justice Harlan once pointed, the choice is between amputation and a skin graft.

Warren E. Burger

That's what he suggest in Welsh but --

Ruth Bader Ginsburg

Yes.

Warren E. Burger

-- this Court has never done that, has it? That was his point of view?

Ruth Bader Ginsburg

That was a concurring opinion --

Warren E. Burger

Yes. Well, that was the Fifth vote in determining this.

Ruth Bader Ginsburg

Yes.

Warren E. Burger

But it's definitely, I gather you recognize. You suggested at page 25 of your brief that if we agree that the statute is unconstitutional that we should remand for consideration whether consistent with the dominant legislative purpose constitutional infirmity this should be remedied by holding the exemption available to all widowed property owners. We wouldn't do that but we only would do --

Ruth Bader Ginsburg

It will be my --

Warren E. Burger

It will be simply remand from proceedings not inconsistent --

Ruth Bader Ginsburg

Exactly right.

Warren E. Burger

-- without making any suggestion.

Ruth Bader Ginsburg

That's quite so.

Yes.

What we seek in this Court is a declaration of the gender line is unconstitutional, that it is unconstitutional to exclude widowers, and then a remand before the proceedings not inconsistent with that opinion.

Warren E. Burger

Is that the only way we could do it or could we simply say the statute is invalid. If we --

Ruth Bader Ginsburg

I think that you would be clearer and provide more precise instruction to the Florida Supreme Court if you said that the statute was unconstitutional insofar as it excluded widowers.

Warren E. Burger

Right. You take the risk of you, I am speaking in broad terms, a litigant takes the risk of destroying an entire statutory scheme, when they attack it in this Court as one of the risks, is that not so?

Ruth Bader Ginsburg

Justice Brandeis once made that point that when a taxpayer is in this situation.

That taxpayer cannot be expected to have a situation equalize by asking the taxpayer to increase the taxes of others similarly situated.

So that when a taxpayer is subject to a discriminatory tax through favoring others.

The only equalization possible is to grant that taxpayer the exemption afforded to others and then change for the future can be made so that all persons similarly situated will either be included or excluded from the exemption.

Thurgood Marshall

But you don't -- you still -- we cannot do that.

Ruth Bader Ginsburg

I think it's the province of the Florida Supreme Court to decide what should be done with that Florida statute.

Thurgood Marshall

But are we obliged to suggest to them what they should do or can we do anything more than hold that statute unconstitutional? Can we do anything more?

Ruth Bader Ginsburg

Well, you can do what Justice Brandeis suggested in the Iowa-Des Moines case 284 U.S. and that is to say that this appellant must be granted the exemption because there is no other way that his claim of the denial of equal protection can be redressed.

Thurgood Marshall

Which is entirely different from this case? The exemption in that case is --

Ruth Bader Ginsburg

It wasn't a different kind of exemption but the same situation that --

Thurgood Marshall

That is not a member. But wouldn't we be rewriting the statute?

Ruth Bader Ginsburg

No, you wouldn't be rewriting the statute.

You would be holding that the statute contains a constitutional defect at the classification.

Thurgood Marshall

No. If we say that you must include the others. We wouldn't be rewriting the statute?

Ruth Bader Ginsburg

You would not be rewriting the statute for anyone other than our claimant who made a timely claim for this exemption and whose denial -- to whom the denial of equal protection cannot be redressed in any other way.

Warren E. Burger

Or that a minor repair of the statute?

Ruth Bader Ginsburg

Would call the extension of the statute to widowers a minor repair. Yes.

Thurgood Marshall

Necessary repair.

Ruth Bader Ginsburg

A necessary repair to preserve its constitutionality. Yes.

Warren E. Burger

I think we'll not ask you to spend one minute dividing your argument counsel.

We'll let you start fresh in the morning.

Sydney H. McKenzie, III

Pretty good, Your Honor.

ORAL ARGUMENT - FEBRUARY 26, 1974

Warren E. Burger

We'll resume arguments in 73-78.

Mr. McKenzie.

Sydney H. McKenzie, III

Mr. Chief Justice, and may it please the Court. Because of that part of the argument yesterday, I feel that it's necessary this time to clarify some of the facts of this case. This is a claim by a widower that he has been denied equal protection of the law both by a mandatory, self-executing provision of a Florida constitution and by a statute providing exemption from ad valorem taxation of properties with a value of $500 yearly for widows but not for widowers. Now, that's important for two reasons. One, first of all, counsel in argument yesterday stated that this was a deduction from taxation. In fact, it's not a deduction. It's an exemption to the amount of $500 which, in dollar terms translated through the assessment laws of Florida, comes out to about a $15 amount. Secondly, --

William J. Brennan, Jr.

What difference does that make?

Sydney H. McKenzie, III

We don't make a de minimis argument. I simply wanted to clarify the fact that it's not a $500 deduction from tax but --

William J. Brennan, Jr.

I thought you were making a distinction between a deduction and an exemption.

Sydney H. McKenzie, III

That's right.

William J. Brennan, Jr.

And I ask, is there a difference?

Sydney H. McKenzie, III

Yes, there is a difference. The exemption--

William J. Brennan, Jr.

If there's a difference, is there a significant --

Sydney H. McKenzie, III

The exemption is from the ad valorem value of the property. In other words, if property is worth --

William J. Brennan, Jr.

I know what it is, but I'm asking what difference does it make?

Sydney H. McKenzie, III

It makes a difference --

Potter Stewart

It makes a difference about $485. Is that right?

Sydney H. McKenzie, III

That's right, Your Honor.

William J. Brennan, Jr.

But what legal difference does it make is what I'm trying to --

Sydney H. McKenzie, III

No legal difference as far as this particular case. I merely wanted to clarify the fact, Your Honor. Secondly --

Potter Stewart

It's a $15-benefit.

Sydney H. McKenzie, III

It's a $15-benefit and I was merely trying to put it in perspective.

William H. Rehnquist

Actually, if the $500 were actually deductible from the taxable you refer to it as a tax credit, wouldn't you?

Sydney H. McKenzie, III

Yes.

Warren E. Burger

Yesterday, we had another case involving all kinds of millions of claims $3-10, but the case was here just as well.

Sydney H. McKenzie, III

Yes, Your Honor, and we're not making an argument that the case should not be here. The other question -- I'm sure you'd rather that it weren't.

Sydney H. McKenzie, III

Yes, Your Honor. The other question though is of more significance and that's the fact that we are dealing with, as I say, not simply a statute but a provision of the Florida constitution. And this is significant in that, as we noted in our brief, we know of no case providing for this Court or the Florida Court to expand a provision of the constitution to include members of a class who are not included in the class where there is no ambiguity, and I think that's important in the discussion yesterday of whether it could be sent back to the Florida Supreme Court for the purpose of expanding the class in the statute. It isn't simply a statute. It's a Florida constitutional provision that we're dealing with.

Potter Stewart

As I understand it, the ultimate conclusion was that Mrs. Ginsburg, I think, acknowledged that that wasn't for us to do that. The limit of our function here was to uphold the provision of the Florida constitution and statute or to invalidate it and, if it's invalidated, it would be remanded to the Florida Supreme Court to do with our decision what it will.

Sydney H. McKenzie, III

Very good. They've made a strong argument in their briefs --

Potter Stewart

As to what the Supreme Court ought to do, but that's not for us.

Sydney H. McKenzie, III

Basically, the State of Florida has two positions. First of all, that the compelling interest tests of the Frontiero plurality should not be applied to sex classifications and, secondly, that the classification of widows to the exclusion of widowers in view of the purpose and the factual realities of this situation does not, as applied to the appellant here, violate the equal protection either,-- whether tested by Frontiero in the plurality or by the standard in Reed, if in fact that's different from traditional standards, or by traditional tax classification in sex standards. And I'll address myself first to the traditional test because I feel that, under that test, it's clear that the distinction here meets the test. First of all, the classification we have is a classification of widows and widowers, and the question is, what is the purpose of that classification? The State of Florida, as noted by the Florida Supreme Court, recognizes by this classification that women and especially widows are an economically disadvantaged class in our society. This is not in line with past cases where stereotypes were developed for the purpose of so-called protective legislation for denying women something on a basis of a stereotype that wasn't backed up by facts but was backed up by beliefs that people had, by mythology, really. It's not based --

William J. Brennan, Jr.

(Inaudible)economically disadvantaged?

Sydney H. McKenzie, III

What?

Potter Stewart

Widows.

William J. Brennan, Jr.

Widows?

Sydney H. McKenzie, III

Widows, yes, I would say that widows is --

William J. Brennan, Jr.

I thought the statistics were all over the country.

Sydney H. McKenzie, III

The statistics of the country -- the widows are to the country -- I think the widows are economically disadvantaged.

William J. Brennan, Jr.

Anything but an economically disadvantaged.

Potter Stewart

Well, I think my brother Brennan is referring to the fact that widows own a great deal of the property in the country but that is because there are many, many, many more widows than there are widowers.

Sydney H. McKenzie, III

That's right. I would agree with that.

Byron R. White

And it's somewhat those are --

Sydney H. McKenzie, III

Well, if they--

Byron R. White

-- don't have any money and others do.

Sydney H. McKenzie, III

Well, I think that --

Byron R. White

Like widowers.

Sydney H. McKenzie, III

I think-- but, basically, the fact is that taking a widow and a widower, the general facts are that a widow has a likelihood if she must transfer into the job market of not being able to earn as much as the widower simply, if for no other reason, then the fact is that women in general can only earn -- are only earning 60% of what men earn. William O. Douglas You mean they are discriminated against?

Sydney H. McKenzie, III

They are discriminated against, and I think it's a recognition of that fact. The Florida statute really wrecking and constitutional provision merely recognizes the women not because of any inherent problem with women but with an inherent problem with our society that hasn't been corrected yet are, in fact, discriminated against.

Thurgood Marshall

Does Florida give any other provision in benefit of women in their taxation other than this?

Sydney H. McKenzie, III

Other than this particular --

Thurgood Marshall

Yes, sir.

Sydney H. McKenzie, III

Provision? I'm not --

Thurgood Marshall

Because I would assume that the widow before she becomes a widow, if what you say is true, she suffers a lot too. Does Florida recognize that in this taxing scheme?

Sydney H. McKenzie, III

Women other than widowers?

Thurgood Marshall

Yes.

Sydney H. McKenzie, III

I am not familiar with any provisions that --

Thurgood Marshall

Well, why single out the widows?

Sydney H. McKenzie, III

Well, it was the wills of people in adopting the constitution of Florida.

Thurgood Marshall

Well, our fact says when the constitution was adopted the same as they are today?

Sydney H. McKenzie, III

Pardon, Your Honor?

Thurgood Marshall

Were women allowed to make contracts when this constitution was first adopted?

Sydney H. McKenzie, III

This constitution was adopted in 1968, Your Honor.

Thurgood Marshall

Wasn't there a provision before then in the old constitution?

Sydney H. McKenzie, III

Yes.

Thurgood Marshall

And it was just carried over.

Sydney H. McKenzie, III

It was --

Thurgood Marshall

When was it originally in the constitution?

Sydney H. McKenzie, III

1885, Your Honor.

Thurgood Marshall

Well, aren't women in a little disposition now than they were in 1885, little?

Sydney H. McKenzie, III

In a better position now than they were in 1885?

Thurgood Marshall

Yes.

Sydney H. McKenzie, III

Yes, Your Honor. But, clearly, they are not by any means have been given economic equality in society, and I think this is a recognition of that.

Thurgood Marshall

But how can you put them in a class? I would assume that there are some widows in the Palm Beach area that are little better off than some widowers in upper part of Florida.

Sydney H. McKenzie, III

Well, I think the law has always recognized that no class is going to be perfect even if we took $4,000 limen than anyone who earns $4,000 or less should get $500 exemption but still have the --

Thurgood Marshall

That's especially true in taxation I assume.

Sydney H. McKenzie, III

Yes, Your Honor. We still have the problem of saying that there are people who earn $4,000 who have no dependents and there are people who earn $4,001 who have 10 dependents and are much more needy. Obviously, for the purpose of taxation, states have never been called on to treat every case on an individual basis. And, I think that --

Thurgood Marshall

Well, of course --

Sydney H. McKenzie, III

The Court will recognize that that's not a practical possibility.

Thurgood Marshall

I'm just trying to get the reason for this singling out. You agree this is solely on sex?

Sydney H. McKenzie, III

I would say it's sex as tied to economic reality. In other words, the class is not simply actually --

Thurgood Marshall

It's strictly, well --

Sydney H. McKenzie, III

The fact, the class isn't--

Lewis F. Powell, Jr.

This isn't between a widow and a widower other than sex.

Sydney H. McKenzie, III

Other than sex?

Thurgood Marshall

Yes.

Sydney H. McKenzie, III

One, the fact that a widower being a man is recognized as having greater earning potential in our society --

Thurgood Marshall

Is there any way for a widower to become a widow?

Sydney H. McKenzie, III

Pardon?

Thurgood Marshall

There's no way for a widower to become a widow.

Sydney H. McKenzie, III

No, there is no way --

Thurgood Marshall

So, it's sex. What's wrong with admitting that it's based on sex?

Sydney H. McKenzie, III

It's based -- Let's say that it's based on sex is accurate, but it's based on sex plus an underlying recognition of factual difference between the sexes are not simply a stereotype difference between men and women.

Thurgood Marshall

The same constitution also that prevented women from serving on juries, didn't it?

Sydney H. McKenzie, III

Yes, it did, Your Honor. The law of Florida prevented women from serving on juries.

Thurgood Marshall

And now they do.

Sydney H. McKenzie, III

But it didn't prevent them from showing on juries.

Thurgood Marshall

Now, they've been persuaded to let women serve on juries, haven't they?

Sydney H. McKenzie, III

Women were not prevented from serving on juries. They had to take affirmative action to indicate a desire to serve on juries.

Thurgood Marshall

Back in the 19th century? In the original --

Sydney H. McKenzie, III

At the time of the Hoyt case, Your Honor.

Thurgood Marshall

In time of the original constitution?

Sydney H. McKenzie, III

At the time the original constitution of Florida. I'm not prepared to say, Your Honor.

Warren E. Burger

Mr. McKenzie, are you suggesting that this is based on economic need?

Sydney H. McKenzie, III

Yes, Your Honor. I'm suggesting that this case is very little and different than Gruenwald versus Gardner which was --

Warren E. Burger

Well if it was based on economic need, why doesn't it say so instead of putting it on widowhood?

Sydney H. McKenzie, III

Well, because I think it recognizes the underlying rationale. The class is not simply widows. The class is widows, the blind, and the totally and permanently disabled. I think that all those have the same line of reasoning running through them for different reasons. But disabled or --

Warren E. Burger

And the works --

Sydney H. McKenzie, III

All are economically disabled.

Warren E. Burger

It works to benefit the wealthy widow in Palm Beach.

Sydney H. McKenzie, III

It works to benefit the wealthy --

Warren E. Burger

Widow and --

Sydney H. McKenzie, III

Blind person also.

Warren E. Burger

The wealthy widow in Palm Beach and to disadvantage the poor spinster in Tallahassee.

Sydney H. McKenzie, III

Right, but the fact is that, as a general objective analysis, women and widows are not in the same economic classification as our widowers. They don't have the same opportunities. First of all, a woman who is a widow is either one of two possibilities. One, she's the head of the household, the same as the widower and, in that case, the distinction is exactly as I've said that she has to -- she does not have, as a general rule, the job opportunity that the male does. The other case is where she has been -- she has not been the head of the household and a widow -- then the husband is the one that dies. And, in that case, she not only has to move over into the job market but she has to get someone to replace her and take over the duties that she had, which is really a double burden compared to the man whose wife dies who simply has to replace the functions that his wife had in the family unit. She has to do both that and move over into the job market.

William H. Rehnquist

And if she moves over in the job market for the first time at age 55, I suppose her lower earnings compared to a widower who may have been in the market for 30 years aren't necessarily attributable to discrimination. She simply hasn't been in the market.

Sydney H. McKenzie, III

She hasn't -- well, I would agree that they aren't -- that that's true but they're even compounded by discrimination and that the job opportunities not only to an elderly person but to her particularly are greatly lessened both by her age and by her sex. Now, as to the general classification, the traditional test, first of all, if the Court is to use that test, then we would submit that it would be appropriate in all the tax cases where there are tax classifications, there's a presumption of constitutionality, a heavy burden on one challenging the classification to show no conceivable permissible basis and it's been recognized that the classification need not be exact or have mathematical nicety. Clearly, if the no conceivable rationale purpose test is to be used, I'd submit that the appellant here has not met that burden. Not only is there a conceivable rational purpose, I submit, but the purpose that we've offered to the court is in accordance with proper tax purpose concerned for the economically disadvantaged groups in society, and that that's a valid social concern. Secondly, under Reed versus Reed, it's possible that that case could be read to say that there is an additional burden that the court is going to place on the state where it makes a classification, and that's the burden of justifying a rational classification. And, I submit again that we have not relied on stereotypes that women are either physically not capable of doing the work that men are capable of doing or the women are in some way, because they're the creator of children, that they should stay at home. We're not saying that. We believe that women have all the rights that men have, but that the facts of our society are that women have not yet been given those economic rights and that, until they do, it's appropriate for the State of Florida to have legislation which recognizes that and gives them an affirmative chance to pull themselves to attain equality.

Thurgood Marshall

Of $15?

Sydney H. McKenzie, III

Well, Your Honor, the fact that it's a small amount is true. But, to argue that the State of Florida should give more, the determination of the people of Florida was that it was an appropriate --

Thurgood Marshall

Gesture.

Sydney H. McKenzie, III

Gesture, and it is the --

Potter Stewart

It might enable her to retain the ownership of the property rather than make a distressed sale of it.

Sydney H. McKenzie, III

The fact is that someone at a low level of income, $15 -

Potter Stewart

Well, $15 annually on taxes on a real estate.

Sydney H. McKenzie, III

Annually, may enable them to retain property which they would otherwise not be able --

Potter Stewart

To sell.

Sydney H. McKenzie, III

-- to retain. While we submit that the plurality opinion in Frontiero, Frontiero should not be applied. I would submit that based on that decision, the classification that we've established is sufficient. That case specifically, in a footnote, refers to in footnote 22 I believe it is, states it should be noted that these statutes and those are the statutes in Frontiero are not in any sense designed to rectify the effects of past discrimination against women citing Gruenwald versus Gardner and Jones versus Mayer and South Carolina versus Katzenbach. And, on the contrary, these statutes seize upon a group of women who have historically suffered discrimination in employment and rely on the effects of this past discrimination as a justification for heaping on additional economic disadvantages. That isn't the case that we have here. There's no -- there is -- I mean, the second is not the case that we have here. There is no purpose, nor result of heaping additional economic disadvantages on women. There is a purpose of taking affirmative action if indeed women are to be determined to be a suspect classification to reduce the results of past historic discrimination, so that even under Frontiero I would submit that it would be appropriate to approve this classification. However, I think it's well to point out to the Court, and we submit, that this Court has, in general, limited suspect classifications to groups which sense that have been described since carrying products as discrete and insular minorities. And, I would submit that a classification based on sex does not have within it a discrete and insular minority whether be it the plaintiff here who is a male seeking to have the statute applied to him or else struck down all together. Clearly, the male is not a minority in a group where men and women are equal and if women are anything, it would be, I guess, a philosophical minority and that they've been discriminated against. But, I know of no case where the court has found that a philosophical minority qualifies for a strict scrutiny and I think it's proper because any group that is an interest group is a minority and it may not get everything at once out of the judicial process and it's not for the court, every time some group other than a racial classification or an easily identifiable classification like that comes before the court to give strict scrutiny to something that doesn't -- to a statute that doesn't give that interest group what it wants. And, on those grounds, Your Honor, I would submit that this classification should be upheld.

Potter Stewart

Mr. McKenzie.

Sydney H. McKenzie, III

Yes.

Potter Stewart

Is a property tax -- is this tax imposed on both real and personal property and as well as mixed or is this just a real property tax we're talking about?

Sydney H. McKenzie, III

This is -- no, it's a tax on both real and personal property. It's on any ad valorem taxation which, in ad valorem taxes in Florida are both on real and personal property.

Potter Stewart

Real and personal property. And how is it -- how is property appraised down there? How is it -- what's the assessed evaluation? How close to realistic market value?

Sydney H. McKenzie, III

It's assessed at 100 -- by constitution, it's to be assessed at full market value, 100%.

Potter Stewart

Well, what's the practice? We all know about those constitutional issues.

Sydney H. McKenzie, III

Well, that's in the court's now as to whether in fact it is assessed at 100% of market value. In fact, it's -- I would say, assessed between 80% and 100% of market value. That's --

Potter Stewart

Does it vary by counties?

Sydney H. McKenzie, III

It varies by counties. That's right.

Potter Stewart

It usually does.

Sydney H. McKenzie, III

The assessors of the counties do the assessing.

Potter Stewart

So, this wouldn't--

Sydney H. McKenzie, III

However, to add to that, all assessments are reviewed for the purpose of equalization by the Department of Revenue of the State of Florida. So that, theoretically, when they approve it, it's a determination that that county is at 100% of assessed value.

Potter Stewart

The reason for my question is, I was wondering whether this exemption could validly be supported as a provision where they might enable the widow to keep their family home after widowhood rather than having to sell it at a distressed sale if this were a real relief from the real estate taxes on that home. But, it hardly is enough, is it?

Sydney H. McKenzie, III

Well, the question is really limited. It might be enough for one widow. It might not be enough for another.

Potter Stewart

Well, $500 is -- and that's the reason I asked how close to realistic market prices are your actual appraisals and assessments.

Sydney H. McKenzie, III

It is directly at 100% of assessed value, Your Honor.

William H. Rehnquist

What's your typical tax rate on real property, say, in Dade County?

Sydney H. McKenzie, III

The rate would generally be 30 Mills which would translate into -- the 30 Mills would translate into a $15 exemption under this.

William H. Rehnquist

Well, on a house assessed at $20,000, what property tax would you pay in Dade County?

Sydney H. McKenzie, III

That's right.

William H. Rehnquist

$600.

Sydney H. McKenzie, III

$600.

William H. Rehnquist

A month?

Sydney H. McKenzie, III

$600.

William H. Rehnquist

At 30 Mills, that $600.

Sydney H. McKenzie, III

That's right.

Lewis F. Powell, Jr.

Mr. McKenzie, in your brief you point out relying on Bureau of the Census figures that 35.8% of the families in Florida in which a female is a head of the family below the poverty level whereas, I think, about of about 9 --

Sydney H. McKenzie, III

7% --

Lewis F. Powell, Jr.

9% of the men who had families --

Sydney H. McKenzie, III

That's right, Your Honor.

Lewis F. Powell, Jr.

Are below poverty level.

Sydney H. McKenzie, III

That's right and I think that's just --

Lewis F. Powell, Jr.

Are those figures unique to Florida or how would they be compared with national figures?

Sydney H. McKenzie, III

I would imagine they would -- I really can't answer that, Your Honor. Those figures were drawn out because we were especially concerned with the Florida situation. I imagine that they would probably be typical. I know of no situation in Florida that would make them a typical on a national basis, but I can't represent that to the Court.

Thurgood Marshall

Well, you don't have many of those owning homes, do you?

Sydney H. McKenzie, III

Pardon?

Thurgood Marshall

You don't have many of those owning homes.

Sydney H. McKenzie, III

The ones below the poverty level, Your Honor?

Thurgood Marshall

Yes, they're mostly renters, aren't they?

Sydney H. McKenzie, III

Not necessarily in Florida, Your Honor, because you have a lot of very poor people that own property and that they own mobile homes. That's the typical situation in Florida. Much more so than any other state. I'd say a much larger percentage of those than in a typical state would be in a position where they were in property ownership.

Thurgood Marshall

That wouldn't be true up in the Turpentine area.

Sydney H. McKenzie, III

I'm sorry?

Thurgood Marshall

Up in the Turpentine area, up near the Georgia boarder. They don't own anything up there.

Sydney H. McKenzie, III

Well, I live in the Turpentine area, Your Honor, and it's not so much as the rest of the state but, certainly, it's a mobile home area the same as the other part of the state, although it's not so much of the elderly living there. So, that's part of the problem.

Thurgood Marshall

But it's still at rage from the lower person to the highest anywhere you go. You admit that and I --

Sydney H. McKenzie, III

Yes, Your Honor.

Thurgood Marshall

You say that's normal for taxation and, in some areas, it is. It's the question of whether it's normal here where you draw the line on sex. Isn't that the real problem?

Sydney H. McKenzie, III

We submit that this statute is a wreck. This statute and constitutional provision are a recognition of the economic realities of the State of Florida. Thank you, Gentlemen.

Warren E. Burger

Thank you, Mr. McKenzie. Mrs. Ginsburg, do you have anything further?

Ruth Bader Ginsburg

Yes, I do.

Warren E. Burger

You have about two minutes remaining.

Ruth Bader Ginsburg

First, I would like to qualify that mobile homes are not subject to the ad valorem property tax.

Article VII, Section 1 of the Constitution exempts, along with motor vehicles, mobile homes.

Then, in --

Potter Stewart

With wheels or without? This probably isn't very important but I know in many states there's an argument about what is a mobile home. After it comes to rest --

Ruth Bader Ginsburg

Yes.

Potter Stewart

And if the wheels come off it, is it still a mobile home?

Ruth Bader Ginsburg

Also, I would like to qualify the statement made that this tax is subject -- real property and personal property are subject to this tax.

That's true in the constitutional description, but a statute exempts all household goods and all personal effects for all persons whether or not they're heads of family, and that's Florida statute 196.181.

In fact, the legislature has twice extended this constitutional provision that we're talking about by ordinary statute.

And then, finally, with respect to a point that came out yesterday, recent models for the disposition that appellant seeks in this case include the per curiam opinion last term in New Jersey Welfare Rights Organization against Cahill and early on, Mr. Justice Blackmun's opinion in Graham against Richardson.

Both of those opinions dealt with constitutionally under-inclusive state rather than federal benefit statutes, and both are cited at page 27 of our main brief and in a footnote at page 8 of our reply brief.

Warren E. Burger

Professor Ginsburg, could I ask a question. You're familiar with the DeFunis case to be argued this afternoon?

Ruth Bader Ginsburg

Yes.

Warren E. Burger

This, perhaps, is an unfair question but does your position in this case with respect to the Florida classifications bear in any way on the issues in DeFunis?

Ruth Bader Ginsburg

Not at all.

The DeFunis case raises a very different issue.

DeFunis is a program of a law school that is designed to open doors to equal opportunity, to assure a law student body with diverse backgrounds and experience and to what defy the conspicuous absence of minority groups in the profession.

It is not a welfare, though assumed, based on the assumed inferior capabilities of any population group.

No rigid race line is presented, as we have here, a rigid sex line.

Race is merely one of the many characteristics assessed in that case.

But most significantly, DeFunis involves no general law classification.

It's a measure addressed to very special selection problem that law schools have.

Law schools have the very hard task of choosing some from among many applicants that are fit to pursue their educational program.

By contrast, here we are dealing with the law, general application of the law with respect to property owners where there can be no justification for the crude device of labeling any group: racial, ethnic, or sexual as needy persons.

And, income tax is readily available to a legislature that wishes to distinguish on the basis of need, and immutable birth characteristic should be irrelevant for general law purposes.

Warren E. Burger

Thank you, Mrs. Ginsburg.

Thank you.

The case is submitted.

CASPAR WEINBERGER, SECRETARY OF HEALTH, EDUCATION, AND WELFARE v. STEPHEN WIESENFELD

Facts of the Case: Stephen Wiesenfeld and Paula Polatschek married in 1970. Polatschek had worked for the several years prior to their marriage and continued working after they were married. Her salary was the primary source of the couple's income, and social security contributions were regularly deducted. In 1972, Polatschek died, which left Wiesenfeld with the care of their newborn child. Wiesenfeld applied for social security benefits for himself and the child, and was told that his son could receive them but that he could not. The Social Security Act provides benefits based on the earnings of a deceased husband and father that are available to both the children and the widow. The benefits for a deceased wife and mother, however, are only available to the children. In 1973, Wiesenfeld sued on behalf of himself and similarly affected widowers. His claim was that the relevant section of the Social Security Act unfairly discriminated on the basis of sex and asked for a summary judgment. A three-judge panel of the district court granted Wiesenfeld's motion for summary judgment.

Question: Is the Due Process Clause of the Fifth Amendment violated by the gender-based distinction in Social Security benefits?

Conclusion: Yes. Justice William J. Brennan, Jr. wrote the opinion for the 8-0 majority. The Supreme Court decided that the purpose of the social security benefits for the surviving spouse and children is to enable the surviving spouse to adequately care for the children, regardless of the gender of the parent. Gender-based discrimination regarding these benefits is therefore both counter-productive and illogical. Justice Lewis F. Powell, Jr. wrote a concurring opinion (joined by the Chief Justice) in which he argued that the gender-based classification of the social security benefits doesn't serve any government interest. In his concurring opinion, Justice William H. Rehnquist wrote that the majority's opinion overreached the bounds of the question by ruling on whether the statute violated the Fifth Amendment. It was his argument that the statute does not serve a valid legislative purpose and could be overturned on that basis alone.

Burger Majority	Stewart Majority	White Majority
Douglas Abstain	Marshall Majority	Blackmun Majority
Brennan Majority	Powell Dissent	Rehnquist Majority

Weinberger v. Wiesenfeld Oral Arguments - January 20, 1975

Warren E. Burger

We'll hear arguments next in 73-1892, Weinberger against Wiesenfeld. Mr. Jones, you may proceed whenever you're ready.

Keith A. Jones

Mr. Chief Justice and may it please the Court. This case involves a claim of sex discrimination under the Social Security Act. Section 202 (g) of that Act provides for the payments of benefits to certain widowed mothers. There is no comparable provision under the Act for payment benefits to widowed fathers. The appellee in this case is a widowed father who claims that he is constitutionally entitled to the payment benefits on the same basis as if he were a widowed mother. It is the Government's position as I will elaborate that at some length later that this statute like the property tax exemption in favor of widows in Kahn against Shevin, serves a permissible legislative objective of ameliorating the harsh economic consequences of economic job discrimination against women and that it should be sustained on that basis. A description of the operation of the Act is essential to an understanding of this case. The benefits payable under Section 202 (g) are paid out or on account of the Social Security Account of the diseased wage earner. The widowed mother receives, I think, a benefit equal to three quarters of the primary insurance benefit that the diseased husband would have received had he lived and retired, reduced $0.50 cents for each dollar that the widow earns in excess of $2,400.00 per year. The payments are made to the widowed mother so long as she has a minor child in her care and remains unmarried. Similar benefits are provided under the Act to the child of a diseased wage earner. A child receives benefits on the basis of the Social Security Account of his or her diseased parent, whether or not the parent is the father or the mother, it makes no difference. But there is no provision under the Act for the payment of benefits to widowed fathers under the age of 60 on the basis of the account of their diseased wives. The appellee in this case is a young unemployed widower. After the death of his wife his child began receiving benefits based upon her Social Security Account. He however, was not entitled to benefits, he I mean the appellee, was not entitled to benefits himself under the Act. In view of this, he brought present suit for the declaratory and injunctive relief contending that he was constitutionally entitled to a distribution of benefits on the same basis as if he were a widow rather than a widower. A three-judge court was convened. The court determined that all sex based classifications are inherently suspect under this Court's two tiered equal protection analysis that is applied in recent years. The court analyzed the statute and concluded that it did not served a compelling governmental interest. And accordingly, the court held the statute on constitutional and ordered the payment of benefits to the appellee as if he were a widow. The court stayed its order pending this appeal and the case is now here on the government's direct appeal. At the outset, I think it can be said that the District Court clearly erred in applying the compelling governmental interest standard of review. It has become clear in these Court's decisions in Kahn against Shevin and last week in Schlesinger against Ballard, that sex based classifications are not inherently suspect. They're not subject to justification only on the basis of a so-called compelling governmental interest. They are not invalid per se. This is not to suggest that the traditionally permissive rational basis standard of review is fully appropriate in all sex discrimination cases. Sex based classifications we believe do merit close judicial scrutiny and they've received it by this Court in the past in Frontiero against Richardson and Reed against Reed. This Court struck down the sex classifications that merely served the purpose of administrative convenience. Plus the Court has applied a standard of review which involves a close scrutiny, a scrutiny which is not so strict as to be inevitably fatal. The rule that the Court seems to be applying is simply that sex based classifications must rest upon some substantial reasonable basis, or as Chief Justice Burger said in the Reed opinion, "Upon some ground of difference having a fair and substantial relation to the object of the legislation as I will now show the statute here in question easily meets that test." Appellee's principle attack on the statute is curiously enough, not from the point of view of the widower who has been denied benefits but rather from the point of view of the female wager who it is alleged is denied of social security coverage for her spouse that would have been granted to a male wager earner. The appellee's argument proceeds so logistically. First, the appellee analogizes the payment of Social Security taxes to the purchase of private insurance coverage and the appellee contends that female wager earners are not granted the right to purchase the same insurance coverage that a male wage earner purchases for his spouse under the system. And appellee's concludes that this discrepancy and treatment -- this discrepancy in insurance coverage is in permissible. We believe, there are two fatal flaws to this chain of reasoning. First, the analogy to a private insurance scheme is itself fundamentally erroneous. As this Court noted in Flemming against Nestor, the Social Security Act comprehends this scheme not of private but of Social Insurance under which, benefits are distributed and coverage provided in large part on the basis of probable need rather than on the basis of strict compe -- rather than strictly on the basis of the contributions that the insured wage earner has paid. We even, accepting for the moment the private insurer paradigm on which the appellee relies, we think it's nevertheless clear that the female wage earner is not entitled to any additional insurance coverage under the Act that the female wage earner has not been disadvantaged in anyway. As we pointed out on pages 21 and 22 of our brief, female wage earners under the Social Security system pay in only 28% of all Social Security taxes whereas 34% of the benefits paid out in the system are paid out on the basis of the Social Security accounts of female wage earners. I'm not talking about the benefits that are paid to women I'm talking about the benefits that are paid out solely on the basis of the women's account as workers. Now this means that the Social Security System is already out of actuarial balance in favor of female wage earner as against the male wage earner. If my rough estimatical calculations are correct, right now, the female wage earners receives a 33% greater coverage under the Act, in terms of dollars than does male wage earner. To grant the additional insurance coverage for which appellee contents here, would simply further tilt the scales in favor of the female wage earner as against her male counter part.

Potter Stewart

How do you account for the existing disparity?

Keith A. Jones

I think, in large part the disparity flows from the fact that women have longer life expectancies and that their retirement benefits are spread out over a longer period of time. They may also be attributable in part to the fact that lower wage earners are entitled to somewhat great return under the Act than are higher wage earners and women statistically are lower wage earners. Like for those two reasons and I'm not sure which is more important, women do received on the basis of their accounts far greater return than the men. And our position with respect to this argument, this insurance coverage argument by the appellee is that to grant further coverage, to further tilt the scales in favor of women, obviously would not serve the purposes of the Equal Protection Clause. It therefore, seems to us that appellee's insurance coverage argument simply reduces to the complaint that appellee's individual wife as a wage earner, unlike the average female wage earner has been somehow disadvantaged that the payments made on the basis of her account are in some sense constitutionally insufficient. There's no merit to this argument either legally or factually. As a factual matter, I think that you can deduce from the record and that it is clear that appellee's son has already or will soon have received greater benefits under the Social Security Act than his wife ever paid into the system, that there is no ground for reviewing her account as being somehow disadvantaged but more fundamental is a legal matter. There's no basis for an argument that a Social Security contributor has a vested interest in his or her Social Security account. That argument which obviously is not a sex discrimination argument was firmly rejected by this Court in Flemming against Nestor in language which, I think is equally appropriate here and I would like to quote, "The Social Security System maybe accurately describe as a form of Social Insurance whereby person's gainfully employed and those who employ them are taxed, to permit the payment of benefits to the retired and the disabled and their dependents." A non-contractual interest of an employee covered by the Act cannot be soundly analogized to that of a holder of an annuity. His right to benefit is bottomed on his contractual premium payments. And therefore, I think its clear that appellee's wife as a female wage earner, was not disadvantaged either in her individual capacity or as a member of a class under the Act, that she was not the subject -- was not the victim of any cognizable discrimination under Act. For that reason, I now turn to the appellee's alternative argument which is based upon the contention that the denial of benefits to a widower constitutes a denial of equal protection to men as an impermissible discrimination against men. That argument it seems to us, is foreclosed by this Court's decision in Kahn against Shevin. In that case, this Court upheld a special Florida property tax exemption that was granted only to widows and not to widowers. The objective of that legislation is like that of the statute here was to ameliorate some degree the economic difficulties that uniquely confront the lone woman who has lost her husband. The Court in that opinion recited statistics showing that the average female workers are in approximately 40% of the income of the average male worker. And the Court noted that this disparity in the economic capabilities would be exacerbated in the case of a widow vis-a-vis a widower and that the difference in earning power between a widow and widower was probably even greater to that between women and men generally. Mr. Justice Douglas writing for the Court in that case observed that while the widower can usually continue in his occupation, in many cases, the widow will suddenly find herself forced into a job market with which she is unfamiliar and in which, because of her former economic dependency, she will have fewer skills to offer. And it's also clear that, the discrimination inherent in such a statute between widows and widowers is not impermissible. As Mr. Justice Brennan, who is dissenting on other grounds in that case, observed it's permissible to distinguish between widows and widowers because only the former and not the latter are subject to discrimination as a class. And if I may quote again from the descending opinion, "Inclusion of needy widowers would not further the state's overriding interest in remedying the economic effects of past sex discrimination of needy victims of that discrimination. No doubt some widowers are in financial need, no one suggests that such need results from sex discrimination." On the basis of these considerations, the Court in this case, Kahn against Shevin, upheld the Florida statute as resting upon some ground of difference having a fair and substantial relation to the object of the legislation. Well, precisely the same considerations govern this case. Congress recognized that the probable need of widows is greater than that of widowers and then enacted

Section 202 (g) to provide for that need. In doing so, Congress merely acted as it has also done in behalf of other persons such as aged dependent parents, who cannot be fairly expected to replace by their own efforts in the job market the loss of support that has been occasioned by the death of a family wage earner. Moreover, this provision, Section 202 (g), does not suffer from the vice of over inclusiveness that led two justices of this Court to descent from the ruling in Kahn. The amount of the benefits payable under Section 202 (g) is inversely correlated to the amount of the widow's earnings. So that the women, who has in fact successfully surmounted, sexual job discrimination is not provided benefits under this Act. Similarly, benefits are provided only to the widow with a minor child in her care for whom the economic consequences or job discrimination are heightened by the fact that she must additionally provide competent child care during the working hours. At the same time, the benefits provided under the statute are considerably more substantial than those that were granted by the property tax exemption in Kahn. Therefore, it seems clear to us that Section 202 (g) serves the permissible legislative objective of ameliorating the economic consequences of the employment discrimination that widows with children suffer with heightened severity, and that does both more thoroughly, and more carefully than the statute at Kahn against Shevin. I would add at this point only one final point. At the bottom, the appellee's argument here is that benefits under the Social Security Act must be distributed without regard to sex equally to men and women in all cases. Although, we realize that program costs cannot be determined even a case such as this, we feel that it is nevertheless not without some significance that the cost of achieving this objective of paying out all benefits without regards to sex would be approximately $350,000,000.00 additional dollars per year. Now these statistics are set fort on page 15 of the appendix. This additional money would have to come from somewhere. The Social Security System is supposed to remain in actuarial balance. Therefore, to pay out these additional benefits either Social Security taxes would have to be increased or some other benefit group with the benefits payable to some other group would have to be reduced. In this context, that we feel that this Court's statement in Dandridge against Williams is particularly appropriate. That is that it does not sit to second guess officials charged with difficult responsibility of allocating scarce public welfare funds among the merit of potential recipients. Now, to apply a judicial restrain of this kind in a case like this is not however to place the Social Security System in the iron grip of the status quo. Congress has recently considered sex based classifications under the Act and it has amended the statute to eliminate one of the major sex based classifications like providing for the equalization of the method of computing retirement benefits for men and women. And it may well act to further reduce or ultimately entirely eliminate all sex classifications under the Act. But for the present we feel that it's clear that the exclusion of widowers under Section 202 (g) lies well within Congress' constitutional power to allocate welfare funds. For these reasons we respectfully submit that the judgment below should be reversed.

Potter Stewart

Mr. Jones --

Keith A. Jones

Yes.

Potter Stewart

Do they remain in this Act any differentials based upon gender as to age, another basic one as eliminated in 1972?

Keith A. Jones

That was the only one that I am aware of. I don't think they are anymore that remain. It -- well, on age exclusively now there are some provisions that discriminate between men and women on the basis of age. For example, a widower over age 60, I mean, in some cases may be entitled to benefits for as a widow might be entitled to benefits at an earlier age.

Potter Stewart

Without regard the children?

Keith A. Jones

Without regard to children, that's right. But I don't think there are many significant age qualifications in the Act of --

William J. Brennan, Jr.

Well, apart from widows and widowers is there another distinction that women beneficiaries on retirement that there is computed -- may retire at age 62 for as on male is at age 65?

Keith A. Jones

This was the difference that was eliminated in the 1972 Act.

Potter Stewart

Who did that?

Keith A. Jones

The Congress.

Potter Stewart

It's on page 15 of your appendix, under the --

Keith A. Jones

That's correct. Pages 14 through 16 discussed the --

William J. Brennan, Jr.

Well, it might be but haven't you brought a case here and that we having for pending cert?

Keith A. Jones

Well, we have moved to affirm the judgment of the three judges from the Court.

William J. Brennan, Jr.

I know but there is such a case here, isn't it?

Keith A. Jones

That's correct. That that's on a basis of a claim of man who are retired earlier and the --

William J. Brennan, Jr.

Before the -- the 1972 Amendment has now become effective until this year?

Keith A. Jones

They're not retroactive. That's correct.

William J. Brennan, Jr.

And it may become effective in 1975?

Keith A. Jones

I think they were phased in over a period of time.

William J. Brennan, Jr.

This rather petition this morning and what you tell us there is that it become effective this year.

Potter Stewart

Now, let's say a new provision will become effective starting January 1973 and will be fully effective in January 1975.

Keith A. Jones

Yes. I think that it is phased in over three years. It does become fully effective this year, that's correct.

Warren E. Burger

The Congress there elected to ignore the difference in longevity of women over men?

Keith A. Jones

Well, in fact men were disfavored under the old law and --

Warren E. Burger

But the point is, they ignored the fact that women as category live longer than men?

Keith A. Jones

That's correct.

Warren E. Burger

And that's within their legislative discussion, I supposed you would say --

Keith A. Jones

Yes.

Warren E. Burger

They can ignore it or they act on it?

Keith A. Jones

That's right Mr. Chief Justice Burger. We don't think the constitutional places Congress in a straight jacket with respect to the determination of distribution this wealth for benefits. We think either alternative is acceptable under the constitution.

Potter Stewart

Through the old -- the old law was more commensurate with the idea that men lived longer than women.

Keith A. Jones

Yes, an assumption which, if ever true, is no longer --

Warren E. Burger

Well, that isn't supported that the American experience table of mortality or never has been, is it?

Keith A. Jones

Not that I know of.

William J. Brennan, Jr.

Well, what was it the basis that they argued the distinction between 62 and 65 under the old law is to favor compensated disfavored class?

Keith A. Jones

It did have the effect of providing women --

William J. Brennan, Jr.

Was it that the Government's argument?

Warren E. Burger

Congressional theory?

Keith A. Jones

I'm not sure exactly what the Government's argue was in the motion to -- we maybe speaking of different cases. The one I have in mind is called Kohr against Weinberger.

William J. Brennan, Jr.

I remember it by name.

Keith A. Jones

But of course, Congress doesn't have to locked into favoring disadvantaged classes. If there are no further questions I would like to reserve my remaining time.

Warren E. Burger

Thank you, Mr. Jones. Mrs. Ginsburg.

Ruth Bader Ginsburg

Mr. Chief Justice and may it please the Court.

Steven Wiesenfeld's case concerns the entitlement of a female wage earner, a female wage earners family to Social Insurance of the same quality as that accorded to the family of a male wage earner.

Four prime facts of the Wiesenfeld family's life situation bears special emphasis.

Paula Wiesenfeld, the diseased insured worker, was gainfully employed at all times during the seven years immediately preceding her death.

Throughout this period, maximum contributions were deducted from her salary and paid to Social Security.

During Paula's marriage to Steven Wiesenfeld, both were employed.

Neither was attending school and Paula was the family's principal income earner.

In 1972, Paula died giving birth to her son Jason Paul, leaving the child's father Steven Wiesenfeld with the sole responsibility for the care of Jason Paul.

For the eight months, immediately following his wife's death and for all but the seventh month period thereafter, Steven Wiesenfeld did not engage in substantial gainful employment.

Instead, he devoted himself to the care of the infant Jason Paul.

At issue is the constitutionality of the gender line drawn by 42 U.S.C. 402 (g), the child in care provision of the Social Security Act.

However, it's established this child and care insurance in 1939, as part of that year's conversion of Social Security from a system that insured only the worker to a system that provided a family basis of coverage.

The specific purpose of 402 (g) was to protect families of deceased insured workers, by supplementing the child's benefit provided in 42 U.S.C. 402 (d) with the deceased insured worker as male.

The family is afforded the full measure of protection, a child's benefit under 402 (d), and a child in care benefit under 402 (g).

Whether deceased worker is female, family protection is subject to a 50% discount.

A child in care benefit for survivors of a female insured worker is absolutely excluded even though as here the deceased mother was the family's principle bread winner.

This absolutely exclusion, based on gender per se, operates to the disadvantage of female workers, their surviving spouses and their children.

It denies the female worker social insurance family coverage of the same quality as the coverage available under the account of a make worker.

It denies the surviving spouse of the female worker.

The opportunity to care personally for his child and opportunity afforded the surviving spouse of a male worker and it denies the motherless child an opportunity for parental care, afforded the fatherless child.

It is appellee's position that this three-fold discrimination violates the constitutional rights of Paula, Steven, and Jason Paul Wiesenfeld to the equal protection of the laws, guaranteed to them with respect to federal legislation by the Fifth Amendment.

The care with which the judiciary should assess gender lines drawn by legislation is currently a matter of widespread uncertainty.

The District of Columbia Court of Appeals recently observed in while Waldie v. Schlesinger, decided November 20, 1974, precedent is still evolving and existing decisions of this Court are variously interpreted by the Lower Courts.

Appellant had urged in his brief, that it would be sufficient if any rationality can be conceived for the overt sex discrimination operating against the Wiesenfeld family.

But this Court acknowledged in Reed v. Reed, 404 US that the legislative objective there in question, producing probate court work loads did not lack legitimacy.

Yet, in light of the differential, based on gender per se the Court required a more substantial relationship between legislative ends and means so that men and women similarly circumstanced would be treated alike.

Again, in the Court's eight to one judgment in Frontiero v. Richardson, 411 US requiring the same fringe benefits for married men and women in the military, the Court evidenced a concern to analyze gender classifications with a view to the modern world and to be weary of gross, archaic, overbroad generalizations.

As in the case at Bar, in Frontiero, the underlying assumption was wives are typically dependent, husbands are not.

Hence, the statutory scheme in this case, as this scheme in Frontiero, favors one type of family unit over another and in both cases, the basis for the distinction is that in the favored unit the husband's employment attracts the benefit in question.

Where the bread winner is male, the family gets more, and where the bread winner is female, the family gets less.

Kahn v. Shevin, 416 US and Schlesinger v. Ballad, this Court's most recent expression, are viewed by some as reestablishing a slack or a cursory review standard, at least when the defender of the discrimination packages his argument with the protective or remedial libel.

Kahn approved Florida's $15.00 real property tax saving for widows.

The decision reflects this Court's consistent difference to State policy in areas of local concern such as State tax systems, domestic relations, zoning, disposition of property within the state's boarders.

By contrast national workers insurance and no issue of local concern, is in question here.

The differential in Schlesinger v. Ballard, this Court appointed out, did not reflect archaic, overbroad generalizations of the kind involved in Frontiero or in the instance case.

Indeed, there might have been a certain irony to a ruling in Lt. Ballard's favor.

To this day, women seeking careers in the uniform services are barred by Federal Statute and regulations from enlistment training and promotion opportunities open to men.

The Courts majority thought it a mismatch for Federal Law to mandate unequal treatment of women officers, denial to them of training and promotion opportunities open to men, a denial not challenged by Lt. Ballard, but to ignore that anterior discrimination for promotion and tenure purposes.

Perhaps most significantly, Kahn and Ballard are among the very few situations where a discriminatory advantage accorded some women is not readily perceived as a double-edged sword, a weapon that strikes directly against women who chose to be wives and mothers and at the same time to participate as full and equal individuals in a work centered world.

But there could not be a clear a case then this one of the double-edged sword in operation of differential treatment accorded similarly situated persons based grossly and solely on gender.

Paula Wiesenfeld, in fact the principal wage earner, is treated as though her use of work were of only secondary value to her family.

Steven Wiesenfeld, in fact the nurturing parent, is treated as though he did not perform that function and Jason Paul, a motherless infant with the child -- with the father, able and willing to provide care for him personally is treated as an infant not entitled to the personal care of his sole surviving parent.

The line drawn is absolute, not merely a more onerous test for one sex than the other as in Frontiero and Stanley v. Illinois, 405 US.

And a shout out is more extreme then it was in Reed, where a woman could qualify as administrator, if the man who opposed her, were closely related to the decedent.

This case, more than any other, yet heard by this Court, illustrates the critical importance of careful judicial assessment of law reinforced sex role pigeon-holing defended as a remedy.

For any degree of scrutiny that is more than cursory.

402 (g)'s conclusive presumption, automatically and irrebuttably ragging husband principal bread winner displays the pattern, Justice Brennan identified in Frontiero.

In practical effect, laws of this quality help to keep women not on the pedestal but in a cage.

They reinforced not remedy, women's inferior position in the labor force.

Appellant has pointed out that women do not earn as much as man and urges that 402 (g) response to this condition by rectifying past and present economic discrimination against women.

This attempt to wrap a remedial rational around a 1939 statute, originating in and reinforcing traditional sex based assumptions should attract strong suspicion.

In fact, Congress had in view male bread winners, male heads of household, and the women and children depended upon them.

Its attention to the families of insured male workers, their wives, and children is expressed in the scheme that heaps further disadvantage on the woman worker far from rectifying economic discrimination against women.

The scheme conspicuously discriminates against women workers by discounting the value to their family of their gainful employment and it intrudes on private decision making in an area in which the law should maintain strict neutrality for when federal law provides a family benefit base on a husband's gainful employment, but absolutely bars that benefit base on a wife's gainful employment.

The impact is to encourage the traditional division of labor between man and woman to underscore twin assumptions; first, that level for paying including attendant benefits is the prerogative of men; and second, that women but not men, appropriately reduce their contributions in the working life to care for children.

On another day, the pernicious impact of gender lines, like the one drawn by 402 (g), was precisely an accurately discerned by appellant, in common with every Government agency genuinely determined to breakdown artificial barriers and hindrances to woman's economic advancement.

Appellant has instructed that employer's fringe benefit and pension schemes must not presume, as 402 (g) does, that husband is head of household or principal wage earner.

It is surely irrational to condemn this sex line as discriminating against women when it appears in an employer's pension scheme while asserting that it rectifies such discrimination, when it appears in workers social insurance.

Potter Stewart

You say the appellant has taken these inconsistent positions. I assuming, he was -- it wasn't just his idea --

Ruth Bader Ginsburg

He was --

Potter Stewart

-- promulgating that for private pension schemes, but that he was carrying out his understanding of a federal statute?

Ruth Bader Ginsburg

He was carrying out inconsistent congressional commands.

Guidelines that he issued pursuant to Title IX of the Education Amendments of 1972 --

Potter Stewart

Right.

Ruth Bader Ginsburg

-- forbid recipients of federal money from making distinctions of this kind.

In sum, the prime generator of discrimination accounted by women in the economic sector is the pervasive attitude, now lacking functional justification that pairs women with children, men with work.

This attitude is short of and reinforced by laws of the 402 (g) variety, laws that tell a woman how employment is less valuable to and supportive of the family then the employment of a male worker.

Surely, Paula Wiesenfeld would find unfathomable, it's attempt to cast the compensatory cloak over the denial to her family of benefits available to the family of a male insured nor does appellant's rationalization for discrimination even attempt to explain why Jason Paul, child of a fully insured deceased worker can have the personal care of his sole surviving parent only if the deceased wage earning parent was male.

Appellant has asserted that providing child and care benefits under a female worker's account would involve fiscal considerations.

The amount involved is considerably less than was indicated some moments ago.

He estimates the cost for this particular benefit to be 0.01% of taxable payroll in the appendix at 16, and other differentials are not now before this Court.

At the same time he maintains --

Potter Stewart

Are you familiar, Mrs. Ginsburg with the little of chart on the top of page 15 on the appendix?

Ruth Bader Ginsburg

Yes, I am.

Potter Stewart

Could you tell us which one of these are we talking about?

Ruth Bader Ginsburg

We are talking about --

Potter Stewart

Which number?

Ruth Bader Ginsburg

Three.

Potter Stewart

Three?

Ruth Bader Ginsburg

We are talking about three, that's right.

The number of person affected 15,000 thousand, estimated benefit --

Potter Stewart

$20 million.

Ruth Bader Ginsburg

$20 million, right and that is the only one we're talking about in this case.

Potter Stewart

And the -- well --

Ruth Bader Ginsburg

Of course, there is someone in consistent argument made and that is that the bulk of widowed fathers would not qualify for child and care benefits in any event according to appellant because unlike Stephen Wiesenfeld, they would not devote themselves to child care, but rather to gainful employment.

Budgetary considerations --

Potter Stewart

And the children have to be under what, 18?

Ruth Bader Ginsburg

Yes.

A child has to be a child entitled to child's benefit under the Act.

Potter Stewart

Which means among other things that he is under 18?

Ruth Bader Ginsburg

Yes.

Budgetary considerations to justify invidious discrimination should fair no better in this case than such considerations faired in cases in which relatively larger cost savings were involved.

For example, New Jersey Welfare Rights Organization against Cahill, 411 US summarily reversing 349 federal supplement.

Warren E. Burger

What is the justification for benefits with respect to children, persons under age 18 as distinguished from having a line at 21 or 24 or some other age?

Ruth Bader Ginsburg

I don't know why the age line was set, but it's for all benefit purposes under the Social Security Act.

I think a distinction is made if a child is attending school after 18, but I'm not certain of that.

Warren E. Burger

But you don't need a baby sitter for --

Ruth Bader Ginsburg

No, you certainly don't.

Warren E. Burger

While at 14, 16, and 18 year old people, do you?

Ruth Bader Ginsburg

That's right.

And whether that Congress has gone too far in that direction is not of concern here.

Certainly, it has not gone too far when it considers that an infant such as Jason Paul Wiesenfeld, might benefit from the personal care of a parent.

Warren E. Burger

Well, is there any possibility that the reasoning for his claim depends somewhat on this age factor?

Ruth Bader Ginsburg

The reasoning for --

Warren E. Burger

The justification? If the justification is not warranted would that enter into it?

Ruth Bader Ginsburg

Presumably, the greatest need is for very young children, preschools children, and in many cases, the sole surviving parent, male or female, may not avail herself as the statute now stands of this benefit once the child gets beyond preschool age or school age.

Remember that this is not a benefit that is paid automatically no matter what.

There is an income limitation.

Once you earn beyond, it was $2,400.00, $1.00 a benefit is removed for ever $2.00 earned.

So, the parent who receives this benefit must be performing that function, must be performing the child care function.

Warren E. Burger

I suppose we're not confronted with that each problem unless a 19 year old brings at equal protection benefit sometime?

Ruth Bader Ginsburg

Well, but 18 years as the voting age now, I think that that is probably unlikely, but in any event, comparing the cost analysis here with the New Jersey Welfare Rights Organization case, that case involved a wholly state funded program for aid to families of the working poor.

This Court declared unconstitutional limitation of benefits under that program to families with wed parents.

Unlike New Jersey Welfare Rights Organization, the case at Bar presents no issue of federal difference arguably due to state family law policy or any other local concern.

And surely, leeway for cost saving is no broader in federal workers insurance than it is in a wholly state financed and operated welfare program, a program funded by general state revenues rather than by contributions of insured workers and their employers.

Budgetary policy like administrative convenience simply cannot provide a fair and substantial basis for a scheme that establishes two classes of insured workers, both subject to the same contributions work rate.

Male workers, whose families receive bulk protection and female workers whose families receive diminished protection.

Finally, the appropriate remedy is correctly specified in the judgment below.

That judgment declares the gender line at issue unconstitutional because it discriminates in violation of the Fifth Amendment against gainfully employed women such as Paula Wiesenfeld as well as against men and children who have lost their wives and mothers.

The judgment enjoins enforcement of the statute insofar as it discriminates on the basis of sex.

Extension of child and care benefits under Paula Wiesenfeld's account is unquestionably the cause consistent with the dominant congressional purpose to insure the family of deceased workers and the express congressional concern to ameliorate the plight of the deceased worker's child by facilitating a close relationship with the sole surviving parent.

Unequal treatment of male and female workers surely is not a vital part of the congressional plan.

Withdrawal of benefits from female parents who now receive them would conflict with the primary statutory objectives, to compensate the family unit for the lost of the insured individual, and to facilitate parental care of the child.

Under the circumstances, extension of benefits to the surviving spouse of female insured workers, to the father who devotes himself to child rearing is the only suitable remedy.

It accords with the express remedial preference of Congress in all recent matches of eliminating gender base differentials.

For example, 5 U.S.C. 7152 cited at pages 39 to 40 of our brief and with this Court's precedent in such cases as US Department of Agriculture v. Moreno, 413 US, New Jersey Welfare Right Organization against Cahill, 411 US and Frontiero v. Richardson, 411 US.

I did want to comment very briefly on the point made with respect to woman receiving social security benefits that exceed the amount of their contribution.

The reason for this, the prime reason of course, is that women live longer than men.

Most benefits are paid to retirement age beneficiaries and women happened to be 58% of the population of persons over 65 that increases in time there about 54.5% of the 65-year olds, 58.5% of the 75-year olds, and about 64.5% of the 85-year olds.

But the critical point here is that payments to the elderly are based on the individual's life span not on his or her sex.

So, that if a man should live to a 100, he will continue to receive benefits and he won't be told, "Oh!

Too bad, you should have died earlier, only women receives payments for that length of time."

In sum, appellee respectfully requests that the judgment below be affirmed, thereby establishing that under this nation's fundamental law, the Woman Workers National Social Insurance is no less valuable to her family than is the social insurance of the working man.

Warren E. Burger

Thank you, Mrs. Ginsburg. Do you have any further Mr. Jones?

Keith A. Jones

Yes, thank you Mr. Chief Justice. First, I would like to correct the typographical error on page 15 of the appendix. In item number two, it says eliminate the dependency requirement of Section 202 (d) that should be 202 (f). I point out that the appellee here is distinguished Kahn against Shevin which we rely or tried to distinguish it only on two basis. One is by relying upon the private insurance paradigm that female wage earners are entitled to a certain amount of insurance coverage. I discussed that at length in my opening argument. Second is that, Kahn in some sense of represents difference towards state taxing policies that appellee claims would not be due to federal welfare policies. I don't understand it's now analytical matter by federal distribution of public welfare funds should not be entitled to the same difference, state taxing policies. Appellee also argues that, the child here somehow has rights independent from that of either parent. I see no basis for that. The child has his own benefits under the Act. His only claim here is that one of his parents didn't get benefits. That claim is derivative from the claim of the parent, cannot be analyzed separately.

Potter Stewart

The thought of a third party beneficiary, you mean?

Keith A. Jones

That's right.

Potter Stewart

You mean the purpose of giving benefits to the parent is so that he can stay home and take care of the child, right?

Keith A. Jones

Well, I don't think that this legislative history backs that up necessarily that legislative --

Potter Stewart

What is its purpose then?

Keith A. Jones

Well, legislative history shows that the purpose of the statute was to distribute benefits in accordance with the probable new of beneficiaries and was made on the individual and not on the family basis. And it simply represents the judgment that women who seek employment or less likely to find it than do men and that if they do find it, they likely to earn less than do men.

Potter Stewart

Yes, but this doesn't unless I can -- if there were no children?

Keith A. Jones

If there were no children there --

Potter Stewart

At those -- those conditions, those presumptive conditions would still prevail, wouldn't they?

Keith A. Jones

If there are no children. The problems of job discrimination at least would not be exacerbated by the need to provide child care during the working hours. There is, I think, the justifiable difference between treatment of widows generally and the widows with minor children. If there are no further questions. Thank you.

Warren E. Burger

Thank you, Mr. Jones.

Thank you, Mrs. Ginsburg.

The case is submitted.

EDWIN EDWARDS, GOVERNOR OF LOUISIANA, et al. v. MARSHA B. HEALY, et al.

Facts of the Case: The Louisiana Constitution and statutes exempted women from service on juries unless they filed a written declaration of their desire to serve. This benign dispensation has resulted in jury panels that, in the parishes involved, had never included more than five percent females, and frequently less. When this case was being argued before the Supreme Court, recent changes to the Louisiana Constitution rendered the subject of the class action moot.

Question: Do exemption provisions for jury service on the basis of gender violate the rights of women to Equal Protection and Due Process of the Law?

Conclusion: The judgment of the District Court for the Eastern District of Louisiana was vacated and the case was remanded to that court to consider whether in the light of changes in the state constitutional, statutory, and other rules applicable to the case, the cause became moot.

Burger Majority	Stewart Majority	White Majority
Douglas Abstain	Marshall Majority	Blackmun Majority
Brennan Majority	Powell Majority	Rehnquist Majority

Edwards v. Healy Oral Arguments - October 16, 1974

Warren E. Burger

We'll hear arguments next in number 73-759, Edwards against Healy and Others. Mr. Vick, you may proceed whenever you're ready.

Kendall L. Vick

Mr. Chief Justice, may I please the Court. I'm Kendall Vick Assistant Attorney General, State of Louisiana for Governor Edwards and others. This case was brought by Miss Healy and others to challenge the Louisiana Constitution and Statutes, exempting women from service on juries unless they filed a written declaration of desire to serve. This matter was heard before a three-judge panel in the Eastern District of Louisiana comprised of Judges Wisdom from the Fifth Circuit, Judges Rubin and Blake West from the Eastern District of Louisiana. They found Hoyt Florida decided by this Court in 1961, a sterile precedent, no longer binding and held that the Constitution and statutory provisions of Louisiana unconstitutional as a denial of due process. After appeal in this case had been perfected, the people of the State of Louisiana adopted a New Constitution which the Attorney General believes will moot the issue presently before the Court, January 1, 1975. We filed a supplemental memorandum and type written and a supplemental brief printed reflecting those changes. Article V, Section 33 (a) of the New Constitution of Louisiana, makes every citizen who has attained majority eligible to serve on a jury and 33 (b) of Article V of the New Constitution of Louisiana, leaves exemptions to the Supreme Court of Louisiana. In the supplemental brief that I've supplied to the Court suggesting mootness, Exhibit One, starting on page five of the supplemental brief, which is a verbatim transcript of the convention's proceedings on the 36-day on August 24, 1973, which deals with this particular Section of the New Constitution clearly evidences, the overwhelming intention of that body made up of a 132 citizens of the State of Louisiana, that women be called for jury duty on the same basis as men. Exhibit Two in the supplemental brief to be found starting on page 25 is a draft order of the Supreme Court of the State of Louisiana implementing the intention of the convention.

William H. Rehnquist

Mr. Vick, what's the status of that draft order? Does that the word draft, I mean, it hasn't really been promulgated yet?

Kendall L. Vick

I dare say, if I please the Court, is very much like a draft opinion that you would circulate to your brother and I checked with the Director of the judicial counsel and also with Justice Tate, who is the author of this order, on Friday and he said they was still being circularized to his brother. I might add in an further answer to your question Your Honor, I was a delegate to the constitutional convention. Justice Tate, Associate Justice of the Supreme Court of Louisiana was a delegate to the convention. He is the author of this draft order and I have no doubt in my mind that this order will be in substantial form the way it appears here. Furthermore, on Friday --

Thurgood Marshall

I don't know where can you speak the Supreme Court of Louisiana?

Kendall L. Vick

I don't presume to do so.

Thurgood Marshall

Well, I thought you said --

Kendall L. Vick

I don't presume to do so. I was only reflecting --

Thurgood Marshall

Is that so, that one man has drafted an order, one member of the Court and it circulated period, is that the facts?

Kendall L. Vick

That is a fact.

Thurgood Marshall

Do we have anything more than that?

Kendall L. Vick

As of Friday, I have nothing more Your Honor.

Thurgood Marshall

Well, as of today --

Kendall L. Vick

As of today, nothing more. This morning --

Byron R. White

We still have your opinion as to what's going to happen?

Kendall L. Vick

Yes, Your Honor I do. I was about to say that on Friday the Attorney General issued an opinion to all clerks of Court in the State of Louisiana, directing them to put women in the wheel and in anticipation of January 1. I do not obviously have a -- did not have time to--

William J. Brennan, Jr.

What's the selection from voter's list or something?

Kendall L. Vick

Yes, Your Honor.

William J. Brennan, Jr.

Primarily or?

Kendall L. Vick

Yes, Your Honor. This morning, I was served with a reply to our brief suggesting mootness and I would like, if the Court please, to reject those portions that the Miss Ginsburg has raised out of hand because she has said, "While the volunteers only provision for female jury services not retained in the text of the New Constitution, nothing there in precludes continuation of the same exemption." I direct the Court's attention to the intention of the convention and furthermore, it directs the Louisiana's Supreme Court to provide by rule for exemption of jurors. No provision to become operative at midnight on December 31, 1974, caused change in existing system. I disagree, I think it most certainly does and the Attorney General has already taken steps in that direction as indeed the Supreme Court of State of Louisiana. And on page 2, she says, "the Louisiana Supreme Court has held time and again that exemption at issue in the instant case is neither a rational nor discriminatory." May it please the Court, the Supreme Court Louisiana was following the guidelines set down in Hoyt and I don't think they could do anymore or any less.

Potter Stewart

Mr. Vick, what's the practical importance of question of whether or not this case is moot to the? You're going to be arguing the next case which involves a conviction --

Kendall L. Vick

Well, that's --

Potter Stewart

And whether the same question arises and where no question of mootness could possibly exist. So, what is the practical importance of this?

Kendall L. Vick

Practical importance is to bring the Court to the Court's attention pursuant of the rules of this Court.

Potter Stewart

Which we appreciated --

Kendall L. Vick

Any change.

Potter Stewart

But I just wondered what -

-

Kendall L. Vick

Now, our position is whatever the Court has of course is a matter for --

Potter Stewart

Let's say --

Kendall L. Vick

Court.

Potter Stewart

Let's say, we agree that this particular case was moot but the same issue exist in the next case, where there can be no question with mootness, isn't that?

Kendall L. Vick

That's correct. But of course the appellants in that cases seeking reversal of a conviction.

Potter Stewart

Right.

Byron R. White

But don't you think that the defendant in the next case could loose that case and excluded potential women's jurors could win this case as an equal protection matter --

Potter Stewart

Depart from mootness, you mean?

Kendall L. Vick

It's possible. That's always a possibility.

Byron R. White

Well, I mean just legally and logically it could happen I take it?

Kendall L. Vick

Yes.

Byron R. White

So, it doesn't make some difference to whether this case is moot or not?

Kendall L. Vick

The only problem --

Byron R. White

But the other case may not determine this one?

Kendall L. Vick

Indeed. The only problem I have with that Your Honor is that when this man was tried Hoyt was good law and I assume its still is good law. Now, that's the only promise the State of Louisiana would have.

Byron R. White

What ground do you think the -- in this case, didn't the Court find this settled down on the -- on potential litigants as the ones with standing?

Kendall L. Vick

In the District Court?

Byron R. White

Yes.

Kendall L. Vick

Yes, You Honor.

Byron R. White

And wasn't the rationale of the Court that there was such an opportunity for bias, for biased jurors that the exclusion of women was unconstitutional?

Kendall L. Vick

Indeed, they did.

Byron R. White

Isn't that a due process matter?

Kendall L. Vick

It is indeed.

Byron R. White

Don't -- most due process decisions retroactive?

Kendall L. Vick

Well, they have been from time to time. Conversely Your Honor, the facts surrounding the conviction in the other case, I think might lend itself to a cry of passion of prejudice if indeed there were women in the jury, but I suppose we'll get into that then.

Byron R. White

That could be a Sixth Amendment decision?

Kendall L. Vick

It could indeed.

Byron R. White

Not a due process, isn't it?

Kendall L. Vick

Yes sir.

Byron R. White

Well, I mean it could be a Sixth Amendment through the due processes, isn't it?

Kendall L. Vick

Yes, You Honor.

Byron R. White

Which may be different than a -- the due process decision that has been rendered by the three-judge District Court, isn't it?

Kendall L. Vick

Yes, Your Honor.

William H. Rehnquist

Well, there could be a question of standing in this -- in the appeal from the criminal conviction, whether or not as to whether a man has standing to raise this claim?

Kendall L. Vick

Well, Your Honor. I'm almost prepared to concede that on the basis some decisions that have been handed by this Court recently. However, it is an arguable point.

Thurgood Marshall

What in Louisiana -- could the legislature give exemptions with the --

Kendall L. Vick

Not.

Thurgood Marshall

With the present 11.28?

Kendall L. Vick

Not under the present Constitution. May it please Your Honor, if you will read that is the entire purpose of taking out the legislators' hands. Mr. Ambrose Lamprey, who introduced the resolution making it a reflecting what it does now in the present and in the New Constitution, was the President of the Clerks of Court Association. He said unequivocally that he want to take out the hands of the legislature and putting it in the hands to the Supreme Court.

Thurgood Marshall

That word, I mean on the language itself doesn't it preclude the legislature?

Kendall L. Vick

Unequivocally.

Thurgood Marshall

That's what I thought.

Kendall L. Vick

Thank you.

Warren E. Burger

Very well. Mrs. Ginsburg.

Ruth Bader Ginsburg

Mr. Chief Justice, may it please the Court.

I will address first appellant's mootness suggestion.

In a judgment entered in September 1973, the Louisiana Constitution, Article VII, Section 41 and legislation enacted pursuant to it where declared unconstitutional by the Federal District Court for the Eastern District of Louisiana sitting as a three-judge court.

Article VII, Section 41, precludes jury service by women who do not file with the clerk of the Court, a written declaration of their desire to serve.

On April 20, 1974 while this appeal was pending, Louisiana adopted a New Constitution to become affective at the start of 1975.

On the basis of that development, appellant suggests that this controversy, although, not now moot will become moot on January 1, 1975.

The New Constitution as appellate has pointed out provides that all citizens who have reached the age of majority are eligible for jury service.

It authorizes the legislature to provide additional qualifications.

The legislature has not yet had its session to implement the constitutional divisions and it directs the Louisiana Supreme Court to provide by rule for exemption.

The draft order on exemptions under the New Constitution and next to appellant's memorandum suggesting mootness is at this stage merely a proposal.

It's interesting to note that it was drafted by Justice Tate, who has been a consistent dissenter from the

Louisiana's Supreme Court opinions upholding the jury service exemption for women.

The volunteer's only scheme remains fully operative until that system is discarded and replaced by a system that renders women and men equally amenable to jury service.

William J. Brennan, Jr.

Would that be true after January the 1st?

Ruth Bader Ginsburg

There is no way unknowing that --

Byron R. White

Is that volunteers only, would that continue after January 1st, until there was a Supreme Court rule?

Ruth Bader Ginsburg

Unless and until something comes from the Supreme Court or from the legislature there is nothing on which to base a change.

There's just a constitutional provision, is absence of a constitutional provision where there was one before.

In Hoyt v. Florida there was no constitutional provision involved, there was just a statute.

William H. Rehnquist

What is -- what will the New Constitution say about jury service Mrs. Ginsburg?

Ruth Bader Ginsburg

It will say, "Simply," this is practically verbatim from the text, "all citizens who have reached the age of majority are eligible for jury service."

The women are not eligible for jury service and then it authorizes the legislature to provide and the expression is additional qualifications and it directs the Louisiana Supreme Court to provide by rule for exemption.

William H. Rehnquist

What if neither of those bodies act and you simply have the constitutional provision and nothing else? What's the court of a typical --

Ruth Bader Ginsburg

Likely still to follow the statute and Louisiana Code of Criminal Procedure 402, which says that we don't put women on the list unless they register, the statute would still be enforced unless the legislature acts to ignore it.

William H. Rehnquist

Well, wouldn't it be inconsistent with the constitutional provision, it says all persons are eligible?

Ruth Bader Ginsburg

All persons are eligible for jury service or all citizens are eligible for jury service in Louisiana.

Now, it isn't a question of women's ineligibility.

Question is whether they are to be accorded an exemption under which they are not put on the list unless they affirmatively come in and volunteer for service.

Appellees and the class they represent, all female citizens of Louisiana engaged in State Court litigation in which trial by jury is sought.

They maintain that the Louisiana jury selection system which effectively excludes more than half of the population eligible for jury service, impacts adversely upon the state's adjudicatory system and denies all litigants jury trials consistent with representative Government and a democratic society composed of men and women.

More particularly, they assert that the Louisiana jury selection system denies them the equal protection of the laws and due process of law because the system precludes any possibility that their cases will be tried by a jury drawn from a representative cross-section of the community.

Rather the system assures that their peers, members of their sex, 53 % of the population of persons eligible for service are almost totally absent from the jury pool.

Appellees standing to challenge the absence of members of their class is evident.

Women are surely a cognizable group within the community.

They are a readily identifiable class similarly constant in membership.

As litigants, women are no less entitled to maintain a challenge of this kind than on members of a racial, national origin or religious group as --

Potter Stewart

The class -- the class was what? The plaintiff's --

Ruth Bader Ginsburg

There are three classes in the action as instituted in a District Court.

Judge Rubin left open the question of a standing of two of those classes.

He declared that the class of women litigants had standing and therefore, it was unnecessary to decide whether the class of woman as potential jurors or of men as potential jurors had standing.

Potter Stewart

So, that he allowed the class of women litigants or potential women litigants?

Ruth Bader Ginsburg

Yes.

Byron R. White

Only potential? Just potential, none of them are accidentally --

Ruth Bader Ginsburg

Oh, yes they were.

In fact Judge Rubin point specifically to Jenny Lee Smith Baggett, one of he named representatives of the cause of litigants.

She had filed a civil damage action.

Potter Stewart

Civil and/or criminal litigants?

Ruth Bader Ginsburg

That presented a certain problem.

The difficulty of joining women who are enmeshed in the criminal process, in a civil litigation report of three-judge Court, so our named representatives are all civil litigants, not criminal litigants.

However, they assert the interest of women litigants generally in both proceedings.

This Court noted in Ballard against United --

Potter Stewart

What is that claimed damage? What is their claimed injury?

Ruth Bader Ginsburg

Two claims.

One, that they are denied equal protection as any other well defined group would be by the total absence of their peers from the jury.

And --

Potter Stewart

Why -- I thought the new theory was that there's very little difference between men and women and so why wouldn't a men jury be there --

Ruth Bader Ginsburg

Well, I am not aware of that new theory. I subscribe and I think most people do to a theory announced by one of the justices some years ago in Ballard against the Unites States, that the two sexes are not fungible, that the absence of either may make the jury even less representative of the community than it would be if an economic or a racial group were excluded.

Potter Stewart

What was the other's injury? You said, one was denial of the equal protection to --

Ruth Bader Ginsburg

And the other is denial of due process.

The right of every litigant who is subject to jury trial to a jury that is drawn from a representative cross-section of the community and that is the right of all litigants male or female to that jury composed of a representative cross-section.

The difficulty for the three-judge court was this Court's 1961 --

Byron R. White

What's the source of that?

Potter Stewart

Yes.

Ruth Bader Ginsburg

What is the source of that?

Byron R. White

Provision of the Constitution 21.08?

Ruth Bader Ginsburg

Well, due process, yes.

William H. Rehnquist

What decision?

Ruth Bader Ginsburg

This Court has expressed in, for example, appeal against Southern Pacific Company 328 --

William H. Rehnquist

It was a Federal Court case?

Ruth Bader Ginsburg

Yes, but the proposition expressed that went beyond supervision of the Federal Judicial system.

The Court said that the American tradition of trial by jury in criminal or civil cases necessarily contemplates an impartial jury drawn from a cross-section of the community.

Byron R. White

Well, what -- the state could try these civil cases without any jury at all as far as any decision this Court is concerned?

Ruth Bader Ginsburg

Yes the -- well, at least I should put it even if there is no Seventh Amendment right to jury trial in a state court, once the State does provide a jury trial Justice White, the State does provide a grand jury though it's not required, then its selection and procedures become subject to equal protection and due process scrutiny as does any other state action.

On the merits, Hoyt against Florida upheld the statute virtually identical to the scheme at issue here and indeed this court has not yet explicitly reconsidered its 1880 dictum in Strauder against West Virginia, 100 U.S. at 310, that a state may constitutionally confine jury duty to males after Strauder, but before Hoyt in 1947 and Fay v. New York, 332 U.S.

The "blue ribbon" jury was contested but also in New York's automatic exemption of women, the Court upheld that women don't need exemption and in the process indicated that women might be beyond the pale of the Fourteenth Amendment.

The majority opinion in Fay assert that though, there maybe no logical reasoning for differential treatment of men and women for jury service purposes, the states are constitutionally compelled to acknowledge only one aspect of women's full membership in the political community, her Nineteenth Amendment right to vote.

The Fay Court was relying exclusively on the fact that well into the 20th Century, it was the virtually universal practice in the United States to allow only men to sit on juries.

Appellants had asserted in their jurisdictional statement and appellees agree, that this case presents an appropriate occasion for the Court to articulate guidelines and standards with respect to the equal amenability of women and men to jury service.

Because this Court's own past pronouncements have operated not merely to sanction women only jury service exemptions, devious from the start, but to impede change long over due though a majority of States now treat jury service as a basic civil right as well as a fundamental civic responsibility.

Potter Stewart

Is Louisiana -- Louisiana is unique as I understand it from the briefs, is it not?

Ruth Bader Ginsburg

In the registration system.

There are six other States that have one slight variant on that.

Women are placed in the jury pool but they are exempt simply because they are women and then there are several other States that have a range of women only exemptions and these exemptions persist well into the 1970's and challenges to them are rejected summarily by both federal and state courts.

Potter Stewart

For the basis of Hoyt, isn't it?

Ruth Bader Ginsburg

Yes, and Hoyt is precedent.

Potter Stewart

What's the present status Mrs. Ginsburg of the proposed equal rights amendment to the Constitution of the United States?

Ruth Bader Ginsburg

The proposed amendment has been ratified by 33 States.

The period in which ratification is open runs until 1979.

Potter Stewart

79?

Ruth Bader Ginsburg

Yes.

Potter Stewart

And it requires a how many States?

Ruth Bader Ginsburg

38.

Potter Stewart

38 and it's been ratified by 30?

Ruth Bader Ginsburg

33.

Potter Stewart

33.

William J. Brennan, Jr.

That include the two that have drawn?

Ruth Bader Ginsburg

No.

No, it adds a question not appropriate to go into at this point, but two have purported to withdraw their ratification.

Potter Stewart

Two and you're including those two in the 33?

Ruth Bader Ginsburg

I know I'm not.

It would be 31 if those withdrawals were effective.

Potter Stewart

Well, you're including those two in the 33?

Ruth Bader Ginsburg

I am including them, yes correct, yes.

Potter Stewart

So, there are at least five to go between now and 1979?

Ruth Bader Ginsburg

At least five and if you accept the argument that withdrawal is effective than seven. The --

Potter Stewart

How many have affirmatively rejected?

Ruth Bader Ginsburg

I don't know what the counties on that.

A number of States have rejected it but that doesn't -- that's not binding.

If a State that once rejects, I think that's --

Potter Stewart

Can later approve?

Ruth Bader Ginsburg

Yes.

Potter Stewart

So, long it is done before 1979 --

Ruth Bader Ginsburg

Yes.

Potter Stewart

By the date of 1979?

Ruth Bader Ginsburg

Yes and of course, that as would be expected, the States that have already ratified with States in which the ratification campaigns were easier than the remaining states.

Potter Stewart

The -- I asked that because I'm reminded that there is some discussion of that proposal amendment in the Frontiero opinion and --

Ruth Bader Ginsburg

Yes, yes.

The progress has been slow since the Frontiero opinion on ratification.

William J. Brennan, Jr.

Since or because of it?

Ruth Bader Ginsburg

I think it unrelated.

Potter Stewart

You think what?

Ruth Bader Ginsburg

Unrelated.

Potter Stewart

Oh.

Ruth Bader Ginsburg

Well, I'm -- I might have say with it -- that with respect to this Strauder dictum and without regard to any bold dynamic development of that dictum is totally understandable in it's historic context.

The common more jury was composed of three unlawful men not women and Blackstone had explained in the third volume of his commentary that, though the Latin word "homo" are referred to members of both sexes, the female was, of course, excluded from jury service because of the defects of her sex and that pattern was accepted in 19th Century even early 20th Century United States.

Why should the women serve on juries when they couldn't vote or hold office, when many of them, a married woman, were subject to a range of legal disabilities that drastically curtailed their scope of activity.

Hoyt decided just 13 years ago is not susceptible to the same kind of historical interpretation, but it maybe explained on the basis of an assumption apparently indulged by the Court, that the volunteers' only system might yet yield substantial female participation.

The system had been in effect in Florida only some 10 years at the time Hoyt was tried. Until 1949, Florida (Inaudible) jury said, "This is exclusively to men."

The three concurring justices were unable to say based on the Hoyt record that Florida failed to make an effort to have women perform jury duty and the majority opinion suggests that appellant Hoyt had not ruled out other circumstances for chance as one of the reasons for the porosity of women jurors.

But in the instant case, it is not disputed that the Louisiana selection system and only that system not other circumstances and not chance, produces jury list that rarely include any woman's name.

Based on the stipulated facts, the court below found that Louisiana's benign dispensation, not chance yields jury panels that never include more than 5% women and frequently less.

Significantly Mr. Justice Douglas, who concurred in Hoyt later acknowledged that inevitably, a volunteer's only system results in almost as total an exclusion as would obtain in women were not permitted to serve at all for --

Potter Stewart

In there any variation among the counties or parishes is I guess you call them in Louisiana?

Ruth Bader Ginsburg

I had not made a survey but I think that the stipulation was generous that not more than 10% are I think, I suppose less.

Potter Stewart

Anywhere, in the state?

Ruth Bader Ginsburg

Within in the State, Yes.

Byron R. White

Let assume but by the time this case is decided there's a new rule in Louisiana that does not exclude with women amenity that exactly like with respect jury duty, would this case of the moot or not?

Ruth Bader Ginsburg

By the time this case is decided?

In other words, if an exemption similar to the one attached to the memorandum is adopted and if the legislator doesn't put on additional qualifications and if the list, that's an important thing the implementation of it.

Byron R. White

Well, just answer my question. Let's assume that women and men are treat exactly alike under whatever new rules adopted with it.

Ruth Bader Ginsburg

Yes.

Then, there is a difficulty in my case that is not present in Taylor that is in showing injury.

If you're --

Byron R. White

All of your women plaintiffs would be eligible -- will be treated just like men.

Ruth Bader Ginsburg

Yes.

Byron R. White

And your --

Ruth Bader Ginsburg

And they are not claiming the damages for the past.

Byron R. White

And do your litigants and your civil litigants would have a right your potential litigants and litigants will have had their cases tried --

Ruth Bader Ginsburg

That's right.

Byron R. White

Would have -- have --

Ruth Bader Ginsburg

That's right.

Byron R. White

So, your case would be pretty empty, wouldn't it?

Ruth Bader Ginsburg

If that happens well, we don't -- its mere speculation whether it will happen --

Byron R. White

Oh, I understand that.

Ruth Bader Ginsburg

Yes.

It would be certainly difficult --

William J. Brennan, Jr.

Well, do you have any idea Mrs. Ginsberg what state plans in that regard? Is this the plan of the circulated Supreme Court document and whatever legislature is going to do or accomplish before the first of January?

Ruth Bader Ginsburg

It should be accomplished before the first of January because that's one that when the New Constitution goes into an effect whether it will be I don't know.

I was told at the Court --

William J. Brennan, Jr.

But the plan is to have it by then --

Ruth Bader Ginsburg

Yes.

I think that is right.

Byron R. White

And is true that the rule that is circulating is what represented to the circulating report?

Ruth Bader Ginsburg

Yes.

There is -- that is a draft rule drafted by Justice Tate that is now circulating.

What --

Byron R. White

Assume that rule becomes the law?

Ruth Bader Ginsburg

That rule, I might say is a model with jury exemptions.

It makes no distinction whatever between men and women.

It permits for excuses based on individualized circumstances and so that, in fact, is the rule of that appellees wished Louisiana had.

Byron R. White

Have any of you -- have any of your actual women litigants have their cases tried yet?

Ruth Bader Ginsburg

No.

No, not at this time.

Byron R. White

And you don't have --

Ruth Bader Ginsburg

And they can't ask --

Byron R. White

If you don't ask this to pass on the standing of any other group here --

Ruth Bader Ginsburg

Since the standing of the other groups --

Byron R. White

You're supporting the decision below?

Ruth Bader Ginsburg

Well, the decision below was to recognize clearly the standing of one group.

The standing of another group, I think, women as potential jurors is also clear in Judge Rubin's opinion at page 1114.

He does find unequivocally that women as jurors are denied equal protection.

Since the system conspicuously fails to meet the equal protection requirements for women as potential jurors because he made that finding on the merits, it's difficult to understand why he left over is the standing question and indeed appellees --

Byron R. White

Well, it is not difficult if he says, a potential woman who wants to serve on the jury claiming she's denied equal protection of the law. All she has to do is go ahead.

Ruth Bader Ginsburg

That was not his position and I suppose it wasn't because that's -- we could make an analogy to voting.

Suppose there was a requirement that all women were eligible to vote but they must come in and register, while the men automatically added to the list when they reached the age of 18.

I suppose that would also be saying that women could do if they wanted to do but that additional burden I think would be --

Byron R. White

But he did pass up their standing. The standing --

Ruth Bader Ginsburg

On the basis of the size of the class.

Not on the basis that they could register to service.

Thurgood Marshall

What difference does it make it? You got one class and you win, will you be satisfied?

Ruth Bader Ginsburg

Yes, of course, I'd be delighted.

Finally, I'd like to deal with the purported justifications for Hoyt that I heard in the Louisiana and in Federal State courts, passing on similar to those likely less extreme exceptions.

Two points are made.

One, it's administratively convenient to exclude the women as a class, and the other is we must be concerned with family stability.

As far as the administrative convenience of a lump exemption of an individual project excuse is concerned, this Court's decisions in Reed v. Reed 404 U.S. and Frontiero v. Richardson 411 U.S., should be dispositive administrative ease is not sufficient to justify legislative resort to a gender criteria.

With respect to ensuring the care of dependence, particularly small children, the women only exemption is a appallingly overbroad, and stereotypically underinclusive.

Overboard because it includes the childless woman, the woman whose children are grown, the woman who can provide without hardship or care consistent with her family's needs while she's away from home and underinclusive because it does not encompass men among them without fathers husbands with incapacitated wives whose presence at home maybe essential to the family's well-being, but the total rationality of the Louisiana classification is demonstrated by census data and labor market statistics.

Focusing on the statistics for Louisiana set out at pages 18 and 19 of our brief, in 1970, 59% of Louisiana's total adult female population had no children under 18 and of the 41% with children under 18, 37% were in the labor force.

Thus, for nearly three quarters of the population covered by this benign dispensation, child care is not a factor determining involvement in civic responsibility or in employment outside of home.

National statistics are similar.

Potter Stewart

Hoyt against Florida was decided less than 13 years ago?

Ruth Bader Ginsburg

Yes.

Potter Stewart

And it was a unanimous Court?

Ruth Bader Ginsburg

Yes.

Potter Stewart

You seem to could it really cavalierly, talking about it's purported justification and so on --

Ruth Bader Ginsburg

Well, I think they were two reasons I did not tend to be cavalier.

There was the point that -- no, two points.

One, there was no assurance at that time that this system would in fact produced no women.

The three concurring justices indicated that, that maybe if Florida makes it a good faith effort to try and get women, women will serve.

Later, I think it's been acknowledged that as a practical matter a volunteer's only system whether it's offered to men or women will lead to virtual absence of that group from the jury people simply do not, most people, do not volunteer for what they might regard as a burdensome civic responsibility.

That was one aspect of it.

The other aspect of it was that the statistics in Hoyt not the same as those presented here in addition to the tremendous increase even initial period of time, women's participation in the labor force.

Hoyt court, never adverted to all the unemployed women, who do not have childcare responsibilities, that was another factor and the third factor was the concentration in Hoyt on the woman as potential juror.

This was a benign dispensation of favor to her, she could serve if she wanted to, but she had no responsibility to serve.

Warren E. Burger

In my respect it was somewhat like Shevin against Kahn, wasn't it?

Ruth Bader Ginsburg

Well, if I may take a cue from Mr. Justice Brennan on that on his remark yesterday, Kahn against Shevin was a tax case and the dominant theme of that opinion is the large leeway, the line drawing permitted to the states in making tax classifications.

But what the focus on women jurors caused the Court to lose sight of what should have been the principle focus.

Now that action -- in that action, the defendant's crime was committed after an altercation in which she claimed her husband had insulted and humiliated her to the breaking point, convicted of second degree murder by an all-male jury.

She believed that women jurors might better understand her state of mind when she picked up a baseball bat and administered the blow that led to the litigation.

The Court did not focus on the denials of equal protection due process to Mrs. Hoyt.

The focus was on the benign nature of a classification to women as jurors rather than the unfairness to the litigant.

And that viewed in that light, the overriding consideration really should not be the burden or the benefit of jury service to perspective jurors, but the fairness of the system to litigants.

Potter Stewart

Louisiana has age limits against it, doesn't it?

Ruth Bader Ginsburg

No.

It provides an -- I think it --

Potter Stewart

Can a two-year-old child serve --

Ruth Bader Ginsburg

Oh!

Oh I'm sorry.

I though you meant upper age limits.

Yes, certainly than 18 is the age limit.

Potter Stewart

18?

Ruth Bader Ginsburg

Yes.

Potter Stewart

And under the draft proposal I think it says some 70, over 70?

Ruth Bader Ginsburg

The 70 would be the basis for an exemption, I think.

I don't --

Potter Stewart

Yes.

Ruth Bader Ginsburg

People are off the list.

Potter Stewart

So, there's a -- if a 75-year-old man is a litigant? Does he have a lawsuit? That he --

Ruth Bader Ginsburg

At 75 --

Potter Stewart

That he didn't got any jury of his peers --

Ruth Bader Ginsburg

Of course, there is a tremendous difference between age, which is something that happens to all of us --

Potter Stewart

75-year-old man or a woman?

Ruth Bader Ginsburg

-- and sex which is immutable and doesn't change.

And that's why age classifications should not properly be considered in the same light as classification based on a factor like race or sex or national origin something that is not going to happen to everybody.

You put in that status at birth and you can't get out of it.

Potter Stewart

Well, it's some few exemptions.

Ruth Bader Ginsburg

Which from (Inaudible) – [Attempt to Laughter]

Potter Stewart

Worry about the favor sometime?

Ruth Bader Ginsburg

Yes.

Well, --

Byron R. White

At least Hoyt put a rest of any claims at that time anyway that there was something bias about juries without women on it?

Ruth Bader Ginsburg

I don't think that it put --

Byron R. White

And in that respect -- in that respect the Hoyt can't hardly be squared can it with this three-judge court decision?

Ruth Bader Ginsburg

But Hoyt cannot be squared with these three judge court decision.

This three judge court said in Hoyt was --

Byron R. White

And you can talk about --

Ruth Bader Ginsburg

Sterile precedent and --

Byron R. White

You can talk about, I mean, there are other reasons, that if it talked about Hoyt another jury cases, will you focus on the equal protection ramifications of excluding some potential jurors from serving on the jury without records to who the defendant is or what the consequences to the defendant might be --

Ruth Bader Ginsburg

Yes.

Byron R. White

-- but Hoyt involved the woman defendant in a criminal charge?

Ruth Bader Ginsburg

Yes.

And I think that --

Byron R. White

And the question was -- one of the questions was, whether exclusion of women -- that there was an unfair jury not whether there are some other --

Ruth Bader Ginsburg

Well, there after all women are like men so they represented a cross section so it can be achieved by having men represent women.

Byron R. White

I know, but the judge -- the judgment you're defending is that excluding women means they are unfair bias juries?

Ruth Bader Ginsburg

Now, this, --

Byron R. White

Now, what's happen since Hoyt?Did they think --

Ruth Bader Ginsburg

This point has acknowledged that this --

Byron R. White

-- that juries without women on are more unfair today than they were 15 years ago?

Ruth Bader Ginsburg

If it were necessary to prove the unfairness in any particular case that would be virtually impossible standard --

Byron R. White

But what's happened to say, that in enough cases it happened that you want to have a general rule about it?

Ruth Bader Ginsburg

But it is a general rule I believe, I mean not only from (Inaudible) but from Williams case --

Byron R. White

But it wasn't in Hoyt?

Ruth Bader Ginsburg

No, it certainly wasn't in Hoyt, but there been a lot of jury cases in this Court, Carter against Jury Commission, Williams against Florida, talking about the essential attributes of a jury trial and one of the critical attributes is that it would be drawn from a representative cross section of the community, something that cannot be achieved if women are absent --

Byron R. White

Can I suggest to you that the representative cross section requirements more related to equal protection than the due process in the sense of unfairness, equal protection and the sense of protecting members of the community from exclusion from jury service?

Ruth Bader Ginsburg

Well, I think that it has come up in at least three context equal protection, due process, and then specifically, in the context of the Sixth Amendment.

Byron R. White

Well, do you know of a case that says because of the -- because of the lack of a fair cross section just generally unfair cross section that you conclude that there is a unfair and unfairness in the jury in the sense that it is biased or that there could be an unreliable result?

Ruth Bader Ginsburg

A case in this Court?

There are several District Court decisions.

All men --

Byron R. White

There's a lot of them -- there are a lot of them that say that you have to have fair cross sections.

Ruth Bader Ginsburg

Yes.

Byron R. White

But what interest you're taking about that requirement furthers? Now, this --

Ruth Bader Ginsburg

Well, --

Byron R. White

-- this district judge didn't say that the problem here was a cross section problem and it was a problem excluding women and then --

Ruth Bader Ginsburg

And this -- I think --

Byron R. White

And a jury without women on it trying a woman defendant would be unfair.

Ruth Bader Ginsburg

If the Court -- I think said that in due process discussion in the context of the cross section requirement.

What it did say was that, the absence of women makes impossible this cross section.

The cross section is essential to the integrity of the jury system, is inherent in due process of law and therefore as a safeguard for all litigants.

That was the determination of the court below similar to the position taken by Justice Marshal in Peters v. Kiff.

I think, I've got no time --

Warren E. Burger

I'm not sure you need any defense Mrs. Ginsburg, but your brief and argument is much less cavalier toward Hoyt than the three judges of the Fifth Circuit. Mr. Vick, do you have anything further?

Kendall L. Vick

No, Mr. Chief Justice.

JOSEPH CALIFANO v. LEON GOLDFARB

Facts of the Case: Leon Goldfarb was a widower who applied for Social Security survivor's benefits. His application was denied even though his wife had paid Social Security taxes for 25 years. To be eligible for benefits (under 42 U.S.C. Section 402), he had to have been receiving half his support from his wife at her time of death. Section 402 did not require this of widows whose husbands had recently passed away. Goldfarb challenged this statute under the Due Process Clause of the Fifth Amendment in the United States District Court for the Eastern District of New York. The District Court decided that the statute was unconstitutional. The Government appealed to the Supreme Court.

Question: Is the Due Process Clause of the Fifth Amendment violated by the gender-based requirements for survivor's benefits in Section 402?

Conclusion: Yes. In a 5-4 decision, the Court affirmed the District Court's decision that the statute was unconstitutional. Writing for a four-justice plurality, Justice William J. Brennan, Jr. described this situation as "indistinguishable" from the one in Weinberger v. Wiesenfeld, where a similar statute was struck down. In this case, a female worker's family was less protected than the family of a male worker. The court rejected the "archaic and overbroad" generalizations that a wife is more likely to be dependent on her husband than a husband on his wife. These "old notions" of gender roles weren't sufficient to justify the disparate treatment of widows and widowers, and was therefore in violation of the Due Process Clause.

Burger Dissent	White Majority	Marshall Majority
Brennan Majority	Blackmun Dissent	Powell Majority
Stewart Dissent	Rehnquist Dissent	Stevens Majority

Califano v. Goldfarb Oral Arguments - October 5, 1976

Warren E. Burger

We will hear argument next in 75-699 Mathews against Goldfarb. Mr. Jones, you may proceed whenever you are ready.

Keith A. Jones

Mr. Chief Justice and may it please the Court. This case is here on appeal from the United States District Court for the Eastern District of New York. The issue concerns the imposition of a support test on widowers, but not widows as a condition on eligibility for Social Cecurity survivors' benefits. The appellee is a retired federal employee and a widower. Following the death of his wife he applied for Social Security widower's benefits, under his deceased wife's earnings account. That is he sought to tack Social Security retirements benefits, Social Security survivors' benefits on to his existing civil service pension. If appellee had been a private employee rather than a civil servant, he would not have been able to tack benefits in this way even without regards of the support test he challenges here. Reason for this is that both widows and widowers to be eligible for survivors' benefits must pass what may for convenience be called the PIA test. PIA refers to the Primary Insurance Amount, which is the maximum monthly old age benefit to which a veteran is entitled under his or her own earnings account. Only a survivor whose PIA is less than that of the deceased spouse is entitled to a survivors' benefits and it is undisputed that if appellee's lifetime earnings have been covered by Social Security, he could not have passed this test. The PIA test bars a widower from tacking a smaller survivors' benefit on to an existing Social Security old age benefit. The theory behind this rule is that Social Security benefits are not vested rights, but are payable on the basis of probable need. If a widower is already receiving old age benefits in access of the survivors' benefits to which he would otherwise be entitled, he probably is not needy. But the PIA test standing alone is insufficient, inadequate to weed out non-needy federal pensioners, such as appellee. It is inadequate to weed out this category of non-needy widowers. To achieve this end of weeding out such widowers, Congress has imposed a second test, the support test that is at issue in this case. Under this test a widower must prove that he was receiving more than one half of his support from his wife at the time of her death, disability or retirement. The practical effect of the support test is suggested in the Appendix to our Brief. In short, if the support test were eliminated, approximately $447 million annually would be required to be distributed to non-needy widowers and out of this from $300 million to $350 million would be required to be distributed to non-needy pensioners such as appellee.

Potter Stewart

Mr. Jones, it is been a while that I have read these briefs in this case, they might write in understanding that the basic PIA test is applicable alike to males and females.

Keith A. Jones

That is correct Mr. Justice Stewart.

Potter Stewart

That is only this additional test that differentiates...

Keith A. Jones

That is correct, it is correct.

Potter Stewart

...between men and women.

Keith A. Jones

The problem in this case is that the support test does not apply to women. A widow age 60 year older who passes the PIA test is entitled to survivors' benefits without regard to support. Thats is a woman, similarly situated to appellee that is a retired female civil servant whose husband's lifetime employment had been covered by Social Security, would be entitled to survivors' benefits and this loophole in the Social Security law does not appear ever to have received explicit congressional attention. And it is upon the existence of this loophole that creates different treatment for this small narrow class of men and women upon which appellee's case largely depends.

John Paul Stevens

Mr. Jones I am also a little rusty on the case. This $440 million figure which applies to the small narrow class, is that based anything on the record or is that something you have developed subsequently just in the briefs here?

Keith A. Jones

It is not in the record Mr. Justice Stevens. The methodology underlying the estimate is spelled out in the Appendix to our Brief on the merits. The amount involved was not for an issue in the District Courts as far as I understood it. The appellee could not pass the support test, he had not in fact been dependent upon his wife and for that reason he was denied widower's benefits. He then brought this suit in District Court and the District Court declared the support test as to widowers unconstitutional. Relying in large part upon this Court's opinions in Wiesenfeld that is Weinberger against Wiesenfeld and Frontiero against Richardson. Before turning to a discussion of those two cases which underpin the appellee's arguments here, I would like to make some general observations about the appellee's arguments on the merits. Although appellee is a man and it is the denial of benefits to himself that he complains of, he has sought to portray the statutory classification as discriminating principally against women. He contends that the real discrimination here is against the deceased working wives whose widowers must now prove support. That is largely against the deceased working wives of civil servants. Of course, as an analytical matter the discrimination if any, bears equally upon these widowers and their deceased working wives. These two categories, one male and one female, necessarily are present here in a one to one ratio. That suggests that this case does not involve sex discrimination at all, but rather discrimination, if any, against certain kinds of families that is appellee's kind of family. But putting that aside at a minimum, all other things being equal, the choice of which sex to characterize is the disadvantage class here would appear to a matter of purely rhetorical significance, yet all other things are not equal. There is no legislative motive here to discriminate against women. Congress plainly designed the support test, simply to deny benefits to non-needy widowers, such as appellee. The difference in treatment is aimed at men not at women. Since this is so it may seem all the more puzzling, why the appellee has worked so hard to characterize the support test as discriminating principally against women. But there are suspect three good reasons for this approach. First, appellee is attempting to obscure the fact that what he seeks here is a double benefit that is it is a windfall in a nature of Social Security survivors' benefits on top of the civil service pension.

Potter Stewart

Yeah, but if he were -- if the genders were reversed she would get this windfall, right?

Keith A. Jones

That is correct Mr. Justice Stewart that is the loophole. Widows would get the benefit.

Potter Stewart

Well, anytime if somebody does not like a provision of the law he calls it a loophole, this is a provision of the law.

Keith A. Jones

Sometimes they call it unconstitutional. But it does seem to me that the appellee understandably seeks to divert the Court's attention away from the obvious rationality of Congress' decision to deny him this double benefit. In that purpose I would like to frustrate that it is claimed here that what he seeks is a windfall. It is true, it is a windfall that is available to women and of a special narrow class, but that does not mean it is a constitutional matter. It should also be made available to him.

Potter Stewart

Well that is the question in this case, isn't it?

Keith A. Jones

That is correct Mr. Justice Stewart. I think the second reason that the appellee seeks to characterize this as a women's rights case, but that the cause of women's is now a fashionable one and the appellee seeks to ride on its skirt tails, but it is the responsibility of this Court to act on the basis of what reflects a proper accommodation of the respective roles of Congress and the Courts and not to act on the basis of what maybe favored by the shifting tides of extra judicial legal fashion. But the third reason by appellee maybe characterizing this as a women's rights case is the one that disturbs me the most. Appellee maybe implicitly suggesting, that the rights of women are constitutionally entitled to higher protection than the rights of men. As a lawyer and as a member of the class that would thereby be disadvantaged I would urge this Court to reject any such settled suggestion. Women constitute a majority of the voting age population in this country, unlike racial minorities for example, women have the political power, if they choose to use it to remedy any statutory inequality of which they perceive themselves to be the victims. In short, women are not a discrete insular minority that requires special judicial protection against an indifferent or a hostile legislature. This is not to say that women have not been subject to legal and social discrimination in the past. That history of discrimination justifies remedial legislation that extends to women certain benefits or opportunities that may not be made available on the same basis to men. This Court so held in Kahn against Shevin, but further than that, the Courts may not go. Men and women are entitled to the same stature under the constitution. The ssame constitutional analysis must apply whether the discrimination of which appellee complaints is directed against men or against women. With these preliminary thoughts in mind, I would now turn to discussion of this Court's opinions in Frontiero and Wiesenfeld. Statutory classification at issue in Frontiero was conceitedly, superficially quite similar to the one involved here. But superficial similarities of that kind are largely irrelevant to equal protection analysis. At the heart of any equal protection inquiry is whether the challenge classification is rationally related to a permissible and a substantial legislative objective. In Frontiero the differential treatment accorded men and women, furthered no objective other than mere administrative convenience. The Government so conceited and this Court so held, and that objective the Court held was insufficiently substantial that justified the difference in treatment. That rationale is not applicable here. The statutory classification challenged here is not routed in mere administrative convenience. Instead, as I will show momentarily, the classification reflects Congress' legitimate efforts rationally to allocate source that scarce, Social Security's moneys on the basis of the probable needs of competing classes, special beneficiaries. Yes Mr. Justice Stevens.

John Paul Stevens

Would it not be correct that the decision not to require a support test in the converse situation is just justified by administrative convenience?

Keith A. Jones

It is justified by several factors and administrative convenience is one of them.

John Paul Stevens

What are the others?

Keith A. Jones

It is not rooted in the administrative convenience. Well, the rational bases or the social welfare considerations on which the Government relies here are spelled out at length at Pages 15 to 36 of our main Brief. But I can summarize them here. The Social Security provisions for widows and widowers have a separate and different history. In 1939, Congress determined to pay monthly benefits to those groups of survivors whose probable need was the greatest and it identified those groups, its elderly widows, dependent children and aged dependent parents and although a major purpose of the support test, excuse me, of the survivors' benefits was to replace the support lost by a dependant upon the death of the wage earner. Congress did not restrict widow's benefits to those women who were in fact dependant upon their husbands and the reasons for this Mr. Justice Stevens were too full. First, in 1939 and for many years thereafter, very few aged women were in fact economically dependent upon their husbands and to impose the support test, would have placed a substantial burden upon all of those widows and upon the administrative agency as well. That burden would have been incurred to weed out a very small percentage of non-dependent women. The appellee here conceits, that the imposition of the support test upon widows would entail, and I quote from Pages 65 and 68 of his Brief, "an exorbitant administrative burden, a potentially monstrous proportion". That is the appellee's language that is not our language, so that to some extent Mr. Justice Stevens, you are correct that the extension of benefits to women does have some basis at administrative convenience, but at the same time, the non-dependent women who would have been weeded out by a support test, are very likely to have been needy in any event. Then the women who had passed the support test that is the women who receive less than half their support from their husbands are very likely to have been either deserted or to have been living in other circumstances of substantial need. Very few aged widows were truly self sufficient and it was both reasonable and should remain for Congress to extend widow's benefits to these women without regard to dependency.

John Paul Stevens

Does not your argument suggest that there is not necessarily a correlation between the ability to pass the support test and probable need at the time of the applicant applies for benefits?

Keith A. Jones

That is certainly true as to widows and it was truer perhaps, in 1939 than it is today. But at that time -- and I must confess that these statistics are very rough, but at that time, it is a fair inference that considerably fewer then 10% of all women would have passed the support test at any given point in time. Not only…

John Paul Stevens

Would have thought for support test.

Keith A. Jones

Would have thought for support test, that is correct. They would have been non dependent, that is correct. At any given point in time, at any point during their employment history. As to women age 55 and older, there was a decrease in their participation in the job market. So that, it would be considerably less than 10% for this age group, but not only that, these are women who probably did not work over the full course of their working lives, who may have worked sporadically, but who probably did not build up substantial social earnings, entitlements or other retirement benefits, so that has to these -- as to this class of working women, it is a fair assumption I think that even those women who were non dependent at the critical point, still existed in circumstances of need. Now, the same is not true I submit generally as to widowers. A program of widower's benefits was established later in 1950 and at that time, Congress reasonably identifies as presumptively needy only those widowers who had been dependent upon their wives for support. With few exceptions, non-dependent men either had substantial Social Security entitlements or they had been gainfully employed in positions outside the Social Security systems like the appellee, and they therefore, fell outside the category of probable need. The support test served to weed out approximately 97% of all widowers, whereas they would have only weeded out less than 10% of widows, and if the support test had not been imposed from 75 to 90% of the additional moneys, that would have been required to be paid out, would have been paid to non-needy pensioners such as the appellee, and Congress rationally chose not to spend its scarce Social Security moneys in that manner.

Byron R. White

But I suppose there are some widowers who are needy, but who cannot pass the support test.

Keith A. Jones

It depends upon what you mean by needy Mr. Justice White, it is conceivable that there may…

Byron R. White

I mean what is considerable as a support test, what is the purpose of the support test in the first place?

Keith A. Jones

To weed out the non needy basically.

Byron R. White

Oh, yes to weed out the needy which implies that there are some that are not needy or you would not have to weed anybody out.

Keith A. Jones

Well, I think as a practical matter -- well, it implies that some are not -- excuse me, I misunderstand you, implies that some widowers are not needy…

Byron R. White

Well, my additional question was, aren't there some widowers who are needy even though they can not pass the support test?

Keith A. Jones

Again, Mr. Justice White, I say that that may well depend upon the standard of neediness that you use in a welfare system. It is certainly hypothetically possible that there are some men who were self supporting, who nevertheless were needy. Now, there are of course, supplementary programs which are designed to alleviate the need of those people whose need has not been entirely met by the Social Security action.

Byron R. White

Has the man involved in this case ever indicated that he was needy?

Keith A. Jones

He has not, it was our understanding that…

Byron R. White

Would the case here be any different if he had?

Keith A. Jones

Well, it would certainly be more attractive on facts for the other side. But as a statistical matter Mr. Justice White, 85% roughly of the benefits that we are talking about, go to civil service pensioners. They are plainly not needy and of the other percentages where we can not say with certainty that no needy person would thereby be given benefits, but as a practical matter, it is a rare member of the so-called disadvantaged class here who in fact is needy. Maybe I misunderstood, but as I understood my Brother White's question it was directed, or at least my question is directed to this proposition. Why is the fact that a widow or a widower may have received more than one half of his support during the lifetime of his spouse, from his spouse relevant to his present neediness?

Keith A. Jones

Well, the time in which it is measured is not during the lifetime, that is the time of the death, retirement or disability of spouse. At the time of the spouse's death, why is that fact relevant to his present state of need?

Keith A. Jones

If he was dependent upon his wife at that point and if he is a retired widower, then it is unlikely that he has extrinsic sources of support and the retirement, excuse me, the survivors' benefit serves to replace the support he has in fact lost. We may say that he is presumed needy by virtual impact. It is really equivalence, isn't it, or it could be non-equivalence, isn't that the case?

Keith A. Jones

Well, I do not think it could be said to be a non-equivalence except in those rare instances of perhaps not so rare, but in those instances where the woman has substantial independent wealth which the man will inherit upon her death. But, other than, in those situations, if he was in fact dependent upon her at the time of her death, it is very probable that he has lost support, support which the Congress has deemed, he needs to have replaced.

Byron R. White

Well then how about the consequences if he was not dependent upon her at the time of her death.

Keith A. Jones

Then he is ineligible for benefits.

Byron R. White

Well, I know but what has that got to do with need now?

Keith A. Jones

If he were not dependent upon her at the time of her death, then he has lost little in the way of support and can be presumed to be continuing on whatever sources of support that he had in the past. Now, it is true that this is not a means test; it does not definitively distinguish between those persons acutely in need and those who are not.

Byron R. White

Weel, to that extent, it is an administrative convenience argument, I suppose.

Keith A. Jones

Well, I think that any support test, any dependency test is only roughly equivalent to need, for example, in Mathews against Lucas, last term, this Court upheld a statute which imposed upon illegitimate children a dependency test or support test, even though a similar test was not imposed upon legitimate children. The criterion was considered substantially, rationally related to a need to distinguish between those who would need additional support and those who did not and this statute serves exactly the same purpose. Now, it is true that we have here, as we did in Lucas, a problem of overinclusiveness. The statute provides benefits to certain women, federal, retired, civil servants and certainly other women that are not made available, benefits are not made available to similar situated men. But mere overinclusiveness, without more, does not render a statute unconstitutional. Well, let me backtrack for a moment to make a few comments about the Wiesenfeld opinion on which appellee and the Court below had partially relied. The Wiesenfeld opinion must be conceded contains language that have taken a face value, but requires a widower support test to be struck down. The Court stated that "The constitution forbids gender based differentiation that results in the efforts of female workers producing less protection for their families and as produced by the efforts of men." But that statement can not be lifted bodily and applied out of context. In the first place, the statement was made with regard to a statute that the Court found have no rational basis. The Court's rationale in Wiesenfeld was that the statutory bar against father's benefits was inconsistent with the legislative purpose providing children deprived with one parent with the opportunity for the personal attention of the other. Neither that rationale, nor any similar rationale, is available here. The support test for widowers is fully consistent, I submit with the underlined legislative purpose of restricting benefits to those groups that may largely be presumed to be non-need, excuse me, to be needy. But secondly, if the statement in Wiesenfeld were detached from its factual context, it would amount to a per se constitutional rule, that is what appellee suggest that it is. But the Due Process Clause affords no basis for such a rule, such a flat declaration of what Congress may not do in the Social Security Act would, I submit, constitute a radical and unwise departure from historical principles of equal protection that would allow no way to be given to governmental interest that might be served by a particular gender based classification. This Court has always given way to such interest in equal protection cases in the past and it should do so here. Mr. Chief Justice, I would like to reserve my remaining time.

Warren E. Burger

Very well. Mrs. Bader, Mrs. Ginsburg.

Ruth Bader Ginsburg

Mr. Chief Justice and may it please the Court.

Leon Goldfarb's case concerns a differential in the quality of social insurance accorded men and women.

Pursuant to the Federal Insurance Contributions Act, payments into Social Security's old age and survivors' insurance program are exacted from gainfully employed men and women without regard to the sex of the contributor, whether the wage earner is a man or a woman, equal earnings require equal contributions.

In contrast to the gender neutral contribution system the program draws a sharp line between the sexes amid pay outside.

Benefits to a spouse available under a male wage earner's account are not equally available under a female wage earner's account.

The Court below ruled that this separate and unequal payout system discriminates invidiously against

the wage earning woman and her spouse.

That decision and all other, five other, the Federal Court judgments on the same point. Solidly anchored to this Court's 1973 judgment in Frontiero v. Richardson and 1975 decision in Weinberger v. Wiesenfeld.

Thus the issue on which this appeal turns is cleanly posed, do Frontiero and Wiesenfeld impart principled cses for deciding gender discrimination cases formed from the same mould or all the Frontiero and Wiesenfeld precedence shallow and evanescent as the Secretary would have it today.

In Wiesenfeld the Court declared unconstitutional, the Social Security Act's provision of a mother's benefit, but no father's benefit.

When Wiesenfeld was presented to this Court, the Solicitor General described the gender differential varied issue as very closely analogous to the one at par, and in Frontiero the Court held unconstitutional a military fringe benefit arrangement displaying a gender line, virtually identical to the one at par.

In defending the Frontiero classification, the Solicitor General noted similar distinctions are found in other federal laws.

He supplied as a sole example, 42 U. S. C. Section 402 the very Social Security provision now before the Court.

Like Stephen Wiesenfeld and Sharron and Joseph Frontiero, Leon Goldfarb challenged an employment related benefit scheme that attributes to the male wage earner, status, dignity and importance not attributed to the female wage earner.

As the Secretary recites the old age and survivors' insurance at issue, took shape in two stages: First, in 1939, Congress ordered that the male workers' Social Security account should attract benefits for his spouse without regard to husband's and wife's respective contributions to family income.

Potter Stewart

Mrs. Bader may I interrupt for a moment. You heard about what is your -- what our friend Mr. Jones had to say preliminarily about whether or not this is anti-female discrimination or anti-male discrimination, and I suppose you would agree that it can be cast either way you cast it as anti-female discrimination, anti-female wage earner discrimination that could be equally cast as anti-male beneficiary discrimination, but in any event, do you think there is any constitutional difference? Let us say the statute wherever it says widow, it said widower and vice versa, let us just turn the coin around and say the statute was the other way, would it make any constitutional difference? Would you have just as strong or and no more strong or any constitutional argument?

Ruth Bader Ginsburg

At the lines what he has like virtually, every gender discrimination is a two edged sword.

It works both ways.

Potter Stewart

Because some of the opinions of this Court and other Courts have when they have seen anti-female discrimination have relied for their constitutional decisions upon the history of anti-female discrimination, there has been so such history of anti male discrimination. I guess as a matter of historic fact.

Ruth Bader Ginsburg

Because most anti-female discrimination was dressed up as discrimination favoring the woman.

Potter Stewart

I know that, but should the Courts through help of those advocates such of you as a view I have been able to see through that?

Ruth Bader Ginsburg

The point is that the discriminatory line almost inevitably hurts women.

Potter Stewart

No, my question is if this were purely an anti-male discrimination and let us assume it were, would you have a stronger constitutional argument in your view?

Ruth Bader Ginsburg

My argument would be the same because I do not know of any purely anti-male discrimination.

In the end, the women are the ones who end up hurting.

I should point out that in 1950, when Congress authorized these benefits under the female workers account, the dependency test that was attached was very stringent dependency test.

It was not a question of whether the woman…

John Paul Stevens

Can I interrupt you just to be sure to understand your position in response to Justice Stewart, is it your view that there is no discrimination against males?

Ruth Bader Ginsburg

I think there is discrimination against males.

John Paul Stevens

Now, if there is such a discrimination is it to be tested by the same or by a different standard from discrimination against female?

Ruth Bader Ginsburg

My response to that Mr. Justice Stevens is that almost every discrimination that operates against males operates against females as well.

John Paul Stevens

Is that a yes or a no answer? I just do not understand you and are you trying to avoid the question or…

Ruth Bader Ginsburg

No, I am not trying to avoid the question.

I am trying to clarify the position that I do not know of any line that does not work as a two edged sword as we heard both…

John Paul Stevens

But we hear a case this morning just to be pre-involving a law that would not permit males to make certain purchases that females could make. It was attacked as a discrimination against male.

Ruth Bader Ginsburg

Yes.

John Paul Stevens

My question is whether we should examine that law under a same or a different standard when if it were a discrimination against the other sex?

Ruth Bader Ginsburg

My answer to that question is no, in part because such a law has an insidious impact against females.

It stands then docile compliance and safe to be trusted.

John Paul Stevens

If your answer always depends on their finding some discrimination against females, you seem put that in every answer to this question.

Ruth Bader Ginsburg

My answer was that I have not yet come across the statute.

It does not have that effect.

John Paul Stevens

But if there were one you would say it should be tested under a different standard?

Ruth Bader Ginsburg

If there were such a statute, I would reserve judgment on what the standards should be.

In any case I have not come across such a statute in my...

John Paul Stevens

So, your case depends then on our analyzing this case as a discrimination against female?

Ruth Bader Ginsburg

No, my case depends on your recognition that using gender as a classification resorting to that classification is highly questionable and should be closely reviewed.

Justice

There is always in fact a discrimination against females.

Ruth Bader Ginsburg

Yes, as far as I have seen.

Justice

That is your position.

Ruth Bader Ginsburg

That is the ultimate effect of such line drawing.

Justice

How, in fact you should use this Court's opinion in Shevin against Kahn into this follow through you are having with my brothers.

Ruth Bader Ginsburg

In Kahn against Shevin, that the Court analyzes that classification as helpful to some women harmful to none.

If you accept that analysis well then you might rationalize that as a compensatory classification that could survive constitutional review, in addition, it was a very small matter involved in Kahn v. Shevin.

Justice

But it did survive a constitutional certainly here.

Ruth Bader Ginsburg

Yes, but what we have in this case is a classification that is harmful for women.

Justice

Mrs. Ginsburg speaking of the test which is to be of my understanding that has not been a holding or a decision of a majority of the full Court that says in so many words that sex is a suspect classification. Would you say that the existing precedents from this Court requires sex to be scrutinized more or less carefully than a classification based on illegitimacy such as the one in Mathews against Lucas last term?

Ruth Bader Ginsburg

Yes, I think that was a clear indication of the Mathews against Lucas decision.

Justice

Well, but the question is which is the strictest scrutiny, sex or illegitimacy in your construction of our case?

Ruth Bader Ginsburg

Sex and let me say that has been a very recent development because as we know at the time these lines came into Social Security in 1939 and 1950 virtually, anything goes within the state of equal protection law with respect to gender classification.

But anything always is certainly not the law as to gender classification today.

Equal Protection Principle is part of our Constitution, intended to govern American society as it evolves overtime and inevitably, keeping pace with the Nation's progress toward maturity, notions of what constitutes the equal protection of the laws do change and as to sex discrimination, they have changed.

Thus the gender line in question here is no more secure because it solidified in 1950 than it would be if a program had taken shape in 1970.

The Court has not yet acknowledged sex as a suspect criterion, but it has plainly identified the vice of legislative resort to gender pigeonholing.

Last term, in Mathews v. Lucas Mr. Justice Blackmun writing for the Court referred to the severity and pervasiveness of the historic, legal and political discrimination against women, discrimination made ever so easy because sex like race.

Justice

Yeah that case upheld the classification largely on a justification of administrative convenience, doesn't it?

Ruth Bader Ginsburg

Mathews v. Lucas did not involve a sex classification.

Justice

No, the classification of illegitimacy.

Ruth Bader Ginsburg

And in the process of so doing distinguished sex classifications and race classifications, both of which present, as Mr. Justice Blackmun said an obvious badge.

Yet women's history has been a history of purposeful, unequal treatment. women have been subjected to unique disabilities based on stereotype characteristics, not truly indicative of their abilities.

Further in Mathews v. Lucas, the Court pointed to the generalization harmful to women underlining this one way three to one support test.

The woman spouse does not qualify unless the woman supplied all of her own support plus half of his at the 75% as support test, at issue here, it is not enough that she earns 51% of the family's income, but the Court pointed out in Mathews v. Lucas that such a gender specific classification reflects the familiar over broad stereotypical assumption that earnings of men are vital to the family and earnings of women are not, but the Secretary has told you that this discrimination in the old age and survivors' insurance is discrimination helpful to women discrimination rationally responsive to the low economic status of many wives and widows?

Yes, Congress did attend to the man's wife in 1939 in the same paternalistic spirit it attended to his children.

But the warranted congressional attention to wives and widows is expressed in his scheme that heaps further disadvantage on the gainfully employed woman.

A law that benefits a woman as wife or widow but does not denigrate woman as wager and that might be rationalized as benign and the gender criteria in ranks as an appropriate means to a legitimate end.

But the Section 402 differential can not be rationalized as favorable to some women, harmful to none.

The wage earning woman is disfavored, her worked is devalued, when the earnings dollar she contributes to Social Security is worth lifetime protection for her family than the earnings dollar of an identically situated male worker.

In sum, the line Congress drew with Section 402 does not ameliorate gender discrimination, it does not alter conditions that relegate women to an inferior place in political and economic endeavor, rather the gender line drawn in the old days and survivors' insurance program reflects and reinforces constraining stereotypes.

The differential favors and rewards men's employment more than women's.

It casts the law's weight on the side of arrangements in which man's work comes first, woman's second, together with other incentives.

It helps steer the married couple in one direction and discourages independent choice by the pair.

Justice

Mrs. Ginsburg let me come back to Kahn and Shevin again, really it was not too clear on whether yourself you have decided that case strongly or what is your view is. That is not too important but in that case did we not hold that the state had enacted there the special benefit for women which was not given to, it is for widows, not given to widowers because -- and this is the language of the opinion it was reasonably designed to further a state policy of questioning the financial impact of spousal loss on the sex for which that loss imposes a disproportionately heavy burden. Now, isn't there something of that same undertone in this case?

Ruth Bader Ginsburg

The critical difference is that in Kahn that small tax break was unlikely to reinforce significantly.

Justice

What does it make, what is the difference whether it is small or large on a constitutional basis?

Ruth Bader Ginsburg

The question, the critical issue is whether the distinction reinforces stereotype characterizations of the way women or men are or whether such align influences men and women's...

Justice

I think such a small benefit might be more invidious as a sex stereotype than a large benefit, wouldn't it?

Ruth Bader Ginsburg

It is unlikely to affect the decisions of men and women concerning the work that they do a, $15 annual tax benefit is not likely to have such an impact but it is also security differential if it is a question of which one will be the dominant bread winner and if it is a question of thousands of dollars that can sway decisions one way or another, $15 tax break is not likely to have that.

Justice

Well, what you are saying is that Congress cannot legislate on the basis of the assumption that in the great majority of cases, the man is the primary, is the dominant bread winner in the society?

Ruth Bader Ginsburg

Congress can use a gender neutral standard but it cannot simply assume that the men are the bread winners and that the women are the dependents.

Justice

What is the fact statistically?

Ruth Bader Ginsburg

The fact statistically as to this three to one dependency test I think it is quite clear that millions of American women could not meet such a test.

It is not a small group of women involved here.

The Secretary has noted that the median average computation of the wife's family income is 27%, when she works fulltime it is 38% but even 27% is too high to qualify her under this three to one dependency test.

So, most women could not meet that test.

Secretary's ultimate...

Justice

Mrs. Ginsburg can I ask -- would you find objection of all on equal protection or due process grounds an application of support test across the board to both men and women?

Ruth Bader Ginsburg

If that is the line Congress chose to draw there would be no problem with such a line.

The question whether the legislature should do it...

Justice

That is another -- that is a different question, but you would not -- if Congress said, "Our overall aim is to provide for need and we are going to have a simple rule to serve that and namely a support test and we are going to apply to both men and women." You would not find that objected?

Ruth Bader Ginsburg

There would not be a constitutional infirmity with that line.

Justice

Thank you.

Ruth Bader Ginsburg

Secretary's position here is that -- although this is not clearly stated as justification for discrimination, it is cheaper to adhere to this gender criterion, but that is not necessarily true nor is it material to this Court's function.

It should be underscored that the remedial issue in this case calls for tentative adjudication, not final resolution by this Court, authority and responsibility for the punitive disposition remain with Congress.

Striking the gender criterion leads to the legislature, the full range of gender neutral options, Congress may extend benefits, it may retract them, it may apply across the board that have support test or a less blunt limitation.

This Court's interim disposition should be guided by the preference, Congress has consistently indicated when a gender line infects a benefit program.

The reshaping has taken the same form on each occasion, removal of the gender based differential by dropping the dependency test.

That is the course unexceptionally recommended in every official report recently made regarding gender lines in Social Security including the reports so extensively quoted in the Secretary's Brief.

Justice

Well, what does -- suppose you win the case what kind of a judgment should the Court enter? Just the declaration that the...

Ruth Bader Ginsburg

Court should affirm the judgment below.

Justice

Which is just the declaration that the distinction is unconstitutional on equal protection grounds?

Ruth Bader Ginsburg

Affirm the decision below which held the one way dependency test unconstitutional, the consequence of that was that Leon Goldfarb qualified for benefits and is presently receiving them.

An application of across the board dependency test, though open to Congress is unlikely in view of the very drastic program change that approach would effect.

It would remove from the beneficiary category, not a small percentage of wives and widows as the Secretary asserted.

But based on that 27% figure clearly, millions of wives and widows would fail that three to one dependency test.

Nor has the Secretary supplied a shred of evidence in this case as to dollars saved by presuming the wife's dependence as -- there was a reference to a lower Court hearing in Maryland in the Jablon case in which the Government Counsel did tender a guess that the administrative expense could run as high as a billion dollars, but in a subsequent hearing, Government Counsel stated if there was no factual basis whatever for that figure or any other figure.

In short there is no factual basis in this record, nor in the record of any other case for comparison of administrative dollars saved as against benefit dollars paid out to wives and widows who would be ineligible under the three to one dependency test.

The Congress never attempted to determine whether any saving would be effected by assuming men independent and women dependent.

It appears that what Congress did have in mind in 1939 and 1950 was not so much administrative convenience as the notion that husband whatever his actual earnings ought to be ranked the family's dominant bread winner.

Further, as even the Secretary's Brief reveals albeit sotto voce, most of the husbands and widowers who would qualify where this three to one support test eliminated are not their family's principal bread winners.

Rather, on the basis of the Secretary's projections, the majority of these men earned less than their wives, the life's partner of these men, are women whose earnings ranged from over 50% to just under 75% of the family income.

Finally, as to that cost computation, the computation introduced for the first time in the Secretary's Brief to this Court.

It is a one eye illusive estimate that both exaggerates and obscures.

It does not offset against new secondary beneficiaries with ever increasing extent to which wives and widows are removed from that category because they qualify as primary beneficiaries.

Entitled to maximum benefits under their own accounts, does not take account of the probability of continued movement towards the announced congressional goal of universal Social Security primary coverage for all gainfully employed persons.

It does not place the estimates in context, the total sum of Secretary conjunctions amount to just about two thirds of 1% of annual Social Security receipts.

In 1975 those receipts exceeded $66.7 billion.

As significantly it appears to hypothesize the condition that does not correspond to reality.

The projections suppose that every newly eligible man would retire forthwith as early as age 60 or 62 and take full advantage of his eligibility, left out of the calculation is the Social Security Act's vitally important retirement test.

Most individuals do not retire at ages 60 to 64.

Many potential Social Security recipients worked well past the age of 65.

Leon Goldfarb for example retired when he was approaching 67.

All potential Social Security beneficiaries under age 72 are subject to the ex-retirement test, otherwise, eligible individuals under 72 if they have earnings in excess of the income ceiling will receive no benefits.

Under the retirement test a high percentage of the husbands and widowers counted by the Secretary as eligible likely would receive no benefits at all or would have their benefits cut down substantially because they earn an excessive $2760, the current income ceiling for full benefits.

Justice

Do we have any reliable figures on that Mrs. Ginsburg?

Ruth Bader Ginsburg

I have no access to figures concerning these tentative people who could not get full of benefits or whose benefits would be reduced.

Justice

Wouldn't that be likely a fluctuating group?

Ruth Bader Ginsburg

But, we know that the computation appears to count every person who is eligible in that estimate and we know that it does not appear to take account of anybody, not retiring at the first available opportunity. We do...

Justice

Is it possible that is why they have revised their figures downward from a billion dollars to four hundred and some million?

Ruth Bader Ginsburg

No, they have never revised the figures downward.

The billion dollars was suggested once as the cost of applying the dependency test to wives, requiring wives to prove that they supplied less than a quarter of the total family income.

That is another -- that billion dollars have nothing to do with this estimate.

This estimate has constantly escalated.

In the Wiesenfeld case, it was suggested that it was 300 million and now it is up to 447 million.

But, it appears that no account was taken over the retirement test and that is the significant omission and it is underscored by the emphasis that the Social Security administration has placed on the enormous expense of eliminating or scaling down the retirement test through legislative provision.

In any event, it is impossible to rationalize a gender criterion allocating benefits on the ground that it is cheaper to perceive that way.

If all that is required to uphold the statutory classification is the conclusion that it affects economies, then any statutory scheme can be established and no arbitrarily excluded group can complain.

That case ago, now senior Federal District Court Judge Burnita Shelton Matthews in her days at the Bar as Counsel to the National Women's Party, explained like why a gender line, such as the one at par, helps to keep women not on a pedestal, but in a cage.

Such classification she said fortifies the assumption, harmful to women that label full pay with attendant benefits for one's family is primarily the prerogative of men.

Appellee Goldfarb respectfully requests that the judgment below be affirmed thereby establishing that under the equal protection principle, the women workers' national social insurance is of no less value than is the social insurance of the working man.

Warren E. Burger

Thank you Mrs. Ginsburg. Mr. Jones do you have anything further?

Keith A. Jones

Yes, thank you Mr. Chief Justice. I would like to point out that the beneficiaries with which we are largely concerned here are retired civil servants who receive government pensions and that this Court should not likely require a largely irrational distribution of benefits that the appellee seeks. Now, the appellee's arguments here largely depend on changing employment statistics. His reliance is upon the fact that today very much unlike 1939 and 1950, there is a substantial proportion of non-dependent women in the job market, perhaps aside has 20% at this point or roughly in that area.

John Paul Stevens

Mr. Jones, do you think that constitutionality of this statute turns on the statistic says they existed in 1939, 1950 or today?

Keith A. Jones

Mr. Justice Stevens, if you believe that this statute was constitutional when first enacted and that recent social history has largely eroded the factual basis on which the classification originally depended, I would think that the appropriate remedy would not be to determine in the first instance that this statute is unconstitutional. I do not think that this Court should sit as a committee of revision on the Social Security Act in the first instance. It seems to me that if you believe that recent social history has undercut the foundation of the act in this respect, you should advice Congress of the fact that changing events have cast serious doubt upon the continued viability of this distinction. But you should give to Congress the opportunity to sort out this very complicated matter which -- no matter how this Court would dispose off it -- would result in an irrational and unfair allocation of Social Security moneys.

John Paul Stevens

Let me change the question a little bit. Supposing we were convinced that the statute was constitutional in 1950 and that conditions have totally changed, whenever we get to the case, would we be bound to say it is still constitutional?

Keith A. Jones

I think that to give due deference to Congress which has a primary responsibility of sorting out the difficult questions of the proper allocations Social Security moneys, it would be appropriate for this Court to hold at this point that the statute remains constitutional but advice Congress that if current social trends continue, the factual basis for that final constitutionality would have been completely eroded, but give to Congress some opportunity to sort this matter out.

Thurgood Marshall

(Inaudible).

Keith A. Jones

Well, I think that that opinion to the effect would sufficiently apprise Congress of -- to solve this matter. Do you do (Inaudible).

John Paul Stevens

This is an odd role which you are recommending to this Court.

Keith A. Jones

Well, it is not unlike the role you played in the Federal Election Commission case. Well, in the half a dozen cases...

John Paul Stevens

Sorry to hear that. Half a dozen cases have been decided where the Court has done almost precisely what you are suggesting and making recommendations about legislature.

Keith A. Jones

Well, I think that in the matter such as this where to affirm the decision below, would require an irrational allocation of benefits, that it just makes plain good sense to give Congress the primary opportunity to take care of, what seem to be an unfair...

Thurgood Marshall

Do you say that the statute is constitutional or unconstitutional?

Keith A. Jones

Constitutional.

Thurgood Marshall

You would say that it is constitutional despite the fact that we think it is unconstitutional.

Keith A. Jones

Well, I submit that the fact that more women are now in the job market than in 1939 does not, at this point, standing alone, necessitate our finding of unconstitutionality. I do not think we have yet reached that point, my submission is that... Mr. Jones, what do you think your primary -- what are your points anyway, earlier in your argument was that, merely in the fact that they are paying widows something you are not paying widowers, did not prove unconstitutionality. You just said accessed over...

Keith A. Jones

That is quite right, I stand by it... ...overinclusiveness...

Keith A. Jones

That is correct. Is that Congress' aim as to pay this to take care of needy people?

Keith A. Jones

The appellee's argument, as I understand it, is that what was once overinclusiveness as to 5 to 10% of the women is now overinclusiveness as to perhaps 20 or 25% of women. It may well be that -- and I would submit to the contrary, but it may well be that if the Court concludes that that kind of broad overinclusiveness is of doubtful constitutionality that might apprise Congress of that fact, that my submission would be that mere overinclusiveness without more does not render the statute unconstitutional. That the statute need not be mathematically precise as to the categories of beneficiaries... Why does that worth 30% instead of 2%? Would you say that degree of overinclusiveness is not a matter?

Keith A. Jones

Well, it is a matter of degree, if it were 100%, then obviously, it would be very difficult to sustain. Where 30% stands in relation to that other than being about 30% toward 100%, I am not sure I am prepared to say at this moment. Thank you.

Warren E. Burger

Thank you Mr. Jones.

Thank you Mrs. Ginsburg.

The case is submitted.

BILLY DUREN v. MISSOURI

Facts of the Case: A jury convicted Billy Duren of first degree murder and first degree robbery. Duren alleged that the selection of this jury violated his Sixth and Fourteenth Amendment right to a trial by a jury chosen from a fair selection of the community. Specifically, Jackson County allowed an automatic exemption from jury service for women upon request. While women made up 54% of the population in the Jackson County, only 26.7% of people summoned were women. Duren had an all-male jury selected from a panel of 48 men and 5 women. The Missouri Supreme Court affirmed the conviction, questioning the validity of Duren's statistics. The court also held that, even if women were disproportionally excluded from jury service, the amount of women who participated in the process was well above constitutional standards.

Question: Does Jackson County's automatic exemption of women from jury duty on request violate the Sixth and Fourteenth Amendment guarantees to a trial by a jury chosen from a fair cross section of the community?

Conclusion: Yes. The state court was reversed and remanded by Justice Byron R. White, writing for an 8-1 majority. The Supreme Court held that Duren's statistical evidence proved that Jackson County's jury selection process violated his constitutional rights. Duren demonstated an underrepresented "distinctive" group resulting from Jackson County's practice of exempting women. Additionally, there was no significant state interest to justify exempting women from jury service. Justice William H. Rehnquist dissented, arguing that the majority wrongly used an combination of the Due Process clause and Equal Protection clause to make their decision.

Burger Majority	White Majority	Marshall Majority
Brennan Majority	Blackmun Majority	Powell Majority
Stewart Majority	Rehnquist Dissent	Stevens Majority

Duren v. Missouri Oral Arguments - November 1, 1978

Warren E. Burger

We'll hear arguments next in 6067, Duren against Missouri. Mr. Nation, you may proceed whenever you're ready.

Lee M. Nation

Mr. Chief Justice, may it please the Court. In March of 1976, petitioner Billy Duren appeared for trial on the Jackson County Circuit Court. Appearing with Mr. Duren was a jury panel. That panel of 53 people included only five women. Billy Duren moved to quash the jury panel on the basis that the Missouri procedure for selecting jurors violates his right to a reasonably representative cross-sectional jury.

Thurgood Marshall

Mr. Nation, if you excuse me, there's a crank on the side that you'd -- lift it up.

Lee M. Nation

Okay, thank you. I think I'm okay.

Thurgood Marshall

What I mean that microphone.

Potter Stewart

We can hear you better.

Thurgood Marshall

That microphone.

Warren E. Burger

No, up the other way.

Lee M. Nation

Mr. Duren's motion to quash filed before trial was overruled and he was convicted of murder in the first degree by an all male jury. Of course, our challenge here is bottomed upon Taylor versus Louisiana. Taylor holds first that petitioner Billy Duren can raise such a challenge concerning women on juries. And second, that if women are not on juries in sufficient numbers, Billy Duren's right to a fair cross-sectional jury panel has been defeated. The Missouri Court --

Warren E. Burger

Wait a minute, did you say the on the jury or on the jury panel?

Lee M. Nation

On the jury panel.

Warren E. Burger

Not the jury.

Lee M. Nation

Jury panel. The Missouri Court and the state here attempt to distinguish Taylor in two ways. First, that the effect of the Missouri system is different than the effect of the Taylor system. I will speak to that issue. My co-counsel Professor Ginsburg will speak to the distinction the state makes with respect to the operation of the women's exemption. The facts of this case speak strongly. Jackson County is 54% women. Voters -- the voter registration roles are used to pick the master jury wheel and we would assume that the voter registration roles through the statistics in our brief would mirror the population characteristic of 54%. Each year, the voter registrations roles are subjected to a random computer search which draws out 70,000 names. These names are then sent questionnaires to determine whether or not the 70,000 names meet Missouri's law as to eligibility for service. The questionnaire also contains the women's exemption. The first question on the questionnaire is "State your sex" and parenthetically, "If you are a woman, and do not desire to serve, see the bottom of the page."Missouri makes it very easy at this stage for women to opt off and they do in significant numbers. This questionnaire procedure unquestionably causes the diminution from 54% women in the community to the panel which is 30% women, excuse me, the master jury wheel which is 30% women. Our inquiry does not stop there however, because women are given a second opportunity to opt off juries. Each week before trials, summonses are sent out. These summonses compel only the attendants of men to serve on the juries. The questionnaire in red -- excuse me, the summons in red states, "Women, if you do not desire to serve, contact the jury commissioner." The jury commissioner John Fitzgerald also testified that if women just ignored the summons, she would be deemed to have exercised her exemption. She was in Mr. Fitzgerald's words, "an excused female." Men, however, their names, if they failed to appear would be -- their names would be sent to the bail for the presiding judge who would attempt to contact them. These summons procedure is the only reason for the diminution between the master jury wheel which is 30% and the number of women appearing for trial week after week.

William H. Rehnquist

Mr. Nation, the Supreme Court of Missouri expressed some dissatisfaction with your numerical claims. Oh, in what posture do you think we find that factual question?

Lee M. Nation

Well, the Missouri Supreme Court cited new -- can you be specific as to which claim they -- you're referring to?

William H. Rehnquist

Well, I am -- I think it's the court's majority and I don't have the opinion directly before me, but it's a phrase that casts some -- gives some indication it is not satisfied in it that you have satisfactorily demonstrated the facts in which you're relying but goes on to treat it --

Lee M. Nation

Yes.

William H. Rehnquist

-- as if you had nothing left.

Lee M. Nation

There are several things. First, they didn't like the fact that we used 1970 population statistics which of course are the only statistics that are available. They didn't like the fact that in the opinion that the master jury wheel count was as they said only an unverified pencil sketch. Apparently, they forgot to read the transcript because there was testimony concerning the actual count of the jury wheel week after week after week prior to Billy Duren's trial, the panel's average 14.5% women. They questioned the statistics but I believe the statistics in this case are in such a posture that we can reach the merits certainly. Further, a woman is again given an opportunity to opt off jury service even after she appears, even after she appears at any point before she has sworn as a juror, she can decide to go home. Petitioner Billy Duren's jury panel in this case of 53 people with five women, there were almost ten times as many men on the jury panel as there were women. Now, the state and the Missouri Supreme Court have said that these facts are not conclusive. In some, what they want petitioner to do is to prove that there is no conceivable or even inconceivable reason which would cause this underrepresentation. As was noted in the amicus brief filed by the Solicitor General, the constitutional provision allowing women to opt off juries is the only possible explanation for the under-representation. Further, petitioner --

William H. Rehnquist

You mean a federal constitutional provision of your Missouri (Voice Overlap)?

Lee M. Nation

The Missouri constitutional provision. Further, it is petitioner's position that we have made a prima facie case that we have shown first that the jury selection procedure in Jackson County is non-neutral, that women are given an exemption which men are not. And second, we have shown that in week after week, jury panels appear for jury service that are only 14.5% women in a community that is 54% women.

Warren E. Burger

Is that because of some lesser registration in the voting process by women?

Lee M. Nation

Well, the statistics that are in our brief indicate that in Missouri, men registered to vote -- 71% of the men were registered to vote and 69.9% of the women registered to vote. Therefore we -- I think, can assume that right around 54% will be what the voter role is. Further the --

Warren E. Burger

Then when their -- when the wheel is made up, it doesn't reflect the voter population on your figures, you've got definitely 70 to 60.

Lee M. Nation

That's correct.

Warren E. Burger

Any explanation for that in the record?

Lee M. Nation

70 to 69%.

Warren E. Burger

Well, roughly 70.

Lee M. Nation

Excuse me, I didn't -- what was your question?

Warren E. Burger

Any explanation for why the drawings don't average out fairly close to the --

Lee M. Nation

I imagine the -- the computer selects people from the voter registration rolls and we don't know exactly what percentage of those people selected or those people who were sent questionnaires are men and women because obviously, some of the questionnaires never returned. People either ignore them or they're lost or people have moved away or died. So we have no way of knowing who is mailed questionnaires. But presumably, if it is randomly drawn from voter registration roles, it would be about again 54% female. Petitioner Billy Duren asserts here that we have made a prima facie case, that we have shown a non-neutral jury selection method and that we have shown underrepresentation. Thus, it is now incumbent upon the state, upon the respondent to give some constitutionally permissible reason for the fact that Billy Duren's jury panel was 9% women. There is one point that I agree with respondent and with the Missouri Supreme Court. Jackson County is not as bad as Taylor. Taylor's panel of 1% was very, very low. But I don't believe a fair reading of Taylor that Taylor stands for the proposition that anything above 1% is constitutionally permissible. Instead, the thrust of Taylor is obviously that any system which denies an accused his right to a panel with reasonably representative participation of the elements of society also violates his right to jury trial under the Sixth Amendment. The importance of a jury, Your Honor, as everyone knows is -- it is the body that is interposed between the accused and the accuser. It is our way of guaranteeing a man a fair trial and thus it must be woven from the fabric of the community that we cannot exclude any identifiable group that they must be represented on jury panels so that an individual can have a possibility of having these people on his final jury.

William H. Rehnquist

Where do you get that from that you -- the const -- the federal constitution prohibits a state from excluding any identifiable group?

Lee M. Nation

From the past precedents of this Court.

William H. Rehnquist

Such as?

Lee M. Nation

Such as Taylor.

William H. Rehnquist

Is that what Taylor said?

Lee M. Nation

That it -- a state cannot exclude an identifiable group by -- on juries.

William H. Rehnquist

Would you carry that beyond discrimination between the sexes or what other identifiable groups?

Lee M. Nation

Blacks, Mexican-Americans.

William H. Rehnquist

How beyond that?

Lee M. Nation

That's -- I think that's about as far as we've gone.

Potter Stewart

How about lawyers and judges and dentists and doctors and clergymen and teachers?

Lee M. Nation

That doesn't -- the prior cases in the federal circuits have not held those to be identifiable groups.

Potter Stewart

But they are, and that even in the common meaning of that phrase.

Lee M. Nation

Well, they're identifiable groups in a common sense language but as in terms of jury, in the jury cases, they have not been recognized as important enough that we need to include them on juries. Also they make up of --

William H. Rehnquist

Don't you think a lawyer can make a much bigger impact if he's a member of a jury than a woman as a woman or a Mexican-American as a Mexican-American?

Lee M. Nation

Well, perhaps he might be able to. However, lawyers are very small percentage of the community and they're -- even the possibility of they're being on juries is de minimis. Finally, the system which denies a defendant his right to a reasonably representative cross sectional jury panel violates the Sixth Amendment and should be reversed. Thank you.

Warren E. Burger

Mrs. Ginsburg, you may lower the lectern if you would like.

Ruth Bader Ginsburg

Yes, I could do that.

Mr. Chief Justice and may it please the Court.

My argument addresses the citizen's duty tied to a defendant's fair cross section right and the complete absence of justification for exempting any woman.

Though Jackson County jury panels are dominated by men, the Missouri Supreme Court said that the right affected is unimpaired.

That reasoning in two key respects is topsy-turvy.

First, the right central in this case, the right secured by the Sixth Amendment is the criminal defendants.

Here Billy Duren's right to a fair chance for a jury genuinely representative of the community's complexion and second, the vaunted woman's privilege viewed against history's backdrop simply reflects and perpetuates a certain way of thinking about women.

Women traditionally were deemed lesser citizens.

Warren E. Burger

That wouldn't concern Mr. Duren, would it?

Ruth Bader Ginsburg

Mr. Duren has a right to a jury drawn from a panel reasonably representative of the community.

Warren E. Burger

Now, as --

Ruth Bader Ginsburg

And as this --

Warren E. Burger

-- to who wouldn't -- he wouldn't be interested in the factor you mentioned whether this is fair or unfair to the women, they're called for --

Ruth Bader Ginsburg

Yes.

Warren E. Burger

-- a jury service or not called, would it?

Ruth Bader Ginsburg

But that was the traditional justification given by states.

First, for excluding women altogether and then second -- the second step was providing an exemption for any women the notion being that the women are not really needed, not really wanted for participation in the democratic processes of Government.

Viewed in that light, this is hardly a privilege.

This is hardly a favor to the supposedly favored class.

But as to the quo right at stake, Judge Saylor dissenting below pointed out a defendant's fair cross section right can be meaningful only if it hinges on a correlative duty, the duty of the citizen to show up for jury service when summoned.

A privilege to avoid service at whim, prominently advertised and readily available to any woman or any man or any other large, stable, distinctive population group, the basis, the defendant's cross section right, that right is real only when the obligation to serve is placed on citizens without automatic exemption based solely on their race, national origin or sex.

Warren E. Burger

I take it that very few doctors serve on juries in Missouri State Courts as is true in most states which -- would you regard that a -- as a --

Ruth Bader Ginsburg

Exemptions that apply on the basis of one's occupations reflect determinations by the state that certain occupations for the good of the community should be pursued uninterrupted and it makes no difference whether a person is male/female, black or white, it's the neutral, functional category that is excluded, doctor, lawyer, dentist, clergy not any woman --

Warren E. Burger

Would that preclude the state from saying that without getting into that old cliché about women's places in the home, if the state said in effect, mothers of small children should belong at home not serving on juries. Now, suppose it were narrowed to housewives with children under 16 --

Ruth Bader Ginsburg

There are several --

Warren E. Burger

-- would you still have the same problem?

Ruth Bader Ginsburg

There are several states that have exemptions for persons primarily responsible for the care of young children.

Warren E. Burger

So that'd be husbands or wives then.

Ruth Bader Ginsburg

It could be husband or wife, yes.

Warren E. Burger

And do --

Ruth Bader Ginsburg

But by using the term assuming that it will be the woman here or in a more general, any woman excuse, the state is providing an ineludible message that the male citizens are counted by Government as the essential participants of the administration of justice but the female citizens are not so counted, this service is expendable. I would like to stress --

John Paul Stevens

Mrs. Ginsburg, may I ask you a question. If we look at from the point of view of the defendant and you take the view as I think you do that men and women are essentially fungible for purposes of jury service, how is the cross section heard if women are excluded?

Ruth Bader Ginsburg

That was an issue that the Court addressed in Taylor against Louisiana.

Yes, men and women are persons of equal dignity and they should count equally before the law but they are not the same.

There are differences between them that most of us value highly.

This Court said twice, first in Ballard against United States and then in Taylor against Louisiana that there is a certain quality that would certainly be missing from that jury --

John Paul Stevens

What is the relevant difference between men and women for the purposes of jury service, from the point of view of the defendant?

Ruth Bader Ginsburg

What is the rele --

John Paul Stevens

Yes.

Ruth Bader Ginsburg

Is that indefinable something --

John Paul Stevens

That sounds kind of like a stereotype answer to me.

Ruth Bader Ginsburg

I think that we -- perhaps all understand it when we see it and we feel it but it is not that easy to describe, yes, there is a difference.

In any event, Missouri's insistence that 9 to 15% representation of women is quite enough although it is an exorbitant argument is understandable for the state to this day has urged no justification whatever for exempting any woman.

Missouri makes no claim that this women's excuse is even minimally rational, though to overcome a defendant's Sixth Amendment right as Taylor held merely rational grounds would not suffice.

The Court said in Taylor that is untenable to suggest it would be a special hardship for a woman to perform jury duty simply because of her sex.

Post Taylor then, a woman's work whether at home or on the job and the administrative convenience of treating all women as expendable, these are not even arguable basis for diminishing the defendant's Sixth Amendment right by diluting the quality of community judgment a jury trial provides.

Moreover, eliminating the exemption for any woman clouds no reasonable jury service exemption.

Only two states, Missouri and Tennessee today maintain a solely sex-based exemption.

Other Missouri exemptions are tied to occupation, prior service, individual hardship, not to an unalterable identification each of us is marked with at birth and identification bearing no necessary relationship to one's capacity or life situation and therefore inherently unreasonable as a basis for jury duty avoidance.

In some, no sense at all nourishes Missouri's solely sex-based exemption implemented by Jackson County's prominent invitations to any woman to sign off and the jury commissioner's assumption from a woman's inaction that she doesn't want to serve.

Have it?

Yes.

Surely not analysis or actual reflection accounts for an excuse based simply on a woman's sex and not on what she does or is capable of doing.

Finally, the Court's eight to one judgment in Taylor leaves no room for the Missouri argument that Billy Duren must show how he in particular might have been disadvantaged by a violation of the fair cross-section requirement.

Selection of a criminal trial jury from a representative cross-section, the Court held in Taylor is an essential component of a defendant's Sixth Amendment right.

Neither Missouri nor this Court is at liberty to apply or dispense with the cross-section rule based on the view of prosecutor or of judge of the strength of the evidence against a defendant.

Full respect for the cross-section command is required of the state because the constitutional safeguard is guaranteed to all and it may be relied upon by every person, the most low and the least deserving to the same extent as the most upright and virtuous.

Harry A. Blackmun

Mrs. Ginsburg, somewhere in these briefs, the opposing brief says a suggestion that if Mr. Duren prevails here, the Missouri jailhouse doors might be open, do you have any comment? What is your response to that suggestion?

Ruth Bader Ginsburg

I think it's certainly the case that this objection is available only the defendants who have properly raised it below and pursued it on appeal.

Moreover, it would be relevant only the case of Jackson County.

That questionnaire and that summons in the record that flags and signals repeatedly that women may take themselves off.

Those are used only in Jackson County and no other county in Missouri, so I would say we are talking about one county only, about trials post this Court's decision in Taylor against Louisiana an only in cases where the objection has been properly raised and pursued under Missouri law.

Harry A. Blackmun

Do you know what the follow through in the Louisiana case was?

Ruth Bader Ginsburg

Yes.

Billy Joe Taylor was retried and reconvicted.

Harry A. Blackmun

But was that ruling specifically held not retroactive?

Ruth Bader Ginsburg

But you held that it was not retroactive.

Harry A. Blackmun

And so the result is that the Louisiana jails were not open and you think this would follow here also?

Ruth Bader Ginsburg

In Taylor against Louisiana, you overturn a fairly, a 1961 precedent, Hoyt against Florida.

Byron R. White

But you would think -- you would argue, I suppose that Taylor mandated the invalidation of the Missouri law.

Ruth Bader Ginsburg

I certainly think so.

Byron R. White

And that this ought to go back at least to Taylor.

Ruth Bader Ginsburg

At least -- yes.
To --

Byron R. White

Yes.

Ruth Bader Ginsburg

Although that's not necessary part of the case that's here today, yes, that was a message that New York got and other states, all states except Missouri and Tennessee got that message.

To conclude, the unconstitutionality of Missouri's excuse for any woman as it operates to distort Jackson County jury panels is plainly established.

Any sensible reading of this record juxtaposed with this Court's eight to one judgment in Taylor leads ineluctably to that conclusion.

William H. Rehnquist

You won't settle for putting Susan B. Anthony on the new dollar, right?

Warren E. Burger

I think you have no jurisdiction to make that concession, Mrs. Ginsburg. Thank you. Ms. Laughrey.

Nanette Laughrey

Mr. Chief Justice and may it please the Court. I think there are three issues that we have to address here. First of all, this Missouri's jury selection system systematically excludes women which I believe is what was held in Taylor versus Louisiana to be unconstitutional if it resulted in jury panels which are almost totally male. I think we also have to find out what degree of disparity must be proven in order to make out a violation of the Sixth Amendment and I think there's also a question as to the allocation of the burden of proof in these cases. I will first address the question as to whether Missouri's jury selection system systematically excludes women. I think there is a distinct factual difference between our system and the Louisiana system and that in Louisiana, women were not included in the jury wheel unless they took affirmative action. There was an assumption that they were not interested. In Missouri on the other hand, women are treated at the inception of the process in exactly the same way as are men. The voter registration lists are used and names are selected at random from those list and questionnaires are sent out.

Warren E. Burger

Are you suggesting that there are generally in the category of physicians and others who's as -- who was conceded by I think your friends in the other side of the table was permissible exclusion on the part of the state for reasons of public policy?

Nanette Laughrey

I think an exemption does not exclude women or doctors.

Warren E. Burger

Well --

Nanette Laughrey

It gives them the opportunity not to participate if they choose.

Warren E. Burger

Well, what do you call it, exemption or exclusion? Since it gives the woman the opportunity to get off the jury more readily than it goes to other people, carpenters and bookkeepers, then why is it different? Do you suggest it is essentially the same as that dispensation given the physicians, is that your -- part of your argument?

Nanette Laughrey

Yes, Your Honor it is essentially the same as any exemption which the State of Missouri Courts.

Thurgood Marshall

Is it true that they have -- the woman has two, a woman doctor has two exemptions?

Nanette Laughrey

That is correct Your Honor.

Thurgood Marshall

And you don't see any thing wrong with that?

Nanette Laughrey

I think it is wrong if there is a violation of the Sixth Amendment. I don't think the question is whether the fact that we give women special privilege is wrong. I think it's a question of whether as a result of that; Billy Duren's Sixth Amendment Rights were violated.

Thurgood Marshall

Well, isn't that the direct result of them having only 0.9 women on the jury, the direct result of the Missouri practice?

Nanette Laughrey

Your Honor we would submit that no it is not and the --

Thurgood Marshall

And what --

Nanette Laughrey

If petitioner has not shown it to be.

Thurgood Marshall

What would cause it? What would cause this? Where you have 54% population, what would make it possible to have such as small amount, lets say among juries?

Nanette Laughrey

Petition -- Your Honor, we do not believe that it is the obligation of the state to show why there was so few women on the jury but rather that the burden of proof was on the petitioner.

Thurgood Marshall

-- if you're unreasonably requested to do so, can you?

Nanette Laughrey

No Your Honor because we --

Thurgood Marshall

You can't justify it, can you?

Nanette Laughrey

What do you mean by justification?

Thurgood Marshall

What the word it says.

Nanette Laughrey

The reduction in the number of women available or the reason for the exemption?

Thurgood Marshall

The reason for the exemption, one.

Nanette Laughrey

One, no. The exemption originally was given because of the presumed role of women in the home and that there were so many women in that situation that they should be given an exemption. Also, there was some intimation that women should be given a choice as to whether they wanted to participate in the selection of juries where certain details might be describe that they were uncomfortable in hearing.

Thurgood Marshall

And at a time when --

Nanette Laughrey

Those --

Thurgood Marshall

They weren't even qualified to vote?

Nanette Laughrey

Yes Your Honor, that is true and I think this Court in the past has characterized those as --

Thurgood Marshall

Oh, they make contracts. Or to make contracts?

Nanette Laughrey

Yes Your Honor and I think --

Thurgood Marshall

They just couldn't do anything but tend a home.

Nanette Laughrey

I think the question Your Honor is not whether we can justify the exemption because we only need to justify the exemption once it has been shown to be a violation of the Sixth Amendment and once it has been shown to operate in such a way that there are so few women on the jury panel that it is no longer fairly representative of the community. And it is our belief that the figures in this case are sufficient to show that there was a fair cross-section of women on the community, on the panel. We would point to the fact that there were 29% women on the master jury wheel even after women were given the opportunity to fill out the questionnaire and take their exemption there were still 29% women which is three times more than the situation in Taylor versus Louisiana. There were 15 times more women on the venires than there were in Taylor versus Louisiana. In Taylor, you stated that it would be a violation if we could -- if it were shown that the exemption or the exclusion resulted in almost totally male panels. We submit to you that almost totally male is not an accurate characterization of the panels which tried Billy Duren and which are used in Jackson County, Missouri. As I said before, I agree that what once were justifications for our exemption maybe outmoded in archaic. And yet it seems to me that the basis of the petitioner's position is that Billy Duren somehow was deprived of a fair and impartial trial because the indefinable something that distinguishes men and women. I submit that is equally outmoded in archaic and not a basis for finding a violation of the defendant's Sixth Amendment.

Thurgood Marshall

Didn't Taylor say so?

Nanette Laughrey

Yes Your Honor, Taylor did say so.

John Paul Stevens

Taylor is based on an outmoded stereotype is what you're saying. That's your argument? I think it is.

Nanette Laughrey

I submit that that is in fact. I think an important question here also is where the burden of proof is going to be allocated in these cases. In other cases which are pending before this Court on petitions for cert, you are aware that there has been evidence introduced to show that the reduction from 54% to 29% on the jury wheel was the basis of the questionnaires and the exemptions for women. This however is not in the record before this Court and we submit that it should not be considered by this Court since it was not considered by the Missouri Supreme Court in making of their decision. Even however, if you do consider that evidence, there is still no explanation for the diminution of the amount of women from 29% to 15% because we submit that if a woman has a right to check the questionnaire and say, "I don't want to serve" and she doesn't then we can assume that she's later when she's called to serve going to say, "Well, the only reason I'm not interested in serving it's because I am a woman." And there is no proof in the record here as to why women were excused for cause by the judge as evidenced in the tables which are in the appendix.

William H. Rehnquist

Ms. Laughrey, let me get back for a moment if I may to your comment about the outmoded stereotype in response to Justice Stevens' question. Actually, a jury -- lawyers who pick juries operate largely on stereotypes, don't they? In the sense that, you know people of certain nationalities are believed to award higher personal injury verdicts than others. And others -- there's types that are supposed to be more favorable to criminal defendants, others are kind of hard hearted and favorable to the prosecution, there maybe very little to them, to the stereotypes, perhaps, they're not justified but certainly a lot of lawyers use them in picking juries in using their preemptory challenge.

Nanette Laughrey

That may be Your Honor, I don't know, is there a question?

William H. Rehnquist

Well, the question, you say in effect that it didn't make any difference to Billy Duren that there weren't that many women on the jury because there really isn't much -- the concept that women would react differently than men is outmoded or did I misinterpretation your --?

Nanette Laughrey

No, that was correct Your Honor. I think though that when we're talking about a violation of the Sixth Amendment and saying that he did not have a fair and impartial trial that -- and not allowing the State of Missouri to justify their exemption on the basis of outmoded in archaic ideas. It seems inconsistent to rely on those kinds of ideas to fashion the Sixth Amendment violation. I'd like to discuss the question of burden of proof for a minute as it relates to the reduction of women from 29% to 15% and from 54% to 29%. The Solicitor General would like this Court to say that there some kind of a prima facie case made out when you show a non-neutral selection process. And you show underrepresentation and they try to relate this to the situation in which this Court has found discrimination and exclusion of a particular group from a jury on the basis of a lower representation of that group and a non-neutral selection process a subjective selection process. And if shifted, the burden to the state, we submit that there is no reason to make such an allocation of the burden of proof in these cases because of the fact that the same situation is simply inapplicable here that is applicable in a discrimination case. When you're talking about trying to point at some place in a subjective process where discrimination has occurred, it is impossible for the defendant to go into that process and find out at what point that happens and therefore there is a reason for developing these rules about the prima facie case in shifting the burden of going forward with the evidence of the state. We submit that there is no similar reason here that there is nothing in our process which makes it easier for the state to show why it is not the exemption for women than it is for the defendant to show that it is the exemption for women that results in the underrepresentation. As evidenced by the fact that they have counted the questionnaires, they have found out the reason as far as other cases go.

Byron R. White

Suppose, it was sought that prima facie case had been made out, does the state -- what's the state's strongest argument in justification or do you have one?

Nanette Laughrey

Are you talking about justification for the exemption?

Byron R. White

Yes, for treating women different than men and in terms of excuse.

Nanette Laughrey

We recognize that women still play a primary role in the home that even though women may in fact be working mothers does not mean that they have been relieved of the responsibilities of their obligations to the home or to their family. And that just because their work is not a sufficient reason for saying that they no longer carry the responsibilities that they were once thought to have.

Byron R. White

Is that -- is that a -- do you think that's the legislative decision?

Nanette Laughrey

The justification for this exemption? I don't know what the legislative justification was. We do not have any evidence. I submit that that is the strongest justification that the State of Missouri can make for the exemption.

Warren E. Burger

Well, under McGowan against Maryland if there was any rational reason for it, we'd give that considerable weight I suppose, would we, should we?

Nanette Laughrey

Yes, but again, it's not an equal protection case. I don't think the question is whether our exemption is good or bad. It's a question of whether it fits in to the mold of Taylor versus Louisiana. And in Taylor versus Louisiana, there were certain statements about what made out a violation of the Sixth Amendment. There had to be systematic exclusion of women. We submit that there was not exclusion of women here because we did not assume that they were not going to serve on juries merely because they did not opt in to the jury selection process. I would like to point to one place in the petitioner's reply brief that I think it's an inaccurate characterization of the fact. On page 3, they indicate that if women do not return their questionnaires and do not respond to the jury service summons it is assumed that they will -- that they do not want to serve and that is not true. If a woman does not return her questionnaire, she is automatically put in the pool from which juries are selected. Second part of that statement is true. If a woman does not respond to the summons, they do assume that she's going to exercise her right to an exemption. But I think there is a distinct difference between a process which at the beginning does not include women in the jury selection system. And a process at the end which does not send the police out to arrest women because they may use their exemption is a distinct factual deference. I think also if you look at the statistics in the appendix and the tables which the petitioner has provided, you will see that the number of women who do not respond to summons is insignificant in comparison to the number who have appeared for jury duty who are excused and for other reasons and end up appearing on the jury wheel (Voice Overlap).

Potter Stewart

What happens to a man who does not respond to the summons?

Nanette Laughrey

The testimony is that the police will make an attempt to find out why he has not responding.

Potter Stewart

Well, (Voice Overlap) if they find out, I just -- if they didn't want to serve.

Nanette Laughrey

There is a distinction at that point.

Potter Stewart

And he tells the police I just didn't want to serve, that's a reason I didn't respond. Then what happens to him?

Nanette Laughrey

He is subject to be in held in contempt of court. Now, in the record in this case there is no great discussion about how many men in fact are found to be held in contempt of court whether they do anything about it. I would point you however to a footnote in the petitioner's reply brief at page 2, footnote 1, when they talk about the Saint Louis jury system and state that if we were to amplify we would indicate that in Saint Louis they do not assume from the fact that women do not answer the summons that they do not want to serve. In talking with Mr. Ruland (ph) who is the author of the Authority which they cite, the situation in Saint Louis is that for a period of time, they experimented and they went out and try to find out why people did not show up. And if a woman did not show up, they did nothing to her in exactly the same as in Jackson County. What they really --

Potter Stewart

Is Jackson County a Kansas city?

Nanette Laughrey

Jackson County is Kansas City, Missouri.

William H. Rehnquist

How many counties are there in Missouri?

Nanette Laughrey

Your Honor I do not have the answer to that question. There are more than a hundred. Jackson County, Missouri of course is one of the largest population areas.

William H. Rehnquist

So a case based on statistics from Jackson County although it would affect the substantial number of people in Missouri would not be determinative of other convictions obtained in other counties, I take it?

Nanette Laughrey

I think that is the -- certainly the import of Taylor is that it is only when it results and in underrepresentation in a particular case and if it doesn't result in under representation in Saint Louis or Boom County, does that mean that, you know the exemption is still valid.

William H. Rehnquist

So a federal habeas judge sitting in the Western District of Missouri maybe scanning convictions of -- if the Supreme Court of Missouri has reversed 50 different counties and he's going to have to get evidence as to the functioning of the jury system and each of those counties before he can decide.

Nanette Laughrey

Well, that's true Your Honor but we would submit that even if the Missouri Supreme Court were reversed in this case that this is not a situation that should be made retroactive that we think that the rules which were applicable in Taylor versus Louisiana are equally applicable in this case for two reasons. Number one, because of the factual distinctions between Taylor versus Louisiana and the situation of Missouri. We do not think that Taylor is so dispositive of the question that we can just say, "This is an application of Taylor." We submit that it is an extension of the rational in Taylor largely because it's based on statistics. We never know what is going to be a fair-cross-section of the community Your Honors. We know that 1% is too small and we know that 54% would be in exact mirror. We never know where in between that the Sixth Amendment violation occurs and therefore, to say that it's merely an application of Taylor I do not think it's correct. And before you have stated in Daniels and in Stovall versus Daniels the standards that you want to consider when you're deciding whether something is retroactive or not to the standards in addition to our reliance on prior law would be the interest that the constitutional provision was intending to protect and as you stated in Daniel, you're not submitting that Billy Duren was prejudiced in any way that you know, it may not have made one iota a difference of Billy Duren whether there were women in his pool or in his jury or whatever. So, there's not the kind of inherent prejudice and problems that would be where a defendant is denied the right to an attorney during the process of a trial.

Warren E. Burger

Are you hinting at a harmless error even assuming all that your friends say that it's harmless error?

Nanette Laughrey

No Your Honor. We of course submit that we do not think --

Warren E. Burger

No, but --

Nanette Laughrey

-- that there is any prejudice in this case.

Warren E. Burger

-- an alternate, I wonder whether you're making an alternative argument that this is harmless error even if otherwise (Voice Overlap) --

Nanette Laughrey

No, I'm saying that if you decide that it was error and it was unconstitutional and you're considering whether it is retroactive or not you look at the question of what did the constitutional provision protect. And in Daniels, you indicated that what the Sixth Amendment fair-cross-section protects is not of the kind that would necessitate a retroactive application. The third most important thing is what happens if you make this retroactive. That if petitioner has tried to minimize the effect that it would have on the administration of justice in Jackson County by saying that it is only one county in Missouri. I'm sure that this Court is aware of that half of the population in the State of Missouri is in the metropolitan Kansas City area. And that there is going to be a substantial undermining of the administration of justice in Jackson County, Missouri.

Byron R. White

And does a -- what percentage of the convicts who were convicted in Jackson County -- what percentage of those are still in -- who've been convicted since Taylor are still there?

Nanette Laughrey

Your Honor we of course do not have those statistics at this time. You are aware though of how many petitions for cert have already been filed in this Court that they are in Limbo at this time that the petitioner can certainly tell you that there is certainly more than 150 cases in which this issue has been raised and in which the statistics have been made out. And one of the issues that you indicated that you would consider in Stovall versus Denno and in Daniels versus Louisiana is the effect on the administration of justice and to make the State of Missouri we try all of those cases would have a devastating effect on the administration of justice in our state.

Potter Stewart

Daniels against Louisiana was the case that held the Taylor doctrine not retroactive?

Nanette Laughrey

That is correct Your Honor.

Potter Stewart

I don't -- is it cited in your brief?

Nanette Laughrey

No it is not. We did not discuss it --

Potter Stewart

Do you remember the citation, 400 and something, 15 or --

Nanette Laughrey

I do not have the citation with me.

Potter Stewart

After Taylor, 420 something.

Nanette Laughrey

If there are no further questions, thank you very much.

Warren E. Burger

Very well. Do you have anything further Mr. Nation?

Lee M. Nation

Yes.

Warren E. Burger

You seem didn't have -- there seems to be disagreement on the factual situation between you and the state about the women who do not return their questionnaires. She says they are automatically put -- and you said they were automatically out --

Lee M. Nation

The statement made in our reply brief was that women who do not return the questionnaires and who do not follow the request of the summons do not appear for jury service.

Warren E. Burger

That isn't quite the way you put it in your argument. I think there was a little difference --

Lee M. Nation

It was something like that in the brief that -- yes, and that's the reason that the wheel is as high as it is. That's the reason that there is 29% women on the wheel it's because if they don't return the questionnaire, they're put onto the wheel and then, they opt off when they receive the summons. I'm not sure what we could further prove prior to trial. To prove a case I believe under the precedence of this Court of prima facie case has been made. We showed a non-neutral selection procedure and we showed marked underrepresentation of women. Now, it is incumbent upon the state to come up with some reasonable explanation and attributing the fact that 14.5% of jury panels could possibly be random chance or something else. The possibility of that happening is infinitesimal.

William H. Rehnquist

You don't claim the Missouri statute though is unconstitutional in all situations. It has to be accompanied by your Jackson County statistical showing?

Lee M. Nation

Well, under Taylor, you have to prove that there is an exemption and that there is underrepresentation. No statute is would -- is per se unconstitutional but in its effect here in Jackson County it is. Further, the only reason --

Potter Stewart

That is because of your statistical showing as well as because of the practices and procedures in Jackson County?

Lee M. Nation

Yes. The exemption is the same for other counties in the state but other people hide the exemption from their women.

Warren E. Burger

In the -- in a specific case, could this ever -- in your view be harmless error?

Lee M. Nation

Only in a case where there is absolutely no question of credibility for the jury. In any case where the jury has to determine the credibility of witnesses it is impossible to say that it's harmless error or harmless constitutional error.

Warren E. Burger

Well, what if a defendant on the stand under cross-examination has as it has happened in some cases, testified in a way that its added up to essentially a judicial confession of the crime, would you think that'd be the kind that could be harmless error?

Lee M. Nation

Well, Your Honor as a criminal defense lawyer, I have occasionally had instances where my client -- the only reason where a trial is not to contest the facts but to try and receive a light sentence because in Missouri the jury sentences and it's my experience that women are much more sympathetic towards defendants than men are. So, in that instance, even in that situation --

Warren E. Burger

(Voice Overlap) fungible, it's a -- was --

Lee M. Nation

I don't think they're fungible.

Thurgood Marshall

I think we're going to give a lot of trouble cause that wasn't my experience.

Lee M. Nation

There is -- I don't know how many, there are seven I believe petitions for certiorari on this issue before the Court. And I have nowhere near 150 cases. I'm not sure what the number is. But we believe as far as retroactivity that this case falls squarely under Taylor and that anyone who raised it prior to trial introduced evidence requested the court to quash the jury panel and give him a reasonably representative jury at trial should be afforded a new trial. Thank you.

Warren E. Burger

Thank you counsel.

The case is submitted.

Selected Majority Opinions

- ORRIN S. REED v. ROBERT FARLEY, SUPERINTENDENT, INDIANA STATE PRISON, et al.

- CARL THOMPSON v. PATRICK KEOHANE, WARDEN, et al.

- UNITED STATES v. VIRGINIA, et al.

- CATERPILLAR INC. v. JAMES DAVID LEWIS

- AMCHEM PRODUCTS, INC., et al. v. GEORGE WINDSOR et al.

- UNITED STATES v. JAMES HERMAN O'HAGAN

- MARGARET KAWAAUHAU, et vir, PETITIONERS v. PAUL W. GEIGER

- RUHRGAS AG v. MARATHON OIL CO. et al.

- TOMMY OLMSTEAD, COMMISSIONER, GEORGIA DEPT. OF HUMAN RESOURCES, et al. v. L. C., by JONATHAN ZIMRING, et al.

- FRIENDS OF THE EARTH, INC., et al. v. LAIDLAW ENVIRONMENTAL SERVICES (TOC), INC.

- CORRECTION OFFICER PORTER, et al. v. RONALD NUSSLE

- ERIC ELDRED, et al. v. JOHN D. ASHCROFT, ATTORNEY GENERAL

- ERICK CORNELL CLAY v. UNITED STATES

- EXXON MOBIL CORP. et al. v. SAUDI BASIC INDUSTRIES CORP.

- JENIFER ARBAUGH v. Y & H CORPORATION, DBA THE MOONLIGHT CAFE

- PATRICK A. DAY v. JAMES McDONOUGH, INTERIM SECRETARY, FLORIDA DEPARTMENT OF CORRECTIONS

- JOHN CUNNINGHAM v. CALIFORNIA

- TELLABS, INC., et al. v. MAKOR ISSUES & RIGHTS, LTD., et al.

- DERRICK KIMBROUGH v. UNITED STATES

- NATIONAL FEDERATION OF INDEPENDENT BUSINESS, et al. v. KATHLEEN SEBELIUS, SECRETARY OF HHS, et al.

- GREG McQUIGGIN, WARDEN v. FLOYD PERKINS

- DAIMLER AG v. BARBARA BAUMAN et al.

- STEPHANIE C. ARTIS v. DISTRICT OF COLUMBIA

ORRIN S. REED v. ROBERT FARLEY, SUPERINTENDENT, INDIANA STATE PRISON, et al.

No. 93-5418, June 20, 1994

ON WRIT OF CERTIORARI TO THE UNITED STATES COURT OF APPEALS FOR THE SEVENTH CIRCUIT

The Interstate Agreement on Detainers Act (IAD), a compact among 48 States, the District of Columbia, and the Federal Government, provides that the trial of a prisoner transferred from one participating jurisdiction to another shall commence within 120 days of the prisoner's arrival in the receiving State, Article IV(c), and directs dismissal with prejudice when trial does not occur within the time prescribed, Article V(c). Petitioner Reed was transferred in April 1983 from a federal prison in Indiana to state custody pursuant to an IAD detainer lodged by Indiana officials. Trial on the state charges was originally set for a date 19 days beyond the 120-day IAD period and was subsequently postponed for an additional 35 days. Although Reed's many and wide-ranging pretrial motions contained a few general references to the IAD time limit, he did not specifically object to his trial date until four days after the 120-day period expired. The trial court denied Reed's petition for discharge on the grounds that the judge had previously been unaware of the 120-day limitation and that Reed had not earlier objected to the trial date or requested a speedier trial. Reed then successfully moved for a continuance to enable him to prepare his defense. Mter his trial and conviction in October 1983, Reed unsuccesfully pursued an appeal and sought postconviction relief in Indiana's courts. He then petitioned for a federal writ of habeas corpus under 28 U. S. C. § 2254. The District Court denied relief, and the Court of Appeals affirmed.

Ginsburg, J., announced the judgment of the Court and delivered the opinion of the Court with respect to Parts I, III, and all but the final paragraph of Part IV, in which Rehnquist, C. J., and O'Connor, Scalia, and Thomas, JJ., joined, and an opinion with respect to Part II and the final paragraph of Part IV, in which Rehnquist, C. J., and O'Connor, J., joined. Scalia, J., filed an opinion concurring in part and concurring in the judgment, in which Thomas, J., joined, post, p. 355. Blackmun, J., filed a dissenting opinion, in which Stevens, Kennedy, and Souter, JJ., joined, post, p. 359.

Jerold S. Solovy argued the cause for petitioner. With him on the briefs were Barry Levenstam, Ellen R. Kordik, and Douglas A. Graham.

Arend J. Abel, Deputy Attorney General of Indiana, argued the cause for respondents. With him on the brief were Pamela Carter, Attorney General, and Matthew R. Gutwein, Wayne E. Uhl, and Suzann Weber Lupton, Deputy Attorneys General.[*]

Justice Ginsburg announced the judgment of the Court and delivered the opinion of the Court with respect to Parts I, III, and all but the final paragraph of Part IV, and an opinion with respect to Part II and the final paragraph of Part IV, in which The Chief Justice and Justice O'Connor join.

The Interstate Agreement on Detainers (IAD), 18 U. S. C. App. §2, is a compact among 48 States, the District of Columbia, and the Federal Government. It enables a participating State to gain custody of a prisoner incarcerated in another jurisdiction, in order to try him on criminal charges. Article IV(c) of the IAD provides that trial of a transferred prisoner "shall be commenced within one hundred and twenty days of the arrival of the prisoner in the receiving State, but for good cause shown in open court, . . . the court having jurisdiction of the matter may grant any necessary or reasonable continuance." IAD Article V(c) states that when trial does not occur within the time prescribed, the charges shall be dismissed with prejudice.

The petitioner in this case, Orrin Scott Reed, was transferred in April 1983 from a federal prison in Indiana to state custody pursuant to an IAD request made by Indiana officials. Reed was tried in October of that year, following postponements made and explained in his presence in open court. Reed's petition raises the question whether a state prisoner, asserting a violation of IAD Article IV(c)'s 120-day limitation, may enforce that speedy trial prescription in a federal habeas corpus action under 28 U.S.C. § 2254.

We hold that a state court's failure to observe the 120-day rule of IAD Article IV(c) is not cognizable under §2254 when the defendant registered no objection to the trial date at the time it was set, and suffered no prejudice attributable to the delayed commencement. Accordingly, we affirm the judgment of the Court of Appeals.

I

In December 1982, while petitioner Reed was serving time in a Terre Haute, Indiana, federal prison, the State of Indiana charged him with theft and habitual offender status. Indiana authorities lodged a detainer [n.1] against Reed and, on April 27, 1983, took custody of him. The 120-day rule of IAD Article IV(c) thus instructed that, absent any continuance, Reed's trial was to commence on or before August 25, 1983.

At two pretrial conferences, one on June 27, the other on August 1, the trial judge discussed with Reed (who chose to represent himself) and the prosecutor the number of days needed for the trial, and the opening date. At the June 27 conference, the court set a July 18 deadline for submission of the many threshold motions Reed said he wished to file, and September 13 as the trial date. That trial date exceeded IAD Article IV(c)'s120-day limit, but neither the prosecutor nor Reed called the IAD limit to the attention of the judge, and neither asked for a different trial date. Reed did indicate a preference for trial at a time when he would be out of jail on bond (or on his own recognizance); he informed the court that he would be released from federal custody two weeks before September 13, unless federal authorities revoked his "good days" credits, in which case he would be paroled on September 14. App. 39; see id., at 76.

At the August 1 pretrial conference, Reed noted his imminent release from federal custody and asked the court to set bond. Id., at 76-79. In response, the court set bond at $25,000. Also, because of a calendar conflict, the court reset the trial date to September 19. Id., at 79-81. [n.2] Reed inquired about witness subpoenas and requested books on procedure, but again, he said nothing at the conference to alert the judge to Article IV(c)'s 120-day limit, nor did he express any other objection to the September 19 trial date.

Interspersed in Reed's many written and oral pretrial motions are references to IAD provisions other than Article IV(c). See App. 28-31, 44 (alleging illegality of transfer from federal to state custody without a pre-transfer hearing); id., at 46 (asserting failure to provide hygienic care in violation of IAD Article V). Reed did refer to the IAD prescription on trial commencement in three of the written motions he filed during the 120-day period; indeed, one of these motions was filed on the very day of the August 1 pretrial conference. [n.3] In noneof the three motions, however, did Reed mention Article IV(c) or the September 13 trial date previously set. In contrast, on August 29, four days after the 120-day period expired, Reed presented a clear statement and citation. In a "Petition for Discharge," he alleged that Indiana had failed to try him within 120 days of his transfer to state custody, and therefore had violated Article IV(c); [n.4] consequently, he urged, the IAD mandated his immediate release. [n.5] The trial judge denied the petition, explaining:

> "Today is the first day I was aware that there was a 120 day limitation on the Detainer Act. The Court made its setting and while there has been a request for moving the trial forward, there has not been any speedy trial request filed, nor has there been anything in the nature of an objection to the trial setting, but only an urging that it be done within the guidelines that have been set out." App. 113-114.

The morning trial was to commence, September 19, Reed filed a motion for continuance, saying he needed additional time for trial preparation. Id., at 128. A newspaper article published two days earlier had listed the names of persons called for jury duty and the 1954 to 1980 time frame of Reed's alleged prior felony convictions. Concerned that the article might jeopardize the fairness of the trial, the judge offered Reed three options: (1) start the trial on schedule; (2) postpone it for one week; or (3) continue it to a late October date. Reed chose the third option, id., at 134, 142, and the trial began on October 18; the jury convicted Reed of theft, and found him a habitual offender. He received a sentence of four years in prison on the theft conviction, and 30 years on the habitual offender conviction, the terms to run consecutively.

The Indiana Supreme Court affirmed the convictions. Reed v. State, 491 N. E. 2d 182 (1986). Concerning Reed's objection that the trial commenced after the 120-day period specified in IAD Article IV(c), the Indiana Supreme Court stressed the timing of Reed's pleas in court: Reed had vigorously urged at the August 1 pretrial conference other alleged IAD violations (particularly, his asserted right to a hearing in advance of the federal transfer to state custody), but he did not then object to the trial date. Id., at 184-185; see App. 67-74. "The relevant times when [Reed] should have objected were on June 27, 1983, the date the trial was set, and August 1, 1983, the date the trial was reset," the Indiana Supreme Court concluded. 491 N. E. 2d, at 185.

Reed unsuccessfully sought postconviction relief in the Indiana courts, and then petitioned under 28 U.S.C. § 2254 for a federal writ of habeas corpus. The District Court denied the petition. Examining the record, that court concluded that "a significant amount of the delay of trial is attributable to the many motions filed by[Reed] or filed on [Reed's] behalf"; delay chargeable to Reed, the court held, was excludable from the 120-day period. Reed v. Clark, Civ. No. S 90-226 (ND Ind., Sept. 21, 1990), App. 188, 195-196.

The Court of Appeals for the Seventh Circuit affirmed. Reed v. Clark, 984 F. 2d 209 (1993). Preliminarily, the Court of Appeals recognized that the IAD, although state law, is also a "law of the United States" within the meaning of §2254(a). Id., at 210. Nonetheless, that court held collateral relief unavailable because Reed's IAD speedy trial arguments and remedial contentions had been considered and rejected by the Indiana courts. Stone v. Powell, 428 U.S. 465 (1976), the Court of Appeals concluded, "establishes the proper framework for evaluating claims under the IAD." 984 F. 2d, at 213. In Stone, this Court held that the exclusionary rule, devised to promote police respect for the Fourth Amendment rights of suspects, should not be applied on collateral review unless the state court failed to consider the defendant's arguments. We granted certiorari, 510 U. S. ___ (1993), to resolve a conflict among the Courts of Appeals on the availability of habeas review of IAD speedy trial claims. [n.6]

II

A state prisoner may obtain federal habeas corpus relief "only on the ground that he is in custody in violation of the Constitution or laws or treaties of the United States." 28 U.S.C. § 2254(a) (emphasis added). Respondent Indiana initially argues that the IAD is a voluntary interstate agreement, not a "la[w] . . . of the United States" within the meaning of §2254(a). Our precedent, however, has settled that issue: while the IAD is indeed state law, it is a law of the United States as well. See Carchman v. Nash, 473 U.S. 716, 719 (1985) (§2254 case, holding that the IAD "is a congressionally sanctioned interstate compact within the Compact Clause, U. S. Const., Art. I, §10, cl. 3, and thus is a federal law subject to federal construction"); Cuyler v. Adams, 449 U.S. 433, 438-442 (1981) ("congressional consent transforms an interstate compact . . . into a law of the United States").

The Court of Appeals recognized that the IAD is both a law of Indiana and a federal statute. 984 F. 2d, at 210. Adopting Stone v. Powell, 428 U.S. 465 (1976), asits framework, however, that court held relief under §2254 unavailable to Reed. 984 F. 2d, at 213. Stone holdsthat a federal court may not, under §2254, consider a claim that evidence from an unconstitutional search was introduced at a state prisoner's trial if the prisoner had "an opportunity for full and fair litigation of [the] claim in the state courts." 428 U. S., at 469. Our opinion in Stone concentrated on "the nature and purpose of the Fourth Amendment exclusionary rule." Id., at 481. The Court emphasized that its decision confined the exclusionary rule, not the scope of §2254 generally:

> "Our decision today is not concerned with the scope of the habeas corpus statute as authority for litigating constitutional claims generally. We do reaffirm that the exclusionary rule is a judicially created remedy rather than a personal constitutional right, . . . and we emphasize the minimal utility of the rule when sought to be applied to Fourth Amendment claims in a habeas corpus proceeding." Id., at 495, n. 37 (emphasis in original).

We have "repeatedly declined to extend the rule in Stone beyond its original bounds." Withrow v. Williams, 507 U. S. ___, ___ (slip op., at 5) (1993) (holding that Stone does not apply to a state prisoner's claim that his conviction rests on statements obtained in violation of the safeguards set out in Miranda v. Arizona, 384 U.S. 436 (1966)). [n.7] Because precedent already in place suffices to resolve Reed's case, we do not adopt the Seventh Circuit's Stone%based rationale.

We have stated that habeas review is available to check violations of federal laws when the error qualifies as "a fundamental defect which inherently results in a complete miscarriage of justice, [or] an omission inconsistent with the rudimentary demands of fair procedure. Hill v. United States, 368 U.S. 424, 428 (1962); accord, United States v. Timmreck, 441 U.S. 780, 783 (1979); Davis v. United States, 417 U.S. 333, 346 (1974). The IAD's purpose--providing a nationally uniform means of transferring prisoners between jurisdictions--can be effectuated only by nationally uniform interpretation. See 984 F. 2d, at 214 (Ripple, J., dissenting from denial of rehearing in banc). Therefore, the argument that the compact would be undermined if a State's courts resisted steadfast enforcement, with total insulation from §2254 review, is not without force. Cf. Stone v. Powell, supra, at 526 (Brennan, J., dissenting) (institutional constraints preclude Supreme Court from overseeing adequately whether state courts have properly applied federal law). This case, however, gives us no cause to consider whether we would confront an omission of the kind contemplated in Hill, Timmreck, or Davis, if a state court, presented with a timely request to set a trial date within the IAD's 120-day period, nonetheless refused to comply with Article IV(c).

When a defendant obscures Article IV(c)'s time prescription and avoids clear objection until the clock has run, cause for collateral review scarcely exists. An unwitting judicial slip of the kind involved here ranks with the nonconstitutional lapses we have held not cognizable in a postconviction proceeding. In Hill, for example, a federal prisoner sought collateral relief,under 28 U.S.C. § 2255 [n.8] based on the trial court's failure at sentencing to afford him an opportunity to make a statement and present information in mitigation of punishment, as required by Rule 32(a) of the Federal Rules of Criminal Procedure. The petitioner, however, had not sought to assert his Rule 32(a) rights at the time of sentencing, a point we stressed:

> "[W]e are not dealing here with a case where the defendant was affirmatively denied an opportunity to speak during the hearing at which his sentence was imposed. Nor is it suggested that in imposing the sentence the District Judge was either misinformed or uninformed as to any relevant circumstances. Indeed, there is no

claim that the defendant would have had anything at all to say if he had been formally invited to speak." 368 U. S., at 429.

"[W]hen all that is shown is a failure to comply with the formal requirements" of Rule 32(a), we held, "collateral relief is not available." Ibid. But we left open the question whether "[collateral] relief would be available if a violation of Rule 32(a) occurred in the context of other aggravating circumstances." Ibid.

Hill controlled our decision in United States v. Timmreck, supra, where a federal prisoner sought collateral review, under §2255, to set aside a conviction based on a guilty plea. The complainant in Timmreck alleged that the judge who accepted his plea failed to inform him, in violation of Rule 11 of the Federal Rules of Criminal Procedure, that he faced a mandatory postincarceration special parole term. We rejected the collateral attack, observing that the violation of Rule 11 was technical, and did not "resul[t] in a `complete miscarriage of justice' or in a proceeding `inconsistent withthe rudimentary demands of fair procedure.' " Id., at 784, quoting Hill, supra, at 428. "As in Hill," we found it unnecessary to consider whether "[postconviction] relief would be available if a violation of Rule 11 occurred in the context of other aggravating circum stances." Id., at 784-785.

Reed's case similarly lacks "aggravating circumstances" rendering " `the need for the remedy afforded by the writ of habeas corpus . . . apparent.' " Hill, supra, at 428, quoting Bowen v. Johnston, 306 U.S. 19, 27 (1939). Reed had two clear chances to alert the trial judge in open court if he indeed wanted his trial to start on or before August 25, 1993. He let both opportunities pass by. At the pretrial hearings at which the trial date was set and rescheduled, on June 27 and August 1, Reed not only failed to mention the 120-day limit; he indicated a preference for holding the trial after his release from federal imprisonment, which was due to occur after the 120 days expired. See supra, at 2-3. Then, on the 124th day, when it was no longer possible to meet Article IV(c)'s deadline, Reed produced his meticulously precise "Petition for Discharge." See supra, at 4, and n. 4. [n.9]

As the Court of Appeals observed, had Reed objected to the trial date on June 27 or August 1 "instead of burying his demand in a flood of other documents, the [trial] court could have complied with the IAD's requirements." 984 F. 2d, at 209-210. The Court of Appeals further elaborated:

"During the pretrial conference of August 1, 1983, Reed presented several arguments based on the IAD, including claims that the federal government should have held a hearing before turning him over to the state and that his treatment in Indiana fell short of the state's obligations under Art. V(d) and (h). Reed did not mention the fact that the date set for trial would fall outside the 120 days allowed by Art. IV(c). Courts often require litigants to flag important issues orally rather than bury vital (and easily addressed) problems in reams of paper, as Reed did. E.g., Fed. R. Crim. P. 30 (requiring a distinct objection to jury instructions); cf. Fed. R. Crim. P. 12(b) (a district judge may require motions to be made orally). It would not have been difficult for the judge to advance the date of the trial or make a finding on the record of good cause, either of which would have satisfied Art. IV(c). Because the subject never came up, however, the trial judge overlooked the problem." 984 F. 2d, at 213.

Reed regards the Court of Appeals' description of his litigation conduct, even if true, as irrelevant. He maintains that the IAD dictates the result we must reach, for Article V(c) directs dismissal with prejudice when Article IV(c)'s time limit has passed. [n.10] Article V(c) instructs only that "the appropriate court of the jurisdiction where the indictment . . . has been pending"--i.e., the original trial court--shall dismiss the charges iftrial does not commence within the time Article IV(c) prescribes. Article V(c) does not address the discrete question whether relief for violations of the IAD's speedy trial provisions is available on collateral review. That matter is governed instead by the principles and precedent generally controlling availability of the great writ. See 984 F. 2d, at 212. Referring to those guides, and particularly the Hill and Timmreck decisions, we conclude that a state court's failure to observe the 120-day rule of IAD Article IV(c) is not cognizable under §2254 when the defendant registered no objection to the trial date at the time it was set, and suffered no prejudice attributable to the delayed commencement.

III

Reed argues that he is entitled to habeas relief because the IAD's speedy trial provision "effectuates a constitutional right," the Sixth Amendment guarantee of a speedy trial. Brief for Petitioner 26. Accordingly, he maintains, the alleged IAD violation should be treated as a constitutional violation or as a "fundamental defect" satisfying the Hill standard, not as a mere technical error. Reed's argument is insubstantial for, as he concedes, his constitutional right to a speedy trial was in no way violated. See Tr. of Oral Arg. 7.

Reed's trial commenced 54 days after the 120-day period expired. He does not suggest that his ability to present a defense was prejudiced by the delay. Nor could he plausibly make such a claim. [n.11] Indeed, asserting a need for more time to prepare for a trial thatwould be "fair and meaningful," App. 128, Reed himself requested a delay beyond the scheduled September 19 opening. A showing of prejudice is required to establish a violation of the Sixth Amendment Speedy Trial Clause, and that necessary ingredient is entirely missing here. See Barker v. Wingo, 407 U.S. 514, 530 (1972) (four factors figure in the determination of Sixth Amendment speedy trial claims; one of the four is "prejudice to the defendant").

IV

More strenuously, Reed argues that Hill and similar decisions establish a standard for federal prisoners seeking relief under 28 U.S.C. § 2255 [n.12] not for state prisoners seeking relief under §2254. But it is scarcely doubted that, at least where mere statutory violations are at issue, "§2255 was intended to mirror §2254 in operative effect." Davis v. United States, 417 U.S. 333, 344 (1974). Far from suggesting that the Hill standard is inapplicable to §2254 cases, our decisions assume that Hill controls collateral review--under both §§2254 and 2255--when a federal statute, but not the Constitution, is the basis for the postconviction attack. For example, in Stone v. Powell, a §2254 case, we recalled "the established rule with respect to nonconstitutional claims" as follows: "[N]onconstitutional claims . . . can be raised on collateral review only if the alleged error constituted a ` "fundamental defect which inherently results in a complete miscarriage of justice." ' " 428 U. S., at 477,n. 10, quoting Davis, 417 U. S., at 346, quoting Hill, 368 U. S., at 428. [n.13]

Reed nevertheless suggests that we invoked the fundamental defect standard in Hill and Timmreck for this sole reason: "So far as convictions obtained in the federal courts are concerned, the general rule is that the writ of habeas corpus will not be allowed to do service for an appeal." Sunal v. Large, 332 U.S. 174, 178 (1947) (emphasis added). The same "general rule," however, applies to §2254. Where the petitioner--whether a state or federal prisoner--failed properly to raise his claim on direct review, the writ is available only if the petitioner establishes "cause" for the waiver and shows "actual prejudice resulting from the alleged . . . violation." Wainwright v. Sykes, 433 U.S. 72, 84 (1977); id., at 87.

We see no reason to afford habeas review to a state prisoner like Reed, who let a time clock run without alerting the trial court, yet deny collateral review to a federal prisoner similarly situated. See Francis v. Henderson, 425 U.S. 536, 542 (1976) (" `Plainly the interest in finality is the same with regard to both federal and state prisoners. . . . There is no reason to . . . give greater preclusive effect to procedural defaults by federal defendants than to similar defaults by state defendants.' ") (quoting Kaufman v. United States, 394 U.S. 217, 228 (1969)); see also United States v. Frady,456 U.S. 152, 167-168 (1982) (collateral review of procedurally defaulted claims is subject to same "cause and actual prejudice" standard, whether the claim is brought by a state prisoner under §2254 or a federal prisoner under §2255).

Reed contends that the scope of review should be broader under §2254 than under §2255, because state prisoners, unlike their federal counterparts, have "had no meaningful opportunity to have a federal court consider any federal claim." Brief for Petitioner 34. But concern that state courts might be hostile to the federal law here at stake is muted by two considerations. First, we have reserved the question whether federal habeas review is available to check violations of the IAD's speedy trial prescriptions when the state court disregards timely pleas for their application. See supra, at 9. Second, the IAD is both federal law, and the law of Indiana. Ind. Code §35-33-10-4 (1993). As the Court of Appeals noted: "We have no more reason to suppose that the Supreme Court of Indiana seeks to undermine the IAD than we have to suppose that it seeks to undermine any other law of Indiana." 984 F. 2d, at 211.

For the reasons stated, the judgment of the Court of Appeals is Affirmed.

NOTES

* Solicitor General Days, Assistant Attorney General Harris, Deputy Solicitor General Bryson, and Richard H. Seamon filed a brief for the United States as amicus curiae urging affirmance.

[1] A detainer is "a request filed by a criminal justice agency with the institution in which a prisoner is incarcerated, asking either to hold the prisoner for the agency or to notify the agency when release of the prisoner is imminent." Carchman v. Nash, 473 U.S. 716, 719 (1985).

[2] Reed posted bond by corporate surety on September 28 and was thereupon released from pretrial incarceration. See App. 148.

[3] See Petition for Relief of Violations (filed July 25, 1983), id. at 56 (requesting that "trial be held within the legal guidelines of the [IAD]" and asserting that the State was "forcing [him] to be tried beyond the limits as set forth in the [IAD]"); Petition for Revision ofPre trial Procedure and Relief of Violations (filed August 1, 1983), id., at 88 (seeking dismissal of charges, referring, inter alia, to "the limited time left for trial within the laws"); Petition for Subpoena for Depositions upon Oral Examination, and for Production of Documentary Evidence (filed August 11, 1983), id., at 91 (requesting action "as soon as possible due to approaching trial date and Detainer Act time limits").

[4] App. 94. Specifically, Reed wrote: "That petitioner is being detained contrary to Indiana law and procedure: 35-33-10-4, Article 4(c) . . . trial shall be commenced within one hundred twenty (120) days of arrival of the prisoner in the receiving state . . . ."

[5] The prosecutor, in response, pointed out that Article IV(c) permits "any necessary or reasonable continuance," and that Reed had not objected at the time the trial court set the date. App. 113. He also expressed confusion about the effect of the 120-day rule and its relationship to the 180-day time limit prescribed by a different IAD provision. Id., at 114; see n. 6, infra.

[6] The IAD's other speedy trial provision, Article III(a), requires that a prisoner against whom a detainer has been lodged be tried within 180 days of the prosecuting State's receipt of the prisoner's notice requesting speedy disposition of the charges. Fex v. Michigan, 507 U. S. ___ (1993).

The Seventh Circuit's rationale is one of several approaches taken by Courts of Appeals addressing the availability of habeas review for violations of Articles IV(c) and III(a). Some courts have denied relief without regard to whether the petitioner alerted the trial court to the IAD's speedy trial provisions. In this category, some decisions state that IAD speedy trial claims are never cognizable under §2254, because IAD speedy trial violations do not constitute a "fundamental defect which inherently results in a complete miscarriage of justice," under Hill v. United States, 368 U.S. 424, 428 (1962). See, e.g., Reilly v. Warden, FCI Petersburg, 947 F. 2d 43, 44-45 (CA2 1991) (per curiam); Fasano v.Hall, 615 F. 2d 555, 558-559 (CA1 1980). Other courts applying the Hill standard have said §2254 is not available for failure to meet IAD speedy trial specifications unless the petitioner shows actual prejudice. See, e.g., Seymore v. Alabama, 846 F. 2d 1355, 1359-1360 (CA11 1988); Kerr v. Finkbeiner, 757 F. 2d 604, 607 (CA4 1985). Still other courts have reached the merits of IAD speedy trial contentions raised in habeas actions under §2254. See, e.g., Birdwell v. Skeen, 983 F. 2d 1332 (CA5 1993) (affirming District Court's grant of the writ, where state court failed to comply with IAD Article III(a) in spite of petitioner's repeated request for compliance with the 180-day rule); Cody v. Morris, 623 F. 2d 101, 103 (CA9 1980) (remanding to District Court for resolution of factual dispute over whether habeas petitioner had been tried within Article IV(c)'s 120-day limit); United States ex rel. Esola v. Groomes, 520 F. 2d 830, 839 (CA3 1975) (remanding to District Court for determination on whether state trial court had granted continuance for good cause pursuant to Article IV(c)).

[7] See also Kimmelman v. Morrison, 477 U.S. 365, 375-377 (1986) (Stone does not bar habeas review of claim of ineffective assistance of counsel based on counsel's failure to file a timely suppression motion); Rose v. Mitchell, 443 U.S. 545, 559-564 (1979) (refusing to extend Stone to equal protection claim of racial discrimination in selection of state grand jury foreman); Jackson v. Virginia, 443 U.S. 307, 321-324 (1979) (Stone does not bar habeas review of due process claim of insufficiency of evidence supporting conviction).

[8] The text of §2255, in relevant part, is set out at n. 11, infra.

[9] In contrast, the defendant in United States v. Ford, 550 F. 2d 732 (CA2 1977), aff'd sub nom. United

States v. Mauro, 436 U.S. 340 (1978), made "[timely and] vigorous protests," to several government requested continuances, yet was tried 13 months after Article IV(c)'s 120-day period expired. 550 F. 2d, at 735. Reed's trial occurred within 2 months of the period's expiration. See infra, at 13.

[10] Article V(c) provides in relevant part:

%[I]n the event that an action on the indictment, information, or complaint on the basis of which the detainer has been lodged is not brought to trial within the period provided in article III or article IV hereof, the appropriate court of the jurisdiction where the indictment, information, or complaint has been pending shall enter an order dismissing the same with prejudice, and any detainer based thereon shall cease to be of any force or effect."

[11] As the Court of Appeals noted:

%Had Indiana put Reed to trial within 120 days of his transfer from federal prison, everything would have proceeded as it did. Reed does not contend that vital evidence fell into the prosecutor's hands (or slipped through his own fingers) between August 26 and September 19, 1983." 984 F. 2d, at 212.

[12] Section 2255 provides in pertinent part:

%A prisoner in custody under sentence of a court established by Act of Congress claiming the right to be released upon the ground that the sentence was imposed in violation of the Constitution or laws of the United States, . . . may move the court which imposed the sentence to vacate, set aside or correct the sentence."

[13] See also United States v. Addonizio, 442 U.S. 178 (1979), in which we reiterated that the Hill standard governs habeas review of all claims of federal statutory error, citing Stone:

%[U]nless the claim alleges a lack of jurisdiction or constitutional error, the scope of collateral attack has remained far more limited. Stone v. Powell, 428 U.S. 465, 477, n. 10. The Court has held that an error of law does not provide a basis for collateral attack unless the claimed error constituted `a fundamental defect which inherently results in a complete miscarriage of justice.' " 442 U. S., at 185, quoting Hill, 368 U. S., at 428.

CARL THOMPSON v. PATRICK KEOHANE, WARDEN, et al.

No. 94-6615, November 29, 1995

ON WRIT OF CERTIORARI TO THE UNITED STATES COURT OF APPEALS FOR THE NINTH CIRCUIT

Justice Ginsburg, delivered the opinion of the Court.

During a two-hour, tape-recorded session at Alaska state trooper headquarters, petitioner Carl Thompson confessed that he killed his former wife. Thompson's confession was placed in evidence at the ensuing Alaska state-court trial, and he was convicted of first-degree murder. Challenging his conviction in a federal habeas corpus proceeding, Thompson maintained that the Alaska troopers gained his confession without according him the warnings Miranda v. Arizona, 384 U. S. 436 (1966), requires: that he could remain silent; that anything he said could be used against him in court; and that he was entitled to an attorney, either retained or appointed.

Miranda warnings are due only when a suspect interrogated by the police is "in custody." The state trial and appellate courts determined that Thompson was not "in custody" when he confessed. The statute governing federal habeas corpus proceedings, 28 U. S. C. § 2254, directs that, ordinarily, state-court fact findings "shall be presumed to be correct." § 2254(d). The question before this Court is whether the state-court determination that Thompson was not "in custody" when he confessed is a finding of fact warranting a presumption of correctness, or a matter of law calling for independent review in federal court. We hold that the issue whether a suspect is "in custody," and therefore entitled to Miranda warnings, presents a mixed question of law and fact qualifying for independent review.

I

On September 10, 1986, two moose hunters discovered the body of a dead woman floating in a gravel pit lake on the outskirts of Fairbanks, Alaska. The woman had been stabbed 29 times. Notified by the hunters, the Alaska state troopers issued a press release seeking assistance in identifying the body. Thompson called the troopers on September 11 to inform them that his former wife, Dixie Thompson, fit the description in the press release and that she had been missing for about a month. Through a dental examination, the troopers conclusively established that the corpse was Dixie Thompson. On September 15, a trooper called Thompson and asked him to come to headquarters, purportedly to identify personal items the troopers thought belonged to Dixie Thompson. It is now undisputed, however, that the trooper's primary reason for contacting Thompson was to question him about the murder.

Thompson drove to the troopers' headquarters in his pickup truck and, upon arriving, immediately identified the items as Dixie's. He remained at headquarters, however, for two more hours while two unarmed troopers continuously questioned him in a small interview room and tape-recorded the exchange. The troopers did not inform Thompson of his Miranda rights. Although they constantly assured Thompson he was free to leave, they also told him repeatedly that they knew he had killed his former wife. Informing Thompson that execution of a search warrant was underway at his home, and that his truck was about to be searched pursuant to another warrant, the troopers asked questions that invited a confession. App. 43-79.[1] Eventually, Thompson told the troopers he killed Dixie.

As promised, the troopers permitted Thompson to leave, but impounded his truck. Left without transportation, Thompson accepted the troopers' offer of a ride to his friend's house. Some two hours later, the troopers arrested Thompson and charged him with first-degree murder.

The Alaska trial court, without holding an evidentiary hearing, denied Thompson's motion to suppress his September 15 statements. Tr. 118 (Dec. 12, 1986); Tr. 142 (Mar. 18, 1987). Deciding the motion on the papers submitted, the trial court ruled that Thompson was not "in custody" for Miranda purposes, therefore the troopers had no obligation to inform him of his Miranda rights. App. 8-9.[2] Applying an objective test to resolve the "in custody" question, the court asked whether "'a reasonable person would feel he was not free to leave and break off police questioning.' " Id. , at 7 (quoting Hunter v. State, 590 P. 2d 888, 895 (Alaska 1979)). These features, the court indicated, were key: Thompson arrived at the station in response to a trooper's request; two unarmed troopers in plain clothes questioned him; Thompson was told he was free to go at any time; and he was not arrested at the conclusion of the interrogation. App. 7-8. Although the trial court held that, under the totality of the circumstances, a reasonable person would have felt free to leave, it also observed that the troopers' subsequent actions—releasing and shortly thereafter arresting Thompson—rendered the question "very close." Id. , at 8-9.

After a trial, at which the prosecution played the taperecorded confession, the jury found Thompson guilty of first-degree murder and tampering with evidence. The Court of Appeals of Alaska affirmed Thompson's conviction, concluding, among other things, that the troopers had not placed Thompson "in custody," and therefore had no obligation to give him Miranda warnings. Thompson v. State, 768 P. 2d 127, 131 (Alaska App. 1989).[3] The Alaska Supreme Court denied discretionary review. App. 24.

Thompson filed a petition for a writ of habeas corpus in the United States District Court for the District of Alaska. The District Court denied the writ, according a presumption of correctness under 28 U. S. C. § 2254(d) to the state court's conclusion that, when Thompson confessed, he was not yet "in custody" for Miranda purposes. App. 37. The Court of Appeals for the Ninth Circuit affirmed without publishing an opinion. 34 F. 3d 1073 (1994). Based on Circuit precedent,[4] the court held that "a state court's determination that a defendant was not in custody for purposes of Miranda is a question of fact entitled to the presumption of correctness under 28 U. S. C. § 2254(d)." App. 41.

Federal Courts of Appeals disagree on the issue Thompson asks us to resolve: whether state-court "in custody" determinations are matters of fact entitled to a presumption of correctness under 28 U. S. C. § 2254(d), or mixed questions of law and fact warranting independent review by the federal habeas court. Compare Feltrop v. Delo, 46 F. 3d 766, 773 (CA8 1995) (applying presumption of correctness), with Jacobs v. Singletary, 952 F. 2d 1282, 1291 (CA11 1992) (conducting independent review). Because uniformity among federal courts is important on questions of this order, we granted certiorari to end the division of authority. 513 U. S. 1126 (1995). We now hold that the 28 U. S. C. § 2254(d) presumption does not apply to "in custody" rulings; accordingly, we vacate the Ninth Circuit's judgment.

II

"[I]n-custody interrogation[s]," this Court recognized in Miranda v. Arizona, place "inherently compelling pressures" on the persons interrogated. 384 U. S., at 467. To safeguard the uncounseled individual's Fifth Amendment privilege against self-incrimination, the Miranda Court held, suspects interrogated while in police custody must be told that they have a right to remain silent, that anything they say may be used against them in court, and that they are entitled to the presence of an attorney, either retained or appointed, at the interrogation. Id. , at 444. The Court defined "custodial interrogation" as "questioning initiated by law enforcement officers after a person has been taken into custody or otherwise deprived of his freedom of action in any significant way." Ibid.; see also Oregon v. Mathiason, 429 U. S. 492, 495 (1977) (per curiam) (duty to give Miranda warnings is triggered "only where there has been such a restriction on a person's freedom as to render him `in custody' ") (quoted in Stansbury v. California, 511 U. S. 318, 322 (1994) (per curiam)). Our task in petitioner Thompson's case is to identify the standard governing federal habeas courts' review of state-court "in custody" determinations.[5]

A

Section 2254 governs federal habeas corpus proceedings instituted by persons in custody pursuant to the judgment of a state court. In such proceedings, § 2254(d) declares, state-court determinations of "a factual issue" "shall be presumed to be correct" absent one of the enumerated exceptions.[6] This provision, added in a 1966 amendment, Act of Nov. 2, 1966, Pub. L. 89-711, 80 Stat. 1105-1106, received the Court's close attention in Miller v. Fenton, 474 U. S. 104 (1985). As the Miller Court observed, § 2254(d) "was an almost verbatim codification of the standards delineated in Townsend v. Sain, 372 U. S. 293 (1963), for determining when a district court must hold an evidentiary hearing before acting on a habeas petition." Miller, 474 U. S., at 111.[7] Townsend counseled that, if the habeas petitioner has had in state court "a full and fair hearing . . . resulting in reliable findings," the federal court "ordinarily should . . . accept the facts as found" by the state tribunal. 372 U. S., at 318. Section 2254(d) essentially "elevated [the Townsend Court's] exhortation into a mandatory presumption of correctness." Miller , 474 U. S., at 111-112; see also id. , at 112 (emphasizing respect appropriately accorded "a coequal state judiciary" and citing Culombe v. Connecticut, 367 U. S. 568, 605 (1961) (opinion of Frankfurter, J.)).

Just as Townsend `s instruction on the respect appropriately accorded state-court fact findings is now captured in the § 2254(d) presumption, so we have adhered to Townsend `s definition of the § 2254(d) term "factual issue."[8] The Townsend Court explained that by "`issues of fact,' " it meant "basic, primary, or historical facts: facts `in the sense of a recital of external events and the credibility of their narrators . . . .' " 372 U. S., at 309, n. 6 (quoting Brown v. Allen, 344 U. S. 443, 506 (1953) (opinion of Frankfurter, J.)). "Socalled mixed questions of fact and law, which require the application of a legal standard to the historical-fact determinations," the Townsend Court added, "are not facts in this sense." 372 U. S., at 309, n. 6.[9] In applying § 2254(d), we have reaffirmed that "basic, primary, or historical facts" are the "factual issue[s]" to which the statutory presumption of correctness dominantly relates. See, e. g., Miller, 474 U. S., at 112 (" [S]ubsidiary factual questions" in alleged involuntariness of confession cases are subject to the § 2254(d) presumption, but "the ultimate question"—requiring a "totality of the circumstances" assessment—"is a matter for independent federal determination."); Cuyler v. Sullivan, 446 U. S. 335, 342 (1980) ("mixed determination[s] of law and fact" generally are not subject to the § 2254(d) presumption of correctness).

It must be acknowledged, however, "that the Court has not charted an entirely clear course in this area." Miller, 474 U. S., at 113. In regard to § 2254(d), as in other contexts,[10] the proper characterization of a question as one of fact or law is sometimes slippery. See ibid.; Wainwright v. Witt, 469 U. S. 412, 429 (1985) ("It will not always be easy to separate questions of `fact' from `mixed questions of law and fact' for § 2254(d) purposes . . . ."). Two lines of decisions compose the Court's § 2254(d) law/fact jurisprudence.

In several cases, the Court has classified as "factual issues" within § 2254(d)'s compass questions extending beyond the determination of "what happened." This category notably includes: competency to stand trial (e. g., Maggio v. Fulford, 462 U. S. 111, 117 (1983) (per curiam)); and juror impartiality (e. g., Witt , 469 U. S., at 429; Patton v. Yount, 467 U. S.

1025, 1036 (1984); Rushen v. Spain, 464 U. S. 114, 120 (1983)). While these issues encompass more than "basic, primary, or historical facts," their resolution depends heavily on the trial court's appraisal of witness credibility and demeanor. See, e. g., Witt, 469 U. S., at 429 (Although the trial court is "applying some kind of legal standard to what [it] sees and hears," its "predominant function in determining juror bias involves credibility findings whose basis cannot be easily discerned from an appellate record."). This Court has reasoned that a trial court is better positioned to make decisions of this genre, and has therefore accorded the judgment of the jurist-observer "presumptive weight." Miller, 474 U. S., at 114 (when an "issue involves the credibility of witnesses and therefore turns largely on an evaluation of demeanor, there are compelling and familiar justifications for leaving the process of applying law to fact to the trial court").

On the other hand, the Court has ranked as issues of law for § 2254(d) purposes: the voluntariness of a confession (Miller, 474 U. S., at 116); the effectiveness of counsel's assistance (Strickland v. Washington, 466 U. S. 668, 698 (1984)); and the potential conflict of interest arising out of an attorney's representation of multiple defendants (Cuyler, 446 U. S., at 341-342). "What happened" issues in these cases warranted a presumption of correctness, but the Court declared "the ultimate question" outside § 2254(d)'s domain because of its "uniquely legal dimension." Miller, 474 U. S., at 116; see also Sumner v. Mata, 455 U. S. 591, 597 (1982) (per curiam) ("[T]he constitutionality of the pretrial identification procedures used in this case is a mixed question of law and fact that is not governed by § 2254(d)."); Brewer v. Williams, 430 U. S. 387, 397, and n. 4, 403-404 (1977) (waiver of Sixth Amendment right to assistance of counsel is not a question of historical fact, but rather requires application of constitutional principles to facts).

B

The ultimate "in custody" determination for Miranda purposes, we are persuaded, fits within the latter class of cases. Two discrete inquiries are essential to the determination: first, what were the circumstances surrounding the interrogation; and second, given those circumstances,[11] would a reasonable person have felt he or she was not at liberty to terminate the interrogation and leave. Once the scene is set and the players' lines and actions are reconstructed, the court must apply an objective test to resolve "the ultimate inquiry": "[was] there a `formal arrest or restraint on freedom of movement' of the degree associated with a formal arrest." California v. Beheler, 463 U. S. 1121, 1125 (1983) (per curiam) (quoting Mathiason, 429 U. S., at 495). The first inquiry, all agree, is distinctly factual. State-court findings on these scene- and action-setting questions attract a presumption of correctness under 28 U. S. C. § 2254(d). The second inquiry, however, calls for application of the controlling legal standard to the historical facts. This ultimate determination, we hold, presents a "mixed question of law and fact" qualifying for independent review.

The practical considerations that have prompted the Court to type questions like juror bias and competency as "factual issue[s]," and therefore governed by § 2254(d)'s presumption of correctness, are not dominant here. As this case illustrates, the trial court's superior capacity to resolve credibility issues is not dispositive of the "in custody" inquiry.[12] Credibility determinations, as in the case of the alleged involuntariness of a confession, see Miller, 474 U. S., at 112, may sometimes contribute to the establishment of the historical facts and thus to identification of the "totality of the circumstances." But the crucial question entails an evaluation made after determination of those circumstances: if encountered by a "reasonable person," would the identified circumstances add up to custody as defined in Miranda?[13] See Berkemer v. McCarty, 468 U. S. 420, 442 (1984) (court must assess "how a reasonable man in the suspect's position would have understood his situation"); cf. Miller, 474 U. S., at 116-117 ("[A]ssessments of credibility and demeanor are not crucial to the proper resolution of the ultimate issue of `voluntariness.' ").

Unlike the voir dire of a juror, Patton, 467 U. S., at 1038, or the determination of a defendant's competency, Maggio, 462 U. S., at 117, which "take[s] place in open court on a full record," Miller, 474 U. S., at 117, the trial court does not have a first-person vantage on whether a defendant was "in custody" for Miranda purposes. See 474 U. S., at 117 (police interrogations yielding confessions ordinarily occur, not in court, but in an "inherently more coercive environment"). Furthermore, in fathoming the state of mind of a potential juror or a defendant in order to answer the questions, "Is she free of bias?," "Is he competent to stand trial?," the trial court makes an individual-specific decision, one unlikely to have precedential value.[14] In contrast, "in custody" determinations do guide future decisions.[15] We thus conclude that once the historical facts are resolved, the state court is not "in an appreciably better position than the federal habeas court to make [the ultimate] determination" of the consistency of the law enforcement officer's conduct with the federal Miranda warning requirement. See 474 U. S., at 117.

Notably, we have treated the "in custody" question as one of law when States complained that their courts had erroneously expanded the meaning of "custodial interrogation." See Beheler, 463 U. S., at 1121-1125 (summarily reversing California Court of Appeal's judgment that respondent was "in custody"); Mathiason, 429 U. S., at 494-496 (summarily reversing Oregon Supreme Court's determination that respondent was "in custody"); cf. Oregon v. Hass, 420 U. S. 714, 719 (1975) ("[A] State may not impose . . . greater restrictions [on police activity] as a matter of federal constitutional law when this Court specifically refrains from imposing them."). It would be anomalous to type the question differently when an individual complains that the state courts had erroneously constricted the circumstances that add up to an "in custody" conclusion.

Classifying "in custody" as a determination qualifying for independent review should serve legitimate law enforcement interests as effectively as it serves to ensure protection of the right against self-incrimination. As our decisions bear out, the law declaration aspect of independent review potentially may guide police, unify precedent, and stabilize the law. See, e. g., Berkemer, 468 U. S., at 436-439 (routine traffic stop—typically temporary, brief, and public—does not place driver "in custody" for Miranda warning purposes); see also Monaghan, Constitutional Fact Review, 85 Colum. L. Rev.

229, 273-276 (1985) ("norm elaboration occurs best when the Court has power to consider fully a series of closely related situations"; case-by-case elaboration when a constitutional right is implicated may more accurately be described as law declaration than as law application).

* * *

Applying § 2254(d)'s presumption of correctness to the Alaska court's "in custody" determination, both the District Court and the Court of Appeals ruled that Thompson was not "in custody" and thus not entitled to Miranda warnings. Because we conclude that state-court "in custody" determinations warrant independent review by a federal habeas court, the judgment of the United States Court of Appeals for the Ninth Circuit is vacated, and the case is remanded for further proceedings consistent with this opinion.

It is so ordered.

NOTES

[1] These passages from the transcript of the tape-recorded interrogation indicate the tenor of the questioning:

"Q Do you know—of course, I don't mean to take up a lot of your time, you—you can leave any time that you want to, if you've got something else going on.

"A Oh no (indiscernible) around here, no.

"Q I know we called you and probably woke you up and. . . .

"A No, I was just laying there.

"Q Okay. But you know, you can go any time you want to. We got a—you know, we're trying to—trying to crack on this thing, and I—I don't imagine it's any secret to you that there are some of your—your friends or associates who have been kind of calling up and saying, you know, they've been pointing at you. . . .

"A Yeah, that (indiscernible) guy you know and we've been friends for ten years, you know, and this guy is starting to say stuff that I never even said. . . ." App. 44-45.

"Q . . . And I'm willing to work with you on this thing to make the best of a bad situation. I can't tell you that this isn't a bad situation. I mean you're free to get up and walk out of here now and—and never talk to me again. But what I'm telling you now is this is probably the last chance we'll have to—for you to say something that other people are gonna believe because let's just—let's just say that there's enough (indiscernible) here already that we can—we can prove conclusively beyond a reasonable doubt that —that you were responsible for this thing—this thing. Well really there's a lot that she's responsible for, but you're the guy that's stuck with the problem. . . .

"A I've already told you the story.

"Q . . . Well you haven't told me the critical part and you haven't told me the part about where Dixie gets killed.

"A And I don't know about that. That's your guys' job. You're supposed to know that.

"Q Well like I told you, we know the who, the

where, the when, the how. The thing we don't know
is the why. And that's—that's the thing we've got
to kind of get straight here today between you
and I. See I know that you did this thing.
There's—there's no question in my mind about
that. I can see it. I can see it when I'm looking
at you. And I know that you care about Dixie. I
mean this isn't something that you wanted to
happen. . . .

. . . . .

"Q . . . I think that now it's the time for you
to come honest about this thing, because if you
turn around later and try to. . . .

"A I am being honest about it.

"Q No, you haven't. You told part of the truth
and you told a lot of it, but you haven't told
all of it. . . . I mean your—you're not probably
lying directly to me, but you're lying by
omission . . . . I can tell you that right now
there's a search warrant being served out at
[your home] and a search warrant for your truck
is gonna be served and we've got a forensic
expert up from—from Anchorage . . . .

"A Huh.

"Q . . . And I don't believe that you're a bad
person. I really don't. . . . [W]hat happened
here was never planned, what happened here was
one of these things that just happen. . . . And
when it happened you're stuck with this—I mean
you're stuck with a hell of a mess now. She's got
—she's finally got you into more trouble than she
can possibly imagine. I mean she's brought this
thing on you. She causes that. . . . I mean I
don't know whether she started the thing by
grabbing the knife and saying she was gonna
(indiscernible) at you and it got turned around
or just what happened. I mean I don't know those
things. . . ." Id. , at 49–51.

[2] The trial court also rejected Thompson's contention that his confession was involuntary. On both
direct and habeas review, Thompson unsuccessfully asserted the involuntariness of his confession.
His petition to this Court, however, does not present that issue.

[3] It is unclear in this case what deference the Alaska appellate court accorded to the trial court's
conclusion that petitioner was not "in custody"; in later decisions, the Alaska Court of Appeals
reviewed the trial courts' "in custody" determinations for "clear error." See Higgins v. State, 887 P. 2d
966, 971 (Alaska App. 1994); McKillop v. State, 857 P. 2d 358, 361 (Alaska App. 1993).

[4] The panel relied on Krantz v. Briggs, 983 F. 2d 961, 964 (CA9 1993), which held that state-court "in
custody" determinations warrant a presumption of correctness under § 2254(d) if the state court made
factfindings after a hearing on the merits.

[5] Claims that state courts have incorrectly decided Miranda issues, as Withrow v. Williams, 507 U. S.
680 (1993), confirms, are appropriately considered in federal habeas review.

[6] Section 2254(d) lists eight exceptions to the presumption of correctness. In full, 28 U. S. C. §
2254(d) reads:

"In any proceeding instituted in a Federal court
by an application for a writ of habeas corpus by
a person in custody pursuant to the judgment of a
State court, a determination after a hearing on

the merits of a factual issue, made by a State court of competent jurisdiction in a proceeding to which the applicant for the writ and the State or an officer or agent thereof were parties, evidenced by a written finding, written opinion, or other reliable and adequate written indicia, shall be presumed to be correct, unless the applicant shall establish or it shall otherwise appear, or the respondent shall admit—

"(1) that the merits of the factual dispute were not resolved in the State court hearing;

"(2) that the factfinding procedure employed by the State court was not adequate to afford a full and fair hearing;

"(3) that the material facts were not adequately developed at the State court hearing;

"(4) that the State court lacked jurisdiction of the subject matter or over the person of the applicant in the State court proceeding;

"(5) that the applicant was an indigent and the State court, in deprivation of his constitutional right, failed to appoint counsel to represent him in the State court proceeding;

"(6) that the applicant did not receive a full, fair, and adequate hearing in the State court proceeding; or

"(7) that the applicant was otherwise denied due process of law in the State court proceeding;

"(8) or unless that part of the record of the State court proceeding in which the determination of such factual issue was made, pertinent to a determination of the sufficiency of the evidence to support such factual determination, is produced as provided for hereinafter, and the Federal court on a consideration of such part of the record as a whole concludes that such factual determination is not fairly supported by the record: "And in an evidentiary hearing in the proceeding in the Federal court, when due proof of such factual determination has been made, unless the existence of one or more of the circumstances respectively set forth in paragraphs numbered (1) to (7), inclusive, is shown by the applicant, otherwise appears, or is admitted by the respondent, or unless the court concludes pursuant to the provisions of paragraph numbered (8) that the record in the State court proceeding, considered as a whole, does not fairly support such factual determination, the burden shall rest upon the applicant to establish by convincing evidence that the factual determination by the State court was erroneous."

[7] The list of circumstances warranting an evidentiary hearing in a federal habeas proceeding set out in H. R. Rep. No. 1384, 88th Cong., 2d Sess., 25 (1964), is similar to the list set out in Townsend v. Sain, 372 U. S. 293, 313 (1963). The legislative history further indicates that the House Judiciary Committee, in framing its recommendations, was mindful of the Court's recent precedent, including Townsend. H. R. Rep. No. 1384, supra, at 24-25. See also 1 J. Liebman & R. Hertz, Federal Habeas Corpus Practice and Procedure § 20.1a, pp. 537-538 (2d ed. 1994) (description of interplay between habeas statute and Townsend).

[8] Keeney v. Tamayo-Reyes, 504 U. S. 1 (1992), partially overruled Townsend on a point not relevant

here; Keeney held that a "cause-andprejudice" standard, rather than the "deliberate by-pass" standard, is the correct standard for excusing a habeas petitioner's failure to develop a material fact in state-court proceedings. 504 U. S., at 5-6.

[9] See also Brown v. Allen, 344 U. S. 443, 507 (1953) (opinion of Frankfurter, J.) ("Where the ascertainment of the historical facts does not dispose of the claim but calls for interpretation of the legal significance of such facts, the District Judge must exercise his own judgment on this blend of facts and their legal values. Thus, so-called mixed questions or the application of constitutional principles to the facts as found leave the duty of adjudication with the federal judge.") (citation omitted).

[10] See, e. g., Cooter & Gell v. Hartmarx Corp. , 496 U. S. 384, 401 (1990) (observing in regard to appellate review of sanctions imposed under Fed. Rule Civ. Proc. 11: "The Court has long noted the difficulty of distinguishing between legal and factual issues."); Pullman-Standard v. Swint, 456 U. S. 273, 288 (1982) (acknowledging, in relation to appellate review of intent determinations in Title VII cases, "the vexing nature of the distinction between questions of fact and questions of law").

[11] The "totality of the circumstances" cast of the "in custody" determination, contrary to respondents' suggestions, does not mean deferential review is in order. See, e. g., Miller v.Fenton, 474 U. S.104, 117 (1985) (state-court determination "whether, under the totality of the circumstances, the confession was obtained in a manner consistent with the Constitution" qualifies for independent review by federal habeas court).

[12] As earlier observed, see supra, at 105, the trial court decided Thompson's motion to suppress his September 15 statements on the papers submitted without holding an evidentiary hearing.

[13] Respondents observe that "reasonable person" assessments, most prominently to gauge negligence in personal injury litigation, fall within the province of fact triers. See, e. g., Cooter & Gell , 496 U. S., at 402 (negligence determinations "generally reviewed deferentially"); McAllister v. United States, 348 U. S. 19, 20-23 (1954) (District Court finding of negligence was not "clearly erroneous"); 9A C. Wright & A. Miller, Federal Practice and Procedures § 2590 (2d ed. 1995). Traditionally, our legal system has entrusted negligence questions to jurors, inviting them to apply community standards. See W. Keeton, D. Dobbs, R. Keeton, & D. Owen, Prosser and Keeton on Law of Torts § 37, pp. 235-237 (5th ed. 1984). For that reason, "[t]he question usually is said to be one of fact," although "it should be apparent that the function of the jury in fixing the standard differs from that of the judge only in that it cannot be reduced to anything approaching a definite rule." Id. , at 237.

Judges alone make "in custody" assessments for Miranda purposes, and they do so with a view to identifying recurrent patterns, and advancing uniform outcomes. If they cannot supply "a definite rule," they nonetheless can reduce the area of uncertainty. See, e. g., Illinois v. Perkins, 496 U. S. 292, 296 (1990) (Miranda warnings not required prior to questioning of incarcerated individual by undercover agent because suspect, unaware of police presence, is not coerced); Berkemer v. McCarty, 468 U. S. 420, 436-439 (1984) (nature of suspected offense is irrelevant to duty to administer Miranda warnings); Oregon v. Mathiason, 429 U. S. 492, 495-496 (1977) (per curiam) (fact that interrogation occurs at police station does not, in itself, require Miranda warnings).

[14] In other contexts, we have similarly concluded that the likely absence of precedential value cuts against requiring plenary appellate review of a district court's determination. For example, in Cooter & Gell v. Hartmarx Corp., a decision confirming that the abuse-of-discretion standard applies to appellate review of sanctions under Federal Rule of Civil Procedure 11, we observed that plenary review would likely "'fail to produce the normal law-clarifying benefits that come from an appellate decision on a question of law . . . .'" 496 U. S., at 404 (quoting Pierce v. Underwood, 487 U. S. 552, 561 (1988)).

[15] See, e. g., Stansbury v. California, 511 U. S. 318, 322-324 (1994) (per curiam) (review of precedent demonstrated a "well settled" principle: officer's undisclosed, subjective belief that person questioned is a suspect is irrelevant to objective "in custody" determination); Pennsylvania v. Bruder, 488 U. S. 9, 11 (1988) (per curiam) (summary reversal appropriate because state-court decision was contrary to rule of Berkemer v. McCarty, 468 U. S. 420 (1984), that ordinary traffic stops do not involve "custody" for purposes of Miranda).

UNITED STATES v. VIRGINIA, et al.

NoS. 94-1941 & 94-2107, June 26, 1996

ON WRITS OF CERTIORARI TO THE UNITED STATES COURT OF APPEALS FOR THE FOURTH CIRCUIT

Justice Ginsburg delivered the opinion of the Court.

Virginia's public institutions of higher learning include an incomparable military college, Virginia Military Institute (VMI). The United States maintains that the Constitution's equal protection guarantee precludes Virginia from reserving exclusively to men the unique educational opportunities VMI affords. We agree.

I

Founded in 1839, VMI is today the sole single sex school among Virginia's 15 public institutions of higher learning. VMI's distinctive mission is to produce "citizen soldiers," men prepared for leadership in civilian life and in military service. VMI pursues this mission through pervasive training of a kind not available anywhere else in Virginia. Assigning prime place to character development, VMI uses an "adversative method" modeled on English public schools and once characteristic of military instruction. VMI constantly endeavors to instill physical and mental discipline in its cadets and impart to them a strong moral code. The school's graduates leave VMI with heightened comprehension of their capacity to deal with duress and stress, and a large sense of accomplishment for completing the hazardous course.

VMI has notably succeeded in its mission to produce leaders; among its alumni are military generals, Members of Congress, and business executives. The school's alumni overwhelmingly perceive that their VMI training helped them to realize their personal goals. VMI's endowment reflects the loyalty of its graduates; VMI has the largest per student endowment of all undergraduate institutions in the Nation.

Neither the goal of producing citizen soldiers nor VMI's implementing methodology is inherently unsuitable to women. And the school's impressive record in producing leaders has made admission desirable to some women. Nevertheless, Virginia has elected to preserve exclusively for men the advantages and opportunities a VMI education affords.

II

A

From its establishment in 1839 as one of the Nation's first state military colleges, see 1839 Va. Acts, ch. 20, VMI has remained financially supported by Virginia and "subject to the control of the [Virginia] General Assembly," Va. Code Ann. §23-92 (1993). First southern college to teach engineering and industrial chemistry, see H. Wise, Drawing Out the Man: The VMI Story 13 (1978) (The VMI Story), VMI once provided teachers for the State's schools, see 1842 Va. Acts, ch. 24, §2 (requiring every cadet to teach in one of the Commonwealth's schools for a 2 year period). [n.1] Civil War strife threatened the school's vitality, but a resourceful superintendent regained legislative support by highlighting "VMI's great potential[,] through its technical know how," to advance Virginia's postwar recovery. The VMI Story 47.

VMI today enrolls about 1,300 men as cadets. [n.2] Its academic offerings in the liberal arts, sciences, and engineering are also available at other public colleges and universities in Virginia. But VMI's mission is special. It is the mission of the school

```
" `to produce educated and honorable men,
prepared for the varied work of civil life,
imbued with love of learning, confident in the
functions and attitudes of leadership,
possessing a high sense of public service,
advocates of the American democracy and free
enterprise system, and ready as citizen soldiers
to defend their country in time of national
peril.' " 766 F. Supp. 1407, 1425 (WD Va. 1991)
(quoting Mission Study Committee of the VMI
```

Board of Visitors, Report, May 16, 1986).

In contrast to the federal service academies, institutions maintained "to prepare cadets for career service in the armed forces," VMI's program "is directed at preparation for both military and civilian life"; "[o]nly about 15% of VMI cadets enter career military service." 766 F. Supp., at 1432.

VMI produces its "citizen soldiers" through "an adversative, or doubting, model of education" which features "[p]hysical rigor, mental stress, absolute equality of treatment, absence of privacy, minute regulation of behavior, and indoctrination in desirable values." *Id.*, at 1421. As one Commandant of Cadets described it, the adversative method "dissects the young student," and makes him aware of his "limits and capabilities," so that he knows "how far he can go with his anger, . . . how much he can take under stress, . . . exactly what he can do when he is physically exhausted." *Id.*, at 1421-1422 (quoting Col. N. Bissell).

VMI cadets live in spartan barracks where surveillance is constant and privacy nonexistent; they wear uniforms, eat together in the mess hall, and regularly participate in drills. *Id.*, at 1424, 1432. Entering students are incessantly exposed to the rat line, "an extreme form of the adversative model," comparable in intensity to Marine Corps boot camp. *Id.*, at 1422. Tormenting and punishing, the rat line bonds new cadets to their fellow sufferers and, when they have completed the 7 month experience, to their former tormentors. *Ibid.*

VMI's "adversative model" is further characterized by a hierarchical "class system" of privileges and responsibilities, a "dyke system" for assigning a senior class mentor to each entering class "rat," and a stringently enforced "honor code," which prescribes that a cadet " `does not lie, cheat, steal nor tolerate those who do.' " *Id.*, at 1422-1423.

VMI attracts some applicants because of its reputation as an extraordinarily challenging military school, and "because its alumni are exceptionally close to the school." *Id.*, at 1421. "[W]omen have no opportunity anywhere to gain the benefits of [the system of education at VMI]." *Ibid.*

B

In 1990, prompted by a complaint filed with the Attorney General by a female high school student seeking admission to VMI, the United States sued the Commonwealth of Virginia and VMI, alleging that VMI's exclusively male admission policy violated the Equal Protection Clause of the Fourteenth Amendment. *Id.*, at 1408. [n.3] Trial of the action consumed six days and involved an array of expert witnesses on each side. *Ibid.*

In the two years preceding the lawsuit, the District Court noted, VMI had received inquiries from 347 women, but had responded to none of them. *Id.*, at 1436. "[S]ome women, at least," the court said, "would want to attend the school if they had the opportunity." *Id.*, at 1414. The court further recognized that, with recruitment, VMI could "achieve at least 10% female enrollment"--"a sufficient `critical mass' to provide the female cadets with a positive educational experience." *Id.*, at 1437-1438. And it was also established that "some women are capable of all of the individual activities required of VMI cadets." *Id.*, at 1412. In addition, experts agreed that if VMI admitted women, "the VMI ROTC experience would become a better training program from the perspective of the armed forces, because it would provide training in dealing with a mixed gender army." *Id.*, at 1441.

The District Court ruled in favor of VMI, however, and rejected the equal protection challenge pressed by the United States. That court correctly recognized that *Mississippi Univ. for Women* v. *Hogan*, 458 U.S. 718(1982), was the closest guide. 766 F. Supp., at 1410. There, this Court underscored that a party seeking to uphold government action based on sex must establish an "exceedingly persuasive justification" for the classification. *Mississippi Univ. for Women*, 458 U. S., at 724 (internal quotation marks omitted). To succeed, the defender of the challenged action must show "at least that the classification serves important governmental objectives and that the discriminatory means employed are substantially related to the achievement of those objectives." *Ibid.* (internal quotation marks omitted).

The District Court reasoned that education in "a single gender environment, be it male or female," yields substantial benefits. 766 F. Supp., at 1415. VMI's school for men brought diversity to an otherwise coeducational Virginia system, and that diversity was "enhanced by VMI's unique method of instruction." *Ibid.* If single gender education for males ranks as an important governmental objective, it becomes obvious, the District Court concluded, that the *only* means of achieving the objective "is to exclude women from the all male institution--VMI." *Ibid.*

"Women are [indeed] denied a unique educational opportunity that is available only at VMI," the District Court acknowledged. *Id.*, at 1432. But "[VMI's] single sex status would be lost, and some aspects of the [school's] distinctive method would be altered" if women were admitted, *id.*, at 1413: "Allowance for personal privacy would have to be made," *id.*, at 1412; "[p]hysical education requirements would have to be altered, at least for the women," *id.*, at 1413; the adversative environment could not survive unmodified, *id.*, at 1412-1413. Thus, "sufficient constitutional justification" had been shown, the District Court held, "for continuing [VMI's] single sex policy." *Id.*, at 1413.

The Court of Appeals for the Fourth Circuit disagreed and vacated the District Court's judgment. The appellate court held: "The Commonwealth of Virginia has not. . . advanced any state policy by which it can justify its determination, under an announced policy of diversity, to afford VMI's unique type of program to men and not to women." 976 F. 2d 890, 892 (1992).

The appeals court greeted with skepticism Virginia's assertion that it offers single sex education at VMI as a facet of the State's overarching and undisputed policy to advance "autonomy and diversity." The court underscored Virginia's nondiscrimination commitment: " `[I]t is extremely important that [colleges and universities] deal with faculty, staff, and students *without regard to sex, race, or ethnic origin.*' " *Id.*, at 899 (quoting 1990 Report of the Virginia Commission on the University of the 21st Century). "That statement," the Court of Appeals said, "is the only explicit one that we have found in the record in which the Commonwealth has expressed itself with respect to gender distinctions." *Ibid.* Furthermore, the appeals court observed, in urging "diversity" to justify an all male VMI, the State had supplied "no explanation for the movement away from [single sex education] in Virginia by public colleges and universities." *Ibid.* In short, the court concluded, "[a] policy of diversity which aims to provide an array of educational opportunities, including single gender institutions, must do more than favor one gender." *Ibid.*

The parties agreed that "*some* women can meet the physical standards now imposed on men," *id.*, at 896, and the court was satisfied that "neither the goal of producing citizen soldiers nor VMI's implementing methodology is inherently unsuitable to women," *id.*, at 899. The Court of Appeals, however, accepted the District Court's finding that "at least these three aspects of VMI's program--physical training, the absence of privacy, and the adversarial approach--would be materially affected by coeducation." *Id.*, at 896-897. Remanding the case, the appeals court assigned to Virginia, in the first instance, responsibility for selecting a remedial course. The court suggested these options for the State: Admit women to VMI; establish parallel institutions or programs; or abandon state support, leaving VMI free to pursue its policies as a private institution. *Id.*, at 900. In May 1993, this Court denied certiorari. See 508 U.S. 946; see also *ibid.* (opinion of Scalia, J., noting the interlocutory posture of the litigation).

C

In response to the Fourth Circuit's ruling, Virginia proposed a parallel program for women: Virginia Women's Institute for Leadership (VWIL). The 4 year, state sponsored undergraduate program would be located at Mary Baldwin College, a private liberal arts school for women, and would be open, initially, to about 25 to 30 students. Although VWIL would share VMI's mission--to produce "citizen soldiers"--the VWIL program would differ, as does Mary Baldwin College, from VMI in academic offerings, methods of education, and financial resources. See 852 F. Supp. 471, 476-477 (WD Va. 1994).

The average combined SAT score of entrants at Mary Baldwin is about 100 points lower than the score for VMI freshmen. See *id.*, at 501. Mary Baldwin's faculty holds "significantly fewer Ph.D.'s than the faculty at VMI," *id.*, at 502, and receives significantly lower salaries, see Tr. 158 (testimony of James Lott, Dean of Mary Baldwin College), reprinted in 2 App. in Nos. 94-1667 and 94-1717 (CA4) (hereinafter Tr.). While VMI offers degrees in liberal arts, the sciences, and engineering, Mary Baldwin, at the time of trial, offered only bachelor of arts degrees. See 852 F. Supp., at 503. A VWIL student seeking to earn an engineering degree could gain one, without public support, by attending Washington University in St. Louis, Missouri, for two years, paying the required private tuition. See *ibid.*

Experts in educating women at the college level composed the Task Force charged with designing the VWIL program; Task Force members were drawn from Mary Baldwin's own faculty and staff. *Id.*, at 476. Training its attention on methods of instruction appropriate for "most women," the Task Force determined that a military model would be "wholly inappropriate" for VWIL. *Ibid.*; see 44 F. 3d 1229, 1233 (CA4 1995).

VWIL students would participate in ROTC programs and a newly established, "largely ceremonial" Virginia Corps of Cadets, *id.*, at 1234, but the VWIL House would not have a military format, 852 F. Supp., at 477, and VWIL would not require its students to eat meals together or to wear uniforms during the school day, *id.*, at 495. In lieu of VMI's adversarial method, the VWIL Task Force favored "a cooperative method which reinforces self esteem." *Id.*, at 476. In addition to the standard bachelor of arts program offered at Mary Baldwin, VWIL students would take courses in leadership, complete an off campus leadership externship, participate in community service projects, and assist in arranging a speaker series. See 44 F. 3d, at 1234.

Virginia represented that it will provide equal financial support for in state VWIL students and VMI cadets, 852 F. Supp., at 483, and the VMI Foundation agreed to supply a $5.4625 million endowment for the VWIL program, *id.*, at 499. Mary Baldwin's own endowment is about $19 million; VMI's is $131 million. *Id.*, at 503. Mary Baldwin will add $35 million to its endowment based on future commitments; VMI will add $220 million. *Ibid.* The VMI Alumni Association has developed a network of employers interested in hiring VMI graduates. The Association has agreed to open its network to VWIL graduates, *id.*, at 499, but those graduates will not have the advantage afforded by a VMI degree.

D

Virginia returned to the District Court seeking approval of its proposed remedial plan, and the court decided the plan met the requirements of the Equal Protection Clause. *Id.*, at 473. The District Court again acknowledged evidentiary support for these determinations: "[T]he VMI methodology could be used to educate women and, in fact, some women . . . may prefer the VMI methodology to the VWIL methodology." *Id.*, at 481. But the "controlling legal principles," the District Court decided, "do not require the Commonwealth to provide a mirror image VMI for women." *Ibid.* The court anticipated that the two schools would "achieve substantially similar outcomes." *Ibid.* It concluded: "If VMI marches to the beat of a drum, then Mary Baldwin marches to the melody of a fife and when the march is over, both will have arrived at the same destination." *Id.*, at 484.

A divided Court of Appeals affirmed the District Court's judgment. 44 F. 3d 1229 (CA4 1995). This time, the appellate court determined to give "greater scrutiny to the selection of means than to the [State's] proffered objective." *Id.*, at 1236. The official objective or purpose, the court said, should be reviewed deferentially. *Ibid.* Respect for the "legislative will," the court reasoned, meant that the judiciary should take a "cautious approach," inquiring into the "legitima[cy]" of the governmental objective and refusing approval for any purpose revealed to be "pernicious." *Ibid.*

"[P]roviding the option of a single gender college education may be considered a legitimate and important aspect of a public system of higher education," the appeals court observed, *id.*, at 1238; that objective, the court added, is "not pernicious," *id.*, at 1239. Moreover, the court continued, the adversative method vital to a VMI education "has never been tolerated in a sexually heterogeneous environment." *Ibid.* The method itself "was not designed to exclude women," the court noted, but women could not be accommodated in the VMI program, the court believed, for female participation in VMI's adversative training "would destroy . . . any sense of decency that still permeates the relationship between the sexes." *Ibid.*

Having determined, deferentially, the legitimacy of Virginia's purpose, the court considered the question of means. Exclusion of "men at Mary Baldwin College and women at VMI," the court said, was essential to Virginia's purpose, for without such exclusion, the State could not "accomplish [its] objective of providing single gender education." *Ibid.*

The court recognized that, as it analyzed the case, means merged into end, and the merger risked "bypass[ing] any equal protection scrutiny." *Id.*, at 1237. The court therefore added another inquiry, a decisive test it called "substantive comparability." *Ibid.* The key question, the court said, was whether men at VMI and women at VWIL would obtain "substantively comparable benefits at their institution or through other means offered by the [S]tate." *Ibid.* Although the appeals court recognized that the VWIL degree "lacks the historical benefit and prestige" of a VMI degree, it nevertheless found the educational opportunities at the two schools "sufficiently comparable." *Id.*, at 1241.

Senior Circuit Judge Phillips dissented. The court, in his judgment, had not held Virginia to the burden of showing an " `exceedingly persuasive [justification]' " for the State's action. *Id.*, at 1247 (quoting *Mississippi University for Women*, 458 U. S., at 724). In Judge Phillips' view, the court had accepted "rationalizations compelled by the exigencies of this litigation," and had not confronted the State's "actual overriding purpose." *Ibid.* That purpose, Judge Phillips said, was clear from the historical record; it was "not to create a new type of educational opportunity for women, . . . nor to further diversify the Commonwealth's higher education system[,] . . . but [was] simply . . . to allow VMI to continue to exclude women in order to preserve its historic character and mission." *Ibid.*

Judge Phillips suggested that the State would satisfy the Constitution's equal protection requirement if it "simultaneously opened single gender undergraduate institutions having substantially comparable curricular and extra curricular programs, funding, physical plant, administration and support services, and faculty and library resources." *Id.*, at 1250. But he thought it evident that the proposed VWIL program, in comparison to VMI, fell "far short . . . from providing substantially equal tangible and intangible educational benefits to men and women." *Ibid.*

The Fourth Circuit denied rehearing en banc. 52 F. 3d 90 (1995). Circuit Judge Motz, joined by Circuit Judges Hall, Murnaghan, and Michael, filed a dissenting opinion. [n.4] Judge Motz agreed with Judge Phillips that Virginia had not shown an " `exceedingly persuasive justification' " for the disparate opportunities the State supported. *Id.*, at 92 (quoting *Mississippi Univ. for Women*, 458 U. S., at 724). She asked: "[H]ow can a degree from a yet to be implemented supplemental program at Mary Baldwin be held `substantively comparable' to a degree from a venerable Virginia military institution that was established more than 150 years ago?" *Id.*, at 93. "Women need not be guaranteed equal `results,' " Judge Motz said, "but the Equal Protection Clause does require equal opportunity . . . [and] that opportunity is being denied here." *Ibid.*

III

The cross petitions in this case present two ultimate issues. First, does Virginia's exclusion of women from the educational opportunities provided by VMI--extraordinary opportunities for military training and civilian leadership development--deny to women "capable of all of the individual activities required of VMI cadets," 766F. Supp., at 1412, the equal protection of the laws guaranteed by the Fourteenth Amendment? Second, if VMI's "unique" situation, *id.*, at 1413-- as Virginia's sole single sex public institution of higher education--offends the Constitution's equal protection principle, what is the remedial requirement?

IV

We note, once again, the core instruction of this Court's pathmarking decisions in *J. E. B.* v. *Alabama ex rel. T. B.*, 511 U. S. 127, 136-137, and n. 6 (1994), and *Mississippi Univ. for Women*, 458 U. S., at 724 (internal quotation marks omitted): Parties who seek to defend gender based government action must demonstrate an "exceedingly persuasive justification" for that action.

Today's skeptical scrutiny of official action denying rights or opportunities based on sex responds to volumes of history. As a plurality of this Court acknowledged a generation ago, "our Nation has had a long and unfortunate history of sex discrimination." *Frontiero* v. *Richardson*, 411 U.S. 677, 684 (1973). Through a century plus three decades and more of that history, women did not count among voters composing "We the People"; [n.5] not until 1920 did women gain a constitutional right to the franchise. *Id.*, at 685. And for a half century thereafter, it remained the prevailing doctrine that government, both federal and state, could withhold from women opportunities accorded men so long as any "basis in reason" could be conceived for the discrimination. See, *e.g.*, *Goesaert* v. *Cleary*, 335 U.S. 464, 467 (1948) (rejecting challenge of female tavern owner and her daughter to Michigan law denying bartender licenses to females--except for wives and daughters of male tavern owners; Court would not "give ear" to the contention that "an unchivalrous desire of male bartenders to . . . monopolize the calling" prompted the legislation).

In 1971, for the first time in our Nation's history, this Court ruled in favor of a woman who complained that her State had denied her the equal protection of its laws. *Reed* v. *Reed*, 404 U.S. 71, 73 (holding unconstitutional Idaho Code prescription that, among " `several persons claiming and equally entitled to administer [a decedent's estate], males must be preferred to females' "). Since *Reed*, the Court has repeatedly recognized that neither federal nor state government acts compatibly with the equal protection principle when a law or official policy denies to women, simply because they are women, full citizenship stature--equal opportunity to aspire, achieve, participate in and contribute to society based on their individual talents and capacities. See, *e.g.*, *Kirchberg* v. *Feenstra*, 450 U.S. 455, 462-463 (1981) (affirming invalidity of Louisiana law that made husband "head and master" of property jointly owned with his wife, giving him unilateral right to dispose of such property without his wife's consent); *Stanton* v. *Stanton*, 421 U.S. 7 (1975) (invalidating Utah requirement that parents support boys until age 21, girls only until age 18).

Without equating gender classifications, for all purposes, to classifications based on race or national origin, [n.6] the Court, in post-*Reed* decisions, has carefully inspected official action that closes a door or denies opportunity to women (or to men). See *J. E. B.*, 511 U. S., at 152 (Kennedy, J., concurring in judgment) (case law evolving since 1971 "reveal[s] a strong presumption that gender classifications are invalid"). To summarize the Court's current directions for cases of official classification based on gender: Focusing on the differential treatment or denial of opportunity for which relief is sought, the reviewing court must determine whether the proffered justification is "exceedingly persuasive." The burden of justification is demanding and it rests entirely on the State. See *Mississippi Univ. for Women*, 458 U. S., at 724. The State must show "at least that the [challenged] classification serves `important governmental objectives and that the discriminatory means employed' are `substantially related to the achievement of those objectives.' " *Ibid.* (quoting *Wengler* v. *Druggists Mutual Ins. Co.*, 446 U.S. 142, 150 (1980)). The justification must be genuine, not hypothesized or invented *post hoc* in response to litigation. And it must not rely on overbroad generalizations about the different talents, capacities, or preferences of males and females. See *Weinberger* v. *Wiesenfeld*, 420 U.S. 636, 643, 648 (1975); *Califano* v. *Goldfarb*, 430 U.S. 199, 223-224 (1977) (Stevens, J., concurring in judgment).

The heightened review standard our precedent establishes does not make sex a proscribed classification. Supposed "inherent differences" are no longer accepted as a ground for race or national origin classifications. See *Loving* v. *Virginia*, 388 U.S. 1 (1967). Physical differences between men and women, however, are enduring: "[T]he two sexes are not fungible; a community made up exclusively of one [sex] is different from a community composed of both." *Ballard* v. *United States*, 329 U.S. 187, 193 (1946).

"Inherent differences" between men and women, we have come to appreciate, remain cause for celebration, but not for denigration of the members of either sex or for artificial constraints on an individual's opportunity. Sex classifications may be used to compensate women "for particular economic disabilities [they have] suffered," *Califano* v. *Webster*, 430 U.S. 313, 320 (1977) *(per curiam)*, to "promot[e] equal employment opportunity," see *California Federal Sav. & Loan Assn.* v. *Guerra*, 479 U.S. 272, 289 (1987), to advance full development of the talent and capacities of our Nation's people. [n.7] But such classifications may not be used, as they once were, see *Goesaert*, 335 U. S., at 467, to create or perpetuate the legal, social, and economic inferiority of women.

Measuring the record in this case against the review standard just described, we conclude that Virginia has shown no "exceedingly persuasive justification" for excluding all women from the citizen soldier training afforded by VMI. We therefore affirm the Fourth Circuit's initial judgment, which held that Virginia had violated the Fourteenth Amendment's Equal Protection Clause. Because the remedy proffered by Virginia--the Mary Baldwin VWIL program--does not cure the constitutional violation, *i.e.*, it does not provide equal opportunity, we reverse the Fourth Circuit's final judgment in this case.

V

The Fourth Circuit initially held that Virginia had advanced no state policy by which it could justify, under equal protection principles, its determination "to afford VMI's unique type of program to men and not to women." 976 F. 2d, at 892. Virginia challenges that "liability" ruling and asserts two justifications in defense of VMI's exclusion of women. First, the Commonwealth contends, "single sex education provides important educational benefits," Brief for Cross Petitioners 20, and the option of single sex education contributes to "diversity in educational approaches," *id.*, at 25. Second, the Commonwealth argues, "the unique VMI method of character development and leadership training," the school's adversative approach, would have to be modified were VMI to admit women. *Id.*, at 33-36. We consider these two justifications in turn.

A

Single sex education affords pedagogical benefits to at least some students, Virginia emphasizes, and that reality is uncontested in this litigation. [n.8] Similarly, it is not disputed that diversity among public educational institutions can serve the public good. But Virginia has not shown that VMI was established, or has been maintained, with a view to diversifying, by its categorical exclusion of women, educational opportunities within the State. In cases of this genre, our precedent instructs that "benign" justifications proffered in defense of categorical exclusions will not be accepted automatically; a tenable justification must describe actual state purposes, not rationalizations for actions in fact differently grounded. See *Wiesenfeld*, 420 U. S., at 648, and n. 16 ("mere recitation of a benign [or] compensatory purpose" does not block "inquiry into the actual purposes" of government maintained gender based classifications); *Goldfarb*, 430 U. S., at 212-213 (rejecting government proffered purposes after "inquiry into the actual purposes") (internal quotation marks omitted).

Mississippi Univ. for Women is immediately in point. There the State asserted, in justification of its exclusion of men from a nursing school, that it was engaging in "educational affirmative action" by "compensat[ing] for discrimination against women." 458 U. S., at 727. Undertaking a "searching analysis," *id.*, at 728, the Court found no close resemblance between "the alleged objective" and "the actual purpose underlying the discriminatory classification," *id.*, at 730. Pursuing a similar inquiry here, we reach the same conclusion.

Neither recent nor distant history bears out Virginia's alleged pursuit of diversity through single sex educational options. In 1839, when the State established VMI, a range of educational opportunities for men and women was scarcely contemplated. Higher education at the time was considered dangerous for women; [n.9] reflecting widely held views about women's proper place, the Nation's first universities and colleges--for example, Harvard in Massachusetts, William and Mary in Virginia-- admitted only men. See E. Farello, A History of the Education of Women in the United States 163 (1970). VMI was not at all novel in this respect: In admitting no women, VMI followed the lead of the State's flagship school, the University of Virginia, founded in 1819.

"[N]o struggle for the admission of women to a state university," a historian has recounted, "was longer drawn out, or developed more bitterness, than that at the University of Virginia." 2 T. Woody, A History of Women's Education in the United States 254 (1929) (History of Women's Education). In 1879, the State Senate resolved to look into the possibility of higher education for women, recognizing that Virginia " `has never, at any period of her history,' " provided for the higher education of her daughters, though she " `has liberally provided for the higher education of her sons.' " *Ibid.* (quoting 10 Educ. J. Va. 212 (1879)). Despite this recognition, no new opportunities were instantly open to women. [n.10]

Virginia eventually provided for several women's seminaries and colleges. Farmville Female Seminary became a public institution in 1884. See *supra*, at 3, n. 2. Two women's schools, Mary Washington College and James Madison University, were founded in 1908; another, Radford University, was founded in 1910. 766 F. Supp., at 1418-1419. By the mid 1970's, all four schools had become coeducational. *Ibid.*

Debate concerning women's admission as undergraduates at the main university continued well past the century's midpoint. Familiar arguments were rehearsed. If women were admitted, it was feared, they "would encroach on the rights of men; there would be new problems of government, perhaps scandals; the old honor system would have to be changed; standards would be lowered to those of other coeducational schools; and the glorious reputation of the university, as a school for men, would be trailed in the dust." 2 History of Women's Education 255.

Ultimately, in 1970, "the most prestigious institution of higher education in Virginia," the University of Virginia, introduced coeducation and, in 1972, began to admit women on an equal basis with men. See *Kirstein* v. *Rector and Visitors of Univ. of Virginia*, 309 F. Supp. 184, 186 (ED Va. 1970). A three judge Federal District Court confirmed: "Virginia may not now deny to women, on the basis of sex, educational opportunities at the Charlottesville campus that are not afforded in other institutions operated by the [S]tate." *Id.*, at 187.

Virginia describes the current absence of public single sex higher education for women as "an historical anomaly." Brief for Cross Petitioners 30. But the historical record indicates action more deliberate than anomalous: First, protection of women against higher education; next, schools for women far from equal in resources and stature to schools for men; finally, conversion of the separate schools to coeducation. The state legislature, prior to the advent of this controversy, had repealed "[a]ll Virginia statutes requiring individual institutions to admit only men or women." 766 F. Supp., at 1419. And in 1990, an official commission, "legislatively established to chart the future goals of higher education in Virginia," reaffirmed the policy "of affording broad access" while maintaining "autonomy and diversity." 976 F. 2d, at 898-899 (quoting Report of the Virginia Commission on the University of the 21st Century). Significantly, the Commission reported:

> " `Because colleges and universities provide opportunities for students to develop values and learn from role models, it is extremely important that they deal with faculty, staff, and students without regard to sex, race, or ethnic origin.' " *Id.*, at 899 (emphasis supplied by Court of Appeals deleted).

This statement, the Court of Appeals observed, "is the only explicit one that we have found in the record in which the Commonwealth has expressed itself with respect to gender distinctions." *Ibid.*

Our 1982 decision in *Mississippi Univ. for Women* prompted VMI to reexamine its male only admission policy. See 766 F. Supp., at 1427-1428. Virginia relies on that reexamination as a legitimate basis for maintaining VMI's single sex character. See Reply Brief for Cross Petitioners 6. A Mission Study Committee, appointed by the VMI Board of Visitors, studied the problem from October 1983 until May 1986, and in that month counseled against "change of VMI status as a single sex college." See 766 F. Supp., at 1429 (internal quotation marks omitted). Whatever internal purpose the Mission

Study Committee served--and however well meaning the framers of the report--we can hardly extract from that effort any state policy evenhandedly to advance diverse educational options. As the District Court observed, the Committee's analysis "primarily focuse[d] on anticipated difficulties in attracting females to VMI," and the report, overall, supplied "very little indication of how th[e] conclusion was reached." *Ibid*.

In sum, we find no persuasive evidence in this record that VMI's male only admission policy "is in furtherance of a state policy of `diversity.' " See 976 F. 2d, at 899. No such policy, the Fourth Circuit observed, can be discerned from the movement of all other public colleges and universities in Virginia away from single sex education. See *ibid*. That court also questioned "how one institution with autonomy, but with no authority over any other state institution, can give effect to a state policy of diversity among institutions." *Ibid*. A purpose genuinely to advance an array of educational options, as the Court of Appeals recognized, is not served by VMI's historic and constant plan--a plan to "affor[d] a unique educational benefit only to males." *Ibid*. However "liberally" this plan serves the State's sons, it makes no provision whatever for her daughters. That is not *equal* protection.

B

Virginia next argues that VMI's adversative method of training provides educational benefits that cannot be made available, unmodified, to women. Alterations to accommodate women would necessarily be "radical," so "drastic," Virginia asserts, as to transform, indeed "destroy," VMI's program. See Brief for Cross Petitioners 34-36. Neither sex would be favored by the transformation, Virginia maintains: Men would be deprived of the unique opportunity currently available to them; women would not gain that opportunity because their participation would "eliminat[e] the very aspects of [the] program that distinguish [VMI] from . . . other institutions of higher education in Virginia." *Id.*, at 34 (internal quotation marks omitted).

The District Court forecast from expert witness testimony, and the Court of Appeals accepted, that coeducation would materially affect "at least these three aspects of VMI's program--physical training, the absence of privacy, and the adversative approach." 976 F. 2d, at 896-897. And it is uncontested that women's admission would require accommodations, primarily in arranging housing assignments and physical training programs for female cadets. See Brief for Cross Respondent 11, 29-30. It is also undisputed, however, that "the VMI methodology could be used to educate women." 852 F. Supp., at 481. The District Court even allowed that some women may prefer it to the methodology a women's college might pursue. See *ibid*. "[S]ome women, at least, would want to attend [VMI] if they had the opportunity," the District Court recognized, 766 F. Supp., at 1414, and "some women," the expert testimony established, "are capable of all of the individual activities required of VMI cadets," *id.*, at 1412. The parties, furthermore, agree that "*some* women can meet the physical standards [VMI] now impose[s] on men." 976 F. 2d, at 896. In sum, as the Court of Appeals stated, "neither the goal of producing citizen soldiers," VMI's *raison d'être*, "nor VMI's implementing methodology is inherently unsuitable to women." *Id.*, at 899.

In support of its initial judgment for Virginia, a judgment rejecting all equal protection objections presented by the United States, the District Court made "findings" on "gender based developmental differences." 766 F. Supp., at 1434-1435. These "findings" restate the opinions of Virginia's expert witnesses, opinions about typically male or typically female "tendencies." *Id.*, at 1434. For example, "[m]ales tend to need an atmosphere of adversativeness," while "[f]emales tend to thrive in a cooperative atmosphere." *Ibid*. "I'm not saying that some women don't do well under [the] adversative model," VMI's expert on educational institutions testified, "undoubtedly there are some [women] who do"; but educational experiences must be designed "around the rule," this expert maintained, and not "around the exception." *Ibid*. (internal quotation marks omitted).

The United States does not challenge any expert witness estimation on average capacities or preferences of men and women. Instead, the United States emphasizes that time and again since this Court's turning point decision in *Reed* v. *Reed*, 404 U.S. 71 (1971), we have cautioned reviewing courts to take a "hard look" at generalizations or "tendencies" of the kind pressed by Virginia, and relied upon by the District Court. See O'Connor, Portia's Progress, 66 N. Y. U. L. Rev. 1546, 1551 (1991). State actors controlling gates to opportunity, we have instructed, may not exclude qualified individuals based on "fixed notions concerning the roles and abilities of males and females." *Mississippi Univ. for Women*, 458 U. S., at 725; see *J. E. B.*, 511 U. S., at 139, n. 11 (equal protection principles, as applied to gender classifications, mean state actors may not rely on "overbroad" generalizations to make "judgments about people that are likely to . . . perpetuate historical patterns of discrimination").

It may be assumed, for purposes of this decision, that most women would not choose VMI's adversative method. As Fourth Circuit Judge Motz observed, however, in her dissent from the Court of Appeals' denial of rehearing en banc, it is also probable that "many men would not want to be educated in such an environment." 52 F. 3d, at 93. (On that point, even our dissenting colleague might agree.) Education, to be sure, is not a "one size fits all" business. The issue, however, is not whether "women--or men--should be forced to attend VMI"; rather, the question is whether the State can constitutionally deny to women who have the will and capacity, the training and attendant opportunities that VMI uniquely affords. *Ibid*.

The notion that admission of women would downgrade VMI's stature, destroy the adversative system and, with it, even the school, [n.11] is a judgment hardly proved, [n.12] a prediction hardly different from other "self fulfilling prophec[ies]," see *Mississippi Univ. for Women*, 458 U. S., at 730, once routinely used to deny rights or opportunities. When women first sought admission to the bar and access to legal education, concerns of the same order were expressed. For example, in 1876, the Court of Common Pleas of Hennepin County, Minnesota, explained why women were thought ineligible for the practice of law. Women train and educate the young, the court said, which

"forbids that they shall bestow that time (early and late) and labor, so essential in attaining to the eminence to which the true lawyer should ever aspire. It cannot therefore be said that the opposition of courts to the admission of females to practice . . . is to any extent the outgrowth of . . . `old fogyism[.]' . . . [I]t arises rather from a comprehension of the magnitude of the responsibilities connected with the successful practice of law, and a desire to *grade up* the profession." In re Application of Martha Angle Dorsett to Be Admitted to Practice as Attorney and Counselor at Law (Minn. C. P. Hennepin Cty., 1876), in The Syllabi, Oct. 21, 1876, pp. 5, 6 (emphasis added).

A like fear, according to a 1925 report, accounted for Columbia Law School's resistance to women's admission, although "[t]he faculty . . . never maintained that women could not master legal learning . . . . No, its argument has been . . . more practical. If women were admitted to the Columbia Law School, [the faculty] said, then the choicer, more manly and red blooded graduates of our great universities would go to the Harvard Law School!" The Nation, Feb. 18, 1925, p. 173.

Medical faculties similarly resisted men and women as partners in the study of medicine. See R. Morantz Sanchez, Sympathy and Science: Women Physicians in American Medicine 51-54, 250 (1985); see also M. Walsh, "Doctors Wanted: No Women Need Apply" 121-122 (1977) (quoting E. Clarke, Medical Education of Women, 4 Boston Med. & Surg. J. 345, 346 (1869) (" `God forbid that I should ever see men and women aiding each other to display with the scalpel the secrets of the reproductive system . . . .' ")); cf. *supra*, at 18-19, n. 9. More recently, women seeking careers in policing encountered resistance based on fears that their presence would "undermine male solidarity," see F. Heidensohn, Women in Control? 201 (1992); deprive male partners of adequate assistance, see *id.*, at 184-185; and lead to sexual misconduct, see C. Milton et al., Women in Policing 32-33 (1974). Field studies did not confirm these fears. See Women in Control? *supra*, at 92-93; P. Bloch & D. Anderson, Policewomen on Patrol: Final Report (1974).

Women's successful entry into the federal military academies, [n.13] and their participation in the Nation's military forces, [n.14] indicate that Virginia's fears for the future of VMI may not be solidly grounded. [n.15] The State's justification for excluding all women from "citizen soldier" training for which some are qualified, in any event, cannot rank as "exceedingly persuasive," as we have explained and applied that standard.

Virginia and VMI trained their argument on "means" rather than "end," and thus misperceived our precedent. Single sex education at VMI serves an "important governmental objective," they maintained, and exclusion of women is not only "substantially related," it is essential to that objective. By this notably circular argument, the "straightforward" test *Mississippi Univ. for Women* described, see 458 U. S., at 724-725, was bent and bowed.

The State's misunderstanding and, in turn, the District Court's, is apparent from VMI's mission: to produce "citizen soldiers," individuals

" `imbued with love of learning, confident in the functions and attitudes of leadership, possessing a high sense of public service, advocates of the American democracy and free enterprise system, and ready . . . to defend their country in time of national peril.' " 766 F. Supp., at 1425 (quoting Mission Study Committee of the VMI Board of Visitors, Report, May 16, 1986).

Surely that goal is great enough to accommodate women, who today count as citizens in our American democracy equal in stature to men. Just as surely, the State's great goal is not substantially advanced by women's categorical exclusion, in total disregard of their individual merit, from the State's premier "citizen soldier" corps. [n.16] Virginia, in sum, "has fallen far short of establishing the `exceedingly persuasive justification,' " *Mississippi Univ. for Women*, 458 U. S., at 731, that must be the solid base for any gender defined classification.

VI

In the second phase of the litigation, Virginia presented its remedial plan--maintain VMI as a male only college and create VWIL as a separate program for women. The plan met District Court approval. The Fourth Circuit, in turn, deferentially reviewed the State's proposal and decided that the two single sex programs directly served Virginia's reasserted purposes: single gender education, and "achieving the results of an adversative method in a military environment." See 44 F. 3d, at 1236, 1239. Inspecting the VMI and VWIL educational programs to determine whether they "afford[ed] to both genders benefits comparable in substance, [if] not in form and detail," *id.*, at 1240, the Court of Appeals concluded that Virginia had arranged for men and women opportunities "sufficiently comparable" to survive equal protection evaluation, *id.*, at 1240-1241. The United States challenges this "remedial" ruling as pervasively misguided.

A

A remedial decree, this Court has said, must closely fit the constitutional violation; it must be shaped to place persons unconstitutionally denied an opportunity or advantage in "the position they would have occupied in the absence of [discrimination]." See *Milliken* v. *Bradley*, 433 U.S. 267, 280 (1977) (internal quotation marks omitted). The constitutional violation in this case is the categorical exclusion of women from an extraordinary educational opportunity afforded men. A proper remedy for an unconstitutional exclusion, we have explained, aims to "eliminate [so far as possible] the discriminatory effects of the past" and to "bar like discrimination in the future." *Louisiana* v. *United States*, 380 U.S. 145, 154 (1965).

Virginia chose not to eliminate, but to leave untouched, VMI's exclusionary policy. For women only, however, Virginia proposed a separate program, different in kind from VMI and unequal in tangible and intangible facilities. [n.17] Having violated the Constitution's equal protection requirement, Virginia was obliged to show that its remedial proposal "directly address[ed] and relate[d] to" the violation, see *Milliken*, 433 U. S., at 282, *i.e.*, the equal protection denied to women ready, willing, and able to benefit from educational opportunities of the kind VMI offers. Virginia described VWIL as a "parallel program," and asserted that VWIL shares VMI's mission of producing "citizen soldiers" and VMI's goals of providing "education, military training, mental and physical discipline, character . . . and leadership development." Brief for Respondents 24 (internal quotation marks omitted). If the VWIL program could not "eliminate the discriminatory effects of the past," could it at least "bar like discrimination in the future"? See *Louisiana*, 380 U. S., at 154. A comparison of the programs said to be "parallel" informs our answer. In exposing the character of, and differences in, the VMI and VWIL programs, we recapitulate facts earlier presented. See *supra*, at 2-5, 8-9.

VWIL affords women no opportunity to experience the rigorous military training for which VMI is famed. See 766 F. Supp., at 1413-1414 ("No other school in Virginia or in the United States, public or private, offers the same kind of rigorous military training as is available at VMI."); *id.*, at 1421 (VMI "is known to be the most challenging military school in the United States"). Instead, the VWIL program "deemphasize[s]" military education, 44 F. 3d, at 1234, and uses a "cooperative method" of education "which reinforces self esteem," 852 F. Supp., at 476.

VWIL students participate in ROTC and a "largely ceremonial" Virginia Corps of Cadets, see 44 F. 3d, at 1234, but Virginia deliberately did not make VWIL a military institute. The VWIL House is not a military style residence and VWIL students need not live together throughout the 4 year program, eat meals together, or wear uniforms during the school day. See 852 F. Supp.,at 477, 495. VWIL students thus do not experience the "barracks" life "crucial to the VMI experience," the spartan living arrangements designed to foster an "egalitarian ethic." See 766 F. Supp., at 1423-1424. "[T]he most important aspects of the VMI educational experience occur in the barracks," the District Court found, *id.*, at 1423, yet Virginia deemed that core experience nonessential, indeed inappropriate, for training its female citizen soldiers.

VWIL students receive their "leadership training" in seminars, externships, and speaker series, see 852 F. Supp., at 477, episodes and encounters lacking the "[p]hysical rigor, mental stress, . . . minute regulation of behavior, and indoctrination in desirable values" made hallmarks of VMI's citizen soldier training, see 766 F. Supp., at 1421. [n.18] Kept away from the pressures, hazards, and psychological bonding characteristic of VMI's adversative training, see *id.*, at 1422, VWIL students will not know the "feeling of tremendous accomplishment" commonly experienced by VMI's successful cadets, *id.*, at 1426.

Virginia maintains that these methodological differences are "justified pedagogically," based on "important differences between men and women in learning and developmental needs," "psychological and sociological differences" Virginia describes as "real" and "not stereotypes." Brief for Respondents 28 (internal quotation marks omitted). The Task Force charged with developing the leadership program for women, drawn from the staff and faculty at Mary Baldwin College, "determined that a military model and, especially VMI's adversative method, would be wholly inappropriate for educating and training *most women*." 852 F. Supp., at 476 (emphasis added). See also 44 F. 3d, at 1233-1234 (noting Task Force conclusion that, while "some women would be suited to and interested in [a VMI style experience]," VMI's adversative method "would not be effective for *women as a group*") (emphasis added). The Commonwealth embraced the Task Force view, as did expert witnesses who testified for Virginia. See 852 F. Supp., at 480-481.

As earlier stated, see *supra*, at 24, generalizations about "the way women are," estimates of what is appropriate for *most women*, no longer justify denying opportunity to women whose talent and capacity place them outside the average description. Notably, Virginia never asserted that VMI's method of education suits *most men*. It is also revealing that Virginia accounted for its failure to make the VWIL experience "the entirely militaristic experience of VMI" on the ground that VWIL "is planned for women who do not necessarily expect to pursue military careers." 852 F. Supp., at 478. By that reasoning, VMI's "entirely militaristic" program would be inappropriate for men in general or *as a group*, for "[o]nly about 15% of VMI cadets enter career military service." See 766 F. Supp., at 1432.

In contrast to the generalizations about women on which Virginia rests, we note again these dispositive realties: VMI's "implementing methodology" is not "inherently unsuitable to women," 976 F. 2d, at 899; "some women . . . do well under [the] adversative model," 766 F. Supp., at 1434 (internal quotation marks omitted); "some women, at least, would want to attend [VMI] if they had the opportunity," *id.*, at 1414; "some women are capable of all of the individual activities required of VMI cadets," *id.*, at 1412, and "can meet the physical standards [VMI] now impose[s] on men," 976 F. 2d, at 896. It is on behalf of these women that the United States has instituted this suit, and it is for them that a remedy must be crafted, [n.19] a remedy that will end their exclusion from a state supplied educational opportunity for which they are fit, a decree that will "bar like discrimination in the future." *Louisiana*, 380 U. S., at 154.

B

In myriad respects other than military training, VWIL does not qualify as VMI's equal. VWIL's student body, faculty, course offerings, and facilities hardly match VMI's. Nor can the VWIL graduate anticipate the benefits associated with VMI's 157-year history, the school's prestige, and its influential alumni network.

Mary Baldwin College, whose degree VWIL students will gain, enrolls first year women with an average combined SAT score about 100 points lower than the average score for VMI freshmen. 852 F. Supp., at 501. The Mary Baldwin faculty holds "significantly fewer Ph.D.'s," *id.*, at 502, and receives substantially lower salaries, see Tr. 158 (testimony of James Lott, Dean of Mary Baldwin College), than the faculty at VMI.

Mary Baldwin does not offer a VWIL student the range of curricular choices available to a VMI cadet. VMI awards baccalaureate degrees in liberal arts, biology, chemistry, civil engineering, electrical and computer engineering, and mechanical engineering. See 852 F. Supp., at 503; Virginia Military Institute: More than an Education 11 (Govt. exh. 75, lodged with Clerk of this Court). VWIL students attend a school that "does not have a math and science focus," 852 F. Supp., at 503; they cannot take at Mary Baldwin any courses in engineering or the advanced math and physics courses VMI offers, see *id.*, at 477.

For physical training, Mary Baldwin has "two multi purpose fields" and "[o]ne gymnasium." *Id.*, at 503. VMI has "an NCAA competition level indoor track and field facility; a number of multi purpose fields; baseball, soccer and lacrosse fields; an obstacle course; large boxing, wrestling and martial arts facilities; an 11-laps to the mile indoor running course; an indoor pool; indoor and outdoor rifle ranges; and a football stadium that also contains a practice field and outdoor track." *Ibid.*

Although Virginia has represented that it will provide equal financial support for in state VWIL students and VMI cadets, *id.*, at 483, and the VMI Foundation has agreed to endow VWIL with $5.4625 million, *id.*, at 499, the difference between the two schools' financial reserves is pronounced. Mary Baldwin's endowment, currently about $19 million, will gain an additional $35 million based on future commitments; VMI's current endowment, $131 million--the largest per student endowment in the Nation--will gain $220 million. *Id.*, at 503.

The VWIL student does not graduate with the advantage of a VMI degree. Her diploma does not unite her with the legions of VMI "graduates [who] have distinguished themselves" in military and civilian life. See 976 F. 2d, at 892-893. "[VMI] alumni are exceptionally close to the school," and that closeness accounts, in part, for VMI's success in attracting applicants. See 766F. Supp., at 1421. A VWIL graduate cannot assume that the "network of business owners, corporations, VMI graduates and non graduate employers . . . interested in hiring VMI graduates," 852 F. Supp., at 499, will be equally responsive to her search for employment, see 44 F. 3d, at 1250 (Phillips, J., dissenting) ("the powerful political and economic ties of the VMI alumni network cannot be expected to open" for graduates of the fledgling VWIL program).

Virginia, in sum, while maintaining VMI for men only, has failed to provide any "comparable single gender women's institution." *Id.*, at 1241. Instead, the Commonwealth has created a VWIL program fairly appraised as a "pale shadow" of VMI in terms of the range of curricular choices and faculty stature, funding, prestige, alumni support and influence. See *id.*, at 1250 (Phillips, J., dissenting).

Virginia's VWIL solution is reminiscent of the remedy Texas proposed 50 years ago, in response to a state trial court's 1946 ruling that, given the equal protection guarantee, African Americans could not be denied a legal education at a state facility. See *Sweatt* v. *Painter*, 339 U.S. 629 (1950). Reluctant to admit African Americans to its flagship University of Texas Law School, the State set up a separate school for Herman Sweatt and other black law students. *Id.*, at 632. As originally opened, the new school had no independent faculty or library, and it lacked accreditation. *Id.*, at 633. Nevertheless, the state trial and appellate courts were satisfied that the new school offered Sweatt opportunities for the study of law "substantially equivalent to those offered by the State to white students at the University of Texas." *Id.*, at 632 (internal quotation marks omitted).

Before this Court considered the case, the new school had gained "a faculty of five full time professors; a student body of 23; a library of some 16,500 volumes serviced by a full time staff; a practice court and legal aid association; and one alumnus who ha[d] become a member of the Texas Bar." *Id.*, at 633. This Court contrasted resources at the new school with those at the school from which Sweatt had been excluded. The University of Texas Law School had a full time faculty of 16, a student body of 850, a library containing over 65,000 volumes, scholarship funds, a law review, and moot court facilities. *Id.*, at 632-633.

More important than the tangible features, the Court emphasized, are "those qualities which are incapable of objective measurement but which make for greatness" in a school, including "reputation of the faculty, experience of the administration, position and influence of the alumni, standing in the community, traditions and prestige." *Id.*, at 634. Facing the marked differences reported in the *Sweatt* opinion, the Court unanimously ruled that Texas had not shown "substantial equality in the [separate] educational opportunities" the State offered. *Id.*, at 633. Accordingly, the Court held, the Equal Protection Clause required Texas to admit African Americans to the University of Texas Law School. *Id.*, at 636. In line with *Sweatt*, we rule here that Virginia has not shown substantial equality in the separate educational opportunities the State supports at VWIL and VMI.

C

When Virginia tendered its VWIL plan, the Fourth Circuit did not inquire whether the proposed remedy, approved by the District Court, placed women denied the VMI advantage in "the position they would have occupied in the absence of [discrimination]." *Milliken*, 433 U.S., at 280 (internal quotation marks omitted). Instead, the Court of Appeals considered whether the State could provide, with fidelity to the equal protection principle, separate and unequal educational programs for men and women.

The Fourth Circuit acknowledged that "the VWIL degree from Mary Baldwin College lacks the historical benefit and prestige of a degree from VMI." 44 F. 3d, at 1241. The Court of Appeals further observed that VMI is "an ongoing and successful institution with a long history," and there remains no "comparable single gender women's institution." *Ibid.* Nevertheless, the appeals court declared the substantially different and significantly unequal VWIL program satisfactory. The court reached that result by revising the applicable standard of review. The Fourth Circuit displaced the standard developed in our precedent, see *supra*, at 13-16, and substituted a standard of its own invention.

We have earlier described the deferential review in which the Court of Appeals engaged, see *supra*, at 10-11, a brand of review inconsistent with the more exacting standard our precedent requires, see *supra*, at 13-16. Quoting in part from *Mississippi Univ. for Women*, the Court of Appeals candidly described its own analysis as one capable of checking a legislative purpose ranked as "pernicious," but generally according "deference to [the] legislative will." 44 F. 3d, at 1235, 1236. Recognizing that it had extracted from our decisions a test yielding "little or no scrutiny of the effect of a classification directed at [single gender education]," the Court of Appeals devised another test, a "substantive comparability" inquiry, *id.*, at 1237, and proceeded to find that new test satisfied, *id.*, at 1241.

The Fourth Circuit plainly erred in exposing Virginia's VWIL plan to a deferential analysis, for "all gender based classifications today" warrant "heightened scrutiny." See *J. E. B.*, 511 U. S., at 136. Valuable as VWIL may prove for students who seek the program offered, Virginia's remedy affords no cure at all for the opportunities and advantages withheld from women who want a VMI education and can make the grade. See *supra*, at 31-36. [n.20] In sum, Virginia's remedy does not match the constitutional violation; the State has shown no "exceedingly persuasive justification" for withholding from women qualified for the experience premier training of the kind VMI affords.

VII

A generation ago, "the authorities controlling Virginia higher education," despite long established tradition, agreed "to innovate and favorably entertain[ed] the [then] relatively new idea that there must be no discrimination by sex in offering educational opportunity." *Kirstein*, 309 F. Supp., at 186. Commencing in 1970, Virginia opened to women "educational opportunities at the Charlottesville campus that [were] not afforded in other [State operated] institutions." *Id.*, at 187; see *supra*, at 20. A federal court approved the State's innovation, emphasizing that the University of Virginia "offer[ed] courses of instruction . . . not available elsewhere." 309 F. Supp., at 187. The court further noted: "[T]here exists at Charlottesville a `prestige' factor [not paralleled in] other Virginia educational institutions." *Ibid.*

VMI, too, offers an educational opportunity no other Virginia institution provides, and the school's "prestige"--associated with its success in developing "citizen soldiers"--is unequaled. Virginia has closed this facility to its daughters and, instead, has devised for them a "parallel program," with a faculty less impressively credentialed and less well paid, more limited course offerings, fewer opportunities for military training and for scientific specialization. Cf. *Sweatt*, 339 U. S., at 633. VMI, beyond question, "possesses to a far greater degree" than the VWIL program "those qualities which are incapable of objective measurement but which make for greatness in a . . . school," including "position and influence of the alumni, standing in the community, traditions and prestige." *Id.*, at 634. Women seeking and fit for a VMI quality education cannot be offered anything less, under the State's obligation to afford them genuinely equal protection.

A prime part of the history of our Constitution, historian Richard Morris recounted, is the story of the extension of constitutional rights and protections to people once ignored or excluded. [n.21] VMI's story continued as our comprehension of "We the People" expanded. See *supra*, at 29, n. 16. There is no reason to believe that the admission of women capable of all the activities required of VMI cadets would destroy the Institute rather than enhance its capacity to serve the "more perfect Union."

* * *

For the reasons stated, the initial judgment of the Court of Appeals, 976 F. 2d 890 (CA4 1992), is affirmed, the final judgment of the Court of Appeals, 44 F. 3d 1229 (CA4 1995), is reversed, and the case is remanded for further proceedings consistent with this opinion.

It is so ordered.

Justice Thomas took no part in the consideration or decision of this case.

NOTES

[1] During the Civil War, school teaching became a field dominated by women. See A. Scott, The Southern Lady: From Pedestal to Politics, 1830-1930, p. 82 (1970).

[2] Historically, most of Virginia's public colleges and universities were single sex; by the mid 1970's, however, all except VMI had become coeducational. 766 F. Supp. 1407, 1418-1419 (WD Va. 1991). For example, Virginia's legislature incorporated Farmville Female Seminary Association in 1839, the year VMI opened. 1839 Va. Acts, ch. 167. Originally providing instruction in "English, Latin, Greek, French, and piano" in a "home atmosphere," R. Sprague, Longwood College: A History 7-8, 15 (1989) (Longwood College), Farmville Female Seminary became a public institution in 1884 with a mission to train "white female teachers for public schools," 1884 Va. Acts, ch. 311. The school became Longwood College in 1949, Longwood College 136, and introduced coeducation in 1976, *id.*, at 133.

[3] The District Court allowed the VMI Foundation and the VMI Alumni Association to intervene as

defendants. 766 F. Supp., at 1408.

[4] Six judges voted to rehear the case en banc, four voted against rehearing, and three were recused. The Fourth Circuit's local rule permits rehearing en banc only on the vote of a majority of the Circuit's judges in regular active service (currently 13) without regard to recusals. See 52 F. 3d, at 91, and n. 1.

[5] As Thomas Jefferson stated the view prevailing when the Constitution was new:

> "Were our State a pure democracy . . . there would yet be excluded from their deliberations . . . women, who, to prevent depravation of morals and ambiguity of issue, should not mix promiscuously in the public meetings of men." Letter from Thomas Jefferson to Samuel Kercheval (Sept. 5, 1816), in 10 Writings of Thomas Jefferson 45-46, n. 1 (P. Ford ed. 1899).

[6] The Court has thus far reserved most stringent judicial scrutiny for classifications based on race or national origin, but last Term observed that strict scrutiny of such classifications is not inevitably "fatal in fact." *Adarand Constructors, Inc.* v. *Pena*, 515 U. S. __, __ (1995) (slip op., at 35) (internal quotation marks omitted).

[7] Several *amici* have urged that diversity in educational opportunities is an altogether appropriate governmental pursuit and that single sex schools can contribute importantly to such diversity. Indeed, it is the mission of some single sex schools "to dissipate, rather than perpetuate, traditional gender classifications." See Brief for Twenty Six Private Women's Colleges as *Amici Curiae* 5. We do not question the State's prerogative evenhandedly to support diverse educational opportunities. We address specifically and only an educational opportunity recognized by the District Court and the Court of Appeals as "unique," see 766 F. Supp., at 1413, 1432; 976 F. 2d, at 892, an opportunity available only at Virginia's premier military institute, the State's sole single sex public university or college. Cf. *Mississippi Univ. for Women* v. *Hogan*, 458 U.S. 718, 720, n. 1 (1982) ("Mississippi maintains no other single sex public university or college. Thus, we are not faced with the question of whether States can provide 'separate but equal' undergraduate institutions for males and females.").

[8] On this point, the dissent sees fire where there is no flame. See *post*, at 33-34, 35-37. "Both men and women can benefit from a single sex education," the District Court recognized, although "the beneficial effects" of such education, the court added, apparently "are stronger among women than among men." 766 F. Supp., at 1414. The United States does not challenge that recognition. Cf. C. Jencks & D. Riesman, The Academic Revolution 297-298 (1968):

> "The pluralistic argument for preserving all male colleges is uncomfortably similar to the pluralistic argument for preserving all white colleges . . . . The all male college would be relatively easy to defend if it emerged from a world in which women were established as fully equal to men. But it does not. It is therefore likely to be a whiting or unwitting device for preserving tacit assumptions of male superiority--assumptions for which women must eventually pay."

[9] Dr. Edward H. Clarke of Harvard Medical School, whose influential book, Sex in Education, went through 17 editions, was perhaps the most well known speaker from the medical community opposing higher education for women. He maintained that the physiological effects of hard study and academic competition with boys would interfere with the development of girls' reproductive organs. See E. Clarke, Sex in Education 38-39, 62-63 (1873); *id.*, at 127 ("identical education of the two sexes is a crime before God and humanity, that physiology protests against, and that experience weeps over"); see also H. Maudsley, Sex in Mind and in Education 17 (1874) ("It is not that girls have not ambition,

nor that they fail generally to run the intellectual race [in coeducational settings], but it is asserted that they do it at a cost to their strength and health which entails life long suffering, and even incapacitates them for the adequate performance of the natural functions of their sex."); C. Meigs, Females and Their Diseases 350 (1848) (after five or six weeks of "mental and educational discipline," a healthy woman would "lose . . . the habit of menstruation" and suffer numerous ills as a result of depriving her body for the sake of her mind).

[10] Virginia's Superintendent of Public Instruction dismissed the coeducational idea as " `repugnant to the prejudices of the people' " and proposed a female college similar in quality to Girton, Smith, or Vassar. 2 History of Women's Education 254 (quoting 1 Report of the Commissioner of Education, H. R. Doc. No. 5, 58th Cong., 2d Sess., 438 (1904)).

[11] See *post*, at 1, 35, 40. Forecasts of the same kind were made regarding admission of women to the federal military academies. See, *e.g.*, Hearings on H. R. 9832 et al. before Subcommittee No. 2 on Military Personnel of the House Committee on Armed Services, 93d Cong., 2d Sess., 137 (1975) (statement of Lt. Gen. A. P. Clark, Superintendent of U. S. Air Force Academy) ("It is my considered judgment that the introduction of female cadets will inevitably erode this vital atmosphere."); *id.*, at 165 (statement of Hon. H. H. Callaway, Secretary of the Army) ("Admitting women to West Point would irrevocably change the Academy. . . . The Spartan atmosphere--which is so important to producing the final product--would surely be diluted, and would in all probability disappear.").

[12] See 766 F. Supp., at 1413 (describing testimony of expert witness David Riesman: "[I]f VMI were to admit women, it would eventually find it necessary to drop the adversative system altogether, and adopt a system that provides more nurturing and support for the students."). Such judgments have attended, and impeded, women's progress toward full citizenship stature throughout our Nation's history. Speaking in 1879 in support of higher education for females, for example, Virginia State Senator C. T. Smith of Nelson recounted that legislation proposed to protect the property rights of women had encountered resistance. 10 Educ. J. Va. 213 (1879). A Senator opposing the measures objected that "there [was] no formal call for the [legislation]," and "depicted in burning eloquence the terrible consequences such laws would produce." *Ibid*. The legislation passed, and a year or so later, its sponsor, C. T. Smith, reported that "not one of [the forecast "terrible consequences"] has or ever will happen, even unto the sounding of Gabriel's trumpet." *Ibid*. See also *supra*, at 20.

[13] Women cadets have graduated at the top of their class at every federal military academy. See Brief for Lieutenant Colonel Rhonda Cornum et al. as *Amici Curiae* 11, n. 25; cf. Defense Advisory Committee on Women in the Services, Report on the Integration and Performance of Women at West Point 64 (1992).

[14] Brief for Lieutenant Colonel Rhonda Cornum, *supra*, at 5-9 (reporting the vital contributions and courageous performance of women in the military); see J. Mintz, President Nominates 1st Woman to Rank of Three Star General, Washington Post, Mar. 27, 1996, p. A19, col. 1 (announcing President's nomination of Marine Corps Major General Carol Mutter to rank of Lieutenant General; Mutter will head Corps manpower and planning); M. Tousignant, A New Era for the Old Guard, Washington Post, Mar. 23, 1996, p. C1, col. 2 (reporting admission of Sergeant Heather Johnsen to elite Infantry unit that keeps round the clock vigil at Tomb of the Unknowns in Arlington National Cemetery).

[15] Inclusion of women in settings where, traditionally, they were not wanted inevitably entails a period of adjustment. As one West Point cadet squad leader recounted: "[T]he classes of '78 and '79 see the women as women, but the classes of '80 and '81 see them as classmates." U. S. Military Academy, A. Vitters, Report of Admission of Women (Project Athena II) 84 (1978) (internal quotation marks omitted).

[16] VMI has successfully managed another notable change. The school admitted its first African American cadets in 1968. See The VMI Story 347-349 (students no longer sing "Dixie," salute the Confederate flag or the tomb of General Robert E. Lee at ceremonies and sports events). As the District Court noted, VMI established a Program on "retention of black cadets" designed to offer academic and social cultural support to "minority members of a dominantly white and tradition oriented student body." 766 F. Supp., at 1436-1437. The school maintains a "special recruitment program for blacks" which, the District Court found, "has had little, if any, effect on VMI's method of accomplishing its mission." *Id.*, at 1437.

[17] As earlier observed, see *supra*, at 11-12, Judge Phillips, in dissent, measured Virginia's plan against a paradigm arrangement, one that "could survive equal protection scrutiny": single sex schools with "substantially comparable curricular and extra curricular programs, funding, physical plant, administration and support services, . . . faculty[,] and library resources." 44 F. 3d, at 1250. Cf. *Bray* v. *Lee*, 337 F. Supp. 934 (D. Mass. 1972) (holding inconsistent with the Equal Protection Clause admission of males to Boston's Boys Latin School with a test score of 120 or higher (up to a top score of 200) while requiring a score, on the same test, of at least 133 for admission of females to Girls Latin School, but not ordering coeducation). Measuring VMI/VWIL against the paradigm, Judge Phillips said, "reveals how far short the [Virginia] plan falls from providing substantially equal tangible and intangible educational benefits to men and women." 44 F. 3d, at 1250.

[18] Both programs include an honor system. Students at VMI are expelled forthwith for honor code violations, see 766 F. Supp., at 1423; the system for VWIL students, see 852 F. Supp., at 496-497, is less severe, see Tr. 414-415 (testimony of Mary Baldwin College President Cynthia Tyson).

[19] Admitting women to VMI would undoubtedly require alterations necessary to afford members of each sex privacy from the other sex in living arrangements, and to adjust aspects of the physical training programs. See Brief for Petitioner 27-29; cf. note following 10 U.S.C. § 4342 (academic and other standards for women admitted to the Military, Naval, and Air Force Academies "shall be the same as those required for male individuals, except for those minimum essential adjustments in such standards required because of physiological differences between male and female individuals"). Experience shows such adjustments are manageable. See U. S. Military Academy, A. Vitters, N. Kinzer, & J. Adams, Report of Admission of Women (Project Athena I IV) (1977-1980) (4 year longitudinal study of the admission of women to West Point); Defense Advisory Committee on Women in the Services, Report on the Integration and Performance of Women at West Point 17-18 (1992).

[20] Virginia's prime concern, it appears, is that "plac[ing] men and women into the adversative relationship inherent in the VMI program . . . would destroy, at least for that period of the adversative training, any sense of decency that still permeates the relationship between the sexes." 44 F. 3d, at 1239; see *supra*, at 22-27. It is an ancient and familiar fear. Compare *In re Lavinia Goodell*, 39 Wis. 232, 246 (1875) (denying female applicant's motion for admission to the bar of its court, Wisconsin Supreme Court explained: "Discussions are habitually necessary in courts of justice, which are unfit for female ears. The habitual presence of women at these would tend to relax the public sense of decency and propriety."), with Levine, Closing Comments, 6 Law & Inequality 41, 41 (1988) (presentation at Eighth Circuit Judicial Conference, Colorado Springs, Colorado, July 17, 1987) (footnotes omitted):

> "Plato questioned whether women should be afforded equal opportunity to become guardians, those elite Rulers of Platonic society. Ironically, in that most undemocratic system of government, the Republic, women's native ability to serve as guardians was not seriously questioned. The concern was over the wrestling and exercise class in which all candidates for guardianship had to participate, for rigorous physical and mental training were prerequisites to attain the exalted status of guardian. And in accord with Greek custom, those exercise classes were conducted in the nude. Plato concluded that their virtue would clothe the women's nakedness and that Platonic society would not thereby be deprived of the talent of qualified citizens for reasons of mere gender."

For Plato's full text on the equality of women, see 2 The Dialogues of Plato 302-312 (B. Jowett transl., 4th ed. 1953). Virginia, not bound to ancient Greek custom in its "rigorous physical and mental training" programs, could more readily make the accommodations necessary to draw on "the talent of [all] qualified citizens." Cf. *supra*, at 34, n. 19.

[21] R. Morris, The Forging of the Union, 1781-1789, p. 193 (1987); see *id.*, at 191, setting out letter to a friend from Massachusetts patriot (later second President) John Adams, on the subject of qualifications for voting in his home state:

"[I]t is dangerous to open so fruitful a source of controversy and altercation as would be opened by attempting to alter the qualifications of voters; there will be no end of it. New claims will arise; women will demand a vote; lads from twelve to twenty one will think their rights not enough attended to; and every man who has not a farthing, will demand an equal voice with any other, in all acts of state. It tends to confound and destroy all distinctions, and prostrate all ranks to one common level." Letter from John Adams to James Sullivan (May 26, 1776), in 9 Works of John Adams 378 (C. Adams ed. 1854).

CATERPILLAR INC. v. JAMES DAVID LEWIS

No. 95-1263, December 10, 1996

ON WRIT OF CERTIORARI TO THE UNITED STATES COURT OF APPEALS FOR THE SIXTH CIRCUIT

Justice Ginsburg delivered the opinion of the Court.

This case, commenced in a state court, involves personal injury claims arising under state law. The case was removed to a federal court at a time when, the Court of Appeals concluded, complete diversity of citizenship did not exist among the parties. Promptly after the removal, the plaintiff moved to remand the case to the state court, but the District Court denied that motion. Before trial of the case, however, all claims involving the nondiverse defendant were settled, and that defendant was dismissed as a party to the action. Complete diversity thereafter existed. The case proceeded to trial, jury verdict, and judgment for the removing defendant. The Court of Appeals vacated the judgment, concluding that, absent complete diversity at the time of removal, the District Court lacked subject-matter jurisdiction.

The question presented is whether the absence of complete diversity at the time of removal is fatal to federal court adjudication. We hold that a district court's error in failing to remand a case improperly removed is not fatal to the ensuing adjudication if federal jurisdictional requirements are met at the time judgment is entered.

I

Respondent James David Lewis, a resident of Kentucky, filed this lawsuit in Kentucky state court on June 22, 1989, after sustaining injuries while operating a bulldozer. Asserting state law claims based on defective manufacture, negligent maintenance, failure to warn, and breach of warranty, Lewis named as defendants both the manufacturer of the bulldozer--petitioner Caterpillar Inc., a Delaware corporation with its principal place of business in Illinois--and the company that serviced the bulldozer--Whayne Supply Company, a Kentucky corporation with its principal place of business in Kentucky.

Several months later, Liberty Mutual Insurance Group, the insurance carrier for Lewis' employer, intervened in the lawsuit as a plaintiff. A Massachusetts corporation with its principal place of business in that State, Liberty Mutual asserted subrogation claims against both Caterpillar and Whayne Supply for workers' compensation benefits Liberty Mutual had paid to Lewis on behalf of his employer.

Lewis entered into a settlement agreement with defendant Whayne Supply less than a year after filing his complaint. Shortly after learning of this agreement, Caterpillar filed a notice of removal, on June 21, 1990, in the United States District Court for the Eastern District of Kentucky. Grounding federal jurisdiction on diversity of citizenship, see 28 U.S.C. § 1332 Caterpillar satisfied with only a day to spare the statutory requirement that a diversity based removal take place within one year of a lawsuit's commencement, see 28 U.S.C. § 1446(b). Caterpillar's notice of removal explained that the case was nonremovable at the lawsuit's start: Complete diversity was absent then because plaintiff Lewis and defendant Whayne Supply shared Kentucky citizenship. App. 31. Proceeding on the understanding that the settlement agreement between these two Kentucky parties would result in the dismissal of Whayne Supply from the lawsuit, Caterpillar stated that the settlement rendered the case removable. Id., at 31-32.

Lewis objected to the removal and moved to remand the case to state court. Lewis acknowledged that he had settled his own claims against Whayne Supply. But Liberty Mutual had not yet settled its subrogation claim against Whayne Supply, Lewis asserted. Whayne Supply's presence as a defendant in the lawsuit, Lewis urged, defeated diversity of citizenship. Id., at 36. Without addressing this argument, the District Court denied Lewis' motion to remand on September 24, 1990, treating as dispositive Lewis' admission that he had settled his own claims against Whayne Supply. Id., at 55.

Discovery, begun in state court, continued in the now federal lawsuit, and the parties filed pretrial conference papers beginning in July 1991. In June 1993, plaintiff Liberty Mutual and defendant Whayne Supply entered into a settlement of Liberty Mutual's subrogation claim, and the District Court dismissed Whayne Supply from the lawsuit. With Caterpillar as the sole defendant adverse to Lewis, [n.1] the case proceeded to a 6 day jury trial in November 1993, ending in a unanimous verdict for Caterpillar. The District Court entered judgment for Caterpillar on November 23, 1993, and denied Lewis' motion for a new trial on February 1, 1994.

On appeal, the Court of Appeals for the Sixth Circuit accepted Lewis' argument that, at the time of removal, Whayne Supply remained a defendant in the case due to Liberty Mutual's subrogation claim against it. App. to Pet. for Cert. 8a. Because the party lineup, on removal, included Kentucky plaintiff Lewis and Kentucky defendant Whayne Supply, the Court of Appeals observed that diversity was not complete when Caterpillar took the case from state court to federal court. Id., at 8a 9a. Consequently, the Court of Appeals concluded, the District Court "erred in denying [Lewis'] motion to remand this case to the state court for lack of subject matter jurisdiction." Id., at 9a. That error, according to the Court of

Appeals, made it necessary to vacate the District Court's judgment. *Ibid.* [n.2]

Caterpillar petitioned for this Court's review. Caterpillar stressed that the nondiverse defendant, Whayne Supply, had been dismissed from the lawsuit prior to trial. It was therefore improper, Caterpillar urged, for the Court of Appeals to vacate the District Court's judgment--entered after several years of litigation and a 6 day trial--on account of a jurisdictional defect cured, all agreed, by the time of trial and judgment. Pet. for Cert. 8. We granted certiorari, 517 U. S. ___ (1996), and now reverse.

II

The Constitution provides, in Article III, §2, that "[t]he judicial Power [of the United States] shall extend . . . to Controversies . . . between Citizens of different States." Commencing with the Judiciary Act of 1789, ch. 20, §11, 1 Stat. 78, Congress has constantly authorized the federal courts to exercise jurisdiction based on the diverse citizenship of parties. In *Strawbridge* v. *Curtiss,* 3 Cranch 267 (1806), this Court construed the original Judiciary Act's diversity provision to require complete diversity of citizenship. *Id.,* at 267. We have adhered to that statutory interpretation ever since. See *Carden* v. *Arkoma Associates,* 494 U.S. 185, 187 (1990). The current general diversity statute, permitting federal district court jurisdiction over suits for more than $50,000 "between . . . citizens of different States," 28 U.S.C. § 1332(a), thus applies only to cases in which the citizenship of each plaintiff is diverse from the citizenship of each defendant. [n.3]

When a plaintiff files in state court a civil action over which the federal district courts would have original jurisdiction based on diversity of citizenship, the defendant or defendants may remove the action to federal court, 28 U.S.C. § 1441(a), provided that no defendant "is a citizen of the State in which such action is brought," §1441(b). [n.4] In a case not originally removable, a defendant who receives a pleading or other paper indicating the post-commencement satisfaction of federal jurisdictional requirements--for example, by reason of the dismissal of a nondiverse party--may remove the case to federal court within 30 days of receiving such information. §1446(b). No case, however, may be removed from state to federal court based on diversity of citizenship "more than 1 year after commencement of the action." *Ibid.* [n.5]

Once a defendant has filed a notice of removal in the federal district court, a plaintiff objecting to removal "on the basis of any defect in removal procedure" may, within 30 days, file a motion asking the district court to remand the case to state court. §1447(c). This 30-day limit does not apply, however, to jurisdictional defects: "If at any time before final judgment it appears that the district court lacks subject matter jurisdiction, the case shall be remanded." *Ibid.* [n.6]

III

We note, initially, two "givens" in this case as we have accepted it for review. First, the District Court, in its decision denying Lewis' timely motion to remand, incorrectly treated Whayne Supply, the nondiverse defendant, as effectively dropped from the case prior to removal. See App. 55. Second, the Sixth Circuit correctly determined that the complete diversity requirement was not satisfied at the time of removal. App. to Pet. for Cert. 8a 9a. [n.7] We accordingly home in on this question: Does the District Court's initial misjudgment still burden and run with the case, or is it overcome by the eventual dismissal of the nondiverse defendant?

Petitioner Caterpillar relies heavily on our decisions in *American Fire & Casualty Co.* v. *Finn,* 341 U.S. 6 (1951), and *Grubbs* v. *General Elec. Credit Corp.,* 405 U.S. 699 (1972), urging that these decisions "long ago settled the proposition that remand to the state court is unnecessary even if jurisdiction did not exist at the time of removal, so long as the district court had subject matter jurisdiction at the time of judgment." Brief for Petitioner 8-9. Caterpillar is right that *Finn* and *Grubbs* are key cases in point and tend in Caterpillar's favor. Each suggests that the existence of subject matter jurisdiction at time of judgment may shield a judgment against later jurisdictional attack. But neither decision resolves dispositively a controversy of the kind we face, for neither involved a plaintiff who moved promptly, but unsuccessfully, to remand a case improperly removed from state court to federal court, and then challenged on appeal a judgment entered by the federal court.

In *Finn,* two defendants removed a case to federal court on the basis of diversity of citizenship. 341 U. S., at 7-8. Eventually, final judgment was entered for the plaintiff against one of the removing defendants. *Id.,* at 8. The losing defendant urged on appeal, and before this Court, that the judgment could not stand because the requisite diversity jurisdiction, it turned out, existed neither at the time of removal nor at the time of judgment. Agreeing with the defendant, we held that the absence of federal jurisdiction at the time of judgment required the Court of Appeals to vacate the District Court's judgment. *Id.,* at 17-18. [n.8]

Finn's holding does not speak to the situation here, where the requirement of complete diversity was satisfied at the time of judgment. But Caterpillar points to well known dicta in *Finn* more helpful to its cause. "There are cases," the Court observed, "which uphold judgments in the district courts even though there was no right to removal." *Id.,* at 16. [n.9] "In those cases," the *Finn* Court explained, "the federal trial court would have had original jurisdiction of the controversy had it been brought in the federal court in the posture it had at the time of the actual trial of the cause or of the entry of the judgment." *Ibid.*

The discussion in *Finn* concentrated on cases in which courts held *removing defendants* estopped from challenging final judgments on the basis of removal errors. See *id.,* at 17. The *Finn* Court did not address the situation of a plaintiff such as Lewis, who chose a state court as the forum for his lawsuit, timely objected to removal before the District Court, and then challenged the removal on appeal from an adverse judgment.

In *Grubbs,* a civil action filed in state court was removed to federal court on the petition of the United States, which had been named as a party defendant in a "cross action" filed by the original defendant. 405 U. S., at 700-701; see 28 U.S.C. § 1444 (authorizing removal of actions brought against the United States, pursuant to 28 U.S.C. § 2410 with respect to property on which the United States has or claims a lien). No party objected to the removal before trial or judgment. See *Grubbs,* 405 U. S., at 701. The Court of Appeals nonetheless held, on its own motion, that the "interpleader" of the United States was spurious, and that removal had therefore been improper under 28 U.S.C. § 1444. See *Grubbs,* 405 U. S., at 702. On this basis, the Court of Appeals concluded that the District Court's judgment should be vacated and the case remanded to state court. See *ibid.*

This Court reversed. *Id.,* at 700. We explained:

> "Longstanding decisions of this Court make clear . . . that where after removal a case is tried on the merits without objection and the federal court enters judgment, the issue in subsequent proceedings on appeal is not whether the case was properly removed, but whether the federal district court would have had original jurisdiction of the case had it been filed in that court." *Id.,* at 702.

We concluded that, "whether or not the case was properly removed, the District Court did have jurisdiction of the parties at the time it entered judgment." *Id.,* at 700. "Under such circumstances," we held, "the validity of the removal procedure followed *may not be raised for the first time on appeal.*" *Ibid.* (emphasis added). *Grubbs* instructs that an erroneous removal need not cause the destruction of a final judgment, if the requirements of federal subject matter jurisdiction are met at the time the judgment is entered. *Grubbs, however,* dealt with a case removed without objection. The decision is not dispositive of the question whether a plaintiff, who timely objects to removal, may later successfully challenge an adverse judgment on the ground that the removal did not comply with statutory prescriptions.

Beyond question, as Lewis acknowledges, there was in this case complete diversity, and therefore federal subject matter jurisdiction, at the time of trial and judgment. See Brief for Respondent 18-19 (diversity became complete "when Liberty Mutual settled its subrogation claim with Whayne Supply and the latter was formally dismissed from the case"). The case had by then become, essentially, a two party lawsuit: Lewis, a citizen of Kentucky, was the sole plaintiff; Caterpillar, incorporated in Delaware with its principal place of business in Illinois, was the sole defendant Lewis confronted. Caterpillar maintains that this change cured the threshold *statutory* misstep, *i.e.,* the removal of a case when diversity was incomplete. Brief for Petitioner 7, 13.

Caterpillar moves too quickly over the terrain we must cover. The *jurisdictional* defect was cured, *i.e.,* complete diversity was established before the trial commenced. Therefore, the Sixth Circuit erred in resting its decision on the absence of subject matter jurisdiction. But a statutory flaw--Caterpillar's failure to meet the §1441(a) requirement that the case be fit for federal adjudication at the time the removal petition is filed--remained in the unerasable history of the case.

And Lewis, by timely moving for remand, did all that was required to preserve his objection to removal. An order denying a motion to remand, "standing alone," is "[o]bviously . . . not final and [immediately] appealable" as of right. *Chicago, R. I. & P. R. Co. v. Stude,* 346 U.S. 574, 578 (1954). Nor is a plaintiff required to seek permission to take an interlocutory appeal pursuant to 28 U.S.C. § 1292(b) [n.10] in order to avoid waiving whatever ultimate appeal right he may have. [n.11] Indeed, if a party had to invoke §1292(b) in order to preserve an objection to an interlocutory ruling, litigants would be obliged to seek §1292(b) certifications constantly. Routine resort to §1292(b) requests would hardly comport with Congress' design to reserve interlocutory review for " `exceptional' " cases while generally retaining for the federal courts a firm final judgment rule. *Coopers & Lybrand* v. *Livesay,* 437 U.S. 463, 475 (1978) (quoting *Fisons, Ltd.* v. *United States,* 458 F. 2d 1241, 1248 (CA7), cert. denied, 405 U.S. 1041 (1972)).

Having preserved his objection to an improper removal, Lewis urges that an "all's well that ends well" approach is inappropriate here. He maintains that ultimate satisfaction of the subject matter jurisdiction requirement ought not swallow up antecedent statutory violations. The course Caterpillar advocates, Lewis observes, would disfavor diligent plaintiffs who timely, but unsuccessfully, move to check improper removals in district court. Further, that course would allow improperly removing defendants to profit from their disregard of Congress' instructions, and their ability to lead district judges into error.

Concretely, in this very case, Lewis emphasizes, adherence to the rules Congress prescribed for removal would have kept the case in state court. Only by removing prematurely was Caterpillar able to get to federal court inside the 1 year limitation set in §1446(b). [n.12] Had Caterpillar waited until the case was ripe for removal, *i.e.,* until Whayne Supply was dismissed as a defendant, the 1 year limitation would have barred the way, [n.13] and plaintiff's choice of forum would have been preserved. [n.14]

These arguments are hardly meritless, but they run up against an overriding consideration. Once a diversity case has been tried in federal court, with rules of decision supplied by state law under the regime of *Erie R. Co.* v. *Tompkins,* 304

U.S. 64 (1938), considerations of finality, efficiency, and economy become overwhelming.

Our decision in *Newman Green, Inc.* v. *Alfonzo Larrain*, 490 U.S. 826 (1989), is instructive in this regard. *Newman Green* did not involve removal, but it did involve the federal courts' diversity jurisdiction and a party defendant whose presence, like Whayne Supply's in this case, blocked complete diversity. *Newman Green* proceeded to summary judgment with the jurisdictional flaw--the absence of complete diversity--undetected. See *id.*, at 828-829. The Court of Appeals noticed the flaw, invited the parties to address it, and, en banc, returned the case to the District Court "to determine whether it would be prudent to drop [the jurisdiction spoiler] from the litigation." *Id.*, at 830. We held that the Court of Appeals itself had authority "to dismiss a dispensable nondiverse party," although we recognized that, ordinarily, district courts are better positioned to make such judgments. *Id.*, at 837-838. "[R]equiring dismissal after years of litigation," the Court stressed in *Newman Green*, "would impose unnecessary and wasteful burdens on the parties, judges, and other litigants waiting for judicial attention." *Id.*, at 836. The same may be said of the remand to state court Lewis seeks here. Cf. *Knop* v. *McMahan*, 872 F. 2d 1132, 1139, n. 16 (CA3 1989) ("To permit a case in which there is complete diversity throughout trial to proceed to judgment and then cancel the effect of that judgment and relegate the parties to a new trial in a state court because of a brief lack of complete diversity at the beginning of the case would be a waste of judicial resources.").

Our view is in harmony with a main theme of the removal scheme Congress devised. Congress ordered a procedure calling for expeditious superintendence by district courts. The lawmakers specified a short time, 30 days, for motions to remand for defects in removal procedure, 28 U.S.C. § 1447(c), and district court orders remanding cases to state courts generally are "not reviewable on appeal or otherwise," §1447(d). Congress did not similarly exclude appellate review of refusals to remand. But an evident concern that may explain the lack of symmetry relates to the federal courts' subject matter jurisdiction. Despite a federal trial court's threshold denial of a motion to remand, if, at the end of the day and case, a *jurisdictional* defect remains uncured, the judgment must be vacated. See Fed. Rule Civ. Proc. 12(h)(3) ("Whenever it appears by suggestion of the parties or otherwise that the court lacks jurisdiction of the subject matter, the court shall dismiss the action."); *Finn,* 341 U. S., at 18. In this case, however, no jurisdictional defect lingered through judgment in the District Court. To wipe out the adjudication post-judgment, and return to state court a case now satisfying all federal jurisdictional requirements, would impose an exorbitant cost on our dual court system, a cost incompatible with the fair and unprotracted administration of justice.

Lewis ultimately argues that, if the final judgment against him is allowed to stand, "all of the various procedural requirements for removal will become unenforceable"; therefore, "defendants will have an enormous incentive to attempt wrongful removals." Brief for Respondent 9. In particular, Lewis suggests that defendants will remove prematurely "in the hope that some subsequent developments, such as the eventual dismissal of nondiverse defendants, will permit th[e] case to be kept in federal court." *Id.*, at 21. We do not anticipate the dire consequences Lewis forecasts.

The procedural requirements for removal remain enforceable by the federal trial court judges to whom those requirements are directly addressed. Lewis' prediction that rejection of his petition will "encourag[e] state court defendants to remove cases improperly," *id.*, at 19, rests on an assumption we do not indulge--that district courts generally will not comprehend, or will balk at applying, the rules on removal Congress has prescribed. The prediction furthermore assumes defendants' readiness to gamble that any jurisdictional defect, for example, the absence of complete diversity, will first escape detection, then disappear prior to judgment. The well advised defendant, we are satisfied, will foresee the likely outcome of an unwarranted removal--a swift, and nonreviewable remand order, see 28 U.S.C. § 1447(c), (d), attended by the displeasure of a district court whose authority has been improperly invoked. The odds against any gain from a wrongful removal, in sum, render improbable Lewis' projection of increased resort to the maneuver.

* * *

For the reasons stated, the judgment of the Court of Appeals is reversed, and the case is remanded for proceedings consistent with this opinion.

It is so ordered.

NOTES

[1] In accord with 28 U.S.C. § 1367 and Rule 14 of the Federal Rules of Civil Procedure, Caterpillar, after removing the case to federal court, impleaded Lewis' employer, Gene Wilson Enterprises, a Kentucky corporation, as a third party defendant. See App. 2. Gene Wilson Enterprises, so far as the record shows, remained a named third party defendant, adverse solely to third party plaintiff Caterpillar, through judgment. See Brief for Respondent 5. No dispute ran between Lewis and his employer, and Caterpillar's third party complaint against Gene Wilson Enterprises had no bearing on the authority of the federal court to adjudicate the diversity claims Lewis asserted against Caterpillar. See, *e.g., Wichita Railroad & Light Co.* v. *Public Util. Comm'n of Kan.*, 260 U.S. 48, 54 (1922) (federal jurisdiction once acquired on the ground of complete diversity of citizenship is unaffected by the subsequent intervention "of a party whose presence is not essential to a decision of the controversy between the original parties"). As elaborated in 3 J. Moore, Moore's Federal Practice ¶14.26, p. 14-

116 (2d ed. 1996) (footnotes omitted): "Once federal subject matter jurisdiction is established over the underlying case between [plaintiff] and [defendant], the jurisdictional propriety of each additional claim is to be assessed individually. Thus, assuming that jurisdiction is based upon diversity of citizenship between [plaintiff] and [defendant], the question concerning impleader is whether there is a jurisdictional basis for the claim by [defendant] against [third party defendant]. The fact that [plaintiff] and [third party defendant] may be co citizens is completely irrelevant. Unless [plaintiff] chooses to amend his complaint to assert a claim against [third party defendant], [plaintiff] and [third party defendant] are simply not adverse, and there need be no basis of jurisdiction between them."

2 Because the Court of Appeals held the District Court lacked jurisdiction over the case, it did not reach several other issues Lewis raised on appeal. See App. to Pet. for Cert. 2a, 9a, n. 3.

3 This "complete diversity" interpretation of the general diversity provision is a matter of statutory construction. "Article III poses no obstacle to the legislative extension of federal jurisdiction, founded on diversity, so long as any two adverse parties are not co citizens." *State Farm Fire & Casualty Co.* v. *Tashire,* 386 U.S. 523, 531 (1967).

4 In relevant part, 28 U.S.C. § 1441 provides:

"(a) Except as otherwise expressly provided by Act of Congress, any civil action brought in a State court of which the district courts of the United States have original jurisdiction, may be removed by the defendant or the defendants, to the district court of the United States for the district and division embracing the place where such action is pending. For purposes of removal under this chapter, the citizenship of defendants sued under fictitious names shall be disregarded. (b) Any civil action of which the district courts have original jurisdiction founded on a claim or right arising under the Constitution, treaties or laws of the United States shall be removable without regard to the citizenship or residence of the parties. Any other such action shall be removable only if none of the parties in interest properly joined and served as defendants is a citizen of the State in which such action is brought."

5 In full, 28 U.S.C. § 1446(b) provides:

"The notice of removal of a civil action or proceeding shall be filed within thirty days after the receipt by the defendant, through service or otherwise, of a copy of the initial pleading setting forth the claim for relief upon which such action or proceeding is based, or within thirty days after the service of summons upon the defendant if such initial pleading has then been filed in court and is not required to be served on the defendant, whichever period is shorter. If the case stated by the initial pleading is not removable, a notice of removal may be filed within thirty days after receipt by the defendant, through service or otherwise, of a copy of an amended pleading, motion, order or other paper from which it may first be ascertained that the case is one which is or has become removable, except that a case may not be removed on the basis of jurisdiction conferred by section 1332 of this title more than 1 year after commencement of the action."

[6] In relevant part, 28 U.S.C. § 1447(c) provides:

"A motion to remand the case on the basis of any defect in removal procedure must be made within 30 days after the filing of the notice of removal under section 1446(a). If at any time before final judgment it appears that the district court lacks subject matter jurisdiction, the case shall be remanded. . . . The State court may thereupon proceed with such case."

[7] Caterpillar's petition for certiorari raised the question whether the subrogation claim asserted by Liberty Mutual, and thus the citizenship of Whayne Supply, should be disregarded for purposes of determining diversity of citizenship, in view of the settlement agreed upon between Lewis and Whayne Supply. See Pet. for Cert. i, 18-23. Our order granting review did not encompass that question, see 517 U. S. ___ (1996), and we express no opinion on it.

[8] The Court left open in *Finn* the question whether, on remand to the District Court, "a new judgment [could] be entered on the old verdict without a new trial" if the nondiverse defendant were dismissed from the case. 341 U. S., at 18, n. 18. In the litigation's second round, the District Court allowed the plaintiff to dismiss all claims against the nondiverse defendant. See *Finn* v. *American Fire & Casualty Co.,* 207 F. 2d 113, 114 (CA5 1953), cert. denied, 347 U.S. 912 (1954). Thereafter, the District Court granted a new trial, on the assumption that the original judgment could not stand for lack of jurisdiction. See *ibid.* Ultimately, the Court of Appeals for the Fifth Circuit set aside the judgment entered after the second trial and ordered the original judgment reinstated. *Id.,* at 117.

[9] The Court cited *Baggs* v. *Martin,* 179 U.S. 206 (1900), and three lower federal court cases. *Finn,* 341 U. S., at 16, n. 14.

[10] Section 1292(b) provides for interlocutory appeals from otherwise not immediately appealable orders, if conditions specified in the section are met, the district court so certifies, and the court of appeals exercises its discretion to take up the request for review.

[11] On brief, Caterpillar argued that "Lewis effectively waived his objection to removal by failing to seek an immediate appeal of the district court's refusal to remand." Brief for Petitioner 13. We reject this waiver argument, though we recognize that it has attracted some support in Court of Appeals opinions. See, *e.g., Able* v. *Upjohn Co.,* 829 F. 2d 1330, 1333-1334 (CA4 1987), cert. denied, 485 U.S. 963 (1988).

[12] Congress amended §1446(b) in 1988 to include the 1 year limitation in order to "reduc[e] the opportunity for removal after substantial progress has been made in state court." H. R. Rep. No. 100-889, p. 72 (1988).

[13] On appeal, Lewis raised only the absence of diversity. He did not refer to the 1 year limitation prior to his brief on the merits in this Court. See Tr. of Oral Arg. 17, 30-31. Under this Court's Rule 15.2, a nonjurisdictional argument not raised in a respondent's brief in opposition to a petition for a writ of certiorari "may be deemed waived." Under the facts of this case, however, addressing the implications of §1446(b)'s 1 year limitation is " `predicate to an intelligent resolution' of the question presented." *Ohio* v. *Robinette,* 519 U. S. ___, ___ (1996) (slip op., at 4) (quoting *Vance* v. *Terrazas,* 444 U.S. 252, 258-259, n. 5 (1980)). We therefore regard the issue as one "fairly included" within the question presented. This Court's Rule 14.1. The parties addressed the issue in their briefs and at oral argument, and we exercise our discretion to decide it.

[14] Lewis preferred state court to federal court based on differences he perceived in, *inter alia,* the state and federal jury systems and rules of evidence. See Brief for Respondent 22-23.

AMCHEM PRODUCTS, INC., et al. v. GEORGE WINDSOR et al.

No. 96-270, June 25, 1997

ON WRIT OF CERTIORARI TO THE UNITED STATES COURT OF APPEALS FOR THE THIRD CIRCUIT

Justice Ginsburg delivered the opinion of the Court.

This case concerns the legitimacy under Rule 23 of the Federal Rules of Civil Procedure of a class action certification sought to achieve global settlement of current and future asbestos related claims. The class proposed for certification potentially encompasses hundreds of thousands, perhaps millions, of individuals tied together by this commonality: each was, or some day may be, adversely affected by past exposure to asbestos products manufactured by one or more of 20 companies. Those companies, defendants in the lower courts, are petitioners here.

The United States District Court for the Eastern District of Pennsylvania certified the class for settlement only, finding that the proposed settlement was fair and that representation and notice had been adequate. That court enjoined class members from separately pursuing asbestos related personal injury suits in any court, federal or state, pending the issuance of a final order. The Court of Appeals for the Third Circuit vacated the District Court's orders, holding that the class certification failed to satisfy Rule 23's requirements in several critical respects. We affirm the Court of Appeals' judgment.

The settlement class certification we confront evolved in response to an asbestos litigation crisis. See *Georgine* v. *Amchem Products, Inc.*, 83 F. 3d 610, 618, and n. 2 (CA3 1996) (citing commentary). A United States Judicial Conference Ad Hoc Committee on Asbestos Litigation, appointed by The Chief Justice in September 1990, described facets of the problem in a 1991 report:

> "[This] is a tale of danger known in the 1930s, exposure inflicted upon millions of Americans in the 1940s and 1950s, injuries that began to take their toll in the 1960s, and a flood of lawsuits beginning in the 1970s. On the basis of past and current filing data, and because of a latency period that may last as long as 40 years for some asbestos related diseases, a continuing stream of claims can be expected. The final toll of asbestos related injuries is unknown. Predictions have been made of 200,000 asbestos disease deaths before the year 2000 and as many as 265,000 by the year 2015.

"The most objectionable aspects of asbestos litigation can be briefly summarized: dockets in both federal and state courts continue to grow; long delays are routine; trials are too long; the same issues are litigated over and over; transaction costs exceed the victims' recovery by nearly two to one; exhaustion of assets threatens and distorts the process; and future claimants may lose altogether." Report of The Judicial Conference Ad Hoc Committee on Asbestos Litigation 2-3 (Mar. 1991).

Real reform, the report concluded, required federal legislation creating a national asbestos dispute resolution scheme. See *id.*, at 3, 27-35; see also *id.*, at 42 (dissenting statement of Hogan, J.) (agreeing that "a national solution is the only answer" and suggesting-passage by Congress of an administrative claims procedure similar to the Black Lung legislation"). As recommended by the Ad Hoc Committee, the Judicial Conference of the United States urged Congress to act. See Report of the Proceedings of the Judicial Conference of the United States 33 (Mar. 12, 1991). To this date, no congressional response has emerged.

In the face of legislative inaction, the federal courts--lacking authority to replace state tort systems with a national toxic tort compensation regime--endeavored to work with the procedural tools available to improve management of federal asbestos litigation. Eight federal judges, experienced in the superintendence of asbestos cases, urged the Judicial Panel on Multidistrict Litigation (MDL Panel), to consolidate in a single district all asbestos complaints then pending in federal courts. Accepting the recommendation, the MDL Panel transferred all asbestos cases then filed, but not yet on trial in federal courts to a single district, the United States District Court for the Eastern District of Pennsylvania; pursuant to the transfer order, the collected cases were consolidated for pretrial proceedings before Judge Weiner. See *In re Asbestos Products Liability Litigation (No. VI)*, 771 F. Supp. 415, 422-424 (JPML 1991). [n.1] The order aggregated pending cases only; no authority resides in the MDL Panel to license for consolidated proceedings claims not yet filed.

After the consolidation, attorneys for plaintiffs and defendants formed separate steering committees and began settlement negotiations. Ronald L. Motley and Gene Locks--later appointed, along with Motley's law partner Joseph F. Rice, to represent the plaintiff class in this action--co chaired the Plaintiffs' Steering Committee. Counsel for the Center for Claims Resolution (CCR), the consortium of 20 former asbestos manufacturers now before us as petitioners, participated in the Defendants' Steering Committee. [n.2] Although the MDL order collected, transferred, and consolidated only cases already commenced in federal courts, settlement negotiations included efforts to find a "means of resolving . . . future cases." Record, Doc. 3, p. 2 (Memorandum in Support of Joint Motion for Conditional Class Certification); see also *Georgine* v. *Amchem Products, Inc.*, 157 F. R. D. 246, 266 (ED Pa. 1994) ("primary purpose of the settlement talks in the consolidated MDL litigation was to craft a national settlement that would provide an alternative resolution mechanism for asbestos claims," including claims that might be filed in the future).

In November 1991, the Defendants' Steering Committee made an offer designed to settle all pending and future asbestos cases by providing a fund for distribution by plaintiffs' counsel among asbestos exposed individuals. The Plaintiffs' Steering Committee rejected this offer, and negotiations fell apart. CCR, however, continued to pursue "a workable administrative system for the handling of future claims." *Id.*, at 270.

To that end, CCR counsel approached the lawyers who had headed the Plaintiffs' Steering Committee in the unsuccessful negotiations, and a new round of negotiations began; that round yielded the mass settlement agreement now in controversy. At the time, the former heads of the Plaintiffs' Steering Committee represented thousands of plaintiffs with then pending asbestos related claims--claimants the parties to this suit call "inventory" plaintiffs. CCR indicated in these discussions that it would resist settlement of inventory cases absent "some kind of protection for the future." *Id.*, at 294; see also *id.*, at 295 (CCR communicated to the inventory plaintiffs' attorneys that once the CCR defendants saw a rational way to deal with claims expected to be filed in the future, those defendants would be prepared to address the settlement of pending cases).

Settlement talks thus concentrated on devising an administrative scheme for disposition of asbestos claims not yet in litigation. In these negotiations, counsel for masses of inventory plaintiffs endeavored to represent the interests of the anticipated future claimants, although those lawyers then had no attorney client relationship with such claimants.

Once negotiations seemed likely to produce an agreement purporting to bind potential plaintiffs, CCR agreed to settle, through separate agreements, the claims of plaintiffs who had already filed asbestos related lawsuits. In one such agreement, CCR defendants promised to pay more than $200 million to gain release of the claims of numerous inventory plaintiffs. After settling the inventory claims, CCR, together with the plaintiffs' lawyers CCR had approached, launched this case, exclusively involving persons outside the MDL Panel's province--plaintiffs without already pending lawsuits. [n.3]

The class action thus instituted was not intended to be litigated. Rather, within the space of a single day, January 15, 1993, the settling parties--CCR defendants and the representatives of the plaintiff class described below--presented to the District Court a complaint, an answer, a proposed settlement agreement, and a joint motion for conditional class certification. [n.4]

The complaint identified nine lead plaintiffs, designating them and members of their families as representatives of a class comprising all persons who had not filed an asbestos-related lawsuit against a CCR defendant as of the date the class action commenced, but who (1) had been exposed--occupationally or through the occupational exposure of a spouse or household member--to asbestos or products containing asbestos attributable to a CCR defendant, or (2) whose spouse or family member had been so exposed. [n.5] Untold numbers of individuals may fall within this description. All named plaintiffs alleged that they or a member of their family had been exposed to asbestos containing products of CCR defendants. More than half of the named plaintiffs alleged that they or their family members had already suffered various physical injuries as a result of the exposure. The others alleged that they had not yet manifested any asbestos related condition. The complaint delineated no subclasses; all named plaintiffs were designated as representatives of the class as a whole.

The complaint invoked the District Court's diversity jurisdiction and asserted various state law claims for relief, including (1) negligent failure to warn, (2) strict liability, (3) breach of express and implied warranty, (4) negligent infliction of emotional distress, (5) enhanced risk of disease, (6) medical monitoring, and (7) civil conspiracy. Each plaintiff requested unspecified damages in excess of $100,000. CCR defendants' answer denied the principal allegations of the complaint and asserted 11 affirmative defenses.

A stipulation of settlement accompanied the pleadings;

it proposed to settle, and to preclude nearly all class members from litigating against CCR companies, all claims not filed before January 15, 1993, involving compensation for present and future asbestos related personal injury or death. An exhaustive document exceeding 100 pages, the stipulation presents in detail an administrative mechanism and a schedule of payments to compensate class members who meet defined asbestos exposure and medical requirements. The stipulation describes four categories of compensable disease: mesothelioma; lung cancer; certain "other cancers" (colon-rectal, laryngeal, esophageal, and stomach cancer); and "non-malignant conditions" (asbestosis and bilateral pleural thickening). Persons with "exceptional" medical claims--claims that do not fall within the four described diagnostic categories--may in some instances qualify for compensation, but the settlement caps the number of "exceptional" claims CCR must cover.

For each qualifying disease category, the stipulation specifies the range of damages CCR will pay to qualifying claimants. Payments under the settlement are not adjustable for inflation. Mesothelioma claimants--the most highly compensated category--are scheduled to receive between $20,000 and $200,000. The stipulation provides that CCR is to propose the level of compensation within the prescribed ranges; it also establishes procedures to resolve disputes over medical diagnoses and levels of compensation.

Compensation above the fixed ranges may be obtained for "extraordinary" claims. But the settlement places both numerical caps and dollar limits on such claims. [n.6] The settlement also imposes "case flow maximums," which cap the number of claims payable for each disease in a given year.

Class members are to receive no compensation for certain kinds of claims, even if otherwise applicable state law recognizes such claims. Claims that garner no compensation under the settlement include claims by family members of asbestos exposed individuals for loss of consortium, and claims by so called "exposure only" plaintiffs for increased risk of cancer, fear of future asbestos-related injury, and medical monitoring. "Pleural" claims, which might be asserted by persons with asbestos-related plaques on their lungs but no accompanying physical impairment, are also excluded. Although not entitled to present compensation, exposure only claimants and pleural claimants may qualify for benefits when and if they develop a compensable disease and meet the relevant exposure and medical criteria. Defendants forgo defenses to liability, including statute of limitations pleas.

Class members, in the main, are bound by the settlement in perpetuity, while CCR defendants may choose to withdraw from the settlement after ten years. A small number of class members--only a few per year--may reject the settlement and pursue their claims in court. Those permitted to exercise this option, however, may not assert any punitive damages claim or any claim for increased risk of cancer. Aspects of the administration of the settlement are to be monitored by the AFL-CIO and class counsel. Class counsel are to receive attorneys' fees in an amount to be approved by the District Court.

On January 29, 1993, as requested by the settling parties, the District Court conditionally certified, under Federal Rule of Civil Procedure 23(b)(3), an encompassing opt out class. The certified class included persons occupationally exposed to defendants' asbestos products, and members of their families, who had not filed suit as of January 15. Judge Weiner appointed Locks, Motley, and Rice as class counsel, noting that "[t]he Court may in the future appoint additional counsel if it is deemed necessary and advisable." Record, Doc. 11, p. 3 (Class Certification Order). At no stage of the proceedings, however, were additional counsel in fact appointed. Nor was the class ever divided into subclasses. In a separate order, Judge Weiner assigned to Judge Reed, also of the Eastern District of Pennsylvania, "the task of conducting fairness proceedings and of determining whether the proposed settlement is fair to the class." See 157 F. R. D., at 258. Various class members raised objections to the settlement stipulation, and Judge Weiner granted the objectors full rights to participate in the subsequent proceedings. Ibid. [n.7]

In preliminary rulings, Judge Reed held that the District Court had subject matter jurisdiction, see *Carlough* v. *Amchem Products, Inc.*, 834 F. Supp. 1437,1467-1468 (ED Pa. 1993), and he approved the settling parties' elaborate plan for giving notice to the class, see *Carlough* v. *Amchem Products, Inc.*, 158 F. R. D. 314, 336 (ED Pa. 1993). The court approved notice informed recipients that they could exclude themselves from the class, if they so chose, within a three month opt out period.

Objectors raised numerous challenges to the settlement. They urged that the settlement unfairly disadvantaged those without currently compensable conditions in that it failed to adjust for inflation or to account for changes, over time, in medical understanding. They maintained that compensation levels were intolerably low in comparison to awards available in tort litigation or payments received by the inventory plaintiffs. And they objected to the absence of any compensation for certain claims, for example, medical monitoring, compensable under the tort law of several States. Rejecting these and all other objections, Judge Reed concluded that the settlement terms were fair and had been negotiated without collusion. See 157 F. R. D., at 325, 331-332. He also found that adequate notice had been given to class members, see *id.*, at 332-334, and that final class certification under Rule 23(b)(3) was appropriate, see *id.*, at 315.

As to the specific prerequisites to certification, the District Court observed that the class satisfied Rule 23(a)(1)'s numerosity requirement, [n.8] see *ibid.*, a matter no one debates. The Rule 23(a)(2) and (b)(3) requirements of commonality [n.9] and preponderance [n.10] were also satisfied, the District Court held, in that

"[t]he members of the class have all been exposed to asbestos products supplied by the defendants and all share an interest in receiving prompt and fair compensation for their claims, while minimizing the risks and transaction costs inherent in the asbestos litigation process as it occurs presently in the tort system. Whether the proposed settlement satisfies this interest and is otherwise a fair, reasonable and adequate compromise of the claims of the class is a predominant issue for purposes of Rule 23(b)(3)." *Id.*, at 316.

The District Court held next that the claims of the class representatives were "typical" of the class as a whole, a requirement of Rule 23(a)(3), [n.11] and that, as Rule 23(b)(3) demands, [n.12] the class settlement was "superior" to other methods of adjudication. See *ibid.*

Strenuous objections had been asserted regarding the adequacy of representation, a Rule 23(a)(4) requirement. [n.13] Objectors maintained that class counsel and class representatives had disqualifying conflicts of interests. In particular, objectors urged, claimants whose injuries had become manifest and claimants without manifest injuries should not have common counsel and should not be aggregated in a single class. Furthermore, objectors argued, lawyers representing inventory plaintiffs should not represent the newly formed class.

Satisfied that class counsel had ably negotiated the settlement in the best interests of all concerned, and that the named parties served as adequate representatives, the District Court rejected these objections. See *id.,* at 317-319, 326-332. Subclasses were unnecessary, the District Court held, bearing in mind the added cost and confusion they would entail and the ability of class members to exclude themselves from the class during the three month opt out period. See *id.,* at 318-319. Reasoning that the representative plaintiffs "have a strong interest that recovery for *all* of the medical categories be maximized because they may have claims in *any,* or several categories," the District Court found "no antagonism of interest between class members with various medical conditions, or between persons with and without currently manifest asbestos impairment." *Id.,* at 318. Declaring class certification appropriate and the settlement fair, the District Court preliminarily enjoined all class members from commencing any asbestos related suit against the CCR defendants in any state or federal court. See *Georgine* v. *Amchem Products, Inc.,* 878 F. Supp. 716, 726-727 (ED Pa. 1994).

The objectors appealed. The United States Court of Appeals for the Third Circuit vacated the certification, holding that the requirements of Rule 23 had not been satisfied. See *Georgine* v. *Amchem Products, Inc.,* 83 F. 3d 610 (1996).

The Court of Appeals, in a long, heavily detailed opinion by Judge Becker, first noted several challenges by objectors to justiciability, subject matter jurisdiction, and adequacy of notice. These challenges, the court said, raised "serious concerns." *Id.,* at 623. However, the court observed, "the jurisdictional issues in this case would not exist but for the [class action] certification." *Ibid.* Turning to the class certification issues and finding them dispositive, the Third Circuit declined to decide other questions.

On class action prerequisites, the Court of Appeals referred to an earlier Third Circuit decision, *In re General Motors Corp. Pick-Up Truck Fuel Tank Products Liability Litigation,* 55 F. 3d 768 (CA3), cert. denied, 516 U. S. ___ (1995) (hereinafter *GM Trucks*), which held that although a class action may be certified for settlement purposes only, Rule 23(a)'s requirements must be satisfied as if the case were going to be litigated. 55 F. 3d, at 799-800. The same rule should apply, the Third Circuit said, to class certification under Rule 23(b)(3). See 83 F. 3d, at 625. But cf. *In re Asbestos Litigation,* 90 F. 3d 963, 975-976, and n. 8 (CA5 1996), cert. pending, Nos. 96-1379, 96-1394. While stating that the requirements of Rule 23(a) and (b)(3) must be met "without taking into account the settlement," 83 F. 3d, at 626, the Court of Appeals in fact closely considered the terms of the settlement as it examined aspects of the case under Rule 23 criteria. See *id.,* at 630-634.

The Third Circuit recognized that Rule 23(a)(2)'s "commonality" requirement is subsumed under, or superseded by, the more stringent Rule 23(b)(3) requirement that questions common to the class "predominate over" other questions. The court therefore trained its attention on the "predominance" inquiry. See *id.,* at 627. The harmfulness of asbestos exposure was indeed a prime factor common to the class, the Third Circuit observed. See *id.,* at 626, 630. But uncommon questions abounded.

In contrast to mass torts involving a single accident, class members in this case were exposed to different asbestos containing products, in different ways, over different periods, and for different amounts of time; some suffered no physical injury, others suffered disabling or deadly diseases. See *id.,* at 626, 628. "These factual differences," the Third Circuit explained, "translate[d] into significant legal differences." *Id.,* at 627. State law governed and varied widely on such critical issues as "viability of [exposure only] claims [and] availability of causes of action for medical monitoring, increased risk of cancer, and fear of future injury." *Ibid.* [n.14] "[T]he number of uncommon issues in this humongous class action," the Third Circuit concluded, *ibid.,* barred a determination, under existing tort law, that common questions predominated, see *id.,* at 630.

The Court of Appeals next found that "serious intra class conflicts preclude[d] th[e] class from meeting the adequacy of representation requirement" of Rule 23(a)(4). *Ibid.* Adverting to, but not resolving charges of attorney conflict of interests, the Third Circuit addressed the question whether the named plaintiffs could adequately advance the interests of all class members. The Court of Appeals acknowledged that the District Court was certainly correct to this extent: " `[T]he members of the class are united in seeking the maximum possible recovery for their asbestos related claims.' " *Ibid.* (quoting 157 F. R. D., at 317). "But the settlement does more than simply provide a general recovery fund," the Court of Appeals immediately added; "[r]ather, it makes important judgments on how recovery is to be *allocated* among different kinds of plaintiffs, decisions that necessarily favor some claimants over others." 83 F. 3d, at 630.

In the Third Circuit's view, the "most salient" divergence of interests separated plaintiffs already afflicted with an asbestos related disease from plaintiffs without manifest injury (exposure only plaintiffs). The latter would rationally want protection against inflation for distant recoveries. See *ibid.* They would also seek sturdy back end opt out rights and "causation provisions that can keep pace with changing science and medicine, rather than freezing in place the science of 1993." *Id.,* at 630-631. Already injured parties, in contrast, would care little about such provisions and would rationally trade them for higher current payouts. See *id.,* at 631. These and other adverse interests, the Court of Appeals carefully explained, strongly suggested that an undivided set of representatives could not adequately protect the discrete interests of both currently afflicted and exposure only claimants.

The Third Circuit next rejected the District Court's determination that the named plaintiffs were "typical" of the class, noting that this Rule 23(a)(3) inquiry overlaps the adequacy of representation question: "both look to the potential for conflicts in the class." *Id.*, at 632. Evident conflict problems, the court said, led it to hold that "no set of representatives can be `typical' of this class." *Ibid.*

The Court of Appeals similarly rejected the District Court's assessment of the superiority of the class action. The Third Circuit initially noted that a class action so large and complex "could not be tried." *Ibid.* The court elaborated most particularly, however, on the unfairness of binding exposure only plaintiffs who might be unaware of the class action or lack sufficient information about their exposure to make a reasoned decision whether to stay in or opt out. See *id.*, at 633. "A series of statewide or more narrowly defined adjudications, either through consolidation under Rule 42(a) or as class actions under Rule 23, would seem preferable," the Court of Appeals said. *Id.*, at 634.

The Third Circuit, after intensive review, ultimately ordered decertification of the class and vacation of the District Court's anti suit injunction. *Id.*, at 635. Judge Wellford concurred, "fully subscrib[ing] to the decision of Judge Becker that the plaintiffs in this case ha[d] not met the requirements of Rule 23." *Ibid.* He added that in his view, named exposure only plaintiffs had no standing to pursue the suit in federal court, for their depositions showed that "[t]hey claimed no damages and no present injury." *Id.*, at 638.

We granted certiorari, 519 U. S. ___ (1996), and now affirm.

Objectors assert in this Court, as they did in the District Court and Court of Appeals, an array of jurisdictional barriers. Most fundamentally, they maintain that the settlement proceeding instituted by class counsel and CCR is not a justiciable case or controversy within the confines of Article III of the Federal Constitution. In the main, they say, the proceeding is a nonadversarial endeavor to impose on countless individuals without currently ripe claims an administrative compensation regime binding on those individuals if and when they manifest injuries.

Furthermore, objectors urge that exposure only claimants lack standing to sue: Either they have not yet sustained any cognizable injury or, to the extent the complaint states claims and demands relief for emotional distress, enhanced risk of disease, and medical monitoring, the settlement provides no redress. Objectors also argue that exposure only claimants did not meet the then current amount in controversy requirement (in excess of $50,000) specified for federal court jurisdiction based upon diversity of citizenship. See 28 U.S.C. § 1332(a).

As earlier recounted, see *supra*, at 13, the Third Circuit declined to reach these issues because they would not exist but for the [class action] certification." 83 F. 3d, at 623. We agree that "[t]he class certification issues are dispositive," *ibid.*; because their resolution here is logically antecedent to the existence of any Article III issues, it is appropriate to reach them first, cf. *Arizonans for Official English* v. *Arizona*, 520 U. S. ___, ___ (1997) (slip op., at 21) (declining to resolve definitively question whether petitioners had standing because mootness issue was dispositive of the case). We therefore follow the path taken by the Court of Appeals, mindful that Rule 23's requirements must be interpreted in keeping with Article III constraints, and with the Rules Enabling Act, which instructs that rules of procedure "shall not abridge, enlarge or modify any substantive right," 28 U.S.C. § 2072(b). See also Fed. Rule Civ. Proc. 82 ("rules shall not be construed to extend . . . the [subject matter] jurisdiction of the United States district courts"). [n.15]

To place this controversy in context, we briefly describe the characteristics of class actions for which the Federal Rules provide. Rule 23, governing federal court class actions, stems from equity practice and gained its current shape in an innovative 1966 revision. See generally Kaplan, Continuing Work of the Civil Committee: 1966 Amendments of the Federal Rules of Civil Procedure (I), 81 Harv. L. Rev. 356, 375-400 (1967) (hereinafter Kaplan, Continuing Work). Rule 23(a) states four threshold requirements applicable to all class actions: (1) numerosity (a "class [so large] that joinder of all members is impracticable"); (2) commonality ("questions of law or fact common to the class"); (3) typicality (named parties' claims or defenses "are typical . . . of the class"); and (4) adequacy of representation (representatives "will fairly and adequately protect the interests of the class").

In addition to satisfying Rule 23(a)'s prerequisites, parties seeking class certification must show that the action is maintainable under Rule 23(b)(1), (2), or (3). Rule 23(b)(1) covers cases in which separate actions by or against individual class members would risk establishing "incompatible standards of conduct for the party opposing the class," Fed. Rule Civ. Proc. 23(b)(1)(A), or would "as a practical matter be dispositive of the interests" of nonparty class members "or substantially impair or impede their ability to protect their interests," Fed. Rule Civ. Proc. 23(b)(1)(B). Rule 23(b)(1)(A) "takes in cases where the party is obliged by law to treat the members of the class alike (a utility acting toward customers; a government imposing a tax), or where the party must treat all alike as a matter of practical necessity (a riparian owner using water as against down river owners)." Kaplan, Continuing Work 388 (footnotes omitted). Rule 23(b)(1)(B) includes, for example, "limited fund" cases, instances in which numerous persons make claims against a fund insufficient to satisfy all claims. See Advisory Committee's Notes on Fed. Rule Civ. Proc. 23, 28 U. S. C. App., pp. 696-697 (hereinafter Adv. Comm. Notes).

Rule 23(b)(2) permits class actions for declaratory or injunctive relief where "the party opposing the class has acted or refused to act on grounds generally applicable to the class." Civil rights cases against parties charged with unlawful, class based discrimination are prime examples. Adv. Comm. Notes, 28 U. S. C. App., p. 697; see Kaplan, Continuing Work 389 (subdivision (b)(2) "build[s] on experience mainly, but not exclusively, in the civil rights field").

In the 1966 class action amendments, Rule 23(b)(3), the category at issue here, was "the most adventuresome" innovation. See Kaplan, A Prefatory Note, 10 B. C. Ind. & Com. L. Rev. 497, 497 (1969) (hereinafter Kaplan, Prefatory Note). Rule 23(b)(3) added to the complex litigation arsenal class actions for damages designed to secure judgments binding all class members save those who affirmatively elected to be excluded. See 7A C. Wright, A. Miller, & M. Kane, Federal Practice and Procedure §1777, p. 517 (2d ed. 1986) (hereinafter Wright, Miller, & Kane); see generally Kaplan,

Continuing Work 379-400. Rule 23(b)(3) "opt out" class actions superseded the former "spurious" class action, so characterized because it generally functioned as a permissive joinder ("opt in") device. See 7A Wright, Miller, & Kane §1753, at 28-31, 42-44; see also Adv. Comm. Notes, 28 U. S. C. App., p. 695.

Framed for situations in which "class-action treatment is not as clearly called for" as it is in Rule 23(b)(1) and (b)(2) situations, Rule 23(b)(3) permits certification where class suit "may nevertheless be convenient and desirable." Adv. Comm. Notes, 28 U. S. C. App., p. 697. To qualify for certification under Rule 23(b)(3), a class must meet two requirements beyond the Rule 23(a) prerequisites: Common questions must "predominate over any questions affecting only individual members"; and class resolution must be "superior to other available methods for the fair and efficient adjudication of the controversy." In adding "predominance" and "superiority" to the qualification for certification list, the Advisory Committee sought to cover cases "in which a class action would achieve economies of time, effort, and expense, and promote . . . uniformity of decision as to persons similarly situated, without sacrificing procedural fairness or bringing about other undesirable results." *Ibid.* Sensitive to the competing tugs of individual autonomy for those who might prefer to go it alone or in a smaller unit, on the one hand, and systemic efficiency on the other, the Reporter for the 1966 amendments cautioned: "The new provision invites a close look at the case before it is accepted as a class action . . . ." Kaplan, Continuing Work 390.

Rule 23(b)(3) includes a nonexhaustive list of factors pertinent to a court's "close look" at the predominance and superiority criteria:

> "(A) the interest of members of the class in individually controlling the prosecution or defense of separate actions; (B) the extent and nature of any litigation concerning the controversy already commenced by or against members of the class; (C) the desirability or undesirability of concentrating the litigation of the claims in the particular forum; (D) the difficulties likely to be encountered in the management of a class action."

In setting out these factors, the Advisory Committee for the 1966 reform anticipated that in each case, courts would "consider the interests of individual members of the class in controlling their own litigations and carrying them on as they see fit." Adv. Comm. Notes, 28 U. S. C. App., p. 698. They elaborated:

> "The interests of individuals in conducting separate lawsuits may be so strong as to call for denial of a class action. On the other hand, these interests may be theoretic rather than practical; the class may have a high degree of cohesion and prosecution of the action through representatives would be quite unobjectionable, or the amounts at stake for individuals may be so small that separate suits would be impracticable." *Ibid.*

See also Kaplan, Continuing Work 391 ("Th[e] interest [in individual control] can be high where the stake of each member bulks large and his will and ability to take care of himself are strong; the interest may be no more than theoretic where the individual stake is so small as to make a separate action impracticable.") (footnote omitted). As the Third Circuit observed in the instant case: "Each plaintiff [in an action involving claims for personal injury and death] has a significant interest in individually controlling the prosecution of [his case]"; each "ha[s] a substantial stake in making individual decisions on whether and when to settle." 83 F. 3d, at 633.

While the text of Rule 23(b)(3) does not exclude from certification cases in which individual damages run high, the Advisory Committee had dominantly in mind vindication of "the rights of groups of people who individually would be without effective strength to bring their opponents into court at all." Kaplan, Prefatory Note 497. As concisely recalled in a recent Seventh Circuit opinion:

> "The policy at the very core of the class action mechanism is to overcome the problem that small recoveries do not provide the incentive for any individual to bring a solo action prosecuting his or her rights. A class action solves this problem by aggregating the relatively paltry

potential recoveries into something worth
someone's (usually an attorney's) labor." *Mace*
v. *Van Ru Credit Corp.*, 109 F. 3d 338, 344
(1997).

To alert class members to their right to "opt out" of a(b)(3) class, Rule 23 instructs the court to "direct to the members of the class the best notice practicable under the circumstances, including individual notice to all members who can be identified through reasonable effort." Fed. Rule Civ. Proc. 23(c)(2); see *Eisen* v. *Carlisle & Jacquelin*, 417 U.S. 156, 173-177 (1974) (individual notice to class members identifiable through reasonable effort is mandatory in (b)(3) actions; requirement may not be relaxed based on high cost).

No class action may be "dismissed or compromised without [court] approval," preceded by notice to class members. Fed. Rule Civ. Proc. 23(e). The Advisory Committee's sole comment on this terse final provision of Rule 23 restates the rule's instruction without elaboration: "Subdivision (e) requires approval of the court, after notice, for the dismissal or compromise of any class action." Adv. Comm. Notes, 28 U. S. C. App., p. 699.

In the decades since the 1966 revision of Rule 23, class action practice has become ever more "adventuresome" as a means of coping with claims too numerous to secure their "just, speedy, and inexpensive determination" one by one. See Fed. Rule Civ. Proc. 1. The development reflects concerns about the efficient use of court resources and the conservation of funds to compensate claimants who do not line up early in a litigation queue. See generally J. Weinstein, Individual Justice in Mass Tort Litigation: The Effect of Class Actions, Consolidations, and Other Multiparty Devices (1995); Schwarzer, Settlement of Mass Tort Class Actions: Order out of Chaos, 80 Cornell L. Rev. 837 (1995).

Among current applications of Rule 23(b)(3), the "settlement only" class has become a stock device. See, *e.g.*, T. Willging, L. Hooper, & R. Niemic, Empirical Study of Class Actions in Four Federal District Courts: Final Report to the Advisory Committee on Civil Rules 61-62 (1996) (noting large number of such cases in districts studied). Although all Federal Circuits recognize the utility of Rule 23(b)(3) settlement classes, courts have divided on the extent to which a proffered settlement affects court surveillance under Rule 23's certification criteria.

In *GM Trucks*, 55 F. 3d, at 799-800, and in the instant case, 83 F. 3d, at 624-626, the Third Circuit held that a class cannot be certified for settlement when certification for trial would be unwarranted. Other courts have held that settlement obviates or reduces the need to measure a proposed class against the enumerated Rule 23 requirements. See, *e.g.*, *In re Asbestos Litigation*, 90 F. 3d, at 975 (CA5) ("in settlement class context, common issues arise from the settlement itself ") (citing H. Newberg & A. Conte, 2 Newberg on Class Actions §11.28, at 11-58 (3d ed. 1992)); *White* v. *National Football League*, 41 F. 3d 402, 408 (CA8 1994) ("adequacy of class representation . . . is ultimately determined by the settlement itself"), cert. denied, 515 U.S. 1137 (1995); *In re A. H. Robins Co.*, 880 F. 2d 709, 740 (CA4) ("[i]f not a ground for certification *per se*, certainly settlement should be a factor, and an important factor, to be considered when determining certification"), cert. denied *sub nom. Anderson* v. *Aetna Casualty & Surety Co.*, 493 U.S. 959 (1989); *Malchman* v. *Davis*, 761 F. 2d 893, 900 (CA2 1985) (certification appropriate, in part, because "the interests of the members of the broadened class in the settlement agreement were commonly held"), cert. denied, 475 U.S. 1143 (1986).

A proposed amendment to Rule 23 would expressly authorize settlement class certification, in conjunction with a motion by the settling parties for Rule 23(b)(3) certification, "even though the requirements of subdivision (b)(3) might not be met for purposes of trial." Proposed Amendment to Fed. Rule Civ. Proc. 23(b), 117 S. Ct. No. 1 CXIX, CLIV to CLV (Aug. 1996) (Request for Comment). In response to the publication of this proposal, voluminous public comments--many of them opposed to, or skeptical of, the amendment--were received by the Judicial Conference Standing Committee on Rules of Practice and Procedure. See, *e.g.*, Letter from Steering Committee to Oppose Proposed Rule 23, signed by 129 law professors (May 28, 1996); Letter from Paul D. Carrington (May 21, 1996). The Committee has not yet acted on the matter. We consider the certification at issue under the rule as it is currently framed.

We granted review to decide the role settlement may play, under existing Rule 23, in determining the propriety of class certification. The Third Circuit's opinion stated that each of the requirements of Rule 23(a) and (b)(3) "must be satisfied without taking into account the settlement." 83 F. 3d, at 626 (quoting *GM Trucks*, 55 F. 3d, at 799). That statement, petitioners urge, is incorrect.

We agree with petitioners to this limited extent: settlement is relevant to a class certification. The Third Circuit's opinion bears modification in that respect. But, as we earlier observed, see *supra*, at 14, the Court of Appeals in fact did not ignore the settlement; instead, that court homed in on settlement terms in explaining why it found the absentees' interests inadequately represented. See 83 F. 3d, at 630-631. The Third Circuit's close inspection of the settlement in that regard was altogether proper.

Confronted with a request for settlement only class certification, a district court need not inquire whether the case, if tried, would present intractable management problems, see Fed. Rule Civ. Proc. 23(b)(3)(D), for the proposal is that there be no trial. But other specifications of the rule--those designed to protect absentees by blocking unwarranted or overbroad class definitions-- demand undiluted, even heightened, attention in the settlement context. Such attention is of vital importance, for a court asked to certify a settlement class will lack the opportunity, present when a case is litigated, to adjust the class, informed by the proceedings as they unfold. See Fed. Rule Civ. Proc. 23(c), (d). [n.16]

And, of overriding importance, courts must be mindful that the rule as now composed sets the requirements they are bound to enforce. Federal Rules take effect after an extensive deliberative process involving many reviewers: a Rules Advisory Committee, public commenters, the Judicial Conference, this Court, the Congress. See 28 U.S.C. §§ 2073 2074. The text of a rule thus proposed and reviewed limits judicial inventiveness. Courts are not free to amend a rule outside the process Congress ordered, a process properly tuned to the instruction that rules of procedure "shall not abridge . . . any substantive right." §2072(b).

Rule 23(e), on settlement of class actions, reads in its entirety: "A class action shall not be dismissed or compromised without the approval of the court, and notice of the proposed dismissal or compromise shall be given to all members of the class in such manner as the court directs." This prescription was designed to function as an additional requirement, not a superseding direction, for the "class action" to which Rule 23(e) refers is one qualified for certification under Rule 23(a) and (b). Cf. *Eisen*, 417 U. S., at 176-177 (adequate representation does not eliminate additional requirement to provide notice). Subdivisions (a) and (b) focus court attention on whether a proposed class has sufficient unity so that absent members can fairly be bound by decisions of class representatives. That dominant concern persists when settlement, rather than trial, is proposed.

The safeguards provided by the Rule 23(a) and (b) class qualifying criteria, we emphasize, are not impractical impediments--checks shorn of utility--in the settlement class context. First, the standards set for the protection of absent class members serve to inhibit appraisals of the chancellor's foot kind--class certifications dependent upon the court's gestalt judgment or overarching impression of the settlement's fairness.

Second, if a fairness inquiry under Rule 23(e) controlled certification, eclipsing Rule 23(a) and (b), and permitting class designation despite the impossibility of litigation, both class counsel and court would be disarmed. Class counsel confined to settlement negotiations could not use the threat of litigation to press for a better offer, see Coffee, Class Wars: The Dilemma of the Mass Tort Class Action, 95 Colum. L. Rev. 1343, 1379-1380 (1995), and the court would face a bargain proffered for its approval without benefit of adversarial investigation, see, e.g., *Kamilewicz v. Bank of Boston Corp.*, 100 F. 3d 1348, 1352 (CA7 1996) (Easterbrook, J., dissenting from denial of rehearing en banc) (parties "may even put one over on the court, in a staged performance"), cert. denied, 520 U. S. ___ (1997).

Federal courts, in any case, lack authority to substitute for Rule 23's certification criteria a standard never adopted--that if a settlement is "fair," then certification is proper. Applying to this case criteria the rulemakers set, we conclude that the Third Circuit's appraisal is essentially correct. Although that court should have acknowledged that settlement is a factor in the calculus, a remand is not warranted on that account. The Court of Appeals' opinion amply demonstrates why--with or without a settlement on the table--the sprawling class the District Court certified does not satisfy Rule 23's requirements. [n.17]

We address first the requirement of Rule 23(b)(3) that "[common] questions of law or fact . . . predominate over any questions affecting only individual members." The District Court concluded that predominance was satisfied based on two factors: class members' shared experience of asbestos exposure and their common "interest in receiving prompt and fair compensation for their claims, while minimizing the risks and transaction costs inherent in the asbestos litigation process as it occurs presently in the tort system." 157 F. R. D., at 316. The settling parties also contend that the settlement's fairness is a common question, predominating over disparate legal issues that might be pivotal in litigation but become irrelevant under the settlement.

The predominance requirement stated in Rule 23(b)(3), we hold, is not met by the factors on which the District Court relied. The benefits asbestos exposed persons might gain from the establishment of a grand scale compensation scheme is a matter fit for legislative consideration, see *supra*, at 2-3, but it is not pertinent to the predominance inquiry. That inquiry trains on the legal or factual questions that qualify each class member's case as a genuine controversy, questions that preexist any settlement. [n.18]

The Rule 23(b)(3) predominance inquiry tests whether proposed classes are sufficiently cohesive to warrant adjudication by representation. See 7A Wright, Miller, & Kane 518-519. [n.19] The inquiry appropriate under Rule 23(e), on the other hand, protects unnamed class members "from unjust or unfair settlements affecting their rights when the representatives become fainthearted before the action is adjudicated or are able to secure satisfaction of their individual claims by a compromise." See 7B Wright, Miller, & Kane §1797, at 340-341. But it is not the mission of Rule 23(e) to assure the class cohesion that legitimizes representative action in the first place. If a common interest in a fair compromise could satisfy the predominance requirement of Rule 23(b)(3), that vital prescription would be stripped of any meaning in the settlement context.

The District Court also relied upon this commonality: "The members of the class have all been exposed to asbestos products supplied by the defendants . . . ." 157 F. R. D., at 316. Even if Rule 23(a)'s commonality requirement may be satisfied by that shared experience, the predominance criterion is far more demanding. See 83 F. 3d, at 626-627. Given the greater number of questions peculiar to the several categories of class members, and to individuals within each category, and the significance of those uncommon questions, any overarching dispute about the health consequences of asbestos exposure cannot satisfy the Rule 23(b)(3) predominance standard.

The Third Circuit highlighted the disparate questions undermining class cohesion in this case:

> "Class members were exposed to different asbestos- containing products, for different amounts of time, in different ways, and over different periods. Some class members suffer no physical injury or have only asymptomatic pleural changes, while others suffer from lung cancer, disabling asbestosis, or from

> mesothelioma . . . . Each has a different
> history of cigarette smoking, a factor that
> complicates the causation inquiry.

"The [exposure only] plaintiffs especially share little in common, either with each other or with the presently injured class members. It is unclear whether they will contract asbestos-related disease and, if so, what disease each will suffer. They will also incur different medical expenses because their monitoring and treatment will depend on singular circumstances and individual medical histories." *Id.*, at 626.

Differences in state law, the Court of Appeals observed, compound these disparities. See *id.*, at 627 (citing *Phillips Petroleum Co.* v. *Shutts*, 472 U.S. 797, 823 (1985)).

No settlement class called to our attention is as sprawling as this one. Cf. *In re Asbestos Litigation*, 90 F. 3d, at 976, n. 8 ("We would likely agree with the Third Circuit that a class action requesting individual damages for members of a global class of asbestos claimants would not satisfy [Rule 23] requirements due to the huge number of individuals and their varying medical expenses, smoking histories, and family situations."). Predominance is a test readily met in certain cases alleging consumer or securities fraud or violations of the antitrust laws. See Adv. Comm. Notes, 28 U. S. C. App., p. 697; see also *supra*, at 21-22. Even mass tort cases arising from a common cause or disaster may, depending upon the circumstances, satisfy the predominance requirement. The Advisory Committee for the 1966 revision of Rule 23, it is true, noted that "mass accident" cases are likely to present "significant questions, not only of damages but of liability and defenses of liability, . . . affecting the individuals in different ways." *Ibid.* And the Committee advised that such cases are "ordinarily not appropriate" for class treatment. *Ibid.* But the text of the rule does not categorically exclude mass tort cases from class certification, and district courts, since the late 1970s, have been certifying such cases in increasing number. See Resnik, From "Cases" to "Litigation," 54 Law & Contemp. Prob. 5, 17-19 (Summer 1991) (describing trend). The Committee's warning, however, continues to call for caution when individual stakes are high and disparities among class members great. As the Third Circuit's opinion makes plain, the certification in this case does not follow the counsel of caution. That certification cannot be upheld, for it rests on a conception of Rule 23(b)(3)'s predominance requirement irreconcilable with the rule's design.

Nor can the class approved by the District Court satisfy Rule 23(a)(4)'s requirement that the named parties "will fairly and adequately protect the interests of the class." The adequacy inquiry under Rule 23(a)(4) serves to uncover conflicts of interest between named parties and the class they seek to represent. See General *Telephone Co. of Southwest* v. *Falcon*, 457 U.S. 147, 157-158, n. 13 (1982). "[A] class representative must be part of the class and `possess the same interest and suffer the same injury' as the class members." *East Tex. Motor Freight System, Inc.* v. *Rodriguez*, 431 U.S. 395, 403 (1977) (quoting *Schlesinger* v. *Reservists Comm. to Stop the War*, 418 U.S. 208, 216 (1974)). [n.20]

As the Third Circuit pointed out, named parties with diverse medical conditions sought to act on behalf of a single giant class rather than on behalf of discrete subclasses. In significant respects, the interests of those within the single class are not aligned. Most saliently, for the currently injured, the critical goal is generous immediate payments. That goal tugs against the interest of exposure only plaintiffs in ensuring an ample, inflation protected fund for the future. Cf. *General Telephone Co. of Northwest* v. *EEOC*, 446 U.S. 318, 331 (1980) ("In employment discrimination litigation, conflicts might arise, for example, between employees and applicants who were denied employment and who will, if granted relief, compete with employees for fringe benefits or seniority. Under Rule 23, the same plaintiff could not represent these classes.").

The disparity between the currently injured and exposure only categories of plaintiffs, and the diversity within each category are not made insignificant by the District Court's finding that petitioners' assets suffice to pay claims under the settlement. See 157 F. R. D., at 291. Although this is not a "limited fund" case certified under Rule 23(b)(1)(B), the terms of the settlement reflect essential allocation decisions designed to confine compensation and to limit defendants' liability. For example, as earlier described, see *supra*, at 8-9, the settlement includes no adjustment for inflation; only a few claimants per year can opt out at the back end; and loss of consortium claims are extinguished with no compensation.

The settling parties, in sum, achieved a global compromise with no structural assurance of fair and adequate representation for the diverse groups and individuals affected. Although the named parties alleged a range of complaints, each served generally as representative for the whole, not for a separate constituency. In another asbestos class action, the Second Circuit spoke precisely to this point:

> "[W]here differences among members of a class
> are such that subclasses must be established, we
> know of no authority that permits a court to
> approve a settlement without creating subclasses
> on the basis of consents by members of a unitary
> class, some of whom happen to be members of the
> distinct subgroups. The class representatives
> may well have thought that the settlement serves
> the aggregate interests of the entire class. But
> the adversity among subgroups requires that the
> members of each subgroup cannot be bound to a

settlement except by consents given by those who
understand that their role is to represent
solely the members of their respective
subgroups." *In re Joint Eastern and Southern
Dist. Asbestos Litigation*, 982 F. 2d 721, 742-
743 (CA2 1992), modified on reh'g *sub nom. Inre
Findley*, 993 F. 2d 7 (CA2 1993).

The Third Circuit found no assurance here--either in the terms of the settlement or in the structure of the negotiations--that the named plaintiffs operated under a proper understanding of their representational responsibilities. See 83 F. 3d, at 630-631. That assessment, we conclude, is on the mark.

Impediments to the provision of adequate notice, the Third Circuit emphasized, rendered highly problematic any endeavor to tie to a settlement class persons with no perceptible asbestos related disease at the time of the settlement. *Id.*, at 633; cf. *In re Asbestos Litigation*, 90 F. 3d, at 999-1000 (Smith, J., dissenting). Many persons in the exposure only category, the Court of Appeals stressed, may not even know of their exposure, or realize the extent of the harm they may incur. Even if they fully appreciate the significance of class notice, those without current afflictions may not have the information or foresight needed to decide, intelligently, whether to stay in or opt out.

Family members of asbestos exposed individuals may themselves fall prey to disease or may ultimately have ripe claims for loss of consortium. Yet large numbers of people in this category--future spouses and children of asbestos victims--could not be alerted to their class membership. And current spouses and children of the occupationally exposed may know nothing of that exposure.

Because we have concluded that the class in this case cannot satisfy the requirements of common issue predominance and adequacy of representation, we need not rule, definitively, on the notice given here. In accord with the Third Circuit, however, see 83 F. 3d, at 633-634, we recognize the gravity of the question whether class action notice sufficient under the Constitution and Rule 23 could ever be given to legions so unselfconscious and amorphous.

The argument is sensibly made that a nationwide administrative claims processing regime would provide the most secure, fair, and efficient means of compensating victims of asbestos exposure. [n.21] Congress, however, has not adopted such a solution. And Rule 23, which must be interpreted with fidelity to the Rules Enabling Act and applied with the interests of absent class members in close view, cannot carry the large load CCR, class counsel, and the District Court heaped upon it. As this case exemplifies, the rulemakers' prescriptions for class actions may be endangered by "those who embrace [Rule 23] too enthusiastically just as [they are by] those who approach [the rule] with distaste." C. Wright, Law of Federal Courts 508 (5th ed. 1994); cf. 83 F. 3d, at 634 (suggesting resort to less bold aggregation techniques, including more narrowly defined class certifications).

* * *

For the reasons stated, the judgment of the Court of Appeals for the Third Circuit is Affirmed.

Justice O'Connor took no part in the consideration or decision of this case.

NOTES

[1] In a series of orders, the MDL Panel had previously denied other asbestos case transfer requests. See *In re Asbestos and Asbestos Insulation Material Products Liability Litigation*, 431 F. Supp. 906, 910 (JPML 1977); *In re Asbestos Products Liability Litigation (No. II)*, MDL-416 (JPML Mar. 13, 1980) (unpublished order); *In re Asbestos School Products Liability Litigation*, 606 F. Supp. 713, 714 (JPML 1985); *In re Ship Asbestos Products Liability Litigation*, MDL-676 (JPML Feb. 4, 1986) (unpublished order); *In re Leon Blair Asbestos Products Liability Litigation*, MDL-702 (JPML Feb. 6, 1987) (unpublished order).

[2] The CCR Companies are Amchem Products, Inc.; A. P. Green Industries, Inc.; Armstrong World Industries, Inc.; Asbestos Claims Management Corp.; Certainteed Corp.; C. E. Thurston & Sons, Inc.; Dana Corp.; Ferodo America, Inc.; Flexitallic, Inc.; GAF Building Materials, Inc.; I. U. North America, Inc.; Maremont Corp.; National Services Industries, Inc.; Nosroc Corp.; Pfizer Inc.; Quigley Co.; Shook & Fletcher Insulation Co.; T & N, PLC; Union Carbide Corp.; and United States Gypsum Co. All of the CCR petitioners stopped manufacturing asbestos products around 1975.

[3] It is basic to comprehension of this proceeding to notice that no transferred case is included in the settlement at issue, and no case covered by the settlement existed as a civil action at the time of the MDL Panel transfer.

4 Also on the same day, the CCR defendants filed a third party action against their insurers, seeking a declaratory judgment holding the insurers liable for the costs of the settlement. The insurance litigation, upon which implementation of the settlement is conditioned, is still pending in the District Court. See, *e.g., Georgine* v. *Amchem Prods., Inc.*, No. 93-0215, 1994 WL 502475 (ED Pa., Sept. 2, 1994) (denying motion of insurers to compel discovery).

5 The complaint defines the class as follows:

```
"(a) All persons (or their legal
representatives) who have been exposed in the
United States or its territories (or while
working aboard U. S. military, merchant, or
passenger ships), either occupationally or
through the occupational exposure of a spouse or
household member, to asbestos or to asbestos-
containing products for which one or more of the
Defendants may bear legal liability and who, as
of January 15, 1993, reside in the United States
or its territories, and who have not, as of
January 15, 1993, filed a lawsuit for asbestos-
related personal injury, or damage, or death in
any state or federal court against the
Defendant(s) (or against entities for whose
actions or omissions the Defendant(s) bear legal
liability). (b) All spouses, parents, children,
and other relatives (or their legal
representatives) of the class members described
in paragraph (a) above who have not, as of
January 15, 1993, filed a lawsuit for the
asbestos-related personal injury, or damage, or
death of a class member described in paragraph
(a) above in any state or federal court against
the Defendant(s) (or against entities for whose
actions or omissions the Defendant(s) bear legal
liability)." 1 App. 13-14.
```

6 Only three percent of the qualified mesothelioma, lung cancer, and "other cancer" claims, and only one percent of the total number of qualified "non-malignant condition" claims can be designated "extraordinary." Average expenditures are specified for claims found "extraordinary"; mesothelioma victims with compensable extraordinary claims, for example, receive, on average, $300,000.

7 These objectors, now respondents before this Court, include three groups of individuals with overlapping interests, designated as the "Windsor Group," the New Jersey "White Lung Group," and the "Cargile Group." Margaret Balonis, an individual objector, is also a respondent before this Court. Balonis states that her husband, Casimir, was exposed to asbestos in the late 1940s and was diagnosed with mesothelioma in May 1994, after expiration of the opt out period, see *infra*, at 11, 13. The Balonises sued CCR members in Maryland state court, but were charged with civil contempt for violating the federal District Court's anti suit injunction. Casimir Balonis died in October 1996. See Brief for Balonis Respondents 9-11.

8 Rule 23(a)(1) requires that the class be "so numerous that joinder of all members is impracticable."

9 Rule 23(a)(2) requires that there be "questions of law or fact common to the class."

10 Rule 23(b)(3) requires that "the [common] questions of law or fact . . . predominate over any questions affecting only individual members."

11 Rule 23(a)(3) states that "the claims . . . of the representative parties [must be] typical of the claims . . . of the class."

12

Rule 23(b)(3) requires that "a class action [be] superior to other available methods for the fair and efficient adjudication of the controversy."

[13] Rule 23(a)(4) requires that "the representative parties will fairly and adequately protect the interests of the class."

[14] Recoveries under the laws of different States spanned a wide range. Objectors assert, for example, that 15% of current mesothelioma claims arise in California, where the statewide average recovery is $419,674--or more than 209% above the $200,000 maximum specified in the settlement for mesothelioma claims not typed "extraordinary." See Brief for Respondents George Windsor et al. 5-6, n. 5 (citing 2 App. 461).

[15] The opinion dissenting in part does not find the class certification issues dispositive--at least not yet, and would return the case to the Third Circuit for a second look. See *post*, at 2, 13. If certification issues were genuinely in doubt, however, the jurisdictional issues would loom larger. Concerning objectors' assertions that exposure only claimants do not satisfy the $50,000 amount-in-controversy and may have no currently ripe claim, see *Metro-North Commuter R. Co.* v. *Buckley, ante*, p. __ (Federal Employers' Liability Act, 35 Stat. 65, as amended, 45 U.S.C. § 51 *et seq.*, interpreted in light of common law principles, does not permit "exposure only" railworker to recover for negligent infliction of emotional distress or lump sum damages for costs of medical monitoring).

[16] Portions of the opinion dissenting in part appear to assume that settlement counts only one way--in favor of certification. See *post*, at 1-2, 13. But see *post*, at 7. To the extent that is the dissent's meaning, we disagree. Settlement, though a relevant factor, does not inevitably signal that class action certification should be granted more readily than it would be were the case to be litigated. For reasons the Third Circuit aired, see 83 F. 3d 610, 626-635 (1996), proposed settlement classes sometimes warrant more, not less caution on the question of certification.

[17] We do not inspect and set aside for insufficient evidence district court findings of fact. Cf. *post*, at 5, 9-10. Rather, we focus on the requirements of Rule 23, and endeavor to explain why those requirements cannot be met for a class so enormously diverse and problematic as the one the District Court certified.

[18] In this respect, the predominance requirement of Rule 23(b)(3) is similar to the requirement of Rule 23(a)(3) that "claims or defenses" of the named representatives must be "typical of the claims or defenses of the class." The words "claims or defenses" in this context--just as in the context of Rule 24(b)(2) governing permissive intervention--"manifestly refer to the kinds of claims or defenses that can be raised in courts of law as part of an actual or impending law suit." *Diamond* v. *Charles*, 476 U.S. 54, 76-77 (1986) (O'Connor, J., concurring in part and concurring in judgment).

[19] This case, we note, involves no "limited fund" capable of supporting class treatment under Rule 23(b)(1)(B), which does not have a predominance requirement. See *Georgine* v. *Amchem Products, Inc.*, 157 F. R. D. 246, 318 (ED Pa. 1994); see also *id.*, at 291, and n. 40. The settling parties sought to proceed exclusively under Rule 23(b)(3).

[20] The adequacy of representation requirement "tend[s] to merge" with the commonality and typicality criteria of Rule 23(a), which "serve as guideposts for determining whether . . . maintenance of a class action is economical and whether the named plaintiff's claim and the class claims are so interrelated that the interests of the class members will be fairly and adequately protected in their absence." *General Telephone Co. of Southwest* v. *Falcon*, 457 U.S. 147, 157, n. 13 (1982). The adequacy heading also factors in competency and conflicts of class counsel. See *id.*, at 157-158, n. 13. Like the Third Circuit, we decline to address adequacy of counsel issues discretely in light of our conclusions that common questions of law or fact do not predominate and that the named plaintiffs cannot adequately represent the interests of this enormous class.

[21] The opinion dissenting in part is a forceful statement of that argument.

UNITED STATES v. JAMES HERMAN O'HAGAN

No. 96-842, June 25, 1997

ON WRIT OF CERTIORARI TO THE UNITED STATES COURT OF APPEALS FOR THE EIGHTH CIRCUIT

Justice Ginsburg delivered the opinion of the Court.

This case concerns the interpretation and enforcement of §10(b) and §14(e) of the Securities Exchange Act of 1934, and rules made by the Securities and Exchange Commission pursuant to these provisions, Rule 10b-5 and Rule 14e-3(a). Two prime questions are presented. The first relates to the misappropriation of material, nonpublic information for securities trading; the second concerns fraudulent practices in the tender offer setting. In particular, we address and resolve these issues: (1) Is a person who trades in securities for personal profit, using confidential information misappropriated in breach of a fiduciary duty to the source of the information, guilty of violating §10(b) and Rule 10b-5? (2) Did the Commission exceed its rulemaking authority by adopting Rule 14e-3(a), which proscribes trading on undisclosed information in the tender offer setting, even in the absence of a duty to disclose? Our answer to the first question is yes, and to the second question, viewed in the context of this case, no.

Respondent James Herman O'Hagan was a partner in the law firm of Dorsey & Whitney in Minneapolis, Minnesota. In July 1988, Grand Metropolitan PLC (Grand Met), a company based in London, England, retained Dorsey & Whitney as local counsel to represent Grand Met regarding a potential tender offer for the common stock of the Pillsbury Company, headquartered in Minneapolis. Both Grand Met and Dorsey & Whitney took precautions to protect the confidentiality of Grand Met's tender offer plans. O'Hagan did no work on the Grand Met representation. Dorsey & Whitney withdrew from representing Grand Met on September 9, 1988. Less than a month later, on October 4, 1988, Grand Met publicly announced its tender offer for Pillsbury stock.

On August 18, 1988, while Dorsey & Whitney was still representing Grand Met, O'Hagan began purchasing call options for Pillsbury stock. Each option gave him the right to purchase 100 shares of Pillsbury stock by a specified date in September 1988. Later in August and in September, O'Hagan made additional purchases of Pillsbury call options. By the end of September, he owned 2,500 unexpired Pillsbury options, apparently more than any other individual investor. See App. 85, 148. O'Hagan also purchased, in September 1988, some 5,000 shares of Pillsbury common stock, at a price just under $39 per share. When Grand Met announced its tender offer in October, the price of Pillsbury stock rose to nearly $60 per share. O'Hagan then sold his Pillsbury call options and common stock, making a profit of more than $4.3 million.

The Securities and Exchange Commission (SEC or Commission) initiated an investigation into O'Hagan's transactions, culminating in a 57 count indictment. The indictment alleged that O'Hagan defrauded his law firm and its client, Grand Met, by using for his own trad ing purposes material, nonpublic information regarding Grand Met's planned tender offer. *Id.*, at 8.[1] According to the indictment, O'Hagan used the profits he gained through this trading to conceal his previous embezzlement and conversion of unrelated client trust funds. *Id.*, at 10.[2] O'Hagan was charged with 20 counts of mail fraud, in violation of 18 U.S.C. § 1341; 17 counts of securities fraud, in violation of §10(b) of the Securities Exchange Act of 1934 (Exchange Act), 48 Stat. 891, 15 U.S.C. § 78j(b), and SEC Rule 10b-5, 17 CFR § 240.10b-5 (1996); 17 counts of fraudulent trading in connection with a tender offer, in violation of §14(e) of the Exchange Act, 15 U.S.C. § 78n(e), and SEC Rule 14e-3(a), 17 CFR § 240.14e-3(a) (1996); and 3 counts of violating federal money laundering statutes, 18 U.S.C. §§ 1956(a)(1)(B)(i), 1957. See App. 13-24. A jury convicted O'Hagan on all 57 counts, and he was sentenced to a 41 month term of imprisonment.

A divided panel of the Court of Appeals for the Eighth Circuit reversed all of O'Hagan's convictions. 92 F. 3d 612 (1996). Liability under §10(b) and Rule 10b-5, the Eighth Circuit held, may not be grounded on the-misappropriation theory" of securities fraud on which the prosecution relied. *Id.*, at 622. The Court of Appeals also held that Rule 14e-3(a)--which prohibits trading while in possession of material, nonpublic information relating to a tender offer--exceeds the SEC's §14(e) rulemaking authority because the rule contains no breach of fiduciary duty requirement. *Id.*, at 627. The Eighth Circuit further concluded that O'Hagan's mail fraud and money laundering convictions rested on violations of the securities laws, and therefore could not stand once the securities fraud convictions were reversed. *Id.*, at 627-628. Judge Fagg, dissenting, stated that he would recognize and enforce the misappropriation theory, and would hold that the SEC did not exceed its rulemaking authority when it adopted Rule 14e-3(a) without requiring proof of a breach of fiduciary duty. *Id.*, at 628.

Decisions of the Courts of Appeals are in conflict on the propriety of the misappropriation theory under §10(b) and Rule 10b-5, see *infra* this page and n. 3, and on the legitimacy of Rule 14e-3(a) under §14(e), see *infra*, at 25. We granted certiorari, 519 U. S. ___ (1997), and now reverse the Eighth Circuit's judgment.

We address first the Court of Appeals' reversal of O'Hagan's convictions under §10(b) and Rule 10b-5. Following the Fourth Circuit's lead, see *United States* v. *Bryan,* 58 F. 3d 933, 943-959 (1995), the Eighth Circuit rejected the misappropriation theory as a basis for §10(b) liability. We hold, in accord with several other Courts of Appeals,[3] that criminal liability under §10(b) may be predicated on the misappropriation theory.[4]

In pertinent part, §10(b) of the Exchange Act provides:

> It shall be unlawful for any person, directly or indirectly, by the use of any means or instrumentality of interstate commerce or of the mails, or of any facility of any national securities exchange- "(b) To use or employ, in connection with the purchase or sale of any security registered on a national securities exchange or any security not so registered, any manipulative or deceptive device or contrivance in contravention of such rules and regulations as the [Securities and Exchange] Commission may prescribe as necessary or appropriate in the public interest or for the protection of investors." 15 U.S.C. § 78j(b).

The statute thus proscribes (1) using any deceptive device (2) in connection with the purchase or sale of securities, in contravention of rules prescribed by the Commission. The provision, as written, does not confine its coverage to deception of a purchaser or seller of securities, see *United States* v. *Newman,* 664 F. 2d 12, 17 (CA2 1981); rather, the statute reaches any deceptive device used "in connection with the purchase or sale of any security."

Pursuant to its §10(b) rulemaking authority, the Commission has adopted Rule 10b-5, which, as relevant here, provides:

> "It shall be unlawful for any person, directly or indirectly, by the use of any means or instrumentality of interstate commerce, or of the mails or of any facility of any national securities exchange,
>
> "(a) To employ any device, scheme, or artifice to defraud, [or]
>
> "(c) To engage in any act, practice, or course of business which operates or would operate as a fraud or deceit upon any person,
>
> "in connection with the purchase or sale of any security." 17 CFR § 240.10b-5 (1996).

Liability under Rule 10b-5, our precedent indicates, does not extend beyond conduct encompassed by §10(b)'s prohibition. See *Ernst & Ernst* v. *Hochfelder,* 425 U.S. 185, 214 (1976) (scope of Rule 10b-5 cannot exceed power Congress granted Commission under §10(b)); see also *Central Bank of Denver, N. A.* v. *First Interstate Bank of Denver, N. A.,* 511 U.S. 164, 173 (1994) ("We have refused to allow [private] 10b-5 challenges to conduct not prohibited by the text of the statute.").

Under the "traditional" or "classical theory" of insider trading liability, §10(b) and Rule 10b-5 are violated when a corporate insider trades in the securities of his corporation on the basis of material, nonpublic information. Trading on such information qualifies as a "deceptive device" under §10(b), we have affirmed, because "a relationship of trust and confidence [exists] between the shareholders of a corporation and those insiders who have obtained confidential information by reason of their position with that corporation." *Chiarella* v. *United States,* 445 U.S. 222, 228 (1980). That relationship, we recognized, "gives rise to a duty to disclose [or to abstain from trading] because of the `necessity of preventing a corporate insider from . . . tak[ing] unfair advantage of . . . uninformed . . . stockholders.' " *Id.,* at 228-229 (citation omitted). The classical theory applies not only to officers, directors, and other permanent insiders of a corporation, but also to attorneys, accountants, consultants, and others who temporarily become fiduciaries of a corporation. See *Dirks* v. *SEC,* 463 U.S. 646, 655, n. 14 (1983).

The "misappropriation theory" holds that a person commits fraud "in connection with" a securities transaction, and thereby violates §10(b) and Rule 10b-5, when he misappropriates confidential information for securities trading purposes, in breach of a duty owed to the source of the information. See Brief for United States 14. Under this theory, a fiduciary's undisclosed, self serving use of a principal's information to purchase or sell securities, in breach of a duty of loyalty and confidentiality, defrauds the principal of the exclusive use of that information. In lieu of premising liability on a fiduciary relationship between company insider and purchaser or seller of the company's stock, the misappropriation theory premises liability on a fiduciary turned trader's deception of those who entrusted him with access to confidential information.

The two theories are complementary, each addressing efforts to capitalize on nonpublic information through the purchase or sale of securities. The classical theory targets a corporate insider's breach of duty to shareholders with whom the insider transacts; the misappropriation theory outlaws trading on the basis of nonpublic information by a corporate "outsider" in breach of a duty owed not to a trading party, but to the source of the information. The misappropriation theory is thus designed to "protec[t] the integrity of the securities markets against abuses by `outsiders' to a corporation who have access to confidential information that will affect th[e] corporation's security price when revealed, but who owe no fiduciary or other duty to that corporation's shareholders." *Ibid.*

In this case, the indictment alleged that O'Hagan, in breach of a duty of trust and confidence he owed to his law firm, Dorsey & Whitney, and to its client, Grand Met, traded on the basis of nonpublic information regarding Grand Met's planned tender offer for Pillsbury common stock. App. 16. This conduct, the Government charged, constituted a fraudulent device in connection with the purchase and sale of securities.[5]

We agree with the Government that misappropriation, as just defined, satisfies §10(b)'s requirement that chargeable conduct involve a "deceptive device or contrivance" used "in connection with" the purchase or sale of securities. We observe, first, that misappropriators, as the Government describes them, deal in deception. A fiduciary who "[pretends] loyalty to the principal while secretly converting the principal's information for personal gain," Brief for United States 17, "dupes" or defrauds the principal. See Aldave, Misappropriation: A General Theory of Liability for Trading on Nonpublic Information, 13 Hofstra L. Rev. 101, 119 (1984).

We addressed fraud of the same species in *Carpenter* v. *United States,* 484 U.S. 19 (1987), which involved the mail fraud statute's proscription of "any scheme or artifice to defraud," 18 U.S.C. § 1341. Affirming convictions under that statute, we said in *Carpenter* that an employee's undertaking not to reveal his employer's confidential information "became a sham" when the employee provided the information to his co conspirators in a scheme to obtain trading profits. 484 U. S., at 27. A company's confidential information, we recognized in *Carpenter*, qualifies as property to which the company has a right of exclusive use. *Id.,* at 25-27. The undisclosed misappropriation of such information, in violation of a fiduciary duty, the Court said in *Carpenter,* constitutes fraud akin to embezzlement--" `the fraudulent appropriation to one's own use of the money or goods entrusted to one's care by another.' " *Id.,* at 27 (quoting *Grin* v. *Shine,* 187 U.S. 181, 189 (1902)); see Aldave, 13 Hofstra L. Rev., at 119. *Carpenter's* discussion of the fraudulent misuse of confidential information, the Government notes, "is a particularly apt source of guidance here, because [the mail fraud statute] (like Section 10(b)) has long been held to require deception, not merely the breach of a fiduciary duty." Brief for United States 18, n. 9 (citation omitted).

Deception through nondisclosure is central to the theory of liability for which the Government seeks recognition. As counsel for the Government stated in explanation of the theory at oral argument: "To satisfy the common law rule that a trustee may not use the property that [has] been entrusted [to] him, there would have to be consent. To satisfy the requirement of the Securities Act that there be no deception, there would only have to be disclosure." Tr. of Oral Arg. 12; see generally Restatement (Second) of Agency §§390, 395 (1958) (agent's disclosure obligation regarding use of confidential information).[6]

The misappropriation theory advanced by the Government is consistent with *Santa Fe Industries, Inc.* v. *Green,* 430 U.S. 462 (1977), a decision underscoring that §10(b) is not an all purpose breach of fiduciary duty ban; rather, it trains on conduct involving manipulation or deception. See *id.,* at 473-476. In contrast to the Government's allegations in this case, in *Santa Fe Industries,* all pertinent facts were disclosed by the persons charged with violating §10(b) and Rule 10b-5, see *id.,* at 474; therefore, there was no deception through nondisclosure to which liability under those provisions could attach, see *id.,* at 476. Similarly, full disclosure forecloses liability under the misappropriation theory: Because the deception essential to the misappropriation theory involves feigning fidelity to the source of information, if the fiduciary discloses to the source that he plans to trade on the nonpublic information, there is no "deceptive device" and thus no §10(b) violation--although the fiduciary turned trader may remain liable under state law for breach of a duty of loyalty.[7]

We turn next to the §10(b) requirement that the misappropriator's deceptive use of information be "in connection with the purchase or sale of [a] security." This element is satisfied because the fiduciary's fraud is consummated, not when the fiduciary gains the confidential information, but when, without disclosure to his principal, he uses the information to purchase or sell securities. The securities transaction and the breach of duty thus coincide. This is so even though the person or entity defrauded is not the other party to the trade, but is, instead, the source of the nonpublic information. See Aldave, 13 Hofstra L. Rev., at 120 ("a fraud or deceit can be practiced on one person, with resultant harm to another person or group of persons"). A misappropriator who trades on the basis of material, nonpublic information, in short, gains his advantageous market position through deception; he deceives the source of the information and simultaneously harms members of the investing public. See *id.,* at 120-121, and n. 107.

The misappropriation theory targets information of a sort that misappropriators ordinarily capitalize upon to gain no risk profits through the purchase or sale of securities. Should a misappropriator put such information to other use, the statute's prohibition would not be implicated. The theory does not catch all conceivable forms of fraud involving confidential information; rather, it catches fraudulent means of capitalizing on such information through securities transactions.

The Government notes another limitation on the forms of fraud §10(b) reaches: "The misappropriation theory would not . . . apply to a case in which a person defrauded a bank into giving him a loan or embezzled cash from another, and then used the proceeds of the misdeed to purchase securities." Brief for United States 24, n. 13. In such a case, the Government states, "the proceeds would have value to the malefactor apart from their use in a securities transaction, and the fraud would be complete as soon as the money was obtained." *Ibid.* In other words, money can buy, if not anything, then at least many things; its misappropriation may thus be viewed as sufficiently detached from a subsequent securities transaction that §10(b)'s "in connection with" requirement would not be met. *Ibid.*

The dissent's charge that the misappropriation theory is incoherent because information, like funds, can be put to multiple uses, see *post,* at 4-8, misses the point. The Exchange Act was enacted in part "to insure the maintenance of fair and honest markets," 15 U.S.C. § 78b and there is no question that fraudulent uses of confidential information fall within §10(b)'s prohibition if the fraud is "in connection with" a securities transaction. It is hardly remarkable that a rule suitably applied to the fraudulent uses of certain kinds of information would be stretched beyond reason were it applied to the fraudulent use of money.

The dissent does catch the Government in overstatement. Observing that money can be used for all manner of purposes and purchases, the Government urges that confidential information of the kind at issue derives its value *only* from its utility in securities trading. See Brief for United States 10, 21; *post,* at 4-6 (several times emphasizing the word "only"). Substitute "ordinarily" for "only," and the Government is on the mark.[8]

Our recognition that the Government's "only" is an overstatement has provoked the dissent to cry "new theory." See *post,* at 9-11. But the very case on which the dissent relies, *Motor Vehicle Mfrs. Assn. of United States, Inc.* v. *State Farm Mut. Automobile Ins. Co.,* 463 U.S. 29 (1983), shows the extremity of that charge. In *State Farm,* we reviewed an agency's rescission of a rule under the same "arbitrary and capricious" standard by which the promulgation of a rule under the relevant statute was to be judged, see *id.,* at 41-42; in our decision concluding that the agency had not adequately explained its regulatory action, see *id.,* at 57, we cautioned that a "reviewing court should not attempt itself to make up for such deficiencies," *id.,* at 43. Here, by contrast, Rule 10b-5's promulgation has not been challenged; we consider only the Government's charge that O'Hagan's alleged fraudulent conduct falls within the prohibitions of the rule and §10(b). In this context, we acknowledge simply that, in defending the Government's interpretation of the rule and statute in this Court, the Government's lawyers have pressed a solid point too far, something lawyers, occasionally even judges, are wont to do.

The misappropriation theory comports with §10(b)'s language, which requires deception "in connection with the purchase or sale of any security," not deception of an identifiable purchaser or seller. The theory is also well tuned to an animating purpose of the Exchange Act: to insure honest securities markets and thereby promote investor confidence. See 45 Fed. Reg. 60412 (1980) (trading on misappropriated information "undermines the integrity of, and investor confidence in, the securities markets"). Although informational disparity is inevitable in the securities markets, investors likely would hesitate to venture their capital in a market where trading based on misappropriated nonpublic information is unchecked by law. An investor's informational disadvantage vis á vis a misappropriator with material, nonpublic information stems from contrivance, not luck; it is a disadvantage that cannot be overcome with research or skill. See Brudney, Insiders, Outsiders, and Informational Advantages Under the Federal Securities Laws, 93 Harv. L. Rev. 322, 356 (1979) ("If the market is thought to be systematically populated with . . . transactors [trading on the basis of misappropriated information] some investors will refrain from dealing altogether, and others will incur costs to avoid dealing with such transactors or corruptly to overcome their unerodable informational advantages."); Aldave, 13 Hofstra L. Rev., at 122-123.

In sum, considering the inhibiting impact on market participation of trading on misappropriated information, and the congressional purposes underlying §10(b), it makes scant sense to hold a lawyer like O'Hagan a §10(b) violator if he works for a law firm representing the target of a tender offer, but not if he works for a law firm representing the bidder. The text of the statute requires no such result.[9] The misappropriation at issue here was properly made the subject of a §10(b) charge because it meets the statutory requirement that there be "deceptive" conduct "in connection with" securities transactions.

The Court of Appeals rejected the misappropriation theory primarily on two grounds. First, as the Eighth Circuit comprehended the theory, it requires neither misrepresentation nor nondisclosure. See 92 F. 3d, at 618. As we just explained, however, see *supra,* at 8-10, deceptive nondisclosure is essential to the §10(b) liability at issue. Concretely, in this case, "it [was O'Hagan's] failure to disclose his personal trading to Grand Met and Dorsey, in breach of his duty to do so, that ma[de] his conduct 'deceptive' within the meaning of [§]10(b)." Reply Brief 7.

Second and "more obvious," the Court of Appeals said, the misappropriation theory is not moored to §10(b)'s requirement that "the fraud be 'in connection with the purchase or sale of any security.'" See 92 F. 3d, at 618 (quoting 15 U.S.C. § 78j(b)). According to the Eighth Circuit, three of our decisions reveal that §10(b) liability cannot be predicated on a duty owed to the source of nonpublic information: *Chiarella* v. *United States,* 445 U.S. 222 (1980); *Dirks* v. *SEC,* 463 U.S. 646 (1983); and *Central Bank of Denver, N. A.* v. *First Interstate Bank of Denver, N. A.,* 511 U.S. 164 (1994). "[O]nly a breach of a duty to parties to the securities transaction," the Court of Appeals concluded, "or, at the most, to other market participants such as investors, will be sufficient to give rise to §10(b) liability." 92 F. 3d, at 618. We read the statute and our precedent differently, and note again that §10(b) refers to "the purchase or sale of any security," not to identifiable purchasers or sellers of securities.

Chiarella involved securities trades by a printer employed at a shop that printed documents announcing corporate takeover bids. See 445 U. S., at 224. Deducing the names of target companies from documents he handled, the printer bought shares of the targets before takeover bids were announced, expecting (correctly) that the share prices would rise upon announcement. In these transactions, the printer did not disclose to the sellers of the securities (the target companies' shareholders) the nonpublic information on which he traded. See *ibid.* For that trading, the printer was convicted of violating §10(b) and Rule 10b-5. We reversed the Court of Appeals judgment that had affirmed the conviction. See *id.,* at 225.

The jury in *Chiarella* had been instructed that it could convict the defendant if he willfully failed to inform sellers of target company securities that he knew of a takeover bid that would increase the value of their shares. See *id.*, at 226. Emphasizing that the printer had no agency or other fiduciary relationship with the sellers, we held that liability could not be imposed on so broad a theory. See *id.*, at 235. There is under §10(b), we explained, no "general duty between all participants in market transactions to forgo actions based on material, nonpublic information." *Id.*, at 233. Under established doctrine, we said, a duty to disclose or abstain from trading "arises from a specific relationship between two parties." *Ibid.*

The Court did not hold in *Chiarella* that the *only* relationship prompting liability for trading on undisclosed information is the relationship between a corporation's insiders and shareholders. That is evident from our response to the Government's argument before this Court that the printer's misappropriation of information from his employer for purposes of securities trading--in violation of a duty of confidentiality owed to the acquiring companies--constituted fraud in connection with the purchase or sale of a security, and thereby satisfied the terms of §10(b). *Id.*, at 235-236. The Court declined to reach that potential basis for the printer's liability, because the theory had not been submitted to the jury. See *id.*, at 236-237. But four Justices found merit in it. See *id.*, at 239 (Brennan, J., concurring in judgment); *id.*, at 240-243 (Burger, C. J., dissenting); *id.*, at 245 (Blackmun, J., joined by Marshall, J., dissenting). And a fifth Justice stated that the Court "wisely le[ft] the resolution of this issue for another day." *Id.*, at 238 (Stevens, J., concurring).

Chiarella thus expressly left open the misappropriation theory before us today. Certain statements in *Chiarella*, however, led the Eighth Circuit in the instant case to conclude that §10(b) liability hinges exclusively on a breach of duty owed to a purchaser or seller of securities. See 92 F. 3d, at 618. The Court said in *Chiarella* that §10(b) liability "is premised upon a duty to disclose arising from a relationship of trust and confidence *between parties to a transaction,*" 445 U. S., at 230 (emphasis added), and observed that the print shop employee defendant in that case "was not a person in whom the sellers had placed their trust and confidence," see *id.*, at 232. These statements rejected the notion that §10(b) stretches so far as to impose "a general duty between all participants in market transactions to forgo actions based on material, nonpublic information," *id.*, at 233, and we confine them to that context. The statements highlighted by the Eighth Circuit, in short, appear in an opinion carefully leaving for future resolution the validity of the misappropriation theory, and therefore cannot be read to foreclose that theory.

Dirks, too, left room for application of the misappropriation theory in cases like the one we confront.[10] *Dirks* involved an investment analyst who had received information from a former insider of a corporation with which the analyst had no connection. See 463 U. S., at 648-649. The information indicated that the corporation had engaged in a massive fraud. The analyst investigated the fraud, obtaining corroborating information from employees of the corporation. During his investigation, the analyst discussed his findings with clients and investors, some of whom sold their holdings in the company the analyst suspected of gross wrongdoing. See *id.*, at 649.

The SEC censured the analyst for, *inter alia,* aiding and abetting §10(b) and Rule 10b-5 violations by clients and investors who sold their holdings based on the nonpublic information the analyst passed on. See *id.*, at 650-652. In the SEC's view, the analyst, as a "tippee" of corporation insiders, had a duty under §10(b) and Rule 10b-5 to refrain from communicating the nonpublic information to persons likely to trade on the basis of it. See *id.*, at 651, 655-656. This Court found no such obligation, see *id.*, at 665-667, and repeated the key point made in *Chiarella:* There is no " `general duty between all participants in market transactions to forgo actions based on material, nonpublic information.' " *Id.*, at 655 (quoting *Chiarella,* 445 U. S., at 233); see Aldave, 13 Hofstra L. Rev., at 122 (misappropriation theory bars only "trading on the basis of information that the wrongdoer converted to his own use in violation of some fiduciary, contractual, or similar obligation to the owner or rightful possessor of the information").

No showing had been made in *Dirks* that the "tippers" had violated any duty by disclosing to the analyst nonpublic information about their former employer. The insiders had acted not for personal profit, but to expose a massive fraud within the corporation. See *Dirks,* 463 U. S., at 666-667. Absent any violation by the tippers, there could be no derivative liability for the tippee. See *id.*, at 667. Most important for purposes of the instant case, the Court observed in *Dirks:* "There was no expectation by [the analyst's] sources that he would keep their information in confidence. Nor did [the analyst] misappropriate or illegally obtain the information . . . ." *Id.*, at 665. *Dirks* thus presents no suggestion that a person who gains nonpublic information through misappropriation in breach of a fiduciary duty escapes §10(b) liability when, without alerting the source, he trades on the information.

Last of the three cases the Eighth Circuit regarded as warranting disapproval of the misappropriation theory, *Central Bank* held that "a private plaintiff may not maintain an aiding and abetting suit under §10(b)." 511 U. S., at 191. We immediately cautioned in *Central Bank* that secondary actors in the securities markets may sometimes be chargeable under the securities Acts: "Any person or entity, including a lawyer, accountant, or bank, who employs a manipulative device or makes a material misstatement (or omission) *on which a purchaser or seller of securities relies* may be liable as a primary violator under 10b-5, assuming . . . the requirements for primary liability under Rule 10b-5 are met." *Ibid.* (emphasis added). The Eighth Circuit isolated the statement just quoted and drew from it the conclusion that §10(b) covers only deceptive statements or omissions on which purchasers and sellers, and perhaps other market participants, rely. See 92 F. 3d, at 619. It is evident from the question presented in *Central Bank,* however, that this Court, in the quoted passage, sought only to clarify that secondary actors, although not subject to aiding and abetting liability, remain subject to primary liability under §10(b) and Rule 10b-5 for certain conduct.

Furthermore, *Central Bank*'s discussion concerned only private civil litigation under §10(b) and Rule 10b-5, not criminal liability. *Central Bank*'s reference to purchasers or sellers of securities must be read in light of a longstanding limitation on private §10(b) suits. In *Blue Chip Stamps* v. *Manor Drug Stores,* 421 U.S. 723 (1975), we held that only actual purchasers or sellers of securities may maintain a private civil action under §10(b) and Rule 10b-5. We so confined the §10(b) private right of action because of "policy considerations." *Id.*, at 737. In particular, *Blue Chip Stamps* recognized the abuse potential and proof problems inherent in suits by investors who neither bought nor sold, but asserted they would have traded absent fraudulent conduct by others. See *id.*, at 739-747; see also *Holmes* v. *Securities Investor Protection Corporation,* 503 U.S. 258, 285 (1992) (O'Connor, J., concurring in part and concurring in judgment); *id.,* at 289-290 (Scalia, J., concurring in judgment). Criminal prosecutions do not present the dangers the Court addressed in *Blue Chip Stamps,* so that decision is "inapplicable" to indictments for violations of §10(b) and Rule 10b-5. *United States* v. *Naftalin,* 441 U.S. 768, 774, n. 6 (1979); see also *Holmes,* 503 U. S., at 281 (O'Connor, J., concurring in part and concurring in judgment) ("[T]he purchaser/seller standing requirement for private civil actions under §10(b) and Rule 10b-5 is of no import in criminal prosecutions for willful violations of those provisions.").

In sum, the misappropriation theory, as we have examined and explained it in this opinion, is both consistent with the statute and with our precedent.[11] Vital to our decision that criminal liability may be sustained under the misappropriation theory, we emphasize, are two sturdy safeguards Congress has provided regarding scienter. To establish a criminal violation of Rule 10b-5, the Government must prove that a person "willfully" violated the provision. See 15 U.S.C. § 78ff(a).[12] Furthermore, a defendant may not be imprisoned for violating Rule 10b-5 if he proves that he had no knowledge of the rule. See *ibid.*[13] O'Hagan's charge that the misappropriation theory is too indefinite to permit the imposition of criminal liability, see Brief for Respondent 30-33, thus fails not only because the theory is limited to those who breach a recognized duty. In addition, the statute's "requirement of the presence of culpable intent as a necessary element of the offense does much to destroy any force in the argument that application of the [statute]" in circumstances such as O'Hagan's is unjust. *Boyce Motor Lines, Inc.* v. *United States,* 342 U.S. 337, 342 (1952).

The Eighth Circuit erred in holding that the misappropriation theory is inconsistent with §10(b). The Court of Appeals may address on remand O'Hagan's other challenges to his convictions under §10(b) and Rule 10b-5.

We consider next the ground on which the Court of Appeals reversed O'Hagan's convictions for fraudulent trading in connection with a tender offer, in violation of §14(e) of the Exchange Act and SEC Rule 14e-3(a). A sole question is before us as to these convictions: Did the Commission, as the Court of Appeals held, exceed its rulemaking authority under §14(e) when it adopted Rule 14e-3(a) without requiring a showing that the trading at issue entailed a breach of fiduciary duty? We hold that the Commission, in this regard and to the extent relevant to this case, did not exceed its authority.

The governing statutory provision, §14(e) of the Exchange Act, reads in relevant part:

> "It shall be unlawful for any person . . . to engage in any fraudulent, deceptive, or manipulative acts or practices, in connection with any tender offer . . . .The [SEC] shall, for the purposes of this subsection, by rules and regulations define, and prescribe means reasonably designed to prevent, such acts and practices as are fraudulent, deceptive, or manipulative." 15 U.S.C. § 78n(e).

Section 14(e)'s first sentence prohibits fraudulent acts in connection with a tender offer. This self operating proscription was one of several provisions added to the Exchange Act in 1968 by the Williams Act, 82 Stat. 454. The section's second sentence delegates definitional and prophylactic rulemaking authority to the Commission. Congress added this rulemaking delegation to §14(e) in 1970 amendments to the Williams Act. See §5, 84 Stat. 1497.

Through §14(e) and other provisions on disclosure in the Williams Act,[14] Congress sought to ensure that shareholders "confronted by a cash tender offer for their stock [would] not be required to respond without adequate information." *Rondeau* v. *Mosinee Paper Corp.*, 422 U.S. 49, 58 (1975); see *Lewis* v. *McGraw,* 619 F. 2d 192, 195 (CA2 1980) *(per curiam)* ("very purpose" of Williams Act was "informed decisionmaking by shareholders"). As we recognized in *Schreiber* v. *Burlington Northern, Inc.,* 472 U.S. 1 (1985), Congress designed the Williams Act to make "disclosure, rather than court imposed principles of `fairness' or `artificiality,' . . . the preferred method of market regulation." *Id.,* at 9, n. 8. Section 14(e), we explained, "supplements the more precise disclosure provisions found elsewhere in the Williams Act, while requiring disclosure more explicitly addressed to the tender offer context than that required by §10(b)." *Id.,* at 10-11.

Relying on §14(e)'s rulemaking authorization, the Commission, in 1980, promulgated Rule 14e-3(a). That measure provides:

> "(a) If any person has taken a substantial step or steps to commence, or has commenced, a tender offer (the `offering person'), it shall constitute a fraudulent, deceptive or manipulative act or practice within the meaning of section 14(e) of the [Exchange] Act for any other person who is in possession of material information relating to such tender offer which information he knows or has reason to know is nonpublic and which he knows or has reason to know has been acquired directly or indirectly from:

"(1) The offering person,

"(2) The issuer of the securities sought or to be sought by such tender offer, or

"(3) Any officer, director, partner or employee or any other person acting on behalf of the offering person or such issuer, to purchase or sell or cause to be purchased or sold any of such securities or any securities convertible into or exchangeable for any such securities or any option or right to obtain or to dispose of any of the foregoing securities, unless within a reasonable time prior to any purchase or sale such information and its source are publicly disclosed by press release or otherwise." 17 CFR § 240.14e-3(a) (1996).

As characterized by the Commission, Rule 14e-3(a) is a-disclose or abstain from trading" requirement. 45 Fed. Reg. 60410 (1980).[15] The Second Circuit concisely described the rule's thrust:

"One violates Rule 14e-3(a) if he trades on the basis of material nonpublic information concerning a pending tender offer that he knows or has reason to know has been acquired `directly or indirectly' from an insider of the offeror or issuer, or someone working on their behalf. Rule 14e-3(a) is a disclosure provision. It creates a duty in those traders who fall within its ambit to abstain or disclose, *without regard to whether the trader owes a pre-existing fiduciary duty* to respect the confidentiality of the information." *United States* v. *Chestman*, 947 F. 2d 551, 557 (1991) (en banc) (emphasis added), cert. denied, 503 U.S. 1004 (1992).

See also *SEC* v. *Maio*, 51 F. 3d 623, 635 (CA7 1995) ("Rule 14e-3 creates a duty to disclose material non public information, or abstain from trading in stocks implicated by an impending tender offer, *regardless of whether such information was obtained through a breach of fiduciary duty*.") (emphasis added); *SEC* v. *Peters*, 978 F. 2d 1162, 1165 (CA10 1992) (as written, Rule 14e-3(a) has no fiduciary duty requirement).

In the Eighth Circuit's view, because Rule 14e-3(a) applies whether or not the trading in question breaches a fiduciary duty, the regulation exceeds the SEC's §14(e) rulemaking authority. See 92 F. 3d, at 624, 627. Contra, *Maio*, 51 F. 3d, at 634-635 (CA7); *Peters*, 978 F. 2d, at 1165-1167 (CA10); *Chestman*, 947 F. 2d, at 556-563 (CA2) (all holding Rule 14e-3(a) a proper exercise of SEC's statutory authority). In support of its holding, the Eighth Circuit relied on the text of §14(e) and our decisions in *Schreiber* and *Chiarella*. See 92 F. 3d, at 624-627.

The Eighth Circuit homed in on the essence of §14(e)'s rulemaking authorization: "[T]he statute empowers the SEC to `define' and `prescribe means reasonably designed to prevent' `acts and practices' which are `fraudulent.' " *Id.*, at 624. All that means, the Eighth Circuit found plain, is that the SEC may "identify and regulate," in the tender offer context, "acts and practices" the law already defines as "fraudulent"; but, the Eighth Circuit maintained, the SEC may not "create its own definition of fraud." *Ibid.* (internal quotation marks omitted).

This Court, the Eighth Circuit pointed out, held in *Schreiber* that the word "manipulative" in the §14(e) phrase "fraudulent, deceptive, or manipulative acts or practices" means just what the word means in §10(b): Absent misrepresentation or nondisclosure, an act cannot be indicted as manipulative. See 92 F. 3d, at 625 (citing *Schreiber*, 472 U. S., at 7-8, and n. 6). Section 10(b) interpretations guide construction of §14(e), the Eighth Circuit added, see 92 F. 3d, at 625, citing this Court's acknowledgment in *Schreiber* that §14(e)'s " `broad antifraud prohibition' . . . [is] modeled on the antifraud provisions of §10(b) . . . and Rule 10b-5," 472 U. S., at 10 (citation omitted); see *id.*, at 10-11, n. 10.

For the meaning of "fraudulent" under §10(b), the Eighth Circuit looked to *Chiarella*. See 92 F. 3d, at 625. In that case, the Eighth Circuit recounted, this Court held that a failure to disclose information could be "fraudulent" under §10(b) only when there was a duty to speak arising out of " `a fiduciary or other similar relationship of trust and confidence.' " *Chiarella*, 445 U. S., at 228 (quoting Restatement (Second) of Torts §551(2)(a) (1976)). Just as §10(b) demands a showing of a breach of fiduciary duty, so such a breach is necessary to make out a §14(e) violation, the Eighth Circuit concluded.

As to the Commission's §14(e) authority to "prescribe means reasonably designed to prevent" fraudulent acts, the Eighth Circuit stated: "Properly read, this provision means simply that the SEC has broad regulatory powers in the field of tender offers, but the statutory terms have a fixed meaning which the SEC cannot alter by way of an administrative rule." 92 F. 3d, at 627.

The United States urges that the Eighth Circuit's reading of §14(e) misapprehends both the Commission's authority to define fraudulent acts and the Commission's power to prevent them. "The `defining' power," the United States submits, "would be a virtual nullity were the SEC not permitted to go beyond common law fraud (which is separately prohibited in the first [self operative] sentence of Section 14(e))." Brief for United States 11; see id., at 37.

In maintaining that the Commission's power to define fraudulent acts under §14(e) is broader than its rulemaking power under §10(b), the United States questions the Court of Appeals' reading of Schreiber. See id., at 38-40. Parenthetically, the United States notes that the word before the Schreiber Court was "manipulative"; unlike "fraudulent," the United States observes, " `manipulative' . . . is `virtually a term of art when used in connection with the securities markets.' " Id., at 38, n. 20 (quoting Schreiber, 472 U. S., at 6). Most tellingly, the United States submits, Schreiber involved acts alleged to violate the self operative provision in §14(e)'s first sentence, a sentence containing language similar to §10(b). But §14(e)'s second sentence, containing the rulemaking authorization, the United States points out, does not track §10(b), which simply authorizes the SEC to proscribe "manipulative or deceptive device[s] or contrivance[s]." Brief for United States 38. Instead, §14(e)'s rulemaking prescription tracks §15(c)(2)(D) of the Exchange Act, 15 U.S.C. § 78o(c)(2)(D), which concerns the conduct of broker dealers in over the counter markets. See Brief for United States 38-39. Since 1938, see 52 Stat. 1075, §15(c)(2) has given the Commission authority to "define, and prescribe means reasonably designed to prevent, such [broker dealer] acts and practices as are fraudulent, deceptive, or manipulative." 15 U.S.C. § 78o(c)(2)(D). When Congress added this same rulemaking language to §14(e) in 1970, the Government states, the Commission had already used its §15(c)(2) authority to reach beyond common law fraud. See Brief for United States 39, n. 22.[16]

We need not resolve in this case whether the Commission's authority under §14(e) to "define . . . such acts and practices as are fraudulent" is broader than the Commission's fraud defining authority under §10(b), for we agree with the United States that Rule 14e-3(a), as applied to cases of this genre, qualifies under §14(e) as a "means reasonably designed to prevent" fraudulent trading on material, nonpublic information in the tender offer context.[17] A prophylactic measure, because its mission is to prevent, typically encompasses more than the core activity prohibited. As we noted in Schreiber, §14(e)'s rulemaking authorization gives the Commission "latitude," even in the context of a term of art like "manipulative," "to regulate nondeceptive activities as a `reasonably designed' means of preventing manipulative acts, without suggesting any change in the meaning of the term `manipulative' itself." 472 U. S., at 11, n. 11. We hold, accordingly, that under §14(e), the Commission may prohibit acts, not themselves fraudulent under the common law or §10(b), if the prohibition is "reasonably designed to prevent . . . acts and practices [that] are fraudulent." 15 U.S.C. § 78n(e).[18]

Because Congress has authorized the Commission, in §14(e), to prescribe legislative rules, we owe the Commission's judgment "more than mere deference or weight." Batterton v. Francis, 432 U.S. 416, 424-426 (1977). Therefore, in determining whether Rule 14e-3(a)'s "disclose or abstain from trading" requirement is reasonably designed to prevent fraudulent acts, we must accord the Commission's assessment "controlling weight unless [it is] arbitrary, capricious, or manifestly contrary to the statute." Chevron U. S. A. Inc. v. Natural Resources Defense Council, Inc., 467 U.S. 837, 844 (1984). In this case, we conclude, the Commission's assessment is none of these.[19]

In adopting the "disclose or abstain" rule, the SEC explained:

> "The Commission has previously expressed and continues to have serious concerns about trading by persons in possession of material, nonpublic information relating to a tender offer. This practice results in unfair disparities in market information and market disruption. Security holders who purchase from or sell to such persons are effectively denied the benefits of disclosure and the substantive protections of the Williams Act. If furnished with the information, these security holders would be able to make an informed investment decision, which could involve deferring the purchase or sale of the securities until the material information had been disseminated or until the tender offer has been commenced or terminated." 45 Fed. Reg. 60412 (1980) (footnotes omitted).

The Commission thus justified Rule 14e-3(a) as a means necessary and proper to assure the efficacy of Williams Act protections.

The United States emphasizes that Rule 14e-3(a) reaches trading in which "a breach of duty is likely but difficult to prove." Reply Brief 16. "Particularly in the context of a tender offer," as the Tenth Circuit recognized, "there is a fairly wide circle of people with confidential information," Peters, 978 F. 2d, at 1167, notably, the attorneys, investment bankers, and accountants involved in structuring the transaction. The availability of that information may lead to abuse, for "even a hint of an upcoming tender offer may send the price of the target company's stock soaring." SEC v. Materia, 745 F. 2d 197,

199 (CA2 1984). Individuals entrusted with nonpublic information, particularly if they have no long term loyalty to the issuer, may find the temptation to trade on that information hard to resist in view of "the very large short term profits potentially available [to them]." *Peters*, 978 F. 2d, at 1167.

"[I]t may be possible to prove circumstantially that a person [traded on the basis of material, nonpublic information], but almost impossible to prove that the trader obtained such information in breach of a fiduciary duty owed either by the trader or by the ultimate insider source of the information." *Ibid*. The example of a "tippee" who trades on information received from an insider illustrates the problem. Under Rule 10b-5, "a tippee assumes a fiduciary duty to the shareholders of a corporation not to trade on material nonpublic information only when the insider has breached his fiduciary duty to the shareholders by disclosing the information to the tippee and the tippee knows or should know that there has been a breach." *Dirks*, 463 U. S., at 660. To show that a tippee who traded on nonpublic information about a tender offer had breached a fiduciary duty would require proof not only that the insider source breached a fiduciary duty, but that the tippee knew or should have known of that breach. "Yet, in most cases, the only parties to the [information transfer] will be the insider and the alleged tippee." *Peters*, 978 F. 2d, at 1167.[20]

In sum, it is a fair assumption that trading on the basis of material, nonpublic information will often involve a breach of a duty of confidentiality to the bidder or target company or their representatives. The SEC, cognizant of the proof problem that could enable sophisticated traders to escape responsibility, placed in Rule 14e-3(a) a "disclose or abstain from trading" command that does not require specific proof of a breach of fiduciary duty. That prescription, we are satisfied, applied to this case, is a "means reasonably designed to prevent" fraudulent trading on material, nonpublic information in the tender offer context. See *Chestman*, 947 F. 2d, at 560 ("While dispensing with the subtle problems of proof associated with demonstrating fiduciary breach in the problematic area of tender offer insider trading, [Rule 14e-3(a)] retains a close nexus between the prohibited conduct and the statutory aims."); accord, *Maio*, 51 F. 3d, at 635, and n. 14; *Peters*, 978 F. 2d, at 1167.[21] Therefore, insofar as it serves to prevent the type of misappropriation charged against O'Hagan, Rule 14e-3(a) is a proper exercise of the Commission's prophylactic power under §14(e).[22]

As an alternate ground for affirming the Eighth Circuit's judgment, O'Hagan urges that Rule 14e-3(a) is invalid because it prohibits trading in advance of a tender offer--when "a substantial step . . . to commence" such an offer has been taken-- while §14(e) prohibits fraudulent acts "in connection with any tender offer." See Brief for Respondent 41-42. O'Hagan further contends that, by covering pre-offer conduct, Rule 14e-3(a) "fails to comport with due process on two levels": The rule does not "give fair notice as to when, in advance of a tender offer, a violation of §14(e) occurs," *id.*, at 42; and it "disposes of any scienter requirement," *id.*, at 43. The Court of Appeals did not address these arguments, and O'Hagan did not raise the due process points in his briefs before that court. We decline to consider these contentions in the first instance.[23] The Court of Appeals may address on remand any arguments O'Hagan has preserved.

Based on its dispositions of the securities fraud convictions, the Court of Appeals also reversed O'Hagan's convictions, under 18 U.S.C. § 1341 for mail fraud. See 92 F. 3d, at 627-628. Reversal of the securities convictions, the Court of Appeals recognized, "d[id] not as a matter of law require that the mail fraud convictions likewise be reversed." *Id.*, at 627 (citing *Carpenter*, 484 U. S., at 24, in which this Court unanimously affirmed mail and wire fraud convictions based on the same conduct that evenly divided the Court on the defendants' securities fraud convictions). But in this case, the Court of Appeals said, the indictment was so structured that the mail fraud charges could not be disassociated from the securities fraud charges, and absent any securities fraud, "there was no fraud upon which to base the mail fraud charges." 92 F. 3d, at 627-628.[24]

The United States urges that the Court of Appeals' position is irreconcilable with *Carpenter*: Just as in *Carpenter*, so here, the "mail fraud charges are independent of [the] securities fraud charges, even [though] both rest on the same set of facts." Brief for United States 46-47. We need not linger over this matter, for our rulings on the securities fraud issues require that we reverse the Court of Appeals judgment on the mail fraud counts as well.[25]

O'Hagan, we note, attacked the mail fraud convictions in the Court of Appeals on alternate grounds; his other arguments, not yet addressed by the Eighth Circuit, remain open for consideration on remand.

* * *

The judgment of the Court of Appeals for the Eighth Circuit is reversed, and the case is remanded for further proceedings consistent with this opinion.

It is so ordered.

NOTES

[1] As evidence that O'Hagan traded on the basis of nonpublic information misappropriated from his law firm, the Government relied on a conversation between O'Hagan and the Dorsey & Whitney partner heading the firm's Grand Met representation. That conversation allegedly took place shortly before August 26, 1988. See Brief for United States 4. O'Hagan urges that the Government's evidence does not show he traded on the basis of nonpublic information. O'Hagan points to news reports on August 18 and 22, 1988, that Grand Met was interested in acquiring Pillsbury, and to an earlier, August 12,

1988, news report that Grand Met had put up its hotel chain for auction to raise funds for an acquisition. See Brief for Respondent 4 (citing App. 73-74, 78-80). O'Hagan's challenge to the sufficiency of the evidence remains open for consideration on remand.

[2] O'Hagan was convicted of theft in state court, sentenced to 30 months' imprisonment, and fined. See *State* v. *O'Hagan,* 474 N. W. 2d 613, 615, 623 (Minn. App. 1991). The Supreme Court of Minnesota disbarred O'Hagan from the practice of law. See *In re O'Hagan,* 450 N. W. 2d 571 (Minn. 1990).

[3] See, *e.g., United States* v. *Chestman,* 947 F. 2d 551, 566 (CA2 1991) (en banc), cert. denied, 503 U.S. 1004 (1992); *SEC* v. *Cherif,* 933 F. 2d 403, 410 (CA7 1991), cert. denied, 502 U.S. 1071 (1992); *SEC* v. *Clark,* 915 F. 2d 439, 453 (CA9 1990).

[4] Twice before we have been presented with the question whether criminal liability for violation of §10(b) may be based on a misappropriation theory. In *Chiarella* v. *United States,* 445 U.S. 222, 235-237 (1980), the jury had received no misappropriation theory instructions, so we declined to address the question. See *infra,* at 17. In *Carpenter* v. *United States,* 484 U.S. 19, 24 (1987), the Court divided evenly on whether, under the circumstances of that case, convictions resting on the misappropriation theory should be affirmed. See Aldave, The Misappropriation Theory: *Carpenter* and Its Aftermath, 49 Ohio St. L. J. 373, 375 (1988) (observing that "*Carpenter* was, by any reckoning, an unusual case," for the information there misappropriated belonged not to a company preparing to engage in securities transactions, *e.g.,* a bidder in a corporate acquisition, but to the Wall Street Journal).

[5] The Government could not have prosecuted O'Hagan under the classical theory, for O'Hagan was not an "insider" of Pillsbury, the corporation in whose stock he traded. Although an "outsider" with respect to Pillsbury, O'Hagan had an intimate association with, and was found to have traded on confidential information from, Dorsey & Whitney, counsel to tender offeror Grand Met. Under the misappropriation theory, O'Hagan's securities trading does not escape Exchange Act sanction, as it would under the dissent's reasoning, simply because he was associated with, and gained nonpublic information from, the bidder, rather than the target.

[6] Under the misappropriation theory urged in this case, the disclosure obligation runs to the source of the information, here, Dorsey & Whitney and Grand Met. Chief Justice Burger, dissenting in *Chiarella,* advanced a broader reading of §10(b) and Rule 10b-5; the disclosure obligation, as he envisioned it, ran to those with whom the misappropriator trades. 445 U. S., at 240 ("a person who has misappropriated nonpublic information has an absolute duty to disclose that information or to refrain from trading"); see also *id.,* at 243, n. 4. The Government does not propose that we adopt a misappropriation theory of that breadth.

[7] Where, however, a person trading on the basis of material, nonpublic information owes a duty of loyalty and confidentiality to two entities or persons--for example, a law firm and its client--but makes disclosure to only one, the trader may still be liable under the misappropriation theory.

[8] The dissent's evident struggle to invent other uses to which O'Hagan plausibly might have put the nonpublic information, see *post,* at 7, is telling. It is imaginative to suggest that a trade journal would have paid O'Hagan dollars in the millions to publish his information. See Tr. of Oral Arg. 36-37. Counsel for O'HAGAN hypothesized, as a nontrading use, that O'Hagan could have "misappropriat[ed] this information of [his] law firm and its client, deliver[ed] it to [Pillsbury], and suggest[ed] that [Pillsbury] in the future . . . might find it very desirable to use [O'Hagan] for legal work." *Id.,* at 37. But Pillsbury might well have had large doubts about engaging for its legal work a lawyer who so stunningly displayed his readiness to betray a client's confidence. Nor is the Commission's theory "incoherent" or "inconsistent," *post,* at 1, 14, for failing to inhibit use of confidential information for "personal amusement . . . in a fantasy stock trading game," *post,* at 7.

[9] As noted earlier, however, see *supra,* at 9-10, the textual requirement of deception precludes §10(b) liability when a person trading on the basis of nonpublic information has disclosed his trading plans to, or obtained authorization from, the principal--even though such conduct may affect the securities markets in the same manner as the conduct reached by the misappropriation theory. Contrary to the dissent's suggestion, see *post,* at 11-13, the fact that §10(b) is only a partial antidote to the problems it was designed to alleviate does not call into question its prohibition of conduct that falls within its textual proscription. Moreover, once a disloyal agent discloses his imminent breach of duty, his

principal may seek appropriate equitable relief under state law. Furthermore, in the context of a tender offer, the principal who authorizes an agent's trading on confidential information may, in the Commission's view, incur liability for an Exchange Act violation under Rule 14e-3(a).

[10] The Eighth Circuit's conclusion to the contrary was based in large part on *Dirks*'s reiteration of the *Chiarella* language quoted and discussed above. See 92 F. 3d 612, 618-619 (1996).

[11] The United States additionally argues that Congress confirmed the validity of the misappropriation theory in the Insider Trading and Securities Fraud Enforcement Act of 1988 (ITSFEA), §2(1), 102 Stat. 4677, note following 15 U.S.C. § 78u 1. See Brief for United States 32-35. ITSFEA declares that "the rules and regulations of the Securities and Exchange Commission under the Securities Exchange Act of 1934 . . . governing trading while in possession of material, nonpublic information are, as required by such Act, necessary and appropriate in the public interest and for the protection of investors." Note following 15 U.S.C. § 78u 1. ITSFEA also includes a new §20A(a) of the Exchange Act expressly providing a private cause of action against persons who violate the Exchange Act "by purchasing or selling a security while in possession of material, nonpublic information"; such an action may be brought by "any person who, contemporaneously with the purchase or sale of securities that is the subject of such violation, has purchased . . . or sold . . . securities of the same class." 15 U.S.C. § 78t 1(a). Because we uphold the misappropriation theory on the basis of §10(b) itself, we do not address ITSFEA's significance for cases of this genre.

[12] In relevant part, §32 of the Exchange Act, as set forth in 15 U.S.C. § 78ff(a), provides:

```
"Any person who willfully violates any provision
of this chapter . . . or any rule or regulation
thereunder the violation of which is made
unlawful or the observance of which is required
under the terms of this chapter . . . shall upon
conviction be fined not more than $1,000,000, or
imprisoned not more than 10 years, or both . .
.; but no person shall be subject to
imprisonment under this section for the
violation of any rule or regulation if he proves
that he had no knowledge of such rule or
regulation."
```

[13] The statute provides no such defense to imposition of monetary fines. See *ibid.*

[14] In addition to §14(e), the Williams Act and the 1970 amendments added to the Exchange Act the following provisions concerning disclosure: §13(d), 15 U.S.C. § 78m(d) (disclosure requirements for persons acquiring more than five percent of certain classes of securities); §13(e), 15 U.S.C. § 78m(e) (authorizing Commission to adopt disclosure requirements for certain repurchases of securities by issuer); §14(d), 15 U.S.C. § 78n(d) (disclosure requirements when tender offer results in offeror owning more than five percent of a class of securities); §14(f), 15 U.S.C. § 78n(f) (disclosure requirements when tender offer results in new corporate directors constituting a majority).

[15] The rule thus adopts for the tender offer context a requirement resembling the one Chief Justice Burger would have adopted in *Chiarella* for misappropriators under §10(b). See *supra,* at 10, n. 6.

[16] The Government draws our attention to the following measures: 17 CFR § 240.15c2-1 (1970) (prohibiting a broker dealer's hypothecation of a customer's securities if hypothecated securities would be commingled with the securities of another customer, absent written consent); §240.15c2-3 (1970) (prohibiting transactions by broker dealers in unvalidated German securities); §240.15c2-4 (1970) (prohibiting broker dealers from accepting any part of the sale price of a security being distributed unless the money received is promptly transmitted to the persons entitled to it); §240.15c2-5 (1970) (requiring broker dealers to provide written disclosure of credit terms and commissions in connection with securities sales in which broker dealers extend credit, or participate in arranging for loans, to the purchasers). See Brief for United States 39, n. 22.

[17] We leave for another day, when the issue requires decision, the legitimacy of Rule 14e-3(a) as

applied to "warehousing," which the Government describes as "the practice by which bidders leak advance information of a tender offer to allies and encourage them to purchase the target company's stock before the bid is announced." Reply Brief 17. As we observed in *Chiarella*, one of the Commission's purposes in proposing Rule 14e-3(a) was "to bar warehousing under its authority to regulate tender offers." 445 U. S., at 234. The Government acknowledges that trading authorized by a principal breaches no fiduciary duty. See Reply Brief 17. The instant case, however, does not involve trading authorized by a principal; therefore, we need not here decide whether the Commission's proscription of warehousing falls within its §14(e) authority to define or prevent fraud.

[18] The Commission's power under §10(b) is more limited. See *supra,* at 6 (Rule 10b-5 may proscribe only conduct that §10(b) prohibits).

[19] The dissent urges that the Commission must be precise about the authority it is exercising--that it must say whether it is acting to "define" or to "prevent" fraud--and that in this instance it has purported only to define, not to prevent. See *post,* at 18-19. The dissent sees this precision in Rule 14e-3(a)'s words: "it shall constitute a fraudulent . . . act . . . within the meaning of section 14(e) . . . ." We do not find the Commission's rule vulnerable for failure to recite as a regulatory preamble: We hereby exercise our authority to "define, and prescribe means reasonably designed to prevent, . . . [fraudulent] acts." Sensibly read, the rule is an exercise of the Commission's full authority. Logically and practically, such a rule may be conceived and defended, alternatively, as definitional or preventive.

[20] The dissent opines that there is no reason to anticipate difficulties in proving breach of duty in "misappropriation" cases. "Once the source of the [purloined] information has been identified," the dissent asserts, "it should be a simple task to obtain proof of any breach of duty." *Post,* at 20. To test that assertion, assume a misappropriating partner at Dorsey & Whitney told his daughter or son and a wealthy friend that a tender for Pillsbury was in the offing, and each tippee promptly purchased Pillsbury stock, the child borrowing the purchase price from the wealthy friend. The dissent's confidence, *post,* at 20, n. 12, that "there is no reason to suspect that the tipper would gratuitously protect the tippee," seems misplaced.

[21] The dissent insists that even if the misappropriation of information from the bidder about a tender offer is fraud, the Commission has not explained why such fraud is "in connection with" a tender offer. *Post,* at 19. What else, one can only wonder, might such fraud be "in connection with"?

[22] Repeating the argument it made concerning the misappropriation theory, see *supra,* at 21, n. 11, the United States urges that Congress confirmed Rule 14e-3(a)'s validity in ITSFEA, 15 U.S.C. § 78u 1. See Brief for United States 44-45. We uphold Rule 14e-3(a) on the basis of §14(e) itself and need not address ITSFEA's relevance to this case.

[23] As to O'Hagan's scienter argument, we reiterate that 15 U.S.C. § 78ff(a) requires the Government to prove "willful[l] violat[ion]" of the securities laws, and that lack of knowledge of the relevant rule is an affirmative defense to a sentence of imprisonment. See *supra,* at 21-22.

[24] The Court of Appeals reversed respondent's money laundering convictions on similar reasoning. See 92 F. 3d, at 628. Because the United States did not seek review of that ruling, we leave undisturbed that portion of the Court of Appeals' judgment.

[25] The dissent finds O'Hagan's convictions on the mail fraud counts, but not on the securities fraud counts, sustainable. *Post,* at 23-24. Under the dissent's view, securities traders like O'Hagan would escape SEC civil actions and federal prosecutions under legislation targeting securities fraud, only to be caught for their trading activities in the broad mail fraud net. If misappropriation theory cases could proceed only under the federal mail and wire fraud statutes, practical consequences for individual defendants might not be large, see Aldave, 49 Ohio St. L. J., at 381, and n. 60; however, "proportionally more persons accused of insider trading [might] be pursued by a U. S. Attorney, and proportionally fewer by the SEC," *id.,* at 382. Our decision, of course, does not rest on such enforcement policy considerations.

MARGARET KAWAAUHAU, et vir v. PAUL W. GEIGER

No. 97-115, March 3, 1998

ON WRIT OF CERTIORARI TO THE UNITED STATES COURT OF APPEALS FOR THE EIGHTH CIRCUIT

Justice Ginsburg delivered the opinion of the Court.

Section 523(a)(6) of the Bankruptcy Code provides that a debt "for willful and malicious injury by the debtor to another" is not dischargeable. 11 U.S.C. § 523(a)(6). The question before us is whether a debt arising from a medical malpractice judgment, attributable to negligent or reckless conduct, falls within this statutory exception. We hold that it does not and that the debt is dischargeable.

I

In January 1983, petitioner Margaret Kawaauhau sought treatment from respondent Dr. Paul Geiger for a foot injury. Geiger examined Kawaauhau and admitted her to the hospital to attend to the risk of infection resulting from the injury. Although Geiger knew that intravenous penicillin would have been more effective, he prescribed oral penicillin, explaining in his testimony that he understood his patient wished to minimize the cost of her treatment.

Geiger then departed on a business trip, leaving Kawaauhau in the care of other physicians, who decided she should be transferred to an infectious disease specialist. When Geiger returned, he canceled the transfer and discontinued all antibiotics because he believed the infection had subsided. Kawaauhau's condition deteriorated over the next few days, requiring the amputation of her right leg below the knee.

Kawaauhau, joined by her husband Solomon, sued Geiger for malpractice. After a trial, the jury found Geiger liable and awarded the Kawaauhaus approximately $355,000 in damages.[1] Geiger, who carried no malpractice insurance,[2] moved to Missouri, where his wages were garnished by the Kawaauhaus. Geiger then petitioned for bankruptcy. The Kawaauhaus requested the Bankruptcy Court to hold the malpractice judgment nondischargeable on the ground that it was a debt "for willful and malicious injury" excepted from discharge by 11 U.S.C. § 523(a)(6). The Bankruptcy Court concluded that Geiger's treatment fell far below the appropriate standard of care and therefore ranked as "willful and malicious." Accordingly, the Bankruptcy Court held the debt nondischargeable. *In re Geiger*, 172 B. R. 916, 922—923 (Bkrtcy. Ct. ED Mo. 1994). In an unpublished order, the District Court affirmed. App. to Pet. for Cert. A—18 to A—22.

A three-judge panel of the Court of Appeals for the Eighth Circuit reversed, 93 F.3d 443 (1996), and a divided en banc court adhered to the panel's position, 113 F.3d 848 (1997) (en banc). Section 523(a)(6)'s exemption from discharge, the en banc court held, is confined to debts "based on what the law has for generations called an intentional tort." *Id.*, at 852. On this view, a debt for malpractice, because it is based on conduct that is negligent or reckless, rather than intentional, remains dischargeable.

The Eighth Circuit acknowledged that its interpretation of §523(a)(6) diverged from previous holdings of the Sixth and Tenth Circuits. See *id.*, at 853 (citing *Perkins* v. *Scharffe*, 817 F.2d 392, 394 (CA6), cert. denied, 484 U.S. 853 (1987), and *In re Franklin*, 726 F.2d 606, 610 (CA10 1984)). We granted certiorari to resolve this conflict, 521 U.S. ___ (1997), and now affirm the Eighth Circuit's judgment.

II

Section 523(a)(6) of the Bankruptcy Code provides:

> "(a) A discharge under Section 727, 1141, 1228(a), 1228(b), or 1328(b) of this title does not discharge an individual debtor from any debt–
>
> . . .
>
> "(6) for willful and malicious injury by the debtor to another entity or to the property of another entity."

The Kawaauhaus urge that the malpractice award fits within this exception because Dr. Geiger intentionally rendered inadequate medical care to Margaret Kawaauhau that necessarily led to her injury. According to the Kawaauhaus, Geiger deliberately chose less effective treatment because he wanted to cut costs, all the while knowing that he was providing substandard care. Such conduct, the Kawaauhaus assert, meets the "willful and malicious" specification of §523(a)(6).

We confront this pivotal question concerning the scope of the "willful and malicious injury" exception: Does §523(a)(6)'s compass cover acts, done intentionally,[3] that cause injury (as the Kawaauhaus urge), or only acts done with the actual intent to cause injury (as the Eighth Circuit ruled)? The words of the statute strongly support the Eighth Circuit's reading.

The word "willful" in (a)(6) modifies the word "injury," indicating that nondischargeability takes a deliberate or intentional *injury*, not merely a deliberate or intentional *act* that leads to injury. Had Congress meant to exempt debts resulting from unintentionally inflicted injuries, it might have described instead "willful acts that cause injury." Or, Congress might have selected an additional word or words, *i.e.*, "reckless" or "negligent," to modify "injury." Moreover, as the Eighth Circuit observed, the (a)(6) formulation triggers in the lawyer's mind the category "intentional torts," as distinguished from negligent or reckless torts. Intentional torts generally require that the actor intend "the *consequences* of an act," not simply "the act itself." Restatement (Second) of Torts §8A, comment *a*, p. 15 (1964) (emphasis added).

The Kawaauhaus' more encompassing interpretation could place within the excepted category a wide range of situations in which an act is intentional, but injury is unintended, *i.e.*, neither desired nor in fact anticipated by the debtor. Every traffic accident stemming from an initial intentional act–for example, intentionally rotating the wheel of an automobile to make a left-hand turn without first checking oncoming traffic–could fit the description. See 113 F.3d, at 852. A "knowing breach of contract" could also qualify. See *ibid.* A construction so broad would be incompatible with the "well-known" guide that exceptions to discharge "should be confined to those plainly expressed." *Gleason* v. *Thaw*, 236 U.S. 558, 562 (1915).

Furthermore, "we are hesitant to adopt an interpretation of a congressional enactment which renders superfluous another portion of that same law." *Mackey* v. *Lanier Collection Agency & Service, Inc.*, 486 U.S. 825, 837 (1988). Reading §523(a)(6) as the Kawaauhaus urge would obviate the need for §523(a)(9), which specifically exempts debts "for death or personal injury caused by the debtor's operation of a motor vehicle if such operation was unlawful because the debtor was intoxicated from using alcohol, a drug, or another substance." 11 U.S.C. § 523(a)(9); see also 11 U.S.C. § 523(a)(12) (exempting debts for "malicious or reckless failure" to fulfill certain commitments owed to a federal depository institutions regulatory agency).[4]

The Kawaauhaus heavily rely on *Tinker* v. *Colwell*, 193 U.S. 473 (1904), which presented this question: Does an award of damages for "criminal conversation" survive bankruptcy under the 1898 Bankruptcy Act's exception from discharge for judgments in civil actions for "'willful and malicious injuries to the person or property of another'"? *Id.*, at 480. The *Tinker* Court held such an award a nondischargeable debt. The Kawaauhaus feature certain statements in the *Tinker* opinion, in particular: "[An] act is willful ... in the sense that it is intentional and voluntary" even if performed "without any particular malice," *id.*, at 485; an act that "necessarily causes injury and is done intentionally, may be said to be done willfully and maliciously, so as to come within the [bankruptcy discharge] exception," *id.*, at 487. See also *id.*, at 486 (the statute exempts from discharge liability for "'a wrongful act, done intentionally, without just cause or excuse'") (quoting from definition of malice in *Bromage* v. *Prosser*, 4 Barn. & Cress. 247, 107 Eng. Rep. 1051 (K. B. 1825)).

The exposition in the *Tinker* opinion is less than crystalline. Counterbalancing the portions the Kawaauhaus emphasize, the *Tinker* Court repeatedly observed that the tort in question qualified in the common law as trespassory. Indeed, it ranked as "trespass *vi et armis*." 193 U.S., at 482, 483. Criminal conversation, the Court noted, was an action akin to a master's "action of trespass and assault ... for the battery of his servant," *id.*, at 482. *Tinker* thus placed criminal conversation solidly within the traditional intentional tort category, and we so confine its holding. That decision, we clarify, provides no warrant for departure from the current statutory instruction that, to be nondischargeable, the judgment debt must be "for willful and malicious *injury*."

Subsequent decisions of this Court are in accord with our construction. In *McIntyre* v. *Kavanaugh*, 242 U.S. 138 (1916), a broker "deprive[d] another of his property forever by deliberately disposing of it without semblance of authority." *Id.*, at 141. The Court held that this act constituted an intentional injury to property of another, bringing it within the discharge exception. But in *Davis* v. *Aetna Acceptance Co.*, 293 U.S. 328 (1934), the Court explained that not every tort judgment for conversion is exempt from discharge. Negligent or reckless acts, the Court held, do not suffice to establish that a resulting injury is "wilful and malicious." See *id.*, at 332.

Finally, the Kawaauhaus maintain that, as a policy matter, malpractice judgments should be excepted from discharge, at least when the debtor acted recklessly or carried no malpractice insurance. Congress, of course, may so decide. But unless and until Congress makes such a decision, we must follow the current direction §523(a)(6) provides.

* * *

We hold that debts arising from recklessly or negligently inflicted injuries do not fall within the compass of §523(a)(6). For the reasons stated, the judgment of the Court of Appeals for the Eighth Circuit is Affirmed.

NOTES

[1] The jury awarded Margaret Kawaauhau $203,040 in special damages and $99,000 in general

damages. *In re Geiger*, 172 B. R. 916, 919 (Bkrtcy. Ct. ED Mo. 1994). In addition, the jury awarded Solomon Kawaauhau $18,000 in general damages for loss of consortium and $35,000 for emotional distress. Ibid.

[2] Although the record is not clear on this point, it appears that Dr. Geiger was not required by state law to carry medical malpractice insurance. See Tr. of Oral Arg. 19.

[3] The word "willful" is defined in Black's Law Dictionary as "volun-tary" or "intentional." Black's Law Dictionary 1434 (5th ed. 1979). Consistently, legislative reports note that the word "willful" in §523(a)(6) means "deliberate or intentional." See S. Rep. No. 95—989, p. 79 (1978); H. R. Rep. No. 95—595, p. 365 (1977).

[4] Sections 523(a)(9) and (12) were added to the Bankruptcy Code in 1984 and 1990 respectively. See Pub. L. No. 98—353, 98 Stat. 364 (1984) and Pub. L. No. 101—647, 104 Stat. 4865 (1990).

RUHRGAS AG v. MARATHON OIL CO. et al.

No. 98-470, May 17, 1999

ON WRIT OF CERTIORARI TO THE UNITED STATES COURT OF APPEALS FOR THE FIFTH CIRCUIT

Justice Ginsburg delivered the opinion of the Court.

This case concerns the authority of the federal courts to adjudicate controversies. Jurisdiction to resolve cases on the merits requires both authority over the category of claim in suit (subject-matter jurisdiction) and authority over the parties (personal jurisdiction), so that the court's decision will bind them. In *Steel Co.* v. *Citizens for Better Environment,* 523 U.S. 83 (1998), this Court adhered to the rule that a federal court may not hypothesize subject-matter jurisdiction for the purpose of deciding the merits. *Steel Co.* rejected a doctrine, once approved by several Courts of Appeals, that allowed federal tribunals to pretermit jurisdictional objections "where (1) the merits question is more readily resolved, and (2) the prevailing party on the merits would be the same as the prevailing party were jurisdiction denied." *Id.,* at 93. Recalling "a long and venerable line of our cases," *id.,* at 94, *Steel Co.* reiterated: "The requirement that jurisdiction be established as a threshold matter ... is 'inflexible and without exception,'" *id.,* at 94—95 (quoting *Mansfield, C. & L. M. R. Co.* v. *Swan,* 111 U.S. 379, 382 (1884)); for "[j]urisdiction is power to declare the law," and "'[w]ithout jurisdiction the court cannot proceed at all in any cause,'" 523 U.S., at 94 (quoting *Ex parte McCardle,* 7 Wall. 506, 514 (1869)). The Court, in *Steel Co.,* acknowledged that "the absolute purity" of the jurisdiction-first rule had been diluted in a few extraordinary cases, 523 U.S., at 101, and Justice O'Connor, joined by Justice Kennedy, joined the majority on the understanding that the Court's opinion did not catalog "an exhaustive list of circumstances" in which exceptions to the solid rule were appropriate, *id.,* at 110.

Steel Co. is the backdrop for the issue now before us: If, as *Steel Co.* held, jurisdiction generally must precede merits in dispositional order, must subject-matter jurisdiction precede personal jurisdiction on the decisional line? Or, do federal district courts have discretion to avoid a difficult question of subject-matter jurisdiction when the absence of personal jurisdiction is the surer ground? The particular civil action we confront was commenced in state court and removed to federal court. The specific question on which we granted certiorari asks "[w]hether a federal district court is absolutely barred in all circumstances from dismissing a removed case for lack of personal jurisdiction without first deciding its subject-matter jurisdiction." Pet. for Cert. i.

We hold that in cases removed from state court to federal court, as in cases originating in federal court, there is no unyielding jurisdictional hierarchy. Customarily, a federal court first resolves doubts about its jurisdiction over the subject matter, but there are circumstances in which a district court appropriately accords priority to a personal jurisdiction inquiry. The proceeding before us is such a case.

I

The underlying controversy stems from a venture to produce gas in the Heimdal Field of the Norwegian North Sea. In 1976, respondents Marathon Oil Company and Marathon International Oil Company acquired Marathon Petroleum Company (Norway) (MPCN) and respondent Marathon Petroleum Norge (Norge). See App. 26. [1] Before the acquisition, Norge held a license to produce gas in the Heimdal Field; following the transaction, Norge assigned the license to MPCN. See Record, Exhs. 61 and 62 to Document 64. In 1981, MPCN contracted to sell 70% of its share of the Heimdal gas production to a group of European buyers, including petitioner Ruhrgas AG. See Record, Exh. 1 to Document 63, pp. 90, 280. The parties' agreement was incorporated into the Heimdal Gas Sales Agreement (Heimdal Agreement), which is "governed by and construed in accordance with Norwegian Law," Record, Exh. B, Tab 1 to Pet. for Removal, Heimdal Agreement, p. 102; disputes thereunder are to be "exclusively and finally ... settled by arbitration in Stockholm, Sweden, in accordance with" International Chamber of Commerce rules, *id.,* at 100.

II

Marathon Oil Company, Marathon International Oil Company, and Norge (collectively, Marathon) filed this lawsuit against Ruhrgas in Texas state court on July 6, 1995, asserting state-law claims of fraud, tortious interference with prospective business relations, participation in breach of fiduciary duty, and civil conspiracy. See App. 33—40. Marathon Oil Company and Marathon International Oil Company alleged that Ruhrgas and the other European buyers induced them with false promises of "premium prices" and guaranteed pipeline tariffs to invest over $300 million in MPCN for the development of the Heimdal Field and the erection of a pipeline to Ruhrgas' plant in Germany. See *id.,* at 26—28; Brief for Respondents 1—2. Norge alleged that Ruhrgas' effective monopolization of the Heimdal gas diminished the value of the license Norge had assigned to MPCN. See App. 31, 33, 357; Brief for Respondents 2. Marathon asserted that Ruhrgas had furthered its plans at three meetings in Houston, Texas, and through a stream of correspondence directed to Marathon in Texas. See App. 229, 233.

Ruhrgas removed the case to the District Court for the Southern District of Texas. See 145 F.3d 211, 214 (CA5 1998). In its notice of removal, Ruhrgas asserted three bases for federal jurisdiction: diversity of citizenship, see 28 U.S.C. § 1332 (1994 ed. and Supp. III), on the theory that Norge, the only nondiverse plaintiff, had been fraudulently joined;[2] federal question, see §1331, because Marathon's claims "raise[d] substantial questions of foreign and international relations, which are incorporated into and form part of the federal common law," App. 274; and 9 U.S.C. § 205 which authorizes removal of cases "relat[ing] to" international arbitration agreements.[3] See 145 F.3d, at 214—215; 115 F.3d 315, 319—321 (CA5), vacated and rehearing en banc granted, 129 F.3d 746 (1997). Ruhrgas moved to dismiss the complaint for lack of personal jurisdiction. Marathon moved to remand the case to the state court for lack of federal subject-matter jurisdiction. See 145 F.3d, at 215.

After permitting jurisdictional discovery, the District Court dismissed the case for lack of personal jurisdiction. See App. 455. In so ruling, the District Court relied on Fifth Circuit precedent allowing district courts to adjudicate personal jurisdiction without first establishing subject-matter jurisdiction. See id., at 445. Texas' long-arm statute, see Tex. Civ. Prac. & Rem. Code Ann. §17.042 (1997), authorizes personal jurisdiction to the extent allowed by the Due Process Clause of the Federal Constitution. See App. 446; Kawasaki Steel Corp. v. Middleton, 699 S.W. 2d 199, 200 (Tex. 1985). The District Court addressed the constitutional question and concluded that Ruhrgas' contacts with Texas were insufficient to support personal jurisdiction. See App. 445—454. Finding "no evidence that Ruhrgas engaged in any tortious conduct in Texas," id., at 450, the court determined that Marathon's complaint did not present circumstances adequately affiliating Ruhrgas with Texas, see id., at 448. [4]

A panel of the Court of Appeals for the Fifth Circuit concluded that "respec[t]" for "the proper balance of federalism" impelled it to turn first to "the formidable subject matter jurisdiction issue presented." 115 F.3d, at 318. After examining and rejecting each of Ruhrgas' asserted bases of federal jurisdiction, see id., at 319—321,[5] the Court of Appeals vacated the judgment of the District Court and ordered the case remanded to the state court, see id., at 321. This Court denied Ruhrgas' petition for a writ of certiorari, which was limited to the question whether subject-matter jurisdiction existed under 9 U.S.C. § 205. See 522 U.S. 967 (1997).

The Fifth Circuit, on its own motion, granted rehearing en banc, thereby vacating the panel decision. See 129 F.3d 746 (1997). In a 9-to-7 decision, the en banc court held that, in removed cases, district courts must decide issues of subject-matter jurisdiction first, reaching issues of personal jurisdiction "only if subject-matter jurisdiction is found to exist." 145 F.3d, at 214. Noting Steel Co.'s instruction that subject-matter jurisdiction must be "'established as a threshold matter,'" 145 F.3d, at 217 (quoting 523 U.S., at 94), the Court of Appeals derived from that decision "counsel against" recognition of judicial discretion to proceed directly to personal jurisdiction. 145 F.3d, at 218. The court limited its holding to removed cases; it perceived in those cases the most grave threat that federal courts would "usur[p] … state courts' residual jurisdiction." Id., at 219.[6]

Writing for the seven dissenters, Judge Higginbotham agreed that subject-matter jurisdiction ordinarily should be considered first. See id., at 231. If the challenge to personal jurisdiction involves no complex state-law questions, however, and is more readily resolved than the challenge to subject-matter jurisdiction, the District Court, in the dissenters' view, should take the easier route. See ibid. Judge Higginbotham regarded the District Court's decision dismissing Marathon's case as illustrative and appropriate: While Ruhrgas' argument under 9 U.S.C. § 205 presented a difficult issue of first impression, its personal jurisdiction challenge raised "[n]o substantial questions of purely state law," and "could be resolved relatively easily in [Ruhrgas'] favor." 145 F.3d, at 232—233.

We granted certiorari, 525 U.S. __ (1998), to resolve a conflict between the Circuits[7] and now reverse.

III

Steel Co. held that Article III generally requires a federal court to satisfy itself of its jurisdiction over the subject matter before it considers the merits of a case. "For a court to pronounce upon [the merits] when it has no jurisdiction to do so," Steel Co. declared, "is … for a court to act ultra vires." 523 U.S., at 101—102. The Fifth Circuit incorrectly read Steel Co. to teach that subject-matter jurisdiction must be found to exist, not only before a federal court reaches the merits, but also before personal jurisdiction is addressed. See 145 F.3d, at 218.

A

The Court of Appeals accorded priority to the requirement of subject-matter jurisdiction because it is nonwaiv-able and delimits federal-court power, while restrictions on a court's jurisdiction over the person are waivable and protect individual rights. See id., at 217—218. The character of the two jurisdictional bedrocks unquestionably differs. Subject-matter limitations on federal jurisdiction serve institutional interests. They keep the federal courts within the bounds the Constitution and Congress have prescribed. Accordingly, subject-matter delineations must be policed by the courts on their own initiative even at the highest level. See Steel Co., 523 U.S., at 94—95; Fed. Rule Civ. Proc.12(h)(3) ("Whenever it appears … that the court lacks jurisdiction of the subject matter, the court shall dismiss the action."); 28 U.S.C. § 1447(c) (1994 ed., Supp. III) ("If at any time before final judgment [in a removed case] it appears that the district court lacks subject matter jurisdiction, the case shall be remanded.").

Personal jurisdiction, on the other hand, "represents a restriction on judicial power ... as a matter of individual liberty." *Insurance Corp. of Ireland* v. *Compagnie des Bauxites de Guinee,* 456 U.S. 694, 702 (1982). Therefore, a party may insist that the limitation be observed, or he may forgo that right, effectively consenting to the court's exercise of adjudicatory authority. See Fed. Rule Civ. Proc.12(h)(1) (defense of lack of jurisdiction over the person waivable); *Insurance Corp. of Ireland,* 456 U.S., at 703 (same).

These distinctions do not mean that subject-matter jurisdiction is ever and always the more "fundamental." Personal jurisdiction, too, is "an essential element of the jurisdiction of a district ... court," without which the court is "powerless to proceed to an adjudication." *Employers Reinsurance Corp.* v. *Bryant,* 299 U.S. 374, 382 (1937). In this case, indeed, the impediment to subject-matter jurisdiction on which Marathon relies–lack of complete diversity–rests on statutory interpretation, not constitutional command. Marathon joined an alien plaintiff (Norge) as well as an alien defendant (Ruhrgas). If the joinder of Norge is legitimate, the complete diversity required by 28 U.S.C. § 1332 (1994 ed. and Supp. III), but not by Article III, see *State Farm Fire & Casualty Co.* v. *Tashire,* 386 U.S. 523, 530—531 (1967), is absent. In contrast, Ruhrgas relies on the constitutional safeguard of due process to stop the court from proceeding to the merits of the case. See *Insurance Corp. of Ireland,* 456 U.S., at 702 ("The requirement that a court have personal jurisdiction flows ... from the Due Process Clause.").

While *Steel Co.* reasoned that subject-matter jurisdiction necessarily precedes a ruling on the merits, the same principle does not dictate a sequencing of jurisdictional issues. "[A] court that dismisses on ... non-merits grounds such as ... personal jurisdiction, before finding subject-matter jurisdiction, makes no assumption of law-declaring power that violates the separation of powers principles underlying *Mansfield* and *Steel Company*." *Inre Papandreou,* 139 F.3d 247, 255 (CADC 1998). It is hardly novel for a federal court to choose among threshold grounds for denying audience to a case on the merits. Thus, as the Court observed in *Steel Co.*, district courts do not overstep Article III limits when they decline jurisdiction of state-law claims on discretionary grounds without determining whether those claims fall within their pendent jurisdiction, see *Moor* v. *County of Alameda,* 411 U.S. 693, 715—716 (1973), or abstain under *Younger* v. *Harris,* 401 U.S. 37 (1971), without deciding whether the parties present a case or controversy, see *Ellis* v. *Dyson,* 421 U.S. 426, 433 —434 (1975). See *Steel Co.,* 523 U.S., at 100—101, n.3; cf. *Arizonans for Official English* v. *Arizona,* 520 U.S. 43, 66— 67 (1997) (pretermitting challenge to appellants' standing and dismissing on mootness grounds).

B

Maintaining that subject-matter jurisdiction must be decided first even when the litigation originates in federal court, see Tr. of Oral Arg. 21; Brief for Respondents 13, Marathon sees removal as the more offensive case, on the ground that the dignity of state courts is immediately at stake. If a federal court dismisses a removed case for want of personal jurisdiction, that determination may preclude the parties from relitigating the very same personal jurisdiction issue in state court. See *Baldwin* v. *Iowa State Traveling Men's Assn.,* 283 U.S. 522, 524—527 (1931) (personal jurisdiction ruling has issue-preclusive effect).

Issue preclusion in subsequent state-court litigation, however, may also attend a federal court's subject-matter determination. Ruhrgas hypothesizes, for example, a defendant who removes on diversity grounds a state-court suit seeking $50,000 in compensatory and $1 million in punitive damages for breach of contract. See Tr. of Oral Arg. 10—11. If the district court determines that state law does not allow punitive damages for breach of contract and therefore remands the removed action for failure to satisfy the amount in controversy, see 28 U.S.C. § 1332(a) (1994 ed., Supp. III) ($75,000), the federal court's conclusion will travel back with the case. Assuming a fair airing of the issue in federal court, that court's ruling on permissible state-law damages may bind the parties in state court, although it will set no precedent otherwise governing state-court adjudications. See *Chicot County Drainage Dist.* v. *Baxter State Bank,* 308 U.S. 371, 376 (1940) ("[Federal courts'] determinations of [whether they have jurisdiction to entertain a case] may not be assailed collaterally."); Restatement (Second) of Judgments §12, p. 115 (1980) ("When a court has rendered a judgment in a contested action, the judgment [ordinarily] precludes the parties from litigating the question of the court's subject matter jurisdiction in subsequent litigation."). Similarly, as Judge Higginbotham observed, our "dualistic ... system of federal and state courts" allows federal courts to make issue-preclusive rulings about state law in the exercise of supplemental jurisdiction under 28 U.S.C. § 1367. 145 F.3d, at 231, and n.7.

Most essentially, federal and state courts are complementary systems for administering justice in our Nation. Cooperation and comity, not competition and conflict, are essential to the federal design. A State's dignitary interest bears consideration when a district court exercises discretion in a case of this order. If personal jurisdiction raises "difficult questions of [state] law," and subject-matter jurisdiction is resolved "as eas[ily]" as personal jurisdiction, a district court will ordinarily conclude that "federalism concerns tip the scales in favor of initially ruling on the motion to remand." *Allen* v. *Ferguson,* 791 F.2d 611, 616 (CA7 1986). In other cases, however, the district court may find that concerns of judicial economy and restraint are overriding. See, *e.g., Asociacion Nacional de Pescadores* v. *Dow Quimica,* 988 F.2d 559, 566 —567 (CA5 1993) (if removal is nonfrivolous and personal jurisdiction turns on federal constitutional issues, "federal intrusion into state courts' authority ... is minimized"). The federal design allows leeway for sensitive judgments of this sort. "'Our Federalism'"

"does not mean blind deference to 'States' Rights' any more than it means centralization of control over every important issue in our National Government and its courts. The Framers rejected both these courses. What the concept does represent is a system in which there is sensitivity to the legitimate interests of both State and National Governments."

Younger, 401 U.S., at 44.

The Fifth Circuit and Marathon posit that state-court defendants will abuse the federal system with opportunistic removals. A discretionary rule, they suggest, will encourage manufactured, convoluted federal subject-matter theories designed to wrench cases from state court. See 145 F.3d, at 219; Brief for Respondents 28—29. This specter of unwarranted removal, we have recently observed, "rests on an assumption we do not indulge–that district courts generally will not comprehend, or will balk at applying, the rules on removal Congress has prescribed…. The well-advised defendant … will foresee the likely outcome of an unwarranted removal–a swift and nonreviewable remand order, see 28 U.S.C. § 1447(c), (d), attended by the displeasure of a district court whose authority has been improperly invoked." *Caterpillar Inc.* v. *Lewis*, 519 U.S. 61, 77—78 (1996).

C

In accord with Judge Higginbotham, we recognize that in most instances subject-matter jurisdiction will involve no arduous inquiry. See 145 F.3d, at 229 ("engag[ing]" subject-matter jurisdiction "at the outset of a case … [is] often … the most efficient way of going"). In such cases, both expedition and sensitivity to state courts' coequal stature should impel the federal court to dispose of that issue first. See *Cantor Fitzgerald, L. P.* v. *Peaslee*, 88 F.3d 152, 155 (CA2 1996) (a court disposing of a case on personal jurisdiction grounds "should be convinced that the challenge to the court's subject-matter jurisdiction is not easily resolved"). Where, as here, however, a district court has before it a straightforward personal jurisdiction issue presenting no complex question of state law, and the alleged defect in subject-matter jurisdiction raises a difficult and novel question, the court does not abuse its discretion by turning directly to personal jurisdiction.[8]

* * *

For the reasons stated, the judgment of the Court of Appeals is reversed, and the case is remanded for proceedings consistent with this opinion.

It is so ordered.

NOTES

[1] Ruhrgas is a German corporation; Norge is a Norwegian corporation. See App. 21, 22. Marathon Oil Company, an Ohio corporation, and Marathon International Oil Company, a Delaware corporation, moved their principal places of business from Ohio to Texas while the venture underlying this case was in formation. See *id.*, at 21, 239, and n.11.

[2] A suit between "citizens of a State and citizens or subjects of a foreign state" lies within federal diversity jurisdiction. 28 U.S.C. § 1332(a)(2). Section 1332 has been interpreted to require "complete diversity." See *Strawbridge* v. *Curtiss*, 3 Cranch 267 (1806); R. Fallon, D. Meltzer, & D. Shapiro, Hart and Wechsler's The Federal Courts and the Federal System 1528—1531 (4th ed. 1996). The foreign citizenship of defendant Ruhrgas, a German corporation, and plaintiff Norge, a Norwegian corporation, rendered diversity incomplete.

[3] Title 9 U.S.C. § 205 allows removal "[w]here the subject matter of an action or proceeding pending in a State court relates to an arbitration agreement or award falling under the Convention [on the Recognition and Enforcement of Foreign Arbitral Awards of June 10, 1958]."

[4] Respecting the three meetings Ruhrgas attended in Houston, Texas, see *supra*, at 4, the District Court concluded that Marathon had not shown that Ruhrgas pursued the alleged pattern of fraud and misrepresentation during the Houston meetings. See App. 449. The court further found that Ruhrgas attended those meetings "due to the [Heimdal Agreement] with MPCN." *Id.*, at 450. As the Heimdal Agreement provides for arbitration in Sweden, the court reasoned, "Ruhrgas could not have expected to be haled into Texas courts based on these meetings." *Ibid.* The court also determined that Ruhrgas did not have "systematic and continuous contacts with Texas" of the kind that would "subject it to general jurisdiction in Texas." *Id.*, at 453 (citing *Helicopteros Nacionales de Colombia, S. A.* v. *Hall*, 466 U.S. 408 (1984)).

[5] The Court of Appeals concluded that whether Norge had a legal interest in the Heimdal license notwithstanding its assignment to MPCN likely turned on difficult questions of Norwegian law; Ruhrgas therefore could not show, at the outset, that Norge had been fraudulently joined as a plaintiff to defeat diversity. See 115 F.3d 315, 319— 320 (CA5), vacated and rehearing en banc granted, 129 F.3d 746

(1997). The appeals court also determined that Marathon's claims did not "strike at the sovereignty of a foreign nation," so as to raise a federal question on that account. 115 F.3d, at 320. Finally, the court concluded that Marathon asserted claims independent of the Heimdal Agreement and that the case therefore did not "relat[e] to" an international arbitration agreement under 9 U.S.C. § 205. See 115 F.3d, at 320—321.

[6] The Fifth Circuit remanded the case to the District Court for it to consider the "nove[l]" subject-matter jurisdiction issues presented. 145 F.3d 211, 225 (CA5 1998). The appeals court "express[ed] no opinion" on the vacated panel decision which had held that the District Court lacked subject-matter jurisdiction. *Id.*, at 225, n. 23.

[7] The Court of Appeals for the Second Circuit has concluded that district courts have discretion to dismiss a removed case for want of personal jurisdiction without reaching the issue of subject-matter jurisdiction. See *Cantor Fitzgerald, L.P.* v. *Peaslee*, 88 F.3d 152, 155 (1996).

[8] Ruhrgas suggests that it would be appropriate simply to affirm the District Court's holding that it lacked personal jurisdiction over Ruhrgas. See Brief for Petitioner 38—39, and n.20. That issue is not within the question presented and is properly considered by the Fifth Circuit on remand.

TOMMY OLMSTEAD, COMMISSIONER, GEORGIA DEPARTMENT OF HUMAN RESOURCES, et al. v. L. C., by JONATHAN ZIMRING, guardian ad litem and next friend, et al.

No. 98-536, June 22, 1999

ON WRIT OF CERTIORARI TO THE UNITED STATES COURT OF APPEALS FOR THE ELEVENTH CIRCUIT

Justice Ginsburg announced the judgment of the Court and delivered the opinion of the Court with respect to Parts I, II, and III—A, and an opinion with respect to Part III—B, in which O'Connor, Souter, and Breyer, JJ., joined.

This case concerns the proper construction of the anti-discrimination provision contained in the public services portion (Title II) of the Americans with Disabilities Act of 1990, 104 Stat. 337, 42 U.S.C. § 12132. Specifically, we confront the question whether the proscription of discrimination may require placement of persons with mental disabilities in community settings rather than in institutions. The answer, we hold, is a qualified yes. Such action is in order when the State's treatment professionals have determined that community placement is appropriate, the transfer from institutional care to a less restrictive setting is not opposed by the affected individual, and the placement can be reasonably accommodated, taking into account the resources available to the State and the needs of others with mental disabilities. In so ruling, we affirm the decision of the Eleventh Circuit in substantial part. We remand the case, however, for further consideration of the appropriate relief, given the range of facilities the State maintains for the care and treatment of persons with diverse mental disabilities, and its obligation to administer services with an even hand.

I

This case, as it comes to us, presents no constitutional question. The complaints filed by plaintiffs-respondents L. C. and E. W. did include such an issue; L. C. and E. W. alleged that defendants-petitioners, Georgia health care officials, failed to afford them minimally adequate care and freedom from undue restraint, in violation of their rights under the Due Process Clause of the Fourteenth Amendment. See Complaint ¶¶87—91; Intervenor's Complaint ¶¶30—34. But neither the District Court nor the Court of Appeals reached those Fourteenth Amendment claims. See Civ. No. 1:95—cv—1210—MHS (ND Ga., Mar. 26, 1997), pp. 5—6, 11—13, App. to Pet. for Cert. 34a—35a, 40a—41a; 138 F.3d 893, 895, and n. 3 (CA11 1998). Instead, the courts below resolved the case solely on statutory grounds. Our review is similarly confined. Cf. *Cleburne* v. *Cleburne Living Center, Inc.*, 473 U.S. 432, 450 (1985) (Texas city's requirement of special use permit for operation of group home for mentally retarded, when other care and multiple-dwelling facilities were freely permitted, lacked rational basis and therefore violated Equal Protection Clause of Fourteenth Amendment). Mindful that it is a statute we are construing, we set out first the legislative and regulatory prescriptions on which the case turns.

In the opening provisions of the ADA, Congress stated findings applicable to the statute in all its parts. Most relevant to this case, Congress determined that

> "(2) historically, society has tended to isolate and segregate individuals with disabilities, and, despite some improvements, such forms of discrimination against individuals with disabilities continue to be a serious and pervasive social problem;
>
> "(3) discrimination against individuals with disabilities persists in such critical areas as . . . institutionalization . . . ;
>
> "(5) individuals with disabilities continually encounter various forms of discrimination, including outright intentional exclusion, . . . failure to make modifications to existing facilities and practices, . . . [and] segregation . . . ." 42 U.S.C. § 12101(a)(2), (3), (5).[1]

Congress then set forth prohibitions against discrimination in employment (Title I, §§12111—12117), public services furnished by governmental entities (Title II, §§12131—12165), and public accommodations provided by private entities (Title III, §§12181—12189). The statute as a whole is intended "to provide a clear and comprehensive national mandate for the elimination of discrimination against individuals with disabilities." §12101(b)(1).[2]

This case concerns Title II, the public services portion of the ADA.[3] The provision of Title II centrally at issue reads:

"Subject to the provisions of this subchapter, no qualified individual with a disability shall, by reason of such disability, be excluded from participation in or be denied the benefits of the services, programs, or activities of a public entity, or be subjected to discrimination by any such entity." §12132.

Title II's definition section states that "public entity" includes "any State or local government," and "any department, agency, [or] special purpose district." §§12131(1)(A), (B). The same section defines "qualified individual with a disability" as

"an individual with a disability who, with or without reasonable modifications to rules, policies, or practices, the removal of architectural, communication, or transportation barriers, or the provision of auxiliary aids and services, meets the essential eligibility requirements for the receipt of services or the participation in programs or activities provided by a public entity." §12131(2).

On redress for violations of §12132's discrimination prohibition, Congress referred to remedies available under §505 of the Rehabilitation Act of 1973, 92 Stat. 2982, 29 U.S.C. § 794a. See 42 U.S.C. § 12133 ("The remedies, procedures, and rights set forth in [§505 of the Rehabilitation Act] shall be the remedies, procedures, and rights this subchapter provides to any person alleging discrimination on the basis of disability in violation of section 12132 of this title.").[4]

Congress instructed the Attorney General to issue regulations implementing provisions of Title II, including §12132's discrimination proscription. See §12134(a) ("[T]he Attorney General shall promulgate regulations in an accessible format that implement this part.").[5] The Attorney General's regulations, Congress further directed, "shall be consistent with this chapter and with the coordination regulations . . . applicable to recipients of Federal financial assistance under [§504 of the Rehabilitation Act]." 42 U.S.C. § 12134(b). One of the §504 regulations requires recipients of federal funds to "administer programs and activities in the most integrated setting appropriate to the needs of qualified handicapped persons." 28 CFR § 41.51(d) (1998).

As Congress instructed, the Attorney General issued Title II regulations, see 28 CFR pt. 35 (1998), including one modeled on the §504 regulation just quoted; called the "integration regulation," it reads:

"A public entity shall administer services, programs, and activities in the most integrated setting appropriate to the needs of qualified individuals with disabilities." 28 CFR § 35.130(d) (1998).

The preamble to the Attorney General's Title II regulations defines "the most integrated setting appropriate to the needs of qualified individuals with disabilities" to mean "a setting that enables individuals with disabilities to interact with non-disabled persons to the fullest extent possible." 28 CFR pt. 35, App. A, p. 450 (1998). Another regulation requires public entities to "make reasonable modifications" to avoid "discrimination on the basis of disability," unless those modifications would entail a "fundamenta[l] alter[ation]"; called here the "reasonable-modifications regulation," it provides:

"A public entity shall make reasonable modifications in policies, practices, or procedures when the modifications are necessary to avoid discrimination on the basis of disability, unless the public entity can demonstrate that making the modifications would fundamentally alter the nature of the service, program, or activity." 28 CFR § 35.130(b)(7) (1998).

We recite these regulations with the caveat that we do not here determine their validity. While the parties differ on the proper construction and enforcement of the regulations, we do not understand petitioners to challenge the regulatory formulations themselves as outside the congressional authorization. See Brief for Petitioners 16—17, 36, 40—41; Reply Brief 15—16 (challenging the Attorney General's interpretation of the integration regulation).

II

With the key legislative provisions in full view, we summarize the facts underlying this dispute. Respondents L. C. and E. W. are mentally retarded women; L. C. has also been diagnosed with schizophrenia, and E. W., with a personality disorder. Both women have a history of treatment in institutional settings. In May 1992, L. C. was voluntarily admitted to Georgia Regional Hospital at Atlanta (GRH), where she was confined for treatment in a psychiatric unit. By May 1993, her psychiatric condition had stabilized, and L. C.'s treatment team at GRH agreed that her needs could be met appropriately in one of the community-based programs the State supported. Despite this evaluation, L. C. remained institutionalized until February 1996, when the State placed her in a community-based treatment program.

E. W. was voluntarily admitted to GRH in February 1995; like L. C., E. W. was confined for treatment in a psychiatric unit. In March 1995, GRH sought to discharge E. W. to a homeless shelter, but abandoned that plan after her attorney filed an administrative complaint. By 1996, E. W.'s treating psychiatrist concluded that she could be treated appropriately in a community-based setting. She nonetheless remained institutionalized until a few months after the District Court issued its judgment in this case in 1997.

In May 1995, when she was still institutionalized at GRH, L. C. filed suit in the United States District Court for the Northern District of Georgia, challenging her continued confinement in a segregated environment. Her complaint invoked 42 U.S.C. § 1983 and provisions of the ADA, §§12131—12134, and named as defendants, now petitioners, the Commissioner of the Georgia Department of Human Resources, the Superintendent of GRH, and the Executive Director of the Fulton County Regional Board (collectively, the State). L. C. alleged that the State's failure to place her in a community-based program, once her treating professionals determined that such placement was appropriate, violated, *inter alia,* Title II of the ADA. L. C.'s pleading requested, among other things, that the State place her in a community care residential program, and that she receive treatment with the ultimate goal of integrating her into the mainstream of society. E. W. intervened in the action, stating an identical claim.[6]

The District Court granted partial summary judgment in favor of L. C. and E. W. See App. to Pet. for Cert. 31a—42a. The court held that the State's failure to place L. C. and E. W. in an appropriate community-based treatment program violated Title II of the ADA. See *id.,* at 39a, 41a. In so ruling, the court rejected the State's argument that inadequate funding, not discrimination against L. C. and E. W. "by reason of" their disabilities, accounted for their retention at GRH. Under Title II, the court concluded, "unnecessary institutional segregation of the disabled constitutes discrimination *per se,* which cannot be justified by a lack of funding." *Id.,* at 37a.

In addition to contending that L. C. and E. W. had not shown discrimination "by reason of [their] disabilit[ies]," the State resisted court intervention on the ground that requiring immediate transfers in cases of this order would "fundamentally alter" the State's activity. The State reasserted that it was already using all available funds to provide services to other persons with disabilities. See *id.,* at 38a. Rejecting the State's "fundamental alteration" defense, the court observed that existing state programs provided community-based treatment of the kind for which L. C. and E. W. qualified, and that the State could "provide services to plaintiffs in the community at considerably *less* cost than is required to maintain them in an institution." *Id.,* at 39a.

The Court of Appeals for the Eleventh Circuit affirmed the judgment of the District Court, but remanded for reassessment of the State's cost-based defense. See 138 F.3d, at 905. As the appeals court read the statute and regulations: When "a disabled individual's treating professionals find that a community-based placement is appropriate for that individual, the ADA imposes a duty to provide treatment in a community setting–the most integrated setting appropriate to that patient's needs"; "[w]here there is no such finding [by the treating professionals], nothing in the ADA requires the deinstitutionalization of th[e] patient." *Id.,* at 902.

The Court of Appeals recognized that the State's duty to provide integrated services "is not absolute"; under the Attorney General's Title II regulation, "reasonable modifications" were required of the State, but fundamental alterations were not demanded. *Id.,* at 904. The appeals court thought it clear, however, that "Congress wanted to permit a cost defense only in the most limited of circumstances." *Id.,* at 902. In conclusion, the court stated that a cost justification would fail "[u]nless the State can prove that requiring it to [expend additional funds in order to provide L. C. and E. W. with integrated services] would be so unreasonable given the demands of the State's mental health budget that it would fundamentally alter the service [the State] provides." *Id.,* at 905. Because it appeared that the District Court had entirely ruled out a "lack of funding" justification, see App. to Pet. for Cert. 37a, the appeals court remanded, repeating that the District Court should consider, among other things, "whether the additional expenditures necessary to treat L. C. and E. W. in community-based care would be unreasonable given the demands of the State's mental health budget." 138 F.3d, at 905.[7]

We granted certiorari in view of the importance of the question presented to the States and affected individuals. See 525 U.S. ___ (1998).[8]

III

Endeavoring to carry out Congress' instruction to issue regulations implementing Title II, the Attorney General, in the integration and reasonable-modifications regulations, see *supra,* at 5—7, made two key determinations. The first concerned the scope of the ADA's discrimination proscription, 42 U.S.C. § 12132; the second concerned the obligation of the States to counter discrimination. As to the first, the Attorney General concluded that unjustified placement or retention of persons in institutions, severely limiting their exposure to the outside community, constitutes a form of discrimination based on disability prohibited by Title II. See 28 CFR § 35.130(d) (1998) ("A public entity shall administer services . . . in the most integrated setting appropriate to the needs of qualified individuals with disabilities."); Brief for United States as *Amicus Curiae* in *Helen L.* v. *DiDario,* No. 94—1243 (CA3 1994), pp. 8, 15—16 (unnecessary segregation of persons with disabilities constitutes a form of discrimination prohibited by the ADA and the integration regulation). Regarding the States' obligation to avoid unjustified isolation of individuals with disabilities, the Attorney General provided that States could resist modifications that "would fundamentally alter the nature of the service, program, or activity." 28 CFR § 35.130(b)(7) (1998).

The Court of Appeals essentially upheld the Attorney General's construction of the ADA. As just recounted, see *supra,* at 9—10, the appeals court ruled that the unjustified institutionalization of persons with mental disabilities violated Title II; the court then remanded with instructions to measure the cost of caring for L. C. and E. W. in a community-based facility against the State's mental health budget.

We affirm the Court of Appeals' decision in substantial part. Unjustified isolation, we hold, is properly regarded as discrimination based on disability. But we recognize, as well, the States' need to maintain a range of facilities for the care and treatment of persons with diverse mental disabilities, and the States' obligation to administer services with an even hand. Accordingly, we further hold that the Court of Appeals' remand instruction was unduly restrictive. In evaluating a State's fundamental-alteration defense, the District Court must consider, in view of the resources available to the State, not only the cost of providing community-based care to the litigants, but also the range of services the State provides others with mental disabilities, and the State's obligation to mete out those services equitably.

A

We examine first whether, as the Eleventh Circuit held, undue institutionalization qualifies as discrimination "by reason of . . . disability." The Department of Justice has consistently advocated that it does.[9] Because the Department is the agency directed by Congress to issue regulations implementing Title II, see *supra*, at 5—6, its views warrant respect. We need not inquire whether the degree of deference described in *Chevron U.S.A. Inc.* v. *Natural Resources Defense Council, Inc.*, 467 U.S. 837, 844 (1984), is in order; "[i]t is enough to observe that the well-reasoned views of the agencies implementing a statute 'constitute a body of experience and informed judgment to which courts and litigants may properly resort for guidance.'" *Bragdon* v. *Abbott*, 524 U.S. 624, 642 (1998) (quoting *Skidmore* v. *Swift & Co.*, 323 U.S. 134, 139—140 (1944)).

The State argues that L. C. and E. W. encountered no discrimination "by reason of" their disabilities because they were not denied community placement on account of those disabilities. See Brief for Petitioners 20. Nor were they subjected to "discrimination," the State contends, because "'discrimination' necessarily requires uneven treatment of similarly situated individuals," and L. C. and E. W. had identified no comparison class, *i.e.*, no similarly situated individuals given preferential treatment. *Id.*, at 21. We are satisfied that Congress had a more comprehensive view of the concept of discrimination advanced in the ADA.[10]

The ADA stepped up earlier measures to secure opportunities for people with developmental disabilities to enjoy the benefits of community living. The Developmentally Disabled Assistance and Bill of Rights Act (DDABRA), a 1975 measure, stated in aspirational terms that "[t]he treatment, services, and habilitation for a person with developmental disabilities . . . *should be* provided in the setting that is least restrictive of the person's personal liberty." 89 Stat. 502, 42 U.S.C. § 6010(2) (1976 ed.) (emphasis added); see also *Pennhurst State School and Hospital* v. *Halderman*, 451 U.S. 1, 24 (1981) (concluding that the §6010 provisions of the DDABRA "were intended to be hortatory, not mandatory"). In a related legislative endeavor, the Rehabilitation Act of 1973, Congress used mandatory language to proscribe discrimination against persons with disabilities. See 87 Stat. 394, as amended, 29 U.S.C. § 794 (1976 ed.) ("No otherwise qualified individual with a disability in the United States . . . *shall*, solely by reason of her or his disability, be excluded from the participation in, be denied the benefits of, or be subjected to discrimination under any program or activity receiving Federal financial assistance." (Emphasis added)). Ultimately, in the ADA, enacted in 1990, Congress not only required all public entities to refrain from discrimination, see 42 U.S.C. § 12132; additionally, in findings applicable to the entire statute, Congress explicitly identified unjustified "segregation" of persons with disabilities as a "for[m] of discrimination." See §12101(a)(2) ("historically, society has tended to isolate and segregate individuals with disabilities, and, despite some improvements, such forms of discrimination against individuals with disabilities continue to be a serious and pervasive social problem"); §12101(a)(5) ("individuals with disabilities continually encounter various forms of discrimination, including . . . segregation").[11]

Recognition that unjustified institutional isolation of persons with disabilities is a form of discrimination reflects two evident judgments. First, institutional placement of persons who can handle and benefit from community settings perpetuates unwarranted assumptions that persons so isolated are incapable or unworthy of participating in community life. Cf. *Allen* v. *Wright*, 468 U.S. 737, 755 (1984) ("There can be no doubt that [stigmatizing injury often caused by racial discrimination] is one of the most serious consequences of discriminatory government action."); *Los Angeles Dept. of Water and Power* v. *Manhart*, 435 U.S. 702, 707, n. 13 (1978) ("'In forbidding employers to discriminate against individuals because of their sex, Congress intended to strike at the entire spectrum of disparate treatment of men and women resulting from sex stereotypes.'" (quoting *Sprogis* v. *United Air Lines, Inc.*, 444 F.2d 1194, 1198 (CA7 1971)). Second, confinement in an institution severely diminishes the everyday life activities of individuals, including family relations, social contacts, work options, economic independence, educational advancement, and cultural enrichment. See Brief for American Psychiatric Association et al. as *Amici Curiae* 20—22. Dissimilar treatment correspondingly exists in this key respect: In order to receive needed medical services, persons with mental disabilities must, because of those disabilities, relinquish participation in community life they could enjoy given reasonable accommodations, while persons without mental disabilities can receive the medical services they need without similar sacrifice. See Brief for United States as *Amicus Curiae* 6—7, 17.

The State urges that, whatever Congress may have stated as its findings in the ADA, the Medicaid statute "reflected a congressional policy preference for treatment in the institution over treatment in the community." Brief for Petitioners 31. The State correctly used the past tense. Since 1981, Medicaid has provided funding for state-run home and community-based care through a waiver program. See 95 Stat. 812—813, as amended, 42 U.S.C. § 1396n(c); Brief for United States as *Amicus Curiae* 20—21.[12] Indeed, the United States points out that the Department of Health and Human Services (HHS) "has a policy of encouraging States to take advantage of the waiver program, and often approves more waiver slots than a State ultimately uses." *Id.*, at 25—26 (further observing that, by 1996, "HHS approved up to 2109 waiver slots for Georgia, but Georgia used only 700").

We emphasize that nothing in the ADA or its implementing regulations condones termination of institutional settings for persons unable to handle or benefit from community settings. Title II provides only that "qualified individual[s] with a disability" may not "be subjected to discrimination." 42 U.S.C. § 12132. "Qualified individuals," the ADA further explains, are persons with disabilities who, "with or without reasonable modifications to rules, policies, or practices, . . . mee[t] the essential eligibility requirements for the receipt of services or the participation in programs or activities provided by a public entity." §12131(2).

Consistent with these provisions, the State generally may rely on the reasonable assessments of its own professionals in determining whether an individual "meets the essential eligibility requirements" for habilitation in a community-based program. Absent such qualification, it would be inappropriate to remove a patient from the more restrictive setting. See 28 CFR § 35.130(d) (1998) (public entity shall administer services and programs in "the most integrated setting *appropriate* to the needs of qualified individuals with disabilities" (emphasis added)); cf. *School Bd. of Nassau Cty.* v. *Arline*, 480 U.S. 273, 288 (1987) ("[C]ourts normally should defer to the reasonable medical judgments of public health officials.").[13] Nor is there any federal requirement that community-based treatment be imposed on patients who do not desire it. See 28 CFR § 35.130(e)(1) (1998) ("Nothing in this part shall be construed to require an individual with a disability to accept an accommodation . . . which such individual chooses not to accept."); 28 CFR pt. 35, App. A, p. 450 (1998) ("[P]ersons with disabilities must be provided the option of declining to accept a particular accommodation."). In this case, however, there is no genuine dispute concerning the status of L. C. and E. W. as individuals "qualified" for noninstitutional care: The State's own professionals determined that community-based treatment would be appropriate for L. C. and E. W., and neither woman opposed such treatment. See *supra*, at 7—8.[14]

B

The State's responsibility, once it provides community-based treatment to qualified persons with disabilities, is not boundless. The reasonable-modifications regulation speaks of "reasonable modifications" to avoid discrimination, and allows States to resist modifications that entail a "fundamenta[l] alter[ation]" of the States' services and programs. 28 CFR § 35.130(b)(7) (1998). The Court of Appeals construed this regulation to permit a cost-based defense "only in the most limited of circumstances," 138 F.3d, at 902, and remanded to the District Court to consider, among other things, "whether the additional expenditures necessary to treat L. C. and E. W. in community-based care would be unreasonable given the demands of the State's mental health budget," *id.*, at 905.

The Court of Appeals' construction of the reasonable-modifications regulation is unacceptable for it would leave the State virtually defenseless once it is shown that the plaintiff is qualified for the service or program she seeks. If the expense entailed in placing one or two people in a community-based treatment program is properly measured for reasonableness against the State's entire mental health budget, it is unlikely that a State, relying on the fundamental-alteration defense, could ever prevail. See Tr. of Oral Arg. 27 (State's attorney argues that Court of Appeals' understanding of the fundamental-alteration defense, as expressed in its order to the District Court, "will always preclude the State from a meaningful defense"); cf. Brief for Petitioners 37—38 (Court of Appeals' remand order "mistakenly asks the district court to examine [the fundamental-alteration] defense based on the cost of providing community care to just two individuals, not all Georgia citizens who desire community care"); 1:95—cv—1210—MHS (ND Ga., Oct. 20, 1998), p. 3, App. 177 (District Court, on remand, declares the impact of its decision beyond L. C. and E. W. "irrelevant"). Sensibly construed, the fundamental-alteration component of the reasonable-modifications regulation would allow the State to show that, in the allocation of available resources, immediate relief for the plaintiffs would be inequitable, given the responsibility the State has undertaken for the care and treatment of a large and diverse population of persons with mental disabilities.

When it granted summary judgment for plaintiffs in this case, the District Court compared the cost of caring for the plaintiffs in a community-based setting with the cost of caring for them in an institution. That simple comparison showed that community placements cost less than institutional confinements. See App. to Pet. for Cert. 39a. As the United States recognizes, however, a comparison so simple overlooks costs the State cannot avoid; most notably, a "State . . . may experience increased overall expenses by funding community placements without being able to take advantage of the savings associated with the closure of institutions." Brief for United States as *Amicus Curiae* 21.[15]

As already observed, see *supra*, at 17, the ADA is not reasonably read to impel States to phase out institutions, placing patients in need of close care at risk. Cf. *post*, at 2—3 (Kennedy, J., concurring in judgment). Nor is it the ADA's mission to drive States to move institutionalized patients into an inappropriate setting, such as a homeless shelter, a placement the State proposed, then retracted, for E. W. See *supra*, at 8. Some individuals, like L. C. and E. W. in prior years, may need institutional care from time to time "to stabilize acute psychiatric symptoms." App. 98 (affidavit of Dr. Richard L. Elliott); see 138 F.3d, at 903 ("[T]here may be times [when] a patient can be treated in the community, and others whe[n] an institutional placement is necessary."); Reply Brief 19 (placement in a community-based treatment program does not mean the State will no longer need to retain hospital accommodations for the person so placed). For other individuals, no placement outside the institution may ever be appropriate. See Brief for American Psychiatric Association et al. as *Amici Curiae* 22—23 ("Some individuals, whether mentally retarded or mentally ill, are not prepared at particular times—perhaps in the short run, perhaps in the long run—for the risks and exposure of the less protective environment of community settings"; for these persons, "institutional settings are needed and must remain available."); Brief for Voice of the Retarded et al. as *Amici Curiae* 11 ("Each disabled person is entitled to treatment in the most integrated setting possible for that person—recognizing that, on a case-by-case basis, that setting may be in an institution."); *Youngberg* v. *Romeo*, 457 U.S. 307, 327 (1982) (Blackmun, J., concurring) ("For many mentally retarded people, the difference between the capacity to do things for themselves within an institution and total dependence on the institution for all of their needs is as much liberty as they ever will know.").

To maintain a range of facilities and to administer services with an even hand, the State must have more leeway than the courts below understood the fundamental-alteration defense to allow. If, for example, the State were to demonstrate that it had a comprehensive, effectively working plan for placing qualified persons with mental disabilities in less restrictive settings, and a waiting list that moved at a reasonable pace not controlled by the State's endeavors to keep its institutions fully populated, the reasonable-modifications standard would be met. See Tr. of Oral Arg. 5 (State's attorney urges that, "by asking [a] person to wait a short time until a community bed is available, Georgia does not exclude [that] person by reason of disability, neither does Georgia discriminate against her by reason of disability"); see also *id.*, at 25 ("[I]t is reasonable for the State to ask someone to wait until a community placement is available."). In such circumstances, a court would have no warrant effectively to order displacement of persons at the top of the community-based treatment waiting list by individuals lower down who commenced civil actions.[16]

* * *

For the reasons stated, we conclude that, under Title II of the ADA, States are required to provide community-based treatment for persons with mental disabilities when the State's treatment professionals determine that such placement is appropriate, the affected persons do not oppose such treatment, and the placement can be reasonably accommodated, taking into account the resources available to the State and the needs of others with mental disabilities. The judgment of the Eleventh Circuit is therefore affirmed in part and vacated in part, and the case is remanded for further proceedings consistent with this opinion.

It is so ordered.

NOTES

[1] The ADA, enacted in 1990, is the Federal Government's most recent and extensive endeavor to address discrimination against persons with disabilities. Earlier legislative efforts included the Rehabilitation Act of 1973, 87 Stat. 355, 29 U.S.C. § 701 *et seq.* (1976 ed.), and the Developmentally Disabled Assistance and Bill of Rights Act, 89 Stat. 486, 42 U.S.C. § 6001 *et seq.* (1976 ed.), enacted in 1975. In the ADA, Congress for the first time referred expressly to "segregation" of persons with disabilities as a "for[m] of discrimination," and to discrimination that persists in the area of "institutionalization." §§12101(a)(2), (3), (5).

[2] The ADA defines "disability," "with respect to an individual," as "(A) a physical or mental impairment that substantially limits one or more of the major life activities of such individual; "(B) a record of such an impairment; or "(C) being regarded as having such an impairment." §12102(2). There is no dispute that L. C. and E. W. are disabled within the meaning of the ADA.

[3] In addition to the provisions set out in Part A governing public services generally, see §§12131—12134, Title II contains in Part B a host of provisions governing public transportation services, see §§12141—12165.

[4] Section 505 of the Rehabilitation Act incorporates the remedies, rights, and procedures set forth in Title VI of the Civil Rights Act of 1964 for violations of §504 of the Rehabilitation Act. See 29 U.S.C. § 794a(a)(2). Title VI, in turn, directs each federal department authorized to extend financial assistance to any department or agency of a State to issue rules and regulations consistent with achievement of the objectives of the statute authorizing financial assistance. See 78 Stat. 252, 42 U.S.C. § 2000d—1. Compliance with such requirements may be effected by the termination or denial of federal funds, or "by any other means authorized by law." *Ibid.* Remedies both at law and in equity are available for violations of the statute. See §2000d—7(a)(2).

[5] Congress directed the Secretary of Transportation to issue regulations implementing the portion of Title II concerning public transportation. See 42 U.S.C. § 12143(b), 12149, 12164. As stated in the regulations, a person alleging discrimination on the basis of disability in violation of Title II may seek to enforce its provisions by commencing a private lawsuit, or by filing a complaint with (a) a federal agency that provides funding to the public entity that is the subject of the complaint, (b) the Department of Justice for referral to an appropriate agency, or (c) one of eight federal agencies responsible for investigating complaints arising under Title II: the Department of Agriculture, the Department of Education, the Department of Health and Human Services, the Department of Housing and Urban Development, the Department of the Interior, the Department of Justice, the Department of

Labor, and the Department of Transportation. See 28 CFR §§35.170(c), 35.172(b), 35.190(b) (1998). The ADA contains several other provisions allocating regulatory and enforcement responsibility. Congress instructed the Equal Employment Opportunity Commission (EEOC) to issue regulations implementing Title I, see 42 U.S.C. § 12116; the EEOC, the Attorney General, and persons alleging discrimination on the basis of disability in violation of Title I may enforce its provisions, see §12117(a). Congress similarly instructed the Secretary of Transportation and the Attorney General to issue regulations implementing provisions of Title III, see §§12186(a)(1), (b); the Attorney General and persons alleging discrimination on the basis of disability in violation of Title III may enforce its provisions, see §§12188(a)(1), (b). Each federal agency responsible for ADA implementation may render technical assistance to affected individuals and institutions with respect to provisions of the ADA for which the agency has responsibility. See §12206(c)(1).

[6] L. C. and E. W. are currently receiving treatment in community-based programs. Nevertheless, the case is not moot. As the District Court and Court of Appeals explained, in view of the multiple institutional placements L. C. and E. W. have experienced, the controversy they brought to court is "capable of repetition, yet evading review." No. 1:95—cv—1210—MHS (ND Ga., Mar. 26, 1997), p. 6, App. to Pet. for Cert. 35a (internal quotation marks omitted); see 138 F.3d 893, 895, n. 2 (CA11 1998) (citing Honig v. Doe, 484 U.S. 305, 318—323 (1988), and Vitek v. Jones, 445 U.S. 480, 486—487 (1980)).

[7] After this Court granted certiorari, the District Court issued a decision on remand rejecting the State's fundamental-alteration defense. See 1:95—cv—1210—MHS (ND Ga., Jan. 29, 1999), p. 1. The court concluded that the annual cost to the State of providing community-based treatment to L. C. and E. W. was not unreasonable in relation to the State's overall mental health budget. See id., at 5. In reaching that judgment, the District Court first declared "irrelevant" the potential impact of its decision beyond L. C. and E. W. 1:95—cv—1210-MHS (ND Ga., Oct. 20, 1998), p. 3, App. 177. The District Court's decision on remand is now pending appeal before the Eleventh Circuit.

[8] Twenty-two States and the Territory of Guam joined a brief urging that certiorari be granted. Seven of those States filed a brief in support of petitioners on the merits.

[9] See Brief for United States in Halderman v. Pennhurst State School and Hospital, Nos. 78—1490, 78—1564, 78—1602 (CA3 1978), p. 45 ("[I]nstitutionalization result[ing] in separation of mentally retarded persons for no permissible reason . . . . is 'discrimination,' and a violation of Section 504 [of the Rehabilitation Act] if it is supported by federal funds."); Brief for United States in Halderman v. Pennhurst State School and Hospital, Nos. 78—1490, 78—1564, 78—1602 (CA3 1981), p. 27 ("Pennsylvania violates Section 504 by indiscriminately subjecting handicapped persons to [an institution] without first making an individual reasoned professional judgment as to the appropriate placement for each such person among all available alternatives."); Brief for United States as Amicus Curiae in Helen L. v. DiDario, No. 94—1243 (CA3 1994), p. 7 ("Both the Section 504 coordination regulations and the rest of the ADA make clear that the unnecessary segregation of individuals with disabilities in the provision of public services is itself a form of discrimination within the meaning of those statutes."); id., at 8—16.

[10] The dissent is driven by the notion that "this Court has never endorsed an interpretation of the term 'discrimination' that encompassed disparate treatment among members of the *same* protected class," post, at 1 (opinion of Thomas, J.), that "[o]ur decisions construing various statutory prohibitions against 'discrimination' have not wavered from this path," post, at 2, and that "a plaintiff cannot prove 'discrimination' by demonstrating that one member of a particular protected group has been favored over another member of that same group," post, at 4. The dissent is incorrect as a matter of precedent and logic. See O'Connor v. Consolidated Coin Caterers Corp., 517 U.S. 308, 312 (1996) (The Age Discrimination in Employment Act of 1967 "does not ban discrimination against employees because they are aged 40 or older; it bans discrimination against employees because of their age, but limits the protected class to those who are 40 or older. The fact that one person in the protected class has lost out to another person in the protected class is thus irrelevant, so long as he has lost out *because of his age*."); cf. Oncale v. Sundowner Offshore Services, Inc., 523 U.S. 75, 76 (1998) ("[W]orkplace harassment can violate Title VII's prohibition against 'discriminat[ion] . . . because of . . . sex,' 42 U.S.C. § 2000e—2(a)(1), when the harasser and the harassed employee are of the same sex."); Jefferies v. Harris County Community Action Assn., 615 F.2d 1025, 1032 (CA5 1980) ("[D]iscrimination against black females can exist even in the absence of discrimination against black

men or white women.").

[11] Unlike the ADA, §504 of the Rehabilitation Act contains no express recognition that isolation or segregation of persons with disabilities is a form of discrimination. Section 504's discrimination proscription, a single sentence attached to vocational rehabilitation legislation, has yielded divergent court interpretations. See Brief for United States as *Amicus Curiae* 23—25.

[12] The waiver program provides Medicaid reimbursement to States for the provision of community-based services to individuals who would otherwise require institutional care, upon a showing that the average annual cost of such services is not more than the annual cost of institutional services. See §1396n(c).

[13] Georgia law also expresses a preference for treatment in the most integrated setting appropriate. See Ga. Code Ann. §37—4—121 (1995) ("It is the policy of the state that the least restrictive alternative placement be secured for every client at every stage of his habilitation. It shall be the duty of the facility to assist the client in securing placement in noninstitutional community facilities and programs.").

[14] We do not in this opinion hold that the ADA imposes on the States a "standard of care" for whatever medical services they render, or that the ADA requires States to "provide a certain level of benefits to individuals with disabilities." Cf. *post*, at 9, 10 (Thomas, J., dissenting). We do hold, however, that States must adhere to the ADA's non-discrimination requirement with regard to the services they in fact provide.

[15] Even if States eventually were able to close some institutions in response to an increase in the number of community placements, the States would still incur the cost of running partially full institutions in the interim. See Brief for United States as *Amicus Curiae* 21.

[16] We reject the Court of Appeals' construction of the reasonable-modifications regulation for another reason. The Attorney General's Title II regulations, Congress ordered, "shall be consistent with" the regulations in part 41 of Title 28 of the Code of Federal Regulations implementing §504 of the Rehabilitation Act. 42 U.S.C. § 12134(b). The §504 regulation upon which the reasonable-modifications regulation is based provides now, as it did at the time the ADA was enacted: "A recipient shall make reasonable accommodation to the known physical or mental limitations of an otherwise qualified handicapped applicant or employee unless the recipient can demonstrate that the accommodation would impose an undue hardship on the operation of its program." 28 CFR § 41.53 (1990 and 1998 eds.). While the part 41 regulations do not define "undue hardship," other §504 regulations make clear that the "undue hardship" inquiry requires not simply an assessment of the cost of the accommodation in relation to the recipient's overall budget, but a "case-by-case analysis weighing factors that include: (1) [t]he overall size of the recipient's program with respect to number of employees, number and type of facilities, and size of budget; (2) [t]he type of the recipient's operation, including the composition and structure of the recipient's workforce; and (3) [t]he nature and cost of the accommodation needed." 28 CFR § 42.511(c) (1998); see 45 CFR § 84.12(c) (1998) (same). Under the Court of Appeals' restrictive reading, the reasonable-modifications regulation would impose a standard substantially more difficult for the State to meet than the "undue burden" standard imposed by the corresponding §504 regulation.

FRIENDS OF THE EARTH, INC., et al. v. LAIDLAW ENVIRONMENTAL SERVICES (TOC), INC.

No. 98-822, January 12, 2000

ON WRIT OF CERTIORARI TO THE UNITED STATES COURT OF APPEALS FOR THE FOURTH CIRCUIT

Justice Ginsburg delivered the opinion of the Court.

This case presents an important question concerning the operation of the citizen-suit provisions of the Clean Water Act. Congress authorized the federal district courts to entertain Clean Water Act suits initiated by "a person or persons having an interest which is or may be adversely affected." 33 U.S.C. § 1365(a), (g). To impel future compliance with the Act, a district court may prescribe injunctive relief in such a suit; additionally or alternatively, the court may impose civil penalties payable to the United States Treasury. §1365(a). In the Clean Water Act citizen suit now before us, the District Court determined that injunctive relief was inappropriate because the defendant, after the institution of the litigation, achieved substantial compliance with the terms of its discharge permit. 956 F.Supp. 588, 611 (SC 1997). The court did, however, assess a civil penalty of $405,800. *Id.*, at 610. The "total deterrent effect" of the penalty would be adequate to forestall future violations, the court reasoned, taking into account that the defendant "will be required to reimburse plaintiffs for a significant amount of legal fees and has, itself, incurred significant legal expenses." *Id.*, at 610—611.

The Court of Appeals vacated the District Court's order. 149 F.3d 303 (CA4 1998). The case became moot, the appellate court declared, once the defendant fully complied with the terms of its permit and the plaintiff failed to appeal the denial of equitable relief. "[C]ivil penalties payable to the government," the Court of Appeals stated, "would not redress any injury Plaintiffs have suffered." *Id.*, at 307. Nor were attorneys' fees in order, the Court of Appeals noted, because absent relief on the merits, plaintiffs could not qualify as prevailing parties. *Id.*, at 307, n.5.

We reverse the judgment of the Court of Appeals. The appellate court erred in concluding that a citizen suitor's claim for civil penalties must be dismissed as moot when the defendant, albeit after commencement of the litigation, has come into compliance. In directing dismissal of the suit on grounds of mootness, the Court of Appeals incorrectly conflated our case law on initial standing to bring suit, see, *e.g.*, *Steel Co.* v. *Citizens for Better Environment*, 523 U.S. 83 (1998), with our case law on post-commencement mootness, see, *e.g.*, *City of Mesquite* v. *Aladdin's Castle, Inc.*, 455 U.S. 283 (1982). A defendant's voluntary cessation of allegedly unlawful conduct ordinarily does not suffice to moot a case. The Court of Appeals also misperceived the remedial potential of civil penalties. Such penalties may serve, as an alternative to an injunction, to deter future violations and thereby redress the injuries that prompted a citizen suitor to commence litigation.

I

A

In 1972, Congress enacted the Clean Water Act (Act), also known as the Federal Water Pollution Control Act, 86 Stat. 816, as amended, 33 U.S.C. § 1251 *et seq.* Section 402 of the Act, 33 U.S.C. § 1342 provides for the issuance, by the Administrator of the Environmental Protection Agency (EPA) or by authorized States, of National Pollutant Discharge Elimination System (NPDES) permits. NPDES permits impose limitations on the discharge of pollutants, and establish related monitoring and reporting requirements, in order to improve the cleanliness and safety of the Nation's waters. Noncompliance with a permit constitutes a violation of the Act. §1342(h).

Under §505(a) of the Act, a suit to enforce any limitation in an NPDES permit may be brought by any "citizen," defined as "a person or persons having an interest which is or may be adversely affected." 33 U.S.C. § 1365(a), (g). Sixty days before initiating a citizen suit, however, the would-be plaintiff must give notice of the alleged violation to the EPA, the State in which the alleged violation occurred, and the alleged violator. §1365(b)(1)(A). "[T]he purpose of notice to the alleged violator is to give it an opportunity to bring itself into complete compliance with the Act and thus ... render unnecessary a citizen suit." *Gwaltney of Smithfield, Ltd.* v. *Chesapeake Bay Foundation, Inc.*, 484 U.S. 49, 60 (1987). Accordingly, we have held that citizens lack statutory standing under §505(a) to sue for violations that have ceased by the time the complaint is filed. *Id.*, at 56—63. The Act also bars a citizen from suing if the EPA or the State has already commenced, and is "diligently prosecuting," an enforcement action. 33 U.S.C. § 1365(b)(1)(B).

The Act authorizes district courts in citizen-suit proceedings to enter injunctions and to assess civil penalties, which are payable to the United States Treasury. §1365(a). In determining the amount of any civil penalty, the district court must take into account "the seriousness of the violation or violations, the economic benefit (if any) resulting from the violation, any history of such violations, any good-faith efforts to comply with the applicable requirements, the economic impact of the penalty on the violator, and such other matters as justice may require." §1319(d). In addition, the court "may award costs of litigation (including reasonable attorney and expert witness fees) to any prevailing or substantially prevailing party, whenever the court determines such award is appropriate." §1365(d).

B

In 1986, defendant-respondent Laidlaw Environmental Services (TOC), Inc., bought a hazardous waste incinerator facility in Roebuck, South Carolina, that included a wastewater treatment plant. (The company has since changed its name to Safety-Kleen (Roebuck), Inc., but for simplicity we will refer to it as "Laidlaw" throughout.) Shortly after Laidlaw acquired the facility, the South Carolina Department of Health and Environmental Control (DHEC), acting under 33 U.S.C. § 1342(a)(1), granted Laidlaw an NPDES permit authorizing the company to discharge treated water into the North Tyger River. The permit, which became effective on January 1, 1987, placed limits on Laidlaw's discharge of several pollutants into the river, including–of particular relevance to this case–mercury, an extremely toxic pollutant. The permit also regulated the flow, temperature, toxicity, and pH of the effluent from the facility, and imposed monitoring and reporting obligations.

Once it received its permit, Laidlaw began to discharge various pollutants into the waterway; repeatedly, Laidlaw's discharges exceeded the limits set by the permit. In particular, despite experimenting with several technological fixes, Laidlaw consistently failed to meet the permit's stringent 1.3 ppb (parts per billion) daily average limit on mercury discharges. The District Court later found that Laidlaw had violated the mercury limits on 489 occasions between 1987 and 1995. 956 F.Supp., at 613—621.

On April 10, 1992, plaintiff-petitioners Friends of the Earth (FOE) and Citizens Local Environmental Action Network, Inc. (CLEAN) (referred to collectively in this opinion, together with later joined plaintiff-petitioner Sierra Club, as "FOE") took the preliminary step necessary to the institution of litigation. They sent a letter to Laidlaw notifying the company of their intention to file a citizen suit against it under §505(a) of the Act after the expiration of the requisite 60-day notice period, *i.e.*, on or after June 10, 1992. Laidlaw's lawyer then contacted DHEC to ask whether DHEC would consider filing a lawsuit against Laidlaw. The District Court later found that Laidlaw's reason for requesting that DHEC file a lawsuit against it was to bar FOE's proposed citizen suit through the operation of 33 U.S.C. § 1365(b)(1)(B). 890 F.Supp. 470, 478 (SC 1995). DHEC agreed to file a lawsuit against Laidlaw; the company's lawyer then drafted the complaint for DHEC and paid the filing fee. On June 9, 1992, the last day before FOE's 60-day notice period expired, DHEC and Laidlaw reached a settlement requiring Laidlaw to pay $100,000 in civil penalties and to make "'every effort'" to comply with its permit obligations. 890 F.Supp., at 479—481.

On June 12, 1992, FOE filed this citizen suit against Laidlaw under §505(a) of the Act, alleging noncompliance with the NPDES permit and seeking declaratory and injunctive relief and an award of civil penalties. Laidlaw moved for summary judgment on the ground that FOE had failed to present evidence demonstrating injury in fact, and therefore lacked Article III standing to bring the lawsuit. Record, Doc. No. 43. In opposition to this motion, FOE submitted affidavits and deposition testimony from members of the plaintiff organizations. Record, Doc. No. 71 (Exhs. 41—51). The record before the District Court also included affidavits from the organizations' members submitted by FOE in support of an earlier motion for preliminary injunctive relief. Record, Doc. No. 21 (Exhs. 5—10). After examining this evidence, the District Court denied Laidlaw's summary judgment motion, finding–albeit "by the very slimmest of margins"–that FOE had standing to bring the suit. App. in No. 97—1246 (CA4), pp. 207—208 (Tr. of Hearing 39—40 (June 30, 1993)).

Laidlaw also moved to dismiss the action on the ground that the citizen suit was barred under 33 U.S.C. § 1365(b)(1)(B) by DHEC's prior action against the company. The United States, appearing as *amicus curiae*, joined FOE in opposing the motion. After an extensive analysis of the Laidlaw-DHEC settlement and the circumstances under which it was reached, the District Court held that DHEC's action against Laidlaw had not been "diligently prosecuted"; consequently, the court allowed FOE's citizen suit to proceed. 890 F.Supp., at 499.[1] The record indicates that after FOE initiated the suit, but before the District Court rendered judgment, Laidlaw violated the mercury discharge limitation in its permit 13 times. 956 F.Supp., at 621. The District Court also found that Laidlaw had committed 13 monitoring and 10 reporting violations during this period. *Id.*, at 601. The last recorded mercury discharge violation occurred in January 1995, long after the complaint was filed but about two years before judgment was rendered. *Id.*, at 621.

On January 22, 1997, the District Court issued its judgment. 956 F.Supp. 588 (SC 1997). It found that Laidlaw had gained a total economic benefit of $1,092,581 as a result of its extended period of noncompliance with the mercury discharge limit in its permit. *Id.*, at 603. The court concluded, however, that a civil penalty of $405,800 was adequate in light of the guiding factors listed in 33 U.S.C. § 1319(d). 956 F.Supp., at 610. In particular, the District Court stated that the lesser penalty was appropriate taking into account the judgment's "total deterrent effect." In reaching this determination, the court "considered that Laidlaw will be required to reimburse plaintiffs for a significant amount of legal fees." *Id.*, at 610—611. The court declined to grant FOE's request for injunctive relief, stating that an injunction was inappropriate because "Laidlaw has been in substantial compliance with all parameters in its NPDES permit since at least August 1992." *Id.*, at 611.

FOE appealed the District Court's civil penalty judgment, arguing that the penalty was inadequate, but did not appeal the denial of declaratory or injunctive relief. Laidlaw cross-appealed, arguing, among other things, that FOE lacked standing to bring the suit and that DHEC's action qualified as a diligent prosecution precluding FOE's litigation. The United States continued to participate as *amicus curiae* in support of FOE.

On July 16, 1998, the Court of Appeals for the Fourth Circuit issued its judgment. 149 F.3d 303. The Court of Appeals assumed without deciding that FOE initially had standing to bring the action, *id.,* at 306, n.3, but went on to hold that the case had become moot. The appellate court stated, first, that the elements of Article III standing–injury, causation, and redressability–must persist at every stage of review, or else the action becomes moot. *Id.,* at 306. Citing our decision in *Steel Co.,* the Court of Appeals reasoned that the case had become moot because "the only remedy currently available to [FOE]–civil penalties payable to the government–would not redress any injury [FOE has] suffered." *Id.,* at 306—307. The court therefore vacated the District Court's order and remanded with instructions to dismiss the action. In a footnote, the Court of Appeals added that FOE's "failure to obtain relief on the merits of [its] claims precludes any recovery of attorneys' fees or other litigation costs because such an award is available only to a 'prevailing or substantially prevailing party.'" *Id.,* at 307, n.5 (quoting 33 U.S.C. § 1365(d)).

According to Laidlaw, after the Court of Appeals issued its decision but before this Court granted certiorari, the entire incinerator facility in Roebuck was permanently closed, dismantled, and put up for sale, and all discharges from the facility permanently ceased. Respondent's Suggestion of Mootness 3.

We granted certiorari, 525 U.S. 1176 (1999), to resolve the inconsistency between the Fourth Circuit's decision in this case and the decisions of several other Courts of Appeals, which have held that a defendant's compliance with its permit after the commencement of litigation does not moot claims for civil penalties under the Act. See, *e.g., Atlantic States Legal Foundation, Inc.* v. *Stroh Die Casting Co.,* 116 F.3d 814, 820 (CA7), cert. denied, 522 U.S. 981 (1997); *Natural Resources Defense Council, Inc.* v. *Texaco Rfg. and Mktg., Inc.,* 2 F.3d 493, 503—504 (CA3 1993); *Atlantic States Legal Foundation, Inc.* v. *Pan American Tanning Corp.,* 993 F.2d 1017, 1020—1021 (CA2 1993); *Atlantic States Legal Foundation, Inc.* v. *Tyson Foods, Inc.,* 897 F.2d 1128, 1135—1136 (CA11 1990).

II

A

The Constitution's case-or-controversy limitation on federal judicial authority, Art. III, §2, underpins both our standing and our mootness jurisprudence, but the two inquiries differ in respects critical to the proper resolution of this case, so we address them separately. Because the Court of Appeals was persuaded that the case had become moot and so held, it simply assumed without deciding that FOE had initial standing. See *Arizonans for Official English* v. *Arizona,* 520 U.S. 43, 66—67 (1997) (court may assume without deciding that standing exists in order to analyze mootness). But because we hold that the Court of Appeals erred in declaring the case moot, we have an obligation to assure ourselves that FOE had Article III standing at the outset of the litigation. We therefore address the question of standing before turning to mootness.

In *Lujan* v. *Defenders of Wildlife,* 504 U.S. 555, 560—561 (1992), we held that, to satisfy Article III's standing requirements, a plaintiff must show (1) it has suffered an "injury in fact" that is (a) concrete and particularized and (b) actual or imminent, not conjectural or hypothetical; (2) the injury is fairly traceable to the challenged action of the defendant; and (3) it is likely, as opposed to merely speculative, that the injury will be redressed by a favorable decision. An association has standing to bring suit on behalf of its members when its members would otherwise have standing to sue in their own right, the interests at stake are germane to the organization's purpose, and neither the claim asserted nor the relief requested requires the participation of individual members in the lawsuit. *Hunt* v. *Washington State Apple Advertising Comm'n,* 432 U.S. 333, 343 (1977).

Laidlaw contends first that FOE lacked standing from the outset even to seek injunctive relief, because the plaintiff organizations failed to show that any of their members had sustained or faced the threat of any "injury in fact" from Laidlaw's activities. In support of this contention Laidlaw points to the District Court's finding, made in the course of setting the penalty amount, that there had been "no demonstrated proof of harm to the environment" from Laidlaw's mercury discharge violations. 956 F.Supp., at 602; see also *ibid.* ("[T]he NPDES permit violations at issue in this citizen suit did not result in any health risk or environmental harm.").

The relevant showing for purposes of Article III standing, however, is not injury to the environment but injury to the plaintiff. To insist upon the former rather than the latter as part of the standing inquiry (as the dissent in essence does, *post,* at 2—3) is to raise the standing hurdle higher than the necessary showing for success on the merits in an action alleging noncompliance with an NPDES permit. Focusing properly on injury to the plaintiff, the District Court found that FOE had demonstrated sufficient injury to establish standing. App. in No. 97—1246 (CA4), pp. 207—208 (Tr. of Hearing 39—40 (June 30, 1993)). For example, FOE member Kenneth Lee Curtis averred in affidavits that he lived a half-mile from Laidlaw's facility; that he occasionally drove over the North Tyger River, and that it looked and smelled polluted; and that he would like to fish, camp, swim, and picnic in and near the river between 3 and 15 miles downstream from the facility, as he did when he was a teenager, but would not do so because he was concerned that the water was polluted by Laidlaw's discharges. Record, Doc. No. 71 (Exhs. 41, 42). Curtis reaffirmed these statements in extensive deposition testimony. For example, he testified that he would like to fish in the river at a specific spot he used as a boy, but that he would not do so now because of his concerns about Laidlaw's discharges. *Ibid.* (Exh. 43, at 52—53; Exh. 44, at 33).

Other members presented evidence to similar effect. CLEAN member Angela Patterson attested that she lived two miles from the facility; that before Laidlaw operated the facility, she picnicked, walked, birdwatched, and waded in and along the North Tyger River because of the natural beauty of the area; that she no longer engaged in these activities in or near the river because she was concerned about harmful effects from discharged pollutants; and that she and her husband would like to purchase a home near the river but did not intend to do so, in part because of Laidlaw's discharges. Record, Doc. No. 21 (Exh. 10). CLEAN member Judy Pruitt averred that she lived one-quarter mile from Laidlaw's facility and would like to fish, hike, and picnic along the North Tyger River, but has refrained from those activities because of the discharges. *Ibid.* (Exh. 7). FOE member Linda Moore attested that she lived 20 miles from Roebuck, and would use the North Tyger River south of Roebuck and the land surrounding it for recreational purposes were she not concerned that the water contained harmful pollutants. Record, Doc. No. 71 (Exhs. 45, 46). In her deposition, Moore testified at length that she would hike, picnic, camp, swim, boat, and drive near or in the river were it not for her concerns about illegal discharges. *Ibid.* (Exh. 48, at 29, 36—37, 62—63, 72). CLEAN member Gail Lee attested that her home, which is near Laidlaw's facility, had a lower value than similar homes located further from the facility, and that she believed the pollutant discharges accounted for some of the discrepancy. Record, Doc. No. 21 (Exh. 9). Sierra Club member Norman Sharp averred that he had canoed approximately 40 miles downstream of the Laidlaw facility and would like to canoe in the North Tyger River closer to Laidlaw's discharge point, but did not do so because he was concerned that the water contained harmful pollutants. *Ibid.* (Exh. 8).

These sworn statements, as the District Court determined, adequately documented injury in fact. We have held that environmental plaintiffs adequately allege injury in fact when they aver that they use the affected area and are persons "for whom the aesthetic and recreational values of the area will be lessened" by the challenged activity. *Sierra Club* v. *Morton*, 405 U.S. 727, 735 (1972). See also *Defenders of Wildlife*, 504 U.S., at 562—563 ("Of course, the desire to use or observe an animal species, even for purely esthetic purposes, is undeniably a cognizable interest for purposes of standing.").

Our decision in *Lujan* v. *National Wildlife Federation*, 497 U.S. 871 (1990), is not to the contrary. In that case an environmental organization assailed the Bureau of Land Management's "land withdrawal review program," a program covering millions of acres, alleging that the program illegally opened up public lands to mining activities. The defendants moved for summary judgment, challenging the plaintiff organization's standing to initiate the action under the Administrative Procedure Act, 5 U.S.C. § 702. We held that the plaintiff could not survive the summary judgment motion merely by offering "averments which state only that one of [the organization's] members uses unspecified portions of an immense tract of territory, on some portions of which mining activity has occurred or probably will occur by virtue of the governmental action." 497 U.S., at 889.

In contrast, the affidavits and testimony presented by FOE in this case assert that Laidlaw's discharges, and the affiant members' reasonable concerns about the effects of those discharges, directly affected those affiants' recreational, aesthetic, and economic interests. These submissions present dispositively more than the mere "general averments" and "conclusory allegations" found inadequate in *National Wildlife Federation. Id.,* at 888. Nor can the affiants' conditional statements–that they would use the nearby North Tyger River for recreation if Laidlaw were not discharging pollutants into it–be equated with the speculative "'some day' intentions" to visit endangered species halfway around the world that we held insufficient to show injury in fact in *Defenders of Wildlife*. 504 U.S., at 564.

Los Angeles v. *Lyons,* 461 U.S. 95 (1983), relied on by the dissent, *post,* at 3, does not weigh against standing in this case. In *Lyons*, we held that a plaintiff lacked standing to seek an injunction against the enforcement of a police chokehold policy because he could not credibly allege that he faced a realistic threat from the policy. 461 U.S., at 107, n.7. In the footnote from *Lyons* cited by the dissent, we noted that "[t]he reasonableness of Lyons' fear is dependent upon the likelihood of a recurrence of the allegedly unlawful conduct," and that his "subjective apprehensions" that such a recurrence would even *take place* were not enough to support standing. *Id.*, at 108, n.8. Here, in contrast, it is undisputed that Laidlaw's unlawful conduct–discharging pollutants in excess of permit limits–was occurring at the time the complaint was filed. Under *Lyons*, then, the only "subjective" issue here is "[t]he reasonableness of [the] fear" that led the affiants to respond to that concededly ongoing conduct by refraining from use of the North Tyger River and surrounding areas. Unlike the dissent, *post*, at 3, we see nothing "improbable" about the proposition that a company's continuous and pervasive illegal discharges of pollutants into a river would cause nearby residents to curtail their recreational use of that waterway and would subject them to other economic and aesthetic harms. The proposition is entirely reasonable, the District Court found it was true in this case, and that is enough for injury in fact.

Laidlaw argues next that even if FOE had standing to seek injunctive relief, it lacked standing to seek civil penalties. Here the asserted defect is not injury but redressability. Civil penalties offer no redress to private plaintiffs, Laidlaw argues, because they are paid to the government, and therefore a citizen plaintiff can never have standing to seek them.

Laidlaw is right to insist that a plaintiff must demonstrate standing separately for each form of relief sought. See, *e.g., Lyons*, 461 U.S., at 109 (notwithstanding the fact that plaintiff had standing to pursue damages, he lacked standing to pursue injunctive relief); see also *Lewis* v. *Casey*, 518 U.S. 343, 358, n.6 (1996) ("[S]tanding is not dispensed in gross."). But it is wrong to maintain that citizen plaintiffs facing ongoing violations never have standing to seek civil penalties.

We have recognized on numerous occasions that "all civil penalties have some deterrent effect." *Hudson* v. *United States,* 522 U.S. 93, 102 (1997); see also, *e.g., Department of Revenue of Mont.* v. *Kurth Ranch,* 511 U.S. 767, 778 (1994). More specifically, Congress has found that civil penalties in Clean Water Act cases do more than promote immediate compliance by limiting the defendant's economic incentive to delay its attainment of permit limits; they also deter future violations. This congressional determination warrants judicial attention and respect. "The legislative history of the Act reveals that Congress wanted the district court to consider the need for retribution and deterrence, in addition to restitution, when it imposed civil penalties. ... [The district court may] seek to deter future violations by basing the penalty on its economic impact." *Tull* v. *United States*, 481 U.S. 412, 422—423 (1987).

It can scarcely be doubted that, for a plaintiff who is injured or faces the threat of future injury due to illegal conduct ongoing at the time of suit, a sanction that effectively abates that conduct and prevents its recurrence provides a form of redress. Civil penalties can fit that description. To the extent that they encourage defendants to discontinue current violations and deter them from committing future ones, they afford redress to citizen plaintiffs who are injured or threatened with injury as a consequence of ongoing unlawful conduct.

The dissent argues that it is the *availability* rather than the *imposition* of civil penalties that deters any particular polluter from continuing to pollute. *Post*, at 11—12. This argument misses the mark in two ways. First, it overlooks the interdependence of the availability and the imposition; a threat has no deterrent value unless it is credible that it will be carried out. Second, it is reasonable for Congress to conclude that an actual award of civil penalties does in fact bring with it a significant quantum of deterrence over and above what is achieved by the mere prospect of such penalties. A would-be polluter may or may not be dissuaded by the existence of a remedy on the books, but a defendant once hit in its pocketbook will surely think twice before polluting again.[2]

We recognize that there may be a point at which the deterrent effect of a claim for civil penalties becomes so insubstantial or so remote that it cannot support citizen standing. The fact that this vanishing point is not easy to ascertain does not detract from the deterrent power of such penalties in the ordinary case. Justice Frankfurter's observations for the Court, made in a different context nearly 60 years ago, hold true here as well:

"How to effectuate policy–the adaptation of means to legitimately sought ends–is one of the most intractable of legislative problems. Whether proscribed conduct is to be deterred by *qui tam* action or triple damages or injunction, or by criminal prosecution, or merely by defense to actions in contract, or by some, or all, of these remedies in combination, is a matter within the legislature's range of choice. Judgment on the deterrent effect of the various weapons in the armory of the law can lay little claim to scientific basis." *Tigner* v. *Texas,* 310 U.S. 141, 148 (1940).[3]

In this case we need not explore the outer limits of the principle that civil penalties provide sufficient deterrence to support redressability. Here, the civil penalties sought by FOE carried with them a deterrent effect that made it likely, as opposed to merely speculative, that the penalties would redress FOE's injuries by abating current violations and preventing future ones–as the District Court reasonably found when it assessed a penalty of $405,800. 956 F.Supp., at 610—611.

Laidlaw contends that the reasoning of our decision in *Steel Co.* directs the conclusion that citizen plaintiffs have no standing to seek civil penalties under the Act. We disagree. *Steel Co.* established that citizen suitors lack standing to seek civil penalties for violations that have abated by the time of suit. 523 U.S., at 106—107. We specifically noted in that case that there was no allegation in the complaint of any continuing or imminent violation, and that no basis for such an allegation appeared to exist. *Id.,* at 108; see also *Gwaltney,* 484 U.S., at 59 ("the harm sought to be addressed by the citizen suit lies in the present or the future, not in the past"). In short, *Steel Co.* held that private plaintiffs, unlike the Federal Government, may not sue to assess penalties for wholly past violations, but our decision in that case did not reach the issue of standing to seek penalties for violations that are ongoing at the time of the complaint and that could continue into the future if undeterred.[4]

B

Satisfied that FOE had standing under Article III to bring this action, we turn to the question of mootness.

The only conceivable basis for a finding of mootness in this case is Laidlaw's voluntary conduct–either its achievement by August 1992 of substantial compliance with its NPDES permit or its more recent shutdown of the Roebuck facility. It is well settled that "a defendant's voluntary cessation of a challenged practice does not deprive a federal court of its power to determine the legality of the practice." *City of Mesquite*, 455 U.S., at 289. "[I]f it did, the courts would be compelled to leave '[t]he defendant ... free to return to his old ways.'" *Id.,* at 289, n.10 (citing *United States* v. *W. T. Grant Co.,* 345 U.S. 629, 632 (1953)). In accordance with this principle, the standard we have announced for determining whether a case has been mooted by the defendant's voluntary conduct is stringent: "A case might become moot if subsequent events made it absolutely clear that the allegedly wrongful behavior could not reasonably be expected to recur." *United States* v. *Concentrated Phosphate Export Assn., Inc.,* 393 U.S. 199, 203 (1968). The "heavy burden of persua[ding]" the court that the challenged conduct cannot reasonably be expected to start up again lies with the party asserting mootness. *Ibid.*

The Court of Appeals justified its mootness disposition by reference to *Steel Co.*, which held that citizen plaintiffs lack standing to seek civil penalties for wholly past violations. In relying on *Steel Co.*, the Court of Appeals confused mootness with standing. The confusion is understandable, given this Court's repeated statements that the doctrine of mootness can be described as "the doctrine of standing set in a time frame: The requisite personal interest that must exist at the commencement of the litigation (standing) must continue throughout its existence (mootness)." *Arizonans for Official English,* 520 U.S., at 68, n. 22 (quoting *United States Parole Comm'n* v. *Geraghty,* 445 U.S. 388, 397 (1980), in turn quoting Monaghan, Constitutional Adjudication: The Who and When, 82 Yale L.J. 1363, 1384 (1973)) (internal quotation marks omitted).

Careful reflection on the long-recognized exceptions to mootness, however, reveals that the description of mootness as "standing set in a time frame" is not comprehensive. As just noted, a defendant claiming that its voluntary compliance moots a case bears the formidable burden of showing that it is absolutely clear the allegedly wrongful behavior could not reasonably be expected to recur. *Concentrated Phosphate Export Assn.,* 393 U.S., at 203. By contrast, in a lawsuit brought to force compliance, it is the plaintiff's burden to establish standing by demonstrating that, if unchecked by the litigation, the defendant's allegedly wrongful behavior will likely occur or continue, and that the "threatened injury [is] certainly impending." *Whitmore* v. *Arkansas*, 495 U.S. 149, 158 (1990) (citations and internal quotation marks omitted). Thus, in *Lyons*, as already noted, we held that a plaintiff lacked initial standing to seek an injunction against the enforcement of a police chokehold policy because he could not credibly allege that he faced a realistic threat arising from the policy. 461 U.S., at 105—110. Elsewhere in the opinion, however, we noted that a citywide moratorium on police chokeholds–an action that surely diminished the already slim likelihood that any particular individual would be choked by police–would not have mooted an otherwise valid claim for injunctive relief, because the moratorium by its terms was not permanent. *Id.*, at 101. The plain lesson of these cases is that there are circumstances in which the prospect that a defendant will engage in (or resume) harmful conduct may be too speculative to support standing, but not too speculative to overcome mootness.

Furthermore, if mootness were simply "standing set in a time frame," the exception to mootness that arises when the defendant's allegedly unlawful activity is "capable of repetition, yet evading review" could not exist. When, for example, a mentally disabled patient files a lawsuit challenging her confinement in a segregated institution, her postcomplaint transfer to a community-based program will not moot the action, *Olmstead* v. *L. C.*, 527 U.S. ___, ___, n.6 (1999) (slip. op., at 8, n.6), despite the fact that she would have lacked initial standing had she filed the complaint after the transfer. Standing admits of no similar exception; if a plaintiff lacks standing at the time the action commences, the fact that the dispute is capable of repetition yet evading review will not entitle the complainant to a federal judicial forum. See *Steel Co.*, 523 U.S., at 109 (" 'the mootness exception for disputes capable of repetition yet evading review . . . will not revive a dispute which became moot before the action commenced' ") (quoting *Renne* v. *Geary*, 501 U.S. 312, 320 (1991)).

We acknowledged the distinction between mootness and standing most recently in *Steel Co.*:

"The United States ... argues that the injunctive relief does constitute remediation because 'there is a presumption of [future] injury when the defendant has voluntarily ceased its illegal activity in response to litigation,' even if that occurs before a complaint is filed. ... This makes a sword out of a shield. The 'presumption' the Government refers to has been applied to refute the assertion of mootness by a defendant who, when sued in a complaint that alleges present or threatened injury, ceases the complained-of activity. ... It is an immense and unacceptable stretch to call the presumption into service as a substitute for the allegation of present or threatened injury upon which initial standing must be based." 523 U.S., at 109.

Standing doctrine functions to ensure, among other things, that the scarce resources of the federal courts are devoted to those disputes in which the parties have a concrete stake. In contrast, by the time mootness is an issue, the case has been brought and litigated, often (as here) for years. To abandon the case at an advanced stage may prove more wasteful than frugal. This argument from sunk costs[5] does not license courts to retain jurisdiction over cases in which one or both of the parties plainly lacks a continuing interest, as when the parties have settled or a plaintiff pursuing a nonsurviving claim has died. See, *e.g.*, *DeFunis* v. *Odegaard*, 416 U.S. 312 (1974) *(per curiam)* (non-class-action challenge to constitutionality of law school admissions process mooted when plaintiff, admitted pursuant to preliminary injunction, neared graduation and defendant law school conceded that, as a matter of ordinary school policy, plaintiff would be allowed to finish his final term); *Arizonans*, 520 U.S., at 67 (non-class-action challenge to state constitutional amendment declaring English the official language of the State became moot when plaintiff, a state employee who sought to use her bilingual skills, left state employment). But the argument surely highlights an important difference between the two doctrines. See generally *Honig* v. *Doe*, 484 U.S. 305, 329—332 (1988) (Rehnquist, C.J., concurring).

In its brief, Laidlaw appears to argue that, regardless of the effect of Laidlaw's compliance, FOE doomed its own civil penalty claim to mootness by failing to appeal the District Court's denial of injunctive relief. Brief for Respondent 14—17. This argument misconceives the statutory scheme. Under §1365(a), the district court has discretion to determine which form of relief is best suited, in the particular case, to abate current violations and deter future ones. "[A] federal judge sitting as chancellor is not mechanically obligated to grant an injunction for every violation of law." *Weinberger* v. *Romero-Barcelo*, 456 U.S. 305, 313 (1982). Denial of injunctive relief does not necessarily mean that the district court has concluded there is no prospect of future violations for civil penalties to deter. Indeed, it meant no such thing in this case. The District Court denied injunctive relief, but expressly based its award of civil penalties on the need for deterrence. See 956 F.Supp., at 610—611. As the dissent notes, *post*, at 8, federal courts should aim to ensure " 'the framing of relief no broader than required by the precise facts.' " *Schlesinger* v. *Reservists Comm. to Stop the War*, 418 U.S. 208, 222 (1974). In accordance with this aim, a district court in a Clean Water Act citizen suit properly may conclude that an injunction would be an excessively intrusive remedy, because it could entail continuing superintendence of the permit holder's activities by a federal court–a process burdensome to court and permit holder alike. See *City of Mesquite*, 455 U.S., at 289 (although the defendant's voluntary cessation of the challenged practice does not moot the case, "[s]uch abandonment is an important factor bearing on the question whether a court should exercise its power to enjoin the defendant from renewing the practice").

Laidlaw also asserts, in a supplemental suggestion of mootness, that the closure of its Roebuck facility, which took place after the Court of Appeals issued its decision, mooted the case. The facility closure, like Laidlaw's earlier achievement of substantial compliance with its permit requirements, might moot the case, but–we once more reiterate–only if one or the other of these events made it absolutely clear that Laidlaw's permit violations could not reasonably be expected to recur. *Concentrated Phosphate Export Assn.*, 393 U.S., at 203. The effect of both Laidlaw's compliance and the facility closure on the prospect of future violations is a disputed factual matter. FOE points out, for example–and Laidlaw does not appear to contest–that Laidlaw retains its NPDES permit. These issues have not been aired in the lower courts; they remain open for consideration on remand.[6]

C

FOE argues that it is entitled to attorneys' fees on the theory that a plaintiff can be a "prevailing party" for purposes of 33 U.S.C. § 1365(d) if it was the "catalyst" that triggered a favorable outcome. In the decision under review, the Court of Appeals noted that its Circuit precedent construed our decision in *Farrar* v. *Hobby*, 506 U.S. 103 (1992), to require rejection of that theory. 149 F.3d, at 307, n.5 (citing *S—1 & S—2* v. *State Bd. of Ed. of N.C.*, 21 F.3d 49, 51 (CA4 1994) (en banc)). Cf. *Foreman* v. *Dallas County*, 193 F.3d 314, 320 (CA5 1999) (stating, in dicta, that "[a]fter *Farrar* ... the continuing validity of the catalyst theory is in serious doubt").

Farrar acknowledged that a civil rights plaintiff awarded nominal damages may be a "prevailing party" under 42 U.S.C. § 1988. 506 U.S., at 112. The case involved no catalytic effect. Recognizing that the issue was not presented for this Court's decision in *Farrar*, several Courts of Appeals have expressly concluded that *Farrar* did not repudiate the catalyst theory. See *Marbley* v. *Bane*, 57 F.3d 224, 234 (CA2 1995); *Baumgartner* v. *Harrisburg Housing Authority*, 21 F.3d 541, 546—550 (CA3 1994); *Zinn* v. *Shalala*, 35 F.3d 273, 276 (CA7 1994); *Little Rock School Dist.* v. *Pulaski County Special Sch. Dist., #1*, 17 F.3d 260, 263, n.2 (CA8 1994); *Kilgour* v. *Pasadena*, 53 F.3d 1007, 1010 (CA9 1995); *Beard* v. *Teska*, 31 F.3d 942, 951—952 (CA10 1994); *Morris* v. *West Palm Beach*, 194 F.3d 1203, 1207 (CA11 1999). Other Courts of Appeals have likewise continued to apply the catalyst theory notwithstanding *Farrar*. *Paris* v. *United States Dept. of Housing and Urban Development*, 988 F.2d 236, 238 (CA1 1993); *Citizens Against Tax Waste* v. *Westerville City School*, 985 F.2d 255, 257 (CA6 1993).

It would be premature, however, for us to address the continuing validity of the catalyst theory in the context of this case. The District Court, in an order separate from the one in which it imposed civil penalties against Laidlaw, stayed the time for a petition for attorneys' fees until the time for appeal had expired or, if either party appealed, until the appeal was resolved. See 149 F.3d, at 305 (describing order staying time for attorneys' fees petition). In the opinion accompanying its order on penalties, the District Court stated only that "this court has considered that Laidlaw will be required to reimburse plaintiffs for a significant amount of legal fees," and referred to "potential fee awards." 956 F.Supp., at 610—611. Thus, when the Court of Appeals addressed the availability of counsel fees in this case, no order was before it either denying or awarding fees. It is for the District Court, not this Court, to address in the first instance any request for reimbursement of costs, including fees.

* * *

For the reasons stated, the judgment of the United States Court of Appeals for the Fourth Circuit is reversed, and the case is remanded for further proceedings consistent with this opinion.

It is so ordered.

NOTES

[1] The District Court noted that "Laidlaw drafted the state court complaint and settlement agreement, filed the lawsuit against itself, and paid the filing fee." 890 F.Supp., at 489. Further, "the settlement agreement between DHEC and Laidlaw was entered into with unusual haste, without giving the Plaintiffs the opportunity to intervene." *Ibid.* The court found "most persuasive" the fact that "in imposing the civil penalty of $100,000 against Laidlaw, DHEC failed to recover, or even to calculate, the economic benefit that Laidlaw received by not complying with its permit." *Id.,* at 491.

[2] The dissent suggests that there was little deterrent work for civil penalties to do in this case because the lawsuit brought against Laidlaw by DHEC had already pushed the level of deterrence to "near the top of the graph." *Post,* at 11. This suggestion ignores the District Court's specific finding that the penalty agreed to by Laidlaw and DHEC was far too low to remove Laidlaw's economic benefit from noncompliance, and thus was inadequate to deter future violations. 890 F.Supp. 470, 491—494, 497 —498 (SC 1995). And it begins to look especially farfetched when one recalls that Laidlaw itself prompted the DHEC lawsuit, paid the filing fee, and drafted the complaint. See *supra,* at 5, 6, n.1.

[3] In *Tigner* the Court rejected an equal protection challenge to a statutory provision exempting agricultural producers from the reach of the Texas antitrust laws.

[4] In insisting that the redressability requirement is not met, the dissent relies heavily on *Linda R. S.* v. *Richard D.,* 410 U.S. 614 (1973). That reliance is sorely misplaced. In *Linda R. S.*, the mother of an out-of-wedlock child filed suit to force a district attorney to bring a criminal prosecution against the absentee father for failure to pay child support. *Id.,* at 616. In finding that the mother lacked standing to seek this extraordinary remedy, the Court drew attention to "the special status of criminal prosecutions in our system," *id.,* at 619, and carefully limited its holding to the "unique context of a

challenge to [the non-enforcement of] a criminal statute," *id.,* at 617. Furthermore, as to redressability, the relief sought in *Linda R. S.*–a prosecution which, if successful, would automatically land the delinquent father in jail for a fixed term, *id.,* at 618, with predictably negative effects on his earning power–would scarcely remedy the plaintiff's lack of child support payments. In this regard, the Court contrasted "the civil contempt model whereby the defendant 'keeps the keys to the jail in his own pocket' and may be released whenever he complies with his legal obligations." *Ibid.* The dissent's contention, *post* at 7, that "precisely the same situation exists here" as in *Linda R. S.* is, to say the least, extravagant. Putting aside its mistaken reliance on *Linda R. S.*, the dissent's broader charge that citizen suits for civil penalties under the Act carry "grave implications for democratic governance," *post*, at 6, seems to us overdrawn. Certainly the federal Executive Branch does not share the dissent's view that such suits dissipate its authority to enforce the law. In fact, the Department of Justice has endorsed this citizen suit from the outset, submitting *amicus* briefs in support of FOE in the District Court, the Court of Appeals, and this Court. See *supra*, at 6, 7. As we have already noted, *supra*, at 3, the Federal Government retains the power to foreclose a citizen suit by undertaking its own action. 33 U.S.C. § 1365(b)(1)(B). And if the Executive Branch opposes a particular citizen suit, the statute allows the Administrator of the EPA to "intervene as a matter of right" and bring the Government's views to the attention of the court. §1365(c)(2).

[5] Of course we mean sunk costs to the judicial system, not to the litigants. *Lewis* v. *Continental Bank Corp.,* 494 U.S. 472 (1990) (cited by the dissent, *post*, at 17) dealt with the latter, noting that courts should use caution to avoid carrying forward a moot case solely to vindicate a plaintiff's interest in recovering attorneys' fees.

[6] We note that it is far from clear that vacatur of the District Court's judgment would be the appropriate response to a finding of mootness on appeal brought about by the voluntary conduct of the party that lost in the District Court. See *U.S. Bancorp Mortgage Co.* v. *Bonner Mall Partnership,* 513 U.S. 18 (1994) (mootness attributable to a voluntary act of a nonprevailing party ordinarily does not justify vacatur of a judgment under review); see also *Walling* v. *James V. Reuter, Inc.,* 321 U.S. 671 (1944).

CORRECTION OFFICER PORTER, et al. v. RONALD NUSSLE

No. 00-853, February 26, 2002

ON WRIT OF CERTIORARI TO THE UNITED STATES COURT OF APPEALS FOR THE SECOND CIRCUIT

Justice Ginsburg delivered the opinion of the Court.

This case concerns the obligation of prisoners who claim denial of their federal rights while incarcerated to exhaust prison grievance procedures before seeking judicial relief. Plaintiff-respondent Ronald Nussle, an inmate in a Connecticut prison, brought directly to court, without filing an inmate grievance, a complaint charging that corrections officers singled him out for a severe beating, in violation of the Eighth Amendment's ban on "cruel and unusual punishments." Nussle bypassed the grievance procedure despite a provision of the Prison Litigation Reform Act of 1995 (PLRA), 110 Stat. 1321—73, as amended, 42 U.S.C. § 1997e(a) (1994 ed., Supp.V), that directs: "No action shall be brought with respect to prison conditions under section 1983 of this title, or any other Federal law, by a prisoner confined in any jail, prison, or other correctional facility until such administrative remedies as are available are exhausted."

The Court of Appeals for the Second Circuit held that §1997e(a) governs only conditions affecting prisoners generally, not single incidents, such as corrections officers' use of excessive force, actions that immediately affect only particular prisoners. Nussle defends the Second Circuit's judgment, but urges that the relevant distinction is between excessive force claims, which, he says, need not be pursued administratively, and all other claims, which, he recognizes, must proceed first through the prison grievance process. We reject both readings and hold, in line with the text and purpose of the PLRA, our precedent in point, and the weight of lower court authority, that §1997e(a)'s exhaustion requirement applies to all prisoners seeking redress for prison circumstances or occurrences.

I

Respondent Ronald Nussle is an inmate at the Cheshire Correctional Institution in Connecticut. App. 38. According to his complaint, corrections officers at the prison subjected him to "a prolonged and sustained pattern of harassment and intimidation" from the time of his arrival there in May 1996. *Id.*, at 39. Nussle alleged that he was singled out because he was "perceived" to be a friend of the Governor of Connecticut, with whom corrections officers were feuding over labor issues. Ibid.

Concerning the episode in suit, Nussle asserted that, on or about June 15, 1996, several officers, including defendant-petitioner Porter, ordered Nussle to leave his cell, "placed him against a wall and struck him with their hands, kneed him in the back, [and] pulled his hair." *Ibid.* Nussle alleged that the attack was unprovoked and unjustified, and that the officers told him they would kill him if he reported the beating. Ibid.

Then, as now, the Connecticut Department of Correction provided a grievance system for prisoners. See *id.*, at 5—18. Under that system, grievances must be filed within 30 days of the "occurrence." *Id.*, at 11. Rules governing the grievance process include provisions on confidentiality and against reprisals. *Id.*, at 17—18.

Without filing a grievance, on June 10, 1999, Nussle commenced an action in federal district court under 42 U.S.C. § 1983; he filed suit days before the three-year statute of limitations ran out on the §1983 claim.[1] Nussle charged, principally, that the corrections officers' assault violated his right to be free from cruel and unusual punishment under the Eighth Amendment, as made applicable to the States by the Fourteenth Amendment. App. 38. The District Court, relying on §1997e(a), dismissed Nussle's complaint for failure to exhaust administrative remedies. *Nussle* v. *Willette*, 3:99CV1091(AHN) (DConn., Nov. 22, 1999), App.43.

Construing §1997e(a) narrowly because it is an exception "to the general rule of non-exhaustion in §1983 cases," the Court of Appeals for the Second Circuit reversed the District Court's judgment; the appeals court held that "exhaustion of administrative remedies is not required for [prisoner] claims of assault or excessive force brought under §1983." *Nussle* v. *Willette*, 224 F.3d 95, 106 (2000). Section 1997e(a) requires administrative exhaustion of inmates' claims "with respect to prison conditions," but contains no definition of the words "prison conditions." The appeals court found the term "scarcely free of ambiguity." *Id.*, at 101.[2] For purposes of the PLRA's exhaustion requirement, the court concluded, the term was most appropriately read to mean "'circumstances affecting everyone in the area,'" rather than "'single or momentary matter[s],' such as beatings ... directed at particular individuals." *Ibid.* (quoting *Booth* v. *Churner*, 206 F.3d 289, 300—301 (CA3 2000) (Noonan, J., concurring and dissenting), aff'd on other grounds, 532 U.S. 731 (2001)).

The Court of Appeals found support for its position in the PLRA's legislative history. Floor statements "overwhelmingly suggest[ed]" that Congress sought to curtail suits qualifying as "frivolous" because of their "subject matter," *e.g.*, suits over "insufficient storage locker space," "a defective haircut," or "being served chunky peanut butter instead of the creamy variety." 224 F.3d, at 105 (internal quotation marks omitted). Actions seeking relief from corrections officer brutality, the Second Circuit stressed, are not of that genre. Further, the Court of Appeals referred to pre-PLRA decisions in which this Court had "disaggregate[d] the broad category of Eighth Amendment claims so as to distinguish [for proof of injury and *mens rea* purposes] between 'excessive force' claims, on the one hand, and 'conditions of confinement' claims, on the other." *Id.*, at 106 (citing *Hudson* v. *McMillian,* 503 U.S. 1 (1992), and *Farmer* v. *Brennan,* 511 U.S. 825 (1994)).

In conflict with the Second Circuit, other Federal Courts of Appeals have determined that prisoners alleging assaults by prison guards must meet §1997e(a)'s exhaustion requirement before commencing a civil rights action. See *Smith* v. *Zachary,* 255 F.3d 446 (CA7 2001); *Higginbottom* v. *Carter,* 223 F.3d 1259 (CA11 2000); *Booth* v. *Churner,* 206 F.3d 289 (CA3 2000); *Freeman* v. *Francis,* 196 F.3d 641 (CA6 1999). We granted certiorari to resolve the intercircuit conflict, 532 U.S. 1065 (2001), and now reverse the Second Circuit's judgment.

II

Ordinarily, plaintiffs pursuing civil rights claims under 42 U.S.C. § 1983 need not exhaust administrative remedies before filing suit in court. See *Patsy* v. *Board of Regents of Fla.,* 457 U.S. 496, 516 (1982). Prisoner suits alleging constitutional deprivations while incarcerated once fell within this general rule. See *Wilwording* v. *Swenson,* 404 U.S. 249, 251 (1971) *(per curiam).*

In 1980, however, Congress introduced an exhaustion prescription for suits initiated by state prisoners. See Civil Rights of Institutionalized Persons Act, 94 Stat. 352, as amended, 42 U.S.C. § 1997e (1994 ed.). This measure authorized district courts to stay a state prisoner's §1983 action "for a period not to exceed 180 days" while the prisoner exhausted available "plain, speedy, and effective administrative remedies." §1997e(a)(1). Exhaustion under the 1980 prescription was in large part discretionary; it could be ordered only if the State's prison grievance system met specified federal standards, and even then, only if, in the particular case, the court believed the requirement "appropriate and in the interests of justice." §§1997e(a) and (b). We described this provision as a "limited exhaustion requirement" in *McCarthy* v. *Madigan,* 503 U.S. 140, 150—151 (1992), and thought it inapplicable to prisoner suits for damages when monetary relief was unavailable through the prison grievance system.

In 1995, as part of the PLRA, Congress invigorated the exhaustion prescription. The revised exhaustion provision, titled "Suits by prisoners," states: "No action shall be brought with respect to prison conditions under section 1983 of this title, or any other Federal law, by a prisoner confined in any jail, prison, or other correctional facility until such administrative remedies as are available are exhausted." 42 U.S.C. § 1997e(a) (1994 ed., Supp.V).

The current exhaustion provision differs markedly from its predecessor. Once within the discretion of the district court, exhaustion in cases covered by §1997e(a) is now mandatory. See *Booth* v. *Churner,* 532 U.S. 731, 739 (2001). All "available" remedies must now be exhausted; those remedies need not meet federal standards, nor must they be "plain, speedy, and effective." See *ibid.*; see also *id.,* at 740, n.5. Even when the prisoner seeks relief not available in grievance proceedings, notably money damages, exhaustion is a prerequisite to suit. See *id.,* at 741. And unlike the previous provision, which encompassed only §1983 suits, exhaustion is now required for all "action[s] ... brought with respect to prison conditions," whether under §1983 or "any other Federal law." Compare 42 U.S.C. § 1997e (1994 ed.) with 42 U.S.C. § 1997e(a) (1994 ed., Supp.V). Thus federal prisoners suing under *Bivens* v. *Six Unknown Fed. Narcotics Agents,* 403 U.S. 388 (1971), must first exhaust inmate grievance procedures just as state prisoners must exhaust administrative processes prior to instituting a §1983 suit.

Beyond doubt, Congress enacted §1997e(a) to reduce the quantity and improve the quality of prisoner suits; to this purpose, Congress afforded corrections officials time and opportunity to address complaints internally before allowing the initiation of a federal case. In some instances, corrective action taken in response to an inmate's grievance might improve prison administration and satisfy the inmate, thereby obviating the need for litigation. *Booth,* 532 U.S., at 737. In other instances, the internal review might "filter out some frivolous claims." *Ibid.* And for cases ultimately brought to court, adjudication could be facilitated by an administrative record that clarifies the contours of the controversy. See *ibid.*; see also *Madigan,* 503 U.S., at 146.

Congress described the cases covered by §1997e(a)'s exhaustion requirement as "action[s] ... brought with respect to prison conditions." Nussle's case requires us to determine what the §1997e(a) term "prison conditions" means, given Congress' failure to define the term in the text of the exhaustion provision.[3] We are guided in this endeavor by the PLRA's text and context, and by our prior decisions relating to "[s]uits by prisoners," §1997e.[4]

As to precedent, the pathmarking opinion is *McCarthy* v. *Bronson,* 500 U.S. 136 (1991), which construed 28 U.S.C. § 636(b)(1)(B) (1988 ed.), a Judicial Code provision authorizing district judges to refer to magistrate judges, *inter alia,* "prisoner petitions challenging conditions of confinement."[5] The petitioning prisoner in *McCarthy* argued that §636(b)(1)(B) allowed nonconsensual referrals "only when a prisoner challenges ongoing prison conditions." 500 U.S., at 138. The complaint in *McCarthy* targeted no "ongoing prison conditions"; it homed in on "an isolated incident" of excessive force. *Ibid.* For that reason, according to the *McCarthy* petitioner, nonconsensual referral of his case was impermissible. *Id.,* at 138—139.

We did not "quarrel with" the prisoner's assertion in *McCarthy* that "the most natural reading of the phrase 'challenging conditions of confinement,' when viewed in isolation, would not include suits seeking relief from isolated episodes of unconstitutional conduct." *Id.*, at 139. We nonetheless concluded that the petitioner's argument failed upon reading the phrase "in its proper context." *Ibid.* We found no suggestion in §636(b)(1)(B) that Congress meant to divide prisoner petitions "into subcategories." *Ibid.* "On the contrary," we observed, "when the relevant section is read in its entirety, it suggests that Congress intended to authorize the nonconsensual reference of *all* prisoner petitions to a magistrate." *Ibid.* The Federal Magistrates Act, we noted, covers actions of two kinds: challenges to "conditions of confinement"; and "applications for habeas corpus relief." *Id.*, at 140. Congress, we concluded, "intended to include in their entirety th[ose] two primary categories of suits brought by prisoners." Ibid.

"Just three years before [§636(b)(1)(B)] was drafted," we explained in *McCarthy*, "our opinion in *Preiser* v. *Rodriguez*, 411 U.S. 475 (1973), had described [the] two broad categories of prisoner petitions: (1)those challenging the fact or duration of confinement itself; and (2)those challenging the conditions of confinement." *Ibid. Preiser* v. *Rodriguez*, 411 U.S. 475 (1973), left no doubt, we further stated in *McCarthy*, that "the latter category unambiguously embraced the kind of single episode cases that petitioner's construction would exclude." 500 U.S., at 141. We found it telling that Congress, in composing the Magistrates Act, chose language "that so clearly parallel[ed] our *Preiser* opinion." *Id.*, at 142. We considered it significant as well that the purpose of the Magistrates Act–to lighten the caseload of overworked district judges–would be thwarted by opening the door to satellite litigation over "the precise contours of [the] suggested exception for single episode cases." *Id.*, at 143.

As in *McCarthy*, we here read the term "prison conditions" not in isolation, but "in its proper context." *Id.*, at 139. The PLRA exhaustion provision is captioned "Suits by prisoners," see §1997e; this unqualified heading scarcely aids the argument that Congress meant to bi-sect the universe of prisoner suits. See *ibid.*; see also *Almendarez-Torres* v. *United States,* 523 U.S. 224, 234 (1998) ("[T]he title of a statute and the heading of a section are tools available for the resolution of a doubt about the meaning of a statute." (internal quotation marks omitted)).

This Court generally "presume[s] that Congress expects its statutes to be read in conformity with th[e] Court's precedents." *United States* v. *Wells,* 519 U.S. 482, 495 (1997). That presumption, and the PLRA's dominant concern to promote administrative redress, filter out groundless claims, and foster better prepared litigation of claims aired in court, see *Booth*, 532 U.S., at 737, persuade us that §1997e(a)'s key words "prison conditions" are properly read through the lens of *McCarthy* and *Preiser*. Those decisions tug strongly away from classifying suits about prison guards' use of excessive force, one or many times, as anything other than actions "with respect to prison conditions."

Nussle places principal reliance on *Hudson* v. *McMillian,* 503 U.S. 1 (1992), and *Farmer* v. *Brennan,* 511 U.S. 825, 835—836 (1994), and the Second Circuit found support for its position in those cases as well, 224 F.3d, at 106. *Hudson* held that to sustain a claim of excessive force, a prisoner need not show significant injury. 503 U.S., at 9. In so ruling, the Court did indeed distinguish excessive force claims from "conditions of confinement" claims; to sustain a claim of the latter kind "significant injury" must be shown. *Id.*, at 8—9. *Hudson* also observed that a "conditions of confinement" claim may succeed if a prisoner demonstrates that prison officials acted with "deliberate indifference," *id.*, at 8 (citing *Wilson* v. *Seiter,* 501 U.S. 294, 298 (1991)), while a prisoner alleging excessive force must demonstrate that the defendant acted "maliciously and sadistically to cause harm." *Hudson*, 503 U.S., at 7. *Farmer* similarly distinguished the mental state that must be shown to prevail on an excessive force claim, *i.e.*, "purposeful or knowing conduct," from the lesser *mens rea* requirement governing "conditions of confinement" claims, *i.e.*, "deliberate indifference." 511 U.S., at 835—836. We do not question those decisions and attendant distinctions in the context in which they were made. But the question presented here is of a different order.

Hudson and *Farmer* trained solely and precisely on proof requirements: what injury must a plaintiff allege and show; what mental state must a plaintiff plead and prove. Proof requirements once a case is in court, however, do not touch or concern the threshold inquiry before us: whether resort to a prison grievance process must precede resort to a court. We have no reason to believe that Congress meant to release the evidentiary distinctions drawn in *Hudson* and *Farmer* from their moorings and extend their application to the otherwise invigorated exhaustion requirement of §1997e(a). Such an extension would be highly anomalous given Congress' elimination of judicial discretion to dispense with exhaustion and its deletion of the former constraint that administrative remedies must be "plain, speedy, and effective" before exhaustion could be required. See *supra*, at 6; *Booth*, 532 U.S., at 739; cf. *id.*, at 740—741 ("Congress's imposition of an obviously broader exhaustion requirement makes it highly implausible that it meant to give prisoners a strong inducement to skip the administrative process simply by limiting prayers for relief to money damages not offered through administrative grievance mechanisms.").

Nussle contends that Congress added the words "prison conditions" to the text of §1997e(a) specifically to exempt excessive force claims from the now mandatory exhaustion requirement; he sees that requirement as applicable mainly to "'prison conditions'claims that may be frivolous as to subject matter," 224 F.3d, at 106. See Brief for Respondent 2, 26—27. It is at least equally plausible, however, that Congress inserted "prison conditions" into the exhaustion provision simply to make it clear that preincarceration claims fall outside §1997e(a), for example, a TitleVII claim against the prisoner's preincarceration employer, or, for that matter, a §1983 claim against his arresting officer.

Furthermore, the asserted distinction between excessive force claims that need not be exhausted, on the one hand, and exhaustion-mandatory "frivolous" claims on the other, see *id.*, at 2, 26—27, is untenable, for "[e]xcessive force claims can be frivolous," *Smith*, 255 F.3d, at 452 ("Inmates can allege they were subject to vicious nudges."), and exhaustion serves purposes beyond weeding out frivolous allegations, see *supra*, at 6—7.

Other infirmities inhere in the Second Circuit's disposition. See *McCarthy*, 500 U.S., at 143 ("Petitioner's definition would generate additional work for the district courts because the distinction between cases challenging ongoing conditions and those challenging specific acts of alleged misconduct will often be difficult to identify."). As *McCarthy* emphasized, in the prison environment a specific incident may be symptomatic rather than aberrational. *Id.*, at 143—144. An unwarranted assault by a corrections officer may be reflective of a systemic problem traceable to poor hiring practices, inadequate training, or insufficient supervision. See *Smith*, 255 F.3d, at 449. Nussle himself alleged in this very case not only the beating he suffered on June 15, 1996; he also alleged, extending before and after that date, "a prolonged and sustained pattern of harassment and intimidation by correction officers." App. 39. Nussle urges that his case could be placed in the isolated episode category, but he might equally urge that his complaint describes a pattern or practice of harassment climaxing in the alleged beating. It seems unlikely that Congress, when it included in the PLRA a firm exhaustion requirement, meant to leave the need to exhaust to the pleader's option. Cf.*Preiser*, 411 U.S., at 489—490 ("It would wholly frustrate explicit congressional intent to hold that [prisoners] could evade this [exhaustion] requirement by the simple expedient of putting a different label on their pleadings.").

Under Nussle's view and that of the Second Circuit, moreover, bifurcation would be normal when a prisoner sues both a corrections officer alleged to have used excessive force and the supervisor who allegedly failed adequately to monitor those in his charge. Tr. of Oral Arg. 31. The officer alone could be taken directly to court; the charge against the supervisor would proceed first through the internal grievance process. Similarly split proceedings apparently would be in order, under the Second Circuit's decision, when the prisoner elects to pursue against the same officers both discrete instance and ongoing conduct charges.

Finally, we emphasize a concern over and above the complexity augured by the Second Circuit's disposition: Scant sense supports the single occurrence, prevailing circumstance dichotomy. Why should a prisoner have immediate access to court when a guard assaults him on one occasion, but not when beatings are widespread or routine? See *Smith*, 255 F.3d, at 450. Nussle's distinction between excessive force claims and all other prisoner suits, see *supra*, at 2, presents a similar anomaly. Do prison authorities have an interest in receiving prompt notice of, and opportunity to take action against, guard brutality that is somehow less compelling than their interest in receiving notice and an opportunity to stop other types of staff wrongdoing? See *Preiser*, 411 U.S., at 492 ("Since [the] internal problems of state prisons involve issues so peculiarly within state authority and expertise, the States have an important interest in not being bypassed in the correction of those problems.").[6]

* * *

For the reasons stated, we hold that the PLRA's exhaustion requirement applies to all inmate suits about prison life, whether they involve general circumstances or particular episodes, and whether they allege excessive force or some other wrong. Cf. *Wilson,* 501 U.S., at 299, n.1. Accordingly, the judgment of the Court of Appeals is reversed, and the case is remanded for further proceedings consistent with this opinion.

It is so ordered.

NOTES

[1] The Second Circuit has held that §1983 actions in Connecticut are governed by that State's three-year statute of limitations for tort actions. *Williams* v. *Walsh*, 558 F.2d 667, 670 (1977).

[2] Another provision of the PLRA, 18 U.S.C. § 3626(g)(2) (1994 ed., Supp.V), the court observed, does define "prison conditions." *Nussle* v. *Willette*, 224 F.3d 95, 101 (CA2 2000). That provision, which concerns prospective relief, defines "prison conditions" to mean "the conditions of confinement or the effects of actions by government officials on the lives of persons confined in prison." The Second Circuit found the §3626(g)(2) definition "no less ambiguous" than the bare text of §1997e(a). Neither of the alternative §3626(g)(2) formulations, the court said, would be used in "everyday" speech to describe "particular instances of assault or excessive force." *Id.*, at 102. But see *Booth* v. *Churner*, 206 F.3d 289, 294—295 (CA3 2000), aff'd on other grounds, 532 U.S. 731 (2001) (reading §3626(g)(2) to cover all prison conditions and corrections officer actions that "make [prisoners'] lives worse"). The Second Circuit ultimately concluded that it would be improper, in any event, automatically to import §3626(g)(2)'s "definition of 'civil actions brought with respect to prison conditions' into 42 U.S.C. § 1997e(a)" because the two provisions had "distinct statutory purposes." 224 F.3d, at 105.

[3] The parties dispute the meaning of a simultaneously enacted provision, §3626(g)(2), which concerns prospective relief, and for that purpose, defines the expression "civil action with respect to prison conditions." See *supra*, at 3, n.2 (noting, *inter alia*, divergent constructions of Second and Third Circuits). We rest our decision on the meaning of "prison conditions" in the context of §1997e, and express no definitive opinion on the proper reading of §3626(g)(2).

[4] In reaching its decision, the Second Circuit referred to its "obligation to construe statutory exceptions narrowly, in order to give full effect to the general rule of non-exhaustion in §1983." 224 F.3d, at 106 (citing *City of Edmonds* v. *Oxford House, Inc.,* 514 U.S. 725, 731—732 (1995), and *Patsy* v. *Board of*

Regents of Fla., 457 U.S. 496, 508 (1982)). The Second Circuit did not then have available to it our subsequently rendered decision in *Booth* v. *Churner,* 532 U.S. 731 (2001). *Booth* held that §1997e(a) mandates initial recourse to the prison grievance process even when a prisoner seeks only money damages, a remedy not available in that process. See *id.,* at 741. In so ruling, we observed that "Congress … may well have thought we were shortsighted" in failing adequately to recognize the utility of the administrative process to satisfy, reduce, or clarify prisoner grievances. *Id.,* at 737. While the canon on which the Second Circuit relied may be dependable in other contexts, the PLRA establishes a different regime. For litigation within §1997e(a)'s compass, Congress has replaced the "general rule of non-exhaustion" with a general rule of exhaustion.

[5] Title 28 U.S.C. § 636(b)(1)(B) provides in relevant part: "(b)(1) Notwithstanding any provision of law to the contrary– . . . "a judge may … designate a magistrate to conduct hearings, including evidentiary hearings, and to submit to a judge of the court proposed findings of fact and recommendations for the disposition, by a judge of the court, … of applications for posttrial relief made by individuals convicted of criminal offenses and of prisoner petitions challenging conditions of confinement."

[6] Other provisions of §1997e that refer to "prison conditions" would have less scope under the Second Circuit's construction of the term. Section 1997e(c)(1) provides for dismissal on the court's own initiative of "any action brought with respect to prison conditions" that is "frivolous [or] malicious." No specific incident complaint would be subject to that prescription under the view that such suits do not implicate "prison conditions." Further, §1997e(f)(1) provides that pretrial proceedings in "any action brought with respect to prison conditions" may be held at the prison via telephone, video conference, or other telecommunications technology so that the prisoner need not be physically transferred to participate. Surely such arrangements would be appropriate in Nussle's case and others of its genre. But on what authority would these practical procedures rest if cases like Nussle's do not qualify as actions regarding "prison conditions"?

ERIC ELDRED, et al. v. JOHN D. ASHCROFT, ATTORNEY GENERAL

No. 01-618, January 15, 2003

ON WRIT OF CERTIORARI TO THE UNITED STATES COURT OF APPEALS FOR THE DISTRICT OF COLUMBIA CIRCUIT

Justice Ginsburg delivered the opinion of the Court.

This case concerns the authority the Constitution assigns to Congress to prescribe the duration of copyrights. The Copyright and Patent Clause of the Constitution, Art. I, §8, cl. 8, provides as to copyrights: "Congress shall have Power … [t]o promote the Progress of Science … by securing [to Authors] for limited Times … the exclusive Right to their … Writings." In 1998, in the measure here under inspection, Congress enlarged the duration of copyrights by 20 years. Copyright Term Extension Act (CTEA), Pub. L. 105—298, §102(b) and (d), 112 Stat. 2827—2828 (amending 17 U.S.C. § 302 304). As in the case of prior extensions, principally in 1831, 1909, and 1976, Congress provided for application of the enlarged terms to existing and future copyrights alike.

Petitioners are individuals and businesses whose products or services build on copyrighted works that have gone into the public domain. They seek a determination that the CTEA fails constitutional review under both the Copyright Clause's "limited Times" prescription and the First Amendment's free speech guarantee. Under the 1976 Copyright Act, copyright protection generally lasted from the work's creation until 50 years after the author's death. Pub. L. 94—553, §302(a), 90 Stat. 2572 (1976 Act). Under the CTEA, most copyrights now run from creation until 70 years after the author's death. 17 U.S.C. § 302(a). Petitioners do not challenge the "life-plus-70-years" time span itself. "Whether 50 years is enough, or 70 years too much," they acknowledge, "is not a judgment meet for this Court." Brief for Petitioners 14.[1] Congress went awry, petitioners maintain, not with respect to newly created works, but in enlarging the term for published works with existing copyrights. The "limited Tim[e]" in effect when a copyright is secured, petitioners urge, becomes the constitutional boundary, a clear line beyond the power of Congress to extend. See *ibid.* As to the First Amendment, petitioners contend that the CTEA is a content-neutral regulation of speech that fails inspection under the heightened judicial scrutiny appropriate for such regulations.

In accord with the District Court and the Court of Appeals, we reject petitioners' challenges to the CTEA. In that 1998 legislation, as in all previous copyright term extensions, Congress placed existing and future copyrights in parity. In prescribing that alignment, we hold, Congress acted within its authority and did not transgress constitutional limitations.

I

A

We evaluate petitioners' challenge to the constitutionality of the CTEA against the backdrop of Congress' previous exercises of its authority under the Copyright Clause. The Nation's first copyright statute, enacted in 1790, provided a federal copyright term of 14 years from the date of publication, renewable for an additional 14 years if the author survived the first term. Act of May 31, 1790, ch. 15, §1, 1 Stat. 124 (1790 Act). The 1790 Act's renewable 14-year term applied to existing works (*i.e.*, works already published and works created but not yet published) and future works alike. *Ibid.* Congress expanded the federal copyright term to 42 years in 1831 (28 years from publication, renewable for an additional 14 years), and to 56 years in 1909 (28 years from publication, renewable for an additional 28 years). Act of Feb. 3, 1831, ch. 16, §§1, 16, 4 Stat. 436, 439 (1831 Act); Act of Mar. 4, 1909, ch. 320, §§23—24, 35 Stat. 1080—1081 (1909 Act). Both times, Congress applied the new copyright term to existing and future works, 1831 Act §§1, 16; 1909 Act §§23—24; to qualify for the 1831 extension, an existing work had to be in its initial copyright term at the time the Act became effective, 1831 Act §§1, 16.

In 1976, Congress altered the method for computing federal copyright terms. 1976 Act §§302—304. For works created by identified natural persons, the 1976 Act provided that federal copyright protection would run from the work's creation, not–as in the 1790, 1831, and 1909 Acts–its publication; protection would last until 50 years after the author's death. §302(a). In these respects, the 1976 Act aligned United States copyright terms with the then-dominant international standard adopted under the Berne Convention for the Protection of Literary and Artistic Works. See H. R. Rep. No. 94—1476, p. 135 (1976). For anonymous works, pseudonymous works, and works made for hire, the 1976 Act provided a term of 75 years from publication or 100 years from creation, whichever expired first. §302(c).

These new copyright terms, the 1976 Act instructed, governed all works not published by its effective date of January 1, 1978, regardless of when the works were created. §§302—303. For published works with existing copyrights as of that date, the 1976 Act granted a copyright term of 75 years from the date of publication, §304(a) and (b), a 19-year increase over the 56-year term applicable under the 1909 Act.

The measure at issue here, the CTEA, installed the fourth major duration extension of federal copyrights.[2] Retaining the general structure of the 1976 Act, the CTEA enlarges the terms of all existing and future copyrights by 20 years. For works created by identified natural persons, the term now lasts from creation until 70 years after the author's death. 17 U.S.C. § 302(a). This standard harmonizes the baseline United States copyright term with the term adopted by the European Union in 1993. See Council Directive 93/98/EEC of 29 October 1993 Harmonizing the Term of Protection of Copyright and Certain Related Rights, 1993 Official J. Eur. Cmty. 290 (EU Council Directive 93/98). For anonymous works, pseudonymous works, and works made for hire, the term is 95 years from publication or 120 years from creation, whichever expires first. 17 U.S.C. § 302(c).

Paralleling the 1976 Act, the CTEA applies these new terms to all works not published by January 1, 1978. §§302(a), 303(a). For works published before 1978 with existing copyrights as of the CTEA's effective date, the CTEA extends the term to 95 years from publication. §304(a) and (b). Thus, in common with the 1831, 1909, and 1976 Acts, the CTEA's new terms apply to both future and existing copyrights.[3]

B

Petitioners' suit challenges the CTEA's constitutionality under both the Copyright Clause and the First Amendment. On cross-motions for judgment on the pleadings, the District Court entered judgment for the Attorney General (respondent here). 74 F. Supp. 2d 1 (DC 1999). The court held that the CTEA does not violate the "limited Times" restriction of the Copyright Clause because the CTEA's terms, though longer than the 1976 Act's terms, are still limited, not perpetual, and therefore fit within Congress' discretion. Id., at 3. The court also held that "there are no First Amendment rights to use the copyrighted works of others." Ibid.

The Court of Appeals for the District of Columbia Circuit affirmed. 239 F.3d 372 (2001). In that court's unanimous view, Harper & Row, Publishers, Inc. v. Nation Enterprises, 471 U.S. 539 (1985), foreclosed petitioners' First Amendment challenge to the CTEA. 239 F.3d, at 375. Copyright, the court reasoned, does not impermissibly restrict free speech, for it grants the author an exclusive right only to the specific form of expression; it does not shield any idea or fact contained in the copyrighted work, and it allows for "fair use" even of the expression itself. Id., at 375—376.

A majority of the Court of Appeals also upheld the CTEA against petitioners' contention that the measure exceeds Congress' power under the Copyright Clause. Specifically, the court rejected petitioners' plea for interpretation of the "limited Times" prescription not discretely but with a view to the "preambular statement of purpose" contained in the Copyright Clause: "To promote the Progress of Science." Id., at 377—378. Circuit precedent, Schnapper v. Foley, 667 F.2d 102 (CADC 1981), the court determined, precluded that plea. In this regard, the court took into account petitioners' acknowledgment that the preamble itself places no substantive limit on Congress' legislative power. 239 F.3d, at 378.

The appeals court found nothing in the constitutional text or its history to suggest that "a term of years for a copyright is not a 'limited Time' if it may later be extended for another 'limited Time.'" Id., at 379. The court recounted that "the First Congress made the Copyright Act of 1790 applicable to subsisting copyrights arising under the copyright laws of the several states." Ibid. That construction of Congress' authority under the Copyright Clause "by [those] contemporary with [the Constitution's] formation," the court said, merited "very great" and in this case "almost conclusive" weight. Ibid. (quoting Burrow-Giles Lithographic Co. v. Sarony, 111 U.S. 53, 57 (1884)). As early as McClurg v. Kingsland, 1 How. 202 (1843), the Court of Appeals added, this Court had made it "plain" that the same Clause permits Congress to "amplify the terms of an existing patent." 239 F.3d, at 380. The appeals court recognized that this Court has been similarly deferential to the judgment of Congress in the realm of copyright. Ibid. (citing Sony Corp. of America v. Universal City Studios, Inc., 464 U.S. 417 (1984); Stewart v. Abend, 495 U.S. 207 (1990)).

Concerning petitioners' assertion that Congress might evade the limitation on its authority by stringing together "an unlimited number of 'limited Times,'" the Court of Appeals stated that such legislative misbehavior "clearly is not the situation before us." 239 F.3d, at 379. Rather, the court noted, the CTEA "matches" the baseline term for "United States copyrights [with] the terms of copyrights granted by the European Union." Ibid. "[I]n an era of multinational publishers and instantaneous electronic transmission," the court said, "harmonization in this regard has obvious practical benefits" and is "a 'necessary and proper' measure to meet contemporary circumstances rather than a step on the way to making copyrights perpetual." Ibid.

Judge Sentelle dissented in part. He concluded that Congress lacks power under the Copyright Clause to expand the copyright terms of existing works. Id., at 380—384. The Court of Appeals subsequently denied rehearing and rehearing en banc. 255 F.3d 849 (2001).

We granted certiorari to address two questions: whether the CTEA's extension of existing copyrights exceeds Congress' power under the Copyright Clause; and whether the CTEA's extension of existing and future copyrights violates the First Amendment. 534 U.S. 1126 and 1160 (2002). We now answer those two questions in the negative and affirm.

II

A

We address first the determination of the courts below that Congress has authority under the Copyright Clause to extend the terms of existing copyrights. Text, history, and precedent, we conclude, confirm that the Copyright Clause empowers Congress to prescribe "limited Times" for copyright protection and to secure the same level and duration of protection for all copyright holders, present and future.

The CTEA's baseline term of life plus 70 years, petitioners concede, qualifies as a "limited Tim[e]" as applied to future copyrights.[4] Petitioners contend, however, that existing copyrights extended to endure for that same term are not "limited." Petitioners' argument essentially reads into the text of the Copyright Clause the command that a time prescription, once set, becomes forever "fixed" or "inalterable." The word "limited," however, does not convey a meaning so constricted. At the time of the Framing, that word meant what it means today: "confine[d] within certain bounds," "restrain[ed]," or "circumscribe[d]." S. Johnson, A Dictionary of the English Language (7th ed. 1785); see T. Sheridan, A Complete Dictionary of the English Language (6th ed. 1796) ("confine[d] within certain bounds"); Webster's Third New International Dictionary 1312 (1976) ("confined within limits"; "restricted in extent, number, or duration"). Thus understood, a time span appropriately "limited" as applied to future copyrights does not automatically cease to be "limited" when applied to existing copyrights. And as we observe, *infra*, at 18, there is no cause to suspect that a purpose to evade the "limited Times" prescription prompted Congress to adopt the CTEA.

To comprehend the scope of Congress' power under the Copyright Clause, "a page of history is worth a volume of logic." *New York Trust Co.* v. *Eisner,* 256 U.S. 345, 349 (1921) (Holmes, J.). History reveals an unbroken congressional practice of granting to authors of works with existing copyrights the benefit of term extensions so that all under copyright protection will be governed evenhandedly under the same regime. As earlier recounted, see *supra,* at 3, the First Congress accorded the protections of the Nation's first federal copyright statute to existing and future works alike. 1790 Act §1.[5] Since then, Congress has regularly applied duration extensions to both existing and future copyrights. 1831 Act §§1, 16; 1909 Act §§23—24; 1976 Act §§302—303; 17 U.S.C. § 302—304.[6]

Because the Clause empowering Congress to confer copyrights also authorizes patents, congressional practice with respect to patents informs our inquiry. We count it significant that early Congresses extended the duration of numerous individual patents as well as copyrights. See, *e.g.,* Act of Jan. 7, 1808, ch. 6, 6 Stat. 70 (patent); Act of Mar. 3, 1809, ch. 35, 6 Stat. 80 (patent); Act of Feb. 7, 1815, ch. 36, 6 Stat. 147 (patent); Act of May 24, 1828, ch. 145, 6 Stat. 389 (copyright); Act of Feb. 11, 1830, ch. 13, 6 Stat. 403 (copyright); see generally Ochoa, Patent and Copyright Term Extension and the Constitution: A Historical Perspective, 49 J. Copyright Society 19 (2001). The courts saw no "limited Times" impediment to such extensions; renewed or extended terms were upheld in the early days, for example, by Chief Justice Marshall and Justice Story sitting as circuit justices. See *Evans* v. *Jordan,* 8 F. Cas. 872, 874 (No. 4,564) (CC Va. 1813) (Marshall, J.) ("Th[e] construction of the constitution which admits the renewal of a patent is not controverted. A renewed patent ... confers the same rights, with an original."), aff'd, 9 Cranch 199 (1815); *Blanchard* v. *Sprague,* 3 F. Cas. 648, 650 (No. 1,518) (CC Mass. 1839) (Story, J.) ("I never have entertained any doubt of the constitutional authority of congress" to enact a 14-year patent extension that "operates retrospectively"); see also *Evans* v. *Robinson,* 8 F. Cas. 886, 888 (No. 4,571) (CC Md. 1813) (Congresses "have the exclusive right ... to limit the times for which a patent right shall be granted, and are not restrained from renewing a patent or prolonging" it.).[7]

Further, although prior to the instant case this Court did not have occasion to decide whether extending the duration of existing copyrights complies with the "limited Times" prescription, the Court has found no constitutional barrier to the legislative expansion of existing patents.[8] *McClurg* v. *Kingsland,* 1 How. 202 (1843), is the pathsetting precedent. The patentee in that case was unprotected under the law in force when the patent issued because he had allowed his employer briefly to practice the invention before he obtained the patent. Only upon enactment, two years later, of an exemption for such allowances did the patent become valid, retroactive to the time it issued. *McClurg* upheld retroactive application of the new law. The Court explained that the legal regime governing a particular patent "depend[s] on the law as it stood at the emanation of the patent, together with such changes as have been since made; for though they may be retrospective in their operation, that is not a sound objection to their validity." *Id.,* at 206.[9] Neither is it a sound objection to the validity of a copyright term extension, enacted pursuant to the same constitutional grant of authority, that the enlarged term covers existing copyrights.

Congress' consistent historical practice of applying newly enacted copyright terms to future and existing copyrights reflects a judgment stated concisely by Representative Huntington at the time of the 1831 Act: "[J]ustice, policy, and equity alike forb[id]" that an "author who had sold his [work] a week ago, be placed in a worse situation than the author who should sell his work the day after the passing of [the] act." 7 Cong. Deb. 424 (1831); accord Symposium, The Constitutionality of Copyright Term Extension, 18 Cardozo Arts & Ent. L. J. 651, 694 (2000) (Prof. Miller) ("[S]ince 1790, it has indeed been Congress's policy that the author of yesterday's work should not get a lesser reward than the author of tomorrow's work just because Congress passed a statute lengthening the term today."). The CTEA follows this historical practice by keeping the duration provisions of the 1976 Act largely in place and simply adding 20 years to each of them. Guided by text, history, and precedent, we cannot agree with petitioners' submission that extending the duration of existing copyrights is categorically beyond Congress' authority under the Copyright Clause.

Satisfied that the CTEA complies with the "limited Times" prescription, we turn now to whether it is a rational exercise of the legislative authority conferred by the Copyright Clause. On that point, we defer substantially to Congress. *Sony,* 464 U.S., at 429 ("[I]t is Congress that has been assigned the task of defining the scope of the limited monopoly that should be granted to authors ... in order to give the public appropriate access to their work product.").[10]

The CTEA reflects judgments of a kind Congress typically makes, judgments we cannot dismiss as outside the

Legislature's domain. As respondent describes, see Brief for Respondent 37—38, a key factor in the CTEA's passage was a 1993 European Union (EU) directive instructing EU members to establish a copyright term of life plus 70 years. EU Council Directive 93/98, p. 4; see 144 Cong. Rec. S12377—S12378 (daily ed. Oct. 12, 1998) (statement of Sen. Hatch). Consistent with the Berne Convention, the EU directed its members to deny this longer term to the works of any non-EU country whose laws did not secure the same extended term. See Berne Conv. Art. 7(8); P. Goldstein, International Copyright §5.3, p. 239 (2001). By extending the baseline United States copyright term to life plus 70 years, Congress sought to ensure that American authors would receive the same copyright protection in Europe as their European counterparts.[11] The CTEA may also provide greater incentive for American and other authors to create and disseminate their work in the United States. See Perlmutter, Participation in the International Copyright System as a Means to Promote the Progress of Science and Useful Arts, 36 Loyola (LA) L. Rev. 323, 330 (2002) ("[M]atching th[e] level of [copyright] protection in the United States [to that in the EU] can ensure stronger protection for U.S. works abroad and avoid competitive disadvantages vis-à-vis foreign rightholders."); see also id., at 332 (the United States could not "play a leadership role" in the give-and-take evolution of the international copyright system, indeed it would "lose all flexibility," "if the only way to promote the progress of science were to provide incentives to create new works").[12]

In addition to international concerns,[13] Congress passed the CTEA in light of demographic, economic, and technological changes, Brief for Respondent 25—26, 33, and nn. 23 and 24,[14] and rationally credited projections that longer terms would encourage copyright holders to invest in the restoration and public distribution of their works, id., at 34—37; see H. R. Rep. No. 105—452, p. 4 (1998) (term extension "provide[s] copyright owners generally with the incentive to restore older works and further disseminate them to the public").[15]

In sum, we find that the CTEA is a rational enactment; we are not at liberty to second-guess congressional determinations and policy judgments of this order, however debatable or arguably unwise they may be. Accordingly, we cannot conclude that the CTEA–which continues the unbroken congressional practice of treating future and existing copyrights in parity for term extension purposes–is an impermissible exercise of Congress' power under the Copyright Clause.

B

Petitioners' Copyright Clause arguments rely on several novel readings of the Clause. We next address these arguments and explain why we find them unpersuasive.

1

Petitioners contend that even if the CTEA's 20-year term extension is literally a "limited Tim[e]," permitting Congress to extend existing copyrights allows it to evade the "limited Times" constraint by creating effectively perpetual copyrights through repeated extensions. We disagree.

As the Court of Appeals observed, a regime of perpetual copyrights "clearly is not the situation before us." 239 F.3d, at 379. Nothing before this Court warrants construction of the CTEA's 20-year term extension as a congressional attempt to evade or override the "limited Times" constraint.[16] Critically, we again emphasize, petitioners fail to show how the CTEA crosses a constitutionally significant threshold with respect to "limited Times" that the 1831, 1909, and 1976 Acts did not. See supra, at 3—5; Austin, supra, n. 13, at 56 ("If extending copyright protection to works already in existence is constitutionally suspect," so is "extending the protections of U. S copyright law to works by foreign authors that had already been created and even first published when the federal rights attached."). Those earlier Acts did not create perpetual copyrights, and neither does the CTEA.[17]

2

Petitioners dominantly advance a series of arguments all premised on the proposition that Congress may not extend an existing copyright absent new consideration from the author. They pursue this main theme under three headings. Petitioners contend that the CTEA's extension of existing copyrights (1) overlooks the requirement of "originality," (2) fails to "promote the Progress of Science," and (3) ignores copyright's quid pro quo.

Petitioners' "originality" argument draws on Feist Publications, Inc. v. Rural Telephone Service Co., 499 U.S. 340 (1991). In Feist, we observed that "[t]he sine qua non of copyright is originality," id., at 345, and held that copyright protection is unavailable to "a narrow category of works in which the creative spark is utterly lacking or so trivial as to be virtually nonexistent," id., at 359. Relying on Feist, petitioners urge that even if a work is sufficiently "original" to qualify for copyright protection in the first instance, any extension of the copyright's duration is impermissible because, once published, a work is no longer original.

Feist, however, did not touch on the duration of copyright protection. Rather, the decision addressed the core question of copyrightability, i.e., the "creative spark" a work must have to be eligible for copyright protection at all. Explaining the originality requirement, Feist trained on the Copyright Clause words "Authors" and "Writings." Id., at 346—347. The decision did not construe the "limited Times" for which a work may be protected, and the originality requirement has no bearing on that prescription.

More forcibly, petitioners contend that the CTEA's extension of existing copyrights does not "promote the Progress of Science" as contemplated by the preambular language of the Copyright Clause. Art. I, §8, cl. 8. To sustain this objection, petitioners do not argue that the Clause's preamble is an independently enforceable limit on Congress' power. See 239 F.3d, at 378 (Petitioners acknowledge that "the preamble of the Copyright Clause is not a substantive limit on Congress' legislative power." (internal quotation marks omitted)). Rather, they maintain that the preambular language identifies the sole end to which Congress may legislate; accordingly, they conclude, the meaning of "limited Times" must be "determined in light of that specified end." Brief for Petitioners 19. The CTEA's extension of existing copyrights categorically fails to "promote the Progress of Science," petitioners argue, because it does not stimulate the creation of new works but merely adds value to works already created.

As petitioners point out, we have described the Copyright Clause as "both a grant of power and a limitation," *Graham* v. *John Deere Co. of Kansas City,* 383 U.S. 1, 5 (1966), and have said that "[t]he primary objective of copyright" is "[t]o promote the Progress of Science," *Feist,* 499 U.S., at 349. The "constitutional command," we have recognized, is that Congress, to the extent it enacts copyright laws at all, create a "system" that "promote[s] the Progress of Science." *Graham,* 383 U.S., at 6.[18]

We have also stressed, however, that it is generally for Congress, not the courts, to decide how best to pursue the Copyright Clause's objectives. See *Stewart* v. *Abend,* 495 U.S., at 230 ("Th[e] evolution of the duration of copyright protection tellingly illustrates the difficulties Congress faces ... . [I]t is not our role to alter the delicate balance Congress has labored to achieve."); *Sony,* 464 U.S., at 429 ("[I]t is Congress that has been assigned the task of defining the scope of [rights] that should be granted to authors or to inventors in order to give the public appropriate access to their work product."); *Graham,* 383 U.S., at 6 ("Within the limits of the constitutional grant, the Congress may, of course, implement the stated purpose of the Framers by selecting the policy which in its judgment best effectuates the constitutional aim."). The justifications we earlier set out for Congress' enactment of the CTEA, *supra,* at 14—17, provide a rational basis for the conclusion that the CTEA "promote[s] the Progress of Science."

On the issue of copyright duration, Congress, from the start, has routinely applied new definitions or adjustments of the copyright term to both future works and existing works not yet in the public domain.[19] Such consistent congressional practice is entitled to "very great weight, and when it is remembered that the rights thus established have not been disputed during a period of [over two] centur[ies], it is almost conclusive." *Burrow-Giles Lithographic Co.* v. *Sarony,* 111 U.S., at 57. Indeed, "[t]his Court has repeatedly laid down the principle that a contemporaneous legislative exposition of the Constitution when the founders of our Government and framers of our Constitution were actively participating in public affairs, acquiesced in for a long term of years, fixes the construction to be given [the Constitution's] provisions." *Myers* v. *United States,* 272 U.S. 52, 175 (1926). Congress' unbroken practice since the founding generation thus overwhelms petitioners' argument that the CTEA's extension of existing copyrights fails *per se* to "promote the Progress of Science."[20]

Closely related to petitioners' preambular argument, or a variant of it, is their assertion that the Copyright Clause "imbeds a quid pro quo." Brief for Petitioners 23. They contend, in this regard, that Congress may grant to an "Autho[r]" an "exclusive Right" for a "limited Tim[e]," but only in exchange for a "Writin[g]." Congress' power to confer copyright protection, petitioners argue, is thus contingent upon an exchange: The author of an original work receives an "exclusive Right" for a "limited Tim[e]" in exchange for a dedication to the public thereafter. Extending an existing copyright without demanding additional consideration, petitioners maintain, bestows an unpaid-for benefit on copyright holders and their heirs, in violation of the *quid pro quo* requirement.

We can demur to petitioners' description of the Copyright Clause as a grant of legislative authority empowering Congress "to secure a bargain–this for that." Brief for Petitioners 16; see *Mazer* v. *Stein,* 347 U.S. 201, 219 (1954) ("The economic philosophy behind the clause empowering Congress to grant patents and copyrights is the conviction that encouragement of individual effort by personal gain is the best way to advance public welfare through the talents of authors and inventors in 'Science and useful Arts.'"). But the legislative evolution earlier recalled demonstrates what the bargain entails. Given the consistent placement of existing copyright holders in parity with future holders, the author of a work created in the last 170 years would reasonably comprehend, as the "this" offered her, a copyright not only for the time in place when protection is gained, but also for any renewal or extension legislated during that time.[21] Congress could rationally seek to "promote ... Progress" by including in every copyright statute an express guarantee that authors would receive the benefit of any later legislative extension of the copyright term. Nothing in the Copyright Clause bars Congress from creating the same incentive by adopting the same position as a matter of unbroken practice. See Brief for Respondent 31—32.

Neither *Sears, Roebuck & Co.* v. *Stiffel Co.,* 376 U.S. 225 (1964), nor *Bonito Boats, Inc.* v. *Thunder Craft Boats, Inc.,* 489 U.S. 141 (1989), is to the contrary. In both cases, we invalidated the application of certain state laws as inconsistent with the federal patent regime. *Sears,* 376 U.S., at 231—233; *Bonito,* 489 U.S., at 152. Describing Congress' constitutional authority to confer patents, *Bonito Boats* noted: "The Patent Clause itself reflects a balance between the need to encourage innovation and the avoidance of monopolies which stifle competition without any concomitant advance in the 'Progress of Science and useful Arts.'" *Id.,* at 146. *Sears* similarly stated that "[p]atents are not given as favors ... but are meant to encourage invention by rewarding the inventor with the right, limited to a term of years fixed by the patent, to exclude others from the use of his invention." 376 U.S., at 229. Neither case concerned the extension of a patent's duration. Nor did either suggest that such an extension might be constitutionally infirm. Rather, *Bonito Boats* reiterated the Court's unclouded understanding: "It is for Congress to determine if the present system" effectuates the goals of the Copyright and Patent Clause. 489 U.S., at 168. And as we have documented, see *supra,* at 10—13, Congress has many times sought to effectuate those goals by extending existing patents.

215

We note, furthermore, that patents and copyrights do not entail the same exchange, and that our references to a *quid pro quo* typically appear in the patent context. See, *e.g., J. E. M. Ag Supply, Inc.* v. *Pioneer Hi-Bred International, Inc.,* 534 U.S. 124, 142 (2001) ("The disclosure required by the Patent Act is 'the *quid pro quo* of the right to exclude.'" (quoting *Kewanee Oil Co.* v. *Bicron Corp.,* 416 U.S. 470, 484 (1974))); *Bonito Boats,* 489 U.S., at 161 ("the *quid pro quo* of substantial creative effort required by the federal [patent] statute"); *Brenner* v. *Manson,* 383 U.S. 519, 534 (1966) ("The basic *quid pro quo* … for granting a patent monopoly is the benefit derived by the public from an invention with substantial utility."); *Pennock* v. *Dialogue,* 2 Pet. 1, 23 (1829) (If an invention is already commonly known and used when the patent is sought, "there might be sound reason for presuming, that the legislature did not intend to grant an exclusive right," given the absence of a "*quid pro quo.*"). This is understandable, given that immediate disclosure is not the objective of, but is *exacted from*, the patentee. It is the price paid for the exclusivity secured. See *J. E. M. Ag Supply,* 534 U.S., at 142. For the author seeking copyright protection, in contrast, disclosure is the desired objective, not something exacted from the author in exchange for the copyright. Indeed, since the 1976 Act, copyright has run from creation, not publication. See 1976 Act §302(a); 17 U.S.C. § 302(a).

Further distinguishing the two kinds of intellectual property, copyright gives the holder no monopoly on any knowledge. A reader of an author's writing may make full use of any fact or idea she acquires from her reading. See §102(b). The grant of a patent, on the other hand, does prevent full use by others of the inventor's knowledge. See Brief for Respondent 22; *Alfred Bell & Co.* v. *Catalda Fine Arts,* 191 F.2d 99, 103, n. 16 (CA2 1951) (The monopoly granted by a copyright "is not a monopoly of knowledge. The grant of a patent does prevent full use being made of knowledge, but the reader of a book is not by the copyright laws prevented from making full use of any information he may acquire from his reading." (quoting W. Copinger, Law of Copyright 2 (7th ed. 1936))). In light of these distinctions, one cannot extract from language in our patent decisions–language not trained on a grant's duration–genuine support for petitioners' bold view. Accordingly, we reject the proposition that a *quid pro quo* require-ment stops Congress from expanding copyright's termin a manner that puts existing and future copyrights in parity.[22]

3

As an alternative to their various arguments that extending existing copyrights violates the Copyright Clause *per se*, petitioners urge heightened judicial review of such extensions to ensure that they appropriately pursue the purposes of the Clause. See Brief for Petitioners 31—32. Specifically, petitioners ask us to apply the "congruence and proportionality" standard described in cases evaluating exercises of Congress' power under §5 of the Fourteenth Amendment. See, *e.g., City of Boerne* v. *Flores,* 521 U.S. 507 (1997). But we have never applied that standard outside the §5 context; it does not hold sway for judicial review of legislation enacted, as copyright laws are, pursuant to Article I authorization.

Section 5 authorizes Congress to *enforce* commands contained in and incorporated into the Fourteenth Amendment. Amdt. 14, §5 ("The Congress shall have power to *enforce*, by appropriate legislation, the provisions of this article." (emphasis added)). The Copyright Clause, in contrast, empowers Congress to *define* the scope of the substantive right. See *Sony,* 464 U.S., at 429. Judicial deference to such congressional definition is "but a corollary to the grant to Congress of any Article I power." *Graham,* 383 U.S., at 6. It would be no more appropriate for us to subject the CTEA to "congruence and proportionality" review under the Copyright Clause than it would be for us to hold the Act unconstitutional *per se*.

For the several reasons stated, we find no Copyright Clause impediment to the CTEA's extension of existing copyrights.

III

Petitioners separately argue that the CTEA is a content-neutral regulation of speech that fails heightened judicial review under the First Amendment.[23] We reject petitioners' plea for imposition of uncommonly strict scrutiny on a copyright scheme that incorporates its own speech-protective purposes and safeguards. The Copyright Clause and First Amendment were adopted close in time. This proximity indicates that, in the Framers' view, copyright's limited monopolies are compatible with free speech principles. Indeed, copyright's purpose is to *promote* the creation and publication of free expression. As *Harper & Row* observed: "[T]he Framers intended copyright itself to be the engine of free expression. By establishing a marketable right to the use of one's expression, copyright supplies the economic incentive to create and disseminate ideas." 471 U.S., at 558.

In addition to spurring the creation and publication of new expression, copyright law contains built-in First Amendment accommodations. See *id.,* at 560. First, it distinguishes between ideas and expression and makes only the latter eligible for copyright protection. Specifically, 17 U.S.C. § 102(b) provides: "In no case does copyright protection for an original work of authorship extend to any idea, procedure, process, system, method of operation, concept, principle, or discovery, regardless of the form in which it is described, explained, illustrated, or embodied in such work." As we said in *Harper & Row*, this "idea/expression dichotomy strike[s] a definitional balance between the First Amendment and the Copyright Act by permitting free communication of facts while still protecting an author's expression." 471 U.S., at 556 (internal quotation marks omitted). Due to this distinction, every idea, theory, and fact in a copyrighted work becomes instantly available for public exploitation at the moment of publication. See *Feist,* 499 U.S., at 349—350.

Second, the "fair use" defense allows the public to use not only facts and ideas contained in a copyrighted work, but also expression itself in certain circumstances. Codified at 17 U.S.C. § 107 the defense provides: "[T]he fair use of a copyrighted work, including such use by reproduction in copies ... , for purposes such as criticism, comment, news reporting, teaching (including multiple copies for classroom use), scholarship, or research, is not an infringement of copyright." The fair use defense affords considerable "latitude for scholarship and comment," *Harper & Row*, 471 U.S., at 560, and even for parody, see *Campbell* v. *Acuff-Rose Music, Inc.,* 510 U.S. 569 (1994) (rap group's musical parody of Roy Orbison's "Oh, Pretty Woman" may be fair use).

The CTEA itself supplements these traditional First Amendment safeguards. First, it allows libraries, archives, and similar institutions to "reproduce" and "distribute, display, or perform in facsimile or digital form" copies of certain published works "during the last 20 years of any term of copyright ... for purposes of preservation, scholarship, or research" if the work is not already being exploited commercially and further copies are unavailable at a reasonable price. 17 U.S.C. § 108(h); see Brief for Respondent 36. Second, Title II of the CTEA, known as the Fairness in Music Licensing Act of 1998, exempts small businesses, restaurants, and like entities from having to pay performance royalties on music played from licensed radio, television, and similar facilities. 17 U.S.C. § 110(5)(B); see Brief for Representative F. James Sensenbrenner, Jr., et al. as *Amici Curiae* 5—6, n. 3.

Finally, the case petitioners principally rely upon for their First Amendment argument, *Turner Broadcasting System, Inc.* v. *FCC,* 512 U.S. 622 (1994), bears little on copyright. The statute at issue in *Turner* required cable operators to carry and transmit broadcast stations through their proprietary cable systems. Those "must-carry" provisions, we explained, implicated "the heart of the First Amendment," namely, "the principle that each person should decide for himself or herself the ideas and beliefs deserving of expression, consideration, and adherence." *Id.,* at 641.

The CTEA, in contrast, does not oblige anyone to reproduce another's speech against the carrier's will. Instead, it protects authors' original expression from unrestricted exploitation. Protection of that order does not raise the free speech concerns present when the government compels or burdens the communication of particular facts or ideas. The First Amendment securely protects the freedom to make--or decline to make--one's own speech; it bears less heavily when speakers assert the right to make other people's speeches. To the extent such assertions raise First Amendment concerns, copyright's built-in free speech safeguards are generally adequate to address them. We recognize that the D. C. Circuit spoke too broadly when it declared copyrights "categorically immune from challenges under the First Amendment." 239 F.3d, at 375. But when, as in this case, Congress has not altered the traditional contours of copyright protection, further First Amendment scrutiny is unnecessary. See *Harper & Row*, 471 U.S., at 560; cf. *San Francisco Arts & Athletics, Inc.* v. *United States Olympic Comm.,* 483 U.S. 522 (1987).[24]

IV

If petitioners' vision of the Copyright Clause held sway, it would do more than render the CTEA's duration extensions unconstitutional as to existing works. Indeed, petitioners' assertion that the provisions of the CTEA are not severable would make the CTEA's enlarged terms invalid even as to tomorrow's work. The 1976 Act's time extensions, which set the pattern that the CTEA followed, would be vulnerable as well.

As we read the Framers' instruction, the Copyright Clause empowers Congress to determine the intellectual property regimes that, overall, in that body's judgment, will serve the ends of the Clause. See *Graham*, 383 U.S., at 6 (Congress may "implement the stated purpose of the Framers by selecting the policy which *in its judgment* best effectuates the constitutional aim." (emphasis added)). Beneath the facade of their inventive constitutional interpretation, petitioners forcefully urge that Congress pursued very bad policy in prescribing the CTEA's long terms. The wisdom of Congress' action, however, is not within our province to second guess. Satisfied that the legislation before us remains inside the domain the Constitution assigns to the First Branch, we affirm the judgment of the Court of Appeals.

It is so ordered.

NOTES

[1] Justice Breyer's dissent is not similarly restrained. He makes no effort meaningfully to distinguish existing copyrights from future grants. See, *e.g., post*, at 1, 13—19, 23—25. Under his reasoning, the CTEA's 20-year extension is globally unconstitutional.

[2] Asserting that the last several decades have seen a proliferation of copyright legislation in departure from Congress' traditional pace of legislative amendment in this area, petitioners cite nine statutes passed between 1962 and 1974, each of which incrementally extended existing copyrights for brief periods. See Pub. L. 87—668, 76 Stat. 555; Pub. L. 89—142, 79 Stat. 581; Pub. L. 90—141, 81 Stat. 464; Pub. L. 90—416, 82 Stat. 397; Pub. L. 91—147, 83 Stat. 360; Pub. L. 91—555, 84 Stat. 1441; Pub. L. 92—170, 85 Stat. 490; Pub. L. 92—566, 86 Stat. 1181; Pub. L. 93—573, Title I, 88 Stat. 1873. As respondent (Attorney General Ashcroft) points out, however, these statutes were all temporary placeholders subsumed into the systemic changes effected by the 1976 Act. Brief for Respondent 9.

[3] Petitioners argue that the 1790 Act must be distinguished from the later Acts on the ground that it covered existing *works* but did not extend existing *copyrights*. Reply Brief 3—7. The parties disagree

on the question whether the 1790 Act's copyright term should be regarded in part as compensation for the loss of any then existing state- or common-law copyright protections. See Brief for Petitioners 28 —30; Brief for Respondent 17, n. 9; Reply Brief 3—7. Without resolving that dispute, we underscore that the First Congress clearly did confer copyright protection on works that had already been created.

[4] We note again that Justice Breyer makes no such concession. See *supra*, at 2, n. 1. He does not train his fire, as petitioners do, on Congress' choice to place existing and future copyrights in parity. Moving beyond the bounds of the parties' presentations, and with abundant policy arguments but precious little support from precedent, he would condemn Congress' entire product as irrational.

[5] This approach comported with English practice at the time. The Statute of Anne, 1710, 8 Ann. c. 19, provided copyright protection to books not yet composed or published, books already composed but not yet published, and books already composed and published. See *ibid.* ("[T]he author of any book or books already composed, and not printed and published, or that shall hereafter be composed, and his assignee or assigns, shall have the sole liberty of printing and reprinting such book and books for the term of fourteen years, to commence from the day of the first publishing the same, and no longer."); *ibid.* ("[T]he author of any book or books already printed … or the bookseller or booksellers, printer or printers, or other person or persons, who hath or have purchased or acquired the copy or copies of any book or books, in order to print or reprint the same, shall have the sole right and liberty of printing such book and books for the term of one and twenty years, to commence from the said tenth day of April, and no longer."). Justice Stevens stresses the rejection of a proposed amendment to the Statute of Anne that would have extended the term of existing copyrights, and reports that opponents of the extension feared it would perpetuate the monopoly position enjoyed by English booksellers. *Post*, at 12, and n. 9. But the English Parliament confronted a situation that never existed in the United States. Through the late 17th century, a government-sanctioned printing monopoly was held by the Stationers' Company, "the ancient London guild of printers and booksellers." M. Rose, Authors and Owners: The Invention of Copyright 4 (1993); see L. Patterson, Copyright in Historical Perspective ch. 3 (1968). Although that legal monopoly ended in 1695, concerns about monopolistic practices remained, and the 18th century English Parliament was resistant to any enhancement of booksellers' and publishers' entrenched position. See Rose, *supra*, at 52—56. In this country, in contrast, competition among publishers, printers, and booksellers was "intens[e]" at the time of the founding, and "there was not even a rough analog to the Stationers' Company on the horizon." Nachbar, Constructing Copyright's Mythology, 6 Green Bag 2d 37, 45 (2002). The Framers guarded against the future accumulation of monopoly power in booksellers and publishers by authorizing Congress to vest copyrights only in "Authors." Justice Stevens does not even attempt to explain how Parliament's response to England's experience with a publishing monopoly may be construed to impose a constitutional limitation on Congress' power to extend copyrights granted to "Authors."

[6] Moreover, the precise duration of a federal copyright has never been fixed at the time of the initial grant. The 1790 Act provided a federal copyright term of 14 years from the work's publication, renewable for an additional 14 years *if* the author survived and applied for an additional term. §1. Congress retained that approach in subsequent statutes. See *Stewart* v. *Abend*, 495 U.S. 207, 217 (1990) ("Since the earliest copyright statute in this country, the copyright term of ownership has been split between an original term and a renewal term."). Similarly, under the method for measuring copyright terms established by the 1976 Act and retained by the CTEA, the baseline copyright term is measured in part by the life of the author, rendering its duration indeterminate at the time of the grant. See 1976 Act §302(a); 17 U.S.C. § 302(a).

[7] Justice Stevens would sweep away these decisions, asserting that *Graham* v. *John Deere Co. of Kansas City*, 383 U.S. 1 (1966), "flatly contradicts" them. *Post*, at 17. Nothing but wishful thinking underpins that assertion. The controversy in *Graham* involved no patent extension. *Graham* addressed an invention's very eligibility for patent protection, and spent no words on Congress' power to enlarge a patent's duration.

[8] Justice Stevens recites words from *Sears, Roebuck & Co.* v. *Stiffel Co.*, 376 U.S. 225 (1964), supporting the uncontroversial proposition that a State may not "extend the life of a patent beyond its expiration date," *id.*, at 231, then boldly asserts that for the same reasons Congress may not do so either. See *post*, at 1, 5. But *Sears* placed no reins on Congress' authority to extend a patent's life. The full sentence in *Sears*, from which Justice Stevens extracts words, reads: "Obviously a State could not, consistently with the Supremacy Clause of the Constitution, extend the life of a patent

beyond its expiration date or give a patent on an article which lacked the level of invention required for federal patents." 376 U.S., at 231. The point insistently made in *Sears* is no more and no less than this: *States* may not enact measures inconsistent with the federal patent laws. *Ibid.* ("[A] State cannot encroach upon the federal patent laws directly ... [and] cannot ... give protection of a kind that clashes with the objectives of the federal patent laws."). A decision thus rooted in the Supremacy Clause cannot be turned around to shrink congressional choices. Also unavailing is Justice Stevens' appeal to language found in a private letter written by James Madison. *Post*, at 9, n. 6; see also dissenting opinion of Breyer, J., *post*, at 5, 20. Respondent points to a better "demonstrat[ion]," *post*, at 5, n. 3 (Stevens, J., dissenting), of Madison's and other Framers' understanding of the scope of Congress' power to extend patents: "[T]hen-President Thomas Jefferson–the first administrator of the patent system, and perhaps the Founder with the narrowest view of the copyright and patent powers–signed the 1808 and 1809 patent term extensions into law; ... James Madison, who drafted the Constitution's 'limited Times' language, issued the extended patents under those laws as Secretary of State; and ... Madison as President signed another patent term extension in 1815." Brief for Respondent 15.

[9] Justice Stevens reads *McClurg* to convey that "Congress cannot change the bargain between the public and the patentee in a way that disadvantages the patentee." *Post*, at 19. But *McClurg* concerned no such change. To the contrary, as Justice Stevens acknowledges, *McClurg* held that use of an invention by the patentee's employer did not invalidate the inventor's 1834 patent, "even if it might have had that effect prior to the amendment of the patent statute in 1836." *Post*, at 18. In other words, *McClurg* evaluated the patentee's rights not simply in light of the patent law in force at the time the patent issued, but also in light of "such changes as ha[d] been since made." 1 How., at 206. It is thus inescapably plain that *McClurg* upheld the application of expanded patent protection to an existing patent.

[10] Justice Breyer would adopt a heightened, three-part test for the constitutionality of copyright enactments. *Post*, at 3. He would invalidate the CTEA as irrational in part because, in his view, harmonizing the United States and European Union baseline copyright terms "apparent[ly]" fails to achieve "significant" uniformity. *Post*, at 23. But see *infra*, at 15. The novelty of the "rational basis" approach he presents is plain. Cf. *Board of Trustees of Univ. of Ala.* v. *Garrett*, 531 U.S. 356, 383 (2001) (Breyer, J., dissenting) ("Rational-basis review–with its presumptions favoring constitutionality–is 'a paradigm of *judicial* restraint.' ") (quoting *FCC* v. *Beach Communications, Inc.*, 508 U.S. 307, 314 (1993)). Rather than subjecting Congress' legislative choices in the copyright area to heightened judicial scrutiny, we have stressed that "it is not our role to alter the delicate balance Congress has labored to achieve." *Stewart* v. *Abend*, 495 U.S., at 230; see *Sony Corp. of America* v. *Universal City Studios, Inc.*, 464 U.S. 417, 429 (1984). Congress' exercise of its Copyright Clause authority must be rational, but Justice Breyer's stringent version of rationality is unknown to our literary property jurisprudence.

[11] Responding to an inquiry whether copyrights could be extended "forever," Register of Copyrights Marybeth Peters emphasized the dominant reason for the CTEA: "There certainly are proponents of perpetual copyright: We heard that in our proceeding on term extension. The Songwriters Guild suggested a perpetual term. However, our Constitution says limited times, but there really isn't a very good indication on what limited times is. The reason why you're going to life-plus-70 today is because Europe has gone that way . . . ." Copyright Term, Film Labeling, and Film Preservation Legislation: Hearings on H. R. 989 et al. before the Subcommittee on Courts and Intellectual Property of the House Committee on the Judiciary, 104th Cong., 1st Sess., 230 (1995) (hereinafter House Hearings).

[12] The author of the law review article cited in text, Shira Perlmutter, currently a vice president of AOL Time Warner, was at the time of the CTEA's enactment Associate Register for Policy and International Affairs, United States Copyright Office.

[13] See also Austin, Does the Copyright Clause Mandate Isolationism? 26 Colum.—VLA J. L. & Arts 17, 59 (2002) (cautioning against "an isolationist reading of the Copyright Clause that is in tension with ... America's international copyright relations over the last hundred or so years").

[14] Members of Congress expressed the view that, as a result of increases in human longevity and in parents' average age when their children are born, the pre-CTEA term did not adequately secure "the right to profit from licensing one's work during one's lifetime and to take pride and comfort in knowing that one's children–and perhaps their children–might also benefit from one's posthumous popularity."

141 Cong. Rec. 6553 (1995) (statement of Sen. Feinstein); see 144 Cong. Rec. S12377 (daily ed. Oct. 12, 1998) (statement of Sen. Hatch) ("Among the main developments [compelling reconsideration of the 1976 Act's term] is the effect of demographic trends, such as increasing longevity and the trend toward rearing children later in life, on the effectiveness of the life-plus-50 term to provide adequate protection for American creators and their heirs."). Also cited was "the failure of the U.S. copyright term to keep pace with the substantially increased commercial life of copyrighted works resulting from the rapid growth in communications media." *Ibid.* (statement of Sen. Hatch); cf. *Sony,* 464 U.S., at 430 —431 ("From its beginning, the law of copyright has developed in response to significant changes in technology… . [A]s new developments have occurred in this country, it has been the Congress that has fashioned the new rules that new technology made necessary.").

[15] Justice Breyer urges that the economic incentives accompanying copyright term extension are too insignificant to "mov[e]" any author with a "rational economic perspective." *Post,* at 14; see *post,* at 13 —16. Calibrating rational economic incentives, however, like "fashion[ing] … new rules [in light of] new technology," *Sony,* 464 U.S., at 431, is a task primarily for Congress, not the courts. Congress heard testimony from a number of prominent artists; each expressed the belief that the copyright system's assurance of fair compensation for themselves and their heirs was an incentive to create. See, *e.g.,* House Hearings 233—239 (statement of Quincy Jones); Copyright Term Extension Act of 1995: Hearings before the Senate Committee on the Judiciary, 104th Cong., 1st Sess., 55—56 (1995) (statement of Bob Dylan); *id.,* at 56—57 (statement of Don Henley); *id.,* at 57 (statement of Carlos Santana). We would not take Congress to task for crediting this evidence which, as Justice Breyer acknowledges, reflects general "propositions about the value of incentives" that are "undeniably true." *Post,* at 14. Congress also heard testimony from Register of Copyrights Marybeth Peters and others regarding the economic incentives created by the CTEA. According to the Register, extending the copyright for existing works "could … provide additional income that would finance the production and distribution of new works." House Hearings 158. "Authors would not be able to continue to create," the Register explained, "unless they earned income on their finished works. The public benefits not only from an author's original work but also from his or her further creations. Although this truism may be illustrated in many ways, one of the best examples is Noah Webster[,] who supported his entire family from the earnings on his speller and grammar during the twenty years he took to complete his dictionary." *Id.,* at 165.

[16] Justice Breyer agrees that "Congress did not intend to act unconstitutionally" when it enacted the CTEA, *post,* at 15, yet in his very next breath, he seems to make just that accusation, *ibid.* What else is one to glean from his selection of scattered statements from individual members of Congress? He does not identify any statement in the statutory text that installs a perpetual copyright, for there is none. But even if the statutory text were sufficiently ambiguous to warrant recourse to legislative history, Justice Breyer's selections are not the sort to which this Court accords high value: "In surveying legislative history we have repeatedly stated that the authoritative source for finding the Legislature's intent lies in the Committee Reports on the bill, which 'represen[t] the considered and collective understanding of those [members of Congress] involved in drafting and studying proposed legislation.' " *Garcia* v. *United States,* 469 U.S. 70, 76 (1984) (quoting *Zuber* v. *Allen,* 396 U.S. 168, 186 (1969)). The House and Senate Reports accompanying the CTEA reflect no purpose to make copyright a forever thing. Notably, the Senate Report expressly acknowledged that the Constitution "clearly precludes Congress from granting unlimited protection for copyrighted works," S. Rep. No. 104—315, p. 11 (1996), and disclaimed any intent to contravene that prohibition, *ibid.* Members of Congress instrumental in the CTEA's passage spoke to similar effect. See, *e.g.,* 144 Cong. Rec. H1458 (daily ed. Mar. 25, 1998) (statement of Rep. Coble) (observing that "copyright protection should be for a limited time only" and that "[p]erpetual protection does not benefit society"). Justice Breyer nevertheless insists that the "economic effect" of the CTEA is to make the copyright term "virtually perpetual." *Post,* at 1. Relying on formulas and assumptions provided in an *amicus* brief supporting petitioners, he stresses that the CTEA creates a copyright term worth 99.8% of the value of a perpetual copyright. *Post,* at 13—15. If Justice Breyer's calculations were a basis for holding the CTEA unconstitutional, then the 1976 Act would surely fall as well, for–under the same assumptions he indulges–the term set by that Act secures 99.4% of the value of a perpetual term. See Brief for George A. Akerloff et al. as *Amici Curiae* 6, n. 6 (describing the relevant formula). Indeed, on that analysis even the "limited" character of the 1909 (97.7%) and 1831 (94.1%) Acts might be suspect. Justice Breyer several times places the Founding Fathers on his side. See, *e.g., post,* at 5, 20. It is doubtful, however, that those architects of our Nation, in framing the "limited Times" prescription,

thought in terms of the calculator rather than the calendar.

[17] Respondent notes that the CTEA's life-plus-70-years baseline term is expected to produce an average copyright duration of 95 years, and that this term "resembles some other long-accepted durational practices in the law, such as 99-year leases of real property and bequests within the rule against perpetuities." Brief for Respondent 27, n. 18. Whether such referents mark the outer boundary of "limited Times" is not before us today. Justice Breyer suggests that the CTEA's baseline term extends beyond that typically permitted by the traditional rule against perpetuities. *Post*, at 15—16. The traditional common-law rule looks to lives in being plus 21 years. Under that rule, the period before a bequest vests could easily equal or exceed the anticipated average copyright term under the CTEA. If, for example, the vesting period on a deed were defined with reference to the life of an infant, the sum of the measuring life plus 21 years could commonly add up to 95 years.

[18] Justice Stevens' characterization of reward to the author as "a secondary consideration" of copyright law, *post*, at 6, n. 4 (internal quotation marks omitted), understates the relationship between such rewards and the "Progress of Science." As we have explained, "[t]he economic philosophy behind the [Copyright] [C]lause ... is the conviction that encouragement of individual effort by personal gain is the best way to advance public welfare through the talents of authors and inventors." *Mazer* v. *Stein,* 347 U.S. 201, 219 (1954). Accordingly, "copyright law *celebrates* the profit motive, recognizing that the incentive to profit from the exploitation of copyrights will redound to the public benefit by resulting in the proliferation of knowledge.... The profit motive is the engine that ensures the progress of science." *American Geophysical Union* v. *Texaco Inc.*, 802 F. Supp. 1, 27 (SDNY 1992), aff'd, 60 F.3d 913 (CA2 1994). Rewarding authors for their creative labor and "promot[ing] ... Progress" are thus complementary; as James Madison observed, in copyright "[t]he public good fully coincides ... with the claims of individuals." The Federalist No. 43, p. 272 (C. Rossiter ed. 1961). Justice Breyer's assertion that "copyright statutes must serve public, not private, ends" *post*, at 6, similarly misses the mark. The two ends are not mutually exclusive; copyright law serves public ends by providing individuals with an incentive to pursue private ones.

[19] As we have noted, see *supra*, at 5, n. 3, petitioners seek to distinguish the 1790 Act from those that followed. They argue that by requiring authors seeking its protection to surrender whatever rights they had under state law, the 1790 Act enhanced uniformity and certainty and thus "promote[d] ... Progress." See Brief for Petitioners 28—31. This account of the 1790 Act simply confirms, however, thatthe First Congress understood it could "promote ... Progress" by extending copyright protection to existing works. Every subsequent adjustment of copyright's duration, including the CTEA, reflects a similar understanding.

[20] Justice Stevens, *post*, at 15, refers to the "legislative veto" held unconstitutional in *INS* v. *Chadha,* 462 U.S. 919 (1983), and observes that we reached that decision despite its impact on federal laws geared to our "contemporary political system," *id.*, at 967 (White, J., dissenting). Placing existing works in parity with future works for copyright purposes, in contrast, is not a similarly pragmatic endeavor responsive to modern times. It is a measure of the kind Congress has enacted under its Patent and Copyright Clause authority since the founding generation. See *supra*, at 3—5.

[21] Standard copyright assignment agreements reflect this expectation. See, *e.g.*, A. Kohn & B. Kohn, Music Licensing 471 (3d ed. 1992—2002) (short form copyright assignment for musical composition, under which assignor conveys all rights to the work, "including the copyrights and proprietary rights therein and in any and all versions of said musical composition(s), and any renewals and extensions thereof (whether presently available *or subsequently available as a result of intervening legislation*)" (emphasis added)); 5 M. Nimmer & D. Nimmer, Copyright §21.11[B], p. 21—305 (2002) (short form copyright assignment under which assignor conveys all assets relating to the work, "including without limitation, copyrights and renewals and/or extensions thereof"); 6 *id.*, §30.04[B][1], p. 30—325 (form composer-producer agreement under which composer "assigns to Producer all rights (copyrights, rights under copyright and otherwise, whether now or hereafter known) and all renewals and extensions (as may now or hereafter exist)").

[22] The fact that patent and copyright involve different exchanges does not, of course, mean that we may not be guided in our "limited Times" analysis by Congress' repeated extensions of existing patents. See *supra*, at 10—13. If patent's *quid pro quo* is more exacting than copyright's, then Congress' repeated extensions of existing patents without constitutional objection suggests even

more strongly that similar legislation with respect to copyrights is constitutionally permissible.

23 Petitioners originally framed this argument as implicating the CTEA's extension of both existing and future copyrights. See Pet. for Cert. i. Now, however, they train on the CTEA's extension of existing copyrights and urge against consideration of the CTEA's First Amendment validity as applied to future copyrights. See Brief for Petitioners 39—48; Reply Brief 16—17; Tr. of Oral Arg. 11—13. We therefore consider petitioners' argument as so limited. We note, however, that petitioners do not explain how their First Amendment argument is moored to the prospective/retrospective line they urge us to draw, nor do they say whether or how their free speech argument applies to copyright duration but not to other aspects of copyright protection, notably scope.

24 We are not persuaded by petitioners' attempt to distinguish *Harper & Row* on the ground that it involved an infringement suit rather than a declaratory action of the kind here presented. As respondent observes, the same legal question can arise in either posture. See Brief for Respondent 42. In both postures, it is appropriate to construe copyright's internal safeguards to accommodate First Amendment concerns. Cf. *United States* v. *X-Citement Video, Inc.,* 513 U.S. 64, 78 (1994) ("It is … incumbent upon us to read the statute to eliminate [serious constitutional] doubts so long as such a reading is not plainly contrary to the intent of Congress.").

ERICK CORNELL CLAY v. UNITED STATES

No. 01-1500, March 4, 2003

ON WRIT OF CERTIORARI TO THE UNITED STATES COURT OF APPEALS FOR THE SEVENTH CIRCUIT

Justice Ginsburg delivered the opinion of the Court.

A motion by a federal prisoner for postconviction relief under 28 U. S. C. §2255 is subject to a one-year time limitation that generally runs from "the date on which the judgment of conviction becomes final." §2255, ¶6(1). This case concerns the starting date for the one-year limitation. It presents a narrow but recurring question on which courts of appeals have divided: When a defendant in a federal prosecution takes an unsuccessful direct appeal from a judgment of conviction, but does not next petition for a writ of certiorari from this Court, does the judgment become "final" for postconviction relief purposes (1) when the appellate court issues its mandate affirming the conviction, or, instead, (2) on the date, ordinarily 69 days later, when the time for filing a petition for certiorari expires?

In accord with this Court's consistent understanding of finality in the context of collateral review, and the weight of lower court authority, we reject the issuance of the appellate court mandate as the triggering date. For the purpose of starting the clock on §2255's one-year limitation period, we hold, a judgment of conviction becomes final when the time expires for filing a petition for certiorari contesting the appellate court's affirmation of the conviction.

I

In 1997, petitioner Erick Cornell Clay was convicted of arson and distribution of cocaine base in the United States District Court for the Northern District of Indiana. On November 23, 1998, the Court of Appeals for the Seventh Circuit affirmed his convictions. That court's mandate issued on December 15, 1998. See Fed. Rules App. Proc. 40(a)(1) and 41(b) (when no petition for rehearing is filed, a court of appeals' mandate issues 21 days after entry of judgment). Clay did not file a petition for a writ of certiorari. The time in which he could have petitioned for certiorari expired on February 22, 1999, 90 days after entry of the Court of Appeals' judgment, see this Court's Rule 13(1), and 69 days after the issuance of the appellate court's mandate.

On February 22, 2000—one year and 69 days after the Court of Appeals issued its mandate and exactly one year after the time for seeking certiorari expired—Clay filed a motion in the District Court, pursuant to 28 U. S. C. §2255, to vacate, set aside, or correct his sentence. Congress has prescribed "[a] 1-year period of limitation" for such motions "run[ning] from the latest of" four specified dates. §2255, ¶6. Of the four dates, the only one relevant in this case, as in the generality of cases, is the first: "the date on which the judgment of conviction becomes final." §2255, ¶6(1).

Relying on Gendron v. United States , 154 F. 3d 672, 674 (CA7 1998) (per curiam) , the District Court stated that "when a federal prisoner in this circuit does not seek certiorari ... , the conviction becomes 'final' on the date the appellate court issues the mandate in the direct appeal." App. to Pet. for Cert. 8a. Because Clay filed his §2255 motion more than one year after that date, the court denied the motion as time barred.

The Seventh Circuit affirmed. That court declined Clay's "invitation to reconsider our holding in Gendron ," although it acknowledged that Gendron 's "construction of section 2255 represents the minority view." 30 Fed. Appx. 607, 609 (2002). "Bowing to stare decisis ," the court expressed "reluctan[ce] to overrule [its own] recently-reaffirmed precedent without guidance from the Supreme Court." Ibid.

The Fourth Circuit has agreed with Gendron 's interpretation of §2255. See United States v. Torres , 211 F. 3d 836, 838–842 (2000) (when a federal prisoner does not file a petition for certiorari, his judgment of conviction becomes final for §2255 purposes upon issuance of the court of appeals' mandate). Six Courts of Appeals have parted ways with the Seventh and Fourth Circuits. These courts hold that, for federal prisoners like Clay who do not file petitions for certiorari following affirmance of their convictions, §2255's one-year limitation period begins to run when the defendant's time for seeking review by this Court expires.[1] To secure uniformity in the application of §2255's time constraint, we granted certiorari, 536 U. S. 957 (2002) , and now reverse the Seventh Circuit's judgment.[2]

II

Finality is variously defined; like many legal terms, its precise meaning depends on context. Typically, a federal judgment becomes final for appellate review and claim preclusion purposes when the district court disassociates itself from the case, leaving nothing to be done at the court of first instance save execution of the judgment. See, e.g., Quackenbush v. Allstate Ins. Co., 517 U. S. 706, 712 (1996) ; Restatement (Second) of Judgments §13, Comment b (1980). For other purposes, finality attaches at a different stage. For example, for certain determinations under the Speedy Trial Act of 1974, 18 U. S. C. §3161 et seq. , and under a now-repealed version of Federal Rule of Criminal Procedure 33, several lower courts have held that finality attends issuance of the appellate court's mandate. See Brief for Amicus Curiae by Invitation of the Court 22–28 (hereinafter DeBruin Brief) (citing cases). For the purpose of seeking review by this Court, in contrast, "[t]he time to file a petition for a writ of certiorari runs from the date of entry of the judgment or order sought to be reviewed, and not from the issuance date of the mandate (or its equivalent under local practice)." This Court's Rule 13(3).

Here, the relevant context is postconviction relief, a context in which finality has a long-recognized, clear meaning: Finality attaches when this Court affirms a conviction on the merits on direct review or denies a petition for a writ of certiorari, or when the time for filing a certiorari petition expires. See, e.g., Caspari v. Bohlen, 510 U. S. 383, 390 (1994) ; Griffith v. Kentucky, 479 U. S. 314, 321, n. 6 (1987) ; Barefoot v. Estelle, 463 U. S. 880, 887 (1983) ; United States v. Johnson, 457 U. S. 537, 542, n. 8 (1982) ; Linkletter v. Walker, 381 U. S. 618, 622, n. 5 (1965) . Because "we presume that Congress expects its statutes to be read in conformity with this Court's precedents," United States v. Wells, 519 U. S. 482, 495 (1997) , our unvarying understanding of finality for collateral review purposes would ordinarily determine the meaning of "becomes final" in §2255.

Amicus urges a different determinant, relying on verbal differences between §2255 and a parallel statutory provision, 28 U. S. C. §2244(d)(1), which governs petitions for federal habeas corpus by state prisoners. See DeBruin Brief 8–20. Sections 2255 and 2244(d)(1), as now formulated, were reshaped by the Antiterrorism and Effective Death Penalty Act of 1996. See §§101, 105, 110Stat. 1217, 1220. Prior to that Act, no statute of limitations governed requests for federal habeas corpus or §2255 habeas-like relief. See Vasquez v. Hillery, 474 U. S. 254, 265 (1986) ; United States v. Nahodil , 36 F. 3d 323, 328 (CA3 1994). Like §2255, §2244(d)(1) establishes a one-year limitation period, running from the latest of four specified dates. Three of the four time triggers under §2244(d)(1) closely track corresponding portions of §2255. Compare §§2244(d)(1)(B)–(D), with §2255, ¶¶6(2)–(4). But where §2255, ¶6(1), refers simply to "the date on which the judgment of conviction becomes final," §2244(d)(1)(A) speaks of "the date on which the judgment became final by the conclusion of direct review or the expiration of the time for seeking such review."[3]

When "Congress includes particular language in one section of a statute but omits it in another section of the same Act," we have recognized, "it is generally presumed that Congress acts intentionally and purposely in the disparate inclusion or exclusion." Russello v. United States, 464 U. S. 16, 23 (1983) (quoting United States v. Wong Kim Bo , 472 F. 2d 720, 722 (CA5 1972)). Invoking the maxim recited in Russello , amicus asserts that "becomes final" in §2255, ¶6(1), cannot mean the same thing as "became final" in §2244(d)(1)(A); reading the two as synonymous, amicus maintains, would render superfluous the words "by the conclusion of direct review or the expiration of the time for seeking such review"— words found only in the latter provision. DeBruin Brief 8–20. We can give effect to the discrete wording of the two prescriptions, amicus urges, if we adopt the following rule: When a convicted defendant does not seek certiorari on direct review, §2255's limitation period starts to run on the date the court of appeals issues its mandate. Id., at 36.[4]

Amicus would have a stronger argument if §2255, ¶6(1), explicitly incorporated the first of §2244(d)(1)(A)'s finality formulations but not the second, so that the §2255 text read "becomes final by the conclusion of direct review ." Had §2255 explicitly provided for the first of the two finality triggers set forth in §2244(d)(1)(A), one might indeed question the soundness of interpreting §2255 implicitly to incorporate §2244(d)(1)(A)'s second trigger as well. As written, however, §2255 does not qualify "becomes final" at all. Using neither of the disjunctive phrases that follow the words "became final" in §2244(d)(1)(A), §2255 simply leaves "becomes final" undefined.

Russello , we think it plain, hardly warrants the decision amicus urges, one that would hold the §2255 petitioner to a tighter time constraint than the petitioner governed by §2244(d)(1)(A). Russello concerned the meaning of a provision in the Racketeer Influenced and Corrupt Organizations Act (RICO), 18 U. S. C. §1961 et seq. , that directed forfeiture to the United States of "any interest [a convicted defendant] has acquired ... in violation of [the Act]." §1963(a)(1). The petitioner in Russello urged a narrow construction of the unqualified words "any interest ... acquired." Rejecting that argument, we observed that a succeeding subsection, §1963(a)(2), reached "any interest in ... any enterprise" the defendant conducted in violation of RICO's proscriptions. At that point, we referred to the maxim invoked by amicus . See supra , at 6. The qualifying words "in ... any enterprise" narrowed §1963(a)(2), but in no way affected §1963(a)(1). The comparison of the two subsections, we said, "fortified" the broad construction we approved for the unmodified words "any interest ... acquired." Russello , 464 U. S., at 22–23 (internal quotation marks omitted); see id. , at 23 ("Had Congress intended to restrict §1963(a)(1) to an interest in an enterprise, it presumably would have done so expressly as it did in the immediately following subsection (a)(2).").

Far from supporting the Seventh Circuit's constricted reading of §2255, ¶6(1), Russello 's reasoning tends in Clay's favor. An unqualified term—here "becomes final"— Russello indicates, calls for a reading surely no less broad than a pinpointed one—here, §2244(d)(1)(A)'s specification "became final by the conclusion of direct review or the expiration of the time for seeking such review."

Moreover, as Clay and the Government urge, see Brief for Petitioner 22; Reply Brief for United States 7–8, one can readily comprehend why Congress might have found it appropriate to spell out the meaning of "final" in §2244(d)(1)(A) but not in §2255. Section 2244(d)(1) governs petitions by state prisoners. In that context, a bare reference to "became final" might have suggested that finality assessments should be made by reference to state law rules that may differ from the general federal rule and vary from State to State. Cf. Artuz v. Bennett, 531 U. S. 4, 8 (2000) (an application for state postconviction relief is "properly filed" for purposes of 28 U. S. C. §2244(d)(2) "when its delivery and acceptance are in compliance with the applicable [state] laws and rules governing filings"). The words "by the conclusion of direct review or the expiration of the time for seeking such review" make it clear that finality for the purpose of §2244(d)(1)(A) is to be determined by reference to a uniform federal rule. Section 2255, however, governs only petitions by federal prisoners; within the federal system there is no comparable risk of varying rules to guard against.

Amicus also submits that 28 U. S. C. §2263 "reinforces" the Seventh Circuit's understanding of §2255. DeBruin Brief 20; accord, Torres , 211 F. 3d, at 840. Chapter 154 of Title 28 governs certain habeas petitions filed by death-sentenced state prisoners. Section 2263(a) prescribes a 180-day limitation period for such petitions running from "final State court affirmance of the conviction and sentence on direct review or the expiration of the time for seeking such review." That period is tolled, however, "from the date that a petition for certiorari is filed in the Supreme Court until the date of final disposition of the petition if a State prisoner files the petition to secure review by the Supreme Court of the affirmance of a capital sentence on direct review by the court of last resort of the State or other final State court decision on direct review." §2263(b)(1).

We do not find in §2263 cause to alter our reading of §2255. First, amicus ' reliance on §2263 encounters essentially the same problem as does his reliance on §2244(d)(1)(A): Section 2255, ¶6(1), refers to neither of the two events that §2263(a) identifies as possible starting points for the limitation period—"affirmance of the conviction and sentence on direct review" and "the expiration of the time for seeking such review." Thus, reasoning by negative implication from §2263 does not justify the conclusion that §2255, ¶6(1)'s limitation period begins to run at one of those times rather than the other. Cf. supra , at 6–8. Second, §2263(a) ties the applicable limitation period to "affirmance of the conviction and sentence," while §2255, ¶6(1), ties the limitation period to the date when "the judgment of conviction becomes final." See Torres , 211 F. 3d, at 845 (Hamilton, J., dissenting). "The Russello presumption—that the presence of a phrase in one provision and its absence in another reveals Congress' design—grows weaker with each difference in the formulation of the provisions under inspection." Columbus v. Ours Garage & Wrecker Service, Inc., 536 U. S. 424, 435–436 (2002).

* * *

We hold that, for federal criminal defendants who do not file a petition for certiorari with this Court on direct review, §2255's one-year limitation period starts to run when the time for seeking such review expires. Under this rule, Clay's §2255 petition was timely filed. The judgment of the United States Court of Appeals for the Seventh Circuit is therefore reversed, and the case is remanded for further proceedings consistent with this opinion.

It is so ordered.

NOTES

[1] See Derman v. United States, 298 F. 3d 34, 39–42 (CA1 2002); Kapral v. United States, 166 F. 3d 565, 567–577 (CA3 1999); United States v. Gamble, 208 F. 3d 536, 537 (CA5 2000) (per curiam); United States v. Garcia, 210 F. 3d 1058, 1059–1061 (CA9 2000); United States v. Burch, 202 F. 3d 1274, 1275–1279 (CA10 2000); Kaufmann v. United States, 282 F. 3d 1336, 1337–1339 (CA11 2002).

[2] Agreeing with the position advanced by the majority of the courts of appeals that have ruled on the question, the United States joins petitioner Clay in urging that Clay's §2255 motion was timely filed. We therefore invited David W. DeBruin to brief and argue this case, as amicus curiae, in support of the Seventh Circuit's judgment. Mr. DeBruin's able advocacy permits us to decide the case satisfied that the relevant issues have been fully aired.

[3] The Courts of Appeals have uniformly interpreted "direct review" in §2244(d)(1)(A) to encompass review of a state conviction by this Court. See Derman v. United States, 298 F. 3d, at 40–41; Williams v. Artuz, 237 F. 3d 147, 151 (CA2 2001); Kapral v. United States, 166 F. 3d, at 575; Hill v. Braxton, 277 F. 3d 701, 704 (CA4 2002); Ott v. Johnson, 192 F. 3d 510, 513 (CA5 1999); Bronaugh v. Ohio, 235 F. 3d 280, 283 (CA6 2000); Anderson v. Litscher, 281 F. 3d 672, 674–675 (CA7 2002); Smith v. Bowersox, 159 F. 3d 345, 347–348 (CA8 1998); Bowen v. Roe, 188 F. 3d 1157, 1159 (CA9 1999); Locke v. Saffle, 237 F. 3d 1269, 1273 (CA10 2001); Bond v. Moore, 309 F. 3d 770, 774 (CA11 2002).

[4] Although recognizing that "the question is not presented in this case," Tr. of Oral Arg. 27, amicus suggests that §2255's limitation period starts to run upon issuance of the court of appeals' mandate even in cases in which the defendant does petition for certiorari. Id., at 27–28, 36–38, 41–42. As amicus also recognizes, however, id., at 41, courts of appeals "have uniformly concluded that, if a prisoner petitions for certiorari, the contested conviction becomes final when the Supreme Court either denies the writ or issues a decision on the merits," United States v. Hicks, 283 F. 3d 380, 387 (CADC 2002).

EXXON MOBIL CORP. et al. v. SAUDI BASIC INDUSTRIES CORP.

No. 03-1696, March 30, 2005

ON WRIT OF CERTIORARI TO THE UNITED STATES COURT OF APPEALS FOR THE THIRD CIRCUIT

Justice Ginsburg delivered the opinion of the Court.

This case concerns what has come to be known as the *Rooker-Feldman* doctrine, applied by this Court only twice, first in *Rooker* v. *Fidelity Trust Co.*, 263 U.S. 413 (1923), then, 60 years later, in *District of Columbia Court of Appeals* v. *Feldman*, 460 U.S. 462 (1983). Variously interpreted in the lower courts, the doctrine has sometimes been construed to extend far beyond the contours of the *Rooker* and *Feldman* cases, overriding Congress' conferral of federal-court jurisdiction concurrent with jurisdiction exercised by state courts, and superseding the ordinary application of preclusion law pursuant to 28 U.S.C. § 1738. See, *e.g., Moccio* v. *New York State Office of Court Admin.*, 95 F.3d 195, 199—200 (CA2 1996).

Rooker was a suit commenced in Federal District Court to have a judgment of a state court, adverse to the federal court plaintiffs, "declared null and void." 263 U.S., at 414. In *Feldman*, parties unsuccessful in the District of Columbia Court of Appeals (the District's highest court) commenced a federal-court action against the very court that had rejected their applications. Holding the federal suits impermissible, we emphasized that appellate jurisdiction to reverse or modify a state-court judgment is lodged, initially by §25 of the Judiciary Act of 1789, 1 Stat. 85, and now by 28 U.S.C. § 1257 exclusively in this Court. Federal district courts, we noted, are empowered to exercise original, not appellate, jurisdiction. Plaintiffs in *Rooker* and *Feldman* had litigated and lost in state court. Their federal complaints, we observed, essentially invited federal courts of first instance to review and reverse unfavorable state-court judgments. We declared such suits out of bounds, *i.e.*, properly dismissed for want of subject-matter jurisdiction.

The *Rooker-Feldman* doctrine, we hold today, is confined to cases of the kind from which the doctrine acquired its name: cases brought by state-court losers complaining of injuries caused by state-court judgments rendered before the district court proceedings commenced and inviting district court review and rejection of those judgments. *Rooker-Feldman* does not otherwise override or supplant preclusion doctrine or augment the circumscribed doctrines that allow federal courts to stay or dismiss proceedings in deference to state-court actions.

In the case before us, the Court of Appeals for the Third Circuit misperceived the narrow ground occupied by *Rooker-Feldman*, and consequently erred in ordering the federal action dismissed for lack of subject-matter jurisdiction. We therefore reverse the Third Circuit's judgment.

I

In *Rooker* v. *Fidelity Trust Co.*, 263 U.S. 413, the parties defeated in state court turned to a Federal District Court for relief. Alleging that the adverse state-court judgment was rendered in contravention of the Constitution, they asked the federal court to declare it "null and void." *Id.*, at 414—415. This Court noted preliminarily that the state court had acted within its jurisdiction. *Id.*, at 415. If the state-court decision was wrong, the Court explained, "that did not make the judgment void, but merely left it open to reversal or modification in an appropriate and timely appellate proceeding." *Ibid.* Federal district courts, the *Rooker* Court recognized, lacked the requisite appellate authority, for their jurisdiction was "strictly original." *Id.*, at 416. Among federal courts, the *Rooker* Court clarified, Congress had empowered only this Court to exercise appellate authority "to reverse or modify" a state-court judgment. *Ibid.* Accordingly, the Court affirmed a decree dismissing the suit for lack of jurisdiction. *Id.*, at 415, 417.

Sixty years later, the Court decided *District of Columbia Court of Appeals* v. *Feldman*, 460 U.S. 462. The two plaintiffs in that case, Hickey and Feldman, neither of whom had graduated from an accredited law school, petitioned the District of Columbia Court of Appeals to waive a court Rule that required D.C. bar applicants to have graduated from a law school approved by the American Bar Association. After the D.C. court denied their waiver requests, Hickey and Feldman filed suits in the United States District Court for the District of Columbia. *Id.*, at 465—473. The District Court and the Court of Appeals for the District of Columbia Circuit disagreed on the question whether the federal suit could be maintained, and we granted certiorari. *Id.*, at 474—475.

Recalling *Rooker*, this Court's opinion in *Feldman* observed first that the District Court lacked authority to review a final judicial determination of the D.C. high court. "Review of such determinations," the *Feldman* opinion reiterated, "can be obtained only in this Court." 460 U.S., at 476. The "crucial question," the Court next stated, was whether the proceedings in the D.C. court were "judicial in nature." *Ibid.* Addressing that question, the Court concluded that the D.C. court had acted both judicially and legislatively.

In applying the accreditation Rule to the Hickey and Feldman waiver petitions, this Court determined, the D.C. court had acted judicially. *Id.,* at 479—482. As to that adjudication, *Feldman* held, this Court alone among federal courts had review authority. Hence, "to the extent that Hickey and Feldman sought review in the District Court of the District of Columbia Court of Appeals' denial of their petitions for waiver, the District Court lacked subject-matter jurisdiction over their complaints." *Id.,* at 482. But that determination did not dispose of the entire case, for in promulgating the bar admission rule, this Court said, the D.C. court had acted legislatively, not judicially. *Id.,* at 485—486. "Challenges to the constitutionality of state bar rules," the Court elaborated, "do not necessarily require a United States district court to review a final state-court judgment in a judicial proceeding." *Id.,* at 486. Thus, the Court reasoned, 28 U.S.C. § 1257 did not bar District Court proceedings addressed to the validity of the accreditation Rule itself. *Feldman,* 460 U.S., at 486. The Rule could be contested in federal court, this Court held, so long as plaintiffs did not seek review of the Rule's application in a particular case. Ibid.

The Court endeavored to separate elements of the Hickey and Feldman complaints that failed the jurisdictional threshold from those that survived jurisdictional inspection. Plaintiffs had urged that the District of Columbia Court of Appeals acted arbitrarily in denying the waiver petitions of Hickey and Feldman, given that court's "former policy of granting waivers to graduates of unaccredited law schools." *Ibid.* That charge, the Court held, could not be pursued, for it was "inextricably intertwined with the District of Columbia Court of Appeals' decisions, in judicial proceedings, to deny [plaintiffs'] petitions." *Id.,* at 486—487.[1]

On the other hand, the Court said, plaintiffs could maintain "claims that the [bar admission] rule is unconstitutional because it creates an irrebuttable presumption that only graduates of accredited law schools are fit to practice law, discriminates against those who have obtained equivalent legal training by other means, and impermissibly delegates the District of Columbia Court of Appeals' power to regulate the bar to the American Bar Association," for those claims "do not require review of a judicial decision in a particular case." *Id.,* at 487. The Court left open the question whether the doctrine of res judicata foreclosed litigation of the elements of the complaints spared from dismissal for want of subject-matter jurisdiction. *Id.,* at 487—488.

Since *Feldman,* this Court has never applied *Rooker-Feldman* to dismiss an action for want of jurisdiction. The few decisions that have mentioned *Rooker* and *Feldman* have done so only in passing or to explain why those cases did not dictate dismissal. See *Verizon Md. Inc.* v. *Public Serv. Comm'n of Md.,* 535 U.S. 635, 644, n. 3 (2002) (*Rooker-Feldman* does not apply to a suit seeking review of state agency action); *Johnson* v. *De Grandy,* 512 U.S. 997, 1005—1006 (1994) (*Rooker-Feldman* bars a losing party in state court "from seeking what in substance would be appellate review of the state judgment in a United States district court, based on the losing party's claim that the state judgment itself violates the loser's federal rights," but the doctrine has no application to a federal suit brought by a nonparty to the state suit.); *Howlett* v. *Rose,* 496 U.S. 356, 370, n. 16 (1990) (citing *Rooker* and *Feldman* for "the rule that a federal district court cannot entertain an original action alleging that a state court violated the Constitution by giving effect to an unconstitutional state statute"); *ASARCO Inc.* v. *Kadish,* 490 U.S. 605, 622—623 (1989) (If, instead of seeking review of an adverse state supreme court decision in the Supreme Court, petitioners sued in federal district court, the federal action would be an attempt to obtain direct review of the state supreme court decision and would "represent a partial inroad on *Rooker-Feldman*'s construction of 28 U.S.C. § 1257.");[2] *Pennzoil Co.* v. *Texaco Inc.,* 481 U.S. 1, 6—10 (1987) (abstaining under *Younger* v. *Harris,* 401 U.S. 37 (1971), rather than dismissing under *Rooker-Feldman,* in a suit that challenged Texas procedures for enforcing judgments); 481 U.S., at 18 (Scalia, J., concurring) (The "so-called *Rooker-Feldman* doctrine" does not deprive the Court of jurisdiction to decide Texaco's challenge to the Texas procedures); *id.,* at 21 (Brennan, J., concurring in judgment) (*Rooker* and *Feldman* do not apply; Texaco filed its federal action to protect its "right to a meaningful opportunity for appellate review, not to challenge the merits of the Texas suit."). But cf. 481 U.S., at 25—26 (Marshall, J., concurring in judgment) (*Rooker-Feldman* would apply because Texaco's claims necessarily called for review of the merits of its state appeal). See also *Martin* v. *Wilks,* 490 U.S. 755, 784, n. 21 (1989) (Stevens, J., dissenting) (it would be anomalous to allow courts to sit in review of judgments entered by courts of equal, or greater, authority (citing *Rooker* and *Feldman*)).[3]

II

In 1980, two subsidiaries of petitioner Exxon Mobil Corporation (then the separate companies Exxon Corp. and Mobil Corp.) formed joint ventures with respondent Saudi Basic Industries Corp. (SABIC) to produce polyethylene in Saudi Arabia. 194 F.Supp. 2d 378, 384 (NJ 2002). Two decades later, the parties began to dispute royalties that SABIC had charged the joint ventures for sublicenses to a polyethylene manufacturing method. 364 F.3d 102, 103 (CA3 2004).

SABIC preemptively sued the two ExxonMobil subsidiaries in Delaware Superior Court in July 2000 seeking a declaratory judgment that the royalty charges were proper under the joint venture agreements. 194 F.Supp. 2d, at 385—386. About two weeks later, ExxonMobil and its subsidiaries countersued SABIC in the United States District Court for the District of New Jersey, alleging that SABIC overcharged the joint ventures for the sublicenses. *Id.,* at 385; App. 3. ExxonMobil invoked subject-matter jurisdiction in the New Jersey action under 28 U.S.C. § 1330 which authorizes district courts to adjudicate actions against foreign states. 194 F.Supp. 2d, at 401.[4]

In January 2002, the ExxonMobil subsidiaries answered SABIC's state-court complaint, asserting as counterclaims the same claims ExxonMobil had made in the federal suit in New Jersey. 364 F.3d, at 103. The state suit went to trial in March 2003, and the jury returned a verdict of over $400 million in favor of the ExxonMobil subsidiaries. *Ibid.; Saudi Basic Industries Corp.* v. *Mobil Yanbu Petrochemical Co.,* 866 A.2d 1, 11 (Del. 2005). SABIC appealed the judgment entered on the verdict to the Delaware Supreme Court.

Before the state-court trial, SABIC moved to dismiss the federal suit, alleging, *inter alia*, immunity under the Foreign Sovereign Immunities Act of 1976, 28 U.S.C. § 1602 *et seq.* (2000 ed. and Supp. II). The Federal District Court denied SABIC's motion to dismiss. 194 F.Supp. 2d, at 401—407, 416—417. SABIC took an interlocutory appeal, and the Court of Appeals heard argument in December 2003, over eight months after the state-court jury verdict. 364 F.3d, at 103—104.[5]

The Court of Appeals, on its own motion, raised the question whether "subject matter jurisdiction over this case fails under the *Rooker-Feldman* doctrine because ExxonMobil's claims have already been litigated in state court." *Id.,* at 104.[6] The court did not question the District Court's possession of subject-matter jurisdiction at the outset of the suit, but held that federal jurisdiction terminated when the Delaware Superior Court entered judgment on the jury verdict. *Id.,* at 104—105. The court rejected ExxonMobil's argument that *Rooker-Feldman* could not apply because ExxonMobil filed its federal complaint well before the state-court judgment. The only relevant consideration, the court stated, "is whether the state judgment precedes a federal judgment on the same claims." 364 F.3d, at 105. If *Rooker-Feldman* did not apply to federal actions filed prior to a state-court judgment, the Court of Appeals worried, "we would be encouraging parties to maintain federal actions as 'insurance policies' while their state court claims were pending." 364 F.3d, at 105. Once ExxonMobil's claims had been litigated to a judgment in state court, the Court of Appeals held, *Rooker-Feldman* "preclude[d] [the] federal district court from proceeding." 364 F.3d, at 104 (internal quotation marks omitted).

ExxonMobil, at that point prevailing in Delaware, was not seeking to overturn the state-court judgment. Nevertheless, the Court of Appeals hypothesized that, if SABIC won on appeal in Delaware, ExxonMobil would be endeavoring in the federal action to "invalidate" the state-court judgment, "the very situation," the court concluded, "contemplated by *Rooker-Feldman*'s 'inextricably intertwined' bar." *Id.,* at 106.

We granted certiorari, 543 U.S. ___ (2004), to resolve conflict among the Courts of Appeals over the scope of the *Rooker-Feldman* doctrine. We now reverse the judgment of the Court of Appeals for the Third Circuit.[7]

III

Rooker and *Feldman* exhibit the limited circumstances in which this Court's appellate jurisdiction over state-court judgments, 28 U.S.C. § 1257 precludes a United States district court from exercising subject-matter jurisdiction in an action it would otherwise be empowered to adjudicate under a congressional grant of authority, *e.g.,* §1330 (suits against foreign states), §1331 (federal question), and §1332 (diversity). In both cases, the losing party in state court filed suit in federal court after the state proceedings ended, complaining of an injury caused by the state-court judgment and seeking review and rejection of that judgment.Plaintiffs in both cases, alleging federal-question jurisdiction, called upon the District Court to overturn an injurious state-court judgment. Because §1257, as long interpreted, vests authority to review a state court's judgment solely in this Court, *e.g., Feldman,* 460 U.S., at 476; *Atlantic Coast Line R. Co.* v. *Locomotive Engineers,* 398 U.S. 281, 286 (1970); *Rooker,* 263 U.S., at 416, the District Courts in *Rooker* and *Feldman* lacked subject-matter jurisdiction. See *Verizon Md. Inc.,* 535 U.S., at 644, n.3 ("The *Rooker-Feldman* doctrine merely recognizes that 28 U.S.C. § 1331 is a grant of original jurisdiction, and does not authorize district courts to exercise appellate jurisdiction over state-court judgments, which Congress has reserved to this Court, see §1257(a).").[8]

When there is parallel state and federal litigation, *Rooker-Feldman* is not triggered simply by the entry of judgment in state court. This Court has repeatedly held that "the pendency of an action in the state court is no bar to proceedings concerning the same matter in the Federal court having jurisdiction." *McClellan* v. *Carland,* 217 U.S. 268, 282 (1910); accord *Doran* v. *Salem Inn, Inc.,* 422 U.S. 922, 928 (1975); *Atlantic Coast Line R. Co.,* 398 U.S., at 295. Comity or abstention doctrines may, in various circumstances, permit or require the federal court to stay or dismiss the federal action in favor of the state-court litigation.See, *e.g., Colorado River Water Conservation Dist.* v. *United States,* 424 U.S. 800 (1976); *Younger* v. *Harris,* 401 U.S. 37 (1971); *Burford* v. *Sun Oil Co.,* 319 U.S. 315 (1943); *Railroad Comm'n of Tex.* v. *Pullman Co.,* 312 U.S. 496 (1941). But neither *Rooker* nor *Feldman* supports the notion that properly invoked concurrent jurisdiction vanishes if a state court reaches judgment on the same or related question while the case remains *sub judice* in a federal court.

Disposition of the federal action, once the state-court adjudication is complete, would be governed by preclusion law. The Full Faith and Credit Act, 28 U.S.C. § 1738 originally enacted in 1790, ch. 11, 1 Stat. 122, requires the federal court to "give the same preclusive effect to a state-court judgment as another court of that State would give." *Parsons Steel, Inc.* v. *First Alabama Bank,* 474 U.S. 518, 523 (1986); accord *Matsushita Elec. Industrial Co.* v. *Epstein,* 516 U.S. 367, 373 (1996); *Marrese* v. *American Academy of Orthopaedic Surgeons,* 470 U.S. 373, 380—381 (1985). Preclusion, of course, is not a jurisdictional matter.See Fed. Rule Civ. Proc. 8(c) (listing res judicata as an affirmative defense). In parallel litigation, a federal court may be bound to recognize the claim- and issue-preclusive effects of a state-court judgment, but federal jurisdiction over an action does not terminate automatically on the entry of judgment in the state court.

Nor does §1257 stop a district court from exercising subject-matter jurisdiction simply because a party attempts to litigate in federal court a matter previously litigated in state court. If a federal plaintiff "present[s] some independent claim, albeit one that denies a legal conclusion that a state court has reached in a case to which he was a party ..., then there is jurisdiction and state law determines whether the defendant prevails under principles of preclusion." *GASH Assocs.* v. *Village of Rosemont,* 995 F.2d 726, 728 (CA7 1993); accord *Noel* v. *Hall,* 341 F.3d 1148, 1163—1164 (CA9 2003).

This case surely is not the "paradigm situation in which *Rooker-Feldman* precludes a federal district court from proceeding." 364 F.3d, at 104 (quoting *E.B.* v. *Verniero*, 119 F.3d 1077, 1090—1091 (CA3 1997)).ExxonMobil plainly has not repaired to federal court to undo the Delaware judgment in its favor. Rather, it appears ExxonMobil filed suit in Federal District Court (only two weeks after SABIC filed in Delaware and well before any judgment in state court) to protect itself in the event it lost in state court on grounds (such as the state statute of limitations) that might not preclude relief in the federal venue. Tr. of Oral Arg. 46; App. 35—36.[9] *Rooker-Feldman* did not prevent the District Court from exercising jurisdiction when ExxonMobil filed the federal action, and it did not emerge to vanquish jurisdiction after ExxonMobil prevailed in the Delaware courts.

* * *

For the reasons stated, the judgment of the Court of Appeals for the Third Circuit is reversed, and the case is remanded for further proceedings consistent with this opinion.

It is so ordered.

NOTES

[1] Earlier in the opinion the Court had used the same expression. In a footnote, the Court explained that a district court could not entertain constitutional claims attacking a state-court judgment, even if the state court had not passed directly on those claims, when the constitutional attack was "inextricably intertwined" with the state court's judgment.*District of Columbia Court of Appeals* v. *Feldman,* 460 U.S. 462, 482, n. 16 (1983).

[2] Respondent Saudi Basic Industries Corp. urges that *ASARCO Inc.* v. *Kadish,* 490 U.S. 605 (1989), expanded *Rooker-Feldman*'s jurisdictional bar to include federal actions that simply raise claims previously litigated in state court. Brief for Respondent 20—22. This is not so. In *ASARCO*, the petitioners (defendants below in the state-court action) sought review in this Court of the Arizona Supreme Court's invalidation of a state statute governing mineral leases on state lands. 490 U.S., at 610. This Court dismissed the suggestion of the United States that the petitioners should have pursued their claim as a new action in federal district court. Such an action, we said, "in essence, would be an attempt to obtain direct review of the Arizona Supreme Court's decision in the lower federal courts" in contravention of 28 U.S.C. § 1257. 490 U.S., at 622—623. The injury of which the petitioners (the losing parties in state court) could have complained in the hypothetical federal suit would have been caused by the state court's invalidation of their mineral leases, and the relief they would have sought would have been to undo the state court's invalidation of the statute. The hypothetical suit in *ASARCO*, therefore, shares the characteristics of the suits in *Rooker* and *Feldman, i.e.,* loser in state court invites federal district court to overturn state-court judgment.

[3] Between 1923, when the Court decided *Rooker*, and 1983, when it decided *Feldman*, the Court cited *Rooker* in one opinion, *Fishgold* v. *Sullivan Drydock & Repair Corp.,* 328 U.S. 275, 283 (1946), in reference to the finality of prior judgments. See *Rooker* v. *Fidelity Trust Co.,* 263 U.S. 413, 415 (1923) ("Unless and until ... reversed or modified, [the state-court judgment] would be an effective and conclusive adjudication.").*Rooker*'s only other appearance in the United States Reports before 1983 occurs in Justice White's dissent from denial of certiorari in *Florida State Bd. of Dentistry* v. *Mack*, 401 U.S. 960, 961 (1971).

[4] SABIC is a Saudi Arabian corporation, 70% owned by the Saudi Government and 30% owned by private investors. 194 F.Supp. 2d, at 384.

[5] At ExxonMobil's request, the Court of Appeals initially stayed its consideration of the appeal to await resolution of the proceedings in Delaware. App. 9—10. In November 2003, shortly after SABIC filed its appeal in the Delaware Supreme Court, the Court of Appeals, on SABIC's motion, lifted the stay and set the appeal for argument. *Id.,* at 11—13.

[6] One day before argument, the Court of Appeals directed the parties to be prepared to address whether the *Rooker-Feldman* doctrine deprived the District Court of jurisdiction over the case.App. 17.

[7] SABIC contends that this case is moot because the Delaware Supreme Court has affirmed the trial-court judgment in favor of ExxonMobil, *Saudi Basic Industries Corp.* v. *Mobil Yanbu Petrochemical Co.,* 866 A.2d 1 (2005), and has denied reargument en banc, *Saudi Basic Industries Corp.* v. *Mobil Yanbu Petrochemical Co.,* No. 493,2003 (Feb. 22, 2005). Brief for Respondent 10—13.SABIC

continues to oppose the Delaware judgment, however, and has represented that it will petition this Court for a writ of certiorari. Tr. of Oral Arg. 22—23. The controversy therefore remains live.

[8] Congress, if so minded, may explicitly empower district courts to oversee certain state-court judgments and has done so, most notably, in authorizing federal habeas review of state prisoners' petitions. 28 U.S.C. § 2254(a).

[9] The Court of Appeals criticized ExxonMobil for pursuing its federal suit as an "insurance policy" against an adverse result in state court.364 F.3d 102, 105—106 (CA3 2004). There is nothing necessarily inappropriate, however, about filing a protective action. See, *e.g., Rhines* v. *Weber, ante*, at 7—8 (permitting a federal district court to stay a federal habeas action and hold the petition in abeyance while a petitioner exhausts claims in state court); *Union Pacific R.Co.* v. *Dept. of Revenue of Ore.*, 920 F.2d 581, 584, and n.9 (CA9 1990) (noting that the railroad company had filed protective actions in state court to prevent expiration of the state statute of limitations); *Government of Virgin Islands* v. *Neadle*, 861 F.Supp. 1054, 1055 (MD Fla. 1994) (staying an action brought by plaintiffs to "to protect themselves" in the event that personal jurisdiction over the defendants failed in the United States District Court for the Virgin Islands); see also *England* v. *Louisiana Bd. of Medical Examiners*, 375 U.S. 411, 421 (1964) (permitting a party to reserve litigation of federal constitutional claims for federal court while a state court resolves questions of state law).

JENIFER ARBAUGH v. Y & H CORPORATION, DBA THE MOONLIGHT CAFE

No. 04-944, February 22, 2006

ON WRIT OF CERTIORARI TO THE UNITED STATES COURT OF APPEALS FOR THE FIFTH CIRCUIT

Justice Ginsburg delivered the opinion of the Court.

This case concerns the distinction between two sometimes confused or conflated concepts: federal-court "subject-matter" jurisdiction over a controversy; and the essential ingredients of a federal claim for relief. Title VII of the Civil Rights Act of 1964 makes it unlawful "for an employer . . . to discriminate," inter alia, on the basis of sex. 42 U. S. C. §2000e–2(a)(1). The Act's jurisdictional provision empowers federal courts to adjudicate civil actions "brought under" Title VII. §2000e–5(f)(3). Covering a broader field, the Judicial Code gives federal courts subject-matter jurisdiction over all civil actions "arising under" the laws of the United States. 28 U. S. C. §1331. Title VII actions fit that description. In a provision defining 13 terms used in Title VII, 42 U. S. C. §2000e, Congress limited the definition of "employer" to include only those having "fifteen or more employees," §2000e(b). The question here presented is whether the numerical qualification contained in Title VII's definition of "employer" affects federal-court subject-matter jurisdiction or, instead, delineates a substantive ingredient of a Title VII claim for relief.

The question arises in this context. Jenifer Arbaugh, plaintiff below, petitioner here, brought a Title VII action in federal court against her former employer, defendant-respondent Y&H Corporation (hereinafter Y&H), charging sexual harassment. The case was tried to a jury, which returned a verdict for Arbaugh in the total amount of $40,000. Two weeks after the trial court entered judgment on the jury verdict, Y&H moved to dismiss the entire action for want of federal subject-matter jurisdiction. For the first time in the litigation, Y&H asserted that it had fewer than 15 employees on its payroll and therefore was not amenable to suit under Title VII.

Although recognizing that it was "unfair and a waste of judicial resources" to grant the motion to dismiss, App. to Pet. for Cert. 47, the trial court considered itself obliged to do so because it believed that the 15-or-more-employees requirement was jurisdictional. We reject that categorization and hold that the numerical threshold does not circumscribe federal-court subject-matter jurisdiction. Instead, the employee-numerosity requirement relates to the substantive adequacy of Arbaugh's Title VII claim, and therefore could not be raised defensively late in the lawsuit, i.e., after Y&H had failed to assert the objection prior to the close of trial on the merits.

I

We set out below statutory provisions and rules that bear on this case. Title VII makes it "an unlawful employment practice for an employer ... to fail or refuse to hire or to discharge any individual, or otherwise to discriminate against any individual with respect to his compensation, terms, conditions, or privileges of employment, because of such individual's race, color, religion, sex, or national origin." 42 U. S. C. §2000e–2(a)(1). To spare very small businesses from Title VII liability, Congress provided that:

> "[t]he term 'employer' means a person engaged in an industry affecting commerce who has fifteen or more employees for each working day in each of twenty or more calendar weeks in the current or preceding calendar year, and any agent of such a person ... ." §2000e(b).[1]

This employee-numerosity requirement[2] appears in a section headed "Definitions," §2000e, which also prescribes the meaning, for Title VII purposes, of 12 other terms used in the Act.[3]

Congress has broadly authorized the federal courts to exercise subject-matter jurisdiction over "all civil actions arising under the Constitution, laws, or treaties of the United States." 28 U. S. C. §1331. Title VII surely is a "la[w] of the United States." Ibid. In 1964, however, when Title VII was enacted, §1331's umbrella provision for federal-question jurisdiction contained an amount-in-controversy limitation: Claims could not be brought under §1331 unless the amount in controversy exceeded $10,000. See §1331(a) (1964 ed.). Title VII, framed in that light, assured that the amount-in-controversy limitation would not impede an employment-discrimination complainant's access to a federal forum. The Act thus contains its own jurisdiction-conferring provision, which reads:

"Each United States district court and each United States court of a place subject to the jurisdiction of the United States shall have jurisdiction of actions brought under this subchapter." 42 U. S. C. §2000e-5(f)(3).[4]

Congress amended 28 U. S. C. §1331 in 1980 to eliminate the amount-in-controversy threshold. See Federal Question Jurisdictional Amendments Act of 1980, §2, 94 Stat. 2369. Since that time, Title VII's own jurisdictional provision, 42 U. S. C. §2000e–5(f)(3), has served simply to underscore Congress' intention to provide a federal forum for the adjudication of Title VII claims. See Brief for United States as Amicus Curiae 13; Tr. of Oral Arg. 4.

We note, too, that, under 28 U. S. C. §1367, federal courts may exercise "supplemental" jurisdiction over state-law claims linked to a claim based on federal law.[5] Plaintiffs suing under Title VII may avail themselves of the opportunity §1367 provides to pursue complete relief in a federal-court lawsuit. Arbaugh did so in the instant case by adding to her federal complaint pendent claims arising under state law that would not independently qualify for federal-court adjudication.

The objection that a federal court lacks subject-matter jurisdiction, see Fed. Rule Civ. Proc. 12(b)(1), may be raised by a party, or by a court on its own initiative, at any stage in the litigation, even after trial and the entry of judgment. Rule 12(h)(3) instructs: "Whenever it appears by suggestion of the parties or otherwise that the court lacks jurisdiction of the subject matter, the court shall dismiss the action." See Kontrick v. Ryan, 540 U. S. 443, 455 (2004). By contrast, the objection that a complaint "fail[s] to state a claim upon which relief can be granted," Rule 12(b)(6), may not be asserted post trial. Under Rule 12(h)(2), that objection endures up to, but not beyond, trial on the merits: "A defense of failure to state a claim upon which relief can be granted … may be made in any pleading … or by motion for judgment on the pleadings, or at the trial on the merits." Cf. Kontrick, 540 U. S., at 459.

II

From May 2000 through February 2001, Jenifer Arbaugh worked as a bartender and waitress at the Moonlight Cafe, a New Orleans restaurant owned and operated by Y&H. Arbaugh alleged that Yalcin Hatipoglu, one of the company's owners, sexually harassed her and precipitated her constructive discharge.[6] In November 2001, Arbaugh filed suit against Y&H in the United States District Court for the Eastern District of Louisiana. Her complaint asserted claims under Title VII and Louisiana law. App. to Pet. for Cert. 1–2.

Arbaugh's pleadings alleged that her federal claim "ar[o]se under Title VII" and that the Federal District Court had jurisdiction over this claim under §1331 plus supplemental jurisdiction over her state-law claims under §1367. Record in No. 01–3376 (ED La.), Doc. 3, p. 1 (Amended Complaint). Y&H's responsive pleadings admitted Arbaugh's "jurisdictional" allegations but denied her contentions on the merits. Id., Doc. 4, p. 1 (Answer to Complaint). The pretrial order submitted and signed by the parties, and later subscribed by the presiding judge, reiterated that the court was "vested with jurisdiction over [Arbaugh's Title VII claim] pursuant to 28 U. S. C. §1331," and "ha[d] supplemental jurisdiction over [her] state law claims pursuant to 28 U. S. C. §1367." Id., Doc. 19, p. 2. The order listed "Uncontested Material Facts," including: "Plaintiff was employed as a waitress/bartender at the Moonlight for Defendants from May, 2000 through February 10, 2001 when she terminated her employment with the company." Id., p. 3. It did not list among "Contested Issues of Fact" or "Contested Legal Issues" the question whether Y&H had the requisite number of employees under 42 U. S. C. §2000e(b). Record, Doc. 19, pp. 4–5. Nor was the issue raised at any other point pretrial or at trial.

The parties consented to trial before a Magistrate Judge. See 28 U. S. C. §636(c). After a two-day trial, the jury found that Arbaugh had been sexually harassed and constructively discharged in violation of Title VII and Louisiana antidiscrimination law. The verdict awarded Arbaugh $5,000 in backpay, $5,000 in compensatory damages, and $30,000 in punitive damages. The trial court entered judgment for Arbaugh on November 5, 2002.

Two weeks later, Y&H filed a motion under Federal Rule 12(h)(3) to dismiss Arbaugh's complaint for lack of subject-matter jurisdiction. Record, Doc. 44. As sole ground for the motion, Y&H alleged, for the first time in the proceedings, that it "did not employ fifteen or more employees [during the relevant period] and thus is not an employer for Title VII purposes." Id., p. 2 (Memorandum in Support of Rule 12(h)(3) Motion to Dismiss for Lack of Subject Matter Jurisdiction). The trial court commented that "[i]t is unfair and a waste of judicial resources to permit [Y&H] to admit Arbaugh's allegations of jurisdiction, try the case for two days and then assert a lack of subject matter jurisdiction in response to an adverse jury verdict." App. to Pet. for Cert. 47. Nevertheless, reciting the text of Rule 12(h)(3), see supra, at 5, the trial court allowed Y&H to plead that it did not qualify as an "employer" under Title VII's definition of that term. App. to Pet. for Cert. 47–48; see supra, at 3.

Discovery ensued. The dispute over the employee count turned on the employment status of Y&H's eight drivers, engaged to make deliveries for the restaurant, and the company's four owners (the Moonlight Cafe's two managers and their shareholder spouses). As the trial court noted, "[i]f either the delivery drivers or the four owners are counted with the persons shown on the payroll journals, then Y&H employed fifteen or more persons for the requisite time." App. to Pet. for Cert. 27. After reviewing the parties' submissions, however, the trial court concluded that neither the delivery drivers nor the owner-managers nor their shareholder spouses qualified as "employees" for Title VII purposes. Id., at 32–43.

Based on that determination, the trial court vacated its prior judgment in favor of Arbaugh, dismissed her Title VII claim with prejudice, and her state-law claims without prejudice. Id., at 23.

The Court of Appeals for the Fifth Circuit affirmed. 380 F. 3d 219 (2004). Bound by its prior decisions, the Court of Appeals held that a defendant's "failure to qualify as an 'employer' under Title VII deprives a district court of subject matter jurisdiction." Id., at 224 (citing, e.g., Dumas v. Mt. Vernon, 612 F. 2d 974, 980 (1980)). Dismissal for want of subject-matter jurisdiction was proper, the Court of Appeals ruled, for the record warranted the conclusion that Y&H's delivery drivers, its owner-managers, and their shareholder wives were not "employees" for Title VII purposes, 380 F. 3d, at 225–230, and it was undisputed that Y&H "did not employ the requisite 15 employees without the inclusion of" those persons, id., at 231.

We granted certiorari, 544 U. S. 1031 (2005), to resolve conflicting opinions in Courts of Appeals on the question whether Title VII's employee-numerosity requirement, 42 U. S. C. §2000e(b), is jurisdictional or simply an element of a plaintiff's claim for relief. Compare, e.g., 380 F. 3d, at 223–225 (Title VII's employee-numerosity requirement is jurisdictional), and Armbruster v. Quinn, 711 F. 2d 1332, 1335 (CA6 1983) (same), with, e.g., Da Silva v. Kinsho International Corp., 229 F. 3d 358, 361–366 (CA2 2000) (Title VII's employee-numerosity requirement is not jurisdictional); Nesbit v. Gears Unlimited, Inc., 347 F. 3d 72, 76–83 (CA3 2003) (same); EEOC v. St. Francis Xavier Parochial School, 117 F. 3d 621, 623–624 (CADC 1997) (Americans with Disabilities Act's employee-numerosity requirement, 42 U. S. C. §12111(5)(A), resembling Title VII's requirement, is not jurisdictional).

III

"Jurisdiction," this Court has observed, "is a word of many, too many, meanings." Steel Co. v. Citizens for Better Environment, 523 U. S. 83, 90 (1998) (internal quotation marks omitted). This Court, no less than other courts, has sometimes been profligate in its use of the term. For example, this Court and others have occasionally described a nonextendable time limit as "mandatory and jurisdictional." See, e.g., United States v. Robinson, 361 U. S. 220, 229 (1960). But in recent decisions, we have clarified that time prescriptions, however emphatic, "are not properly typed 'jurisdictional.'" Scarborough v. Principi, 541 U. S. 401, 414 (2004); accord Eberhart v. United States, 546 U. S. ___, ___ (2005) (per curiam) (slip op., at 4–7); Kontrick, 540 U. S., at 454–455. See also Carlisle v. United States, 517 U. S. 416, 434–435 (1996) (Ginsburg, J., concurring).

The dispute now before us concerns the proper classification of Title VII's statutory limitation of covered employers to those with 15 or more employees. If the limitation conditions subject-matter jurisdiction, as the lower courts held it did, then a conclusion that Y&H had fewer than 15 employees would require erasure of the judgment for Arbaugh entered on the jury verdict. But if the lower courts' subject-matter jurisdiction characterization is incorrect, and the issue, instead, concerns the merits of Arbaugh's case, then Y&H raised the employee-numerosity requirement too late. Its pretrial stipulations, see supra, at 6, and its failure to speak to the issue prior to the conclusion of the trial on the merits, see Fed. Rule Civ. Proc. 12(h)(2), supra, at 5, would preclude vacation of the $40,000 judgment in Arbaugh's favor.

On the subject-matter jurisdiction/ingredient-of-claim-for-relief dichotomy, this Court and others have been less than meticulous. "Subject matter jurisdiction in federal-question cases is sometimes erroneously conflated with a plaintiff's need and ability to prove the defendant bound by the federal law asserted as the predicate for relief—a merits-related determination." 2 J. Moore et al., Moore's Federal Practice §12.30[1], p. 12–36.1 (3d ed. 2005) (hereinafter Moore). Judicial opinions, the Second Circuit incisively observed, "often obscure the issue by stating that the court is dismissing 'for lack of jurisdiction' when some threshold fact has not been established, without explicitly considering whether the dismissal should be for lack of subject matter jurisdiction or for failure to state a claim." Da Silva, 229 F. 3d, at 361. We have described such unrefined dispositions as "drive-by jurisdictional rulings" that should be accorded "no precedential effect" on the question whether the federal court had authority to adjudicate the claim in suit. Steel Co., 523 U. S., at 91.

Cases of this genre include Hishon v. King & Spalding, 467 U. S. 69 (1984), and EEOC v. Arabian American Oil Co., 499 U. S. 244 (1991). Hishon involved a Title VII claim brought by a lawyer denied partnership in a law firm. The District Court ruled that Title VII did not apply to the selection of partners and dismissed the case for lack of subject-matter jurisdiction. The Court of Appeals affirmed that judgment. We noted that the District Court's reasoning "ma[de] clear that it dismissed petitioner's complaint on the ground that her allegations did not state a claim cognizable under Title VII." 467 U. S., at 73, n. 2. Disagreeing with the lower courts, we held that Title VII applies to partnership decisions. Id., at 73–78. That holding, we said, "ma[de] it unnecessary to consider the wisdom of the District Court's invocation of Rule 12(b)(1), as opposed to Rule 12(b)(6)." Id., at 73, n. 2. The former Rule concerns subject-matter jurisdiction, the latter, "failure to state a claim upon which relief can be granted." See supra, at 5. Our opinion in Hishon thus raised, but did not decide, the question whether subject-matter jurisdiction was the proper rubric for the District Court's decisions.[7]

In Arabian American Oil Co., we affirmed the judgment of the courts below that Title VII, as then composed, did not apply to a suit by a United States employee working abroad for a United States employer.[8] That judgment had been placed under a lack of subject-matter jurisdiction label. We agreed with the lower courts' view of the limited geographical reach of the statute. 499 U. S., at 246–247. En passant, we copied the petitioners' characterizations of terms included in Title VII's "Definitions" section, 42 U. S. C. §2000e, as "jurisdictional." See 499 U. S., at 249, 251, 253. But our decision did not turn on that characterization, and the parties did not cross swords over it. See Steel Co., 523 U. S., at 91 (declining to follow a decision treating an issue as jurisdictional because nothing "turned upon whether [the issue] was technically jurisdictional" in that case). In short, we were not prompted in Arabian American Oil Co. to home in on whether the dismissal had been properly based on the absence of subject-matter jurisdiction rather than on the plaintiff's failure to state a claim. 499 U. S., at 247.[9]

The basic statutory grants of federal-court subject-matter jurisdiction are contained in 28 U. S. C. §§1331 and 1332. Section 1331 provides for "[f]ederal-question" jurisdiction, §1332 for "[d]iversity of citizenship" jurisdiction. A plaintiff properly invokes §1331 jurisdiction when she pleads a colorable claim "arising under" the Constitution or laws of the United States. See Bell v. Hood, 327 U. S. 678, 681–685 (1946).[10] She invokes §1332 jurisdiction when she presents a claim between parties of diverse citizenship that exceeds the required jurisdictional amount, currently $75,000. See §1332(a).

Arbaugh invoked federal-question jurisdiction under §1331, but her case "aris[es]" under a federal law, Title VII, that specifies, as a prerequisite to its application, the existence of a particular fact, i.e., 15 or more employees. We resolve the question whether that fact is "jurisdictional" or relates to the "merits" of a Title VII claim mindful of the consequences of typing the 15-employee threshold a determinant of subject-matter jurisdiction, rather than an element of Arbaugh's claim for relief.

First, "subject-matter jurisdiction, because it involves the court's power to hear a case, can never be forfeited or waived." United States v. Cotton, 535 U. S. 625, 630 (2002). Moreover, courts, including this Court, have an independent obligation to determine whether subject-matter jurisdiction exists, even in the absence of a challenge from any party. Ruhrgas AG v. Marathon Oil Co., 526 U. S. 574, 583 (1999). Nothing in the text of Title VII indicates that Congress intended courts, on their own motion, to assure that the employee-numerosity requirement is met.

Second, in some instances, if subject-matter jurisdiction turns on contested facts, the trial judge may be authorized to review the evidence and resolve the dispute on her own. See 5B C. Wright & A. Miller, Federal Practice and Procedure §1350, pp. 243–249 (3d ed. 2004); 2 Moore §12.30[3], pp. 12–37 to 12–38. If satisfaction of an essential element of a claim for relief is at issue, however, the jury is the proper trier of contested facts. Reeves v. Sanderson Plumbing Products, Inc., 530 U. S. 133, 150–151 (2000).

Third, when a federal court concludes that it lacks subject-matter jurisdiction, the court must dismiss the complaint in its entirety. See 16 Moore §106.66[1], pp. 106–88 to 106–89. Thus in the instant case, the trial court dismissed, along with the Title VII claim, pendent state-law claims, see supra, at 4, fully tried by a jury and determined on the merits, see App. to Pet. for Cert. 23, 47. In contrast, when a court grants a motion to dismiss for failure to state a federal claim, the court generally retains discretion to exercise supplemental jurisdiction, pursuant to 28 U. S. C. §1367, over pendent state-law claims. See 16 Moore §106.66[1], pp. 106–86 to 106–89.

Of course, Congress could make the employee-numerosity requirement "jurisdictional," just as it has made an amount-in-controversy threshold an ingredient of subject-matter jurisdiction in delineating diversity-of-citizenship jurisdiction under 28 U. S. C. §1332. But neither §1331, nor Title VII's jurisdictional provision, 42 U. S. C. §2000e–5(f)(3) (authorizing jurisdiction over actions "brought under" Title VII), specifies any threshold ingredient akin to 28 U. S. C. §1332's monetary floor. Instead, the 15-employee threshold appears in a separate provision that "does not speak in jurisdictional terms or refer in any way to the jurisdiction of the district courts." Zipes v. Trans World Airlines, Inc., 455 U. S. 385, 394 (1982). Given the "unfair[ness]" and "waste of judicial resources," App. to Pet. for Cert. 47, entailed in tying the employee-numerosity requirement to subject-matter jurisdiction, we think it the sounder course to refrain from constricting §1331 or Title VII's jurisdictional provision, 42 U. S. C. §2000e–5(f)(3), and to leave the ball in Congress' court. If the Legislature clearly states that a threshold limitation on a statute's scope shall count as jurisdictional,[11] then courts and litigants will be duly instructed and will not be left to wrestle with the issue. See Da Silva, 229 F. 3d, at 361 ("Whether a disputed matter concerns jurisdiction or the merits (or occasionally both) is sometimes a close question."). But when Congress does not rank a statutory limitation on coverage as jurisdictional, courts should treat the restriction as nonjurisdictional in character. Applying that readily administrable bright line to this case, we hold that the threshold number of employees for application of Title VII is an element of a plaintiff's claim for relief, not a jurisdictional issue.

* * *

For the reasons stated, the judgment of the Court of Appeals is reversed, and the case is remanded for further proceedings consistent with this opinion.

It is so ordered.

Justice Alito took no part in the consideration or decision of this case.

NOTES

[1] The same provision further states that the term "employer" does not include the United States, corporations wholly owned by the United States, Indian Tribes, certain departments and agencies of the District of Columbia, or tax-exempt "bona fide private membership club[s]" (other than labor organizations). §2000e(b).

[2] Congress originally prescribed a 25-or-more-employee threshold, Civil Rights Act of 1964, §701, 78 Stat. 253, but lowered the minimum number of employees to 15 in the Equal Employment Opportunity

Act of 1972, §2, 86 Stat. 103.

3 The other terms defined in §2000e are: "person," "employment agency," "labor organization," "employee," "commerce," "industry affecting commerce," "State," "religion," "because of sex," "complaining party," "demonstrates," and "respondent."

4 Title VII contains a separate jurisdictional provision, 42 U. S. C. §2000e–6(b), authorizing suits by the Government to enjoin "pattern or practice" discrimination.

5 Section 1367(a) states: "Except as provided in subsections (b) and (c) or as expressly provided otherwise by Federal statute, in any civil action of which the district courts have original jurisdiction, the district courts shall have supplemental jurisdiction over all other claims that are so related to claims in the action within such original jurisdiction that they form part of the same case or controversy under Article III of the United States Constitution. Such supplemental jurisdiction shall include claims that involve the joinder or intervention of additional parties."

6 See Pennsylvania State Police v. Suders, 542 U. S. 129, 147 (2004) (constructive discharge compensable under Title VII includes an employee's departure due to sexual harassment that renders "working conditions so intolerable that a reasonable person would have felt compelled to resign").

7 Y&H features Walters v. Metropolitan Ed. Enterprises, Inc., 519 U. S. 202 (1997), as supportive of the jurisdictional character of the employee-numerosity requirement. Brief for Respondent 8–10. Y&H urges that the Court must have considered the requirement jurisdictional, for Walters held definitively that, under the correct legal standard, the defendant had more than 15 employees. If the requirement had been seen as a merits issue, Y&H contends, the Court would have remanded the employee count for determination by the trier of fact. But the parties in Walters apparently stipulated to all relevant facts, leaving nothing for a fact trier to resolve on remand. Cf. 519 U. S., at 211–212.

8 Congress subsequently amended Title VII to extend protection to United States citizens working overseas. See Civil Rights Act of 1991, §109(a), 105 Stat. 1077, codified at 42 U. S. C. §2000e(f) ("With respect to employment in a foreign country," the term "employee" "includes an individual who is a citizen of the United States.").

9 In EEOC v. Commercial Office Products Co., 486 U. S. 107 (1988), also featured by Y&H, see Brief for Respondent 12, a plurality of this Court noted that "[r]eactivation of state proceedings after the conclusion of federal proceedings serves [a] useful function," in part because "Title VII does not give the EEOC jurisdiction to enforce the Act against employers of fewer than 15 employees." 486 U. S., at 119, n. 5. That fleeting footnote addressed the relative administrative provinces of the EEOC and state agencies. It did not speak of federal-court subject-matter jurisdiction, which was not at issue in the case.

10 A claim invoking federal-question jurisdiction under 28 U. S. C. §1331, Bell held, may be dismissed for want of subject-matter jurisdiction if it is not colorable, i.e., if it is "immaterial and made solely for the purpose of obtaining jurisdiction" or is "wholly insubstantial and frivolous." 327 U. S., at 682–683; see Steel Co. v. Citizens for Better Environment, 523 U. S. 83, 89 (1998). Arbaugh's case surely does not belong in that category.

11 Congress has exercised its prerogative to restrict the subject-matter jurisdiction of federal district courts based on a wide variety of factors, some of them also relevant to the merits of a case. Certain statutes confer subject-matter jurisdiction only for actions brought by specific plaintiffs, e.g., 28 U. S. C. §1345 (United States and its agencies and officers), 49 U. S. C. §24301(l)(2) (Amtrak), or for claims against particular defendants, e.g., 7 U. S. C. §2707(e)(3) (persons subject to orders of the Egg Board); 28 U. S. C. §1348 (national banking associations), or for actions in which the amount in controversy exceeds, e.g., 16 U. S. C. §814, or falls below, e.g., 22 U. S. C. §6713(a)(1)(B), 28 U. S. C. §1346(a)(2), a stated amount. Other jurisdiction-conferring provisions describe particular types of claims. See, e.g., §1339 ("any civil action arising under any Act of Congress relating to the postal service"); §1347 ("any civil action commenced by any tenant in common or joint tenant for the partition of lands where the United States is one of the tenants in common or joint tenants"). In a few instances, Congress has enacted a separate provision that expressly restricts application of a jurisdiction-conferring statute. See, e.g., Weinberger v. Salfi, 422 U. S. 749, 756–761 (1975) (42 U. S. C. §405(h) bars §1331 jurisdiction over suits to recover Social Security benefits).

PATRICK A. DAY v. JAMES McDONOUGH, INTERIM SECRETARY, FLORIDA DEPARTMENT OF CORRECTIONS

No. 04-1324, April 25, 2006

ON WRIT OF CERTIORARI TO THE UNITED STATES COURT OF APPEALS FOR THE ELEVENTH CIRCUIT

Justice Ginsburg delivered the opinion of the Court.

This case concerns the authority of a U. S. District Court, on its own initiative, to dismiss as untimely a state prisoner's petition for a writ of habeas corpus. The Antiterrorism and Effective Death Penalty Act of 1996 (AEDPA), 110 Stat. 1214, sets a one-year limitation period for filing such petitions, running from "the date on which the judgment became final by the conclusion of direct review or the expiration of the time for seeking such review." 28 U. S. C. §2244(d)(1)(A). The one-year clock is stopped, however, during the time the petitioner's "properly filed" application for state postconviction relief "is pending." §2244(d)(2). Under Eleventh Circuit precedent, that tolling period does not include the 90 days in which a petitioner might have sought certiorari review in this Court challenging state-court denial of postconviction relief. Coates v. Byrd, 211 F. 3d 1225, 1227 (2000).

In the case before us, the State's answer to the federal habeas petition "agree[d] the petition [was] timely" because it was "filed after 352 days of untolled time." App. 24. Inspecting the pleadings and attachments, a Federal Magistrate Judge determined that the State had miscalculated the tolling time. Under Circuit precedent, the untolled time was 388 days, rendering the petition untimely by some three weeks. After affording the petitioner an opportunity to show cause why the petition should not be dismissed for failure to meet the statutory deadline, and finding petitioner's responses inadequate, the Magistrate Judge recommended dismissal of the petition. The District Court adopted the Magistrate Judge's recommendation, and the Court of Appeals affirmed, concluding that "[a] concession of timeliness by the state that is patently erroneous does not compromise the authority of a district court sua sponte to dismiss a habeas petition as untimely, under AEDPA." Day v. Crosby, 391 F. 3d 1192, 1195 (CA11 2004).

The question presented is whether a federal court lacks authority, on its own initiative, to dismiss a habeas petition as untimely, once the State has answered the petition without contesting its timeliness. Ordinarily in civil litigation, a statutory time limitation is forfeited if not raised in a defendant's answer or in an amendment thereto. Fed. Rules Civ. Proc. 8(c), 12(b), and 15(a). And we would count it an abuse of discretion to override a State's deliberate waiver of a limitations defense. In this case, however, the federal court confronted no intelligent waiver on the State's part, only an evident miscalculation of the elapsed time under a statute designed to impose a tight time constraint on federal habeas petitioners.[1] In the circumstances here presented, we hold, the federal court had discretion to correct the State's error and, accordingly, to dismiss the petition as untimely under AEDPA's one-year limitation.

I

Petitioner Patrick A. Day was convicted of second-degree murder and sentenced to 55 years in prison by a Florida trial court. Day unsuccessfully appealed the sentence, which was affirmed on December 21, 1999. Day did not seek this Court's review of the final state-court decision; his time to do so expired on March 20, 2000.

Three hundred and fifty-three (353) days later, Day unsuccessfully sought state postconviction relief. The Florida trial court's judgment denying relief was affirmed on appeal, and the appellate court issued its mandate on December 3, 2002. See Nyland v. Moore, 216 F. 3d 1264, 1267 (CA11 2000) (under Florida law, appellate order "is pending" until the mandate issues). Thirty-six (36) days thereafter, on January 8, 2003, Day petitioned for federal habeas relief asserting several claims of ineffective assistance of trial counsel. A Magistrate Judge, finding the petition "in proper form," App. 21, ordered the State to file an answer, id., at 21–22. In its responsive pleading, the State failed to raise AEDPA's one-year limitation as a defense. See supra, at 2. Overlooking controlling Eleventh Circuit precedent, see Coates, 211 F. 3d, at 1227, the State calculated that the petition had been "filed after 352 days of untolled time," and was therefore "timely." App. 24. The State's answer and attachments, however, revealed that, had the State followed the Eleventh Circuit's instruction on computation of elapsed time, the timeliness concession would not have been made: Under the Circuit's precedent, more than one year, specifically, 388 days of untolled time, had passed between the finality of Day's state-court conviction and the filing of his federal habeas petition.[2]

A newly assigned Magistrate Judge noticed the State's computation error and ordered Day to show cause why his federal habeas petition should not be dismissed as untimely. Id., at 26–30. Determining that Day's responses did not overcome the time bar, the Magistrate Judge recommended dismissal of the petition, App. to Pet. for Cert. 8a–15a, and the District Court adopted that recommendation, id., at 7a.

The Eleventh Circuit granted Day a certificate of appealability on the question "[w]hether the district court erred in addressing the timeliness of [Day's] habeas corpus petition ... after the [State] had conceded that [the] petition was timely." App. 37. In a decision rendered two years earlier, Jackson v. Secretary for Dept. of Corrections, 292 F. 3d 1347 (2002), the Eleventh Circuit had ruled that, "even though the statute of limitations is an affirmative defense, the district court may review sua sponte the timeliness of [a federal habeas] petition." Id., at 1349. Adhering to Jackson, and satisfied that the State's concession of timeliness "was patently erroneous," the Eleventh Circuit affirmed the dismissal of Day's petition. 391 F. 3d, at 1192–1195.[3]

We granted certiorari sub nom. Day v. Crosby, 545 U. S. __ (2005), in view of the division among the Circuits on the question whether a district court may dismiss a federal habeas petition as untimely under AEDPA, despite the State's failure to raise the one-year limitation in its answer to the petition or its erroneous concession of the timeliness issue. Compare, e.g., Long v. Wilson, 393 F. 3d 390, 401–404 (CA3 2004), and 391 F. 3d, at 1194–1195 (case below), with Scott v. Collins, 286 F. 3d 923, 930–931 (CA6 2002), and Nardi v. Stewart, 354 F. 3d 1134, 1141–1142 (CA9 2004).

II

A statute of limitations defense, the State acknowledges, is not "jurisdictional," hence courts are under no obligation to raise the time bar sua sponte. See, e.g., Acosta v. Artuz, 221 F. 3d 117, 122 (CA2 2000); Hill v. Braxton, 277 F. 3d 701, 705 (CA4 2002); Davis v. Johnson, 158 F. 3d 806, 810 (CA5 1998); cf. Kontrick v. Ryan, 540 U. S. 443, 458 (2004) (defendant forfeited untimeliness argument "by failing to raise the issue until after [the] complaint was adjudicated on the merits"). In this respect, the limitations defense resembles other threshold barriers—exhaustion of state remedies, procedural default, nonretroactivity—courts have typed "nonjurisdictional," although recognizing that those defenses "implicat[e] values beyond the concerns of the parties." Acosta, 221 F. 3d, at 123 ("The AEDPA statute of limitation promotes judicial efficiency and conservation of judicial resources, safeguards the accuracy of state court judgments by requiring resolution of constitutional questions while the record is fresh, and lends finality to state court judgments within a reasonable time.").

On the exhaustion of state remedies doctrine, requiring state prisoners, before invoking federal habeas jurisdiction, to pursue remedies available in state court, Granberry v. Greer, 481 U. S. 129 (1987), is the pathmarking case. We held in Granberry that federal appellate courts have discretion to consider the issue of exhaustion despite the State's failure to interpose the defense at the district-court level. Id., at 133.[4] Later, in Caspari v. Bohlen, 510 U. S. 383, 389 (1994), we similarly held that "a federal court may, but need not, decline to apply [the nonretroactivity rule announced in Teague v. Lane, 489 U. S. 288, 310 (1989),] if the State does not argue it." See also Schiro v. Farley, 510 U. S. 222, 229 (1994) (declining to address nonretroactivity defense that State raised only in Supreme Court merits brief, "[a]lthough we undoubtedly have the discretion to reach" the argument).

While the issue remains open in this Court, see Trest v. Cain, 522 U. S. 87, 90 (1997),[5] the Courts of Appeals have unanimously held that, in appropriate circumstances, courts, on their own initiative, may raise a petitioner's procedural default, i.e., a petitioner's failure properly to present an alleged constitutional error in state court, and the consequent adequacy and independence of state-law grounds for the state-court judgment. See Brewer v. Marshall, 119 F. 3d 993, 999 (CA1 1997); Rosario v. United States, 164 F. 3d 729, 732 (CA2 1998); Sweger v. Chesney, 294 F. 3d 506, 520 (CA3 2002); Yeatts v. Angelone, 166 F. 3d 255, 261 (CA4 1999); Magouirk v. Phillips, 144 F. 3d 348, 358 (CA5 1998); Sowell v. Bradshaw, 372 F. 3d 821, 830 (CA6 2004); Kurzawa v. Jordan, 146 F. 3d 435, 440 (CA7 1998); King v. Kemna, 266 F. 3d 816, 822 (CA8 2001) (en banc); Vang v. Nevada, 329 F. 3d 1069, 1073 (CA9 2003); United States v. Wiseman, 297 F. 3d 975, 979 (CA10 2002); Moon v. Head, 285 F. 3d 1301, 1315, n. 17 (CA11 2002).

Petitioner Day relies heavily on Rule 4 of the Rules Governing Section 2254 Cases in the United States District Courts (Habeas Rules), i.e., the procedural Rules governing federal habeas petitions from state prisoners, in urging that AEDPA's limitation may be raised by a federal court sua sponte only at the preanswer, initial screening stage. Habeas Rule 4 provides that district courts "must promptly examine" state prisoner habeas petitions and must dismiss the petition "[i]f it plainly appears ... that the petitioner is not entitled to relief." Once an answer has been ordered and filed, Day maintains, the court loses authority to rule the petition untimely sua sponte.[6] At that point, according to Day, the Federal Rules of Civil Procedure hold sway. See Habeas Rule 11 ("The Federal Rules of Civil Procedure, to the extent that they are not inconsistent with any statutory provisions or these rules, may be applied to a proceeding under these rules.").[7] Under the Civil Procedure Rules, a defendant forfeits a statute of limitations defense, see Fed. Rule Civ. Proc. 8(c), not asserted in its answer, see Rule 12(b), or an amendment thereto, see Rule 15(a).

The State, on the other hand, points out that the statute of limitations is akin to other affirmative defenses to habeas petitions, notably exhaustion of state remedies, procedural default, and nonretroactivity. Indeed, the statute of limitations is explicitly aligned with those other defenses under the current version of Habeas Rule 5(b), which provides that the State's answer to a habeas petition "must state whether any claim in the petition is barred by a failure to exhaust state remedies, a procedural bar, non-retroactivity, or a statute of limitations." The considerations of comity, finality, and the expeditious handling of habeas proceedings that motivated AEDPA,[8] the State maintains, counsel against an excessively rigid or formal approach to the affirmative defenses now listed in Habeas Rule 5. Citing Granberry, 481 U. S., at 131–134, as the instructive case, the State urges express recognition of an "intermediate approach." Brief for Respondent 14 (internal quotation marks omitted); see also id., at 25. In lieu of an inflexible rule requiring dismissal whenever AEDPA's one-year clock has run, or, at the opposite extreme, a rule treating the State's failure initially to plead the one-year bar as an absolute waiver, the State reads the statutes, Rules, and decisions in point to permit the "exercise [of] discretion in each case to decide whether the administration of justice is better served by dismissing the case on statute of limitations grounds or by reaching the merits of the petition." Id., at 14. Employing that "intermediate approach" in this particular case, the State argues, the petition should not be deemed timely simply because a government attorney calculated the days in between petitions incorrectly.

We agree, noting particularly that the Magistrate Judge, instead of acting sua sponte, might have informed the State of its obvious computation error and entertained an amendment to the State's answer. See Fed. Rule Civ. Proc. 15(a) (leave to amend "shall be freely given when justice so requires"); see also 28 U. S. C. §2243 (State's response to habeas petition may be amended by leave of court); cf. Long, 393 F. 3d, at 402–404 (District Court raised the statute of limitations sua sponte, the State agreed with that disposition, and the Court of Appeals treated that agreement as a constructive amendment to the State's answer). Recognizing that an amendment to the State's answer might have obviated this controversy,[9] we see no dispositive difference between that route, and the one taken here. See Brief for Respondent 24 ("Here, the State did not respond to the show cause order because its concession of timeliness was based on an erroneous calculation and it agreed the petition should be dismissed as untimely."); cf. Slack v. McDaniel, 529 U. S. 473, 487 (2000) (admonishing against interpretation of procedural prescriptions in federal habeas cases to "trap the unwary pro se prisoner" (quoting Rose v. Lundy, 455 U. S. 509, 520 (1982))).

In sum, we hold that district courts are permitted, but not obliged, to consider, sua sponte, the timeliness of a state prisoner's habeas petition. We so hold, noting that it would make scant sense to distinguish in this regard AEDPA's time bar from other threshold constraints on federal habeas petitioners. See supra, at 6–7; Habeas Rule 5(b) (placing "a statute of limitations" defense on a par with "failure to exhaust state remedies, a procedural bar, [and] non-retroactivity"); Long, 393 F. 3d, at 404 ("AEDPA's statute of limitations advances the same concerns as those advanced by the doctrines of exhaustion and procedural default, and must be treated the same."). We stress that a district court is not required to double-check the State's math. If, as this Court has held, "[d]istrict judges have no obligation to act as counsel or paralegal to pro se litigants," Pliler v. Ford, 542 U. S. 225, 231 (2004),[10] then, by the same token, they surely have no obligation to assist attorneys representing the State. Nevertheless, if a judge does detect a clear computation error, no Rule, statute, or constitutional provision commands the judge to suppress that knowledge. Cf. Fed. Rule Civ. Proc. 60(a) (clerical errors in the record "arising from oversight or omission may be corrected by the court at any time of its own initiative or on the motion of any party").

Of course, before acting on its own initiative, a court must accord the parties fair notice and an opportunity to present their positions. See, e.g., Acosta, 221 F. 3d, at 124–125; McMillan v. Jarvis, 332 F. 3d 244, 250 (CA4 2003). Further, the court must assure itself that the petitioner is not significantly prejudiced by the delayed focus on the limitation issue, and "determine whether the interests of justice would be better served" by addressing the merits or by dismissing the petition as time barred. See Granberry, 481 U. S., at 136.[11] Here, the Magistrate Judge gave Day due notice and a fair opportunity to show why the limitation period should not yield dismissal of the petition. The notice issued some nine months after the State answered the petition. No court proceedings or action occurred in the interim, and nothing in the record suggests that the State "strategically" withheld the defense or chose to relinquish it. From all that appears in the record, there was merely an inadvertent error, a miscalculation that was plain under Circuit precedent, and no abuse of discretion in following this Court's lead in Granberry and Caspari, described supra, at 6–7.

* * *

For the reasons stated, the judgment of the Court of Appeals is Affirmed.

[1] Until AEDPA took effect in 1996, no statute of limitations applied to habeas petitions. See Mayle v. Felix, 545 U. S. ___, ___ (2005) (slip op., at 7). Courts invoked the doctrine of "prejudicial delay" to screen out unreasonably late filings. See generally 2 R. Hertz & J. Liebman, Federal Habeas Corpus Practice and Procedure §24 (4th ed. 2001). In AEDPA, Congress prescribed a uniform rule: "A 1-year period of limitation shall apply to an application for a writ of habeas corpus by a person in custody pursuant to the judgment of a State court." 28 U. S. C. §2244(d)(1).

[2] Day urges this Court to find his petition timely. He asserts that the Eleventh Circuit misinterpreted §2244(d)(2) in holding that AEDPA's time limitation was not tolled during the 90-day period he could have petitioned this Court to review the denial of his motion for state postconviction relief. See Brief for Petitioner 45–50. This question was not "set out in the petition [for certiorari], or fairly included therein," and we therefore do not consider it here. This Court's Rule 14.1(a). We note, however, that the Court recently granted certiorari in Lawrence v. Florida, No. 05–8820 (cert. granted, Mar. 27, 2006), which presents the question whether AEDPA's time limitation is tolled during the pendency of a petition for certiorari from a judgment denying state postconviction relief. The instant opinion, we emphasize, addresses only the authority of the District Court to raise AEDPA's time bar, not the correctness of its decision that the limitation period had run.

[3] Day reads the Eleventh Circuit's opinion in this case as rendering mandatory a district court's sua sponte application of AEDPA's one-year limitation, even when the respondent elects to waive the

limitation and oppose the petition solely on the merits. See Tr. of Oral Arg. 6–8. He points to a sentence in the Eleventh Circuit's brief per curiam opinion stating: "A federal court that sits in collateral review of a criminal judgment of a state court has an obligation to enforce the federal statute of limitations." 391 F. 3d, at 1194. We read the Eleventh Circuit's summary disposition in line with that court's description of its controlling precedent: "We ... ruled that, 'even though the statute of limitations is an affirmative defense, the district court may review sua sponte the timeliness of [a federal habeas] petition.' " Ibid. (referring to Jackson v. Secretary for Dept. of Corrections, 292 F. 3d, at 1349 (emphasis added)); see also 391 F. 3d, at 1195 (State's "patently erroneous" concession of timeliness "does not compromise the authority of a district court sua sponte to dismiss a habeas petition as untimely" under AEDPA's one-year limitation (emphasis added)).

[4] In AEDPA, enacted nearly a decade after Granberry, Congress expressly provided that "[a] State shall not be deemed to have waived the exhaustion requirement or be estopped from reliance upon the requirement unless the State, through counsel, expressly waives the requirement." 28 U. S. C. §2254(b)(3).

[5] Trest held that a Court of Appeals was not obliged to raise procedural default on its own initiative, but declined to decide whether courts have discretion to do so. 522 U. S., at 89.

[6] Were we to accept Day's position, courts would never (or, at least, hardly ever) be positioned to raise AEDPA's time bar sua sponte. As this Court recognized in Pliler v. Ford, 542 U. S. 225, 232 (2004), information essential to the time calculation is often absent—as it was in this case—until the State has filed, along with its answer, copies of documents from the state-court proceedings.

[7] The Habeas Rules were amended after the proceedings below. We cite the current version because both parties agree that the amendments to Rules 4 and 11, effective December 1, 2004, wrought no relevant substantive change.

[8] See Rhines v. Weber, 544 U. S. 269, 276 (2005) (AEDPA's time bar "quite plainly serves the well-recognized interest in the finality of state court judgments"; it "reduces the potential for delay on the road to finality[.]" (quoting Duncan v. Walker, 533 U. S. 167, 179 (2001))).

[9] The Court is unanimous on this point. See post, at 5, n. 2 (Scalia, J., dissenting).

[10] The procedural hindrance in Pliler was the petitioner's failure to exhaust state remedies. The Court in that case declined to rule on the propriety of the stay-and-abeyance procedure that would enable a habeas petitioner to remain in federal court while exhausting unexhausted claims in state court. 542 U. S., at 231. In a later decision, Rhines, 544 U. S., at 278–279, this Court held that a district court has discretion to stay a mixed petition (i.e., one that includes both exhausted and unexhausted claims) to allow a habeas petitioner to present his unexhausted claims to the state court in the first instance, then return to federal court for review of his perfected petition.

[11] A district court's discretion is confined within these limits. As earlier noted, should a State intelligently choose to waive a statute of limitations defense, a district court would not be at liberty to disregard that choice. See supra, at 2. But see post, at 7 (Scalia, J., dissenting).

JOHN CUNNINGHAM v. CALIFORNIA

No. 05–6551, January 22, 2007

ON WRIT OF CERTIORARI TO THE COURT OF APPEAL OF CALIFORNIA, FIRST APPELLATE DISTRICT

Justice Ginsburg delivered the opinion of the Court.

California's determinate sentencing law (DSL) assigns to the trial judge, not to the jury, authority to find the facts that expose a defendant to an elevated "upper term" sentence. The facts so found are neither inherent in the jury's verdict nor embraced by the defendant's plea, and they need only be established by a preponderance of the evidence, not beyond a reasonable doubt. The question presented is whether the DSL, by placing sentence-elevating factfinding within the judge's province, violates a defendant's right to trial by jury safeguarded by the Sixth and Fourteenth Amendment s. We hold that it does.

As this Court's decisions instruct, the Federal Constitution's jury-trial guarantee proscribes a sentencing scheme that allows a judge to impose a sentence above the statutory maximum based on a fact, other than a prior conviction, not found by a jury or admitted by the defendant. *Apprendi* v. *New Jersey*, 530 U.S. 466 (2000) ; *Ring* v. *Arizona*, 536 U.S. 584 (2002) ; *Blakely* v. *Washington*, 542 U.S. 296 (2004) ; *United States* v. *Booker*, 543 U.S. 220 (2005) . "[T]he relevant 'statutory maximum,'" this Court has clarified, "is not the maximum sentence a judge may impose after finding additional facts, but the maximum he may impose *without* any additional findings." *Blakely*, 542 U.S., at 303–304 (emphasis in original). In petitioner's case, the jury's verdict alone limited the permissible sentence to 12 years. Additional factfinding by the trial judge, however, yielded an upper term sentence of 16 years. The California Court of Appeal affirmed the harsher sentence. We reverse that disposition because the four-year elevation based on judicial factfinding denied petitioner his right to a jury trial.

I

A

Petitioner John Cunningham was tried and convicted of continuous sexual abuse of a child under the age of 14. Under the DSL, that offense is punishable by imprisonment for a lower term sentence of 6 years, a middle term sentence of 12 years, or an upper term sentence of 16 years. Cal. Penal Code Ann. §288.5(a) (West 1999) (hereinafter Penal Code). As further explained below, see *infra*, at 4–7, the DSL obliged the trial judge to sentence Cunningham to the 12-year middle term unless the judge found one or more additional facts in aggravation. Based on a post-trial sentencing hearing, the trial judge found by a preponderance of the evidence six aggravating circumstances, among them, the particular vulnerability of Cunningham's victim, and Cunningham's violent conduct, which indicated a serious danger to the community. Tr. of Sentencing (Aug. 1, 2003), App. 22.[1] In mitigation, the judge found one fact: Cunningham had no record of prior criminal conduct. *Ibid*. Concluding that the aggravators outweighed the sole mitigator, the judge sentenced Cunningham to the upper term of 16 years. *Id*., at 23.

A panel of the California Court of Appeal affirmed the conviction and sentence; one judge dissented in part, urging that this Court's precedent precluded the judge-determined four-year increase in Cunningham's sentence. No. A103501 (Apr. 18, 2005), App. 43–48; *id*., at 48–50 (Jones, J., concurring in part and dissenting in part).[2] The California Supreme Court denied review. No. S133971 (June 29, 2005) (en banc), *id*., at 52. In a reasoned decision published nine days earlier, that court considered the question here presented and held that the DSL survived Sixth Amendment inspection. *People* v. *Black*, 35 Cal. 4th 1238, 113 P.3d 534 (June 20, 2005).

B

Enacted in 1977, the DSL replaced an indeterminate sentencing regime in force in California for some 60 years. See *id*., at 1246, 113 P.3d, at 537; Cassou & Taugher, Determinate Sentencing in California: The New Numbers Game, 9 Pac. L.J. 5, 6–22 (1978) (hereinafter Cassou & Taugher). Under the prior regime, courts imposed open-ended prison terms (often one year to life), and the parole board—the Adult Authority—determined the amount of time a felon would ultimately spend in prison. *Black*, 35 Cal. 4th, at 1246, 1256, 113 P.3d, at 537, 544; *In re Roberts*, 36 Cal. 4th 575, 588, n.6, 115 P.3d 1121, 1129, n.6 (2005); Cassou & Taugher 5–9. In contrast, the DSL fixed the terms of imprisonment for most offenses, and eliminated the possibility of early release on parole. See Penal Code §3000 *et seq*. (West Supp. 2006); 3 B. Witkin & N. Epstein, California Criminal Law §610, p. 809 (3d ed. 2000); Brief for Respondent 7.[3] Through the

DSL, California's lawmakers aimed to promote uniform and proportionate punishment. Penal Code §1170(a)(1); *Black*, 35 Cal. 4th, at 1246, 113 P.3d, at 537.

For most offenses, including Cunningham's, the DSL regime is implemented in the following manner. The statute defining the offense prescribes three precise terms of imprisonment—a lower, middle, and upper term sentence. *E.g.*, Penal Code §288.5(a) (West 1999) (a person convicted of continuous sexual abuse of a child "shall be punished by imprisonment in the state prison for a term of 6, 12, or 16 years"). See also *Black*, 35 Cal. 4th, at 1247, 113 P.3d, at 538. Penal Code §1170(b) (West Supp. 2006) controls the trial judge's choice; it provides that "the court shall order imposition of the middle term, unless there are circumstances in aggravation or mitigation of the crime." "[C]ircumstances in aggravation or mitigation" are to be determined by the court after consideration of several items: the trial record; the probation officer's report; statements in aggravation or mitigation submitted by the parties, the victim, or the victim's family; "and any further evidence introduced at the sentencing hearing." *Ibid.*

The DSL directed the State's Judicial Council[4] to adopt Rules guiding the sentencing judge's decision whether to "[i]mpose the lower or upper prison term." Penal Code §1170.3(a)(2) (West 2004).[5] Restating §1170(b), the Council's Rules provide that "[t]he middle term shall be selected unless imposition of the upper or lower term is justified by circumstances in aggravation or mitigation." Rule 4.420(a). "Circumstances in aggravation," as crisply defined by the Judicial Council, means "*facts* which justify the imposition of the upper prison term." Rule 4.405(d) (emphasis added). Facts aggravating an offense, the Rules instruct, "shall be established by a preponderance of the evidence," Rule 4.420(b),[6] and must be "stated orally on the record." Rule 4.420(e).

The Rules provide a nonexhaustive list of aggravating circumstances, including "[f]acts relating to the crime," Rule 4.421(a),[7] "[f]acts relating to the defendant," Rule 4.421(b),[8] and "[a]ny other facts statutorily declared to be circumstances in aggravation," Rule 4.421(c). Beyond the enumerated circumstances, "the judge is free to consider any 'additional criteria reasonably related to the decision being made.'" *Black*, 35 Cal. 4th, at 1247, 113 P.3d, at 538 (quoting Rule 4.408(a)). "A fact that is an element of the crime," however, "shall not be used to impose the upper term." Rule 4.420(d). In sum, California's DSL, and the rules governing its application, direct the sentencing court to start with the middle term, and to move from that term only when the court itself finds and places on the record facts—whether related to the offense or the offender—beyond the elements of the charged offense.

Justice Alito maintains, however, that a circumstance in aggravation need not be a fact at all. In his view, a policy judgment, or even a judge's "subjective belief" regarding the appropriate sentence, qualifies as an aggravating circumstance. *Post*, at 11–12 (dissenting opinion). California's Rules, however, constantly refer to "facts." As just noted, the Rules define "circumstances in aggravation" as "*facts* which justify the imposition of the upper prison term." Rule 4.405(d) (emphasis added).[9] And "circumstances in aggravation," the Rules unambiguously declare, "shall be established by a preponderance of the evidence," Rule 4.420(b), a clear factfinding directive to which there is no exception. See *People* v. *Hall*, 8 Cal. 4th 950, 957, 883 P.2d 974, 978 (1994) ("Selection of the upper term is justified *only* if circumstances in aggravation are established by a preponderance of evidence . . . ." (emphasis added)).

While the Rules list "[g]eneral objectives of sentencing," Rule 4.410(a), nowhere are these objectives cast as "circumstances in aggravation" that alone authorize an upper term sentence. The Rules also state that "[t]he enumeration . . . of some criteria for the making of discretionary sentencing decisions does not prohibit the application of additional criteria reasonably related to the decision being made." Rule 4.408(a). California courts have not read this language to unmoor "circumstances in aggravation" from any factfinding anchor.

In line with the Rules, the California Supreme Court has repeatedly referred to circumstances in aggravation as facts. See, *e.g.*, *Black*, 35 Cal. 4th, at 1256, 113 P.3d, at 544 ("The Legislature did not identify all of the particular *facts* that could justify the upper term." (emphasis added)); *People* v. *Wiley*, 9 Cal. 4th 580, 587, 889 P.2d 541, 545 (1995) ("[T]rial courts are assigned the task of deciding whether to impose an upper or lower term of imprisonment based upon their determination whether there are circumstances in aggravation or mitigation of the crime, *a determination that invariably requires numerous factual findings*." (emphasis added and internal quotation marks omitted)).

It is unsurprising, then, that State's counsel, at oral argument, acknowledged that he knew of no case in which a California trial judge had gone beyond the middle term based not on any fact the judge found, but solely on the basis of a policy judgment or subjective belief. See Tr. of Oral Arg. 49–50.

Notably, the Penal Code permits elevation of a sentence above the upper term based on specified statutory enhancements relating to the defendant's criminal history or circumstances of the crime. See, *e.g.*, Penal Code §667 *et seq.* (West Supp. 2006); §12022 *et seq.* See also *Black*, 35 Cal. 4th, at 1257, 113 P.3d, at 545. Unlike aggravating circumstances, statutory enhancements must be charged in the indictment, and the underlying facts must be proved to the jury beyond a reasonable doubt. Penal Code §1170.1(e); *Black*, 35 Cal. 4th, at 1257, 113 P.3d, at 545. A fact underlying an enhancement cannot do double duty; it cannot be used to impose an upper term sentence and, on top of that, an enhanced term. Penal Code §1170(b). Where permitted by statute, however, a judge may use a fact qualifying as an enhancer to impose an upper term rather than an enhanced sentence. *Ibid.*; Rule 4.420(c).

II

This Court has repeatedly held that, under the Sixth Amendment , any fact that exposes a defendant to a greater potential sentence must be found by a jury, not a judge, and established beyond a reasonable doubt, not merely by a preponderance of the evidence. While this rule is rooted in longstanding common-law practice, its explicit statement in our decisions is recent. In *Jones* v. *United States*, 526 U.S. 227 (1999), we examined the Sixth Amendment's historical and doctrinal foundations, and recognized that judicial factfinding operating to increase a defendant's otherwise maximum punishment posed a grave constitutional question. *Id.*, at 239–252. While the Court construed the statute at issue to avoid the question, the *Jones* opinion presaged our decision, some 15 months later, in *Apprendi* v. *New Jersey*, 530 U.S. 466 (2000).

Charles Apprendi was convicted of possession of a firearm for an unlawful purpose, a second-degree offense under New Jersey law punishable by five to ten years' imprisonment. *Id.*, at 468. A separate "hate crime" statute authorized an "extended term" of imprisonment: Ten to twenty years could be imposed if the trial judge found, by a preponderance of the evidence, that "'[t]he defendant in committing the crime acted with a purpose to intimidate an individual or group of individuals because of race, color, gender, handicap, religion, sexual orientation or ethnicity.'" *Id.*, at 468–469 (quoting N.J. Stat. Ann. §2C:44–3(e) (West Supp. 1999–2000)). The judge in Apprendi's case so found, and therefore sentenced the defendant to 12 years' imprisonment. This Court held that the Sixth Amendment proscribed the enhanced sentence. 530 U.S., at 471. Other than a prior conviction, see *Almendarez-Torres* v. *United States*, 523 U.S. 224, 239–247 (1998), we held in *Apprendi*, "any fact that increases the penalty for a crime beyond the prescribed statutory maximum must be submitted to a jury, and proved beyond a reasonable doubt." 530 U.S., at 490. See also *Harris* v. *United States*, 536 U.S. 545, 557–566 (2002) (plurality opinion) ("*Apprendi* said that any fact extending the defendant's sentence beyond the maximum authorized by the jury's verdict would have been considered an element of an aggravated crime—and thus the domain of the jury—by those who framed the Bill of Rights.").

We have since reaffirmed the rule of *Apprendi*, applying it to facts subjecting a defendant to the death penalty, *Ring* v. *Arizona*, 536 U.S. 584, 602, 609 (2002), facts permitting a sentence in excess of the "standard range" under Washington's Sentencing Reform Act, *Blakely* v. *Washington*, 542 U.S. 296, 304–305 (2004), and facts triggering a sentence range elevation under the then-mandatory Federal Sentencing Guidelines, *United States* v. *Booker*, 543 U.S. 220, 243–244 (2005). *Blakely* and *Booker* bear most closely on the question presented in this case.

Ralph Howard Blakely was convicted of second-degree kidnapping with a firearm, a class B felony under Washington law. *Blakely*, 542 U.S., at 298–299. While the overall statutory maximum for a class B felony was ten years, the State's Sentencing Reform Act (Reform Act) added an important qualification: If no facts beyond those reflected in the jury's verdict were found by the trial judge, a defendant could not receive a sentence above a "standard range" of 49 to 53 months. *Id.*, at 299–300. The Reform Act permitted but did not require a judge to exceed that standard range if she found "'substantial and compelling reasons justifying an exceptional sentence.'" *Ibid.* (quoting Wash. Rev. Code Ann. §9.94A.120(2) (2000)). The Reform Act set out a nonexhaustive list of aggravating facts on which such a sentence elevation could be based. It also clarified that a fact taken into account in fixing the standard range—*i.e.*, any fact found by the jury—could under no circumstances count in the determination whether to impose an exceptional sentence. 542 U.S., at 299–300. Blakely was sentenced to 90 months' imprisonment, more than three years above the standard range, based on the trial judge's finding that he had acted with deliberate cruelty. *Id.*, at 300.

Applying the rule of *Apprendi*, this Court held Blakely's sentence unconstitutional. The State in *Blakely* had endeavored to distinguish *Apprendi* on the ground that "[u]nder the Washington guidelines, an exceptional sentence is within the court's discretion as a result of a guilty verdict." Brief for Respondent in *Blakely* v. *Washington*, O.T. 2003, No. 02–1632, p.15. We rejected that argument. The judge could not have sentenced Blakely above the standard range without finding the additional fact of deliberate cruelty. Consequently, that fact was subject to the Sixth Amendment's jury-trial guarantee. 542 U.S., at 304–314. It did not matter, we explained, that Blakely's sentence, though outside the standard range, was within the 10-year maximum for class B felonies:

"Our precedents make clear . . . that the 'statutory maximum' for *Apprendi* purposes is the maximum sentence a judge may impose *solely on the basis of the facts reflected in the jury verdict or admitted by the defendant* . . . . In other words, the relevant 'statutory maximum' is not the maximum sentence a judge may impose after finding additional facts, but the maximum he may impose *without* any additional findings. When a judge inflicts punishment that the jury's verdict alone does not allow, the jury has not found all the facts 'which the law makes essential to the punishment,' . . . and the judge exceeds his proper authority." *Id.*, at 303 (emphasis in original) (quoting 1 J. Bishop, Criminal Procedure §87, p. 55 (2d ed. 1872)).

Because the judge in Blakely's case could not have imposed a sentence outside the standard range without finding an additional fact, the top of that range—53 months, and not 10 years—was the relevant statutory maximum. 542 U.S., at 304.

The State had additionally argued in *Blakely* that *Apprendi*'s rule was satisfied because Washington's Reform Act did not specify an exclusive catalog of potential facts on which a judge might base a departure from the standard range. This Court rejected that argument as well. "Whether the judge's authority to impose an enhanced sentence depends on finding a specified fact... one of several specified facts . . . or *any* aggravating fact (as here)," we observed, "it remains the case that the jury's verdict alone does not authorize the sentence." 542 U.S., at 305 (emphasis in original). Further, we held it irrelevant that the Reform Act ultimately left the decision whether or not to depart to the judge's discretion: "Whether the judicially determined facts *require* a sentence enhancement or merely *allow* it," we noted, "the verdict alone does not authorize the sentence." *Ibid.*, n.8 (emphasis in original).

Freddie Booker was convicted of possession with intent to distribute crack cocaine and was sentenced under the Federal Sentencing Guidelines. The facts found by Booker's jury yielded a base Guidelines range of 210 to 262 months' imprisonment, a range the judge could not exceed without undertaking additional factfinding. *Booker*, 543 U.S., at 227, 233–234. The judge did so, finding by a preponderance of the evidence that Booker possessed an amount of drugs in excess of the amount determined by the jury's verdict. That finding boosted Booker into a higher Guidelines range.

Booker was sentenced at the bottom of the higher range, to 360 months in prison. *Id.*, at 227.

In an opinion written by Justice Stevens for a five-Member majority, the Court held Booker's sentence impermissible under the Sixth Amendment . In the majority's judgment, there was "no distinction of constitutional significance between the Federal Sentencing Guidelines and the Washington procedures at issue in *[Blakely]*." *Id.*, at 233. Both systems were "mandatory and impose[d] binding requirements on all sentencing judges." *Ibid.*[10] Justice Stevens' opinion for the Court, it bears emphasis, next expressed a view on which there was no disagreement among the Justices. He acknowledged that the Federal Guidelines would not implicate the Sixth Amendment were they advisory:

"If the Guidelines as currently written could be read as merely advisory provisions that recommended, rather than required, the selection of particular sentences in response to differing sets of facts, their use would not implicate the Sixth Amendment . We have never doubted the authority of a judge to exercise broad discretion in imposing a sentence within a statutory range. Indeed, everyone agrees that the constitutional issues presented by [this case] would have been avoided entirely if Congress had omitted from the [federal Sentencing Reform Act] the provisions that make the Guidelines binding on district judges . . . . For when a trial judge exercises his discretion to select a specific sentence within a defined range, the defendant has no right to a jury determination of the facts that the judge deems relevant.

"The Guidelines as written, however, are not advisory; they are mandatory and binding on all judges." *Ibid.* (citations omitted).

In an opinion written by Justice Breyer, also garnering a five-Member majority, the Court faced the remedial question, which turned on an assessment of legislative intent: What alteration would Congress have intended had it known that the Guidelines were vulnerable to a Sixth Amendment challenge? Three choices were apparent: the Court could invalidate in its entirety the Sentencing Reform Act of 1984 (SRA), the law comprehensively delineating the federal sentencing system; or it could preserve the SRA, and the mandatory Guidelines regime the SRA established, by attaching a jury-trial requirement to any fact increasing a defendant's base Guidelines range; finally, the Court could render the Guidelines advisory by severing two provisions of the SRA, 18 U.S.C. §3553(b)(1) and 3742(e) (2000 ed. and Supp. IV). 543 U.S., at 246–249.[11] Recognizing that "reasonable minds can, and do, differ" on the remedial question, the majority concluded that the advisory Guidelines solution came closest to the congressional mark. *Id.*, at 248–258.

Under the system described in Justice Breyer's opinion for the Court in *Booker*, judges would no longer be tied to the sentencing range indicated in the Guidelines. But they would be obliged to "take account of" that range along with the sentencing goals Congress enumerated in the SRA at 18 U.S.C. §3553(a). 543 U.S., at 259, 264.[12] Having severed §3742(e), the provision of the SRA governing appellate review of sentences under the mandatory Guidelines scheme, see *supra*, at 13, and n.11, the Court installed, as consistent with the Act and the sound administration of justice, a "reasonableness" standard of review. 543 U.S., at 261. Without attempting an elaborate discussion of that standard, Justice Breyer's remedial opinion for the Court observed: "Section 3553(a) remains in effect, and sets forth numerous factors that guide sentencing. Those factors in turn will guide appellate courts, as they have in the past, in determining whether a sentence is reasonable." *Ibid.*[13] The Court emphasized the provisional character of the *Booker* remedy. Recognizing that authority to speak "the last word" resides in Congress, the Court said:

"The ball now lies in Congress' court. The National Legislature is equipped to devise and install, long term, the sentencing system, compatible with the Constitution, that Congress judges best for the federal system of justice." *Id.*, at 265.

We turn now to the instant case in light of both parts of the Court's *Booker* opinion, and our earlier decisions in point.

III

Under California's DSL, an upper term sentence may be imposed only when the trial judge finds an aggravating circumstance. See *supra*, at 4–5. An element of the charged offense, essential to a jury's determination of guilt, or admitted in a defendant's guilty plea, does not qualify as such a circumstance. See *supra*, at 5–6. Instead, aggravating circumstances depend on facts found discretely and solely by the judge. In accord with *Blakely*, therefore, the middle term prescribed in California's statutes, not the upper term, is the relevant statutory maximum. 542 U.S., at 303 ("[T]he 'statutory maximum' for *Apprendi* purposes is the maximum sentence a judge may impose *solely on the basis of the facts reflected in the jury verdict or admitted by the defendant*." (emphasis in original)). Because circumstances in aggravation are found by the judge, not the jury, and need only be established by a preponderance of the evidence, not beyond a reasonable doubt, see *supra*, at 5, the DSL violates *Apprendi*'s bright-line rule: Except for a prior conviction, "any fact that increases the penalty for a crime beyond the prescribed statutory maximum must be submitted to a jury, and proved beyond a reasonable doubt." 530 U.S., at 490.

While "[t]hat should be the end of the matter," *Blakely*, 542 U.S., at 313, in *People* v. *Black*, the California Supreme Court held otherwise. In that court's view, the DSL survived examination under our precedent intact. See 35 Cal. 4th, at 1254–1261, 113 P.3d, at 543–548. The *Black* court acknowledged that California's system appears on surface inspection to be in tension with the rule of *Apprendi*. But in "operation and effect," the court said, the DSL "simply authorize[s] a sentencing court to engage in the type of factfinding that traditionally has been incident to the judge's selection of an appropriate sentence within a statutorily prescribed sentencing range." 35 Cal. 4th, at 1254, 113 P.3d, at 543. Therefore, the court concluded, "the upper term is the 'statutory maximum' and a trial court's imposition of an upper term sentence does not violate a defendant's right to a jury trial under the principles set forth in *Apprendi, Blakely*, and *Booker*." *Ibid.* But see *id.*, at 1270, 113 P.3d, at 554 (Kennard, J., concurring and dissenting) ("Nothing in the high court's majority opinions in *Apprendi*, *Blakely*, and *Booker* suggests that the constitutionality of a state's sentencing scheme turns on whether, in the words of the majority here, it involves the type of factfinding 'that traditionally has been performed by a judge.'" (quoting *id.*, at 1253, 113 P.3d, at 542)).

The *Black* court's conclusion that the upper term, and not the middle term, qualifies as the relevant statutory maximum, rested on several considerations. First, the court reasoned that, given the ample discretion afforded trial judges to identify aggravating facts warranting an upper term sentence, the DSL

"does not represent a legislative effort to shift the proof of particular facts from elements of a crime (to be proved to a jury) to sentencing factors (to be decided by a judge). . . . Instead, it afforded the sentencing judge the discretion to decide, with the guidance of rules and statutes, whether the facts of the case and the history of the defendant justify the higher sentence. Such a system does not diminish the traditional power of the jury." *Id.*, at 1256, 113 P.3d, at 544 (footnote omitted).

We cautioned in *Blakely*, however, that broad discretion to decide what facts may support an enhanced sentence, or to determine whether an enhanced sentence is warranted in any particular case, does not shield a sentencing system from the force of our decisions. If the jury's verdict alone does not authorize the sentence, if, instead, the judge must find an additional fact to impose the longer term, the Sixth Amendment requirement is not satisfied. *Blakely*, 542 U.S., at 305, and n.8.

The *Black* court also urged that the DSL is not cause for concern because it reduced the penalties for most crimes over the prior indeterminate sentencing regime. 35 Cal. 4th, at 1256–1258, 113 P.3d, at 544–545. But see *id.*, at 1271–1272, 113 P.3d, at 555 (Kennard, J., concurring and dissenting) ("This aspect of our sentencing law does not differ significantly from the Washington sentencing scheme [the high court invalidated in *Blakely*.]"); *supra*, at 10. Furthermore, California's system is not unfair to defendants, for they "cannot reasonably expect a guarantee that the upper term will not be imposed" given judges' broad discretion to impose an upper term sentence or to keep their punishment at the middle term. 35 Cal. 4th, at 1258–1259, 113 P.3d, at 545–546. The *Black* court additionally noted that the DSL requires statutory enhancements (as distinguished from aggravators)—*e.g.*, the use of a firearm or other dangerous weapon, infliction of great bodily injury, Penal Code §§12022, 12022.7–.8 (West 2000 and Supp. 2006)—to be charged in the indictment and proved to a jury beyond a reasonable doubt. 35 Cal. 4th, at 1257, 113 P.3d, at 545.

The *Black* court's examination of the DSL, in short, satisfied it that California's sentencing system does not implicate significantly the concerns underlying the Sixth Amendment's jury-trial guarantee. Our decisions, however, leave no room for such an examination. Asking whether a defendant's basic jury-trial right is preserved, though some facts essential to punishment are reserved for determination by the judge, we have said, is the *very* inquiry *Apprendi*'s "bright-line rule" was designed to exclude. See *Blakely*, 542 U.S., at 307–308. But see *Black*, 35 Cal. 4th, at 1260, 113 P.3d, at 547 (stating, remarkably, that "[t]he high court precedents do not draw a bright line").[14]

Ultimately, the *Black* court relied on an equation of California's DSL system to the post-*Booker* federal system. "The level of discretion available to a California judge in selecting which of the three available terms to impose," the court said, "appears comparable to the level of discretion that the high court has chosen to permit federal judges in post-*Booker* sentencing." 35 Cal. 4th, at 1261, 113 P.3d, at 548. The same equation drives Justice Alito's dissent. See *post*, at 1 ("The California sentencing law . .. is indistinguishable in any constitutionally significant respect from the advisory Guidelines scheme that the Court approved in *[Booker]*.").

The attempted comparison is unavailing. As earlier explained, see *supra*, at 12–13, this Court in *Booker* held the Federal Sentencing Guidelines incompatible with the Sixth Amendment because the Guidelines were "mandatory and imposed binding requirements on all sentencing judges." 543 U.S., at 233. "[M]erely advisory provisions," recommending but not requiring "the selection of particular sentences in response to differing sets of facts," all Members of the Court agreed, "would not implicate the Sixth Amendment ." *Ibid.* To remedy the constitutional infirmity found in *Booker*, the Court's majority excised provisions that rendered the system mandatory, leaving the Guidelines in place as advisory only. *Id.*, at 245–246. See also *supra*, at 13–14.

California's DSL does not resemble the advisory system the *Booker* Court had in view. Under California's system, judges are not free to exercise their "discretion to select a specific sentence within a defined range." *Booker*, 543 U.S., at 233. California's Legislature has adopted sentencing triads, three fixed sentences with no ranges between them. Cunningham's sentencing judge had no discretion to select a sentence within a range of 6 to 16 years. His instruction was to select 12 years, nothing less and nothing more, unless he found facts allowing the imposition of a sentence of 6 or 16 years. Factfinding to elevate a sentence from 12 to 16 years, our decisions make plain, falls within the province of the jury employing a beyond-a-reasonable-doubt standard, not the bailiwick of a judge determining where the preponderance of the evidence lies.

Nevertheless, the *Black* court attempted to rescue the DSL's judicial factfinding authority by typing it simply a reasonableness constraint, equivalent to the constraint operative in the federal system post-*Booker*. See 35 Cal. 4th, at 1261, 113 P.3d, at 548 ("Because an aggravating factor under California law may include any factor that the judge reasonably deems relevant, the [DSL's] requirement that an upper term sentence be imposed only if an aggravating factor exists is comparable to *Booker*'s requirement that a federal judge's sentencing decision not be unreasonable."). Reasonableness, however, is not, as the *Black* court would have it, the touchstone of Sixth Amendment analysis. The reasonableness requirement *Booker* anticipated for the federal system operates *within* the Sixth Amendment constraints delineated in our precedent, not as a substitute for those constraints. Because the DSL allocates to judges sole authority to find facts permitting the imposition of an upper term sentence, the system violates the Sixth Amendment . It is comforting, but beside the point, that California's system requires judge-determined DSL sentences to be reasonable.

Booker's remedy for the Federal Guidelines, in short, is not a recipe for rendering our Sixth Amendment case law toothless.[15]

To summarize: Contrary to the *Black* court's holding, our decisions from *Apprendi* to *Booker* point to the middle term specified in California's statutes, not the upper term, as the relevant statutory maximum. Because the DSL authorizes the judge, not the jury, to find the facts permitting an upper term sentence, the system cannot withstand measurement against our Sixth Amendment precedent.[16]

IV

As to the adjustment of California's sentencing system in light of our decision, "[t]he ball . . . lies in [California's] court." *Booker*, 543 U.S., at 265; cf. *supra*, at 15. We note that several States have modified their systems in the wake of *Apprendi* and *Blakely* to retain determinate sentencing. They have done so by calling upon the jury— either at trial or in a separate sentencing proceeding—to find any fact necessary to the imposition of an elevated sentence.[17] As earlier noted, California already employs juries in this manner to determine statutory sentencing enhancements. See *supra*, at 7, 18. Other States have chosen to permit judges genuinely "to exercise broad discretion . . . within a statutory range,"[18] which, "everyone agrees," encounters no Sixth Amendment shoal. *Booker*, 543 U.S., at 233. California may follow the paths taken by its sister States or otherwise alter its system, so long as the State observes Sixth Amendment limitations declared in this Court's decisions.

* * *

For the reasons stated, the judgment of the California Court of Appeal is reversed in part, and the case is remanded for further proceedings not inconsistent with this opinion.

It is so ordered.

NOTES

[1] The particular vulnerability of the victim is listed in Cal. Rule of Court 4.421(a)(3) (Criminal Cases) (West 2006) (hereinafter Rule), as a fact "relating to the crime." Violent conduct indicating a serious danger to society is listed in Rule 4.421(b)(1) as a fact "relating to the defendant."

[2] In addition to a Sixth Amendment challenge, Cunningham disputed the substance of five of the six findings made by the trial judge. The appellate panel affirmed the trial judge's vulnerable victim and violent conduct findings, but rejected the finding that Cunningham abused a position of trust (because that finding overlapped with the vulnerable victim finding). The panel did not decide whether the judge's other findings were warranted, concluding that he properly relied on at least two aggravating facts in imposing the upper term, and that it was not "reasonably probable" that a different sentence would have been imposed absent any improper findings. App. 43–46; id., at 51 (May 4, 2005, order modifying opinion and denying rehearing).

[3] Murder and certain other grave offenses still carry lengthy indeterminate terms with the possibility of early release on parole. Brief for Respondent 7, n.2. See, e.g., Penal Code §190 (West Supp. 2006).

[4] The Judicial Council includes the chief justice and another justice of the California Supreme Court, three judges sitting on the Courts of Appeal, ten judges from the Superior Courts, and other nonvoting members. Cal. Const., Art. 6, §6(a) (West Supp. 2006). The California Constitution grants the Council authority, inter alia, "to adopt rules for court administration, practice and procedure, and perform other functions prescribed by statute." Art. 6, §6(d).

[5] The Rules were amended on January 1, 2007. Those amendments made technical changes, none of them material to the constitutional question before us. We refer in this opinion to the prior text of the Rules, upon which the parties and principal authorities rely.

[6] The judge must provide a statement of reasons for a sentence only when a lower or upper term sentence is imposed. Rules 4.406(b), 4.420(e).

[7] E.g., Rule 4.421(a)(1) ("[T]he fact that . . . [t]he crime involved great violence, great bodily harm, threat of great bodily harm, or other acts disclosing a high degree of cruelty, viciousness, or callousness.").

8

E.g., Rule 4.421(b)(1) ("[T]he fact that . . . [t]he defendant has engaged in violent conduct which indicates a serious danger to society.").

[9] See also, e.g., Rule 4.420(b) ("Selection of the upper term is justified only if, after a consideration of all the relevant facts, the circumstances in aggravation outweigh the circumstances in mitigation." (emphasis added)); Rule 4.420(e) (court must provide "a concise statement of the ultimate facts that the court deemed to constitute circumstances in aggravation or mitigation" (emphasis added)).

[10] California's DSL, we note in this context, resembles pre-Booker federal sentencing in the same ways Washington's sentencing system did: The key California Penal Code provision states that the sentencing court "shall order imposition of the middle term" absent "circumstances in aggravation or mitigation of the crime," §1170(b) (emphasis added), and any move to the upper or lower term must be justified by "a concise statement of the ultimate facts" on which the departure rests, Rule 4.420(e) (emphasis added). But see post, at 7 (Alito, J., dissenting) (characterizing California's DSL as indistinguishable from post-Booker sentencing).

[11] Title 18 U.S.C. §3553(b)(1) mandated the imposition of a Guidelines sentence unless the district court found "an aggravating or mitigating circumstance of a kind, or to a degree, not adequately taken into consideration by the Sentencing Commission in formulating the guidelines." Section 3742(e) directed the court of appeals to determine, inter alia, whether the district court correctly applied the Guidelines, §3742(e)(2), and, if the sentence imposed fell outside the applicable Guidelines range, whether the sentencing judge had provided a written statement of reasons, whether §3553(b) and the facts of the case warranted the departure, and whether the degree of departure was reasonable, §3742(e)(3).

[12] Section 3553(a) instructs sentencing judges to consider "the nature and circumstances of the offense and the history and characteristics of the defendant," "the kinds of sentences available," and the Guidelines and policy statements issued by the United States Sentencing Commission. §3553(a) (1), (3)–(5). Avoidance of unwarranted sentencing disparities, and the need to provide restitution, are also listed as concerns to which the judge should respond. §3553(a)(6)–(7).

In a further enumeration, §3553(a) calls for the imposition of "a sentence sufficient, but not greater than necessary" to "reflect the seriousness of the offense," "promote respect for the law," "provide just punishment for the offense," "afford adequate deterrence to criminal conduct," "protect the public from further crimes of the defendant," and "provide the defendant with needed educational or vocational training, medical care, or other correctional treatment in the most effective manner." §3553(a)(2).

[13] While this case does not call for elaboration of the reasonableness check on federal sentencing post-Booker, we note that the Court has granted review in two cases raising questions trained on that matter: Claiborne v. United States, No. 06–5618 (cert. granted, Nov. 3, 2006); and Rita v. United States, No. 06–5754 (cert. granted, Nov. 3, 2006). In Claiborne, the Court will consider whether it is consistent with the advisory cast of the Guidelines system post-Booker to require that extraordinary circumstances attend a sentence varying substantially from the Guidelines. Rita includes the question whether is it consistent with Booker to accord a presumption of reasonableness to a within-Guidelines sentence.

In this regard, we note Justice Alito's view that California's DSL is essentially the same as post-Booker federal sentencing. Post, at 1–10. To maintain that position, his dissent previews, without benefit of briefing or argument, how "reasonableness review," post-Booker, works. Post, at 13–15. It is neither necessary nor proper now to join issue with Justice Alito on this matter.

[14] Justice Kennedy urges a distinction between facts concerning the offense, where Apprendi would apply, and facts concerning the offender, where it would not. Post, at 1–2 (dissenting opinion). Apprendi itself, however, leaves no room for the bifurcated approach Justice Kennedy proposes. See 530 U. S., at 490 ("[A]ny fact that increases the penalty for a crime beyond the prescribed statutory maximum must be submitted to a jury, and proved beyond a reasonable doubt." (emphasis added)).

[15] Justice Alito, however, would do just that. His opinion reads the remedial portion of the Court's opinion in Booker to override Blakely, and to render academic the entire first part of Booker itself. Post, at 13–15. There would have been no majority in Booker for the revision of Blakely essayed in his dissent. Grounded in a notion of how federal reasonableness review operates in practice, Justice Alito "necessarily anticipates" a question that will be aired later this Term in Rita and Claiborne. See supra,

at 14, n.13. While we do not forecast the Court's responses in those cases, we affirm the continuing vitality of our prior decisions in point.

16 Respondent and its amici argue that whatever this Court makes of California's sentencing law, the Black court's "construction" of that law as consistent with the Sixth Amendment is authoritative. Brief for Respondent 6, 18, 33; Brief for Hawaii etal. as Amici Curiae 17, 29. We disagree. The Black court did not modify California law so as to align it with this Court's Sixth Amendment precedent. See 35 Cal. 4th, at 1273, 113 P.3d, at 555–556 (Kennard, J., concurring and dissenting). Rather, it construed this Court's decisions in an endeavor to render them consistent with California law. The Black court's interpretation of federal constitutional law plainly does not qualify for this Court's deference.

17 States that have so altered their systems are Alaska, Arizona, Kansas, Minnesota, North Carolina, Oregon, and Washington. Alaska Stat. §§12.55.155(f), 12.55.125(c) (2004); Ariz. Rev. Stat. Ann. §13–702.01 (West Supp. 2006); Kan. Stat. Ann. §§21–4716(b), 21–4718(b) (2005 Supp.); Minn. Stat. §244.10, subd. 5 (2005 Supp.); N.C. Gen. Stat. Ann. §15A–1340.16(a1) (Lexis 2005); 2005 Ore. Sess. Laws, ch. 463, §§3(1), 4(1); Wash. Rev. Code §§9.94A.535, 9.94A.537 (2006). The Colorado Supreme Court has adopted this approach as an interim solution. Lopez v. People, 113 P.3d 713, 716 (Colo. 2005) (en banc). See also Stemen & Wilhelm, Finding the Jury: State Legislative Responses to Blakely v. Washington, 18 Fed. Sentencing Rptr. 7 (Oct. 2005) (majority of affected States have retained determinate sentencing systems).

18 See Ind. Code Ann. §35–50–2–1.3(a) (West 2006); Tenn. Code Ann. §40–35–210(c) (2005 Supp.).

TELLABS, INC., et al. v. MAKOR ISSUES & RIGHTS, LTD., et al.

No. 06–484, June 21, 2007

ON WRIT OF CERTIORARI TO THE UNITED STATES COURT OF APPEALS FOR THE SEVENTH CIRCUIT

Justice Ginsburg delivered the opinion of the Court.

This Court has long recognized that meritorious private actions to enforce federal antifraud securities laws are an essential supplement to criminal prosecutions and civil enforcement actions brought, respectively, by the Department of Justice and the Securities and Exchange Commission (SEC). See, *e.g.*, *Dura Pharmaceuticals, Inc.* v. *Broudo*, 544 U.S. 336, 345 (2005); *J. I. Case Co.* v. *Borak*, 377 U.S. 426, 432 (1964). Private securities fraud actions, however, if not adequately contained, can be employed abusively to impose substantial costs on companies and individuals whose conduct conforms to the law. See *Merrill Lynch, Pierce, Fenner & Smith Inc.* v. *Dabit*, 547 U.S. 71, 81 (2006). As a check against abusive litigation by private parties, Congress enacted the Private Securities Litigation Reform Act of 1995 (PSLRA), 109 Stat. 737.

Exacting pleading requirements are among the control measures Congress included in the PSLRA. The Act requires plaintiffs to state with particularity both the facts constituting the alleged violation, and the facts evidencing scienter, *i.e.*, the defendant's intention "to deceive, manipulate, or defraud." *Ernst & Ernst* v. *Hochfelder*, 425 U.S. 185, and n. 12 (1976); see 15 U.S.C. §78u–4(b)(1),(2). This case concerns the latter requirement. As set out in §21D(b)(2) of the PSLRA, plaintiffs must "state with particularity facts giving rise to a strong inference that the defendant acted with the required state of mind." 15 U. S. C. §78u–4(b)(2).

Congress left the key term "strong inference" undefined, and Courts of Appeals have divided on its meaning. In the case before us, the Court of Appeals for the Seventh Circuit held that the "strong inference" standard would be met if the complaint "allege[d] facts from which, if true, a reasonable person could infer that the defendant acted with the required intent." 437 F.3d 588, 602 (2006). That formulation, we conclude, does not capture the stricter demand Congress sought to convey in §21D(b)(2). It does not suffice that a reasonable factfinder plausibly could infer from the complaint's allegations the requisite state of mind. Rather, to determine whether a complaint's scienter allegations can survive threshold inspection for sufficiency, a court governed by §21D(b)(2) must engage in a comparative evaluation; it must consider, not only inferences urged by the plaintiff, as the Seventh Circuit did, but also competing inferences rationally drawn from the facts alleged. An inference of fraudulent intent may be plausible, yet less cogent than other, nonculpable explanations for the defendant's conduct. To qualify as "strong" within the intendment of §21D(b)(2), we hold, an inference of scienter must be more than merely plausible or reasonable—it must be cogent and at least as compelling as any opposing inference of nonfraudulent intent.

I

Petitioner Tellabs, Inc., manufactures specialized equipment used in fiber optic networks. During the time period relevant to this case, petitioner Richard Notebaert was Tellabs' chief executive officer and president. Respondents (Shareholders) are persons who purchased Tellabs stock between December 11, 2000, and June 19, 2001. They accuse Tellabs and Notebaert (as well as several other Tellabs executives) of engaging in a scheme to deceive the investing public about the true value of Tellabs' stock. See 437 F.3d, at 591; App. 94–98.[1]

Beginning on December 11, 2000, the Shareholders allege, Notebaert (and by imputation Tellabs) "falsely reassured public investors, in a series of statements ... that Tellabs was continuing to enjoy strong demand for its products and earning record revenues," when, in fact, Notebaert knew the opposite was true. *Id.*, at 94–95, 98. From December 2000 until the spring of 2001, the Shareholders claim, Notebaert knowingly misled the public in four ways. 437 F.3d, at 596. First, he made statements indicating that demand for Tellabs' flagship networking device, the TITAN 5500, was continuing to grow, when in fact demand for that product was waning. *Id.*, at 596, 597. Second, Notebaert made statements indicating that the TITAN 6500, Tellabs' next-generation networking device, was available for delivery, and that demand for that product was strong and growing, when in truth the product was not ready for delivery and demand was weak. *Id.*, at 596, 597–598. Third, he falsely represented Tellabs' financial results for the fourth quarter of 2000 (and, in connection with those results, condoned the practice of "channel stuffing," under which Tellabs flooded its customers with unwanted products). *Id.*, at 596, 598. Fourth, Notebaert made a series of overstated revenue projections, when demand for the TITAN 5500 was drying up and production of the TITAN 6500 was behind schedule. *Id.*, at 596, 598–599. Based on Notebaert's sunny assessments, the Shareholders contend, market analysts recommended that investors buy Tellabs' stock. See *id.*, at 592.

The first public glimmer that business was not so healthy came in March 2001 whenTellabs modestly reduced its first quarter sales projections. *Ibid.* In the next months, Tellabs made progressively more cautious statements about its projected sales. On June 19, 2001, the last day of the class period, Tellabs disclosed that demand for the TITAN 5500 had significantly dropped. *Id.*, at 593. Simultaneously, the company substantially lowered its revenue projections for the second quarter of 2001. The next day, the price of Tellabs stock, which had reached a high of $67 during the period, plunged to a low of $15.87. *Ibid.*

On December 3, 2002, the Shareholders filed a class action in the District Court for the Northern District of Illinois. *Ibid.* Their complaint stated, *inter alia*, that Tellabs and Notebaert had engaged in securities fraud in violation of §10(b) of the Securities Exchange Act of 1934, 48 Stat. 891, 15 U.S.C. §78j(b), and SEC Rule 10b–5, 17 CFR §240.10b–5 (2006), also that Notebaert was a "controlling person" under §20(a) of the 1934 Act, 15 U.S.C. §78t(a), and therefore derivatively liable for the company's fraudulent acts. See App. 98–101, 167–171. Tellabs moved to dismiss the complaint on the ground that the Shareholders had failed to plead their case with the particularity the PSLRA requires. The District Court agreed, and therefore dismissed the complaint without prejudice. App. to Pet. for Cert. 80a–117a; see *Johnson* v. *Tellabs, Inc.*, 303 F.Supp. 2d 941, 945 (ND Ill. 2004).

The Shareholders then amended their complaint, adding references to 27 confidential sources and making further, more specific, allegations concerning Notebaert's mental state. See 437 F.3d, at 594; App. 91–93, 152–160. The District Court again dismissed, this time with prejudice. 303 F.Supp. 2d, at 971. The Shareholders had sufficiently pleaded that Notebaert's statements were misleading, the court determined, *id.*, at 955–961, but they had insufficiently alleged that he acted with scienter, *id.*, at 954–955, 961–969.

The Court of Appeals for the Seventh Circuit reversed in relevant part. 437 F.3d, at 591. Like the District Court, the Court of Appeals found that the Shareholders had pleaded the misleading character of Notebaert's statements with sufficient particularity. *Id.*, at 595–600.Unlike the District Court, however, the Seventh Circuit concluded that the Shareholders had sufficiently alleged that Notebaert acted with the requisite state of mind. *Id.*, at 603–605.

The Court of Appeals recognized that the PSLRA "unequivocally raise[d] the bar for pleading scienter" by requiring plaintiffs to "plea[d] sufficient facts to create a strong inference of scienter." *Id.*, at 601 (internal quotation marks omitted). In evaluating whether that pleading standard is met, the Seventh Circuit said, "courts [should] examine all of the allegations in the complaint and then ... decide whether collectively they establish such an inference." *Ibid.* "[W]e will allow the complaint to survive," the court next and critically stated, "if it alleges facts from which, if true, a reasonable person could infer that the defendant acted with the required intent .... If a reasonable person could not draw such an inference from the alleged facts, the defendants are entitled to dismissal." *Id.*, at 602.

In adopting its standard for the survival of a complaint, the Seventh Circuit explicitly rejected a stiffer standard adopted by the Sixth Circuit, *i.e.*, that "plaintiffs are entitled only to the most plausible of competing inferences." *Id.*, at 601, 602 (quoting *Fidel* v. *Farley*, 392 F.3d 220, 227 (CA6 2004)). The Sixth Circuit's standard, the court observed, because it involved an assessment of competing inferences, "could potentially infringe upon plaintiffs' Seventh Amendment rights." 437 F.3d, at 602. We granted certiorari to resolve the disagreement among the Circuits on whether, and to what extent, a court must consider competing inferences in determining whether a securities fraud complaint gives rise to a "strong inference" of scienter.[2] 549 U.S. ___ (2007).

II

Section 10(b) of the Securities Exchange Act of 1934 forbids the "use or employ, in connection with the purchase or sale of any security ... , [of] any manipulative or deceptive device or contrivance in contravention of such rules and regulations as the [SEC] may prescribe as necessary or appropriate in the public interest or for the protection of investors." 15 U.S.C. §78j(b). SEC Rule 10b–5 implements §10(b) by declaring it unlawful:

> "(a) To employ any device, scheme, or artifice to defraud,
>
> "(b) To make any untrue statement of a material fact or to omit to state a material fact necessary in order to make the statements made ... not misleading, or
>
> "(c) To engage in any act, practice, or course of business which operates or would operate as a fraud or deceit upon any person, in connection with the purchase or sale of any security." 17 CFR §240.10b–5.

Section 10(b), this Court has implied from the statute's text and purpose, affords a right of action to purchasers or sellers of securities injured by its violation. See, *e.g.*, *Dura Pharmaceuticals*, 544 U.S., at 341. See also *id.*, at 345 ("The securities statutes seek to maintain public confidence in the marketplace ... . by deterring fraud, in part, through the availability of private securities fraud actions."); *Borak*, 377 U.S., at 432 (private securities fraud actions provide "a most effective weapon in the enforcement" of securities laws and are "a necessary supplement to Commission action"). To establish liability under §10(b) and Rule 10b–5, a private plaintiff must prove that the defendant acted with scienter, "a mental state embracing intent to deceive, manipulate, or defraud." *Ernst & Ernst*, 425 U.S., at 193–194, and n. 12.[3]

In an ordinary civil action, the Federal Rules of Civil Procedure require only "a short and plain statement of the claim showing that the pleader is entitled to relief." Fed. Rule Civ. Proc. 8(a)(2). Although the rule encourages brevity, the complaint must say enough to give the defendant "fair notice of what the plaintiff's claim is and the grounds upon which it rests." *Dura Pharmaceuticals*, 544 U.S., at 346 (internal quotation marks omitted). Prior to the enactment of the PSLRA, the sufficiency of a complaint for securities fraud was governed not by Rule 8, but by the heightened pleading standard set forth in Rule 9(b). See *Greenstone* v. *Cambex Corp.*, 975 F.2d 22, 25 (CA1 1992) (Breyer, J.) (collecting cases). Rule 9(b) applies to "all averments of fraud or mistake"; it requires that "the circumstances constituting fraud … be stated with particularity" but provides that "[m]alice, intent, knowledge, and other condition of mind of a person, may be averred generally."

Courts of Appeals diverged on the character of the Rule 9(b) inquiry in §10(b) cases: Could securities fraud plaintiffs allege the requisite mental state "simply by stating that scienter existed," *Inre GlenFed, Inc. Securities Litigation*, 42 F.3d 1541, 1546–1547 (CA9 1994) (en banc), or were they required to allege with particularity facts giving rise to an inference of scienter? Compare *id.*, at 1546 ("We are not permitted to add new requirements to Rule 9(b) simply because we like the effects of doing so."), with, *e.g.*, *Greenstone*, 975 F.2d, at 25 (were the law to permit a securities fraud complaint simply to allege scienter without supporting facts, "a complaint could evade too easily the 'particularity' requirement in Rule 9(b)'s first sentence"). Circuits requiring plaintiffs to allege specific facts indicating scienter expressed that requirement variously. See 5A C. Wright & A. Miller, Federal Practice and Procedure §1301.1, pp.300–302 (3d ed. 2004) (hereinafter Wright & Miller). The Second Circuit's formulation was the most stringent. Securities fraud plaintiffs in that Circuit were required to "specifically plead those [facts] which they assert give rise to a *strong inference* that the defendants had" the requisite state of mind. *Ross* v. *A. H. Robins Co.*, 607 F.2d 545, 558 (1979) (emphasis added). The "strong inference" formulation was appropriate, the Second Circuit said, to ward off allegations of "fraud by hindsight." See, *e.g.*, *Shields* v. *Citytrust Bancorp, Inc.*, 25 F.3d 1124, 1129 (1994) (quoting *Denny* v. *Barber*, 576 F.2d 465, 470 (CA2 1978) (Friendly, J.)).

Setting a uniform pleading standard for §10(b) actions was among Congress' objectives when it enacted the PSLRA. Designed to curb perceived abuses of the §10(b) private action—"nuisance filings, targeting of deep-pocket defendants, vexatious discovery requests and manipulation by class action lawyers," *Dabit*, 547 U.S., at 81 (quoting H.R. Conf. Rep. No. 104–369, p.31 (1995) (hereinafter H.R. Conf. Rep.))—the PSLRA installed both substantive and procedural controls.[4] Notably, Congress prescribed new procedures for the appointment of lead plaintiffs and lead counsel. This innovation aimed to increase the likelihood that institutional investors—parties more likely to balance the interests of the class with the long-term interests of the company—would serve as lead plaintiffs. See *id.*, at 33–34; S.Rep. No. 104–98, p.11 (1995). Congress also "limit[ed] recoverable damages and attorney's fees, provide[d] a 'safe harbor' for forward-looking statements, … mandate[d] imposition of sanctions for frivolous litigation, and authorize[d] a stay of discovery pending resolution of any motion to dismiss." *Dabit*, 547 U.S., at 81. And in §21D(b) of the PSLRA, Congress "impose[d] heightened pleading requirements in actions brought pursuant to §10(b) and Rule 10b–5." Ibid.

Under the PSLRA's heightened pleading instructions, any private securities complaint alleging that the defendant made a false or misleading statement must: (1) "specify each statement alleged to have been misleading [and] the reason or reasons why the statement is misleading," 15 U.S.C. §78u–4(b)(1); and (2) "state with particularity facts giving rise to a strong inference that the defendant acted with the required state of mind," §78u–4(b)(2). In the instant case, as earlier stated, see supra, at 5, the District Court and the Seventh Circuit agreed that the Shareholders met the first of the two requirements: The complaint sufficiently specified Notebaert's alleged misleading statements and the reasons why the statements were misleading. 303 F.Supp. 2d, at 955–961; 437 F.3d, at 596–600. But those courts disagreed on whether the Shareholders, as required by §21D(b)(2), "state[d] with particularity facts giving rise to a strong inference that [Notebaert] acted with [scienter]," §78u–4(b)(2). See *supra*, at 5.

The "strong inference" standard "unequivocally raise[d] the bar for pleading scienter," 437 F.3d, at 601, and signaled Congress' purpose to promote greater uniformity among the Circuits, see H.R. Conf. Rep., p. 41. But "Congress did not … throw much light on what facts … suffice to create [a strong] inference," or on what "degree of imagination courts can use in divining whether" the requisite inference exists. 437 F.3d, at 601.While adopting the Second Circuit's "strong inference" standard, Congress did not codify that Circuit's case law interpreting the standard. See §78u–4(b)(2). See also Brief for United States as *Amicus Curiae* 18. With no clear guide from Congress other than its "inten[tion] to strengthen existing pleading requirements," H.R. Conf. Rep., p. 41, Courts of Appeals have diverged again, this time in construing the term "strong inference." Among the uncertainties, should courts consider competing inferences in determining whether an inference of scienter is "strong"? See 437 F.3d, at 601–602 (collecting cases). Our task is to prescribe a workable construction of the "strong inference" standard, a reading geared to the PSLRA's twin goals:to curb frivolous, lawyer-driven litigation, while preserving investors' ability to recover on meritorious claims.

III

A

We establish the following prescriptions: *First*, faced with a Rule 12(b)(6) motion to dismiss a §10(b) action, courts must, as with any motion to dismiss for failure to plead a claim on which relief can be granted, accept all factual allegations in the complaint as true. See *Leatherman* v. *Tarrant County Narcotics Intelligence and Coordination Unit*, 507 U.S. 163, 164 (1993). On this point, the parties agree. See Reply Brief 8; Brief for Respondents 26; Brief for United States as *Amicus Curiae* 8, 20, 21.

Second, courts must consider the complaint in its entirety, as well as other sources courts ordinarily examine when ruling on Rule 12(b)(6) motions to dismiss, in particular, documents incorporated into the complaint by reference, and matters of which a court may take judicial notice. See 5B Wright & Miller §1357 (3d ed. 2004 and Supp. 2007). The inquiry, as several Courts of Appeals have recognized, is whether *all* of the facts alleged, taken collectively, give rise to a strong inference of scienter, not whether any individual allegation, scrutinized in isolation, meets that standard. See, *e.g.*, *Abrams* v. *Baker Hughes Inc.*, 292 F.3d 424, 431 (CA5 2002); *Gompper* v. *VISX, Inc.*, 298 F.3d 893, 897 (CA9 2002). See also Brief for United States as *Amicus Curiae* 25.

Third, in determining whether the pleaded facts give rise to a "strong" inference of scienter, the court must take into account plausible opposing inferences. The Seventh Circuit expressly declined to engage in such a comparative inquiry. A complaint could survive, that court said, as long as it "alleges facts from which, if true, a reasonable person could infer that the defendant acted with the required intent"; in other words, only "[i]f a reasonable person could not draw such an inference from the alleged facts" would the defendant prevail on a motion to dismiss. 437 F.3d, at 602. But in §21D(b)(2), Congress did not merely require plaintiffs to "provide a factual basis for [their] scienter allegations," *ibid.* (quoting *Inre Cerner Corp. Securities Litigation*, 425 F.3d 1079, 1084, 1085 (CA8 2005)), *i.e.*, toallege facts from which an inference of scienter rationally *could* be drawn. Instead, Congress required plaintiffs to plead with particularity facts that give rise to a "strong"—*i.e.*, a powerful or cogent—inference. See American Heritage Dictionary 1717 (4th ed. 2000) (defining "strong" as "[p]ersuasive, effective, and cogent"); 16 Oxford English Dictionary 949 (2d ed. 1989) (defining "strong" as "[p]owerful to demonstrate or convince" (definition 16b)); cf. 7 *id.*, at 924 (defining "inference" as "a conclusion [drawn] from known or assumed facts or statements"; "reasoning from something known or assumed to something else which follows from it").

The strength of an inference cannot be decided in a vacuum. The inquiry is inherently comparative: How likely is it that one conclusion, as compared to others, follows from the underlying facts? To determine whether the plaintiff has alleged facts that give rise to the requisite "strong inference" of scienter, a court must consider plausible nonculpable explanations for the defendant's conduct, as well as inferences favoring the plaintiff. The inference that the defendant acted with scienter need not be irrefutable, *i.e.*, of the "smoking-gun" genre, or even the "most plausible of competing inferences," *Fidel*, 392 F.3d, at 227 (quoting *Helwig* v. *Vencor, Inc.*, 251 F.3d 540, 553 (CA6 2001) (en banc)). Recall in this regard that §21D(b)'s pleading requirements are but one constraint among many the PSLRA installed to screen out frivolous suits, while allowing meritorious actions to move forward. See *supra*, at 9, and n.4. Yet the inference of scienter must be more than merely "reasonable" or "permissible"—it must be cogent and compelling, thus strong in light of other explanations. A complaint will survive, we hold, only if a reasonable person would deem the inference of scienter cogent and at least as compelling as any opposing inference one could draw from the facts alleged.[5]

B

Tellabs contends that when competing inferences are considered, Notebaert's evident lack of pecuniary motive will be dispositive. The Shareholders, Tellabs stresses, did not allege that Notebaert sold any shares during the class period. See Brief for Petitioners 50 ("The absence of any allegations of motive color all the other allegations putatively giving rise to an inference of scienter.").While it is true that motive can be a relevant consideration, and personal financial gain may weigh heavily in favor of a scienter inference, we agree with the Seventh Circuit that the absence of a motive allegation is not fatal. See 437 F.3d, at 601. As earlier stated, *supra*, at 11, allegations must be considered collectively; the significance that can be ascribed to an allegation of motive, or lack thereof, depends on the entirety of the complaint.

Tellabs also maintains that several of the Shareholders' allegations are too vague or ambiguous to contribute to a strong inference of scienter. For example, the Shareholders alleged that Tellabs flooded its customers with unwanted products, a practice known as "channel stuffing." See *supra*, at 3. But theyfailed, Tellabs argues, to specify whether the channel stuffing allegedly known to Notebaert was the illegitimate kind (*e.g.*, writing orders for products customers had not requested) or the legitimate kind (*e.g.*, offering customers discounts as an incentive to buy). Brief for Petitioners 44–46; Reply Brief 8. See also *id.*, at 8–9 (complaint lacks precise dates of reports critical to distinguish legitimate conduct from culpable conduct). But see 437 F.3d, at 598, 603–604 (pointing to multiple particulars alleged by the Shareholders, including specifications as to timing). We agree that omissions and ambiguities count against inferring scienter, for plaintiffs must "state with particularity facts giving rise to a strong inference that the defendant acted with the required state of mind." §78u–4(b)(2). We reiterate, however, that the court's job is not to scrutinize each allegation in isolation but to assess all the allegations holistically. See *supra*, at 11; 437 F.3d, at 601. In sum, the reviewing court must ask: When the allegations are accepted as true and taken collectively, would a reasonable person deem the inference of scienter at least as strong as any opposing inference?[6]

IV

Accounting for its construction of §21D(b)(2), the Seventh Circuit explained that the court "th[ought] it wis[e] to adopt an approach that [could not] be misunderstood as a usurpation of the jury's role." 437 F.3d, at 602. In our view, the Seventh Circuit's concern was undue.[7] A court's comparative assessment of plausible inferences, while constantly assuming the plaintiff's allegations to be true, we think it plain, does not impinge upon the Seventh Amendment right to jury trial.[8]

Congress, as creator of federal statutory claims, has power to prescribe what must be pleaded to state the claim, just as it has power to determine what must be proved to prevail on the merits. It is the federal lawmaker's prerogative, therefore, to allow, disallow, or shape the contours of—including the pleading and proof requirements for—§10(b) private actions. No decision of this Court questions that authority in general, or suggests, in particular, that the Seventh Amendment inhibits Congress from establishing whatever pleading requirements it finds appropriate for federal statutory claims. Cf. *Swierkiewicz* v. *Sorema N.A.*, 534 U.S. 506, 512–513 (2002) ; *Leatherman*, 507 U.S., at 168 (both recognizing that heightened pleading requirements can be established by Federal Rule, citing Fed. Rule Civ. Proc. 9(b), which requires that fraud or mistake be pleaded with particularity).[9]

Our decision in *Fidelity & Deposit Co. of Md.* v. *United States*, 187 U.S. 315 (1902), is instructive. That case concerned a rule adopted by the Supreme Court of the District of Columbia in 1879 pursuant to rulemaking power delegated by Congress. The rule required defendants, in certain contract actions, to file an affidavit "specifically stating ... , in precise and distinct terms, the grounds of his defen[s]e." *Id.*, at 318 (internal quotation marks omitted). The defendant's affidavit was found insufficient, and judgment was entered for the plaintiff, whose declaration and supporting affidavit had been found satisfactory. *Ibid.* This Court upheld the District's rule against the contention that it violated the Seventh Amendment . *Id.*, at 320. Just as the purpose of §21D(b) is to screen out frivolous complaints, the purpose of the prescription at issue in *Fidelity & Deposit Co.* was to "preserve the courts from frivolous defen[s]es," *ibid.* Explaining why the Seventh Amendment was not implicated, this Court said that the heightened pleading rule simply "prescribes the means of making an issue," and that, when "[t]he issue [was] made as prescribed, the right of trial by jury accrues." *Ibid.*; accord *Ex parte Peterson*, 253 U.S. 300, 310 (1920) (Brandeis, J.) (citing *Fidelity & Deposit Co.*, and reiterating: "It does not infringe the constitutional right to a trial by jury [in a civil case], to require, with a view to formulating the issues, an oath by each party to the facts relied upon."). See also *Walker* v. *New Mexico & Southern Pacific R. Co.*, 165 U.S. 593, 596 (1897) (Seventh Amendment "does not attempt to regulate matters of pleading").

In the instant case, provided that the Shareholders have satisfied the congressionally "prescribe[d] ... means of making an issue," *Fidelity & Deposit Co.*, 187 U.S., at 320, the case will fall within the jury's authority to assess the credibility of witnesses, resolve any genuine issues of fact, and make the ultimate determination whether Notebaert and, by imputation, Tellabs acted with scienter. We emphasize, as well, that under our construction of the "strong inference" standard, a plaintiff is not forced to plead more than she would be required to prove at trial. A plaintiff alleging fraud in a §10(b) action, we hold today, must plead facts rendering an inference of scienter *at least as likely as* any plausible opposing inference. At trial, she must then prove her case by a "preponderance of the evidence." Stated otherwise, she must demonstrate that it is *more likely* than not that the defendant acted with scienter. See *Herman & MacLean* v. *Huddleston*, 459 U.S. 375, 390 (1983).

* * *

While we reject the Seventh Circuit's approach to §21D(b)(2), we do not decide whether, under the standard we have described, see *supra*, at 11–14, the Shareholders' allegations warrant "a strong inference that [Notebaert and Tellabs] acted with the required state of mind," 15 U.S.C. §78u–4(b)(2). Neither the District Court nor the Court of Appeals had the opportunity to consider the matter in light of the prescriptions we announce today. We therefore vacate the Seventh Circuit's judgment so that the case may be reexamined in accord with our construction of §21D(b)(2).

The judgment of the Court of Appeals is vacated, and the case is remanded for further proceedings consistent with this opinion.

It is so ordered.

NOTES

[1] The Shareholders brought suit against Tellabs executives other than Notebaert, including Richard Birck, Tellabs' chairman and former chief executive officer. Because the claims against the other executives, many of which have been dismissed, are not before us, we focus on the allegations as they relate to Notebaert. We refer to the defendant-petitioners collectively as "Tellabs."

[2] See, e.g., 437 F.3d 588, 602 (CA7 2006) (decision below); Inre Credit Suisse First Boston Corp., 431 F.3d 36, 49, 51 (CA1 2005); Ottmann v. Hanger Orthopedic Group, Inc., 353 F.3d 338, 347–349 (CA4 2003); Pirraglia v. Novell, Inc., 339 F.3d 1182, 1187–1188 (CA10 2003); Gompper v. VISX, Inc., 298 F.3d 893, 896–897 (CA9 2002); Helwig v. Vencor, Inc., 251 F.3d 540, 553 (CA6 2001) (en banc).

[3] We have previously reserved the question whether reckless behavior is sufficient for civil liability under §10(b) and Rule 10b–5. See Ernst & Ernst v. Hochfelder, 425 U.S. 185, 194, n. 12 (1976). Every Court of Appeals that has considered the issue has held that a plaintiff may meet the scienter requirement by showing that the defendant acted intentionally or recklessly, though the Circuits differ on the degree of recklessness required. See Ottmann, 353 F.3d, at 343 (collecting cases). The question whether and when recklessness satisfies the scienter requirement is not presented in this case.

[4] Nothing in the Act, we have previously noted, casts doubt on the conclusion "that private securities

litigation [i]s an indispensable tool with which defrauded investors can recover their losses"—a matter crucial to the integrity of domestic capital markets. See Merrill Lynch, Pierce, Fenner & Smith Inc. v. Dabit, 547 U.S. 71, 81 (2006) (internal quotation marks omitted).

[5] Justice Scalia objects to this standard on the ground that "[i]f a jade falcon were stolen from a room to which only A and B had access," it could not "possibly be said there was a 'strong inference' that B was the thief." Post, at 1 (opinion concurring in judgment) (emphasis in original). I suspect, however, that law enforcement officials as well as the owner of the precious falcon would find the inference of guilt as to B quite strong—certainly strong enough to warrant further investigation. Indeed, an inference at least as likely as competing inferences can, in some cases, warrant recovery. See Summers v. Tice, 33 Cal. 2d 80, 84–87, 199 P.2d 1, 3–5 (1948) (in bank) (plaintiff wounded by gunshot could recover from two defendants, even though the most he could prove was that each defendant was at least as likely to have injured him as the other); Restatement (Third) of Torts §28(b), Comment e, p. 504 (Proposed Final Draft No. 1, Apr. 6, 2005) ("Since the publication of the Second Restatement in 1965, courts have generally accepted the alternative-liability principle of [Summers v. Tice, adopted in] §433B(3), while fleshing out its limits."). In any event, we disagree with Justice Scalia that the hardly stock term "strong inference" has only one invariably right ("natural" or "normal") reading—his. See post, at 3.

Justice Alito agrees with Justice Scalia, and would transpose to the pleading stage "the test that is used at the summary-judgment and judgment-as-a-matter-of-law stages." Post, at 3 (opinion concurring in judgment). But the test at each stage is measured against a different backdrop. It is improbable that Congress, without so stating, intended courts to test pleadings, unaided by discovery, to determine whether there is "no genuine issue as to any material fact." See Fed. Rule Civ. Proc. 56(c). And judgment as a matter of law is a post-trial device, turning on the question whether a party has produced evidence "legally sufficient" to warrant a jury determination in that party's favor. See Rule 50(a)(1).

[6] The Seventh Circuit held that allegations of scienter made against one defendant cannot be imputed to all other individual defendants. 437 F.3d, at 602–603. See also id., at 603 (to proceed beyond the pleading stage, the plaintiff must allege as to each defendant facts sufficient to demonstrate a culpable state of mind regarding his or her violations) (citing Phillips v. Scientific-Atlanta, Inc., 374 F.3d 1015, 1018 (CA11 2004)). Though there is disagreement among the Circuits as to whether the group pleading doctrine survived the PSLRA, see, e.g., Southland Securities Corp. v. Inspire Ins. Solutions Inc., 365 F.3d 353, 364 (CA5 2004), the Shareholders do not contest the Seventh Circuit's determination, and we do not disturb it.

[7] The Seventh Circuit raised the possibility of a Seventh Amendment problem on its own initiative. The Shareholders did not contend below that dismissal of their complaint under §21D(b)(2) would violate their right to trial by jury. Cf. Monroe Employees Retirement System v. Bridgestone Corp., 399 F.3d 651, 683, n. 25 (CA6 2005) (noting possible Seventh Amendment argument but declining to address it when not raised by plaintiffs).

[8] In numerous contexts, gatekeeping judicial determinations prevent submission of claims to a jury's judgment without violating the Seventh Amendment . See, e.g., Daubert v. Merrell Dow Pharmaceuticals, Inc., 509 U.S. 579, 589 (1993) (expert testimony can be excluded based on judicial determination of reliability); Neely v. Martin K. Eby Constr. Co., 386 U.S. 317, 321 (1967) (judgment as a matter of law); Pease v. Rathbun-Jones Engineering Co., 243 U.S. 273, 278 (1917) (summary judgment).

[9] Any heightened pleading rule, including Fed. Rule Civ. Proc. 9(b), could have the effect of preventing a plaintiff from getting discovery on a claim that might have gone to a jury, had discovery occurred and yielded substantial evidence. In recognizing Congress' or the Federal Rule makers' authority to adopt special pleading rules, we have detected no Seventh Amendment impediment.

DERRICK KIMBROUGH v. UNITED STATES

No. 06-6330, December 10, 2007

ON WRIT OF CERTIORARI TO THE UNITED STATES COURT OF APPEALS FOR THE FOURTH CIRCUIT

Justice Ginsburg delivered the opinion of the Court.

This Court's remedial opinion in *United States* v. *Booker*, 543 U.S. 220, 244 (2005), instructed district courts to read the United States Sentencing Guidelines as "effectively advisory," *id.*, at245. In accord with 18 U.S.C. §3553(a), the Guidelines, formerly mandatory, now serve as one factor among several courts must consider in determining an appropriate sentence. *Booker* further instructed that "reasonableness" is the standard controlling appellate review of the sentences district courts impose.

Under the statute criminalizing the manufacture and distribution of crack cocaine, 21 U.S.C. §841, and the relevant Guidelines prescription, §2D1.1, a drug trafficker dealing in crack cocaine is subject to the same sentence as one dealing in 100 times more powder cocaine. The question here presented is whether, as the Court of Appeals held in this case, "a sentence ... outside the guidelines range is per se unreasonable when it is based on a disagreement with the sentencing disparity for crack and powder cocaine offenses." 174 Fed. Appx. 798, 799 (CA4 2006) *(per curiam)*. We hold that, under *Booker*, the cocaine Guidelines, like all other Guidelines, are advisory only, and that the Court of Appeals erred in holding the crack/powder disparity effectively mandatory. A district judge must include the Guidelines range in the array of factors warranting consideration. The judge may determine, however, that, in the particular case, a within-Guidelines sentence is "greater than necessary" to serve the objectives of sentencing. 18 U.S.C. §3553(a) (2000 ed. and Supp. V). In making that determination, the judge may consider the disparity between the Guidelines' treatment of crack and powder cocaine offenses.

I

In September 2004, petitioner Derrick Kimbrough was indicted in the United States District Court for the Eastern District of Virginia and charged with four offenses: conspiracy to distribute crack and powder cocaine; possession with intent to distribute more than 50 grams of crack cocaine; possession with intent to distribute powder cocaine; and possession of a firearm in furtherance of a drug-trafficking offense. Kimbrough pleaded guilty to all four charges.

Under the relevant statutes, Kimbrough's plea subjected him to an aggregate sentence of 15 years to life in prison: 10 years to life for the three drug offenses, plus a consecutive term of 5 years to life for the firearm offense.[1] In order to determine the appropriate sentence within this statutory range, the District Court first calculated Kimbrough's sentence under the advisory Sentencing Guidelines.[2] Kimbrough's guilty plea acknowledged that he was accountable for 56 grams of crack cocaine and 92.1 grams of powder cocaine. This quantity of drugs yielded a base offense level of 32 for the three drug charges. See United States Sentencing Commission, Guidelines Manual §2D1.1(c) (Nov. 2004) (USSG). Finding that Kimbrough, by asserting sole culpability for the crime, had testified falsely at his codefendant's trial, the District Court increased his offense level to 34. See §3C1.1. In accord with the presentence report, the court determined that Kimbrough's criminal history category was II. An offense level of 34 and a criminal history category of II yielded a Guidelines range of 168 to 210 months for the three drug charges. See *id.*, ch.5, pt.A, Sentencing Table. The Guidelines sentence for the firearm offense was the statutory minimum, 60 months. See USSG§2K2.4(b). Kimbrough's final advisory Guidelines range was thus 228 to 270 months, or 19 to 22.5 years.

A sentence in this range, in the District Court's judgment, would have been "greater than necessary" to accomplish the purposes of sentencing set forth in 18 U.S.C. §3553(a). App.72. As required by §3553(a), the court took into account the "nature and circumstances" of the offense and Kimbrough's "history and characteristics." *Id.*, at72–73. The court also commented that the case exemplified the "disproportionate and unjust effect that crack cocaine guidelines have in sentencing." *Id.*, at72. In this regard, the court contrasted Kimbrough's Guidelines range of 228 to 270 months with the range that would have applied had he been accountable for an equivalent amount of powder cocaine: 97 to 106 months, inclusive of the 5-year mandatory minimum for the firearm charge, see USSG §2D1.1(c); *id.*, ch.5, pt.A, Sentencing Table. Concluding that the statutory minimum sentence was "clearly long enough" to accomplish the objectives listed in §3553(a), the court sentenced Kimbrough to 15 years, or 180 months, in prison plus 5 years of supervised release. App.74–75.[3]

In an unpublished *per curiam* opinion, the Fourth Circuit vacated the sentence. Under Circuit precedent, the Court of Appeals observed, a sentence "outside the guidelines range is per se unreasonable when it is based on a disagreement with the sentencing disparity for crack and powder cocaine offenses." 174 Fed. Appx., at 799 (citing *United States* v. *Eura*, 440 F.3d 625, 633–634 (CA4 2006)).

We granted certiorari, 551 U.S. ___ (2007), to determine whether the crack/powder disparity adopted in the United States Sentencing Guidelines has been rendered "advisory" by our decision in *Booker*.[4]

II

We begin with some background on the different treatment of crack and powder cocaine under the federal sentencing laws. Crack and powder cocaine are two forms of the same drug. Powder cocaine, or cocaine hydrochloride, is generally inhaled through the nose; it may also be mixed with water and injected. See United States Sentencing Commission, Special Report to Congress: Cocaine and Federal Sentencing Policy 5, 12 (Feb. 1995), available at http://www.ussc.gov/crack/exec.htm (hereinafter 1995 Report). (All Internet materials as visited Dec. 7, 2007, and included in Clerk of Court's case file.) Crack cocaine, a type of cocaine base, is formed by dissolving powder cocaine and baking soda in boiling water. *Id.*, at14. The resulting solid is divided into single-dose "rocks" that users smoke. *Ibid.* The active ingredient in powder and crack cocaine is the same. *Id.*, at9. The two forms of the drug also have the same physiological and psychotropic effects, but smoking crack cocaine allows the body to absorb the drug much faster than inhaling powder cocaine, and thus produces a shorter, more intense high. *Id.*, at 15–19.[5]

Although chemically similar, crack and powder cocaine are handled very differently for sentencing purposes. The 100-to-1 ratio yields sentences for crack offenses three to six times longer than those for powder offenses involving equal amounts of drugs. See United States Sentencing Commission, Report to Congress: Cocaine and Federal Sentencing Policy iv (May 2002), available at http://www.ussc.gov/r_congress/02crack/2002crackrpt.pdf (hereinafter 2002 Report).[6] This disparity means that a major supplier of powder cocaine may receive a shorter sentence than a low-level dealer who buys powder from the supplier but then converts it to crack. See 1995 Report193–194.

A

The crack/powder disparity originated in the Anti-Drug Abuse Act of 1986 (1986 Act), 100 Stat. 3207. The 1986 Act created a two-tiered scheme of five- and ten-year mandatory minimum sentences for drug manufacturing and distribution offenses. Congress sought "to link the ten-year mandatory minimum trafficking prison term to major drug dealers and to link the five-year minimum term to serious traffickers." 1995 Report119. The 1986 Act uses the weight of the drugs involved in the offense as the sole proxy to identify "major" and "serious" dealers. For example, any defendant responsible for 100 grams of heroin is subject to the five-year mandatory minimum, see 21 U.S.C. §841(b)(1)(B)(i) (2000 ed. and Supp V), and any defendant responsible for 1,000 grams of heroin is subject to the ten-year mandatory minimum, see §841(b)(1)(A)(i).

Crack cocaine was a relatively new drug when the 1986 Act was signed into law, but it was already a matter of great public concern: "Drug abuse in general, and crack cocaine in particular, had become in public opinion and in members' minds a problem of overwhelming dimensions." 1995 Report121. Congress apparently believed that crack was significantly more dangerous than powder cocaine in that: (1) crack was highly addictive; (2) crack users and dealers were more likely to be violent than users and dealers of other drugs; (3) crack was more harmful to users than powder, particularly for children who had been exposed by their mothers' drug use during pregnancy; (4) crack use was especially prevalent among teenagers; and (5) crack's potency and low cost were making it increasingly popular. See 2002 Report90.

Based on these assumptions, the 1986 Act adopted a "100-to-1 ratio" that treated every gram of crack cocaine as the equivalent of 100 grams of powder cocaine. The Act's five-year mandatory minimum applies to any defendant accountable for 5 grams of crack or 500 grams of powder, 21 U.S.C. §841(b)(1)(B)(ii), (iii); its ten-year mandatory minimum applies to any defendant accountable for 50 grams of crack or 5,000 grams of powder, §841(b)(1)(A)(ii), (iii).

While Congress was considering adoption of the 1986 Act, the Sentencing Commission was engaged in formulating the Sentencing Guidelines.[7] In the main, the Commission developed Guidelines sentences using an empirical approach based on data about past sentencing practices, including 10,000 presentence investigation reports. See USSG §1A.1, intro. comment., pt.A, ¶3. The Commission "modif[ied] and adjust[ed] past practice in the interests of greater rationality, avoiding inconsistency, complying with congressional instructions, and the like." *Rita* v. *United States*, 551 U.S. ___, ___ (2007) (slip op., at10).

The Commission did not use this empirical approach in developing the Guidelines sentences for drug-trafficking offenses. Instead, it employed the 1986 Act's weight-driven scheme. The Guidelines use a drug quantity table based on drug type and weight to set base offense levels for drug trafficking offenses. See USSG §2D1.1(c). In setting offense levels for crack and powder cocaine, the Commission, in line with the 1986 Act, adopted the 100-to-1 ratio. The statute itself specifies only two quantities of each drug, but the Guidelines "go further and set sentences for the full range of possible drug quantities using the same 100-to-1 quantity ratio." 1995 Report1. The Guidelines' drug quantity table sets base offense levels ranging from 12, for offenses involving less than 250 milligrams of crack (or 25 grams of powder), to 38, for offenses involving more than 1.5 kilograms of crack (or 150 kilograms of powder). USSG §2D1.1(c).[8]

B

Although the Commission immediately used the 100-to-1 ratio to define base offense levels for all crack and powder offenses, it later determined that the crack/powder sentencing disparity is generally unwarranted. Based on additional research and experience with the 100-to-1 ratio, the Commission concluded that the disparity "fails to meet the sentencing objectives set forth by Congress in both the Sentencing Reform Act and the 1986 Act." 2002 Report91. In a series of reports, the Commission identified three problems with the crack/powder disparity.

First, the Commission reported, the 100-to-1 ratio rested on assumptions about "the relative harmfulness of the two drugs and the relative prevalence of certain harmful conduct associated with their use and distribution that more recent research and data no longer support." *Ibid.;* see United States Sentencing Commission, Report to Congress: Cocaine and Federal Sentencing Policy 8 (May 2007), available at http://www.ussc.gov/r_congress/cocaine2007.pdf (hereinafter 2007 Report) (ratio Congress embedded in the statute far "overstate[s]" both "the relative harmfulness" of crack cocaine, and the "seriousness of most crack cocaine offenses"). For example, the Commission found that crack is associated with "significantly less trafficking-related violence … than previously assumed." 2002 Report 100. It also observed that "the negative effects of prenatal crack cocaine exposure are identical to the negative effects of prenatal powder cocaine exposure." *Id.,* at 94. The Commission furthermore noted that "the epidemic of crack cocaine use by youth never materialized to the extent feared." *Id.,* at96.

Second, the Commission concluded that the crack/powder disparity is inconsistent with the 1986 Act's goal of punishing major drug traffickers more severely than low-level dealers. Drug importers and major traffickers generally deal in powder cocaine, which is then converted into crack by street-level sellers. See 1995 Report66–67. But the 100-to-1 ratio can lead to the "anomalous" result that "retail crack dealers get longer sentences than the wholesale drug distributors who supply them the powder cocaine from which their crack is produced." *Id.,* at 174.

Finally, the Commission stated that the crack/powder sentencing differential "fosters disrespect for and lack of confidence in the criminal justice system" because of a "widely-held perception" that it "promotes unwarranted disparity based on race." 2002 Report 103. Approximately 85 percent of defendants convicted of crack offenses in federal court are black; thus the severe sentences required by the 100-to-1 ratio are imposed "primarily upon black offenders." Ibid.

Despite these observations, the Commission's most recent reports do not urge identical treatment of crack and powder cocaine. In the Commission's view, "some differential in the quantity-based penalties" for the two drugs is warranted, id., at 102, because crack is more addictive than powder, crack offenses are more likely to involve weapons or bodily injury, and crack distribution is associated with higher levels of crime, see *id.,* at 93–94, 101–102. But the 100-to-1 crack/powder ratio, the Commission concluded, significantly overstates the differences between the two forms of the drug. Accordingly, the Commission recommended that the ratio be "substantially" reduced. *Id.,* at viii.

C

The Commission has several times sought to achieve a reduction in the crack/powder ratio. In 1995, it proposed amendments to the Guidelines that would have replaced the 100-to-1 ratio with a 1-to-1 ratio. Complementing that change, the Commission would have installed special enhancements for trafficking offenses involving weapons or bodily injury. See Amendments to the Sentencing Guidelines for United States Courts, 60 Fed. Reg. 25075–25077 (1995). Congress, acting pursuant to 28 U.S.C. §994(p),[9] rejected the amendments. See Pub. L. 104–38, §1, 109 Stat. 334. Simultaneously, however, Congress directed the Commission to "propose revision of the drug quantity ratio of crack cocaine to powder cocaine under the relevant statutes and guidelines." §2(a)(2), *id.,* at335.

In response to this directive, the Commission issued reports in 1997 and 2002 recommending that Congress change the 100-to-1 ratio prescribed in the 1986 Act. The 1997 Report proposed a 5-to-1 ratio. See United States Sentencing Commission, Special Report to Congress: Cocaine and Federal Sentencing Policy 2 (Apr. 1997), http://www.ussc.gov/r_congress/newcrack.pdf. The 2002 Report recommended lowering the ratio "at least" to 20 to 1. 2002 Reportviii. Neither proposal prompted congressional action.

The Commission's most recent report, issued in 2007, again urged Congress to amend the 1986 Act to reduce the 100-to-1 ratio. This time, however, the Commission did not simply await congressional action. Instead, the Commission adopted an ameliorating change in the Guidelines. See 2007 Report 9. The alteration, which became effective on November 1, 2007, reduces the base offense level associated with each quantity of crack by two levels. See Amendments to the Sentencing Guidelines for United States Courts, 72 Fed. Reg. 28571–28572 (2007).[10] This modest amendment yields sentences for crack offenses between two and five times longer than sentences for equal amounts of powder. See *ibid.*[11] Describing the amendment as "only … a partial remedy" for the problems generated by the crack/powder disparity, the Commission noted that "[a]ny comprehensive solution requires appropriate legislative action by Congress." 2007 Report10.

III

With this history of the crack/powder sentencing ratio in mind, we next consider the status of the Guidelines tied to the ratio after our decision in *United States* v. *Booker*, 543 U.S. 220 (2005). In *Booker*, the Court held that the mandatory Sentencing Guidelines system violated the Sixth Amendment. See *id.,* at226–227. The *Booker* remedial opinion determined that the appropriate cure was to sever and excise the provision of the statute that rendered the Guidelines mandatory, 18 U.S.C. §3553(b)(1) (2000 ed., Supp. IV).[12] This modification of the federal sentencing statute, we explained, "makes the Guidelines effectively advisory." 543 U.S., at 245.

The statute, as modified by *Booker*, contains an overarching provision instructing district courts to "impose a sentence sufficient, but not greater than necessary" to accomplish the goals of sentencing, including "to reflect the seriousness of the offense," "to promote respect for the law," "to provide just punishment for the offense," "to afford adequate deterrence to criminal conduct," and "to protect the public from further crimes of the defendant." 18 U.S.C. §3553(a) (2000 ed. and Supp. V). The statute further provides that, in determining the appropriate sentence, the court should consider a number of factors, including "the nature and circumstances of the offense," "the history and characteristics of the defendant," "the sentencing range established" by the Guidelines, "any pertinent policy statement" issued by the Sentencing Commission pursuant to its statutory authority, and "the need to avoid unwarranted sentence disparities among defendants with similar records who have been found guilty of similar conduct." *Ibid.* In sum, while the statute still requires a court to give respectful consideration to the Guidelines, see *Gall* v. *United States*, *ante*, at 7, 11, *Booker* "permits the court to tailor the sentence in light of other statutory concerns as well," 543 U.S., at245–246.

The Government acknowledges that the Guidelines "are now advisory" and that, as a general matter, "courts may vary [from Guidelines ranges] based solely on policy considerations, including disagreements with the Guidelines." Brief for United States16; cf. *Rita* v. *United States*, 551 U.S. ___, ___ (2007) (slip op., at12) (a district court may consider arguments that "the Guidelines sentence itself fails properly to reflect §3553(a) considerations"). But the Government contends that the Guidelines adopting the 100-to-1 ratio are an exception to the "general freedom that sentencing courts have to apply the [§3553(a)] factors." Brief for United States 16. That is so, according to the Government, because the ratio is a "specific policy determinatio[n] that Congress has directed sentencing courts to observe." *Id.*, at25. The Government offers three arguments in support of this position. We consider each in turn.

A

As its first and most heavily pressed argument, the Government urges that the 1986 Act itself prohibits the Sentencing Commission and sentencing courts from disagreeing with the 100-to-1 ratio.[13] The Government acknowledges that the "Congress did not *expressly* direct the Sentencing Commission to incorporate the 100:1 ratio in the Guidelines." Brief for United States33 (brackets and internal quotation marks omitted). Nevertheless, it asserts that the Act "[i]mplicit[ly]" requires the Commission and sentencing courts to apply the 100-to-1 ratio. *Id.*, at 32. Any deviation, the Government urges, would be "logically incoherent" when combined with mandatory minimum sentences based on the 100-to-1 ratio. *Id.*, at33.

This argument encounters a formidable obstacle: It lacks grounding in the text of the 1986 Act. The statute, by its terms, mandates only maximum and minimum sentences: A person convicted of possession with intent to distribute 5 grams or more of crack cocaine must be sentenced to a minimum of 5 years and the maximum term is 40 years. A person with 50 grams or more of crack cocaine must be sentenced to a minimum of 10 years and the maximum term is life. The statute says nothing about the appropriate sentences within these brackets, and we decline to read any implicit directive into that congressional silence. See *Jama* v. *Immigration and Customs Enforcement*, 543 U.S. 335, 341 (2005) ("We do not lightly assume that Congress has omitted from its adopted text requirements that it nonetheless intends to apply ...."). Drawing meaning from silence is particularly inappropriate here, for Congress has shown that it knows how to direct sentencing practices in express terms. For example, Congress has specifically required the Sentencing Commission to set Guidelines sentences for serious recidivist offenders "at or near" the statutory maximum. 28 U.S.C. §994(h). See also §994(i) ("The Commission shall assure that the guidelines specify a sentence to a substantial term of imprisonment" for specified categories of offenders.).

Our cautious reading of the 1986 Act draws force from *Neal* v. *United States*, 516 U.S. 284 (1996). That case involved different methods of calculating lysergic acid diethylamide (LSD) weights, one applicable in determining statutory minimum sentences, the other controlling the calculation of Guidelines ranges. The 1986 Act sets mandatory minimum sentences based on the weight of "a mixture or substance containing a detectable amount" of LSD. 21 U.S.C. §841(b)(1)(A)(v), (B)(v). Prior to *Neal*, we had interpreted that language to include the weight of the carrier medium (usually blotter paper) on which LSD is absorbed even though the carrier is usually far heavier than the LSD itself. See *Chapman* v. *United States*, 500 U.S. 453, 468 (1991). Until 1993, the Sentencing Commission had interpreted the relevant Guidelines in the same way. That year, however, the Commission changed its approach and "instructed courts to give each dose of LSD on a carrier medium a constructive or presumed weight of 0.4 milligrams." *Neal*, 516 U.S., at287 (citing USSG §2D1.1(c), n.(H) (Nov. 1995)). The Commission's change significantly lowered the Guidelines range applicable to most LSD offenses, but defendants remained subject to higher statutory minimum sentences based on the combined weight of the pure drug and its carrier medium. The defendant in *Neal* argued that the revised Guidelines and the statute should be interpreted consistently and that the "presumptive-weight method of the Guidelines should also control the mandatory minimum calculation." 516 U.S., at287. We rejected that argument, emphasizing that the Commission had not purported to interpret the statute and could not in any event overrule our decision in *Chapman*. See 516 U.S., at293–295.

If the Government's current position were correct, then the Guidelines involved in *Neal* would be in serious jeopardy. We have just recounted the reasons alleged to justify reading into the 1986 Act an implicit command to the Commission and sentencing courts to apply the 100-to-1 ratio to all quantities of crack cocaine. Those same reasons could be urged in support of an argument that the 1986 Act requires the Commission to include the full weight of the carrier medium in calculating the weight of LSD for Guidelines purposes. Yet our opinion in *Neal* never questioned the validity of the altered Guidelines. To the contrary, we stated: "Entrusted within its sphere to make policy judgments, the Commission may abandon its old methods in favor of what it has deemed a more desirable 'approach' to calculating LSD quantities." *Id.*, at295.[14] If the 1986 Act does not require the Commission to adhere to the Act's method for determining LSD weights, it does not require the Commission—or, after *Booker*, sentencing courts—to adhere to the 100-to-1 ratio for crack cocaine quantities other than those that trigger the statutory mandatory minimum sentences.

B

In addition to the 1986 Act, the Government relies on Congress' disapproval of the Guidelines amendment that the Sentencing Commission proposed in 1995. Congress "not only disapproved of the 1:1 ratio," the Government urges; it also made clear "that the 1986 Act required the Commission (and sentencing courts) to take drug quantities into account, and to do so in a manner that respects the 100:1 ratio." Brief for United States35.

It is true that Congress rejected the Commission's 1995 proposal to place a 1-to-1 ratio in the Guidelines, and that Congress also expressed the view that "the sentence imposed for trafficking in a quantity of crack cocaine should generally exceed the sentence imposed for trafficking in a like quantity of powder cocaine." Pub. L. 104–38, §2(a)(1)(A), 109 Stat. 334. But nothing in Congress' 1995 reaction to the Commission-proposed 1-to-1 ratio suggested that crack sentences must exceed powder sentences by a ratio of 100 to 1. To the contrary, Congress' 1995 action required the Commission to recommend a "revision of the drug quantity ratio of crack cocaine to powder cocaine." §2(a)(2), *id.*, at 335.

The Government emphasizes that Congress required the Commission to propose changes to the 100-to-1 ratio in *both* the 1986 Act and the Guidelines. This requirement, the Government contends, implicitly foreclosed any deviation from the 100-to-1 ratio in the Guidelines (or by sentencing courts) in the absence of a corresponding change in the statute. See Brief for United States 35–36. But it does not follow as the night follows the day that, by calling for recommendations to change the statute, Congress meant to bar any Guidelines alteration in advance of congressional action. The more likely reading is that Congress sought proposals to amend both the statute and the Guidelines because the Commission's criticisms of the 100-to-1 ratio, see Part II–B, *supra*, concerned the exorbitance of the crack/powder disparity in both contexts.

Moreover, as a result of the 2007 amendment, see *supra*, at 10–11,the Guidelines now advance a crack/powder ratio that varies (at different offense levels) between 25 to 1 and 80 to 1. See Amendments to the Sentencing Guidelines for United States Courts, 72 Fed. Reg. 28571–28572. Adopting the Government's analysis, the amended Guidelines would conflict with Congress' 1995 action, and with the 1986 Act, because the current Guidelines ratios deviate from the 100-to-1 statutory ratio. Congress, however, did not disapprove or modify the Commission-initiated 2007 amendment. Ordinarily, we resist reading congressional intent into congressional inaction. See *Bob Jones Univ.* v. *United States*, 461 U.S. 574, 600 (1983). But in this case, Congress failed to act on a proposed amendment to the Guidelines in a high-profile area in which it had previously exercised its disapproval authority under 28 U.S.C. §994(p). If nothing else, this tacit acceptance of the 2007 amendment undermines the Government's position, which is itself based on implications drawn from congressional silence.

C

Finally, the Government argues that if district courts are free to deviate from the Guidelines based on disagreements with the crack/powder ratio, unwarranted disparities of two kinds will ensue. See 18 U.S.C. §3553(a)(6) (sentencing courts shall consider "the need to avoid unwarranted sentence disparities"). First, because sentencing courts remain bound by the mandatory minimum sentences prescribed in the 1986 Act, deviations from the 100-to-1 ratio could result in sentencing "cliffs" around quantities that trigger the mandatory minimums. Brief for United States33 (internal quotation marks omitted). For example, a district court could grant a sizable downward variance to a defendant convicted of distributing 49 grams of crack but would be required by the statutory minimum to impose a much higher sentence on a defendant responsible for only 1 additional gram. Second, the Government maintains that, if district courts are permitted to vary from the Guidelines based on their disagreement with the crack/powder disparity, "defendants with identical real conduct will receive markedly different sentences, depending on nothing more than the particular judge drawn for sentencing." *Id.*, at40.

Neither of these arguments persuades us to hold the crack/powder ratio untouchable by sentencing courts. As to the first, the LSD Guidelines we approved in *Neal* create a similar risk of sentencing "cliffs." An offender who possesses LSD on a carrier medium weighing ten grams is subject to the ten-year mandatory minimum, see 21 U.S.C. §841(b)(1)(A)(v), but an offender whose carrier medium weighs slightly less may receive a considerably lower sentence based on the Guidelines' presumptive-weight methodology. Concerning the second disparity, it is unquestioned that uniformity remains an important goal of sentencing. As we explained in *Booker*, however, advisory Guidelines combined with appellate review for reasonableness and ongoing revision of the Guidelines in response to sentencing practices will help to "avoid excessive sentencing disparities." 543 U.S., at 264. These measures will not eliminate variations between district courts, but our opinion in *Booker* recognized that some departures from uniformity were a necessary cost of the remedy we adopted. See *id.*, at263 ("We cannot and do not claim that use of a 'reasonableness' standard will provide the uniformity that Congress originally sought to secure [through mandatory Guidelines]."). And as to crack cocaine sentences in particular, we note a congressional control on disparities: possible variations among district courts are constrained by the mandatory minimums Congress prescribed in the 1986 Act.[15]

Moreover, to the extent that the Government correctly identifies risks of "unwarranted sentence disparities" within the meaning of 18 U.S.C. §3353(a)(6), the proper solution is not to treat the crack/powder ratio as mandatory. Section 3553(a)(6) directs *district courts* to consider the need to avoid unwarranted disparities—along with other §3553(a) factors —when imposing sentences. See *Gall, ante,* at 11, n.6, 16. Under this instruction, district courts must take account of sentencing practices in other courts and the "cliffs" resulting from the statutory mandatory minimum sentences. To reach an appropriate sentence, these disparities must be weighed against the other §3553(a) factors and any unwarranted disparity created by the crack/powder ratio itself.

IV

While rendering the Sentencing Guidelines advisory, *United States* v. *Booker,* 543 U.S. 220, 245 (2005) , we have nevertheless preserved a key role for the Sentencing Commission. As explained in *Rita* and *Gall,* district courts must treat the Guidelines as the "starting point and the initial benchmark," *Gall* v. *United States, ante,* at 11. Congress established the Commission to formulate and constantly refine national sentencing standards. See *Rita* v. *United States,* 551 U.S. ___, ___–___ (2007) (slip op., at 9–11). Carrying out its charge, the Commission fills an important institutional role: It has the capacity courts lack to "base its determinations on empirical data and national experience, guided by a professional staff with appropriate expertise." *United States* v. *Pruitt,* 502 F.3d 1154, 1171 (CA10 2007) (McConnell, J., concurring); see *supra,* at 7.

We have accordingly recognized that, in the ordinary case, the Commission's recommendation of a sentencing range will "reflect a rough approximation of sentences that might achieve §3553(a)'s objectives." *Rita,* 551 U.S., at ___ (slip op., at 11). The sentencing judge, on the other hand, has "greater familiarity with … the individual case and the individual defendant before him than the Commission or the appeals court." *Id.,* at ___ (slip op., at 18). He is therefore "in a superior position to find facts and judge their import under §3353(a)" in each particular case. *Gall, ante,* at 13 (internal quotation marks omitted). In light of these discrete institutional strengths, a district court's decision to vary from the advisory Guidelines may attract greatest respect when the sentencing judge finds a particular case "outside the 'heartland' to which the Commission intends individual Guidelines to apply." *Rita,* 551 U.S., at ___ (slip op., at 12). On the other hand, while the Guidelines are no longer binding, closer review may be in order when the sentencing judge varies from the Guidelines based solely on the judge's view that the Guidelines range "fails properly to reflect §3553(a) considerations" even in a mine-run case. *Ibid.* Cf. Tr. of Oral Arg. in *Gall* v. *United States,* O. T. 2007, No. 06-7949, pp. 38–39.

The crack cocaine Guidelines, however, present no occasion for elaborative discussion of this matter because those Guidelines do not exemplify the Commission's exercise of its characteristic institutional role. In formulating Guidelines ranges for crack cocaine offenses, as we earlier noted, the Commission looked to the mandatory minimum sentences set in the 1986 Act, and did not take account of "empirical data and national experience." See *Pruitt,* 502 F.3d, at 1171 (McConnell, J., concurring). Indeed, the Commission itself has reported that the crack/powder disparity produces disproportionately harsh sanctions, *i.e.,* sentences for crack cocaine offenses "greater than necessary" in light of the purposes of sentencing set forth in §3553(a). See *supra,* at 8–9. Given all this, it would not be an abuse of discretion for a district court to conclude when sentencing a particular defendant that the crack/powder disparity yields a sentence "greater than necessary" to achieve §3553(a)'s purposes, even in a mine-run case.

V

Taking account of the foregoing discussion in appraising the District Court's disposition in this case, we conclude that the 180-month sentence imposed on Kimbrough should survive appellate inspection. The District Court began by properly calculating and considering the advisory Guidelines range. It then addressed the relevant §3553(a) factors. First, the court considered "the nature and circumstances" of the crime, see 18 U.S.C. §3553(a)(1), which was an unremarkable drug-trafficking offense. App.72–73 ("[T]his defendant and another defendant were caught sitting in a car with some crack cocaine and powder by two police officers—that's the sum and substance of it—[and they also had] a firearm."). Second, the court considered Kimbrough's "history and characteristics." §3553(a)(1). The court noted that Kimbrough had no prior felony convictions, that he had served in combat during Operation Desert Storm and received an honorable discharge from the Marine Corps, and that he had a steady history of employment.

Furthermore, the court alluded to the Sentencing Commission's reports criticizing the 100-to-1 ratio, cf. §3553(a)(5) (Supp. V), noting that the Commission "recognizes that crack cocaine has not caused the damage that the Justice Department alleges it has." App.72. Comparing the Guidelines range to the range that would have applied if Kimbrough had possessed an equal amount of powder, the court suggested that the 100-to-1 ratio itself created an unwarranted disparity within the meaning of §3553(a). Finally, the court did not purport to establish a ratio of its own. Rather, it appropriately framed its final determination in line with §3553(a)'s overarching instruction to "impose a sentence sufficient, but not greater than necessary" to accomplish the sentencing goals advanced in §3553(a)(2). See *supra,* at 12. Concluding that "the crack cocaine guidelines [drove] the offense level to a point higher than is necessary to do justice in this case," App. 72, the District Court thus rested its sentence on the appropriate considerations and "committed no procedural error," *Gall* v. *United States, ante,* at 17.

The ultimate question in Kimbrough's case is "whether the sentence was reasonable—*i.e.,* whether the District Judge abused his discretion in determining that the §3553(a) factors supported a sentence of [15 years] and justified a substantial deviation from the Guidelines range." *Ibid.* The sentence the District Court imposed on Kimbrough was 4.5 years below the bottom of the Guidelines range. But in determining that 15 years was the appropriate prison term, the District Court properly homed in on the particular circumstances of Kimbrough's case and accorded weight to the Sentencing Commission's consistent and emphatic position that the crack/powder disparity is at odds with §3553(a). See Part II–B, *supra.* Indeed, aside from its claim that the 100-to-1 ratio is mandatory, the Government did not attack the District Court's downward variance as unsupported by §3553(a).Giving due respect to the District Court's reasoned appraisal, a reviewing court could not rationally conclude that the 4.5-year sentence reduction Kimbrough received qualified as an abuse of discretion. See *Gall, ante,* at 20–21; *Rita* v. *United States,* 551 U.S. ___, ___ (2007) (slip op., at19–20).

* * *

For the reasons stated, the judgment of the United States Court of Appeals for the Fourth Circuit is reversed, and the case is remanded for further proceedings consistent with this opinion.

It is so ordered.

NOTES

[1] The statutory range for possession with intent to distribute more than 50 grams of crack is ten years to life. See 21 U.S.C. §841(b)(1)(A)(iii) (2000 ed. and Supp. V). The same range applies to the conspiracy offense. See §846 (2000 ed.). The statutory range for possession with intent to distribute powder cocaine is 0 to 20 years. See §841(b)(1)(C) (Supp. V). Finally, the statutory range for possession of a firearm in furtherance of a drug-trafficking offense is five years to life. See 18 U.S.C. §924(c)(1)(A)(i). The sentences for the three drug crimes may run concurrently, see §3584(a), but the sentence for the firearm offense must be consecutive, see §924(c)(1)(A).

[2] Kimbrough was sentenced in April 2005, three months after our decision in Booker v. United States, 543 U.S. 220 (2005), rendered the Guidelines advisory. The District Court employed the version of the Guidelines effective November 1, 2004.

[3] The prison sentence consisted of 120 months on each of the three drug counts, to be served concurrently, plus 60 months on the firearm count, to be served consecutively.

[4] This question has divided the Courts of Appeals. Compare United States v. Pickett, 475 F.3d 1347, 1355–1356 (CADC 2007) (District Court erred when it concluded that it had no discretion to consider the crack/powder disparity in imposing a sentence), and United States v. Gunter, 462 F.3d 237, 248–249 (CA3 2006) (same), with United States v. Leatch, 482 F.3d 790, 791 (CA5 2007) (per curiam) (sentencing court may not impose a sentence outside the Guidelines range based on its disagreement with the crack/powder disparity), United States v. Johnson, 474 F.3d 515, 522 (CA8 2007) (same), United States v. Castillo, 460 F.3d 337, 361 (CA2 2006) (same), United States v. Williams, 456 F.3d 1353, 1369 (CA11 2006) (same), United States v. Miller, 450 F.3d 270, 275–276 (CA7 2006) (same), United States v. Eura, 440 F.3d 625, 633–634 (CA4 2006) (same), and United States v. Pho, 433 F.3d 53, 62–63 (CA1 2006) (same).

[5] Injecting powder cocaine produces effects similar to smoking crack cocaine, but very few powder users inject the drug. See 1995 Report18.

[6] As explained in Part II–C, infra, the Sentencing Commission amended the Guidelines and reduced sentences for crack offenses effective November 1, 2007. Except as noted, this opinion refers to the 2004 Guidelines in effect at the time of Kimbrough's sentencing.

[7] Congress created the Sentencing Commission and charged it with promulgating the Guidelines in the Sentencing Reform Act of 1984, 98 Stat. 1987, 18 U.S.C. §3551 et seq. (2000 ed. and Supp. V), but the first version of the Guidelines did not become operative until November 1987, see 1995 Report ii–iv.

[8] An offense level of 12 results in a Guidelines range of 10 to 16 months for a first-time offender; an offense level of 38 results in a range of 235 to 293 months for the same offender. See USSG ch.5, pt.A, Sentencing Table.

[9] Subsection 994(p) requires the Commission to submit Guidelines amendments to Congress and

provides that such amendments become effective unless "modified or disapproved by Act of Congress."

[10] The amended Guidelines still produce sentencing ranges keyed to the mandatory minimums in the 1986 Act. Under the pre-2007 Guidelines, the 5- and 50-gram quantities that trigger the statutory minimums produced sentencing ranges that slightly exceeded those statutory minimums. Under the amended Guidelines, in contrast, the 5- and 50-gram quantities produce "base offense levels corresponding to guideline ranges that include the statutory mandatory minimum penalties." 2007 Report9.

[11] The Commission has not yet determined whether the amendment will be retroactive to cover defendants like Kimbrough. Even under the amendment, however, Kimbrough's Guidelines range would be 195 to 218 months—well above the 180-month sentence imposed by the District Court. See Amendments to the Sentencing Guidelines for United States Courts, 72 Fed. Reg. 28571–28572 (2007); USSG ch.5, pt.A, Sentencing Table.

[12] The remedial opinion also severed and excised the provision of the statute requiring de novo review of departures from the Guidelines, 18 U.S.C. §3742(e), because that provision depended on the Guidelines' mandatory status. Booker, 543 U.S., at 245.

[13] The Government concedes that a district court may vary from the 100-to-1 ratio if it does so "based on the individualized circumstance[s]" of a particular case. Brief for United States 45. But the Government maintains that the 100-to-1 ratio is binding in the sense that a court may not give any weight to its own view that the ratio itself is inconsistent with the §3553(a) factors.

[14] At oral argument, the Government sought to distinguish Neal v. United States, 516 U.S. 284 (1996), on the ground that the validity of the amended Guidelines was not before us in that case. See Tr. of Oral Arg.25. That is true, but only because the Government did not challenge the amendment. In fact, the Government's brief appeared to acknowledge that the Commission may legitimately deviate from the policies and methods embodied in the 1986 Act, even if the deviation produces some inconsistency. See Brief for United States in Neal v. United States, O.T. 1995, No. 94–9088, p.26 ("When the Commission's views about sentencing policy depart from those of Congress, it may become difficult to achieve entirely consistent sentencing, but that is a matter for Congress, not the courts, to address."). Moreover, our opinion in Neal assumed that the amendment was a legitimate exercise of the Commission's authority. See 516 U.S., at 294 (noting with apparent approval the Commission's position that "the Guidelines calculation is independent of the statutory calculation").

[15] The Sentencing Commission reports that roughly 70% of crack offenders are responsible for drug quantities that yield base offense levels at or only two levels above those that correspond to the statutory minimums. See 2007 Report 25.

NATIONAL FEDERATION OF INDEPENDENT BUSINESS, et al. v. KATHLEEN SEBELIUS, SECRETARY OF HEALTH AND HUMAN SERVICES, et al.

No. 11-393, June 28, 2012

ON WRIT OF CERTIORARI TO THE UNITED STATES COURT OF APPEALS FOR THE ELEVENTH CIRCUIT

Justice Ginsburg,with whom Justice Sotomayor joins, and with whom Justice Breyer and Justice Kagan join as to Parts I, II, III, and IV, concurring in part, concurring in the judgment in part, and dissenting in part.

I agree with The Chief Justice that the Anti-Injunction Act does not bar the Court's consideration of this case,and that the minimum coverage provision is a proper exercise of Congress' taxing power. I therefore join Parts I, II, and III–C of The Chief Justice's opinion.Unlike The Chief Justice, however, I would hold, alternatively, that the Commerce Clause authorizes Congress to enact the minimum coverage provision. I would also hold that the Spending Clause permits the Medicaid expansion exactly as Congress enacted it.

I

The provision of health care is today a concern of national dimension, just as the provision of old-age and survivors' benefits was in the 1930's. In the Social Secu-rity Act, Congress installed a federal system to provide monthly benefits to retired wage earners and, eventually, to their survivors. Beyond question, Congress could have adopted a similar scheme for health care. Congress chose, instead, to preserve a central role for private insurers and state governments. According to The Chief Justice, the Commerce Clause does not permit that preservation. This rigid reading of the Clause makes scant sense and is stunningly retrogressive.

Since 1937, our precedent has recognized Congress' large authority to set the Nation's course in the economic and social welfare realm. See *United States* v. *Darby*, 312 U. S. 100, 115 (1941) (overruling *Hammer* v. *Dagenhart* 247 U. S. 251 (1918), and recognizing that "regulations of commerce which do not infringe some constitutional prohibi-tion are within the plenary power conferred on Congress by the Commerce Clause"); *NLRB* v. *Jones & Laughlin Steel Corp.*, 301 U. S. 1, 37 (1937) ("[The commerce]power is plenary and may be exerted to protect interstate commerce no matter what the source of the dangers which threaten it." (internal quotation marks omitted)). The Chief Justice's crabbed reading of the Commerce Clause harks back to the era in which the Court routinely thwarted Congress' efforts to regulate the national economy inthe interest of those who labor to sustain it. See, *e.g.*, *Railroad Retirement Bd.* v. *Alton R. Co.*, 295 U. S. 330, 362, 368 (1935) (invalidating compulsory retirement and pension plan for employees of carriers subject to the Interstate Commerce Act; Court found law related essentially "to the social welfare of the worker, and therefore remote from any regulation of commerce as such"). It is a reading that should not have staying power.

A

In enacting the Patient Protection and Affordable Care Act (ACA), Congress comprehensively reformed thenational market for health-care products and services.By any measure, that market is immense. Collectively, Americans spent $2.5 trillion on health care in 2009, accounting for 17.6% of our Nation's economy. 42 U. S. C. §18091(2)(B) (2006 ed., Supp. IV). Within the next decade, it is anticipated, spending on health care will nearly double. *Ibid*.

The health-care market's size is not its only distinctive feature. Unlike the market for almost any other product or service, the market for medical care is one in which all individuals inevitably participate. Virtually every person residing in the United States, sooner or later, will visita doctor or other health-care professional. See Dept. of Health and Human Services, National Center for Health Statistics, Summary Health Statistics for U. S. Adults: National Health Interview Survey 2009, Ser. 10, No. 249, p. 124, Table 37 (Dec. 2010) (Over 99.5% of adults above 65 have visited a health-care professional.). Most people will do so repeatedly. See *id.*, at 115, Table 34 (In 2009 alone, 64% of adults made two or more visits to a doctor's office.).

When individuals make those visits, they face another reality of the current market for medical care: its high cost. In 2010, on average, an individual in the United States incurred over $7,000 in health-care expenses. Dept. of Health and Human Services, Centers for Medicare and Medicaid Services, Historic National Health Expenditure Data, National Health Expenditures: Se-lected Calendar Years 1960–2010 (Table 1). Over a lifetime, costs mount to hundreds of thousands of dollars. See Alemayahu & Warner, The Lifetime Distribution of Health Care Costs, in 39 Health Service

Research 627, 635 (June 2004). When a person requires nonroutine care, the cost will generally exceed what he or she can afford to pay. A single hospital stay, for instance, typically costs upwards of $10,000. See Dept. of Health and Human Services, Office of Health Policy, ASPE Research Brief: The Value of Health Insurance 5 (May 2011). Treatments for many serious, though not uncommon, conditions similarly cost a substantial sum. Brief for Economic Scholars as *Amici Curiae* in No. 11–398, p. 10 (citing a study indicating that, in 1998, the cost of treating a heart attack for the first 90 days exceeded $20,000, while the annual cost of treating certain cancers was more than $50,000).

Although every U. S. domiciliary will incur significant medical expenses during his or her lifetime, the time when care will be needed is often unpredictable. An accident, a heart attack, or a cancer diagnosis commonly occurs without warning. Inescapably, we are all at peril of needing medical care without a moment's notice. See, *e.g.,* Campbell, Down the Insurance Rabbit Hole, N. Y. Times, Apr. 5, 2012, p. A23 (telling of an uninsured 32-year-old woman who, healthy one day, became a quadriplegic the next due to an auto accident).

To manage the risks associated with medical care—its high cost, its unpredictability, and its inevitability—most people in the United States obtain health insurance. Many (approximately 170 million in 2009) are insured by private insurance companies. Others, including thoseover 65 and certain poor and disabled persons, rely on government-funded insurance programs, notably Medicare and Medicaid. Combined, private health insurers and State and Federal Governments finance almost 85% of the medical care administered to U. S. residents. See Congressional Budget Office, CBO's 2011 Long-Term Budget Outlook 37 (June 2011).

Not all U. S. residents, however, have health insurance. In 2009, approximately 50 million people were uninsured, either by choice or, more likely, because they could not afford private insurance and did not qualify for government aid. See Dept. of Commerce, Census Bureau, C.DeNavas-Walt, B. Proctor, & J. Smith, Income, Poverty, and Health Insurance Coverage in the United States: 2009, p. 23, Table 8 (Sept. 2010). As a group, uninsured individuals annually consume more than $100 billion in health-care services, nearly 5% of the Nation's total. Hidden Health Tax: Americans Pay a Premium 2 (2009), avail-able at http://www.familiesusa.org (all Internet mate-rial as visited June 25, 2012, and included in Clerk of Court's case file). Over 60% of those without insurance visit a doctor's office or emergency room in a given year. See Dept. of Health and Human Services, National Cen-ter for Health Statistics, Health—United States—2010, p. 282, Table 79 (Feb. 2011).

B

The large number of individuals without health insurance, Congress found, heavily burdens the national health-care market. See 42 U. S. C. §18091(2). As just noted, the cost of emergency care or treatment for a serious illness generally exceeds what an individual can afford to pay on her own. Unlike markets for most products, however, the inability to pay for care does not mean that an uninsured individual will receive no care. Federal and state law, as well as professional obligations and embedded social norms, require hospitals and physicians to provide care when it is most needed, regardless of the patient's ability to pay. See, *e.g.,* 42 U. S. C. §1395dd; Fla. Stat. §395.1041(3)(f) (2010); Tex. Health & Safety Code Ann. §§311.022(a) and (b) (West 2010); American Medical Association, Council on Ethical and Judicial Affairs,Code of Medical Ethics, Current Opinions: Opinion 8.11—Neglect of Patient, p. 70 (1998–1999 ed.).

As a consequence, medical-care providers deliver sig-nificant amounts of care to the uninsured for which the providers receive no payment. In 2008, for example, hospi-tals, physicians, and other health-care professionalsreceived no compensation for $43 billion worth of the $116 billion in care they administered to those without insurance. 42 U. S. C. §18091(2)(F) (2006 ed., Supp. IV).

Health-care providers do not absorb these bad debts. Instead, they raise their prices, passing along the costof uncompensated care to those who do pay reliably: the government and private insurance companies. In response, private insurers increase their premiums, shifting thecost of the elevated bills from providers onto those who carry insurance. The net result: Those with health insurance subsidize the medical care of those without it. As economists would describe what happens, the uninsured "free ride" on those who pay for health insurance.

The size of this subsidy is considerable. Congress found that the cost-shifting just described "increases family [insurance] premiums by on average over $1,000 a year." *Ibid.* Higher premiums, in turn, render health insurance less affordable, forcing more people to go without insurance and leading to further cost-shifting.

And it is hardly just the currently sick or injured among the uninsured who prompt elevation of the price of health care and health insurance. Insurance companies and health-care providers know that some percentage of healthy, uninsured people will suffer sickness or injury each year and will receive medical care despite their inability to pay. In anticipation of this uncompensated care, health-care companies raise their prices, and insurers their premiums. In other words, because any uninsured person may need medical care at any moment and because health-care companies must account for that risk, every uninsured person impacts the market price of medical care and medical insurance.

The failure of individuals to acquire insurance has other deleterious effects on the health-care market. Because those without insurance generally lack access to preventative care, they do not receive treatment for conditions—like hypertension and diabetes—that can be successfully and affordably treated if diagnosed early on. See Institute of Medicine, National Academies, Insuring America's Health: Principles and Recommendations 43 (2004). When sickness finally drives the uninsured to seek care, once treatable conditions have escalated into grave health problems, requiring more costly and extensive intervention. *Id.,* at 43–44. The extra time and resources providers spend serving the uninsured lessens the providers' ability to care for those who do have insurance. See Kliff, High Uninsured Rates Can Kill You—Even if You Have Coverage, Washington Post (May 7, 2012) (describing a study of California's health-care market which foundthat, when hospitals divert time and resources to provide uncompensated care, the quality of care the hospitals deliver to those with insurance drops significantly), availa-ble at http://www.washingtonpost.com/blogs/ezra-klein/post/high-uninsured-rates-can-kill-you-even-if-you-have-coverage/2012/05/07/gIQALNHN8T_print.html.

C

States cannot resolve the problem of the uninsured on their own. Like Social Security benefits, a universal health-care system, if adopted by an individual State, would be "bait to the needy and dependent elsewhere, encouraging them to migrate and seek a haven of repose." *Helvering* v. *Davis*, 301 U. S. 619, 644 (1937) . See also Brief for Commonwealth of Massachusetts as *Amicus Curiae* in No. 11–398, p. 15 (noting that, in 2009, Massachusetts' emergency rooms served thousands of uninsured, out-of-state residents). An influx of unhealthy individuals into a State with universal health care would result in increased spending on medical services. To cover the increased costs, a State would have to raise taxes, and private health-insurance companies would have to increase premiums. Higher taxes and increased insurance costs would, in turn, encourage businesses and healthy individuals to leave the State.

States that undertake health-care reforms on their own thus risk "placing themselves in a position of economic disadvantage as compared with neighbors or competitors." *Davis*, 301 U. S., at 644. See also Brief for Health Care for All, Inc., et al. as *Amici Curiae* in No. 11–398, p. 4 ("[O]ut-of-state residents continue to seek and receive millions of dollars in uncompensated care in Massachusetts hospitals, limiting the State's efforts to improve its health care system through the elimination of uncompensated care."). Facing that risk, individual States are unlikely to take the initiative in addressing the problem of the uninsured, even though solving that problem is in all States' best interests. Congress' intervention was needed to overcome this collective- action impasse.

D

Aware that a national solution was required, Congress could have taken over the health-insurance market by establishing a tax-and-spend federal program like Social Security. Such a program, commonly referred to as a single-payer system (where the sole payer is the Federal Government), would have left little, if any, room for private enterprise or the States. Instead of going this route, Congress enacted the ACA, a solution that retains a robust role for private insurers and state governments. To make its chosen approach work, however, Congress had to use some new tools, including a requirement that most individuals obtain private health insurance coverage. See 26 U. S. C. §5000A (2006 ed., Supp. IV) (the minimum coverage provision). As explained below, by employing these tools, Congress was able to achieve a practical, alto-gether reasonable, solution.

A central aim of the ACA is to reduce the number of uninsured U. S. residents. See 42 U. S. C. §18091(2)(C) and (I) (2006 ed., Supp. IV). The minimum coverage provision advances this objective by giving potential recipients of health care a financial incentive to acquire insurance. Per the minimum coverage provision, an individual must either obtain insurance or pay a toll constructed as a tax penalty. See 26 U. S. C. §5000A.

The minimum coverage provision serves a further purpose vital to Congress' plan to reduce the number of uninsured. Congress knew that encouraging individuals to purchase insurance would not suffice to solve the problem, because most of the uninsured are not uninsured by choice.[1] Of particular concern to Congress were people who, though desperately in need of insurance, often cannot acquire it: persons who suffer from preexisting medical conditions.

Before the ACA's enactment, private insurance companies took an applicant's medical history into account when setting insurance rates or deciding whether to insure an individual. Because individuals with preexisting med-ical conditions cost insurance companies significantly more than those without such conditions, insurers routinely re-fused to insure these individuals, charged them substantially higher premiums, or offered only limited coverage that did not include the preexisting illness. See Dept. of Health and Human Services, Coverage Denied: How the Current Health Insurance System Leaves Millions Behind 1 (2009) (Over the past three years, 12.6 million non-elderly adults were denied insurance coverage or charged higher premiums due to a preexisting condition.).

To ensure that individuals with medical histories have access to affordable insurance, Congress devised a three-part solution. First, Congress imposed a "guaranteed is-sue" requirement, which bars insurers from denyingcoverage to any person on account of that person's medical condition or history. See 42 U. S. C. §§300gg–1, 300gg–3, 300gg–4(a) (2006 ed., Supp. IV). Second, Congress required insurers to use "community rating" to price their insurance policies. See §300gg. Community rating, in effect, bars insurance companies from charging higher premiumsto those with preexisting conditions.

But these two provisions, Congress comprehended, could not work effectively unless individuals were given a powerful incentive to obtain insurance. See Hearings before the House Ways and Means Committee, 111th Cong., 1st Sess., 10, 13 (2009) (statement of Uwe Reinhardt) ("[I]m-position of *community-rated premiums* and *guaranteed* issue on a market of competing private health insurers will inexorably drive that market into extinction, unless these two features are coupled with . . . *a mandate on individual[s] to be insured.*" (emphasis in original)).

In the 1990's, several States—including New York, New Jersey, Washington, Kentucky, Maine, New Hampshire, and Vermont—enacted guaranteed-issue and community-rating laws without requiring universal acquisition of insurance coverage. The results were disastrous. "All seven states suffered from skyrocketing insurance pre-mium costs, reductions in individuals with coverage, and reductions in insurance products and providers." Brief for American

Association of People with Disabilities et al. as *Amici Curiae* in No. 11–398, p. 9 (hereinafter AAPD Brief). See also Brief for Governor of Washington Christine Gregoire as *Amicus Curiae* in No. 11–398, pp. 11–14 (describing the "death spiral" in the insurance market Washington experienced when the State passed a law requiring coverage for preexisting conditions).

Congress comprehended that guaranteed-issue and community-rating laws alone will not work. When insurance companies are required to insure the sick at affordable prices, individuals can wait until they become ill to buy insurance. Pretty soon, those in need of immediate medical care—*i.e.*, those who cost insurers the most—become the insurance companies' main customers. This "adverse selection" problem leaves insurers with two choices: They can either raise premiums dramatically to cover their ever-increasing costs or they can exit the market. In the seven States that tried guaranteed-issue and community-rating requirements without a minimum coverage provision, that is precisely what insurance companies did. See, *e.g.*, AAPD Brief 10 ("[In Maine,] [m]any insurance providers doubled their premiums in just three years or less."); *id.*, at 12 ("Like New York, Vermont saw substantial increases in premiums after its . . . insurance reform measures took effect in 1993."); Hall, An Evaluation of New York's Reform Law, 25 J. Health Pol. Pol'y & L. 71, 91–92 (2000) (Guaranteed-issue and community-rating laws resulted in a "dramatic exodus of indemnity insurers from New York's individual [insurance] market."); Brief for Barry Friedman et al. as *Amici Curiae* in No. 11–398, p. 17 ("In Kentucky, all but two insurers (one State-run) abandoned the State.").

Massachusetts, Congress was told, cracked the adverse selection problem. By requiring most residents to obtain insurance, see Mass. Gen. Laws, ch. 111M, §2 (West 2011), the Commonwealth ensured that insurers would not be left with only the sick as customers. As a result, federal lawmakers observed, Massachusetts succeeded where other States had failed. See Brief for Commonwealth of Massachusetts as *Amicus Curiae* in No. 11–398, p. 3 (noting that the Commonwealth's reforms reduced the number of uninsured residents to less than 2%, the lowest rate in the Nation, and cut the amount of uncompensated careby a third); 42 U. S. C. §18091(2)(D) (2006 ed., Supp. IV) (noting the success of Massachusetts' reforms).[2] In coupling the minimum coverage provision with guaranteed-issue and community-rating prescriptions, Congressfollowed Massachusetts' lead.

* * *

In sum, Congress passed the minimum coverage provision as a key component of the ACA to address an economic and social problem that has plagued the Nation for decades: the large number of U. S. residents who are unable or unwilling to obtain health insurance. Whatever one thinks of the policy decision Congress made, it was Congress' prerogative to make it. Reviewed with appropriate deference, the minimum coverage provision, allied to the guaranteed-issue and community-rating prescriptions, should survive measurement under the Commerce and Necessary and Proper Clauses.

II

A

The Commerce Clause, it is widely acknowledged, "was the Framers' response to the central problem that gave rise to the Constitution itself." *EEOC* v. *Wyoming*, 460 U. S. 226, n. 1 (1983) (Stevens, J., concurring) (citing sources). Under the Articles of Confederation, the Constitution's precursor, the regulation of commerce was left to the States. This scheme proved unworkable, because the individual States, understandably focused on their own economic interests, often failed to take actions critical to the success of the Nation as a whole. See Vices of the Political System of the United States, in James Madison: Writings 69, 71, ¶5 (J. Rakove ed. 1999) (As a result of the "want of concert in matters where common interest requires it," the "national dignity, interest, and reve-nue [have] suffered.").[3]

What was needed was a "national Government . . . armed with a positive & compleat authority in all cases where uniform measures are necessary." See Letter from James Madison to Edmund Randolph (Apr. 8, 1787), in 9 Papers of James Madison 368, 370 (R. Rutland ed. 1975). See also Letter from George Washington to James Madison (Nov. 30, 1785), in 8 *id.*, at 428, 429 ("We are either a United people, or we are not. If the former, let us, in all matters of general concern act as a nation, which ha[s] national objects to promote, and a national characterto support."). The Framers' solution was the Commerce Clause, which, as they perceived it, granted Congress the authority to enact economic legislation "in all Cases for the general Interests of the Union, and also in those Cases to which the States are separately incompetent." 2 Records of the Federal Convention of 1787, pp. 131–132, ¶8 (M. Farrand rev. 1966). See also *North American Co.* v. *SEC*, 327 U. S. 686, 705 (1946) ("[The commerce power]is an affirmative power commensurate with the national needs.").

The Framers understood that the "general Interests of the Union" would change over time, in ways they could not anticipate. Accordingly, they recognized that the Constitution was of necessity a "great outlin[e]," not a detailed blueprint, see *McCulloch* v. *Maryland*, 4 Wheat. 316, 407 (1819), and that its provisions included broad concepts, to be "explained by the context or by the facts of the case," Letter from James Madison to N. P. Trist (Dec. 1831), in 9 Writings of James Madison 471, 475 (G. Hunt ed. 1910). "Nothing . . . can be more fallacious," Alexander Hamilton emphasized, "than to infer the extent of any power, proper to be lodged in the national government, from . . . its immediate necessities. There ought to be a capacity to provide for future contingencies[,] as they may happen; and as these are illimitable in their nature, it is impossible safely to limit that capacity." The Federalist No. 34, pp. 205, 206 (John Harvard Library ed. 2009).

See also *McCulloch*, 4 Wheat., at 415 (The Necessary and Proper Clause is lodged "in a constitution[,] intended to endure for ages to come, and consequently, to be adapted to the various *crises* of human affairs.").

B

Consistent with the Framers' intent, we have repeatedly emphasized that Congress' authority under the Commerce Clause is dependent upon "practical" considerations, including "actual experience." *Jones & Laughlin Steel Corp.*, 301 U. S., at 41–42; see *Wickard* v. *Filburn*, 317 U. S. 111, 122 (1942) ; *United States* v. *Lopez*, 514 U. S. 549, 573 (1995) (Kennedy, J., concurring) (emphasizing "the Court's definitive commitment to the practical conception of the commerce power"). See also *North American Co.*, 327 U. S., at 705 ("Commerce itself is an intensely practical matter. To deal with it effectively, Congress must be able to act in terms of economic and financial realities." (citation omitted)). We afford Congress the leeway "to undertake to solve national problems directly and realistically." *American Power & Light Co.* v. *SEC*, 329 U. S. 90, 103 (1946) .

Until today, this Court's pragmatic approach to judging whether Congress validly exercised its commerce power was guided by two familiar principles. First, Congress has the power to regulate economic activities "that substantially affect interstate commerce." *Gonzales* v. *Raich*, 545 U. S. 1, 17 (2005) . This capacious power extends even to local activities that, viewed in the aggregate, have a substantial impact on interstate commerce. See *ibid.* See also *Wickard*, 317 U. S., at 125 ("[E]ven if appellee's activ-ity be local and though it may not be regarded as commerce, it may still, *whatever its nature*, be reached by Congress if it exerts a substantial economic effect on interstate commerce." (emphasis added)); *Jones & Laughlin Steel Corp.*, 301 U. S., at 37.

Second, we owe a large measure of respect to Congress when it frames and enacts economic and social legislation. See *Raich*, 545 U. S., at 17. See also *Pension Benefit Guaranty Corporation* v. *R. A. Gray & Co.*, 467 U. S. 717, 729 (1984) ("[S]trong deference [is] accorded legislation in the field of national economic policy."); *Hodel* v. *Indiana*, 452 U. S. 314, 326 (1981) ("This [C]ourt will certainly not substitute its judgment for that of Congress unless the relation of the subject to interstate commerce and its ef-fect upon it are clearly non-existent." (internal quotation marks omitted)). When appraising such legislation, we ask only (1) whether Congress had a "rational basis" for concluding that the regulated activity substantially affects interstate commerce, and (2) whether there is a "reasonable connection between the regulatory means selected and the asserted ends." *Id.*, at 323–324. See also *Raich*, 545 U. S., at 22; *Lopez*, 514 U. S., at 557; *Hodel* v. *Virginia Surface Mining & Reclamation Assn., Inc.*, 452 U. S. 264, 277 (1981) ; *Katzenbach* v. *McClung*, 379 U. S. 294, 303 (1964) ; *Heart of Atlanta Motel, Inc.* v. *United States*, 379 U. S. 241, 258 (1964) ; *United States* v. *Carolene Products Co.*, 304 U. S. 144–153 (1938). In answering these questions, we presume the statute under review is constitutional and may strike it down only on a "plain showing" that Congress acted irrationally. *United States* v. *Morrison*, 529 U. S. 598, 607 (2000) .

C

Straightforward application of these principles would require the Court to hold that the minimum coverage provision is proper Commerce Clause legislation. Beyond dispute, Congress had a rational basis for concluding that the uninsured, as a class, substantially affect interstate commerce. Those without insurance consume billions of dollars of health-care products and services each year. See *supra*, at 5. Those goods are produced, sold, and delivered largely by national and regional companies who routinely transact business across state lines. The uninsured also cross state lines to receive care. Some have medical emergencies while away from home. Others, when sick, go to a neighboring State that provides better care for those who have not prepaid for care. See *supra*, at 7–8.

Not only do those without insurance consume a large amount of health care each year; critically, as earlier explained, their inability to pay for a significant portion of that consumption drives up market prices, foists costs on other consumers, and reduces market efficiency and stability. See *supra*, at 5–7. Given these far-reaching effects on interstate commerce, the decision to forgo insurance is hardly inconsequential or equivalent to "doing nothing," *ante*, at 20; it is, instead, an economic decision Congress has the authority to address under the Commerce Clause. See *supra*, at 14–16. See also *Wickard*, 317 U. S., at 128 ("It is well established by decisions of this Court thatthe power to regulate commerce includes the power to regulate the prices at which commodities in that commerce are dealt in and *practices affecting such prices*." (emphasis added)).

The minimum coverage provision, furthermore, bears a "reasonable connection" to Congress' goal of protecting the health-care market from the disruption caused by individuals who fail to obtain insurance. By requiring those who do not carry insurance to pay a toll, the minimum coverage provision gives individuals a strong incentive to insure. This incentive, Congress had good reason to believe, would reduce the number of uninsured and, correspondingly, mitigate the adverse impact the uninsured have on the national health-care market.

Congress also acted reasonably in requiring uninsured individuals, whether sick or healthy, either to obtain insurance or to pay the specified penalty. As earlier observed, because every person is at risk of needing care at any moment, all those who lack insurance, regardless of their current health status, adversely affect the price of health care and health insurance. See *supra*, at 6–7. Moreover, an insurance-purchase requirement limited to those in need of immediate care simply could not work. Insurance companies would either charge these individuals prohibitively expensive premiums, or, if community-rating regulations were in place, close up shop. See *supra*, at 9–11. See also Brief for State of Maryland and 10 Other States et al. as *Amici Curiae* in No. 11–398, p. 28 (hereinafter Maryland Brief) ("No insurance regime can survive if people can opt out when the risk insured against is only a risk, but opt in when the risk materializes.").

"[W]here we find that the legislators . . . have a rational basis for finding a chosen regulatory scheme necessary to the protection of commerce, our investigation is at an end." *Katzenbach*, 379 U. S., at 303–304. Congress' enactment of the minimum coverage provision, which addresses a specific interstate problem in a practical, experience-informed manner, easily meets this criterion.

D

Rather than evaluating the constitutionality of the minimum coverage provision in the manner established by our precedents, The Chief Justice relies on a newly minted constitutional doctrine. The commerce power does not, The Chief Justice announces, permit Congressto "compe[l] individuals to become active in commerceby purchasing a product." *Ante,* at 20 (emphasis deleted).

1

A

The Chief Justice's novel constraint on Congress' commerce power gains no force from our precedent and for that reason alone warrants disapprobation. See *infra,* at 23–27. But even assuming, for the moment, that Congress lacks authority under the Commerce Clause to "compel individuals not engaged in commerce to purchase an unwanted product," *ante,* at 18, such a limitation would be inapplicable here. Everyone will, at some point, consume health-care products and services. See *supra,* at 3. Thus, if The Chief Justice is correct that an insurance-purchase requirement can be applied only to those who "actively" consume health care, the minimum coverage provision fits the bill.

The Chief Justice does not dispute that all U. S. residents participate in the market for health services over the course of their lives. See *ante,* at 16 ("Everyone will eventually need health care at a time and to an extent they cannot predict."). But, The Chief Justice insists, the uninsured cannot be considered active in the market for health care, because "[t]he proximity and degree of connection between the [uninsured today] and [their] subsequent commercial activity is too lacking." *Ante,*at 27.

This argument has multiple flaws. First, more than 60% of those without insurance visit a hospital or doctor's office each year. See *supra,* at 5. Nearly 90% will within five years.[4] An uninsured's consumption of health care is thus quite proximate: It is virtually certain to occur in the next five years and more likely than not to occur this year.

Equally evident, Congress has no way of separating those uninsured individuals who will need emergency medi-cal care today (surely their consumption of medical careis sufficiently imminent) from those who will not need medical services for years to come. No one knows when an emergency will occur, yet emergencies involving the uninsured arise daily. To capture individuals who unexpect-edly will obtain medical care in the very near future, then, Congress needed to include individuals who will not go to a doctor anytime soon. Congress, our decisions instruct, has authority to cast its net that wide. See *Perez* v. *United States*, 402 U. S. 146, 154 (1971) ("[W]hen it is necessary in order to prevent an evil to make the law embrace more than the precise thing to be prevented it may do so." (internal quotation marks omitted)).[5]

Second, it is Congress' role, not the Court's, to delineate the boundaries of the market the Legislature seeks to regulate. The Chief Justice defines the health-care mar-ket as including only those transactions that will occur either in the next instant or within some (unspecified) proximity to the next instant. But Congress could reasonably have viewed the market from a long-term perspective, encompassing all transactions virtually certain to occur over the next decade, see *supra,* at 19, not just those occurring here and now.

Third, contrary to The Chief Justice's contention, our precedent does indeed support "[t]he proposition that Congress may dictate the conduct of an individual today because of prophesied future activity." *Ante,* at 26. In *Wickard*, the Court upheld a penalty the Federal Government imposed on a farmer who grew more wheat than he was permitted to grow under the Agricultural Adjustment Act of 1938 (AAA). 317 U. S., at 114–115. He could notbe penalized, the farmer argued, as he was growing the wheat for home consumption, not for sale on the open market. *Id.,* at 119. The Court rejected this argument. *Id.,* at 127–129. Wheat intended for home consumption, the Court noted, "overhangs the market, and if induced by rising prices, tends to flow into the market and check price increases [intended by the AAA]." *Id.,* at 128.

Similar reasoning supported the Court's judgment in *Raich*, which upheld Congress' authority to regulate marijuana grown for personal use. 545 U. S., at 19. Homegrown marijuana substantially affects the interstate mar-ket for marijuana, we observed, for "the high demand in the interstate market will [likely] draw such marijuana into that market." *Ibid.*

Our decisions thus acknowledge Congress' authority, under the Commerce Clause, to direct the conduct of an individual today (the farmer in *Wickard*, stopped from growing excess wheat; the plaintiff in *Raich*, ordered to cease cultivating marijuana) because of a prophesied future transaction (the eventual sale of that wheat or marijuana in the interstate market). Congress' actions are even more rational in this case, where the future activity (the consumption of medical care) is certain to occur, the sole uncertainty being the time the activity will take place.

Maintaining that the uninsured are not active in the health-care market, The Chief Justice draws an analogy to the car market. An individual "is not 'active in the car market,' " The Chief Justice observes, simply because he or she may someday buy a car. *Ante,* at 25. The analogy is inapt. The inevitable yet unpredictable need for medical care and the guarantee that emergency care will be provided when required are conditions nonexistent in other markets. That is so of the market for cars, and of the market for broccoli as well. Although an individual *might* buy a car or a crown of broccoli one day, there is no certainty she will ever do so. And if she eventually wants a car or has a craving for broccoli, she will be obliged to pay at the counter before receiving the vehicle or nourishment. She will get no free ride or food, at the expense of another consumer forced to pay an inflated price. See *Thomas More Law Center* v. *Obama*, 651 F. 3d 529, 565 (CA6 2011) (Sutton, J., concurring in part) ("Regulating how citizens pay for what they already receive (health care), never quite know when they will need, and in the case of severe illnesses or emergencies generally will not be able to afford, has few (if any) parallels in modern life."). Upholding the minimum coverage provision on the ground that all are participants or will be participants in the health-care market would therefore carry no implication that Congress may justify under the Commerce Clause a mandate to buy other products and services.

Nor is it accurate to say that the minimum coverage provision "compel[s] individuals . . . to purchase an unwanted product," *ante,* at 18, or "suite of products," *post,* at 11, n. 2 (joint opinion of Scalia, Kennedy, Thomas, and Alito, JJ.). If unwanted today, medical service secured by insurance may be desperately needed tomorrow. Virtually everyone, I reiterate, consumes health care at some point in his or her life. See *supra,* at 3. Health insurance is a means of paying for this care, nothing more. In requiring individuals to obtain insurance, Congress is therefore not mandating the purchase of a discrete, unwanted product. Rather, Congress is merely defining the terms on which individuals pay for an interstate good they consume: Persons subject to the mandate must now pay for medical care in advance (instead of at the point of service) and through insurance (instead of out of pocket). Establishing payment terms for goods in or affecting interstate commerce is quintessential economic regulation well within Congress' domain. See, *e.g., United States* v. *Wrightwood Dairy Co.*, 315 U. S. 110, 118 (1942) . Cf. *post,* at 13 (joint opinion of Scalia, Kennedy, Thomas, and Alito, JJ.) (recognizing that "the Federal Government can prescribe [a commodity's] quality . . . and even [its price]").

The Chief Justice also calls the minimum coverage provision an illegitimate effort to make young, healthy individuals subsidize insurance premiums paid by the less hale and hardy. See *ante,* at 17, 25–26. This complaint, too, is spurious. Under the current health-care system, healthy persons who lack insurance receive a benefit for which they do not pay: They are assured that, if they need it, emergency medical care will be available, although they cannot afford it. See *supra,* at 5–6. Those who have insurance bear the cost of this guarantee. See *ibid.* By requiring the healthy uninsured to obtain insurance or pay a penalty structured as a tax, the minimum coverage provision ends the free ride these individuals currently enjoy.

In the fullness of time, moreover, today's young and healthy will become society's old and infirm. Viewed over a lifespan, the costs and benefits even out: The young who pay more than their fair share currently will pay less than their fair share when they become senior citizens. And even if, as undoubtedly will be the case, some individuals, over their lifespans, will pay more for health insurance than they receive in health services, they have little to complain about, for that is how insurance works. Every insured person receives protection against a catastrophic loss, even though only a subset of the covered class will ultimately need that protection.

B

In any event, The Chief Justice's limitation of the commerce power to the regulation of those actively engaged in commerce finds no home in the text of the Constitution or our decisions. Article I, §8, of the Constitution grants Congress the power "[t]o regulate Commerce . . . among the several States." Nothing in this language im-plies that Congress' commerce power is limited to regu-lating those actively engaged in commercial transactions. Indeed, as the D. C. Circuit observed, "[a]t the time the Constitution was [framed], to 'regulate' meant," among other things, "to require action." See *Seven-Sky* v. *Holder*, 661 F. 3d 1, 16 (2011).

Arguing to the contrary, The Chief Justice notes that "the Constitution gives Congress the power to 'coinMoney,' in addition to the power to 'regulate the Value thereof,' " and similarly "gives Congress the power to 'raise and support Armies' and to 'provide and maintain a Navy,' in addition to the power to 'make Rules for the Government and Regulation of the land and naval Forces.' " *Ante,* at 18–19 (citing Art. I, §8, cls. 5, 12–14). In separating the power to regulate from the power to bring the subject of the regulation into existence, The Chief Justice asserts, "[t]he language of the Constitution reflects the natural understanding that the power to regulate assumes there is already something to be regulated." *Ante,* at 19.

This argument is difficult to fathom. Requiring individuals to obtain insurance unquestionably regulates the inter-state health-insurance and health-care markets, both of them in existence well before the enactment of the ACA. See *Wickard*, 317 U. S., at 128 ("The stimulation of commerce is a use of the regulatory function quite as definitely as prohibitions or restrictions thereon."). Thus, the "something to be regulated" was surely there when Congress created the minimum coverage provision.[6]

Nor does our case law toe the activity versus inactiv-ity line. In *Wickard*, for example, we upheld the penalty imposed on a farmer who grew too much wheat, even though the regulation had the effect of compelling farmers to purchase wheat in the open market. *Id.,* at 127–129. "[F]orcing some farmers into the market to buy what they could provide for themselves" was, the Court held, a valid means of regulating commerce. *Id.,* at 128–129. In an-other context, this Court similarly upheld Congress' authority under the commerce power to compel an "inactive" land-holder to submit to an unwanted sale. See *Monongahela Nav. Co.* v. *United States*, 148 U. S. 312–337 (1893) ("[U]pon *the [great] power to regulate commerce*[,]" Congress has the authority to mandate the sale of real prop-erty to the Government, where the sale is essential to the improvement of a navigable waterway (emphasis added)); *Cherokee Nation* v. *Southern Kansas R. Co.*, 135 U. S. 641, 657–659 (1890) (similar reliance on the commerce power regarding mandated sale of private property for railroad construction).

In concluding that the Commerce Clause does not permit Congress to regulate commercial "inactivity," and there-fore does not allow Congress to adopt the practical solution it devised for the health-care problem, The Chief Justice views the Clause as a "technical legal conception," precisely what our case law tells us not to do. *Wickard*, 317 U. S., at 122 (internal quotation marks omitted). See also *supra,* at 14–16. This Court's former endeavors to impose categorical limits on the commerce power have not fared well. In several pre-New Deal cases, the Court attempted to cabin Congress' Commerce Clause authority by distinguishing "commerce" from activity once conceived to be noncommercial, notably, "production," "mining," and "manufacturing." See, *e.g., United States* v. *E. C. Knight Co.*, 156 U. S. 1, 12 (1895) ("Commerce succeeds to manufacture, and is not a part of it."); *Carter* v. *Carter Coal Co.*, 298 U. S. 238, 304 (1936) ("Mining brings the subject matter of commerce into existence. Commerce disposes of it."). The Court also sought to distinguish activities having a "direct" effect on interstate commerce, and for that reason, subject to federal regulation, from those having only an "indirect" effect, and therefore not amenable to federal control. See, *e.g., A. L. A. Schechter Poultry Corp.* v. *United States*, 295 U. S. 495, 548 (1935) ("[T]he dis-tinction between direct and indirect effects of intrastate transactions upon interstate commerce must be recognized as a fundamental one.").

These line-drawing exercises were untenable, and the Court long ago abandoned them. "[Q]uestions of the power of Congress [under the Commerce Clause]," we held in *Wickard*, "are not to be decided by reference to any for-mula which would give controlling force to nomenclature such as 'production' and 'indirect' and foreclose consideration of the actual effects of the activity in question upon interstate commerce." 317 U. S., at 120. See also *Morrison*, 529 U. S., at 641–644 (Souter, J., dissenting) (recounting the Court's "nearly disastrous experiment" with formalistic limits on Congress' commerce power). Failing to learn from this history, The Chief Justice plows ahead with his formalistic distinction between those who are "active in commerce," *ante,* at 20, and those who are not.

It is not hard to show the difficulty courts (and Congress) would encounter in distinguishing statutes that reg-ulate "activity" from those that regulate "inactivity." As Judge Easterbrook noted, "it is possible to restate most actions as corresponding inactions with the same effect." *Archie* v. *Racine*, 847 F. 2d 1211, 1213 (CA7 1988) (en banc). Take this case as an example. An individual who opts not to purchase insurance from a private insurer can be seen as actively selecting another form of insurance: self-insurance. See *Thomas More Law Center*, 651 F. 3d, at 561 (Sutton, J., concurring in part) ("No one is in-active when deciding how to pay for health care, as self-insurance and private insurance are two forms of action for addressing the same risk."). The minimum coverage provision could therefore be described as regulating activists in the self-insurance market.[7] *Wickard* is another example. Did the statute there at issue target activity (the growing of too much wheat) or inactivity (the farmer's failure to purchase wheat in the marketplace)? If anything, the Court's analysis suggested the latter. See 317 U. S., at 127–129.

At bottom, The Chief Justice's and the joint dissenters' "view that an individual cannot be subject to Commerce Clause regulation absent voluntary, affirmative acts that enter him or her into, or affect, the interstate mar-ket expresses a concern for individual liberty that [is] more redolent of Due Process Clause arguments." *Seven-Sky*, 661 F. 3d, at 19. See also *Troxel* v. *Granville*, 530 U. S. 57, 65 (2000) (plurality opinion) ("The [Due Process] Clause also includes a substantive component that provides heightened protection against government interference with certain fundamental rights and liberty interests." (internal quotation marks omitted)). Plaintiffs have abandoned any argument pinned to substantive due process, however, see 648 F. 3d 1235, 1291, n. 93 (CA11 2011), and now concede that the provisions here at issue do not offend the Due Process Clause.[8]

2

Underlying The Chief Justice's view that the Commerce Clause must be confined to the regulation of active participants in a commercial market is a fear that the commerce power would otherwise know no limits. See, *e.g., ante,* at 23 (Allowing Congress to compel an individ-ual not engaged in commerce to purchase a product would "permi[t] Congress to reach beyond the natural extentof its authority, everywhere extending the sphere of its activity, and drawing all power into its impetuous vortex." (internal quotation marks omitted)). The joint dissenters express a similar apprehension. See *post,* at 8 (If the minimum coverage provision is upheld under the commerce power then "the Commerce Clause becomes a font of unlimited power, . . . the hideous monster whose devouring jaws . . . spare neither sex nor age, nor high nor low, nor sacred nor profane." (internal quotation marks omitted)). This concern is unfounded.

First, The Chief Justice could certainly uphold the individual mandate without giving Congress *carte blanche* to enact any and all purchase mandates. As several times noted, the unique attributes of the health-care market render everyone active in that market and give rise to a significant free-riding problem that does not occur in other markets. See *supra,* at 3–7, 16–18, 21.

Nor would the commerce power be unbridled, absent The Chief Justice's "activity" limitation. Congress wouldremain unable to regulate noneconomic conduct that has only an attenuated effect on interstate commerce and is traditionally left to state law. See *Lopez*, 514 U. S., at567; *Morrison*, 529 U. S., at 617–619. In *Lopez*, forexample, the Court held that the Federal Government lacked power, under the Commerce Clause, to criminalize the possession of a gun in a local school zone. Possessinga gun near a school, the Court reasoned, "is in no sensean economic activity that might, through repetition elsewhere, substantially affect any sort of interstate commerce." 514 U. S., at 567; *ibid.* (noting that the Court would have "to pile inference upon inference" to conclude that gun possession has a substantial effect on commerce). Relying on similar logic, the Court concluded in *Morrison* that Congress could not regulate gender-motivated violence, which the Court deemed to have too "attenuated [an] effect upon interstate commerce." 529 U. S., at 615.

An individual's decision to self-insure, I have explained, is an economic act with the requisite connection to interstate commerce. See *supra,* at 16–17. Other choices individuals make are unlikely to fit the same or similar description. As an example of the type of regulation he fears, The Chief Justice cites a Government mandate to purchase green vegetables. *Ante,* at 22–23. One could call this concern "the broccoli horrible." Congress, The Chief Justice posits, might adopt such a mandate, reasoning that an individual's failure to eat a healthy diet, like the failure to purchase health insurance, imposes costs on others. See *ibid.*

Consider the chain of inferences the Court would have to accept to conclude that a vegetable-purchase mandate was likely to have a substantial effect on the health-care costs borne by lithe Americans. The Court would have to believe that individuals forced to buy vegetables would then eat them (instead of throwing or giving them away), would prepare the vegetables in a healthy way (steamed or raw, not deep-fried), would cut back on unhealthy foods, and would not allow other factors (such as lack of exercise or little sleep) to trump the improved diet.[9] Such "pil[ing of] inference upon inference" is just what the Court refused to do in *Lopez* and *Morrison.*

Other provisions of the Constitution also check congressional overreaching. A mandate to purchase a particu-lar product would be unconstitutional if, for example, the edict impermissibly abridged the freedom of speech, interfered with the free exercise of religion, or infringed on a liberty interest protected by the Due Process Clause.

Supplementing these legal restraints is a formidable check on congressional power: the democratic process. See *Raich,* 545 U. S., at 33; *Wickard,* 317 U. S., at 120 (repeating Chief Justice Marshall's "warning that effective restraints on [the commerce power's] exercise must proceed from political rather than judicial processes" (citing *Gibbons* v. *Ogden,* 9 Wheat. 1, 197 (1824)). As the controversy surrounding the passage of the Affordable Care Act attests, purchase mandates are likely to engender political resistance. This prospect is borne out by the behavior of state legislators. Despite their possession of unquestioned authority to impose mandates, state governments have rarely done so. See Hall, Commerce Clause Challenges to Health Care Reform, 159 U. Pa. L. Rev. 1825, 1838 (2011).

When contemplated in its extreme, almost any power looks dangerous. The commerce power, hypothetically, would enable Congress to prohibit the purchase and home production of all meat, fish, and dairy goods, effectively compelling Americans to eat only vegetables. Cf. *Raich,* 545 U. S., at 9; *Wickard,* 317 U. S., at 127–129. Yet no one would offer the "hypothetical and unreal possibilit[y]," *Pullman Co.* v. *Knott,* 235 U. S. 23, 26 (1914) , of a vegetarian state as a credible reason to deny Congress the authority ever to ban the possession and sale of goods. The Chief Justice accepts just such specious logic when he cites the broccoli horrible as a reason to deny Congressthe power to pass the individual mandate. Cf. R. Bork, The Tempting of America 169 (1990) ("Judges and lawyers live on the slippery slope of analogies; they are not supposed to ski it to the bottom."). But see, *e.g., post,* at 3 (joint opinion of Scalia, Kennedy, Thomas, and Alito, JJ.) (asserting, outlandishly, that if the minimum coverage provision is sustained, then Congress could make "breathing in and out the basis for federal prescription").

3

To bolster his argument that the minimum coverage provision is not valid Commerce Clause legislation, The Chief Justice emphasizes the provision's novelty. See *ante,* at 18 (asserting that "sometimes the most telling indication of [a] severe constitutional problem . . . is the lack of historical precedent for Congress's action" (internal quotation marks omitted)). While an insurance-purchase mandate may be novel, The Chief Justice's argument certainly is not. "[I]n almost every instance of the exer-cise of the [commerce] power differences are asserted from previous exercises of it and made a ground of attack." *Hoke* v. *United States*, 227 U. S. 308, 320 (1913) . See, *e.g.,* Brief for Petitioner in *Perez* v. *United States*, O. T. 1970, No. 600, p. 5 ("unprecedented exercise of power"); Sup-plemental Brief for Appellees in *Katzenbach* v. *McClung,* O. T. 1964, No. 543, p. 40 ("novel assertion of federal power"); Brief for Appellee in *Wickard* v. *Filburn,* O. T. 1941, No. 59, p. 6 ("complete departure"). For decades, the Court has declined to override legislation because of its novelty, and for good reason. As our national economy grows and changes, we have recognized, Congress must adapt to the changing "economic and financial realities." See *supra,* at 14–15. Hindering Congress' ability to do so is shortsighted; if history is any guide, today's constriction of the Commerce Clause will not endure. See *supra,* at 25–26.

III

A

For the reasons explained above, the minimum coverage provision is valid Commerce Clause legislation. See *supra,* Part II. When viewed as a component of the entire ACA, the provision's constitutionality becomes even plainer.

The Necessary and Proper Clause "empowers Congress to enact laws in effectuation of its [commerce] powe[r]that are not within its authority to enact in isolation." *Raich,* 545 U. S., at 39 (Scalia, J., concurring in judgment). Hence, "[a] complex regulatory program . . . can survive a Commerce Clause challenge without a showing that every single facet of the program is independently and directly related to a valid congressional goal." *Indiana,* 452 U. S., at 329, n. 17. "It is enough that the challenged provisions are an integral part of the regulatory program and that the regulatory scheme when considered as a whole satisfies this test." *Ibid.* (collecting cases). See also *Raich,*545 U. S., at 24–25 (A challenged statutory provisionfits within Congress' commerce authority if it is an "essential par[t] of a larger regulation of economic activity,"such that, in the absence of the provision, "the regulatory scheme could be undercut." (quoting *Lopez*, 514 U. S., at 561)); *Raich*, 545 U. S., at 37 (Scalia, J., concurring in judgment) ("Congress may regulate even noneconomic local activity if that regulation is a necessary part ofa more general regulation of interstate commerce. The relevant question is simply whether the means chosen are 'reasonably adapted' to the attainment of a legitimate end under the commerce power." (citation omitted)).

Recall that one of Congress' goals in enacting the Affordable Care Act was to eliminate the insurance industry's practice of charging higher prices or denying coverage to individuals with preexisting medical conditions. See *supra,* at 9–10. The commerce power allows Congress to ban this practice, a point no one disputes. See *United States* v. *South-Eastern Underwriters Assn.*, 322 U. S. 533–553 (1944) (Congress may regulate "the methods by which interstate insurance companies do business.").

Congress knew, however, that simply barring insurance companies from relying on an applicant's medical history would not work in practice. Without the individual mandate, Congress learned, guaranteed-issue and community-rating requirements would trigger an adverse-selection death-spiral in the health-insurance market: Insurance premiums would skyrocket, the number of uninsured would increase, and insurance companies would exit the market. See *supra,* at 10–11. When complemented by an insurance mandate, on the other hand, guaranteed issue and community rating would work as intended, increasing access to insurance and reducing uncompensated care. See *supra,* at 11–12. The minimum coverage provision is thus an "essential par[t] of a larger regulation of economic activity"; without the provision, "the regulatory scheme [w]ould be undercut." *Raich*, 545 U. S., at 24–25 (inter-nal quotation marks omitted). Put differently, the minimum coverage provision, together with the guaranteed-issue and community-rating requirements, is " 'reasonably adapted' to the attainment of a legitimate end underthe commerce power": the elimination of pricing andsales practices that take an applicant's medical history into account. See *id.*, at 37 (Scalia, J., concurring in judgment).

B

Asserting that the Necessary and Proper Clause does not authorize the minimum coverage provision, The Chief Justice focuses on the word "proper." A mandate to purchase health insurance is not "proper" legislation, The Chief Justice urges, because the command "undermine[s] the structure of government established by the Constitution." *Ante,* at 28. If long on rhetoric, The Chief Justice's argument is short on substance.

The Chief Justice cites only two cases in which this Court concluded that a federal statute impermissibly transgressed the Constitution's boundary between state and federal authority: *Printz* v. *United States*, 521 U. S. 898 (1997) , and *New York* v. *United States*, 505 U. S.144 (1992). See *ante,* at 29. The statutes at issue inboth cases, however, compelled *state officials* to act on the Federal Government's behalf. 521 U. S., at 925–933 (holding unconstitutional a statute obligating state law enforcement officers to implement a federal gun-control law); *New York*, 505 U. S., at 176–177 (striking down a statute requiring state legislators to pass regulations pursuant to Congress' instructions). "[Federal] laws conscripting state officers," the Court reasoned, "violate state sovereignty and are thus not in accord with the Constitution." *Printz*, 521 U. S., at 925, 935; *New York*, 505 U. S., at 176.

The minimum coverage provision, in contrast, acts "directly upon individuals, without employing the States as intermediaries." *New York*, 505 U. S., at 164. The provision is thus entirely consistent with the Consti-tution's design. See *Printz*, 521 U. S., at 920 ("[T]he Framers explicitly chose a Constitution that confers upon Congress the power to regulate individuals, not States." (internal quotation marks omitted)).

Lacking case law support for his holding, The Chief Justice nevertheless declares the minimum coverage provision not "proper" because it is less "narrow in scope" than other laws this Court has upheld under the Necessary and Proper Clause. *Ante,* at 29 (citing *United States* v. *Comstock*, 560 U. S. ___ (2010); *Sabri* v. *United States*, 541 U. S. 600 (2004) ; *Jinks* v. *Richland County*, 538 U. S. 456 (2003)). The Chief Justice's reliance on cases in which this Court has *affirmed* Congress' "broad authority to enact federal legislation" under the Necessary and Proper Clause, *Comstock*, 560 U. S., at ___ (slip op., at 5), is underwhelming.

Nor does The Chief Justice pause to explain *why* the power to direct either the purchase of health insurance or, alternatively, the payment of a penalty collectible as a tax is more far-reaching than other implied powers this Court has found meet under the Necessary and Proper Clause. These powers include the power to enact criminal laws, see, *e.g., United States* v. *Fox*, 95 U. S. 670, 672 (1878) ; the power to imprison, including civil imprisonment, see, *e.g., Comstock*, 560 U. S., at ___ (slip op., at 1); and the power to create a national bank, see *McCulloch*, 4 Wheat., at 425. See also *Jinks*, 538 U. S., at 463 (affirming Congress' power to alter the way a state law is applied in state court, where the alteration "promotes fair and efficient operation of the federal courts").[10]

In failing to explain why the individual mandate threatens our constitutional order, The Chief Justice disserves future courts. How is a judge to decide, when ruling on the constitutionality of a federal statute, whether Congress employed an "independent power," *ante,* at 28, or merely a "derivative" one, *ante,* at 29. Whether the power used is "substantive," *ante,* at 30, or just "incidental," *ante,* at 29? The instruction The Chief Justice, in effect, provides lower courts: You will know it when you see it.

It is more than exaggeration to suggest that the minimum coverage provision improperly intrudes on "essential attributes of state sovereignty." *Ibid.* (internal quotation marks omitted). First, the Affordable Care Act does not operate "in [an] are[a] such as criminal law enforcement or education where States historically have been sovereign." *Lopez,* 514 U. S., at 564. As evidenced by Medicare, Medicaid, the Employee Retirement Income Security Act of 1974 (ERISA), and the Health Insurance Portability and Accountability Act of 1996 (HIPAA), the Federal Government plays a lead role in the health-care sector, both as a direct payer and as a regulator.

Second, and perhaps most important, the minimum coverage provision, along with other provisions of the ACA, addresses the very sort of interstate problem that made the commerce power essential in our federal system. See *supra,* at 12–14. The crisis created by the large number of U. S. residents who lack health insurance is one of national dimension that States are "separately incompetent" to handle. See *supra,* at 7–8, 13. See also Maryland Brief 15–26 (describing "the impediments to effective state policymaking that flow from the interconnectedness of each state's healthcare economy" and emphasizing that "state-level reforms cannot fully address the problems associated with uncompensated care"). Far from trampling on States' sovereignty, the ACA attempts a federal solution for the very reason that the States, acting separately, cannot meet the need. Notably, the ACA serves the general welfare of the people of the United States while retaining a prominent role for the States. See *id.,* at 31–36 (explaining and illustrating how the ACA affords States wide latitude in implementing key elements of the Act's reforms).[11]

IV

In the early 20th century, this Court regularly struck down economic regulation enacted by the peoples' representatives in both the States and the Federal Government. See, *e.g., Carter Coal Co.,* 298 U. S., at 303–304, 309–310; *Dagenhart,* 247 U. S., at 276–277; *Lochner* v. *New York,* 198 U. S. 45, 64 (1905) . The Chief Justice's Commerce Clause opinion, and even more so the joint dissenters' reasoning, see *post,* at 4–16, bear a disquieting resemblance to those long-overruled decisions.

Ultimately, the Court upholds the individual mandate as a proper exercise of Congress' power to tax and spend "for the . . . general Welfare of the United States." Art. I, §8, cl. 1; *ante,* at 43–44. I concur in that determination, which makes The Chief Justice's Commerce Clause essay all the more puzzling. Why should The Chief Justice strive so mightily to hem in Congress' capacity to meet the new problems arising constantly in our ever-developing modern economy? I find no satisfying response to that question in his opinion.[12]

V

Through Medicaid, Congress has offered the States an opportunity to furnish health care to the poor with the aid of federal financing. To receive federal Medicaid funds, States must provide health benefits to specified categories of needy persons, including pregnant women, children, parents, and adults with disabilities. Guaranteed eligibility varies by category: for some it is tied to the federal poverty level (incomes up to 100% or 133%); for others it depends on criteria such as eligibility for designated state or federal assistance programs. The ACA enlarges the population of needy people States must cover to include adults under age 65 with incomes up to 133% of the fed-eral poverty level. The spending power conferred by the Constitution, the Court has never doubted, permits Congress to define the contours of programs financed with federal funds. See, *e.g., Pennhurst State School and Hospital* v. *Halderman,* 451 U. S. 1, 17 (1981) . And to expand coverage, Congress could have recalled the existing legislation, and replaced it with a new law making Medicaid as embracive of the poor as Congress chose.

The question posed by the 2010 Medicaid expansion, then, is essentially this: To cover a notably larger population, must Congress take the repeal/reenact route, or may it achieve the same result by amending existing law? The answer should be that Congress may expand by amendment the classes of needy persons entitled to Medicaid benefits. A ritualistic requirement that Congress repeal and reenact spending legislation in order to enlarge the population served by a federally funded program would advance no constitutional principle and would scarcely serve the interests of federalism. To the contrary, such a requirement would rigidify Congress' efforts to empower States by partnering with them in the implementation of federal programs.

Medicaid is a prototypical example of federal-state cooperation in serving the Nation's general welfare. Rather than authorizing a federal agency to administer a uni-form national health-care system for the poor, Con-gress offered States the opportunity to tailor Medicaid grants to their particular needs, so long as they remain within bounds set by federal law. In shaping Medicaid, Congress did not endeavor to fix permanently the terms participating states must meet; instead, Congress reserved the "right to alter, amend, or repeal" any provision of the Medicaid Act. 42 U. S. C. §1304. States, for their part, agreed to amend their own Medicaid plans consistent with changes from time to time made in the federal law. See 42 CFR §430.12(c)(i) (2011). And from 1965 to the present, States have regularly conformed to Congress' alterations of the Medicaid Act.

The Chief Justice acknowledges that Congress may "condition the receipt of [federal] funds on the States' complying with restrictions on the use of those funds," *ante,* at 50, but nevertheless concludes that the 2010 expansion is unduly coercive. His conclusion rests on three premises, each of them essential to his theory. First, the Medicaid expansion is, in The Chief Justice's view, a new grant program, not an addition to the Medicaid program existing before the ACA's enactment. Congress, The Chief Justice maintains, has threatened States with the loss of funds from an old program in an effort to get them to adopt a new one. Second, the expansion was unforeseeable by the States when they first signed on to Medicaid. Third, the threatened loss of funding is so large that the States have no real choice but to participate in the Medicaid expansion. The Chief Justice therefore—*for the first time ever*—finds an exercise of Congress' spending power unconstitutionally coercive.

Medicaid, as amended by the ACA, however, is not two spending programs; it is a single program with a constant aim—to enable poor persons to receive basic health care when they need it. Given past expansions, plus express statutory warning that Congress may change the requirements participating States must meet, there can be no tenable claim that the ACA fails for lack of notice. Moreover, States have no entitlement to receive any Medicaid funds; they enjoy only the opportunity to accept funds on Congress' terms. Future Congresses are not boundby their predecessors' dispositions; they have authority to spend federal revenue as they see fit. The Federal Government, therefore, is not, as The Chief Justice charges, threatening States with the loss of "existing" funds from one spending program in order to induce them to opt into another program. Congress is simply requiring States to do what States have long been required to do to receive Medicaid funding: comply with the conditions Congress prescribes for participation.

A majority of the Court, however, buys the argument that prospective withholding of funds formerly available exceeds Congress' spending power. Given that holding, I entirely agree with The Chief Justice as to the appropriate remedy. It is to bar the withholding found impermissible—not, as the joint dissenters would have it, to scrap the expansion altogether, see *post*, at 46–48. The dissenters' view that the ACA must fall in its entirety is a radical departure from the Court's normal course. When a constitutional infirmity mars a statute, the Court ordinarily removes the infirmity. It undertakes a salvage operation; it does not demolish the legislation. See, *e.g., Brockett* v. *Spokane Arcades, Inc.*, 472 U. S. 491, 504 (1985) (Court's normal course is to declare a statute invalid "to the extent that it reaches too far, but otherwise [to leave the statute] intact"). That course is plainly in order where, as in this case, Congress has expressly instructed courts to leave untouched every provision not found invalid. See 42 U. S. C. §1303. Because The Chief Justice finds the withholding—not the granting—of federal funds incom-patible with the Spending Clause, Congress' extension of Medicaid remains available to any State that affirms its willingness to participate.

A

Expansion has been characteristic of the Medicaid program. Akin to the ACA in 2010, the Medicaid Act as passed in 1965 augmented existing federal grant programs jointly administered with the States.[13] States were not required to participate in Medicaid. But if they did, the Federal Government paid at least half the costs. To qual-ify for these grants, States had to offer a minimum level of health coverage to beneficiaries of four federally funded, state-administered welfare programs: Aid to Families with Dependent Children; Old Age Assistance; Aid to the Blind; and Aid to the Permanently and Totally Disabled. See Social Security Amendments of 1965, §121(a), 79Stat. 343; *Schweiker* v. *Gray Panthers*, 453 U. S. 34, 37 (1981) . At their option, States could enroll additional "medically needy" individuals; these costs, too, were partially borne by the Federal Government at the same, at least 50%, rate. *Ibid.*

Since 1965, Congress has amended the Medicaid program on more than 50 occasions, sometimes quite sizably. Most relevant here, between 1988 and 1990, Congress required participating States to include among their beneficiaries pregnant women with family incomes up to 133% of the federal poverty level, children up to age 6 at the same income levels, and children ages 6 to 18 with family incomes up to 100% of the poverty level. See 42 U. S. C. §§1396a(a)(10)(A)(i), 1396a(*l*); Medicare Catastrophic Cov-erage Act of 1988, §302, 102Stat. 750; Omnibus Budget Reconciliation Act of 1989, §6401, 103Stat. 2258; Om-nibus Budget Reconciliation Act of 1990, §4601, 104Stat. 1388–166. These amendments added millions to the Medicaid-eligible population. Dubay & Kenney, Lessons from the Medicaid Expansions for Children and Pregnant Women 5 (Apr. 1997).

Between 1966 and 1990, annual federal Medicaid spending grew from $631.6 million to $42.6 billion; statespending rose to $31 billion over the same period. See Dept. of Health and Human Services, National Health Expenditures by Type of Service and Source of Funds: Calendar Years 1960 to 2010 (table).[14] And between 1990 and 2010, federal spending increased to $269.5 billion. *Ibid.* Enlargement of the population and services covered by Medicaid, in short, has been the trend.

Compared to past alterations, the ACA is notable for the extent to which the Federal Government will pick up the tab. Medicaid's 2010 expansion is financed largely by federal outlays. In 2014, federal funds will cover 100%of the costs for newly eligible beneficiaries; that rate will gradually decrease before settling at 90% in 2020. 42 U. S. C. §1396d(y) (2006 ed., Supp. IV). By comparison, federal contributions toward the care of beneficiaries eligible pre-ACA range from 50% to 83%, and averaged 57% between 2005 and 2008. §1396d(b) (2006 ed., Supp. IV); Dept. of Health and Human Services, Centers for Medicare and Medicaid Services, C. Truffer et al., 2010 Actuarial Report on the Financial Outlook for Medicaid, p. 20.

Nor will the expansion exorbitantly increase state Medicaid spending. The Congressional Budget Office (CBO) projects that States will spend 0.8% more than they would have, absent the ACA. See CBO, Spending & Enrollment Detail for CBO's March 2009 Baseline. But see *ante*, at 44–45 ("[T]he Act dramatically increases state obligations under Medicaid."); *post*, at 45 (joint opinion of Scalia, Kennedy, Thomas, and Alito, JJ.) ("[A]cceptance of the [ACA expansion] will impose very substantial costs on participating States."). Whatever the increase in state obligations after the ACA, it will pale in comparison to the increase in federal funding.[15]

Finally, any fair appraisal of Medicaid would require acknowledgment of the considerable autonomy States enjoy under the Act. Far from "conscript[ing] state agencies into the national bureaucratic army," *ante*, at 55 (citing *FERC* v. *Mississippi*, 456 U. S. 742, 775 (1982) (O'Connor, J., concurring in judgment in part and dissenting in part) (brackets in original and internal quotation marks omitted)), Medicaid "is designed to advance cooperative federalism." *Wisconsin Dept. of Health and Family Servs.* v. *Blumer,* 534 U. S. 473, 495 (2002) (citing *Harris* v. *McRae,* 448 U. S. 297, 308 (1980)). Subject to its basic requirements, the Medicaid Act empowers States to "select dramatically different levels of funding and coverage,alter and experiment with different financing and delivery modes, and opt to cover (or not to cover) a range of parti-cular procedures and therapies. States have leveraged this policy discretion to generate a myriad of dramatically different Medicaid programs over the past several decades." Ruger, Of Icebergs and Glaciers, 75 Law & Contemp. Probs. 215, 233 (2012) (footnote omitted). The ACA does not jettison this approach. States, as first-line administrators, will continue to guide the distribution of substantial resources among their needy populations.

The alternative to conditional federal spending, it bears emphasis, is not state autonomy but state marginalization.[16] In 1965, Congress elected to nationalize health coverage for seniors through Medicare. It could similarly have established Medicaid as an exclusively federal program. Instead, Congress gave the States the opportunity to partner in the program's administration and development. Absent from the nationalized model, of course, is the state-level policy discretion and experimentation that is Medicaid's hallmark; undoubtedly the interests of federalism are better served when States retain a meaning-ful role in the implementation of a program of suchimportance. See Caminker, State Sovereignty and Sub-ordinacy, 95 Colum. L. Rev. 1001, 1002–1003 (1995) (coopera-tive federalism can preserve "a significant role for state discretion in achieving specified federal goals, where the alternative is complete federal preemption of any state regulatory role"); Rose-Ackerman, Cooperative Federalism and Co-optation, 92 Yale L. J. 1344, 1346 (1983) ("Ifthe federal government begins to take full responsibility for social welfare spending and preempts the states, the result is likely to be weaker . . . state governments.").[17]

Although Congress "has no obligation to use its Spending Clause power to disburse funds to the States," *College Savings Bank* v. *Florida Prepaid Postsecondary Ed. Expense Bd.,* 527 U. S. 666, 686 (1999) , it has provided Medicaid grants notable for their generosity and flexibility. "[S]uch funds," we once observed, "are gifts," *id.,* at 686–687, and so they have remained through decades of expansion in their size and scope.

B

The Spending Clause authorizes Congress "to pay the Debts and provide for the . . . general Welfare of theUnited States." Art. I, §8, cl. 1. To ensure that federal funds granted to the States are spent "to 'provide for the . . . general Welfare' in the manner Congress intended," *ante,* at 46, Congress must of course have authority to impose limitations on the States' use of the federal dollars. This Court, time and again, has respected Congress' prescription of spending conditions, and has required States to abide by them. See, *e.g., Pennhurst,* 451 U. S., at 17 ("[O]ur cases have long recognized that Congress may fix the terms on which it shall disburse federal money to the States."). In particular, we have recognized Congress' prerogative to condition a State's receipt of Medicaid funding on compliance with the terms Congress set for participation in the program. See, *e.g., Harris,* 448 U. S., at 301 ("[O]nce a State elects to participate [in Medicaid], it must comply with the requirements of [the Medicaid Act]."); *Arkansas Dept. of Health and Human Servs.* v. *Ahlborn,* 547 U. S. 268, 275 (2006) ; *Frew* v. *Hawkins,* 540 U. S. 431, 433 (2004) ; *Atkins* v. *Rivera,* 477 U. S. 154–157 (1986).

Congress' authority to condition the use of federal funds is not confined to spending programs as first launched. The legislature may, and often does, amend the law, imposing new conditions grant recipients henceforth must meet in order to continue receiving funds. See *infra,* at 54 (describing *Bennett* v. *Kentucky Dept. of Ed.,* 470 U. S. 656–660 (1985) (enforcing restriction added five years after adoption of educational program)).

Yes, there are federalism-based limits on the use of Congress' conditional spending power. In the leading decision in this area, *South Dakota* v. *Dole,* 483 U. S. 203 (1987) , the Court identified four criteria. The conditions placed on federal grants to States must (a) promote the "general welfare," (b) "unambiguously" inform States what is demanded of them, (c) be germane "to the federal interest in particular national projects or programs," and (d) not "induce the States to engage in activities that would themselves be unconstitutional." *Id.,* at 207–208, 210 (internal quotation marks omitted).[18]

The Court in *Dole* mentioned, but did not adopt, a further limitation, one hypothetically raised a half-century earlier: In "some circumstances," Congress might be prohibited from offering a "financial inducement . . . so coercive as to pass the point at which 'pressure turns into compulsion.' " *Id.,* at 211 (quoting *Steward Machine Co.* v. *Davis,* 301 U. S. 548, 590 (1937)). Prior to today's decision, however, the Court has never ruled that the terms of any grant crossed the indistinct line between temptation and coercion.

Dole involved the National Minimum Drinking Age Act, 23 U. S. C. §158, enacted in 1984. That Act directed the Secretary of Transportation to withhold 5% of the federal highway funds otherwise payable to a State if the State permitted purchase of alcoholic beverages by personsless than 21 years old. Drinking age was not within the authority of Congress to regulate, South Dakota argued, because the Twenty-First Amendment gave the States exclusive power to control the manufacture, transportation, and consumption of alcoholic beverages. The small percentage of highway-construction funds South Dakota stood to lose by adhering to 19 as the age of eligibility to purchase 3.2% beer, however, was not enough to qualify as coercion, the Court concluded.

This case does not present the concerns that led the Court in *Dole* even to consider the prospect of coercion. In *Dole,* the condition—set 21 as the minimum drinking age—did not tell the States how to use funds Congress pro-vided for highway construction. Further, in view of the Twenty-First Amendment, it was an open question whether Congress could directly impose a national minimumdrinking age.

The ACA, in contrast, relates solely to the federally funded Medicaid program; if States choose not to comply, Congress has not threatened to withhold funds earmarked for any other program. Nor does the ACA use Medicaid funding to induce States to take action Congress itself could not undertake. The Federal Government undoubtedly could operate its own health-care program for poor persons, just as it operates Medicare for seniors' health care. See *supra,* at 44.

That is what makes this such a simple case, and the Court's decision so unsettling. Congress, aiming to assist the needy, has appropriated federal money to subsidize state health-insurance programs that meet federal standards. The principal standard the ACA sets is that the state program cover adults earning no more than 133% of the federal poverty line. Enforcing that prescription ensures that federal funds will be spent on health care for the poor in furtherance of Congress' present perception of the general welfare.

C

The Chief Justice asserts that the Medicaid expan-sion creates a "new health care program." *Ante,* at 54. Moreover, States could "hardly anticipate" that Congress would "transform [the program] so dramatically." *Ante,*at 55. Therefore, The Chief Justice maintains, Congress' threat to withhold "old" Medicaid funds based on a State's refusal to participate in the "new" program is a "threa[t] to terminate [an]other . . . independent gran[t]." *Ante,* at 50, 52–53. And because the threat to withhold a large amount of funds from one program "leaves the States with no real option but to acquiesce [in a newly created program]," The Chief Justice concludes, the Medicaid expansion is unconstitutionally coercive. *Ante,* at 52.

1

The starting premise on which The Chief Justice's coercion analysis rests is that the ACA did not really "extend" Medicaid; instead, Congress created an entirely new program to co-exist with the old. The Chief Justice calls the ACA new, but in truth, it simply reaches more of America's poor than Congress originally covered.

Medicaid was created to enable States to provide medical assistance to "needy persons." See S. Rep. No. 404, 89th Cong., 1st Sess., pt. 1, p. 9 (1965). See also §121(a), 79Stat. 343 (The purpose of Medicaid is to enable States "to furnish . . . medical assistance on behalf of [certain persons] whose income and resources are insufficient to meet the costs of necessary medical services."). By bringing health care within the reach of a larger population of Americans unable to afford it, the Medicaid expansion is an extension of that basic aim.

The Medicaid Act contains hundreds of provisions governing operation of the program, setting conditions ranging from "Limitation on payments to States for expend-itures attributable to taxes," 42 U. S. C. §1396a(t) (2006 ed.), to "Medical assistance to aliens not lawfully admitted for permanent residence," §1396b(v) (2006 ed. and Supp. IV). The Medicaid expansion leaves unchanged the vast majority of these provisions; it adds beneficiaries to the existing program and specifies the rate at which States will be reimbursed for services provided to the added bene-ficiaries. See ACA §§2001(a)(1), (3), 124Stat. 271–272. The ACA does not describe operational aspects of the program for these newly eligible persons; for that information, one must read the existing Medicaid Act. See 42 U. S. C. §§1396–1396v(b) (2006 ed. and Supp. IV).

Congress styled and clearly viewed the Medicaid expansion as an amendment to the Medicaid Act, not as a "new" health-care program. To the four categories of beneficiaries for whom coverage became mandatory in 1965, and the three mandatory classes added in the late 1980's, see *supra,* at 41–42, the ACA adds an eighth: individuals under 65 with incomes not exceeding 133% of the federal poverty level. The expansion is effectuated by §2001 of the ACA, aptly titled: "Medicaid Coverage for the Lowest Income Populations." 124Stat. 271. That section amends Title 42, Chapter 7, Subchapter XIX: Grants to States for Medical Assistance Programs. Commonly known as the Medicaid Act, Subchapter XIX filled some 278 pages in 2006. Section 2001 of the ACA would add approximately three pages.[19]

Congress has broad authority to construct or adjust spending programs to meet its contemporary understanding of "the general Welfare." *Helvering* v. *Davis,* 301 U. S. 619–641 (1937). Courts owe a large measure of respect to Congress' characterization of the grant programs it establishes. See *Steward Machine,* 301 U. S., at 594. Even if courts were inclined to second-guess Congress' conception of the character of its legislation, how would reviewing judges divine whether an Act of Congress, purporting to amend a law, is in reality not an amendment, but a new creation? At what point does an extension become so large that it "transforms" the basic law?

Endeavoring to show that Congress created a new program, The Chief Justice cites three aspects of the expansion. First, he asserts that, in covering those earning no more than 133% of the federal poverty line, the Medicaid expansion, unlike pre-ACA Medicaid, does not "care for the neediest among us." *Ante,* at 53. What makesthat so? Single adults earning no more than $14,856 per year—133% of the current federal poverty level—surely rank among the Nation's poor.

Second, according to The Chief Justice, "Congress mandated that newly eligible persons receive a level of coverage that is less comprehensive than the traditional Medicaid benefit package." *Ibid.* That less comprehensive benefit package, however, is not an innovation introduced by the ACA; since 2006, States have been free to use it for many of their Medicaid beneficiaries.[20] The level of benefits offered therefore does not set apart post-ACA Medicaid recipients from all those entitled to benefits pre-ACA.

Third, The Chief Justice correctly notes that the reimbursement rate for participating States is differ-ent regarding individuals who became Medicaid-eligible through the ACA. *Ibid.* But the rate differs only in its generosity to participating States. Under pre-ACA Medicaid, the Federal Government pays up to 83% of the costs of coverage for current enrollees, §1396d(b) (2006 ed. and Supp. IV); under the ACA, the federal contribution starts at 100% and will eventually settle at 90%, §1396d(y). Even if one agreed that a change of as little as 7 percentage points carries constitutional significance, is it not passing strange to suggest that the purported incursion on state sovereignty might have been averted, or at least mitigated, had Congress offered States *less* money to carry out the same obligations?

Consider also that Congress could have repealed Medicaid. See *supra,* at 38–39 (citing 42 U. S. C. §1304); Brief for Petitioners in No. 11–400, p. 41. Thereafter, Congress could have enacted Medicaid II, a new program combin-ing the pre-2010 coverage with the expanded coverage required by the ACA. By what right does a court stop Congress from building up without first tearing down?

2

The Chief Justice finds the Medicaid expansion vulnerable because it took participating States by surprise. *Ante,* at 54. "A State could hardly anticipate that Congres[s]" would endeavor to "transform [the Medicaid program] so dramatically," he states. *Ante,* at 54–55. For the notion that States must be able to foresee, when they sign up, alterations Congress might make later on, The Chief Justice cites only one case: *Pennhurst State School and Hospital* v. *Halderman*, 451 U. S. 1.

In *Pennhurst*, residents of a state-run, federally funded institution for the mentally disabled complained of abusive treatment and inhumane conditions in alleged violation of the Developmentally Disabled Assistance and Bill of Rights Act. 451 U. S., at 5–6. We held that the State was not answerable in damages for violating conditionsit did not "voluntarily and knowingly accep[t]." *Id.,* at 17, 27. Inspecting the statutory language and legislative his-tory, we found that the Act did not "unambiguously" impose the requirement on which the plaintiffs relied: that they receive appropriate treatment in the least restrictive environment. *Id.,* at 17–18. Satisfied that Congress had not clearly conditioned the States' receipt of federal funds on the States' provision of such treatment, we declined to read such a requirement into the Act. Congress' spending power, we concluded, "does not include surprising participating States with postacceptance or 'retroactive' conditions." *Id.,* at 24–25.

Pennhurst thus instructs that "if Congress intends to impose a condition on the grant of federal moneys, it must do so unambiguously." *Ante,* at 53 (quoting *Pennhurst*, 451 U. S., at 17). That requirement is met in this case. Section 2001 does not take effect until 2014. The ACA makes perfectly clear what will be required of States that accept Medicaid funding after that date: They must extend eligibility to adults with incomes no more than 133% of the federal poverty line. See 42 U. S. C. §1396a(a)(10)(A) (i)(VIII) (2006 ed. and Supp. IV).

The Chief Justice appears to find in *Pennhurst* a requirement that, when spending legislation is first passed, or when States first enlist in the federal program, Congress must provide clear notice of conditions it might later impose. If I understand his point correctly, it was incumbent on Congress, in 1965, to warn the States clearly of the size and shape potential changes to Medicaid might take. And absent such notice, sizable changes could not be made mandatory. Our decisions do not support such a requirement.[21]

In *Bennett* v. *New Jersey*, 470 U. S. 632 (1985) , the Secretary of Education sought to recoup Title I funds[22] based on the State's noncompliance, from 1970 to 1972, with a 1978 amendment to Title I. Relying on *Pennhurst*, we rejected the Secretary's attempt to recover funds based on the States' alleged violation of a rule that did not exist when the State accepted and spent the funds. See 470 U. S., at 640 ("New Jersey[,] when it applied for and received Title I funds for the years 1970–1972[,] had no basis to believe that the propriety of the expenditures would be judged by any standards other than the ones in effect *at the time*." (citing *Pennhurst,* 451 U. S., at 17, 24–25; emphasis added)).

When amendment of an existing grant program has no such retroactive effect, however, we have upheld Congress' instruction. In *Bennett* v. *Kentucky Dept. of Ed.*, 470 U. S. 656 (1985) , the Secretary sued to recapture Title I funds based on the Commonwealth's 1974 violation of a spending condition Congress added to Title I in 1970. Rejecting Kentucky's argument pinned to *Pennhurst*, we held that the Commonwealth suffered no surprise after accepting the federal funds. Kentucky was therefore obliged to re-turn the money. 470 U. S., at 665–666, 673–674. The conditions imposed were to be assessed as of 1974, in light of "the legal requirements in place when the grants were made," *id.,* at 670, not as of 1965, when Title I was originally enacted.

As these decisions show, *Pennhurst*'s rule demands that conditions on federal funds be unambiguously clear at the time a State receives and uses the money—not at the time, perhaps years earlier, when Congress passed the law establishing the program. See also *Dole*, 483 U. S., at 208 (finding *Pennhurst* satisfied based on the clarity of the Federal Aid Highway Act as amended in 1984, without looking back to 1956, the year of the Act's adoption).

In any event, from the start, the Medicaid Act put States on notice that the program could be changed: "The right to alter, amend, or repeal any provision of [Medicaid]," the statute has read since 1965, "is hereby reserved to the Congress." 42 U. S. C. §1304. The "effect of these few simple words" has long been settled. See *National Railroad Passenger Corporation* v. *Atchison, T. & S. F. R. Co.*, 470 U. S. 451–468, n. 22 (1985) (citing *Sinking Fund Cases*, 99 U. S. 700, 720 (1879)). By reserving the right to "alter, amend, [or] repeal" a spending program, Congress "has given special notice of its intention to retain . . . full and complete power to make such alterations and amendments . . . as come within the just scope of legislative power." *Id.,* at 720.

Our decision in *Bowen* v. *Public Agencies Opposed to Social Security Entrapment*, 477 U. S. 41–52 (1986), is guiding here. As enacted in 1935, the Social Security Act did not cover state employees. *Id.,* at 44. In response to pressure from States that wanted coverage for their employees, Congress, in 1950, amended the Act to allow States to opt into the program. *Id.,* at 45. The statutory provision giving States this option expressly permitted them to withdraw from the program. *Ibid.*

Beginning in the late 1970's, States increasingly exercised the option to withdraw. *Id.,* at 46. Concerned that withdrawals were threatening the integrity of Social Security, Congress repealed the termination provision. Congress thereby changed Social Security from a program voluntary for the States to one from which they could not escape. *Id.,* at 48. California objected, arguing that the change impermissibly deprived it of a right to withdraw from Social Security. *Id.,* at 49–50. We unanimously rejected California's argument. *Id.,* at 51–53. By including in the Act "a clause expressly reserving to it '[t]he right to alter, amend, or repeal any provision' of the Act," we held, Congress put States on notice that the Act "created no contractual rights." *Id.,* at 51–52. The States therefore had no law-based ground on which to complain about the amendment, despite the significant character of the change.

The Chief Justice nevertheless would rewrite §1304 to countenance only the "right to alter *somewhat,*" or "amend, *but not too much.*" Congress, however, did not so qualify §1304. Indeed, Congress retained discretion to "repeal" Medicaid, wiping it out entirely. Cf. *Delta Air Lines, Inc.* v. *August,* 450 U. S. 346, 368 (1981) (Rehnquist, J., dissenting) (invoking "the common-sense maxim that the greater includes the lesser"). As *Bowen* indicates, no State could reasonably have read §1304 as reserving to Congress authority to make adjustments only if modestly sized.

In fact, no State proceeded on that understanding. In com-pliance with Medicaid regulations, each State expressly undertook to abide by future Medicaid changes. See 42 CFR §430.12(c)(1) (2011) ("The [state Medicaid] plan must provide that it will be amended whenever necessary to reflect . . . [c]hanges in Federal law, regulations, policy interpretations, or court decisions."). Whenever a State notifies the Federal Government of a change in its own Medicaid program, the State certifies both that it knows the federally set terms of participation may change, and that it will abide by those changes as a condition of continued participation. See, *e.g.,* Florida Agency for Health Care Admin., State Plan Under Title XIX of the Social Security Act Medical Assistance Program §7.1, p. 86 (Oct. 6, 1992).

The Chief Justice insists that the most recent expansion, in contrast to its predecessors, "accomplishes a shift in kind, not merely degree." *Ante,* at 53. But why was Medicaid altered only in degree, not in kind, when Congress required States to cover millions of children and pregnant women? See *supra,* at 41–42. Congress did not "merely alte[r] and expan[d] the boundaries of" the Aid to Families with Dependent Children program. But see *ante,* at 53–55. Rather, Congress required participating States to provide coverage tied to the federal poverty level (as it later did in the ACA), rather than to the AFDC program. See Brief for National Health Law Program et al. as *Amici Curiae* 16–18. In short, given §1304, this Court's construction of §1304's language in *Bowen,* and the enlargement of Medicaid in the years since 1965,[23] a State would be hard put to complain that it lacked fair notice when, in 2010, Congress altered Medicaid to embrace a larger portion of the Nation's poor.

3

The Chief Justice ultimately asks whether "the financial inducement offered by Congress . . . pass[ed] the point at which pressure turns into compulsion." *Ante,* at 50 (internal quotation marks omitted). The financial inducement Congress employed here, he concludes, crosses that threshold: The threatened withholding of "existing Medicaid funds" is "a gun to the head" that forces States to acquiesce. *Ante,* at 50–51 (citing 42 U. S. C. §1396c).[24]

The Chief Justice sees no need to "fix the outermost line," *Steward Machine,* 301 U. S., at 591, "where persuasion gives way to coercion," *ante,* at 55. Neither do the joint dissenters. See *post,* at 36, 38.[25] Notably, the decision on which they rely, *Steward Machine,* found the statute at issue inside the line, "wherever the line may be." 301 U. S., at 591.

When future Spending Clause challenges arrive, as they likely will in the wake of today's decision, how will litigants and judges assess whether "a State has a legitimate choice whether to accept the federal conditions in exchange for federal funds"? *Ante,* at 48. Are courts to measure the number of dollars the Federal Government might withhold for noncompliance? The portion of the State's budget at stake? And which State's—or States'—budget is determinative: the lead plaintiff, all challenging States (26 in this case, many with quite different fiscal situations), or some national median? Does it matter that Florida, unlike most States, imposes no state income tax, and therefore might be able to replace foregone federal funds with new state revenue?[26] Or that the coercion state officials in fact fear is punishment at the ballot box for turning down a politically popular federal grant?

The coercion inquiry, therefore, appears to involve polit-ical judgments that defy judicial calculation. See *Baker* v. *Carr,* 369 U. S. 186, 217 (1962) . Even commentators sympathetic to robust enforcement of *Dole*'s limitations, see *supra,* at 46, have concluded that conceptions of "impermissible coercion" premised on States' perceived inability to decline federal funds "are just too amorphous to be judicially administrable." Baker & Berman, Getting off the *Dole,* 78 Ind. L. J. 459, 521, 522, n. 307 (2003) (citing, *e.g.,* Scalia, The Rule of Law as a Law of Rules, 56 U. Chi. L. Rev. 1175 (1989)).

At bottom, my colleagues' position is that the States' reliance on federal funds limits Congress' authority to alter its spending programs. This gets things backwards: Congress, not the States, is tasked with spending federal money in service of the general welfare. And each successive Congress is empowered to appropriate funds as it sees fit. When the 110th Congress reached a conclusion about Medicaid funds that differed from its predecessors' view, it abridged no State's right to "existing," or "pre-existing," funds. But see *ante,* at 51–52; *post,* at 47–48 (joint opinion of Scalia, Kennedy, Thomas, and Alito, JJ.). For, in fact, there are no such funds. There is only money States *anticipate* receiving from future Congresses.

D

Congress has delegated to the Secretary of Health and Human Services the authority to withhold, in whole orin part, federal Medicaid funds from States that fail to comply with the Medicaid Act as originally composed and as subsequently amended. 42 U. S. C. §1396c.[27] The Chief Justice, however, holds that the Constitution precludes the Secretary from withholding "existing" Medicaid funds based on States' refusal to comply with the expanded Medi-caid program. *Ante,* at 55. For the foregoing reasons, I disagree that any such withholding would violate the Spending Clause. Accordingly, I would affirm the decision of the Court of Appeals for the Eleventh Circuit in this regard.

But in view of The Chief Justice's disposition, I agree with him that the Medicaid Act's severability clause determines the appropriate remedy. That clause provides that "[i]f any provision of [the Medicaid Act], or the application thereof to any person or circumstance, is held in-valid, the remainder of the chapter, and the application of such provision to other persons or circumstances shall not be affected thereby." 42 U. S. C. §1303.

The Court does not strike down any provision of the ACA. It prohibits only the "application" of the Secretary's authority to withhold Medicaid funds from States that decline to conform their Medicaid plans to the ACA's requirements. Thus the ACA's authorization of funds to finance the expansion remains intact, and the Secretary's authority to withhold funds for reasons other than noncompliance with the expansion remains unaffected.

Even absent §1303's command, we would have no warrant to invalidate the Medicaid expansion, contra *post,* at 46–48 (joint opinion of Scalia, Kennedy, Thomas, and Alito, JJ.), not to mention the entire ACA, *post,* at 49–64 (same). For when a court confronts an unconstitutional statute, its endeavor must be to conserve, not destroy,the legislature's dominant objective. See, *e.g., Ayotte* v. *Planned Parenthood of Northern New Eng.,* 546 U. S. 320–330 (2006). In this case, that objective was to increase access to health care for the poor by increasing the States' access to federal funds. The Chief Justice is undoubtedly right to conclude that Congress may offer States funds "to expand the availability of health care, and requir[e] that States accepting such funds comply with the conditions on their use." *Ante,* at 55. I therefore concurin the judgment with respect to Part IV–B of The Chief Justice's opinion.

* * *

For the reasons stated, I agree with The Chief Justice that, as to the validity of the minimum coverage provi-sion, the judgment of the Court of Appeals for the Eleventh Circuit should be reversed. In my view, the provision en-counters no constitutional obstruction. Further, I would uphold the Eleventh Circuit's decision that the Medicaid expansion is within Congress' spending power.

NOTES

[1] According to one study conducted by the National Center for Health Statistics, the high cost of insurance is the most common reason why individuals lack coverage, followed by loss of one's job, an employer's unwillingness to offer insurance or an insurers' unwillingness to cover those with preexisting medical conditions, and loss of Medicaid coverage. See Dept. of Health and Human Services, National Center for Health Statistics, Summary Health Statistics for the U. S. Population: National Health Interview Survey—2009, Ser. 10, No. 248, p. 71, Table 25 (Dec. 2010). "[D]id not want or need coverage" received too few re-sponses to warrant its own category. See *ibid.,* n. 2.

[2] Despite its success, Massachusetts' medical-care providers still administer substantial amounts of uncompensated care, much of that to uninsured patients from out-of-state. See *supra,* at 7–8.

[3] Alexander Hamilton described the problem this way: "[Often] it would be beneficial to all the states to encourage, or suppress[,] a particular branch of trade, while it would be detrimental . . . to attempt it without the concurrence of the rest." The Continentalist No. V, in 3 Papers of Alexander Hamilton 75, 78 (H. Syrett ed. 1962). Because the concurrence of all States was exceedingly difficult to obtain, Hamilton observed, "the experiment would probably be left untried." *Ibid.*

[4] See Dept. of Health and Human Services, National Center for Health Statistics, Summary Health Statistics for U. S. Adults: National Health Interview Survey 2009, Ser. 10, No. 249, p. 124, Table 37 (Dec. 2010).

[5] Echoing The Chief Justice, the joint dissenters urge that the minimum coverage provision impermissibly regulates young people who "have no intention of purchasing [medical care]" and are too far "removed from the [health-care] market." See *post,* at 8, 11. This criticism ignores the reality

that a healthy young person may be a day away from needing health care. See *supra,* at 4. A victim of an accident or unforeseen illness will consume extensive medical care immediately, though scarcely expecting to do so.

[6] The Chief Justice's reliance on the quoted passages of the Constitution, see *ante,* at 18–19, is also dubious on other grounds. The power to "regulate the Value" of the national currency presumably includes the power to increase the currency's worth—*i.e.,* to create value where none previously existed. And if the power to "[r]egulat[e] . . . the land and naval Forces" presupposes "there is already [in existence] something to be regulated," *i.e.,* an Army and a Navy, does Congress lack authority to create an Air Force?

[7] The Chief Justice's characterization of individuals who choose not to purchase private insurance as "doing nothing," *ante,* at 20, is simi-larly questionable. A person who self-insures opts against prepayment for a product the person will in time consume. When aggregated, exercise of that option has a substantial impact on the health-care market. See *supra,* at 5–7, 16–17.

[8] Some adherents to the joint dissent have questioned the existence of substantive due process rights. See *McDonald* v. *Chicago,* 561 U. S. ___, ___ (2010) (Thomas, J., concurring) (slip op., at 7) (The notion that the Due Process Clause "could define the substance of th[e] righ[t to liberty] strains credulity."); *Albright* v. *Oliver,* 510 U. S. 266, 275 (1994) (Scalia, J., concurring) ("I reject the proposition that the Due Process Clause guarantees certain (unspecified) liberties[.]"). Given these Justices' reluctance to interpret the Due Process Clause as guaranteeing liberty interests, their willingness to plant such protections in the Commerce Clause is striking.

[9] The failure to purchase vegetables in The Chief Justice's hypothetical, then, is *not* what leads to higher health-care costs for others; rather, it is the failure of individuals to maintain a healthy diet, and the resulting obesity, that creates the cost-shifting problem. See *ante,* at 22–23. Requiring individuals to purchase vegetables is thusseveral steps removed from solving the problem. The failure to obtain health insurance, by contrast, is the *immediate cause* of the cost-shifting Congress sought to address through the ACA. See *supra,* at 5–7. Requiring individuals to obtain insurance attacks the source of the problem directly, in a single step.

[10] Indeed, Congress regularly and uncontroversially requires individuals who are "doing nothing," see *ante,* at 20, to take action. Exam-ples include federal requirements to report for jury duty, 28 U. S. C. §1866(g) (2006 ed., Supp. IV); to register for selective service, 50 U. S. C. App. §453; to purchase firearms and gear in anticipation of service in the Militia, 1Stat. 271 (Uniform Militia Act of 1792); to turn gold currency over to the Federal Government in exchange for paper currency, see *Nortz* v. *United States,* 294 U. S. 317, 328 (1935) ; and to file a tax return, 26 U. S. C. §6012 (2006 ed., Supp. IV).

[11] In a separate argument, the joint dissenters contend that the minimum coverage provision is not necessary and proper because it was not the "only . . . way" Congress could have made the guaranteed-issue and community-rating reforms work. *Post,* at 9–10. Congress could also have avoided an insurance-market death spiral, the dissenters maintain, by imposing a surcharge on those who did not previously purchase insurance when those individuals eventually enter the health-insurance system. *Post,* at 10. Or Congress could "den[y] a full income tax credit" to those who do not purchase insurance. *Ibid.*

Neither a surcharge on those who purchase insurance nor the denial of a tax credit to those who do not would solve the problem created by guaranteed-issue and community-rating requirements. Neither would prompt the purchase of insurance before sickness or injury occurred.

But even assuming there were "practicable" alternatives to the minimum coverage provision, "we long ago rejected the view that the Necessary and Proper Clause demands that an Act of Congress be '*absolutely* necessary' to the exercise of an enumerated power." *Jinks*v. *Richland County,* 538 U. S. 456, 462 (2003) (quoting *McCulloch*v. *Maryland,* 4 Wheat. 316, 414–415 (1819)). Rather, the statutory provision at issue need only be "conducive" and "[reasonably] adapted" to the goal Congress seeks to achieve. *Jinks,* 538 U. S., at 462 (internal quotation marks omitted). The minimum coverage provision meets this requirement. See *supra,* at 31–33.

[12] The Chief Justice states that he must evaluate the constitution-ality of the minimum coverage provision under the Commerce Clause because the provision "reads more naturally as a command to

buy insurance than as a tax." *Ante,* at 44. The Chief Justice ultimately concludes, however, that interpreting the provision as a tax is a "fairly possible" construction. *Ante,* at 32 (internal quotation marks omitted). That being so, I see no reason to undertake a Commerce Clause analysis that is not outcome determinative.

[13] Medicaid was "plainly an extension of the existing Kerr-Mills" grant program. Huberfeld, Federalizing Medicaid, 14 U. Pa. J. Const. L. 431, 444–445 (2011). Indeed, the "section of the Senate report dealing with Title XIX"—the title establishing Medicaid—"was entitled, 'Improvement and Extension of Kerr-Mills Medical Assistance Program.' " Stevens & Stevens, Welfare Medicine in America 51 (1974) (quoting S. Rep. No. 404, 89th Cong., 1st Sess., pt. 1, p. 9 (1965)). Setting the pattern for Medicaid, Kerr-Mills reimbursed States for a portion of the cost of health care provided to welfare recipients ifStates met conditions specified in the federal law, *e.g.,* participating States were obliged to offer minimum coverage for hospitalization and physician services. See Huberfeld, *supra,* at 443–444.

[14] Available online at http://www.cms.gov/Research-Statistics-Data-and-Systems/Statistics-Trends-and-Reports/NationalHealthExpendData/NationalHealthAccountsHistorical.html.

[15] Even the study on which the plaintiffs rely, see Brief for Petitioners 10, concludes that "[w]hile most states will experience some increase in spending, this is quite small relative to the federal matching payments and low relative to the costs of uncompensated care that [the states] would bear if the[re] were no health reform." See Kaiser Commission on Medicaid & the Uninsured, Medicaid Coverage & Spending in Health Reform 16 (May 2010). Thus there can be no objection to the ACA's expansion of Medicaid as an "unfunded mandate." Quite the contrary, the program is impressively well funded.

[16] In 1972, for example, Congress ended the federal cash-assistance program for the aged, blind, and disabled. That program previously had been operated jointly by the Federal and State Governments, asis the case with Medicaid today. Congress replaced the cooperative federal program with the nationalized Supplemental Security In-come (SSI) program. See *Schweiker* v. *Gray Panthers*, 453 U. S. 34, 38 (1981).

[17] The Chief Justice and the joint dissenters perceive in cooperative federalism a "threa[t]" to "political accountability." *Ante,* at 48; see *post,* at 34–35. By that, they mean voter confusion: Citizens upset by unpopular government action, they posit, may ascribe to state officials blame more appropriately laid at Congress' door. But no such confusion is apparent in this case: Medicaid's status as a federally funded, state-administered program is hardly hidden from view.

[18] Although the plaintiffs, in the proceedings below, did not contest the ACA's satisfaction of these criteria, see 648 F. 3d 1235, 1263 (CA11 2011), The Chief Justice appears to rely heavily on the second crite-rion. Compare *ante,* at 52, 54, with *infra,* at 52–54.

[19] Compare Subchapter XIX, 42 U. S. C. §§1396–1396v(b) (2006 ed. and Supp. IV) with §§1396a(a)(10)(A)(i)(VIII) (2006 ed. and Supp.IV); 1396a(a) (10)(A)(ii)(XX), 1396a(a)(75), 1396a(k), 1396a(gg) to (hh), 1396d(y), 1396r–1(e), 1396u–7(b)(5) to (6).

[20] The Deficit Reduction Act of 2005 authorized States to provide "benchmark coverage" or "benchmark equivalent coverage" to certain Medicaid populations. See §6044, 120Stat. 88, 42 U. S. C. §1396u–7 (2006 ed. and Supp. IV). States may offer the same level of coverage to persons newly eligible under the ACA. See §1396a(k).

[21] The Chief Justice observes that "Spending Clause legislation[i]s much in the nature of a *contract.*" *Ante,* at 46 (internal quotation marks omitted). See also *post,* at 33 (joint opinion of Scalia, Kennedy, Thomas, and Alito, JJ.) (same). But the Court previously has rec-ognized that "[u]nlike normal contractual undertakings, federal grant programs originate in and remain governed by statutory provisions expressing the judgment of Congress concerning desirable public policy." *Bennett* v. *Kentucky Dept. of Ed.*, 470 U. S. 656, 669 (1985).

[22] Title I of the Elementary and Secondary Education Act of 1965 provided federal grants to finance supplemental educational programs in school districts with high concentrations of children from low-income families. See *Bennett* v. *New Jersey*, 470 U. S. 632–635 (1985) (citing Pub. L. No. 89–10, 79Stat. 27).

23

Note, in this regard, the extension of Social Security, which began in 1935 as an old-age pension program, then expanded to include sur-vivor benefits in 1939 and disability benefits in 1956. See Social Security Act, ch. 531, 49Stat. 622–625; Social Security Act Amendments of 1939, 53Stat. 1364–1365; Social Security Amendments of 1956, ch. 836, §103, 70Stat. 815–816.

[24] The joint dissenters, for their part, would make this the entire inquiry. "[I]f States really have no choice other than to accept the package," they assert, "the offer is coercive." *Post,* at 35. The Chief Justice recognizes Congress' authority to construct a single federal program and "condition the receipt of funds on the States' complying with restrictions on the use of those funds." *Ante,* at 50. For the joint dissenters, however, all that matters, it appears, is whether States can resist the temptation of a given federal grant. *Post,* at 35. On this logic, any federal spending program, sufficiently large and well-funded, would be unconstitutional. The joint dissenters point to smaller programs States might have the will to refuse. See *post,* at 40–41 (elementary and secondary education). But how is a court to judge whether "only 6.6% of all state expenditures," *post,* at 41, is an amount States could or would do without?

Speculations of this genre are characteristic of the joint dissent. See, *e.g., post,* at 35 ("it *may* be state officials who will bear the brunt of public disapproval" for joint federal-state endeavors); *ibid.,* ("federal officials . . . *may* remain insulated from the electoral ramifications of their decision"); *post,* at 37 ("a heavy federal tax . . . levied to support a federal program that offers large grants to the States . . . *may,* as a practical matter, [leave States] unable to refuse to participate"); *ibid.* (withdrawal from a federal program "would *likely* force the State to impose a huge tax increase"); *post,* at 46 (state share of ACA expansion costs "*may* increase in the future") (all emphasis added; some internal quotation marks omitted). The joint dissenters are long on conjecture and short on real-world examples.

[25] The joint dissenters also rely heavily on Congress' perceived intent to coerce the States. *Post,* at 42–46; see, *e.g., post,* at 42 ("In crafting the ACA, Congress clearly expressed its informed view that no State could possibly refuse the offer that the ACA extends."). We should not lightly ascribe to Congress an intent to violate the Constitution (at least as my colleagues read it). This is particularly true when the ACA could just as well be comprehended as demonstrating Congress' mere expectation, in light of the uniformity of past participation and the generosity of the federal contribution, that States would not withdraw. Cf. *South Dakota* v. *Dole,* 483 U. S. 203, 211 (1987) ("We cannot conclude . . . that a con-ditional grant of federal money . . . is unconstitutional simply byreason of its success in achieving the congressional objective.").

[26] Federal taxation of a State's citizens, according to the joint dissenters, may diminish a State's ability to raise new revenue. This, in turn, could limit a State's capacity to replace a federal program with an "equivalent" state-funded analog. *Post,* at 40. But it cannot be true that "the amount of the federal taxes extracted from the taxpayers of a State to pay for the program in question is relevant in determining whether there is impermissible coercion." *Post,* at 37. When the United States Government taxes United States citizens, it taxes them "in their individual capacities" as "the people of America"—not as residents of a particular State. See *U. S. Term Limits, Inc.* v. *Thornton,* 514 U. S. 779, 839 (1995) (Kennedy, J., concurring). That is because the "Framers split the atom of sovereignty[,] . . . establishing two orders of government"—"one state and one federal"—"each with its own direct relationship" to the people. *Id.,* at 838.

A State therefore has no claim on the money its residents pay in federal taxes, and federal "spending programs need not help people in all states in the same measure." See Brief for David Satcher et al. as *Amici Curiae* 19. In 2004, for example, New Jersey received 55 centsin federal spending for every dollar its residents paid to the Federal Government in taxes, while Mississippi received $1.77 per tax dollar paid. C. Dubay, Tax Foundation, Federal Tax Burdens and Expenditures by State: Which States Gain Most from Federal Fiscal Operations? 2 (Mar. 2006). Thus no constitutional problem was created when Arizona declined for 16 years to participate in Medicaid, even though its residents' tax dollars financed Medicaid programs in every other State.

[27] As The Chief Justice observes, the Secretary is authorized to withhold all of a State's Medicaid funding. See *ante,* at 51. But total withdrawal is what the Secretary *may,* not must, do. She has discretion to withhold only a portion of the Medicaid funds otherwise due a noncompliant State. See §1396c; cf. 45 CFR §80.10(f) (2011) (Secretary may enforce Title VI's nondiscrimination requirement through "refusal to grant or continue Federal financial assistance, *in whole or in part.*" (emphasis added)). The Secretary, it is worth noting, may herself experience political pressures, which would

make her all the more reluctant to cut off funds Congress has appropriated for a State's needy citizens.

GREG McQUIGGIN, WARDEN v. FLOYD PERKINS

No. 12-126, May 28, 2013

ON WRIT OF CERTIORARI TO THE UNITED STATES COURT OF APPEALS FOR THE SIXTH CIRCUIT

Justice Ginsburg delivered the opinion of the Court.

This case concerns the "actual innocence" gateway to federal habeas review applied in *Schlup* v. *Delo*, 513 U. S. 298 (1995), and further explained in *House* v. *Bell*, 547 U.S. 518 (2006). In those cases, a convincing showing of actual innocence enabled habeas petitioners to overcomea procedural bar to consideration of the merits of their constitutional claims. Here, the question arises in the context of 28 U. S. C. §2244(d)(1), the statute of limitations on federal habeas petitions prescribed in the Antiterrorism and Effective Death Penalty Act of 1996. Specifically,if the petitioner does not file her federal habeas peti-tion, at the latest, within one year of "the date on whichthe factual predicate of the claim or claims presented could have been discovered through the exercise of due diligence," §2244(d)(1)(D), can the time bar be overcome by a convincing showing that she committed no crime?

We hold that actual innocence, if proved, serves as a gateway through which a petitioner may pass whether the impediment is a procedural bar, as it was in *Schlup* and *House*, or, as in this case, expiration of the statute of limitations. We caution, however, that tenable actual-innocence gateway pleas are rare: "[A] petitioner does not meet the threshold requirement unless he persuades the district court that, in light of the new evidence, no juror, acting reasonably, would have voted to find him guilty beyond a reasonable doubt." *Schlup*, 513 U. S., at 329; see *House*, 547 U. S., at 538 (emphasizing that the *Schlup* standard is "demanding" and seldom met). And in making an assessment of the kind *Schlup* envisioned, "the timing of the [petition]" is a factor bearing on the "reliability of th[e] evidence" purporting to show actual innocence. *Schlup*, 513 U. S., at 332.

In the instant case, the Sixth Circuit acknowledged that habeas petitioner Perkins (respondent here) had filed his petition after the statute of limitations ran out, and had "failed to diligently pursue his rights." Order in No. 09–1875, (CA6, Feb. 24, 2010), p.2 (Certificate of Appealability). Nevertheless, the Court of Appeals reversed the decision of the District Court denying Perkins' petition, and held that Perkins' actual-innocence claim allowed him to pursue his habeas petition as if it had been filed on time. 670 F.3d 665, 670 (2012). The appeals court ap-parently considered a petitioner's delay irrelevant to ap-praisal of an actual-innocence claim. See *ibid.*

We vacate the Court of Appeals' judgment and remand the case. Our opinion clarifies that a federal habeascourt, faced with an actual-innocence gateway claim, should count unjustifiable delay on a habeas petitioner's part,not as an absolute barrier to relief, but as a factor indetermining whether actual innocence has been re-liably shown. See Brief for Respondent 45 (habeas court "could ... hold the unjustified delay *against the petitioner* when making credibility findings as to whether the [actual-innocence] exception has been met").

I

A

On March 4, 1993, respondent Floyd Perkins attendeda party in Flint, Michigan, in the company of his friend, Rodney Henderson, and an acquaintance, Damarr Jones. The three men left the party together. Henderson was later discovered on a wooded trail, murdered by stab wounds to his head.

Perkins was charged with the murder of Henderson. At trial, Jones was the key witness for the prosecution. He testified that Perkins alone committed the murder while Jones looked on. App. 55.

Chauncey Vaughn, a friend of Perkins and Henderson, testified that, prior to the murder, Perkins had told himhe would kill Henderson, *id.*, at 39, and that Perkins later called Vaughn, confessing to his commission of the crime. *Id.*, at 36–38. A third witness, Torriano Player, also a friend of both Perkins and Henderson, testified that Perkins told him, had he known how Player felt about Henderson, he would not have killed Henderson. *Id.*, at 74.

Perkins, testifying in his own defense, offered a different account of the episode. He testified that he left Hender-son and Jones to purchase cigarettes at a convenience store. When he exited the store, Perkins related, Jones and Henderson were gone. *Id.*, at 84. Perkins said that he then visited his girlfriend. *Id.*, at 87. About an hour later, Perkins recalled, he saw Jones standing under a streetlight with blood on his pants, shoes, and plaid coat. *Id.*,at 90.

The jury convicted Perkins of first-degree murder. He was sentenced to life in prison without the possibility of parole on October 27, 1993. The Michigan Court of Appeals affirmed Perkins' conviction and sentence, and the Michigan Supreme Court denied Perkins leave to appeal on January 31, 1997. Perkins' conviction became final on May 5, 1997.

B

Under the Antiterrorism and Effective Death Penalty Act of 1996 (AEDPA), 110Stat. 1214, a state prisoner ordinarily has one year to file a federal petition for habeas corpus, starting from "the date on which the judgment became final by the conclusion of direct review or the ex-piration of the time for seeking such review." 28 U.S.C. §2244(d)(1)(A). If the petition alleges newly discovered evidence, however, the filing deadline is one year from "the date on which the factual predicate of the claim or claims presented could have been discovered through the exercise of due diligence." §2244(d)(1)(D).

Perkins filed his federal habeas corpus petition on June 13, 2008, more than 11 years after his conviction became final. He alleged, *inter alia*, ineffective assistance on the part of his trial attorney, depriving him of his Sixth Amendment right to competent counsel. To overcome AEDPA's time limitations, Perkins asserted newly discovered evidence of actual innocence. He relied on three affidavits, each pointing to Jones, not Perkins, as Henderson's murderer.

The first affidavit, dated January 30, 1997, was submitted by Perkins' sister, Ronda Hudson. Hudson stated that she had heard from a third party, Louis Ford, that Jones bragged about stabbing Henderson and had taken his clothes to the cleaners after the murder. App. to Pet. for Cert. 54a–55a. The second affidavit, dated March 16, 1999, was subscribed to by Demond Louis, Chauncey Vaughn's younger brother. Louis stated that, on the night of the murder, Jones confessed to him that he had just killed Henderson. Louis also described the clothes Jones wore that night, bloodstained orange shoes and orange pants, and a colorful shirt. *Id.*, at 50a–53a. The next day, Louis added, he accompanied Jones, first to a dumpster where Jones disposed of the bloodstained shoes, and then to the cleaners. Finally, Perkins presented the July 16, 2002 affidavit of Linda Fleming, an employee at Pro-Clean Cleaners in 1993. She stated that, on or about March 4, 1993, a man matching Jones's description entered the shop and asked her whether bloodstains could be removed from the pants and a shirt he brought in. The pants were orange, she recalled, and heavily stained with blood, as was the multicolored shirt left for cleaning along with the pants. *Id.*, at 48a–49a.

The District Court found the affidavits insufficient to entitle Perkins to habeas relief. Characterizing the affidavits as newly discovered evidence was "dubious," the District Court observed, in light of what Perkins knew about the underlying facts at the time of trial. *Id.*, at 29a. But even assuming qualification of the affidavits as evidence newly discovered, the District Court next explained, "[Perkins'] petition [was] untimely under §2244(d)(1)(D)." *Ibid.* "[If] the statute of limitations began to run as ofthe date of the latest of th[e] affidavits, July 16, 2002," the District Court noted, then "absent tolling, [Perkins] had until July 16, 2003 in which to file his habeas petition." *Ibid.* Perkins, however, did not file until nearly five years later, on June 13, 2008.

Under Sixth Circuit precedent, the District Court stated, "a habeas petitioner who demonstrates a credible claimof actual innocence based on new evidence may, in ex-ceptional circumstances, be entitled to equitable tollingof habeas limitations." *Id.*, at 30a. But Perkins had not established exceptional circumstances, the District Court determined. In any event, the District Court observed, equitable tolling requires diligence and Perkins "ha[d] failed utterly to demonstrate the necessary diligence in exercising his rights." *Id.*, at 31a. Alternatively, the Dis-trict Court found that Perkins had failed to meet the strict standard by which pleas of actual innocence are mea-sured: He had not shown that, taking account of allthe evidence, "it is more likely than not that no reasonable juror would have convicted him," or even that the evidence was new. *Id.*, at 30a–31a.

Perkins appealed the District Court's judgment. Al-though recognizing that AEDPA's statute of limitations had expired and that Perkins had not diligently pursued his rights, the Sixth Circuit granted a certificate of appealability limited to a single question: Is reasonable diligence a precondition to relying on actual innocence as a gateway to adjudication of a federal habeas petition on the merits? Certificate of Appealability 2–3.

On consideration of the certified question, the Court of Appeals reversed the District Court's judgment. Adhering to Circuit precedent, *Souter* v. *Jones*, 395 F.3d 577, 597–602 (2005), the Sixth Circuit held that Perkins' gateway actual-innocence allegations allowed him to present his ineffective-assistance-of-counsel claim as if it were filedon time. On remand, the Court of Appeals instructed, "the [D]istrict [C]ourt [should] fully consider whether Perkins assert[ed] a credible claim of actual innocence." 670 F.3d, at 676.

We granted certiorari to resolve a Circuit conflict on whether AEDPA's statute of limitations can be overcome by a showing of actual innocence. 568 U.S. ___ (2012). Compare, *e.g.*, *San Martin* v. *McNeil*, 633 F.3d 1257, 1267–1268 (CA11 2011) ("A court . . . may consider an untimely §2254 petition if, by refusing to consider the petition for untimeliness, the court thereby would endorse a 'fundamental miscarriage of justice' because it would require that an individual who is actually innocent remain imprisoned."), with, *e.g.*, *Escamilla* v. *Jungwirth*, 426 F.3d 868, 871–872 (CA7 2005) ("Prisoners claiming to be innocent, like those contending that other events spoil the conviction, must meet the statutory requirement of timely action."). See also *Rivas* v. *Fischer*, 687 F.3d 514, 548 (CA2 2012) (collecting cases).

II

A

In *Holland* v. *Florida*, 560 U.S. ___ (2010), this Court addressed the circumstances in which a federal habeas petitioner could invoke the doctrine of "equitable tolling." *Holland* held that "a [habeas] petitioner is entitled to equitable tolling only if he shows (1) that he has been pursuing his rights diligently, and (2) that some extraordinary circumstance stood in his way and prevented timely filing." *Id.*, at ___ (slip op., at 16–17) (internal quotation marks omitted). As the courts below comprehended, Perkins does not qualify for equitable tolling. In possession of all three affidavits by July 2002, he waited nearly six years to seek federal postconviction relief. "Such a delay falls far short of demonstrating the . . . diligence" required to entitle a petitioner to equitable tolling. App. to Pet. for Cert. 31a (District Court opinion). See also Certificate of Appealability 2.

Perkins, however, asserts not an excuse for filing after the statute of limitations has run. Instead, he maintains that a plea of actual innocence can overcome AEDPA's one-year statute of limitations. He thus seeks an equi-table *exception* to §2244(d)(1), not an extension of the time statutorily prescribed. See *Rivas*, 687 F.3d, at 547, n. 42 (distinguishing from "equitable tolling" a plea to override the statute of limitations when actual innocence is shown).

Decisions of this Court support Perkins' view of the significance of a convincing actual-innocence claim. We have not resolved whether a prisoner may be entitled to habeas relief based on a freestanding claim of actual innocence. *Herrera* v. *Collins*, 506 U.S. 390–405 (1993). We have recognized, however, that a prisoner "otherwise subject to defenses of abusive or successive use of the writ [of habeas corpus] may have his federal constitutional claim considered on the merits if he makes a proper showing of actual innocence." *Id.*, at 404 (citing *Sawyer* v. *Whitley*, 505 U.S. 333 (1992)). See also *Murray* v. *Carrier*, 477 U.S. 478, 496 (1986)("[W]e think that in an extraordinary case, where a constitutional violation has probably resulted in the conviction of one who is actually innocent, a federal habeas court may grant the writ even in the absence of a showing of cause for the procedural default."). In other words, a credible showing of actual innocence may allow a prisoner to pursue his constitu-tional claims (here, ineffective assistance of counsel) on the merits notwithstanding the existence of a procedural bar to relief. "This rule, or fundamental miscarriage of justice exception, is grounded in the 'equitable discretion' of habeas courts to see that federal constitutional errors do not result in the incarceration of innocent persons." *Herrera*, 506 U.S., at 404.

We have applied the miscarriage of justice exception to overcome various procedural defaults. These include "successive" petitions asserting previously rejected claims, see *Kuhlmann* v. *Wilson*, 477 U.S. 436, 454 (1986) (plurality opinion), "abusive" petitions asserting in a second petition claims that could have been raised in a first petition, see *McCleskey* v. *Zant*, 499 U.S. 467–495(1991), failure to develop facts in state court, see *Keeney* v. *Tamayo-Reyes*, 504 U.S. 1–12 (1992), and failure to observe state procedural rules, including filing deadlines, see *Coleman* v. *Thompson*, 501 U.S. 722, 750 (1991); *Carrier*, 477 U.S., at 495–496.

The miscarriage of justice exception, our decisions bear out, survived AEDPA's passage. In *Calderon* v. *Thompson*, 523 U.S. 538 (1998), we applied the exception to hold that a federal court may, consistent with AEDPA, recall its mandate in order to revisit the merits of a decision. *Id.*, at 558 ("The miscarriage of justice standard is altogether consistent . . . with AEDPA's central concern that the merits of concluded criminal proceedings not be revisited in the absence of a strong showing of actual innocence."). In *Bousley* v. *United States*, 523 U.S. 614, 622 (1998), we held, in the context of §2255, that actual in-nocence may overcome a prisoner's failure to raise a constitutional objection on direct review. Most recently, in *House*, we reiterated that a prisoner's proof of actual innocence may provide a gateway for federal habeas review of a procedurally defaulted claim of constitutional error. 547 U.S., at 537–538.

These decisions "see[k] to balance the societal interests in finality, comity, and conservation of scarce judicial re-sources with the individual interest in justice that arises in the extraordinary case." *Schlup*, 513 U.S., at 324. Sensitivity to the injustice of incarcerating an innocent individual should not abate when the impediment is AEDPA's statute of limitations.

As just noted, see *supra*, at 8, we have held that the miscarriage of justice exception applies to state procedural rules, including filing deadlines. *Coleman*, 501 U.S., at 750. A federal court may invoke the miscarriage of justice exception to justify consideration of claims defaulted in state court under state timeliness rules. See *ibid*. The State's reading of AEDPA's time prescription would thus accord greater force to a federal deadline than to a simi-larly designed state deadline. It would be passing strange to interpret a statute seeking to promote federalism and comity as requiring stricter enforcement of federal procedural rules than procedural rules established and enforced by the *States*.

B

The State ties to §2244(d)'s text its insistence that AEDPA's statute of limitations precludes courts from considering late-filed actual-innocence gateway claims. "Section 2244(d)(1)(D)," the State contends, "forecloses any argument that a habeas petitioner has unlimited time to present new evidence in support of a constitutional claim." Brief for Petitioner 17. That is so, the State maintains, because AEDPA prescribes a comprehensive system for determining when its one-year limitations period begins to run. "Included within that system," the State observes, "is a specific trigger for the precise circumstance presented here: a constitutional claim based on new evidence." *Ibid.* Section 2244(d)(1)(D) runs the clock from "the date on which the factual predicate of the claim . . . could have been discovered through the exercise of due diligence." In light of that provision, the State urges, "there is no need for the courts to act in equity to provide additional time for persons who allege actual innocence as a gateway to their claims of constitutional error." *Ibid.* Perkins' request for an equitable exception to the statute of limitations, the State charges, would "rende[r] superfluous this carefully scripted scheme." *Id.*, at 18.

The State's argument in this regard bears blinders. AEDPA's time limitations apply to the typical case in which no allegation of actual innocence is made. The miscarriage of justice exception, we underscore, applies to a severely confined category: cases in which new evidence shows "it is more likely than not that no reasonable ju-ror would have convicted [the petitioner]." *Schlup*, 513 U.S., at 329 (internal quotation marks omitted). Section 2244(d)(1)(D) is both modestly more stringent (because it requires diligence) and dramatically less stringent (because it requires no showing of innocence). Many petitions that could not pass through the actual-innocence gateway will be timely or not measured by §2244(d)(1)(D)'s triggering provision. That provision, in short, will hardly be rendered superfluous by recognition of the miscarriage of justice exception.

The State further relies on provisions of AEDPA other than §2244(d)(1)(D), namely, §§2244(b)(2)(B) and 2254(e) (2), to urge that Congress knew how to incorporate the miscarriage of justice exception when it was so minded. Section 2244(b)(2)(B), the State observes, provides thata petitioner whose first federal habeas petition has already been adjudicated when new evidence comes to light may file a second-or-successive petition when, and only when, the facts underlying the new claim would "es-tablish by clear and convincing evidence that, but for constitutional error, no reasonable factfinder would have found the applicant guilty of the underlying offense." §2244(b)(2)(B)(ii). And §2254(e)(2), which generally bars evidentiary hearings in federal habeas proceedings ini-tiated by state prisoners, includes an exception for pris-oners who present new evidence of their innocence. See §§2254(e)(2)(A)(ii), (B) (permitting evidentiary hearings in federal court if "the facts underlying the claim would be sufficient to establish by clear and convincing evidence that but for constitutional error, no reasonable factfinder would have found the applicant guilty of the underlying offense").

But Congress did not simply incorporate the miscarriage of justice exception into §§2244(b)(2)(B) and 2254(e)(2). Rather, Congress constrained the application of the exception. Prior to AEDPA's enactment, a court could grant relief on a second-or-successive petition, then known asan "abusive" petition, if the petitioner could show that "a fundamental miscarriage of justice would result from a failure to entertain the claim." *McCleskey*, 499 U.S., at 495. Section 2244(b)(2)(B) limits the exception to cases in which "the factual predicate for the claim could not have been discovered previously through the exercise of due diligence," and the petitioner can establish that no reasonable factfinder "would have found [her] guilty of the underlying offense" by "clear and convincing evidence." Congress thus required second-or-successive habeas petitioners attempting to benefit from the miscarriage of justice exception to meet a higher level of proof ("clear and convincing evidence") and to satisfy a diligence requirement that did not exist prior to AEDPA's passage.

Likewise, petitioners asserting actual innocence pre-AEDPA could obtain evidentiary hearings in federal court even if they failed to develop facts in state court. See *Keeney*, 504 U.S., at 12 ("A habeas petitioner's failure to develop a claim in state-court proceedings will be excused and a hearing mandated if he can show that a fundamental miscarriage of justice would result from failure to hold a federal evidentiary hearing."). Under AEDPA, a petitioner seeking an evidentiary hearing must show diligence and, in addition, establish her actual innocence by clear and convincing evidence. §§2254(e)(2)(A)(ii), (B).

Sections 2244(b)(2)(B) and 2254(e)(2) thus reflect Congress' will to *modify* the miscarriage of justice exception with respect to second-or-successive petitions and the hold-ing of evidentiary hearings in federal court. These pro-visions do not demonstrate Congress' intent to preclude courts from applying the exception, unmodified, to "the type of petition at issue here"—an untimely first federal habeas petition alleging a gateway actual-innocence claim. *House*, 547 U.S., at 539.[1] The more rational inference to draw from Congress' incorporation of a modified version of the miscarriage of justice exception in §§2244(b)(2)(B) and 2254(e)(2) is simply this: In a case not governed by those provisions, *i.e.*, a first petition for federal habeas relief, the miscarriage of justice exception survived AEDPA's passage intact and unrestricted.[2]

Our reading of the statute is supported by the Court's opinion in *Holland*. "[E]quitable principles have traditionally governed the substantive law of habeas corpus," *Holland* reminded, and affirmed that "we will not construe a statute to displace courts' traditional equitable authority absent the clearest command." 560 U.S., at ___ (slipop., at 13) (internal quotation marks omitted). The textof §2244(d)(1) contains no clear command countering the courts' equitable authority to invoke the miscarriage of justice exception to overcome expiration of the statute of limitations governing a first federal habeas petition. As we observed in *Holland*,

> "AEDPA seeks to eliminate delays in the federal habeas review process. But AEDPA seeks to do so without undermining basic habeas corpus principles and while seeking to harmonize the new statute with prior law .... When Congress codified new rules governing this previously judicially managed area of law, it did so without losing sight of the fact that the writ of habeas corpus plays a vital role in protecting constitutional rights." *Id.*, at ___ (slip op., at 16) (citations and internal quotation marks omitted).[3]

III

Having rejected the State's argument that §2244(d) (1)(D) precludes a court from entertaining an un-timely first federal habeas petition raising a convincing claim of actual innocence, we turn to the State's further objection to the Sixth Circuit's opinion. Even if a habeas petitioner asserting a credible claim of actual innocence may overcome AEDPA's statute of limitations, the State argues, the Court of Appeals erred in finding that no threshold diligence requirement at all applies to Perkins' petition.

While formally distinct from its argument that §2244(d)(1)(D)'s text forecloses a late-filed claim alleging actual innocence, the State's contention makes scant sense. Section 2244(d)(1)(D) requires a habeas petitioner to file a claim within one year of the time in which new evidence "could have been discovered through the exercise of due diligence." It would be bizarre to hold that a habeas

petitioner who asserts a convincing claim of actual innocence may overcome the statutory time bar §2244(d)(1)(D) erects, yet simultaneously encounter a court-fashioned diligence barrier to pursuit of her petition. See 670 F.3d, at 673 ("Requiring reasonable diligence effectively makes the concept of the actual innocence gateway redundant, since petitioners ... seek [an equitable exception only] when they were not reasonably diligent in complying with §2244(d)(1)(D).").

While we reject the State's argument that habeas petitioners who assert convincing actual-innocence claims must prove diligence to cross a federal court's threshold, we hold that the Sixth Circuit erred to the extent that it eliminated timing as a factor relevant in evaluating the reliability of a petitioner's proof of innocence. To invoke the miscarriage of justice exception to AEDPA's statute of limitations, we repeat, a petitioner "must show that it is more likely than not that no reasonable juror would have convicted him in the light of the new evidence." *Schlup*, 513 U.S., at 327. Unexplained delay in presenting new evidence bears on the determination whether the petitioner has made the requisite showing. Perkins so acknowl-edges. See Brief for Respondent 52 (unjustified delay may figure in determining "whether a petitioner has made a sufficient showing of innocence"). As we stated in *Schlup*, "[a] court may consider how the timing of the submission and the likely credibility of [a petitioner's] affiants bear on the probable reliability of ... evidence [of actual innocence]." 513 U.S., at 332. See also *House*, 547 U.S., at 537.

Considering a petitioner's diligence, not discretely, but as part of the assessment whether actual innocence has been convincingly shown, attends to the State's concern that it will be prejudiced by a prisoner's untoward delay in proffering new evidence. The State fears that a prisoner might "lie in wait and use stale evidence to collaterally attack his conviction ... when an elderly witness has died and cannot appear at a hearing to rebut new evidence." Brief for Petitioner 25. The timing of such a petition, however, should seriously undermine the credibility of the actual-innocence claim. Moreover, the deceased witness' prior testimony, which would have been subject to cross-examination, could be introduced in the event of a new trial. See *Crawford* v. *Washington*, 541 U.S. 36–54 (2004) (recognizing exception to the Confrontation Clause where witness is unavailable and the defendant had a prior opportunity for cross-examination). And frivolous petitions should occasion instant dismissal. See 28 U.S.C. §2254 Rule 4. Focusing on the merits of a petitioner's actual-innocence claim and taking account of delay in that context, rather than treating timeliness as a threshold inquiry, is tuned to the rationale underlying the miscarriage of justice exception—*i.e.*, ensuring "that federal constitutional errors do not result in the incarceration of innocent persons." *Herrera*, 506 U.S., at 404.[4]

IV

We now return to the case at hand. The District Court proceeded properly in first determining that Perkins' claim was filed well beyond AEDPA's limitations period and that equitable tolling was unavailable to Perkins because he could demonstrate neither exceptional circumstances nor diligence. See *supra*, at 5. The District Court then found that Perkins' alleged newly discovered evidence, *i.e.*, the information contained in the three affidavits, was "substantially available to [Perkins] at trial."

App. to Pet. for Cert. 31a. Moreover, the proffered evidence, even if "new," was hardly adequate to show that, had it been presented at trial, no reasonable juror would have convicted Perkins. *Id.*, at 30a–31a.

The Sixth Circuit granted a certificate of appealability limited to the question whether reasonable diligence is a precondition to reliance on actual innocence as a gateway to adjudication of a federal habeas petition on the merits. We have explained that untimeliness, although not an unyielding ground for dismissal of a petition, does bear on the credibility of evidence proffered to show actual innocence. On remand, the District Court's appraisal of Perkins' petition as insufficient to meet *Schlup*'s actual-innocence standard should be dispositive, absent cause, which we do not currently see, for the Sixth Circuit to upset that evaluation. We stress once again that the *Schlup* standard is demanding. The gateway should open only when a petition presents "evidence of innocence so strong that a court cannot have confidence in the outcome of the trial unless the court is also satisfied that the trial was free of nonharmless constitutional error." 513 U.S., at 316.

* * *

For the reasons stated, the judgment of the Sixth Circuit is vacated, and the case is remanded for further proceedings consistent with this opinion.

It is so ordered.

NOTES

[1] In *House*, we rejected the analogous argument that AEDPA re-placed the standard for actual-innocence gateway claims prescribed in *Schlup* v. *Delo*, 513 U. S. 298, 327 (1995) (petitioner "must show that it is more likely than not that no reasonable juror would have convicted him in the light of the new evidence"), with a "clear and convincing" evidence requirement. 547 U.S., at 539 (internal quotation marks omitted). As here, the State relied on §§2244(b)(2)(B)(ii) and 2254(e)(2) to support its argument. But "[n]either provision address[ed] the type of petition at issue ... [,] a first federal habeas petition seeking consideration of defaulted claims based on a showing of actual innocence." *Ibid.* Consequently, we held inapplicable to first petitions the stricter standard AEDPA prescribed for second-or-successive petitions. *Ibid.*

[2] Prior to AEDPA, it is true, this Court had not ruled that a credible claim of actual innocence could supersede a federal statute of limitations. The reason why that is so is evident: Pre-AEDPA, petitions for federal habeas relief were not governed by any statute of limitations. Notably, we said in *Coleman* v. *Thompson*, 501 U.S. 722 (1991), that a petitioner who failed to comply with a timeliness requirement in *state* court could nevertheless plead her claims on the merits in federal court if she could show that "failure to consider the claims [would] result in a fundamental miscarriage of justice." *Id.*, at 750.

[3] For eight pages, the dissent stridently insists that federal (although not state) statutes of limitations allow no exceptions not contained in the text. Well, not quite so, the dissent ultimately acknowledges. *Post*, at 8. Even AEDPA's statute of limitations, the dissent admits, is subject to equitable tolling. But that is because equitable tolling "can be seen as a reasonable assumption of genuine legislative intent." *Post*, at 9. Why is it not an equally reasonable assumption that Congress would want a limitations period to yield when what is at stake is a State's incarceration of an individual for a crime, it has become clear, no reasonable person would find he committed? For all its bluster, the dissent agrees with the Court on a crucial point: Congress legis-lates against the backdrop of existing law. *Post*, at 10. At the time of AEDPA's enactment, multiple decisions of this Court applied the miscarriage of justice exception to overcome various threshold barriers to relief. See *supra*, at 7–9. It is hardly "unprecedented," therefore, to conclude that "Congress intended or could have anticipated [a miscarriage of justice] exception" when it enacted AEDPA. *Post*, at 10–11.

[4] We note one caveat: A showing that delay was part of a deliberate attempt to manipulate the case, say by waiting until a key prosecution witness died or was deported, might raise a different ground for withholding equitable relief. No such contention was presented here, however, so we do not discuss the point.

DAIMLER AG v. BARBARA BAUMAN et al.

No. 11-965, January 14, 2014

ON WRIT OF CERTIORARI TO THE UNITED STATES COURT OF APPEALS FOR THE NINTH CIRCUIT

Justice Ginsburg delivered the opinion of the Court.

This case concerns the authority of a court in the United States to entertain a claim brought by foreign plaintiffs against a foreign defendant based on events occurring entirely outside the United States. The litigation commenced in 2004, when twenty-two Argentinian residents[1] filed a complaint in the United States District Court for the Northern District of California against DaimlerChrysler Aktiengesellschaft (Daimler),[2] a German public stock company, headquartered in Stuttgart, that manufactures Mercedes-Benz vehicles in Germany. The complaint alleged that during Argentina's 1976–1983 "Dirty War," Daimler's Argentinian subsidiary, Mercedes-Benz Argentina (MB Argentina) collaborated with state security forces to kidnap, detain, torture, and kill certain MB Argentina workers, among them, plaintiffs or persons closely related to plaintiffs. Damages for the alleged human-rights violations were sought from Daimler under the laws of the United States, California, and Argentina. Jurisdiction over the lawsuit was predicated on the California contacts of Mercedes-Benz USA, LLC (MBUSA),a subsidiary of Daimler incorporated in Delaware withits principal place of business in New Jersey. MBUSA distributes Daimler-manufactured vehicles to independ-ent dealerships throughout the United States, including California.

The question presented is whether the Due Process Clause of the Fourteenth Amendment precludes the District Court from exercising jurisdiction over Daimler in this case, given the absence of any California connectionto the atrocities, perpetrators, or victims described in the complaint. Plaintiffs invoked the court's general or all-purpose jurisdiction. California, they urge, is a place where Daimler may be sued on any and all claims against it, wherever in the world the claims may arise. For example, as plaintiffs' counsel affirmed, under the proffered jurisdictional theory, if a Daimler-manufactured vehicle overturned in Poland, injuring a Polish driver and passenger, the injured parties could maintain a design defect suit in California. See Tr. of Oral Arg. 28–29. Exercises of personal jurisdiction so exorbitant, we hold, are barred by due process constraints on the assertion of adjudicatory authority.

In *Goodyear Dunlop Tires Operations, S.A. v. Brown*, 564 U.S. ___ (2011), we addressed the distinction between general or all-purpose jurisdiction, and specific or conduct-linked jurisdiction. As to the former, we held that a court may assert jurisdiction over a foreign corporation "to hear any and all claims against [it]" only when the corporation's affiliations with the State in which suit is brought areso constant and pervasive "as to render [it] essentially at home in the forum State." *Id.*, at ___ (slip op., at 2). Instructed by *Goodyear*, we conclude Daimler is not "at home" in California, and cannot be sued there for injuries plaintiffs attribute to MB Argentina's conduct in Argentina.

I

In 2004, plaintiffs (respondents here) filed suit in the United States District Court for the Northern District of California, alleging that MB Argentina collaborated with Argentinian state security forces to kidnap, detain, torture, and kill plaintiffs and their relatives during the military dictatorship in place there from 1976 through 1983, a period known as Argentina's "Dirty War." Based on those allegations, plaintiffs asserted claims under the Alien Tort Statute, 28 U.S.C. §1350, and the Torture Victim Protection Act of 1991, 106Stat. 73, note following 28 U.S.C. §1350, as well as claims for wrongful death and intentional infliction of emotional distress under the laws of California and Argentina. The incidents recounted in the complaint center on MB Argentina's plant in Gonzalez Catan, Argentina; no part of MB Argentina's alleged col-laboration with Argentinian authorities took place in Cali-fornia or anywhere else in the United States.

Plaintiffs' operative complaint names only one corporate defendant: Daimler, the petitioner here. Plaintiffs seek to hold Daimler vicariously liable for MB Argentina's alleged malfeasance. Daimler is a German *Aktiengesellschaft* (public stock company) that manufactures Mercedes-Benz vehicles in Germany and has its headquarters in Stuttgart. At times relevant to this case, MB Argentina was a subsidiary wholly owned by Daimler's predecessor in interest.

Daimler moved to dismiss the action for want of personal jurisdiction. Opposing the motion, plaintiffs submitted declarations and exhibits purporting to demonstrate the presence of Daimler itself in California. Alternatively, plaintiffs maintained that jurisdiction over Daimler could be founded on the California contacts of MBUSA, a distinct corporate entity that, according to plaintiffs, should be treated as Daimler's agent for jurisdictional purposes.

MBUSA, an indirect subsidiary of Daimler, is a Delaware limited liability corporation.[3] MBUSA serves as Daimler's exclusive importer and distributor in the United States, purchasing Mercedes-Benz automobiles from Daimler in Germany, then importing those vehicles, and ultimately distributing them to independent dealerships located throughout the Nation. Although MBUSA's principal place of business is in New Jersey, MBUSA has multiple California-based facilities, including a regional office in Costa Mesa, a Vehicle Preparation Center in Carson, and a Classic Center in Irvine. According to the record developed below, MBUSA is the largest supplier of luxury vehicles to the California market. In particular, over 10% of all sales of new vehicles in the United States take place in California, and MBUSA's California sales account for 2.4% of Daimler's worldwide sales.

The relationship between Daimler and MBUSA is delineated in a General Distributor Agreement, which sets forth requirements for MBUSA's distribution of Mercedes-Benz vehicles in the United States. That agreementestablished MBUSA as an "independent contracto[r]"that "buy[s] and sell[s] [vehicles] ... as an independent business for [its] own account." App. 179a. The agreement "does not make [MBUSA] ... a general or special agent, partner, joint venturer or employee of DAIMLERCHRYSLER or any DaimlerChrysler Group Company"; MBUSA "ha[s] no authority to make binding obligations for or act on behalf of DAIMLERCHRYSLER or any DaimlerChrysler Group Company." *Ibid.*

After allowing jurisdictional discovery on plaintiffs' agency allegations, the District Court granted Daimler's motion to dismiss. Daimler's own affiliations with California, the court first determined, were insufficient to support the exercise of all-purpose jurisdiction over the corporation. *Bauman* v. *DaimlerChrysler AG*, No. C–04–00194 RMW (ND Cal., Nov. 22, 2005), App. to Pet. for Cert. 111a–112a, 2005 WL 3157472, *9–*10. Next, the court declined to attribute MBUSA's California contacts to Daimler on an agency theory, concluding that plaintiffs failed to demonstrate that MBUSA acted as Daimler's agent. *Id.,* at 117a, 133a, 2005 WL 3157472, *12, *19; *Bauman* v. *DaimlerChrysler AG*, No. C–04–00194 RMW (ND Cal., Feb. 12, 2007), App. to Pet. for Cert. 83a–85a, 2007 WL 486389, *2.

The Ninth Circuit at first affirmed the District Court's judgment. Addressing solely the question of agency, the Court of Appeals held that plaintiffs had not shown the existence of an agency relationship of the kind that might warrant attribution of MBUSA's contacts to Daimler. *Bauman* v. *DaimlerChrysler Corp.*, 579 F.3d 1088, 1096–1097 (2009). Judge Reinhardt dissented. In his view, the agency test was satisfied and considerations of "reason-ableness" did not bar the exercise of jurisdiction. *Id.,* at 1098–1106. Granting plaintiffs' petition for rehearing, the panel withdrew its initial opinion and replaced it with one authored by Judge Reinhardt, which elaborated on reasoning he initially expressed in dissent. *Bauman* v. *Daimler-Chrysler Corp.*, 644 F.3d 909 (CA9 2011).

Daimler petitioned for rehearing and rehearing en banc, urging that the exercise of personal jurisdiction over Daimler could not be reconciled with this Court's decision in *Goodyear Dunlop Tires Operations, S.A.* v. *Brown*, 564 U.S. ___ (2011). Over the dissent of eight judges, the Ninth Circuit denied Daimler's petition. See *Bauman* v. *DaimlerChrysler Corp.*, 676 F.3d 774 (2011) (O'Scannlain, J., dissenting from denial of rehearing en banc).

We granted certiorari to decide whether, consistent with the Due Process Clause of the Fourteenth Amendment, Daimler is amenable to suit in California courts for claims involving only foreign plaintiffs and conduct occurring entirely abroad. 569 U.S. ___ (2013).

II

Federal courts ordinarily follow state law in determining the bounds of their jurisdiction over persons. See Fed. Rule Civ. Proc. 4(k)(1)(A) (service of process is effective to establish personal jurisdiction over a defendant "who is subject to the jurisdiction of a court of general jurisdiction in the state where the district court is located"). Under California's long-arm statute, California state courts may exercise personal jurisdiction "on any basis not inconsistent with the Constitution of this state or of the United States." Cal. Civ. Proc. Code Ann. §410.10 (West 2004). California's long-arm statute allows the exercise of personal jurisdiction to the full extent permissible under the U.S. Constitution. We therefore inquire whether the Ninth Circuit's holding comports with the limits imposed by federal due process. See, *e.g., Burger King Corp.* v. *Rudzewicz*, 471 U.S. 462, 464 (1985) .

III

In *Pennoyer* v. *Neff*, 95 U.S. 714 (1878) , decided shortly after the enactment of the Fourteenth Amendment, the Court held that a tribunal's jurisdiction over persons reaches no farther than the geographic bounds of the forum. See *id.,* at 720 ("The authority of every tribunal is necessarily restricted by the territorial limits of the State in which it is established."). See also *Shaffer* v. *Heitner*, 433 U.S. 186, 197 (1977) (Under *Pennoyer*, "any attempt 'directly' to assert extraterritorial jurisdiction over persons or property would offend sister States and exceed the inherent limits of the State's power."). In time, however, that strict territorial approach yielded to a less rigid understanding, spurred by "changes in the technology of transportation and communication, and the tremendous growth of interstate business activity." *Burnham* v. *Superior Court of Cal., County of Marin*, 495 U.S. 604, 617 (1990) (opinion of Scalia, J.).

"The canonical opinion in this area remains *International Shoe [Co.* v. *Washington]*, 326 U.S. 310 [(1945)], in which we held that a State may authorize its courts to exercise personal jurisdiction over an out-of-state defendant if the defendant has 'certain minimum contacts with [the State] such that the maintenance of the suit does not offend "traditional notions of fair play and substantial justice.""" *Goodyear*, 564 U.S., at ___ (slip op., at 6) (quoting *International Shoe*, 326 U.S., at 316). Following *International Shoe*, "the relationship among the defendant, the forum, and the litigation, rather than the mutually exclusive sovereignty of the States on which the rules of *Pennoyer* rest, became the central concern of the inquiry into personal jurisdiction." *Shaffer*, 433 U.S., at 204.

International Shoe's conception of "fair play and substantial justice" presaged the development of two categories of personal jurisdiction. The first category is represented by *International Shoe* itself, a case in which the in-state activities of the corporate defendant "ha[d] not only been continuous and systematic, but also g[a]ve rise to the liabilities sued on." 326 U.S., at 317.[4] *International Shoe* recognized, as well, that "the commission of some single or occasional acts of the corporate agent in a state" may sometimes be enough to subject the corporation to jurisdiction in that State's tribunals with respect to suits relating to that in-state activity. *Id.,* at 318. Adjudicatory author-ity of this order, in which the suit "aris[es] out of orrelate[s] to the defendant's contacts with the forum," *Heli-copteros Nacionales de Colombia, S.A.* v. *Hall,* 466 U.S. 408, n.8 (1984), is today called "specific jurisdiction." See *Goodyear,* 564 U.S., at ___ (slip op., at 7) (citing von Mehren & Trautman, Jurisdiction to Adjudicate: A Suggested Analysis, 79 Harv. L.Rev. 1121, 1144–1163 (1966) (hereinafter von Mehren & Trautman)).

International Shoe distinguished between, on the one hand, exercises of specific jurisdiction, as just described, and on the other, situations where a foreign corporation's "continuous corporate operations within a state [are] so substantial and of such a nature as to justify suit against it on causes of action arising from dealings entirely distinct from those activities." 326 U.S., at 318. As we have since explained, "[a] court may assert general jurisdiction over foreign (sister-state or foreign-country) corporations to hear any and all claims against them when their affiliations with the State are so 'continuous and systematic' as to render them essentially at home in the forum State." *Goodyear,* 564 U.S., at ___ (slip op., at 2); see *id.,* at ___ (slip op., at 7); *Helicopteros,* 466 U.S., at 414, n.9.[5]

Since *International Shoe,* "specific jurisdiction has become the centerpiece of modern jurisdiction theory, while general jurisdiction [has played] a reduced role." *Goodyear,* 564 U.S., at ___ (slip op., at 8) (quoting Twitchell, The Myth of General Jurisdiction, 101 Harv. L.Rev. 610, 628 (1988)). *International Shoe's* momentous departure from *Pennoyer's* rigidly territorial focus, we have noted, unleashed a rapid expansion of tribunals' ability to hear claims against out-of-state defendants when the episode-in-suit occurred in the forum or the defendant purposefully availed itself of the forum.[6] Our subsequent decisions have continued to bear out the prediction that "specific jurisdiction will come into sharper relief and form a considerably more significant part of the scene." von Mehren & Trautman 1164.[7]

Our post-*International Shoe* opinions on general jurisdiction, by comparison, are few. "[The Court's] 1952 decision in *Perkins* v. *Benguet Consol. Mining Co.* remains the textbook case of general jurisdiction appropriately exercised over a foreign corporation that has not consented to suit in the forum." *Goodyear,* 564 U.S., at ___ (slip op., at 11) (internal quotation marks and brackets omitted). The defendant in *Perkins,* Benguet, was a company incorporated under the laws of the Philippines, where it operated gold and silver mines. Benguet ceased its mining operations during the Japanese occupation of the Philippines in World War II; its president moved to Ohio, where he kept an office, maintained the company's files, and oversaw the company's activities. *Perkins* v. *Benguet Consol. Mining Co.,* 342 U.S. 437, 448 (1952) . The plaintiff, an Ohio resident, sued Benguet on a claim that neither arose in Ohio nor related to the corporation's activities in that State. We held that the Ohio courts could exercise general jurisdiction over Benguet without offending due process. *Ibid.* That was so, we later noted, because "Ohio was the corporation's principal, if temporary, place of business." *Keeton* v. *Hustler Magazine, Inc.,* 465 U.S. 770, n.11 (1984).[8]

The next case on point, *Helicopteros,* 466 U.S. 408, arose from a helicopter crash in Peru. Four U.S. citizens perished in that accident; their survivors and representatives brought suit in Texas state court against the helicopter's owner and operator, a Colombian corporation. That company's contacts with Texas were confined to "sending its chief executive officer to Houston for a contract-negotiation session; accepting into its New York bank account checks drawn on a Houston bank; purchasing helicopters, equipment, and training services from [a Texas-based helicopter company] for substantial sums; and sending personnel to [Texas] for training." *Id.,* at 416. Notably, those contacts bore no apparent relationship to the accident that gave rise to the suit. We held that the company's Texas connections did not resemble the "continuous and systematic general business contacts ... found to exist in *Perkins.*" *Ibid.* "[M]ere purchases, even if occurring at regular intervals," we clarified, "are not enough to warrant a State's assertion of *in personam* jurisdiction over a nonresident corporation in a cause of action not related to those purchase transactions." *Id.,* at 418.

Most recently, in *Goodyear,* we answered the question: "Are foreign subsidiaries of a United States parent corporation amenable to suit in state court on claims unrelated to any activity of the subsidiaries in the forum State?" 564 U.S., at ___ (slip op., at 1). That case arose from a bus accident outside Paris that killed two boys from North Carolina. The boys' parents brought a wrongful-death suit in North Carolina state court alleging that the bus's tire was defectively manufactured. The complaint named as defendants not only The Goodyear Tire and Rubber Company (Goodyear), an Ohio corporation, but also Goodyear's Turkish, French, and Luxembourgian subsidiaries. Those foreign subsidiaries, which manufactured tires for sale in Europe and Asia, lacked any affiliation with North Caro-lina. A small percentage of tires manufactured by the foreign subsidiaries were distributed in North Carolina, however, and on that ground, the North Carolina Court of Appeals held the subsidiaries amenable to the general jurisdiction of North Carolina courts.

We reversed, observing that the North Carolina court's analysis "elided the essential difference between case-specific and all-purpose (general) jurisdiction." *Id.,* at ___ (slip op., at 10). Although the placement of a product into the stream of commerce "may bolster an affiliation germane to *specific* jurisdiction," we explained, such contacts "do not warrant a determination that, based on those ties, the forum has *general* jurisdiction over a defendant." *Id.,* at ___ (slip op., at 10–11). As *International Shoe* itself teaches, a corporation's "continuous activity of some sorts within a state is not enough to support the demand that the corporation be amenable to suits unrelated to that activity." 326 U.S., at 318. Because Goodyear's foreign subsidiaries were "in no sense at home in North Carolina," we held, those subsidiaries could not be required to submit to the general jurisdiction of that State's courts. 564 U.S., at ___ (slip op., at 13). See also *J. McIntyre Machinery, Ltd.* v. *Nicastro,* 564 U.S. ___, ___ (2011) (Ginsburg, J., dissenting) (slip op., at 7) (noting unanimous agreement that a foreign manufacturer, which engaged an independent U.S.-based distributor to sell its machines throughout the United States, could not be exposed to all-purpose jurisdiction in New Jersey courts based on those contacts).

As is evident from *Perkins, Helicopteros,* and *Goodyear,* general and specific jurisdiction have followed markedly different trajectories post-*International Shoe.* Specific jurisdiction has been cut loose from *Pennoyer*'s sway, but we have declined to stretch general jurisdiction beyond limits traditionally recognized.[9] As this Court has increasingly trained on the "relationship among the defendant, the forum, and the litigation," *Shaffer,* 433 U.S., at 204, *i.e.,* specific jurisdiction,[10] general jurisdiction has come to occupy a less dominant place in the contemporary scheme.[11]

IV

With this background, we turn directly to the question whether Daimler's affiliations with California are sufficient to subject it to the general (all-purpose) personal jurisdiction of that State's courts. In the proceedings below, the parties agreed on, or failed to contest, certain points we now take as given. Plaintiffs have never attempted to fit this case into the *specific* jurisdiction category. Nor did plaintiffs challenge on appeal the District Court's holding that Daimler's own contacts with California were, by themselves, too sporadic to justify the exercise of general jurisdiction. While plaintiffs ultimately persuaded the Ninth Circuit to impute MBUSA's California contacts to Daimler on an agency theory, at no point have they maintained that MBUSA is an alter ego of Daimler.

Daimler, on the other hand, failed to object below to plaintiffs' assertion that the California courts could exercise all-purpose jurisdiction over MBUSA.[12] But see Brief for Petitioner 23, n.4 (suggestion that in light of *Goodyear,* MBUSA may not be amenable to general jurisdiction in California); Brief for United States as *Amicus Curiae* 16, n.5 (hereinafter U.S. Brief) (same). We will assume then, for purposes of this decision only, that MBUSA qualifies as at home in California.

A

In sustaining the exercise of general jurisdiction over Daimler, the Ninth Circuit relied on an agency theory, determining that MBUSA acted as Daimler's agent for jurisdictional purposes and then attributing MBUSA's California contacts to Daimler. The Ninth Circuit's agency analysis derived from Circuit precedent considering principally whether the subsidiary "performs services that are sufficiently important to the foreign corporation that if it did not have a representative to perform them, the corporation's own officials would undertake to perform substantially similar services." 644 F.3d, at 920 (quoting *Doe* v. *Unocal Corp.,* 248 F.3d 915, 928 (CA9 2001); emphasis deleted).

This Court has not yet addressed whether a foreign corporation may be subjected to a court's general jurisdiction based on the contacts of its in-state subsidiary. Daimler argues, and several Courts of Appeals have held, that a subsidiary's jurisdictional contacts can be imputed to its parent only when the former is so dominated by the latter as to be its alter ego. The Ninth Circuit adopted a less rigorous test based on what it described as an "agency" relationship. Agencies, we note, come in many sizes and shapes: "One may be an agent for some business purposes and not others so that the fact that one may be an agent for one purpose does not make him or her an agent for every purpose." 2A C. J. S., Agency §43, p. 367 (2013) (footnote omitted).[13] A subsidiary, for example, might be its parent's agent for claims arising in the place where the subsidiary operates, yet not its agent regarding claims arising elsewhere. The Court of Appeals did not advert to that prospect. But we need not pass judgment on invocation of an agency theory in the context of general jurisdiction, for in no event can the appeals court's analysis be sustained.

The Ninth Circuit's agency finding rested primarily on its observation that MBUSA's services were "important" to Daimler, as gauged by Daimler's hypothetical readiness to perform those services itself if MBUSA did not exist. Formulated this way, the inquiry into importance stacks the deck, for it will always yield a pro-jurisdiction answer: "Anything a corporation does through an independent contractor, subsidiary, or distributor is presumably something that the corporation would do 'by other means' if the independent contractor, subsidiary, or distributor did not exist." 676 F.3d, at 777 (O'Scannlain, J., dissenting from denial of rehearing en banc).[14] The Ninth Circuit's agency theory thus appears to subject foreign corporations to general jurisdiction whenever they have an in-state subsidiary or affiliate, an outcome that would sweep beyond even the "sprawling view of general jurisdiction" we rejected in *Goodyear.* 564 U.S., at ___ (slip op., at 12).[15]

B

Even if we were to assume that MBUSA is at home in California, and further to assume MBUSA's contacts are imputable to Daimler, there would still be no basis to subject Daimler to general jurisdiction in California, for Daimler's slim contacts with the State hardly render it at home there.[16]

Goodyear made clear that only a limited set of affiliations with a forum will render a defendant amenable to all-purpose jurisdiction there. "For an individual, the paradigm forum for the exercise of general jurisdiction is the individual's domicile; for a corporation, it is an equivalent place, one in which the corporation is fairly regarded as at home." 564 U.S., at ___ (slip op., at 7) (citing Brilmayer et al., A General Look at General Jurisdiction, 66 Texas L.Rev. 721, 728 (1988)). With respect to a corporation, the place of incorporation and principal place of business are "paradig[m] ... bases for general jurisdiction." *Id.,* at 735. See also Twitchell, 101 Harv. L.Rev., at 633. Those affiliations have the virtue of being unique—that is, each ordinarily indicates only one place—as well as easily ascertainable. Cf. *Hertz Corp.* v. *Friend,* 559 U.S. 77, 94 (2010) ("Simple jurisdictional rules ... promote greater predictability."). These bases afford plaintiffs recourse to at least one clear and certain forum in which a corporate defendant may be sued on any and all claims.

Goodyear did not hold that a corporation may be subject to general jurisdiction *only* in a forum where it is incor-porated or has its principal place of business; it simply typed those places paradigm all-purpose forums. Plaintiffs would have us look beyond the exemplar bases *Goodyear* identified, and approve the exercise of general jurisdiction in every State in which a corporation "engages in a substantial, continuous, and systematic course of business." Brief for Respondents 16–17, and nn.7–8. That formulation, we hold, is unacceptably grasping.

As noted, see *supra*, at 7–8, the words "continuous and systematic" were used in *International Shoe* to describe instances in which the exercise of *specific* jurisdiction would be appropriate. See 326 U.S., at 317 (jurisdiction can be asserted where a corporation's in-state activities are not only "continuous and systematic, but also give rise to the liabilities sued on").[17] Turning to all-purpose jurisdiction, in contrast, *International Shoe* speaks of "instances in which the continuous corporate operations within a state [are] so substantial and of such a nature as to justify suit ... *on causes of action arising from dealings en-tirely distinct from those activities.*" *Id.*, at 318 (emphasis added). See also Twitchell, Why We Keep Doing Business With Doing-Business Jurisdiction, 2001 U. Chi. Legal Forum 171, 184 (*International Shoe* "is clearly not saying that dispute-blind jurisdiction exists whenever 'continuous and systematic' contacts are found.").[18] Accordingly, the inquiry under *Goodyear* is not whether a foreign corporation's in-forum contacts can be said to be in some sense "continuous and systematic," it is whether that corporation's "affiliations with the State are so 'continuous and systematic' as to render [it] essentially at home in the forum State." 564 U.S., at ___ (slip op., at 2).[19]

Here, neither Daimler nor MBUSA is incorporated in California, nor does either entity have its principal place of business there. If Daimler's California activities sufficed to allow adjudication of this Argentina-rooted case in California, the same global reach would presumably be available in every other State in which MBUSA's sales are sizable. Such exorbitant exercises of all-purpose jurisdiction would scarcely permit out-of-state defendants "to structure their primary conduct with some minimum assurance as to where that conduct will and will not render them liable to suit." *Burger King Corp.*, 471 U.S., at 472 (internal quotation marks omitted).

It was therefore error for the Ninth Circuit to conclude that Daimler, even with MBUSA's contacts attributed to it, was at home in California, and hence subject to suit there on claims by foreign plaintiffs having nothing to do with anything that occurred or had its principal impact in California.[20]

C

Finally, the transnational context of this dispute bears attention. The Court of Appeals emphasized, as supportive of the exercise of general jurisdiction, plaintiffs' assertion of claims under the Alien Tort Statute (ATS), 28 U.S.C. §1350, and the Torture Victim Protection Act of 1991 (TVPA), 106Stat. 73, note following 28 U.S.C. §1350. See 644 F.3d, at 927 ("American federal courts, be they in California or any other state, have a strong interest in adjudicating and redressing international human rights abuses."). Recent decisions of this Court, however, have rendered plaintiffs' ATS and TVPA claims infirm. See *Kiobel* v. *Royal Dutch Petroleum Co.*, 569 U.S. ___, ___ (2013) (slip op., at 14) (presumption against extra-territorial application controls claims under the ATS); *Mohamad* v. *Palestinian Authority*, 566 U.S. ___, ___ (2012) (slip op., at 1) (only natural persons are subject to liability under the TVPA).

The Ninth Circuit, moreover, paid little heed to the risks to international comity its expansive view of general jurisdiction posed. Other nations do not share the uninhibited approach to personal jurisdiction advanced by the Court of Appeals in this case. In the European Union, for example, a corporation may generally be sued in the nation in which it is "domiciled," a term defined to refer only to the location of the corporation's "statutory seat," "central administration," or "principal place of business." European Parliament and Council Reg. 1215/2012, Arts. 4(1), and 63(1), 2012 O. J. (L. 351) 7, 18. See also *id.*, Art. 7(5), 2012 O. J. 7 (as to "a dispute *arising out of the operations of a branch, agency or other establishment*," a corporation may be sued "in the courts for the place where the branch, agency or other establishment is situated" (emphasis added)). The Solicitor General informs us, in this regard, that "foreign governments' objections to some domestic courts' expansive views of general jurisdiction have in the past impeded negotiations of international agreements on the reciprocal recognition and enforcement of judgments." U.S. Brief 2 (citing Juenger, The American Law of General Jurisdiction, 2001 U. Chi. Legal Forum 141, 161–162). See also U.S. Brief 2 (expressing concern thatunpredictable applications of general jurisdiction based on activities of U.S.-based subsidiaries could discourage foreign investors); Brief for Respondents 35 (acknowledging that "doing business" basis for general jurisdiction has led to "international friction"). Considerations of international rapport thus reinforce our determination that subjecting Daimler to the general jurisdiction of courts in California would not accord with the "fair play and substantial justice" due process demands. *International Shoe*, 326 U.S., at 316 (quoting *Milliken* v. *Meyer*, 311 U.S. 457, 463 (1940)).

* * *

For the reasons stated, the judgment of the United States Court of Appeals for the Ninth Circuit is Reversed.

NOTES

[1] One plaintiff is a resident of Argentina and a citizen of Chile; all other plaintiffs are residents and

citizens of Argentina.

[2] Daimler was restructured in 2007 and is now known as Daimler AG. No party contends that any postsuit corporate reorganization bears on our disposition of this case. This opinion refers to members of the Daimler corporate family by the names current at the time plaintiffs filed suit.

[3] At times relevant to this suit, MBUSA was wholly owned by Daimler-Chrysler North America Holding Corporation, a Daimler subsidiary.

[4] *International Shoe* was an action by the State of Washington to collect payments to the State's unemployment fund. Liability for the payments rested on in-state activities of resident sales solicitors engaged by the corporation to promote its wares in Washington. See 326 U.S., at 313–314.

[5] Colloquy at oral argument illustrated the respective provinces of general and specific jurisdiction over persons. Two hypothetical scenarios were posed: *First*, if a California plaintiff, injured in a California accident involving a Daimler-manufactured vehicle, sued Daimler in California court alleging that the vehicle was defectively designed, that court's adjudicatory authority would be premised on specific juris-diction. See Tr. of Oral Arg. 11 (Daimler's counsel acknowledgedthat specific jurisdiction "may well be ... available" in such a case, de-pending on whether Daimler purposefully availed itself of the forum). *Second*, if a similar accident took place in Poland and injured Polish plaintiffs sued Daimler in California court, the question would be one of general jurisdiction. See *id.*, at 29 (on plaintiffs' view, Daimler would be amenable to such a suit in California).

[6] See *Shaffer* v. *Heitner*, 433 U.S. 186, 204 (1977) ("The immediate effect of [*International Shoe*'s] departure from *Pennoyer*'s conceptual apparatus was to increase the ability of the state courts to obtain personal jurisdiction over nonresident defendants."); *McGee* v. *International Life Ins. Co.*, 355 U.S. 220, 222 (1957) ("[A] trend is clearly discernible toward expanding the permissible scope of state jurisdiction over foreign corporations and other nonresidents."). For an early codification, see Uniform Interstate and International Procedure Act §1.02 (describing jurisdiction based on "[e]nduring [r]elationship" to encompass a person's domicile or a corporation's place of incorporation or principal place of business, and providing that "any ... claim for relief" may be brought in such a place), §1.03 (describing jurisdiction "[b]ased upon [c]onduct," limited to claims arising from the enumerated acts, *e.g.*, "transacting any business in th[e] state," "contracting to supply services or things in th[e] state," or "causing tortious injury by an act or omission in th[e] state"), 9B U.L.A. 308, 310 (1966).

[7] See, *e.g.*, *Asahi Metal Industry Co.* v. *Superior Court of Cal., Solano Cty.*, 480 U.S. 102, 112 (1987) (opinion of O'Connor, J.) (specific jurisdiction may lie over a foreign defendant that places a product into the "stream of commerce" while also "designing the product for the market in the forum State, advertising in the forum State, establishing channels for providing regular advice to customers in the forum State, or marketing the product through a distributor who has agreed to serve as the sales agent in the forum State"); *World-Wide Volkswagen Corp.* v. *Woodson*, 444 U.S. 286, 297 (1980) ("[I]f the sale of a product of a manufacturer or distributor such as Audi or Volkswagen is not simply an isolated occurrence, but arises from the efforts of the manufacturer or distributor to serve, directly or indirectly, the market for its product in other States, it is not unreasonable to subject it to suit in one of those States if its allegedly defective merchandise has there been the source of injury to its owner or to others."); *Calder* v. *Jones*, 465 U.S. 783–790 (1984) (California court had specific jurisdiction to hear suit brought by California plaintiff where Florida-based publisher of a newspaper having its largest circulation in California published an article allegedly defaming the complaining Californian; under those circumstances, defendants "must 'reasonably anticipate being haled into [a California] court'"); *Keeton* v. *Hustler Magazine, Inc.*, 465 U.S. 770–781 (1984) (New York resident may maintain suit for libel in New Hampshire state court against California-based magazine that sold 10,000 to 15,000 copies in New Hampshire each month; as long as the defendant "continuously and deliberately exploited the New Hampshire market," it could reasonably be expected to answer a libel suit there).

[8] Selectively referring to the trial court record in *Perkins* (as summarized in an opinion of the intermediate appellate court), Justice Sotomayor posits that Benguet may have had extensive operations in places other than Ohio. See *post*, at 11–12, n.8 (opinion concurring in judgment) ("By the time the suit [in *Perkins*] was commenced, the company had resumed its considerable operations in the Philippines," "rebuilding its properties there" and "purchasing machinery, supplies and equipment." (internal quotation marks omitted)). See also *post*, at 7–8, n.5 (many of the corporation's "key management decisions" were made by the out-of-state purchasing agent and chief of staff).

Justice Sotomayor's account overlooks this Court's opinion in *Perkins* and the point on which that opinion turned: All of Benguet's activities were directed by the company's president from within Ohio. See *Perkins* v. *Benguet Consol. Mining Co.*, 342 U.S. 437–448 (1952) (company's Philippine mining operations "were completely halted during the occupation ... by the Japanese"; and the company's president, from his Ohio office, "supervised policies dealing with the rehabilitation of the corporation's properties in the Philippines and ... dispatched funds to cover purchases of machinery for such rehabilitation"). On another day, Justice Sotomayor joined a unanimous Court in recognizing: "To the extent that the company was conducting any business during and immediately after the Japanese occupation of the Philippines, it was doing so in Ohio ...." *Goodyear Dunlop Tires Operations, S.A.* v. *Brown*, 564 U.S. ___, ___ (2011) (slip op., at 11). Given the wartime circumstances, Ohio could be considered "a surrogate for the place of incorporation or head office." von Mehren & Trautman 1144. See also *ibid.* (*Perkins* "should be regarded as a decision on its exceptional facts, not as a significant reaffirmation of obsolescing notions of general jurisdiction" based on nothing more than a corporation's "doing business" in a forum). Justice Sotomayor emphasizes *Perkins'* statement that Benguet's Ohio contacts, while "continuous and systematic," were but a "limited ... part of its general business." 342 U.S., at 438. Describing the company's "wartime activities" as "necessarily limited," *id.,* at 448, however, this Court had in mind the diminution in operations resulting from the Japanese occupation and the ensuing shutdown of the com-pany's Philippine mines. No fair reader of the full opinion in *Perkins* could conclude that the Court meant to convey anything other than that Ohio was the center of the corporation's wartime activities. But cf. *post,* at 9 ("If anything, [*Perkins*] intimated that the defendant's Ohio contacts were *not* substantial in comparison to its contacts elsewhere.").

[9] See generally von Mehren & Trautman 1177–1179. See also Twitchell, The Myth of General Jurisdiction, 101 Harv. L. Rev. 610, 676 (1988) ("[W]e do not need to justify broad exercises of dispute-blind jurisdiction unless our interpretation of the scope of specific jurisdiction unreasonably limits state authority over nonresident defendants."); Borchers, The Problem With General Jurisdiction, 2001 U. Chi. Legal Forum 119, 139 ("[G]eneral jurisdiction exists as an imperfect safety valve that sometimes allows plaintiffs access to a reasonable forum in cases when specific jurisdiction would deny it.").

[10] Remarkably, Justice Sotomayor treats specific jurisdiction as though it were barely there. Given the many decades in which specific jurisdiction has flourished, it would be hard to conjure up an example of the "deep injustice" Justice Sotomayor predicts as a consequence of our holding that California is not an all-purpose forum for suits against Daimler. *Post,* at 16. Justice Sotomayor identifies "the concept of reciprocal fairness" as the "touchstone principle of due process in this field." *Post,* at 10 (citing *International Shoe*, 326 U.S., at 319). She over-looks, however, that in the very passage of *International Shoe* on which she relies, the Court left no doubt that it was addressing specific—not general—jurisdiction. See *id.,* at 319 ("The exercise of th[e]privilege [of conducting corporate activities within a State] may give rise to obligations, and, *so far as those obligations arise out of or are connected with the activities within the state*, a procedure which requires the corporation to respond to a suit brought to enforce them can, in most instances, hardly be said to be undue." (emphasis added)).

[11] As the Court made plain in *Goodyear* and repeats here, general jurisdiction requires affiliations "so 'continuous and systematic' as to render [the foreign corporation] essentially at home in the forum State." 564 U. S., at ___ (slip op., at 2), *i.e.,* comparable to a domestic enterprise in that State.

[12] MBUSA is not a defendant in this case.

[13] Agency relationships, we have recognized, may be relevant to the existence of *specific* jurisdiction. "[T]he corporate personality," *International Shoe Co.* v. *Washington*, 326 U.S. 310 (1945) , observed, "is a fiction, although a fiction intended to be acted upon as though it were a fact." *Id.,* at 316. See generally 1 W. Fletcher, Cyclopedia of the Law of Corporations §30, p.30 (Supp. 2012–2013) ("A corporation is a distinct legal entity that can act only through its agents."). As such, a corporation can purposefully avail itself of a forum by directing its agents or distributors to take action there. See, *e.g.,* *Asahi*, 480 U.S., at 112 (opinion of O'Connor, J.) (defendant's act of "marketing [a] product through a distributor who has agreed to serve as the sales agent in the forum State" may amount to purposeful availment); *International Shoe*, 326 U.S., at 318 ("the commission of some single or occasional acts of the corporate agent in a state" may sometimes "be deemed sufficient to render the corporation liable to suit" on related claims). See also Brief for Petitioner 24 (acknowledging that "an agency relationship

may be sufficient in some circumstances to give rise to *specific* jurisdiction"). It does not inevitably follow, however, that similar reasoning applies to *general* jurisdiction. Cf. *Goodyear*, 564 U.S., at ___ (slip op., at 10) (faulting analysis that "elided the essential difference between case-specific and all-purpose (general) jurisdiction").

[14] Indeed, plaintiffs do not defend this aspect of the Ninth Circuit's analysis. See Brief for Respondents 39, n.18 ("We do not believe that this gloss is particularly helpful.").

[15] The Ninth Circuit's agency analysis also looked to whether the parent enjoys "the right to substantially control" the subsidiary's activities. *Bauman* v. *DaimlerChrysler Corp.*, 644 F.3d 909, 924 (2011). The Court of Appeals found the requisite "control" demon-strated by the General Distributor Agreement between Daimler and MBUSA, which gives Daimler the right to oversee certain of MBUSA's operations, even though that agreement expressly disavowed the creation of any agency relationship. Thus grounded, the separate inquiry into control hardly curtails the overbreadth of the Ninth Circuit's agency holding.

[16] By addressing this point, Justice Sotomayor asserts, we have strayed from the question on which we granted certiorari to decide an issue not argued below. *Post,* at 5–6. That assertion is doubly flawed. First, the question on which we granted certiorari, as stated in Daimler's petition, is "whether it violates due process for a court to exercise general personal jurisdiction over a foreign corporation based solely on the fact that an indirect corporate subsidiary performs services on behalf of the defendant in the forum State." Pet. for Cert. i. That question fairly encompasses an inquiry into whether, in light of *Goodyear*, Daimler can be considered at home in California based on MBUSA's in-state activities. See also this Court's Rule 14.1(a) (a party's statement of the question presented "is deemed to comprise every subsidiary question fairly included therein"). Moreover, both in the Ninth Circuit, see, *e.g.*, Brief for Federation of German Industries etal. as *Amici Curiae* in No. 07–15386 (CA9), p.3, and in this Court, see, *e.g.*, U.S. Brief 13–18; Brief for Chamber of Commerce of United States of America etal. as *Amici Curiae* 6–23; Brief for Lea Brilmayer as *Amica Curiae* 10–12, *amici* in support of Daimler homed in on the insufficiency of Daimler's California contacts for general jurisdiction purposes. In short, and in light of our pathmarking opinion in *Goodyear*, we perceive no unfairness in deciding today that California is not an all-purpose forum for claims against Daimler.

[17] *International Shoe* also recognized, as noted above, see *supra,* at 7–8, that "some single or occasional acts of the corporate agent in a state... , because of their nature and quality and the circumstances of their commission, may be deemed sufficient to render the corporation liable to suit." 326 U.S., at 318.

[18] Plaintiffs emphasize two decisions, *Barrow S.S. Co.* v. *Kane*, 170 U.S. 100 (1898) , and *Tauza* v. *Susquehanna Coal Co.*, 220 N.Y. 259, 115 N.E. 915 (1917) (Cardozo, J.), both cited in *Perkins* v. *Benguet Consol. Mining Co.*, 342 U.S. 437 (1952) , just after the statement that a corporation's continuous operations in-state may suffice to establish general jurisdiction. *Id.*, at 446, and n.6. See also *International Shoe*, 326 U.S., at 318 (citing *Tauza*). *Barrow* and *Tauza* indeed upheld the exercise of general jurisdiction based on the presence of a local office, which signaled that the corporation was "doing business" in the forum. *Perkins'* unadorned citations to these cases, both decided in the era dominated by *Pennoyer*'s territorial thinking, see *supra,* at 6–7, should not attract heavy reliance today. See generally Feder, *Goodyear,* "Home," and the Uncertain Future of Doing Business Jurisdiction, 63 S.C. L.Rev. 671 (2012) (questioning whether "doing business" should persist as a basis for general jurisdiction).

[19] We do not foreclose the possibility that in an exceptional case, see, *e.g., Perkins*, described *supra,* at 10–12, and n.8, a corporation's operations in a forum other than its formal place of incorporation or principal place of business may be so substantial and of such a nature as to render the corporation at home in that State. But this case presents no occasion to explore that question, because Daimler's activities in California plainly do not approach that level. It is one thing to hold a corporation answerable for operations in the forum State, see *infra*, at 23, quite another to expose it to suit on claims having no connection whatever to the forum State.

[20] To clarify in light of Justice Sotomayor's opinion concurring in the judgment, the general jurisdiction inquiry does not "focu[s] solely on the magnitude of the defendant's in-state contacts." *Post,* at 8. General jurisdiction instead calls for an appraisal of a corporation's activities in their entirety, nationwide and worldwide. A corporation that operates in many places can scarcely be deemed at

home in all of them. Otherwise, "at home" would be synonymous with "doing business" tests framed before specific jurisdiction evolved in the United States. See von Mehren & Trautman 1142–1144. Nothing in *International Shoe* and its progeny suggests that "a particular quantum of local activity" should give a State authority over a "far larger quantum of ... activity" having no connection to any in-state activity. Feder, *supra,* at 694.Justice Sotomayor would reach the same result, but for a different reason. Rather than concluding that Daimler is not at home in Cali-fornia, Justice Sotomayor would hold that the exercise of general jurisdiction over Daimler would be unreasonable "in the unique circumstances of this case." *Post,* at 1. In other words, she favors a resolution fit for this day and case only. True, a multipronged reasonableness check was articulated in *Asahi,* 480 U.S., at 113–114, but not as a free-floating test. Instead, the check was to be essayed when *specific* jurisdiction is at issue. See also *Burger King Corp.* v. *Rudzewicz,* 471 U.S. 462–478 (1985). First, a court is to determine whether the connection between the forum and the episode-in-suit could justify the exercise of specific jurisdiction. Then, in a second step, the court is to consider several additional factors to assess the reasonableness of entertaining the case. When a corporation is genuinely at home in the forum State, however, any second-step inquiry would be superfluous.Justice Sotomayor fears that our holding will "lead to greater unpredictability by radically expanding the scope of jurisdictional dis-covery." *Post,* at 14. But it is hard to see why much in the way of discovery would be needed to determine where a corporation is at home. Justice Sotomayor's proposal to import *Asahi*'s "reasonableness" check into the general jurisdiction determination, on the other hand, would indeed compound the jurisdictional inquiry. The reasonableness factors identified in *Asahi* include "the burden on the defendant," "the interests of the forum State," "the plaintiff's interest in obtaining relief," "the interstate judicial system's interest in obtaining the most efficient resolution of controversies," "the shared interest of the several States in furthering fundamental substantive social policies," and, in the international context, "the procedural and substantive policies of other *nations* whose interests are affected by the assertion of jurisdiction." 480 U.S., at 113–115 (some internal quotation marks omitted). Imposing such a checklist in cases of general jurisdiction would hardly promote the efficient disposition of an issue that should be resolved expeditiously at the outset of litigation.

STEPHANIE C. ARTIS v. DISTRICT OF COLUMBIA

No. 16-460, January 22, 2018

ON WRIT OF CERTIORARI TO THE DISTRICT OF COLUMBIA COURT OF APPEALS

Justice Ginsburg delivered the opinion of the Court.

The Supplemental Jurisdiction statute, 28 U. S. C. §1367, enables federal district courts to entertain claims not otherwise within their adjudicatory authority when those claims "are so related to claims . . . within [federal-court competence] that they form part of the same case or controversy." §1367(a). Included within this supplemental jurisdiction are state claims brought along with federal claims arising from the same episode. When district courts dismiss all claims independently qualifying for the exercise of federal jurisdiction, they ordinarily dismiss as well all related state claims. See §1367(c)(3). A district court may also dismiss the related state claims if there is a good reason to decline jurisdiction. See §1367(c)(1), (2), and (4). This case concerns the time within which state claims so dismissed may be refiled in state court.

Section 1367(d), addressing that issue, provides:

"The period of limitations for any [state] claim [joined with a claim within federal-court competence] shall be tolled while the claim is pending [in federal court] and for a period of 30 days after it is dismissed unless State law provides for a longer tolling period."

The question presented: Does the word "tolled," as used in §1367(d), mean the state limitations period is suspended during the pendency of the federal suit; or does "tolled" mean that, although the state limitations period continues to run, a plaintiff is accorded a grace period of 30 days to refile in state court post dismissal of the federal case? Petitioner urges the first, or stop-the-clock, reading. Respondent urges, and the District of Columbia Court of Appeals adopted, the second, or grace-period, reading.

In the case before us, plaintiff-petitioner Stephanie C. Artis refiled her state-law claims in state court 59 days after dismissal of her federal suit.[1] Reading §1367(d) as a grace-period prescription, her complaint would be time barred. Reading §1367(d) as stopping the limitations clock during the pendency of the federal-court suit, her complaint would be timely. We hold that §1367(d)'s instruction to "toll" a state limitations period means to hold it in abeyance, *i.e.,* to stop the clock. Because the D. C. Court of Appeals held that §1367(d) did not stop the D. C. Code's limitations clock, but merely provided a 30-day grace period for refiling in D. C. Superior Court, we reverse the D. C. Court of Appeals' judgment.

I

A

Section 1367, which Congress added to Title 28 as part of the Judicial Improvements Act of 1990, 104Stat. 5089, codifies the court-developed pendent and ancillary jurisdiction doctrines under the label "supplemental jurisdiction." See *Exxon Mobil Corp.* v. *Allapattah Services, Inc.,* 545 U. S. 546, 552–558 (2005) (describing the development of pendent and ancillary jurisdiction doctrines and subsequent enactment of §1367); *id.,* at 579–584 (Ginsburg, J., dissenting) (same). The House Report accompanying the Act explains that Congress sought to clarify the scope of federal courts' authority to hear claims within their supplemental jurisdiction, appreciating that "[s]upplemental jurisdiction has enabled federal courts and litigants to . . . deal economically—in single rather than multiple litigation—with related matters." H. R. Rep. No. 101–734, p. 28 (1990) (H. R. Rep.). Section 1367(a) provides, in relevant part, that a district court with original jurisdiction over a claim "shall have supplemental jurisdiction over all other claims . . . form[ing] part of the same case or controversy."

"[N]ot every claim within the same 'case or controversy' as the claim within the federal courts' original jurisdiction will be decided by the federal court." *Jinks* v. *Richland County,* 538 U. S. 456, 459 (2003). Section 1367(c) states:

"The district courts may decline to exercise supplemental jurisdiction over a claim under subsection (a) if—

"(1) the claim raises a novel or complex issue of State law,

"(2) the claim substantially predominates over the claim or claims over which the district court has original jurisdiction,

"(3) the district court has dismissed all claims over which it has original jurisdiction, or

> "(4) in exceptional circumstances, there are other
> compelling reasons for declining jurisdiction."

If a district court declines to exercise jurisdiction over a claim asserted under §1367(a) and the plaintiff wishes to continue pursuing it, she must refile the claim in state court. If the state court would hold the claim time barred, however, then, absent a curative provision, the district court's dismissal of the state-law claim without prejudice would be tantamount to a dismissal with prejudice. See, *e.g., Carnegie-Mellon Univ.* v. *Cohill*, 484 U. S. 343, 352 (1988) (under the doctrine of pendent jurisdiction, if the statute of limitations on state-law claims expires before the federal court "relinquish[es] jurisdiction[,] . . . a dismissal will foreclose the plaintiff from litigating his claims"). To prevent that result, §1367(d) supplies "a tolling rule that must be applied by state courts." *Jinks*, 538 U. S., at 459. Section 1367(d) provides:

> "The period of limitations for any claim asserted under
> subsection (a), and for any other claim in the same action
> that is voluntarily dismissed at the same time as or after
> the dismissal of the claim under subsection (a), shall be
> tolled while the claim is pending and for a period of 30
> days after it is dismissed unless State law provides for a
> longer tolling period."

This case requires us to determine how §1367(d)'s tolling rule operates.

B

Petitioner Artis worked as a health inspector for respondent, the District of Columbia (the "District"). In November 2010, Artis was told she would lose her job. Thirteen months later, Artis sued the District in the United States District Court for the District of Columbia, alleging that she had suffered employment discrimination in violation of Title VII of the Civil Rights Act of 1964, 78Stat. 253, as amended, 42 U. S. C. §2000e *et seq.* She also asserted three allied claims under D. C. law: retaliation in violation of the District of Columbia Whistleblower Act, D. C. Code §1–615.54 (2001); termination in violation of the District of Columbia False Claims Act, §2–381.04; and wrongful termination against public policy, a common-law claim. Artis alleged that she had been subjected to gender discrimination by her supervisor, and thereafter encountered retaliation for reporting the supervisor's unlawful activities. See *Artis* v. *District of Columbia*, 51 F. Supp. 3d 135, 137 (2014).

On June 27, 2014, the District Court granted the District's motion for summary judgment on the Title VII claim. Having dismissed Artis' sole federal claim, the District Court, pursuant to §1367(c)(3), declined to exercise supplemental jurisdiction over her remaining state-law claims. "Artis will not be prejudiced," the court noted, "because 28 U. S. C. §1367(d) provides for a tolling of the statute of limitations during the period the case was here and for at least 30 days thereafter." *Id.,* at 142.

Fifty-nine days after the dismissal of her federal action, Artis refiled her state-law claims in the D. C. Superior Court, the appropriate local court. The Superior Court granted the District's motion to dismiss, holding that Artis' claims were time barred, because they were filed 29 days too late. See App. to Pet. for Cert. 14a. When Artis first asserted her state-law claims in the District Court, nearly two years remained on the applicable three-year statute of limitations.[2] But two and a half years passed before the federal court relinquished jurisdiction. Unless §1367(d) paused the limitations clock during that time, Artis would have had only 30 days to refile. The Superior Court rejected Artis' stop-the-clock reading of §1367(d), reasoning that Artis could have protected her state-law claims by "pursuing [them] in a state court while the federal court proceeding [was] pending." *Ibid.* In tension with that explanation, the court noted that duplicative filings in federal and state court are "generally disfavored . . . as 'wasteful' and . . . 'against [the interests of] judicial efficiency.' " *Id.,* at 14a, n. 1 (quoting *Stevens* v. *Arco Management of Wash. D.C., Inc.,* 751 A. 2d 995, 1002 (D. C. 2000); alteration in original).

The D. C. Court of Appeals affirmed. That court began by observing that two "competing approaches [to §1367(d)] have evolved nationally": the stop-the-clock reading and the grace-period reading. 135 A. 3d 334, 337 (2016).[3] Without further comment on §1367(d)'s text, the D. C. Court of Appeals turned to the legislative history. Section 1367(d)'s purpose, the court noted, was "to prevent the loss of claims to statutes of limitations where state law might fail to toll the running of the period of limitations while a supplemental claim was pending in federal court." *Id.,* at 338 (quoting H. R. Rep., at 30; internal quotation marks omitted). Following the lead of the California Supreme Court, the D. C. Court of Appeals determined that Congress had intended to implement a 1969 recommendation by the American Law Institute (ALI) to allow refiling in state court "within 30 days after dismissal." 135 A. 3d, at 338 (quoting *Los Angeles* v. *County of Kern,* 59 Cal. 4th 618, 629, 328 P. 3d 56, 63 (2014)).

The D. C. Court of Appeals also concluded that the grace-period approach "better accommodates federalism concerns," by trenching significantly less on state statutes of limitations than the stop-the-clock approach. 135 A. 3d, at 338–339. Construing §1367(d) as affording only a 30-day grace period, the court commented, was "consistent with [its] presumption favoring narrow interpretations of federal preemption of state law." *Id.,* at 339.

To resolve the division of opinion among State Supreme Courts on the proper construction of §1367(d), see *supra,* at 6, n. 3, we granted certiorari. 580 U. S. ___ (2017).

II

A

As just indicated, statutes that shelter from time bars claims earlier commenced in another forum generally employ one of two means.

First, the period (or statute) of limitations may be "tolled" while the claim is pending elsewhere.[4] Ordinarily, "tolled," in the context of a time prescription like §1367(d), means that the limitations period is suspended (stops running) while the claim is *sub judice* elsewhere, then starts running again when the tolling period ends, picking up where it left off. See Black's Law Dictionary 1488 (6th ed. 1990) ("toll," when paired with the grammatical object "statute of limitations," means "to suspend or stop temporarily"). This dictionary definition captures the rule generally applied in federal courts. See, *e.g., Chardon* v. *Fumero Soto*, 462 U. S. 650, 652, n. 1 (1983) (Court's opinion "use[d] the word 'tolling' to mean that, during the relevant period, the statute of limitations ceases to run").[5] Our decisions employ the terms "toll" and "suspend" interchangeably. For example, in *American Pipe & Constr. Co.* v. *Utah*, 414 U. S. 538 (1974), we characterized as a "tolling" prescription a rule "suspend[ing] the applicable statute of limitations," *id.*, at 554; accordingly, we applied the rule to stop the limitations clock, *id.*, at 560–561.[6] We have similarly comprehended what tolling means in decisions on equitable tolling. See, *e.g., CTS Corp.* v. *Waldburger*, 573 U. S. ___, ___ (2014) (slip op., at 7) (describing equitable tolling as "a doctrine that pauses the running of, or 'tolls' a statute of limitations" (some internal quotation marks omitted)); *United States* v. *Ibarra*, 502 U. S. 1, 4, n. 2 (1991) (*per curiam*) ("Principles of equitable tolling usually dictate that when a time bar has been suspended and then begins to run again upon a later event, the time remaining on the clock is calculated by subtracting from the full limitations period whatever time ran before the clock was stopped.").

In lieu of "tolling" or "suspending" a limitations period by pausing its progression, a legislature might elect sim-ply to provide a grace period. When that mode is adopted, the statute of limitations continues to run while the claim is pending in another forum. But the risk of a time bar is averted by according the plaintiff a fixed period in which to refile. A federal statute of that genre is 28 U. S. C. §2415. That provision prescribes a six-year limitations period for suits seeking money damages from the United States for breach of contract. §2415(a). The statute further provides: "In the event that any action . . . is timely brought and is thereafter dismissed without prejudice, the action may be recommenced within one year after such dismissal, regardless of whether the action would otherwise then be barred by this section." §2415(e).[7] Many States have enacted similar grace-period provisions. See App. to Brief for National Conference of State Legislatures et al. as *Amici Curiae* 1a–25a. For example, Georgia law provides:

> "when any case has been commenced in either a state or federal court within the applicable statute of limitations and the plaintiff discontinues or dismisses the same, it may be recommenced in a court of this state or in a federal court either within the original applicable period of limitations or within six months after the discontinuance or dismissal, whichever is later . . . ." Ga. Code Ann. §9-2-61(a) (2007).

Tellingly, the District has not identified any federal statute in which a grace-period meaning has been ascribed to the word "tolled" or any word similarly rooted. Nor has the dissent, for all its mighty strivings, identified even one federal statute that fits its bill, *i.e.*, a federal statute that says "tolled" but means something other than "suspended," or "paused," or "stopped." From what statutory text, then, does the dissent start? See *post*, at 5.[8]

Turning from statutory texts to judicial decisions, only once did an opinion of this Court employ tolling language to describe a grace period: *Hardin* v. *Straub*, 490 U. S. 536 (1989). In *Hardin*, we held that, in 42 U. S. C. §1983 suits, federal courts should give effect to state statutes sheltering claims from time bars during periods of a plaintiff's legal disability. We there characterized a state statute providing a one-year grace period as "tolling" or "suspend[ing]" the limitations period "until one year after the disability has been removed." 490 U. S., at 537. This atypical use of "tolling" or "suspending" to mean something other than stopping the clock on a limitations period is a feather on the scale against the weight of decisions in which "tolling" a statute of limitations signals stopping the clock.

B

In determining the meaning of a statutory provision, "we look first to its language, giving the words used their ordinary meaning." *Moskal* v. *United States*, 498 U. S. 103, 108 (1990) (citation and internal quotation marks omitted). Section 1367(d) is phrased as a tolling provision. It suspends the statute of limitations for two adjacent time periods: while the claim is pending in federal court and for 30 days postdismissal. Artis urges that the phrase "shall be tolled" in §1367(d) has the same meaning it does in the statutes cited *supra*, at 7, n. 4. That is, the limitations clock stops the day the claim is filed in federal court and, 30 days postdismissal, restarts from the point at which it had stopped.

The District reads "tolled" for §1367(d)'s purposes differently. To "toll," the District urges, means to "remove or take away an effect." Brief for Respondent 12–13. To "toll" a limitations period, then, would mean to "remov[e] the bar that ordinarily would accompany its expiration." *Id.,* at 14.[9] "[T]here is nothing special," the District maintains, "about tolling limitations periods versus tolling any other fact, right, or consequence." *Id.,* at 13. But the District offers no reason why, in interpreting "tolled" as used in §1367(d), we should home in only on the word itself, ignoring the information about the verb's ordinary meaning gained from its grammatical object. Just as when the object of "tolled" is "bell" or "highway traveler," the object "period of limitations" sheds light on what it means to "be tolled."

The District's reading, largely embraced by the dissent, is problematic for other reasons as well. First, it tenders a strained interpretation of the phrase "period of limitations." In the District's view, "period of limitations" means "the effect of the period of limitations as a time bar." See *id.,* at 18 ("Section 1367(d) . . . provides that 'the period of limitations'— here its effect as a time bar—'shall be [removed or taken away] while the claim is pending [in federal court] and for a period of 30 days after it is dismissed.' " (alterations in original)). Second, the first portion of the tolling period, the duration of the claim's pendency in federal court, becomes superfluous under the District's construction. The "effect" of the limitations period as a time bar, on the District's reading, becomes operative only after the case has been dismissed. That being so, what need would there be to remove anything while the claim is pending in federal court?

Furthermore, the District's reading could yield an absurdity: It could permit a plaintiff to refile in state court even if the limitations period on her claim had expired before she filed in federal court. To avoid that result, the District's proposed construction of "tolled" as "removed" could not mean simply "removed." Instead, "removed" would require qualification to express "removed, unless the period of limitations expired before the claim was filed in federal court." In sum, the District's interpretation maps poorly onto the language of §1367(d), while Artis' interpretation is a natural fit.

C

The D. C. Court of Appeals adopted the District's grace-period construction primarily because it was convinced that in drafting §1367(d), Congress embraced an ALI recommendation. 135 A. 3d, at 338. Two decades before the enactment of §1367(d), the ALI, in its 1969 Study of the Division of Jurisdiction Between State and Federal Courts, did recommend a 30-day grace period for refiling certain claims. The ALI proposed the following statutory language:

> "If any claim in an action timely commenced in a federal court is dismissed for lack of jurisdiction over the subject matter of the claim, a new action on the same claim brought in another court shall not be barred by a statute of limitations that would not have barred the original action had it been commenced in that court, if such new action is brought in a proper court, federal or State, within thirty days after dismissal of the original claim has become final or within such longer period as may be available under applicable State law." ALI, Study of the Division of Jurisdiction Between State and Federal Courts §1386(b), p. 65 (1969) (ALI Study).

Congress, however, did not adopt the ALI's grace-period formulation. Instead, it ordered tolling of the state limitations period "while the claim is pending" in federal court. Although the provision the ALI proposed, like §1367(d), established a 30-day federal floor on the time allowed for refiling, it did not provide for tolling the period of limitations while a claim is pending.[10] True, the House Report contained a citation to the ALI Study, but only in reference to a different provision, 28 U. S. C. §1391 (the general venue statute). There, Congress noted that its approach was "taken from the ALI Study." H. R. Rep., at 23. Had Congress similarly embraced the ALI's grace-period formulation in §1367(d), one might expect the House Report to have said as much.[11]

D

The District asks us to zero in on §1367(d)'s "express inclusion" of the "period of 30 days after the claim is dismissed" within the tolling period. Brief for Respondent 20 (internal quotation marks omitted). Under Artis' stop-the-clock interpretation, the District contends, "the inclusion of 30 days within the tolling period would be relegated to insignificance in the mine-run of cases." *Id.,* at 21 (citation and internal quotation marks omitted). In §1367(d), Congress did provide for tolling not only while the claim is pending in federal court, but also for 30 days thereafter. Including the 30 days within §1367(d)'s tolling period accounts for cases in which a federal action is commenced close to the expiration date of the relevant state statute of limitations. In such a case, the added days give the plaintiff breathing space to refile in state court.

Adding a brief span of days to the tolling period is not unusual in stop-the-clock statutes. In this respect, §1367(d) closely resembles 46 U. S. C. §53911, which provides, in a subsection titled "Tolling of limitations period," that if a plaintiff submits a claim for war-related vessel damage to the Secretary of Transportation, "the running of the limitations period for bringing a civil action is suspended until the Secretary denies the claim, and for 60 days thereafter." §53911(d). Numerous other statutes similarly append a fixed number of days to an initial tolling period. See, *e.g.,* 22 U. S. C.

§1631k(c) ("Statutes of limitations on assessments . . . shall be suspended with respect to any vested property . . . while vested and for six months thereafter. . . ."); 26 U. S. C. §6213(f)(1) ("In any case under title 11 of the United States Code, the running of the time prescribed by subsection (a) for filing a petition in the Tax Court with respect to any deficiency shall be suspended for the period during which the debtor is prohibited by reason of such case from filing a petition in the Tax Court with respect to such deficiency, and for 60 days thereafter."); §6503(a)(1) ("The running of the period of limitations provided in section 6501 or 6502 . . . shall . . . be suspended for the period during which the Secretary is prohibited from making the assessment . . . and for 60 days thereafter."); 50 U. S. C. §4000(c) ("The running of a statute of limitations against the collection of tax deferred under this section . . . shall be suspended for the period of military service of the servicemember and for an addi-tional period of 270 days thereafter."). Thus, the "30 days" provision casts no large shadow on Artis' interpretation.

Section 1367(d)'s proviso, "unless State law provides for a longer tolling period," could similarly aid a plaintiff who filed in federal court just short of the expiration of the state limitations period. She would have the benefit of §1367(d)'s 30-days-to-refile prescription, or such longer time as state law prescribes.[12] It may be that, in most cases, the state-law tolling period will not be longer than §1367(d)'s. But in some cases it undoubtedly will. For example, Indiana permits a plaintiff to refile within three years of dismissal. See Ind. Code §34–11–8–1 (2017). And Louisiana provides that after dismissal the limitations period "runs anew." La. Civ. Code Ann., Arts. 3462, 3466 (West 2007).

III

Satisfied that Artis' text-based arguments overwhelm the District's, we turn to the District's contention that the stop-the-clock interpretation of §1367(d) raises a significant constitutional question: Does the statute exceed Congress' authority under the Necessary and Proper Clause, Art. I, §8, cl. 18, because its connection to Congress' enumerated powers is too attenuated or because it is too great an incursion on the States' domain? Brief for Respondent 46–49. To avoid constitutional doubt, the District urges, we should adopt its reading. "[W]here an alternative interpretation of [a] statute is fairly possible," the District reminds, we have construed legislation in a manner that "avoid[s] [serious constitutional] problems" raised by "an otherwise acceptable construction." INS v. St. Cyr, 533 U. S. 289, 299–300 (2001) (internal quotation marks omitted). But even if we regarded the District's reading of §1367(d) as "fairly possible," our precedent would undermine the proposition that §1367(d) presents a serious constitutional problem. See Jinks, 538 U. S., at 461–465.

In Jinks, we unanimously rejected an argument that §1367(d) impermissibly exceeds Congress' enumerated powers.[13] Section 1367(d), we held, "is necessary and proper for carrying into execution Congress's power '[t]o constitute Tribunals inferior to the supreme Court,' . . . and to assure that those tribunals may fairly and effi-ciently exercise '[t]he judicial Power of the United States.' " Id., at 462 (quoting U. S. Const., Art. I, §8, cl. 9, and Art. III, §1).

In two principal ways, we explained, §1367(d) is "conducive to the due administration of justice in federal court." 538 U. S., at 462 (internal quotation marks omitted). First, "it provides an alternative to the unsatisfactory options that federal judges faced when they decided whether to retain jurisdiction over supplemental state-law claims that might be time barred in state court." Ibid. Section 1367(d) thus "unquestionably promotes fair and efficient operation of the federal courts." Id., at 463. Second, §1367(d) "eliminates a serious impediment to access to the federal courts on the part of plaintiffs pursuing federal- and state-law claims" arising from the same episode. Ibid. With tolling available, a plaintiff disinclined to litigate simultaneously in two forums is no longer impelled to choose between forgoing either her federal claims or her state claims.

Moreover, we were persuaded that §1367(d) was "plainly adapted" to Congress' exercise of its enumerated power: there was no cause to suspect that Congress had enacted §1367(d) as a " 'pretext' for 'the accomplishment of objects not entrusted to [it],' "; nor was there reason to believe that the connection between §1367(d) and Congress' authority over the federal courts was too attenuated. Id., at 464 (quoting McCulloch v. Maryland, 4 Wheat. 316, 423 (1819)).

Our decision in Jinks also rejected the argument that §1367(d) was not "proper" because it violates principles of state sovereignty by prescribing a procedural rule for state courts' adjudication of purely state-law claims. 538 U. S., at 464–465. "Assuming [without deciding] that a principled dichotomy can be drawn, for purposes of determining whether an Act of Congress is 'proper,' between federal laws that regulate state-court 'procedure' and laws that change the 'substance' of state-law rights of action," we concluded that the tolling of state limitations periods "falls on the [permissible] 'substantive' side of the line." Ibid.

The District's contention that a stop-the-clock prescription serves "no federal purpose" that could not be served by a grace-period prescription is unavailing. Brief for Respondent 49. Both devices are standard, off-the-shelf means of accounting for the fact that a claim was timely pressed in another forum. Requiring Congress to choose one over the other would impose a tighter constraint on Congress' discretion than we have ever countenanced.

The concern that a stop-the-clock prescription entails a greater imposition on the States than a grace-period prescription, moreover, may be more theoretical than real. Consider the alternative suggested by the D. C. Superior Court. Plaintiffs situated as Artis was could simply file two actions and ask the state court to hold the suit filed there in abeyance pending disposition of the federal suit. See supra, at 6. Were the dissent's position to prevail, cautious plaintiffs would surely take up the D. C. Superior Court's suggestion. How it genuinely advances federalism concerns to drive plaintiffs to resort to wasteful, inefficient duplication to preserve their state-law claims is far from apparent. See, e.g., Stevens, 751 A. 2d, at 1002 (it "work[s] against judicial efficiency . . . to compel prudent federal litigants who present state claims to file duplicative and wasteful protective suits in state court").

We do not gainsay that statutes of limitations are "fundamental to a well-ordered judicial system." *Board of Regents of Univ. of State of N. Y.* v. *Tomanio*, 446 U. S. 478, 487 (1980). We note in this regard, however, that a stop-the-clock rule is suited to the primary purposes of limitations statutes: "preventing surprises" to defendants and "barring a plaintiff who has slept on his rights." *American Pipe & Constr. Co.* v. *Utah*, 414 U. S. 538, 554 (1974) (internal quotation marks omitted). Whenever §1367(d) applies, the defendant will have notice of the plaintiff's claims within the state-prescribed limitations period. Likewise, the plaintiff will not have slept on her rights. She will have timely asserted those rights, endeavoring to pursue them in one litigation.

* * *

For the reasons stated, we resist unsettling the usual understanding of the word "tolled" as it appears in legislative time prescriptions and court decisions thereon. The judgment of the D. C. Court of Appeals is therefore reversed, and the case is remanded for further proceedings not inconsistent with this opinion.

It is so ordered.

NOTES

[1] The nonfederal claims Artis asserted arose under the D. C. Code and common law; on dismissal of her federal-court suit, she refiled those claims in D. C. Superior Court. For the purpose at hand, District of Columbia law and courts are treated as state law and courts. See 28 U. S. C. §1367(e) ("As used in this section, the term 'State' includes the District of Columbia, the Commonwealth of Puerto Rico, and any territory or possession of the United States.").

[2] The D. C. False Claims Act and the tort of wrongful termination each have a three-year statute of limitations that started to run on the day Artis lost her job in November 2010. See D. C. Code §2–381.04(c) (2001) (D. C. False Claims Act); *Stephenson* v. *American Dental Assn.*, 789 A. 2d 1248, 1249, 1252 (D. C. 2002) (tort of wrongful termination governed by D. C.'s catchall three-year limitations period and claim accrues on the date when plaintiff has unequivocal notice of termination). Artis' whistleblower claim had a one-year limitations period, which began to accrue when Artis "first bec[a]m[e] aware" that she had been terminated for reporting her supervisor's misconduct. D. C. Code §1–615.54(a)(2). The parties dispute the date the whistleblower claim accrued. See Brief for Petitioner 10, n. 2; Brief for Respondent 8, n. 2.

[3] The high courts of Maryland and Minnesota, along with the Sixth Circuit, have held that §1367(d)'s tolling rule pauses the clock on the statute of limitations until 30 days after the state-law claim is dismissed. See *In re Vertrue Inc. Marketing & Sales Practices Litigation*, 719 F. 3d 474, 481 (CA6 2013); *Goodman* v. *Best Buy, Inc.*, 777 N. W. 2d 755, 759–760 (Minn. 2010); *Turner* v. *Kight*, 406 Md. 167, 180–182, 957 A. 2d 984, 992–993 (2008). In addition to the D. C. Court of Appeals, the high courts of California and the Northern Mariana Islands have held that §1367(d) provides only a 30-day grace period for the refiling of otherwise time-barred claims. See *Los Angeles* v. *County of Kern*, 59 Cal. 4th 618, 622, 328 P. 3d 56, 58 (2014); *Juan* v. *Commonwealth*, 2001 MP 18, 6 N. Mar. I. 322, 327 (2001).

[4] Among illustrations: 21 U. S. C. §1604 (allowing suits to proceed against certain biomaterial providers and providing that "[a]ny applicable statute of limitations shall toll during the period from the time a claimant files a petition with the Secretary under this paragraph until such time as either (i) the Secretary issues a final decision on the petition, or (ii) the petition is withdrawn," §1604(b)(3)(C)); 28 U. S. C. §1332 (permitting the removal of "mass actions" to federal court and providing that "[t]he limitations periods on any claims asserted in a mass action that is removed to Federal court pursuant to this subsection shall be deemed tolled during the period that the action is pending in Federal court," §1332(d)(11)(D)); 42 U. S. C. §233 (providing a remedy against the United States for certain injuries caused by employees of the Public Health Service, and stating that "[t]he time limit for filing a claim under this subsection . . . shall be tolled during the pendency of a[n] [administrative] request for benefits," §233(p)(3)(A)(ii)). See also Wis. Stat. §893.15(3) (2011–2012) ("A Wisconsin law limiting the time for commencement of an action on a Wisconsin cause of action is tolled from the period of commencement of the action in a non-Wisconsin forum until the time of its final disposition in that forum."). The dissent maintains that "stop clock examples [from the U. S. Code] often involve situations where some disability prevents the plaintiff from proceeding to court." *Post,* at 12, n. 7. Plainly, however, the several statutes just set out do not fit that description: They do not involve

"disabilities." Instead, like §1367(d), they involve claims earlier commenced in another forum.

[5] As we recognized in *Chardon* v. *Fumero Soto*, 462 U. S. 650 (1983), there may be different ways of "calculating the amount of time avail-able to file suit *after tolling has ended*." *Id.,* at 652, n. 1 (emphasis added). In addition to the "common-law" stop-the-clock effect, *id.,* at 655, under which the plaintiff must file within the amount of time left in the limitations period, a statute might either provide for the limitations period to be "renewed," so that "the plaintiff has the benefit of a new period as long as the original," or "establish a fixed period such as six months or one year during which the plaintiff may file suit, without regard to the length of the original limitations period or the amount of time left when tolling began." *Id.,* at 652, n. 1. Notably, under each of the "tolling effect[s]" enumerated in *Chardon*, *ibid.,* the word "tolled" means that the progression of the limitations clock is stopped for the duration of "tolling."

[6] The dissent's notion that federal tolling periods may be understood as grace periods, not stop-the-clock periods, see *post,* at 7–8, is entirely imaginative.

[7] Also illustrative, the Equal Credit Opportunity Act prescribes a five-year limitations period for certain suits. 15 U. S. C. §1691e(f). Where a government agency has brought a timely suit, however, an individual may bring an action "not later than one year after the commencement of that proceeding or action." *Ibid.*

[8] Reasons of history, context, and policy, the dissent maintains, would have made it sensible for Congress to have written a grace-period statute. See *post,* at 4–5. But "[t]he controlling principle in this case is the basic and unexceptional rule that courts must give effect to the clear meaning of statutes as written[,] . . . giving each word its ordinary, contemporary, common meaning." *Star Athletica, L. L. C.* v. *Varsity Brands, Inc.,* 580 U. S. ___, ___ (2017) (slip op., at 6) (internal quotation marks omitted).

[9] This is indeed a definition sometimes used in reference to a right. See, *e.g., Ricard* v. *Williams*, 7 Wheat. 59, 120 (1822) ("[A]n adverse possession . . . toll[s] the right of entry of the heirs, and, consequently, extinguish[es], by the lapse of time, their right of action for the land."). See also Black's Law Dictionary 1488 (6th ed. 1990) ("toll" can mean "bar, defeat, or take away; thus, to toll the entry means to deny or take away the right of entry"). The dissent, also relying on this sense of the word "toll," cites *Chardon* as support for the proposition that §1367(d)'s tolling instruction is ambiguous. See *post,* at 3; *supra,* at 8, n. 5. But, importantly, the grace-period statutes noted in *Chardon*, 462 U. S., at 660, n. 13, were precise about their operation. *Chardon* provides no support for the notion that a statute's instruction that a "period of limitations shall be tolled" plausibly could mean that the limitations clock continues to run but its effect as a bar is removed during the tolling. See *post,* at 2–3.

[10] The District emphasizes that the Reporter's note accompanying the ALI's proposed statute stated: "[A]ny governing statute of limitations is tolled by the commencement of an action in a federal court, and for at least thirty days following dismissal . . . in any case in which the dismissal was for lack of jurisdiction." ALI Study 66. The similarity between *this* language and §1367(d), the District argues, rebuts any argument that Congress did not adopt the ALI's recommendation. We are unpersuaded. The District offers no explanation why, if Congress wanted to follow the substance of the ALI's grace-period recommendation, it would neither cite the ALI Study in the legislative history of §1367(d), see *infra* this page, nor adopt the precise language of either the proposed statute or the Reporter's note. The ALI Study, moreover, cautions that the Reporter's notes reflect "the Reporter's work alone," not a position taken by the Institute. ALI Study, p. x.

[11] The dissent offers a history lesson on the ancient common-law principle of "journey's account," see *post,* at 5–6, and n. 4, but nothing suggests that the 101st Congress had any such ancient law in mind when it drafted §1367(d). Cf. *post,* at 9. More likely, Congress was mindful that "suspension" during the pendency of other litigation is "the common-law rule." *Chardon*, 462 U. S., at 655.

[12] The dissent, *post,* at 8–9, conjures up absurdities not presented by this case, for the District of Columbia has no law of the kind the dissent describes. All agree that the phrase "unless State law provides for a longer tolling period" leaves room for a more generous state-law regime. The dissent posits a comparison between the duration of the federal suit, plus 30 days, and a state-law grace period. But of course, as the dissent recognizes, *post,* at 9, the more natural comparison is between the amount of time a plaintiff has left to refile, given the benefit of §1367(d)'s tolling rule, and the

amount of time she would have to refile under the applicable state law. Should the extraordinary circumstances the dissent envisions in fact exist in a given case, the comparison the dissent makes would be far from inevitable.

[13] The dissent refers to an "understanding," *post,* at 14, by the Court in *Jinks* v. *Richland County,* 538 U. S. 456 (2003), that §1367(d) accords only a 30-day "window" for refiling in state court. Scattered characterizations in the *Jinks* briefing might be seen as conveying that understanding. See *post,* at 14, n. 9. The opinion itself, however, contains nary a hint of any such understanding. And indeed, one year earlier, we described §1367(d) as having the effect of stopping the clock, *i.e.,* "toll[ing] the state statute of limitations for 30 days in addition to however long the claim had been pending in federal court." *Raygor* v. *Regents of Univ. of Minn.,* 534 U. S. 533, 542 (2002).

Selected Dissents

- HONDA MOTOR COMPANY, LTD., et al. v. KARL L. OBERG

- CITY OF CHICAGO, et al. v. INTERNATIONAL COLLEGE OF SURGEONS, et al.

- AMOCO PRODUCTION CO., et al. v. SOUTHERN UTE INDIAN TRIBE, et al.

- ANTHONY PALAZZOLO v. RHODE ISLAND, et al.

- JENNIFER GRATZ & PATRICK HAMACHER v. LEE BOLLINGER, et al.

- RICHARD CHENEY, VICE PRESIDENT OF THE UNITED STATES, et al. v. UNITED STATES DISTRICT COURT FOR THE DISTRICT OF COLUMBIA, et al.

- COOPER INDUSTRIES, INC. v. AVIALL SERVICES, INC.

- LILLY LEDBETTER v. GOODYEAR TIRE & RUBBER CO., INC.

- ALBERTO R. GONZALES, ATTORNEY GENERAL v. LEROY CARHART et al. /// ALBERTO R. GONZALES, ATTORNEY GENERAL v. PLANNED PARENTHOOD FEDERATION OF AMERICA, INC., et al.

- DONALD C. WINTER, SECRETARY OF THE NAVY, et al. v NATURAL RESOURCES DEFENSE COUNCIL, INC., et al.

- FRANK RICCI, et al. v. JOHN DeSTEFANO, et al.

- BURLINGTON NORTHERN & SANTA FE RAILWAY CO., et al. v. UNITED STATES, et al. /// SHELL OIL CO. v. UNITED STATES

- COEUR ALASKA, INC. v. SOUTHEAST ALASKA CONSERVATION COUNCIL, et al. /// ALASKA v. SOUTHEAST ALASKA CONSERVATION COUNCIL, et al.

- GEORGE W. BUSH, et al. v. ALBERT GORE, Jr., et al.

- HARRY CONNICK SR., DISTRICT ATTORNEY, et al. v. JOHN THOMPSON

- UNITED STATES v. TOHONO O'ODHAM NATION

- KENTUCKY v. HOLLIS DESHAUN KING

- DANIEL COLEMAN v. COURT OF APPEALS OF MARYLAND

- SUPAP KIRTSAENG v. JOHN WILEY & SONS, INC.

- ABIGAIL NOEL FISHER v. UNIVERSITY OF TEXAS AT AUSTIN, et al.

- SHELBY COUNTY, ALABAMA v. ERIC H. HOLDER, JR., ATTORNEY GENERAL, et al.

- MAETTA VANCE v. BALL STATE UNIVERSITY

- SYLVIA BURWELL, SECRETARY OF HEALTH AND HUMAN SERVICES, et al. v. HOBBY LOBBY STORES, INC., et al. /// CONESTOGA WOOD SPECIALTIES CORPORATION, et al. v. SYLVIA BURWELL, SECRETARY OF HEALTH AND HUMAN SERVICES, et al.

- CTS CORPORATION v. PETER WALDBURGER, et al.

HONDA MOTOR COMPANY, LTD., et al. v. KARL L. OBERG

No. 93-644, June 24, 1994

ON WRIT OF CERTIORARI TO THE SUPREME COURT OF OREGON

Justice Ginsburg , with whom the Chief Justice joins, dissenting.

In product liability cases, Oregon guides and limits the factfinder's discretion on the availability and amount of punitive damages. The plaintiff must establish entitlement to punitive damages, under specific substantive criteria, by clear and convincing evidence. Where the factfinder is a jury, its decision is subject to judicial review to this extent:

The trial court, or an appellate court, may nullify the verdict if reversible error occurred during the trial, if the jury was improperly or inadequately instructed, or if there is no evidence to support the verdict. Absent trial error, and if there is evidence to support the award of punitive damages, however, Oregon's Constitution, Article VII, § 3, provides that a properly instructed jury's verdict shall not be reexamined.[1] Oregon's procedures, I conclude, are adequate to pass the Constitution's due process threshold. I therefore dissent from the Court's judgment upsetting Oregon's disposition in this case.

I

A

To assess the constitutionality of Oregon's scheme, I turn first to this Court's recent opinions in *Pacific Mut. Life Ins. Co. v. Haslip*, 499 U.S. 1 (1991), and *TXO Production Corp. v. Alliance Resources Corp.*, 509 U. S. ___ (1993). The Court upheld punitive damage awards in both cases, but indicated that due process imposes an outer limit on remedies of this type. Significantly, neither decision declared any specific procedures or substantive criteria essential to satisfy due process. In *Haslip*, the Court expressed concerns about "unlimited jury discretion--or unlimited judicial discretion for that matter--in the fixing of punitive damages," but refused to "draw a mathematical bright line between the constitutionally acceptable and the constitutionally unacceptable." 499 U. S., at 18. Regarding the components of "the constitutional calculus," the Court simply referred to "general concerns of reasonableness and [the need for] adequate guidance from the court when the case is tried to a jury." *Ibid*.

And in *TXO*, a majority agreed that a punitive damage award may be so grossly excessive as to violate the Due Process Clause. 509 U. S., at ___ (slip op., at 8-9, 13) (plurality opinion); *id.*, at ___ (slip op., at 1-2) (Kennedy, J., concurring in part and concurring in judgment); *id.*, at ___ (slip op., at 8) (O'Connor, J., dissenting). In the plurality's view, however, "a judgment that is a product" of "fair procedures . . . is entitled to a strong presumption of validity"; this presumption, "persuasive reasons" indicated, "should be irrebuttable, . . . or virtually so." *Id.*, at ___ (slip op., at 12), citing *Haslip, supra*, at 24-40 (Scalia, J., concurring in judgment), and *id.*, at 40-42 (Kennedy, J., concurring in judgment). The opinion stating the plurality position recalled *Haslip*'s touchstone: A "concern [for] reasonableness" is what due process essentially requires. 509 U. S., at ___ (slip op., at 13), quoting *Haslip, supra*, at 18. Writing for the plurality, Justice Stevens explained:

> "[W]e do not suggest that a defendant has a substantive due process right to a correct determination of the `reasonableness' of a punitive damages award. As Justice O'Connor points out, state law generally imposes a requirement that punitive damages be `reasonable.' A violation of a state law `reasonableness' requirement would not, however, necessarily establish that the award is so `grossly excessive' as to violate the Federal Constitution." 509 U. S., at ___, n. 24 (slip op., at 13, n. 24) (citation omitted).

B

The procedures Oregon's courts followed in this case satisfy the due process limits indicated in *Haslip* and *TXO;* the jurors were adequately guided by the trial court's instructions, and Honda has not maintained, in its full presentation to this Court, that the award in question was "so 'grossly excessive' as to violate the Federal Constitution." *TXO, supra,* at ___, n. 24 (slip op., at 13, n. 24).[2]

1

Several preverdict mechanisms channeled the jury's discretion more tightly in this case than in either *Haslip* or *TXO.* First, providing at least some protection against unguided, utterly arbitrary jury awards, respondent Karl Oberg was permitted to recover no more than the amounts specified in the complaint, $919,390.39 in compensatory damages and $5 million in punitive damages. See Ore. Rule Civ. Proc. 18B (1994); *Wiebe* v. *Seely,* 215 Ore. 331, 355-358, 335 P. 2d 379, 391 (1959); *Lovejoy Specialty Hosp.* v. *Advocates for Life, Inc.,* 121 Ore. App. 160, 167, 855 P. 2d 159, 163 (1993). The trial court properly instructed the jury on this damage cap. See 316 Ore. 263, 282, n. 11, 851 P. 2d 1084, 1095, n. 11 (1993). No provision of Oregon law appears to preclude the defendant from seeking an instruction setting a lower cap, if the evidence at trial cannot support an award in the amount demanded. Additionally, if the trial judge relates the incorrect maximum amount, a defendant who timely objects may gain modification or nullification of the verdict. See *Timber Access Industries Co.* v. *U. S. Plywood Champion Papers, Inc.,* 263 Ore. 509, 525-528, 503 P. 2d 482, 490-491 (1972).[3]

Second, Oberg was not allowed to introduce evidence regarding Honda's wealth until he "presented evidence sufficient to justify to the court a prima facie claim of punitive damages." Ore. Rev. Stat. §41.315(2) (1991); see also §30.925(2) ("During the course of trial, evidence of the defendant's ability to pay shall not be admitted unless and until the party entitled to recover establishes a prima facie right to recover [punitive damages]."). This evidentiary rule is designed to lessen the risk "that juries will use their verdicts to express biases against big businesses." *Ante,* at 16; see also Ore. Rev. Stat. §30.925(3)(g) (1991) (requiring factfinder to take into account "[t]he total deterrent effect of other punishment imposed upon the defendant as a result of the misconduct").

Third, and more significant, as the trial court instructed the jury, Honda could not be found liable for punitive damages unless Oberg established by "clear and convincing evidence" that Honda "show[ed] wanton disregard for the health, safety and welfare of others." Ore. Rev. Stat. §30.925 (1991) (governing product liability actions); see also §41.315(1) ("Except as otherwise specifically provided by law, a claim for punitive damages shall be established by clear and convincing evidence."). "[T]he clear and convincing evidence requirement," which is considerably more rigorous than the standards applied by Alabama in *Haslip*[4] and West Virginia in *TXO,*[5] "constrain[s] the jury's discretion, limiting punitive damages to the more egregious cases." *Haslip, supra,* at 58 (O'Connor, J., dissenting). Nothing in Oregon law appears to preclude a new trial order if the trial judge, informed by the jury's verdict, determines that his charge did not adequately explain what the "clear and convincing" standard means. See Ore. Rule Civ. Proc. 64G (1994) (authorizing court to grant new trial "on its own initiative").

Fourth, and perhaps most important, in product liability cases, Oregon requires that punitive damages, if any, be awarded based on seven substantive criteria, set forth in Ore. Rev. Stat. §30.925(3) (1991):

"(a) The likelihood at the time that serious harm would arise from the defendant's misconduct;
%(b) The degree of the defendant's awareness of that likelihood;
%(c) The profitability of the defendant's misconduct;
%(d) The duration of the misconduct and any concealment of it;
%(e) The attitude and conduct of the defendant upon discovery of the misconduct;
%(f) The financial condition of the defendant; and
%(g) The total deterrent effect of other punishment imposed upon the defendant as a result of the misconduct, including, but not limited to, punitive damage awards to persons in situations similar to the claimant's and the severity of criminal penalties to which the defendant has been or may be subjected."

These substantive criteria, and the precise instructions detailing them,[6] gave the jurors "adequate guidance" in making their award, see *Haslip,* 499 U. S., at 18, far more guidance than their counterparts in *Haslip*[7] and *TXO*[8] received. In *Haslip,* for example, the jury was told only the purpose of punitive damages (punishment and deterrence) and that an award was discretionary, not compulsory. We deemed those instructions, notable for their generality, constitutionally sufficient. 499 U. S., at 19-20.

The Court's opinion in *Haslip* went on to describe the checks Alabama places on the jury's discretion *postverdict*--through excessiveness review by the trial court, and appellate review, which tests the award against specific substantive criteria. *Id.*, at 20-23. While postverdict review of that character is not available in Oregon, the seven factors against which Alabama's Supreme Court tests punitive awards[9] strongly resemble the statutory criteria Oregon's juries are instructed to apply. 316 Ore., at 283, and n. 12, 851 P. 2d, at 1095-1096, and n. 12. And this Court has often acknowledged, and generally respected, the presumption that juries follow the instructions theyare given. See, *e.g.*, *Shannon* v. *United States*, ___ U. S. ___, ___ (1994) (slip op., at 11-12); *Richardson* v. *Marsh*, 481 U.S. 200, 206 (1987).

As the Supreme Court of Oregon observed, *Haslip* "determined only that the Alabama procedure, as a whole and in its net effect, did not violate the Due Process Clause." 316 Ore., at 284, 851 P. 2d, at 1096. The Oregon court also observed, correctly, that the Due Process Clause does not require States to subject punitive damage awards to a form of postverdict review "that includes the possibility of remittitur."[10] 316 Ore., at 284, 851 P. 2d, at 1096. Because Oregon requires the factfinder to apply §30.925's objective criteria, moreover, its procedures are perhaps more likely to prompt rational and fair punitive damage decisions than are the *post hoc* checks employed in jurisdictions following Alabama's pattern. See *Haslip, supra*, at 52 (O'Connor, J., dissenting) ("[T]he standards [applied by the Alabama Supreme Court] could assist juries to make fair, rational decisions. Unfortunately, Alabama courts do not give the[se] factors to the jury. Instead, the jury has standardless discretion to impose punitive damages whenever and in whatever amount it wants."). As the Oregon court concluded, "application of objective criteria ensures that sufficiently definite and meaningful constraints are imposed on the finder of fact." 316 Ore., at 283, 851 P. 2d, at 1096. The Oregon court also concluded that the statutory criteria, by adequately guiding the jury, worked to "ensur[e] that the resulting award is not disproportionate to a defendant's conduct and to the need to punish and deter." *Ibid.*[11]

2

The Supreme Court of Oregon's conclusions are buttressed by the availability of at least some postverdict judicial review of punitive damage awards. Oregon's courts ensure that there is evidence to support the verdict:

> "If there is no evidence to support the jury's decision--in this context, no evidence that the statutory prerequisites for the award of punitive damages were met--then the trial court or the appellate courts can intervene to vacate the award. See ORCP 64B(5) (trial court may grant a new trial if the evidence is insufficient to justify the verdict or is against law); *Hill* v. *Garner*, 561 P. 2d 1016 (1977) (judgment notwithstanding the verdict is to be granted when there is no evidence to support the verdict); *State* v. *Brown*, 761 P. 2d 1300 (1988) (a fact decided by a jury may be re examined when a reviewing court can say affirmatively that there is no evidence to support the jury's decision)." 316 Ore., at 285, 851 P. 2d, at 1096-1097 (parallel citations omitted).

The State's courts have shown no reluctance to strike punitive damage awards in cases where punitive liability is not established, so that defendant qualifies for judgment on that issue as a matter of law. See, *e.g.*, *Badger* v. *Paulson Investment Co.*, 311 Ore. 14, 28-30, 803 P. 2d 1178, 1186-1187 (1991); *Andor* v. *United Airlines*, 303 Ore. 505, 739 P. 2d 18 (1987); *Schmidt* v. *Pine Tree Land Development Co.*, 291 Ore. 462, 631 P. 2d 1373 (1981).

In addition, punitive damage awards may be set aside because of flaws in jury instructions. 316 Ore., at 285, 851 P. 2d, at 1097. See, *e.g.*, *Honeywell* v. *Sterling Furniture Co.*, 310 Ore. 206, 210-214, 797 P. 2d 1019, 1021-1023 (1990) (setting aside punitive damage award because it was prejudicial error to instruct jury that a portion of any award would be used to pay plaintiff's attorney fees and that another portion would go toState's common injury fund). As the Court acknowledges, "proper jury instructio[n] is a well established and, of course, important check against excessive awards." *Ante*, at 17.

II

In short, Oregon has enacted legal standards confining punitive damage awards in product liability cases. These state standards are judicially enforced by means of comparatively comprehensive preverdict procedures but markedly limited postverdict review, for Oregon has elected to make factfinding, once supporting evidence is produced, the province of the jury. Cf. *Chicago, R. I. & P. R. Co. v. Cole*, 251 U.S. 54, 56 (1919) (upholding against due process challenge Oklahoma Constitution's assignment of contributory negligence and assumption of risk defenses to jury's unreviewable decision; Court recognized State's prerogative to "confer larger powers upon a jury than those that generally prevail"); *Minnesota v. Clover Leaf Creamery Co.*, 449 U.S. 456, 479 (1981) (Stevens, J., dissenting) (observing that "allocation of functions within the structure of a state government" is ordinarily "a matter for the State to determine"). The Court today invalidates this choice, largely because it concludes that English and early American courts generally provided judicial reviewof the size of punitive damage awards. See *ante*, at 5-10. The Court's account of the relevant history is not compelling.

A

I am not as confident as the Court about either the clarity of early American common law, or its import. Tellingly, the Court barely acknowledges the large authority exercised by American juries in the 18th and 19th centuries. In the early years of our Nation, juries "usually possessed the power to determine both law and fact." Nelson, The Eighteenth Century Background of John Marshall's Constitutional Jurisprudence, 76 Mich. L. Rev. 893, 905 (1978); see, *e.g.*, *Georgia v. Brailsford*, 3 Dall. 1, 4 (1794) (Chief Justice John Jay, trying case in which State was party, instructed jury it had authority "to determine the law as well as the fact in controversy").[12] And at the time trial by jury was recognized as the constitutional right of parties "[i]n [s]uits at common law," U. S. Const., Amdt. 7, the assessment of "uncertain damages" was regarded, generally, as exclusively a jury function. See Note, Judicial Assessment of Punitive Damages, the Seventh Amendment, and the Politics of Jury Power, 91 Colum. L. Rev. 142, 156, and n. 69 (1991); see also *id.*, at 156-158, 163, and n. 112.

More revealing, the Court notably contracts the scope of its inquiry. It asks: Did common law judges claim the power to overturn jury verdicts they viewed as excessive? But full and fair historical inquiry ought to be wider. The Court should inspect, comprehensively and comparatively, the procedures employed--at trial *and* on appeal--to fix the amount of punitive damages.[13] Evaluated in this manner, Oregon's scheme affords defendants like Honda *more* procedural safeguards than 19th century law provided.

As detailed *supra*, at 5-6, Oregon instructs juries to decide punitive damage issues based on seven substantive factors and a clear and convincing evidence standard. When the Fourteenth Amendment was adopted in 1868, in contrast, "no particular procedures were deemed necessary to circumscribe a jury's discretion regarding the award of [punitive] damages, or their amount." *Haslip*, 499 U. S., at 27 (Scalia, J., concurring in judgment). The responsibility entrusted to the jury surely was not guided by instructions of the kind Oregon has enacted. Compare 1 J. Sutherland, Law of Damages 720 (1882) ("If, in committing the wrong complained of, [the defendant] acted recklessly, or wilfully and maliciously, with a design to oppress and injure the plaintiff, the jury in fixing the damages may disregard the rule of compensation; and, beyond that, may, as a punishment of the defendant, and as a protection to society against a violation of personal rights and social order, award such additional damages as in their discretion they may deem proper."), with Ore. Rev. Stat. §30-925 (1991) (requiring jury to consider, *inter alia*, "likelihood at the time that serious harm would arise from the defendant's misconduct"; "degree of the defendant's awareness of that likelihood"; "profitability of the defendant's misconduct"; "duration of the misconduct and any concealment of it").

Furthermore, common law courts reviewed punitive damage verdicts extremely deferentially, if at all. See, *e.g.*, *Day v. Woodworth*, 13 How. 363, 371 (1852) (assessment of "exemplary, punitive, or vindictive damages . . . has been always left to the discretion of the jury, as the degree of punishment to be thus inflicted must depend on the peculiar circumstances of each case"); *Missouri Pacific R. Co. v. Humes*, 115 U.S. 512, 521 (1885) ("[t]he discretion of the jury in such cases is notcontrolled by any very definite rules"); *Barry v. Edmunds*, 116 U.S. 550, 565 (1886) (in "actions for torts where no precise rule of law fixes the recoverable damages, it is the peculiar function of the jury to determine the amount by their verdict"). True, 19th century judges occasionally asserted that they had authority to overturn damage awards upon concluding, from the size of an award, that the jury's decision must have been based on "partiality" or "passion and prejudice." *Ante*, at 8-9. But courts rarely *exercised* this authority. See T. Sedgwick, Measure of Damages 707 (5th ed. 1869) (power "very sparingly used").

B

Because Oregon's procedures assure "adequate guidance from the court when the case is tried to a jury," *Haslip*, 499 U. S., at 18, this Court has no cause to disturb the judgment in this instance, for Honda presses here only a *procedural* due process claim. True, in a footnote to its petition for certiorari, not repeated in its briefs, Honda attributed to this Court an "assumption that procedural due process requires [judicial] review of *both* federal substantive due process and state law excessiveness challenges to the size of an award." Pet. for Cert. 16, n. 10 (emphasis in original). But the assertion regarding "state law excessiveness challenges" is extraordinary, for this Court has never held that the Due Process Clause requires a State's courts to police jury factfindings to ensure their conformity with state law. See *Chicago, R. I. & P. R. Co. v. Cole*, 251 U. S., at 56. And, as earlier observed, see *supra*, at 3, the plurality opinion in *TXO* disavowed the suggestion that a defendant has a federal due process right to a correct determination under state law of the "reasonableness"of a punitive damages award. 509 U. S., at ___, n. 24 (slip op., at 13, n. 24).

Honda further asserted in its certiorari petition footnote:

> "Surely . . . due process (not to mention
> Supremacy Clause principles) requires, at a
> minimum, that state courts entertain and pass on
> the federal law contention that a particular
> punitive verdict is so grossly excessive as to
> violate substantive due process. Oregon's
> refusal to provide even that limited form of
> review is particularly indefensible." Pet. for
> Cert. 16, n. 10.

But Honda points to no definitive Oregon pronouncement postdating this Court's precedent setting decisions in *Haslip* and *TXO* demonstrating the hypothesized refusal to pass on a federal law contention.[14]

It may be that Oregon's procedures guide juries so well that the "grossly excessive" verdict Honda projects in its certiorari petition footnote never materializes. Cf. n. 11, *supra* (between 1965 and the present, awards of punitive damages in Oregon have been reported in only two products liability cases, including this one). If, however, in some future case, a plea is plausibly made that a particular punitive damage award is not merely excessive, but "so `grossly excessive' as to violate the Federal Constitution," *TXO*, 509 U. S., at ___, n. 24 (slip op., at 13, n. 24), and Oregon's judiciary nevertheless insists that it is powerless to consider the plea, this Court might have cause to grant review. Cf. *Testa* v. *Katt*, 330 U.S. 386 (1947) (ruling on obligation of state courts to enforce federal law). No such case is before us today, nor does Honda, in this Court, maintain otherwise. See 316 Ore., at 286, n. 14, 851 P. 2d, at 1097, n. 14; n. 11, *supra* (size of award against Honda does not appear to be out of line with awards upheld in *Haslip* and *TXO*).

To summarize: Oregon's procedures adequately guide the jury charged with the responsibility to determine a plaintiff's qualification for, and the amount of, punitive damages, and on that account do not deny defendants procedural due process; Oregon's Supreme Court cor rectly refused to rule that "an award of punitivedamages, to comport with the requirements of the Due Process Clause, *always* must be subject to a form of post-verdict or appellate review" for excessiveness, 316 Ore., at 284, 851 P. 2d, at 1096 (emphasis added); the verdict in this particular case, considered in light of this Court's decisions in *Haslip* and *TXO*, hardly appears "so `grossly excessive' as to violate the substantive component of the Due Process Clause," *TXO*, 509 U. S., at ___ (slip op., at 13). Accordingly, the Court's procedural directive to the state court is neither necessary nor proper. The Supreme Court of Oregon has not refused to enforce federal law, and I would affirm its judgment.

NOTES

[1] Article VII, §3 of the Oregon Constitution reads:

%In actions at law, where the value in controversy shall exceed $200, the right of trial by jury shall be preserved, and no fact tried by a jury shall be otherwise re examined in any court of this state, unless the court can affirmatively say there is no evidence to support the verdict."

[2] The Supreme Court of Oregon noted that "procedural due process in the context of an award of punitive damages relates to the requirement that the procedure employed in making that award be fundamentally fair," while the substantive limit declared by this Court relates to the size of the award. 316 Ore. 263, 280, n. 10, 851 P. 2d 1084, 1094, n. 10 (1993).

[3] The Court's contrary suggestion, *ante*, at 17, is based on *Tenold* v. *Weyerhaeuser Co.*, 127 Ore. App. 511, ___ P. 2d ___ (1994), a decision by an intermediate appellate court, in which the defendant does not appear to have objected to the trial court's instructions as inaccurate, incomplete, or insufficient, for failure to inform the jury concerning a statutorily mandated $500,000 cap on noneconomic damages.

[4] The *Haslip* jury was told that it could award punitive damages if "reasonably satisfied from the evidence" that the defendant committed fraud. *Pacific Mut. Life Ins. Co.* v. *Haslip*, 499 U.S. 1, 6, n. 1 (1991).

[5] The *TXO* jury was instructed to apply a preponderance of the evidence standard. See *TXO Production Corp.* v. *Alliance Resources Corp.*, 509 U. S. ___, ___, n. 29 (1993) (slip op., at 18, n. 29).

[6] The trial court instructed the jury:

> "Punitive damages: If you have found that
> plaintiff is entitled to general damages, you
> must then consider whether to award punitive
> damages. Punitive damages may be awarded to the
> plaintiff in addition to general damages to
> punish wrongdoers and to discourage wanton
> misconduct.
> "In order for plaintiff to recover punitive
> damages against the defendant[s], the plaintiff
> must prove by clear and convincing evidence that
> defendant[s have] shown wanton disregard for the
> health, safety, and welfare of others. . . .
> "If you decide this issue against the
> defendant[s], you may award punitive damages,
> although you are not required to do so,
> becausepunitive damages are discretionary.
> "In the exercise of that discretion, you shall
> consider evidence, if any, of the following:
> "First, the likelihood at the time of the sale
> [of the ATV] that serious harm would arise from
> defendants' misconduct.
> "Number two, the degree of the defendants'
> awareness of that likelihood.
> "Number three, the duration of the misconduct.
> "Number four, the attitude and conduct of the
> defendant[s] upon notice of the alleged
> condition of the vehicle.
> "Number five, the financial condition of the
> defendant[s]." 316 Ore., at 282, n. 11, 851 P.
> 2d, at 1095, n. 11.

The trial judge did not instruct the jury on §30.925(3)(c), "profitability of [Honda's] misconduct," or §30.925(3)(g), the "total deterrent effect of other punishment" to which Honda was subject. Honda objected to an instruction on factor (3)(c), which it argued was phrased "to assume the existence of misconduct," and expressly waived an instruction on factor (3)(g), on the ground that it had not previously been subject to punitive damages. App. to Brief for Plaintiff Respondent in Opposition in No. S38436 (Ore.), p. 2. In its argument before the Supreme Court of Oregon, Honda did not contend that the trial court failed to instruct the jury concerning the "[§30.925(3)] criteria," or "that the jury did not properly apply those criteria." 316 Ore., at 282, n. 11, 851 P. 2d, at 1095, n. 11.

[7] The trial judge in *Haslip* instructed the jury:

> "Now, if you find that fraud was perpetrated
> then in addition to compensatory damages you may
> in your discretion, when I use the word
> discretion, I say you don't have to even find
> fraud, you wouldn't have to, but you may, the
> law says you may award an amount of money known
> as punitive damages.
> "This amount of money is awarded to the
> plaintiff but it is not to compensate the
> plaintiff for any injury. It is to punish the
> defendant. Punitive means to punish or it is
> also called exemplary damages, which means to
> make an example. So, if you feel or not feel,
> but if you are reasonably satisfied from the
> evidence that the plaintiff[s] . . . ha[ve] had
> a fraud perpetrated upon them and as a direct

result they were injured [then] in addition to
compensatory damages you may in your discretion
award punitive damages.
"Now, the purpose of awarding punitive or
exemplary damages is to allow money recovery to
the plaintiffs, . . . by way of punishment to
the defendant and for the added purpose of
protecting the public by deterring the defendant
and others from doing such wrong in the future.
Imposition of punitive damages is entirely
discretionary with the jury, that means you
don't have to award it unless this jury feels
that you should do so.
"Should you award punitive damages, in fixing
the amount, you must take into consideration the
character and the degree of the wrong as shown
by the evidence and necessity of preventing
similar wrong." 499 U. S., at 6, n. 1 (internal
quotation marks omitted).

[8] The jury instruction in *TXO* read:

"In addition to actual or compensatory damages,
the law permits the jury, under certain
circumstances, to make an award of punitive
damages, in order to punish the wrongdoer for
his misconduct, to serve as an example or
warning to others not to engage in such conduct
and to provide additional compensation for the
conduct to which the injured parties have been
subjected.
"If you find from a preponderance of the
evidence that TXO Production Corp. is guilty of
wanton, wilful, malicious or reckless conduct
which shows an indifference to the right of
others, then you may make an award of punitive
damages in this case.
"In assessing punitive damages, if any, you
should take into consideration all of the
circumstances surrounding the particular
occurrence, including the nature of the
wrongdoing, the extent of the harm inflicted,
the intent of the party committing the act, the
wealth of the perpetrator, as well as any
mitigating circumstances which may operate to
reduce the amount of the damages. The object of
such punishment is to deter TXO Production Corp.
and others from committing like offenses in the
future. Therefore the law recognizes that to in
fact deter such conduct may require a larger
fine upon one of large means than it would upon
one of ordinary means under the same or similar
circumstances." 509 U. S., at ___, n. 29 (slip
op., at 18-19, n. 29).

[9] The Alabama factors are:

%(a) whether there is a reasonable relationship between the punitive damages award and the harm likely to result from the defendant's conduct as well as the harm that actually has occurred; (b) the degree of reprehensibility of the defendant's conduct, the duration of that conduct, the defendant's awareness, any concealment, and the existence and frequency of similar past conduct; (c) the profitability to the defendant of the wrongful conduct and the desirability of removing that profit and of having the defendant also sustain a loss; (d) the `financial position' of the defendant; (e) all the costs of litigation; (f) the imposition of criminal sanctions on the defendant for its conduct, these to be taken in mitigation; and (g) the existence of other civil awards against the defendant for the same conduct, these also to be taken in mitigation." 499 U. S., at 21-22, citing *Green Oil Co.* v. *Hornsby*, 539 So. 2d 218, 223-224 (Ala. 1989), and *Central Alabama Elec. Cooperative* v. *Tapley*, 546 So. 2d 371, 376-377 (Ala. 1989).

[10] Indeed, the compatibility of the remittitur with the Seventh Amendment was not settled until *Dimick* v. *Schiedt*, 293 U.S. 474 (1935).

[11] Oregon juries, reported decisions indicate, rarely award punitive damages. Between 1965 and the present, awards of punitive damages have been reported in only two product liability cases involving Oregon law, including this one. See Brief for Trial Lawyers for Public Justice as *Amicus Curiae* 10, and n. 7. The punitive award in this case was about 5.4 times the amount of compensatory damages and about 258 times the plaintiff's out of pocket expenses. This amount is not far distant from the award upheld in *Haslip*, which was more than 4 times the amount of compensatory damages and more than 200 times the plaintiff's out of pocket expenses. See 499 U. S., at 23. The $10 million award this Court sustained in *TXO*, in contrast, was more than 526 times greater than the actual damages of $19,000. 509 U. S., at ___ (slip op., at 8).

[12] Not until *Sparf* v. *United States*, 156 U.S. 51, 102 (1895), was the jury's power to decide the law conclusively rejected for the federal courts. See Riggs, Constitutionalizing Punitive Damages: The Limits of Due Process, 52 Ohio St. L. J. 859, 900 (1991).

[13] An inquiry of this order is akin to the one made in *Haslip*. See *supra*, at 8-9.

[14] In its 1949 decision in *Van Lom* v. *Schneiderman*, 187 Ore. 89, 210 P. 2d 461, the Supreme Court of Oregon merely held that it lacked authority to order a new trial even though an award of damages was excessive under *state law*. See *ante*, at 1 (Scalia, J., concurring). No federal limit had yet been recognized, and the *Van Lom* court had no occasion to consider its obligation to check jury verdicts deemed excessive under *federal law*.

CITY OF CHICAGO, et al. v. INTERNATIONAL COLLEGE OF SURGEONS, et al.

No. 96-910, December 15, 1997

ON WRIT OF CERTIORARI TO THE UNITED STATES COURT OF APPEALS FOR THE SEVENTH CIRCUIT

Justice Ginsburg, with whom Justice Stevens joins, dissenting.

This now-federal case originated as an appeal in state court from a municipal agency's denials of demolition permits. The review that state law provides is classically appellate in character—on the agency's record, not *de novo.* Nevertheless, the court decides today that this standard brand of appellate review can be shifted from the appropriate state tribunal to a federal court of first instance at the option of either party—plaintiff originally or defendant by removal. The Court approves this enlargement of district court authority explicitly in federal-question cases, and by inescapable implication in diversity cases, satisfied that "neither the jurisdictional statutes nor our prior decisions suggest that federal jurisdiction is lacking." *Ante,* at 5.

The Court's authorization of cross-system appeals qualifies as a watershed decision. After today, litigants asserting federal-question or diversity jurisdiction may routinely lodge in federal courts direct appeals from the actions of all manner of local (county and municipal) agencies, boards, and commissions. Exercising this cross-system appellate authority, federal courts may now directly superintend local agencies by affirming, reversing, or modifying their administrative rulings.

The Court relies on the statutory words found in both 28 U.S.C. § 1331 and 1332: "The district courts shall have original jurisdiction of all civil actions . . . ." Then, as its linchpin, the Court emphasizes the 1990 codification and expansion, in §1367, of what previously had been known as "ancillary jurisdiction" and "pendent jurisdiction." Specifically, the Court stresses the broad authorization in §1367(a) for district court exercise of "supplemental jurisdiction" over claims "so related" to a "civil action of which the district courts have original jurisdiction" as to "form part of the same [Article III] case or controversy." See *ante,* at 7—11, 14—17.[1] The bare words of §§1331, 1332, and 1367(a) permit the Court's construction. For the reasons advanced in this opinion, however, I do not construe these prescriptions, on allocation of judicial business to federal courts of first instance, to embrace the category of appellate business at issue here.

The Court's expansive reading, in my judgment, takes us far from anything Congress conceivably could have meant. Cf. *Lynch* v. *Overholser,* 369 U.S. 705, 710 (1962) ("The decisions of this Court have repeatedly warned against the dangers of an approach to statutory construction which confines itself to the bare words of a statute, for 'literalness may strangle meaning.'") (citations omitted). Cross-system appeals, if they are to be introduced into our federal system, should stem from the National Legislature's considered and explicit decision. In accord with the views of the large majority of federal judges who have considered the question, I would hold the cross-system appeal unauthorized by Congress, and affirm the Seventh Circuit's judgment.

I

Until now it has been taken almost for granted that federal courts of first instance lack authority under §§1331 and 1332 to displace state courts as forums for on-the-record review of state and local agency actions. In *Chicago, R. I. & P. R. Co.* v. *Stude,* 346 U.S. 574 (1954), we recalled the historic understanding: A federal district court "does not sit to review on appeal action taken administratively or judicially in a state proceeding." *Id.,* at 581.[2] Cross-system appellate authority is entrusted to this Court, we said in *Rooker* v. *Fidelity Trust Co.,* 263 U.S. 413 (1923), but it is outside the domain of the lower federal courts. Interpreting the statutory predecessors of 28 U.S.C. § 1331 and 1257, we held in *Rooker* that a federal district court could not modify a decision of the Indiana Supreme Court, for only this Court could exercise such authority. 263 U.S., at 416.

Today, the Court holds that Congress, by enacting §1367, has authorized federal district courts to conduct deferential, on-the-record review of local agency decisions whenever a federal question is pended to the agency review action. Dismissing, as irrelevant to jurisdiction, the distinction between *de novo* and deferential review, the Court also provides easy access to federal court whenever the dissatisfied party in a local agency proceeding has the requisite diverse citizenship. The Court does all this despite the overwhelming weight of lower federal court decisions disclaiming cross-system appellate authority, and without even a hint from Congress that so startling a reallocation of power from state courts to federal courts was within the national lawmakers' contemplation.[3]

I catalog first the decisions, in addition to the Seventh Circuit's, that the Court today overrides: *Volkswagen de Puerto Rico, Inc.* v. *Puerto Rico Labor Relations Bd.,* 454 F.2d 38, 42 (CA1 1972) (permitting a district court to conduct on-the-record review of a decision of the Puerto Rico Labor Relations Board under §1331 "would place a federal court in an improper posture vis-a-vis a non-federal agency"); *Armistead* v. *C & M Transport, Inc.*, 49 F.3d 43, 47 (CA1 1995) ("As courts of *original* jurisdiction, federal district courts sitting in diversity jurisdiction do not have appellate power, nor the right to exercise supplementary equitable control over original proceedings in the state's administrative tribunals."); *Frison* v. *Franklin County Bd. of Ed.*, 596 F.2d 1192, 1194 (CA4 1979) (District Court should have declined pendent jurisdiction over a state-law claim "because it is essentially a petition for judicial review of the state administrative action rather than a distinct claim for relief"); *Fairfax County Redevelopment & Housing Auth.* v. *W. M. Schlosser Co.*, 64 F.3d 155, 158 (CA4 1995) ("Because the district court is 'a court of original jurisdiction,' not 'an appellate tribunal,' and, thus, is without jurisdiction 'to review on appeal action taken administratively or judicially in a state proceeding,' it was without jurisdiction [under §1332] to conduct such a review of the County Executive's finding.") (citations omitted); *Labiche* v. *Louisiana Patients' Compensation Fund Oversight Bd.*, 69 F.3d 21, 22 (CA5 1995) ("We have reviewed [28 U.S.C. § 1330—1368] and none would authorize appellate review by a United States District Court of any actions taken by a state agency."); *Shamrock Motors, Inc.* v. *Ford Motor Co.*, 120 F.3d 196, 200 (CA9 1997) ("When a state provides for administrative agency review of an appellate nature, rather than administrative review of a de novo nature, federal district courts have neither original jurisdiction nor removal jurisdiction over the review proceedings."); *Trapp* v. *Goetz*, 373 F.2d 380, 383 (CA10 1966) (Under §1332, "a United States District Court could not review an appeal action taken either administratively or judicially in a state proceeding."). Indeed, research discloses only a single Court of Appeals decision that has approved a federal district court's exercise of cross-system appellate review. See *Range Oil Supply Co.* v. *Chicago, R. I. & P. R. Co.*, 248 F.2d 477, 478—479 (CA8 1957) (District Court could exercise removal jurisdiction over an appeal from a state railroad and warehouse commission once that appeal had been perfected in state court). As the Ninth Circuit said in *Shamrock Motors*: "[T]he prospect of a federal court sitting as an appellate court over state administrative proceedings is rather jarring and should not be quickly embraced as a matter of policy." *Shamrock Motors, Inc.* v. *Ford Motor Co.*, 120 F.3d, at 200.

Until today, federal habeas corpus proceedings were the closest we had come to cross-system appellate review. See 28 U.S.C. § 2241—2254.[4] Unlike the jurisdictional reallocation the Court now endorses, habeas corpus jurisdiction does not entail *direct* review of a state or local authority's decision. See *Lambrix* v. *Singletary*, 520 U.S. ___, ___ (1997) (slip op., at 4). Notably, in providing for federal habeas corpus review, Congress has taken great care to avoid interrupting or intruding upon state-court processes. See, *e.g.*, 28 U.S.C. § 2254(b)(1) (requiring exhaustion of state remedies before filing a federal petition for writ of habeas corpus). The Court's holding in this "Chicago" case, however, permits the federal court to supplant the State's entire scheme for judicial review of local administrative actions.

When a local actor or agency violates a person's federal right, it is indeed true that the aggrieved party may bring an action under 42 U.S.C. § 1983 without first exhausting state remedies. See *Patsy* v. *Board of Regents of Fla.*, 457 U.S. 496, 516 (1982). But such an action involves no disregard, as the cross-system appeal does, of the separateness of state and federal adjudicatory systems. In a §1983 action, a federal (or state) court inquires whether a person, acting under color of state law, has subjected another "to the deprivation of any rights, privileges, or immunities secured by the Constitution and [federal] laws." The court exercises original, not appellate, jurisdiction; it proceeds independently, not as substantial evidence reviewer on a nonfederal agency's record. As now-Chief Judge Posner explained:

"[A] suit under 42 U.S.C. § 1983 is not a review proceeding even when . . . it challenges administrative action that has an adjudicative component. Federal courts have no general appellate authority over state courts or state agencies. . . . The case that is in federal court did not begin in the state agency but is an independent as well as an original federal action." *Hameetman* v. *Chicago*, 776 F.2d 636, 640 (CA7 1985).

II

To reach its landmark result, the Court holds that a district court may perform cross-system appellate review of administrative agency decisions so long as the plaintiff's complaint also contains related federal claims, for "[t]hose federal claims suffice to make the actions 'civil actions' within the 'original jurisdiction' of the district courts." *Ante*, at 9. Measuring today's disposition against prior decisions concerning proceedings in federal court following a state administrative decision, the Court, *ante*, at 11—14, takes up *Horton* v. *Liberty Mut. Ins. Co.*, 367 U.S. 348 (1961), and *Stude*, see *supra*, at 3, and n. 2.

Horton was a workers' compensation case proceeding in federal court on the basis of the parties' diverse citizenship. The contending parties were an injured worker and the insurance company that served as compensation carrier for the worker's employer. At the administrative stage, the Texas Industrial Accident Board made an award of $1,050. Neither side was satisfied. The insurer maintained that the worker was entitled to no compensation, while the worker urged his entitlement to the statutory maximum of $14,035. The insurer brought suit first, filing its complaint in federal court; one week later, the worker filed a state-court suit and sought dismissal of the insurer's federal action on alternative grounds: (1) the matter in controversy did not meet §1332's monetary amount requirement (then "in excess of $10,000"); (2) the insurer's suit was "nothing more than an appeal from a state administrative order" and federal courts have "no appellate jurisdiction" over such orders, 367 U.S., at 354.

After concluding that the jurisdictional amount requirement was met, the Court turned to the question whether the federal-court proceeding was in fact an "appeal," and therefore barred under *Stude* which, as the *Horton* Court described it, "held that a United States District Court was without jurisdiction to consider an appeal 'taken administratively or judicially in a state proceeding.'" 367 U.S., at 354 (quoting *Stude*, 346 U.S., at 581). On that matter, the Texas Supreme Court's construction of the State's compensation law left no room for debate. When suit commences, the administrative award is vacated and the court determines liability *de novo.* See 367 U.S., at 355, n. 15. The suit to set aside an award is thus like any other first instance proceeding—it is "'a suit, not an appeal.'" *Id.,* at 354 (quoting *Booth* v. *Texas Employer's Ins. Assn.,* 132 Tex. 237, 246, 123 S. W. 2d 322, 328 (1938)).

Remarkably, the Court today asserts that neither *Stude* nor *Horton* "suggest[ed] that jurisdiction turned on whether judicial review of the administrative determination was deferential or *de novo.*" *Ante,* at 12; see also *ante,* at 13 ("The Court [in *Horton*] did not purport to hold that the *de novo* standard was a precondition to federal jurisdiction."). The Court thus casts aside the critical difference between fresh first instance proceedings not tied to a record made by a tribunal lower in the hierarchy, and on-the-record substantial evidence review, which cannot fairly be described as anything but appellate in character.

If, as the Court reasons today, the distinction between *de novo* and deferential review is inconsequential, then a district court may, indeed must, entertain cross-system, on-the-record appeals from local agency decisions—without regard to the presence or absence of any federal question—whenever the parties meet the diversity of citizenship requirement of §1332. The Court so confirms by noting that, in accord with *Califano* v. *Sanders,* 430 U.S. 99, 105—107 (1977), "district courts routinely conduct deferential review [of federal administrative action] pursuant to their original jurisdiction over federal questions." *Ante,* at 14. Just as routinely, it now appears, district courts must "conduct deferential review [of local administrative action] pursuant to their original jurisdiction over [diversity cases]."

The Court's homogenization of *de novo* proceedings and appellate review rests on a single case, *Califano* v. *Sanders.* In *Sanders,* the Court settled a longstanding division of opinion over whether §10 of the [Federal] Administrative Procedure Act (APA), 5 U.S.C. § 701—704, ranked as an independent grant of subject-matter jurisdiction to federal courts, allowing them to review the actions of federal agencies, without regard to the amount in controversy. The Court held that the APA "does not afford an implied grant of subject-matter jurisdiction permitting federal judicial review of agency action." 430 U.S., at 107. Nevertheless, the Court explained, district court review of federal administrative action—when Congress had not prescribed another review route or specifically excluded review—would persist. Congress had just dropped the amount-in-controversy requirement from §1331, thus "fill[ing] the jurisdictional void." *Id.,* at 106. With the amount-in-controversy deleted, the Court indicated in *Sanders,* §1331 would assure fidelity to the presumption that administrative action is subject to judicial review. See *id.,* at 105—106; *Abbott Laboratories* v. *Gardner,* 387 U.S. 136, 141 (1967) (courts generally hold agency action nonreviewable "only upon a showing of 'clear and convincing evidence' of a contrary legislative intent"); see also *Barlow* v. *Collins,* 397 U.S. 159, 166 (1970) ("[J]udicial review of [federal] administrative action is the rule, and nonreviewability an exception which must be demonstrated.").

Whatever the reason for the rule implicit in *Sanders*—that federal district courts may engage in on-the-record, substantial evidence review of federal agency actions under §1331—Chicago homes in on the statutory language. See Brief for Petitioners 11, 30, 39. Section 1331 reads: "The district courts shall have original jurisdiction of all civil actions arising under the Constitution, laws, or treaties of the United States." If deferential, on-the-record review of a *federal* agency's action qualifies as a "civil action" within a district court's "original jurisdiction," Chicago urges, then deferential, on-the-record review of local agency action must fit the same bill, *i.e.,* such review must qualify as a "civil action" within the district court's "original jurisdiction."

But one of these things is not necessarily like the other. I recognize that the bare and identical words "original jurisdiction" and "civil action" in §§1331 and 1332 comport with Chicago's view and that of the Court. See *supra,* at 2. We would do well, however, to recall in this context a sage and grave warning: "The tendency to assume that a word which appears in two or more legal rules, and so in connection with more than one purpose, has and should have precisely the same scope in all of them, runs all through legal discussions. It has all the tenacity of original sin and must constantly be guarded against." Cook, "Substance" and "Procedure" in the Conflict of Laws, 42 Yale L. J. 333, 337 (1933).

Cases "arising under the Constitution, laws, or treaties of the United States" within the meaning of §1331 compose a collection smaller than the one fitting within the similarly worded Clause in Article III of the Constitution, "Cases ... arising under this Constitution, the Laws of the United States, and Treaties made." See, *e.g., Louisville & Nashville R. Co.* v. *Mottley,* 211 U.S. 149, 152 (1908); *Shoshone Mining Co.* v. *Rutter,* 177 U.S. 505, 513 (1900). Diversity of citizenship must be complete to proceed under §1332, see *Strawbridge* v. *Curtiss,* 3 Cranch 267, 268 (1806), but it may be "minimal" in interpleader cases brought under §1335, see *State Farm Fire & Casualty Co.* v. *Tashire,* 386 U.S. 523, 530—531 (1967).

Significantly, in assuming that §1331 ordinarily would be available when a person complains about arbitrary federal administrative action, the Court in *Sanders* never fixed on the words of §1331, and never even mentioned in relation to that provision the terms "civil action" or "original jurisdiction." The Court simply concluded from the legislative history that Congress meant to fill "an interstitial gap," 430 U.S., at 107, *i.e.,* Congress meant to hold federal agencies accountable by making their actions subject to judicial review.

Statutes like the Illinois Administrative Review Law, Ill. Comp. Stat., ch. 735, §§5/3—103, 5/3—104 (Supp. 1997), explicitly provide for state-court judicial review of state and local agency decisions. Unlike the federal picture the Court confronted in *Sanders,* there is no void to fill. The gap to which *Sanders* attended—the absence of any forum for "nonstatutory" review of federal agency decisions unless §1331 provided one—simply does not exist in a case brought under a state measure like the Illinois Administrative Review Law. I would therefore resist reading *Sanders* out of context to mandate cross-system appellate review of local agency decisions.

III

Just last Term, two Members of today's majority recognized the vital interest States have in developing and elaborating state administrative law, for that law regulates the citizen's contact with state and local government at every turn, for example, in gaining life-sustaining public benefits, obtaining a license or, as in this case, receiving a permit. Last Term's lead opinion observed:

"In the States there is an ongoing process by which state courts and state agencies work to elaborate an administrative law designed to reflect the State's own rules and traditions concerning the respective scope of judicial review and administrative discretion... . [T]he elaboration of administrative law ... is one of the primary responsibilities of the state judiciary. Where, as here, the parties invoke federal principles to challenge state administrative action, the courts of the State have a strong interest in integrating those sources of law within their own system for the proper judicial control of state officials." *Idaho* v. *Coeur d'Alene Tribe of Idaho*, 521 U.S. ___, ___ (1997) (slip op., at 14) (principal opinion of Kennedy, J., joined by Rehnquist, C. J.).

Today's decision jeopardizes the "strong interest" courts of the State have in controlling the actions of local as well as state agencies. State court superintendence can now be displaced or dislodged in any case against a local agency in which the parties are of diverse citizenship and in any case in which a Fourteenth Amendment plea can be made.

The Court insists that there is no escape from this erosion of state-court authority. Its explanation is less than compelling. The Court describes as the alternative "ICS's proposed approach." See *ante*, at 9. That approach, according to the Court, would have us determine first "whether [ICS's] state claims constitute 'civil actions' within a district court's 'original jurisdiction.' " *Ibid.* The Court then demolishes the supposed approach by observing that it "would effectively read the supplemental jurisdiction statute out of the books." *Ibid.*; see also *ante*, at 10—11.

I do not find in ICS's brief the approach the Court constructs, then destructs. Instead, the argument I do find, see Brief for Respondents 21—24, runs as follows. Chicago has tried to persuade the Court that ICS's "Complaints for Administrative Review are no different than civil rights actions." *Id.*, at 21. See Notice of Removal for Petitioner in No. 91 C 1587 (ND Ill.), App. 15 ("it appears from the face of plaintiffs' complaint that this is a civil rights complaint"). ICS acknowledged that it might have chosen to bypass on-the-record administrative review in state court, invoking federal jurisdiction under §1983 instead, without exhausting state remedies. Brief for Respondents 22—24. Had ICS done so, review would have been "plenary in its scope" and would not have been "confined by the administrative record." *Id.*, at 24. But ICS did not take that path. It proceeded under the Illinois Administrative Review Law seeking resolution of both state law and federal constitutional issues "in the context of on-the-record administrative review." *Id.*, at 22. The distinction between the appellate review it sought and the first instance action it did not bring "is crucial," ICS argued. Ibid.

In sum, from start to finish, ICS sought accurately to portray the Seventh Circuit's resistance to "federaliz[ing]," without explicit congressional instruction to do so, "garden-variety appeals from . . . local administrative decisions," *id.*, at 3, appeals in which the federal issues ultimately raised "are inextricably intertwined with [the State's] administrative review scheme," *id.*, at 4. Not a case in which pendent or supplemental jurisdiction has ever been exercised is touched by the argument ICS in fact made, which trained constantly on the impropriety of cross-system appellate review. Far from urging the Court to "read the supplemental jurisdiction statute out of the books," *ante*, at 9, ICS simply asked the Court not to read into §1367 more than any other tribunal has conceived to be there. What ICS sought to convey, the Court obscures: "[T]he City fail[ed] to cite a single case in which a federal court specifically assumed pendent or supplemental jurisdiction over an on-the-record state administrative appeal." Brief for Respondents 24, n. 11.

IV

Even if the Court were correct in maintaining that Congress thrust local administrative agency on-the-record review proceedings into federal court at the option of either party, given diversity or an ultimate constitutional argument, the Court's reluctance to "articulat[e] general standards" for the guidance of the lower courts is puzzling. Cf. *Strickland* v. *Washington*, 466 U.S. 668, 698 (1984) (after "articulat[ing] general standards for judging ineffectiveness [of counsel] claims," the Court considered it "useful to apply those standards to the facts of th[e] case in order to illustrate the meaning of the general principles"). ICS, seeking such guidance, did not simply "allud[e] to" the District Court's extraordinary course. Cf. *ante*, at 17. This is a summary of the points ICS made in urging the impropriety of federal court retention of the case, assuming, *arguendo*, federal court power to keep it. The permits in question were sought under Chicago's Landmarks Ordinance, a measure "Illinois courts have never had an opportunity to interpret." Brief for Respondents 4. "The issues of Illinois constitutional law raised by [ICS] have never been decided by Illinois appellate courts." *Ibid.* Land use cases generally, and landmark designations particularly, implicate "local policies" and "local concerns." *Ibid.* Yet all this Court is willing to say is that "the District Court properly exercised federal-question jurisdiction over the federal claims in ICS's complaints, and properly recognized that it could thus also exercise supplemental jurisdiction over ICS's state law claims." *Ante*, at 8. The Court's opinion expresses "no [further] view." *Ante*, at 17.

The District Court disposed of ICS's federal equal protection and due process claims in less than 13 pages of its 63-page opinion, App. to Pet. for Cert. 33a—46a, and then devoted over 40 pages more to the state-law claims. *Id.*, at 46a—89a. That court wrote at greatest length on whether the Landmarks Commission's conclusions were "Against the Manifest Weight of the Evidence." *Id.*, at 73a—89a. Finally, the District Court "affirm[ed] the Commission's decisions." *Id.*, at 89a. It would have been in order for this Court to have recalled, in face of the District Court's federal-claims-first approach, the "fundamental rule of judicial restraint" that federal courts "will not reach constitutional questions in advance of the necessity of deciding them." *Three Affiliated Tribes of Fort Berthold Reservation* v. *Wold Engineering, P. C.*, 467 U.S. 138, 157 (1984). As a rule, potentially dispositive state-law challenges, not ultimate constitutional questions, should be cleared first. See, *e.g.*, *Hagans* v. *Lavine,* 415 U.S. 528, 546—547 (1974).

When local official actions are contested on state and federal grounds, and particularly when construction of a state measure or local ordinance is at issue, the state questions stand at the threshold. In this case, for example, had ICS's construction of the Landmarks Ordinance prevailed, no federal constitutional question would have ripened. The Court does note that §1367(c) "enumerat[es] the circumstances in which district courts can refuse [to] exercise [supplemental jurisdiction]," *ante,* at 15, but as to that, the Court simply reports: "[T]he District Court decided [judicial economy, convenience, fairness, and comity] would be best served by exercising jurisdiction over ICS's state law claims," *ante,* at 16.[5] The Court also mentions, abstractly, that "district courts may be obligated not to decide state law claims (or to stay their adjudication) where one of the abstention doctrines articulated by this Court applies." *Ibid.*

Section 1367(c), which concerns supplemental jurisdiction, will have no utility in diversity cases where, if jurisdiction exists, it is generally not within the court's discretion to "decline." And lower courts have found our abstention pronouncements "less than pellucid." See R. Fallon, D. Meltzer, & D. Shapiro, Hart and Wechsler's The Federal Courts and the Federal System 1247, 1251 (4th ed. 1996). Which of our "various abstention principles," *ante,* at 17, should the lower federal courts consult when asked to review as an appellate instance, and affirm, modify, or reverse, a local license or permit denial? To dispel confusion and advance comity, should the lower courts endeavor to fashion—and will we eventually declare—a "Chicago" abstention doctrine?

Given the state forum to which ICS resorted, and the questions it raised there, see App. 26—35, 76—77, ICS's primary contention is clear: The Commission should have granted, *under state law,* demolition permits or an economic hardship exception. I do not comprehend the Court's reasons for suggesting that the District Court may have acted properly in holding on to this case, rather than allowing the state courts to proceed in their normal course.

V

In *Ankenbrandt* v. *Richards,* 504 U.S. 689 (1992), we addressed the question whether civil actions for divorce, alimony, or child custody fall within §1332 when the parties are of diverse citizenship. Nothing in the text of the Constitution or in the words of §1332 excluded parties from bringing such "civil actions" in federal court. Historically, however, decrees terminating marriages had been considered wholly within the State's domain. See *Barber* v. *Barber,* 21 How. 582 (1859). That understanding, we noted in *Ankenbrandt,* had prevailed "for nearly a century and a half." 504 U.S., at 694—695. "Given the long passage of time without any expression of congressional dissatisfaction," we reaffirmed the absence of statutory jurisdiction for federal court adjudication of original civil actions for divorce, alimony, and child custody. *Id.,* at 703. The Court explained that its conclusion was also

"supported by sound policy considerations. . . . [S]tate courts are more eminently suited to work of this type than are federal courts, which lack the close association with state and local government organizations dedicated to handling [the] issues [involved]." *Id.,* at 703—704.[6]

History and policy tug strongly here as well. There surely has been no "expression of congressional dissatisfaction" with the near-unanimous view of the Circuits that federal courts may not engage in cross-system appellate review, and "[t]he elaboration of [state] administrative law" is a "prim[e] responsibilit[y] of the state judiciary." *Idaho* v. *Coeur d'Alene Tribe of Idaho,* 521 U.S., at ___ (slip op., at 14).

This Court said in *Finley* v. *United States,* 490 U.S. 545, 547—548 (1989):

"It remains rudimentary law that '[a]s regards all courts of the United States inferior to this tribunal, two things are necessary to create jurisdiction, whether original or appellate. The Constitution must have given to the court the capacity to take it, *and an act of Congress must have supplied it.* . . . To the extent that such action is not taken, the power lies dormant.' " (quoting *Mayor* v. *Cooper,* 6 Wall. 247, 252 (1868)).

As I see it, no Act of Congress adverts to and authorizes any cross-system appeal from state or local administrative agency to lower federal court. I would await express legislative direction before proceeding down that road. Accordingly, I would affirm the Seventh Circuit's judgment.

NOTES

[1] The Court assumes, although §1367 does not expressly so provide, that the section covers cases originating in a state court and removed to a federal court. *Ante,* at 7. Although the point has not been briefed, I do not question that assumption. See Steinman, Supplemental Jurisdiction in §1441 Removed Cases: An Unsurveyed Frontier of Congress' Handiwork, 35 Ariz. L. Rev. 305, 308—310 (1993) (observing that arguments against application of §1367 to removed cases "are weak").

[2] The Court in *Stude* also made the following statement: "When the proceeding has reached the stage of a perfected appeal and the jurisdiction of the state district court is invoked, it then becomes in its nature a civil action and subject to removal by the defendant to the United States District Court." *Chicago, R. I. & P. R. Co.* v. *Stude,* 346 U.S., at 578—579. This statement, made on the way to the Court's conclusion that the District Court *lacked* removal jurisdiction, does not carry great weight. It

suggests that while the plaintiff in *Stude* could not have filed the action in federal court initially under §1332, the defendant could have removed the action to federal court pursuant to §1441(a). That suggestion is incorrect, for "[o]nly state-court actions that originally could have been filed in federal court may be removed to federal court by the defendant." *Caterpillar Inc.* v. *Williams,* 482 U.S. 386, 392 (1987).

3 The Court's holding can embrace the decisions of state, as opposed to local, agencies, only if the State consents to the district court's jurisdiction. In *Pennhurst State School and Hospital* v. *Halderman,* 465 U.S. 89 (1984), the Court held it would violate the Eleventh Amendment for a federal court to entertain, without the State's consent, "a claim that state officials violated state law in carrying out their official responsibilities." *Id.,* at 121. The Court further held that "this principle applies as well to state-law claims brought into federal court under pendent jurisdiction." *Ibid.* Notably, the Court commented in *Pennhurst:* "[I]t is difficult to think of a greater intrusion on state sovereignty than when a federal court instructs state officials on how to conform their conduct to state law." *Id.,* at 106.

4 The Court's citation to the Individuals with Disabilities Education Act (IDEA), *ante,* at 14, is unpersuasive for two reasons. First, IDEA has its own jurisdictional provision, so it does not concern §§1331, 1332, or 1367. See §615 of the Individuals with Disabilities Education Act Amendments of 1997, Pub. L. 105—17, 111 Stat. 92, to be codified at 20 U.S.C. § 1415(i)(3)(A); *Zobrest* v. *Catalina Foothills School Dist.,* 509 U.S. 1, 4 (1993). Second, IDEA creates a *federal* regime. While IDEA may require federal courts to defer to state agency decisions, those decisions are made pursuant to *federal* legislation.

5 But cf. *Pennhurst State School and Hospital* v. *Halderman,* 465 U.S. 89, 122, n. 32 (1984) ("[A]llowing claims against state officials based on state law to be brought in federal court does not necessarily foster the policies of 'judicial economy, convenience and fairness to litigants,' *Mine Workers* v. *Gibbs,* 383 U.S. 715, 726 (1966), on which pendent jurisdiction is founded. For example, when a federal decision on state law is obtained, the federal court's construction often is uncertain and ephemeral. In cases of ongoing oversight of a state program ... the federal intrusion is likely to be extensive. Duplication of effort, inconvenience, and uncertainty may well result.").

6 *Ankenbrandt* clarified and illustrated "that the domestic relations exception encompasses only cases involving the issuance of a divorce, alimony, or child custody decree"; claims of a kind traditionally adjudicated in federal courts, for example, tort or contract claims, are not excepted from federal-court jurisdiction simply because they arise in a domestic relations context. *Ankenbrandt* v. *Richards,* 504 U.S., at 704. In enacting the Violence Against Women Act of 1994, 108 Stat. 1916, 42 U.S.C. § 13931 *et seq.,* Congress reinforced *Ankenbrandt* by providing expressly that §1367 shall not be construed, by reason of a claim arising under the Act, "to confer on the courts of the United States jurisdiction over any State law claim seeking the establishment of a divorce, alimony, equitable distribution of martial property, or child custody decree." §13981(e)(4).

AMOCO PRODUCTION CO., et al. v. SOUTHERN UTE INDIAN TRIBE, et al.

No. 98-830, June 7, 1999

ON WRIT OF CERTIORARI TO THE UNITED STATES COURT OF APPEALS FOR THE TENTH CIRCUIT

Justice Ginsburg, dissenting.

I would affirm the judgment below substantially for the reasons stated by the Court of Appeals and the federal respondents. See 151 F.3d 1251, 1256—1267 (CA10 1998) (en banc); Brief for Federal Respondents 14—16. As the Court recognizes, in 1909 and 1910 coalbed methane gas (CBM) was a liability. See *ante,* at 4, 9—10. Congress did not contemplate that the surface owner would be responsible for it. More likely, Congress would have assumed that the coal owner had dominion over, and attendant responsibility for, CBM. I do not find it clear that Congress understood dominion would shift if and when the liability became an asset. I would therefore apply the canon that ambiguities in land grants are construed in favor of the sovereign. See *Watt* v. *Western Nuclear, Inc.,* 462 U.S. 36, 59 (1983) (noting "established rule that land grants are construed favorably to the Government, that nothing passes except what is conveyed in clear language, and that if there are doubts they are resolved for the Government, not against it" (internal quotation marks omitted)).

ANTHONY PALAZZOLO v. RHODE ISLAND, et al.

No. 99-2047, June 28, 2001

ON WRIT OF CERTIORARI TO THE SUPREME COURT OF RHODE ISLAND

Justice Ginsburg, with whom Justice Souter and Justice Breyer join, dissenting.

A regulatory takings claim is not ripe for adjudication, this Court has held, until the agency administering the regulations at issue, proceeding in good faith, "has arrived at a final, definitive position regarding how it will apply [those regulations] to the particular land in question." *Williamson County Regional Planning Comm'n* v. *Hamilton Bank of Johnson City,* 473 U.S. 172, 191 (1985). Absent such a final decision, a court cannot "kno[w] the nature and extent of permitted development" under the regulations, and therefore cannot say "how far the regulation[s] g[o]," as regulatory takings law requires. *MacDonald, Sommer & Frates* v. *Yolo County,* 477 U.S. 340, 348, 351 (1986). Therefore, even when a landowner seeks and is denied permission to develop property, if the denial does not demonstrate the effective impact of the regulations on the land, the denial does not represent the "final decision" requisite to generate a ripe dispute. *Williamson County,* 473 U.S., at 190.

MacDonald illustrates how a highly ambitious application may not ripen a takings claim. The landowner in that case proposed a 159-home subdivision. 477 U.S., at 342. When that large proposal was denied, the owner complained that the State had appropriated "all beneficial use of its property." *Id.,* at 352, n.8; see also *id.,* at 344. This Court concluded, however, that the landowner's claim was not ripe, for the denial of the massive development left "open the possibility that some development [would] be permitted." *Id.,* at 352. "Rejection of exceedingly grandiose development plans," the Court observed, "does not logically imply that less ambitious plans will receive similarly unfavorable reviews." *Id.,* at 353, n.9.

As presented to the Rhode Island Supreme Court, Anthony Palazzolo's case was a close analogue to *MacDonald.* Palazzolo's land has two components. Approximately 18 acres are wetlands that sustain a rich but delicate ecosystem. See 746 A.2d 707, 710, and n.1 (R.I. 2000). Additional acres are less environmentally sensitive "uplands." (The number of upland acres remains in doubt, see *ibid.,* because Palazzolo has never submitted "an accurate or detailed survey" of his property, see Tr. 190 (June 18—19, 1997).) Rhode Island's administrative agency with ultimate permitting authority over the wetlands, the Coastal Resources Management Council (CRMC), bars residential development of the wetlands, but not the uplands.

Although Palazzolo submitted several applications to develop his property, those applications uniformly sought permission to fill most or all of the wetlands portion of the property. None aimed to develop only the uplands.[1] Upon denial of the last of Palazzolo's applications, Palazzolo filed suit claiming that Rhode Island had taken his property by refusing "to allow any development." App. 45 (Complaint ¶17).

As the Rhode Island Supreme Court saw the case, Palazzolo's claim was not ripe for several reasons, among them, that Palazzolo had not sought permission for "development only of the upland portion of the parcel." 746 A.2d, at 714. The Rhode Island court emphasized the "undisputed evidence in the record that it would be possible to build at least one single-family home on the existing upland area, with no need for additional fill." Ibid.

Today, the Court rejects the Rhode Island court's determination that the case is unripe, finding no "uncertainty as to the [uplands'] permitted use." *Ante,* at 12. The Court's conclusion is, in my view, both inaccurate and inequitable. It is inaccurate because the record is ambiguous. And it is inequitable because, given the claim asserted by Palazzolo in the Rhode Island courts, the State had no cause to pursue further inquiry into potential upland development. But Palazzolo presses other claims here, and at his behest, the Court not only entertains them, but also turns the State's legitimate defense against the claim Palazzolo originally stated into a weapon against the State. I would reject Palazzolo's bait-and-switch ploy and affirm the judgment of the Rhode Island Supreme Court.

* * *

Where physical occupation of land is not at issue, the Court's cases identify two basic forms of regulatory taking. *Ante,* at 7—8. In *Lucas* v. *South Carolina Coastal Council,* 505 U.S. 1003 (1992), the Court held that, subject to "certain qualifications," *ante,* at 7, 20, denial of "*all* economically beneficial or productive use of land" constitutes a taking. 505 U.S., at 1015 (emphasis added). However, if a regulation does not leave the property "economically idle," *id.,* at 1019, to establish the alleged taking the landowner may pursue the multifactor inquiry set out in *Penn Central Transp. Co.* v. *New York City,* 438 U.S. 104, 123—125 (1978).

Like the landowner in *MacDonald,* Palazzolo sought federal constitutional relief *only* under a straightforward application of *Lucas.* See *ante,* at 6; App. 45 (Complaint ¶17) ("As a direct and proximate result of the Defendants' refusal to allow *any* development of the property, there has been a taking" (emphasis added)); Plaintiff's Post Trial Memorandum in No.

88—0297 (Super. Ct., R.I.), p. 6 ("[T]his Court need not look beyond the *Lucas* case as its very lucid and precise standards will determine whether a taking has occurred."); *id.*, at 9—10 ("[T]here is *NO USE* for the property whatsoever.... Not one scintilla of evidence was proffered by the State to prove, intimate or even suggest a theoretical possibility of *any* use for this property—never mind a beneficial use. Not once did the State claim that there *is*, in fact, some use available for the Palazzolo parcel."); Brief of Appellant in No. 98—0333, pp. 5, 7, 9—10 (hereinafter Brief of Appellant) (restating, verbatim, assertions of Post Trial Memorandum quoted above).

Responding to Palazzolo's *Lucas* claim, the State urged as a sufficient defense this now uncontested point: CRMC "would [have been] happy to have [Palazzolo] situate a home" on the uplands, "thus allowing [him] to realize 200,000 dollars." State's Post-Trial Memorandum in No. 88—0297 (Super. Ct., R.I.), p. 81; see also Brief of Appellees in No. 98—0333A, p. 25 (hereinafter Brief of Appellees) (Palazzolo "never even applied for the realistic alternative of using the entire parcel as a single unitary home-site"). The State did present some evidence at trial that more than one lot could be developed. See *infra*, at 8—9. And, in a supplemental post-trial memorandum addressing a then-new Rhode Island Supreme Court decision, the State briefly urged that Palazzolo's claims would fail even under *Penn Central*. See *ante*, at 14. The evidence of additional uses and the post-trial argument directed to *Penn Central*, however, were underdeveloped and unnecessary, for Palazzolo himself, in his pleadings and at trial, pressed only a *Lucas*-based claim that he had been denied *all* economically viable use of his property. Once the State demonstrated that an "economically beneficial" development was genuinely plausible, *Lucas*, 505 U.S., at 1015, the State had established the analogy to *MacDonald*: The record now showed "valuable use might still be made of the land." 477 U.S., at 352, n.8; see Brief of Appellees 24—25 (relying on *MacDonald*). The prospect of real development shown by the State warranted a ripeness dismissal of Palazzolo's complaint.

Addressing the State's *Lucas* defense in *Lucas* terms, Palazzolo insisted that his land had "no use ... as a result of CRMC's application of its regulations." Brief of Appellant 11. The Rhode Island Supreme Court rejected Palazzolo's argument, identifying in the record evidence that Palazzolo could build at least one home on the uplands. 746 A.2d, at 714. The court therefore concluded that Palazzolo's failure to seek permission for "development only of the upland portion of the parcel" meant that Palazzolo could not "maintain a claim that the CRMC ha[d] deprived him of all beneficial use of the property." Ibid.

It is true that the Rhode Island courts, in the course of ruling for the State, briefly touched base with *Penn Central*. Cf. *ante*, at 14. The critical point, however, underplayed by the Court, is that Palazzolo never raised or argued the *Penn Central* issue in the state system: not in his complaint; not in his trial court submissions; not—even after the trial court touched on the *Penn Central* issue—in his briefing on appeal. The state high court decision, raising and quickly disposing of the matter, unquestionably permits us to consider the *Penn Central* issue. See *Raley* v. *Ohio*, 360 U.S. 423, 436—437 (1959). But the ruling below does not change the reality essential here: Palazzolo litigated his takings claim, and it was incumbent on the State to defend against that claim, only under Lucas.

If Palazzolo's arguments in this Court had tracked his arguments in the state courts, his petition for certiorari would have argued simply that the Rhode Island courts got it wrong in failing to see that his land had "no use" at all because of CRMC's rules. Brief of Appellant 11. This Court likely would not have granted certiorari to review the application of *MacDonald* and *Lucas* to the facts of Palazzolo's case. However, aided by new counsel, Palazzolo sought—and in the exercise of this Court's discretion obtained—review of two contentions he did not advance below. The first assertion is that the state regulations take the property under *Penn Central*. See Pet. for Cert. 20; Brief for Petitioner 47—50. The second argument is that the regulations amount to a taking under an expanded rendition of *Lucas* covering cases in which a landowner is left with property retaining only a "few crumbs of value." *Ante*, at 21 (quoting Brief for Petitioner 37); Pet. for Cert. 20—22. Again, it bears repetition, Palazzolo never claimed in the courts below that, if the State were correct that his land could be used for a residence, a taking nonetheless occurred.[2]

In support of his new claims, Palazzolo has conceded the very point on which the State properly relied to resist the simple *Lucas* claim presented below: that Palazzolo can obtain approval for one house of substantial economic value. Palazzolo does not merely accept the argument that the State advanced below. He now contends that the evidence proffered by the State in the Rhode Island courts supports the claims he presents here, by demonstrating that *only* one house would be approved. See Brief for Petitioner 13 ("[T]he uncontradicted evidence was that CRMC ... would not deny [Palazzolo] permission to build one single-family home on the small upland portion of his property." (emphasis deleted)); Pet. for Cert. 15 (the extent of development permitted on the land is "perfectly clear: one single-family home and nothing more").

As a logical matter, Palazzolo's argument does not stand up. The State's submissions in the Rhode Island courts hardly establish that Palazzolo could obtain approval for *only* one house of value. By showing that Palazzolo could have obtained approval for a $200,000 house (rather than, say, two houses worth $400,000), the State's submissions established only a floor, not a ceiling, on the value of permissible development. For a floor value was all the State needed to defeat Palazzolo's simple *Lucas* claim.

Furthermore, Palazzolo's argument is unfair: The argument transforms the State's legitimate defense to the only claim Palazzolo stated below into offensive support for other claims he states for the first time here. Casting away fairness (and fairness to a State, no less), the Court indulges Palazzolo's bait-and-switch maneuver. The Court concludes that "there is no genuine ambiguity in the record as to the extent of permitted development on ... the uplands." *Ante*, at 13—14. Two theories are offered to support this conclusion.

First, the Court asserts, it is "too late in the day" for the State to contend the uplands give the property more than $200,000 in value; Palazzolo "stated" in his petition for certiorari that the property has "an estimated worth of $200,000," and the State cited that contention "as fact" in its Brief in Opposition. *Ante*, as 13. But in the cited pages of its Brief in

Opposition, the State simply said it "would" approve a "single home" worth $200,000. Brief in Opposition 4, 19. That statement does not foreclose the possibility that the State would *also* approve another home, adding further value to the property.

To be sure, the Brief in Opposition did overlook Palazzolo's change in his theory of the case, a change that, had it been asserted earlier, could have rendered insufficient the evidence the State intelligently emphasized below. But the State's failure to appreciate that Palazzolo had moved the pea to a different shell hardly merits the Court's waiver finding. The only precedent cited for the waiver, a footnote in *Lucas*, is not remotely on point. *Ante*, at 13. The landowner in *Lucas* had invoked a "finding" of fact by the state court, and this Court deemed the State's challenge to that finding waived because the challenge was not timely raised. *Lucas*, 505 U.S., at 1020—1022, n.9. There is nothing extraordinary about this Court's deciding a case on the findings made by a state court. Here, however, the "fact" this Court has stopped the State from contesting—that the property has value of *only* $200,000—was never found by any court. That valuation was simply asserted, inaccurately, see *infra*, at 9, in Palazzolo's petition for certiorari. This Court's waiver ruling thus amounts to an unsavory invitation to unscrupulous litigants: Change your theory and misrepresent the record in your petition for certiorari; if the respondent fails to note your machinations, you have created a different record on which this Court will review the case.

The Court bolsters its waiver finding by asserting that the $200,000 figure is "well founded" in the record. *Ante*, at 13. But, as earlier observed, an absence of multiple valuation possibilities in the record cannot be held against the State, for proof of more than the $200,000 development was unnecessary to defend against the *Lucas* claim singularly pleaded below. And in any event, the record does not warrant the Court's conclusion.

The Court acknowledges "testimony at trial suggesting the existence of an additional upland parcel elsewhere on the property" on which a second house might be built. *Ante*, at 13. The Court discounts that prospect, however, on the ground that development of the additional parcel would require a new road forbidden under CRMC's regulations. *Ibid*. Yet the one witness on whose testimony the Court relies, Steven M. Clarke, himself concluded that it *would* be "realistic to apply for" development at more than one location. Tr. 612 (June 25—26, 1997). Clarke added that a state official, Russell Chateauneuf, "gave [Clarke] supporting information saying that [multiple applications] made sense." *Ibid*. The conclusions of Clarke and Chateauneuf are confirmed by the testimony of CRMC's executive director, Grover Fugate, who agreed with Palazzolo's counsel during cross-examination that Palazzolo might be able to build "on two, perhaps three, perhaps four of the lots." *Id.*, at 211 (June 20—23, 1997); see also Tr. of Oral Arg. 27 ("[T]here is ... uncertainty as to what additional upland there is and how many other houses can be built.").The ambiguities in the record thus are substantial. They persist in part because their resolution was not required to address the claim Palazzolo presented below, and in part because Palazzolo failed ever to submit an accurate survey of his property. Under the circumstances, I would not step into the role of supreme topographical factfinder to resolve ambiguities in Palazzolo's favor. Instead, I would look to, and rely on, the opinion of the state court whose decision we now review. That opinion states: "There was undisputed evidence in the record that it would be possible to build *at least* one single-family home on the existing upland area." 746 A.2d, at 714 (emphasis added). This Court cites nothing to warrant amendment of that finding.[3]

* * *

In sum, as I see this case, we still do not know "the nature and extent of permitted development" under the regulation in question, *MacDonald*, 477 U.S., at 351. I would therefore affirm the Rhode Island Supreme Court's judgment.

NOTES

[1] Moreover, none proposed the 74-lot subdivision Palazzolo advances as the basis for the compensation he seeks. Palazzolo's first application sought to fill all 18 acres of wetlands for no stated purpose whatever. See App. 11 (Palazzolo's sworn 1983 answer to the question why he sought to fill uplands) ("Because it's my right to do if I want to to look at it it is my business."). Palazzolo's second application proposed a most disagreeable "beach club." See *ante*, at 5 ("trash bins" and "port-a-johns" sought); Tr. 650 (June 25—26, 1997) (testimony of engineer Steven M. Clarke) (to get to the club's water, *i.e.*, Winnapaug Pond rather than the nearby Atlantic Ocean, "you'd have to walk across the gravel fill, but then work your way through approximately 70, 75 feet of marsh land or conservation grasses"). Neither of the CRMC applications supplied a clear map of the proposed development. See App. 7, 16 (1983 application); Tr. 190 (June 18—19, 1997) (1985 application). The Rhode Island Supreme Court ultimately concluded that the 74-lot development would have been barred by zoning requirements, apart from CRMC regulations, requirements Palazzolo never explored. See 746 A.2d 707, 715, n.7 (2000).

[2] After this Court granted certiorari, in his briefing on the merits, Palazzolo presented still another takings theory. That theory, in tension with numerous holdings of this Court, see, *e.g.*, *Concrete Pipe & Products of Cal., Inc.* v. *Construction Laborers Pension Trust for Southern Cal.*, 508 U.S. 602, 643 —644 (1993), was predicated on treatment of his wetlands as a property separate from the uplands.

The Court properly declines to reach this claim. *Ante*, at 22.

[3] If Palazzolo's claim were ripe and the merits properly presented, I would, at a minimum, agree with Justice O'Connor, *ante*, at 1—5 (concurring opinion), Justice Stevens, *ante*, at 6—7 (opinion concurring in part and dissenting in part), and Justice Breyer, *ante*, at 1—2 (dissenting opinion), that transfer of title can impair a takings claim.

JENNIFER GRATZ & PATRICK HAMACHER v. LEE BOLLINGER, et al.

No. 02-516, June 23, 2003

ON WRIT OF CERTIORARI TO THE UNITED STATES COURT OF APPEALS FOR THE SIXTH CIRCUIT

Justice Ginsburg, with whom Justice Souter joins, dissenting.*

I

Educational institutions, the Court acknowledges, are not barred from any and all consideration of race when making admissions decisions. *Ante*, at 20; see *Grutter* v. *Bollinger, post*, at 13—21. But the Court once again maintains that the same standard of review controls judicial inspection of all official race classifications. *Ante*, at 21 (quoting *Adarand Constructors, Inc.* v. *Peña*, 515 U.S. 200, 224 (1995); *Richmond* v. *J. A. Croson Co.*, 488 U.S. 469, 494 (1989) (plurality opinion)). This insistence on "consistency," *Adarand*, 515 U.S., at 224, would be fitting were our Nation free of the vestiges of rank discrimination long reinforced by law, see *id.*, at 274—276, and n.8 (Ginsburg, J., dissenting). But we are not far distant from an overtly discriminatory past, and the effects of centuries of law-sanctioned inequality remain painfully evident in our communities and schools.

In the wake "of a system of racial caste only recently ended," *id.*, at 273 (Ginsburg, J., dissenting), large disparities endure. Unemployment,[1] poverty,[2] and access to health care[3] vary disproportionately by race. Neighborhoods and schools remain racially divided.[4] African-American and Hispanic children are all too often educated in poverty-stricken and underperforming institutions.[5] Adult African-Americans and Hispanics generally earn less than whites with equivalent levels of education.[6] Equally credentialed job applicants receive different receptions depending on their race.[7] Irrational prejudice is still encountered in real estate markets[8] and consumer transactions.[9] "Bias both conscious and unconscious, reflecting traditional and unexamined habits of thought, keeps up barriers that must come down if equal opportunity and nondiscrimination are ever genuinely to become this country's law and practice." *Id.*, at 274 (Ginsburg, J., dissenting); see generally Krieger, Civil Rights Perestroika: Intergroup Relations After Affirmative Action, 86 Calif. L.Rev. 1251, 1276 —1291 (1998).

The Constitution instructs all who act for the government that they may not "deny to any person … the equal protection of the laws." Amdt. 14, §1. In implementing this equality instruction, as I see it, government decisionmakers may properly distinguish between policies of exclusion and inclusion. See *Wygant* v. *Jackson Bd. of Ed.*, 476 U.S. 267, 316 (1986) (Stevens, J., dissenting). Actions designed to burden groups long denied full citizenship stature are not sensibly ranked with measures taken to hasten the day when entrenched discrimination and its after effects have been extirpated. See Carter, When Victims Happen To Be Black, 97 Yale L.J. 420, 433—434 (1988) ("[T]o say that two centuries of struggle for the most basic of civil rights have been mostly about freedom from racial categorization rather than freedom from racial oppressio[n] is to trivialize the lives and deaths of those who have suffered under racism. To pretend … that the issue presented in [*Regents of Univ. of Cal.* v. *Bakke*, 438 U.S. 265 (1978)] was the same as the issue in [*Brown* v. *Board of Education*, 347 U.S. 483 (1954)] is to pretend that history never happened and that the present doesn't exist.").

Our jurisprudence ranks race a "suspect" category, "not because [race] is inevitably an impermissible classification, but because it is one which usually, to our national shame, has been drawn for the purpose of maintaining racial inequality." *Norwalk Core* v. *Norwalk Redevelopment Agency*, 395 F.2d 920, 931—932 (CA2 1968) (footnote omitted). But where race is considered "for the purpose of achieving equality," *id.*, at 932, no automatic proscription is in order. For, as insightfully explained, "[t]he Constitution is both color blind and color conscious. To avoid conflict with the equal protection clause, a classification that denies a benefit, causes harm, or imposes a burden must not be based on race. In that sense, the Constitution is color blind. But the Constitution is color conscious to prevent discrimination being perpetuated and to undo the effects of past discrimination." *United States* v. *Jefferson County Bd. of Ed.*, 372 F.2d 836, 876 (CA5 1966) (Wisdom, J.); see Wechsler, The Nationalization Of Civil Liberties And Civil Rights, Supp. to 12 Tex. Q. 10, 23 (1968) (*Brown* may be seen as disallowing racial classifications that "impl[y] an invidious assessment" while allowing such classifications when "not invidious in implication" but advanced to "correct inequalities"). Contemporary human rights documents draw just this line; they distinguish between policies of oppression and measures designed to accelerate *de facto* equality. See *Grutter, post*, at 1 (Ginsburg, J., concurring) (citing the United Nations-initiated Conventions on the Elimination of All Forms of Racial Discrimination and on the Elimination of All Forms of Discrimination against Women).

The mere assertion of a laudable governmental purpose, of course, should not immunize a race-conscious measure from careful judicial inspection. See *Jefferson County*, 372 F.2d, at 876 ("The criterion is the relevancy of color to a legitimate governmental purpose."). Close review is needed "to ferret out classifications in reality malign, but masquerading as benign," *Adarand*, 515 U.S., at 275 (Ginsburg, J., dissenting), and to "ensure that preferences are not so large as to trammel unduly upon the opportunities of others or interfere too harshly with legitimate expectations of persons in once-preferred groups," *id.*, at 276.

II

Examining in this light the admissions policy employed by the University of Michigan's College of Literature, Science, and the Arts (College), and for the reasons well stated by Justice Souter, I see no constitutional infirmity. See *ante*, at 3—8 (dissenting opinion). Like other top-ranking institutions, the College has many more applicants for admission than it can accommodate in an entering class. App. to Pet. for Cert. 108a. Every applicant admitted under the current plan, petitioners do not here dispute, is qualified to attend the College. *Id.*, at 111a. The racial and ethnic groups to which the College accords special consideration (African-Americans, Hispanics, and Native-Americans) historically have been relegated to inferior status by law and social practice; their members continue to experience class-based discrimination to this day, see *supra*, at 1—4. There is no suggestion that the College adopted its current policy in order to limit or decrease enrollment by any particular racial or ethnic group, and no seats are reserved on the basis of race. See Brief for Respondents 10; Tr. of Oral Arg. 41—42 (in the range between 75 and 100 points, the review committee may look at applications individually and ignore the points). Nor has there been any demonstration that the College's program unduly constricts admissions opportunities for students who do not receive special consideration based on race. Cf. Liu, The Causation Fallacy: *Bakke* and the Basic Arithmetic of Selective Admissions, 100 Mich. L.Rev. 1045, 1049 (2002) ("In any admissions process where applicants greatly outnumber admittees, and where white applicants greatly outnumber minority applicants, substantial preferences for minority applicants will not significantly diminish the odds of admission facing white applicants.").[10]

The stain of generations of racial oppression is still visible in our society, see Krieger, 86 Calif. L.Rev., at 1253, and the determination to hasten its removal remains vital. One can reasonably anticipate, therefore, that colleges and universities will seek to maintain their minority enrollment—and the networks and opportunities thereby opened to minority graduates —whether or not they can do so in full candor through adoption of affirmative action plans of the kind here at issue. Without recourse to such plans, institutions of higher education may resort to camouflage. For example, schools may encourage applicants to write of their cultural traditions in the essays they submit, or to indicate whether English is their second language. Seeking to improve their chances for admission, applicants may highlight the minority group associations to which they belong, or the Hispanic surnames of their mothers or grandparents. In turn, teachers' recommendations may emphasize who a student is as much as what he or she has accomplished. See, *e.g.*, Steinberg, Using Synonyms for Race, College Strives for Diversity, N.Y. Times, Dec. 8, 2002, section 1, p.1, col. 3 (describing admissions process at Rice University); cf. Brief for United States as *Amicus Curiae* 14—15 (suggesting institutions could consider, *inter alia*, "a history of overcoming disadvantage," "reputation and location of high school," and "individual outlook as reflected by essays"). If honesty is the best policy, surely Michigan's accurately described, fully disclosed College affirmative action program is preferable to achieving similar numbers through winks, nods, and disguises.[11]

* * *

For the reasons stated, I would affirm the judgment of the District Court.

NOTES

[1] See, *e.g.*, U.S. Dept. of Commerce, Bureau of Census, Statistical Abstract of the United States: 2002, p.368 (2002) (Table 562) (hereinafter Statistical Abstract) (unemployment rate among whites was 3.7% in 1999, 3.5% in 2000, and 4.2% in 2001; during those years, the unemployment rate among African-Americans was 8.0%, 7.6%, and 8.7%, respectively; among Hispanics, 6.4%, 5.7%, and 6.6%).

[2] See, *e.g.*, U.S. Dept of Commerce, Bureau of Census, Poverty in the United States: 2000, p.291 (2001) (Table A) (In 2000, 7.5% of non-Hispanic whites, 22.1% of African-Americans, 10.8% of Asian-Americans, and 21.2% of Hispanics were living in poverty); S. Staveteig & A. Wigton, Racial and Ethnic Disparities: Key Findings from the National Survey of America's Families 1 (Urban Institute Report B—5, 2000) ("Blacks, Hispanics, and Native Americans ... each have poverty rates almost twice as high as Asians and almost three times as high as whites.").

[3] See, *e.g.*, U.S. Dept. of Commerce, Bureau of Census, Health Insurance Coverage: 2000, p.391 (2001) (Table A) (In 2000, 9.7% of non-Hispanic whites were without health insurance, as compared

to 18.5% of African-Americans, 18.0% of Asian-Americans, and 32.0% of Hispanics.); Waidmann & Rajan, Race and Ethnic Disparities in Health Care Access and Utilization: An Examination of State Variation, 57 Med. Care Res. and Rev. 55, 56 (2000) ("On average, Latinos and African Americans have both worse health and worse access to effective health care than do non-Hispanic whites ....").

[4] See, e.g., U.S. Dept. of Commerce, Bureau of Census, Racial and Ethnic Residential Segregation in the United States: 1980—2000 (2002) (documenting residential segregation); E. Frankenberg, C. Lee, & G. Orfield, A Multiracial Society with Segregated Schools: Are We Losing the Dream? 4 (Jan. 2003), http://www.civilrightsproject.harvard.edu/research/reseg03/AreWeLosingtheDream.pdf (all Internet materials as visited June 2, 2003, and available in Clerk of Court's case file), ("[W]hites are the most segregated group in the nation's public schools; they attend schools, on average, where eighty percent of the student body is white."); id., at 28 ("[A]lmost three-fourths of black and Latino students attend schools that are predominantly minority .... More than one in six black children attend a school that is 99—100% minority .... One in nine Latino students attend virtually all minority schools.").

[5] See, e.g., Ryan, Schools, Race, and Money, 109 Yale L.J. 249, 273—274 (1999) ("Urban public schools are attended primarily by African-American and Hispanic students"; students who attend such schools are disproportionately poor, score poorly on standardized tests, and are far more likely to drop out than students who attend nonurban schools.).

[6] See, e.g., Statistical Abstract 140 (Table 211).

[7] See, e.g., Holzer, Career Advancement Prospects and Strategies for Low-Wage Minority Workers, in Low-Wage Workers in the New Economy 228 (R. Kazis & M. Miller eds. 2001) ("[I]n studies that have sent matched pairs of minority and white applicants with apparently equal credentials to apply for jobs, whites routinely get more interviews and job offers than either black or Hispanic applicants."); M. Bertrand & S. Mullainathan, Are Emily and Brendan More Employable than Lakisha and Jamal?: A Field Experiment on Labor Market Discrimination (Nov. 18, 2002), http://gsb.uchicago.edu/pdf/bertrand.pdf; Mincy, The Urban Institute Audit Studies: Their Research and Policy Context, in Clear and Convincing Evidence: Measurement of Discrimination in America 165 —186 (M. Fix & R. Struyk eds. 1993).

[8] See, e.g., M. Turner etal., Discrimination in Metropolitan Housing Markets: National Results from Phase I HDS 2000, pp. i, iii (Nov. 2002), http://www.huduser.org/Publications/pdf/Phase1_Report.pdf (paired testing in which "two individuals—one minority and the other white—pose as otherwise identical homeseekers, and visit real estate or rental agents to inquire about the availability of advertised housing units" revealed that "discrimination still persists in both rental and sales markets of large metropolitan areas nationwide"); M. Turner & F. Skidmore, Mortgage Lending Discrimination: A Review of Existing Evidence 2 (1999) (existing research evidence shows that minority homebuyers in the United States "face discrimination from mortgage lending institutions.").

[9] See, e.g., Ayres, Further Evidence of Discrimination in New Car Negotiations and Estimates of its Cause, 94 Mich. L.Rev. 109, 109—110 (1995) (study in which 38 testers negotiated the purchase of more than 400 automobiles confirmed earlier finding "that dealers systematically offer lower prices to white males than to other tester types").

[10] The United States points to the "percentage plans" used in California, Florida, and Texas as one example of a "race-neutral alternativ[e]" that would permit the College to enroll meaningful numbers of minority students. Brief for United States as Amicus Curiae 14; see Commission on Civil Rights, Beyond Percentage Plans: The Challenge of Equal Opportunity in Higher Education 1 (Nov. 2002), http://www.usccr.gov/pubs/percent2/percent2.pdf (percentage plans guarantee admission to state universities for a fixed percentage of the top students from high schools in the State). Calling such 10 or 20% plans "race-neutral" seems to me disingenuous, for they "unquestionably were adopted with the specific purpose of increasing representation of African-Americans and Hispanics in the public higher education system." Brief for Respondents 44; see C. Horn & S. Flores, Percent Plans in College Admissions: A Comparative Analysis of Three States' Experiences 14—19 (2003), http://www.civilrightsproject.harvard.edu/research/affirmativeaction/tristate.pdf. Percentage plans depend for their effectiveness on continued racial segregation at the secondary school level: They can ensure significant minority enrollment in universities only if the majority-minority high school population is large enough to guarantee that, in many schools, most of the students in the top 10 or 20% are minorities. Moreover, because such plans link college admission to a single criterion—high

school class rank—they create perverse incentives. They encourage parents to keep their children in low-performing segregated schools, and discourage students from taking challenging classes that might lower their grade point averages. See Selingo, What States Aren't Saying About the 'X-Percent Solution,' Chronicle of Higher Education, June 2, 2000, p. A31. And even if percentage plans could boost the sheer numbers of minority enrollees at the undergraduate level, they do not touch enrollment in graduate and professional schools.

[11] Contrary to the Court's contention, I do not suggest "changing the Constitution so that it conforms to the conduct of the universities." *Ante*, at 27, n. 22. In my view, the Constitution, properly interpreted, permits government officials to respond openly to the continuing importance of race. See *supra*, at 4—5. Among constitutionally permissible options, those that candidly disclose their consideration of race seem to me preferable to those that conceal it.

RICHARD CHENEY, VICE PRESIDENT OF THE UNITED STATES, et al. v. UNITED STATES DISTRICT COURT FOR THE DISTRICT OF COLUMBIA, et al.

No. 03-475, June 24, 2004

ON WRIT OF CERTIORARI TO THE UNITED STATES COURT OF APPEALS FOR THE DISTRICT OF COLUMBIA CIRCUIT

Justice Ginsburg, with whom Justice Souter joins, dissenting.

The Government, in seeking a writ of mandamus from the Court of Appeals for the District of Columbia, and on brief to this Court, urged that this case should be resolved without *any* discovery. See App. 183—184, 339; Brief for Petitioners 45; Reply Brief 18. In vacating the judgment of the Court of Appeals, however, this Court remands for consideration whether mandamus is appropriate due to the *overbreadth* of the District Court's discovery orders. See *ante*, at 1, 16—20. But, as the Court of Appeals observed, it appeared that the Government "never asked the district court to *narrow* discovery." *Inre Cheney*, 334 F.3d 1096, 1106 (CADC 2003) (emphasis in original). Given the Government's decision to resist all discovery, mandamus relief based on the exorbitance of the discovery orders is at least "premature," *id.*, at 1104. I would therefore affirm the judgment of the Court of Appeals denying the writ,[1] and allow the District Court, in the first instance, to pursue its expressed intention "tightly [to] rei[n] [in] discovery," *Judicial Watch, Inc.* v. *National Energy Policy Dev. Group*, 219 F.Supp. 2d 20, 54 (DC 2002), should the Government so request.

I

A

The discovery at issue here was sought in a civil action filed by respondents Judicial Watch, Inc., and Sierra Club. To gain information concerning the membership and operations of an energy-policy task force, the National Energy Policy Development Group (NEPDG), respondents filed suit under the Federal Advisory Committee Act (FACA), 5 U.S.C. App. §1 *et seq.*; respondents named among the defendants the Vice President and senior Executive Branch officials. See App. 16—40, 139—154; *ante*, at 1—3. After granting in part and denying in part the Government's motions to dismiss, see 219 F.Supp. 2d 20, the District Court approved respondents' extensive discovery plan, which included detailed and far-ranging interrogatories and sweeping requests for production of documents, see App. to Pet. for Cert. 51a; App. 215 —230. In a later order, the District Court directed the Government to "produce non-privileged documents and a privilege log." App. to Pet. for Cert. 47a.

The discovery plan drawn by Judicial Watch and Sierra Club was indeed "unbounded in scope." *Ante*, at 17; accord 334 F.3d, at 1106. Initial approval of that plan by the District Court, however, was not given in stunning disregard of separation-of-powers concerns. Cf. *ante*, at 16—20. In the order itself, the District Court invited "detailed and precise object[ions]" to any of the discovery requests, and instructed the Government to "identify and explain … invocations of privilege with particularity." App. to Pet. for Cert. 51a. To avoid duplication, the District Court provided that the Government could identify "documents or information [responsive to the discovery requests] that [it] ha[d] already released to [Judicial Watch or the Sierra Club] in different fora." *Ibid.*[2] Anticipating further proceedings concerning discovery, the District Court suggested that the Government could "submit [any privileged documents] under seal for the court's consideration," or that "the court [could] appoint the equivalent of a Special Master, maybe a retired judge," to review allegedly privileged documents. App. 247.

The Government did not file specific objections; nor did it supply particulars to support assertions of privilege. Instead, the Government urged the District Court to rule that Judicial Watch and the Sierra Club could have no discovery at all. See *id.*, at 192 ("the governmen[t] position is that … no discovery is appropriate"); *id.*, at 205 (same); 334 F.3d, at 1106 ("As far as we can tell, petitioners never asked the district court to *narrow* discovery to those matters [respondents] need to support their allegation that FACA applies to the NEPDG." (emphasis in original)). In the Government's view, "the resolution of the case ha[d] to flow from the administrative record" *sans* discovery. App. 192. Without taking up the District Court's suggestion of that court's readiness to rein in discovery, see 219 F.Supp. 2d, at 54, the Government, on behalf of the Vice President, moved, unsuccessfully, for a protective order and for certification of an interlocutory appeal pursuant to 28 U.S.C. § 1292(b). See 334 F.3d, at 1100; see App. to Pet. for Cert. 47a (District Court denial of protective order); 233 F.Supp. 2d 16 (DC 2002) (District Court denial of §1292(b) certification).[3] At the District Court's hearing on the Government's motion for a stay pending interlocutory appeal, the Government argued that "the injury is submitting to discovery in the absence of a compelling showing of need by the [respondents]." App. 316; see 230 F.Supp. 2d 12 (DC

2002) (District Court order denying stay).

Despite the absence from this "flurry of activity," *ante*, at 8, of any Government motion contesting the terms of the discovery plan or proposing a scaled-down substitute plan, see 334 F.3d, at 1106, this Court states that the Government "did in fact object to the scope of discovery and asked the District Court to narrow it in some way," *ante*, at 18. In support of this statement, the Court points to the Government's objections to the proposed discovery plan, its response to the interrogatories and production requests, and its contention that discovery would be unduly burdensome. See *ante*, at 18; App. 166—184, 201, 231—234, 274.

True, the Government disputed the definition of the term "meeting" in respondents' interrogatories, and stated, in passing, that "discovery should be [both] limited to written interrogatories" and "limited in scope to the issue of membership." *Id.*, at 179, 181, 233.[4] But as the Court of Appeals noted, the Government mentioned "excessive discovery" in support of its plea to be shielded from any discovery.334 F.3d, at 1106. The Government argument that "the burden of doing a document production is an unconstitutional burden," App. 274, was similarly anchored. The Government so urged at a District Court hearing in which its underlying "position [was] that it's not going to produce anything," *id.*, at 249.[5]

The Government's bottom line was firmly and consistently that "review, limited to the administrative record, should frame the resolution of this case." *Id.*, at 181; accord *id.*, at 179, 233. That administrative record would "consist of the Presidential Memorandum establishing NEPDG, NEPDG's public report, and the Office of the Vice President's response to … Judicial Watch's request for permission to attend NEPDG meetings"; it would not include anything respondents could gain through discovery. *Id.*, at 183. Indeed, the Government acknowledged before the District Court that its litigation strategy involved opposition to the discovery plan as a whole in lieu of focused objections. See *id.*, at 205 (Government stated: "We did not choose to offer written objections to [the discovery plan]….").

Further sounding the Government's leitmotif, in a hearing on the proposed discovery plan, the District Court stated that the Government "didn't file objections" to rein in discovery "because [in the Government's view] no discovery is appropriate." *Id.*, at 192; *id.*, at 205 (same). Without endeavoring to correct any misunderstanding on the District Court's part, the Government underscored its resistance to any and all discovery. *Id.*, at 192—194; *id.*, at 201 (asserting that respondents are "not entitled to discovery to supplement [the administrative record]").And in its motion for a protective order, the Government similarly declared its unqualified opposition to discovery. See Memorandum in Support of Defendants' Motion for a Protective Order and for Reconsideration, C.A. Nos. 01—1530 (EGS), 02—631 (EGS), p.21 (D.D.C., Sept. 3, 2002) ("[Petitioners] respectfully request that the Court enter a protective order relieving them of *any obligation* to respond to [respondents'] discovery [requests]." (emphasis added)); see 334 F.3d, at 1106 (same).[6]

The District Court, in short, "ignored" no concrete pleas to "narrow" discovery. But see *ante*, at 18. That court did, however, voice its concern about the Government's failure to heed the court's instructions:

> "I told the government, if you have precise constitutional objections, let me know what they are so I can determine whether or not this [discovery] plan is appropriate, and … you said, well, it's unconstitutional, without elaborating. You said, because Plaintiff's proposed discovery plan has not been approved by the court, the Defendants are not submitting specific objections to Plaintiff's proposed request…. My rule was, if you have objections, let me know what the objections are, and you chose not to do so." App. 205.

B

Denied §1292(b) certification by the District Court, the Government sought a writ of mandamus from the Court of Appeals. See *id.*, at 339—365. In its mandamus petition, the Government asked the appellate court to "vacate the discovery orders issued by the district court, direct the court to decide the case on the basis of the administrative record and such supplemental affidavits as it may require, and direct that the Vice President be dismissed as a defendant." *Id.*, at 364—365. In support of those requests, the Government again argued that the case should be adjudicated without discovery: "The Constitution and principles of comity preclude discovery of the President or Vice President, especially without a demonstration of compelling and focused countervailing interest."*Id.*, at 360.

The Court of Appeals acknowledged that the discovery plan presented by respondents and approved by the District Court "goes well beyond what [respondents] need." 334 F.3d, at 1106. The appellate court nevertheless denied the mandamus petition, concluding that the Government's separation-of-powers concern "remain[ed] hypothetical." *Id.*, at 1105. Far from ordering immediate "disclosure of communications between senior executive branch officials and those with information relevant to advice that was being formulated for the President," the Court of Appeals observed, the District Court had directed the Government initially to produce only "non-privileged documents and a privilege log." *Id.*, at

7

1104 (citation and internal quotation marks omitted); see App. to Pet. for Cert. 47a.

The Court of Appeals stressed that the District Court could accommodate separation-of-powers concerns short of denying all discovery or compelling the invocation of executive privilege. See 334 F.3d, at 1105—1106. Principally, the Court of Appeals stated, discovery could be narrowed, should the Government so move, to encompass only "whether non-federal officials participated [in NEPDG], and if so, to what extent." *Id.*, at 1106. The Government could identify relevant materials produced in other litigation, thus avoiding undue reproduction. *Id.*, at 1105; see App. to Pet. for Cert. 51a; *supra*, at 3. If, after appropriate narrowing, the discovery allowed still impels "the Vice President ... to claim privilege," the District Court could "entertain [those] privilege claims" and "review allegedly privileged documents in camera." 334 F.3d, at 1107. Mindful of "the judiciary's responsibility to police the separation of powers in litigation involving the executive," the Court of Appeals expressed confidence that the District Court would "respond to petitioners' concern and narrow discovery to ensure that [respondents] obtain no more than they need to prove their case." *Id.*, at 1106.

II

"This Court repeatedly has observed that the writ of mandamus is an extraordinary remedy, to be reserved for extraordinary situations." *Gulfstream Aerospace Corp.* v. *Mayacamas Corp.*, 485 U.S. 271, 289 (1988) (citing *Kerr* v. *United States Dist. Court for Northern Dist. of Cal.*, 426 U.S. 394, 402 (1976)); see *ante*, at 9—10 (same).As the Court reiterates, "the party seeking issuance of the writ [must] have no other adequate means to attain the relief he desires."*Kerr*, 426 U.S., at 403 (citing *Roche* v. *Evaporated Milk Assn.*, 319 U.S. 21, 26 (1943)); *ante*, at 9—10.

Throughout this litigation, the Government has declined to move for reduction of the District Court's discovery order to accommodate separation-of-powers concerns.See *supra*, at 3—7. The Court now remands this case so the Court of Appeals can consider whether a mandamus writ should issue ordering the District Court to "explore other avenues, short of forcing the Executive to invoke privilege," and, in particular, to "narrow, on its own, the scope of [discovery]." *Ante*, at 19—20. Nothing in the District Court's orders or the Court of Appeals' opinion, however, suggests that either of those courts would refuse reasonably to accommodate separation-of-powers concerns. See *supra*, at 3, 7—8. When parties seeking a mandamus writ decline to avail themselves of opportunities to obtain relief from the District Court, a writ of mandamus ordering the same relief—*i.e.*, here, reined-in discovery—is surely a doubtful proposition.

The District Court, moreover, did not err in failing to narrow discovery on its own initiative. Although the Court cites *United States* v. *Poindexter*, 727 F.Supp. 1501 (DC 1989), as "sound precedent" for district-court narrowing of discovery, see *ante*, at 19—20, the target of the subpoena in that case, former President Reagan, unlike petitioners in this case, affirmatively requested such narrowing, 727 F.Supp., at 1503.A district court is not subject to criticism if it awaits a party's motion before tightening the scope of discovery; certainly, that court makes no "clear and indisputable" error in adhering to the principle of party initiation, *Kerr*, 426 U.S., at 403 (internal quotation marks omitted).[8]

* * *

Review by mandamus at this stage of the proceedings would be at least comprehensible as a means to test the Government's position that *no* discovery is appropriate in this litigation. See Brief for Petitioners 45 ("[P]etitioners' separation-of-powers arguments are ... in the nature of a claim of immunity from discovery."). But in remanding for consideration of discovery-tailoring measures, the Court apparently rejects that no-discovery position.Otherwise, a remand based on the overbreadth of the discovery requests would make no sense. Nothing in the record, however, intimates lower-court refusal to reduce discovery. Indeed, the appeals court has already suggested tailored discovery that would avoid "effectively prejudg[ing] the merits of respondents' claim," *ante*, at 2 (Stevens, J., concurring). See 334 F.3d, at 1106 (respondents "need only documents referring to the involvement of non-federal officials"). See also *ante*, at 2, n. (Stevens, J., concurring) ("A few interrogatories or depositions might have determined ... whether any non-Government employees voted on NEPDG recommendations or drafted portions of the committee's report").In accord with the Court of Appeals, I am "confident that [were it moved to do so] the district court here [would] protect petitioners' legitimate interests and keep discovery within appropriate limits." 334 F.3d, at 1107.[9] I would therefore affirm the judgment of the Court of Appeals.

NOTES

[1] The Court of Appeals also concluded, altogether correctly in my view, that it lacked ordinary appellate jurisdiction over the Vice President's appeal. See 334 F.3d, at 1109; cf. *ante*, at 7—8 (leaving appellate-jurisdiction question undecided). In its order addressing the petitioners' motions to dismiss, the District Court stated "it would be premature and inappropriate to determine whether" any relief could be obtained from the Vice President. *Judicial Watch, Inc.* v. *National Energy Policy Dev. Group*, 219 F.Supp. 2d 20, 44 (DC 2002). Immediate review of an interlocutory ruling, allowed in rare cases under the collateral-order doctrine, is inappropriate when an order is, as in this case, "inherently tentative" and not "the final word on the subject." *Gulfstream Aerospace Corp.* v. *Mayacamas Corp.*,

485 U.S. 271, 277 (1988) (internal quotation marks omitted).

[2] Government agencies had produced some relevant documents in related Freedom of Information Act litigation. See 219 F.Supp. 2d, at 27.

[3] Section 1292(b) of Title 28 allows a court of appeals, "in its discretion," to entertain an appeal from an interlocutory order "[w]hen a district judge … shall be of the opinion that such order involves a controlling question of law as to which there is substantial ground for difference of opinion and that an immediate appeal from the order may materially advance the ultimate termination of the litigation."

[4] On limiting discovery to the issue of membership, the Court of Appeals indicated its agreement. See 334 F.3d, at 1106 ("[Respondents] have no need for the names of all persons who participated in [NEPDG]'s activities, nor a description of each person's role in the activities of [NEPDG].They must discover only whether non-federal officials participated, and if so, to what extent." (internal quotation marks, ellipsis, and brackets omitted)).

[5] According to the Government, "24 boxes of documents [are] potentially responsive to [respondents'] discovery requests…. The documents identified as likely to be responsive from those boxes … are contained in approximately twelve boxes." App. 282—283. Each box "requires one or two attorney days to review and prepare a rough privilege log. Following that review, privilege logs must be finalized. Further, once the responsive emails are identified, printed, and numbered, [petitioners] expect that the privilege review and logging process [will] be equally, if not more, time-consuming, due to the expected quantity of individual emails." *Id.*, at 284.

[6] The agency petitioners, in responses to interrogatories, gave rote and hardly illuminating responses refusing "on the basis of executive and deliberative process privileges" to be more forthcoming. See, *e.g.*, Defendant Department of Energy's Response to Plaintiff's First Set of Interrogatories, C.A. Nos. 01—1530 (EGS), 02—631 (EGS) (D.D.C., Sept. 3, 2002); Defendant United States Office of Management and Budget's Response to Plaintiff's First Set of Interrogatories, C. A. Nos. 01—1530 (EGS), 02—631 (EGS) (D.D.C., Sept. 3, 2002).

[7] The Court suggests that the appeals court "labored under the mistaken assumption that the assertion of executive privilege is a necessary precondition to the Government's separation-of-powers objections." *Ante*, at 20. The Court of Appeals, however, described the constitutional concern as "hypothetical," not merely because no executive privilege had been asserted, but also in light of measures the District Court could take to "narrow" and "carefully focu[s]" discovery. See 334 F.3d, at 1105, 1107.

[8] The Court also questions the District Court's invocation of the federal mandamus statute, 28 U.S.C. § 1361 which provides that "[t]he district courts shall have original jurisdiction of any action in the nature of mandamus to compel an officer or employee of the United States or any agency thereof to perform a duty owed to the plaintiff." See *ante*, at 20; 219 F.Supp. 2d, at 41—44.See also *Chandler* v. *Judicial Council of Tenth Circuit*, 398 U.S. 74, 87—89, and n. 8 (1970) (holding mandamus under the All Writs Act, 28 U.S.C. § 1651 improper, but expressing no opinion on relief under the federal mandamus statute, §1361). On the question whether §1361 allows enforcement of the FACA against the Vice President, the District Court concluded it "would be premature and inappropriate to determine whether the relief of mandamus will or will not issue." 219 F.Supp. 2d, at 44. The Government, moreover, contested the propriety of §1361 relief only in passing in its petition to the appeals court for §1651 mandamus relief. See App. 363—364 (Government asserted in its mandamus petition: "The more general writ of mandamus cannot be used to circumvent … limits on the provision directly providing for review of administrative action.").A question not decided by the District Court, and barely raised in a petition for mandamus, hardly qualifies as grounds for "drastic and extraordinary" mandamus relief, *Ex parte Fahey*, 332 U.S. 258, 259—260 (1947). Justice Thomas urges that respondents cannot obtain §1361 relief if "wide-ranging discovery [is needed] to prove that they have *any* right to relief." *Ante*, at 3 (opinion concurring in part and dissenting in part) (emphasis in original). First, as the Court of Appeals recognized, see *supra*, at 8—9; *infra*, at 11, should the Government so move, the District Court could contain discovery so that it would not be "wide-ranging." Second, all agree that an applicant seeking a §1361 mandamus writ must show that "the [federal] defendant owes him a clear, *nondiscretionary* duty." *Heckler* v. *Ringer*, 466 U.S. 602, 616 (1984) (emphasis added). No §1361 writ may issue, in other words, when federal law grants discretion to the federal officer, rather than imposing a duty on him. When federal law imposes an obligation, however, suit under

§1361 is not precluded simply because facts must be developed to ascertain whether a federal command has been dishonored.Congress enacted §1361 to "mak[e] it more convenient for aggrieved persons to file actions in the nature of mandamus," *Stafford* v. *Briggs,* 444 U.S. 527, 535 (1980), not to address the rare instance in which a federal defendant, upon whom the law unequivocally places an obligation, concedes his failure to measure up to that obligation.

[9] While I agree with the Court that an interlocutory appeal may become appropriate at some later juncture in this litigation, see *ante,* at 21, I note that the decision whether to allow such an appeal lies in the first instance in the District Court's sound discretion, see 28 U.S.C. § 1292(b); *supra,* at 4, n.3.

COOPER INDUSTRIES, INC. v. AVIALL SERVICES, INC.

No. 02-1192, December 13, 2004

ON WRIT OF CERTIORARI TO THE UNITED STATES COURT OF APPEALS FOR THE FIFTH CIRCUIT

Justice Ginsburg, with whom Justice Stevens joins, dissenting.

Aviall Services, Inc., purchased from Cooper Industries, Inc., property that was contaminated with hazardous substances. Shortly after the purchase, the Texas Natural Resource Conservation Commission notified Aviall that it would institute enforcement action if Aviall failed to remediate the property. Aviall promptly cleaned up the site and now seeks reimbursement from Cooper. In my view, the Court unnecessarily defers decision on Aviall's entitlement to recover cleanup costs from Cooper.

In *Key Tronic Corp.* v. *United States*, 511 U.S. 809, 818 (1994), all Members of this Court agreed that §107 of the Comprehensive Environmental Response, Compensation, and Liability Act of 1980 (CERCLA), 42 U.S.C. § 9607 "unquestionably provides a cause of action for [potentially responsible persons (PRPs)] to seek recovery of cleanup costs." The Court rested that determination squarely and solely on §107(a)(4)(B), which allows *any* person who has incurred costs for cleaning up a hazardous waste site to recover all or a portion of those costs from any other person liable under CERCLA.[1]

The *Key Tronic* Court divided, however, on the question whether the right to contribution is implicit in §107(a)'s text, as the majority determined, or whether §107(a) expressly confers the right, as the dissenters urged. The majority stated: Section 107 "*implies*—but does not expressly *command*—that [a PRP] may have a claim for contribution against those treated as joint tortfeasors." 511 U.S., at 818, and n.11 ((emphasis added)). The dissent maintained: "Section 107(a)(4)(B) states, as clearly as can be, that '[c]overed persons ... shall be liable for... necessary costs of response incurred by any other person.' Surely to say that A shall be liable to B is the *express* creation of a right of action." *Id.*, at 822. But no Justice expressed the slightest doubt that §107 indeed did enable a PRP to sue other covered persons for reimbursement, in whole or part, of cleanup costs the PRP legitimately incurred.

In its original complaint, Aviall identified §107 as the federal-law basis for an independent cost-recovery claim against Cooper, and §113 as the basis for a contribution claim.App. 8A, 16A—17A. In amended pleadings, Aviall alleged both §§107 and 113 as the federal underpinning for its contribution claim. *Id.*, at 27A, 48A. Aviall's use of §§113 and 107 in tandem to assert a contribution claim conformed its pleading to then-governing Fifth Circuit precedent, which held that a CERCLA contribution action arises through the joint operation of §107(a) and §113(f)(1).See *Geraghty and Miller, Inc.* v. *Conoco, Inc.*, 234 F.3d 917, 924 (2000) ("[W]hile section 113(f) is the vehicle for bringing a contribution action, it does not create a new cause of action or create any new liabilities. Rather, it is a mechanism for apportioning costs that are recoverable under section 107." (footnote omitted)). A party obliged by circuit precedent to plead in a certain way can hardly be deemed to have waived a plea the party could have maintained had the law of the Circuit permitted him to do so. But cf. *ante*, at 9—10.

In the Fifth Circuit's view, §107 supplied the right of action for Aviall's claim, and §113(f)(1) prescribed the procedural framework. 312 F.3d 677, 683, and n.10 (2002) (stating that §107 "impliedly authorizes a cause of action for contribution" and §113(f) "govern[s] and regulate[s]" the action (citing *Geraghty and Miller*, 234 F.3d, at 924) (internal quotation marks omitted)); see §113(f)(1) (calling for the governance of "Federal law" and the application of "the Federal Rules of Civil Procedure," and specifying that "[i]n resolving contribution claims, the court may allocate response costs among liable parties using such equitable factors as the court determines are appropriate"). Notably, Aviall expressly urged in the Court of Appeals that, were the court to conclude that §113(f)(1)'s "during or following" language excluded application of that section to this case, Aviall's suit should be adjudicated independently under §107(a). See Response of Appellant Aviall Services, Inc., to the *Amicus Curiae* Brief of the United States in No. 00—10197 (CA5), p. 24 ("[P]arties who are excluded from seeking contribution under section 113(f)(1) must therefore have available to them the broader right of cost recovery [covering both full recovery and contribution] under section 107(a)."); cf. *Key Tronic*, 511 U.S., at 816 ("[T]he statute now expressly authorizes a cause of action for contribution in §113 and impliedly authorizes a similar and somewhat overlapping remedy in §107.").

I see no cause for protracting this litigation by requiring the Fifth Circuit to revisit a determination it has essentially made already: Federal courts, prior to the enactment of §113(f)(1), had correctly held that PRPs could "recover [under §107] a proportionate share of their costs in actions for contribution against other PRPs," 312 F.3d, at 687;[2] nothing in §113 retracts that right, *ibid.* (noting that §113(f)'s saving clause preserves all preexisting state and federal rights of action for contribution, including the §107 implied right this Court recognized in *Key Tronic*, 511 U.S., at 816). Accordingly, I would not defer a definitive ruling by this Court on the question whether Aviall may pursue a §107 claim for relief against Cooper.

NOTES

[1] Key Tronic, a PRP, asserted a cost-recovery claim under §107(a) to recoup approximately $1.2 million in costs that it allegedly incurred cleaning up its site "at its own initiative." *Key Tronic Corp.* v. *United States*, 984 F.2d 1025, 1026 (CA9 1993).Although Key Tronic settled a portion of its liability with the Environmental Protection Agency (EPA), the claim advanced in Key Tronic's §107(a) suit rested on remedial action taken before the EPA's involvement, remediation that did not figure in the settlement. *Id.*, at 1026—1027; *Key Tronic Corp.* v. *United States*, 511 U.S. 809, 811—812 (1994).

[2] The cases to which the Court refers, *ante*, at 12, *Texas Industries, Inc.* v. *Radcliff Materials, Inc.*, 451 U.S. 630 (1981), and *Northwest Airlines, Inc.* v. *Transport Workers*, 451 U.S. 77 (1981), do not address the implication of a right of action for contribution under CERCLA. *Texas Industries* concerned the Sherman and Clayton Acts, 451 U.S., at 639—646; *Northwest Airlines*, the Equal Pay Act and Title VII, 451 U.S., at 90—99. A determination suitable in one statutory context does not necessarily carry over to a different statutory setting.

LILLY LEDBETTER v. GOODYEAR TIRE & RUBBER CO., INC.

No. 05-1074, May 29, 2007

ON WRIT OF CERTIORARI TO THE UNITED STATES COURT OF APPEALS FOR THE ELEVENTH CIRCUIT

Justice Ginsburg, with whom Justice Stevens, Justice Souter, and Justice Breyer join, dissenting.

Lilly Ledbetter was a supervisor at Goodyear Tire and Rubber's plant in Gadsden, Alabama, from 1979 until her retirement in 1998. For most of those years, she worked as an area manager, a position largely occupied by men. Initially, Ledbetter's salary was in line with the salaries of men performing substantially similar work. Over time, however, her pay slipped in comparison to the pay of male area managers with equal or less seniority. By the end of 1997, Ledbetter was the only woman working as an area manager and the pay discrepancy between Ledbetter and her 15 male counterparts was stark: Ledbetter was paid $3,727 per month; the lowest paid male area manager received $4,286 per month, the highest paid, $5,236. See 421 F.3d 1169, 1174 (CA11 2005); Brief for Petitioner 4.

Ledbetter launched charges of discrimination before the Equal Employment Opportunity Commission (EEOC) in March 1998. Her formal administrative complaint specified that, in violation of Title VII, Goodyear paid her a discriminatorily low salary because of her sex. See 42 U.S.C. §2000e–2(a)(1) (rendering it unlawful for an employer "to discriminate against any individual with respect to [her] compensation … because of such individual's … sex"). That charge was eventually tried to a jury, which found it "more likely than not that [Goodyear] paid [Ledbetter] a[n] unequal salary because of her sex." App. 102. In accord with the jury's liability determination, the District Court entered judgment for Ledbetter for backpay and damages, plus counsel fees and costs.

The Court of Appeals for the Eleventh Circuit reversed. Relying on Goodyear's system of annual merit-based raises, the court held that Ledbetter's claim, in relevant part, was time barred. 421 F.3d, at 1171, 1182–1183. Title VII provides that a charge of discrimination "shall be filed within [180] days after the alleged unlawful employment practice occurred." 42 U.S.C. §2000e–5(e)(1).[1] Ledbetter charged, and proved at trial, that within the 180-day period, her pay was substantially less than the pay of men doing the same work. Further, she introduced evidence sufficient to establish that discrimination against female managers at the Gadsden plant, not performance inadequacies on her part, accounted for the pay differential. See, e.g., App. 36–47, 51–68, 82–87, 90–98, 112–113. That evidence was unavailing, the Eleventh Circuit held, and the Court today agrees, because it was incumbent on Ledbetter to file charges year-by-year, each time Goodyear failed to increase her salary commensurate with the salaries of male peers. Any annual pay decision not contested immediately (within 180 days), the Court affirms, becomes grandfathered, a *fait accompli* beyond the province of Title VII ever to repair.

The Court's insistence on immediate contest overlooks common characteristics of pay discrimination. Pay disparities often occur, as they did in Ledbetter's case, in small increments; cause to suspect that discrimination is at work develops only over time. Comparative pay information, moreover, is often hidden from the employee's view. Employers may keep under wraps the pay differentials maintained among supervisors, no less the reasons for those differentials. Small initial discrepancies may not be seen as meet for a federal case, particularly when the employee, trying to succeed in a nontraditional environment, is averse to making waves.

Pay disparities are thus significantly different from adverse actions "such as termination, failure to promote, … or refusal to hire," all involving fully communicated discrete acts, "easy to identify" as discriminatory. See *National Railroad Passenger Corporation* v. *Morgan*, 536 U.S. 101, 114 (2002) . It is only when the disparity becomes apparent and sizable, e.g., through future raises calculated as a percentage of current salaries, that an employee in Ledbetter's situation is likely to comprehend her plight and, therefore, to complain. Her initial readiness to give her employer the benefit of the doubt should not preclude her from later challenging the then current and continuing payment of a wage depressed on account of her sex.

On questions of time under Title VII, we have identified as the critical inquiries: "What constitutes an 'unlawful employment practice' and when has that practice 'occurred'?" *Id.*, at 110. Our precedent suggests, and lower courts have overwhelmingly held, that the unlawful practice is the *current payment* of salaries infected by gender-based (or race-based) discrimination—a practice that occurs whenever a paycheck delivers less to a woman than to a similarly situated man. See *Bazemore* v. *Friday*, 478 U.S. 385, 395 (1986) (Brennan, J., joined by all other Members of the Court, concurring in part).

I

Title VII proscribes as an "unlawful employment practice" discrimination "against any individual with respect to his compensation ... because of such individual's race, color, religion, sex, or national origin." 42 U.S.C. §2000e–2(a)(1). An individual seeking to challenge an employment practice under this proscription must file a charge with the EEOC within 180 days "after the alleged unlawful employment practice occurred." §2000e–5(e)(1). See *ante*, at 4; *supra*, at 2, n.1.

Ledbetter's petition presents a question important to the sound application of Title VII: What activity qualifies as an unlawful employment practice in cases of discrimination with respect to compensation. One answer identifies the pay-setting decision, and that decision alone, as the unlawful practice. Under this view, each particular salary-setting decision is discrete from prior and subsequent decisions, and must be challenged within 180 days on pain of forfeiture. Another response counts both the pay-setting decision and the actual payment of a discriminatory wage as unlawful practices. Under this approach, each payment of a wage or salary infected by sex-based discrimination constitutes an unlawful employment practice; prior decisions, outside the 180-day charge-filing period, are not themselves actionable, but they are relevant in determining the lawfulness of conduct within the period. The Court adopts the first view, see *ante*, at 1, 4, 9, but the second is more faithful to precedent, more in tune with the realities of the workplace, and more respectful of Title VII's remedial purpose.

A

In *Bazemore*, we unanimously held that an employer, the North Carolina Agricultural Extension Service, committed an unlawful employment practice each time it paid black employees less than similarly situated white employees. 478 U.S., at 395 (opinion of Brennan, J.). Before 1965, the Extension Service was divided into two branches: a white branch and a "Negro branch." *Id.*, at 390. Employees in the "Negro branch" were paid less than their white counterparts. In response to the Civil Rights Act of 1964, which included Title VII, the State merged the two branches into a single organization, made adjustments to reduce the salary disparity, and began giving annual raises based on nondiscriminatory factors. *Id.*, at 390–391, 394–395. Nonetheless, "some pre-existing salary disparities continued to linger on." *Id.*, at 394 (internal quotation marks omitted). We rejected the Court of Appeals' conclusion that the plaintiffs could not prevail because the lingering disparities were simply a continuing effect of a decision lawfully made prior to the effective date of Title VII. See *id.*, at 395–396. Rather, we reasoned, "[e]ach week's paycheck that delivers less to a black than to a similarly situated white is a wrong actionable under Title VII." *Id.*, at 395. Paychecks perpetuating past discrimination, we thus recognized, are actionable not simply because they are "related" to a decision made outside the charge-filing period, cf. *ante*, at 17, but because they discriminate anew each time they issue, see *Bazemore*, 478 U.S., at 395–396, and n.6; *Morgan*, 536 U.S., at 111–112.

Subsequently, in *Morgan*, we set apart, for purposes of Title VII's timely filing requirement, unlawful employment actions of two kinds: "discrete acts" that are "easy to identify" as discriminatory, and acts that recur and are cumulative in impact. See *id.*, at 110, 113–115. "[A] [d]iscrete ac[t] such as termination, failure to promote, denial of transfer, or refusal to hire," *id.*, at 114, we explained, "'occur[s]' on the day that it 'happen[s].'" A party, therefore, must file a charge within ... 180 ... days of the date of the act or lose the ability to recover for it." *Id.*, at 110; see *id.*, at 113 ("[D]iscrete discriminatory acts are not actionable if time barred, even when they are related to acts alleged in timely filed charges. Each discrete discriminatory act starts a new clock for filing charges alleging that act.").

"[D]ifferent in kind from discrete acts," we made clear, are "claims ... based on the cumulative effect of individual acts." *Id.*, at 115. The *Morgan* decision placed hostile work environment claims in that category. "Their very nature involves repeated conduct." *Ibid.* "The unlawful employment practice" in hostile work environment claims, "cannot be said to occur on any particular day. It occurs over a series of days or perhaps years and, in direct contrast to discrete acts, a single act of harassment may not be actionable on its own." *Ibid.* (internal quotation marks omitted). The persistence of the discriminatory conduct both indicates that management should have known of its existence and produces a cognizable harm. *Ibid.* Because the very nature of the hostile work environment claim involves repeated conduct,

> "[i]t does not matter, for purposes of the statute, that some of the component acts of the hostile work environment fall outside the statutory time period. Provided that an act contributing to the claim occurs within the filing period, the entire time period of the hostile environment may be considered by a court for the purposes of determining liability." *Id.*, at 117.

Consequently, although the unlawful conduct began in the past, "a charge may be filed at a later date and still encompass the whole." *Ibid.*

Pay disparities, of the kind Ledbetter experienced, have a closer kinship to hostile work environment claims than to charges of a single episode of discrimination. Ledbetter's claim, resembling Morgan's, rested not on one particular paycheck, but on "the cumulative effect of individual acts." See *id.*, at 115. See also Brief for Petitioner 13, 15–17, and n.9 (analogizing Ledbetter's claim to the recurring and cumulative harm at issue in *Morgan*); Reply Brief for Petitioner 13 (distinguishing pay discrimination from "easy to identify" discrete acts (internal quotation marks omitted)). She charged insidious discrimination building up slowly but steadily. See Brief for Petitioner 5–8. Initially in line with the salaries of men performing substantially the same work, Ledbetter's salary fell 15 to 40 percent behind her male counterparts only after successive evaluations and percentage-based pay adjustments. See *supra*, at 1–2. Over time, she alleged and proved, the repetition of pay decisions undervaluing her work gave rise to the current discrimination of which she complained. Though component acts fell outside the charge-filing period, with each new paycheck, Goodyear contributed incrementally to the accumulating harm. See *Morgan*, 536 U.S., at 117; *Bazemore*, 478 U.S., at 395–396;cf. *Hanover Shoe, Inc.* v. *United Shoe Machinery Corp.*, 392 U.S. 481 , n.15 (1968).[2]

B

The realities of the workplace reveal why the discrimination with respect to compensation that Ledbetter suffered does not fit within the category of singular discrete acts "easy to identify." A worker knows immediately if she is denied a promotion or transfer, if she is fired or refused employment. And promotions, transfers, hirings, and firings are generally public events, known to co-workers. When an employer makes a decision of such open and definitive character, an employee can immediately seek out an explanation and evaluate it for pretext. Compensation disparities, in contrast, are often hidden from sight. It is not unusual, decisions in point illustrate, for management to decline to publish employee pay levels, or for employees to keep private their own salaries. See, *e.g.*, *Goodwin* v. *General Motors Corp.*, 275 F.3d 1005, 1008–1009 (CA10 2002) (plaintiff did not know what her colleagues earned until a printout listing of salaries appeared on her desk, seven years after her starting salary was set lower than her co-workers' salaries); *McMillan* v. *Massachusetts Soc. for the Prevention of Cruelty to Animals*, 140 F.3d 288, 296 (CA1 1998) (plaintiff worked for employer for years before learning of salary disparity published in a newspaper).[3] Tellingly, as the record in this case bears out, Goodyear kept salaries confidential; employees had only limited access to information regarding their colleagues' earnings. App. 56–57, 89.

The problem of concealed pay discrimination is particularly acute where the disparity arises not because the female employee is flatly denied a raise but because male counterparts are given larger raises. Having received a pay increase, the female employee is unlikely to discern at once that she has experienced an adverse employment decision. She may have little reason even to suspect discrimination until a pattern develops incrementally and she ultimately becomes aware of the disparity. Even if an employee suspects that the reason for a comparatively low raise is not performance but sex (or another protected ground), the amount involved may seem too small, or the employer's intent too ambiguous, to make the issue immediately actionable—or winnable.

Further separating pay claims from the discrete employment actions identified in *Morgan*, anemployer gains from sex-based pay disparities in a way it does not from a discriminatory denial of promotion, hiring, or transfer. When a male employee is selected over a female for a higher level position, someone still gets the promotion and is paid a higher salary; the employer is not enriched. But when a woman is paid less than a similarly situated man, the employer reduces its costs each time the pay differential is implemented. Furthermore, decisions on promotions, like decisions installing seniority systems, often implicate the interests of third-party employees in a way that pay differentials do not. Cf. *Teamsters* v. *United States*, 431 U.S. 324, 352–353 (1977) (recognizing that seniority systems involve "vested … rights of employees" and concluding that Title VII was not intended to "destroy or water down" those rights). Disparate pay, by contrast, can be remedied at any time solely at the expense of the employer who acts in a discriminatory fashion.

C

In light of the significant differences between pay disparities and discrete employment decisions of the type identified in *Morgan*, the cases on which the Court relies hold no sway. See *ante*, at 5–10 (discussing *United Air Lines, Inc.* v. *Evans*, 431 U.S. 553 (1977) , *Delaware State College* v. *Ricks*, 449 U.S. 250 (1980) , and *Lorance* v. *AT&T Technologies, Inc.*, 490 U.S. 900 (1989)). *Evans* and *Ricks* both involved a single, immediately identifiable act of discrimination: in *Evans*, a constructive discharge, 431 U.S., at 554; in *Ricks*, a denial of tenure, 449 U.S., at 252. In each case, the employee filed charges well after the discrete discriminatory act occurred: When United Airlines forced Evans to resign because of its policy barring married female flight attendants, she filed no charge; only four years later, when Evans was rehired, did she allege that the airline's former no-marriage rule was unlawful and therefore should not operate to deny her seniority credit for her prior service. See *Evans*,431 U.S., at 554–557. Similarly, when Delaware State College denied Ricks tenure, he did not object until his terminal contract came to an end, one year later. *Ricks*, 449 U.S., at 253–254, 257–258. No repetitive, cumulative discriminatory employment practice was at issue in either case. See *Evans*, 431 U.S., at 557–558; *Ricks*, 449 U.S., at 258.[4]

Lorance is also inapposite, for, in this Court's view, it too involved a one-time discrete act: the adoption of a new seniority system that "had its genesis in sex discrimination." See 490 U.S., at 902, 905 (internal quotation marks omitted). The Court's extensive relianceon *Lorance*, *ante*, at 7–9, 14, 17–18, moreover, is perplexing for that decision is no longer effective: In the 1991 Civil Rights Act, Congress superseded *Lorance*'s holding. §112, 105 Stat. 1079 (codified as amended at 42 U.S.C. §2000e-5(e)(2)). Repudiating our judgment that a facially neutral seniority system adopted with discriminatory intent must be challenged immediately, Congress provided:

"For purposes of this section, an unlawful

employment practice occurs … when the seniority system is adopted, when an individual becomes subject to the seniority system, or when a person aggrieved is injured by the application of the seniority system or provision of the system." Ibid.

Congress thus agreed with the dissenters in *Lorance* that "the harsh reality of [that] decision," was "glaringly at odds with the purposes of Title VII." 490 U.S., at 914 (opinion of Marshall, J.). See also §3, 105 Stat. 1071 (1991 Civil Rights Act was designed "to respond to recent decisions of the Supreme Court by expanding the scope of relevant civil rights statutes in order to provide adequate protection to victims of discrimination").

True, §112 of the 1991 Civil Rights Act directly addressed only seniority systems. See *ante*, at 8, and n.2. But Congress made clear (1) its view that this Court had unduly *contracted* the scope of protection afforded by Title VII and other civil rights statutes, and (2) its aim to generalize the ruling in *Bazemore*. As the Senate Report accompanying the proposed Civil Rights Act of 1990, the precursor to the 1991 Act, explained:

"Where, as was alleged in *Lorance*, an employer adopts a rule or decision with an unlawful discriminatory motive, each application of that rule or decision is a new violation of the law. In *Bazemore* . . ., for example, … the Supreme Court properly held that each application of th[e] racially motivated salary structure, *i.e.*, each new paycheck, constituted a distinct violation of Title VII. Section 7(a)(2) generalizes the result correctly reached in *Bazemore*." Civil Rights Act of 1990, S. Rep. No. 101-315, p. 54 (1990).[5]

See also 137 Cong. Rec. 29046, 29047(1991) (Sponsors' Interpretative Memorandum) ("This legislation should be interpreted as disapproving the extension of *[Lorance]* to contexts outside of seniority systems."). But cf. *ante*, at 18 (relying on *Lorance* to conclude that "when an employer issues paychecks pursuant to a system that is facially nondiscriminatory and neutrally applied" a new Title VII violation does not occur (internal quotation marks omitted)).

Until today, in the more than 15 years since Congress amended Title VII, the Court had not once relied upon *Lorance*. It is mistaken to do so now. Just as Congress' "goals in enacting Title VII … never included conferring absolute immunity on discriminatorily adopted seniority systems that survive their first [180] days," 490 U.S., at 914 (Marshall, J., dissenting), Congress never intended to immunize forever discriminatory pay differentials unchallenged within 180 days of their adoption. This assessment gains weight when one comprehends that even a relatively minor pay disparity will expand exponentially over an employee's working life if raises are set as a percentage of prior pay.

A clue to congressional intent can be found in Title VII's backpay provision. The statute expressly provides that backpay may be awarded for a period of up to two years before the discrimination charge is filed. 42 U.S.C. §2000e–5(g)(1) ("Back pay liability shall not accrue from a date more than two years prior to the filing of a charge with the Commission."). This prescription indicates that Congress contemplated challenges to pay discrimination commencing before, but continuing into, the 180-day filing period. See *Morgan*, 536 U.S., at 119 ("If Congress intended to limit liability to conduct occurring in the period within which the party must file the charge, it seems unlikely that Congress would have allowed recovery for two years of backpay."). As we recognized in *Morgan*, "the fact that Congress expressly limited the amount of recoverable damages elsewhere to a particular time period [*i.e.*, two years]indicates that the [180-day] timely filing provision was not meant to serve as a specific limitation … [on] the conduct that may be considered." *Ibid.*

D

In tune with the realities of wage discrimination, the Courts of Appeals have overwhelmingly judged as a present violation the payment of wages infected by discrimination: Each paycheck less than the amount payable had the employer adhered to a nondiscriminatory compensation regime, courts have held, constitutes a cognizable harm. See, *e.g.*, *Forsyth* v. *Federation Employment and Guidance Serv.*, 409 F.3d 565, 573 (CA2 2005) ("Any paycheck given within the [charge-filing] period … would be actionable, even if based on a discriminatory pay scale set up outside of the statutory period."); *Shea* v. *Rice*, 409 F.3d 448, 452–453 (CADC 2005) ("[An] employer commit[s] a separate unlawful employment practice each time he pa[ys] one employee less than another for a discriminatory reason" (citing *Bazemore*, 478 U.S., at 396)); *Goodwin* v. *General Motors Corp.*, 275 F.3d 1005, 1009–1010 (CA10 2002) ("*[Bazemore]* hastaught a crucial distinction with respect to discriminatory disparities in pay, establishing that a discriminatory salary is not merely a lingering effect of past discrimination—instead it is itself a continually recurring violation…. [E]ach race-based discriminatory salary payment constitutes a fresh violation of Title VII." (footnote omitted)); *Anderson* v. *Zubieta*, 180 F.3d 329, 335 (CADC 1999) ("The Courts of Appeals have repeatedly reached the ... conclusion" that pay discrimination is "actionable upon receipt of each paycheck."); accord *Hildebrandt* v. *Illinois Dept. of Natural Resources*, 347 F.3d 1014, 1025–1029 (CA7 2003); *Cardenas* v. *Massey*, 269 F.3d 251, 257 (CA3 2001); *Ashley* v. *Boyle's Famous Corned Beef Co.*, 66 F.3d 164, 167–168 (CA8 1995) (en banc); *Brinkley-Obu* v. *Hughes Training, Inc.*, 36 F.3d 336, 347–349 (CA4 1994); *Gibbs* v. *Pierce County Law Enforcement Support Agency*, 785 F.2d 1396, 1399–1400 (CA9 1986).

Similarly in line with the real-world characteristics of pay discrimination, the EEOC—the federal agency responsible for enforcing Title VII, see, *e.g.*, 42 U.S.C. §§2000e–5(f)—has interpreted the Act to permit employees to challenge disparate pay each time it is received. The EEOC's Compliance Manual provides that "repeated occurrences of the same discriminatory employment action, such as discriminatory paychecks, can be challenged as long as one discriminatory act occurred within the charge filing period." 2 EEOC Compliance Manual §2–IV–C(1)(a), p. 605:0024, and n. 183 (2006); cf. *id.*, §10–III, p. 633:0002 (Title VII requires an employer to eliminate pay disparities attributable to a discriminatory system, even if that system has been discontinued).

The EEOC has given effect to its interpretation in a series of administrative decisions. See *Albritton* v. *Potter*, No. 01A44063, 2004 WL 2983682, *2 (EEOC Office of Fed. Operations, Dec. 17, 2004) (although disparity arose and employee became aware of the disparity outside the charge-filing period, claim was not time barred because "[e]ach paycheck that complainant receives which is less than that of similarly situated employees outside of her protected classes could support a claim under Title VII if discrimination is found to be the reason for the pay discrepancy." (citing *Bazemore*, 478 U.S., at 396)). See also *Bynum-Doles* v. *Winter*, No. 01A53973, 2006 WL 2096290 (EEOC Office of Fed. Operations, July 18, 2006); *Ward* v. *Potter*, No. 01A60047, 2006 WL 721992 (EEOC Office of Fed. Operations, Mar. 10, 2006). And in this very case, the EEOC urged the Eleventh Circuit to recognize that Ledbetter's failure to challenge any particular pay-setting decision when that decision was made "does not deprive her of the right to seek relief for discriminatory paychecks she received in 1997 and 1998." Brief of EEOC in Support of Petition for Rehearing and Suggestion for Rehearing En Banc, in No. 03–15264–GG (CA11), p. 14 (hereinafter EEOC Brief) (citing *Morgan*, 536 U.S., at 113).[6]

II

The Court asserts that treating pay discrimination as a discrete act, limited to each particular pay-setting decision, is necessary to "protec[t] employers from the burden of defending claims arising from employment decisions that are long past." *Ante*, at 11 (quoting *Ricks*, 449 U.S., at 256–257).But the discrimination of which Ledbetter complained is *not* long past. As she alleged, and as the jury found, Goodyear continued to treat Ledbetter differently because of sex each pay period, with mounting harm. Allowing employees to challenge discrimination "that extend[s] over long periods of time," into the charge-filing period, we have previously explained, "does not leave employers defenseless" against unreasonable or prejudicial delay. *Morgan*, 536 U.S., at 121. Employers disadvantaged by such delay may raise various defenses. *Id.*, at 122. Doctrines such as "waiver, estoppel, and equitable tolling" "allow us to honor Title VII's remedial purpose without negating the particular purpose of the filing requirement, to give prompt notice to the employer." *Id.*, at 121 (quoting *Zipes* v. *Trans World Airlines, Inc.*, 455 U.S. 385, 398 (1982)); see 536 U.S., at 121 (defense of laches may be invoked to block an employee's suit "if he unreasonably delays in filing [charges] and as a result harms the defendant"); EEOC Brief 15 ("[I]f Ledbetter unreasonably delayed challenging an earlier decision, and that delay significantly impaired Goodyear's ability to defend itself ... Goodyear can raise a defense of laches....").[7]

In a last-ditch argument, the Court asserts that this dissent would allow a plaintiff to sue on a single decision made 20 years ago "even if the employee had full knowledge of all the circumstances relating to the ... decision at the time it was made." *Ante*, at 20. It suffices to point out that the defenses just noted would make such a suit foolhardy. No sensible judge would tolerate such inexcusable neglect. See *Morgan*, 536 U.S., at 121 ("In such cases, the federal courts have the discretionary power ... to locate a just result in light of the circumstances peculiar to the case." (internal quotation marks omitted)).

Ledbetter, the Court observes, *ante*, at 21, n.9, dropped an alternative remedy she could have pursued: Had she persisted in pressing her claim under the Equal Pay Act of 1963 (EPA), 29 U.S.C. §206(d), she would not have encountered a time bar.[8] See *ante*, at 21("If Ledbetter had pursued her EPA claim, she would not face the Title VII obstacles that she now confronts."); cf. *Corning Glass Works* v. *Brennan*, 417 U. S. 188, 208–210 (1974) . Notably, the EPA provides no relief when the pay discrimination charged is based on race, religion, national origin, age, or disability. Thus, in truncating the Title VII rule this Court announced in *Bazemore*, the Court does not disarm female workers from achieving redress for unequal pay, but it does impede racial and other minorities from gaining similar relief.[9]

Furthermore, the difference between the EPA's prohibition against paying unequal wages and Title VII's ban on discrimination with regard to compensation is not as large as the Court's opinion might suggest. See *ante*, at 21. The key distinction is that Title VII requires a showing of intent. In practical effect, "if the trier of fact is in equipoise about whether the wage differential is motivated by gender discrimination," Title VII compels a verdict for the employer, while the EPA compels a verdict for the plaintiff. 2 C. Sullivan, M. Zimmer, & R. White, Employment Discrimination: Law and Practice §7.08[F][3], p. 532 (3d ed. 2002). In this case, Ledbetter carried the burden of persuading the jury that the pay disparity she suffered was attributable to intentional sex discrimination. See *supra*, at 1–2; *infra*, this page and 18.

III

To show how far the Court has strayed from interpretation of Title VII with fidelity to the Act's core purpose, I return to the evidence Ledbetter presented at trial. Ledbetter proved to the jury the following: She was a member of a protected class; she performed work substantially equal to work of the dominant class (men); she was compensated less for that work; and the disparity was attributable to gender-based discrimination. See *supra*, at 1–2.

Specifically, Ledbetter's evidence demonstrated that her current pay was discriminatorily low due to a long series of decisions reflecting Goodyear's pervasive discrimination against women managers in general and Ledbetter in particular. Ledbetter's former supervisor, for example, admitted to the jury that Ledbetter's pay, during a particular one-year period, fell below Goodyear's minimum threshold for her position. App. 93–97.Although Goodyear claimed the pay disparity was due to poor performance, the supervisor acknowledged that Ledbetter received a "Top Performance Award" in 1996. *Id.*, at 90–93. The jury also heard testimony that another supervisor—who evaluated Ledbetter in 1997 and whose evaluation led to her most recent raise denial—was openly biased against women. *Id.*, at 46, 77–82. And two women who had previously worked as managers at the plant told the jury they had been subject to pervasive discrimination and were paid less than their male counterparts. One was paid less than the men she supervised. *Id.*, at 51–68. Ledbetter herself testified about the discriminatory animus conveyed to her by plant officials. Toward the end of her career, for instance, the plant manager told Ledbetter that the "plant did not need women, that [women] didn't help it, [and] caused problems." *Id.*, at 36.[10] After weighing all the evidence, the jury found for Ledbetter, concluding that the pay disparity was due to intentional discrimination.

Yet, under the Court's decision, the discrimination Ledbetter proved is not redressable under Title VII. Each and every pay decision she did not immediately challenge wiped the slate clean. Consideration may not be given to the cumulative effect of a series of decisions that, together, set her pay well below that of every male area manager. Knowingly carrying past pay discrimination forward must be treated as lawful conduct. Ledbetter may not be compensated for the lower pay she was in fact receiving when she complained to the EEOC. Nor, were she still employed by Goodyear, could she gain, on the proof she presented at trial, injunctive relief requiring, prospectively, her receipt of the same compensation men receive for substantially similar work. The Court's approbation of these consequences is totally at odds with the robust protection against workplace discrimination Congress intended Title VII to secure. See, *e.g.*, *Teamsters* v. *United States*, 431 U.S., at 348 ("The primary purpose of Title VII was to assure equality of employment opportunities and to eliminate … discriminatory practices and devices…." (internal quotation marks omitted)); *Albemarle Paper Co.* v. *Moody*, 422 U.S. 405, 418 (1975) ("It is … the purpose of Title VII to make persons whole for injuries suffered on account of unlawful employment discrimination.").

This is not the first time the Court has ordered a cramped interpretation of Title VII, incompatible with the statute's broad remedial purpose. See *supra*, at 10–12. See also *Wards Cove Packing Co.* v. *Atonio*, 490 U.S. 642 (1989) (superseded in part by the Civil Rights Act of 1991); *Price Waterhouse* v. *Hopkins*, 490 U.S. 228 (1989) (plurality opinion) (same); 1 B. Lindemann & P. Grossman, Employment Discrimination Law 2 (3d ed. 1996) ("A spate of Court decisions in the late 1980s drew congressional fire and resulted in demands for legislative change[,]" culminating in the 1991 Civil Rights Act (footnote omitted)). Once again, the ball is in Congress' court. As in 1991, the Legislature may act to correct this Court's parsimonious reading of Title VII.

$$* * *$$

For the reasons stated, I would hold that Ledbetter's claim is not time barred and would reverse the Eleventh Circuit's judgment.

NOTES

[1] If the complainant has first instituted proceedings with a state or local agency, the filing period is extended to 300 days or 30 days after the denial of relief by the agency. 42 U.S.C. §2000e–5(e)(1). Because the 180-day period applies to Ledbetter's case, that figure will be used throughout. See ante, at 3, 4.

[2] National Railroad Passenger Corporation v. Morgan, 536 U.S. 101, 117 (2002) , the Court emphasizes, required that "an act contributing to the claim occu[r] within the [charge-]filing period." Ante, at 19, and n.7 (emphasis deleted; internal quotation marks omitted). Here, each paycheck within the filing period compounded the discrimination Ledbetter encountered, and thus contributed to the "actionable wrong," i.e., the succession of acts composing the pattern of discriminatory pay, of which she complained.

[3] See also Bierman & Gely, "Love, Sex and Politics? Sure. Salary? No Way": Workplace Social Norms and the Law, 25 Berkeley J. Emp. & Lab. L. 167, 168, 171 (2004) (one-third of private sector employers have adopted specific rules prohibiting employees from discussing their wages with co-workers; only one in ten employers has adopted a pay openness policy).

[4] The Court also relies on Machinists v. NLRB, 362 U.S. 411 (1960) , which like Evans and Ricks, concerned a discrete act: the execution of a collective bargaining agreement containing a union security clause. 362 U.S., at 412, 417. In Machinists, it was undisputed that under the National Labor Relations Act (NLRA), a union and an employer may not agree to a union security clause "if at the time of original execution the union does not represent a majority of the employees in the [bargaining] unit." Id., at 412–414, 417. The complainants, however, failed to file a charge within the NLRA's six-month charge filing period; instead, they filed charges 10 and 12 months after the execution of the agreement, objecting to its subsequent enforcement. See id., at 412, 414. Thus, as in Evans and Ricks, but in contrast to Ledbetter's case, the employment decision at issue was easily identifiable and occurred on a single day.

[5] No Senate Report was submitted with the Civil Rights Act of 1991, which was in all material respects identical to the proposed 1990 Act.

[6] The Court dismisses the EEOC's considerable "experience and informed judgment," Firefighters v. Cleveland, 478 U.S. 501, 518 (1986) (internal quotation marks omitted), as unworthy of any deference in this case, see ante, at 23–24, n.11. But the EEOC's interpretations mirror workplace realities and merit at least respectful attention. In any event, the level of deference due the EEOC here is an academic question, for the agency's conclusion that Ledbetter's claim is not time barred is the best reading of the statute even if the Court "were interpreting [Title VII] from scratch." See Edelman v. Lynchburg College, 535 U.S. 106, 114 (2002) ; see supra, at 4–14.

[7] Further, as the EEOC appropriately recognized in its brief to the Eleventh Circuit, Ledbetter's failure to challenge particular pay raises within the charge-filing period "significantly limit[s] the relief she can seek. By waiting to file a charge, Ledbetter lost her opportunity to seek relief for any discriminatory paychecks she received between 1979 and late 1997." EEOC Brief 14. See also supra, at 12–13.

[8] Under the EPA 29 U.S.C. §206(d), which is subject to the Fair Labor Standards Act's time prescriptions, a claim charging denial of equal pay accrues anew with each paycheck. 1 B. Lindemann & P. Grossman, Employment Discrimination Law 529 (3d ed. 1996); cf. 29 U.S.C. §255(a) (prescribing a two-year statute of limitations for violations generally, but a three-year limitation period for willful violations).

[9] For example, under today's decision, if a black supervisor initially received the same salary as his white colleagues, but annually received smaller raises, there would be no right to sue under Title VII outside the 180-day window following each annual salary change, however strong the cumulative evidence of discrimination might be. The Court would thus force plaintiffs, in many cases, to sue too soon to prevail, while cutting them off as time barred once the pay differential is large enough to enable them to mount a winnable case.

[10] Given this abundant evidence, the Court cannot tenably maintain that Ledbetter's case "turned principally on the misconduct of a single Goodyear supervisor." See ante, at 12–13, n.4.

ALBERTO R. GONZALES, ATTORNEY GENERAL v. LEROY CARHART et al. /// ALBERTO R. GONZALES, ATTORNEY GENERAL v. PLANNED PARENTHOOD FEDERATION OF AMERICA, INC., et al.

NoS. 05-380 & 05-1382, April 18, 2007

ON WRITS OF CERTIORARI TO THE UNITED STATES COURT OF APPEALS FOR THE EIGHTH CIRCUIT /// NINTH CIRCUIT

Justice Ginsburg, with whom Justice Stevens, Justice Souter, and Justice Breyer join, dissenting.

In *Planned Parenthood of Southeastern Pa.* v. *Casey*, 505 U.S. 833, 844 (1992) , the Court declared that "[l]iberty finds no refuge in a jurisprudence of doubt." There was, the Court said, an "imperative" need to dispel doubt as to "the meaning and reach" of the Court's 7-to-2 judgment, rendered nearly two decades earlier in *Roe* v. *Wade*, 410 U.S. 113 (1973) . 505 U.S., at 845. Responsive to that need, the Court endeavored to provide secure guidance to "[s]tate and federal courts as well as legislatures throughout the Union," by defining "the rights of the woman and the legitimate authority of the State respecting the termination of pregnancies by abortion procedures." *Ibid.*

Taking care to speak plainly, the *Casey* Court restated and reaffirmed *Roe*'s essential holding. 505 U.S., at 845–846. First, the Court addressed the type of abortion regulation permissible prior to fetal viability. It recognized "the right of the woman to choose to have an abortion before viability and to obtain it without undue interference from the State." *Id.*, at 846. Second, the Court acknowledged "the State's power to restrict abortions *after fetal viability*, if the law contains exceptions for pregnancies which endanger the woman's life *or health.*" *Ibid.* (emphasis added). Third, the Court confirmed that "the State has legitimate interests from the outset of the pregnancy in protecting *the health of the woman* and the life of the fetus that may become a child." *Ibid.* (emphasis added).

In reaffirming *Roe*,the *Casey* Court described the centrality of "the decision whether to bear . . . a child," *Eisenstadt* v. *Baird*, 405 U.S. 438, 453 (1972) , to a woman's "dignity and autonomy," her "personhood" and "destiny," her "conception of . . . her place in society." 505 U.S., at 851–852. Of signal importance here, the *Casey* Court stated with unmistakable clarity that state regulation of access to abortion procedures, even after viability, must protect "the health of the woman." *Id.*, at 846.

Seven years ago, in *Stenberg* v. *Carhart*, 530 U.S. 914 (2000) , the Court invalidated a Nebraska statute criminalizing the performance of a medical procedure that, in the political arena, has been dubbed "partial-birth abortion."[1] With fidelity to the *Roe-Casey* line of precedent, the Court held the Nebraska statute unconstitutional in part because it lacked the requisite protection for the preservation of a woman's health. *Stenberg*, 530 U.S., at 930; cf. *Ayotte* v. *Planned Parenthood of Northern New Eng.*, 546 U.S. 320, 327 (2006) .

Today's decision is alarming. It refuses to take *Casey* and *Stenberg* seriously. It tolerates, indeed applauds, federal intervention to ban nationwide a procedure found necessary and proper in certain cases by the American College of Obstetricians and Gynecologists (ACOG). It blurs the line, firmly drawn in *Casey*,between previability and postviability abortions. And, for the first time since *Roe*, the Court blesses a prohibition with no exception safeguarding a woman's health.

I dissent from the Court's disposition. Retreating from prior rulings that abortion restrictions cannot be imposed absent an exception safeguarding a woman's health, the Court upholds an Act that surely would not survive under the close scrutiny that previously attended state-decreed limitations on a woman's reproductive choices.

I

A

As *Casey* comprehended, at stake in cases challenging abortion restrictions is a woman's "control over her [own] destiny." 505 U.S., at 869 (plurality opinion). See also *id.*, at 852 (majority opinion).[2] "There was a time, not so long ago," when women were "regarded as the center of home and family life, with attendant special responsibilities that precluded full and independent legal status under the Constitution." *Id.*, at 896–897 (quoting *Hoyt* v. *Florida*, 368 U.S. 57, 62 (1961)). Those views, this Court made clear in *Casey*, "are no longer consistent with our understanding of the family, the individual, or the Constitution." 505 U.S., at 897. Women, it is now acknowledged, have the talent, capacity, and right "to participate equally in the economic and social life of the Nation." *Id.*, at 856. Their ability to realize their full potential, the

Court recognized, is intimately connected to "their ability to control their reproductive lives." *Ibid.* Thus, legal challenges to undue restrictions on abortion procedures do not seek to vindicate some generalized notion of privacy; rather, they center on a woman's autonomy to determine her life's course, and thus to enjoy equal citizenship stature. See, *e.g.*, Siegel, Reasoning from the Body: A Historical Perspective on Abortion Regulation and Questions ofEqual Protection, 44 Stan. L.Rev. 261 (1992); Law, Rethinking Sex and the Constitution,132 U.Pa. L.Rev. 955, 1002–1028 (1984).

In keeping with this comprehension of the right to reproductive choice, the Court has consistently required that laws regulating abortion, at any stage of pregnancy and in all cases, safeguard a woman's health. See, *e.g.*, Ayotte, 546 U.S., at 327–328 ("[O]ur precedents hold … that a State may not restrict access to abortions that are necessary, in appropriate medical judgment, for preservation of the life or health of the [woman]." (quoting *Casey*, 505 U.S., at 879 (plurality opinion))); *Stenberg*, 530 U.S., at 930 ("Since the law requires a health exception in order to validate even a postviability abortion regulation, it at a minimum requires the same in respect to previability regulation."). See also *Thornburgh* v. *American College of Obstetricians and Gynecologists*, 476 U.S. 747, 768–769 (1986) (invalidating a *post*-viability abortion regulation for "fail[ure] to require that [a pregnant woman's] health be the physician's paramount consideration").

We have thus ruled that a State must avoid subjecting women to health risks not only where the pregnancy itself creates danger, but also where state regulation forces women to resort to less safe methods of abortion. See *Planned Parenthood of Central Mo.* v. *Danforth*, 428 U.S. 52, 79 (1976) (holding unconstitutional a ban on a method of abortion that "force[d] a woman … to terminate her pregnancy by methods more dangerous to her health"). See also *Stenberg*, 530 U.S., at 931 ("[Our cases] make clear that a risk to . . . women's health is the same whether it happens to arise from regulating a particular method of abortion, or from barring abortion entirely."). Indeed, we have applied the rule that abortion regulation must safeguard a woman's health to the particular procedure at issue here—intact dilation and evacuation (D&E).[3]

In *Stenberg*, we expressly held that a statute banning intact D&E was unconstitutional in part because it lacked a health exception. 530 U.S., at 930, 937. We noted that there existed a "division of medical opinion" about the relative safety of intact D&E, *id.*, at 937, but we made clear that as long as "substantial medical authority supports the proposition that banning a particular abortion procedure could endanger women's health," a health exception is required, *id.*, at 938. We explained:

> "The word 'necessary' in *Casey*'s phrase 'necessary, in appropriate medical judgment, for the preservation of the life or health of the [pregnant woman],' cannot refer to an absolute necessity or to absolute proof. Medical treatments and procedures are often considered appropriate (or inappropriate) in light of estimated comparative health risks (and health benefits) in particular cases. Neither can that phrase require unanimity of medical opinion. Doctors often differ in their estimation of comparative health risks and appropriate treatment. And *Casey*'s words 'appropriate medical judgment' must embody the judicial need to tolerate responsible differences of medical opinion …." *Id.*, at 937 (citation omitted).

Thus, we reasoned, division in medical opinion "at most means uncertainty, a factor that signals the presence of risk, not its absence." *Ibid.* "[A] statute that altogether forbids [intact D&E] . . . . consequently must contain a health exception." *Id.*, at 938. See also *id.*, at 948 (O'Connor, J., concurring) ("Th[e] lack of a health exception necessarily renders the statute unconstitutional.").

B

In 2003, a few years after our ruling in *Stenberg*, Congress passed the Partial-Birth Abortion Ban Act—without an exception for women's health. See 18 U.S.C. §1531(a) (2000 ed., Supp. IV).[4] The congressional findings on which the Partial-Birth Abortion Ban Act rests do not withstand inspection, as the lower courts have determined and this Court is obliged to concede. *Ante*, at 35–36. See *National Abortion Federation* v. *Ashcroft*, 330 F.Supp. 2d 436, 482 (SDNY 2004) ("Congress did not … carefully consider the evidence before arriving at its findings."), aff'd *subnom. National Abortion Federation* v. *Gonzales*, 437 F.3d 278 (CA2 2006). See also *Planned Parenthood Federation of Am.* v. *Ashcroft*, 320 F.Supp. 2d 957, 1019 (ND Cal. 2004) ("[N]one of the six physicians who testified before Congress had ever performed an intact D&E. Several did not provide abortion services at all; and one was not even an obgyn…. [T]he oral testimony before Congress was not only unbalanced, but intentionally polemic."), aff'd, 435 F.3d 1163 (CA9 2006); *Carhart* v. *Ashcroft*, 331 F.Supp. 2d 805, 1011 (Neb. 2004) ("Congress arbitrarily relied upon the opinions of doctors who claimed to have no (or very little) recent and relevant experience with surgical abortions, and disregarded the views of doctors who had significant and relevant experience with those procedures."), aff'd,413 F.3d 791 (CA8 2005).

Many of the Act's recitations are incorrect. See *ante,* at 35–36. For example, Congress determined that no medical schools provide instruction on intact D&E. §2(14)(B), 117 Stat. 1204, notes following 18 U.S.C. §1531 (2000 ed., Supp. IV), p.769, ¶(14)(B) (Congressional Findings). But in fact, numerous leading medical schools teach the procedure. See *Planned Parenthood,* 320 F.Supp. 2d, at 1029; *National Abortion Federation,* 330 F.Supp. 2d, at 479. See also Brief for ACOG as *Amicus Curiae* 18 ("Among the schools that now teach the intact variant are Columbia, Cornell, Yale, New York University, Northwestern, University of Pittsburgh, University of Pennsylvania, University of Rochester, and University of Chicago.").

More important, Congress claimed there was a medical consensus that the banned procedure is never necessary. Congressional Findings (1), in notes following 18 U.S.C. §1531 (2000 ed., Supp. IV), p.767. But the evidence "very clearly demonstrate[d] the opposite." *Planned Parenthood,* 320 F.Supp. 2d, at 1025. See also *Carhart,* 331 F.Supp. 2d, at 1008–1009 ("[T]here was no evident consensus in the record that Congress compiled. There was, however, a substantial body of medical opinion presented to Congress in opposition. If anything ... the congressional record establishes that there was a 'consensus' in favor of the banned procedure."); *National Abortion Federation,*330 F.Supp. 2d, at 488 ("The congressional record itself undermines [Congress'] finding" that there is a medical consensus that intact D&E "is never medically necessary and should be prohibited." (internal quotation marks omitted)).

Similarly, Congress found that "[t]here is no credible medical evidence that partial-birth abortions are safe or are safer than other abortion procedures." Congressional Findings (14)(B), in notes following 18 U.S.C. §1531 (2000 ed., Supp. IV), p.769. But the congressional record includes letters from numerous individual physicians stating that pregnant women's health would be jeopardized under the Act, as well as statements from nine professional associations, including ACOG, the American Public Health Association, and the California Medical Association, attesting that intact D&E carries meaningful safety advantages over other methods. See *National Abortion Federation,* 330 F.Supp. 2d, at 490. See also *Planned Parenthood,* 320 F.Supp. 2d, at 1021 ("Congress in its findings . . . chose to disregard the statements by ACOG and other medical organizations."). No comparable medical groups supported the ban. In fact, "all of the government's own witnesses disagreed with many of the specific congressional findings." *Id.,* at 1024.

C

In contrast to Congress, the District Courts made findings after full trials at which all parties had the opportunity to present their best evidence. The courts had the benefit of "much more extensive medical and scientific evidence . . . concerning the safety and necessity of intact D&Es." *Planned Parenthood,* 320 F.Supp. 2d, at 1014; cf. *National Abortion Federation,* 330 F.Supp. 2d, at 482 (District Court "heard more evidence during its trial than Congress heard over the span of eight years.").

During the District Court trials, "numerous" "extraordinarily accomplished" and "very experienced" medical experts explained that, in certain circumstances and for certain women,intact D&E is safer than alternative procedures and necessary to protect women's health. *Carhart,* 331 F.Supp. 2d, at 1024–1027; see *Planned Parenthood,* 320 F.Supp. 2d, at 1001 ("[A]ll of the doctors who actually perform intact D&Es concluded that in their opinion and clinical judgment, intact D&Es remain the safest option for certain individual women under certain individual health circumstances, and are significantly safer for these women than other abortion techniques, and are thus medically necessary."); cf. *ante,* at 31 ("Respondents presented evidence that intact D&E may be the safest method of abortion, for reasons similar to those adduced in *Stenberg.*").

According to the expert testimony plaintiffs introduced, the safety advantages of intact D&E are marked for women with certain medical conditions, for example, uterine scarring, bleeding disorders, heart disease, or compromised immune systems. See *Carhart,* 331 F.Supp. 2d, at 924–929, 1026–1027; *National Abortion Federation,* 330 F.Supp. 2d, at 472–473; *Planned Parenthood,* 320 F.Supp. 2d, at 992–994, 1001.Further, plaintiffs' experts testified that intact D&E is significantly safer for women with certain pregnancy-related conditions, such as placenta previa and accreta, and for women carrying fetuses with certain abnormalities, such as severe hydrocephalus. See *Carhart,* 331 F.Supp. 2d, at 924, 1026–1027; *National Abortion Federation,* 330 F.Supp. 2d, at 473–474; *Planned Parenthood,* 320 F.Supp. 2d, at 992–994, 1001. See also *Stenberg,* 530 U.S., at 929;Brief for ACOG as *Amicus Curiae* 2, 13–16.

Intact D&E, plaintiffs' experts explained, provides safety benefits over D&E by dismemberment for several reasons: *First,*intact D&E minimizes the number of times a physician must insert instruments through the cervix and into the uterus, and thereby reduces the risk of trauma to, and perforation of, the cervix and uterus—the most serious complication associated with nonintact D&E. See *Carhart,* 331 F.Supp. 2d, at 923–928, 1025; *National Abortion Federation,* 330 F.Supp. 2d, at 471; *Planned Parenthood,* 320 F.Supp. 2d, at 982, 1001. *Second,*removing the fetus intact, instead of dismembering it *in utero,* decreases the likelihood that fetal tissue will be retained in the uterus, a condition that can cause infection, hemorrhage, and infertility. See *Carhart,* 331 F.Supp. 2d, at 923–928, 1025–1026; *National Abortion Federation,* 330 F.Supp. 2d, at 472; *Planned Parenthood,* 320 F.Supp. 2d, at 1001. *Third,* intact D&E diminishes the chances of exposing the patient's tissues to sharp bony fragments sometimes resulting from dismemberment of the fetus. See *Carhart,* 331 F.Supp. 2d, at 923–928, 1026; *National Abortion Federation,* 330 F.Supp. 2d, at 471; *Planned Parenthood,* 320 F.Supp. 2d, at 1001. *Fourth,* intact D&E takes less operating time than D&E by dismemberment, and thus may reduce bleeding, the risk of infection, and complications relating to anesthesia. See *Carhart,* 331 F.Supp. 2d, at 923–928, 1026; *National Abortion Federation,* 330 F.Supp. 2d, at 472; *Planned Parenthood,* 320 F.Supp. 2d, at 1001. See also *Stenberg,* 530 U.S., at 928–929, 932; Brief for ACOG as *Amicus Curiae* 2, 11–13.

Based on thoroughgoing review of the trial evidence and the congressional record, each of the District Courts to consider the issue rejected Congress' findings as unreasonable and not supported by the evidence. See *Carhart*, 331 F.Supp. 2d, at 1008–1027; *National Abortion Federation*, 330 F.Supp. 2d, at 482, 488–491; *Planned Parenthood*, 320 F.Supp. 2d, at 1032. The trial courts concluded, in contrast to Congress' findings, that "significant medical authority supports the proposition that in some circumstances, [intact D&E] is the safest procedure." *Id.*, at 1033 (quoting *Stenberg*, 530 U.S., at 932);accord *Carhart*, 331 F.Supp. 2d, at 1008–1009, 1017–1018; *National Abortion Federation*, 330 F.Supp. 2d, at 480–482;[5] cf. *Stenberg*, 530 U.S., at 932 ("[T]he record shows that significant medical authority supports the proposition that in some circumstances, [intact D&E] would be the safest procedure.").

The District Courts' findings merit this Court's respect. See, *e.g.*, Fed. Rule Civ. Proc. 52(a); *Salve Regina College* v. *Russell*, 499 U.S. 225, 233 (1991) . Today's opinion supplies no reason to reject those findings. Nevertheless, despite the District Courts' appraisal of the weight of the evidence, and in undisguised conflict with *Stenberg*, the Court asserts that the Partial-Birth Abortion Ban Act can survive "when ... medical uncertainty persists." *Ante*, at 33. This assertion is bewildering. Not only does it defy the Court's longstanding precedent affirming the necessity of a health exception, with no carve-out for circumstances of medical uncertainty, see *supra*, at 4–5; it gives short shrift to the records before us, carefully canvassed by the District Courts. Those records indicate that "the majority of highly-qualified experts on the subject believe intact D&E to be the safest, most appropriate procedure under certain circumstances." *Planned Parenthood*, 320 F.Supp. 2d, at 1034. See *supra*, at 9–10.

The Court acknowledges some of this evidence, *ante*, at 31,but insists that, because some witnesses disagreed with the ACOG and other experts' assessment of risk, the Act can stand. *Ante*, at 32–33, 37. In this insistence, the Court brushes under the rug the District Courts' well-supported findings that the physicians who testified that intact D&E is never necessary to preserve the health of a woman had slim authority for their opinions. They had no training for, or personal experience with, the intact D&E procedure, and many performed abortions only on rare occasions. See *Planned Parenthood*, 320 F.Supp. 2d, at 980; *Carhart*, 331 F.Supp. 2d, at 1025; cf. *National Abortion Federation*, 330 F.Supp. 2d, at 462–464. Even indulging the assumption that the Government witnesses were equally qualified to evaluate the relative risks of abortion procedures, their testimony could not erase the "significant medical authority support[ing] the proposition that in some circumstances, [intact D&E] would be the safest procedure." *Stenberg*, 530 U.S., at 932.[6]

II

A

The Court offers flimsy and transparent justifications for upholding a nationwide ban on intact D&E *sans* any exception to safeguard a women's health. Today's ruling, the Court declares, advances "a premise central to [*Casey*'s] conclusion"—*i.e.*,the Government's "legitimate and substantial interest in preserving and promoting fetal life." *Ante*, at 14. See also *ante*, at 15 ("[W]e must determine whether the Act furthers the legitimate interest of the Government in protecting the life of the fetus that may become a child."). But the Act scarcely furthers that interest: The law saves not a single fetus from destruction, for it targets only a *method* of performing abortion. See *Stenberg*, 530 U.S., at 930. And surely the statute was not designed to protect the lives or health of pregnant women. *Id.*, at 951 (Ginsburg, J., concurring);cf. *Casey*, 505 U.S., at 846 (recognizing along with the State's legitimate interest in the life of the fetus, its "legitimate interes[t] ... in protecting the *health of the woman*" (emphasis added)). In short, the Court upholds a law that, while doing nothing to "preserv[e] ... fetal life," *ante*, at 14, bars a woman from choosing intact D&E although her doctor "reasonably believes [that procedure] will best protect [her]." *Stenberg*, 530 U.S., at 946 (Stevens, J., concurring).

As another reason for upholding the ban, the Court emphasizes that the Act does not proscribe the nonintact D&E procedure. See *ante*, at 34. But why not, one might ask. Nonintact D&E could equally be characterized as "brutal," *ante*, at 26, involving as it does "tear[ing] [a fetus] apart" and "ripp[ing] off" its limbs, *ante*, at 4, 6. "[T]he notion that either of these two equally gruesome procedures ... is more akin to infanticide than the other, or that the State furthers any legitimate interest by banning one but not the other, is simply irrational." *Stenberg*, 530 U.S., at 946–947 (Stevens, J., concurring).

Delivery of an intact, albeit nonviable, fetus warrants special condemnation, the Court maintains, because a fetus that is not dismembered resembles an infant. *Ante*, at28. But so, too, does a fetus delivered intact after it is terminated by injection a day or two before the surgical evacuation, *ante*, at 5, 34–35, or a fetus delivered through medical induction or cesarean, *ante*, at 9. Yet, the availability of those procedures—along with D&E by dismemberment—the Court says, saves the ban on intact D&E from a declaration of unconstitutionality. *Ante*, at 34–35. Never mind that the procedures deemed acceptable might put a woman's health at greater risk. See *supra*, at 13, and n.6; cf. *ante*, at 5, 31–32.

Ultimately, the Court admits that "moral concerns" are at work, concerns that could yield prohibitions on any abortion. See *ante*, at28 ("Congress could ... conclude that the type of abortion proscribed by the Act requires specific regulation because it implicates additional ethical and moral concerns that justify a special prohibition."). Notably, the concerns expressed are untethered to any ground genuinely serving the Government's interest in preserving life. By allowing such concerns to carry the day and case, overriding fundamental rights, the Court dishonors our precedent. See, *e.g.*, *Casey*, 505 U.S., at 850 ("Some of us as individuals find abortion offensive to our most basic principles of morality, but that cannot control our decision. Our obligation is to define the liberty of all, not to mandate our own moral code."); *Lawrence* v. *Texas*, 539 U.S. 558, 571 (2003) (Though "[f]or many persons [objections to homosexual conduct] are not trivial concerns but profound and deep convictions accepted as ethical and moral principles," the power of the State may not be used "to enforce these views on the whole society through operation of the criminal law." (citing *Casey*, 505 U.S., at 850)).

Revealing in this regard, the Court invokes an antiabortion shibboleth for which it concededly has no reliable evidence: Women who have abortions come to regret their choices, and consequently suffer from "[s]evere depression and loss of esteem." *Ante*, at 29.[7] Because of women's fragile emotional state and because of the "bond of love the mother has for her child," the Court worries, doctors may withhold information about the nature of the intact D&E procedure. *Ante*, at 28–29.[8] The solution the Court approves, then, is *not* to require doctors to inform women, accurately and adequately, of the different procedures and their attendant risks. Cf. *Casey*, 505 U.S., at 873 (plurality opinion) ("States are free to enact laws to provide a reasonable framework for a woman to make a decision that has such profound and lasting meaning."). Instead, the Court deprives women of the right to make an autonomous choice, even at the expense of their safety.[9]

This way of thinking reflects ancient notions about women's place in the family and under the Constitution—ideas that have long since been discredited. Compare, *e.g., Muller* v. *Oregon*, 208 U.S. 412, 422–423 (1908) ("protective" legislation imposing hours-of-work limitations on women only held permissible in view of women's "physical structure and a proper discharge of her maternal funct[ion]"); *Bradwell* v. *State*, 16Wall. 130, 141 (1873) (Bradley, J., concurring) ("Man is, or should be, woman's protector and defender. The natural and proper timidity and delicacy which belongs to the female sex evidently unfits it for many of the occupations of civil life. ... The paramount destiny and mission of woman are to fulfil[l] the noble and benign offices of wife and mother."), with *United States* v. *Virginia*, 518 U.S. 515 , n.12 (1996) (State may not rely on "overbroad generalizations" about the "talents, capacities, or preferences" of women; "[s]uch judgments have ... impeded ... women's progress toward full citizenship stature throughout our Nation's history"); *Califano* v. *Goldfarb*, 430 U.S. 199, 207 (1977) (gender-based Social Security classification rejected because it rested on "archaic and overbroad generalizations" "such as assumptions as to [women's] dependency" (internal quotation marks omitted)).

Though today's majority may regard women's feelings on the matter as "self-evident," *ante*, at 29, this Court has repeatedly confirmed that "[t]he destiny of the woman must be shaped ... on her own conception of her spiritual imperatives and her place in society." *Casey*, 505 U.S., at 852. See also *id.*, at 877 (plurality opinion) ("[M]eans chosen by the State to further the interest in potential life must be calculated to inform the woman's free choice, not hinder it."); *supra*, at 3–4.

B

In cases on a "woman's liberty to determine whether to [continue] her pregnancy," this Court has identified viability as a critical consideration. See *Casey*, 505 U.S., at 869–870 (plurality opinion). "[T]here is no line [more workable] than viability," the Court explained in *Casey*, for viability is "the time at which there is a realistic possibility of maintaining and nourishing a life outside the womb, so that the independent existence of the second life can in reason and all fairness be the object of state protection that now overrides the rights of the woman. ... In some broad sense it might be said that a woman who fails to act before viability has consented to the State's intervention on behalf of the developing child." *Id.*, at 870.

Today, the Court blurs that line, maintaining that "[t]he Act [legitimately] appl[ies] both previability and postviability because ... a fetus is a living organism while within the womb, whether or not it is viable outside the womb." *Ante*, at 17. Instead of drawing the line at viability, the Court refers to Congress' purpose to differentiate "abortion and infanticide" based not on whether a fetus can survive outside the womb, but on where a fetus is anatomically located when a particular medical procedure is performed. See *ante*, at 28 (quoting Congressional Findings (14)(G), in notes following 18 U.S.C. §1531 (2000 ed., Supp. IV), p. 769).

One wonders how long a line that saves no fetus from destruction will hold in face of the Court's "moral concerns." See *supra*, at 15; cf. *ante*, at16 (noting that "[i]n this litigation" the Attorney General "does not dispute that the Act would impose an undue burden if it covered standard D&E"). The Court's hostility to the right *Roe* and *Casey* secured is not concealed. Throughout, the opinion refers to obstetrician-gynecologists and surgeons who perform abortions not by the titles of their medical specialties, but by the pejorative label "abortion doctor." *Ante*, at 14, 24, 25, 31, 33. A fetus is described as an "unborn child," and as a "baby," *ante*, at 3, 8; second-trimester, previability abortions are referred to as "late-term," *ante*, at 26; and the reasoned medical judgments of highly trained doctors are dismissed as "preferences"motivated by "mere convenience," *ante*, at 3, 37. Instead of the heightened scrutiny we have previously applied, the Court determines that a "rational" ground is enough to uphold the Act, *ante*, at28, 37. And, most troubling, *Casey*'s principles, confirming the continuing vitality of "the essential holding of *Roe*," are merely "assume[d]" for the moment, *ante*, at15, 31, rather than "retained" or "reaffirmed," *Casey*, 505 U.S., at 846.

III

A

The Court further confuses our jurisprudence when it declares that "facial attacks" are not permissible in "these circumstances," *i.e.*,where medical uncertainty exists. *Ante*, at 37; see *ibid*. ("In an as-applied challenge the nature of the medical risk can be better quantified and balanced than in a facial attack."). This holding is perplexing given that, in materially identical circumstances we held that a statute lacking a health exception was unconstitutional on its face. *Stenberg*, 530 U.S., at 930; see *id.*, at 937 (in facial challenge, law held unconstitutional because "significant body of medical opinion believes [the] procedure may bring with it greater safety for *some patients*" (emphasis added)). See also *Sabri* v. *United States*, 541 U.S. 600, 609–610 (2004) (identifying abortion as one setting in which we have recognized the validity of facial challenges); Fallon, Making Sense of Overbreadth, 100 Yale L.J. 853, 859, n.29 (1991) ("[V]irtually all of the abortion cases reaching the Supreme Court since *Roe* v. *Wade*, 410 U.S. 113 (1973) , have involved facial attacks on state statutes, and the Court, whether accepting or rejecting the challenges on the merits, has typically accepted this framing of the question presented."). Accord Fallon, As-Applied and Facial Challenges and Third-Party Standing, 113 Harv. L.Rev. 1321, 1356 (2000);Dorf, Facial Challenges to State and Federal Statutes, 46 Stan. L.Rev. 235, 271–276 (1994).

Without attempting to distinguish *Stenberg* and earlier decisions, the majority asserts that the Act survives review because respondents have not shown that the ban on intact D&E would be unconstitutional "in a large fraction of relevant cases." *Ante*, at 38 (citing *Casey*, 505 U.S., at 895). But *Casey* makes clear that, in determining whether any restriction poses an undue burden on a "large fraction" of women, the relevant class is *not* "all women," nor "all pregnant women," nor even all women "seeking abortions." 505 U.S., at 895. Rather, a provision restricting access to abortion, "must be judged by reference to those [women] for whom it is an actual rather than an irrelevant restriction," *ibid.* Thus the absence of a health exception burdens *all* women for whom it is relevant—women who, in the judgment of their doctors, require an intact D&E because other procedures would place their health at risk.[10] Cf. *Stenberg*,530 U.S., at 934 (accepting the "relative rarity" of medically indicated intact D&Es as true but not "highly relevant"—for "the health exception question is whether protecting women's health requires an exception for those infrequent occasions"); *Ayotte*, 546 U.S., at 328 (facial challenge entertained where "[i]n some very small percentage of cases … women … need immediate abortions to avert serious, and often irreversible damage to their health"). It makes no sense to conclude that this facial challenge fails because respondents have not shown that a health exception is necessary for a large fraction of second-trimester abortions, including those for which a health exception is unnecessary: The very purpose of a health *exception* is to protect women in *exceptional* cases.

B

If there is anything at all redemptive to be said of today's opinion, it is that the Court is not willing to foreclose entirely a constitutional challenge to the Act. "The Act is open," the Court states, "to a proper as-applied challenge in a discrete case." *Ante*, at 38; see *ante*, at 37 ("The Government has acknowledged that preenforcement, as-applied challenges to the Act can be maintained."). But the Court offers no clue on what a "proper" lawsuit might look like. See *ante*, at37–38. Nor does the Court explain why the injunctions ordered by the District Courts should not remain in place, trimmed only to exclude instances in which another procedure would safeguard a woman's health at least equally well. Surely the Court cannot mean that no suit may be brought until a woman's health is immediately jeopardized by the ban on intact D&E. A woman "suffer[ing] from medical complications," *ante*, at 38, needs access to the medical procedure at once and cannot wait for the judicial process to unfold. See *Ayotte*, 546 U.S., at 328.

The Court appears, then, to contemplate another lawsuit by the initiators of the instant actions. In such a second round, the Court suggests, the challengers could succeed upon demonstrating that "in discrete and well-defined instances a particular condition has or is likely to occur in which the procedure prohibited by the Act must be used." *Ante*, at 37. One may anticipate that such a preenforcement challenge will be mounted swiftly, to ward off serious, sometimes irremediable harm, to women whose health would be endangered by the intact D&E prohibition.

The Court envisions that in an as-applied challenge, "the nature of the medical risk can be better quantified and balanced." *Ibid.* But it should not escape notice that the record already includes hundreds and hundreds of pages of testimony identifying "discrete and well-defined instances" in which recourse to an intact D&E would better protect the health of women with particular conditions. See *supra*, at 10–11. Record evidence also documents that medical exigencies, unpredictable in advance, may indicate to a well-trained doctor that intact D&E is the safest procedure. See *ibid.* In light of this evidence, our unanimous decision just one year ago in *Ayotte* counsels against reversal. See 546 U.S., at 331 (remanding for reconsideration of the remedy for the absence of a health exception, suggesting that an injunction prohibiting unconstitutional applications might suffice).

The Court's allowance only of an "as-applied challenge in a discrete case," *ante*, at 38—jeopardizes women's health and places doctors in an untenable position. Even if courts were able to carve-out exceptions through piecemeal litigation for "discrete and well-defined instances," *ante*, at 37, women whose circumstances have not been anticipated by prior litigation could well be left unprotected. In treating those women, physicians would risk criminal prosecution, conviction, and imprisonment if they exercise their best judgment as to the safest medical procedure for their patients. The Court is thus gravely mistaken to conclude that narrow as-applied challenges are "the proper manner to protect the health of the woman." Cf. *ibid.*

IV

As the Court wrote in *Casey*, "overruling *Roe*'s central holding would not only reach an unjustifiable result under principles of *stare decisis*, but would seriously weaken the Court's capacity to exercise the judicial power and to function as the Supreme Court of a Nation dedicated to the rule of law." 505 U.S., at 865. "[T]he very concept of the rule of law underlying our own Constitution requires such continuity over time that a respect for precedent is, by definition, indispensable." *Id.*, at 854. See also *id.*, at 867 ("[T]o overrule under fire in the absence of the most compelling reason to reexamine a watershed decision would subvert the Court's legitimacy beyond any serious question.").

Though today's opinion does not go so far as to discard *Roe* or *Casey*, the Court, differently composed than it was when we last considered a restrictive abortion regulation, is hardly faithful to our earlier invocations of "the rule of law" and the "principles of *stare decisis.*" Congress imposed a ban despite our clear prior holdings that the State cannot proscribe an abortion procedure when its use is necessary to protect a woman's health. See *supra*, at 7, n.4. Although Congress' findings could not withstand the crucible of trial, the Court defers to the legislative override of our Constitution-based rulings. See *supra*, at 7–9. A decision so at odds with our jurisprudence should not have staying power.

In sum, the notion that the Partial-Birth Abortion Ban Act furthers any legitimate governmental interest is, quite simply, irrational. The Court's defense of the statute provides no saving explanation. In candor, the Act, and the Court's defense of it, cannot be understood as anything other than an effort to chip away at a right declared again and again by this Court —and with increasing comprehension of its centrality to women's lives. See *supra*, at 3, n.2; *supra*, at 7, n.4. When "a statute burdens constitutional rights and all that can be said on its behalf is that it is the vehicle that legislators have chosen for expressing their hostility to those rights, the burden is undue." *Stenberg*, 530 U.S., at 952 (Ginsburg, J., concurring) (quoting *Hope Clinic* v. *Ryan*, 195 F.3d 857, 881 (CA7 1999) (Posner, C.J., dissenting)).

* * *

For the reasons stated, I dissent from the Court's disposition and would affirm the judgments before us for review.

NOTES

[1] The term "partial-birth abortion" is neither recognized in the medical literature nor used by physicians who perform second-trimester abortions. See Planned Parenthood Federation of Am. v. Ashcroft, 320 F.Supp. 2d 957, 964 (ND Cal. 2004), aff'd, 435 F.3d 1163 (CA9 2006). The medical community refers to the procedure as either dilation & extraction (D&X) or intact dilation and evacuation (intact D&E). See, e.g., ante, at 5; Stenberg v. Carhart, 530 U.S. 914, 927 (2000).

[2] Planned Parenthood of Southeastern Pa. v. Casey, 505 U.S. 833, 851–852 (1992), described more precisely than did Roe v. Wade, 410 U.S. 113 (1973), the impact of abortion restrictions on women's liberty. Roe's focus was in considerable measure on "vindicat[ing] the right of the physician to administer medical treatment according to his professional judgment." Id., at 165.

[3] Dilation and evacuation (D&E) is the most frequently used abortion procedure during the second trimester of pregnancy; intact D&E is a variant of the D&E procedure. See ante, at 4, 6; Stenberg, 530 U.S., at 924, 927; Planned Parenthood, 320 F.Supp. 2d, at 966. Second-trimester abortions (i.e., midpregnancy, previability abortions) are, however, relatively uncommon. Between 85 and 90 percent of all abortions performed in the United States take place during the first three months of pregnancy. See ante, at 3. See also Stenberg, 530 U.S., at 923–927; National Abortion Federation v. Ashcroft, 330 F.Supp. 2d 436, 464 (SDNY 2004), aff'd subnom. National Abortion Federation v. Gonzales, 437 F.3d 278 (CA2 2006); Planned Parenthood, 320 F.Supp. 2d, at 960, and n.4.

Adolescents and indigent women, research suggests, are more likely than other women to have difficulty obtaining an abortion during the first trimester of pregnancy. Minors may be unaware they are pregnant until relatively late in pregnancy, while poor women's financial constraints are an obstacle to timely receipt of services. See Finer, Frohwirth, Dauphinee, Singh, & Moore, Timing of Steps and Reasons for Delays in Obtaining Abortions in the United States, 74 Contraception 334, 341–343 (2006). See also Drey etal., Risk Factors Associated with Presenting for Abortion in the Second Trimester, 107 Obstetrics & Gynecology 128, 133 (Jan. 2006) (concluding that women who have second-trimester abortions typically discover relatively late that they are pregnant). Severe fetal anomalies and health problems confronting the pregnant woman are also causes of second-trimester abortions; many such conditions cannot be diagnosed or do not develop until the second trimester. See, e.g., Finer, supra, at 344; F. Cunningham etal., Williams Obstetrics 242, 290, 328–329, (22d ed. 2005); cf. Schechtman, Gray, Baty, & Rothman, Decision-Making for Termination of Pregnancies with Fetal Anomalies: Analysis of 53,000 Pregnancies, 99 Obstetrics & Gynecology 216, 220–221 (Feb. 2002) (nearly all women carrying fetuses with the most serious central nervous system anomalies chose to abort their pregnancies).

[4] The Act's sponsors left no doubt that their intention was to nullify our ruling in Stenberg, 530 U.S. 914 . See, e.g., 149Cong. Rec. 5731 (2003) (statement of Sen. Santorum) ("Why are we here? We are here because the Supreme Court defended the indefensible…. We have responded to the Supreme Court."). See also 148Cong. Rec. 14273 (2002) (statement of Rep. Linder) (rejecting proposition that Congress has "no right to legislate a ban on this horrible practice because the Supreme Court says [it] cannot").

[5] Even the District Court for the Southern District of New York, which was more skeptical of the health benefits of intact D&E, see ante, at 32, recognized: "[T]he Government's own experts disagreed with almost all of Congress's factual findings"rdquo;; a "significant body of medical opinion" holds that intact D&E has safety advantages over nonintact D&E; "[p]rofessional medical associations have also expressed their view that [intact D&E] may be the safest procedure for some women"; and "[t]he evidence indicates that the same disagreement among experts found by the Supreme Court in Stenberg existed throughout the time that Congress was considering the legislation, despite Congress's findings to the contrary." National Abortion Federation, 330 F.Supp. 2d, at 480–482.

[6] The majority contends that "[i]f the intact D&E procedure is truly necessary in some circumstances, it appears likely an injection that kills the fetus is an alternative under the Act that allows the doctor to perform the procedure." Ante, at 34–35. But a "significant body of medical opinion believes that inducing fetal death by injection is almost always inappropriate to the preservation of the health of women undergoing abortion because it poses tangible risk and provides no benefit to the woman." Carhart v. Ashcroft, 331 F.Supp. 2d 805, 1028 (Neb. 2004) (internal quotation marks omitted), aff'd, 413 F.3d 791 (CA8 2005). In some circumstances, injections are "absolutely [medically] contraindicated." 331 F.Supp. 2d, at 1027. See also id., at 907–912; National Abortion Federation, 330 F.Supp. 2d, at 474–475; Planned Parenthood, 320 F.Supp. 2d, at 995–997. The Court also identifies medical induction of labor as an alternative. See ante, at 9. That procedure, however, requires a hospital stay, ibid., rendering it inaccessible to patients who lack financial resources, and it too is considered less safe for many women, and impermissible for others. See Carhart, 331 F.Supp. 2d, at 940–949, 1017; National Abortion Federation, 330 F.Supp. 2d, at 468–470; Planned Parenthood, 320 F.Supp. 2d, at 961, n.5, 992–994, 1000–1002.

[7] The Court is surely correct that, for most women, abortion is a painfully difficult decision. See ante, at 28. But "neither the weight of the scientific evidence to date nor the observable reality of 33 years of legal abortion in the United States comports with the idea that having an abortion is any more dangerous to a woman's long-term mental health than delivering and parenting a child that she did not intend to have …." Cohen, Abortion and Mental Health: Myths and Realities, 9 Guttmacher Policy Rev. 8 (2006); see generally Bazelon, Is There a Post-Abortion Syndrome? N.Y. Times Magazine, Jan. 21, 2007, p.40. See also, e.g., American Psychological Association, APA Briefing Paper on the Impact of Abortion (2005) (rejecting theory of a postabortion syndrome and stating that "[a]ccess to legal abortion to terminate an unwanted pregnancy is vital to safeguard both the physical and mental health of women"); Schmiege & Russo, Depression and Unwanted First Pregnancy: Longitudinal Cohort Study, 331 British Medical J. 1303 (2005) (finding no credible evidence that choosing to terminate an unwanted first pregnancy contributes to risk of subsequent depression); Gilchrist, Hannaford, Frank, & Kay, Termination of Pregnancy and Psychiatric Morbidity, 167 British J. of Psychiatry 243, 247–248 (1995) (finding, in a cohort of more than 13,000 women, that the rate of psychiatric disorder was no higher among women who terminated pregnancy than among those who carried pregnancy to term); Stodland, The Myth of the Abortion Trauma Syndrome, 268JAMA 2078, 2079 (1992) ("Scientific studies indicate that legal abortion results in fewer deleterious sequelae for women compared with other possible outcomes of unwanted pregnancy. There is no evidence of an abortion trauma syndrome."); American Psychological Association, Council Policy Manual: (N)(I)(3), Public Interest (1989) (declaring assertions about widespread severe negative psychological effects of abortion to be "without fact"). But see Cougle, Reardon, & Coleman, Generalized Anxiety Following Unintended Pregnancies Resolved Through Childbirth and Abortion: A Cohort Study of the 1995 National Survey of Family Growth, 19 J. Anxiety Disorders 137, 142 (2005) (advancing theory of a postabortion syndrome but acknowledging that "no causal relationship between pregnancy outcome and anxiety could be determined" from study); Reardon etal., Psychiatric Admissions of Low-Income Women following Abortion and Childbirth, 168 Canadian Medical Assn. J. 1253, 1255–1256 (May 13, 2003) (concluding that psychiatric admission rates were higher for women who had an abortion compared with women who delivered); cf. Major, Psychological Implications of Abortion—Highly

Charged and Rife with Misleading Research, 168 Canadian Medical Assn. J. 1257, 1258 (May 13, 2003) (critiquing Reardon study for failing to control for a host of differences between women in the delivery and abortion samples).

[8] Notwithstanding the "bond of love" women often have with their children, see ante, at 28, not all pregnancies, this Court has recognized, are wanted, or even the product of consensual activity. See Casey, 505 U.S., at 891 ("[O]n an average day in the United States, nearly 11,000 women are severely assaulted by their male partners. Many of these incidents involve sexual assault."). See also Glander, Moore, Michielutte, & Parsons, The Prevalence of Domestic Violence Among Women Seeking Abortion, 91 Obstetrics & Gynecology 1002 (1998); Holmes, Resnick, Kilpatrick, & Best, Rape-Related Pregnancy; Estimates and Descriptive Characteristics from a National Sample of Women, 175 Am. J. Obstetrics & Gynecology 320 (Aug. 1996).

[9] Eliminating or reducing women's reproductive choices is manifestly not a means of protecting them. When safe abortion procedures cease to be an option, many women seek other means to end unwanted or coerced pregnancies. See, e.g., World Health Organization, Unsafe Abortion: Global and Regional Estimates of the Incidence of Unsafe Abortion and Associated Mortality in 2000, pp.3, 16 (4th ed. 2004) ("Restrictive legislation is associated with a high incidence of unsafe abortion" worldwide; unsafe abortion represents 13% of all "maternal" deaths); Henshaw, Unintended Pregnancy and Abortion: A Public Health Perspective, in A Clinician's Guide to Medical and Surgical Abortion 11, 19 (M. Paul, E. Lichtenberg, L. Borgatta, D. Grimes, & P. Stubblefield eds. 1999) ("Before legalization, large numbers of women in the United States died from unsafe abortions."); H. Boonstra, R. Gold, C. Richards, & L. Finer, Abortion in Women's Lives 13, and fig. 2.2 (2006) ("as late as 1965, illegal abortion still accounted for an estimated … 17% of all officially reported pregnancy-related deaths"; "[d]eaths from abortion declined dramatically after legalization").

[10] There is, in short, no fraction because the numerator and denominator are the same: The health exception reaches only those cases where a woman's health is at risk. Perhaps for this reason, in mandating safeguards for women's health, we have never before invoked the "large fraction" test.

DONALD C. WINTER, SECRETARY OF THE NAVY, et al. v NATURAL RESOURCES DEFENSE COUNCIL, INC., et al.

No. 07-1239, November 12, 2008

ON WRIT OF CERTIORARI TO THE UNITED STATES COURT OF APPEALS FOR THE NINTH CIRCUIT

Justice Ginsburg, with whom Justice Souter joins, dissenting.

The central question in this action under the National Environmental Policy Act of 1969 (NEPA) was whether the Navy must prepare an environmental impact statement (EIS). The Navy does not challenge its obligation to do so, and it represents that the EIS will be complete in January 2009—one month after the instant exercises conclude. If the Navy had completed the EIS before taking action, as NEPA instructs, the parties and the public could have benefited from the environmental analysis—and the Navy's training could have proceeded without interruption. Instead, the Navy acted first, and thus thwarted the very purpose an EIS is intended to serve. To justify its course, the Navy sought dispensation not from Congress, but from an executive council that lacks authority to countermand or revise NEPA's requirements. I would hold that, in imposing manageable measures to mitigate harm until completion of the EIS, the District Court conscientiously balanced the equities and did not abuse its discretion.

I

In December 2006, the Navy announced its intent to prepare an EIS to address the potential environmental effects of its naval readiness activities in the Southern California (SOCAL) Range Complex. See 71Fed. Reg. 76639 (2006). These readiness activities include expansion and intensification of naval training, as well as research, development, and testing of various systems and weapons. Id., at 76639, 76640. The EIS process is underway, and the Navy represents that it will be complete in January 2009. Brief for Petitioners 11; Tr. of Oral Arg. 11.

In February 2007, seeking to commence training before completion of the EIS, the Navy prepared an Environmental Assessment (EA) for the 14 exercises it planned to undertake in the interim. See App. L to Pet. for Cert. 235a.[1] On February 12, the Navy concluded the EA with a finding of no significant impact. App. 225–226. The same day, the Navy commenced its training exercises. Id., at 227 ("The Proposed Action is hereby implemented.").

On March 22, 2007, the Natural Resources Defense Council (NRDC) filed suit in the U.S. District Court for the Central District of California, seeking declaratory and injunctive relief based on the Navy's alleged violations of NEPA and other environmental statutes. As relevant here, the District Court determined that NRDC was likely to succeed on its NEPA claim and that equitable principles warranted preliminary relief. On August 7, 2007, the court enjoined the Navy's use of mid-frequency active (MFA) sonar during the 11 remaining exercises at issue.

On August 31, the Court of Appeals for the Ninth Circuit stayed the injunction pending disposition of the Navy's appeal, and the Navy proceeded with two more exercises. In a November 13 order, the Court of Appeals vacated the stay, stating that NRDC had shown "a strong likelihood of success on the merits" and that preliminary injunctive relief was appropriate. 508 F.3d 885, 886 (2007). The Court of Appeals remanded, however, instructing the District Court to provide mitigation measures under which the Navy could conduct its remaining exercises.

On remand, the District Court received briefing from both parties. In addition, the court "toured the USS Milius at the naval base in San Diego, California, to improve its understanding of the Navy's sonar training procedures and the feasibility of the parties' proposed mitigation measures. Counsel for both [parties] were present." 530 F.Supp. 2d 1110, 1112 (2008). On January 3, 2008, the District Court entered a modified preliminary injunction imposing six mitigation measures. The court revised the modified injunction slightly on January 10 in response to filings by the Navy, and four days later, denied the Navy's application for a stay pending appeal.

On the following day, January 15, the Council on Environmental Quality (CEQ), an advisory body within the Executive Office of the President, responded to the Navy's request for "alternative arrangements" for NEPA compliance. App. L to Pet. for Cert. 233a.The "arrangements" CEQ set out purported to permit the Navy to continue its training without timely environmental review. Id., at 241a–247a.The Navy accepted the arrangements on the same day. App. 228.

The Navy then filed an emergency motion in the Court of Appeals requesting immediate vacatur of the District Court's modified injunction. CEQ's action, the Navy urged, eliminated the injunction's legal foundation. In the alternative, the Navy sought a stay of two aspects of the injunction pending its appeal: the 2,200-yard mandatory shutdown zone and the power-down requirement in significant surface ducting conditions, see ante, at 7–8. While targeting in its stay application only two of the six measures imposed by the District Court, the Navy explicitly reserved the right to challenge on appeal each of the six mitigation measures. Responding to the Navy's emergency motion, the Court of Appeals remanded the matter to allow the District Court to determine in the first instance the effect of the intervening executive action. Pending its own consideration of the Navy's motion, the District Court stayed the injunction, and the Navy conducted its sixth exercise.

On February 4, after briefing and oral argument, the District Court denied the Navy's motion. The Navy appealed, reiterating its position that CEQ's action eliminated all justification for the injunction. The Navy also argued that vacatur of the entire injunction was required irrespective of CEQ's action, in part because the "conditions imposed, in particular the 2,200 yard mandatory shutdown zone and the six decibel (75%) power-down in significant surface ducting conditions, severely degrade the Navy's training." Brief for Appellants in No. 08–55054 (CA9), p. 15. In the February 29 decision now under review, the Court of Appeals affirmed the District Court's judgment. 518 F.3d 658, 703 (2008). The Navy has continued training in the meantime and plans to complete its final exercise in December 2008.

As the procedural history indicates, the courts below determined that an EIS was required for the 14 exercises. The Navy does not challenge that decision in this Court. Instead, the Navy defends its failure to complete an EIS before launching the exercises based upon CEQ's "alternative arrangements"—arrangements the Navy sought and obtained in order to overcome the lower courts' rulings. As explained below, the Navy's actions undermined NEPA and took an extraordinary course.

II

NEPA "promotes its sweeping commitment" to environmental integrity "by focusing Government and public attention on the environmental effects of proposed agency action." *Marsh* v. *Oregon Natural Resources Council*, 490 U.S. 360, 371 (1989) . "By so focusing agency attention, NEPA ensures that the agency will not act on incomplete information, only to regret its decision after it is too late to correct." Ibid.

The EIS is NEPA's core requirement. *Department of Transportation* v. *Public Citizen*, 541 U.S. 752, 757 (2004) . This Court has characterized the requirement as "action-forcing." *Andrus* v. *Sierra Club*, 442 U.S. 347, 350 (1979) (internal quotation marks omitted). Environmental concerns must be "integrated into the very process of agency decisionmaking" and "interwoven into the fabric of agency planning." *Id.*, at 350–351. In addition to discussing potential consequences, an EIS must describe potential mitigation measures and alternatives to the proposed course of action. See *Robertson* v. *Methow Valley Citizens Council*, 490 U.S. 332, 351–352 (1989) (citing 40 CFR §§1508.25(b), 1502.14(f), 1502.16(h), 1505.2(c) (1987)). The EIS requirement "ensures that important effects will not be overlooked or underestimated only to be discovered after resources have been committed or the die otherwise cast." 490 U.S., at 349.

"Publication of an EIS … also serves a larger informational role." *Ibid.* It demonstrates that an agency has indeed considered environmental concerns, and "perhaps more significantly, provides a springboard for public comment." *Ibid.* At the same time, it affords other affected governmental bodies "notice of the expected consequences and the opportunity to plan and implement corrective measures in a timely manner." *Id.*, at 350.

In light of these objectives, the timing of an EIS is critical. CEQ regulations instruct agencies to "integrate the NEPA process with other planning at the earliest possible time to insure that planning and decisions reflect environmental values." 40 CFR §1501.2 (1987). An EIS must be prepared "early enough so that it can serve practically as an important contribution to the decisionmaking process and will not be used to rationalize or justify decisions already made." *Andrus*, 442 U.S., at 351–352, n.3 (quoting 40 CFR §1502.5 (1979)).

The Navy's publication of its EIS in this case, scheduled to occur *after* the 14 exercises are completed, defeats NEPA's informational and participatory purposes. The Navy's inverted timing, it bears emphasis, is the very reason why the District Court had to confront the question of mitigation measures at all. Had the Navy prepared a legally sufficient EIS before beginning the SOCAL exercises, NEPA would have functioned as its drafters intended: The EIS process and associated public input might have convinced the Navy voluntarily to adopt mitigation measures, but NEPA itself would not have impeded the Navy's exercises. See *Public Citizen*, 541 U.S., at 756, 769, n. 2 (noting that NEPA does not mandate particular results, but rather establishes procedural requirements with a "focus on improving agency decisionmaking").

The Navy had other options. Most importantly, it could have requested assistance from Congress. The Government has sometimes obtained congressional authorization to proceed with planned activities without fulfilling NEPA's requirements. See, *e.g.*, Floyd D. Spence National Defense Authorization Act for Fiscal Year 2001, Pub. L. 106–398, §317, 114 Stat. 1654A–57 (exempting the military from preparing a programmatic EIS for low-level flight training); 42 U.S.C. §10141(c) (exempting the Environmental Protection Agency from preparing an EIS for the development of criteria for handling spent nuclear fuel and high-level radioactive waste); 43 U.S.C. §1652(d) (exempting construction of the trans-Alaska oil pipeline from further NEPA compliance).

Rather than resorting to Congress, the Navy "sought relief from the Executive Branch." *Ante*, at 8. On January 10, 2008, the Navy asked CEQ, adviser to the President, to approve alternative arrangements for NEPA compliance pursuant to 40 CFR §1506.11 (1987). App. L to Pet. for Cert. 233a; see *ante*, at 8, n. 3. The next day, the Navy submitted supplementary material to CEQ, including the Navy's EA and after-action reports, the District Court's orders, and two analyses by the National Marine Fisheries Service (NMFS). App. L to Pet. for Cert. 237a–238a. Neither the Navy nor CEQ notified NRDC, and CEQ did not request or consider any of the materials underlying the District Court orders it addressed.

Four days later, on January 15, the Chairman of CEQ issued a letter to the Secretary of the Navy. Repeating the Navy's submissions with little independent analysis, the letter stated that the District Court's orders posed risks to the Navy's training exercises. See *id.*, at 238a ("You have explained that the training restrictions set forth in the … injunctive orders prevent the Navy from providing Strike Groups with adequate proficiency training and create a substantial risk of precluding certification of the Strike Groups as combat ready.").

The letter continued:

> "Discussions between our staffs, your letter and supporting documents, and the classified declaration and briefings I have received, have clearly determined that the Navy cannot ensure the necessary training to certify strike groups for deployment under the terms of the injunctive orders. Based on the record supporting your request … CEQ has concluded that the Navy must be able to conduct the [exercises] … in a timeframe that does not provide sufficient time to complete an EIS. Therefore, emergency circumstances are present for the nine exercises and alternative arrangements for compliance with NEPA under CEQ regulation 40 C.F.R. §1506.11 are warranted." *Id.*, at 240a.

The alternative arrangements CEQ set forth do not vindicate NEPA's objectives. The arrangements provide for "public participation measures," which require the Navy to provide notices of the alternative arrangements. *Id.*, at 242a. The notices must "seek input on the process for reviewing post-exercise assessments" and "include an offer to meet jointly with Navy representatives … and CEQ to discuss the alternative arrangements." *Id.*, at 242a–243a. The alternative arrangements also describe the Navy's existing research and mitigation efforts. *Id.*, at 243a–247a.

CEQ's hasty decision on a one-sided record is no substitute for the District Court's considered judgment based on a two-sided record.[2] More fundamentally, even an exemplary CEQ review could not have effected the short circuit the Navy sought. CEQ lacks authority to absolve an agency of its statutory duty to prepare an EIS. NEPA established CEQ to assist and advise the President on environmental policy, 42 U. S. C. §4342, and a 1977 Executive Order charged CEQ with issuing regulations to federal agencies for implementation of NEPA's procedural provisions, Exec. Order No. 11991, 3 CFR 123 (1977 Comp.). This Court has recognized that CEQ's regulations are entitled to "substantial deference," *Robertson*, 490 U.S., at 355, and §1506.11 indicates that CEQ may play an important consultative role in emergency circumstances, but we have never suggested that CEQ could eliminate the statute's command. If the Navy sought to avoid its NEPA obligations, its remedy lay in the Legislative Branch. The Navy's alternative course—rapid, self-serving resort to an office in the White House—is surely not what Congress had in mind when it instructed agencies to comply with NEPA "to the fullest extent possible." 42 U. S. C. §4332.[3]

III

A

Flexibility is a hallmark of equity jurisdiction. "The essence of equity jurisdiction has been the power of the Chancellor to do equity and to mould each decree to the necessities of the particular case. Flexibility rather than rigidity has distinguished it." *Weinberger* v. *Romero-Barcelo*, 456 U.S. 305, 312 (1982) (quoting *Hecht Co.* v. *Bowles*, 321 U.S. 321, 329 (1944)). Consistent with equity's character, courts do not insist that litigants uniformly show a particular, predetermined quantum of probable success or injury before awarding equitable relief. Instead, courts have evaluated claims for equitable relief on a "sliding scale," sometimes awarding relief based on a lower likelihood of harm when the likelihood of success is very high. 11A C. Wright, A. Miller, & M. Kane, Federal Practice and Procedure §2948.3, p. 195 (2d ed. 1995). This Court has never rejected that formulation, and I do not believe it does so today.

Equity's flexibility is important in the NEPA context. Because an EIS is the tool for *uncovering* environmental harm, environmental plaintiffs may often rely more heavily on their probability of success than the likelihood of harm. The Court is correct that relief is not warranted "simply to prevent the possibility of some remote future injury." *Ante*, at 12 (quoting Wright & Miller, *supra*, §2948.1, at 155). "However, the injury need not have been inflicted when application is made or be certain to occur; a strong threat of irreparable injury before trial is an adequate basis." Wright & Miller, *supra*, §2948.1, at 155–156 (footnote omitted). I agree with the District Court that NRDC made the required showing here.

B

The Navy's own EA predicted substantial and irreparable harm to marine mammals. Sonar is linked to mass strandings of marine mammals, hemorrhaging around the brain and ears, acute spongiotic changes in the central nervous system, and lesions in vital organs. *E.g.*, App. 600–602; 360–362; 478–479. As the Ninth Circuit noted, the EA predicts that the Navy's "use of MFA sonar in the SOCAL exercises will result in 564 instances of physical injury including permanent hearing loss (Level A harassment) and nearly 170,000 behavioral disturbances (Level B harassment), more than 8,000 of which would also involve temporary hearing loss." 518 F.3d, at 696; see App. 223–224. Within those totals,

> "the EA predicts 436 Level A harassments of Cuvier's beaked whales, of which, according to NOAA, as few as 1,121 may exist in California, Oregon and Washington combined. Likewise, the EA predicts 1,092 Level B harassments of bottlenose dolphins, of which only 5,271 may exist in the California Coastal and Offshore stocks." 518 F.3d, at 691–692.

The majority acknowledges the lower courts' findings, *ante*, at 9, but also states that the EA predicted "only eight Level A harassments of common dolphins each year" and "274 Level B harassments of beaked whales per year, none of which would result in permanent injury," *ante*, at 6. Those numbers do not fully capture the EA's predictions.

The EA classified the harassments of beaked whales as Level A, not Level B. The EA does indeed state that "modeling predicts non-injurious Level B exposures." App. 185. But, as the majority correctly notes, *ante*,at 6, the EA also states that "all beaked whale exposures are counted as Level A," App. 185. The EA counted the predicted exposures as Level A "[b]y Navy policy developed in conjunction with NMFS." *Id.*, at 200. The record reflects "the known sensitivity of these species to tactical sonar," *id.*, at 365 (National Oceanic and Atmospheric Administration letter), and as the majority acknowledges, beaked whales are difficult to study, *ante*, at 6. Further, as the Ninth Circuit noted, "the EA … maintained that the methodology used was based on the 'best available science.'" 518 F.3d, at 669.[4]

In my view, this likely harm—170,000 behavioral disturbances, including 8,000 instances of temporary hearing loss; and 564 Level A harms, including 436 injuries to a beaked whale population numbering only 1,121—cannot be lightly dismissed, even in the face of an alleged risk to the effectiveness of the Navy's 14 training exercises. There is no doubt that the training exercises serve critical interests. But those interests do not authorize the Navy to violate a statutory command, especially when recourse to the Legislature remains open. "Of course, military interests do not always trump other considerations, and we have not held that they do." *Ante*, at 16.

In light of the likely, substantial harm to the environment, NRDC's almost inevitable success on the merits of its claim that NEPA required the Navy to prepare an EIS, the history of this litigation, and the public interest, I cannot agree that the mitigation measures the District Court imposed signal an abuse of discretion. Cf. *Amoco Production Co.* v. *Gambell*, 480 U.S. 531, 545 (1987) ("Environmental injury, by its nature, can seldom be adequately remedied by money damages and is often permanent or at least of long duration, *i.e.*, irreparable. If such injury is sufficiently likely, therefore, the balance of harms will usually favor the issuance of an injunction to protect the environment.").

For the reasons stated, I would affirm the judgment of the Ninth Circuit.

NOTES

[1] An EA is used "for determining whether to prepare" an EIS. Department of Transportation v. Public Citizen, 541 U.S. 752, 757 (2004) (quoting 40 CFR §1508.9(a) (2003)); see ante, at 5. By definition, an EA alone does not satisfy an agency's obligation under NEPA if the effects of a proposed action require preparation of a full EIS.

[2] The District Court may well have given too spare an explanation for the balance of hardships in issuing its injunction of August 7, 2007. The court cured any error in this regard, however, when it closely examined each mitigation measure in issuing the modified injunction of January 3, 2008. The Court of Appeals, too, conducted a detailed analysis of the record.

3 On the same day that CEQ issued its letter, the President granted the Navy an exemption from the requirements of the Coastal Zone Management Act of 1972 (CZMA) pursuant to 16 U.S.C. §1456(c)(1)(B). That exemption, expressly authorized by the CZMA, does not affect NRDC's NEPA claim.

[4] The majority reasons that the environmental harm deserves less weight because the training exercises "have been taking place in SOCAL for the last 40 years," such that "this is not a case in which the defendant is conducting a new type of activity with completely unknown effects on the environment." Ante, at 13. But the EA explains that the proposed action is not a continuation of the "status quo training." App. 128. Instead, the EA is based on the Navy's proposal to employ a "surge" training strategy, ibid., in which the commander "would have the option to conduct two concurrent major range events," id., at 124.

FRANK RICCI, et al. v. JOHN DeSTEFANO, et al.

NoS. 07-1428 & 08–328, June 29, 2009

ON WRITS OF CERTIORARI TO THE UNITED STATES COURT OF APPEALS FOR THE SECOND CIRCUIT

Justice Ginsburg, with whom Justice Stevens, Justice Souter, and Justice Breyer join, dissenting.

In assessing claims of race discrimination, "[c]ontext matters." *Grutter* v. *Bollinger*, 539 U.S. 306, 327 (2003). In 1972, Congress extended Title VII of the Civil Rights Act of 1964 to cover public employment. At that time, municipal fire departments across the country, including New Haven's, pervasively discriminated against minorities. The extension of Title VII to cover jobs in firefighting effected no overnight change. It took decades of persistent effort, advanced by Title VII litigation, to open firefighting posts to members of racial minorities.

The white firefighters who scored high on New Haven's promotional exams understandably attract this Court's sympathy. But they had no vested right to promotion. Nor have other persons received promotions in preference to them. New Haven maintains that it refused to certify the test results because it believed, for good cause, that it would be vulnerable to a Title VII disparate-impact suit if it relied on those results. The Court today holds that New Haven has not demonstrated "a strong basis in evidence" for its plea. *Ante*, at 2. In so holding, the Court pretends that "[t]he City rejected the test results solely because the higher scoring candidates were white." *Ante*, at 20. That pretension, essential to the Court's disposition, ignores substantial evidence of multiple flaws in the tests New Haven used. The Court similarly fails to acknowledge the better tests used in other cities, which have yielded less racially skewed outcomes.[1]

By order of this Court, New Haven, a city in which African-Americans and Hispanics account for nearly 60 percent of the population, must today be served—as it was in the days of undisguised discrimination—by a fire department in which members of racial and ethnic minorities are rarely seen in command positions. In arriving at its order, the Court barely acknowledges the pathmarking decision in *Griggs* v. *Duke Power Co.*, 401 U.S. 424 (1971) , which explained the centrality of the disparate-impact concept to effective enforcement of Title VII. The Court's order and opinion, I anticipate, will not have staying power.

I

A

The Court's recitation of the facts leaves out important parts of the story. Firefighting is a profession in which the legacy of racial discrimination casts an especially long shadow. In extending Title VII to state and local government employers in 1972, Congress took note of a U.S. Commission on Civil Rights (USCCR) report finding racial discrimination in municipal employment even "more pervasive than in the private sector." H.R. Rep. No. 92–238, p. 17 (1971). According to the report, overt racism was partly to blame, but so too was a failure on the part of municipal employers to apply merit-based employment principles. In making hiring and promotion decisions, public employers often "rel[ied] on criteria unrelated to job performance," including nepotism or political patronage. 118 Cong. Rec. 1817 (1972). Such flawed selection methods served to entrench preexisting racial hierarchies. The USCCR report singled out police and fire departments for having "[b]arriers to equal employment ... greater ... than in any other area of State or local government," with African-Americans "hold[ing] almost no positions in the officer ranks." *Ibid.* See also National Commission on Fire Prevention and Control, America Burning 5 (1973) ("Racial minorities are under-represented in the fire departments in nearly every community in which they live.").

The city of New Haven (City) was no exception. In the early 1970's, African-Americans and Hispanics composed 30 percent of New Haven's population, but only 3.6 percent of the City's 502 firefighters. The racial disparity in the officer ranks was even more pronounced: "[O]f the 107 officers in the Department only one was black, and he held the lowest rank above private." *Firebird Soc. of New Haven, Inc.* v. *New Haven Bd. of Fire Comm'rs*, 66 F.R.D. 457, 460 (Conn. 1975).

Following a lawsuit and settlement agreement, see *ibid.*, the City initiated efforts to increase minority representation in the New Haven Fire Department (Department). Those litigation-induced efforts produced some positive change. New Haven's population includes a greater proportion of minorities today than it did in the 1970's: Nearly 40 percent of the City's residents are African-American and more than 20 percent are Hispanic. Among entry-level firefighters, minorities are still underrepresented, but not starkly so. As of 2003, African-Americans and Hispanics constituted 30 percent and 16 percent of the City's firefighters, respectively. In supervisory positions, however, significant disparities remain. Overall, the senior officer ranks (captain and higher) are nine percent African-American and nine percent Hispanic. Only one of the Department's 21 fire captains is African-American. See App. in No. 06–4996–cv (CA2), p. A1588 (hereinafter CA2

App.). It is against this backdrop of entrenched inequality that the promotion process at issue in this litigation should be assessed.

B

By order of its charter, New Haven must use competitive examinations to fill vacancies in fire officer and other civil-service positions. Such examinations, the City's civil service rules specify, "shall be practical in nature, shall relate to matters which fairly measure the relative fitness and capacity of the applicants to discharge the duties of the position which they seek, and shall take into account character, training, experience, physical and mental fitness." *Id.*, at A331. The City may choose among a variety of testing methods, including written and oral exams and "[p]erformance tests to demonstrate skill and ability in performing actual work." *Id.*, at A332.

New Haven, the record indicates, did not closely consider what sort of "practical" examination would "fairly measure the relative fitness and capacity of the applicants to discharge the duties" of a fire officer. Instead, the City simply adhered to the testing regime outlined in its two-decades-old contract with the local firefighters' union: a written exam, which would account for 60 percent of an applicant's total score, and an oral exam, which would account for the remaining 40 percent. *Id.*, at A1045. In soliciting bids from exam development companies, New Haven made clear that it would entertain only "proposals that include a written component that will be weighted at 60%, and an oral component that will be weighted at 40%." *Id.*, at A342. Chad Legel, a representative of the winning bidder, Industrial/Organizational Solutions, Inc. (IOS), testified during his deposition that the City never asked whether alternative methods might better measure the qualities of a successful fire officer, including leadership skills and command presence. See *id.*, at A522 ("I was under contract and had responsibility only to create the oral interview and the written exam.").

Pursuant to New Haven's specifications, IOS developed and administered the oral and written exams. The results showed significant racial disparities. On the lieutenant exam, the pass rate for African-American candidates was about one-half the rate for Caucasian candidates; the pass rate for Hispanic candidates was even lower. On the captain exam, both African-American and Hispanic candidates passed at about half the rate of their Caucasian counterparts. See App. 225–226. More striking still, although nearly half of the 77 lieutenant candidates were African-American or Hispanic, none would have been eligible for promotion to the eight positions then vacant. The highest scoring African-American candidate ranked 13th; the top Hispanic candidate was 26th. As for the seven then-vacant captain positions, two Hispanic candidates would have been eligible, but no African-Americans. The highest scoring African-American candidate ranked 15th. See *id.*, at 218–219.

These stark disparities, the Court acknowledges, sufficed to state a prima facie case under Title VII's disparate-impact provision. See *ante*, at 27 ("The pass rates of minorities . . . f[e]ll well below the 80-percent standard set by the [Equal Employment Opportunity Commission (EEOC)] to implement the disparate-impact provision of Title VII."). New Haven thus had cause for concern about the prospect of Title VII litigation and liability. City officials referred the matter to the New Haven Civil Service Board (CSB), the entity responsible for certifying the results of employment exams.

Between January and March 2004, the CSB held five public meetings to consider the proper course. At the first meeting, New Haven's Corporation Counsel, Thomas Ude, described the legal standard governing Title VII disparate-impact claims. Statistical imbalances alone, Ude correctly recognized, do not give rise to liability. Instead, presented with a disparity, an employer "has the opportunity and the burden of proving that the test is job-related and consistent with business necessity." CA2 App. A724. A Title VII plaintiff may attempt to rebut an employer's showing of job-relatedness and necessity by identifying alternative selection methods that would have been at least as valid but with "less of an adverse or disparate or discriminatory effect." *Ibid.* See also *id.*, at A738. Accordingly, the CSB Commissioners understood, their principal task was to decide whether they were confident about the reliability of the exams: Had the exams fairly measured the qualities of a successful fire officer despite their disparate results? Might an alternative examination process have identified the most qualified candidates without creating such significant racial imbalances?

Seeking a range of input on these questions, the CSB heard from test takers, the test designer, subject-matter experts, City officials, union leaders, and community members. Several candidates for promotion, who did not yet know their exam results, spoke at the CSB's first two meetings. Some candidates favored certification. The exams, they emphasized, had closely tracked the assigned study materials. Having invested substantial time and money to prepare themselves for the test, they felt it would be unfair to scrap the results. See, *e.g.*, *id.*, at A772–A773, A785–A789.

Other firefighters had a different view. A number of the exam questions, they pointed out, were not germane to New Haven's practices and procedures. See, *e.g.*, *id.*, at A774–A784. At least two candidates opposed to certification noted unequal access to study materials. Some individuals, they asserted, had the necessary books even before the syllabus was issued. Others had to invest substantial sums to purchase the materials and "wait a month and a half for some of the books because they were on back-order." *Id.*, at A858. These disparities, it was suggested, fell at least in part along racial lines. While many Caucasian applicants could obtain materials and assistance from relatives in the fire service, the overwhelming majority of minority applicants were "first-generation firefighters" without such support networks. See *id.*, at A857–A861, A886–A887.

A representative of the Northeast Region of the International Association of Black Professional Firefighters, Donald Day, also spoke at the second meeting. Statistical disparities, he told the CSB, had been present in the Department's previous promotional exams. On earlier tests, however, a few minority candidates had fared well enough to earn promotions. *Id.*, at A828. See also App. 218–219. Day contrasted New Haven's experience with that of nearby Bridgeport, where minority firefighters held one-third of lieutenant and captain positions. Bridgeport, Day observed, had once used a testing process similar to New Haven's, with a written exam accounting for 70 percent of an applicant's score, an oral exam for 25 percent, and seniority for the remaining five percent. CA2 App. A830. Bridgeport recognized, however, that the oral component, more so than the written component, addressed the sort of "real-life scenarios" fire officers encounter on the job. *Id.*, at A832. Accordingly, that city "changed the relative weights" to give primacy to the oral exam. *Ibid.* Since that time, Day reported, Bridgeport had seen minorities "fairly represented" in its exam results. *Ibid.*

The CSB's third meeting featured IOS representative Legel, the leader of the team that had designed and administered the exams for New Haven. Several City officials also participated in the discussion. Legel described the exam development process in detail. The City, he recounted, had set the "parameters" for the exams, specifically, the requirement of written and oral components with a 60/40 weighting. *Id.*, at A923, A974. For security reasons, Department officials had not been permitted to check the content of the questions prior to their administration. Instead, IOS retained a senior fire officer from Georgia to review the exams "for content and fidelity to the source material." *Id.*, at A936. Legel defended the exams as "facially neutral," and stated that he "would stand by the[ir] validity." *Id.*, at A962. City officials did not dispute the neutrality of IOS's work. But, they cautioned, even if individual exam questions had no intrinsic bias, the selection process as a whole may nevertheless have been deficient. The officials urged the CSB to consult with experts about the "larger picture." *Id.*, at A1012.

At its fourth meeting, CSB solicited the views of three individuals with testing-related expertise. Dr. Christopher Hornick, an industrial/organizational psychology consultant with 25 years' experience with police and firefighter testing, described the exam results as having "relatively high adverse impact." *Id.*, at A1028. Most of the tests he had developed, Hornick stated, exhibited "significantly and dramatically less adverse impact." *Id.*, at A1029. Hornick downplayed the notion of "facial neutrality." It was more important, he advised the CSB, to consider "the broader issue of how your procedures and your rules and the types of tests that you are using are contributing to the adverse impact." *Id.*, at A1038.

Specifically, Hornick questioned New Haven's union-prompted 60/40 written/oral examination structure, noting the availability of "different types of testing procedures that are much more valid in terms of identifying the best potential supervisors in [the] fire department." *Id.*, at A1032. He suggested, for example, "an assessment center process, which is essentially an opportunity for candidates … to demonstrate how they would address a particular problem as opposed to just verbally saying it or identifying the correct option on a written test." *Id.*, at A1039–A1040. Such selection processes, Hornick said, better "identif[y] the best possible people" and "demonstrate dramatically less adverse impacts." *Ibid.* Hornick added:

> "I've spoken to at least 10,000, maybe 15,000 firefighters in group settings in my consulting practice and I have never one time ever had anyone in the fire service say to me, 'Well, the person who answers–gets the highest score on a written job knowledge, multiple-guess test makes the best company officer.' We know that it's not as valid as other procedures that exist." *Id.*, at A1033.

See also *id.*, at A1042–A1043 ("I think a person's leadership skills, their command presence, their interpersonal skills, their management skills, their tactical skills could have been identified and evaluated in a much more appropriate way.").

Hornick described the written test itself as "reasonably good," *id.*, at A1041, but he criticized the decision not to allow Department officials to check the content. According to Hornick, this "inevitably" led to "test[ing] for processes and procedures that don't necessarily match up into the department." *Id.*, at A1034–A1035. He preferred "experts from within the department who have signed confidentiality agreements … to make sure that the terminology and equipment that's being identified from standardized reading sources apply to the department." *Id.*, at A1035.

Asked whether he thought the City should certify the results, Hornick hedged: "There is adverse impact in the test. That will be identified in any proceeding that you have. You will have industrial psychology experts, if it goes to court, on both sides. And it will not be a pretty or comfortable position for anyone to be in." *Id.*, at A1040–A1041. Perhaps, he suggested, New Haven might certify the results but immediately begin exploring "alternative ways to deal with these issues" in the future. *Id.*, at A1041.

The two other witnesses made relatively brief appearances. Vincent Lewis, a specialist with the Department of Homeland Security and former fire officer in Michigan, believed the exams had generally tested relevant material, although he noted a relatively heavy emphasis on questions pertaining to being an "apparatus driver." He suggested that this may have disadvantaged test takers "who had not had the training or had not had an opportunity to drive the apparatus." *Id.*, at A1051. He also urged the CSB to consider whether candidates had, in fact, enjoyed equal access to the study materials. *Ibid.* Cf. *supra*, at 7.

Janet Helms, a professor of counseling psychology at Boston College, observed that two-thirds of the incumbent fire officers who submitted job analyses to IOS during the exam design phase were Caucasian. Members of different racial groups, Helms told the CSB, sometimes do their jobs in different ways, "often because the experiences that are open to white male firefighters are not open to members of these other under-represented groups." CA2 App. A1063–A1064. The heavy reliance on job analyses from white firefighters, she suggested, may thus have introduced an element of bias. *Id.*, at A1063.

The CSB's fifth and final meeting began with statements from City officials recommending against certification. Ude, New Haven's counsel, repeated the applicable disparate-impact standard:

> "[A] finding of adverse impact is the beginning, not the end, of a review of testing procedures. Where a procedure demonstrates adverse impact, you look to how closely it is related to the job that you're looking to fill and you also look at whether there are other ways to test for those qualities, those traits, those positions that are equally valid with less adverse impact." *Id.,* at A1100–A1101.

New Haven, Ude and other officials asserted, would be vulnerable to Title VII liability under this standard. Even if the exams were "facially neutral," significant doubts had been raised about whether they properly assessed the key attributes of a successful fire officer. *Id.,* at A1103. See also *id.,* at A1125 ("Upon close reading of the exams, the questions themselves would appear to test a candidate's ability to memorize textbooks but not necessarily to identify solutions to real problems on the fire ground."). Moreover, City officials reminded the CSB, Hornick and others had identified better, less discriminatory selection methods–such as assessment centers or exams with a more heavily weighted oral component. *Id.,* at A1108–A1109, A1129–A1130.

After giving members of the public a final chance to weigh in, the CSB voted on certification, dividing 2 to 2. By rule, the result was noncertification. Voting no, Commissioner Webber stated, "I originally was going to vote to certify. ... But I've heard enough testimony here to give me great doubts about the test itself and ... some of the procedures. And I believe we can do better." *Id.,* at A1157. Commissioner Tirado likewise concluded that the "flawed" testing process counseled against certification. *Id.,* at A1158. Chairman Segaloff and Commissioner Caplan voted to certify. According to Segaloff, the testimony had not "compelled [him] to say this exam was not job-related," and he was unconvinced that alternative selection processes would be "less discriminatory." *Id.,* at A1159–A1160. Both Segalhoff and Caplan, however, urged the City to undertake civil service reform. *Id.,* at A1150–A1154.

C

Following the CSB's vote, petitioners—17 white firefighters and one Hispanic firefighter, all of whom had high marks on the exams—filed suit in the United States District Court for the District of Connecticut. They named as defendants—respondents here—the City, several City officials, a local political activist, and the two CSB members who voted against certifying the results. By opposing certification, petitioners alleged, respondents had discriminated against them in violation of Title VII's disparate-treatment provision and the Fourteenth Amendment 's Equal Protection Clause. The decision not to certify, respondents answered, was a lawful effort to comply with Title VII's disparate-impact provision and thus could not have run afoul of Title VII's prohibition of disparate treatment. Characterizing respondents' stated rationale as a mere pretext, petitioners insisted that New Haven would have had a solid defense to any disparate-impact suit.

In a decision summarily affirmed by the Court of Appeals, the District Court granted summary judgment for respondents. 554 F.Supp. 2d 142 (Conn. 2006), aff'd, 530 F.3d 87 (CA2 2008) *(per curiam)*. Under Second Circuit precedent, the District Court explained, "the intent to remedy the disparate impact" of a promotional exam "is not equivalent to an intent to discriminate against non-minority applicants." 554 F.Supp. 2d, at 157 (quoting *Hayden* v. *County of Nassau,* 180 F.3d 42, 51 (CA2 1999)). Rejecting petitioners' pretext argument, the court observed that the exam results were sufficiently skewed "to make out a prima facie case of discrimination" under Title VII's disparate-impact provision. 554 F.Supp. 2d, at 158. Had New Haven gone forward with certification and been sued by aggrieved minority test takers, the City would have been forced to defend tests that were presumptively invalid. And, as the CSB testimony of Hornick and others indicated, overcoming that presumption would have been no easy task. *Id.,* at 153–156. Given Title VII's preference for voluntary compliance, the court held, New Haven could lawfully discard the disputed exams even if the City had not definitively "pinpoint[ed]" the source of the disparity and "ha[d] not yet formulated a better selection method." *Id.,* at 156.

Respondents were no doubt conscious of race during their decisionmaking process, the court acknowledged, but this did not mean they had engaged in racially disparate treatment. The conclusion they had reached and the action thereupon taken were race-neutral in this sense: "[A]ll the test results were discarded, no one was promoted, and firefighters of every race will have to participate in another selection process to be considered for promotion." *Id.,* at 158. New Haven's action, which gave no individual a preference, "was 'simply not analogous to a quota system or a minority set-aside where candidates, on the basis of their race, are not treated uniformly.'" *Id.,* at 157 (quoting *Hayden,* 180 F.3d, at 50). For these and other reasons, the court also rejected petitioners' equal protection claim.

II

A

Title VII became effective in July 1965. Employers responded to the law by eliminating rules and practices that explicitly barred racial minorities from "white" jobs. But removing overtly race-based job classifications did not usher in genuinely equal opportunity. More subtle—and sometimes unconscious—forms of discrimination replaced once undisguised restrictions.

In *Griggs* v. *Duke Power Co.*, 401 U.S. 424 (1971) , this Court responded to that reality and supplied important guidance on Title VII's mission and scope. Congress, the landmark decision recognized, aimed beyond "disparate treatment"; it targeted "disparate impact" as well. Title VII's original text, it was plain to the Court, "proscribe[d] not only overt discrimination but also practices that are fair in form, but discriminatory in operation." *Id.*, at 431.[2] Only by ignoring *Griggs* could one maintain that intentionally disparate treatment alone was Title VII's "original, foundational prohibition," and disparate impact a mere afterthought. Cf. *ante*, at 21.

Griggs addressed Duke Power Company's policy that applicants for positions, save in the company's labor department, be high school graduates and score satisfactorily on two professionally prepared aptitude tests. "[T]here was no showing of a discriminatory purpose in the adoption of the diploma and test requirements." 401 U.S., at 428. The policy, however, "operated to render ineligible a markedly disproportionate number of [African-Americans]." *Id.*, at 429. At the time of the litigation, in North Carolina, where the Duke Power plant was located, 34 percent of white males, but only 12 percent of African-American males, had high school diplomas. *Id.*, at 430, n.6. African-Americans also failed the aptitude tests at a significantly higher rate than whites. *Ibid.* Neither requirement had been "shown to bear a demonstrable relationship to successful performance of the jobs for which it was used." *Id.*, at 431.

The Court unanimously held that the company's diploma and test requirements violated Title VII. "[T]o achieve equality of employment opportunities," the Court comprehended, Congress "directed the thrust of the Act to the *consequences* of employment practices, not simply the motivation." *Id.*, at 429, 432. That meant "unnecessary barriers to employment" must fall, even if "neutral on their face" and "neutral in terms of intent." *Id.*, at 430, 431. "The touchstone" for determining whether a test or qualification meets Title VII's measure, the Court said, is not "good intent or the absence of discriminatory intent"; it is "business necessity." *Id.*, at 431, 432. Matching procedure to substance, the *Griggs* Court observed, Congress "placed on the employer the burden of showing that any given requirement … ha[s] a manifest relationship to the employment in question." *Id.*, at 432.

In *Albemarle Paper Co.* v. *Moody*, 422 U.S. 405 (1975) , the Court, again without dissent, elaborated on *Griggs*. When an employment test "select[s] applicants for hire or promotion in a racial pattern significantly different from the pool of applicants," the Court reiterated, the employer must demonstrate a "manifest relationship" between test and job. 422 U.S., at 425. Such a showing, the Court cautioned, does not necessarily mean the employer prevails: "[I]t remains open to the complaining party to show that other tests or selection devices, without a similarly undesirable racial effect, would also serve the employer's legitimate interest in 'efficient and trustworthy workmanship.'" *Ibid.*

Federal trial and appellate courts applied *Griggs* and *Albemarle* to disallow a host of hiring and promotion practices that "operate[d] as 'built in headwinds' for minority groups." *Griggs*, 401 U.S., at 432. Practices discriminatory in effect, courts repeatedly emphasized, could be maintained only upon an employer's showing of "an overriding and compelling business purpose." *Chrisner* v. *Complete Auto Transit, Inc.*, 645 F.2d 1251, 1261, n. 9 (CA6 1981).[3] That a practice served "legitimate management functions" did not, it was generally understood, suffice to establish business necessity. *Williams* v. *Colorado Springs, Colo., School Dist.*, 641 F.2d 835, 840–841 (CA10 1981) (internal quotation marks omitted). Among selection methods cast aside for lack of a "manifest relationship" to job performance were a number of written hiring and promotional examinations for firefighters.[4]

Moving in a different direction, in *Wards Cove Packing Co.* v. *Atonio*, 490 U.S. 642 (1989) , a bare majority of this Court significantly modified the *Griggs-Albemarle* delineation of Title VII's disparate-impact proscription. As to business necessity for a practice that disproportionately excludes members of minority groups, *Wards Cove* held, the employer bears only the burden of production, not the burden of persuasion. 490 U.S., at 659–660. And in place of the instruction that the challenged practice "must have a manifest relationship to the employment in question," *Griggs*, 401 U.S., at 432, *Wards Cove* said that the practice would be permissible as long as it "serve[d], in a significant way, the legitimate employment goals of the employer." 490 U.S., at 659.

In response to *Wards Cove* and "a number of [other] recent decisions by the United States Supreme Court that sharply cut back on the scope and effectiveness of [civil rights] laws," Congress enacted the Civil Rights Act of 1991. H. R. Rep. No. 102–40, pt. 2, p. 2 (1991). Among the 1991 alterations, Congress formally codified the disparate-impact component of Title VII. In so amending the statute, Congress made plain its intention to restore "the concepts of 'business necessity' and 'job related' enunciated by the Supreme Court in Griggs v. Duke Power Co. … and in other Supreme Court decisions prior to Wards Cove Packing Co. v. Atonio." §3(2), 105 Stat. 1071. Once a complaining party demonstrates that an employment practice causes a disparate impact, amended Title VII states, the burden is on the employer "to demonstrate that the challenged practice is job related for the position in question and consistent with business necessity." 42 U.S.C. §2000e–2(k)(1)(A)(i). If the employer carries that substantial burden, the complainant may respond by identifying "an alternative employment practice" which the employer "refuses to adopt." §2000e–2(k)(1)(A)(ii), (C).

B

Neither Congress' enactments nor this Court's Title VII precedents (including the now-discredited decision in *Wards Cove*) offer even a hint of "conflict" between an employer's obligations under the statute's disparate-treatment and disparate-impact provisions. Cf. *ante*, at 20. Standing on an equal footing, these twin pillars of Title VII advance the same objectives: ending workplace discrimination and promoting genuinely equal opportunity. See *McDonnell Douglas Corp.* v. *Green*, 411 U.S. 792, 800 (1973) .

Yet the Court today sets at odds the statute's core directives. When an employer changes an employment practice in an effort to comply with Title VII's disparate-impact provision, the Court reasons, it acts "because of race"—something Title VII's disparate-treatment provision, see §2000e–2(a)(1), generally forbids. *Ante*, at 20. This characterization of an employer's compliance-directed action shows little attention to Congress' design or to the *Griggs* line of cases Congress recognized as pathmarking.

"[O]ur task in interpreting separate provisions of a single Act is to give the Act the most harmonious, comprehensive meaning possible in light of the legislative policy and purpose." *Weinberger* v. *Hynson, Westcott & Dunning, Inc.*, 412 U.S. 609, 631–632 (1973) (internal quotation marks omitted). A particular phrase need not "extend to the outer limits of its definitional possibilities" if an incongruity would result. *Dolan* v. *Postal Service*, 546 U.S. 481, 486 (2006) . Here, Title VII's disparate-treatment and disparate-impact proscriptions must be read as complementary.

In codifying the *Griggs* and *Albemarle* instructions, Congress declared unambiguously that selection criteria operating to the disadvantage of minority group members can be retained only if justified by business necessity.[5] In keeping with Congress' design, employers who reject such criteria due to reasonable doubts about their reliability can hardly be held to have engaged in discrimination "because of" race. A reasonable endeavor to comply with the law and to ensure that qualified candidates of all races have a fair opportunity to compete is simply not what Congress meant to interdict. I would therefore hold that an employer who jettisons a selection device when its disproportionate racial impact becomes apparent does not violate Title VII's disparate-treatment bar automatically or at all, subject to this key condition: The employer must have good cause to believe the device would not withstand examination for business necessity. Cf. *Faragher* v. *Boca Raton*, 524 U.S. 775, 806 (1998) (observing that it accords with "clear statutory policy" for employers "to prevent violations" and "make reasonable efforts to discharge their duty" under Title VII).

EEOC's interpretative guidelines are corroborative. "[B]y the enactment of title VII," the guidelines state, "Congress did not intend to expose those who comply with the Act to charges that they are violating the very statute they are seeking to implement." 29 CFR §1608.1(a) (2008). Recognizing EEOC's "enforcement responsibility" under Title VII, we have previously accorded the Commission's position respectful consideration. See, *e.g., Albemarle*, 422 U.S., at 431; *Griggs*, 401 U.S., at 434. Yet the Court today does not so much as mention EEOC's counsel.

Our precedents defining the contours of Title VII's disparate-treatment prohibition further confirm the absence of any intra-statutory discord. In *Johnson* v. *Transportation Agency, Santa Clara Cty.*, 480 U.S. 616 (1987) , we upheld a municipal employer's voluntary affirmative-action plan against a disparate-treatment challenge. Pursuant to the plan, the employer selected a woman for a road-dispatcher position, a job category traditionally regarded as "male." A male applicant who had a slightly higher interview score brought suit under Title VII. This Court rejected his claim and approved the plan, which allowed consideration of gender as "one of numerous factors." *Id.*, at 638. Such consideration, we said, is "fully consistent with Title VII" because plans of that order can aid "in eliminating the vestiges of discrimination in the workplace." *Id.*, at 642.

This litigation does not involve affirmative action. But if the voluntary affirmative action at issue in *Johnson* does not discriminate within the meaning of Title VII, neither does an employer's reasonable effort to comply with Title VII's disparate-impact provision by refrain- ing from action of doubtful consistency with business necessity.

C

To "reconcile" the supposed "conflict" between disparate treatment and disparate impact, the Court offers an enigmatic standard. *Ante*, at 20. Employers may attempt to comply with Title VII's disparate-impact provision, the Court declares, only where there is a "strong basis in evidence" documenting the necessity of their action. *Ante*, at 22. The Court's standard, drawn from inapposite equal protection precedents, is not elaborated. One is left to wonder what cases would meet the standard and why the Court is so sure this case does not.

1

In construing Title VII, I note preliminarily, equal protection doctrine is of limited utility. The Equal Protection Clause, this Court has held, prohibits only intentional discrimination; it does not have a disparate-impact component. See *Personnel Administrator of Mass.* v. *Feeney*, 442 U.S. 256, 272 (1979) ; *Washington* v. *Davis*, 426 U.S. 229, 239 (1976) . Title VII, in contrast, aims to eliminate all forms of employment discrimination, unintentional as well as deliberate. Until today, cf. *ante*, at 25; *ante*, p. 1 (Scalia, J., concurring), this Court has never questioned the constitutionality of the disparate-impact component of Title VII, and for good reason. By instructing employers to avoid needlessly exclusionary selection processes, Title VII's disparate-impact provision calls for a "race-neutral means to increase minority ... participation"— something this Court's equal protection precedents also encourage. See *Adarand Constructors, Inc.* v. *Peña*, 515 U.S. 200, 238 (1995) (quoting *Richmond* v. *J. A. Croson Co.*, 488 U.S. 469, 507 (1989)). "The very radicalism of holding disparate impact doctrine unconstitutional as a matter of equal protection," moreover, "suggests that only a very uncompromising court would issue such a decision." Primus, Equal Protection and Disparate Impact: Round Three, 117 Harv. L.Rev. 493, 585 (2003).

The cases from which the Court draws its strong-basis-in-evidence standard are particularly inapt; they concern the constitutionality of absolute racial preferences. See *Wygant* v. *Jackson Bd. of Ed.*, 476 U.S. 267, 277 (1986) (plurality opinion) (invalidating a school district's plan to lay off nonminority teachers while retaining minority teachers with less seniority); *Croson*, 488 U.S., at 499–500 (rejecting a set-aside program for minority contractors that operated as "an unyielding racial quota"). An employer's effort to avoid Title VII liability by repudiating a suspect selection method scarcely resembles those cases. Race was not merely a relevant consideration in *Wygant* and *Croson;* it was the decisive factor. Observance of Title VII's disparate-impact provision, in contrast, calls for no racial preference, absolute or otherwise. The very purpose of the provision is to ensure that individuals are hired and promoted based on qualifications manifestly necessary to successful performance of the job in question, qualifications that do not screen out members of any race.[6]

2

The Court's decision in this litigation underplays a dominant Title VII theme. This Court has repeatedly emphasized that the statute "should not be read to thwart" efforts at voluntary compliance. *Johnson*, 480 U.S., at 630. Such compliance, we have explained, is "the preferred means of achieving [Title VII's] objectives." *Firefighters* v. *Cleveland*, 478 U.S. 501, 515 (1986) . See also *Kolstad* v. *American Dental Assn.*, 527 U.S. 526, 545 (1999) ("Dissuading employers from [taking voluntary action] to prevent discrimination in the workplace is directly contrary to the purposes underlying Title VII."); 29 CFR §1608.1(c). The strong-basis-in-evidence standard, however, as barely described in general, and cavalierly applied in this case, makes voluntary compliance a hazardous venture.

As a result of today's decision, an employer who discards a dubious selection process can anticipate costly disparate-treatment litigation in which its chances for success—even for surviving a summary-judgment motion—are highly problematic. Concern about exposure to disparate-impact liability, however well grounded, is insufficient to insulate an employer from attack. Instead, the employer must make a "strong" showing that (1) its selection method was "not job related and consistent with business necessity," or (2) that it refused to adopt "an equally valid, less-discriminatory alternative." *Ante*, at 28. It is hard to see how these requirements differ from demanding that an employer establish "a provable, actual violation" *against itself.* Cf. *ante*, at 24. There is indeed a sharp conflict here, but it is not the false one the Court describes between Title VII's core provisions. It is, instead, the discordance of the Court's opinion with the voluntary compliance ideal. Cf. *Wygant*, 476 U.S., at 290 (O'Connor, J., concurring in part and concurring in judgment) ("The imposition of a requirement that public employers make findings that they have engaged in illegal discrimina- tion before they [act] would severely undermine public employers' incentive to meet voluntarily their civil rights obligations.").[7]

3

The Court's additional justifications for announcing a strong-basis-in-evidence standard are unimpressive. First, discarding the results of tests, the Court suggests, calls for a heightened standard because it "upset[s] an employee's legitimate expectation." *Ante*, at 25. This rationale puts the cart before the horse. The legitimacy of an employee's expectation depends on the legitimacy of the selection method. If an employer reasonably concludes that an exam fails to identify the most qualified individuals and needlessly shuts out a segment of the applicant pool, Title VII surely does not compel the employer to hire or promote based on the test, however unreliable it may be. Indeed, the statute's prime objective is to prevent exclusionary practices from "operat[ing] to 'freeze' the status quo." *Griggs*, 401 U. S., at 430.

Second, the Court suggests, anything less than a strong-basis-in-evidence standard risks creating "a *de facto* quota system, in which ... an employer could discard test results ... with the intent of obtaining the employer's preferred racial balance." *Ante*, at 22. Under a reasonableness standard, however, an employer could not cast aside a selection method based on a statistical disparity alone.[8] The employer must have good cause to believe that the method screens out qualified applicants and would be difficult to justify as grounded in business necessity. Should an employer repeatedly reject test results, it would be fair, I agree, to infer that the employer is simply seeking a racially balanced outcome and is not genuinely endeavoring to comply with Title VII.

D

The Court stacks the deck further by denying respondents any chance to satisfy the newly announced strong-basis-in-evidence standard. When this Court formulates a new legal rule, the ordinary course is to remand and allow the lower courts to apply the rule in the first instance. See, *e.g.*, *Johnson* v. *California*, 543 U.S. 499, 515 (2005) ; *Pullman-Standard* v. *Swint*, 456 U.S. 273, 291 (1982) . I see no good reason why the Court fails to follow that course in this case. Indeed, the sole basis for the Court's peremptory ruling is the demonstrably false pretension that respondents showed "nothing more" than "a significant statistical disparity." *Ante*, at 27–28; see *supra*, at 24, n.8. [9]

III

A

Applying what I view as the proper standard to the record thus far made, I would hold that New Haven had ample cause to believe its selection process was flawed and not justified by business necessity. Judged by that standard, petitioners have not shown that New Haven's failure to certify the exam results violated Title VII's disparate-treatment provision.[10]

The City, all agree, "was faced with a prima facie case of disparate-impact liability," *ante*, at 27: The pass rate for minority candidates was half the rate for nonminority candidates, and virtually no minority candidates would have been eligible for promotion had the exam results been certified. Alerted to this stark disparity, the CSB heard expert and lay testimony, presented at public hearings, in an endeavor to ascertain whether the exams were fair and consistent with business necessity. Its investigation revealed grave cause for concern about the exam process itself and the City's failure to consider alternative selection devices.

Chief among the City's problems was the very nature of the tests for promotion. In choosing to use written and oral exams with a 60/40 weighting, the City simply adhered to the union's preference and apparently gave no consideration to whether the weighting was likely to identify the most qualified fire-officer candidates.[11] There is strong reason to think it was not.

Relying heavily on written tests to select fire officers is a questionable practice, to say the least. Successful fire officers, the City's description of the position makes clear, must have the "[a]bility to lead personnel effectively, maintain discipline, promote harmony, exercise sound judgment, and cooperate with other officials." CA2 App. A432. These qualities are not well measured by written tests. Testifying before the CSB, Christopher Hornick, an exam-design expert with more than two decades of relevant experience, was emphatic on this point: Leadership skills, command presence, and the like "could have been identified and evaluated in a much more appropriate way." *Id.*, at A1042–A1043.

Hornick's commonsense observation is mirrored in case law and in Title VII's administrative guidelines. Courts have long criticized written firefighter promotion exams for being "more probative of the test-taker's ability to recall what a particular text stated on a given topic than of his firefighting or supervisory knowledge and abilities." *Vulcan Pioneers, Inc.* v. *New Jersey Dept. of Civil Serv.*, 625 F.Supp. 527, 539 (NJ 1985). A fire officer's job, courts have observed, "involves complex behaviors, good interpersonal skills, the ability to make decisions under tremendous pressure, and a host of other abilities—none of which is easily measured by a written, multiple choice test." *Firefighters Inst. for Racial Equality* v. *St.Louis*, 616 F.2d 350, 359 (CA8 1980).[12] Interpreting the Uniform Guidelines, EEOC and other federal agencies responsible for enforcing equal opportunity employment laws have similarly recognized that, as measures of "interpersonal relations" or "ability to function under danger (*e.g.*, firefighters)," "[p]encil-and-paper tests ... generally are not close enough approximations of work behaviors to show content validity." 44 Fed. Reg. 12007 (1979). See also 29 CFR §1607.15(C)(4).[13]

Given these unfavorable appraisals, it is unsurprising that most municipal employers do not evaluate their fire-officer candidates as New Haven does. Although comprehensive statistics are scarce, a 1996 study found that nearly two-thirds of surveyed municipalities used assessment centers ("simulations of the real world of work") as part of their promotion processes. P. Lowry, A Survey of the Assessment Center Process in the Public Sector, 25 Public Personnel Management 307, 315 (1996). That figure represented a marked increase over the previous decade, see *ibid.*, so the percentage today may well be even higher. Among municipalities still relying in part on written exams, the median weight assigned to them was 30 percent—half the weight given to New Haven's written exam. *Id.*, at 309.

Testimony before the CSB indicated that these alternative methods were both more reliable and notably less discriminatory in operation. According to Donald Day of the International Association of Black Professional Firefighters, nearby Bridgeport saw less skewed results after switching to a selection process that placed primary weight on an oral exam. CA2 App. A830–A832; see *supra*, at 7–8. And Hornick described assessment centers as "demonstrat[ing] dramatically less adverse impacts" than written exams. CA2 App. A1040.[14] Considering the prevalence of these proven alternatives, New Haven was poorly positioned to argue that promotions based on its outmoded and exclusionary selection process qualified as a business necessity. Cf. *Robinson* v. *Lorillard Corp.*, 444 F.2d 791, 798, n. 7 (CA4 1971) ("It should go without saying that a practice is hardly 'necessary' if an alternative practice better effectuates its intended purpose or is equally effective but less discriminatory.").[15]

Ignoring the conceptual and other defects in New Haven's selection process, the Court describes the exams as "painstaking[ly]" developed to test "relevant" material and on that basis finds no substantial risk of disparate-impact liability. See *ante*, at 28. Perhaps such reasoning would have sufficed under *Wards Cove*, which permitted exclusionary practices as long as they advanced an employer's "legitimate" goals. 490 U.S., at 659. But Congress repudiated *Wards Cove* and reinstated the "business necessity" rule attended by a "manifest relationship" requirement. See *Griggs*, 401 U.S., at 431–432. See also *supra*, at 17. Like the chess player who tries to win by sweeping the opponent's pieces off the table, the Court simply shuts from its sight the formidable obstacles New Haven would have faced in defending against a disparate-impact suit. See *Lanning* v. *Southeastern Pa. Transp. Auth.*, 181 F.3d 478, 489 (CA3 1999) ("Judicial application of a standard focusing solely on whether the qualities measured by an ... exam bear some relationship to the job in question would impermissibly write out the business necessity prong of the Act's chosen standard.").

That IOS representative Chad Legel and his team may have been diligent in designing the exams says little about the exams' suitability for selecting fire officers. IOS worked within the City's constraints. Legel never discussed with the City the propriety of the 60/40 weighting and "was not asked to consider the possibility of an assessment center." CA2 App. A522. See also *id.*, at A467. The IOS exams, Legel admitted, had not even attempted to assess "command presence":

"[Y]ou would probably be better off with an assessment center if you cared to measure that." *Id.*, at A521. Cf. *Boston Chapter, NAACP* v. *Beecher*, 504 F.2d 1017, 1021–1022 (CA1 1974) ("A test fashioned from materials pertaining to the job ... superficially may seem job-related. But what is at issue is whether it demonstrably selects people who will perform better the required on-the-job behaviors.").

In addition to the highly questionable character of the exams and the neglect of available alternatives, the City had other reasons to worry about its vulnerability to disparate-impact liability. Under the City's ground rules, IOS was not allowed to show the exams to anyone in the New Haven Fire Department prior to their administration. This "precluded [IOS] from being able to engage in [its] normal subject matter expert review process"—something Legel described as "very critical." CA2 App. A477, A506. As a result, some of the exam questions were confusing or irrelevant, and the exams may have over-tested some subject-matter areas while missing others. See, *e.g.*, *id.*, at A1034–A1035, A1051. Testimony before the CSB also raised questions concerning unequal access to study materials, see *id.*, at A857–A861, and the potential bias introduced by relying principally on job analyses from nonminority fire officers to develop the exams, see *id.*, at A1063–A1064.[16] See also *supra*, at 7, 10.

The Court criticizes New Haven for failing to obtain a "technical report" from IOS, which, the Court maintains, would have provided "detailed information to establish the validity of the exams." *Ante*, at 29. The record does not substantiate this assertion. As Legel testified during his deposition, the technical report merely summarized "the steps that [IOS] took methodologically speaking," and would not have established the exams' reliability. CA2 App. A461. See also *id.*, at A462 (the report "doesn't say anything that other documents that already existed wouldn't say").

In sum, the record solidly establishes that the City had good cause to fear disparate-impact liability. Moreover, the Court supplies no tenable explanation why the evidence of the tests' multiple deficiencies does not create at least a triable issue under a strong-basis-in-evidence standard.

B

Concurring in the Court's opinion, Justice Alito asserts that summary judgment for respondents would be improper even if the City had good cause for its noncertification decision. A reasonable jury, he maintains, could have found that respondents were not actually motivated by concern about disparate-impact litigation, but instead sought only "to placate a politically important [African-American] constituency." *Ante*, at 3. As earlier noted, I would not oppose a remand for further proceedings fair to both sides. See *supra*, at 26, n. 10. It is the Court that has chosen to short-circuit this litigation based on its pretension that the City has shown, and can show, nothing more than a statistical disparity. See *supra*, at 24, n.8, 25. Justice Alito compounds the Court's error.

Offering a truncated synopsis of the many hours of deliberations undertaken by the CSB, Justice Alito finds evidence suggesting that respondents' stated desire to comply with Title VII was insincere, a mere "pretext" for discrimination against white firefighters. *Ante*, at 2–3. In support of his assertion, Justice Alito recounts at length the alleged machinations of Rev. Boise Kimber (a local political activist), Mayor John DeStefano, and certain members of the mayor's staff. See *ante*, at 3–10.

Most of the allegations Justice Alito repeats are drawn from petitioners' statement of facts they deem undisputed, a statement displaying an adversarial zeal not uncommonly found in such presentations.[17] What cannot credibly be denied, however, is that the decision against certification of the exams was made neither by Kimber nor by the mayor and his staff. The relevant decision was made by the CSB, an unelected, politically insulated body. It is striking that Justice Alito's concurrence says hardly a word about the CSB itself, perhaps because there is scant evidence that its motivation was anything other than to comply with Title VII's disparate-impact provision. Notably, petitioners did not even seek to take depositions of the two commissioners who voted against certification. Both submitted uncontested affidavits declaring unequivocally that their votes were "based solely on [their] good faith belief that certification" would have discriminated against minority candidates in violation of federal law. CA2 App. A1605, A1611.

Justice Alito discounts these sworn statements, suggesting that the CSB's deliberations were tainted by the preferences of Kimber and City officials, whether or not the CSB itself was aware of the taint. Kimber and City officials, Justice Alito speculates, decided early on to oppose certification and then "engineered" a skewed presentation to the CSB to achieve their preferred outcome. *Ante*, at 12.

As an initial matter, Justice Alito exaggerates the influence of these actors. The CSB, the record reveals, designed and conducted an inclusive decisionmaking process, in which it heard from numerous individuals on both sides of the certification question. See, *e.g.*, CA2 App. A1090. Kimber and others no doubt used strong words to urge the CSB not to certify the exam results, but the CSB received "pressure" from supporters of certification as well as opponents. Cf. *ante*, at 6. Petitioners, for example, engaged counsel to speak on their behalf before the CSB. Their counsel did not mince words: "[I]f you discard these results," she warned, "you will get sued. You will force the taxpayers of the city of New Haven into protracted litigation." CA2 App. A816. See also *id.*, at A788.

The local firefighters union—an organization required by law to represent all the City's firefighters—was similarly outspoken in favor of certification. Discarding the test results, the union's president told the CSB, would be "totally ridiculous." *Id.*, at A806. He insisted, inaccurately, that the City was not at risk of disparate-impact liability because the exams were administered pursuant to "a collective bargaining agreement." *Id.*, at A1137. Cf. *supra*, at 26–27, n.11. Never mentioned by Justice Alito in his attempt to show testing expert Christopher Hornick's alliance with the City, *ante*, at 8–9, the CSB solicited Hornick's testimony at the union's suggestion, not the City's. CA2 App. A1128. Hornick's cogent

18

testimony raised substantial doubts about the exams' reliability. See *supra*, at 8–10.

There is scant cause to suspect that maneuvering or overheated rhetoric, from either side, prevented the CSB from evenhandedly assessing the reliability of the exams and rendering an independent, good-faith decision on certification. Justice Alito acknowledges that the CSB had little patience for Kimber's antics. *Ante*, at 6–7.[19] As to petitioners, Chairman Segaloff—who voted to certify the exam results—dismissed the threats made by their counsel as unhelpful and needlessly "inflammatory." CA2 App. A821. Regarding the views expressed by City officials, the CSB made clear that they were entitled to no special weight. *Id.*, at A1080.[20]

In any event, Justice Alito's analysis contains a more fundamental flaw: It equates political considerations with unlawful discrimination. As Justice Alito sees it, if the mayor and his staff were motivated by their desire "to placate a … racial constituency," *ante*, at 3, then they engaged in unlawful discrimination against petitioners. But Justice Alito fails to ask a vital question: "[P]lacate" how? That political officials would have politics in mind is hardly extraordinary, and there are many ways in which a politician can attempt to win over a constituency—including a racial constituency—without engaging in unlawful discrimination. As courts have recognized, "[p]oliticians routinely respond to bad press … , but it is not a violation of Title VII to take advantage of a situation to gain political favor." *Henry* v. *Jones*, 507 F.3d 558, 567 (CA7 2007).

The real issue, then, is not whether the mayor and his staff were politically motivated; it is whether their attempt to score political points was legitimate (*i.e.*, nondiscriminatory). Were they seeking to exclude white firefighters from promotion (unlikely, as a fair test would undoubtedly result in the addition of white firefighters to the officer ranks), or did they realize, at least belatedly, that their tests could be toppled in a disparate-impact suit? In the latter case, there is no disparate-treatment violation. Justice Alito, I recognize, would disagree. In his view, an employer's action to avoid Title VII disparate-impact liability qualifies as a presumptively improper race-based employment decision. See *ante*, at 2. I reject that construction of Title VII. See *supra*, at 18–20. As I see it, when employers endeavor to avoid exposure to disparate-impact liability, they do not thereby encounter liability for disparate treatment.

Applying this understanding of Title VII, supported by *Griggs* and the long line of decisions following *Griggs*, see *supra*, at 16–17, and nn. 3–4, the District Court found no genuine dispute of material fact. That court noted, particularly, the guidance furnished by Second Circuit precedent. See *supra*, at 12. Petitioners' allegations that City officials took account of politics, the District Court determined, simply "d[id] not suffice" to create an inference of unlawful discrimination. 554 F.Supp. 2d, at 160, n.12. The noncertification decision, even if undertaken "in a political context," reflected a legitimate "intent not to implement a promotional process based on testing results that had an adverse impact." *Id.*, at 158, 160. Indeed, the District Court perceived "a total absence of any evidence of discriminatory animus towards [petitioners]." *Id.*, at 158. See also *id.*, at 162 ("Nothing in the record in this case suggests that the City defendants or CSB acted 'because of' discriminatory animus toward [petitioners] or other non-minority applicants for promotion."). Perhaps the District Court could have been more expansive in its discussion of these issues, but its conclusions appear entirely consistent with the record before it.[21]

It is indeed regrettable that the City's noncertification decision would have required all candidates to go through another selection process. But it would have been more regrettable to rely on flawed exams to shut out candidates who may well have the command presence and other qualities needed to excel as fire officers. Yet that is the choice the Court makes today. It is a choice that breaks the promise of *Griggs* that groups long denied equal opportunity would not be held back by tests "fair in form, but discriminatory in operation." 401 U.S., at 431.

* * *

This case presents an unfortunate situation, one New Haven might well have avoided had it utilized a better selection process in the first place. But what this case does not present is race-based discrimination in violation of Title VII. I dissent from the Court's judgment, which rests on the false premise that respondents showed "a significant statistical disparity," but "nothing more." See *ante*, at 27–28.

NOTES

[1] Never mind the flawed tests New Haven used and the better selection methods used elsewhere, Justice Alito's concurring opinion urges. Overriding all else, racial politics, fired up by a strident African-American pastor, were at work in New Haven. See *ante*, at 4–9. Even a detached and disinterested observer, however, would have every reason to ask: Why did such racially skewed results occur in New Haven, when better tests likely would have produced less disproportionate results?

[2] The Court's disparate-impact analysis rested on two provisions of Title VII: §703(a)(2), which made it unlawful for an employer "to limit, segregate, or classify his employees in any way which would deprive or tend to deprive any individual of employment opportunities or otherwise adversely affect his status as an employee, because of such individual's race, color, religion, sex, or national origin"; and §703(h), which permitted employers "to act upon the results of any professionally developed ability

test provided that such test, its administration or action upon the results is not designed, intended or used to discriminate because of race, color, religion, sex or national origin." Griggs v. Duke Power Co., 401 U.S. 424, 426, n. 1 (1971) (quoting 78 Stat.255, 42 U.S.C. §2000e–2(a)(2), (h) (1964 ed.)). See also 401 U.S., at 433–436 (explaining that §703(h) authorizes only tests that are "demonstrably a reasonable measure of job performance").

3 See also Dothard v. Rawlinson, 433 U.S. 321, 332, n. 14 (1977) ("a discriminatory employment practice must be shown to be necessary to safe and efficient job performance to survive a Title VII challenge"); Williams v. Colorado Springs, Colo., School Dist., 641 F.2d 835, 840–841 (CA10 1981) ("The term 'necessity' connotes that the exclusionary practice must be shown to be of great importance to job performance."); Kirby v. Colony Furniture Co., 613 F.2d 696, 705, n. 6 (CA8 1980) ("the proper standard for determining whether 'business necessity' justifies a practice which has a racially discriminatory result is not whether it is justified by routine business considerations but whether there is a compelling need for the employer to maintain that practice and whether the employer can prove there is no alternative to the challenged practice"); Pettway v. American Cast Iron Pipe Co., 494 F.2d 211, 244, n. 87 (CA5 1974) ("this doctrine of business necessity ... connotes an irresistible demand" (internal quotation marks omitted)); United States v. Bethlehem Steel Corp., 446 F.2d 652, 662 (CA2 1971) (an exclusionary practice "must not only directly foster safety and efficiency of a plant, but also be essential to those goals"); Robinson v. Lorillard Corp., 444 F.2d 791, 798 (CA4 1971) ("The test is whether there exists an overriding legitimate business purpose such that the practice is necessary to the safe and efficient operation of the business.").

4 See, e.g., Nash v. Jacksonville, 837 F.2d 1534 (CA11 1988), vacated, 490 U.S. 1103 (1989), opinion reinstated, 905 F.2d 355 (CA11 1990); Vulcan Pioneers, Inc. v. New Jersey Dept. of Civil Serv., 832 F.2d 811 (CA3 (1987); Guardians Assn. of N.Y. City Police Dept. v. Civil Serv. Comm'n, 630 F.2d 79 (CA2 1980); Ensley Branch of NAACP v. Seibels, 616 F.2d 812 (CA5 1980); Firefighters Inst. for Racial Equality v. St.Louis, 616 F.2d 350 (CA8 1980); Boston Chapter, NAACP v. Beecher, 504 F.2d 1017 (CA1 1974).

5 What was the "business necessity" for the tests New Haven used? How could one justify, e.g., the 60/40 written/oral ratio, see supra, at 4–5, 7–8, under that standard? Neither the Court nor the concurring opinions attempt to defend the ratio.

6 Even in Title VII cases involving race-conscious (or gender-conscious) affirmative-action plans, the Court has never proposed a strong-basis-in-evidence standard. In Johnson v. Transportation Agency, Santa Clara Cty., 480 U.S. 616 (1987), the Court simply examined the municipal employer's action for reasonableness: "Given the obvious imbalance in the Skilled Craft category, and given the Agency's commitment to eliminating such imbalances, it was plainly not unreasonable for the Agency ... to consider as one factor the sex of [applicants] in making its decision." Id., at 637. See also Firefighters v. Cleveland, 478 U.S. 501, 516 (1986) ("Title VII permits employers and unions voluntarily to make use of reasonable race-conscious affirmative action.").

7 Notably, prior decisions applying a strong-basis-in-evidence standard have not imposed a burden as heavy as the one the Court imposes today. In Croson, the Court found no strong basis in evidence because the City had offered "nothing approaching a prima facie case." Richmond v. J. A. Croson Co., 488 U.S. 469, 500 (1989). The Court did not suggest that anything beyond a prima facie case would have been required. In the context of race-based electoral districting, the Court has indicated that a "strong basis" exists when the "threshold conditions" for liability are present. Bush v. Vera, 517 U.S. 952, 978 (1996) (plurality opinion).

8 Infecting the Court's entire analysis is its insistence that the City rejected the test results "in sole reliance upon race-based statistics." Ante, at 24. See also ante, at 20, 27–28. But as the part of the story the Court leaves out, see supra, at 2–12, so plainly shows—the long history of rank discrimination against African-Americans in the firefighting profession, the multiple flaws in New Haven's test for promotions—"sole reliance" on statistics certainly is not descriptive of the CSB's decision.

9 The Court's refusal to remand for further proceedings also deprives respondents of an opportunity to invoke 42 U.S.C. §2000e–12(b) as a shield to liability. Section 2000e–12(b) provides:

"In any action or proceeding based on any alleged unlawful employment practice, no person shall be subject to any liability or punishment for or on account of (1) the commission by such person of an unlawful employment practice if he pleads and proves that the act or omission complained of was in good faith, in conformity with, and in reliance on any written interpretation or opinion of the [EEOC] … . Such a defense, if established, shall be a bar to the action or proceeding, notwithstanding that (A) after such act or omission, such interpretation or opinion is modified or rescinded or is determined by judicial authority to be invalid or of no legal effect…."

Specifically, given the chance, respondents might have called attention to the EEOC guidelines set out in 29 CFR §§1608.3 and 1608.4 (2008). The guidelines recognize that employers may "take affirmative action based on an analysis which reveals facts constituting actual or potential adverse impact." §1608.3(a). If "affirmative action" is in order, so is the lesser step of discarding a dubious selection device.

[10] The lower courts focused on respondents' "intent" rather than on whether respondents in fact had good cause to act. See 554 F.Supp. 2d 142, 157 (Conn. 2006). Ordinarily, a remand for fresh consideration would be in order. But the Court has seen fit to preclude further proceedings. I therefore explain why, if final adjudication by this Court is indeed appropriate, New Haven should be the prevailing party.

[11] This alone would have posed a substantial problem for New Haven in a disparate-impact suit, particularly in light of the disparate results the City's scheme had produced in the past. See supra, at 7. Under the Uniform Guidelines on Employee Selection Procedures (Uniform Guidelines), employers must conduct "an investigation of suitable alternative selection procedures." 29 CFR §1607.3(B). See also Officers for Justice v. Civil Serv. Comm'n, 979 F.2d 721, 728 (CA9 1992) ("before utilizing a procedure that has an adverse impact on minorities, the City has an obligation pursuant to the Uniform Guidelines to explore alternative procedures and to implement them if they have less adverse impact and are substantially equally valid"). It is no answer to "presume" that the two-decades-old 60/40 formula was adopted for a "rational reason" because it "was the result of a union-negotiated collective bargaining agreement." Cf. ante, at 30. That the parties may have been "rational" says nothing about whether their agreed-upon selection process was consistent with business necessity. It is not at all unusual for agreements negotiated between employers and unions to run afoul of Title VII. See, e.g., Peters v. Missouri-Pacific R.Co., 483 F.2d 490, 497 (CA5 1973) (an employment practice "is not shielded [from the requirements of Title VII] by the facts that it is the product of collective bargaining and meets the standards of fair representation").

[12] See also Nash, 837 F.2d, at 1538 ("the examination did not test the one aspect of job performance that differentiated the job of firefighter engineer from fire lieutenant (combat): supervisory skills"); Firefighters Inst. for Racial Equality v. St.Louis, 549 F.2d 506, 512 (CA8 1977) ("there is no good pen and paper test for evaluating supervisory skills"); Boston Chapter, NAACP, 504 F.2d, at 1023 ("[T]here is a difference between memorizing … fire fighting terminology and being a good fire fighter. If the Boston Red Sox recruited players on the basis of their knowledge of baseball history and vocabulary, the team might acquire [players] who could not bat, pitch or catch.").

[13] Cf. Gillespie v. Wisconsin, 771 F.2d 1035, 1043 (CA7 1985) (courts must evaluate "the degree to which the nature of the examination procedure approximates the job conditions"). In addition to "content validity," the Uniform Guidelines discuss "construct validity" and "criterion validity" as means by which an employer might establish the reliability of a selection method. See 29 CFR §1607.14(B)–(D). Content validity, however, is the only type of validity addressed by the parties and "the only feasible type of validation in these circumstances." Brief for Industrial-Organizational Psychologists as Amicus Curiae 7, n. 2 (hereinafter I-O Psychologists Brief).

14

See also G. Thornton & D. Rupp, Assessment Centers in Human Resource Management 15 (2006) ("Assessment centers predict future success, do not cause adverse impact, and are seen as fair by participants."); W. Cascio & H. Aguinis, Applied Psychology in Human Resource Management 372 (6th ed. 2005) ("research has demonstrated that adverse impact is less of a problem in an [assessment center] as compared to an aptitude test"). Cf. Firefighters Inst. for Racial Equality, 549 F.2d, at 513 (recommending assessment centers as an alternative to written exams).

[15] Finding the evidence concerning these alternatives insufficiently developed to "create a genuine issue of fact," ante, at 32, the Court effectively confirms that an employer cannot prevail under its strong-basis-in-evidence standard unless the employer decisively proves a disparate-impact violation against itself. The Court's specific arguments are unavailing. First, the Court suggests, changing the oral/written weighting may have violated Title VII's prohibition on altering test scores. Ante, at 31. No one is arguing, however, that the results of the exams given should have been altered. Rather, the argument is that the City could have availed itself of a better option when it initially decided what selection process to use. Second, with respect to assessment centers, the Court identifies "statements to the CSB indicat[ing] that the Department could not have used [them] for the 2003 examinations." Ante, at 31–32. The Court comes up with only a single statement on this subject—an offhand remark made by petitioner Ricci, who hardly qualifies as an expert in testing methods. See ante, at 14. Given the large number of municipalities that regularly use assessment centers, it is impossible to fathom why the City, with proper planning, could not have done so as well.

[16] The I-O Psychologists Brief identifies still other, more technical flaws in the exams that may well have precluded the City from prevailing in a disparate-impact suit. Notably, the exams were never shown to be suitably precise to allow strict rank ordering of candidates. A difference of one or two points on a multiple-choice exam should not be decisive of an applicant's promotion chances if that difference bears little relationship to the applicant's qualifications for the job. Relatedly, it appears that the line between a passing and failing score did not accurately differentiate between qualified and unqualified candidates. A number of fire-officer promotional exams have been invalidated on these bases. See, e.g., Guardians Assn., 630 F.2d, at 105 ("When a cutoff score unrelated to job performance produces disparate racial results, Title VII is violated."); Vulcan Pioneers, Inc. v. New Jersey Dept. of Civil Serv., 625 F.Supp. 527, 538 (NJ 1985) ("[T]he tests here at issue are not appropriate for ranking candidates.").

[17] Some of petitioners' so-called facts find little support in the record, and many others can scarcely be deemed material. Petitioners allege, for example, that City officials prevented New Haven's fire chief and assistant chief from sharing their views about the exams with the CSB. App. to Pet. for Cert. in No. 07–1428, p. 228a. None of the materials petitioners cite, however, "suggests" that this proposition is accurate. Cf. ante, at 5. In her deposition testimony, City official Karen Dubois-Walton specifically denied that she or her colleagues directed the chief and assistant chief not to appear. App. to Pet. for Cert. in No. 07–1428, p. 850a. Moreover, contrary to the insinuations of petitioners and Justice Alito, the statements made by City officials before the CSB did not emphasize allegations of cheating by test takers. Cf. ante, at 7–8. In her deposition, Dubois-Walton acknowledged sharing the cheating allegations not with the CSB, but with a different City commission. App. to Pet. for Cert. in No. 07–1428, p. 837a. Justice Alito also reports that the City's attorney advised the mayor's team that the way to convince the CSB not to certify was "to focus on something other than 'a big discussion re: adverse impact' law." Ante, at 8 (quoting App. to Pet. for Cert. in No. 07–1428, p. 458a). This is a misleading abbreviation of the attorney's advice. Focusing on the exams' defects and on disparate-impact law is precisely what he recommended. See id., at 458a–459a.

[18] City officials, Justice Alito reports, sent Hornick newspaper accounts and other material about the exams prior to his testimony. Ante, at 8. Some of these materials, Justice Alito intimates, may have given Hornick an inaccurate portrait of the exams. But Hornick's testimony before the CSB, viewed in full, indicates that Hornick had an accurate understanding of the exam process. Much of Hornick's analysis focused on the 60/40 weighting of the written and oral exams, something that neither the Court nor the concurrences even attempt to defend. It is, moreover, entirely misleading to say that the City later hired union-proposed Hornick as a "rewar[d]" for his testimony. Cf. Ante, at 9.

[19] To be clear, the Board of Fire Commissioners on which Kimber served is an entity separate from the CSB. Kimber was not a member of the CSB. Kimber, Justice Alito states, requested a private meeting with the CSB. Ante, at 6. There is not a shred of evidence that a private meeting with Kimber

or anyone else took place.

[20] Justice Alito points to evidence that the mayor had decided not to make promotions based on the exams even if the CSB voted to certify the results, going so far as to prepare a press release to that effect. Ante, at 9. If anything, this evidence reinforces the conclusion that the CSB—which made the noncertification decision—remained independent and above the political fray. The mayor and his staff needed a contingency plan precisely because they did not control the CSB.

[21] The District Court, Justice Alito writes, "all but conceded that a jury could find that the City's asserted justification was pretextual" by "admitt[ing] that 'a jury could rationally infer that city officials worked behind the scenes to sabotage the promotional examinations because they knew that, were the exams certified, the Mayor would incur the wrath of [Rev. Boise] Kimber and other influential leaders of New Haven's African-American community.' " Ante, at 3, 13 (quoting 554 F. Supp. 2d, at 162). The District Court drew the quoted passage from petitioners' lower court brief, and used it in reference to a First Amendment claim not before this Court. In any event, it is not apparent why these alleged political maneuvers suggest an intent to discriminate against petitioners. That City officials may have wanted to please political supporters is entirely consistent with their stated desire to avoid a disparate-impact violation. Cf. Ashcroft v. Iqbal, 556 U. S. ___, ___ (2009) (slip op., at 18) (allegations that senior Government officials condoned the arrest and detention of thousands of Arab Muslim men following the September 11 attacks failed to establish even a "plausible inference" of unlawful discrimination sufficient to survive a motion to dismiss).

BURLINGTON NORTHERN & SANTA FE RAILWAY CO., et al. v. UNITED STATES, et al. /// SHELL OIL CO. v. UNITED STATES

No. 07-1601 & 07-1607, May 4, 2009

ON WRITS OF CERTIORARI TO THE UNITED STATES COURT OF APPEALS FOR THE NINTH CIRCUIT

Justice Ginsburg, dissenting.

Although the question is close, I would uphold the determinations of the courts below that Shell qualifies as an arranger within the compass of the Comprehensive Environmental Response, Compensation and Liability Act (CERCLA). See 42 U.S.C. §9607(a)(3). As the facts found by the District Court bear out, App. to Pet. for Cert. in No. 07–1601, pp. 113a–129a, 208a–213a, Shell "arranged for disposal ... of hazardous substances" owned by Shell when the arrangements were made.[1]

In the 1950's and early 1960's, Shell shipped most of its products to Brown and Bryant (B&B) in 55-gallon drums, thereby ensuring against spillage or leakage during delivery and transfer. *Id.,* at 89a, 115a. Later, Shell found it economically advantageous, in lieu of shipping in drums, to require B&B to maintain bulk storage facilities for receipt of the chemicals B&B purchased from Shell. *Id.,* at 115a. By the mid-1960's, Shell was delivering its chemical to B&B in bulk tank truckloads. *Id.,* at 89a, 115a. As the Court recognizes, "bulk storage of the chemical led to numerous tank failures and spills as the chemical rusted tanks and eroded valves." *Ante,* at 2–3, n.1.

Shell furthermore specified the equipment to be used in transferring the chemicals from the delivery truck to B&B's storage tanks. App. to Pet. for Cert. in No. 07–1601, pp. 120a–122a, 124a.[2] In the process, spills and leaks were inevitable, indeed spills occurred every time deliveries were made. 520 F.3d 918, 950–951 (CA9 2008). See also App. to Pet. for Cert. in No. 07–1601, pp. 119a–122a ("It is undisputed that spills were inherent in the delivery process that Shell arranged ....").

That Shell sold B&B useful products, the Ninth Circuit observed, did not exonerate Shell from CERCLA liability, for the sales "necessarily and immediately result[ed] in the leakage of hazardous substances." 520 F.3d, at 950. The deliveries, Shell was well aware, directly and routinely resulted in disposals of hazardous substances (through spills and leaks) for more than 20 years. "[M]ere knowledge" may not be enough, *ante,* at 13, but Shell did not simply know of the spills and leaks without contributing to them. Given the control rein held by Shell over the mode of delivery and transfer, 520 F.3d, at 950–951, the lower courts held and I agree, Shell was properly ranked an arranger. Relieving Shell of any obligation to pay for the cleanup undertaken by the United States and California is hardly commanded by CERCLA's text, and is surely at odds with CERCLA's objective—to place the cost of remediation on persons whose activities contributed to the contamination rather than on the taxpaying public.

As to apportioning costs, the District Court undertook an heroic labor. The Railroads and Shell, the court noted, had pursued a "'scorched earth,' all-or-nothing approach to liability. Neither acknowledged an iota of responsibility .... Neither party offered helpful arguments to apportion liability." App. to Pet. for Cert. in No. 07–1601, p. 236a, ¶455. Consequently, the court strived "independently [to] perform [an] equitable apportionment analysis." *Id.,* at 237a, ¶455. Given the party presentation principle basic to our procedural system, *Greenlaw* v. *United States,* 554 U.S. ___, ___ (2008) (slip op., at 5), it is questionable whether the court should have pursued the matter *sua sponte.* See *Castro* v. *United States,* 540 U.S. 375, 386 (2003) (Scalia, J., concurring) ("Our adversary system is designed around the premise that the parties know what is best for them, and are responsible for advancing the facts and arguments entitling them to relief."). Cf. Kaplan, von Mehren, & Schaefer, Phases of German Civil Procedure I, 71 Harv. L.Rev. 1193, 1224 (1958) (describing court's obligation, under Germany's Code of Civil Procedure, to see to it that the case is fully developed).

The trial court's mode of procedure, the United States urged before this Court, "deprived the government of a fair opportunity to respond to the court's theories of apportionment and to rebut their factual underpinnings—an opportunity the governmen[t] would have had if those theories had been advanced by petitioners themselves." Brief for United States 41.[3] I would return these cases to the District Court to give all parties a fair opportunity to address that court's endeavor to allocate costs. Because the Court's disposition precludes that opportunity, I dissent from the Court's judgment.

NOTES

[1] "Disposal" is defined in 42 U.S.C. §6903(3) to include "spilling [or] leaking" of "any ... hazardous waste into or on any land or water so that [the] ... hazardous waste or any constituent thereof may

enter the environment or be emitted into the air or discharged into any waters."

[2] Shell shipped the chemicals to B&B "F.O.B. Destination." At oral argument, the Court asked Shell's counsel: Suppose there had been "no transfer of ownership until the delivery [was] complete?" In that event, counsel responded, "Shell would have been the owner of the waste." Tr. of Oral Arg. 8. The Court credits the fact that at the time of the spills, the chemicals, having been shipped "F.O.B. Destination," "had come under B&B's stewardship." Ante, at 12. In my view, CERCLA liability, or the absence thereof, should not turn, in any part, on such an eminently shipper-fixable specification as "F.O.B. Destination."

[3] For example, on brief, the United States observed: "[P]etitioners identify no record support for the district court's assumption that each party's contribution to the overall harm is proportional to the relative volume of hazardous substances attributable to it." Brief for United States 45. And at oral argument, counsel for the United States stressed that the District Court "framed the relevant inquiry as what percentage of the contamination was attributable to the railroad parcel, to the Shell-controlled deliveries, and to the B&B parcel. But it made no finding ... as to what the cost of [remediation] would have been ... if the only source of contamination had been the railroad parcel." Tr. of Oral Arg. 52. See also id., at 56 ("[T]he crucial question is what response costs the government would have been required to bear ... if only the railroad parcel's contamination had been at issue ....").

COEUR ALASKA, INC. v. SOUTHEAST ALASKA CONSERVATION COUNCIL, et al. /// ALASKA v. SOUTHEAST ALASKA CONSERVATION COUNCIL, et al.

NoS. 07-984 & 07-990, June 22, 2009

ON WRITS OF CERTIORARI TO THE UNITED STATES COURT OF APPEALS FOR THE NINTH CIRCUIT

Justice Ginsburg, with whom Justice Stevens and Justice Souter join, dissenting.

Petitioner Coeur Alaska, Inc., proposes to discharge 210,000 gallons per day of mining waste into Lower Slate Lake, a 23-acre subalpine lake in Tongass National Forest. The "tailings slurry" would contain concentrations of aluminum, copper, lead, and mercury. Over the life of the mine, roughly 4.5 million tons of solid tailings would enter the lake, raising the bottom elevation by 50 feet. It is undisputed that the discharge would kill all of the lake's fish and nearly all of its other aquatic life.[1]

Coeur Alaska's proposal is prohibited by the Environmental Protection Agency (EPA) performance standard forbidding any discharge of process wastewater from new "froth-flotation" mills into waters of the United States. See 40 CFR §440.104(b)(1) (2008). Section 306 of the Clean Water Act directs EPA to promulgate such performance standards, 33 U.S.C. §1316(a), and declares it unlawful for any discharger to violate them, §1316(e). Ordinarily, that would be the end of the inquiry.

Coeur Alaska contends, however, that its discharge is not subject to EPA's regulatory regime, but is governed, instead, by the mutually exclusive permitting authority of the Army Corps of Engineers. The Corps has authority, under §404 of the Act, §1344(a), to issue permits for discharges of "dredged or fill material." By regulation, a discharge that has the effect of raising a water body's bottom elevation qualifies as "fill material." See 33 CFR §323.2(e) (2008). Discharges properly within the Corps' permitting authority, it is undisputed, are not subject to EPA performance standards. See *ante*, at 20; Brief for Petitioner Coeur Alaska 26; Brief for Respondent Southeast Alaska Conservation Council etal. 37.

The litigation before the Court thus presents a single question: Is a pollutant discharge prohibited under §306 of the Act eligible for a §404 permit as a discharge of fill material? In agreement with the Court of Appeals, I would answer no. The statute's text, structure, and purpose all mandate adherence to EPA pollution-control requirements. A discharge covered by a performance standard must be authorized, if at all, by EPA.

I

A

Congress enacted the Clean Water Act in 1972 "to restore and maintain the chemical, physical, and biological integrity" of the waters of the United States. 33 U.S.C. §1251(a). "The use of any river, lake, stream or ocean as a waste treatment system," the Act's drafters stated, "is unacceptable." S.Rep. No. 92–414, p.7 (1971). Congress announced in the Act itself an ambitious objective: to eliminate, by 1985, the discharge of all pollutants into the Nation's navigable waters. 33 U.S.C. §1251(a).

In service of its goals, Congress issued a core command: "[T]he discharge of any pollutant by any person shall be unlawful," except in compliance with the Act's terms. §1311(a). The Act's substantive requirements—housed primarily in Subchapter III, "Standards and Enforcement"—establish "a comprehensive regulatory program supervised by an expert administrative agency," EPA. *Milwaukee* v. *Illinois*, 451 U.S. 304, 317 (1981) . See also 33 U.S.C. §1251(d) ("Except as otherwise expressly provided…, the Administrator of [EPA] shall administer this [Act].").

The Act instructs EPA to establish various technology-based, increasingly stringent effluent limitations for categories of point sources. *E.g.*, §§1311, 1314. These limitations, formulated as restrictions "on quantities, rates, and concentrations of chemical, physical, biological, and other constituents," §1362(11), were imposed to achieve national uniformity among categories of sources. See, *e.g.* *E.l. du Pont de Nemours & Co.* v. *Train*, 430 U.S. 112, 129–130 (1977) . The limitations for a given discharge depend on the type of pollutant and source at issue.[2]

Of key importance, new sources must meet stringent "standards of performance" adopted by EPA under §306. That section makes it "unlawful for *any* … new source to operate … in violation of" an applicable performance standard. 33 U.S.C. §1316(e) (emphasis added). In line with Congress' aim "to insure …'maximum feasible control of new sources,'" *du Pont*, 430 U.S., at 138, the preferred standard for a new source is one "'permitting *no* discharge of pollutants,'" *id.*, at

137–138 (quoting 33 U.S.C. §1316(a)(1) (emphasis added)). Moreover, new sources, unlike existing sources, are not eligible for EPA-granted variances from applicable limitations. 430 U.S., at 138.[3]

In 1982, EPA promulgated new source performance standards for facilities engaged in mining, including those using a froth-flotation milling process. See Ore Mining and Dressing Point Source Category Effluent Limitations Guidelines and New Source Performance Standards, 47 Fed. Reg. 54598 (1982). Existing mills, the Agency found, were already achieving zero discharge; it was therefore practicable, EPA concluded, for new mills to do as well. *Id.*, at 54602. Accordingly, under 40 CFR §440.104(b)(1), new mines using the froth-flotation method, as Coeur Alaska proposes to do, may not discharge wastewater directly into waters of the United States.

B

The nationwide pollution-control requirements just described are implemented through the National Pollution Discharge Elimination System (NPDES), a permitting scheme set forth in §402 and administered by EPA and the States. The NPDES is the linchpin of the Act, for it transforms generally applicable effluent limitations into the individual obligations of each discharger. *EPA v. California ex rel. State Water Resources Control Bd.*, 426 U.S. 200, 205 (1976) . The discharge of a pollutant is generally prohibited unless the source has obtained a NPDES permit. *E.g., EPA v. National Crushed Stone Assn.*, 449 U.S. 64, 71 (1980) ("Section 402 authorizes the establishment of the [NPDES], under which every discharger of pollutants is required to obtain a permit.").

The Act also establishes a separate permitting scheme, administered by the Corps, for discharges of "dredged or fill material." 33 U.S.C. §1344(a). Section 404 hews to the Corps' established expertise in matters of navigability and construction. The §404 program does not implement the uniform, technology-based pollution-control standards set out, *inter alia*, in §306. Instead, §404 permits are subject to regulatory guidelines based generally on the impact of a discharge on the receiving environment. See §1344(b); *ante*, at 4–5.

As the above-described statutory background indicates, Coeur Alaska's claim to a §404 permit carries weighty implications. If eligible for that permit, Coeur Alaska can evade the exacting performance standard prescribed by EPA for froth-flotation mills. It may, instead, use Lower Slate Lake "as the settling pond and disposal site for the tailings." App. 360a (Corps' Record of Decision).

II

Is a pollutant discharge prohibited under §306(e) eligible to receive a §404 permit as a discharge of fill material? All agree on preliminary matters. Only one agency, the Corps or EPA, can issue a permit for the discharge. See *ante*, at 10, 22. Only EPA, through the NPDES program, issues permits that implement §306. See *supra*, at 2. Further, §306(e) and EPA's froth-flotation performance standard, unless inapplicable here, bar Coeur Alaska's proposed discharge. See *ante*, at 14–15.

No part of the statutory scheme, in my view, calls into question the governance of EPA's performance standard. The text of §306(e) states a clear proscription: "[I]t shall be unlawful for any owner or operator of any new source to operate such source in violation of any standard of performance applicable to such source." 33 U.S.C. §1316(e). Under the standard of performance relevant here, "there shall be no discharge of process wastewater to navigable waters from mills that use the froth-flotation process" for mining gold. 40 CFR §440.104(b)(1). The Act imposes these requirements without qualification.

Section 404, stating that the Corps "may issue permits" for the discharge of "dredged or fill material," does not create an exception to §306(e)'s plain command. 33 U.S.C. §1344(a). Cf. *ante*, at 12. Section 404 neither mentions §306 nor states a contrary requirement. The Act can be home to both provisions, with no words added or omitted, so long as the category of "dredged or fill material" eligible for a §404 permit is read in harmony with §306. Doing so yields a simple rule: Discharges governed by EPA performance standards are subject to EPA's administration and receive permits under the NPDES, not §404.

This reading accords with the Act's structure and objectives. It retains, through the NPDES, uniform application of the Act's core pollution-control requirements, and it respects Congress' special concern for new sources. Leaving pollution-related decisions to EPA, moreover, is consistent with Congress' delegation to that agency of primary responsibility to administer the Act. Most fundamental, adhering to §306(e)'s instruction honors the overriding statutory goal of eliminating water pollution, and Congress' particular rejection of the use of navigable waters as waste disposal sites. See *supra*, at 2–3. See also 33 U.S.C. §1324 (creating "clean lakes" program requiring States to identify and restore polluted lakes).[4]

The Court's reading, in contrast, strains credulity. A discharge of a pollutant, otherwise prohibited by firm statutory command, becomes lawful if it contains sufficient solid matter to raise the bottom of a water body, transformed into a waste disposal facility. Whole categories of regulated industries can thereby gain immunity from a variety of pollution-control standards. The loophole would swallow not only standards governing mining activities, see 40 CFR pt. 440 (effluent limitations and new source performance standards for ore mining and dressing); *id.*, pt. 434 (coal mining); *id.*, pt. 436 (mineral mining), but also standards for dozens of other categories of regulated point sources, see, *e.g., id.*,pt. 411 (cement manufacturing); *id.*,pt. 425 (leather tanning and finishing); *id.*,pt. 432 (meat and poultry products processing). See also Brief for American Rivers etal. as *Amici Curiae* 26–27 (observing that discharges in these categories "typically contain high volumes of solids"). Providing an escape hatch for polluters whose discharges contain solid matter, it bears noting, is particularly perverse; the Act specifically focuses on solids as harmful pollutants. See 33 U.S.C. §1314(a)(4) (requiring EPA to publish information regarding "conventional pollutants," including "suspended solids"); Brief for American Rivers, *supra*, at 28–29, and n.18 (identifying over 50 effluent limitations that restrict total suspended solids).[5]

Congress, we have recognized, does not "alter the fundamental details of a regulatory scheme in vague terms or ancillary provisions—it does not, one might say, hide elephants in mouseholes." *Whitman* v. *American Trucking Assns., Inc.*, 531 U.S. 457, 467–468 (2001) . Yet an alteration of that kind is just what today's decision imagines. Congress, as the Court reads the Act, silently upended, in an ancillary permitting provision, its painstaking pollution-control scheme. See *ante*, at 17.Congress did so, the Court holds, notwithstanding the lawmakers' stated effort "to restore and maintain the chemical, physical, and biological integrity" of the waters of the United States, 33 U.S.C. §1251(a); their assignment to EPA of the Herculean task of setting strict effluent limitations for many categories of industrial sources; and their insistence that new sources meet even more ambitious standards, not subject to exception or variance. Would a rational legislature order exacting pollution limits, yet call all bets off if the pollutant, discharged into a lake, will raise the water body's elevation? To say the least, I am persuaded, that is not how Congress intended the Clean Water Act to operate.

In sum, it is neither necessary nor proper to read the statute as allowing mines to bypass EPA's zero-discharge standard by classifying slurry as "fill material." The use of waters of the United States as "settling ponds" for harmful mining waste, the Court of Appeals correctly held, is antithetical to the text, structure, and purpose of the Clean Water Act.

* * *

For the reasons stated, I would affirm the judgment of the Ninth Circuit.

NOTES

[1] Whether aquatic life will eventually be able to inhabit the lake again is uncertain. Compare ante, at 5, with App. 201a–202a; and Southeast Alaska Conservation Council v. United States Army Corps of Engineers, 486 F.3d 638, 642 (CA9 2007).

[2] In addition, the Act requires States to institute comprehensive water quality standards for intrastate waters, subject to EPA approval. See §1313. This program supplements the technology-based standards, serving to "prevent water quality from falling below acceptable levels" even when point sources comply with effluent limitations. EPA v. California ex rel. State Water Resources Control Bd., 426 U.S. 200, 205, n. 12 (1976) .

[3] Even the provision allowing the President to exempt federal installations from compliance with the Act's requirements—"if he determines it to be in the paramount interest of the United States to do so"—does not extend to new source standards: "[N]o exemption may be granted from the requirements of section [306] or [307] of this [Act]." 33 U.S.C. §1323(a).

[4] The Court asserts that "numerous difficulties" will ensue if a discharge governed by a new source performance standard is ineligible for a §404 permit. Ante, at 12. Namely, the Court notes, the discharger will have to determine whether a performance standard applies to it. Ante, at 13. That is not only the usual inquiry under the Clean Water Act; it is one Coeur Alaska answered, without apparent difficulty, when it sought and obtained an EPA permit for the proposed discharge from the lake into a downstream creek. See ante, at 6. Justice Breyer fears that "litera[l] appl[ication]" of performance standards would interfere with efforts "to build a levee or to replace dirt removed from a lake bottom," and thus "may prove unnecessarily strict." Ante, at 2 (concurring opinion). His concerns are imaginative, but it is questionable whether they are real. Apple juice processors, meatcutters, cement manufacturers, and pharmaceutical producers do not ordinarily build levees—and it is almost inconceivable that they would do so using the waste generated by their highly specific industrial processes. See, e.g., 40 CFR §411.10 (performance standard for particular cement manufacturing process). Levee construction generally is undertaken by developers or government, entities not subject to performance standards for such a project. This litigation, furthermore, does not illustrate the "difficulty" Justice Breyer perceives. See ante, at 1. Coeur Alaska does not seek to build a levee or return dirt to a lake; it simply wants to use Lower Slate Lake as a waste disposal site.

[5] The "safeguards" Justice Breyer identifies are hardly reassuring. See ante, at 3 (concurring opinion). Given today's decision, it is optimistic to expect that EPA or the courts will act vigorously to prevent evasion of performance standards. Nor is EPA's veto power under §404(c) of the Clean Water Act an adequate substitute for adherence to §306. That power—exercised only a dozen times over 36 years encompassing more than one million permit applications, see Brief for American Rivers 14—hinges on

a finding of "unacceptable adverse effect," 33 U.S.C. §1344(c). Destruction of nearly all aquatic life in a pristine lake apparently does not qualify as "unacceptable." Reliance on adhoc vetoes, moreover, undermines Congress' aim to install uniform water-pollution regulation.

GEORGE W. BUSH, et al. v. ALBERT GORE, Jr., et al.

No. 00-949, December 12, 2000

ON WRIT OF CERTIORARI TO THE FLORIDA SUPREME COURT

Justice Ginsburg, with whom Justice Stevens joins, and with whom Justice Souter and Justice Breyer join as to Part I, dissenting.

I

The Chief Justice acknowledges that provisions of Florida's Election Code "may well admit of more than one interpretation." *Ante*, at 3. But instead of respecting the state high court's province to say what the State's Election Code means, The Chief Justice maintains that Florida's Supreme Court has veered so far from the ordinary practice of judicial review that what it did cannot properly be called judging. My colleagues have offered a reasonable construction of Florida's law. Their construction coincides with the view of one of Florida's seven Supreme Court justices. *Gore* v. *Harris*, __ So.2d __, __ (Fla. 2000) (slip op., at 45—55) (Wells, C.J., dissenting); *Palm Beach County Canvassing Bd.* v. *Harris*, __ So.2d __, __ (Fla. 2000) (slip op., at 34) (on remand) (confirming, 6—1, the construction of Florida law advanced in *Gore*). I might join The Chief Justice were it my commission to interpret Florida law. But disagreement with the Florida court's interpretation of its own State's law does not warrant the conclusion that the justices of that court have legislated. There is no cause here to believe that the members of Florida's high court have done less than "their mortal best to discharge their oath of office," *Sumner* v. *Mata*, 449 U.S. 539, 549 (1981), and no cause to upset their reasoned interpretation of Florida law.

This Court more than occasionally affirms statutory, and even constitutional, interpretations with which it disagrees. For example, when reviewing challenges to administrative agencies' interpretations of laws they implement, we defer to the agencies unless their interpretation violates "the unambiguously expressed intent of Congress." *Chevron U.S.A. Inc.* v. *Natural Resources Defense Council, Inc.*, 467 U.S. 837, 843 (1984). We do so in the face of the declaration in Article I of the United States Constitution that "All legislative Powers herein granted shall be vested in a Congress of the United States." Surely the Constitution does not call upon us to pay more respect to a federal administrative agency's construction of federal law than to a state high court's interpretation of its own state's law. And not uncommonly, we let stand state-court interpretations of *federal* law with which we might disagree. Notably, in the habeas context, the Court adheres to the view that "there is 'no intrinsic reason why the fact that a man is a federal judge should make him more competent, or conscientious, or learned with respect to [federal law] than his neighbor in the state courthouse.'" *Stone* v. *Powell*, 428 U.S. 465, 494, n. 35 (1976) (quoting Bator, Finality in Criminal Law and Federal Habeas Corpus For State Prisoners, 76 Harv. L. Rev. 441, 509 (1963)); see *O'Dell* v. *Netherland*, 521 U.S. 151, 156 (1997) ("[T]he *Teague* doctrine validates reasonable, good-faith interpretations of existing precedents made by state courts even though they are shown to be contrary to later decisions.") (citing *Butler* v. *McKellar*, 494 U.S. 407, 414 (1990)); O'Connor, Trends in the Relationship Between the Federal and State Courts from the Perspective of a State Court Judge, 22 Wm. & Mary L.Rev. 801, 813 (1981) ("There is no reason to assume that state court judges cannot and will not provide a 'hospitable forum' in litigating federal constitutionalquestions.").

No doubt there are cases in which the proper application of federal law may hinge on interpretations of state law. Unavoidably, this Court must sometimes examine state law in order to protect federal rights. But we have dealt with such cases ever mindful of the full measure of respect we owe to interpretations of state law by a State's highest court. In the Contract Clause case, *General Motors Corp.* v. *Romein*, 503 U.S. 181 (1992), for example, we said that although "ultimately we are bound to decide for ourselves whether a contract was made," the Court "accord[s] respectful consideration and great weight to the views of the State's highest court." *Id.*, at 187 (citation omitted). And in *Central Union Telephone Co.* v. *Edwardsville*, 269 U.S. 190 (1925), we upheld the Illinois Supreme Court's interpretation of a state waiver rule, even though that interpretation resulted in the forfeiture of federal constitutional rights. Refusing to supplant Illinois law with a federal definition of waiver, we explained that the state court's declaration "should bind us unless so unfair or unreasonable in its application to those asserting a federal right as to obstruct it." *Id.*, at 195.[1]

In deferring to state courts on matters of state law, we appropriately recognize that this Court acts as an " 'outside[r]' lacking the common exposure to local law which comes from sitting in the jurisdiction." *Lehman Brothers* v. *Schein*, 416 U.S. 386, 391 (1974). That recognition has sometimes prompted us to resolve doubts about the meaning of state law by certifying issues to a State's highest court, even when federal rights are at stake. Cf. *Arizonans for Official English* v. *Arizona*, 520 U.S. 43, 79 (1997) ("Warnings against premature adjudication of constitutional questions bear heightened attention when a federal court is asked to invalidate a State's law, for the federal tribunal risks friction-generating error when it endeavors to construe a novel state Act not yet reviewed by the State's highest court."). Notwithstanding our authority to decide issues of state law underlying federal claims, we have used the certification devise to afford state high courts an opportunity to inform us on matters of their own State's law because such restraint "helps build a cooperative judicial federalism." *Lehman Brothers*, 416 U.S., at 391.

Just last Term, in *Fiore* v. *White*, 528 U.S. 23 (1999), we took advantage of Pennsylvania's certification procedure. In that case, a state prisoner brought a federal habeas action claiming that the State had failed to prove an essential element of his charged offense in violation of the Due Process Clause. *Id.*, at 25—26. Instead of resolving the state-law question on which the federal claim depended, we certified the question to the Pennsylvania Supreme Court for that court to "help determine the proper state-law predicate for our determination of the federal constitutional questions raised." *Id.*, at 29; *id.*, at 28 (asking the Pennsylvania Supreme Court whether its recent interpretation of the statute under which Fiore was convicted "was always the statute's meaning, even at the time of Fiore's trial"). The Chief Justice's willingness to *reverse* the Florida Supreme Court's interpretation of Florida law in this case is at least in tension with our reluctance in *Fiore* even to interpret Pennsylvania law before seeking instruction from the Pennsylvania Supreme Court. I would have thought the "cautious approach" we counsel when federal courts address matters of state law, *Arizonans*, 520 U.S., at 77, and our commitment to "build[ing] cooperative judicial federalism," *Lehman Brothers*, 416 U.S., at 391, demanded greater restraint.

Rarely has this Court rejected outright an interpretation of state law by a state high court. *Fairfax's Devisee* v. *Hunter's Lessee*, 7 Cranch 603 (1813), *NAACP* v. *Alabama ex rel. Patterson*, 357 U.S. 449 (1958), and *Bouie* v. *City of Columbia*, 378 U.S. 347 (1964), cited by The Chief Justice, are three such rare instances. See *ante*, at 4, 5, and n.2. But those cases are embedded in historical contexts hardly comparable to the situation here. *Fairfax's Devisee*, which held that the Virginia Court of Appeals had misconstrued its own forfeiture laws to deprive a British subject of lands secured to him by federal treaties, occurred amidst vociferous States' rights attacks on the Marshall Court. G. Gunther & K. Sullivan, Constitutional Law 61—62 (13th ed. 1997). The Virginia court refused to obey this Court's *Fairfax's Devisee* mandate to enter judgment for the British subject's successor in interest. That refusal led to the Court's pathmarking decision in *Martin* v. *Hunter's Lessee*, 1 Wheat. 304 (1816). *Patterson*, a case decided three months after *Cooper* v. *Aaron*, 358 U.S. 1 (1958), in the face of Southern resistance to the civil rights movement, held that the Alabama Supreme Court had irregularly applied its own procedural rules to deny review of a contempt order against the NAACP arising from its refusal to disclose membership lists. We said that "our jurisdiction is not defeated if the nonfederal ground relied on by the state court is without any fair or substantial support." 357 U.S., at 455. *Bouie*, stemming from a lunch counter "sit-in" at the height of the civil rights movement, held that the South Carolina Supreme Court's construction of its trespass laws–criminalizing conduct not covered by the text of an otherwise clear statute–was "unforeseeable" and thus violated due process when applied retroactively to the petitioners. 378 U.S., at 350, 354.

The Chief Justice's casual citation of these cases might lead one to believe they are part of a larger collection of cases in which we said that the Constitution impelled us to train a skeptical eye on a state court's portrayal of state law. But one would be hard pressed, I think, to find additional cases that fit the mold. As Justice Breyer convincingly explains, see *post*, at 5—9 (dissenting opinion), this case involves nothing close to the kind of recalcitrance by a state high court that warrants extraordinary action by this Court. The Florida Supreme Court concluded that counting every legal vote was the overriding concern of the Florida Legislature when it enacted the State's Election Code. The court surely should not be bracketed with state high courts of the Jim Crow South.

The Chief Justice says that Article II, by providing that state legislatures shall direct the manner of appointing electors, authorizes federal superintendence over the relationship between state courts and state legislatures, and licenses a departure from the usual deference we give to state court interpretations of state law. *Ante*, at 5 ("To attach definitive weight to the pronouncement of a state court, when the very question at issue is whether the court has actually departed from the statutory meaning, would be to abdicate our responsibility to enforce the explicit requirements of Article II."). The Framers of our Constitution, however, understood that in a republican government, the judiciary would construe the legislature's enactments. See U.S. Const., Art.III; The Federalist No. 78 (A. Hamilton). In light of the constitutional guarantee to States of a "Republican Form of Government," U.S. Const., Art. IV, §4, Article II can hardly be read to invite this Court to disrupt a State's republican regime. Yet The Chief Justice today would reach out to do just that. By holding that Article II requires our revision of a state court's construction of state laws in order to protect one organ of the State from another, The Chief Justice contradicts the basic principle that a State may organize itself as it sees fit. See, *e.g.*, *Gregory* v. *Ashcroft*, 501 U.S. 452, 460 (1991) ("Through the structure of its government, and the character of those who exercise government authority, a State defines itself as a sovereign."); *Highland Farms Dairy, Inc.* v. *Agnew*, 300 U.S. 608, 612 (1937) ("How power shall be distributed by a state among its governmental organs is commonly, if not always, a question for the state itself.").[2] Article II does not call for the scrutiny undertaken by this Court.

The extraordinary setting of this case has obscured the ordinary principle that dictates its proper resolution: Federal courts defer to state high courts' interpretations of their state's own law. This principle reflects the core of federalism, on which all agree. "The Framers split the atom of sovereignty. It was the genius of their idea that our citizens would have two political capacities, one state and one federal, each protected from incursion by the other." *Saenz* v. *Roe*, 526 U.S. 489, 504, n.17 (1999) (citing *U.S. Term Limits, Inc.* v. *Thornton*, 514 U.S. 779, 838 (1995) (Kennedy, J., concurring)). The Chief Justice's solicitude for the Florida Legislature comes at the expense of the more fundamental solicitude we owe to the legislature's sovereign. U.S. Const., Art.II, §1, cl.2 ("Each *State* shall appoint, in such Manner as the Legislature *thereof* may direct," the electors for President and Vice President) (emphasis added); *ante*, at 1—2 (Stevens, J., dissenting).[3] Were the other members of this Court as mindful as they generally are of our system of dual sovereignty, they would affirm the judgment of the Florida Supreme Court.

II

I agree with Justice Stevens that petitioners have not presented a substantial equal protection claim. Ideally, perfection would be the appropriate standard for judging the recount. But we live in an imperfect world, one in which thousands of votes have not been counted. I cannot agree that the recount adopted by the Florida court, flawed as it may be, would yield a result any less fair or precise than the certification that preceded that recount. See, e.g., *McDonald* v. *Board of Election Comm'rs of Chicago*, 394 U.S. 802, 807 (1969) (even in the context of the right to vote, the state is permitted to reform "'one step at a time'") (quoting *Williamson* v. *Lee Optical of Oklahoma, Inc.*, 348 U.S. 483, 489 (1955)).

Even if there were an equal protection violation, I would agree with Justice Stevens, Justice Souter, and Justice Breyer that the Court's concern about "the December 12 deadline," *ante*, at 12, is misplaced. Time is short in part because of the Court's entry of a stay on December 9, several hours after an able circuit judge in Leon County had begun to superintend the recount process. More fundamentally, the Court's reluctance to let the recount go forward–despite its suggestion that "[t]he search for intent can be confined by specific rules designed to ensure uniform treatment," *ante*, at 8–ultimately turns on its own judgment about the practical realities of implementing a recount, not the judgment of those much closer to the process.

Equally important, as Justice Breyer explains, *post*, at 12 (dissenting opinion), the December 12 "deadline" for bringing Florida's electoral votes into 3 U.S.C. § 5's safe harbor lacks the significance the Court assigns it. Were that date to pass, Florida would still be entitled to deliver electoral votes Congress *must* count unless both Houses find that the votes "ha[d] not been … regularly given." 3 U.S.C. § 15. The statute identifies other significant dates. See, e.g., §7 (specifying December 18 as the date electors "shall meet and give their votes"); §12 (specifying "the fourth Wednesday in December"–this year, December 27–as the date on which Congress, if it has not received a State's electoral votes, shall request the state secretary of state to send a certified return immediately). But none of these dates has ultimate significance in light of Congress' detailed provisions for determining, on "the sixth day of January," the validity of electoral votes. §15.

The Court assumes that time will not permit "orderly judicial review of any disputed matters that might arise." *Ante*, at 12. But no one has doubted the good faith and diligence with which Florida election officials, attorneys for all sides of this controversy, and the courts of law have performed their duties. Notably, the Florida Supreme Court has produced two substantial opinions within 29 hours of oral argument. In sum, the Court's conclusion that a constitutionally adequate recount is impractical is a prophecy the Court's own judgment will not allow to be tested. Such an untested prophecy should not decide the Presidency of the United States.

I dissent.

NOTES

[1] See also *Lucas* v. *South Carolina Coastal Council*, 505 U.S. 1003, 1032, n.18 (1992) (South Carolina could defend a regulatory taking "if an *objectively reasonable application* of relevant precedents [by its courts] would exclude … beneficial uses in the circumstances in which the land is presently found"); *Bishop* v. *Wood*, 426 U.S. 341, 344—345 (1976) (deciding whether North Carolina had created a property interest cognizable under the Due Process Clause by reference to state law as interpreted by the North Carolina Supreme Court). Similarly, in *Gurley* v. *Rhoden*, 421 U.S. 200 (1975), a gasoline retailer claimed that due process entitled him to deduct a state gasoline excise tax in computing the amount of his sales subject to a state sales tax, on the grounds that the legal incidence of the excise tax fell on his customers and that he acted merely as a collector of the tax. The Mississippi Supreme Court held that the legal incidence of the excise tax fell on petitioner. Observing that "a State's highest court is the final judicial arbiter of the meaning of state statutes," we said that "[w]hen a state court has made its own definitive determination as to the operating incidence, … [w]e give this finding great weight in determining the natural effect of a statute, and if it is consistent with the statute's reasonable interpretation it will be deemed conclusive." *Id.*, at 208.

[2] Even in the rare case in which a State's "manner" of making and construing laws might implicate a structural constraint, Congress, not this Court, is likely the proper governmental entity to enforce that constraint. See U.S. Const., amend. XII; 3 U.S.C. § 1—15; cf. *Ohio ex rel. Davis* v. *Hildebrant*, 241 U.S. 565, 569 (1916) (treating as a nonjusticiable political question whether use of a referendum to override a congressional districting plan enacted by the state legislature violates Art. I, §4); *Luther* v. *Borden*, 7 How. 1, 42 (1849).

[3] "[B]ecause the Framers recognized that state power and identity were essential parts of the federal balance, see The Federalist No. 39, the Constitution is solicitous of the prerogatives of the States, even in an otherwise sovereign federal province. The Constitution … grants States certain powers over the times, places, and manner of federal elections (subject to congressional revision), Art.I, §4, cl.1 …, and allows States to appoint electors for the President, Art.II, §1, cl.2." *U.S. Term Limits, Inc.* v. *Thornton*, 514 U.S. 779, 841—842 (1995) (Kennedy, J., concurring).

HARRY CONNICK SR., DISTRICT ATTORNEY, et al. v. JOHN THOMPSON

No. 09-571, March 29, 2011

ON WRIT OF CERTIORARI TO THE UNITED STATES COURT OF APPEALS FOR THE FIFTH CIRCUIT

In *Brady* v. *Maryland* , 373 U.S. 83, 87 (1963) , this Court held that due process requires the prosecution to turn over evidence favorable to the accused and material to his guilt or punishment. That obligation, the parties have stipulated, was dishonored in this case; consequently, John Thompson spent 18 years in prison, 14 of them isolated on death row, before the truth came to light: He was innocent of the charge of attempted armed robbery, and his subsequent trial on a murder charge, by prosecutorial design, was fundamentally unfair.

The Court holds that the Orleans Parish District Attorney's Office (District Attorney's Office or Office) cannot be held liable, in a civil rights action under 42 U.S.C. §1983, for the grave injustice Thompson suffered. That is so, the Court tells us, because Thompson has shown only an aberrant *Brady* violation, not a routine practice of giving short shrift to *Brady* 's requirements. The evidence presented to the jury that awarded compensation to Thompson, however, points distinctly away from the Court's assessment. As the trial record in the §1983 action reveals, the conceded, long-concealed prosecutorial transgressions were neither isolated nor atypical.

From the top down, the evidence showed, members of the District Attorney's Office, including the District At-torney himself, misperceived *Brady* 's compass and therefore inadequately attended to their disclosure obligations. Throughout the pretrial and trial proceedings against Thompson, the team of four engaged in prosecuting him for armed robbery and murder hid from the defense and the court exculpatory information Thompson requested and had a constitutional right to receive. The prosecutors did so despite multiple opportunities, spanning nearly two decades, to set the record straight. Based on the prosecutors' conduct relating to Thompson's trials, a fact trier could reasonably conclude that inattention to *Brady* was standard operating procedure at the District Attorney's Office.

What happened here, the Court's opinion obscures, was no momentary oversight, no single incident of a lone officer's misconduct. Instead, the evidence demonstrated that misperception and disregard of *Brady* 's disclosure requirements were pervasive in Orleans Parish. That evidence, I would hold, established persistent, deliberately indifferent conduct for which the District Attorney's Office bears responsibility under §1983.

I dissent from the Court's judgment mindful that *Brady* violations, as this case illustrates, are not easily detected. But for a chance discovery made by a defense team investigator weeks before Thompson's scheduled execution, the evidence that led to his exoneration might have remained under wraps. The prosecutorial concealment Thompson encountered, however, is bound to be repeated unless municipal agencies bear responsibility—made tangible by §1983 liability—for adequately conveying what *Brady* requires and for monitoring staff compliance. Failure to train, this Court has said, can give rise to municipal liability under §1983 "where the failure ... amounts to deliberate indifference to the rights of persons with whom the [untrained employees] come into contact." *Canton* v. *Harris* , 489 U.S. 378, 388 (1989) . That standard is well met in this case.

I

I turn first to a contextual account of the *Brady* violations that infected Thompson's trials.

A

In the early morning hours of December 6, 1984, an assailant shot and killed Raymond T. Liuzza, Jr., son of a prominent New Orleans business executive, on the street fronting the victim's home. Only one witness saw the assailant. As recorded in two contemporaneous police reports, that eyewitness initially described the assailant as African-American, six feet tall, with "close cut hair." Record EX2–EX3, EX9.[1] Thompson is five feet eight inches tall and, at the time of the murder, styled his hair in a large "Afro." *Id.* , at EX13. The police reports of the witness' immediate identification were not disclosed to Thompson or to the court.

While engaged in the murder investigation, the Orleans Parish prosecutors linked Thompson to another violent crime committed three weeks later. On December 28, an assailant attempted to rob three siblings at gunpoint. During the struggle, the perpetrator's blood stained the oldest child's pant leg. That blood, preserved on a swatch of fabric cut from the pant leg by a crime scene analyst, was eventually tested. The test conclusively established that the perpetrator's blood was type B. *Id.* , at EX151. Thompson's blood is type O. His prosecutors failed to disclose the existence of the swatch or the test results.

B

One month after the Liuzza murder, Richard Perkins, a man who knew Thompson, approached the Liuzza family. Perkins did so after the family's announcement of a $15,000 reward for information leading to the murderer's conviction. Police officers surreptitiously recorded the Perkins-Liuzza conversations.[2] As documented on tape, Perkins told the family, "I don't mind helping [you] catch [the perpetrator], ... but I would like [you] to help me and, you know, I'll help [you]." *Id.* , at EX479, EX481. Once the family assured Perkins, "we're on your side, we want to try and help you," *id.* , at EX481, Perkins intimated that Thompson and another man, Kevin Freeman, had been involved in Liuzza's murder. Perkins thereafter told the police what he had learned from Freeman about the murder, and that information was recorded in a police report. Based on Perkins' account, Thompson and Freeman were arrested on murder charges.

Freeman was six feet tall and went by the name "Kojak" because he kept his hair so closely trimmed that his scalp was visible. Unlike Thompson, Freeman fit the eyewitness' initial description of the Liuzza assailant's height and hair style. As the Court notes, *ante* , at 4, n.2, Freeman became the key witness for the prosecution at Thompson's trial for the murder of Liuzza.

After Thompson's arrest for the Liuzza murder, the father of the armed robbery victims saw a newspaper photo of Thompson with a large Afro hairstyle and showed it to his children. He reported to the District Attorney's Office that the children had identified Thompson as their attacker, and the children then picked that same photo out of a "photographic lineup." Record EX120, EX642–EX643. Indicting Thompson on the basis of these questionable identifications, the District Attorney's Office did not pause to test the pant leg swatch dyed by the perpetrator's blood. This lapse ignored or overlooked a prosecutor's notation that the Office "may wish to do [a] blood test." *Id.* , at EX122.

The murder trial was scheduled to begin in mid-March 1985. Armed with the later indictment against Thompson for robbery, however, the prosecutors made a strategic choice: They switched the order of the two trials, proceeding first on the robbery indictment. *Id.* , at EX128–EX129. Their aim was twofold. A robbery conviction gained first would serve to inhibit Thompson from testifying in his own defense at the murder trial, for the prior conviction could be used to impeach his credibility. In addition, an armed robbery conviction could be invoked at the penalty phase of the murder trial in support of the prosecution's plea for the death penalty. *Id.* , at 682.

Recognizing the need for an effective prosecution team, petitioner Harry F. Connick, District Attorney for the Parish of Orleans, appointed his third-in-command, Eric Dubelier, as special prosecutor in both cases. Dubelier enlisted Jim Williams to try the armed robbery case and to assist him in the murder case. Gerry Deegan assisted Williams in the armed robbery case. Bruce Whittaker, the fourth prosecutor involved in the cases, had approved Thompson's armed robbery indictment.[3]

C

During pretrial proceedings in the armed robbery case, Thompson filed a motion requesting access to all materials and information "favorable to the defendant" and "material and relevant to the issue of guilt or punishment," as well as "any results or reports" of "scientific tests or experiments." *Id.* , at EX144, EX145. Prosecutorial responses to this motion fell far short of *Brady* compliance.[4]

First, prosecutors blocked defense counsel's inspection of the pant leg swatch stained by the robber's blood. Although Dubelier's April 3 response stated, "Inspection to be permitted," *id.* , at EX149, the swatch was signed out from the property room at 10:05 a.m. the next day, and was not returned until noon on April 10, the day before trial, *id.* , at EX43, EX670. Thompson's attorney inspected the evidence made available to him and found no blood evidence. No one told defense counsel about the swatch and its recent removal from the property room. *Id.* , at EX701–EX702; Tr. 400–402. But cf. *ante* , at 17, n.11 (Thompson's attorney had "access to the evidence locker where the swatch was recorded as evidence.").[5]

Second, Dubelier or Whittaker ordered the crime laboratory to rush a pretrial test of the swatch. Tr. 952–954. Whittaker received the lab report, addressed to his attention, two days before trial commenced. Immediately thereafter, he placed the lab report on Williams' desk. Record EX151, EX589. Although the lab report conclusively identified the perpetrator's blood type, *id.* , at EX151, the District Attorney's Office never revealed the report to the defense.[6]

Third, Deegan checked the swatch out of the property room on the morning of the first day of trial, but the prosecution did not produce the swatch at trial. *Id.* , at EX43. Deegan did not return the swatch to the property room after trial, and the swatch has never been found. Tr. of Oral Arg. 37.

"[B]ased solely on the descriptions" provided by the three victims, Record 683, the jury convicted Thompson of attempted armed robbery. The court sentenced him to 49.5 years without possibility of parole—the maximum available sentence.

D

Prosecutors continued to disregard *Brady* during the murder trial, held in May 1985, at which the prosecution's order-of-trial strategy achieved its aim.[7] By prosecuting Thompson for armed robbery first—and withholding blood evidence that might have exonerated Thompson of that charge—the District Attorney's Office disabled Thompson from testifying in his own defense at the murder trial.[8] As earlier observed, see *supra*, at 5, impeaching use of the prior conviction would have severely undermined Thompson's credibility. And because Thompson was effectively stopped from testifying in his own defense, the testimony of the witnesses against him gained force. The prosecution's failure to reveal evidence that could have impeached those witnesses helped to seal Thompson's fate.

First, the prosecution undermined Thompson's efforts to impeach Perkins. Perkins testified that he volunteered information to the police with no knowledge of reward money. Record EX366, EX372–EX373. Because prosecutors had not produced the audiotapes of Perkins' conversations with the Liuzza family (or a police summary of the tapes), Thompson's attorneys could do little to cast doubt on Perkins' credibility. In closing argument, the prosecution emphasized that Thompson presented no "direct evidence" that reward money had motivated any of the witnesses. *Id.*, at EX3171–EX3172.

Second, the prosecution impeded Thompson's impeachment of key witness Kevin Freeman. It did so by failing to disclose a police report containing Perkins' account of what he had learned from Freeman about the murder. See *supra*, at 4. Freeman's trial testimony was materially inconsistent with that report. Tr. 382–384, 612–614; Record EX270–EX274. Lacking any knowledge of the police report, Thompson could not point to the inconsistencies.

Third, and most vital, the eyewitness' initial description of the assailant's hair, see *supra*, at 3, was of prime relevance, for it suggested that Freeman, not Thompson, murdered Liuzza, see *supra*, at 4. The materiality of the eyewitness' contemporaneous description of the murderer should have been altogether apparent to the prosecution. Failure to produce the police reports setting out what the eyewitness first said not only undermined efforts to impeach that witness and the police officer who initially interviewed him. The omission left defense counsel without knowledge that the prosecutors were restyling the killer's "close cut hair" into an "Afro."

Prosecutors finessed the discrepancy between the eyewitness' initial description and Thompson's appearance. They asked leading questions prompting the eyewitness to agree on the stand that the perpetrator's hair was "afro type," yet "straight back." Record EX322–EX323. Corroboratively, the police officer—after refreshing his recollection by reviewing material at the prosecution's table—gave artful testimony. He characterized the witness' initial description of the perpetrator's hair as "black and short, *afro style*." *Id.*, at EX265 (emphasis added). As prosecutors well knew, nothing in the withheld police reports, which described the murderer's hair simply as "close cut," portrayed a perpetrator with an Afro or Afro-style hair.

The jury found Thompson guilty of first-degree murder. Having prevented Thompson from testifying that Freeman was the killer, the prosecution delivered its ultimate argument. Because Thompson was already serving a near-life sentence for attempted armed robbery, the prosecution urged, the only way to punish him for murder was to execute him. The strategy worked as planned; Thompson was sentenced to death.

E

Thompson discovered the prosecutors' misconduct through a serendipitous series of events. In 1994, nine years after Thompson's convictions, Deegan, the assistant prosecutor in the armed robbery trial, learned he was terminally ill. Soon thereafter, Deegan confessed to his friend Michael Riehlmann that he had suppressed blood evidence in the armed robbery case. *Id.*, at EX709. Deegan did not heed Riehlmann's counsel to reveal what he had done. For five years, Riehlmann, himself a former Orleans Parish prosecutor, kept Deegan's confession to himself. *Id.*, at EX712–EX713.

On April 16, 1999, the State of Louisiana scheduled Thompson's execution. *Id.*, at EX1366–EX1367. In an eleventh-hour effort to save his life, Thompson's attorneys hired a private investigator. Deep in the crime lab archives, the investigator unearthed a microfiche copy of the lab report identifying the robber's blood type. The copy showed that the report had been addressed to Whittaker. See *supra*, at 7. Thompson's attorneys contacted Whittaker, who informed Riehlmann that the lab report had been found. Riehlmann thereupon told Whittaker that Deegan "had failed to turn over stuff that might have been exculpatory." Tr. 718. Riehlmann prepared an affidavit describing Deegan's disclosure "that he had intentionally suppressed blood evidence in the armed robbery trial of John Thompson." Record EX583.

Thompson's lawyers presented to the trial court the crime lab report showing that the robber's blood type was B, and a report identifying Thompson's blood type as O. This evidence proved Thompson innocent of the robbery. The court immediately stayed Thompson's execution, *id.*, at EX590, and commenced proceedings to assess the newly discovered evidence.

Connick sought an abbreviated hearing. A full hearing was unnecessary, he urged, because the Office had confessed error and had moved to dismiss the armed robbery charges. See, *e.g.*, *id.*, at EX617. The court insisted on a public hearing. Given "the history of this case," the court said, it "was not willing to accept the representations that [Connick] and [his] office made [in their motion to dismiss]." *id.*, at EX882. After a full day's hearing, the court vacated Thompson's attempted armed robbery conviction and dismissed the charges. Before doing so, the court admonished:

"[A]ll day long there have been a number of young Assistant D.A.'s … sitting in this courtroom watching this, and I hope they take home … and take to heart the message that this kind of conduct cannot go on in this Parish if this Criminal Justice System is going to work." *Id.*, at EX883.

The District Attorney's Office then initiated grand jury proceedings against the prosecutors who had withheld the lab report. Connick terminated the grand jury after just one day. He maintained that the lab report would not be *Brady* material if prosecutors did not know Thompson's blood type. Tr. 986; cf. *supra*, at 7, n.6. And he told the investigating prosecutor that the grand jury "w[ould] make [his] job more difficult." Tr. 978–979. In protest, that prosecutor tendered his resignation.

F

Thereafter, the Louisiana Court of Appeal reversed Thompson's murder conviction. *State* v. *Thompson*, 2002–0361, p. 10 (7/17/02), 825 So.2d 552, 558. The unlawfully procured robbery conviction, the court held, had violated Thompson's right to testify and thus fully present his defense in the murder trial. *Id.*, at 557. The merits of several *Brady* claims arising out of the murder trial, the court observed, had therefore become "moot." 825 So.2d, at 555; see also Record 684.[9] But cf. *ante*, at 10–11, n.7, 16–17, n. 11 (suggesting that there were no *Brady* violations in the murder prosecution because no court had adjudicated any violations).[10]

Undeterred by his assistants' disregard of Thompson's rights, Connick retried him for the Liuzza murder. Thompson's defense was bolstered by evidence earlier unavailable to him: ten exhibits the prosecution had not disclosed when Thompson was first tried. The newly produced items included police reports describing the assailant in the murder case as having "close cut" hair, the police report recounting Perkins' meetings with the Liuzza family, see *supra*, at 3–4, audio recordings of those meetings, and a 35-page supplemental police report. After deliberating for only 35 minutes, the jury found Thompson not guilty.

On May 9, 2003, having served more than 18 years in prison for crimes he did not commit, Thompson was released.

II

On July 16, 2003, Thompson commenced a civil action under 42 U.S.C. §1983 alleging that Connick, other officials of the Orleans Parish District Attorney's Office, and the Office itself, had violated his constitutional rights by wrongfully withholding *Brady* evidence. Thompson sought to hold Connick and the District Attorney's Office liable for failure adequately to train prosecutors concerning their *Brady* obligations. Such liability attaches, I agree with the Court, only when the failure "amount[s] to 'deliberate indifference to the rights of persons with whom the [untrained employees] come into contact.'" *Ante*, at 9 (quoting *Canton* v. *Harris*, 489 U.S. 378, 388 (1989)). I disagree, however, with the Court's conclusion that Thompson failed to prove deliberate indifference.

Having weighed all the evidence, the jury in the §1983 case found for Thompson, concluding that the District Attorney's Office had been deliberately indifferent to Thompson's *Brady* rights and to the need for training and supervision to safeguard those rights. "Viewing the evidence in the light most favorable to [Thompson], as appropriate in light of the verdic[t] rendered by the jury," *Patrick* v. *Burget*, 486 U.S. 94, 98, n. 3 (1988) , I see no cause to upset the District Court's determination, affirmed by the Fifth Circuit, that "ample evidence ... adduced at trial" supported the jury's verdict. Record 1917.

Over 20 years ago, we observed that a municipality's failure to provide training may be so egregious that, even without notice of prior constitutional violations, the failure "could properly be characterized as 'deliberate indifference' to constitutional rights." *Canton*, 489 U.S., at 390, n. 10. "[I]n light of the duties assigned to specific officers or employees," *Canton* recognized, "it may happen that ... the need for more or different training is so obvious, and the inadequacy so likely to result in the violation of constitutional rights, that the policymakers ... can reasonably be said to have been deliberately indifferent to the need." *Id.*, at 390. Thompson presented convincing evidence to satisfy this standard.

A

Thompson's §1983 suit proceeded to a jury trial on two theories of liability: First, the Orleans Parish Office's official *Brady* policy was unconstitutional; and second, Connick was deliberately indifferent to an obvious need to train his prosecutors about their *Brady* obligations. Connick's *Brady* policy directed prosecutors to "turn over what was required by state and federal law, but no more." Brief for Petitioners 6–7. The jury thus understandably rejected Thompson's claim that the official policy itself was unconstitutional. *Ante*, at 5.

The jury found, however, that Connick was deliberately indifferent to the need to train prosecutors about *Brady*'s command. On the special verdict form, the jury answered yes to the following question:

> "Was the *Brady* violation in the armed robbery case or any infringements of John Thompson's rights in the murder trial substantially caused by [Connick's] failure, through deliberate indifference, to establish policies and procedures to protect one accused of a crime from these constitutional violations?" Record 1585.

Consistent with the question put to the jury, and without objection, the court instructed the jurors: "[Y]ou are not limited to the nonproduced blood evidence and the resulting infringement of Mr. Thompson's right to testify at the murder trial. You may consider all of the evidence presented during this trial." Tr. 1099; Record 1620.[11] But cf. *ante* , at 2, 6, 10, n.7, 16; *ante* , at 1 (Scalia, J., concurring) (maintaining that the case involves a single *Brady* violation). That evidence included a stipulation that in his retrial for the Liuzza murder, Thompson had introduced ten exhibits containing relevant information withheld by the prosecution in 1985. See *supra* , at 13.

Abundant evidence supported the jury's finding that additional *Brady* training was obviously necessary to ensure that *Brady* violations would not occur: (1) Connick, the Office's sole policymaker, misunderstood *Brady* . (2) Other leaders in the Office, who bore direct responsibility for training less experienced prosecutors, were similarly uninformed about *Brady* . (3) Prosecutors in the Office received no *Brady* training. (4) The Office shirked its responsibility to keep prosecutors abreast of relevant legal developments concerning *Brady* requirements. As a result of these multiple shortfalls, it was hardly surprising that *Brady* violations in fact occurred, severely undermining the integrity of Thompson's trials.

1

Connick was the Office's sole policymaker, and his testimony exposed a flawed understanding of a prosecutor's *Brady* obligations. First, Connick admitted to the jury that his earlier understanding of *Brady* , conveyed in prior sworn testimony, had been too narrow. Tr. 181–182. Second, Connick confessed to having withheld a crime lab report "one time as a prosecutor and I got indicted by the U.S. Attorney over here for doing it." *Id.* , at 872. Third, even at trial Connick persisted in misstating *Brady* 's requirements. For example, Connick urged that there could be no *Brady* violation arising out of "the inadvertent conduct of [an] assistant under pressure with a lot of case load." Tr. 188–189. The court, however, correctly instructed the jury that, in determining whether there has been a *Brady* violation, the "good or bad faith of the prosecution does not matter." Tr. 1094–1095.

2

The testimony of other leaders in the District Attorney's Office revealed similar misunderstandings. Those misunderstandings, the jury could find, were in large part responsible for the gross disregard of *Brady* rights Thompson experienced. Dubelier admitted that he never reviewed police files, but simply relied on the police to flag any potential *Brady* information. Tr. 542. The court, however, instructed the jury that an individual prosecutor has a "duty ... to learn of any favorable evidence known to others acting on the government's behalf in the case, including the police." *Id.* , at 1095; Record 1614. Williams was asked whether " *Brady* material includes documents in the possession of the district attorney that could be used to impeach a witness, to show that he's lying"; he responded simply, and mistakenly, "No." Tr. 381. The testimony of "high-ranking individuals in the Orleans Parish District Attorney's Office," Thompson's expert explained,[12] exposed "complete errors ... as to what *Brady* required [prosecutors] to do." *Id.* , at 427, 434. "Dubelier had no understanding of his obligations under *Brady* whatsoever," *id.* , at 458, the expert observed, and Williams "is still not sure what his obligations were under *Brady* ," *id.* , at 448. But cf. *ante* , at 4–5 ("[I]t was undisputed at trial that the prosecutors were familiar with the general *Brady* requirement that the State disclose to the defense evidence in its possession that is favorable to the accused.").

The jury could attribute the violations of Thompson's rights directly to prosecutors' misapprehension of *Brady* . The prosecution had no obligation to produce the "close-cut hair" police reports, Williams maintained, because newspaper reports had suggested that witness descrip- tions were not consistent with Thompson's appearance. Therefore, Williams urged, the defense already "had everything." Tr. 139. Dubelier tendered an alternative ex- planation for the nondisclosure. In Dubelier's view, the descriptions were not "inconsistent with [Thompson's] appearance," as portrayed in a police photograph showing Thompson's hair extending at least three inches above his forehead. *Id.* , at 171–172; Record EX73. Williams insisted that he had discharged the prosecution's duty to disclose the blood evidence by mentioning, in a motion hearing, that the prosecution intended to obtain a blood sample from Thompson. Tr. 393–394. During the armed robbery trial, Williams told one of the victims that the results of the blood test made on the swatch had been "inconclusive." *Id.* , at 962. And he testified in the §1983 action that the lab report was not *Brady* material "because I didn't know what the blood type of Mr. Thompson was." Tr. 393. But see *supra* , at 6–7, n.5 (District Court instructed the jury that the lab report was *Brady* material).

3

Connick should have comprehended that Orleans Parish prosecutors lacked essential guidance on *Brady* and its application. In fact, Connick has effectively conceded that *Brady* training in his Office was inadequate. Tr. of Oral Arg. 60. Connick explained to the jury that prosecutors' offices must "make ... very clear to [new prosecutors] what their responsibility [i]s" under *Brady* and must not "giv[e] them a lot of leeway." Tr. 834–835. But the jury heard ample evidence that Connick's Office gave prosecutors no *Brady* guidance, and had installed no procedures to monitor *Brady* compliance.

In 1985, Connick acknowledged, many of his prosecutors "were coming fresh out of law school," and the Office's "[h]uge turnover" allowed attorneys with little experience to advance quickly to supervisory positions. See Tr. 853–854, 832. By 1985, Dubelier and Williams were two of the highest ranking attorneys in the Office, *id.* , at 342, 356–357, yet neither man had even five years of experience as a prosecutor, see *supra* , at 5, n.3; Record EX746; Tr. 55, 571–576.

Dubelier and Williams learned the prosecutorial craft in Connick's Office, and, as earlier observed, see *supra*, at 17–18, their testimony manifested a woefully deficient understanding of *Brady* . Dubelier and Williams told the jury that they did not recall any *Brady* training in the Office. Tr. 170–171, 364.

Connick testified that he relied on supervisors, including Dubelier and Williams, to ensure prosecutors were familiar with their *Brady* obligations. Tr. 805–806. Yet Connick did not inquire whether the supervisors themselves understood the importance of teaching newer prosecutors about *Brady* . Riehlmann could not "recall that [he] was ever trained or instructed by anybody about [his] *Brady* obligations," on the job or otherwise. Tr. 728–729. Whittaker agreed it was possible for "inexperienced lawyers, just a few weeks out of law school with no training," to bear responsibility for "decisions on ... whether material was *Brady* material and had to be produced." *Id.* , at 319.

Thompson's expert characterized Connick's supervision regarding *Brady* as "the blind leading the blind." Tr. 458. For example, in 1985 trial attorneys "sometimes ... went to Mr. Connick" with *Brady* questions, "and he would tell them" how to proceed. Tr. 892. But Connick acknowledged that he had "stopped reading law books ... and looking at opinions" when he was first elected District Attorney in 1974. *Id.* , at 175–176.

As part of their training, prosecutors purportedly attended a pretrial conference with the Office's chief of trials before taking a case to trial. Connick intended the practice to provide both training and accountability. But it achieved neither aim in Thompson's prosecutions, for Dubelier and Williams, as senior prosecutors in the Office, were free to take cases to trial without pretrying them, and that is just how they proceeded in Thompson's prosecutions. *Id.* , at 901–902; Record 685. But cf. *ante* , at 13 ("[T]rial chiefs oversaw the preparation of the cases.").

Prosecutors confirmed that training in the District Attorney's Office, overall, was deficient. Soon after Connick retired, a survey of assistant district attorneys in the Office revealed that more than half felt that they had not received the training they needed to do their jobs. Tr. 178.

Thompson, it bears emphasis, is not complaining about the absence of formal training sessions. Tr. of Oral Arg. 55. But cf. *ante* , at 15–16. His complaint does not demand that *Brady* compliance be enforced in any particular way. He asks only that *Brady* obligations be communicated accurately and genuinely enforced.[13] Because that did not happen in the District Attorney's Office, it was inevitable that prosecutors would misapprehend *Brady* . Had *Brady* 's importance been brought home to prosecutors, surely at least one of the four officers who knew of the swatch and lab report would have revealed their existence to defense counsel and the court.[14]

4

Louisiana did not require continuing legal education at the time of Thompson's trials. Tr. 361. But cf. *ante* , at 12–13. Primary responsibility for keeping prosecutors *au courant* with developments in the law, therefore, resided in the District Attorney's Office. Over the course of Connick's tenure as District Attorney, the jury learned, the Office's chief of appeals circulated memoranda when appellate courts issued important opinions. Tr. 751–754, 798.

The 1987 Office policy manual was a compilation of memoranda on criminal law and practice circulated to prosecutors from 1974, when Connick became District Attorney, through 1987. *Id.* , at 798. The manual contained four sentences, nothing more, on *Brady* .[15] This slim instruction, the jury learned, was notably inaccurate, incomplete, and dated. Tr. 798–804, 911–918. But cf. *ante* , at 13 ("Senior attorneys also circulated court decisions and instructional memoranda to keep the prose-cutors abreast of relevant legal developments."). For example, the manual did not acknowledge what *Giglio* v. *United States* , 405 U.S. 150 (1972) , made plain: Impeachment evidence is *Brady* material prosecutors are obligated to disclose.[16]

In sum, the evidence permitted the jury to reach the following conclusions. First, Connick did not ensure that prosecutors in his Office knew their *Brady* obligations; he neither confirmed their familiarity with *Brady* when he hired them, nor saw to it that training took place on his watch. Second, the need for *Brady* training and monitoring was obvious to Connick. Indeed he so testified. Third, Connick's cavalier approach to his staff's knowledge and observation of *Brady* requirements contributed to a culture of inattention to *Brady* in Orleans Parish.

As earlier noted, see *supra* , at 11, Connick resisted an effort to hold prosecutors accountable for *Brady* compliance because he felt the effort would "make [his] job more difficult." Tr. 978. He never disciplined or fired a single prosecutor for violating *Brady* . Tr. 182–183. The jury was told of this Court's decision in *Kyles* v. *Whitley* , 514 U.S. 419 (1995) , a capital case prosecuted by Connick's Office that garnered attention because it featured "so many instances of the state's failure to disclose exculpatory evidence." *Id.* , at 455 (Stevens, J., concurring). When questioned about *Kyles* , Connick told the jury he was satisfied with his Office's practices and saw no need, occasioned by *Kyles* , to make any changes. Tr. 184–185. In both quantity and quality, then, the evidence canvassed here was more than sufficient to warrant a jury determination that Connick and the prosecutors who served under him were not merely negligent regarding *Brady* . Rather, they were deliberately indifferent to what the law requires.

B

In *Canton* , this Court spoke of circumstances in which the need for training may be "so obvious," and the lack of training "so likely" to result in constitutional violations, that policymakers who do not provide for the requisite training "can reasonably be said to have been deliberately indifferent to the need" for such training. 489 U.S., at 390. This case, I am convinced, belongs in the category *Canton* marked out.

Canton offered an often-cited illustration. "[C]ity policymakers know to a moral certainty that their police officers will be required to arrest fleeing felons." *Ibid* ., n.10. Those policymakers, *Canton* observed, equip police officers with firearms to facilitate such arrests. *Ibid.* The need to instruct armed officers about "constitutional limitations on the use of deadly force," *Canton* said, is "'so obvious,' that failure to [train the officers] could properly be characterized as 'deliberate indifference' to constitutional rights." Ibid.

The District Court, tracking *Canton* 's language, instructed the jury that Thompson could prevail on his "deliberate indifference" claim only if the evidence persuaded the jury on three points. First, Connick "was certain that prosecutors would confront the situation where they would have to decide which evidence was required by the Constitution to be provided to the accused." Tr. 1099. Second, "the situation involved a difficult choice[,] or one that prosecutors had a history of mishandling, such that additional training, supervision or monitoring was clearly needed." *Ibid.* Third, "the wrong choice by a prosecutor in that situation would frequently cause a deprivation of an accused's constitutional rights." *Ibid.* ; Record 1619–1620; see *Canton* , 489 U.S., at 390, and n.10; *Walker* v. *New York* , 974 F.2d 293, 297–298 (CA2 1992).[17]

Petitioners used this formulation of the failure to train standard in pretrial and post-trial submissions, Record 1256–1257, 1662, and in their own proposed jury instruction on deliberate indifference.[18] Nor do petitioners dispute that Connick "kn[e]w to a moral certainty that" his prosecutors would regularly face *Brady* decisions. See *Canton* , 489 U.S., at 390, n.10.

The jury, furthermore, could reasonably find that *Brady* rights may involve choices so difficult that Connick obviously knew or should have known prosecutors needed more than perfunctory training to make the correct choices. See *Canton* , 489 U.S., at 390, and n. 10.[19] As demonstrated earlier, see *supra* , at 16–18, even at trial prosecutors failed to give an accurate account of their *Brady* obligations. And, again as emphasized earlier, see *supra* , at 18–20, the evidence permitted the jury to conclude that Connick should have known *Brady* training in his office bordered on "zero." See Tr. of Oral Arg. 41. Moreover, Connick understood that newer prosecutors needed "very clear" guidance and should not be left to grapple with *Brady* on their own. Tr. 834–835. It was thus "obvious" to him, the jury could find, that constitutional rights would be in jeopardy if prosecutors received slim to no *Brady* training.

Based on the evidence presented, the jury could conclude that *Brady* errors by untrained prosecutors would frequently cause deprivations of defendants' constitutional rights. The jury learned of several *Brady* oversights in Thompson's trials and heard testimony that Connick's Office had one of the worst *Brady* records in the country. Tr. 163. Because prosecutors faced considerable pressure to get convictions, *id.* , at 317, 341, and were instructed to "turn over what was required by state and federal law, but no more," Brief for Petitioners 6–7, the risk was all too real that they would err by withholding rather than revealing information favorable to the defense.

In sum, despite Justice Scalia's protestations to the contrary, *ante* , at 1, 5, the *Brady* violations in Thompson's prosecutions were not singular and they were not aberrational. They were just what one would expect given the attitude toward *Brady* pervasive in the District Attorney's Office. Thompson demonstrated that no fewer than five prosecutors— the four trial prosecutors and Riehlmann—disregarded his *Brady* rights. He established that they kept from him, year upon year, evidence vital to his defense. Their conduct, he showed with equal force, was a foreseeable consequence of lax training in, and absence of monitoring of, a legal requirement fundamental to a fair trial.[20]

C

Unquestionably, a municipality that leaves police officers untrained in constitutional limits on the use of deadly weapons places lives in jeopardy. *Canton* , 489 U.S., at 390, n.10. But as this case so vividly shows, a municipality that empowers prosecutors to press for a death sentence without ensuring that those prosecutors know and honor *Brady* rights may be no less "deliberately indifferent" to the risk to innocent lives.

Brady, this Court has long recognized, is among the most basic safeguards brigading a criminal defendant's fair trial right. See *Cone* v. *Bell* , 556 U.S. ___, ___ (2009) (slip op., at 1). See also *United States* v. *Bagley* , 473 U.S. 667, 695 (1985) (Marshall, J., dissenting). Vigilance in superintending prosecutors' attention to *Brady* 's requirement is all the more important for this reason: A *Brady* violation, by its nature, causes suppression of evidence beyond the defendant's capacity to ferret out. Because the absence of the withheld evidence may result in the conviction of an innocent defendant, it is unconscionable not to impose reasonable controls impelling prosecutors to bring the information to light.

The Court nevertheless holds *Canton* 's example inapposite. It maintains that professional obligations, ethics rules, and training—including on-the-job training—set attorneys apart from other municipal employees, including rookie police officers. *Ante* , at 12–15. Connick "had every incentive at trial to attempt to establish" that he could reasonably rely on the professional education and status of his staff. Cf. *ante* , at 10, n.6. But the jury heard and rejected his argument to that effect. Tr. 364, 576–577, 834–835.

The Court advances Connick's argument with greater clarity, but with no greater support. On what basis can one be confident that law schools acquaint students with prosecutors' unique obligation under *Brady* ? Whittaker told the jury he did not recall covering *Brady* in his criminal procedure class in law school. Tr. 335. Dubelier's *alma mater* , like most other law faculties, does not make criminal procedure a required course.[21]

Connick suggested that the bar examination ensures that new attorneys will know what *Brady* demands. Tr. 835. Research indicates, however, that from 1980 to the present, *Brady* questions have not accounted for even 10% of the total points in the criminal law and procedure section of any administration of the Louisiana Bar Examination.[22] A person sitting for the Louisiana Bar Examination, moreover, need pass only five of the exam's nine sections.[23] One can qualify for admission to the profession with no showing of even passing knowledge of criminal law and procedure.

The majority's suggestion that lawyers do not need *Brady* training because they "are equipped with the tools to find, interpret, and apply legal principles," *ante* , at 17–18, "blinks reality" and is belied by the facts of this case. See Brief for Former Federal Civil Rights Officials and Prosecutors as *Amici Curiae* 13. Connick himself recognized that his prosecutors, because of their inexperience, were not so equipped. Indeed, "understanding and complying with *Brady* obligations are not easy tasks, and the appropriate way to resolve *Brady* issues is not always self-evident." Brief for Former Federal Civil Rights Officials and Prosecutors as *Amici Curiae* 6. " *Brady* compliance," therefore, "is too much at risk, and too fundamental to the fairness of our criminal justice system, to be taken for granted," and "training remains critical." *Id.* , at 3, 7.

The majority further suggests that a prior pattern of similar violations is necessary to show deliberate indifference to defendants' *Brady* rights. See *ante* , at 5–6, and n.4, 11–12.[24] The text of §1983 contains no such limitation.[25] Nor is there any reason to imply such a limitation.[26] A district attorney's deliberate indifference might be shown in several ways short of a prior pattern.[27] This case is one such instance. Connick, who himself had been indicted for suppression of evidence, created a tinderbox in Orleans Parish in which *Brady* violations were nigh inevitable. And when they did occur, Connick insisted there was no need to change anything, and opposed efforts to hold prosecutors accountable on the ground that doing so would make his job more difficult.

A District Attorney aware of his office's high turnover rate, who recruits prosecutors fresh out of law school and promotes them rapidly through the ranks, bears responsibility for ensuring that on-the-job training takes place. In short, the buck stops with him.[28] As the Court recognizes, "the duty to produce *Brady* evidence to the defense" is "[a]mong prosecutors' unique ethical obligations." *Ante* , at 13. The evidence in this case presents overwhelming support for the conclusion that the Orleans Parish Office slighted its responsibility to the profession and to the State's system of justice by providing no on-the-job *Brady* training. Connick was not "entitled to rely on prosecutors' professional training," *ante* , at 14, for Connick himself should have been the principal insurer of that training.

* * *

For the reasons stated, I would affirm the judgment of the U.S. Court of Appeals for the Fifth Circuit. Like that court and, before it, the District Court, I would uphold the jury's verdict awarding damages to Thompson for the gross, deliberately indifferent, and long-continuing violation of his fair trial right.

NOTES

[1] Exhibits entered into evidence in Thompson's §1983 trial are herein cited by reference to the page number in the exhibit binder compiled by the District Court and included in the record on appeal.

[2] The majority endorses the Fifth Circuit's conclusion that, when Thompson was tried for murder, no Brady violation occurred with respect to these audio tapes "[b]ecause defense counsel had knowledge of such evidence and could easily have requested access from the prosecution." Thompson v. Cain, 161 F.3d 802, 806–807 (1998); ante, at 17, n.11. The basis for that asserted "knowledge" is a mystery. The recordings secretly made did not come to light until long after Thompson's trials.

[3] At the time of their assignment, Dubelier had served in the District Attorney's Office for three and a half years, Williams, for four and a half years, Deegan, a recent law school graduate, for less than one year, and Whittaker, for three years.

[4] Connick did not dispute that failure to disclose the swatch and the crime lab report violated Brady. See Tr. 46, 1095. But cf. ante, at 4, 6 (limiting Connick's concession, as Connick himself did not, to failure to disclose the crime lab report). In Justice Scalia's contrary view, "[t]here was probably no Brady violation at all," or, if there was any violation of Thompson's rights, it "was surely on the very frontier of our Brady jurisprudence," such that "Connick could not possibly have been on notice" of the need to train. Ante, at 7. Connick's counsel, however, saw the matter differently. "[A]ny reasonable prosecutor would have recognized blood evidence as Brady material," he said, indeed "the proper response" was "obvious to all." Record 1663, 1665.

[5] The majority assails as "highly suspect" the suggestion that prosecutors violated Brady by failing to

disclose the blood-stained swatch. See ante, at 17, n.11. But the parties stipulated in Thompson's §1983 action, and the jury was so informed, that, "[p]rior to the armed robbery trial, Mr. Thompson and his attorneys were not advised of the existence of the blood evidence, that the evidence had been tested, [or] that a blood type was determined definitively from the swatch ...." Tr. 46. Consistent with this stipulation, Thompson's trial counsel testified that he spoke to "[t]he clerk who maintain[ed] the evidence" and learned that "[t]hey didn't have any blood evidence." Id., at 401. And the District Court instructed the jury, with no objection from Connick, "that the nonproduced blood evidence ... violated [Thompson's] constitutional rights as a matter of law." Id., at 1095.

[6] Justice Scalia questions petitioners' concession that Brady was violated when the prosecution failed to inform Thompson of the blood evidence. He considers the evidence outside Brady because the prosecution did not endeavor to test Thompson's blood, and therefore avoided knowing that the evidence was in fact exculpatory. Ante, at 6–7. Such a "don't ask, don't tell" view of a prosecutor's Brady obligations garners no support from precedent. See also supra, at 6, n. 4; infra, at 21, n.13.

[7] During jury deliberations in the armed robbery case, Williams, the only Orleans Parish trial attorney common to the two prosecutions, told Thompson of his objective in no uncertain terms: "I'm going to fry you. You will die in the electric chair." Tr. 252–253.

[8] The Louisiana Court of Appeal concluded, and Connick does not dispute, that Thompson "would have testified in the absence of the attempted armed robbery conviction." State v. Thompson, 2002–0361, p. 7 (7/17/02), 825 So.2d 552, 556. But cf. ante, at 1, 3 (Thompson "elected" not to testify).

[9] Thompson argued that "the State failed to produce police reports 'and other information' which would have identified 'eye- and ear-witnesses' whose testimony would have exonerated him and inculpated [Freeman], ... and would have shown that [Perkins,] ... who stated [he] heard [Thompson] admit to committing the murder[,] had been promised reward money for [his] testimony." Thompson, 825 So.2d, at 555. In leaving these arguments unaddressed, the Louisiana Court of Appeal surely did not defer to the Fifth Circuit's earlier assessment of those claims, made on an anemic record, in Thompson v. Cain, 161 F.3d 802. Nor did the Louisiana Court of Appeal suggest that Thompson was "belatedly tr[ying] to reverse" the Fifth Circuit's decision. But cf. ante, at 17, n.11.

[10] The Court notes that in Thompson v. Cain, the Fifth Circuit rejected Brady claims raised by Thompson, characterizing one of those claims as "without merit." Ante, at 17, n.11 (quoting Thompson, 161 F.3d, at 807); see supra, at 4, n.2. The Court, however, overlooks the date of that Fifth Circuit decision. It was rendered before revelation of the Brady violations in the armed robbery trial, before Thompson had the opportunity for discovery in his §1983 suit, and before Thompson or any court was aware of the "close cut hair" police reports. See Thompson, 161 F.3d, at 812, n.8. It is these later revelations, not the little Thompson knew in 1998, that should count. For example, the Fifth Circuit, in 1998, believed that Perkins' statement recorded in the police report did not "differ from Freeman's trial testimony." Id., at 808. But evidence put before the jury in 2007 in the §1983 trial showed that the police report, in several material respects, was inconsistent with Freeman's trial testimony. Tr. 382–383.

Connick has never suggested to this Court that the jury in the §1983 trial was bound by the Fifth Circuit's 1998 Brady rulings. That court "afford[ed] great deference to" the state trial court's findings, made after a 1995 post-conviction relief hearing. Thompson, 161 F.3d, at 805. The jury in the §1983 trial, of course, had far more extensive and accurate information on which to reach its decision. Moreover, as earlier noted, the same trial court that made the 1995 findings was, in 1999, outraged by the subsequently discovered Brady violations and by Connick's reluctance to bring those violations to light. See supra, at 10–11. Certainly that judge would not have wanted the jury that assessed Connick's deliberate indifference in the §1983 trial to defer to findings he earlier made on a notably incomplete record.

[11] The court permitted Thompson to introduce evidence of other Brady violations, but because "the blood evidence alone proved the violation [of Thompson's constitutional rights]," the court declined specifically "to ask the jury [whether] this other stuff [was] also Brady." Tr. 1003. The court allowed Thompson to submit proof of other violations to "sho[w] the cumulative nature ... and impact [of] evidence ... as to ... the training and deliberate indifference ...." Ibid. But cf. ante, at 17, n.11 (questioning how "these violations are relevant" to this case). Far from indulging in my own factfindings, but cf. ante, at 16–17, n.11, I simply recite the evidence supporting the jury's verdict in

Thompson's §1983 trial. The Court misleadingly states that "the District Court instructed the jury that the 'only issue' was whether the nondisclosure [of the crime lab report] was caused by either a policy, practice, or custom of the dis-trict attorney's office or a deliberately indifferent failure to train the office's prosecutors." Ante, at 4. The jury instruction the majority cites simply directed the jury that, with regard to the blood evidence, as a matter of law, Thompson's constitutional rights had been violated. Record 1614–1615. The court did not preclude the jury from assessing evidence of other infringements of Thompson's rights. Id., at 1585; see Kyles v. Whitley, 514 U.S. 419, 421 (1995) ("[T]he state's obligation under Brady ... turns on the cumulative effect of all ... evidence suppressed by the government ....").

[12] With no objection from petitioners, the court found Thompson's expert, Joseph Lawless, qualified to testify as an expert in criminal law and procedure. Tr. 419, 426. Lawless has practiced criminal law for 30 years; from 1976 to 1979, he was an assistant district attorney, and thereafter he entered private practice. Id., at 412. He is the author of Prosecutorial Misconduct: Law, Procedure, Forms (4th ed. 2008), first published in 1985. Tr. 414. The text is used in a class on ethics and tactics for the criminal lawyer at Harvard Law School and in the federal defender training program of the Administrative Office of the United States Courts. Id., at 416.

[13] To ward off Brady violations of the kind Connick conceded, for example, Connick could have communicated to Orleans Parish prosecutors, in no uncertain terms, that, "[i]f you have physical evidence that, if tested, can establish the innocence of the person who is charged, you have to turn it over." Tr. of Oral Arg. 34; id., at 36 ("[I]f you have evidence that can conclusively establish to a scientific certainty the innocence of the person being charged, you have to turn it over ...."). Or Connick could have told prosecutors what he told the jury when he was asked whether a prosecutor must disclose a crime lab report to the defense, even if the prosecutor does not know the defendant's blood type: "Under the law it qualifies as Brady material. Under Louisiana law we must turn that over. Under Brady we must turn that over. I [failed to disclose a crime lab report] one time as a prosecutor and I got indicted by the U.S. Attorney over here for doing it." Tr. 872. But cf. ante, at 7 (Scalia, J., concurring) (questioning how Connick could have been on notice of the need to train prosecutors about the Brady violations conceded in this case).

[14] The Court can scarcely disagree with respect to Dubelier, Williams, and Whittaker, for it acknowledges the "flagran[cy]" of Deegan's conduct, see ante, at 7, n. 5, and does not dispute that, pretrial, other prosecutors knew of the existence of the swatch and lab report.

[15] Section 5.25 of the manual, titled "Brady Material," states in full: "In most cases, in response to the request of defense attorneys, the Judge orders the State to produce so called Brady material—that is, information in the possession of the State which is exculpatory regarding the defendant. The duty to produce Brady material is ongoing and continues throughout the entirety of the trial. Failure to produce Brady material has resulted in mistrials and reversals, as well as extended court battles over jeopardy issues. In all cases, a review of Brady issues, including apparently self-serving statements made by the defendant, must be included in a pre-trial conference and each Assistant must be familiar with the law regarding exculpatory information possessed by the State." Record EX427.

[16] During the relevant time period, there were many significant developments in this Court's Brady jurisprudence. Among the Brady-related decisions this Court handed down were United States v. Bagley, 473 U.S. 667, 676 (1985) ("This Court has rejected any ... distinction between impeachment evidence and exculpatory evidence [in the Brady context]."); Weatherford v. Bursey, 429 U.S. 545, 559–560 (1977) ("Brady is not implicated ... where the only claim is that the State should have revealed that it would present the eyewitness testimony of a particular agent against the defendant at trial."); and United States v. Agurs, 427 U.S. 97, 103, 104, 106–107 (1976) (Brady claim may arise when "the undisclosed evidence demonstrates that the prosecution's case includes perjured testimony and that the prosecution knew, or should have known, of the perjury," when defense counsel makes "a pretrial request for specific evidence" and the government fails to accede to that request, and when defense counsel makes no request and the government fails to disclose "obviously exculpatory" evidence). These decisions were not referenced in the manual that compiled circulated memoranda. In the same period, the Louisiana Supreme Court issued dozens of opinions discussing Brady, including State v. Sylvester, 388 So.2d 1155, 1161 (1980) (impeachment evidence must be disclosed in response to a specific request if it would create a "reasonable doubt that did not otherwise exist"); State v. Brooks, 386 So.2d 1348, 1351 (1980) (Brady extends to any material information favorable to

the accused); and State v. Carney, 334 So.2d 415, 418–419 (1976) (reversible error if prosecution fails, even inadvertently, to disclose bargain with a witness).

[17] Justice Scalia contends that this "theory of deliberate indifference would repeal the law of Monell," and creates a danger that "'failure to train' would become a talismanic incantation producing municipal liability [i]n virtually every instance where a person has had his or her constitutional rights violated by a city employee." Ante, at 2–3 (some internal quotation marks omitted). The District Court's charge, however, cautiously cabined the jury's assessment of Connick's deliberate indifference. See, e.g., Tr. 1100 ("Mr. Thompson must prove that more likely than not the Brady material would have been produced if the prosecutors involved in his underlying criminal cases had been properly trained, supervised or monitored regarding the production of Brady evidence."). See also id., at 1096–1097, 1099–1100. The deliberate indifference jury instruction in this case was based on the Second Circuit's opinion in Walker v. New York, 974 F.2d 293, 297–298 (1992), applying Canton to a §1983 complaint alleging that a district attorney failed to train prosecutors about Brady. Justice Scalia's fears should be calmed by post-Walker experience in the Second Circuit. There has been no "litigation flood or even rainfall," Skinner v. Switzer, 562 U.S. ___ (2011) (slip op., at 12), in that Circuit in Walker's wake. See Brief for National Association of Criminal Defense Lawyers as Amicus Curiae 39 ("Tellingly, in the Second Circuit, in the nearly 20 years since the court decided Walker, there have been no successful lawsuits for non-Brady constitutional violations committed by prosecutors at trial (and no reported 'single violation' Brady case)." (citation omitted)); Brief for Center on the Administration of Criminal Law, New York University School of Law, etal. as Amici Curiae 35–36 (Walker has prompted "no flood of §1983 liability").

[18] The instruction Connick proposed resembled the charge given by the District Court. See supra, at 24. Connick's proposed instruction read: "Before a district attorney's failure to train or supervise constitutes deliberate indifference to the constitutional rights of citizens: (1) the plaintiff must show that Harry Connick knew 'to a moral certainty' that his employees will confront a given situation; (2) the plaintiff must show that the situation either presents the employee with a difficult choice ... such that training or supervision will make the choice less difficult or that there is a history of employees mishandling the situation; and (3) the plaintiff must show that the wrong choice by the assistant district attorney will frequently cause the deprivation of a citizen's constitutional rights." Record 992 (citing Canton, 489 U.S., at 390; punctuation altered). But cf. ante, at 3 (Scalia, J., concurring) (criticizing "Thompson's theory" of deliberate indifference). Petitioners, it is true, argued all along that "[t]o prove deliberate indifference, Thompson had to demonstrate a pattern of violations," Brief for Appellants in No. 07–30443 (CA5), p. 41; see ante, at 3–4 (Scalia, J., concurring), but the court rejected their categorical position. Petitioners did not otherwise assail the District Court's formulation of the deliberate indifference instruction. E.g., Record 1662.

[19] Courts have noted the often trying nature of a prosecutor's Brady obligation. See, e.g., State v. Whitlock, 454 So.2d 871, 874 (La. App. 1984) (recognizing, in a case involving Brady issues in Connick's Office, that "it is usually most difficult to determine whether or not inconsistencies or omitted information in witnesses' statements are material to the defendant's guilt" (quoting State v. Davenport, 399 So.2d 201, 204 (La. 1981))).

[20] The jury could draw a direct, causal connection between Connick's deliberate indifference, prosecutors' misapprehension of Brady, and the Brady violations in Thompson's case. See, e.g., supra, at 17 (prosecutors' misunderstandings of Brady "were in large part responsible for the gross disregard of Brady rights Thompson experienced"); supra, at 18 ("The jury could attribute the violations of Thompson's rights directly to prosecutors' misapprehension of Brady."); supra, at 17–18 (Williams did not believe Brady required disclosure of impeachment evidence and did not believe he had any obligation to turn over the impeaching "close-cut hair" police reports); supra, at 18 (At the time of the armed robbery trial, Williams reported that the results of the blood test on the swatch were "inconclusive"); ibid. ("[Williams] testified ... that the lab report was not Brady material ...."); supra, at 19–20 (Dubelier and Williams, the lead prosecutors in Thompson's trials, "learned the prosecutorial craft in Connick's Office," "did not recall any Brady training," demonstrated "a woefully deficient understanding of Brady," and received no supervision during Thompson's trials); supra, at 21 ("Had Brady's importance been brought home to prosecutors, surely at least one of the four officers who knew of the swatch and lab report would have revealed their existence to defense counsel and the court."); supra, at 23 (Connick did not want to hold prosecutors accountable for Brady compliance because he felt that doing so would make his job more difficult); supra, at 23 (Connick never

disciplined a single prosecutor for violating Brady); supra, at 27 ("Because prosecutors faced considerable pressure to get convictions, and were instructed to turn over what was required by state and federal law, but no more, the risk was all too real that they would err by withholding rather than revealing information favorable to the defense." (citations and internal quotation marks omitted)). But cf. ante, at 7, n.5 ("The dissent believes that evidence that the prosecutors allegedly 'misapprehen[ded]' Brady proves causation.").

I note, furthermore, that the jury received clear instructions on the causation element, and neither Connick nor the majority disputes the accuracy or adequacy of the instruction that, to prevail, Thompson must prove "that more likely than not the Brady material would have been produced if the prosecutors involved in his underlying criminal cases had been properly trained, supervised or monitored regarding the production of Brady evidence." Tr. 1100.

The jury was properly instructed that "[f]or liability to attach because of a failure to train, the fault must be in the training program itself, not in any particular prosecutor." Id., at 1098. Under that instruction, in finding Connick liable, the jury necessarily rejected the argument—echoed by Justice Scalia—that Deegan "was the only bad guy." Id., at 1074. See also id., at 1057; ante, at 5. If indeed Thompson had shown simply and only that Deegan deliberately withheld evidence, I would agree that there would be no basis for liability. But, as reams of evidence showed, disregard of Brady occurred, over and over again in Orleans Parish, before, during, and after Thompson's 1985 robbery and murder trials.

[21] See Tulane University Law School, Curriculum, http://www.law.tulane.edu (select "Academics"; select "Curriculum") (as visited Mar. 21, 2011, and in Clerk of Court's case file).

[22] See Supreme Court of Louisiana, Committee on Bar Admissions, Compilation of Louisiana State Bar Examinations, Feb. 1980 through July 2010 (available in Clerk of Court's case file).

[23] See La. State Bar Assn., Articles of Incorporation, Art. 14, §10(A), La. Rev. Stat. Ann. §37, ch. 4, App. (West 1974); ibid. (West 1988).

[24] Board of Comm'rs of Bryan Cty. v. Brown, 520 U.S. 397 (1997) , reaffirmed "that evidence of a single violation of federal rights, accompanied by a showing that a municipality has failed to train its employees to handle recurring situations presenting an obvious potential for such a violation, could trigger municipal liability." Id., at 409. Conducting this inquiry, the Court has acknowledged, "may not be an easy task for the factfinder." Canton v. Harris, 489 U.S. 378, 391 (1989) . Bryan County did not retreat from this Court's conclusion in Canton that "judge and jury, doing their respective jobs, will be adequate to the task." 489 U.S., at 391. See also Bryan County, 520 U.S., at 410 (absent a pattern, municipal liability may be predicated on "a particular glaring omission in a training regimen"). But cf. ante, at 16–18 (suggesting that under no set of facts could a plaintiff establish deliberate indifference for failure to train prosecutors in their Brady obligation without showing a prior pattern of violations).

[25] When Congress sought to render a claim for relief contingent on showing a pattern or practice, it did so expressly. See, e.g., 42 U.S.C. §14141(a) ("It shall be unlawful for any governmental authority ... to engage in a pattern or practice of conduct by law enforcement officers ... that deprives persons of rights ... protected by the Constitution ...."); 15 U.S.C. §6104(a) ("Any person adversely affected by any pattern or practice of telemarketing ... may ... bring a civil action ...."); 49 U.S.C. §306(e) (authorizing the Attorney General to bring a civil action when he "has reason to believe that a person is engaged in a pattern or practice [of] violating this section"). See also 47 U.S.C. §532(e)(2)–(3) (authorizing the Federal Communications Commission to establish additional rules when "the Commission finds that the prior adjudicated violations of this section constitute a pattern or practice of violations").

[26] In the end, the majority leaves open the possibility that something other than "a pattern of violations" could also give a district attorney "specific reason" to know that additional training is necessary. See ante, at 14–15. Connick, by his own admission, had such a reason. See supra, at 18–20.

[27] For example, a prosecutor's office could be deliberately indifferent if it had a longstanding open-file policy, abandoned that policy, but failed to provide training to show prosecutors how to comply with their Brady obligations in the altered circumstances. Or a district attorney could be deliberately indifferent if he had a practice of paring well-trained prosecutors with untrained prosecutors, knew that such supervision had stopped untrained prosecutors from committing Brady violations, but

nevertheless changed the staffing on cases so that untrained prosecutors worked without supervision.

[28] If the majority reads this statement as an endorsement of respondeat superior liability, ante, at 18, n.12, then it entirely "misses [my] point," cf. ante, at 17. Canton recognized that deliberate indifference liability and respondeat superior liability are not one and the same. 489 U.S., at 385, 388–389. Connick was directly responsible for the Brady violations in Thompson's prosecutions not because he hired prosecutors who violated Brady, but because of his own deliberate indifference.

UNITED STATES v. TOHONO O'ODHAM NATION

No. 09-846, April 26, 2011

ON WRIT OF CERTIORARI TO THE UNITED STATES COURT OF APPEALS FOR THE FEDERAL CIRCUIT

Justice Ginsburg, dissenting.

I dissent from the Court's immoderate reading of 28 U.S.C. §1500 and would affirm the Federal Circuit's judgment.

According to the Court, the Court of Federal Claims (CFC) lacks subject-matter jurisdiction over the Tohono O'odham Nation's (Nation) claim because the Tribe was simultaneously pursuing in the D.C. District Court an action with "a common factual basis." *Ante* , at 1. It matters not, the Court holds, that to gain complete relief, the Nation had to launch two suits, for neither of the two courts whose jurisdiction the Tribe invoked could alone provide full redress. See *ante* , at 8–9.

The Court concludes that "claim" or "cause of action," terms the Court considers synonymous as used in §1500,[*] see *ante* , at 5, refers to "operative facts," and not to the remedies a plaintiff seeks. See *ante* , at 4. Section 1500 speaks of "the time when the cause of action ... arose," a time antedating the commencement of suit. The Court infers, therefore, that a "claim" or "cause of action" is discrete from a pleading's request for relief. See *ante* , at 4. In fact, however, entitlement to relief is essential to the existence of a claim or cause of action, which arises when a person suffers a harm capable of judicial redress. See 2 J. Story, Equity Jurisprudence §1521 *a* , p. 741 (8th ed. 1861) ("[T]he cause of action ... arises when ... the party has a right to apply to a court ... for relief.").

A plaintiff may not, §1500 instructs, petition both the CFC and a district court, invoking in each a distinct legal theory appropriate to the forum, but seeking redress for a single injury. When Congress bars a plaintiff from obtaining complete relief in one suit, however, and does not call for an election of remedies, Congress is most sensibly read to have comprehended that the operative facts give rise to two discrete claims. *Casman* v. *United States* , 135 Ct. Cl. 647 (1956), as Justice Sotomayor spells out, see *ante* , at 5, is the paradigm case. There, a discharged federal employee, complaining of wrongful termination, sought reinstatement in a district-court action and backpay in the Court of Claims. Section 1500 does not stand in the way, the Court of Claims held in *Casman* , when the plaintiff suffered two distinct injuries, for which she seeks discrete forms of relief within the exclusive competence of different courts. See 135 Ct. Cl., at 649–650 (claim for backpay "entirely different" from claim for reinstatement). The Federal Circuit, in my view, rightly adhered to *Casman* in *Loveladies Harbor, Inc.* v. *United States* , 27 F.3d 1545 (1994) (en banc), and rightly did so in this case.

While I agree with much of Justice Sotomayor 's opinion concurring in the judgment, I do not agree with her conclusion that §1500 bars the Nation's CFC action. Justice Sotomayor joins the Court's judgment (although not the Court's reasoning) because the "Tohono O'odham Nation seeks in the [CFC] ... *some* of the same relief on the same facts as it does in its pending District Court action." *Ante* , at 1 (emphasis added). But to the extent that "the Nation's two actions seek overlapping relief," *ibid* ., a disposition less harsh would be in order. Ordinarily, when a plaintiff's allegations and demands for relief are excessive, her complaint is not instantly dismissed on that account. Instead, she may seek leave to trim her pleading, permission a court "should freely give ... when justice so requires." Rule 15(a)(2) (CFC 2010). Cf. Rule 54(c) (CFC 2010) (judgment, other than default, need not conform to demand for relief, but "should grant the relief to which each party is entitled").

As Justice Sotomayor and the Nation recognize, to avoid both duplication and the running of the statute of limitations, the CFC suit could be stayed while the companion District Court action proceeds. See *ante* , at 11; Brief for Respondent 35. That is a common practice when a prior action is pending. See *Pennsylvania R. Co.* v. *United States* , 363 U.S. 202, 204–206 (1960) (instructing Court of Claims to stay pending proceedings to enable litigant to obtain District Court review of relevant agency order); *Creppel* v. *United States* , 41 F.3d 627, 633 (CA Fed. 1994) ("[T]he Court of Federal Claims may stay a takings action pending completion of a related action in a district court.").

Why is this Court not positioned to direct the CFC to disregard requests for relief simultaneously sought in a district-court action, or at least to recognize that an amended CFC complaint could save the case? I see no impediment to either course, in §1500 or any other law or rule.

NOTES

[*] "'Cause of action,'" the Court simultaneously states, "is the more technical term." Ante, at 5. If "more technical" means more precise, clear or certain, the Court is incorrect. See United States v. Memphis Cotton Oil Co., 288 U.S. 62, 67–68 (1933) ("A 'cause of action' may mean one thing for one purpose

and something different for another."). In its discourse on the term, the Court has fallen into an old error; the drafters of the Federal Rules endeavored to "eliminate the unfortunate rigidity and confusion surrounding the words 'cause of action.'" 5 C. Wright & A. Miller, Federal Practice and Procedure §1216, p. 207 (3d ed. 2004). Today's invocation of a supposed particular or exact meaning for the phrase risks reviving that confusion.

KENTUCKY v. HOLLIS DESHAUN KING

No. 09-1272, May 16, 2011

ON WRIT OF CERTIORARI TO THE SUPREME COURT OF KENTUCKY

Justice Ginsburg, dissenting.

The Court today arms the police with a way routinely to dishonor the Fourth Amendment 's warrant requirement in drug cases. In lieu of presenting their evidence to a neutral magistrate, police officers may now knock, listen, then break the door down, nevermind that they had ample time to obtain a warrant. I dissent from the Court's reduction of the Fourth Amendment 's force.

The Fourth Amendment guarantees to the people "[t]he right … to be secure in their … houses … against unreasonable searches and seizures." Warrants to search, the Amendment further instructs, shall issue only upon a showing of "probable cause" to believe criminal activity is afoot. These complementary provisions are designed to ensure that police will seek the authorization of a neutral magistrate before undertaking a search or seizure. Exceptions to the warrant requirement, this Court has explained, must be "few in number and carefully delineated," if the main rule is to remain hardy. *United States* v. *United States Dist. Court for Eastern Dist. of Mich.*, 407 U.S. 297, 318 (1972); see *Kyllo* v. *United States*, 533 U.S. 27, 31 (2001).

This case involves a principal exception to the warrant requirement, the exception applicable in "exigent circumstances." See *ante*, at 6–7. "[C]arefully delineated," the exception should govern only in genuine emergency situations. Circumstances qualify as "exigent" when there is an imminent risk of death or serious injury, or danger that evidence will be immediately destroyed, or that a suspect will escape. *Brigham City* v. *Stuart*, 547 U.S. 398, 403 (2006) . The question presented: May police, who could pause to gain the approval of a neutral magistrate, dispense with the need to get a warrant by themselves creating exigent circumstances? I would answer no, as did the Kentucky Supreme Court. The urgency must exist, I would rule, when the police come on the scene, not subsequent to their arrival, prompted by their own conduct.

I

Two pillars of our Fourth Amendment jurisprudence should have controlled the Court's ruling: First, "whenever practical, [the police must] obtain advance judicial approval of searches and seizures through the warrant procedure," *Terry* v. *Ohio* , 392 U.S. 1, 20 (1968) ; second, unwarranted "searches and seizures inside a home" bear heightened scrutiny, *Payton* v. *New York* , 445 U.S. 573, 586 (1980). The warrant requirement, Justice Jackson observed, ranks among the "fundamental distinctions between our form of government, where officers are under the law, and the police-state where they are the law." *Johnson* v. *United States* , 333 U.S. 10, 17 (1948). The Court has accordingly declared warrantless searches, in the main, " *per se* unreasonable." *Mincey* v. *Arizona* , 437 U.S. 385, 390 (1978); see also *Groh* v. *Ramirez* , 540 U.S. 551, 559 (2004) . "[T]he police bear a heavy burden," the Court has cautioned, "when attempting to demonstrate an urgent need that might justify warrantless searches." *Welsh* v. *Wisconsin*, 466 U.S. 740, 749–750 (1984).

That heavy burden has not been carried here. There was little risk that drug-related evidence would have been destroyed had the police delayed the search pending a magistrate's authorization. As the Court recognizes, "[p]ersons in possession of valuable drugs are unlikely to destroy them unless they fear discovery by the police." *Ante* , at 8. Nothing in the record shows that, prior to the knock at the apartment door, the occupants were apprehensive about police proximity.

In no quarter does the Fourth Amendment apply with greater force than in our homes, our most private space which, for centuries, has been regarded as "'entitled to special protection.'" *Georgia* v. *Randolph*, 547 U.S. 103, and n.4 (2006); *Minnesota* v. *Carter* , 525 U.S. 83, 99 (1998) (Kennedy, J., concurring). Home intrusions, the Court has said, are indeed "the chief evil against which … the Fourth Amendment is directed." *Payton* , 445 U.S., at 585 (internal quotation marks omitted); see *Silverman* v. *United States* , 365 U.S. 505, 511 (1961) ("At [the Fourth Amendment 's] very core stands the right of a man to retreat to his own home and there be free from unreasonable governmental intrusion."). "'[S]earches and seizures inside a home without a warrant are [therefore] presumptively unreasonable.'" *Brigham City* , 547 U.S., at 403 (quoting *Groh* , 540 U.S., at 559). How "secure" do our homes remain if police, armed with no warrant, can pound on doors at will and, on hearing sounds indicative of things moving, forcibly enter and search for evidence of unlawful activity?

II

As above noted, to justify the police activity in this case, Kentucky invoked the once-guarded exception for emergencies "in which the delay necessary to obtain a warrant ... threaten[s] 'the destruction of evidence.'" *Schmerber* v. *California* , 384 U.S. 757, 770 (1966) (quoting *Preston* v. *United States* , 376 U.S. 364, 367 (1964)). To fit within this exception, "police action literally must be [taken] 'now or never' to preserve the evidence of the crime." *Roaden* v. *Kentucky*, 413 U.S. 496, 505 (1973).

The existence of a genuine emergency depends not only on the state of necessity at the time of the warrantless search; it depends, first and foremost, on "actions taken by the police *preceding* the warrantless search." *United States* v. *Coles* , 437 F.3d 361, 367 (CA3 2006). See also *United States* v. *Chambers* , 395 F.3d 563, 565 (CA6 2005) ("[O]fficers must seek a warrant based on probable cause when they believe in advance they will find contraband or evidence of a crime."). "[W]asting a clear opportunity to obtain a warrant," therefore, "disentitles the officer from relying on subsequent exigent circumstances." S. Saltzburg & D. Capra, American Criminal Procedure 376 (8th ed. 2007).

Under an appropriately reined-in "emergency" or "exigent circumstances" exception, the result in this case should not be in doubt. The target of the investigation's entry into the building, and the smell of marijuana seeping under the apartment door into the hallway, the Kentucky Supreme Court rightly determined, gave the police "probable cause ... sufficient ... to obtain a warrant to search the ... apartment." 302 S.W. 3d 649, 653 (2010). As that court observed, nothing made it impracticable for the police to post officers on the premises while proceeding to obtain a warrant authorizing their entry. *Id* ., at 654. Before this Court, Kentucky does not urge otherwise. See Brief for Petitioner 35, n.13 (asserting "[i]t should be of no importance whether police could have obtained a warrant").

In *Johnson*, the Court confronted this scenario: standing outside a hotel room, the police smelled burning opium and heard "some shuffling or noise" coming from the room. 333 U.S., at 12 (internal quotation marks omitted). Could the police enter the room without a warrant? The Court answered no. Explaining why, the Court said:

> "The right of officers to thrust themselves into a home is ... a grave concern, not only to the individual but to a society which chooses to dwell in reasonable security and freedom from surveillance. When the right of privacy must reasonably yield to the right of search is, as a rule, to be decided by a judicial officer, not a policeman ....
>
> . . .
>
> "If the officers in this case were excused from the constitutional duty of presenting their evidence to a magistrate, it is difficult to think of [any] case in which [a warrant] should be required." *Id*., at 14–15.

I agree, and would not allow an expedient knock to override the warrant requirement.[*] Instead, I would accord that core requirement of the Fourth Amendment full respect. When possible, "a warrant must generally be secured," the Court acknowledges. *Ante,* at 5. There is every reason to conclude that securing a warrant was entirely feasible in this case, and no reason to contract the Fourth Amendment 's dominion.

NOTES

[*] The Court in Johnson was informed that "when [the officer] knocked on [Johnson's] door the 'first thing that naturally struck [her]' was to conceal the opium and the equipment for smoking it." See Brief for United States in Johnson v. United States, O.T. 1947, No. 329, p.17, n. 6. Had the Government in Johnson urged that the "shuffling or noise" indicated evidence was at risk, would the result have changed? Justice Jackson's recognition of the primacy of the warrant requirement suggests not. But see ante, at 15, n.5 (distinguishing Johnson on the ground that the Government did not contend "that the officers entered the room in order to prevent the destruction of evidence").

DANIEL COLEMAN v. COURT OF APPEALS OF MARYLAND

No. 10-1016, March 20, 2012

ON WRIT OF CERTIORARI TO THE UNITED STATES COURT OF APPEALS FOR THE FOURTH CIRCUIT

Justice Ginsburg, with whom Justice Breyer joins, and with whom Justice Sotomayor and Justice Kagan join as to all but footnote 1, dissenting.

Section 1 of the Fourteenth Amendment provides: "No State shall ... deny to any person within its jurisdiction the equal protection of the laws." Section 5 grants Congress the "power to enforce, by appropriate legislation, the provisions of this article." Congress' §5 enforcement power includes the authority to remedy and deter violations of §1's substantive guarantees by prohibiting conduct "not itself forbidden by the Amendment's text." *Kimel* v. *Flor-ida Bd. of Regents*, 528 U.S. 62, 81 (2000) . "In other words, Congress may enact so-called prophylactic leg-islation that proscribes facially constitutional conduct,in order to prevent and deter unconstitutional conduct." *Nevada Dept. of Human Resources* v. *Hibbs*, 538 U.S. 721–728 (2003).

The Family and Medical Leave Act of 1993 (FMLA or Act) entitles eligible employees to 12 weeks of job-secured leave during any 12-month period: (A) to care for a newborn son or daughter; (B) to care for a newly adopted son or daughter; (C) to care for a spouse, child, or parent with a serious health condition; or (D) because the employee has a serious health condition that makes her unableto perform the functions of her position. 29 U.S.C. §2612(a)(1).

Even accepting this Court's view of the scope of Congress' power under §5 of the Fourteenth Amendment, I would hold that the self-care provision, §2612(a)(1)(D), validly enforces the right to be free from gender discrimination in the workplace.[1]

I

Section 5 legislation "must be targeted at conduct transgressing the Fourteenth Amendment's substantive provisions," *ante*, at 5 (internal quotation marks omitted), "[a]nd '[t]here must be a congruence and proportionality between the injury to be prevented or remedied and the means adopted to that end.'" *Ibid.* (quoting *City of Boerne* v. *Flores*, 521 U.S. 507, 520 (1997)). The first step of the now-familiar *Boerne* inquiry calls for identification of the constitutional right Congress sought to enforce. See, *e.g.*, *Tennessee* v. *Lane*, 541 U.S. 509, 522 (2004) . The FMLA's self-care provision, Maryland asserts, trains not on the right to be free from gender discrimination, but on an "equal protection right to be free from irrational state employment discrimination based on a medical condition." Brief for Respondents 14. The plurality agrees, concluding that the self-care provision reveals "a concern for discrimination on the basis of illness, not sex." *Ante*, at 7. In so declaring, the plurality undervalues the language, purpose, and history of the FMLA, and the self-care provision's important role in the statutory scheme. As well, the plurality underplays the main theme of our decision in *Hibbs*: "The FMLA aims to protect the right to be free from gender-based discrimination in the workplace." 538 U.S., at 728.

I begin with the text of the statute, which repeatedly emphasizes gender discrimination. One of the FMLA's stated purposes is to "entitle employees to take reasonable leave," 29 U.S.C. §2601(b)(2), "in a manner that, consistent with the Equal Protection Clause of the Fourteenth Amendment, minimizes the potential for employment dis-crimination on the basis of sex by ensuring generallythat leave is available for eligible medical reasons (including maternity-related disability) and for compelling family reasons, on a gender-neutral basis." §2601(b)(4). Another identified aim is "to promote the goal of equal employment opportunity for women and men, pursuant to [the Equal Protection Clause]." §2601(b)(5). "[E]mployment standards that apply to one gender only," Congress expressly found, "have serious potential for encouraging employers to discriminate against employees and applicants for employment who are of that gender." §2601(a)(6).

The FMLA's purpose and legislative history reinforce the conclusion that the FMLA, in its entirety, is directed at sex discrimination. Indeed, the FMLA was originally envisioned as a way to guarantee—without singling out women or pregnancy—that pregnant women would not lose their jobs when they gave birth. The self-care provision achieves that aim.

A brief history is in order. In his 1982 congressional campaign, then-candidate Howard Berman pledged to introduce legislation similar to the California law challenged in *California Fed. Sav. & Loan Assn.* v. *Guerra*, 479 U.S. 272 (1987) . S. Wisensale, Family Leave Policy: The Political Economy of Work and Family in America 134 (2001) (hereinafter Wisensale). California's law, enacted in 1978, made it unlawful for an employer to refuse to grant female employees disabled by pregnancy or childbirth up to four months' unpaid, job-protected leave. See 1978 Cal. Stats. ch. 1321, §1, now codified at Cal. Govt. Code Ann. §12945(a)(1) (West Supp. 2012).

The California law sharply divided women's rights ad-vocates. "Equal-treatment" feminists asserted it violated the Pregnancy Discrimination Act's (PDA) commitmentto treating pregnancy the same as other disabilities.[2] It did so by requiring leave only for disability caused by pregnancy and childbirth, thereby treating pregnancy as *sui generis*. See Brief for American Civil Liberties Union et al. as *Amici Curiae* in *California Fed.*, O. T. 1985,No. 85–494, pp.5–10. "Equal-opportunity" feminists dis-agreed, urging that the California law was consistent with the PDA because it remedied the discriminatory burden that inadequate leave policies placed on a woman's right to procreate. See Brief for Coalition for Reproductive Equality in the Workplace et al. as *Amici Curiae* in *id.,*at 2–6. See also Williams, Equality's Riddle: Pregnancy and the Equal Treatment/Special Treatment Debate, 13 N. Y. U. Rev. L. & Soc. Change 325, 326–328 (1984–1985) (hereinafter Williams) (discussing disagreement).

While *California Fed.* moved through the lower federal courts, equal-treatment feminists began work on a gender-neutral leave model, which eventually became the FMLA. See Ross, Legal Aspects of Parental Leave, in Parental Leave and Child Care 97 (J. Hyde & M. Essex eds. 1991) (hereinafter Ross). Then-Congressman Berman met with the Women's Legal Defense Fund's Donna Lenhoff, a drafter of the first FMLA bill. *Id.,* at 114–115, n. 27; Wisensale 136.[3] They agreed that any national bill would focus not only on pregnancy, but on equal treatment for all workers. Ross 114–115, n. 27. See also *Kazmier* v. *Widmann*, 225 F.3d 519, 547 (CA5 2000) (Dennis, J., dissenting) ("Perceiving that enacting the PDA had not achieved the intended result of preventing discrimination against either women or men in the granting of leave time in that the States felt it necessary to affirmatively grant preg-nancy leave to women and not men, in 1985 Congress began considering the issue of family and medical leave.").

Though this Court, in *California Fed.*, eventually upheld California's pregnancy-only leave policy as not preempted by the PDA, equal-treatment feminists continued to believe that viewing pregnancy as *sui generis* perpetuated widespread discrimination against women.[4] They therefore maintained their commitment to gender-neutral leave. See Joint Hearing on H.R. 925 before the Subcommittee on Civil Service and the Subcommittee on Compensation and Employee Benefits of the House Committee on Post Office and Civil Service, 100th Cong., 1st Sess.,36 (1987) (hereinafter 1987 House Hearing) (statement of Prof. Eleanor Holmes Norton, Georgetown University Law Center) ("[If *California Fed.*] becomes the model, employers will provide something for women affected by pregnancy that they are not required to provide for other employees. This gives fodder to those who seek to discriminate against women in employment.... In the *[California Fed.]* case, I would have preferred the interpretation urged by the [equal-treatment feminists].").

Congress agreed. See *infra*, at 14–15. Adhering to equal-treatment feminists' aim, the self-care provision, 29 U.S.C. §2612(a)(1)(D), prescribes comprehensive leave for women disabled during pregnancy or while recuperating from childbirth—without singling out pregnancy or childbirth. See S. Rep. No. 101–77, p. 32 (1989) (A "significant benefit of the temporary medical leave provided by this legislation is the form of protection it offers women workers who bear children. Because the bill treats all employees who are temporarily unable to work due to serious health conditions in the same fashion, it does not create the risk of discrimination against pregnant women posed by legislation which provides job protection only forpregnancy-related disability. Legislation solely protecting pregnant women gives employers an economic incentive to discriminate against women in hiring policies; legislation helping all workers equally does not have this effect."). In view of this history, it is impossible to conclude that "nothing in particular about self-care leave ... connects it to gender discrimination." *Ante,* at 10.

II

A

Boerne next asks "whether Congress had evidence ofa pattern of constitutional violations on the part of the States." *Hibbs*, 538 U.S., at 729. See also *Boerne*, 521 U.S., at 530–532. Beyond question, Congress had evidence of a well-documented pattern of workplace discrimination against pregnant women. Section 2612(a)(1)(D) can therefore "be understood as responsive to, or designed to prevent, unconstitutional behavior." *Id.,* at 532.

Although the PDA proscribed blatant discrimination on the basis of pregnancy, see 42 U.S.C. §§2000e(k), 2000e–2, *supra,* at 4, n.2, the Act is fairly described as a nec-essary, but not a sufficient measure. FMLA hearings conducted between 1986 and 1993 included illustrative testi-mony from women fired after becoming pregnant or giving birth. For example, Beverly Wilkenson was granted seven weeks of leave upon the birth of her child. On the eve of her return to work, a superior informed her that her job had been eliminated. He stated: "Beverly, the best thing for you to do is stay home and take care of your baby and collect your unemployment." Hearing on H.R. 770 before the Subcommittee on Labor-Management Relations of the House Committee on Education and Labor, 101st Cong., 1st Sess., 12 (1989) (hereinafter 1989 House Hearing) (statement of Beverly Wilkenson). See also S.Rep. No. 102–68, p.27 (1991) (hereinafter 1991 Senate Report) (describing Ms. Wilkenson's testimony). Similarly, Linda Pillsbury was notified that she no longer had a job three weeks after her daughter was born.[5] Three secretaries at the same workplace were also forced out of their jobs when they returned to work within weeks of giving birth. See Hearings on S. 249 before the Subcommittee on Children, Family, Drugs and Alcoholism of the Senate Committee on Labor and Human Resources, 100th Cong., 1st Sess., pt.2, pp.16, 23 (1987) (hereinafter 1987 Senate Hearings) (statement of Linda Pillsbury).

These women's experiences, Congress learned, were hardly isolated incidents. A spokeswoman for the Mayor's Commission on Women's Affairs in Chicago testified: "The lack of uniform parental and medical leave policies in the workplace has created an environment where discrimination is rampant. Very often we are contacted by women workers who are at risk of losing their jobs or have lost them because they are pregnant, [or have] given birth." *Id.*, at 170 (statement of Peggy Montes). See also Joint Hearing on The Parental and Medical Leave Act of 1986 before the Subcommittee on Labor-Management Relations and the Subcommittee on Labor Standards of the House Committee on Education and Labor, 99th Cong., 2dSess., 110, n. 18 (1986) (hereinafter 1986 House Hearing) (statement of Women's Legal Defense Fund) ("[W]omen who are temporarily unable to work due to pregnancy, child-birth, and related medical conditions such as morning sickness, threatened miscarriage, or complications arising from childbirth, often lose their jobs because ofthe inadequacy of their employers' leave policies."); 1991 Senate Report 28 (recording that an Atlanta-based job counseling hotline received approximately 100 calls each year from women who were fired, harassed, or forced out of their jobs due to pregnancy or maternity-disability leave); 139 Cong. Rec. 1826 (1993) (remarks of Sen. Edward Kennedy) ("[W]omen who are pregnant are discriminated against as a general rule in our society and have difficulty retaining their jobs."). As summarized by the American Bar Association:

"Historically, denial or curtailment of women's employment opportunities has been traceable directly to the pervasive presumption that women are mothers first, and workers second. This prevailing ideology about women's roles has in turn justified discrimination against women when they are mothers or mothers-to-be." 1989 House Hearing 248 (American BarAssociation Background Report). See also *Hibbs*, 538 U.S., at 736 (quoting same language).

"Many pregnant women have been fired when their em-ployer refused to provide an adequate leave of absence," Congress had ample cause to conclude. See H.R. Rep. No. 99–699, pt. 2, p.22 (1986). Pregnancy, Congress also found, has a marked impact on women's earnings. One year after childbirth, mothers' earnings fell to $1.40 per hour less than those of women who had not given birth. See 1991 Senate Report 28. See also 1989 House Hearing 356–357 (Report of 9to5, National Association of Working Women (citing same study)).

Congress heard evidence tying this pattern of discrimination to the States. A 50-state survey by the Yale Bush Center Infant Care Leave Project concluded that "[t]he proportion and construction of leave policies available to public sector employees differs little from those offered private sector employees." *Hibbs*, 538 U.S., at 730, n.3 (quoting 1986 House Hearing 33 (statement of Meryl Frank)). Roughly 28% of women employed in the public sector did not receive eight weeks of job-protected medical leave to recover from childbirth. See 1987 Senate Hearings, pt. 1, pp. 31, 35, 39 (statement of James T. Bond, National Counsel of Jewish Women). A South Carolina state legislator testified: "[I]n South Carolina, as well as in other states ... no unemployment compensation is paidto a woman who is necessarily absent from her place of employment because of pregnancy or maternity." See *id.*, pt. 2, p. 361 (statement of Rep. Irene Rudnick). According to an employee of the State of Georgia, if state employees took leave, it was held against them when they were considered for promotions: "It is common practice for my Department to compare the balance sheets of workers who have and have not used [leave] benefits in determining who should and should not be promoted." Hearing on H.R. 2 before the Subcommittee on Labor-Management Relations of the House Committee on Education and Labor, 102d Cong., 1st Sess., 36 (1991) (statement of Robert E. Dawkins). See also *id.*, at 33 (One type of leave for Georgia state employees "boils down to whether your supervisor wants you to come back or not."). In short, Congress had every reason to believe that a pattern of workplace discrimination against pregnant women existed in public-sector employment, just as it did in the private sector.

B

"[A] state's refusal to provide pregnancy leave to its employees," Maryland responds, is "not unconstitutional." Brief for Respondents 23 (citing *Geduldig* v. *Aiello*, 417 U.S. 484, 495 (1974)). *Aiello*'s footnote 20 proclaimed that discrimination on the basis of pregnancy is not discrimi-nation on the basis of sex. In my view, this case is a fit occasion to revisit that conclusion. Footnote 20 reads:

> "The dissenting opinion to the contrary, this case is ... a far cry from cases like *Reed* v. *Reed*, 404 U.S. 71 (1971) , and *Frontiero* v. *Richardson*, 411 U.S. 677 (1973) , involving discrimination based upon gender as such. The California insurance program does notexclude anyone from benefit eligibility because of gender but merely removes one physical condition –pregnancy–from the list of compensable disabili-ties. While it is true that only women can become pregnant, it does not follow that every legislativeclassification concerning pregnancy is a sex-based classification ....
> "The lack of identity between the excluded disability and gender as such under this insurance programbecomes clear upon the most cursory analysis. The program divides potential

recipients into two groups—pregnant women and nonpregnant persons. While the first group is exclusively female, the second includes members of both sexes. The fiscal and actuarial benefits of the program thus accrue to members of both sexes." 417 U.S., at 496, n.20.

First, "[a]s an abstract statement," it is "simply false" that "a classification based on pregnancy is gender-neutral." *Bray* v. *Alexandria Women's Health Clinic*, 506 U.S. 263, 327 (1993) (Stevens, J., dissenting). Rather, discriminating on the basis of pregnancy "[b]y definition ... discriminates on account of sex; for it is the capacityto become pregnant which primarily differentiates the fe-male from the male." *General Elec. Co.* v. *Gilbert*, 429 U.S. 125–162 (1976) (Stevens, J., dissenting). See also Issacharoff & Rosenblum, Women and the Workplace: Accommodating the Demands of Pregnancy, 94 Colum. L.Rev. 2154, 2180 (1994) ("[I]t is precisely becausepregnancy is a condition unique to women that the exclusion of pregnancy from disability coverage is a sex-based classification....").

This reality is well illustrated by the facts of *Aiello*. The California disability-insurance program at issue granted disability benefits for virtually any conceivable work disability, including those arising from cosmetic surgery, skiing accidents, and alcoholism. See Brief for EEOC as *Amicus Curiae* in *Aiello*, O. T. 1973, No. 73–640, p.7. It also compensated men for disabilities caused by ailments and procedures that affected men alone: for example, vasectomies, circumcision, and prostatectomies. See Brief for American Civil Liberties Union et al. as *Amici Curiae* in *id.*, at 17–18. Only pregnancy was excluded from the definition of disability. See Cal. Un. Ins. Code Ann. §2626 (West 1972); *Aiello*, 417 U.S., at 489. As Justice Brennan insightfully concluded in dissent, "a limitation is imposed upon the disabilities for which women workers may re-cover, while men receive full compensation for all disabilities suffered .... Such dissimilar treatment of men and women, on the basis of physical characteristics inextricablylinked to one sex, inevitably constitutes sex discrimination." *Id.*, at 501.

Second, pregnancy provided a central justification for the historic discrimination against women this Court chronicled in *Hibbs*. See 538 U.S., at 729 ("[A] proper discharge of [a woman's] maternal functions—having in view not merely her own health, but the well-being of the race—justif[ies] legislation to protect her from the greed as well as the passion of man." (quoting *Muller* v. *Oregon*, 208 U.S. 412, 422 (1908) ; 2d and 3d alterations in *Hibbs*)). See also Siegel, Employment Equality Under the Preg-nancy Discrimination Act of 1978, 94 Yale L.J. 929, 942 (1985) (Pregnancy "is a biological difference central to the definition of gender roles, one traditionally believed to render women unfit for employment."). Relatedly, discrimination against pregnant employees was often "based not on the pregnancy itself but on predictions concerning the future behavior of the pregnant woman when her child was born or on views about what her behavior should be." Williams 355. See also S.Rep. No. 95–331, p.3 (1977) ("[T]he assumption that women will become pregnant and leave the labor market is at the core of the sex stereotyping resulting in unfavorable disparate treatment of women in the workplace.").

In sum, childbearing is not only a biological function unique to women. It is also inextricably intertwined with employers' "stereotypical views about women's commitment to work and their value as employees." *Hibbs*, 538 U.S., at 736. Because pregnancy discrimination is in-evitably sex discrimination, and because discrimination against women is tightly interwoven with society's beliefs about pregnancy and motherhood, I would hold that *Aiello* was egregiously wrong to declare that discrimination on the basis of pregnancy is not discrimination on the basis of sex.

C

Boerne's third step requires "'a congruence and proportionality between the injury to be prevented or remedied and the means adopted to that end.'" *Ante*, at 5 (quoting 521 U.S., at 520). Section 2612(a)(1)(D), I would conclude, is an appropriate response to pervasive discriminatory treatment of pregnant women. In separating self-care leave for the physical disability following childbirth, §2612(a)(1)(D), which affects only women, from family-care leave for parenting a newborn baby, §2612(a)(1)(A), for which men and women are equally suited, Congress could attack gender discrimination and challenge stereotypes of women as lone childrearers. Cf. *Hibbs*, 538 U.S., at 731 (States' extended "maternity" leaves, far exceeding a woman's physical disability following childbirth, were attributable "to the pervasive sex-role stereotype that caring for family members is women's work.").

It would make scant sense to provide job-protected leave for a woman to care for a newborn, but not for her recovery from delivery, a miscarriage, or the birth of a stillborn baby. And allowing States to provide no pregnancy-disability leave at all, given that only women can become pregnant, would obviously "exclude far more women than men from the workplace." *Id.*, at 738.

The plurality's statement that Congress lacked "widespread evidence of sex discrimination ... in the administration of sick leave," *ante*, at 6, misses the point. So too does the plurality's observation that state employees likely "could take leave for pregnancy-related illnesses"—presumably severe morning sickness, toxemia, etc.—under paid sick-leave plans, *ante*, at 7. Congress heard evidence that existing sick-leave plans were inadequate to ensure that women were not fired when they needed to take time out to recover their strength and stamina after childbirth. The self-care provision responds to that evidence by requiring employers to allow leave for "ongoing pregnancy, miscarriages, ... the need for prenatal care, childbirth, and recovery from childbirth." S.Rep. No. 103–3, p.29 (1993).

That §2612(a)(1)(D) entitles all employees to up to 12 weeks of unpaid, job-protected leave for a serious health condition, rather than singling out pregnancy or childbirth, does not mean that the provision lacks the requisite congruence and proportionality to the identified constitutional violations. As earlier noted, *supra,* at 6–7, Congress made plain its rationale for the prescription's broader compass: Congress sought to ward off the unconstitutional discrimination it believed would attend a pregnancy-only leave requirement. Under the caption "Equal protection and non-discrimination," Congress explained:

> "The FMLA addresses the basic leave needs of all employees.... This is an important principle reflected in the bill.
> "A law providing special protection to women ... , in addition to being inequitable, runs the risk of causing discriminatory treatment. Employers might be less inclined to hire women .... For example, legislation addressing the needs of pregnant women only might encourage discriminatory hiring practices against women of child bearing age. Legislation addressing the needs of all workers equally does not have this effect. By addressing the serious leave needs of all employees, the FMLA avoids providing employers the temptation to discriminate [against women].
> . . .
> "The legislation is [thus] based not only on the Commerce Clause, but also on the guarantees of equal protection ... embodied in the Fourteenth Amendment." H.R. Rep. No. 102–135, pt. 1, pp. 27–28 (1991) (hereinafter 1991 House Report).

Congress' concern was solidly grounded in workplace realities. After this Court upheld California's pregnancy-only leave policy in *California Fed.*, Don Butler, President of the Merchants and Manufacturers Association, one of the plaintiffs in that case, told National Public Radio reporter Nina Totenberg that, as a result of the decision, "many employers will be prone to discriminate against women in hiring and hire males instead." 1987 House Hearing 36. Totenberg replied, "But that is illegal, too"—to which Butler responded, "Well, that is illegal, but try to prove it." *Ibid.*

Finally, as in *Hibbs*, it is important to note the moderate cast of the FMLA, in particular, the considerable limi-tations Congress placed on §§2612(a)(1)(A)–(D)'s leave requirement. See 538 U.S., at 738–739. FMLA leave is unpaid. It is limited to employees who have workedat least one year for the employer and at least 1,250hours during the past year. §§2611(2)(A), 2612(c)(1). High-ranking employees, including state elected officials and their staffs, are not within the Act's compass. §§203(e)(2)(C), 2611(3). Employees must provide advance notice of foreseeable leaves. §2612(e). Employers may require a doctor's certification of a serious health condition. §2613(a). And, if an employer violates the FMLA, the employees' recoverable damages are "strictly defined and measured by actual monetary losses." *Hibbs*, 538 U.S., at 740 (citing §§2617(a)(1)(A)(i)–(iii)). The self-care provision, I would therefore hold, is congruent and proportional to the injury to be prevented.

III

But even if *Aiello* senselessly holds sway, and impedes the conclusion that §2612(a)(1)(D) is an appropriate response to the States' unconstitutional discrimination against pregnant women,[6] I would nevertheless conclude that the FMLA is valid §5 legislation. For it is a meet response to "the States' record of unconstitutional participation in, and fostering of, gender-based discrimination in the administration of [parental and family-care] leave benefits." *Hibbs*, 538 U.S., at 735. See also *id.,* at 729–731, and n.5 (Congress adduced evidence "of a pattern of constitutional violations on the part of the States" in granting parental and family-care leave).

Requiring States to provide gender-neutral parental and family-care leave alone, Congress was warned, would promote precisely the type of workplace discrimination Congress sought to reduce. The "pervasive sex-role stereotype that caring for family members is women's work," *id.,* at 731, Congress heard, led employers to regard required parental and family-care leave as a woman's benefit. Carol Ball, speaking on behalf of the U.S. Chamber of Commerce, testified that she did not think "there are going to be many men that take up ... parental leave." See Hearing on S. 345 before the Subcommittee on Children, Family, Drugs, and Alcoholism of the Senate Committee on Labor and Human Resources, 101st Cong., 1st Sess., 39 (1989) (statement of Carol Ball). She frankly admitted that she herself would choose to hire a man over an equally qualified woman if parental leave was required by law. *Id.,* at 30.

Others similarly testified that mandating gender-neutral parental leave would lead to discrimination against women. A representative of the National Federal of Independent Business stated: "Requiring employers to provide parental leave benefits creates clear pressures for subtle discrimination based on ... sex. When choosing between two equally qualified candidates, an employer may be more likely to hire the candidate least likely to take the leave. It is the wage levels and jobs of women of childbearing years which are most at risk in such a situation." Hearing on H.R. 1 before the Subcommittee on Labor-Management Relations of the House Committeeon Education and Labor, 103d Cong., 1st Sess., 95 (1993). See also 1989 House Hearing 169 (statement of Cynthia Simpler, American Society for Personnel Administration) ("Since working women will be viewed as the most likely candidates for parental leave, hidden discrimination will occur if this bill becomes law. Women of child-bearing age will be viewed as risks, potentially disrupting operations through an untimely leave.").

Conversely—unlike perceptions surrounding who takes parental and family-care leave—Congress was told that men and women take medical leave approximately equally. According to one study, male workers missed an average of 4.9 days of work per year due to illness or injury; female workers missed 5.1 days. See 1991 House Report, pt. 1, p. 28. "[T]he incidence of serious medical conditions that would be covered by medical leave under the bill," Congress determined, "is virtually the same for men and women. Employers will find that women and men will take medical leave with equal frequency." *Ibid.* "[P]a-rental and medical leave," Congress was thus alerted,"are inseparable":

> "In the words of an old song, 'You can't have one without the other.'
>
> . . .
>
> "Adoption of parental leave protections without medical leave would ... encourage discrimination against women of child-bearing age, who constitute approximately 73 percent of all the women in the labor force.
> "Employers would tend to hire men, who are much less likely to claim [the parental leave] benefit. . . .
> "Parental leave without medical leave would be the modern version of protective labor laws."
> 1986 House Hearing 33-34 (Statement of Irene Natividad, National Women's Political Caucus).

Congress therefore had good reason to conclude that the self-care provision—which men no doubt would use—would counter employers' impressions that the FMLA would otherwise install female leave. Providing for self-care would thus reduce employers' corresponding incentive to discriminate against women in hiring and promotion. In other words, "[t]he availability of self-care leave to men serves to blunt the force of stereotypes of women as primary caregivers by increasing the odds that men and women will invoke the FMLA's leave provisions in near-equal numbers." See Brief for National Partnership for Women & Families etal. as *Amici Curiae* 26. As Judge Lipez explained:

> "If Congress had drawn a line at leave for caring for other family members, there is greater likelihood that the FMLA would have been perceived as further reason to avoid granting employment opportunities to women. Heretofore, women have provided most of the child and elder care, and legislation that focused on these duties could have had a deleterious impact because of the prevalent notion that women take more advantage of such leave policies. The inclusion of personal medical leave in the scheme, unrelated to any need to care for another person, undermines the assumption that women are the only ones taking leave because men, presumably, are as likely as women to get sick." *Laro* v. *New Hampshire*, 259 F.3d 1, 21 (CA1 2001) (dissenting opinion).

Senator Barbara Boxer advanced a similar point. Responding to assertions that the FMLA would lead employers to discriminate against women, Senator Boxer stated: "[T]o say that women will not be hired by business is a specious argument .... Men also get sick. They get cancer. They get heart disease. They have ailments. And this bill applies to men and women." 139 Cong. Rec. 1697 (1993). See also 1987 Senate Hearings, pt. 2, p. 536 ("I just think it's wrong that there will be a perception that this is something that only women will take and they are, therefore, more expensive. Both men and women have medical conditions ...." (statement of Prof. Susan Deller Ross, Georgetown University Law Center)).

The plurality therefore gets it wrong in concluding that "[o]nly supposition and conjecture support the contention that the self-care provision is necessary to make the family-care provisions effective." *Ante*, at 9. Self-care leave, I would hold, is a key part of Congress' endeavor to make it feasible for women to work and have families. See 1991 Senate Report 25–26 ("This legislation is essential if the nation is to address the dramatic changes that have occurred in the American workforce in recent years.... The once-typical American family, where the father worked for pay and the mother stayed at home with the children, is vanishing.... Today, more than one-half of all mothers with infants under one year of age work outside the home. That figure has doubled since 1970 .... By the year 2000, about three out of every four American children will have mothers in the workforce."). By reducing an employer's perceived incentive to avoid hiring women, §2612(a)(1)(D) lessens the risk that the FMLA as a whole would give rise to the very sex discrimination it was enacted to thwart. The plurality offers no legitimate ground to dilute the force of the Act.

IV

Two additional points. First, this Court reached a different conclusion than the one I reach here in *Board of Trustees of Univ. of Ala.* v. *Garrett*, 531 U.S. 356 (2001) , and *Kimel*, 528 U.S. 62. In those cases, as we observed in *Hibbs*, we reviewed statutes targeting disability and age discrimination, respectively. Neither disability nor age is a suspect classification under this Court's Equal Protection Clause jurisprudence; States may discriminate on the basis of disability or age as long as the classification is rationally related to a legitimate state interest. See *Garrett*, 531 U.S., at 366–367; *Kimel*, 528 U.S., at 83–84. Therefore, for the statutes to be responsive to or designed to prevent unconstitutional discrimination, Congress needed to rely on a pattern of irrational state discrimination on the basis of disability or age. See *Garrett*, 531 U.S., at 368; *Kimel*, 528 U.S., at 89. Here, however, Congress homed in on gender discrimination, which triggers heightened review. See *United States* v. *Virginia*, 518 U.S. 515, 531 (1996) ("Parties who seek to defend gender-based government action must demonstrate an exceedingly persuasive justification for that action." (internal quotation marks omitted)). "[I]t was [therefore] easier for Congress to show a pattern of state constitutional violations." *Hibbs*, 538 U.S., at 736.

Finally, the plurality's opinion does not authorize state employers to violate the FMLA, although it does block injured employees from suing for monetary relief. The self-care provision remains valid Commerce Clause legislation, Maryland concedes, and consequently binds the states, as well as the private sector. Tr. of Oral Arg. 25; Brief for Respondents 32–33. An employee wrongly denied self-care leave, Maryland also acknowledges, may, pursuant to *Ex parte Young*, 209 U.S. 123 (1908) , seek injunctive relief against the responsible state official. See Brief for Respondents 33. Moreover, the U.S. Department of Labor may bring an action against a state for violating the self-care provision and may recover monetary relief on an employee's behalf. 29 U.S.C. §§2617(b)(2)–(3), (d).

V

The plurality pays scant attention to the overarching aim of the FMLA: to make it feasible for women to work while sustaining family life. Over the course of eight years, Congress considered the problem of workplace discrimination against women, and devised the FMLA to reduce sex-based inequalities in leave programs. Essential to its design, Congress assiduously avoided a legislative package that, overall, was or would be seen as geared to women only. Congress thereby reduced employers' incentives to prefer men over women, advanced women's economic opportunities, and laid the foundation for a more egalitarian relationship at home and at work. The self-care provision is a key part of that endeavor, and, in my view, a valid exercise of congressional power under §5 of the Fourteenth Amendment. I would therefore reverse the judgment of the U.S. Court of Appeals for the Fourth Circuit.

NOTES

[1] I remain of the view that Congress can abrogate state sovereign immunity pursuant to its Article I Commerce Clause power. See *Seminole Tribe of Fla.* v. *Florida*, 517 U.S. 44, 100 (1996) (Souter, J., dissenting). Beyond debate, 29 U.S.C. §2612(a)(1)(D) is valid Commerce Clause legislation. See *infra*, at 21. I also share the view that Congress can abrogate state immunity pursuant to §5 of the Fourteenth Amendment where Congress could reasonably conclude that legislation "constitutes an appropriate way to enforce [a] basic equal protection requirement." *Board of Trustees of Univ. of Ala.* v. *Garrett*, 531 U.S. 356, 377 (2001) (Breyer, J., dissenting) (internal quotation marks omitted).

[2] Enacted as an addition to the section defining terms used in Title VII of the Civil Rights Act of 1964, the Pregnancy Discrimination Act of 1978 (PDA) provides: "The terms 'because of sex' or 'on the basis of sex' include, but are not limited to, because of or on the basis of pregnancy, childbirth, or

related medical conditions; and women affected by pregnancy, childbirth, or related medical conditions shall be treated the same for all employment-related purposes, including receipt of benefits under fringe benefit programs, as other persons not so affected but similar in their ability or inability to work...." 92Stat. 2076, 42 U.S.C. §2000e(k).

[3] Lenhoff advanced The Parental and Disability Act of 1985, introduced by Rep. Patricia Schroeder. See S. Wisensale, Family Leave Policy: The Political Economy of Work and Family in America 136–138 (2001). She was later named Vice Chair of the Commission on Leave, created by the FMLA to study family and medical leave policies. See 29 U.S.C. §§2631–2632; U.S. Commission on Family and Medical Leave, A Workable Balance: Report to Congress on Family and Medical Leave Policies 210 (Apr. 30, 1996).

[4] For example, in addition to mandating pregnancy leave, the California statute allowed employers to discriminate against pregnant workers. Employers could refuse to select a pregnant woman for a training program if she would not finish the program at least three months before giving birth. See 1978 Cal. Stats. ch. 1321, §1. The law limited pregnancy disability leave to six weeks, §1, and provided that women were to receive paid disability benefits for only three weeks after childbirth, §2, even if a particular woman remained disabled beyond the three-week period, and even if a man received paid disability benefits throughout his disability. Finally, although it prohibited employers from refusing to *promote* a woman because of pregnancy, it did not forbid refusing to *hire* a woman on that basis. See §1. See also Brief for National Organization for Women etal. as *Amici Curiae* in *California Fed. Sav. & Loan Assn.* v. *Guerra*, O. T. 1985, No. 85–494, pp.14–15. These provisions were all expressly made inapplicable to employers covered by Title VII, "[i]n the event Congress enacts legislation amending Title VII ... to prohibit sex discrimination on the basis of pregnancy," namely, the PDA. See 1978 Cal. Stats. ch. 1321, §4.

[5] The medical recovery period for a normal childbirth is four to eight weeks. See *Nevada Dept. of Human Resources* v. *Hibbs*, 538 U.S. 721, 731, n. 4 (2003) .

[6] Notably, the plurality does not cite or discuss *Geduldig* v. *Aiello*, 417 U.S. 484 (1974), perhaps embarrassed by that opinion's widely criticized conclusion that discrimination based on pregnancy does not involve "discrimination based upon gender as such," *id.,* at 496, n.20. See *supra,* at 10–13; E. Chemerinsky, Constitutional Law 759 (3d ed. 2006) ("It is hard to imagine a clearer sex-based distinction" thanthe one at issue in *Aiello*); Kay, Equality and Difference: The Case of Pregnancy, 1 Berkeley Women's L.J. 1, 31 (1985) ("*[Aiello]* results in unequal treatment of similarly situated women and men who have engaged respectively in reproductive conduct [and wish to continue working]. It should be overruled."); Law, Rethinking Sex and the Constitution, 132 U.Pa. L.Rev. 955, 983–984 (1984) ("Criticizing *[Aiello]* has ... become a cottage industry. Over two dozen law review articles have condemned both the Court's approach and the result.... Even the principal scholarly defense of *[Aiello]* admits that the Court was wrong in refusing to recognize that the classification was sex-based ...."); Karst, The Supreme Court 1976 Term Foreword: Equal Citizenship under the Fourteenth Amendment, 91 Harv. L.Rev. 1, 54, n. 304 (1977) ("[T]he constitutional sport of *[Aiello]* and last Term's even sillier statutory counterpart, *General Elec. Co.* v. *Gilbert*, 429 U.S. 125 (1976) , with their Alice-in-Wonderland view of pregnancy as a sex-neutral phenomenon, are good candidates for early retirement. These decisions are textbook examples of the effects of underrepresentation on "legislative" insensitivity. Imagine what the presence of even one woman Justice would have meant to the Court's conferences.").

SUPAP KIRTSAENG v. JOHN WILEY & SONS, INC.

No. 11-697, March 19, 2013

ON WRIT OF CERTIORARI TO THE UNITED STATES COURT OF APPEALS FOR THE SECOND CIRCUIT

Justice Ginsburg, with whom Justice Kennedy joins, and with whom Justice Scalia joins except as to Parts III and V–B–1, dissenting.

"In the interpretation of statutes, the function of the courts is easily stated. It is to construe the language so as to give effect to the intent of Congress." *United States* v. *American Trucking Assns., Inc.*, 310 U.S. 534, 542 (1940) . Instead of adhering to the Legislature's design, the Court today adopts an interpretation of the Copyright Act at odds with Congress' aim to protect copyright owners against the unauthorized importation of low-priced, foreign-made copies of their copyrighted works. The Court's bold departure from Congress' design is all the more stunning, for it places the United States at the vanguard of the movement for "international exhaustion" of copyrights—a movement the United States has steadfastly resisted on the world stage.

To justify a holding that shrinks to insignificance copyright protection against the unauthorized importation of foreign-made copies, the Court identifies several "practical problems." *Ante*, at 24. The Court's parade of horribles, however, is largely imaginary. Congress' objective in enacting 17 U.S.C. §602(a)(1)'s importation prohibition can be honored without generating the absurd consequences hypothesized in the Court's opinion. I dissent from the Court's embrace of "international exhaustion," and would affirm the sound judgment of the Court of Appeals.

I

Because economic conditions and demand for particular goods vary across the globe, copyright owners have a financial incentive to charge different prices for copies of their works in different geographic regions. Their ability to engage in such price discrimination, however, is under-mined if arbitrageurs are permitted to import copiesfrom low-price regions and sell them in high-price regions. The question in this case is whether the unauthorized importation of foreign-made copies constitutes copyright infringement under U. S. law.

To answer this question, one must examine three provisions of Title 17 of the U.S. Code: §§106(3), 109(a), and 602(a)(1). Section 106 sets forth the "exclusive rights" of a copyright owner, including the right "to distribute copies or phonorecords of the copyrighted work to the public by sale or other transfer of ownership, or by rental, lease, or lending." §106(3). This distribution right is limited by §109(a), which provides: "Notwithstanding the provisions of section 106(3), the owner of a particular copy or phono-record lawfully made under this title ... is entitled,without the authority of the copyright owner, to sell or otherwise dispose of the possession of that copy or phonorecord." Section 109(a) codifies the "first sale doctrine," a doctrine articulated in *Bobbs-Merrill Co.* v. *Straus*, 210 U.S. 339–351 (1908), which held that a copyright owner could not control the price at which retailers sold lawfully purchased copies of its work. The first sale doctrine recognizes that a copyright owner should not be permitted to exercise perpetual control over the distribution of copies of a copyrighted work. At some point—ordinarily the time of the first commercial sale—the copyright owner's exclusive right under §106(3) to control the distribution of a particular copy is exhausted, and from that point forward, the copy can be resold or otherwise redistributed without the copyright owner's authorization.

Section 602(a)(1) (2006 ed., Supp. V)[1] —last, but most critical, of the three copyright provisions bearing on this case—is an importation ban. It reads:

> "Importation into the United States, without the authority of the owner of copyright under this title, of copies or phonorecords of a work that have beenacquired outside the United States is an infringe-ment of the exclusive right to distribute copies or phonorecords under section 106, actionable under section 501."

In *Quality King Distributors, Inc.* v. *L'anza Research Int'l, Inc.*, 523 U.S. 135–154 (1998), the Court held that a copyright owner's right to control importation under §602(a)(1) is a component of the distribution right set forth in §106(3) and is therefore subject to §109(a)'s codification of the first sale doctrine. *Quality King* thus held that the importation of copies *made in the United States* but sold abroad did not rank as copyright infringementunder §602(a)(1). *Id.*, at 143–154. See also *id.*, at 154 (Ginsburg, J., concurring) (*Quality King* "involve[d] a 'round trip' journey, travel of the copies in question from the United States to places abroad, then back again").[2] Important to the Court's holding, the copies at issue in *Quality King* had been "'lawfully made under [Title 17]'"—a prerequisite for application of §109(a). *Id.*, at 143, n.9 (quoting §109(a)). Section 602(a)(1), the Court noted, would apply to "copies that were 'lawfully made' not under the United States Copyright Act, but instead, under the law of some other country." *Id.*, at 147. Drawing on an example discussed during a 1964 public meeting on proposed revisions to the U.S. copyright laws,[3] the Court stated:

> "If the author of [a] work gave the exclusive United States distribution rights—enforceable under the Act—to the publisher of the United States edition and the exclusive British distribution rights to the publisher of the British edition, ... presumably only those [copies] made by the publisher of the United States edition would be 'lawfully made under this title' within the meaning of §109(a). The first sale doctrine would not provide the publisher of the British edition who decided to sell in the American market with a defense to an action under §602(a) (or, for that matter, to an action under §106(3), if there was a distribution of the copies)." *Id.*, at 148.

As the District Court and the Court of Appeals concluded, see 654 F.3d 210, 221–222 (CA2 2011); App. to Pet. for Cert. 70a–73a, application of the *Quality King* analysis to the facts of this case would preclude any invocation of §109(a). Petitioner Supap Kirtsaeng imported and then sold at a profit over 600 copies of copyrighted textbooks printed outside the United States by the Asian subsidiary of respondent John Wiley & Sons, Inc. (Wiley). App. 29–34. See also *ante*, at 3–5 (opinion of the Court). In the words the Court used in *Quality King*, these copies "were 'lawfully made' not under the United States Copyright Act, but instead, under the law of some other country." 523 U.S., at 147. Section 109(a) therefore does not ap-ply, and Kirtsaeng's unauthorized importation constitutes copyright infringement under §602(a)(1).

The Court does not deny that under the language I have quoted from *Quality King*, Wiley would prevail. *Ante*, at 27. Nevertheless, the Court dismisses this language, to which all Members of the *Quality King* Court subscribed, as ill-considered dictum. *Ante*, at 27–28. I agree that the discussion was dictum in the sense that it was not essential to the Court's judgment. See *Quality King*, 523 U.S., at 154 (Ginsburg, J., concurring) ("[W]e do not today resolve cases in which the allegedly infringing imports were manufactured abroad."). But I disagree with the Court's conclusion that this dictum was ill considered. Instead, for the reasons explained below, I would hold, consistently with *Quality King*'s dictum, that §602(a)(1) authorizes a copyright owner to bar the importation of a copy manufactured abroad for sale abroad.

II

The text of the Copyright Act demonstrates that Congress intended to provide copyright owners with a potent remedy against the importation of foreign-made copies of their copyrighted works. As the Court recognizes, *ante*, at 3, this case turns on the meaning of the phrase "lawfully made under this title" in §109(a). In my view, that phrase is most sensibly read as referring to instances in which a copy's creation is governed by, and conducted in compliance with, Title 17 of the U.S. Code. This reading is consistent with the Court's interpretation of similar language in other statutes. See *Florida Dept. of Revenue* v. *Piccadilly Cafeterias, Inc.*, 554 U.S. 33–53 (2008) ("under" in 11 U.S.C. §1146(a), a Bankruptcy Code provision exempting certain asset transfers from stamp taxes, means "pursuant to"); *Ardestani* v. *INS*, 502 U.S. 129, 135 (1991) (the phrase "under section 554" in the Equal Access to Justice Act means "subject to" or "governed by" 5 U.S.C. §554 (internal quotation marks omitted)). It also accords with dictionary definitions of the word "under." See, *e.g.*, American Heritage Dictionary 1887 (5th ed. 2011) ("under" means, among other things, "[s]ubject to the authority, rule, or control of").

Section 109(a), properly read, affords Kirtsaeng no defense against Wiley's claim of copyright infringement. The Copyright Act, it has been observed time and again, does not apply extraterritorially. See *United Dictionary Co.* v. *G. & C. Merriam Co.*, 208 U.S. 260, 264 (1908) (copyright statute requiring that U.S. copyright notices be placed in all copies of a work did not apply to copies published abroad because U.S. copyright laws have no "force" beyond the United States' borders); 4 M. Nimmer & D. Nimmer, Copyright §17.02, p.17–18 (2012) (hereinafter Nimmer) ("[C]opyright laws do not have any extraterritorial operation."); 4 W. Patry, Copyright §13:22, p.13–66 (2012) (hereinafter Patry) ("Copyright laws are rigor-ously territorial."). The printing of Wiley's foreign-manufactured textbooks therefore was not governed by Title 17. The textbooks thus were not "lawfully made under [Title 17]," the crucial precondition for application of §109(a). And if §109(a) does not apply, there is no dispute that Kirtsaeng's conduct constituted copyright infringement under §602(a)(1).

The Court's point of departure is similar to mine. According to the Court, the phrase "'lawfully made under this title' means made 'in accordance with' or 'in compliance with' the Copyright Act." *Ante*, at 8. But the Court overlooks that, according to the very dictionaries it cites, *ante*, at 9, the word "under" commonly signals a relationship of subjection, where one thing is governed or regu-lated by another. See Black's Law Dictionary 1525 (6th ed. 1990) ("under" "frequently" means "inferior" or "subordinate" (internal quotation marks omitted)); 18 Oxford English Dictionary 950 (2d ed. 1989) ("under" means, among other things, "[i]n accordance with (*some regulative power or principle*)" (emphasis added)). See also Webster's Third New International Dictionary 2487 (1961) ("under" means, among other things, "in ... a condition of sub-jection, regulation, or subordination" and "suffering restriction, restraint, or control by"). Only by disregarding this established meaning of "under" can the Court arrive at the conclusion that Wiley's foreign-manufactured textbooks were "lawfully made under" U.S. copyright law, even though that law did not govern their creation. It is anomalous, however, to speak of particular conduct as "lawful" under an inapplicable law. For example, one might say that driving on the right side of the road in England is "lawful" under U.S. law, but that would be so only because U.S. law has nothing to say about the subject. The governing law is English law, and English law demands that driving be done on the left side of the road.[4]

The logical implication of the Court's definition of the word "under" is that *any* copy manufactured abroad—even a piratical one made without the copyright owner's authorization and in violation of the law of the country where it was created—would fall within the scope of §109(a). Any such copy would have been made "in accordance with" or "in compliance with" the U.S. Copyright Act, in the sense that manufacturing the copy did not violate the Act (because the Act does not apply extraterritorially).

The Court rightly refuses to accept such an absurd conclusion. Instead, it interprets §109(a) as applying only to copies whose making actually complied with Title 17, or would have complied with Title 17 had Title 17 been applicable (*i.e.*, had the copies been made in the United States). See *ante*, at 8 ("§109(a)'s 'first sale' doctrine would apply to copyrighted works as long as their manufacture met the requirements of American copyright law."). Congress, however, used express language when it called for such a counterfactual inquiry in 17 U.S.C. §§602(a)(2) and (b). See §602(a)(2) ("Importation into the United States or exportation from the United States, without the authority of the owner of copyright under this title, of copies or phonorecords, the making of which either constituted an infringement of copyright, or *which would have constituted an infringement of copyright if this title had been applicable*, is an infringement of the exclusive right to distribute copies or phonorecords under section 106." (emphasis added)); §602(b) ("In a case where the making of the copies or phonorecords *would have constituted an infringement of copyright if this title had been applicable*, their importation is prohibited." (emphasis added)). Had Congress intended courts to engage in a similarly hypothetical inquiry under §109(a), Congress would pre-sumably have included similar language in that section. See *Russello* v. *United States*, 464 U.S. 16, 23 (1983) ("'[W]here Congress includes particular language in one section of a statute but omits it in another section of the same Act, it is generally presumed that Congress acts intentionally and purposely in the disparate inclusion or exclusion.'" (quoting *United States* v. *Wong Kim Bo*, 472 F.2d 720, 722 (CA5 1972) (*per curiam*); brackets in original)).[5]

Not only does the Court adopt an unnatural construction of the §109(a) phrase "lawfully made under this title." Concomitantly, the Court reduces §602(a)(1) to insignificance. As the Court appears to acknowledge, see *ante*, at 26, the only independent effect §602(a)(1) has under today's decision is to prohibit unauthorized importations carried out by persons who merely have possession of, but do not own, the imported copies. See 17 U.S.C. §109(a) (§109(a) applies to any "*owner* of a particular copy or phonorecord lawfully made under this title" (emphasis added)).[6] If this is enough to avoid rendering §602(a)(1) entirely "superfluous," *ante*, at 26, it hardly suffices to give the owner's importation right the scope Congress intended it to have. Congress used broad language in §602(a)(1); it did so to achieve a broad objective. Had Congress intended simply to provide a copyright remedy against larcenous lessees, licensees, consignees, and bailees of films and other copyright-protected goods, see *ante*, at 13–14, 26, it likely would have used language tailored to that narrow purpose. See 2 Nimmer §8.12[B][6][c], at 8–184.31, n. 432 ("It may be wondered whether . . . potential causes of action [against licensees and the like] are more than theoretical."). See also *ante*, at 2 (Kagan, J., concurring) (the Court's decision limits §602(a)(1) "to a fairly esoteric set of applications").[7]

The Court's decision also overwhelms 17 U.S.C. §602(a)(3)'s exceptions to §602(a)(1)'s importation prohibition. 2 P. Goldstein, Copyright §7.6.1.2(a), p. 7:141 (3d ed. 2012) (hereinafter Goldstein).[8] Those exceptions permit the importation of copies without the copyright owner's authorization for certain governmental, personal, schol-arly, educational, and religious purposes. 17 U.S.C. §602(a)(3). Copies imported under these exceptions "will often be lawfully made gray market goods purchased through normal market channels abroad." 2 Goldstein §7.6.1.2(a), at 7:141.[9] But if, as the Court holds, such copies can in any event be imported by virtue of §109(a), §602(a)(3)'s work has already been done. For example, had Congress conceived of §109(a)'s sweep as the Court does, what earthly reason would there be to provide, as Congress did in §602(a)(3)(C), that a library may import "no more than five copies" of a non-audiovisual work for its "lending or archival purposes"?

The far more plausible reading of §§109(a) and 602(a), then, is that Congress intended §109(a) to apply to copies made in the United States, not to copies manufactured and sold abroad. That reading of the first sale and importation provisions leaves §602(a)(3)'s exceptions with real, meaningful work to do. See *TRW Inc.* v. *Andrews*, 534 U.S. 19, 31 (2001) ("It is a cardinal principle of statutory construction that a statute ought, upon the whole, to be so construed that, if it can be prevented, no clause, sen-tence, or word shall be superfluous, void, or insignificant." (internal quotation marks omitted)). In the range of circum-stances covered by the exceptions, §602(a)(3) frees individuals and entities who purchase foreign-made copies abroad from the requirement they would otherwise face under §602(a)(1) of obtaining the copyright owner's permission to import the copies into the United States.[10]

III

The history of §602(a)(1) reinforces the conclusion I draw from the text of the relevant provisions: §109(a)does not apply to copies manufactured abroad. Section 602(a)(1) was enacted as part of the Copyright Act of 1976, 90Stat. 2589–2590. That Act was the product of a lengthy revision effort overseen by the U.S. Copyright Office. See *Mills Music, Inc.* v. *Snyder*, 469 U.S. 153–160 (1985). In its initial 1961 report on recommended revisions, the Copyright Office noted that publishers had "suggested that the [then-existing] import ban on piratical copies should be extended to bar the importation of ... foreign edition[s]" in violation of "agreements to divide international markets for copyrighted works." Copyright Law Revision: Report of the Register of Copyrights on the General Revision of the U.S. Copyright Law, 87th Cong., 1st Sess., 126 (H.R. Judiciary Comm. Print 1961) (hereinafter Copyright Law Revision). See Copyright Act of 1947, §106, 61Stat. 663 ("The importation into the United States ... of any piratical copies of any work copyrighted in the United States ... is prohibited."). The Copyright Office originally recommended against such an extension of the importation ban, reasoning that enforcement of territorial restrictions was best left to contract law. Copyright Law Revision 126.

Publishing-industry representatives argued strenuously against the position initially taken by the Copyright Office. At a 1962 panel discussion on the Copyright Office's report, for example, Horace Manges of the American Book Publishers Council stated:

> "When a U.S. book publisher enters into a contract with a British publisher to acquire exclusive U.S. rights for a particular book, he often finds that the English edition ... of that particular book finds its way into this country. Now it's all right to say, 'Commence a lawsuit for breach of contract.' But this is expensive, burdensome, and, for the most part, ineffective." Copyright Law Revision Part 2: Discussion and Comments on Report of the Register of Copyrights on the General Revision of the U.S. Copyright Law, 88th Cong., 1st Sess., 212 (H.R. Judiciary Comm. Print 1963).

Sidney Diamond, representing London Records, elaborated on Manges' statement. "There are many situations," he explained, "in which it is not necessarily a question of the inadequacy of a contract remedy—in the sense that it may be difficult or not quick enough to solve the particular problem." *Id.*, at 213. "Very frequently," Diamond stated, publishers "run into a situation where ... copies of [a] work ... produced in a foreign country ... may be shipped [to the United States] without violating any contract of the U.S. copyright proprietor." *Ibid.* To illustrate, Diamond noted, if a "British publisher [sells a copy] to an individual who in turn ship[s] it over" to the United States, the individual's conduct would not "violate [any] contract between the British and the American publisher." *Ibid.* In such a case, "no possibility of any contract remedy" would exist. *Ibid.* The facts of Kirtsaeng's case fit Diamond's example, save that the copies at issue here were printed and initially sold in Asia rather than Great Britain.

After considering comments on its 1961 report, the Copyright Office "prepared a preliminary draft of provisions for a new copyright statute." Copyright Law Revision Part 3: Preliminary Draft for Revised U.S. Copyright Law and Discussions and Comments on the Draft, 88th Cong., 2d Sess., v (H.R. Judiciary Comm. Print 1964). Section 44 of the draft statute addressed the concerns raised by publishing-industry representatives. In particular, §44(a) provided:

> "Importation into the United States of copies or records of a work for the purpose of distribution to the public shall, if such articles are imported without the authority of the owner of the exclusive right to distribute copies or records under this title, constitute an infringement of copyright actionable under section 35 [*i.e.*, the section providing for a private cause of action for copyright infringement]." *Id.*, at 32–33.

In a 1964 panel discussion regarding the draft statute, Abe Goldman, the Copyright Office's General Counsel, left no doubt about the meaning of §44(a). It represented, he explained, a "shif[t]" from the Copyright Office's 1961 report, which had recommended against using copyright law to facilitate publishers' efforts to segment international markets. Copyright Law Revision Part 4: Further Discussions and Comments on Preliminary Draft for Revised U.S. Copyright Law, 88th Cong., 2d Sess., 203 (H.R. Judiciary Comm. Print 1964). Section 44(a), Goldman stated, would allow copyright owners to bring infringement actions against importers of "foreign copies that were made under proper authority." *Ibid.*

See also *id.*, at 205–206 (Goldman agreed with a speaker's comment that §44(a) "enlarge[d]" U.S. copyright law by extending import prohibitions "to works legally produced in Europe" and other foreign countries).[11]

The next step in the copyright revision process was the introduction in Congress of a draft bill on July 20, 1964. See Copyright Law Revision Part 5: 1964 Revision Bill with Discussions and Comments, 89th Cong., 1st Sess., III (H.R. Judiciary Comm. Print 1965). After another round of public comments, a revised bill was introduced on February 4, 1965. See Copyright Law Revision Part 6: Supplementary Report of the Register of Copyrights on the General Revision of the U.S. Copyright Law: 1965 Revision Bill, 89th Cong., 1st Sess., V (H.R. Judiciary Comm. Print 1965) (hereinafter Copyright Law Revision Part 6). In language closely resembling the statutory text later enacted by Congress, §602(a) of the 1965 bill provided:

> "Importation into the United States, without the authority of the owner of copyright under this title, of copies or phonorecords of a work for the purpose of distribution to the public is an infringement of the exclusive right to distribute copies or phonorecords under section 106, actionable under section 501." *Id.*, at 292.[12]

The Court implies that the 1965 bill's "explici[t] refer[ence]" to §106" showed a marked departure from §44(a) of the Copyright Office's prior draft. *Ante*, at 29. The Copyright Office, however, did not see it that way. In its summary of the 1965 bill's provisions, the Copyright Office observed that §602(a) of the 1965 bill, like §44(a) of the Copyright Office's prior draft, see *supra*, at 15–16, permitted copyright owners to bring infringement actions against unauthorized importers in cases "where the copyright owner had authorized the making of [the imported] copies in a foreign country for distribution only in that country." Copyright Law Revision Part 6, at 149–150. See also *id.*, at XXVI (Under §602(a) of the 1965 bill, "[a]n unauthorized importer could be enjoined and sued for damages both where the copies or phonorecords he was importing were 'piratical' (that is, where their making would have constituted an infringement if the U.S. copyright law could have been applied), and where their making was 'lawful.'").

The current text of §602(a)(1) was finally enacted into law in 1976. See Copyright Act of 1976, §602(a), 90 Stat. 2589–2590. The House and Senate Committee Reports on the 1976 Act demonstrate that Congress understood, as did the Copyright Office, just what that text meant. Both Reports state:

> "Section 602 [deals] with two separate situations: importation of 'piratical' articles (that is, copies or phonorecords made without any authorization of the copyright owner), and unauthorized importation of copies or phonorecords that were lawfully made. *The general approach of section 602 is to make unauthorized importation an act of infringement in both cases*, but to permit the Bureau of Customs to prohibit importation only of 'piratical' articles." S. Rep. No. 94-473, p. 151 (1975) (emphasis added). See also H.R. Rep. No. 94-1476, p. 169 (1976) (same).

In sum, the legislative history of the Copyright Act of 1976 is hardly "inconclusive." *Ante*, at 28. To the con-trary, it confirms what the plain text of the Act conveys: Congress intended §602(a)(1) to provide copyright owners with a remedy against the unauthorized importation of foreign-made copies of their works, even if those copies were made and sold abroad with the copyright owner's authorization.[13]

IV

Unlike the Court's holding, my position is consistent with the stance the United States has taken in international-trade negotiations. This case bears on the highly con-tentious trade issue of interterritorial exhaustion. The issue arises because intellectual property law is territorial in nature, see *supra*, at 6, which means that creators of intellectual property "may hold a set of parallel" intellectual property rights under the laws of different nations. Chiappetta, The Desirability of Agreeing to Disagree: The WTO, TRIPS, International IPR Exhaustion and a Few Other Things, 21 Mich. J. Int'l L. 333, 340–341 (2000) (hereinafter Chiappetta). There is no international consensus on whether the sale in one country of a good in-corporating protected intellectual property exhausts the intellectual property owner's right to control the distribution of that good elsewhere. Indeed, the members of the World Trade Organization, "agreeing to disagree,"[14] provided in Article 6 of the Agreement on Trade-Related Aspects of Intellectual Property Rights (TRIPS), Apr. 15, 1994, 33 I. L. M. 1197, 1200, that "nothing in this Agreement shall be used to address the issue of ... exhaustion." See Chiappetta 346 (observing that exhaustion of intellectual property rights was "hotly debated" during the TRIPS negotiations and that Article 6 "reflects [the negotiators'] ultimate inability to agree" on a single international standard). Similar language appears in other treaties to which the United States is a party. See World Intellectual Property Organization (WIPO) Copyright Treaty, Art. 6(2), Dec. 20, 1996, S. Treaty Doc. No. 105–17, p. 7 ("Nothing in this Treaty shall affect the freedom of Contracting Parties to determine the conditions, if any, under which the exhaustion of the right [to control distribution of copies of a copyrighted work] applies after the first sale or other transfer of ownership of the original or a copy of the work with the authorization of the author."); WIPO Performances and Phonograms Treaty, Art. 8(2), Dec. 20, 1996, S. Treaty Doc. No. 105–17, p. 28 (containing language nearly identical to Article 6(2) of the WIPO Copyright Treaty).

In the absence of agreement at the international level, each country has been left to choose for itself the exhaustion framework it will follow. One option is a national-exhaustion regime, under which a copyright owner's right to control distribution of a particular copy is exhausted only within the country in which the copy is sold. See Forsyth & Rothnie, Parallel Imports, in The Interface Between Intellectual Property Rights and Competition Policy 429, 430 (S. Anderman ed. 2007) (hereinafterForsyth & Rothnie). Another option is a rule of international exhaustion, under which the authorized distribution of a particular copy anywhere in the world exhausts the copyright owner's distribution right everywhere with respectto that copy. See *ibid.* The European Union has adopted the intermediate approach of regional exhaustion, under which the sale of a copy anywhere within the European Economic Area exhausts the copyright owner's distribution right throughout that region. See *id.*, at 430, 445. Section 602(a)(1), in my view, ties the United States to a national-exhaustion framework. The Court's decision, in con-trast, places the United States solidly in the international-exhaustion camp.

Strong arguments have been made both in favor of, and in opposition to, international exhaustion. See Chiappetta 360 ("[r]easonable people making valid points can, anddo, reach conflicting conclusions" regarding the desirability of international exhaustion). International exhaustion subjects copyright-protected goods to competition from lower priced imports and, to that extent, benefits con-sumers. Correspondingly, copyright owners profit from a national-exhaustion regime, which also enlarges the monetary incentive to create new copyrightable works. See Forsyth & Rothnie 432–437 (surveying arguments for and against international exhaustion).

Weighing the competing policy concerns, our Government reached the conclusion that widespread adoption of the international-exhaustion framework would be inconsistent with the long-term economic interests of the United States. See Brief for United States as *Amicus Curiae* in *Quality King*, O. T. 1997, No. 96–1470, pp.22–26 (hereinafter *Quality King* Brief).[15] Accordingly, the United States has steadfastly "taken the position in international trade negotiations that domestic copyright owners should ... have the right to prevent the unauthorized importation of copies of their work sold abroad." *Id.*, at22. The United States has "advanced this position in multilateral trade negotiations," including the negotiations on the TRIPS Agreement. *Id.*, at 24. See also D. Gervais, The TRIPS Agreement: Drafting History and Analysis §2.63, p. 199 (3d ed. 2008). It has also taken a dim view of our trading partners' adoption of legislation incorporating elementsof international exhaustion. See Clapperton & Corones, Locking in Customers, Locking Out Competitors: Anti-Circumvention Laws in Australia and Their Potential Effect on Competition in High Technology Markets, 30 Melbourne U. L.Rev. 657, 664 (2006) (United States expressed concern regarding international-exhaustion leg-islation in Australia); Montén, Comment, The Inconsistency Between Section 301 and TRIPS: CounterproductiveWith Respect to the Future of International Protectionof Intellectual Property Rights? 9 Marq. IntellectualProperty L. Rev. 387, 417–418 (2005) (same with respect to New Zealand and Taiwan).

Even if the text and history of the Copyright Act were ambiguous on the answer to the question this case presents— which they are not, see Parts II–III, *supra*[16] —Iwould resist a holding out of accord with the firm position the United States has taken on exhaustion in international negotiations. *Quality King*, I acknowledge, discounted the Government's concerns about potential inconsistency with United States obligations under certain bilateral trade agreements. See 523 U.S., at 153–154. See also *Quality King* Brief 22–24 (listing the agreements). That decision, however, dealt only with copyright-protected products made in the United States. See 523 U.S., at 154 (Ginsburg, J., concurring). *Quality King* left open the question whether owners of U.S. copyrights could retain control over the importation of copies manufactured and sold abroad—a point the Court obscures, see *ante*, at 33 (arguing that *Quality King* "significantly eroded" the national-exhaustion principle that, in my view, §602(a)(1) embraces). The Court today answers that question with a resounding "no," and in doing so, it risks undermining the United States' credibility on the world stage. While the Government has urged our trading partners to refrain from adopting international-exhaustion regimes that could benefit consumers within their borders but would impact adversely on intellectual-property producers in the United States, the Court embraces an international-exhaustion rule that could benefit U.S. consumers but would likely disadvantage foreign holders of U.S. copyrights. This dissonance scarcely enhances the United States' "role as a trusted partner in multilateral endeavors." *Vimar Seguros y Reaseguros, S. A.* v. *M/V Sky Reefer*, 515 U.S. 528,539 (1995).

V

I turn now to the Court's justifications for a decision difficult to reconcile with the Copyright Act's text and history.

A

The Court asserts that its holding "is consistent with antitrust laws that ordinarily forbid market divisions." *Ante*, at 32. See also *ante*, at 18 (again referring to antitrust principles). Section 602(a)(1), however, read as I do and as the Government does, simply facilitates copyright owners' efforts to impose "vertical restraints" on distributors of copies of their works. See Forsyth & Rothnie 435 ("Parallel importation restrictions enable manufacturers and distributors to erect 'vertical restraints' in the market through exclusive distribution agreements."). See gener-ally *Leegin Creative Leather Products, Inc.* v. *PSKS, Inc.*, 551 U.S. 877 (2007) (discussing vertical restraints). We have held that vertical restraints are not *perse* illegal under §1 of the Sherman Act, 15 U.S.C. §1, because such "restraints can have procompetitive effects." 551 U.S., at 881–882.[17]

B

The Court sees many "horribles" following from a holding that the §109(a) phrase "lawfully made under this title" does not encompass foreign-made copies. *Ante*, at 22 (internal quotation marks omitted). If §109(a) excluded foreign-made copies, the Court fears, then copyright owners could exercise perpetual control over the downstream distribution or public display of such copies. A ruling in Wiley's favor, the Court asserts, would shutter libraries, put used-book dealers out of business, cripple art museums, and prevent the resale of a wide range of consumer goods, from cars to calculators. *Ante*, at 19–22. See also *ante*, at 2–3 (Kagan, J., concurring) (expressing concern about "imposing downstream liability on those who purchase and resell in the United States copies that happen to have been manufactured abroad"). Copyright law and precedent, however, erect barriers to the anticipated horribles.[18]

1

Recognizing that foreign-made copies fall outside the ambit of §109(a) would not mean they are forever free of the first sale doctrine. As earlier observed, see *supra*, at 2, the Court stated that doctrine initially in its 1908 *Bobbs-Merrill* decision. At that time, no statutory provision expressly codified the first sale doctrine. Instead, copyright law merely provided that copyright owners had "the sole liberty of printing, reprinting, publishing, completing, copying, executing, finishing, and vending" their works. Copyright Act of 1891, §1, 26Stat. 1107.

In *Bobbs-Merrill*, the Court addressed the scope of the statutory right to "ven[d]." In granting that right, the Court held, Congress did not intend to permit copyright owners "to fasten ... a restriction upon the subsequent alienation of the subject-matter of copyright after the owner had parted with the title to one who had acquired full dominion over it and had given a satisfactory price for it." 210 U.S., at 349–350. "[O]ne who has sold a copyrighted article ... without restriction," the Court explained, "has parted with all right to control the sale of it." *Id.*, at 350. Thus, "[t]he purchaser of a book, once sold by authority of the owner of the copyright, may sell it again, although he could not publish a new edition of it." *Ibid.*

Under the logic of *Bobbs-Merrill*, the sale of a foreign-manufactured copy in the United States carried out with the copyright owner's authorization would exhaust the copyright owner's right to "vend" that copy. The copy could thenceforth be resold, lent out, or otherwise redistributed without further authorization from the copyright owner. Although §106(3) uses the word "distribute" rather than "vend," there is no reason to think Congress intended the word "distribute" to bear a meaning different from the construction the Court gave to the word "vend" in *Bobbs-Merrill*. See *ibid.* (emphasizing that the question before the Court was "purely [one] of statutory construction").[19] Thus, in accord with *Bobbs-Merrill*, the first authorized distribution of a foreign-made copy in the United States exhausts the copyright owner's distribution right under §106(3). After such an authorized distribution, a library may lend, or a used-book dealer may resell, the foreign-made copy without seeking the copyright owner's permission. Cf. *ante*, at 19–21.

For example, if Wiley, rather than Kirtsaeng, hadimported into the United States and then sold the foreign-made textbooks at issue in this case, Wiley's §106(3) distribution right would have been exhausted under the rationale of *Bobbs-Merrill*. Purchasers of the textbooks would thus be free to dispose of the books as they wished without first gaining a license from Wiley.

This line of reasoning, it must be acknowledged, significantly curtails the independent effect of §109(a). If, as I maintain, the term "distribute" in §106(3) incorporates the first sale doctrine by virtue of *Bobbs-Merrill*, then §109(a)'s codification of that doctrine adds little to the regulatory regime.[20] Section 109(a), however, does serve as a statutory bulwark against courts deviating from *Bobbs-Merrill* in a way that increases copyright owners' control over downstream distribution, and legislative history indicates that is precisely the role Congress intended §109(a) to play. Congress first codified the first sale doctrine in §41 of the Copyright Act of 1909, 35Stat. 1084.[21] It did so, the House Committee Report on the 1909 Act explains, "in order to make ... clear that [Congress had] no intention [of] enlarg[ing] in any way the construction to be given to the word 'vend.'" H.R. Rep. No. 2222, 60th Cong., 2d Sess., 19 (1909). According to the Committee Report, §41 was "not intended to change [existing law] in any way." *Ibid.* The position I have stated and explained accords with this expression of congressional intent. In enacting §41 and its successors, I would hold, Congress did not "change . . . existing law," *ibid.*, by stripping the word "vend" (and thus its substitute "distribute") of the limiting construction imposed in *Bobbs-Merrill*.

In any event, the reading of the Copyright Act to which I subscribe honors Congress' aim in enacting §109(a)while the Court's reading of the Act severely diminishes §602(a)(1)'s role. See *supra*, at 10–12. My position in no way tugs against the principle underlying §109(a)—*i.e.*, that certain conduct by the copyright owner exhausts the owner's §106(3) distribution right. The Court, in contrast, fails to give meaningful effect to Congress' manifest intent in §602(a)(1) to grant copyright owners the right to control the importation of foreign-made copies of their works.

2

Other statutory prescriptions provide further protection against the absurd consequences imagined by the Court. For example, §602(a)(3)(C) permits "an organization operated for scholarly, educational, or religious purposes" to import, without the copyright owner's authorization, up to five foreign-made copies of a non-audiovisual work—notably, a book— for "library lending or archival purposes." But cf. *ante*, at 19–20 (suggesting that affirming the Second Circuit's decision might prevent libraries from lending foreign-made books).[22]

The Court also notes that *amici* representing art museums fear that a ruling in Wiley's favor would prevent museums from displaying works of art created abroad. *Ante*, at 22 (citing Brief for Association of Art Museum Directors etal.). These *amici* observe that a museum's right to display works of art often depends on 17 U.S.C. §109(c). See Brief for Association of Art Museum Directors etal. 11–13.[23] That provision addresses exhaustion of a copyright owner's exclusive right under §106(5) topublicly display the owner's work. Because §109(c), like §109(a), applies only to copies "lawfully made under this title," *amici* contend that a ruling in Wiley's favor would prevent museums from invoking §109(c) with respect to foreign-made works of art. *Id.*, at 11–13.[24]

Limiting §109(c) to U.S.-made works, however, does not bar art museums from lawfully displaying works made in other countries. Museums can, of course, seek the copyright owner's permission to display a work. Furthermore, the sale of a work of art to a U.S. museum may carry with it an implied license to publicly display the work. See 2 Patry §5:131, at5– 280 ("[C]ourts have noted the potential availability of an implied nonexclusive licens[e] when the circumstances ... demonstrate that the parties intended that the work would be used for a specific purpose."). Displaying a work of art as part of a museum exhibition might also qualify as a "fair use" under 17 U.S.C. §107. Cf. *Bouchat* v. *Baltimore Ravens Ltd. Partnership*, 619 F.3d 301, 313–316 (CA4 2010) (display of copyrighted logo in museum-like exhibition constituted "fair use").

The Court worries about the resale of foreign-made consumer goods "contain[ing] copyrightable software pro-grams or packaging." *Ante*, at 21. For example, the Court observes that a car might be programmed with diverse forms of software, the copyrights to which might beowned by individuals or entities other than the manu-facturer of the car. *Ibid*. Must a car owner, the Court asks, obtain permission from all of these various copyright owners before reselling her car? *Ibid*. Although this question strays far from the one presented in this case and briefed by the parties, principles of fair use and implied license (to the extent that express licenses do not exist) would likely permit the car to be resold without the copyright owners' authorization.[25]

Most telling in this regard, no court, it appears, has been called upon to answer any of the Court's "horribles" in an actual case. Three decades have passed since a federal court first published an opinion reading §109(a) as applicable exclusively to copies made in the United States. See *Columbia Broadcasting System, Inc.* v. *Scorpio Music Distributors, Inc.*, 569 F.Supp. 47, 49 (ED Pa. 1983), summarily aff'd, 738 F.2d 424 (CA3 1984) (table). Yet Kirtsaeng and his supporting *amici* cite not a single case in which the owner of a consumer good authorized for sale in the United States has been sued for copyright infringement after reselling the item or giving it away as a gift or to charity. The absence of such lawsuits is unsurprising. Routinely suing one's customers is hardly a best business practice.[26] Manufacturers, moreover, may be hesitant to do business with software programmers taken to suing consumers. Manufacturers may also insist that soft-ware programmers agree to contract terms barring such lawsuits.

The Court provides a different explanation for theabsence of the untoward consequences predicted in its opinion— namely, that lower court decisions regarding the scope of §109(a)'s first sale prescription have not been uniform. *Ante*, at 23. Uncertainty generated by these conflicting decisions, the Court notes, may have deterred some copyright owners from pressing infringement claims. *Ante*, at 23–24. But if, as the Court suggests, there are a multitude of copyright owners champing at the bit to bring lawsuits against libraries, art museums, and consumers in an effort to exercise perpetual control over the downstream distribution and public display of foreign-made copies, might one not expect that at least a handful of such lawsuits would have been filed over the past 30 years? The absence of such suits indicates that the "practical problems" hypothesized by the Court are greatly exaggerated. *Ante*, at 24.[27] They surely do not warrant disregarding Congress' intent, expressed in §602(a)(1), to grant copyright owners the authority to bar the importation of foreign-made copies of their works. Cf. *Hartford Underwriters Ins. Co.* v. *Union Planters Bank, N.A.*, 530 U.S. 1, 6 (2000) ("[W]hen the statute's language is plain, the sole function of the courts—at least where the disposition required by the text is not absurd—is to enforce it according to its terms." (internal quotation marks omitted)).

VI

To recapitulate, the objective of statutory interpretation is "to give effect to the intent of Congress." *American Trucking Assns.*, 310 U.S., at 542. Here, two congres-sional aims are evident. First, in enacting §602(a)(1), Con-gress intended to grant copyright owners permission to segment international markets by barring the importation of foreign-made copies into the United States. Second, as codification of the first sale doctrine underscores, Congress did not want the exclusive distribution right conferred in §106(3) to be boundless. Instead of harmonizing these objectives, the Court subordinates the first entirely to the second. It is unsurprising that none of the three major treatises on U.S. copyright law embrace the Court's construction of §109(a). See 2 Nimmer §8.12[B][6][c], at8–184.34 to 8–184.35; 2 Goldstein §7.6.1.2(a), at7:141;

4 Patry §§13:22, 13:44, 13:44.10.

Rather than adopting the very international-exhaustion rule the United States has consistently resisted in international-trade negotiations, I would adhere to the national-exhaustion framework set by the CopyrightAct's text and history. Under that regime, codified in §602(a)(1), Kirtsaeng's unauthorized importation of the foreign-made textbooks involved in this case infringed Wiley's copyrights. I would therefore affirm the Second Circuit's judgment.

NOTES

[1] In 2008, Congress renumbered what was previously §602(a) as §602(a)(1). See Prioritizing Resources and Organization for Intellectual Property Act of 2008 (PROIPA), §105(b)(2), 122Stat. 4259. Like the Court, I refer to the provision by its current numbering.

[2] Although Justice Kagan's concurrence suggests that *Quality King* erred in "holding that §109(a) limits §602(a)(1)," *ante*, at 2, that recent, unanimous holding must be taken as a given. See *John R. Sand & Gravel Co.* v. *United States*, 552 U.S. 130, 139 (2008) ("*[S]tare decisis* in respect to statutory interpretation has 'special force,' for 'Congress remains free to alter what we have done.'" (quoting *Patterson* v. *McLean Credit Union*, 491 U.S. 164–173 (1989))). The Court's objective in this case should be to avoid unduly "constrict[ing] the scope of §602(a)(1)'s ban on unauthorized importation," *ante*, at 1 (opinion of Kagan, J.), while at the same time remaining faithful to *Quality King*'s holding and to the text and history of other Copyright Act provisions. This aim is not difficult to achieve. See Parts II–V, *infra*. Justice Kagan and I appear to agree to this extent: Congress meant the ban on unauthorized importation to have real force. See *ante*, at 3 (acknowledging that "Wiley may have a point about what §602(a)(1) was designed to do").

[3] See *Quality King Distributors, Inc.* v. *L'anza Research Int'l, Inc.*, 523 U.S. 135, 148, n. 20 (1998) (quoting Copyright Law Revision Part 4: Further Discussions and Comments on Preliminary Draft for Revised U.S. Copyright Law, 88th Cong., 2d Sess., 119 (H.R. Judiciary Comm. Print 1964) (hereinafter Copyright Law Revision Part 4) (statement of Harriet Pilpel)).

[4] The Court asserts that my position gives the word "lawfully" in §109(a) "little, if any, linguistic work to do." *Ante*, at 9. That is not so. My reading gives meaning to each word in the phrase "lawfully made under this title." The word "made" signifies that the conduct at issue is the creation or manufacture of a copy. See Webster's Third New International Dictionary 1356 (1961) (defining "made" as "artificially produced by a manufacturing process"). The word "lawfully" indicates that for §109(a) to apply, the copy's creation must have complied with some body of law. Finally, the prepositional phrase "under this title" clarifies what that body of law is—namely, the copyright prescriptions contained in Title 17 of the U.S. Code.

[5] Attempting to show that my reading of §109(a) is susceptible to the same criticism, the Court points to the now-repealed "manufacturing clause," which required "copies of a work consisting preponderantly of nondramatic literary material ... in the English language" to be "manufactured in the United States or Canada." Copyright Act of 1976, §601(a), 90Stat. 2588. Because Congress expressly referred to manufacturing in this provision, the Court contends, the phrase "lawfully made under this title" in §109(a) cannot mean "manufactured in the United States." *Ante*, at 19. This argument is a non sequitur. I do *not* contend that the phrases "lawfully made under this title" and "manufactured in the United States" are interchangeable. To repeat, I read the phrase "lawfully made under this title" as referring to instances in which a copy's creation is governed by, and conducted in compliance with, Title 17 of the U.S. Code. See *supra*, at 6. Not all copies "manufactured in the United States" will satisfy this standard. For example, piratical copies manufactured in the United States without the copyright owner's authorization are not "lawfully made under [Title 17]." Nor would the phrase "lawfully manufactured in the United States" be an exact substitute for "lawfully made under this title." The making of a copy may be lawful under Title 17 yet still violate some other provision of law. Consider, for example, a copy made with the copyright owner's authorization by workers who are paid less than minimum wage. The copy would be "lawfully made under [Title 17]" in the sense that its creation would not violate any provision of that title, but the copy's manufacturing would nonetheless be unlawful due to the violation of the minimum-wage laws.

[6] When §602(a)(1) was originally enacted in 1976, it played an additional role—providing a private cause of action against importers of piratical goods. See *Quality King*, 523 U.S., at 146. In 2008,

however, Congress amended §602 to provide for such a cause of action in §602(a)(2), which prohibits the unauthorized "[i]mportation into the United States ... of copies or phonorecords, the making of which either constituted an infringement of copyright, or which would have constituted an infringement of copyright if [Title 17] had been applicable." See PROIPA, §105(b)(3), 122Stat. 4259–4260. Thus, under the Court's interpretation, the only conduct reached by §602(a)(1) but not §602(a)(2) is a nonowner's unauthorized importation of a nonpiratical copy.

[7] Notably, the Court ignores the history of §602(a)(1), which reveals that the primary purpose of the prescription was not to provide a remedy against rogue licensees, consignees, and bailees, against whom copyright owners could frequently assert breach-of-contract claims even in the absence of §602(a)(1). Instead, the primary purpose of §602(a)(1) was to reach third-party importers, enterprising actors like Kirtsaeng, against whom copyright owners could not assert contract claims due to lack of privity. See Part III, *infra*.

[8] Section 602(a)(3) provides:

> "This subsection [*i.e.*, §602(a)] does not apply to—
> "(A) importation or exportation of copies or phonorecords under the authority or for the use of the Government of the United States or of any State or political subdivision of a State, but not including copies or phonorecords for use in schools, or copies of any audiovisual work imported for purposes other than archival use;
> "(B) importation or exportation, for the private use of the importer or exporter and not for distribution, by any person with respect to no more than one copy or phonorecord of any one work at any one time, or by any person arriving from outside the United States or departing from the United States with respect to copies or phonorecords forming part of such person's personal baggage; or
> "(C) importation by or for an organization operated for scholarly, educational, or religious purposes and not for private gain, with respect to no more than one copy of an audiovisual work solely for its archival purposes, and no more than five copies or phonorecords of any other work for its library lending or archival purposes, unless the importation of such copies or phonorecords is part of an activity consisting of systematic reproduction or distribution, engaged in by such organization in violation of the provisions of section 108(g)(2)."

[9] The term "gray market good" refers to a good that is "imported outside the distribution channels that have been contractually negotiated by the intellectual property owner." Forsyth & Rothnie, Parallel Imports, in The Interface Between Intellectual Property Rights and Competition Policy 429 (S. Anderman ed. 2007). Such goods are also commonly called "parallel imports." *Ibid.*

[10] The Court asserts that its reading of §109(a) is bolstered by §104, which extends the copyright "protection[s]" of Title 17 to a wide variety of foreign works. See *ante*, at 10–11. The "protection under this title" afforded by §104, however, is merely protection against infringing conduct within the United States, the only place where Title 17 applies. See 4 W. Patry, Copyright §13:44.10, pp.13–128 to 13–129 (2012) (hereinafter Patry). Thus, my reading of the phrase "under this title" in §109(a) is consistent with Congress' use of that phrase in §104. Furthermore, §104 describes which *works* are

entitled to copyright protection under U.S. law. But no one disputes that Wiley's copyrights in the works at issue in this case are valid. The only question is whether Kirtsaeng's importation of *copies* of those works infringed Wiley's copyrights. It is basic to copyright law that "[o]wnership of a copyright ... is distinct from ownership of any material object in which the work is embodied." 17 U.S.C. §202. See also §101 ("'Copies' are material objects, other than phonorecords, in which a work is fixed by any method now known or later developed, and from which the work can be perceived, reproduced, or otherwise communicated, either directly or with the aid of a machine or device."). Given the distinction copyright law draws between works and copies, §104 is inapposite to the question here presented. 4 Patry §13:44.10, at13–129 ("There is no connection, linguistically or substantively, between Section[s] 104 and 109: Section 104 deals with national eligibility for the *intangible* work of authorship; Section 109(a) deals with the *tangible*, physical embodiment of the work, the 'copy.'").

[11] As the Court observes, *ante*, at 29, Irwin Karp of the Authors League of America stated at the 1964 panel discussion that §44(a) ran counter to "the very basic concept of copyright law that, once you've sold a copy legally, you can't restrict its resale." Copyright Law Revision Part 4, at 212. When asked if he was "presenting ... an argument against" §44(a), however, Karp responded that he was "neutral on th[e] provision." *Id.*, at 211. There is thus little reason to believe that any changes to the wording of §44(a) before its codification in §602(a) were made in response to Karp's discussion of "the problem of restricting [the] transfer of ... lawfully obtained [foreign] copies." *Ibid.*

[12] There is but one difference between this language from the 1965 bill and the corresponding language in the current version of §602(a)(1): In the current version, the phrase "for the purpose of distribution to the public" is omitted and the phrase "that have been acquired outside the United States" appears in its stead. There are no material differences between the quoted language from the 1965 bill and the corresponding language contained in the 1964 bill. See Copyright Law Revision Part 6: Supplementary Report of the Register of Copyrights on the General Revision of the U.S. Copyright Law: 1965 Revision Bill, 89th Cong., 1st Sess., 292–293 (H.R. Judiciary Comm. Print 1965).

[13] The Court purports to find support for its position in the House and Senate Committee Reports on the 1976 Copyright Act. *Ante*, at 30–31. It fails to come up with anything in the Act's legislative history, how-ever, showing that Congress understood the words "lawfully made under this title" in §109(a) to encompass foreign-made copies.

[14] Chiappetta, The Desirability of Agreeing to Disagree: The WTO, TRIPS, International IPR Exhaustion and a Few Other Things, 21 Mich. J. Int'l L. 333, 340 (2000) (hereinafter Chiappetta) (internal quotation marks omitted).

[15] The Court states that my "reliance on the Solicitor General's position in *Quality King* is undermined by his agreement in that case with [the] reading of §109(a)" that the Court today adopts. *Ante,* at 33. The United States' principal concern in both *Quality King* and this case, however, has been to protect copyright owners' "right to prevent parallel imports." Brief for United States as *Amicus Curiae* in *Quality King,* O. T. 1997, No. 96–1470, p.6 (hereinafter *Quality King* Brief). See also Brief for United States as *Amicus Curiae* 14 (arguing that Kirtsaeng's interpretation of §109(a), which the Court adopts, would "subver[t] Section 602(a)(1)'s ban on unauthorized importation"). In *Quality King*, the Solicitor General urged this Court to hold that §109(a)'s codification of the first sale doctrine does not limit the right to control importation set forth in §602(a). *Quality King* Brief 7–30. After *Quality King* rejected that contention, the United States reconsidered its position, and it now endorses the interpretation of the §109(a) phrase "lawfully made under this title" I would adopt. Brief for United States as *Amicus Curiae* 6–7, 13–14.

[16] Congress hardly lacks capacity to provide for international exhaustion when that is its intent. Indeed, Congress has expressly provided for international exhaustion in the narrow context of semiconductor chips embodying protected "mask works." See 17 U.S.C. §§905(2), 906(b). See also 2 M. Nimmer & D. Nimmer, Copyright §8A.06[E], p.8A–37 (2012) (hereinafter Nimmer) ("[T]he first sale doctrine under [§906(b)] expressly immunizes unauthorized importation.").

[17] Despite the Court's suggestion to the contrary, this case in noway implicates the *per se* antitrust prohibition against *horizontal* "'[a]greements between competitors to allocate territories to minimize competition.'" *Ante*, at 32 (quoting *Palmer* v. *BRG of Ga., Inc.*, 498 U.S. 46, 49 (1990) (*per curiam*)). Wiley is not requesting authority to enter into collusive agreements with other textbook publishers that would, for example, make Wiley the exclusive supplier of textbookson particular subjects within

particular geographic regions. Instead, Wiley asserts no more than the prerogative to impose *vertical* restraints on the distribution of its own textbooks. See Hovenkamp, Post-Sale Restraints and Competitive Harm: The First Sale Doctrine in Perspective, 66 N.Y.U. Ann. Survey Am. L. 487, 488 (2011) ("vertical restraints" include "limits [on] the way a seller's own product can be distributed").

[18] As the Court observes, *ante,* at 32–33, the United States stated at oral argument that the types of "horribles" predicted in the Court's opinion would, if they came to pass, be "worse than the frustration of market segmentation" that will result from the Court's interpretation of §109(a). Tr. of Oral Arg. 51. The United States, however, recognized that this purported dilemma is a false one. As the United States explained, the Court's horribles can be avoided while still giving meaningful effect to §602(a)(1)'s ban on unauthorized importation. *Ibid.*

[19] It appears that the Copyright Act of 1976 omitted the word "vend" and introduced the word "distribute" to avoid the "redundan[cy]" present in pre-1976 law. Copyright Law Revision: Report of the Register of Copyrights on the General Revision of the U.S. Copyright Law, 87th Cong., 1st Sess., 21 (H.R. Judiciary Comm. Print 1961) (noting that the exclusive rights to "publish" and "vend" works under the Copyright Act of 1947, §1(a), 61Stat. 652–653, were "redundant").

[20] My position that *Bobbs-Merrill* lives on as a limiting construction of the §106(3) distribution right does not leave §109(a) with no work to do. There can be little doubt that the books at issue in *Bobbs-Merrill* were published and first sold in the United States. See *Bobbs-Merrill Co.* v. *Straus*, 139 F. 155, 157 (CC SDNY 1905) (the publisher claiming copy-right infringement in *Bobbs-Merrill* was incorporated and had its principal office in Indiana). See also Copyright Act of 1891, §3, 26Stat. 1107–1108 (generally prohibiting importation, even by the copyright owner, of foreign-manufactured copies of copyrighted books); 4 Patry §13:40, at13–111 (under the Copyright Act of 1891, "copies of books by both foreign *and* U.S. authors had to be printed in the United States"). But cf. *ante,* at 18 (asserting, without acknowledging the 1891 Copyright Act's general prohibition against the importation of foreign-made copies of copyrighted books, that the Court is unable to find any "geographical distinctions ... in *Bobbs-Merrill*"). Thus, exhaustion occurs under *Bobbs-Merrill* only when a copy is distributed within the United States with the copyright owner's permission, not when it is distributed abroad. But under §109(a), as interpreted in *Quality King*, any authorized distribution of a U.S.-made copy, even a distribution occurring in a foreign country, exhausts the copyright owner's distribution right under §106(3). See 523 U.S., at 145, n.14. Section 109(a) therefore provides for exhaustion in a circumstance not reached by *Bobbs-Merrill.*

[21] Section 41 of the 1909 Act provided: "[N]othing in this Act shall be deemed to forbid, prevent, or restrict the transfer of any copy of a copyrighted work the possession of which has been lawfully obtained." 35Stat. 1084. This language was repeated without material change in §27 of the Copyright Act of 1947, 61Stat. 660. As noted above, see *supra,* at 2, 17 U.S.C. §109(a) sets out the current codification of the first sale doctrine.

[22] A group of *amici* representing libraries expresses the concernthat lower courts might interpret §602(a)(3)(C) as authorizing onlythe importing, but not the lending, of foreign-made copies ofnon-audiovisual works. See Brief for American Library Associationet al. 20. The United States maintains, and I agree, however, that §602(a)(3)(C) "is fairly (and best) read as implicitly authorizing lending, in addition to importation, of all works other than audiovisual works." Brief for United States as *Amicus Curiae* 30, n.6.

[23] Title 17 U.S.C. §109(c) provides: "Notwithstanding the provisions of section 106(5), the owner of a particular copy lawfully made under this title, or any person authorized by such owner, is entitled, without the authority of the copyright owner, to display that copy publicly, either directly or by the projection of no more than one image at a time, to viewers present at the place where the copy is located."

[24] The word "copy," as it appears in §109(c), applies to the original of a work of art because the Copyright Act defines the term "copies" to "includ[e] the material object ... in which the work is first fixed." §101.

[25] Principles of fair use and implied license may also allow a U.S. tourist "who buys a copyrighted work of art, a poster, or ... a bumper sticker" abroad to publicly "display it in America without the copyright owner's further authorization." *Ante,* at 15. (The tourist could lawfully bring the work of art,

poster, or bumper sticker into the United States under 17 U.S.C. §602(a)(3)(B), which provides that §602(a)(1)'s importation ban does not apply to "importation ... by any person arriving from outside the United States ... with respect to copies ... forming part of such person's personal baggage."). Furthermore, an individual clearly would not incur liability for infringement merely by displaying a foreign-made poster or other artwork in her home. See §106(5) (granting the owners of copyrights in "literary, musical, dramatic, and choreographic works, pantomimes, and pictorial, graphic, or sculptural works" the exclusive right "to display the copyrighted work *publicly*" (emphasis added)). See also §101 (a work is displayed "publicly" if it is displayed "at a place open to the public or at any place where a substantial number of persons *outside of a normal circle of a family and its social acquaintances* is gathered" (emphasis added)). Cf. 2 Nimmer §8.14[C][1], at8–192.2(1) ("[A] performance limited to members ofthe family and invited guests is not a public performance." (footnote omitted)).

[26] Exerting extensive control over secondary markets may not always be in a manufacturer's best interest. Carmakers, for example, often trumpet the resale value of their vehicles. See, *e.g.*, Nolan, UD grad leads Cadillac marketing, Dayton Daily News, Apr. 2, 2009, p. A8 ("Cadillac plays up its warranty coverage and reliable resale value to prospective customers."). If the transaction costs of reselling vehicles were to rise, consumers' perception of a new car's value, and thus the price they are willing to pay for such a car, might fall—an outcome hardly favorable to automobile manufacturers.

[27] It should not be overlooked that the ability to prevent importation of foreign-made copies encourages copyright owners such as Wiley to offer copies of their works at reduced prices to consumers in less developed countries who might otherwise be unable to afford them. The Court's holding, however, prevents copyright owners from barring the importation of such low-priced copies into the United States, where they will compete with the higher priced editions copyright owners make available for sale in this country. To protect their profit margins in the U.S. market, copyright owners may raise prices in less developed countries or may withdraw from such markets altogether. See Brief for United States as *Amicus Curiae* 26; Brief for Text and Academic Authors Association as *Amicus Curiae* 12; Brief for Association of American Publishers as *Amicus Curiae* 37. See also Chiappetta 357–358 (a rule of national exhaustion "encourages entry and participation in developing markets at lower, locally more affordable prices by eliminating them as risky sources of cheaper parallel imports back into premium markets"). Such an outcome would disserve consumers—and especially students—in developing nations and would hardly advance the "American foreign policy goals" of supporting education and economic development in such countries. *Quality King* Brief 25–26.

ABIGAIL NOEL FISHER v. UNIVERSITY OF TEXAS AT AUSTIN, et al.

No. 11-345, June 24, 2013

ON WRIT OF CERTIORARI TO THE UNITED STATES COURT OF APPEALS FOR THE FIFTH CIRCUIT

Justice Ginsburg, dissenting.

The University of Texas at Austin (University) is candid about what it is endeavoring to do: It seeks to achieve student-body diversity through an admissions policy patterned after the Harvard plan referenced as exemplary in Justice Powell's opinion in *Regents of Univ. of Cal.* v. *Bakke*, 438 U.S. 265–317 (1978). The University has steered clear of a quota system like the one struck down in *Bakke*, which excluded all nonminority candidates from competition for a fixed number of seats. See *id.*, at 272–275, 315, 319–320 (opinion of Powell, J.). See also *Gratz* v. *Bollinger*, 539 U.S. 244, 293 (2003) (Souter, J., dissenting) ("Justice Powell's opinion in [*Bakke*] rules out a racial quota or set-aside, in which race is the sole fact of eligibility for certain places in a class."). And, like so many educational institutions across the Nation,[1] the University has taken care to follow the model approved by the Court in *Grutter* v. *Bollinger*, 539 U.S. 306 (2003) . See 645 F.Supp. 2d 587, 609 (WD Tex. 2009) ("[T]he parties agree [that the University's] policy was based on the [admissions] policy [upheld in *Grutter*].").

Petitioner urges that Texas' Top Ten Percent Law and race-blind holistic review of each application achieve significant diversity, so the University must be content with those alternatives. I have said before and reiterate here that only an ostrich could regard the supposedly neutral alternatives as race unconscious. See *Gratz*, 539 U.S., at 303–304, n.10 (dissenting opinion). As Justice Souter observed, the vaunted alternatives suffer from "the disadvantage of deliberate obfuscation." *Id.*, at 297–298 (dissenting opinion).

Texas' percentage plan was adopted with racially segregated neighborhoods and schools front and center stage. See House Research Organization, Bill Analysis, HB 588, pp.4–5 (Apr. 15, 1997) ("Many regions of the state, school districts, and high schools in Texas are still predominantly composed of people from a single racial or ethnic group. Because of the persistence of this segregation, admitting the top 10 percent of all high schools would provide a diverse population and ensure that a large, well qualified pool of minority students was admitted to Texas universities."). It is race consciousness, not blindness to race, that drives such plans.[2] As for holistic review, if universities cannot explicitly include race as a factor, many may "resort to camouflage" to "maintain their minority enrollment." *Gratz*, 539 U.S., at 304 (Ginsburg, J., dissenting).

I have several times explained why government actors, including state universities, need not be blind to the lingering effects of "an overtly discriminatory past," the legacy of "centuries of law-sanctioned inequality." *Id.*, at 298 (dissenting opinion). See also *Adarand Constructors, Inc.* v. *Peña*, 515 U.S. 200–274 (1995) (dissenting opinion). Among constitutionally permissible options, I remain convinced, "those that candidly disclose their consideration of race [are] preferable to those that conceal it." *Gratz*, 539 U.S., at 305, n.11 (dissenting opinion).

Accordingly, I would not return this case for a second look. As the thorough opinions below show, 631 F.3d 213 (CA5 2011); 645 F.Supp. 2d 587, the University's admissions policy flexibly considers race only as a "factor of a factor of a factor of a factor" in the calculus, *id.*, at 608; followed a yearlong review through which the University reached the reasonable, good-faith judgment that supposedly race-neutral initiatives were insufficient to achieve, in appropriate measure, the educational benefits of student-body diversity, see 631 F.3d, at 225–226; and is sub-ject to periodic review to ensure that the consideration of race remains necessary and proper to achieve the Uni-versity's educational objectives, see *id.*, at 226.[3] Justice Powell's opinion in *Bakke* and the Court's decision in *Grutter* require no further determinations. See *Grutter*, 539 U.S., at 333–343; *Bakke*, 438 U.S., at 315–320.

The Court rightly declines to cast off the equal protection framework settled in *Grutter*. See *ante*, at 5. Yet it stops short of reaching the conclusion that framework warrants. Instead, the Court vacates the Court of Appeals' judgment and remands for the Court of Appeals to "assess whether the University has offered sufficient evidence [to] prove that its admissions program is narrowly tailored to obtain the educational benefits of diversity." *Ante*, at 13. As I see it, the Court of Appeals has already completed that inquiry, and its judgment, trained on this Court's *Bakke* and *Grutter* pathmarkers, merits ourapprobation.[4]

* * *

For the reasons stated, I would affirm the judgment of the Court of Appeals.

NOTES

[1] See Brief for Amherst College etal. as *Amici Curiae* 33–35; Brief for Association of American Law Schools as *Amicus Curiae* 6; Brief for Association of American Medical Colleges etal. as *Amici Curiae* 30–32; Brief for Brown University etal. as *Amici Curiae* 2–3, 13; Brief for Robert Post etal. as *Amici Curiae* 24–27; Brief for Fordham University etal. as *Amici Curiae* 5–6; Brief for University of Delaware etal. as *Amici Curiae* 16–21.

[2] The notion that Texas' Top Ten Percent Law is race neutral calls to mind Professor Thomas Reed Powell's famous statement: "If you think that you can think about a thing inextricably attached to something else without thinking of the thing which it is attached to, then you have a legal mind." T. Arnold, The Symbols of Government 101 (1935) (internal quotation marks omitted). Only that kind of legal mind could conclude that an admissions plan specifically designed to produce racial diversity is not race conscious.

[3] As the Court said in *Grutter* v. *Bollinger*, 539 U.S. 306, 339 (2003) , "[n]arrow tailoring ... require[s] serious, good faith consideration of workable race-neutral alternatives that will achieve the diversity the university seeks." But, *Grutter* also explained, it does not "require a university to choose between maintaining a reputation for excellence [and] fulfilling a commitment to provide educational opportunitiesto members of all racial groups." *Ibid.* I do not read the Court tosay otherwise. See *ante*, at 10 (acknowledging that, in determining whether a race-conscious admissions policy satisfies *Grutter*'s narrow-tailoring requirement, "a court can take account of a university's experience and expertise in adopting or rejecting certain admissions processes").

[4] Because the University's admissions policy, in my view, is constitutional under *Grutter*, there is no need for the Court in this case "to revisit whether all governmental classifications by race, whether designed to benefit or to burden a historically disadvantaged group, should be subject to the same standard of judicial review." 539 U.S., at 346, n. (Ginsburg, J., concurring). See also *Gratz* v. *Bollinger*, 539 U.S. 244, 301 (2003) (Ginsburg, J., dissenting) ("Actions designed to burden groups long denied full citizenship stature are not sensibly ranked with measures taken to hasten the day when entrenched discrimination and its aftereffects have been extirpated.").

SHELBY COUNTY, ALABAMA v. ERIC H. HOLDER, JR., ATTORNEY GENERAL, et al.

No. 12-96, June 25, 2013

ON WRIT OF CERTIORARI TO THE UNITED STATES COURT OF APPEALS FOR THE DISTRICT OF COLUMBIA CIRCUIT

Justice Ginsburg, with whom Justice Breyer, Justice Sotomayor, and Justice Kagan join, dissenting.

In the Court's view, the very success of §5 of the Voting Rights Act demands its dormancy. Congress was of another mind. Recognizing that large progress has been made, Congress determined, based on a voluminous record, that the scourge of discrimination was not yet extirpated. The question this case presents is who decides whether, as currently operative, §5 remains justifiable,[1] this Court, or a Congress charged with the obligation to enforce the post-Civil War Amendments "by appropriate legislation." With overwhelming support in both Houses, Congress concluded that, for two prime reasons, §5 should continue in force, unabated. First, continuance would facilitate completion of the impressive gains thus far made; and second, continuance would guard against backsliding. Those assessments were well within Congress' province to make and should elicit this Court's unstinting approbation.

I

"[V]oting discrimination still exists; no one doubts that." *Ante*, at 2. But the Court today terminates the remedy that proved to be best suited to block that discrimination. The Voting Rights Act of 1965 (VRA) has worked to combat voting discrimination where other remedies had been tried and failed. Particularly effective is the VRA's requirement of federal preclearance for all changes to voting laws in the regions of the country with the most aggravated records of rank discrimination against minority voting rights.

A century after the Fourteenth and Fifteenth Amendments guaranteed citizens the right to vote free of discrimination on the basis of race, the "blight of racial discrimination in voting" continued to "infec[t] the electoral process in parts of our country." *South Carolina* v. *Katzenbach*, 383 U.S. 301, 308 (1966). Early attempts to cope with this vile infection resembled battling the Hydra. Whenever one form of voting discrimination was identified and prohibited, others sprang up in its place. This Court repeatedly encountered the remarkable "variety and persistence" of laws disenfranchising minority citizens. *Id.*, at 311. To take just one example, the Court, in 1927, held unconstitutional a Texas law barring black voters from participating in primary elections, *Nixon* v. *Herndon*, 273 U.S. 536, 541; in 1944, the Court struck down a "reenacted" and slightly altered version of the same law, *Smith* v. *Allwright*, 321 U.S. 649, 658; and in 1953, the Court once again confronted an attempt by Texas to "circumven[t]" the Fifteenth Amendment by adopting yet another variant of the all-white primary, *Terry* v. *Adams*, 345 U.S. 461, 469.

During this era, the Court recognized that discrimination against minority voters was a quintessentially political problem requiring a political solution. As Justice Holmes explained: If "the great mass of the white population intends to keep the blacks from voting," "relief from [that] great political wrong, if done, as alleged, by the people of a State and the State itself, must be given by them or by the legislative and political department of the government of the United States." *Giles* v. *Harris*, 189 U.S. 475, 488 (1903).

Congress learned from experience that laws targeting particular electoral practices or enabling case-by-case litigation were inadequate to the task. In the Civil Rights Acts of 1957, 1960, and 1964, Congress authorized and then expanded the power of "the Attorney General to seek injunctions against public and private interference with the right to vote on racial grounds." *Katzenbach*, 383 U.S., at 313. But circumstances reduced the ameliorative potential of these legislative Acts:

> "Voting suits are unusually onerous to prepare, sometimes requiring as many as 6,000 man-hours spent combing through registration records in preparation for trial. Litigation has been exceedingly slow, in part because of the ample opportunities for delay afforded voting officials and others involved in the proceedings. Even when favorable decisions have finally been obtained, some of the States affected have

merely switched to discriminatory devices not covered by the federal decrees or have enacted difficult new tests designed to prolong the existing disparity between white and Negro registration. Alternatively, certain local officials have defied and evaded court orders or have simply closed their registration offices to freeze the voting rolls." *Id.*, at 314 (footnote omitted).

Patently, a new approach was needed.

Answering that need, the Voting Rights Act became one of the most consequential, efficacious, and amply justified exercises of federal legislative power in our Nation's his-tory. Requiring federal preclearance of changes in voting laws in the covered jurisdictions—those States and localities where opposition to the Constitution's commands were most virulent—the VRA provided a fit solution for minority voters as well as for States. Under the preclearance regime established by §5 of the VRA, covered jurisdictions must submit proposed changes in voting laws or procedures to the Department of Justice (DOJ), which has 60 days to respond to the changes. 79Stat. 439, codified at 42 U.S.C. §1973c(a). A change will be approved unless DOJ finds it has "the purpose [or] ... the effect of denying or abridging the right to vote on account of race or color." *Ibid.* In the alternative, the covered jurisdiction may seek approval by a three-judge District Court in the District of Columbia.

After a century's failure to fulfill the promise of the Fourteenth and Fifteenth Amendments, passage of the VRA finally led to signal improvement on this front. "The Justice Department estimated that in the five years after [the VRA's] passage, almost as many blacks registered [to vote] in Alabama, Mississippi, Georgia, Louisiana, North Carolina, and South Carolina as in the entire century before 1965." Davidson, The Voting Rights Act: A Brief History, in Controversies in Minority Voting 7, 21 (B. Grofman & C. Davidson eds. 1992). And in assessing the overall effects of the VRA in 2006, Congress found that "[s]ignificant progress has been made in eliminating first generation barriers experienced by minority voters, including increased numbers of registered minority voters, minority voter turnout, and minority representation in Congress, State legislatures, and local elected offices. This progress is the direct result of the Voting Rights Act of 1965." Fannie Lou Hamer, Rosa Parks, and Coretta Scott King Voting Rights Act Reauthorization and Amendments Act of 2006 (hereinafter 2006 Reauthorization), §2(b)(1), 120Stat. 577. On that matter of cause and effects there can be no genuine doubt.

Although the VRA wrought dramatic changes in the realization of minority voting rights, the Act, to date, surely has not eliminated all vestiges of discrimination against the exercise of the franchise by minority citizens. Jurisdictions covered by the preclearance requirement continued to submit, in large numbers, proposed changes to voting laws that the Attorney General declined to approve, auguring that barriers to minority voting would quickly resurface were the preclearance remedy elimi-nated. *City of Rome* v. *United States*, 446 U.S. 156, 181 (1980). Congress also found that as "registration and voting of minority citizens increas[ed], other measures may be resorted to which would dilute increasing minority voting strength." *Ibid.* (quoting H.R. Rep. No. 94–196, p.10 (1975)). See also *Shaw* v. *Reno*, 509 U.S. 630,640 (1993) ("[I]t soon became apparent that guaranteeing equal access to the polls would not suffice to root out other racially discriminatory voting practices" such as voting dilution). Efforts to reduce the impact of minority votes, in contrast to direct attempts to block access to the bal-lot, are aptly described as "second-generation barriers" to minority voting.

Second-generation barriers come in various forms. One of the blockages is racial gerrymandering, the redrawing of legislative districts in an "effort to segregate the races for purposes of voting." *Id.*, at 642. Another is adoption of a system of at-large voting in lieu of district-by-district voting in a city with a sizable black minority. By switching to at-large voting, the overall majority could control the election of each city council member, effectively eliminating the potency of the minority's votes. Grofman & Davidson, The Effect of Municipal Election Structure on Black Representation in Eight Southern States, inQuiet Revolution in the South 301, 319 (C. Davidson& B. Grofman eds. 1994) (hereinafter Quiet Revolution). A similar effect could be achieved if the city engagedin discriminatory annexation by incorporating majority-white areas into city limits, thereby decreasing the effect of VRA-occasioned increases in black voting. Whatever the device employed, this Court has long recognized that vote dilution, when adopted with a discriminatory purpose, cuts down the right to vote as certainly as denial of access to the ballot. *Shaw*, 509 U.S., at 640–641; *Allen* v. *State Bd. of Elections*, 393 U.S. 544, 569 (1969); *Reynolds* v. *Sims*, 377 U.S. 533, 555 (1964). See also H.R. Rep. No. 109–478, p.6 (2006) (although "[d]iscrimination today is more subtle than the visible methods used in 1965," "the effect and results are the same, namely a diminishing of the minority community's ability to fully participate in the electoral process and to elect their preferred candidates").

In response to evidence of these substituted barriers, Congress reauthorized the VRA for five years in 1970, for seven years in 1975, and for 25 years in 1982. *Ante*, at 4–5. Each time, this Court upheld the reauthorization as a valid exercise of congressional power. *Ante*, at 5. As the 1982 reauthorization approached its 2007 expiration date, Congress again considered whether the VRA's preclearance mechanism remained an appropriate response to the problem of voting discrimination in covered jurisdictions.

Congress did not take this task lightly. Quite the opposite. The 109th Congress that took responsibility for the renewal started early and conscientiously. In October 2005, the House began extensive hearings, which continued into November and resumed in March 2006. S.Rep. No. 109–295, p. 2 (2006). In April 2006, the Senate followed suit, with hearings of its own. *Ibid.* In May 2006, the bills that became the VRA's reauthorization were introduced in both Houses. *Ibid.* The House held further hearings of considerable length, as did the Senate, which continued to hold hearings into June and July. H.R. Rep. 109–478, at 5; S.Rep. 109–295, at 3–4. In mid-July, the House considered and rejected four amendments, then passed the reauthorization by a vote of 390 yeas to 33 nays. 152 Cong. Rec. H5207 (July 13, 2006); Persily, The Promise and Pitfalls of the New Voting Rights Act, 117 Yale L.J. 174, 182–183 (2007) (hereinafter Persily). The bill was read and debated in the Senate, where it passed by a vote of 98 to 0. 152 Cong. Rec. S8012 (July 20, 2006). President Bush signed it a week later, on July 27, 2006, recognizing the need for "further work ... in the fight against injustice," and calling the reauthorization "an example of our continued commitment to a united America where every person is valued and treated with dignity and respect." 152 Cong. Rec. S8781 (Aug. 3, 2006).

In the long course of the legislative process, Congress "amassed a sizable record." *Northwest Austin Municipal Util. Dist. No. One* v. *Holder*, 557 U.S. 193, 205 (2009). See also 679 F.3d 848, 865–873 (CADC 2012) (describing the "extensive record" supporting Congress' determina-tion that "serious and widespread intentional discrimination persisted in covered jurisdictions"). The House and Senate Judiciary Committees held 21 hearings, heard from scores of witnesses, received a number of investigative reports and other written documentation of continuing discrimina-tion in covered jurisdictions. In all, the legislative record Congress compiled filled more than 15,000 pages. H.R. Rep. 109–478, at 5, 11–12; S.Rep. 109–295, at 2–4,15. The compilation presents countless "examples of fla-grant racial discrimination" since the last reauthoriza-tion; Congress also brought to light systematic evidence that "intentional racial discrimination in voting remains so serious and widespread in covered jurisdictions that section 5 preclearance is still needed." 679 F.3d, at 866.

After considering the full legislative record, Congress made the following findings: The VRA has directly caused significant progress in eliminating first-generation barriers to ballot access, leading to a marked increase in minority voter registration and turnout and the number of minority elected officials. 2006 Reauthorization §2(b)(1). But despite this progress, "second generation barriers constructed to prevent minority voters from fully participating in the electoral process" continued to exist, as well as racially polarized voting in the covered jurisdictions, which increased the political vulnerability of racial and language minorities in those jurisdictions. §§2(b)(2)–(3), 120Stat. 577. Extensive "[e]vidence of continued discrimination," Congress concluded, "clearly show[ed] the continued need for Federal oversight" in covered jurisdictions. §§2(b)(4)–(5), *id.*, at 577–578. The overall record demonstrated to the federal lawmakers that, "without the continuation of the Voting Rights Act of 1965 protections, racial and language minority citizens will be deprived of the opportunity to exercise their right to vote, or will have their votes diluted, undermining the significant gains made by minorities in the last 40 years." §2(b)(9), *id.*, at 578.

Based on these findings, Congress reauthorized preclearance for another 25 years, while also undertaking to reconsider the extension after 15 years to ensure that the provision was still necessary and effective. 42 U.S.C. §1973b(a)(7), (8) (2006 ed., Supp. V). The question before the Court is whether Congress had the authority under the Constitution to act as it did.

II

In answering this question, the Court does not write on a clean slate. It is well established that Congress' judgment regarding exercise of its power to enforce the Fourteenth and Fifteenth Amendments warrants substantial deference. The VRA addresses the combination of race discrimination and the right to vote, which is "preservative of all rights." *Yick Wo* v. *Hopkins*, 118 U.S. 356, 370 (1886). When confronting the most constitutionally invidious form of discrimination, and the most fundamental right in our democratic system, Congress' power to act is at its height.

The basis for this deference is firmly rooted in both constitutional text and precedent. The Fifteenth Amendment, which targets precisely and only racial discrimination in voting rights, states that, in this domain, "Congress shall have power to enforce this article by appropriate legislation."[2] In choosing this language, the Amendment's framers invoked Chief Justice Marshall's formulation of the scope of Congress' powers under the Necessary and Proper Clause:

> "Let the end be legitimate, let it be within the scope of the constitution, and *all means which are appropriate, which are plainly adapted to that end*, which are not prohibited, but consist with the letter and spirit of the constitution, are constitutional." *McCulloch* v. *Maryland*, 4 Wheat. 316, 421 (1819) (emphasis added).

It cannot tenably be maintained that the VRA, an Act of Congress adopted to shield the right to vote from racial discrimination, is inconsistent with the letter or spirit of the Fifteenth Amendment, or any provision of the Constitution read in light of the Civil War Amendments. Nowhere in today's opinion, or in *Northwest Austin*,[3] is there clear recognition of the transformative effect the Fifteenth Amendment aimed to achieve. Notably, "the Founders' first successful amendment told Congress that it could 'make no law' over a certain domain"; in contrast, the Civil War Amendments used "language [that] authorized transformative new federal statutes to uproot all vestiges of unfreedom and inequality" and provided "sweeping enforcement powers ... to enact 'appropriate' legislation targeting state abuses." A. Amar, America's Constitution: A Biography 361, 363, 399 (2005). See also McConnell, Institutions and Interpretation: A Critique of *City of Boerne* v. *Flores*, 111 Harv. L.Rev. 153, 182 (1997)(quoting Civil War-era framer that "the remedy for the violation of the fourteenth and fifteenth amendmentswas expressly not left to the courts. The remedy was legislative.").

The stated purpose of the Civil War Amendments was to arm Congress with the power and authority to protect all persons within the Nation from violations of their rights by the States. In exercising that power, then, Congress may use "all means which are appropriate, which are plainly adapted" to the constitutional ends declared by these Amendments. *McCulloch*, 4 Wheat., at 421. So when Congress acts to enforce the right to vote free from racial discrimination, we ask not whether Congress has chosen the means most wise, but whether Congress has rationally selected means appropriate to a legitimate end. "It is not for us to review the congressional resolution of [the need for its chosen remedy]. It is enough that we be able to perceive a basis upon which the Congress might resolve the conflict as it did." *Katzenbach* v. *Morgan*, 384 U.S. 641, 653 (1966).

Until today, in considering the constitutionality of the VRA, the Court has accorded Congress the full measure of respect its judgments in this domain should garner. *South Carolina* v. *Katzenbach* supplies the standard of review: "As against the reserved powers of the States, Congress may use any rational means to effectuate the constitu-tional prohibition of racial discrimination in voting." 383 U.S., at 324. Faced with subsequent reauthorizations of the VRA, the Court has reaffirmed this standard. *E.g., City of Rome*, 446 U.S., at 178. Today's Court does not purport to alter settled precedent establishing that the dispositive question is whether Congress has employed "rational means."

For three reasons, legislation *reauthorizing* an existing statute is especially likely to satisfy the minimal requirements of the rational-basis test. First, when reauthorization is at issue, Congress has already assembled a legislative record justifying the initial legislation. Congress is en-titled to consider that preexisting record as well as the record before it at the time of the vote on reauthorization. This is especially true where, as here, the Court has repeatedly affirmed the statute's constitutionality and Congress has adhered to the very model the Court has upheld. See *id.*, at 174 ("The appellants are asking us to do nothing less than overrule our decision in *South Carolina* v. *Katzenbach* ... , in which we upheld the constitutionality of the Act."); *Lopez* v. *Monterey County*, 525 U.S. 266, 283 (1999) (similar).

Second, the very fact that reauthorization is necessary arises because Congress has built a temporal limitation into the Act. It has pledged to review, after a span of years (first 15, then 25) and in light of contemporary evidence, the continued need for the VRA. Cf. *Grutter* v. *Bollinger*, 539 U.S. 306, 343 (2003) (anticipating, but not guaranteeing, that, in 25 years, "the use of racial preferences [in higher education] will no longer be necessary").

Third, a reviewing court should expect the record supporting reauthorization to be less stark than the record originally made. Demand for a record of violations equivalent to the one earlier made would expose Congress to a catch-22. If the statute was working, there would be less evidence of discrimination, so opponents might argue that Congress should not be allowed to renew the statute. In contrast, if the statute was not working, there would be plenty of evidence of discrimination, but scant reason to renew a failed regulatory regime. See Persily 193–194.

This is not to suggest that congressional power in this area is limitless. It is this Court's responsibility to ensure that Congress has used appropriate means. The question meet for judicial review is whether the chosen means are "adapted to carry out the objects the amendments have in view." *Ex parte Virginia*, 100 U.S. 339, 346 (1880). The Court's role, then, is not to substitute its judgment for that of Congress, but to determine whether the legislative record sufficed to show that "Congress could rationally have determined that [its chosen] provisions were appropriate methods." *City of Rome*, 446 U.S., at 176–177.

In summary, the Constitution vests broad power in Congress to protect the right to vote, and in particular to combat racial discrimination in voting. This Court has repeatedly reaffirmed Congress' prerogative to use any rational means in exercise of its power in this area. And both precedent and logic dictate that the rational-means test should be easier to satisfy, and the burden on the statute's challenger should be higher, when what is at issue is the reauthorization of a remedy that the Court has previously affirmed, and that Congress found, from contemporary evidence, to be working to advance the legislature's legitimate objective.

III

The 2006 reauthorization of the Voting Rights Act fully satisfies the standard stated in *McCulloch*, 4 Wheat., at 421: Congress may choose any means "appropriate" and "plainly adapted to" a legitimate constitutional end. As we shall see, it is implausible to suggest otherwise.

A

I begin with the evidence on which Congress based its decision to continue the preclearance remedy. The surest way to evaluate whether that remedy remains in order is to see if preclearance is still effectively preventing discriminatory changes to voting laws. See *City of Rome*, 446 U.S., at 181 (identifying "information on the number and types of submissions made by covered jurisdictions and the number and nature of objections interposed by the Attorney General" as a primary basis for upholding the 1975 reauthorization). On that score, the record before Congress was huge. In fact, Congress found there were *more* DOJ objections between 1982 and 2004 (626) than there were between 1965 and the 1982 reauthorization (490). 1 Voting Rights Act: Evidence of Continued Need, Hearing before the Subcommittee on the Constitution of the House Committee on the Judiciary, 109th Cong., 2d Sess., p. 172 (2006) (hereinafter Evidence of Continued Need).

All told, between 1982 and 2006, DOJ objections blocked over 700 voting changes based on a determination that the changes were discriminatory. H.R. Rep. No. 109–478, at 21. Congress found that the majority of DOJ objections included findings of discriminatory intent, see 679 F.3d, at 867, and that the changes blocked by preclearance were "calculated decisions to keep minority voters from fully participating in the political process." H.R. Rep. 109–478, at 21. On top of that, over the same time period the DOJ and private plaintiffs succeeded in more than 100 actions to enforce the §5 preclearance requirements. 1 Evidence of Continued Need 186, 250.

In addition to blocking proposed voting changes through preclearance, DOJ may request more information from a jurisdiction proposing a change. In turn, the jurisdiction may modify or withdraw the proposed change. The number of such modifications or withdrawals provides an indication of how many discriminatory proposals are deterred without need for formal objection. Congress received evidence that more than 800 proposed changes were altered or withdrawn since the last reauthorization in 1982. H.R. Rep. No. 109–478, at 40–41.[4] Congress also received empirical studies finding that DOJ's requests for more information had a significant effect on the degree to which covered jurisdictions "compl[ied] with their obligatio[n]" to protect minority voting rights. 2 Evidence of Continued Need 2555.

Congress also received evidence that litigation under §2 of the VRA was an inadequate substitute for preclearance in the covered jurisdictions. Litigation occurs only after the fact, when the illegal voting scheme has already been put in place and individuals have been elected pursuant to it, thereby gaining the advantages of incumbency. 1 Evidence of Continued Need 97. An illegal scheme might be in place for several election cycles before a §2 plaintiff can gather sufficient evidence to challenge it. 1 Voting Rights Act: Section 5 of the Act—History, Scope, and Purpose: Hearing before the Subcommittee on the Constitution of the House Committee on the Judiciary, 109th Cong., 1st Sess., p. 92 (2005) (hereinafter Section 5 Hearing). And litigation places a heavy financial burden on minority voters. See id., at 84. Congress also received evidence that preclearance lessened the litigation burden on covered jurisdictions themselves, because the preclearance process is far less costly than defending against a §2 claim, and clearance by DOJ substantially reduces the likelihood that a §2 claim will be mounted. Reauthorizing the Voting Rights Act's Temporary Provisions: Policy Perspectives and Views From the Field: Hearing before the Subcommittee on the Constitution, Civil Rights and Property Rights of the Senate Committee on the Judiciary, 109th Cong., 2d Sess., pp. 13, 120–121 (2006). See also Brief for States of New York, California, Mississippi, and North Carolina as Amici Curiae 8–9 (Section 5 "reduc[es] the likelihood that a jurisdiction will face costly and protracted Section 2 litigation").

The number of discriminatory changes blocked or deterred by the preclearance requirement suggests that the state of voting rights in the covered jurisdictions would have been significantly different absent this remedy. Sur-veying the type of changes stopped by the preclearance procedure conveys a sense of the extent to which §5 continues to protect minority voting rights. Set out below are characteristic examples of changes blocked in the years leading up to the 2006 reauthorization:

In 1995, Mississippi sought to reenact a dual voter registration system, "which was initially enacted in 1892 to disenfranchise Black voters," and for that reason, was struck down by a federal court in 1987. H.R. Rep. No. 109–478, at 39.

Following the 2000 census, the City of Albany, Georgia, proposed a redistricting plan that DOJ found to be "designed with the purpose to limit and retrogress the increased black voting strength ... in the city as a whole." Id., at 37 (internal quotation marks omitted).

In 2001, the mayor and all-white five-member Board of Aldermen of Kilmichael, Mississippi, abruptly canceled the town's election after "anunprecedented number" of African-American can-didates announced they were running for office. DOJ required an election, and the town elected its first black mayor and three black aldermen. Id., at 36–37.

In 2006, this Court found that Texas' attempt to redraw a congressional district to reduce the strength of Latino voters bore "the mark of intentional discrimination that could give rise to an equal protection violation," and ordered the district redrawn in compliance with the VRA. League of United Latin American Citizens v. Perry, 548 U.S. 399, 440 (2006). In response, Texas sought to undermine this Court's order by curtailing early voting in the district, but was blocked by an action to enforce the §5 preclearance requirement. See Order in League of United Latin American Citizens v. Texas, No.06–cv–1046 (WD Tex.), Doc. 8.

In 2003, after African-Americans won a majority of the seats on the school board for the first time in history, Charleston County, South Carolina, proposed an at-large voting mechanism for the board. The proposal, made without consulting any of the African-American members of the school board,was found to be an "'exact replica'" of an earliervoting scheme that, a federal court had determined, violated the VRA. 811 F.Supp. 2d 424, 483 (DDC 2011). See also S.Rep. No. 109–295, at 309. DOJ invoked §5 to block the proposal.

In 1993, the City of Millen, Georgia, proposed to delay the election in a majority-black district by two years, leaving that district without representation on the city council while the neighboring majority-white district would have three representatives. 1 Section 5 Hearing 744. DOJ blocked the proposal. The county then sought to move a polling placefrom a predominantly black neighborhood in the city to an inaccessible location in a predominantly white neighborhood outside city limits. Id., at 816.

In 2004, Waller County, Texas, threatened to prosecute two black students after they announced their intention to run for office. The county then attempted to reduce the availability of early voting in that election at polling places near a historically black university. 679 F.3d, at 865–866.

In 1990, Dallas County, Alabama, whose county seat is the City of Selma, sought to purge its voter rolls of many black voters. DOJ rejected the purge as discriminatory, noting that it would have disquali-fied many citizens from voting "simply becausethey failed to pick up or return a voter updateform, when there was no valid requirement that they do so." 1 Section 5 Hearing 356.

These examples, and scores more like them, fill the pages of the legislative record. The evidence was indeed sufficient to support Congress' conclusion that "racial discrimination in voting in covered jurisdictions [remained] serious and pervasive." 679 F.3d, at 865.[5]

Congress further received evidence indicating that formal requests of the kind set out above represented only the tip of the iceberg. There was what one commentator described as an "avalanche of case studies of voting rights violations in the covered jurisdictions," ranging from "outright intimidation and violence against minority voters" to "more subtle forms of voting rights deprivations." Persily 202 (footnote omitted). This evidence gave Congress ever more reason to conclude that the time had not yet come for relaxed vigilance against the scourge of race discrimination in voting.

True, conditions in the South have impressively improved since passage of the Voting Rights Act. Congress noted this improvement and found that the VRA was the driving force behind it. 2006 Reauthorization §2(b)(1). But Congress also found that voting discrimination had evolved into subtler second-generation barriers, and that eliminating preclearance would risk loss of the gains that had been made. §§2(b)(2), (9). Concerns of this order, the Court previously found, gave Congress adequate cause to reauthorize the VRA. *City of Rome*, 446 U.S., at 180–182 (congressional reauthorization of the preclearance requirement was justified based on "the number and nature of objections interposed by the Attorney General" sincethe prior reauthorization; extension was "necessary to pre-serve the limited and fragile achievements of the Act and to promote further amelioration of voting discrimination") (internal quotation marks omitted). Facing such evidence then, the Court expressly rejected the argument that disparities in voter turnout and number of elected officials were the only metrics capable of justifying reauthorization of the VRA. *Ibid.*

B

I turn next to the evidence on which Congress based its decision to reauthorize the coverage formula in §4(b). Because Congress did not alter the coverage formula, the same jurisdictions previously subject to preclearance continue to be covered by this remedy. The evidence just described, of preclearance's continuing efficacy in blocking constitutional violations in the covered jurisdictions, itself grounded Congress' conclusion that the remedy should be retained for those jurisdictions.

There is no question, moreover, that the covered jurisdictions have a unique history of problems with racial discrimination in voting. *Ante*, at 12–13. Consideration of this long history, still in living memory, was altogether appropriate. The Court criticizes Congress for failing to recognize that "history did not end in 1965." *Ante*, at 20. But the Court ignores that "what's past is prologue." W. Shakespeare, The Tempest, act 2, sc. 1. And "[t]hose who cannot remember the past are condemned to repeat it." 1 G. Santayana, The Life of Reason 284 (1905). Congress was especially mindful of the need to reinforce the gains already made and to prevent backsliding. 2006 Reauthorization §2(b)(9).

Of particular importance, even after 40 years and thousands of discriminatory changes blocked by preclearance, conditions in the covered jurisdictions demonstrated that the formula was still justified by "current needs." *Northwest Austin*, 557 U.S., at 203.

Congress learned of these conditions through a report, known as the Katz study, that looked at §2 suits between 1982 and 2004. To Examine the Impact and Effectiveness of the Voting Rights Act: Hearing before the Subcommittee on the Constitution of the House Committee on the Judiciary, 109th Cong., 1st Sess., pp. 964–1124 (2005) (hereinafter Impact and Effectiveness). Because the private right of action authorized by §2 of the VRA applies nationwide, a comparison of §2 lawsuits in covered and noncovered jurisdictions provides an appropriate yardstick for measuring differences between covered and noncovered jurisdictions. If differences in the risk of voting discrimination between covered and noncovered jurisdictions had disappeared, one would expect that the rate of successful §2 lawsuits would be roughly the same in both areas.[6] The study's findings, however, indicated that racial discrimination in voting remains "concentrated in the jurisdictions singled out for preclearance." *Northwest Austin*, 557 U.S., at 203.

Although covered jurisdictions account for less than 25 percent of the country's population, the Katz study revealed that they accounted for 56 percent of successful§2 litigation since 1982. Impact and Effectiveness 974. Controlling for population, there were nearly *four* times as many successful §2 cases in covered jurisdictions as there were in noncovered jurisdictions. 679 F.3d, at 874. The Katz study further found that §2 lawsuits are more likely to succeed when they are filed in covered jurisdictions than in noncovered jurisdictions. Impact and Effectiveness 974. From these findings —ignored by the Court—Congress reasonably concluded that the coverage formula continues to identify the jurisdictions of greatest concern.

The evidence before Congress, furthermore, indicated that voting in the covered jurisdictions was more racially polarized than elsewhere in the country. H.R. Rep. No. 109–478, at 34–35. While racially polarized voting alone does not signal a constitutional violation, it is a factor that increases the vulnerability of racial minorities to dis-criminatory changes in voting law. The reason is twofold. First, racial polarization means that racial minorities are at risk of being systematically outvoted and having their interests underrepresented in legislatures. Second, "when political preferences fall along racial lines, the natural inclinations of incumbents and ruling parties to entrench themselves have predictable racial effects. Under circumstances of severe racial polarization, efforts to gain political advantage translate into race-specific disadvantages." Ansolabehere, Persily, & Stewart, Regional Differencesin Racial Polarization in the 2012 Presidential Election: Implications for the Constitutionality of Section 5 of the Voting Rights Act, 126 Harv. L.Rev. Forum 205, 209

(2013).

In other words, a governing political coalition has an incentive to prevent changes in the existing balance of voting power. When voting is racially polarized, efforts by the ruling party to pursue that incentive "will inevitably discriminate against a racial group." *Ibid.* Just as buildings in California have a greater need to be earthquake-proofed, places where there is greater racial polarization in voting have a greater need for prophylactic measures to prevent purposeful race discrimination. This point was understood by Congress and is well recognized in the academic literature. See 2006 Reauthorization §2(b)(3), 120Stat. 577 ("The continued evidence of racially polarized voting in each of the jurisdictions covered by the [preclearance requirement] demonstrates that racial and language minorities remain politically vulnerable"); H.R. Rep. No. 109–478, at 35; Davidson, The Recent Evolution of Voting Rights Law Affecting Racial and Language Minorities, in Quiet Revolution 21, 22.

The case for retaining a coverage formula that met needs on the ground was therefore solid. Congress might have been charged with rigidity had it afforded covered jurisdictions no way out or ignored jurisdictions that needed superintendence. Congress, however, responded to this concern. Critical components of the congressional design are the statutory provisions allowing jurisdictions to "bail out" of preclearance, and for court-ordered "bail ins." See *Northwest Austin*, 557 U.S., at 199. The VRA permits a jurisdiction to bail out by showing that it has complied with the Act for ten years, and has engaged in efforts to eliminate intimidation and harassment of vot-ers. 42 U.S.C. §1973b(a) (2006 ed. and Supp. V). It also authorizes a court to subject a noncovered jurisdiction to federal preclearance upon finding that violations of the Fourteenth and Fifteenth Amendments have occurred there. §1973a(c) (2006 ed.).

Congress was satisfied that the VRA's bailout mechanism provided an effective means of adjusting the VRA's coverage over time. H.R. Rep. No. 109–478, at 25 (the success of bailout "illustrates that: (1) covered status is neither permanent nor over-broad; and (2) covered status has been and continues to be within the control of the jurisdiction such that those jurisdictions that have a genuinely clean record and want to terminate coverage have the ability to do so"). Nearly 200 jurisdictions have successfully bailed out of the preclearance requirement, and DOJ has consented to every bailout application filed by an eligible jurisdiction since the current bailout procedure became effective in 1984. Brief for Federal Respondent 54. The bail-in mechanism has also worked. Several jurisdictions have been subject to federal preclearance by court orders, including the States of New Mexico and Arkansas. App. to Brief for Federal Respondent 1a–3a.

This experience exposes the inaccuracy of the Court's portrayal of the Act as static, unchanged since 1965. Congress designed the VRA to be a dynamic statute, capable of adjusting to changing conditions. True, many covered jurisdictions have not been able to bail out due to recent acts of noncompliance with the VRA, but that truth reinforces the congressional judgment that these jurisdictions were rightfully subject to preclearance, and ought to remain under that regime.

IV

Congress approached the 2006 reauthorization of the VRA with great care and seriousness. The same cannot be said of the Court's opinion today. The Court makes no genuine attempt to engage with the massive legislative record that Congress assembled. Instead, it relies on increases in voter registration and turnout as if that were the whole story. See *supra*, at 18–19. Without evenidentifying a standard of review, the Court dismissively brushes off arguments based on "data from the record," and declines to enter the "debat[e about] what [the] record shows." *Ante*, at 20–21. One would expect more from an opinion striking at the heart of the Nation's signal piece of civil-rights legislation.

I note the most disturbing lapses. First, by what right, given its usual restraint, does the Court even address Shelby County's facial challenge to the VRA? Second, the Court veers away from controlling precedent regarding the "equal sovereignty" doctrine without even acknowledging that it is doing so. Third, hardly showing the respect ordinarily paid when Congress acts to implement the Civil War Amendments, and as just stressed, the Court does not even deign to grapple with the legislative record.

A

Shelby County launched a purely facial challenge to the VRA's 2006 reauthorization. "A facial challenge to a legislative Act," the Court has other times said, "is, of course, the most difficult challenge to mount successfully, since the challenger must establish that no set of circumstances exists under which the Act would be valid." *United States* v. *Salerno*, 481 U.S. 739, 745 (1987).

"[U]nder our constitutional system[,] courts are not roving commissions assigned to pass judgment on the validity of the Nation's laws." *Broadrick* v. *Oklahoma*, 413 U.S. 601, 610–611 (1973). Instead, the "judicial Power" is limited to deciding particular "Cases" and "Controversies." U.S. Const., Art.III, §2. "Embedded in the traditional rules governing constitutional adjudication is the principle that a person to whom a statute may constitutionally be applied will not be heard to challenge that statute on the ground that it may conceivably be applied unconstitutionally to others, in other situations not before the Court." *Broadrick*, 413 U.S., at 610. Yet the Court's opinion in this case contains not a word explaining why Congress lacks the power to subject to preclearance the particular plaintiff that initiated this lawsuit—Shelby County, Alabama. The reason for the Court's silence is apparent, for as applied to Shelby County, the VRA's preclearance requirement is hardly contestable.

Alabama is home to Selma, site of the "Bloody Sunday" beatings of civil-rights demonstrators that served as the catalyst for the VRA's enactment. Following those events, Martin Luther King, Jr., led a march from Selma to Montgomery, Alabama's capital, where he called for passage of the VRA. If the Act passed, he foresaw, progress could be made even in Alabama, but there had to be a steadfast national commitment to see the task through to completion. In King's words, "the arc of the moral universe is long, but it bends toward justice." G. May, Bending Toward Justice: The Voting Rights Act and the Transformation of American Democracy 144 (2013).

History has proved King right. Although circumstances in Alabama have changed, serious concerns remain. Between 1982 and 2005, Alabama had one of the highest rates of successful §2 suits, second only to its VRA-covered neighbor Mississippi. 679 F.3d, at 897 (Williams, J., dissenting). In other words, even while subject to the restraining effect of §5, Alabama was found to have "deni[ed] or abridge[d]" voting rights "on account of race or color" more frequently than nearly all other States in the Union. 42 U.S.C. §1973(a). This fact prompted the dissenting judge below to concede that "a more narrowly tailored coverage formula" capturing Alabama and a handful of other jurisdictions with an established track record of racial discrimination in voting "might be defensible." 679 F.3d, at 897 (opinion of Williams, J.). That is an understatement. Alabama's sorry history of §2 violations alone provides sufficient justification for Congress' determination in 2006 that the State should remain subject to §5's preclearance requirement.[7]

A few examples suffice to demonstrate that, at least in Alabama, the "current burdens" imposed by §5's preclearance requirement are "justified by current needs." *Northwest Austin*, 557 U.S., at 203. In the interim between the VRA's 1982 and 2006 reauthorizations, this Court twice confronted purposeful racial discrimination in Alabama. In *Pleasant Grove* v. *United States*, 479 U.S. 462 (1987), the Court held that Pleasant Grove—a city in Jefferson County, Shelby County's neighbor—engaged in purposeful discrimination by annexing all-white areas while rejecting the annexation request of an adjacent black neighborhood. The city had "shown unambiguous opposition to racial integration, both before and after the passage of the fed-eral civil rights laws," and its strategic annexationsappeared to be an attempt "to provide for the growth ofa monolithic white voting block" for "the impermissible purpose of minimizing future black voting strength." *Id.*, at 465, 471–472.

Two years before *Pleasant Grove*, the Court in *Hunter* v. *Underwood*, 471 U.S. 222 (1985), struck down a provision of the Alabama Constitution that prohibited individuals convicted of misdemeanor offenses "involving moral turpitude" from voting. *Id.*, at 223 (internal quotation marks omitted). The provision violated the Fourteenth Amendment's Equal Protection Clause, the Court unanimously concluded, because "its original enactment was motivated by a desire to discriminate against blacks on account of race[,] and the [provision] continues to this day to have that effect." *Id.*, at 233.

Pleasant Grove and *Hunter* were not anomalies. In 1986, a Federal District Judge concluded that the at-large election systems in several Alabama counties violated §2. *Dillard* v. *Crenshaw Cty.*, 640 F.Supp. 1347, 1354–1363 (MD Ala. 1986). Summarizing its findings, the court stated that "[f]rom the late 1800's through the present, [Alabama] has consistently erected barriers to keep black persons from full and equal participation in the social, economic, and political life of the state." *Id.*, at 1360.

The *Dillard* litigation ultimately expanded to include 183 cities, counties, and school boards employing discriminatory at-large election systems. *Dillard* v. *Baldwin Cty. Bd. of Ed.*, 686 F.Supp. 1459, 1461 (MD Ala. 1988). One of those defendants was Shelby County, which eventually signed a consent decree to resolve the claims against it. See *Dillard* v. *Crenshaw Cty.*, 748 F.Supp. 819 (MD Ala. 1990).

Although the *Dillard* litigation resulted in overhauls of numerous electoral systems tainted by racial discrimination, concerns about backsliding persist. In 2008, for example, the city of Calera, located in Shelby County, requested preclearance of a redistricting plan that "would have eliminated the city's sole majority-black district, which had been created pursuant to the consent decree in *Dillard*." 811 F.Supp. 2d 424, 443 (DC 2011). Although DOJ objected to the plan, Calera forged ahead with elections based on the unprecleared voting changes, resulting in the defeat of the incumbent African-American councilman who represented the former majority-black district. *Ibid.* The city's defiance required DOJ to bring a §5 enforcement action that ultimately yielded appropriate redress, including restoration of the majority-black district. *Ibid.*; Brief for Respondent-Intervenors Earl Cunningham etal. 20.

A recent FBI investigation provides a further window into the persistence of racial discrimination in state politics. See *United States* v. *McGregor*, 824 F.Supp. 2d 1339, 1344–1348 (MD Ala. 2011). Recording devices worn by state legislators cooperating with the FBI's investigation captured conversations between members of the state legislature and their political allies. The recorded conversations are shocking. Members of the state Senate derisively refer to African-Americans as "Aborigines" and talk openly of their aim to quash a particular gambling-related referendum because the referendum, if placed on the ballot, might increase African-American voter turnout. *Id.*, at 1345–1346 (internal quotation marks omitted). See also *id.*, at 1345 (legislators and their allies expressed concern that if the referendum were placed on the ballot, "'[e]very black, every illiterate' would be 'bused [to the polls] on HUD financed buses'"). These conversations oc-curred not in the 1870's, or even in the 1960's, they took place in 2010. *Id.*, at 1344–1345. The District Judge presiding over the criminal trial at which the recorded conversations were introduced commented that the "recordings represent compelling evidence that political exclusion through racism remains a real and enduring problem" in Alabama. *Id.*, at 1347. Racist sentiments, the judge observed, "remain regrettably entrenched in the high echelons of state government." *Ibid.*

These recent episodes forcefully demonstrate that §5's preclearance requirement is constitutional as applied to Alabama and its political subdivisions.[8] And under our case law, that conclusion should suffice to resolve this case. See *United States* v. *Raines*, 362 U.S. 17, 24–25 (1960) ("[I]f the complaint here called for an application of the statute clearly constitutional under the Fifteenth Amendment, that should have been an end to the question of constitutionality."). See also *Nevada Dept. of Human Resources* v. *Hibbs*, 538 U.S. 721, 743 (2003) (Scalia, J., dissenting) (where, as here, a state or local government raises a facial challenge to a federal statute on the ground that it exceeds Congress' enforcement powers under the Civil War Amendments, the challenge fails if the opposing party is able to show that the statute "could constitutionally be applied to *some* jurisdictions").

This Court has consistently rejected constitutional challenges to legislation enacted pursuant to Congress' enforcement powers under the Civil War Amendments upon finding that the legislation was constitutional as applied to the particular set of circumstances before the Court. See *United States* v. *Georgia*, 546 U.S. 151, 159 (2006) (Title II of the Americans with Disabilities Act of 1990 (ADA) validly abrogates state sovereign immunity "insofar as [it] creates a private cause of action ... for conduct that *actually* violates the Fourteenth Amendment"); *Tennessee* v. *Lane*, 541 U.S. 509, 530–534 (2004) (Title II of the ADA is constitutional "as it applies to the class of cases implicating the fundamental right of access to the courts"); *Raines*, 362 U.S., at 24–26 (federal statute proscribing deprivations of the right to vote based on race was constitutional as applied to the state officials before the Court, even if it could not constitutionally be applied to other parties). A similar approach is warranted here.[9]

The VRA's exceptionally broad severability provision makes it particularly inappropriate for the Court to allow Shelby County to mount a facial challenge to §§4(b) and 5 of the VRA, even though application of those provisions to the county falls well within the bounds of Congress' legislative authority. The severability provision states:

> "If any provision of [this Act] or the applicationthereof to any person or circumstances is held invalid, the remainder of [the Act] and the application of the provision to other persons not similarly situated orto other circumstances shall not be affected thereby." 42 U.S.C. §1973p.

In other words, even if the VRA could not constitutionally be applied to certain States—*e.g.*, Arizona and Alaska, see *ante*, at 8—§1973p calls for those unconstitutional applications to be severed, leaving the Act in place for juris-dictions as to which its application does not transgress constitutional limits.

Nevertheless, the Court suggests that limiting the jurisdictional scope of the VRA in an appropriate case would be "to try our hand at updating the statute." *Ante*, at 22. Just last Term, however, the Court rejected this very argument when addressing a materially identical severability provision, explaining that such a provision is "Congress' explicit textual instruction to leave unaffected the remainder of [the Act]" if any particular "application is unconstitutional." *National Federation of Independent Business* v. *Sebelius*, 567 U.S. __, __ (2012) (plurality opinion) (slip op., at 56) (internal quotation marks omitted); *id.*, at __ (Ginsburg, J., concurring in part, concurring in judgment in part, and dissenting in part) (slip op., at 60) (agreeing with the plurality's severability analysis). See also *Raines*, 362 U.S., at 23 (a statute capable of some constitutional applications may nonetheless be susceptible to a facial challenge only in "that rarest of cases where this Court can justifiably think itself able confidently to discern that Congress would not have desired its legislation to stand at all unless it could validly stand in its every application"). Leaping to resolve Shelby County's facial challenge without considering whether application of the VRA to Shelby County is constitutional, or even addressing the VRA's severability provision, the Court's opinion can hardly be described as an exemplar of restrained and moderate decisionmaking. Quite the opposite. Hubris is a fit word for today's demolition of the VRA.

B

The Court stops any application of §5 by holding that §4(b)'s coverage formula is unconstitutional. It pins this result, in large measure, to "the fundamental principle of equal sovereignty." *Ante*, at 10–11, 23. In *Katzenbach*, however, the Court held, in no uncertain terms, that the principle "*applies only to the terms upon which States are admitted to the Union*, and not to the remedies for local evils which have subsequently appeared." 383 U.S., at 328–329 (emphasis added).

Katzenbach, the Court acknowledges, "rejected the notion that the [equal sovereignty] principle operate[s] as a bar on differential treatment outside [the] context [of the admission of new States]." *Ante*, at 11 (citing 383 U.S., at 328–329) (emphasis omitted). But the Court clouds that once clear understanding by citing dictum from *Northwest Austin* to convey that the principle of equal sovereignty "remains highly pertinent in assessing subsequent disparate treatment of States." *Ante*, at 11 (citing 557 U.S., at 203). See also *ante*, at 23 (relying on *Northwest Austin*'s "emphasis on [the] significance" of the equal-sovereignty principle). If the Court is suggesting that dictum in *Northwest Austin* silently overruled *Katzenbach*'s limitation of the equal sovereignty doctrine to "the admission of new States," the suggestion is untenable. *Northwest Austin* cited *Katzenbach*'s holding in the course of *declining to decide* whether the VRA was constitutional or even what standard of review applied to the question. 557 U.S., at 203–204. In today's decision, the Court ratchets up what was pure dictum in *Northwest Austin*, attributing breadth to the equal sovereignty principle in flat contradiction of *Katzenbach*. The Court does so with nary an explanation of why it finds *Katzenbach* wrong, let alone any discussion of whether *stare decisis* nonetheless counsels adherence to *Katzenbach*'s ruling on the limited "significance" of the equal sovereignty principle.

Today's unprecedented extension of the equal sovereignty principle outside its proper domain—the admission of new

States—is capable of much mischief. Federal statutes that treat States disparately are hardly novelties. See, *e.g.,* 28 U.S.C. §3704 (no State may operate or permit a sports-related gambling scheme, unless that State conducted such a scheme "at any time during the period beginning January 1, 1976, and ending August 31, 1990"); 26 U.S.C. §142(*l*) (EPA required to locate green building project in a State meeting specified population criteria); 42 U.S.C. §3796bb (at least 50 percent of rural drug enforcement assistance funding must be allocated to States with "a population density of fifty-two or fewer persons per square mile or a State in which the largest county has fewer than one hundred and fifty thousand people, based on the decennial census of 1990 through fiscal year 1997"); §§13925, 13971 (similar population criteria for funding to combat rural domestic violence); §10136 (specifying rules applicable to Nevada's Yucca Mountain nuclear waste site, and providing that "[n]o State, other than the State of Nevada, may receive financial assistance under this subsection after December 22, 1987"). Do such provisions remain safe given the Court's expansion of equal sovereignty's sway?

Of gravest concern, Congress relied on our pathmarking *Katzenbach* decision in each reauthorization of the VRA. It had every reason to believe that the Act's limited geographical scope would weigh in favor of, not against, the Act's constitutionality. See, *e.g., United States* v. *Morrison,* 529 U.S. 598, 626–627 (2000) (confining preclearance regime to States with a record of discrimination bolstered the VRA's constitutionality). Congress could hardly have foreseen that the VRA's limited geographic reach would render the Act constitutionally suspect. See Persily 195 ("[S]upporters of the Act sought to develop an evidentiary record for the principal purpose of explaining why the covered jurisdictions should remain covered, rather than justifying the coverage of certain jurisdictions but not others.").

In the Court's conception, it appears, defenders of the VRA could not prevail upon showing what the record overwhelmingly bears out, *i.e.,* that there is a need for continuing the preclearance regime in covered States. In addition, the defenders would have to disprove the existence of a comparable need elsewhere. See Tr. of Oral Arg. 61–62 (suggesting that proof of egregious episodes of racial discrimination in covered jurisdictions would not suffice to carry the day for the VRA, unless such episodes are shown to be absent elsewhere). I am aware of no precedent for imposing such a double burden on defenders of legislation.

C

The Court has time and again declined to upset legislation of this genre unless there was no or almost no evidence of unconstitutional action by States. See, *e.g., City of Boerne* v. *Flores,* 521 U.S. 507, 530 (1997) (legislative record "mention[ed] no episodes [of the kind the legislation aimed to check] occurring in the past 40 years"). No such claim can be made about the congressional record for the 2006 VRA reauthorization. Given a record replete with examples of denial or abridgment of a paramount federal right, the Court should have left the matter where it belongs: in Congress' bailiwick.

Instead, the Court strikes §4(b)'s coverage provision because, in its view, the provision is not based on "current conditions." *Ante,* at 17. It discounts, however, that one such condition was the preclearance remedy in place in the covered jurisdictions, a remedy Congress designed both to catch discrimination before it causes harm, and to guard against return to old ways. 2006 Reauthorization §2(b)(3), (9). Volumes of evidence supported Congress' de-termination that the prospect of retrogression was real. Throwing out preclearance when it has worked and is continuing to work to stop discriminatory changes is like throwing away your umbrella in a rainstorm because you are not getting wet.

But, the Court insists, the coverage formula is no good; it is based on "decades-old data and eradicated practices." *Ante,* at 18. Even if the legislative record shows, as engaging with it would reveal, that the formula accurately identifies the jurisdictions with the worst conditions of voting discrimination, that is of no moment, as the Court sees it. Congress, the Court decrees, must "star[t] from scratch." *Ante,* at 23. I do not see why that should be so.

Congress' chore was different in 1965 than it was in 2006. In 1965, there were a "small number of States ... which in most instances were familiar to Congress by name," on which Congress fixed its attention. *Katzenbach,* 383 U.S., at 328. In drafting the coverage formula, "Congress began work with reliable evidence of actual voting discrimination in a great majority of the States" it sought to target. *Id.,* at 329. "The formula [Congress] eventually evolved to describe these areas" also captured a few States that had not been the subject of congressional factfinding. *Ibid.* Nevertheless, the Court upheld the formula in its entirety, finding it fair "to infer a significant danger of the evil" in all places the formula covered. *Ibid.*

The situation Congress faced in 2006, when it took up *re*authorization of the coverage formula, was not the same. By then, the formula had been in effect for many years, and *all* of the jurisdictions covered by it were "familiarto Congress by name." *Id.,* at 328. The question before Congress: Was there still a sufficient basis to support continued application of the preclearance remedy in each of those already-identified places? There was at that point no chance that the formula might inadvertently sweep in new areas that were not the subject of congressionalfindings. And Congress could determine from the record whether the jurisdictions captured by the coverage for-mula still belonged under the preclearance regime. If they did, there was no need to alter the formula. That is why the Court, in addressing prior reauthorizations of the VRA, did not question the continuing "relevance" of the formula.

Consider once again the components of the record before Congress in 2006. The coverage provision identified a known list of places with an undisputed history of serious problems with racial discrimination in voting. Recent evidence relating to Alabama and its counties was there for all to see. Multiple Supreme Court decisions had upheld the coverage provision, most recently in 1999. There was extensive evidence that, due to the preclearance mechanism, conditions in the covered jurisdictions had notably improved. And there was evidence that preclearance was still having a substantial real-world effect, having stopped hundreds of discriminatory voting changes in the covered jurisdictions since the last reauthorization. In addition, there was evidence that racial polarization in voting was higher in covered jurisdictions than elsewhere, increasing the vulnerability of minority citizens in those jurisdictions. And countless witnesses, reports, and case studies documented continuing problems with voting dis-crimination in those jurisdictions. In light of this rec-ord, Congress had more than a reasonable basis toconclude that the existing coverage formula was not out of sync with conditions on the ground in covered areas. And certainly Shelby County was no candidate for release through the mechanism Congress provided. See *supra*, at 22–23, 26–28.

The Court holds §4(b) invalid on the ground that it is "irrational to base coverage on the use of voting tests 40 years ago, when such tests have been illegal since that time." *Ante*, at 23. But the Court disregards what Congress set about to do in enacting the VRA. That extraordinary legislation scarcely stopped at the particular tests and devices that happened to exist in 1965. The grand aim of the Act is to secure to all in our polity equal citizenship stature, a voice in our democracy undiluted by race. As the record for the 2006 reauthorization makes abundantly clear, second-generation barriers to minority voting rights have emerged in the covered jurisdictions as attempted *substitutes* for the first-generation barriers that originally triggered preclearance in those jurisdictions. See *supra*, at 5–6, 8, 15–17.

The sad irony of today's decision lies in its utter failure to grasp why the VRA has proven effective. The Court appears to believe that the VRA's success in eliminating the specific devices extant in 1965 means that preclearance is no longer needed. *Ante*, at 21–22, 23–24. With that belief, and the argument derived from it, history repeats itself. The same assumption—that the problem could be solved when particular methods of voting discrimination are identified and eliminated—was indulged and proved wrong repeatedly prior to the VRA's enactment. Unlike prior statutes, which singled out particular tests or devices, the VRA is grounded in Congress' recognition of the "variety and persistence" of measures designed to impair minority voting rights. *Katzenbach*, 383 U.S., at 311; *supra*, at 2. In truth, the evolution of voting discrimination into more subtle second-generation barriers is powerful evidence that a remedy as effective as preclearance remains vital to protect minority voting rights and prevent backsliding.

Beyond question, the VRA is no ordinary legislation. It is extraordinary because Congress embarked on a mission long delayed and of extraordinary importance: to realize the purpose and promise of the Fifteenth Amendment. For a half century, a concerted effort has been made toend racial discrimination in voting. Thanks to the Voting Rights Act, progress once the subject of a dream has been achieved and continues to be made.

The record supporting the 2006 reauthorization ofthe VRA is also extraordinary. It was described by the Chairman of the House Judiciary Committee as "one of the most extensive considerations of any piece of legislation that the United States Congress has dealt with in the 27½ years" he had served in the House. 152 Cong. Rec. H5143 (July 13, 2006) (statement of Rep. Sensenbrenner). After exhaustive evidence-gathering and deliberative process, Congress reauthorized the VRA, including the coverage provision, with overwhelming bipartisan support. It was the judgment of Congress that "40 years has not been a sufficient amount of time to eliminate the vestiges of discrimination following nearly 100 years of disregard for the dictates of the 15th amendment and to ensure that the right of all citizens to vote is protected as guaranteed by the Constitution." 2006 Reauthorization §2(b)(7), 120Stat. 577. That determination of the body empowered to enforce the Civil War Amendments "by appropriate legislation" merits this Court's utmost respect. In my judgment, the Court errs egregiously by overriding Congress' decision.

* * *

For the reasons stated, I would affirm the judgment of the Court of Appeals.

NOTES

[1] The Court purports to declare unconstitutional only the coverage formula set out in §4(b). See *ante*, at 24. But without that formula, §5 is immobilized.

[2] The Constitution uses the words "right to vote" in five separate places: the Fourteenth, Fifteenth, Nineteenth, Twenty-Fourth, and Twenty-Sixth Amendments. Each of these Amendments contains the same broad empowerment of Congress to enact "appropriate legislation" to enforce the protected right. The implication is unmistakable: Under our constitutional structure, Congress holds the lead rein in making the right to vote equally real for all U.S. citizens. These Amendments are in line with the special role assigned to Congress in protecting the integrity of the democratic process in federal elections. U.S. Const., Art.I, §4 ("[T]he Congress may at any time by Law make or alter" regulations concerning the "Times, Places and Manner of holding Elections for Senators and Representatives."); *Arizona* v. *Inter Tribal Council of Ariz., Inc.*, *ante*, at 5–6.

[3] Acknowledging the existence of "serious constitutional questions," see *ante*, at 22 (internal quotation marks omitted), does not suggest how those questions should be answered.

[4] This number includes only changes actually proposed. Congress also received evidence that many

covered jurisdictions engaged in an "informal consultation process" with DOJ before formally submitting a proposal, so that the deterrent effect of preclearance was far broader than the formal submissions alone suggest. The Continuing Need for Section 5 Pre-Clearance: Hearing before the Senate Committee on the Judiciary, 109th Cong., 2d Sess., pp. 53–54 (2006). All agree that an unsupported assertion about "deterrence" would not be sufficient to justify keeping a remedy in place in perpetuity. See *ante*, at 17. But it was certainly reasonable for Congress to consider the testimony of witnesses who had worked with officials in covered jurisdictions and observed a real-world deterrent effect.

[5] For an illustration postdating the 2006 reauthorization, see *South Carolina* v. *United States*, 898 F.Supp. 2d 30 (DC 2012), which involved a South Carolina voter-identification law enacted in 2011. Concerned that the law would burden minority voters, DOJ brought a §5 enforcement action to block the law's implementation. In the course of the litigation, South Carolina officials agreed to binding interpretations that made it "far easier than some might have expected or feared" for South Carolina citizens to vote. *Id.*, at 37. A three-judge panel precleared the law after adopting both interpretations as an express "condition of preclearance." *Id.*, at 37–38. Two of the judges commented that the case demonstrated "the continuing utility of Section 5 of the Voting Rights Act in deterring problematic, and hence encouraging non-discriminatory, changes in state and local voting laws." *Id.*, at 54 (opinion of Bates, J.).

[6] Because preclearance occurs only in covered jurisdictions and can be expected to stop the most obviously objectionable measures, one would expect a *lower* rate of successful §2 lawsuits in those jurisdictions ifthe risk of voting discrimination there were the same as elsewhere in the country.

[7] This lawsuit was filed by Shelby County, a political subdivision of Alabama, rather than by the State itself. Nevertheless, it is appropriate to judge Shelby County's constitutional challenge in light of instances of discrimination statewide because Shelby County is subject to §5's preclearance requirement by virtue of *Alabama's* designation as a covered jurisdiction under §4(b) of the VRA. See *ante*, at 7. In any event, Shelby County's recent record of employing an at-large electoral system tainted by intentional racial discrimination is by itself sufficient to justify subjecting the county to §5's preclearance mandate. See *infra*, at 26.

[8] Congress continued preclearance over Alabama, including Shelby County, *after* considering evidence of current barriers there to minority voting clout. Shelby County, thus, is no "redhead" caught up in an arbitrary scheme. See *ante*, at 22.

[9] The Court does not contest that Alabama's history of racial discrimination provides a sufficient basis for Congress to require Alabama and its political subdivisions to preclear electoral changes. Nevertheless, the Court asserts that Shelby County may prevail on its facial challenge to §4's coverage formula because it is subject to §5's preclearance requirement by virtue of that formula. See *ante*, at 22 ("The county was selected [for preclearance] based on th[e] [coverage] formula."). This misses the reality that Congress decided to subject Alabama to preclearance based on evidence of continuing constitutional violations in that State. See *supra*, at 28, n.8.

MAETTA VANCE v. BALL STATE UNIVERSITY

No. 11-556, June 24, 2013

ON WRIT OF CERTIORARI TO THE UNITED STATES COURT OF APPEALS FOR THE SEVENTH CIRCUIT

Justice Ginsburg, with whom Justice Breyer, Justice Sotomayor, and Justice Kagan join, dissenting.

In *Faragher* v. *Boca Raton*, 524 U.S. 775 (1998) , and *Burlington Industries, Inc.* v. *Ellerth*, 524 U.S. 742 (1998) , this Court held that an employer can be vicariously liable under Title VII of the Civil Rights Act of 1964 for harassment by an employee given supervisory authority over subordinates. In line with those decisions, in 1999, the Equal Employment Opportunity Commission (EEOC) provided enforcement guidance "regarding employer liability for harassment by supervisors based on sex, race, color, religion, national origin, age, disability, or protected activity." EEOC, Guidance on Vicarious Employer Liability For Unlawful Harassment by Supervisors, 8 BNA FEP Manual 405:7651 (Feb. 2003) (hereinafter EEOC Guidance). Addressing who qualifies as a supervisor, the EEOC answered: (1) an individual authorized "to undertake or recommend tangible employment decisions affecting the employee," including "hiring, firing, promoting, demoting, and reassigning the employee"; *or* (2) an individual authorized "to direct the employee's daily work activities." *Id.*, at 405:7654.

The Court today strikes from the supervisory category employees who control the day-to-day schedules and assignments of others, confining the category to those formally empowered to take tangible employment actions. The limitation the Court decrees diminishes the force of *Faragher* and *Ellerth*, ignores the conditions under which members of the work force labor, and disserves the objective of Title VII to prevent discrimination from infecting the Nation's workplaces. I would follow the EEOC's Guidance and hold that the authority to direct an employee's daily activities establishes supervisory status under Title VII.

I

A

Title VII makes it "an unlawful employment practice for an employer" to "discriminate against any individual with respect to" the "terms, conditions, or privileges of employment, because of such individual's race, color, religion, sex, or national origin." 42 U.S.C. §2000e-2(a). The creation of a hostile work environment through harassment, this Court has long recognized, is a form of proscribed discrimination. *Oncale* v. *Sundowner Offshore Services, Inc.*, 523 U.S. 75, 78 (1998) ; *Meritor Savings Bank, FSB* v. *Vinson*, 477 U.S. 57–65 (1986).

What qualifies as harassment? Title VII imposes no "general civility code." *Oncale*, 523 U.S., at 81. It does not reach "the ordinary tribulations of the workplace," for example, "sporadic use of abusive language" or generally boorish conduct. B. Lindemann & D. Kadue, Sexual Harassment in Employment Law 175 (1992). See also 1 B. Lindemann & P. Grossman, Employment Discrimination Law 1335–1343 (4th ed. 2007) (hereinafter Lindemann & Grossman). To be actionable, charged behavior need not drive the victim from her job, but it must be of such sever-ity or pervasiveness as to pollute the working environment, thereby "alter[ing] the conditions of the victim's employment." *Harris* v. *Forklift Systems, Inc.*, 510 U.S. 17–22 (1993).

In *Faragher* and *Ellerth*, this Court established a framework for determining when an employer may be held liable for its employees' creation of a hostile work environment. Recognizing that Title VII's definition of "employer" includes an employer's "agent[s]," 42 U.S.C. §2000e(b), the Court looked to agency law for guidance in formulating liability standards. *Faragher*, 524 U.S., at 791, 801; *Ellerth*, 524 U.S., at 755–760. In particular, the Court drew upon §219(2)(d) of the Restatement (Second) of Agency (1957), which makes an employer liable for the conduct of an employee, even when that employee acts beyond the scope of her employment, if the employee is "aided in accomplishing" a tort "by the existence of the agency relation." See *Faragher*, 524 U.S., at 801; *Ellerth*, 524 U.S., at 758.

Stemming from that guide, *Faragher* and *Ellerth* distinguished between harassment perpetrated by supervisors, which is often enabled by the supervisor's agency relationship with the employer, and harassment perpetrated by co-workers, which is not similarly facilitated. *Faragher*, 524 U.S., at 801–803; *Ellerth*, 524 U.S., at 763–765. If the harassing employee is a supervisor, the Court held, the employer is vicariously liable whenever the harassment culminates in a tangible employment action. *Far-agher*, 524 U.S., at 807–808; *Ellerth*, 524 U.S., at 764–765. The term "tangible employment action," *Ellerth* observed, "constitutes a significant change in employment status, such as hiring, firing, failing to promote, reassignment with significantly different responsibilities, or a decision causing a significant change in benefits." *Id.*, at 761. Such an action, the Court explained, provides "assurance the injury could not have been inflicted absent the agency relation." *Id.*, at 761–762.

An employer may also be held vicariously liable for a supervisor's harassment that does *not* culminate in a tangible employment action, the Court next determined. In such a case, however, the employer may avoid liability by showing that (1) it exercised reasonable care to pre-vent and promptly correct harassing behavior, and (2)the complainant unreasonably failed to take advantage of preventative or corrective measures made available to her. *Faragher*, 524 U.S., at 807; *Ellerth*, 524 U.S., at 765. The employer bears the burden of establishing this affirmative defense by a preponderance of the evidence. *Faragher*, 524 U.S., at 807; *Ellerth*, 524 U.S., at 765.

In contrast, if the harassing employee is a co-worker, a negligence standard applies. To satisfy that standard, the complainant must show that the employer knew or should have known of the offensive conduct but failed to take appropriate corrective action. See *Faragher*, 524 U.S., at 799; *Ellerth*, 524 U.S., at 758–759. See also 29 CFR §1604.11(d) (2012); EEOC Guidance 405:7652.

B

The distinction *Faragher* and *Ellerth* drew between supervisors and co-workers corresponds to the realities of the workplace. Exposed to a fellow employee's harassment, one can walk away or tell the offender to "buzz off." A supervisor's slings and arrows, however, are not so easily avoided. An employee who confronts her harassing supervisor risks, for example, receiving an undesirable or unsafe work assignment or an unwanted transfer. She may be saddled with an excessive workload or with placement on a shift spanning hours disruptive of her family life. And she may be demoted or fired. Facing suchdangers, she may be reluctant to blow the whistle on her superior, whose "power and authority invests his or her harassing conduct with a particular threatening character." *Ellerth*, 524 U.S., at 763. See also *Faragher*, 524 U.S., at 803; Brief for Respondent 23 ("The potential threat to one's livelihood or working conditions will make the victim think twice before resisting harassment or fighting back."). In short, as *Faragher* and *Ellerth* recognized, harassment by supervisors is more likely to cause palpable harm and to persist unabated than similar conduct by fellow employees.

II

While *Faragher* and *Ellerth* differentiated harassment by supervisors from harassment by co-workers, neither decision gave a definitive answer to the question: Who qualifies as a supervisor? Two views have emerged. One view, in line with the EEOC's Guidance, counts as asupervisor anyone with authority to take tangible employ-ment actions or to direct an employee's daily work activities. *E.g., Mack* v. *Otis Elevator Co.*, 326 F.3d 116, 127 (CA2 2003); *Whitten* v. *Fred's, Inc.*, 601 F.3d 231, 246 (CA4 2010); EEOC Guidance 405:7654. The other view ranks as supervisors only those authorized to take tangible employment actions. *E.g., Noviello* v. *Boston*, 398 F.3d 76, 96 (CA1 2005); *Parkins* v. *Civil Constructors of Ill., Inc.*, 163 F.3d 1027, 1034 (CA7 1998); *Joens* v. *John Morrell & Co.*, 354 F.3d 938, 940–941 (CA8 2004).

Notably, respondent Ball State University agreed with petitioner Vance and the United States, as *amicus curiae*, that the tangible-employment-action-only test "does not necessarily capture all employees who may qualify as supervisors." Brief for Respondent 1. "[V]icarious liability," Ball State acknowledged, "also may be triggered when the harassing employee has the authority to control the victim's daily work activities in a way that materially enables the harassment." *Id.*, at 1–2.

The different view taken by the Court today is out of accord with the agency principles that, *Faragher* and *Ellerth* affirmed, govern Title VII. See *supra*, at 3–4. It is blind to the realities of the workplace, and it discounts the guidance of the EEOC, the agency Congress established to interpret, and superintend the enforcement of, Title VII. Under that guidance, the appropriate question is: Hasthe employer given the alleged harasser authority to take tangible employment actions *or* to control the conditions under which subordinates do their daily work? If the answer to either inquiry is yes, vicarious liability is in order, for the superior-subordinate working arrangement facilitating the harassment is of the employer's making.

A

Until today, our decisions have assumed that employees who direct subordinates' daily work are supervisors. In *Faragher*, the city of Boca Raton, Florida, employed Bill Terry and David Silverman to oversee the city's corps of ocean lifeguards. 524 U.S., at 780. Terry and Silverman "repeatedly subject[ed] Faragher and other female lifeguards to uninvited and offensive touching," and they regularly "ma[de] lewd remarks, and [spoke] of women in offensive terms." *Ibid.* (internal quotation marks omitted). Terry told a job applicant that "female lifeguards had sex with their male counterparts," and then "asked whether she would do the same." *Id.*, at 782. Silverman threatened to assign Faragher to toilet-cleaning duties for a year if she refused to date him. *Id.*, at 780. In words and conduct, Silverman and Terry made the beach a hostile place for women to work.

As Chief of Boca Raton's Marine Safety Division, Terry had authority to "hire new lifeguards (subject to the approval of higher management), to supervise all aspects of the lifeguards' work assignments, to engage in counseling, to deliver oral reprimands, and to make a record of any such discipline." *Id.*, at 781. Silverman's duties as a Marine Safety lieutenant included "making the lifeguards' daily assignments, and . . . supervising their work and fitness training." *Ibid.* Both men "were granted virtually unchecked authority over their subordinates, directly controlling and supervising all aspects of Faragher's day-to-day activities." *Id.*, at 808 (internal quotation marks and brackets omitted).

We may assume that Terry would fall within the definition of supervisor the Court adopts today. See *ante*, at 9.[1] But nothing in the *Faragher* record shows that Silver-man would. Silverman had oversight and assignment responsibilities—he could punish lifeguards who would not date him with full-time toilet-cleaning duty—but there was no evidence that he had authority to take tangible employment actions. See *Faragher*, 524 U.S., at 780–781. Holding that Boca Raton was vicariously liable for Silverman's harassment, *id.*, at 808–809, the Court characterized him as Faragher's supervisor, see *id.*, at 780, and there was no dissent on that point, see *id.*, at 810 (Thomas, J., dissenting).

Subsequent decisions reinforced *Faragher*'s use of the term "supervisor" to encompass employees with authority to direct the daily work of their victims. In *Pennsylvania State Police* v. *Suders*, 542 U.S. 129, 140 (2004) , for example, the Court considered whether a constructive discharge occasioned by supervisor harassment ranks as a tangible employment action. The harassing employees lacked authority to discharge or demote the complainant, but they were "responsible for the day-to-day supervi-sion" of the workplace and for overseeing employee shifts. *Suders* v. *Easton*, 325 F.3d 432, 450, n.11 (CA3 2003). Describing the harassing employees as the complainant's "supervisors," the Court proceeded to evaluate the complainant's constructive discharge claim under the *Ellerth* and *Faragher* framework. *Suders*, 542 U.S., at 134, 140–141.

It is true, as the Court says, *ante*, at 15–17, and n.11, that *Faragher* and later cases did not squarely resolve whether an employee without power to take tangible em-ployment actions may nonetheless qualify as a supervisor. But in laboring to establish that Silverman's supervi-sor status, undisputed in *Faragher*, is not dispositive here, the Court misses the forest for the trees. *Faragher* illustrates an all-too-plain reality: A supervisor with authority to control subordinates' daily work is no less aided in his harassment than is a supervisor with authority to fire, demote, or transfer. That Silverman could threaten Far-agher with toilet-cleaning duties while Terry could orally reprimand her was inconsequential in *Faragher*, and properly so. What mattered was that both men took advantage of the power vested in them as agents of Boca Raton to facilitate their abuse. See *Faragher*, 524 U.S., at 801 (Silverman and Terry "implicitly threaten[ed] to mis-use their supervisory powers to deter any resistance or complaint."). And when, assisted by an agency relationship, in-charge superiors like Silverman perpetuate a discriminatory work environment, our decisions have appropriately held the employer vicariously liable, subject to the above-described affirmative defense. See *supra*, at 3–4.

B

Workplace realities fortify my conclusion that harassment by an employee with power to direct subordinates' day-to-day work activities should trigger vicarious employer liability. The following illustrations, none of them hypothetical, involve in-charge employees of the kind the Court today excludes from supervisory status.[2]

Yasharay Mack: Yasharay Mack, an African-American woman, worked for the Otis Elevator Company as an elevator mechanic's helper at the Metropolitan Life Building in New York City. James Connolly, the "mechanic in charge" and the senior employee at the site, targeted Mack for abuse. He commented frequently on her "fantastic ass," "luscious lips," and "beautiful eyes," and, using deplorable racial epithets, opined that minorities and women did not "belong in the business." Once, he pulled her on his lap, touched her buttocks, and tried to kiss her while others looked on. Connolly lacked authority to take tangible employment actions against mechanic's helpers, but he did assign their work, control their schedules, and direct the particulars of their workdays. When he became angry with Mack, for example, he denied her overtime hours. And when she complained about the mistreatment, he scoffed, "I get away with everything." See *Mack*, 326 F.3d, at 120–121, 125–126 (internal quotation marks omitted).

Donna Rhodes: Donna Rhodes, a seasonal highway maintainer for the Illinois Department of Transportation, was responsible for plowing snow during winter months. Michael Poladian was a "Lead Lead Worker" and Matt Mara, a "Technician" at the maintenance yard where Rhodes worked. Both men assembled plow crews and managed the work assignments of employees in Rhodes's position, but neither had authority to hire, fire, promote, demote, transfer, or discipline employees. In her third season working at the yard, Rhodes was verbally assaulted with sex-based invectives and a pornographic image was taped to her locker. Poladian forced her to wash hertruck in sub-zero temperatures, assigned her undesirable yard work instead of road crew work, and prohibited another employee from fixing the malfunctioning heating system in her truck. Conceding that Rhodes had been subjected to a sex-based hostile work environment, the Department of Transportation argued successfully in the District Court and Court of Appeals that Poladian and Mara were not Rhodes's supervisors because they lacked authority to take tangible employment actions against her. See *Rhodes* v. *Illinois Dept. of Transp.*, 359 F.3d 498, 501–503, 506–507 (CA7 2004).

Clara Whitten: Clara Whitten worked at a discount retail store in Belton, South Carolina. On Whitten's first day of work, the manager, Matt Green, told her to "give [him] what [he] want[ed]" in order to obtain approval for long weekends off from work. Later, fearing what might transpire, Whitten ignored Green's order to join him in an isolated storeroom. Angered, Green instructed Whitten to stay late and clean the store. He demanded that she work over the weekend despite her scheduled day off. Dismissing her as "dumb and stupid," Green threatened to make her life a "living hell." Green lacked authority to fire, promote, demote, or otherwise make decisions affecting Whitten's pocketbook. But he directed her activities, gave her tasks to accomplish, burdened her with undesirable work assignments, and controlled her schedule. He was usually the highest ranking employee in the store, and both Whitten and Green considered him the supervisor. See *Whitten*, 601 F.3d, at 236, 244–247 (internal quotation marks omitted).

Monika Starke: CRST Van Expedited, Inc., an interstate transit company, ran a training program for newly hired truckdrivers requiring a 28-day on-the-road trip. Monika Starke participated in the program. Trainees like Starke were paired in a truck cabin with a single "lead driver" who lacked authority to hire, fire, promote, or demote, but who exercised control over the work environment for the duration of the trip. Lead drivers were responsible for providing instruction on CRST's driving method, assigning specific tasks, and scheduling rest stops. At the end of the trip, lead drivers evaluated trainees' performance with a nonbinding pass or fail recommendation that could lead to full driver status. Over the course of Starke's training trip, her first lead driver, Bob Smith, filled the cabin with vulgar sexual remarks, commenting on her breast size and comparing the gear stick to genitalia. A second lead driver, David Goodman, later forced her into unwanted sex with him, an outrage to which she submitted, believing itnecessary to gain a passing grade. See *EEOC* v. *CRST Van Expedited, Inc.*, 679 F.3d 657, 665–666, 684–685 (CA8 2012).

In each of these cases, a person vested with authority to control the conditions of a subordinate's daily work life used his position to aid his harassment. But in none of them would the Court's severely confined definition of su-pervisor yield vicarious liability for the employer. The senior elevator mechanic in charge, the Court today tells us, was Mack's co-worker, not her supervisor. So was the store manager who punished Whitten with long hours for refusing to give him what he wanted. So were the lead drivers who controlled all aspects of Starke's working environment, and the yard worker who kept other employees from helping Rhodes to control the heat in her truck.

As anyone with work experience would immediately grasp, James Connolly, Michael Poladian, Matt Mara, Matt Green, Bob Smith, and David Goodman wielded employer-conferred supervisory authority over their victims. Each man's discriminatory harassment derived force from, and was facilitated by, the control reins he held. Cf. *Burlington N. & S. F. R. Co.* v. *White*, 548 U.S. 53–71 (2006) ("Common sense suggests that one good way to discourage an employee . . . from bringing discrimination charges would be to insist that she spend more time performing the more arduous duties and less time performing those that are easier or more agreeable."). Under any fair reading of Title VII, in each of the illustrative cases, the superior employee should have been classified a supervisor whose conduct would trigger vicarious liability.[3]

C

Within a year after the Court's decisions in *Faragher* and *Ellerth*, the EEOC defined "supervisor" to include any employee with "authority to undertake or recommend tangible employment decisions," *or* with "authority to di-rect [another] employee's daily work activities." EEOC Guidance 405:7654. That definition should garner "respect proportional to its 'power to persuade.'" *United States* v. *Mead Corp.*, 533 U.S. 218, 235 (2001) (quoting *Skidmore* v. *Swift & Co.*, 323 U.S. 134, 140 (1944)). See also *Crawford* v. *Metropolitan Government of Nashville and Davidson Cty.*, 555 U.S. 271, 276 (2009) (EEOC guidelines merited *Skidmore* deference); *Federal Express Corp.* v. *Holowecki*, 552 U.S. 389–403 (2008) (same); *Meritor*, 477 U.S., at 65 (same).[4]

The EEOC's definition of supervisor reflects the agency's "informed judgment" and "body of experience" in enforcing Title VII. *Id.,* at 65 (internal quotation marks omitted). For 14 years, in enforcement actions and litigation,the EEOC has firmly adhered to its definition. See Brief for United States as *Amicus Curiae* 28 (citing numerous briefs in the Courts of Appeals setting forth the EEOC's understanding).

In developing its definition of supervisor, the EEOC paid close attention to the *Faragher* and *Ellerth* framework. An employer is vicariously liable only when the authority it has delegated enables actionable harassment, the EEOC recognized. EEOC Guidance 405:7654. For that reason, a supervisor's authority must be "of a sufficient magnitude so as to assist the harasser . . . in carrying out the harassment." *Ibid.* Determining whether an employee wields sufficient authority is not a mechanical inquiry, the EEOC explained; instead, specific facts about the employee's job function are critical. *Id.,* at 405:7653 to 405:7654. Thus, an employee with authority to increase another's workload or assign undesirable tasks may rank as a supervisor, for those powers can enable harassment. *Id.,* at 405:7654. On the other hand, an employee "who directs only a limited number of tasks or assignments" ordinarily would not qualify as a supervisor, for her harassing conduct is not likely to be aided materially by the agency relationship. *Id.,* at 405:7655.

In my view, the EEOC's definition, which the Court puts down as "a study in ambiguity," *ante*, at 21, has the ring of truth and, therefore, powerfully persuasive force. As a precondition to vicarious employer liability, the EEOC explained, the harassing supervisor must wield authority of sufficient magnitude to enable the harassment. In other words, the aided-in-accomplishment standard requires "something more than the employment relation itself." *Ellerth*, 524 U.S., at 760. Furthermore, as the EEOC perceived, in assessing an employee's qualification as a supervisor, context is often key. See *infra*, at 16–17. I would accord the agency's judgment due respect.

III

Exhibiting remarkable resistance to the thrust of our prior decisions, workplace realities, and the EEOC's Guidance, the Court embraces a position that relieves scores of employers of responsibility for the behavior of the supervisors they employ. Trumpeting the virtues of simplicity and administrability, the Court restricts supervisor status to those with power to take tangible employment actions. In so restricting the definition of supervisor, the Court once again shuts from sight the "robust protection against workplace discrimination Congress intended Title VII to secure." *Ledbetter* v. *Goodyear Tire & Rubber Co.*, 550 U.S. 618, 660 (2007) (Ginsburg, J., dissenting).

A

The Court purports to rely on the *Ellerth* and *Faragher* framework to limit supervisor status to those capable of taking tangible employment actions. *Ante*, at 10, 18. That framework, we are told, presupposes "a sharp line between co-workers and supervisors." *Ante*, at 18. The definition of supervisor decreed today, the Court insists, is "clear," "readily applied," and "easily workable," *ante*, at 10, 20, when compared to the EEOC's vague standard, *ante*, at 22.

There is reason to doubt just how "clear" and "workable" the Court's definition is. A supervisor, the Court holds, is someone empowered to "take tangible employment actions against the victim, *i.e.*, to effect a 'significant changein employment status, such as hiring, firing, failing to promote, reassignment with significantly different responsi-bilities, or a decision causing a significant change in benefits.'" *Ante*, at 9 (quoting *Ellerth*, 524 U.S., at 761). Whether reassignment authority makes someone a supervisor might depend on whether the reassignment carries economic consequences. *Ante*, at 16, n.9. The power to discipline other employees, when the discipline has economic consequences, might count, too. *Ibid*. So might the power to initiate or make recommendations about tangible employment actions. *Ante*, at 15, n.8. And when an employer "concentrates all decisionmaking authority in a few individuals" who rely on information from "other workers who actually interact with the affected employee," the other workers may rank as supervisors (or maybe not; the Court does not commit one way or the other). *Ante*,at 26.

Someone in search of a bright line might well ask, what counts as "significantly different responsibilities"? Can *any* economic consequence make a reassignment ordisciplinary action "significant," or is there a minimum threshold? How concentrated must the decisionmaking authority be to deem those not formally endowed with that authority nevertheless "supervisors"? The Court leaves these questions unanswered, and its liberal use of "mights" and "mays," *ante*, at 15, n.8, 16, n.9, 26, dims the light it casts.[5]

That the Court has adopted a standard, rather than a clear rule, is not surprising, for no crisp definition of supervisor could supply the unwavering line the Court desires. Supervisors, like the workplaces they manage, come in all shapes and sizes. Whether a pitching coach supervises his pitchers (can he demote them?), or an artistic director supervises her opera star (can she impose significantly different responsibilities?), or a law firm associate supervises the firm's paralegals (can she fire them?) are matters not susceptible to mechanical rules and on-off switches. One cannot know whether an employer has vested supervisory authority in an employee, and whether harassment is aided by that authority, without looking to the particular working relationship between the harasser and the victim. That is why *Faragher* and *Ellerth* crafted an employer liability standard embracive of all whose authority significantly aids in the creation and perpetuation of harassment.

The Court's focus on finding a definition of supervisor capable of instant application is at odds with the Court's ordinary emphasis on the importance of particular circumstances in Title VII cases. See, *e.g.*, *Burlington Northern*, 548 U.S., at 69 ("[T]he significance of any given act of retaliation will often depend upon the particular circumstances."); *Harris*, 510 U.S., at 23 ("[W]hether an environment is 'hostile' or 'abusive' can be determined only by looking at all the circumstances.").[6] The question ofsupervisory status, no less than the question whether retali-ation or harassment has occurred, "depends on a constellation of surrounding circumstances, expectations, and relationships." *Oncale*, 523 U.S., at 81–82. The EEOC's Guidance so perceives.

B

As a consequence of the Court's truncated conception of supervisory authority, the *Faragher* and *Ellerth* framework has shifted in a decidedly employer-friendly direction. This realignment will leave many harassmentvictims without an effective remedy and undermine Title VII's capacity to prevent workplace harassment.

The negligence standard allowed by the Court, see *ante*, at 24, scarcely affords the protection the *Faragher* and *Ellerth* framework gave victims harassed by those in control of their lives at work. Recall that an employer is negligent with regard to harassment only if it knew or should have known of the conduct but failed to take appropriate corrective action. See 29 CFR §1604.11(d); EEOC Guidance 405:7652 to 405:7653. It is not uncommon for employers to lack actual or constructive notice of a harassing employee's conduct. See Lindemann & Grossman 1378–1379. An employee may have a reputation as a harasser among those in his vicinity, but if no complaint makes its way up to management, the employer will escape liability under a negligence standard. *Id.*, at 1378.

Faragher is illustrative. After enduring unrelenting harassment, Faragher reported Terry's and Silverman's conduct informally to Robert Gordon, another immediate supervisor. 524 U.S., at 782–783. But the lifeguards were "completely isolated from the City's higher management," and it did not occur to Faragher to pursue the matter with higher ranking city officials distant from the beach. *Id.*, at 783, 808 (internal quotation marks omitted). Applying a negligence standard, the Eleventh Circuit held that, despite the pervasiveness of the harassment, and despite Gordon's awareness of it, Boca Raton lacked constructive notice and therefore escaped liability. *Id.*, at 784–785. Under the vicarious liability standard, however, Boca Raton could not make out the affirmative defense, for it had failed to disseminate a policy against sexual harassment. *Id.*, at 808–809.

On top of the substantive differences in the negligence and vicarious liability standards, harassment victims, under today's decision, are saddled with the burden of proving the employer's negligence whenever the harasser lacks the power to take tangible employment actions. *Faragher* and *Ellerth*, by contrast, placed the burden squarely on the employer to make out the affirmative defense. See *Suders*, 542 U.S., at 146 (citing *Ellerth*, 524 U.S., at 765; *Faragher*, 524 U.S., at 807). This allocation of the burden was both sensible and deliberate: An employer has superior access to evidence bearing on whether it acted reasonably to prevent or correct harassing behavior, and superior resources to marshal that evidence. See 542 U.S., at 146, n.7 ("The employer is in the best position to know what remedial procedures it offers to employees and how those procedures operate.").

Faced with a steeper substantive and procedural hill to climb, victims like Yasharay Mack, Donna Rhodes, Clara Whitten, and Monika Starke likely will find it impossible to obtain redress. We can expect that, as a consequence of restricting the supervisor category to those formally empowered to take tangible employment actions, victims of workplace harassment with meritorious Title VII claims will find suit a hazardous endeavor.[7]

Inevitably, the Court's definition of supervisor will hinder efforts to stamp out discrimination in the workplace. Because supervisors are comparatively few, and employees are many, "the employer has a greater opportunity to guard against misconduct by supervisors than by common workers," and a greater incentive to "screen [supervisors], train them, and monitor their performance." *Faragher*, 524 U.S., at 803. Vicarious liability for employers serves this end. When employers know they will be answerable for the injuries a harassing jobsite boss inflicts, their incentive to provide preventative instruction is heightened. If vicarious liability is confined to supervisors formally empowered to take tangible employment actions, however, employers will have a diminished incentive to train those who control their subordinates' work activities and schedules, *i.e.*, the supervisors who "actually interact" with employees. *Ante*, at 26.

IV

I turn now to the case before us. Maetta Vance worked as substitute server and part-time catering assistant for Ball State University's Banquet and Catering Division. During the period in question, she alleged, Saundra Davis, a catering specialist, and other Ball State employees subjected her to a racially hostile work environment. Applying controlling Circuit precedent, the District Court and Seventh Circuit concluded that Davis was not Vance's supervisor, and reviewed Ball State's liability for her conduct under a negligence standard. 646 F.3d 461, 470–471 (2011); App. to Pet. for Cert. 53a–55a, 59a–60a. Because I would hold that the Seventh Circuit erred in restrict-ing supervisor status to employees formally empoweredto take tangible employment actions, I would remandfor application of the proper standard to Vance's claim. On this record, however, there is cause to anticipate that Davis would not qualify as Vance's supervisor.[8]

Supervisor status is based on "job function rather than job title," and depends on "specific facts" about the working relationship. EEOC Guidance 405:7654. See *supra*, at 13. Vance has adduced scant evidence that Davis controlled the conditions of her daily work. Vance stated in an affidavit that the general manager of the Catering Division, Bill Kimes, was charged with "overall supervision in the kitchen," including "reassign[ing] people to perform different tasks," and "control[ling] the schedule." App. 431. The chef, Shannon Fultz, assigned tasks by preparing "prep lists" of daily duties. *Id.*, at 277–279, 427. There is no allegation that Davis had a hand in creating these prep lists, nor is there any indication that, in fact, Davis otherwise controlled the particulars of Vance's workday. Vance herself testified that she did not know whether Davis was her supervisor. *Id.*, at 198.

True, Davis' job description listed among her responsibilities "[l]ead[ing] and direct[ing] kitchen part-time, substitute, and student employee helpers via demonstration, coaching, and overseeing their work." *Id.*, at 13. And another employee testified to believing that Davis was "a supervisor." *Id.*, at 386. But because the supervisor-status inquiry should focus on substance, not labels or paper descriptions, it is doubtful that this slim evidence would enable Vance to survive a motion for summary judgment. Nevertheless, I would leave it to the Seventh Circuit to decide, under the proper standard for super-visory status, what impact, if any, Davis' job description and the co-worker's statement should have on the determination of Davis' status.[9]

V

Regrettably, the Court has seized upon Vance's thin case to narrow the definition of supervisor, and thereby manifestly limit Title VII's protections against workplace harassment. Not even Ball State, the defendant-employer in this case, has advanced the restrictive definition the Court adopts. See *supra*, at 5. Yet the Court, insistent on constructing artificial categories where context should be key, proceeds on an immoderate and unrestrained course to corral Title VII.

Congress has, in the recent past, intervened to correct this Court's wayward interpretations of Title VII. See Lilly Ledbetter Fair Pay Act of 2009, 123Stat. 5, superseding *Ledbetter* v. *Goodyear Tire & Rubber Co.*, 550 U.S. 618 (2007) . See also Civil Rights Act of 1991, 105Stat. 1071, superseding in part, *Lorance* v. *AT&T Technologies, Inc.*, 490 U.S. 900 (1989) ; *Martin* v. *Wilks*, 490 U.S. 755 (1989) ; *Wards Cove Packing Co.* v. *Atonio*, 490 U.S. 642(1989); and *Price Waterhouse* v. *Hopkins*, 490 U.S. 228 (1989) . The ball is once again in Congress' court to correct the error into which this Court has fallen, and to restore the robust protections against workplace harassment the Court weakens today.

* * *

For the reasons stated, I would reverse the judgment of the Seventh Circuit and remand the case for application of the proper standard for determining who qualifies as a supervisor.

NOTES

[1] It is not altogether evident that Terry would qualify under the Court's test. His authority to hire was subject to approval by higher management, *Faragher* v. *Boca Raton,* 524 U.S. 775, 781 (1998) , and there is scant indication that he possessed other powers on the Court's list. The Court observes that Terry was able to "recommen[d]," and "initiat[e]" tangible employment actions. *Ante*, at 15, n.8 (internal quotation marks omitted). Nothing in the *Faragher* record, however, shows that Terry had authority to take such actions himself. Far-agher's complaint alleged that Terry said he would never promote a female lifeguard to the rank of lieutenant, 524 U.S., at 780, but that statement hardly suffices to establish that he had ultimate promotional authority. Had Boca Raton anticipated the position the Court today announces, the city might have urged classification of Terry as Far-agher's superior, but not her "supervisor."

[2] The illustrative cases reached the appellate level after grants of summary judgment in favor of the employer. Like the Courts of Appeals in each case, I recount the facts in the light most favorable to the employee, the nonmoving party.

[3] The Court misses the point of the illustrations. See *ante*, at 26–28, and nn. 15–16. Even under a vicarious liability rule, the Court points out, employers might escape liability for reasons other than the harasser's status as supervisor. For example, Rhodes might have avoided summary judgment in favor of her employer; even so, it would have been open to the employer to raise and prove to a jury the *Faragher/Ellerth* affirmative defense, see *supra*, at 3–4. No doubt other bar-riers also might impede an employee from prevailing, for example, Whitten's and Starke's intervening bankruptcies, see *Whitten* v. *Fred's Inc.*, No. 8:08–0218–HMH–BHH, 2010 WL 2757005 (D. SC, July 12, 2010); *EEOC* v. *CRST Van Expedited, Inc.,* 679 F.3d 657, 678, and n.14 (CA8 2012), or Mack's withdrawal of her complaint for reasons not apparent from the record, see *ante*, at 27–28, n.16. That, however, is no reason to restrict the definition of supervisor in a way that leaves out those genuinely in charge.

[4] Respondent's *amici* maintain that the EEOC Guidance is ineligible for deference under *Skidmore* v. *Swift & Co.*, 323 U.S. 134 (1944) , because it interprets *Faragher* and *Burlington Industries, Inc.* v. *Ellerth*, 524 U.S. 742 (1998) , not the text of Title VII. See Brief for Society for Human Resource Management etal. 11–16. They are mistaken. The EEOC Guidance rests on the employer liability framework set forth in *Faragher* and *Ellerth*, but both the framework and EEOC Guidance construe the term "agent" in 42 U.S.C. §2000e(b).

[5] Even the Seventh Circuit, whose definition of supervisor the Court adopts in large measure, has candidly acknowledged that, under its definition, supervisor status is not a clear and certain thing. See *Doe* v. *Oberweis Dairy*, 456 F.3d 704, 717 (2006) ("The difficulty of classification in this case arises from the fact that Nayman, the shift supervisor, was in between the paradigmatic classes [of supervisor and co-worker]. He had supervisory responsibility in the sense of authority to direct the work of the [ice-cream] scoopers, and he was even authorized to issue disciplinary write-ups, but he had no authority to fire them. He was either an elevated coworker or a diminished supervisor.").

[6] The Court worries that the EEOC's definition of supervisor will confound jurors who must first determine whether the harasser is a supervisor and second apply the correct employer liability standard. *Ante*, at 22–24, and nn. 13, 14. But the Court can point to no evidence that jury instructions on supervisor status in jurisdictions following the EEOC Guidance have in fact proved unworkable or confusing to jurors. Moreover, under the Court's definition of supervisor, jurors in many cases will be obliged to determine, as a threshold question, whether the alleged harasser possessed supervisory authority. See *supra*, at 15–16.

[7] Nor is the Court's confinement of supervisor status needed to deter insubstantial claims. Under the EEOC Guidance, a plaintiff must meet the threshold requirement of actionable harassment and then show that her supervisor's authority was of "sufficient magnitude" to assist in the harassment. See EEOC Guidance 405:7652, 405:7654.

[8] In addition to concluding that Davis was not Vance's supervisor, the District Court held that the conduct Vance alleged was "neither sufficiently severe nor pervasive to be considered objectively hostile for the purposes of Title VII." App. to Pet. for Cert. 66a. The Seventh Circuit declined to address this issue. See 646 F.3d 461, 471 (2011). If the case were remanded, the Court of Appeals could resolve the hostile environment issue first, and then, if necessary, Davis' status as supervisor or co-worker.

[9] The Court agrees that Davis "would probably not qualify" as Vance's supervisor under the EEOC's definition. *Ante*, at 28–29. Then why, one might ask, does the Court nevertheless reach out to announce its restrictive standard in this case, one in which all parties, including the defendant-employer, accept the fitness for Title VII of the EEOC's Guidance? See *supra*, at 5.

SYLVIA BURWELL, SECRETARY OF HEALTH AND HUMAN SERVICES, et al. v. HOBBY LOBBY STORES, INC., et al. /// CONESTOGA WOOD SPECIALTIES CORPORATION, et al. v. SYLVIA BURWELL, SECRETARY OF HEALTH AND HUMAN SERVICES, et al.

NoS. 13-354 & 13-356, June 30, 2014

ON WRITS OF CERTIORARI TO THE UNITED STATES COURT OF APPEALS FOR THE TENTH CIRCUIT /// THIRD CIRCUIT

Justice Ginsburg, with whom Justice Sotomayor joins, and with whom Justice Breyer and Justice Kagan join as to all but Part III–C–1, dissenting.

In a decision of startling breadth, the Court holds that commercial enterprises, including corporations, along with partnerships and sole proprietorships, can opt out of any law (saving only tax laws) they judge incompatible with their sincerely held religious beliefs. See *ante,* at 16–49. Compelling governmental interests in uniform compliance with the law, and disadvantages that religion-based opt-outs impose on others, hold no sway, the Court decides, at least when there is a "less restrictive alternative." And such an alternative, the Court suggests, there always will be whenever, in lieu of tolling an enterprise claiming a religion-based exemption, the government, *i.e.,* the general public, can pick up the tab. See *ante,* at 41–43.[1]

The Court does not pretend that the First Amendment's Free Exercise Clause demands religion-based accommodations so extreme, for our decisions leave no doubt on that score. See *infra,* at 6–8. Instead, the Court holds that Congress, in the Religious Freedom Restoration Act of 1993 (RFRA), 42 U.S.C. §2000bb *etseq.,* dictated the extraordinary religion-based exemptions today's decision endorses. In the Court's view, RFRA demands accommodation of a for-profit corporation's religious beliefs no matter the impact that accommodation may have on third parties who do not share the corporation owners' religious faith—in these cases, thousands of women employed by Hobby Lobby and Conestoga or dependents of persons those corporations employ. Persuaded that Congress enacted RFRA to serve a far less radical purpose, and mindful of the havoc the Court's judgment can introduce, I dissent.

I

"The ability of women to participate equally in the economic and social life of the Nation has been facilitated by their ability to control their reproductive lives." *Planned Parenthood of Southeastern Pa.* v. *Casey,* 505 U.S. 833, 856 (1992) . Congress acted on that understanding when, as part of a nationwide insurance program intended to be comprehensive, it called for coverage of preventive care responsive to women's needs. Carrying out Congress' direction, the Department of Health and Human Services (HHS), in consultation with public health experts, promulgated regulations requiring group health plans to cover all forms of contraception approved by the Food and Drug Administration (FDA). The genesis of this coverage should enlighten the Court's resolution of these cases.

A

The Affordable Care Act (ACA), in its initial form, specified three categories of preventive care that health plans must cover at no added cost to the plan participant or beneficiary.[2] Particular services were to be recommended by the U.S. Preventive Services Task Force, an independent panel of experts. The scheme had a large gap, how-ever; it left out preventive services that "many women's health advocates and medical professionals believe are critically important." 155 Cong. Rec. 28841 (2009) (statement of Sen. Boxer). To correct this oversight, Senator Barbara Mikulski introduced the Women's Health Amendment, which added to the ACA's minimum coverage requirements a new category of preventive services specific to women's health.

Women paid significantly more than men for preventive care, the amendment's proponents noted; in fact, cost barriers operated to block many women from obtaining needed care at all. See, *e.g., id.,* at 29070 (statement of Sen. Feinstein) ("Women of childbearing age spend 68 percent more in out-of-pocket health care costs than men."); *id.,* at 29302 (statement of Sen. Mikulski) ("copayments are [often] so high that [women] avoid getting [preventive and screening services] in the first place"). And increased access to contraceptive services, the sponsors comprehended, would yield important public health gains. See, *e.g., id.,* at 29768 (statement of Sen. Durbin) ("This bill will expand health insurance coverage to the vast majority of [the 17 million women of reproductive age in the United States who are uninsured] .... This expanded access will reduce unintended pregnancies.").

As altered by the Women's Health Amendment's passage, the ACA requires new insurance plans to include coverage without cost sharing of "such additional preventive care and screenings ... as provided for in comprehensive guidelines supported by the Health Resources and Services Administration [(HRSA)]," a unit of HHS. 42 U.S.C. §300gg–13(a)(4). Thus charged, the HRSA developed recommendations in consultation with the Institute of Medicine (IOM). See 77 Fed. Reg. 8725–8726 (2012).[3] The IOM convened a group of independent experts, including "specialists in disease prevention [and] women's health"; those experts prepared a report evaluating the efficacy of a number of preventive services. IOM, Clinical Prevention Services for Women: Closing the Gaps 2 (2011) (hereinafter IOM Report). Consistent with the findings of "[n]umerous health professional associations" and other organizations, the IOM experts determined that preventive coverage should include the "full range" of FDA-approved contraceptive methods. Id., at 10. See also id., at 102–110.

In making that recommendation, the IOM's report expressed concerns similar to those voiced by congres-sional proponents of the Women's Health Amendment. The report noted the disproportionate burden women carried for comprehensive health services and the adverse health consequences of excluding contraception from preventive care available to employees without cost sharing. See, e.g., id., at 19 ("[W]omen are consistently more likely than men to report a wide range of cost-related barriers to receiving ... medical tests and treatments and to filling prescriptions for themselves and their families."); id., at 103–104, 107 (pregnancy may be contraindicated forwomen with certain medical conditions, for example, some congenital heart diseases, pulmonary hypertension, and Marfan syndrome, and contraceptives may be used to reduce risk of endometrial cancer, among other serious medical conditions); id., at 103 (women with unintended pregnancies are more likely to experience depression and anxiety, and their children face "increased odds of preterm birth and low birth weight").

In line with the IOM's suggestions, the HRSA adopted guidelines recommending coverage of "[a]ll [FDA-]approved contraceptive methods, sterilization procedures, and patient education and counseling for all women with reproductive capacity."[4] Thereafter, HHS, the Department of Labor, and the Department of Treasury promulgated regulations requiring group health plans to include coverage of the contraceptive services recommended in the HRSA guidelines, subject to certain exceptions, described infra, at 25–27.[5] This opinion refers to these regulations as the contraceptive coverage requirement.

B

While the Women's Health Amendment succeeded, a countermove proved unavailing. The Senate voted down the so-called "conscience amendment," which would have enabled any employer or insurance provider to deny coverage based on its asserted "religious beliefs or moral convictions." 158 Cong. Rec. S539 (Feb. 9, 2012); see id., at S1162–S1173 (Mar. 1, 2012) (debate and vote).[6] That amendment, Senator Mikulski observed, would have "pu[t] the personal opinion of employers and insurers over the practice of medicine." Id., at S1127 (Feb. 29, 2012). Rejecting the "conscience amendment," Congress left health care decisions—including the choice among contraceptive methods—in the hands of women, with the aid of their health care providers.

II

Any First Amendment Free Exercise Clause claim Hobby Lobby or Conestoga[7] might assert is foreclosed by this Court's decision in Employment Div., Dept. of Human Resources of Ore. v. Smith, 494 U.S. 872 (1990) . In Smith, two members of the Native American Church were dismissed from their jobs and denied unemployment benefits because they ingested peyote at, and as an essential element of, a religious ceremony. Oregon law forbade the consumption of peyote, and this Court, relying on that prohibition, rejected the employees' claim that the denial of unemployment benefits violated their free exercise rights. The First Amendment is not offended, Smith held, when "prohibiting the exercise of religion ... is not the object of [governmental regulation] but merely the incidental effect of a generally applicable and otherwise valid provision." Id., at 878; see id., at 878–879 ("an individ-ual's religious beliefs [do not] excuse him from compliance with an otherwise valid law prohibiting conduct that the State is free to regulate"). The ACA's contraceptive coverage requirement applies generally, it is "otherwise valid," it trains on women's well being, not on the exerciseof religion, and any effect it has on such exercise isincidental.

Even if Smith did not control, the Free Exercise Clause would not require the exemption Hobby Lobby and Conestoga seek. Accommodations to religious beliefs or observances, the Court has clarified, must not significantly impinge on the interests of third parties. [8]

The exemption sought by Hobby Lobby and Conestoga would override significant interests of the corporations' employees and covered dependents. It would deny legions of women who do not hold their employers' beliefs access to contraceptive coverage that the ACA would otherwise secure. See Catholic Charities of Sacramento, Inc. v. Superior Court, 32 Cal. 4th 527, 565, 85 P.3d 67, 93 (2004) ("We are unaware of any decision in which ... [the U.S. Supreme Court] has exempted a religious objector from the operation of a neutral, generally applicable law despite the recognition that the requested exemption would detrimentally affect the rights of third parties."). In sum, with respect to free exercise claims no less than free speech claims, "[y]our right to swing your arms ends just where the other man's nose begins." Chafee, Freedom of Speech in War Time, 32 Harv. L.Rev. 932, 957 (1919).

III

A

Lacking a tenable claim under the Free Exercise Clause, Hobby Lobby and Conestoga rely on RFRA, a statute instructing that "[g]overnment shall not substantially burden a person's exercise of religion even if the burden results from a rule of general applicability" unless the government shows that application of the burden is "the least restrictive means" to further a "compelling governmental interest." 42 U.S.C. §2000bb–1(a), (b)(2). In RFRA, Congress "adopt[ed] a statutory rule comparable to the constitutional rule rejected in *Smith*." *Gonzales* v. *O Centro Espírita Beneficente União do Vegetal*, 546 U.S. 418, 424 (2006) .

RFRA's purpose is specific and written into the statute itself. The Act was crafted to "restore the compelling interest test as set forth in *Sherbert* v. *Verner*, 374 U.S. 398 (1963) and *Wisconsin* v. *Yoder*, 406 U.S. 205(1972) and to guarantee its application in all cases where free exercise of religion is substantially burdened." §2000bb(b)(1).[9] See also §2000bb(a) (5) ("[T]he compelling interest test as set forth in prior Federal court rulings isa workable test for striking sensible balances between religious liberty and competing prior governmental in-terests."); *ante*, at 48 (agreeing that the pre-*Smith* compelling interest test is "workable" and "strike[s] sensible balances").

The legislative history is correspondingly emphatic on RFRA's aim. See, *e.g.*, S.Rep. No. 103–111, p.12 (1993) (hereinafter Senate Report) (RFRA's purpose was "only to overturn the Supreme Court's decision in *Smith*," not to "unsettle other areas of the law."); 139 Cong. Rec. 26178 (1993) (statement of Sen. Kennedy) (RFRA was "designed to restore the compelling interest test for deciding free exercise claims."). In line with this restorative purpose, Congress expected courts considering RFRA claims to "look to free exercise cases decided prior to *Smith* for guidance." Senate Report 8. See also H.R. Rep. No. 103–88, pp.6–7 (1993) (hereinafter House Report) (same). In short, the Act reinstates the law as it was prior to *Smith*, without "creat[ing] ... new rights for any religious practice or for any potential litigant." 139 Cong. Rec. 26178 (statement of Sen. Kennedy). Given the Act's moderate purpose, it is hardly surprising that RFRA's enactment in 1993 provoked little controversy. See Brief for Senator Murray etal. as *Amici Curiae* 8 (hereinafter Senators Brief) (RFRA was approved by a 97-to-3 vote in the Senate and a voice vote in the House of Representatives).

B

Despite these authoritative indications, the Court sees RFRA as a bold initiative departing from, rather than restoring, pre-*Smith* jurisprudence. See *ante*, at 6, n.3, 7, 17, 25–27. To support its conception of RFRA as a measure detached from this Court's decisions, one that sets a new course, the Court points first to the Religious Land Use and Institutionalized Persons Act of 2000 (RLUIPA), 42 U.S.C. §2000cc *etseq.*, which altered RFRA's definition of the term "exercise of religion." RFRA, as originally enacted, defined that term to mean "the exercise of religion under the First Amendment to the Constitution." §2000bb–2(4) (1994 ed.). See *ante*, at 6–7. As amended by RLUIPA, RFRA's definition now includes "any exercise of religion, whether or not compelled by, or central to, a system of religious belief." §2000bb–2(4) (2012 ed.) (cross-referencing §2000cc–5). That definitional change, according to the Court, reflects "an obvious effort to effect a complete separation from First Amendment case law." *Ante*, at 7.

The Court's reading is not plausible. RLUIPA's alteration clarifies that courts should not question the centrality of a particular religious exercise. But the amendment in no way suggests that Congress meant to expand the class of entities qualified to mount religious accommodation claims, nor does it relieve courts of the obligation to inquire whether a government action substantially burdens a religious exercise. See *Rasul* v. *Myers*, 563 F.3d 527, 535 (CADC 2009) (Brown, J., concurring) ("There is no doubt that RLUIPA's drafters, in changing the definition of 'exercise of religion,' wanted to broaden the scope of the kinds of practices protected by RFRA, not increase the universe of individuals protected by RFRA."); H.R. Rep. No. 106–219, p.30 (1999). See also *Gilardi* v. *United States Dept. of Health and Human Servs.*, 733 F.3d 1208, 1211 (CADC 2013) (RFRA, as amended, "provides us with no helpful definition of 'exercise of religion.'"); *Henderson* v. *Kennedy*, 265 F.3d 1072, 1073 (CADC 2001) ("The [RLUIPA] amendments did not alter RFRA's basic prohibition that the '[g]overnment shall not substantially burden a person's exercise of religion.'").[10]

Next, the Court highlights RFRA's requirement that the government, if its action substantially burdens a person's religious observance, must demonstrate that it chose the least restrictive means for furthering a compelling interest. "[B]y imposing a least-restrictive-means test," the Court suggests, RFRA "went beyond what was required by our pre-*Smith* decisions." *Ante*, at 17, n.18 (citing *City of Boerne* v. *Flores*, 521 U.S. 507 (1997)). See also *ante*, at 6, n.3. But as RFRA's statements of purpose and legislative history make clear, Congress intended only to restore, not to scrap or alter, the balancing test as this Court had applied it pre-*Smith*. See *supra*, at 8–9. See also Senate Report 9 (RFRA's "compelling interest test generally should not be construed more stringently or more leniently than it was prior to *Smith*."); House Report7 (same).

The Congress that passed RFRA correctly read this Court's pre-*Smith* case law as including within the "compelling interest test" a "least restrictive means" requirement. See, *e.g.*, Senate Report 5 ("Where [a substantial] burden is placed upon the free exercise of religion, the Court ruled [in *Sherbert*], the Government must demonstrate that it is the least restrictive means to achieve a compelling governmental interest."). And the view that the pre-*Smith* test included a "least restrictive means" requirement had been aired in testimony before the Senate Judiciary Committee by experts on religious freedom. See, *e.g.*, Hearing on S. 2969 before the Senate Committee on the Judiciary, 102d Cong., 2d Sess.,

78–79 (1993) (statement of Prof. Douglas Laycock).

Our decision in *City of Boerne*, it is true, states that the least restrictive means requirement "was not used in the pre-*Smith* jurisprudence RFRA purported to codify." See *ante,* at 6, n.3, 17, n.18. As just indicated, however, that statement does not accurately convey the Court's pre-*Smith* jurisprudence. See *Sherbert*, 374 U.S., at 407 ("[I]t would plainly be incumbent upon the [government] to demonstrate that no alternative forms of regulation would combat [the problem] without infringing First Amendment rights."); *Thomas* v. *Review Bd. of Indiana Employment Security Div.*, 450 U.S. 707, 718 (1981) ("The state may justify an inroad on religious liberty by showing that it is the least restrictive means of achieving some compelling state interest."). See also Berg, The New Attacks on Religious Freedom Legislation and Why They Are Wrong, 21 Cardozo L.Rev. 415, 424 (1999) ("In *Boerne*, the Court erroneously said that the least restrictive means test 'was not used in the pre-*Smith* jurisprudence.'").[11]

C

With RFRA's restorative purpose in mind, I turn to the Act's application to the instant lawsuits. That task, in view of the positions taken by the Court, requires consideration of several questions, each potentially dispositive of Hobby Lobby's and Conestoga's claims: Do for-profit corporations rank among "person[s]" who "exercise ... religion"? Assuming that they do, does the contraceptive coverage requirement "substantially burden" their religious exercise? If so, is the requirement "in furtherance of a compelling government interest"? And last, does the requirement represent the least restrictive means for furthering that interest?

Misguided by its errant premise that RFRA moved beyond the pre-*Smith* case law, the Court falters at each step of its analysis.

1

RFRA's compelling interest test, as noted, see *supra,* at 8, applies to government actions that "substantially burden *a person's exercise of religion*." 42 U.S.C. §2000bb–1(a) (emphasis added). This reference, the Court submits, incorporates the definition of "person" found in the Dictionary Act, 1 U.S.C. §1, which extends to "corporations, companies, associations, firms, partnerships, societies, and joint stock companies, as well as individuals." See *ante,* at 19–20. The Dictionary Act's definition, however, controls only where "context" does not "indicat[e] otherwise." §1. Here, context does so indicate. RFRA speaks of "a person's *exercise of religion*." 42 U.S.C. §2000bb–1(a) (emphasis added). See also §§2000bb–2(4), 2000cc–5(7)(a).[12] Whether a corporation qualifies as a "person" capable of exercis-ing religion is an inquiry one cannot answer without reference to the "full body" of pre-*Smith* "free-exercise caselaw." *Gilardi*, 733 F.3d, at 1212. There is in that case law no support for the notion that free exercise rights pertain to for-profit corporations.

Until this litigation, no decision of this Court recognized a for-profit corporation's qualification for a religious exemption from a generally applicable law, whether under the Free Exercise Clause or RFRA.[13] The absence of such precedent is just what one would expect, for the exercise of religion is characteristic of natural persons, not artificial legal entities. As Chief Justice Marshall observed nearly two centuries ago, a corporation is "an artificial being, invisible, intangible, and existing only in contemplation of law." *Trustees of Dartmouth College* v. *Woodward*, 4 Wheat. 518, 636 (1819). Corporations, Justice Stevens more recently reminded, "have no consciences, no beliefs, no feelings, no thoughts, no desires." *Citizens United* v. *Federal Election Comm'n*, 558 U.S. 310, 466 (2010) (opinion concurring in part and dissenting in part).

The First Amendment's free exercise protections, the Court has indeed recognized, shelter churches and other nonprofit religion-based organizations.[14] "For many individuals, religious activity derives meaning in large measure from participation in a larger religious community," and "furtherance of the autonomy of religious organizations often furthers individual religious freedom as well." *Corporation of Presiding Bishop of Church of Jesus Christ of Latter-day Saints* v. *Amos*, 483 U.S. 327, 342 (1987) (Brennan, J., concurring in judgment). The Court's "special solicitude to the rights of religious organizations," *Hosanna-Tabor Evangelical Lutheran Church and School* v. *EEOC*, 565 U.S. ___, ___ (2012) (slip op., at 14), how-ever, is just that. No such solicitude is traditional for com-mercial organizations.[15] Indeed, until today, religious exemptions had never been extended to any entity operating in "the commercial, profit-making world." *Amos*, 483 U.S., at 337.[16]

The reason why is hardly obscure. Religious organizations exist to foster the interests of persons subscribing to the same religious faith. Not so of for-profit corporations. Workers who sustain the operations of those corporations commonly are not drawn from one religious community. Indeed, by law, no religion-based criterion can restrict the work force of for-profit corporations. See 42 U.S.C. §§2000e(b), 2000e–1(a), 2000e–2(a); cf. *Trans World Airlines, Inc.* v. *Hardison*, 432 U.S. 63–81 (1977) (Title VII requires reasonable accommodation of an employee's religious exercise, but such accommodation must not come "at the expense of other[employees]"). The distinction between a community made up of believers in the same religion and one embracing persons of diverse beliefs, clear as it is, constantly escapes the Court's attention.[17] One can only wonder why the Court shuts this key difference from sight.

Reading RFRA, as the Court does, to require extension of religion-based exemptions to for-profit corporations surely is not grounded in the pre-*Smith* precedent Congress sought to preserve. Had Congress intended RFRA to initiate a change so huge, a clarion statement to that effect likely would have been made in the legislation. See *Whitman* v. *American Trucking Assns., Inc.*, 531 U.S. 457, 468 (2001) (Congress does not "hide elephants in mouseholes"). The text of RFRA makes no such statement and the legislative history does not so much as mention for-profit corporations. See *Hobby Lobby Stores, Inc.* v. *Sebelius,* 723 F.3d 1114, 1169 (CA10 2013) (Briscoe, C.J., concurring in part and dissenting in part) (legislative record lacks "any suggestion that Congress foresaw, let alone intended that, RFRA would cover for-profit corporations"). See also Senators Brief 10–13 (none of thecases cited in House or Senate Judiciary Committeereports accompanying RFRA, or mentioned during floor speeches, recognized the free exercise rights of for-profit corporations).

The Court notes that for-profit corporations may support charitable causes and use their funds for religious ends, and therefore questions the distinction between such corporations and religious nonprofit organizations. See *ante,* at 20–25. See also *ante,* at 3 (Kennedy, J., concurring) (criticizing the Government for "distinguishing between different religious believers—burdening one while accommodating the other—when it may treat both equally by offering both of them the same accommodation").[18] Again, the Court forgets that religious organizations exist to serve a community of believers. For-profit corporations do not fit that bill. Moreover, history is not on the Court's side. Recognition of the discrete characters of "ecclesiastical and lay" corporations dates back to Blackstone, see 1 W. Blackstone, Commentaries on the Laws of England 458 (1765), and was reiterated by this Court centuries before the enactment of the Internal Revenue Code. See *Terrett* v. *Taylor,* 9 Cranch 43, 49 (1815) (describing religious corporations); *Trustees of Dartmouth College,* 4 Wheat., at 645 (discussing "eleemosynary" corporations, including those "created for the promotion of religion"). To reiterate, "for-profit corporations are different from religious non-profits in that they use labor to make a profit, rather than to perpetuate [the] religious value[s] [shared by a community of believers]." *Gilardi,* 733 F.3d, at 1242 (Edwards, J., concurring in part and dissenting in part) (emphasis deleted).

Citing *Braunfeld* v. *Brown,* 366 U.S. 599 (1961) , the Court questions why, if "a sole proprietorship that seeks to make a profit may assert a free-exercise claim, [Hobby Lobby and Conestoga] can't ... do the same?" *Ante,* at 22 (footnote omitted). See also *ante,* at 16–17. But even accepting, *arguendo,* the premise that unincorporated business enterprises may gain religious accommodations under the Free Exercise Clause, the Court's conclusion is unsound. In a sole proprietorship, the business and its owner are one and the same. By incorporating a business, however, an individual separates herself from the entity and escapes personal responsibility for the entity's obligations. One might ask why the separation should hold only when it serves the interest of those who control the corporation. In any event, *Braunfeld* is hardly impressive authority for the entitlement Hobby Lobby and Conestoga seek. The free exercise claim asserted there was promptly rejected on the merits.

The Court's determination that RFRA extends to for-profit corporations is bound to have untoward effects. Although the Court attempts to cabin its language to closely held corporations, its logic extends to corporations of any size, public or private.[19] Little doubt that RFRA claims will proliferate, for the Court's expansive notion of corporate personhood—combined with its other errorsin construing RFRA—invites for-profit entities to seek religion-based exemptions from regulations they deem offensive to their faith.

2

Even if Hobby Lobby and Conestoga were deemed RFRA "person[s]," to gain an exemption, they must demonstrate that the contraceptive coverage requirement "substan-tially burden[s] [their] exercise of religion." 42 U.S.C. §2000bb–1(a). Congress no doubt meant the modifier "substantially" to carry weight. In the original draft of RFRA, the word "burden" appeared unmodified. The word "substantially" was inserted pursuant to a clarifying amendment offered by Senators Kennedy and Hatch. See 139 Cong. Rec. 26180. In proposing the amendment, Senator Kennedy stated that RFRA, in accord with the Court's pre-*Smith* case law, "does not require the Government to justify every action that has some effect on religious exercise." *Ibid.*

The Court barely pauses to inquire whether any burden imposed by the contraceptive coverage requirement is substantial. Instead, it rests on the Greens' and Hahns' "belie[f] that providing the coverage demanded by the HHS regulations is connected to the destruction of an embryo in a way that is sufficient to make it immoral for them to provide the coverage." *Ante,* at 36.[20] I agree with the Court that the Green and Hahn families' religious convictions regarding contraception are sincerely held. See *Thomas,* 450 U.S., at 715 (courts are not to question where an individual "dr[aws] the line" in defining which practices run afoul of her religious beliefs). See also 42 U.S.C. §§2000bb–1(a), 2000bb–2(4), 2000cc–5(7)(A).[21] But those beliefs, however deeply held, do not suffice to sustain a RFRA claim. RFRA, properly understood, distinguishes between "factual allegations that [plaintiffs'] beliefs are sincere and of a religious nature," which a court must accept as true, and the "legal conclusion ... that [plaintiffs'] religious exercise is substantially burdened," an inquiry the court must undertake. *Kaemmerling* v. *Lappin,* 553 F.3d 669, 679 (CADC 2008).

That distinction is a facet of the pre-*Smith* jurisprudence RFRA incorporates. *Bowen* v. *Roy,* 476 U.S. 693 (1986) , is instructive. There, the Court rejected a free exercise challenge to the Government's use of a Native American child's Social Security number for purposes of administering benefit programs. Without questioning the sincerity of the father's religious belief that "use of [his daughter's Social Security] number may harm [her] spirit," the Court concluded that the Government's internaluses of that number "place[d] [no] restriction on what [the father] may believe or what he may do." *Id.,* at 699. Recognizing that the father's "religious views may not accept" the position that the challenged uses concerned only the Government's internal affairs, the Court explained that "for the adjudication of a constitutional claim, the Constitution, rather than an individual's religion, must supply the frame of reference." *Id.,* at 700–701, n.6. See also *Hernandez* v. *Commissioner,* 490 U.S. 680, 699 (1989) (distinguishing between, on the one hand, "question[s] [of] the centrality of particular beliefs or practices to a faith, or the validity of particular litigants' interpretations of those creeds," and, on the other, "whether the alleged burden imposed [by the challenged government action] is a substantial one"). Inattentive to this guidance, today's decision elides entirely the distinction between the sincerity of a challenger's religious belief and the substantiality of the burden placed on the challenger.

Undertaking the inquiry that the Court forgoes, I would conclude that the connection between the families' religious objections and the contraceptive coverage requirement is too attenuated to rank as substantial. The requirement carries no command that Hobby Lobby or Conestoga purchase or provide the contraceptives they find objectionable. Instead, it calls on the companies covered by the requirement to direct money into undifferentiated funds that finance a wide variety of benefits under comprehensive health plans. Those plans, in order to comply with the ACA, see *supra*, at 3–6, must offer contraceptive coverage without cost sharing, just as they must cover an array of other preventive services.

Importantly, the decisions whether to claim benefits under the plans are made not by Hobby Lobby or Cones-toga, but by the covered employees and dependents, in consultation with their health care providers. Should an employee of Hobby Lobby or Conestoga share the religious beliefs of the Greens and Hahns, she is of course under no compulsion to use the contraceptives in question. But "[n]o individual decision by an employee and her physician—be it to use contraception, treat an infection, or have a hip replaced—is in any meaningful sense [her employer's] decision or action." *Grote* v. *Sebelius*, 708 F.3d 850, 865 (CA7 2013) (Rovner, J., dissenting). It is doubtful that Congress, when it specified that burdens must be "substantia[l]," had in mind a linkage thus interrupted by independent decisionmakers (the woman and her health counselor) standing between the challenged government action and the religious exercise claimed to be infringed. Any decision to use contraceptives made by a woman covered under Hobby Lobby's or Conestoga's plan will not be propelled by the Government, it will be the wo-man's autonomous choice, informed by the physician she consults.

3

Even if one were to conclude that Hobby Lobby and Conestoga meet the substantial burden requirement, the Government has shown that the contraceptive coverage for which the ACA provides furthers compelling interests in public health and women's well being. Those interests are concrete, specific, and demonstrated by a wealth of empirical evidence. To recapitulate, the mandated contraception coverage enables women to avoid the health problems unintended pregnancies may visit on them and their children. See IOM Report 102–107. The coverage helps safeguard the health of women for whom pregnancy may be hazardous, even life threatening. See Brief for American College of Obstetricians and Gynecologists etal. as *Amici Curiae* 14–15. And the mandate secures benefits wholly unrelated to pregnancy, preventing certain cancers, menstrual disorders, and pelvic pain. Brief for Ovarian Cancer National Alliance etal. as *Amici Curiae* 4, 6–7, 15–16; 78 Fed. Reg. 39872 (2013); IOM Report 107.

That Hobby Lobby and Conestoga resist coverage for only 4 of the 20 FDA-approved contraceptives does not lessen these compelling interests. Notably, the corporations exclude intrauterine devices (IUDs), devices significantly more effective, and significantly more expensive than other contraceptive methods. See *id.*, at 105.[22] Moreover, the Court's reasoning appears to permit commercial enterprises like Hobby Lobby and Conestoga to exclude from their group health plans all forms of contraceptives. See Tr. of Oral Arg. 38–39 (counsel for Hobby Lobby acknowledged that his "argument ... would apply just as well if the employer said 'no contraceptives'" (internal quotation marks added)).

Perhaps the gravity of the interests at stake has led the Court to assume, for purposes of its RFRA analysis, that the compelling interest criterion is met in these cases. See *ante*, at 40.[23] It bears note in this regard that the cost of an IUD is nearly equivalent to a month's full-time pay for workers earning the minimum wage, Brief for Guttmacher Institute etal. as *Amici Curiae* 16; that almost one-third of women would change their contraceptive method if costs were not a factor, Frost & Darroch, Factors Associated With Contraceptive Choice and Inconsistent Method Use, United States, 2004, 40 Perspectives on Sexual & Reproductive Health 94, 98 (2008); and that only one-fourth of women who request an IUD actually have one inserted after finding out how expensive it would be, Gariepy, Simon, Patel, Creinin, & Schwarz, The Impact of Out-of-Pocket Expense on IUD Utilization Among Women With Private Insurance, 84 Contraception e39, e40 (2011). See also Eisenberg, *supra*, at S60 (recent study found that women who face out-of-pocket IUD costs in excess of $50 were "11-times less likely to obtain an IUD than women who had to pay less than $50"); Postlethwaite, Trussell, Zoolakis, Shabear, & Petitti, A Comparison of Contraceptive Procurement Pre- and Post-Benefit Change, 76 Contraception 360, 361–362 (2007) (when one health system eliminated patient cost sharing for IUDs, use of this form of contraception more than doubled).

Stepping back from its assumption that compelling interests support the contraceptive coverage requirement, the Court notes that small employers and grandfathered plans are not subject to the requirement. If there is a compelling interest in contraceptive coverage, the Court suggests, Congress would not have created these exclusions. See *ante*, at 39–40.

Federal statutes often include exemptions for small employers, and such provisions have never been held to undermine the interests served by these statutes. See, *e.g.*, Family and Medical Leave Act of 1993, 29 U. S. C. §2611(4)(A)(i) (applicable to employers with 50 or more employees); Age Discrimination in Employment Act of 1967, 29 U. S. C. §630(b) (originally exempting employers with fewer than 50 employees, 81Stat. 605, the statute now governs employers with 20 or more employees); Americans With Disabilities Act, 42 U.S.C. §12111(5)(A) (applicable to employers with 15 or more employees); Title VII, 42 U.S.C. §2000e(b) (originally exempting employers with fewer than 25 employees, see *Arbaugh* v. *Y&H Corp.*, 546 U.S. 500, n.2 (2006), the statute now governs employers with 15 or more employees).

The ACA's grandfathering provision, 42 U.S.C. §18011, allows a phasing-in period for compliance with a number of the Act's requirements (not just the contraceptive coverage or other preventive services provisions). Once specified changes are made, grandfathered status ceases. See 45 CFR §147.140(g). Hobby Lobby's own situation is illustrative. By the time this litigation commenced, Hobby Lobby did not have grandfathered status. Asked why by the District Court, Hobby Lobby's counsel explained that the "grandfathering requirements mean that you can't make a whole menu of changes to your plan that involve things like the amount of co-pays, the amount of co-insurance, deductibles, that sort of thing." App. in No. 13–354, pp. 39–40. Counsel acknowledged that, "just because of economic realitioo, our plaii has to shift over time I mean, insurance plans, as everyone knows, shif[t] over time." Id., at 40.[24] The percentage of employees in grandfathered plans is steadily declining, having dropped from 56% in 2011 to 48% in 2012 to 36% in 2013. Kaiser Family Foundation & Health Research & Educ. Trust, Employer Benefits 2013 Annual Survey 7, 196. In short, far from ranking as a categorical exemption, the grandfathering provision is "temporary, intended to be a means for gradually transitioning employers into mandatory coverage." Gilardi, 733 F.3d, at 1241 (Edwards, J., concurring in part and dissenting in part).

The Court ultimately acknowledges a critical point: RFRA's application "must take adequate account of the burdens a requested accommodation may impose on nonbeneficiaries." Ante, at 42, n.37 (quoting Cutter v. Wilkinson, 544 U.S. 709, 720 (2005) ; emphasis added). No tradition, and no prior decision under RFRA, allows a religion-based exemption when the accommodation would be harmful to others—here, the very persons the contraceptive coverage requirement was designed to protect. Cf. supra, at 7–8; Prince v. Massachusetts, 321 U.S. 158, 177 (1944) (Jackson, J., dissenting) ("[The] limitations which of necessity bound religious freedom ... begin to operate whenever activities begin to affect or collide with liberties of others or of the public.").

4

After assuming the existence of compelling government interests, the Court holds that the contraceptive coverage requirement fails to satisfy RFRA's least restrictive means test. But the Government has shown that there is no less restrictive, equally effective means that would both (1) satisfy the challengers' religious objections to providing insurance coverage for certain contraceptives (which they believe cause abortions); and (2) carry out the objective of the ACA's contraceptive coverage requirement, to ensure that women employees receive, at no cost to them, the preventive care needed to safeguard their health and well being. A "least restrictive means" cannot require employees to relinquish benefits accorded them by federal law in order to ensure that their commercial employers can adhere unreservedly to their religious tenets. See supra, at 7–8, 27.[25]

Then let the government pay (rather than the employees who do not share their employer's faith), the Court suggests. "The most straightforward [alternative]," the Court asserts, "would be for the Government to assume the cost of providing ... contraceptives ... to any women who are unable to obtain them under their health-insurance policies due to their employers' religious objections." Ante, at 41. The ACA, however, requires coverage of preventive services through the existing employer-based system of health insurance "so that [employees] face minimal logistical and administrative obstacles." 78 Fed. Reg. 39888. Impeding women's receipt of benefits "by requiring them to take steps to learn about, and to sign up for, a new [government funded and administered] health benefit" was scarcely what Congress contemplated. Ibid. More-over, Title X of the Public Health Service Act, 42 U.S.C. §300 et seq., "is the nation's only dedicated source of federal funding for safety net family planning services." Brieffor National Health Law Program etal. as Amici Curiae 23. "Safety net programs like Title X are not designed to absorb the unmet needs of ... insured individuals." Id., at 24. Note, too, that Congress declined to write into law the preferential treatment Hobby Lobby and Conestoga describe as a less restrictive alternative. See supra, at 6.

And where is the stopping point to the "let the government pay" alternative? Suppose an employer's sincerely held religious belief is offended by health coverage of vaccines, or paying the minimum wage, see Tony and Susan Alamo Foundation v. Secretary of Labor, 471 U.S. 290, 303 (1985) , or according women equal pay for substantially similar work, see Dole v. Shenandoah Baptist Church, 899 F.2d 1389, 1392 (CA4 1990)? Does it rank as a less restrictive alternative to require the government to provide the money or benefit to which the employer hasa religion-based objection?[26] Because the Court cannot easily answer that question, it proposes something else: Extension to commercial enterprises of the accommodation already afforded to nonprofit religion-based organizations. See ante, at 3–4, 9–10, 43–45. "At a minimum," according to the Court, such an approach would not "impinge on [Hobby Lobby's and Conestoga's] religious belief." Ante, at 44. I have already discussed the "special solicitude" generally accorded nonprofit religion-based organizations that exist to serve a community of believers, solicitude never before accorded to commercial enterprises comprising employees of diverse faiths. See supra, at 14–17.

Ultimately, the Court hedges on its proposal to align for-profit enterprises with nonprofit religion-based organizations. "We do not decide today whether [the] approach [the opinion advances] complies with RFRA for purposes of all religious claims." Ante, at 44. Counsel for Hobby Lobby was similarly noncommittal. Asked at oral argument whether the Court-proposed alternative was acceptable,[27] counsel responded: "We haven't been offered that accommodation, so we haven't had to decide what kind of objection, if any, we would make to that." Tr. of Oral Arg. 86–87.

Conestoga suggests that, if its employees had to acquire and pay for the contraceptives (to which the corporation objects) on their own, a tax credit would qualify as a less restrictive alternative. See Brief for Petitioners in No. 13–356, p. 64. A tax credit, of course, is one variety of "let the government pay." In addition to departing from the existing employer-based system of health insurance, Conestoga's alternative would require a woman to reach into her own pocket in the first instance, and it would do nothing for the woman too poor to be aided by a tax credit.

In sum, in view of what Congress sought to accomplish, i.e., comprehensive preventive care for women furnished through employer-based health plans, none of the proffered alternatives would satisfactorily serve the compelling interests to which Congress responded.

IV

Among the pathmarking pre-*Smith* decisions RFRA preserved is *United States* v. *Lee*, 455 U.S. 252 (1982) . *Lee*, a sole proprietor engaged in farming and carpentry, was a member of the Old Order Amish. He sincerely believed that withholding Social Security taxes from his employees or paying the employer's share of such taxes would violate the Amish faith. This Court held that, although the obligations imposed by the Social Security system conflicted with Lee's religious beliefs, the burden was not unconstitutional. *Id.*, at 260–261. See also *id.*, at 258 (recognizing the important governmental interest in providing a "nationwide ... comprehensive insurance system with a variety of benefits available to all participants, with costs shared by employers and employees").[28] The Government urges that *Lee* should control the challenges brought by Hobby Lobby and Conestoga. See Brief for Respondents in No. 13–356, p.18. In contrast, today's Court dismisses *Lee* as a tax case. See *ante*, at 46–47. Indeed, it was a tax case and the Court in *Lee* homed in on "[t]he difficulty in attempting to accommodate religious beliefs in the area of taxation." 455 U.S., at 259.

But the *Lee* Court made two key points one cannot confine to tax cases. "When followers of a particular sect enter into commercial activity as a matter of choice," the Court observed, "the limits they accept on their own conduct as a matter of conscience and faith are not to be superimposed on statutory schemes which are binding on others in that activity." *Id.*, at 261. The statutory scheme of employer-based comprehensive health coverage involved in these cases is surely binding on others engaged in the same trade or business as the corporate challengers here, Hobby Lobby and Conestoga. Further, the Court recognized in *Lee* that allowing a religion-based exemption to a commercial employer would "operat[e] to impose the employer's religious faith on the employees." *Ibid.*[29] No doubt the Greens and Hahns and all who share their beliefs may decline to acquire for themselves the contraceptives in question. But that choice may not be imposed on employees who hold other beliefs. Working for Hobby Lobby or Conestoga, in other words, should not deprive employees of the preventive care available to workers at the shop next door,[30] at least in the absence of directions from the Legislature or Administration to do so.

Why should decisions of this order be made by Congress or the regulatory authority, and not this Court? Hobby Lobby and Conestoga surely do not stand alone as commercial enterprises seeking exemptions from generally applicable laws on the basis of their religious beliefs. See, *e.g.*, *Newman* v. *Piggie Park Enterprises, Inc.*, 256 F.Supp. 941, 945 (SC 1966) (owner of restaurant chain refused to serve black patrons based on his religious beliefs opposing racial integration), aff'd in relevant part and rev'd in part on other grounds, 377 F.2d 433 (CA4 1967), aff'd and modified on other grounds, 390 U.S. 400 (1968) ; *In re Minnesota ex rel. McClure*, 370 N.W. 2d 844, 847 (Minn. 1985) (born-again Christians who owned closely held, for-profit health clubs believed that the Bible proscribed hiring or retaining an "individua[l] living with but not married to a person of the opposite sex," "a young, single woman working without her father's consent or a married woman working without her husband's consent," and any person "antagonistic to the Bible," including "fornicators and homosexuals" (internal quotation marks omitted)), appeal dismissed, 478 U.S. 1015 (1986) ; *Elane Photography, LLC* v. *Willock*, 2013–NMSC–040, ___ N.M. ___, 309 P.3d 53 (for-profit photography business owned by a husband and wife refused to photograph a lesbian couple's commitment ceremony based on the religious beliefs of the company's owners), cert. denied, 572 U.S. ___ (2014). Would RFRA require exemptions in cases of this ilk? And if not, how does the Court divine which religious beliefs are worthy of accommodation, and which are not? Isn't the Court disarmed from making such a judgment given its recognition that "courts must not presume to determine ... the plausibility of a religious claim"? *Ante*, at 37.

Would the exemption the Court holds RFRA demands for employers with religiously grounded objections to the use of certain contraceptives extend to employers with religiously grounded objections to blood transfusions (Jehovah's Witnesses); antidepressants (Scientologists); medications derived from pigs, including anesthesia, intravenous fluids, and pills coated with gelatin (certain Muslims, Jews, and Hindus); and vaccinations (Christian Scientists, among others)?[31] According to counsel for Hobby Lobby, "each one of these cases ... would have to be evaluated on its own ... apply[ing] the compelling interest-least restrictive alternative test." Tr. of Oral Arg. 6. Not much help there for the lower courts bound by today's decision.

The Court, however, sees nothing to worry about. Today's cases, the Court concludes, are "concerned solely with the contraceptive mandate. Our decision should not be understood to hold that an insurance-coverage mandate must necessarily fall if it conflicts with an employer's religious beliefs. Other coverage requirements, such as immunizations, may be supported by different interests (for example, the need to combat the spread of infectious diseases) and may involve different arguments about the least restrictive means of providing them." *Ante*, at 46. But the Court has assumed, for RFRA purposes, that the interest in women's health and well being is compelling and has come up with no means adequate to serve that interest, the one motivating Congress to adopt the Women's Health Amendment.

There is an overriding interest, I believe, in keeping the courts "out of the business of evaluating the relative merits of differing religious claims," *Lee*, 455 U.S., at 263, n.2 (Stevens, J., concurring in judgment), or the sincerity with which an asserted religious belief is held. Indeed, approving some religious claims while deeming others unworthy of accommodation could be "perceived as favoring one religion over another," the very "risk the Establishment Clause was designed to preclude." *Ibid.* The Court, I fear, has ventured into a minefield, cf. *Spencer* v. *World Vision, Inc.*, 633 F.3d 723, 730 (CA9 2010) (O'Scannlain, J., concurring), by its immoderate reading of RFRA. I would confine religious exemptions under that Act to organizations formed "for a religious purpose," "engage[d] primarily in carrying out that religious purpose," and not "engaged ... substantially in the exchange of goods or services for money beyond nominal amounts." See *id.,* at 748 (Kleinfeld, J., concurring).

* * *

For the reasons stated, I would reverse the judgment of the Court of Appeals for the Tenth Circuit and affirm the judgment of the Court of Appeals for the Third Circuit.

NOTES

[1] The Court insists it has held none of these things, for another less restrictive alternative is at hand: extending an existing accommodation, currently limited to religious nonprofit organizations, to encompass commercial enterprises. See *ante,* at 3–4. With that accommodation extended, the Court asserts, "women would still be entitled to all [Food and Drug Administration]-approved contraceptives without cost sharing." *Ante,* at 4. In the end, however, the Court is not so sure. In stark contrast to the Court's initial emphasis on this accommodation, it ultimately declines to decide whether the highlighted accommodation is even lawful. See *ante,* at 44 ("We do not decide today whether an approach of this type complies with RFRA ....").

[2] See 42 U.S.C. §300gg–13(a)(1)–(3) (group health plans must provide coverage, without cost sharing, for (1) certain "evidence-based items or services" recommended by the U.S. Preventive Services Task Force; (2) immunizations recommended by an advisory committee of the Centers for Disease Control and Prevention; and (3) "with respect to infants, children, and adolescents, evidence-informed preventive care and screenings provided for in the comprehensive guidelines supported by the Health Resources and Services Administration").

[3] The IOM is an arm of the National Academy of Sciences, an organization Congress established "for the explicit purpose of furnishing advice to the Government." *Public Citizen* v. *Department of Justice,* 491 U.S. 440, n.11 (1989) (internal quotation marks omitted).

[4] HRSA, HHS, Women's Preventive Services Guidelines, available at http://www.hrsa.gov/womensguidelines/ (all Internet materials as visited June 27, 2014, and available in Clerk of Court's case file), reprinted in App. to Brief for Petitioners in No. 13–354, pp. 43–44a. See also 77 Fed. Reg. 8725–8726 (2012).

[5] 45 CFR §147.130(a)(1)(iv) (2013) (HHS); 29 CFR §2590.715–2713(a)(1)(iv) (2013) (Labor); 26 CFR §54.9815–2713(a)(1)(iv) (2013) (Treasury).

[6] Separating moral convictions from religious beliefs would be of questionable legitimacy. See *Welsh* v. *United States,* 398 U.S. 333–358 (1970) (Harlan, J., concurring in result).

[7] As the Court explains, see *ante,* at 11–16, these cases arise from two separate lawsuits, one filed by Hobby Lobby, its affiliated business (Mardel), and the family that operates these businesses (the Greens); the other filed by Conestoga and the family that owns and controls that business (the Hahns). Unless otherwise specified, this opinion refers to the respective groups of plaintiffs as Hobby Lobby and Conestoga.

[8] See *Wisconsin* v. *Yoder,* 406 U.S. 205, 230 (1972) ("This case, of course, is not one in which any harm to the physical or mental health of the child or to the public safety, peace, order, or welfare has been demonstrated or may be properly inferred."); *Estate of Thornton* v. *Caldor, Inc.,* 472 U. S. 703 (1985) (invalidating state statute requiring employers to accommodate an employee's Sabbath observance where that statute failed to take into account the burden such an accommodation would impose on the employer or other employees). Notably, in construing the Religious Land Use and Institutionalized Persons Act of 2000 (RLUIPA), 42 U.S.C. §2000cc *etseq.,* the Court has cautioned that "adequate account" must be taken of "the burdens a requested accommodation may impose on nonbeneficiaries." *Cutter* v. *Wilkinson,* 544 U.S. 709, 720 (2005) ; see *id.,* at 722 ("an accommodation must be measured so that it does not override other significant interests"). A balanced approach is all the more in order when the Free Exercise Clause itself is at stake, not a statute designed to promote accommodation to religious beliefs and practices.

[9] Under *Sherbert* and *Yoder,* the Court "requir[ed] the government to justify any substantial burden on

religiously motivated conduct by a compelling state interest and by means narrowly tailored to achieve that interest." *Employment Div., Dept. of Human Resources of Ore.* v. *Smith*, 494 U.S. 872, 894 (1990) (O'Connor, J., concurring injudgment).

[10] RLUIPA, the Court notes, includes a provision directing that "[t]his chapter [*i.e.*, RLUIPA] shall be construed in favor of a broad protection of religious exercise, to the maximum extent permitted by the terms of [the Act] and the Constitution." 42 U.S.C. §2000cc-3(g); see *ante,* at 6–7, 26. RFRA incorporates RLUIPA's definition of "exercise of religion," as RLUIPA does, but contains no omnibus rule of construction governing the statute in its entirety.

[11] The Court points out that I joined the majority opinion in *City of Boerne* and did not then question the statement that "least restrictive means ... was not used [pre-*Smith*]." *Ante,* at 17, n.18. Concerning that observation, I remind my colleagues of Justice Jackson's sage comment: "I see no reason why I should be consciously wrong today because I was unconsciously wrong yesterday." *Massachusetts* v. *United States*, 333 U.S. 611–640 (1948) (dissenting opinion).

[12] As earlier explained, see *supra,* at 10–11, RLUIPA's amendment of the definition of "exercise of religion" does not bear the weight the Court places on it. Moreover, it is passing strange to attribute to RLUIPA any purpose to cover entities other than "religious assembl[ies] or institution[s]." 42 U.S.C. §2000cc(a)(1). But cf. *ante,* at 26. That law applies to land-use regulation. §2000cc(a)(1). To permit commercial enterprises to challenge zoning and other land-use regulations under RLUIPA would "dramatically expand the statute's reach" and deeply intrude on local prerogatives, contrary to Congress' intent. Brief for National League of Cities etal. as *Amici Curiae* 26.

[13] The Court regards *Gallagher* v. *Crown Kosher Super Market of Mass., Inc.*, 366 U.S. 617 (1961) , as "suggest[ing] ... that for-profit corporations possess [free-exercise] rights." *Ante,* at 26–27. See also *ante,* at 21, n.21. The suggestion is barely there. True, one of the five challengers to the Sunday closing law assailed in *Gallagher* was a corporation owned by four Orthodox Jews. The other challengers were human individuals, not artificial, law-created entities, so there was no need to determine whether the corporation could institute the litigation. Accordingly, the plurality stated it could pretermit the question "whether appellees ha[d] standing" because *Braunfeld* v. *Brown*, 366 U.S. 599 (1961) , which upheld a similar closing law, was fatal to their claim on the merits. 366 U.S., at 631.

[14] See, *e.g., Hosanna-Tabor Evangelical Lutheran Church and School* v. *EEOC*, 565 U.S. ___ (2012); *Gonzales* v. *O Centro Espírita Beneficente União do Vegetal*, 546 U.S. 418 (2006) ; *Church of Lukumi Babalu Aye, Inc.* v. *Hialeah*, 508 U.S. 520 (1993) ; *Jimmy Swaggart Ministries* v. *Board of Equalization of Cal.*, 493 U.S. 378 (1990) .

[15] Typically, Congress has accorded to organizations religious in character religion-based exemptions from statutes of general application. *E.g.,* 42 U.S.C. §2000e-1(a) (Title VII exemption from prohibition against employment discrimination based on religion for "a religious corporation, association, educational institution, or society with respect to the employment of individuals of a particular religion to perform work connected with the carrying on ... of its activities"); 42 U.S.C. §12113(d)(1) (parallel exemption in Americans With Disabilities Act of 1990). It can scarcely be maintained that RFRA enlarges these exemptions to allow Hobby Lobby and Conestoga to hire only persons who share the religious beliefs of the Greens or Hahns. Nor does the Court suggest otherwise. Cf. *ante,* at 28.The Court does identify two statutory exemptions it reads to cover for-profit corporations, 42 U.S.C. §§300a-7(b)(2) and 238n(a), and infers from them that "Congress speaks with specificity when it intends a religious accommodation not to extend to for-profit corporations," *ante,* at 28. The Court's inference is unwarranted. The exemptions the Court cites cover certain medical personnel who object to performing or assisting with abortions. Cf. *ante,* at 28, n.27 ("the protection provided by §238n(a) differs significantly from the protection provided by RFRA"). Notably, the Court does not assert that these exemptions have in fact been afforded to for-profit corporations. See §238n(c) ("health care entity" covered by exemption is a term defined to include "an individual physician, a postgraduate physician training program, and a participant in a program of training in the health professions"); Tozzi, Whither Free Exercise: *Employment Division* v. *Smith* and the Rebirth of State Constitutional Free Exercise Clause Jurisprudence?, 48 J. Catholic Legal Studies 269, 296, n.133 (2009) ("Catholic physicians, but not necessarily hospitals, ... may be able to invoke [§238n(a)] ...."); cf. S. 137, 113th Cong., 1st Sess. (2013) (as introduced) (Abortion Non-Discrimination Act of 2013, which would amend the definition of "health care entity" in §238n to include "hospital[s]," "health insurance plan[s]," and

other health care facilities). These provisions are revealing in a way that detracts from one of the Court's main arguments. They show that Congress is not content to rest on the Dictionary Act when it wishes to ensure that particular entities are among those eligible for a religious accommodation.Moreover, the exemption codified in §238n(a) was not enacted until three years after RFRA's passage. See Omnibus Consolidated Rescissions and Appropriations Act of 1996, §515, 110Stat. 1321–245. If, as the Court believes, RFRA opened all statutory schemes to religion-based challenges by for-profit corporations, there would be no need for a statute-specific, post-RFRA exemption of this sort.

[16] That is not to say that a category of plaintiffs, such as resident aliens, may bring RFRA claims only if this Court expressly "addressed their [free-exercise] rights before *Smith*." *Ante,* at 27. Continuing with the Court's example, resident aliens, unlike corporations, are flesh-and-blood individuals who plainly count as persons sheltered by the First Amendment, see *United States* v. *Verdugo-Urquidez,* 494 U.S. 259, 271 (1990) (citing *Bridges* v. *Wixon,* 326 U.S. 135, 148 (1945)), and *afortiori,* RFRA.

[17] I part ways with Justice Kennedy on the context relevant here. He sees it as the employers' "exercise [of] their religious beliefs within the context of their own closely held, for-profit corporations." *Ante,* at 2 (concurring opinion). See also *ante,* at 45–46 (opinion of the Court) (similarly concentrating on religious faith of employers without reference to the different beliefs and liberty interests of employees). I see as the relevant context the employers' asserted right to exercise religion within a nationwide program designed to protect against health hazards employees who do not subscribe to their employers' religious beliefs.

[18] According to the Court, the Government "concedes" that "nonprofit corporation[s]" are protected by RFRA. *Ante,* at 19. See also *ante,* at 20, 24, 30. That is not an accurate description of the Government's position, which encompasses only "churches," "*religious* institutions," and "*religious* non-profits." Brief for Respondents in No. 13–356, p.28 (emphasis added). See also Reply Brief in No. 13–354, p.8 ("RFRA incorporates the longstanding and common-sense distinction between religious organizations, which sometimes have been accorded accommodations under generally applicable laws in recognition of their accepted religious character, and for-profit corporations organized to do business in the commercial world.").

[19] The Court does not even begin to explain how one might go about ascertaining the religious scruples of a corporation where shares are sold to the public. No need to speculate on that, the Court says, for "it seems unlikely" that large corporations "will often assert RFRA claims." *Ante,* at 29. Perhaps so, but as Hobby Lobby's case demonstrates, such claims are indeed pursued by large corporations, employing thousands of persons of different faiths, whose ownership is not diffuse. "Closely held" is not synonymous with "small." Hobby Lobby is hardly the only enterprise of sizable scale that is family owned or closely held. For example, the family-owned candy giant Mars, Inc., takes in $33 billion in revenues and has some 72,000 employees, and closely held Cargill, Inc., takes in more than $136 billion in reve-nues and employs some 140,000 persons. See Forbes, America's Largest Private Companies 2013, available at http://www.forbes.com/largest-private-companies/.

Nor does the Court offer any instruction on how to resolve the disputes that may crop up among corporate owners over religious values and accommodations. The Court is satisfied that "[s]tate corporate law provides a ready means for resolving any conflicts," *ante,* at 30, but the authorities cited in support of that proposition are hardly helpful. See Del. Code Ann., Tit. 8, §351 (2011) (certificates of incorporation may specify how the business is managed); 1 J. Cox & T. Hazen, Treatise on the Law of Corporations §3:2 (3d ed. 2010) (section entitled "Selecting the state of incorporation"); *id.,* §14:11 (observing that "[d]espite the frequency of dissension and deadlock in close corporations, in some states neither legislatures nor courts have provided satisfactory solutions"). And even if a dispute settlement mechanism is in place, how is the arbiter of a religion-based intracorporate controversy to resolve the disagreement, given this Court's instruction that "courts have no business addressing [whether an asserted religious belief] is substantial," *ante,* at 36?

[20] The Court dismisses the argument, advanced by some *amici,* that the $2,000-per-employee tax charged to certain employers that fail to provide health insurance is less than the average cost of offering health insurance, noting that the Government has not provided the statistics that could support such an argument. See *ante,* at 32–34. The Court overlooks, however, that it is not the Government's obligation to prove that an asserted burden is *in*substantial. Instead, it is incumbent upon plaintiffs to demonstrate, in support of a RFRA claim, the substantial-ity of the alleged burden.

[21] The Court levels a criticism that is as wrongheaded as can be. In no way does the dissent "tell the plaintiffs that their beliefs are flawed." *Ante,* at 37. Right or wrong in this domain is a judgment no Member of this Court, or any civil court, is authorized or equipped to make. What the Court must decide is not "the plausibility of a religious claim," *ante,* at 37 (internal quotation marks omitted), but whether accommodating that claim risks depriving others of rights accorded them by the laws of the United States. See *supra,* at 7–8; *infra,* at 27.

[22] IUDs, which are among the most reliable forms of contraception, generally cost women more than $1,000 when the expenses of the office visit and insertion procedure are taken into account. See Eisenberg, McNicholas, & Peipert, Cost as a Barrier to Long-Acting Reversible Contraceptive (LARC) Use in Adolescents, 52 J. Adolescent Health S59, S60 (2013). See also Winner et al., Effectiveness of Long-Acting Reversible Contraception, 366 New Eng. J. Medicine 1998, 1999 (2012).

[23] Although the Court's opinion makes this assumption grudgingly, see *ante,* at 39–40, one Member of the majority recognizes, without reservation, that "the [contraceptive coverage] mandate serves the Government's compelling interest in providing insurance coverage that is necessary to protect the health of female employees." *Ante,* at 2 (opinion of Kennedy, J.).

[24] Hobby Lobby's *amicus* National Religious Broadcasters similarly states that, "[g]iven the nature of employers' needs to meet changing economic and staffing circumstances, and to adjust insurance coverage accordingly, the actual benefit of the 'grandfather' exclusion is *de minimis* and transitory at best." Brief for National Religious Broadcasters as *Amicus Curiae* in No. 13–354, p. 28.

[25] As the Court made clear in *Cutter,* the government's license to grant religion-based exemptions from generally applicable laws is constrained by the Establishment Clause. 544 U.S., at 720–722. "[W]e are a cosmopolitan nation made up of people of almost every conceivable religious preference," *Braunfeld,* 366 U.S., at 606, a "rich mosaic of religious faiths," *Town of Greece* v. *Galloway,* 572 U.S. ___, ___ (2014) (Kagan, J., dissenting) (slip op., at 15). Consequently, one person's right to free exercise must be kept in harmony with the rights of her fellow citizens, and "some religious practices [must] yield to the common good." *United States* v. *Lee,* 455 U.S. 252, 259 (1982) .

[26] Cf. *Ashcroft* v. *American Civil Liberties Union,* 542 U.S. 656, 666 (2004) (in context of First Amendment Speech Clause challenge to a content-based speech restriction, courts must determine "whether the challenged regulation is the least restrictive means among *available,* effective alternatives" (emphasis added)).

[27] On brief, Hobby Lobby and Conestoga barely addressed the extension solution, which would bracket commercial enterprises with nonprofit religion-based organizations for religious accommodations purposes. The hesitation is understandable, for challenges to the adequacy of the accommodation accorded religious nonprofit organizations are currently *sub judice.* See, *e.g., Little Sisters of the Poor Home for the Aged* v. *Sebelius,* ___ F.Supp.2d ___, 2013 WL 6839900 (Colo., Dec. 27, 2013), injunction pending appeal granted, 571 U.S. ___ (2014). At another point in today's decision, the Court refuses to consider an argument neither "raised below [nor] advanced in this Court by any party," giving Hobby Lobby and Conestoga "[no] opportunity to respond to [that] novel claim." *Ante,* at 33. Yet the Court is content to decide this case (and this case only) on the ground that HHS could make an accommodation never suggested in the parties' presentations. RFRA cannot sensibly be read to "requir[e] the government to ... refute each and every conceivable alternative regulation," *United States* v. *Wilgus,* 638 F.3d 1274, 1289 (CA10 2011), especially where the alternative on which the Court seizes was not pressed by any challenger.

[28] As a sole proprietor, Lee was subject to personal liability for violating the law of general application he opposed. His claim to a religion-based exemption would have been even thinner had he conducted his business as a corporation, thus avoiding personal liability.

[29] Congress amended the Social Security Act in response to *Lee.* The amended statute permits Amish sole proprietors and partnerships (but not Amish-owned corporations) to obtain an exemption from the obligation to pay Social Security taxes only for employees who are co-religionists and who likewise seek an exemption and agree to give up their Social Security benefits. See 26 U.S.C. §3127(a)(2), (b)(1). Thus, employers with sincere religious beliefs have no right to a religion-based exemption that would deprive employees of Social Security benefits without the employee's consent—

an exemption analogous to the one Hobby Lobby and Conestoga seek here.

[30] Cf. *Tony and Susan Alamo Foundation* v. *Secretary of Labor*, 471 U.S. 290, 299 (1985) (disallowing religion-based exemption that "would undoubtedly give [the commercial enterprise seeking the exemption] and similar organizations an advantage over their competitors").

[31] Religious objections to immunization programs are not hypothetical. See *Phillips* v. *New York*, ____ F.Supp.2d ____, 2014 WL 2547584 (EDNY, June 5, 2014) (dismissing free exercise challenges to New York's vaccination practices); Liberty Counsel, Compulsory Vaccinations Threaten Religious Freedom (2007), available at http://www.lc.org/media/9980/attachments/memo_vaccination.pdf.

CTS CORPORATION v. PETER WALDBURGER, et al.

No. 13-339, June 9, 2014

ON WRIT OF CERTIORARI TO THE UNITED STATES COURT OF APPEALS FOR THE FOURTH CIRCUIT

Justice Ginsburg, with whom Justice Breyer joins, dissenting.

North Carolina's law prescribing "periods ... for the commencement of actions [for personal injury or damage to property]," N.C. Gen. Stat. Ann. §§1–46, 1–52 (Lexis 2013), includes in the same paragraph, §1–52(16), both a discovery rule and an absolute period of repose. Section 1–52(16) states that personal injury and property damage claims

> "shall not accrue until bodily harm to the claimant or physical damage to his property becomes apparent or ought reasonably to have become apparent to the claimant .... Provided that no [claim] shall accrue more than 10 years from the last act or omission of the defendant giving rise to the [claim]."

The question presented is whether a federal statute on the timeliness of suits for harm caused by environmental contamination, 42 U.S.C. §9658, preempts North Carolina's 10-year repose provision.

The federal statute concerns hazardous-waste-caused injuries with long latency periods that can run 10 to 40 years. To ensure that latent injury claims would not become time barred during the years in which the injury remained without manifestation, Congress amended the Comprehensive Environmental Response, Compensation, and Liability Act of 1980 (CERCLA), 42 U.S.C. §9601 *etseq.*, to include a provision, §9658, on "actions under state law for damages from exposure to hazardous substances." See H. R. Conf. Rep. No. 99–962, pp. 87–88, 261 (1986) (hereinafter Conference Report) (problem centers on when state limitations periods begin to run rather than the number of years they run; Congress therefore established "a [f]ederally-required commencement date"). Captioned "Exception to State statutes," §9658(a)(1) instructs that when the applicable state limitations period specifies "a commencement date ... earlier than the federally required commencement date," the federal date shall apply "in lieu of the date specified in [state law]."

The Court in the case at hand identifies as the relevant prescriptive period North Carolina's 10-year repose provision. I agree. But as I see it, the later "federally required commencement date," §9658(a)(1), (b)(4), displaces the earlier date state law prescribes.

Section 9658(b)(3) defines "commencement date" as "the date specified in a statute of limitations as the beginning of the applicable limitations period." Under North Caro-lina law, that date is determined by the occurrence of"the last act or omission of the defendant giving rise tothe [claim]." N.C. Gen. Stat. Ann. 1–52(16). The definition key to this controversy, however, appears in §9658(b)(4)(A): "'[F]ederally required commencement date' means the date the plaintiff knew (or reasonably should have known) that [her] injury ... [was] caused ... by the hazardous substance ... concerned." Congress, in short, directed, in §9658(a)(1), that the federally prescribed discovery rule, set out in §9658(b)(4), shall apply "in lieu of" the earlier "commencement date" (the defendant's"last act or omission") specified in N.C. Gen. Stat. Ann. §1–52(16).

Why does the Court fight this straightforward reading? At length, the Court's opinion distinguishes statutes of limitations from statutes of repose. See *ante*, at 5–16. Yet North Carolina itself made its repose period a component of the statute prescribing periods for "the commencement of actions." §§1–46, 1–52(16). What is a repose period, in essence, other than a limitations period unattended by a discovery rule? See Senate Committee on Environment and Public Works, Superfund Section 301(e) Study Group, Injuries and Damages from Hazardous Wastes—Analysis and Improvement of Legal Remedies, 97th Cong., 2d Sess., (pt. 1) 255–256 (Comm. Print 1982) (hereinafter Study Group Report).

The legislative history of §9658, moreover, shows why the distinction the Court draws between statutes of limitations and repose prescriptions cannot be what Congress ordered. As the Court recognizes, *ante*, at 2–3, Congress amended CERCLA to include §9658 in response to the report of an expert Study Group commissioned when CERCLA was enacted. That report directed its proposals to the States rather than to Congress. It "recommend[ed] that the several states enhance and develop common law and statutory remedies, and that they remove unreasonable procedural and other barriers to recovery in court action for personal injuries resulting from exposure to hazardous waste." Study Group Report 255. The report then made specific proposals. Under the heading "Statutes of Limitations," the Study Group proposed (1) "that all [S]tates ... clearly adopt the rule that an action accrues when the plaintiff discovers or should have discovered the injury or disease and its cause" and (2) that States repeal "statutes of repose which, in a number of [S]tates have the same effect as some statutes of limitation in barring plaintiff's claim before he knows he has one." *Id.*, at

255–256. Both measures are necessary, the report explained, because "many of the hazardous wastes are carcinogens" with "latency period[s] for the appearance of injury or disease ... likely to [run] for thirty years or more." *Id.,* at 255.

Beyond question, a repose period, like the 10-year period at issue here, will prevent recovery for injuries with la-tency periods running for decades. Thus, altering statutes of limitations to include a discovery rule would be of little use in States with repose prescriptions.

Rather than await action by the States, Congress decided to implement the Study Group's proposal itself by adopting §9658. *Ante,* at 3. The Conference Report relates the Study Group Report's observation that "certain State statutes deprive plaintiffs of their day in court" because "[i]n the case of a long-latency disease, such as cancer," a limitations period that begins to run before the plaintiff has discovered her injury frequently will make timely suit impossible. Conference Report 261. The Conference Report then states that "[t]his section"—§9658—"addresses the problem identified in the [Study Group Report]." *Ibid.* As the Study Group Report makes clear, "the problem" it identified, to which the Conference Report adverted, cannot be solved when statutes of repose remain operative. The Court's interpretation thus thwarts Congress' clearly expressed intent to fix "the problem" the Study Group described.

In lieu of uniform application of the "federally required commencement date," §9658(b)(4), the Court allows those responsible for environmental contamination, if they are located in the still small number of States with repose periods,[*] to escape liability for the devastating harm they cause, harm hidden from detection for more than 10 years. Instead of encouraging prompt identification and remediation of toxic contamination before it can kill, the Court's decision gives contaminators an incentive to conceal the hazards they have created until the repose period has run its full course.

Far from erring, see *ante,* at 2, 10, the Fourth Circuit, I am convinced, got it exactly right in holding that §9658 supersedes state law contrary to the federally required discovery rule. I would affirm that court's sound judgment.

NOTES

[*] See Conn. Gen. Stat. §§52–577, 52–584 (2013) (three years); Kan. Stat. Ann. §60–513(b) (2005) (10 years); Ore. Rev. Stat. §12.115 (2013) (10 years). See also *Abrams* v. *Ciba Specialty Chemicals Corp.,* 659 F.Supp. 2d 1225, 1228–1240 (SD Ala. 2009) (discussing Alabama's 20-year common-law rule of repose and holding that §9658 preempts it).

Made in United States
Troutdale, OR
12/20/2023

16242858R10255